BLACKBOOK
of
ENGLISH VOCABULARY

Updated till February 2026

First Edition : July 2019; November 2019

Second Edition : August 2020; February 2021; January 2022; March 2023

Third Edition : May 2024

Fourth Edition : March 2026 *(Current Edition)*

Printed on : 15th March 2026 (BN: DB0326)

AF539840

Price : ₹ 449 /-

Co-Edited by : **Ashish Gupta**

Published by : **Gupta EduTech**

For Distributorship : Contact us at **support@qmaths.in**

WhatsApp at **9999 121 127 (Message Only)**

Your constructive feedback and suggestions are most important and our team will be highly obliged if you message/mail us your feedback or suggestions at **support@qmaths.in.**

How to Verify the Authenticity of Your BlackBooks

Step 1: Locate the Hologram

Look for the hologram sticker on the cover of your Blackbook. This hologram contains a QR code that is key to verifying your Blackbook's authenticity.

Step 2: Download a QR Scanner App

To scan the QR code, you will need a QR scanner app on your smartphone. Some phones camera automatically scans QR code. If you don't already have one, here are a few free and reliable options available for both Android and iOS devices:

- **For Android:** QR Code Reader, QR & Barcode Scanner
- **For iOS:** QR Reader for iPhone, QR Code & Barcode Scanner

Download and install one of these apps from your device's app store.

Step 3: Scan the QR Code

Open the QR scanner app on your phone and point your camera at the QR code on the hologram. Ensure the QR code is within the camera's frame and hold your phone steady. The app should automatically recognize and scan the code.

Step 4: Verify the BlackBook

After scanning, the app will redirect you to a webpage (verify.qmaths.in). Here, the authenticity of your book will be displayed. If your book is genuine, you'll see "Genuine Blackbook" in green color.

Step 5: Fill Out the Verification Form

Whether your book is genuine or not, you'll be prompted to fill out a verification form. Please provide the following details:

1. **Select Book:** Choose the book you've purchased from the dropdown menu.
2. **Full Name:** Enter your full name.
3. **Email Address:** Provide a valid email address.
4. **Contact Number:** Enter your contact number.
5. **Pincode:** Provide your area's pincode.
6. **City:** Enter the name of your city.
7. **Retailer:** Select the retailer from whom you purchased the book (Amazon, Flipkart, or a local seller).

You also have the option to give a rating and leave feedback about the Blackbook.

What If My BlackBook Is Not Genuine?

If the webpage displays "Pirated Blackbook" in red color, it indicates that the book is not genuine. We encourage you to fill out the form with the details mentioned above to help us track and take action against counterfeit sellers.

Reasons to Choose Original BlackBooks:

1) Exceptional paper quality for durability and readability.
2) Content is current and free of errors, ensuring reliable information.
3) Premium printing quality for clear text and images.
4) Purchasing original books supports the author's efforts and contributes to government revenue through taxes.
5) Profits are reinvested into creating additional resources like free PDFs, study materials, compilations, regular updates, and more, all provided by our dedicated team.

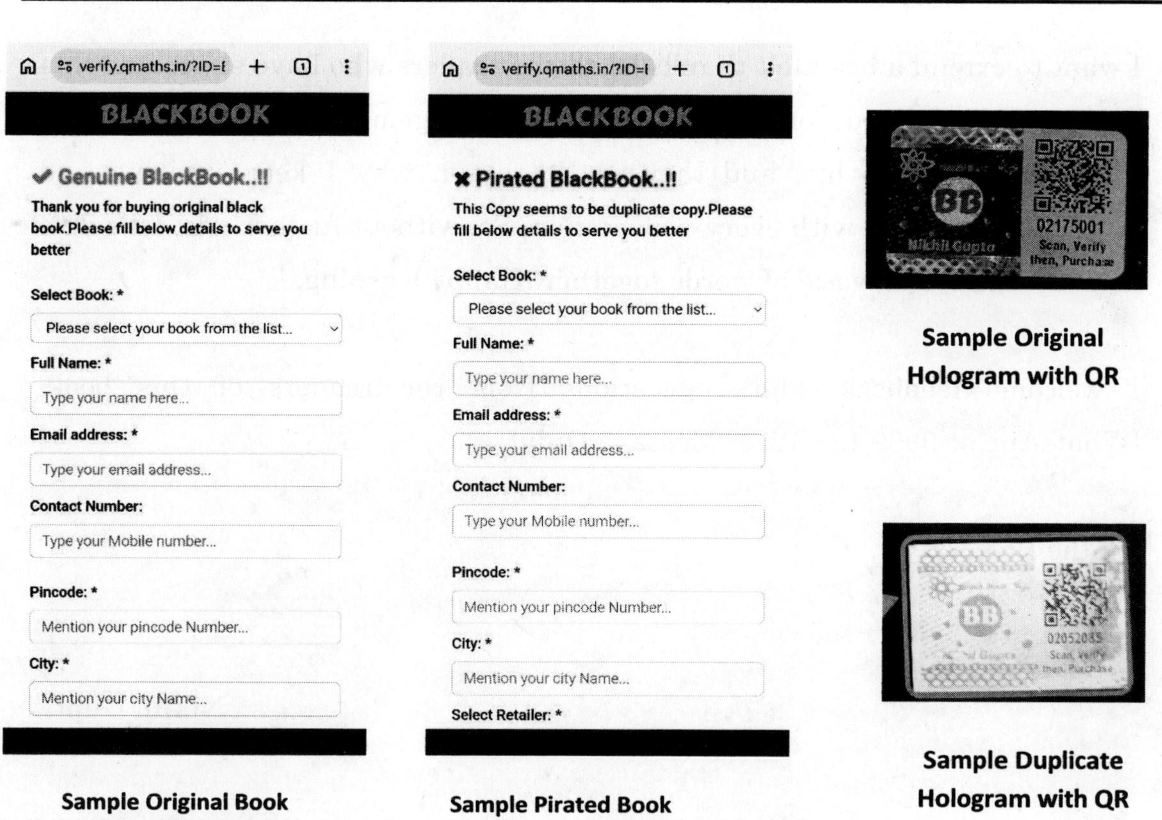

Sample Original Book Verification Page

Sample Pirated Book Verification Page

Sample Original Hologram with QR

Sample Duplicate Hologram with QR

Preface

Welcome to the fourth edition of the "Blackbook of English Vocabulary". If you're flipping through these pages, you're probably on a mission to conquer Vocabulary Section which is crucial for exams like SSC, DSSSB, Defence (CDS, NDA, AFCAT), Bank, and state exams. Well, you've come to the right place!

With each edition of this book, I've aimed to make your vocabulary journey smoother, easier, and smarter. I've scoured through the depths of all competitive vocabularies to bring you a treasure that will not only help you ace SSC and other exams but also enrich your Vocabulary skills for life.

I want to extend a heartfelt thanks to all the readers who have supported this book since its first edition. Your feedback, encouragement, and success stories mean the world to me, and they're the reason why I keep revising and improving this book with every new edition. So, without further ado, let's dive into the wonderful world of words together. Happy learning..!!

I welcome feedback, and suggestions from the readers of this book. (WhatsApp at 9999 121 127 – Message Only)

All the Best. ☺

Nikhil Gupta

INDEX

SECTION: I

(Previous Papers + Practice MCQs)

PART A: ONE WORD SUBSTITUTIONS

PART B: IDIOMS / PHRASES

PART C: SYNONYMS / ANTONYMS

PART D: HOMONYMS & HOMOPHONES

PART E: SPELLING

SECTION: II

PART F: VOCAB BOOSTERS

APPENDIX#

PART G: SPECIAL WORDS

 # Available as Softcopy only

* **Common List**: Words asked as **both Synonyms and Antonyms** in exams. Words asked only as a Synonym are listed under Synonyms, and only as an Antonym under Antonyms.

† **Other Exams include:** IBPS PO, CDS, NDA, CUET UG, AFCAT, UPSC EPFO, DSSSB, DDA, KVS, AAI, SIDBI, IB, AHC, CRPF, BSF, CISF, CBSE, CSIR, ISRO, SCI & other Central/State Govt. Exams.

HOW TO USE THIS BOOK

Brought this book but still confused how to use it? Don't worry, I am here to help you. First things first, trust this book for your vocabulary journey. Many Top Rankers (including AIR 1) have used this book and cracked CGL and various other SSC exams. All you need is dedication and consistency.

One of the main objectives of compiling this book was to provide all vocabularies asked in SSC and other relevant competitive exams. This 2026 edition includes all new vocabulary asked in SSC exams till **February 2026**, along with other relevant competitive exams.

SECTION - I:

This section is your golden ticket, especially for competitive exam aspirants. Around 80–85% of SSC exam questions come from this section alone.

- **Chapters A1, B1, C1, C3, C6, and E2:** Perfect for last-minute revision — containing the most frequently repeated vocabularies in SSC exams, sorted by frequency of appearance.
- **Chapters A2, B2, C2, C4, C7, and E1:** A complete MASTER LIST of all vocabularies asked in SSC exams.
- **Chapters A3, B3, C5, C8, D2, and E3:** Recent SSC PYQ-based practice sets to gauge your preparation. Mandatory for all SSC aspirants.
- **Chapters A4, B4, C9, C10, and C12:** Another MASTER LIST covering vocabularies from recent Non-SSC competitive exams. Vital for both SSC and other exam aspirants. Once you've mastered the SSC vocabulary, tackle these for an extra edge.
- **Chapters A5, B5, C11, and C13:** Practice sets based on recent Non-SSC PYQs, tailored to relevant exams. A must for aspirants aiming beyond SSC.

Section II: Contains essential **Vocab Boosters** — Phrasal Verbs, Fixed Prepositions, The Hindu Editorial Vocabulary, Foreign Words & Phrases, and Important Prefixes, Suffixes & Root Words. Tackle this section only after completing at least the SSC part of Section I.

Appendix: Contains **Part G**, curated word lists across 24 topics (2300+ words). While these words haven't been directly asked in recent exams, they're crucial for well-rounded vocabulary preparation. This section is available in **softcopy format** for convenience, you don't need to memorize every word from it, but diving in when time permits will give your preparation an extra edge.

WHAT'S NEW IN THIS EDITION: -

Updated and Additional Content: -

1. Added new vocabulary from **417 SSC sets** asked after the publication of the last edition (May 2024).
2. Added new vocabulary from **470 sets** of other competitive exams.
3. Expanded chapters: Phrasal Verbs and Homonyms have been expanded and split into PYQ-based and Non-PYQ-based sections.
4. Improved definitions and Hindi meanings added across all chapters.
5. The Hindu Vocabulary: Refreshed with new words; duplicates already present in OWS or Synonyms-Antonyms chapters removed.
6. Foreign Words: Revised and expanded to 197 important foreign words.
7. Root Words: Revised and expanded to cover Root Words, Prefixes, and Suffixes.
8. Fixed Prepositions: Important usage rules and memory aids added.

Topics	*Unique Words*	*Total Words*
OWS -1	2027	5757
OWS -2	545	629
Idioms-1	1887	6981
Idioms-2	413	489
Proverb	219	640
Phrasal Verbs	245	496
Syno-Anto-1	4103	13851
Syno-Anto-2	1231	1565
Homonyms-1	242	738
Spelling	3619	6235
Phrasal Verbs	1028	1028
Homonyms-2	730	730
Fixed Prepositions	532	532
The Hindu	1015	1015
Foreign Words	197	197
Root Words	891	891
Special 24 Word Lists	2300	2300
Grand Total	**21224**	**44074**

Symbols used:
SN: Serial Number
#R: Repetition
* : Also asked as Spelling
~: asked as OWS/Syno-Anto
/ : Either of the words
PoS: Parts of Speech
N.: Noun
V.: Verb
Adj.: Adjective
Adv.: Adverb
P.: Pronoun
P.V.: Phrasal Verb
Prep.: Preposition
Cont.: Contraction
Conj.: Conjunction

BBEV 2026: Study Plan

This study plan will help you cover **every single word list** in this book with just **one focused hour a day**. Don't be intimidated by the word counts. Module I has roughly 9,000 words in total, and completing just this module can help you score **more than 85%** in the vocabulary section of any SSC exam.

Here is the thing most students don't realize: you already know a large number of these words. Even an average student recognizes at least 40-50 % of words on every page. You do not need to memorize the entire list. Just focus on the words you don't know, mark them with a pencil, and keep revising those marked words again and again. Revision is the real game-changer. The more times you see a word, the better it sticks.

The plan is divided into three modules. You start with only 2 topics and gradually add more. No topic overload on Day 1. By the time new topics come in, your earlier ones are already moving fast. There are built-in study gaps for revision so you never fall behind.

How the Plan Works

Module I (Days 1-50): SSC Core Vocabulary

Covers OWS, Idioms, Synonyms-Antonyms (Common List, Synonyms, Antonyms), Proverbs, Phrasal Verbs, and Homonyms. These are the words asked directly in previous SSC exams. This module alone covers **85-90% of vocabulary questions**. Total: 9,116 words across 42 study days + 7 revision days + 1 grand revision day.

Module II (Days 51-70): Other Exams + Spelling

Vocabulary from other competitive exams (CDA, NDA, AFCAT, DDA, DSSSB, CUET, etc.) plus the spelling section. Spelling is fast to scan since you just need to spot the correct or incorrect spelling. Total: 5,808 words in 20 days.

Module III (Days 71-90): Advanced Vocabulary Boosters

Phrasal Verbs, Homonyms, Fixed Prepositions, The Hindu vocabulary, Foreign Words, and Root Words. Essential for advanced preparation and also help with Reading Comprehension and Cloze test passages. Total: 4,267 words in 20 days.

You don't start everything on Day 1. Topics are introduced gradually so you never feel overwhelmed.

Before You Begin

- Keep a pen/pencil handy. Circle or underline every word you don't know. Skip the ones you already know.
- After finishing each day's target, spend 5-10 minutes revising your marked words from the previous days.
- Don't try to memorize everything in one go. Repeated exposure is the key. You will read these lists multiple times.
- Read each word list at least 3 times before the exam. First reading is for exposure, second for recognition, and the third for retention.
- Maintain a small notebook for the toughest words. Write them down with meanings. This helps with retention.
- If you miss a day, don't panic. Just pick up from where you left off. Consistency matters more than perfection.
- This plan is a general guideline. Adjust the daily targets based on your speed and comfort level.

Module I - Core Vocabulary

Topics are introduced gradually. You start with just OWS and Idioms, and new topics are added as you build momentum. Word counts increase step by step so you are comfortable before the load grows. Revision days are placed after every 6 study days.

Day	Daily Tasks	☑ Done
1	OWS: 1-68; Idioms: 1-63	☐
2	OWS: 69-136; Idioms: 64-126	☐
3	OWS: 137-204; Idioms: 127-189	☐
4	OWS: 205-272; Idioms: 190-252	☐
5	OWS: 273-340; Idioms: 253-315	☐
6	OWS: 341-408; Idioms: 316-378	☐
7	**Revision - Review all marked/circled words from Days 1-6**	☐
8	OWS: 409-476; Idioms: 379-441; Syno-Anto Common List: 1-70	☐
9	OWS: 477-544; Idioms: 442-504; Syno-Anto Common List: 71-140	☐
10	OWS: 545-612; Idioms: 505-567; Syno-Anto Common List: 141-210	☐
11	OWS: 613-680; Idioms: 568-630; Syno-Anto Common List: 211-280	☐
12	OWS: 681-748; Idioms: 631-693; Syno-Anto Common List: 281-349	☐
13	OWS: 749-816; Idioms: 694-756; Syno-Anto Common List: 350-418	☐
14	**Revision - Review all marked/circled words from Days 8-13**	☐
15	OWS: 817-884; Idioms: 757-819; Syno-Anto Common List: 419-487; Homonyms: 1-36	☐
16	OWS: 885-952; Idioms: 820-882; Syno-Anto Common List: 488-556; Homonyms: 37-72	☐
17	OWS: 953-1020; Idioms: 883-945; Syno-Anto Common List: 557-625; Homonyms: 73-108	☐
18	OWS: 1021-1088; Idioms: 946-1008; Syno-Anto Common List: 626-694; Homonyms: 109-144	☐
19	OWS: 1089-1156; Idioms: 1009-1071; Syno-Anto Common List: 695-763; Homonyms: 145-180	☐
20	OWS: 1157-1223; Idioms: 1072-1134; Syno-Anto Common List: 764-832; Homonyms: 181-215	☐
21	**Revision - Review all marked/circled words from Days 15-20**	☐
22	OWS: 1224-1290; Idioms: 1135-1197; Syno-Anto Common List: 833-901; Homonyms: 216-250; Proverbs: 1-19; Phrasal Verbs: 1-21	☐
23	OWS: 1291-1357; Idioms: 1198-1260; Syno-Anto Common List: 902-970; Homonyms: 251-285; Proverbs: 20-38; Phrasal Verbs: 22-42	☐
24	OWS: 1358-1424; Idioms: 1261-1323; Syno-Anto Common List: 971-1039; Homonyms: 286-320; Proverbs: 39-57; Phrasal Verbs: 43-63	☐
25	OWS: 1425-1491; Idioms: 1324-1386; Syno-Anto Common List: 1040-1108; Homonyms: 321-355; Proverbs: 58-75; Phrasal Verbs: 64-84	☐
26	OWS: 1492-1558; Idioms: 1387-1449; Syno-Anto Common List: 1109-1177; Homonyms: 356-390; Proverbs: 76-93; Phrasal Verbs: 85-105	☐
27	OWS: 1559-1625; Idioms: 1450-1512; Syno-Anto Common List: 1178-1246; Homonyms: 391-425; Proverbs: 94-111; Phrasal Verbs: 106-125	☐
28	**Revision - Review all marked/circled words from Days 22-27**	☐

29	OWS: 1626-1692; Idioms: 1513-1575; Syno-Anto Common List: 1247-1315; Homonyms: 426-460; Proverbs: 112-129; Phrasal Verbs: 126-145	☐
30	OWS: 1693-1759; Idioms: 1576-1638; Syno-Anto Common List: 1316-1384; Homonyms: 461-495; Proverbs: 130-147; Phrasal Verbs: 146-165	☐
31	OWS: 1760-1826; Idioms: 1639-1701; Syno-Anto Common List: 1385-1453; Homonyms: 496-530; Proverbs: 148-165; Phrasal Verbs: 166-185	☐
32	OWS: 1827-1893; Idioms: 1702-1763; Syno-Anto Common List: 1454-1522; Homonyms: 531-565; Proverbs: 166-183; Phrasal Verbs: 186-205	☐
33	OWS: 1894-1960; Idioms: 1764-1825; Syno-Anto Common List: 1523-1591; Homonyms: 566-600; Proverbs: 184-201; Phrasal Verbs: 206-225	☐
34	OWS: 1961-2027; Idioms: 1826-1887; Syno-Anto Common List: 1592-1660; Homonyms: 601-646; Proverbs: 202-219; Phrasal Verbs: 226-245	☐
35	**Revision - Review all marked/circled words from Days 29-34**	☐
36	Synonyms: 1-109; Antonyms: 1-95	☐
37	Synonyms: 110-218; Antonyms: 96-190	☐
38	Synonyms: 219-327; Antonyms: 191-285	☐
39	Synonyms: 328-436; Antonyms: 286-380	☐
40	Synonyms: 437-545; Antonyms: 381-475	☐
41	Synonyms: 546-654; Antonyms: 476-570	☐
42	**Revision - Review all marked/circled words from Days 36-41**	☐
43	Synonyms: 655-763; Antonyms: 571-665	☐
44	Synonyms: 764-872; Antonyms: 666-760	☐
45	Synonyms: 873-981; Antonyms: 761-855	☐
46	Synonyms: 982-1090; Antonyms: 856-949	☐
47	Synonyms: 1091-1198; Antonyms: 950-1043	☐
48	Synonyms: 1199-1306; Antonyms: 1044-1137	☐
49	**Revision - Review all marked/circled words from Days 43-48**	☐
50	**Grand Revision - Go through ALL of Module I. Focus on circled words.**	☐

Module II - Other Exams + Spelling

After completing Module I, you move on to vocabulary frequently asked in other competitive exams like CDA, NDA, AFCAT, DDA, DSSSB, CUET, etc. This module also covers Spelling, which is fast to go through since you only need to spot the correct or incorrect spelling. Module II strengthens your preparation by exposing you to words that may appear in future SSC exams as well.

Day	Daily Tasks	☑ Done
51	A4: 1-33; B4: 1-25; C9: 1-50; E1: 1-213	☐
52	A4: 34-65; B4: 26-50; C9: 51-99; E1: 214-426	☐
53	A4: 66-97; B4: 51-75; C10: 1-72; E1: 427-639	☐
54	A4: 98-129; B4: 76-100; C10: 73-144; E1: 640-852	☐
55	A4: 130-161; B4: 101-125; C10: 145-216; E1: 853-1065	☐

56	A4: 162-193; B4: 126-149; C10: 217-288; E1: 1066-1278	☐
57	**Revision - Review all marked/circled words from Days 51-56**	☐
58	A4: 194-225; B4: 150-173; C10: 289-360; E1: 1279-1491	☐
59	A4: 226-257; B4: 174-197; C10: 361-431; E1: 1492-1704	☐
60	A4: 258-289; B4: 198-221; C10: 432-502; E1: 1705-1917	☐
61	A4: 290-321; B4: 222-245; C10: 503-573; E1: 1918-2130	☐
62	A4: 322-353; B4: 246-269; C10: 574-644; E1: 2131-2343	☐
63	A4: 354-385; B4: 270-293; C12: 1-82; E1: 2344-2556	☐
64	**Revision - Review all marked/circled words from Days 58-63**	☐
65	A4: 386-417; B4: 294-317; C12: 83-164; E1: 2557-2769	☐
66	A4: 418-449; B4: 318-341; C12: 165-245; E1: 2770-2982	☐
67	A4: 450-481; B4: 342-365; C12: 246-326; E1: 2983-3195	☐
68	A4: 482-513; B4: 366-389; C12: 327-407; E1: 3196-3407	☐
69	A4: 514-545; B4: 390-413; C12: 408-488; E1: 3408-3619	☐
70	**Grand Revision - Go through ALL of Module II. Focus on circled words.**	☐

Module III - Advanced Vocabulary Boosters

Module III is for students who have completed at least one thorough reading of Modules I and II. These topics serve as vocabulary boosters and are essential not only for improving your word power but also for understanding Reading Comprehension and Cloze test passages better. By mastering these lists, you will be better equipped to handle advanced vocabulary questions in various competitive exams.

Day	Daily Tasks	☑ Done
71	F1: 1-62; F2: 1-43; F3.2: 1-53; F4: 1-60; F5.2: 1-11; F6.2: 1-24	☐
72	F1: 63-124; F2: 44-86; F3.2: 54-106; F4: 61-120; F5.2: 12-22; F6.2: 25-48	☐
73	F1: 125-186; F2: 87-129; F3.2: 107-159; F4: 121-180; F5.2: 23-33; F6.2: 49-72	☐
74	F1: 187-247; F2: 130-172; F3.2: 160-212; F4: 181-240; F5.2: 34-44; F6.2: 73-96	☐
75	F1: 248-308; F2: 173-215; F3.2: 213-265; F4: 241-300; F5.2: 45-55; F6.2: 97-120	☐
76	F1: 309-369; F2: 216-258; F3.2: 266-317; F4: 301-360; F5.2: 56-66; F6.2: 121-144	☐
77	**Revision - Review all marked/circled words from Days 71-76**	☐
78	F1: 370-430; F2: 259-301; F3.2: 318-369; F4: 361-420; F5.2: 67-77; F6.2: 145-168	☐
79	F1: 431-491; F2: 302-344; F3.2: 370-421; F4: 421-480; F5.2: 78-88; F6.2: 169-192	☐
80	F1: 492-552; F2: 345-387; F3.2: 422-473; F4: 481-540; F5.2: 89-99; F6.2: 193-216	☐
81	F1: 553-613; F2: 388-430; F3.2: 474-525; F4: 541-600; F5.2: 100-110; F6.2: 217-240	☐
82	F1: 614-674; F2: 431-473; F3.2: 526-577; F4: 601-660; F5.2: 111-121; F6.2: 241-264	☐
83	F1: 675-735; F2: 474-516; F3.2: 578-629; F4: 661-720; F5.2: 122-132; F6.2: 265-288	☐
84	**Revision - Review all marked/circled words from Days 78-83**	☐
85	F1: 736-796; F2: 517-559; F3.2: 630-681; F4: 721-780; F5.2: 133-143; F6.2: 289-312	☐

Blackbook of English Vocabulary: **90 Days Study Plan**

86	F1: 797-857; F2: 560-602; F3.2: 682-733; F4: 781-840; F5.2: 144-153; F6.2: 313-336	☐
87	F1: 858-918; F2: 603-645; F3.2: 734-785; F4: 841-899; F5.2: 154-163; F6.2: 337-360	☐
88	F1: 919-979; F2: 646-688; F3.2: 786-837; F4: 900-958; F5.2: 164-173; F6.2: 361-384	☐
89	F1: 980-1040; F2: 689-730; F3.2: 838-889; F4: 959-1017; F5.2: 174-183; F6.2: 385-408	☐
90	**FINAL Grand Revision - Go through ALL three modules. Focus on circled words.**	☐

Tips

- You don't need to memorize every word. Focus only on the words you don't know. Most students already know 40-50 % of words per page.
- Circle or underline unfamiliar words as you read. These are your revision targets.
- Revision is everything. Spend at least 10 minutes daily revising previously marked words.
- Read each word list at least 3 times before the exam. First reading is for exposure, second for recognition, third for retention.
- If you miss a day, don't restart. Just continue from where you stopped. Consistency beats perfection.
- Test yourself regularly. Cover the answers and try to recall. Active recall is more effective than passive reading.
- This plan is a general guideline. Adjust the daily targets based on your speed and comfort level.

PART - A

(ONE WORD SUBSTITUTION)

Contents:-

Updated and Additional Content: -

1. **New SSC OWS:** Added new OWS from **417 sets** asked by SSC after the publication of the last edition (May 2024).
2. **Expanded OWS Coverage:** Added new OWS from 470 sets of other competitive exams. The 2026 edition now covers a total of 1,277 additional sets (470 + 807) from other exams since the 2023 edition.

Additional Symbols for smarter and efficient preparation: -

1. **#R (Repetition Count):** The #R tag, used to show how many times an OWS has been asked in competitive exams. The number **outside** the bracket shows SSC repetitions; the number **inside** the bracket shows repetitions across the additional 1,277 sets.
2. **Star Symbol (*):** Indicates the word has also been asked as a spelling question in SSC exams.
3. **Tilde Symbol (~):** Indicates the OWS has also been asked as a Synonyms or Antonyms question in SSC exams.

Blackbook's Proven Coverage:

Since the May 2024 edition, SSC and other exams asked approx.1,294 OWS in exams, out of which 1,090 were already present in Blackbook and only 204 were new. That's an impressive **84.2% coverage rate**, powered not just by SSC PYQs but also by our inclusion of other competitive exam vocabulary.

ONE WORD SUBSTITUTION (OWS)

Introduction

One Word Substitution means replacing a phrase or a group of words with a single word that conveys the same meaning. For example, "a book written by a person about their own life" is an Autobiography. "A person who cannot pay his debts" is Insolvent. "An inscription on a tombstone in memory of the dead" is an Epitaph. Instead of writing or saying the full phrase, one word does the job.

OWS is one of the most frequently asked topics in SSC and other competitive exams. It is asked in SSC, CDS, AFCAT, DSSSB and many other exams. Since the questions are direct and fact-based, this is one of the easiest areas to score if you have prepared well.

How Exams Test OWS

The question format is simple. You are given a phrase and asked to pick the correct one word from four options. Here are some real questions from recent SSC papers:

- *"An inscription on a tomb"* Options: espionage, epilogue, epitaph, elegy. Answer: Epitaph
- *"One who is skilled and eloquent in public speaking"* Options: narrator, orator, arbitrator, magistrate. Answer: Orator
- *"A drug or other substance that induces sleep"* Options: steroid, antibiotic, analgesic, sedative. Answer: Sedative
- *"One who walks in sleep"* Options: insomniac, somnambulist, somniloquist, narcissist. Answer: Somnambulist

How to Use This Chapter

This is not just a dictionary or a list of words. Every entry in this chapter has been carefully included based on real exam data, so you know exactly what to focus on and how much attention each word deserves. Here is how to read the symbols:

#R (Repetition Count): The number in the last column shows how many times that word has been asked in SSC exams. The number in brackets shows how many times it appeared in other exams like DSSSB, CDS, AFCAT etc. For example, if a word shows **8 (2)**, it means it was asked 8 times in SSC and 2 times in other exams. Higher the #R, more important the word. Words with high repetition count should be your top priority.

~ (Tilde Symbol): If you see a ~ next to the word, it means that word has also been asked as a Synonym or Antonym in previous exams. The detailed Synonym/Antonym coverage is in a separate chapter, but this marker is here to alert you that this word carries extra weight. Do not take it lightly.

*** (Asterisk on Serial Number):** Serial numbers marked with * and written in **bold** indicate that the word has also been asked as a spelling question in SSC exams. Since the word is already covered here, it has been removed from the Spelling chapter to avoid repetition. Pay special attention to the spelling of these words.

These features are what make this book different from any other vocabulary resource available. You are not just reading a list; you are looking at real exam data telling you exactly what matters and how much. This is one of the key reasons why many toppers, including many Rank 1 holders, have preferred Blackbook as their primary source for vocabulary preparation.

A1 Top 200 OWS (asked in SSC Exams)

SN	Phrases	One Word (PoS)	Hindi	#R
1*	An inscription on a tombstone in memory of the person who has died	**Epitaph (N.)**	समाधि-लेख, स्मृति-लेख	19 (11)
2*	A person who loves mankind and donates money and time to help others	**Philanthropist (N.)~**	मानव प्रेमी; परोपकारी	20 (10)
3*	Something no longer in use	**Obsolete (Adj.)~**	अप्रचलित	19 (9)
4*	A person who endures pain or hardship without showing feelings or complaining	**Stoic (N.)~**	सुख-दुख में समान रहने वाला	18 (10)
5*	One who does not believe in the existence of God	**Atheist (N.)~**	नास्तिक	19 (7)
6*	A speech or presentation made without previous preparation	**Extempore (N.)**	बिना तैयारी के	15 (10)
7	A person who can speak several languages	**Polyglot (N.)**	बहुभाषी	10 (15)
8*	A place for keeping birds in a confined space	**Aviary (N.)**	पक्षीशाला, पक्षी-घर	15 (9)
9	An extreme fear of confined or enclosed spaces	**Claustrophobia (N.)**	बंद या छोटी जगह का भय	15 (8)
10*	Difficult or impossible to read	**Illegible (Adj.)**	अपठनीय	15 (8)
11	A person who loves or collects books	**Bibliophile (N.)~**	पुस्तक प्रेमी	14 (8)
12	An imagined perfect society where everything is ideal	**Utopia (N.)**	आदर्श काल्पनिक समाज	20 (2)
13	A solution for all difficulties or diseases	**Panacea (N.)~**	रामबाण इलाज	16 (5)
14	A person who draws or makes maps	**Cartographer (N.)**	मानचित्रकार	13 (7)
15*	Something that cannot be avoided; certain to happen	**Inevitable (Adj.)~**	अटल	13 (7)
16*	Belonging to or living in the same time period as another	**Contemporary (N.)~**	समकालीन	13 (6)
17*	A person having excessive admiration for oneself, especially one's appearance	**Narcissist (N.)**	आत्ममुग्ध व्यक्ति (स्वयं से अत्यधिक प्रेम करने वाला)	11 (8)
18*	A person who never takes alcoholic drinks	**Teetotaller (N.)**	शराब न पीने वाला व्यक्ति	11 (8)
19	The place where public, government or historical records are kept	**Archive (N.)**	अभिलेखागार	10 (8)
20*	A person who eats human flesh	**Cannibal (N.)**	नरभक्षक	14 (4)
21*	One who is difficult to please	**Fastidious (Adj.)~**	बारीकियों पर अत्यधिक ध्यान देने वाला; बहुत चुनींदा	10 (8)
22*	A person who attacks or criticizes cherished beliefs or institutions	**Iconoclast (N.)~**	स्थापित मान्यताओं का विरोधी	12 (6)
23*	One who cannot make mistakes	**Infallible (Adj.)~**	अचूक	12 (6)
24*	A person who hates and avoids other people	**Misanthrope (N.)**	मानवद्वेषी	10 (8)

[**#R** denotes repetition of word]

[E.g. in SN 13, #R- **16 (5)** denotes this word has been asked 16 times in SSC and 5 times in other exams]

SN	Phrases	One Word (PoS)	Hindi	#R
25	A form of government by a small group of people	**Oligarchy (N.)**	अल्पतंत्र (कुछ लोगों का शासन)	8 (10)
26*	Knowing everything	**Omniscient (Adj.)~**	सर्वज्ञानी	12 (6)
27*	An arrangement of events or dates in the order of their occurrence	**Chronology (N.)**	कालक्रम	11 (6)
28*	Unable to be corrected or reformed	**Incorrigible (Adj.)~**	असंशोधनीय (जो कभी न सुधर सके)	15 (2)
29	One who is unable to pay debts	**Insolvent (Adj.)~**	दिवालिया	6 (11)
30	A person who writes and edits dictionaries	**Lexicographer (N.)**	शब्दकोश निर्माता	12 (5)
31	A person who believes that laws and governments are not necessary	**Anarchist (N.)**	अराजकतावादी	8 (8)
32*	A place where weapons and military equipment are stored	**Arsenal (N.)**	शस्त्रागार	8 (8)
33*	The scientific study of insects	**Entomology (N.)**	कीटविज्ञान	11 (5)
34*	A soldier who fights for any country that pays them	**Mercenary (N.)**	किराये का सैनिक	9 (7)
35	A person who collects or studies stamps	**Philatelist (N.)**	डाक-टिकट संग्रहकर्ता	10 (6)
36*	Having many different skills	**Versatile (Adj.)~**	बहुमुखी (अनेक कार्यों में निपुण)	9 (7)
37	A person who selflessly works for the welfare of others	**Altruist (N.)~**	परोपकारी	11 (4)
38*	One who engages in an activity for pleasure rather than as a profession	**Amateur (N.)~**	शौकिया व्यक्ति	12 (3)
39	Able to use both the left and right hands equally well	**Ambidextrous (Adj.)**	उभयहस्त (दोनों हाथों से समान रूप से काम करने वाला)	12 (3)
40	The story of a person's life written by someone else	**Biography (N.)**	जीवनी	6 (9)
41	The art of beautiful handwriting	**Calligraphy (N.)**	सुलेख	8 (7)
42*	A person employed to drive a private or hired car	**Chauffeur (N.)**	मोटर-चालक	9 (6)
43*	A person who believes that all events are predetermined and inevitable	**Fatalist (N.)**	भाग्यवादी	11 (4)
44	The deliberate killing of a large group of people, especially of a particular nation or ethnic group	**Genocide (N.)**	नरसंहार	11 (4)
45*	Living in groups; tending to associate with others of one's kind	**Gregarious (Adj.)~**	झुण्ड में रहनेवाला, मिलनसार	12 (3)
46*	A sentimental longing for a period in the past	**Nostalgia (N.)~**	पुरानी यादों की तड़प	11 (4)
47	Having unlimited power	**Omnipotent (Adj.)~**	सर्वशक्तिमान	9 (6)
48	A government by the richest people of a country	**Plutocracy (N.)**	धनी लोगों का शासन	9 (6)

SN* (Bold Serial no with * asterisk symbol): Word appeared as a spelling question

~ (Tilde Symbol) next to a word: It appeared as a synonym or antonym question

SN	Phrases	One Word (PoS)	Hindi	#R
49*	Occurring, awarded, or appearing after someone's death	**Posthumous (Adj.)**	मरणोपरांत	8 (7)
50*	A person who lives alone and avoids other people	**Recluse (N.)~**	एकांतवासी	9 (6)
51	An animal that can live both on land and in water	**Amphibian (N.)**	उभयचर जन्तु (जल और स्थल दोनों में रहने वाला जीव)	9 (5)
52*	The study of human history and prehistory through the excavation of sites	**Archaeology (N.)**	पुरातत्व शास्त्र	8 (6)
53*	One who practises severe self-discipline and abstains from bodily pleasures	**Ascetic (N.)~**	तपस्वी व्यक्ति	7 (7)
54	A book written by a person about their own life	**Autobiography (N.)**	आत्मकथा	11 (3)
55*	A person who has expert knowledge and refined taste in a particular subject	**Connoisseur (N.)~**	किसी विषय का पारखी व्यक्ति	8 (6)
56*	A sound that cannot be heard	**Inaudible (Adj.)**	अश्राव्य, सुनाई न देने वाला	11 (3)
57*	A mental condition where a person feels an uncontrollable urge to steal	**Kleptomania (N.)**	चोरी करने की मानसिक बीमारी	8 (6)
58*	A state of disorder due to absence of government or authority	**Anarchy (N.)**	अव्यवस्था, अराजकता	10 (3)
59*	A person who leaves his country to live in another	**Emigrant (N.)**	देश छोड़कर जाने वाला	11 (2)
60*	Lasting for a very short time	**Ephemeral (Adj.)~**	क्षणिक, थोड़े समय के लिए	8 (5)
61*	One who eats excessively	**Glutton (N.)**	अत्यधिक भोजन करने वाला	11 (2)
62*	Holding an office or position as an honour without payment	**Honorary (Adj.)**	अवैतनिक	6 (7)
63	A person who imagines illness or is abnormally anxious about health	**Hypochondriac (N.)**	रोगभ्रमी	7 (6)
64*	A person more focused on their own thoughts than social interaction	**Introvert (N.)~**	अन्तर्मुखी व्यक्ति	8 (5)
65	A place where money is coined by authority of the government	**Mint (N.)**	टकसाल	11 (2)
66*	A person who studies or collects coins	**Numismatist (N.)**	मुद्राशास्त्री	8 (5)
67*	A piece of land or garden in which fruit trees are grown	**Orchard (N.)**	फलदार पेड़ों का बाग	8 (5)
68*	Safe or suitable for drinking	**Potable (Adj.)**	पीने योग्य	7 (6)
69	The killing of a king	**Regicide (N.)**	राज-हत्या	7 (6)
70*	One who walks in sleep	**Somnambulist (N.)**	नींद में चलने वाला	8 (5)
71*	A person who helps another commit a crime; a partner in crime	**Accomplice (N.)**	सह-अपराधी	9 (3)
72	One who is not sure about God's existence	**Agnostic (N.)~**	ईश्वर के बारे में संशयवादी व्यक्ति	3 (9)
73*	The study of human societies, cultures, and their development	**Anthropology (N.)**	मानव विज्ञान	7 (5)

SN	Phrases	One Word (PoS)	Hindi	#R
74*	A government by one person having absolute power	**Autocracy (N.)**	तानाशाही (एक व्यक्ति का निरंकुश शासन)	9 (3)
75	A group of stars that forms a shape in the sky and has a name	**Constellation (N.)**	नक्षत्र (तारों का समूह)	8 (4)
76*	To free somebody from all blame	**Exonerate (V.)~**	दोषमुक्त करना	7 (5)
77*	A person who walks on foot rather than travelling in a vehicle	**Pedestrian (N.)**	पैदल यात्री	8 (4)
78*	The scientific study of sound	**Acoustics (N.)**	ध्वनि-विज्ञान	9 (2)
79*	A place where bees are kept	**Apiary (N.)**	मधुमक्खियों के पालने का स्थान	5 (6)
80	A person who renounces religious or political beliefs	**Apostate (N.)**	धर्म या विश्वास को त्यागने वाला व्यक्ति	7 (4)
81*	A government by the nobles or the highest social class	**Aristocracy (N.)**	श्रेष्ठ जनों का शासन	6 (5)
82*	Hard but easily broken	**Brittle (Adj.)~**	भंगुर, आसानी से टूटने योग्य	9 (2)
83*	A keeper or custodian of a museum or other collection	**Curator (N.)**	संग्रहालय का संरक्षक	7 (4)
84	A poem expressing sorrow for the dead	**Elegy (N.)**	शोकगीत	7 (4)
85	An extreme or irrational fear of water, especially as a symptom of rabies	**Hydrophobia (N.)**	पानी का डर	8 (3)
86*	A person who pretends to be what they are not	**Hypocrite (N.)**	पाखंडी	9 (2)
87	That which cannot be conquered	**Invincible (Adj.)~**	अजेय	6 (5)
88*	A plan of a journey, including the route and the places to be visited	**Itinerary (N.)**	यात्रा कार्यक्रम	7 (4)
89	A document or book written by hand before being printed	**Manuscript (N.)**	हस्तलिखित (हाथ से लिखी हुई)	6 (5)
90*	A person who hates women	**Misogynist (N.)**	स्त्री से घृणा करने वाला	7 (4)
91	The practice of giving unfair advantages to one's relatives	**Nepotism (N.)~**	भाई-भतीजावाद	8 (3)
92*	Well-known for being bad; a person of evil reputation	**Notorious (Adj.)~**	कुख्यात	10 (1)
93*	A person who is new to a profession, without training or experience	**Novice (N.)~**	नौसिखिया	5 (6)
94	The study or collection of coins	**Numismatics (N.)**	मुद्राशास्त्र	6 (5)
95*	One who sees the bright side of things	**Optimist (N.)~**	आशावादी	8 (3)
96*	A person who tends to see the worst aspect of situations	**Pessimist (N.)~**	निराशावादी	9 (2)
97*	Unwilling to speak about one's thoughts or feelings	**Reticent (Adj.)~**	कम बोलने वाला	6 (5)
98*	A speech in which a person talks to themselves, especially in a play	**Soliloquy (N.)**	स्वयं से बोला गया संवाद	5 (6)
99*	One who freely offers to do something	**Volunteer (N.)**	स्वयं सेवक	6 (5)
100*	Open to more than one interpretation	**Ambiguous (Adj.)~**	अस्पष्ट, अनेकार्थी	8 (2)

SN	Phrases	One Word (PoS)	Hindi	#R
101*	A partial or total loss of memory	**Amnesia (N.)**	भूलने की बीमारी	6 (4)
102*	Having an unknown or withheld name or identity	**Anonymous (Adj.)~**	बेनाम, गुमनाम	6 (4)
103*	A person appointed by two parties to settle a dispute	**Arbitrator (N.)**	पंच, मध्यस्थ	6 (4)
104*	A person trained to travel in a spacecraft	**Astronaut (N.)**	अन्तरिक्ष यात्री	7 (3)
105	The act of speaking disrespectfully about sacred or religious things	**Blasphemy (N.)**	ईश्वर की निंदा	9 (1)
106*	A group of travellers journeying together across a desert; a shelter of a gypsy	**Caravan (N.)**	काफिला	8 (2)
107*	A systematic list of items or publications	**Catalogue (N.)**	सूची	8 (2)
108*	A person who regards the whole world as their country	**Cosmopolitan (Adj.)**	सर्वदेशीय	7 (3)
109*	Ready to believe things too easily	**Credulous (Adj.)~**	भोला-भाला	6 (4)
110*	A person who believes people act only from self-interest	**Cynic (N.)**	निंदक, संदेहवादी व्यक्ति	6 (4)
111	A short speech at the end of a play	**Epilogue (N.)**	उपसंहार	6 (4)
112	A formal expression of praise for someone who has died	**Eulogy (N.)~**	प्रशंसा भाषण (अक्सर मृत्यु के बाद)	5 (5)
113	A person who sells and arranges cut flowers	**Florist (N.)**	फूलवाला	9 (1)
114*	Excessively talkative, especially on trivial matters	**Garrulous (Adj.)~**	बातूनी	5 (5)
115*	One who is easily deceived	**Gullible (Adj.)~**	भोला भाला	8 (2)
116*	Unable to read or write	**Illiterate (Adj.)**	अनपढ़	8 (2)
117	The scientific study of birds	**Ornithology (N.)**	पक्षी विज्ञान	3 (7)
118	A person who opposes war or use of military force	**Pacifist (N.)~**	शांतिवादी	8 (2)
119*	The act of using another person's ideas or work as one's own	**Plagiarism (N.)**	साहित्यिक चोरी	5 (5)
120*	The scientific study of the mind and behaviour	**Psychology (N.)**	मनोविज्ञान	9 (1)
121	A large number of fish swimming together	**Shoal (N.)**	मछलियों का झुंड	8 (2)
122	In exactly the same words as were used originally	**Verbatim (Adj.)~**	शब्द-प्रतिशब्द हूबहू	7 (3)
123	A person who is long experienced or practiced in an activity	**Veteran (N.)~**	अनुभवी	8 (2)
124*	The money paid regularly to a former spouse after divorce	**Alimony (N.)**	भूतपूर्व साथी को दिया जाने वाला गुजारा भत्ता	7 (2)
125*	A glass tank where fish and water plants are kept	**Aquarium (N.)**	मछलीघर	7 (2)
126*	Able to speak two languages	**Bilingual (Adj.)**	द्विभाषिक	5 (4)
127*	A funeral procession	**Cortege (N.)**	शव-यात्रा	2 (7)
128	The scientific study of the skin and its diseases	**Dermatology (N.)**	त्वचा विज्ञान	7 (2)

SN	Phrases	One Word (PoS)	Hindi	#R
129*	A man behaving more like a woman than a man	**Effeminate (Adj.)~**	नारी जैसा	6 (3)
130	A widespread outbreak of a disease affecting many people at the same time	**Epidemic (N.)~**	महामारी	5 (4)
131	A person motivated by irrational enthusiasm	**Fanatic (N.)~**	कट्टरपंथी	3 (6)
132	A building in which aircraft are housed	**Hangar (N.)**	विमानशाला	9
133	A person who believes that pleasure is the most important thing in life	**Hedonist (N.)**	सुखवादी	3 (6)
134*	A system of government by a king or queen	**Monarchy (N.)**	राज-तंत्र	6 (3)
135	A place for keeping dead bodies before burial or cremation	**Mortuary (N.)**	शवगृह	5 (4)
136	A notice of a person's death	**Obituary (N.)**	मृत्यु सूचना	7 (2)
137*	That through which light cannot pass	**Opaque (Adj.)~**	अपारदर्शी	8 (1)
138	The belief that God is in everything, including nature	**Pantheism (N.)**	सर्वेश्वरवाद	4 (5)
139*	The violation or misuse of something regarded as sacred	**Sacrilege (N.)~**	अपवित्रीकरण	7 (2)
140	An extreme fear of heights	**Acrophobia (N.)**	ऊँचाई का डर	4 (4)
141	A short, interesting or amusing story about a real person or event	**Anecdote (N.)**	वास्तविक घटना पर आधारित छोटी कहानी	7 (1)
142	One who studies the evolution and development of human societies and cultures	**Anthropologist (N.)**	मानव-विज्ञान का अध्ययन करने वाला	4 (4)
143	The scientific study of celestial bodies	**Astronomy (N.)**	खगोलशास्त्र	6 (2)
144	One who officially examines financial accounts or records	**Auditor (N.)**	लेखा परीक्षक (हिसाब किताब की जांच करने वाला)	6 (2)
145	One who is unable to pay his debts	**Bankrupt (N.)~**	दिवालिया	5 (3)
146	The scientific study of plants and their structure	**Botany (N.)**	वनस्पति विज्ञान	6 (2)
147*	An arrangement of flowers that is usually given as a present	**Bouquet (N.)**	गुलदस्ता	7 (1)
148*	A person with whom one works in a profession or business	**Colleague (N.)~**	सहकर्मी	5 (3)
149*	A group of people gathered for religious worship	**Congregation (N.)~**	धार्मिक सभा	6 (2)
150*	A centre of attraction or attention	**Cynosure (N.)**	आकर्षण-बिंदु	3 (5)
151*	The study of population and its dynamics	**Demography (N.)**	जनसांख्यिकी	7 (1)
152	A doctor who studies and treats skin diseases	**Dermatologist (N.)**	त्वचा रोग विशेषज्ञ	3 (5)
153*	Fit or suitable to be eaten	**Edible (Adj.)~**	खाने योग्य	7 (1)
154*	Causing or ending in death	**Fatal (Adj.)~**	घातक	6 (2)
155*	A person who has escaped from captivity or is in hiding	**Fugitive (N.)~**	भगोड़ा	6 (2)

SN	Phrases	One Word (PoS)	Hindi	#R
156	The scientific study of the Earth, including its structure, rocks, and soil	**Geology (N.)**	भूगर्भशास्त्र	4 (4)
157*	The study of growing garden plants	**Horticulture (N.)**	उद्यान-विज्ञान	7 (1)
158*	Extraordinary or unbelievable	**Incredible (Adj.)~**	अविश्वसनीय	6 (2)
159*	Incapable of feeling tired or exhausted	**Indefatigable (Adj.)~**	न थकने वाला	6 (2)
160	The condition of being unable to sleep over a period of time	**Insomnia (N.)**	अनिद्रा	6 (2)
161*	A person who supervises during an examination	**Invigilator (N.)**	परीक्षा पर्यवेक्षक	7 (1)
162	One who is killed for the cause of religion or faith	**Martyr (N.)**	शहीद	6 (2)
163	A place where dead bodies are kept for identification	**Morgue (N.)**	मुर्दा घर	3 (5)
164*	A person who lacks interest in art, culture, or refined ideas	**Philistine (N.)~**	कला-संस्कृति के प्रति उदासीन व्यक्ति	7 (1)
165	The practice of having more than one husband at the same time	**Polyandry (N.)**	बहुपति प्रथा	3 (5)
166*	An introduction to a literary work	**Prologue (N.)**	प्रस्तावना	4 (4)
167*	A false name used by an author instead of their real one	**Pseudonym (N.)**	उपनाम	7 (1)
168	Not connected with religious or spiritual matters	**Secular (Adj.)**	धर्म निरपेक्ष	4 (4)
169	The study of the nature of God and religious beliefs	**Theology (N.)**	धर्मशास्त्र (धार्मिक विश्वास का अध्ययन)	6 (2)
170	One who lends money at unreasonably high interest	**Usurer (N.)**	सूदखोर	6 (2)
171	A decorative ring of flowers and leaves	**Wreath (N.)**	फूलों की माला	5 (3)
172*	To give up one's authority or throne	**Abdicate (V.)~**	अपना पद (या दावा) छोड़ देना	7
173*	Concerned with beauty or the appreciation of beauty	**Aesthetic (Adj.)~**	सौंदर्य संबंधी	4 (3)
174	A list of items to be discussed at a meeting	**Agenda (N.)**	कार्यसूची	5 (2)
175	An extreme fear of open or public places	**Agoraphobia (N.)**	खुले या भीड़भाड़ वाले सार्वजनिक स्थानों का भय	2 (5)
176*	An annual calendar containing astronomical data and important dates	**Almanac (N.)**	पंचांग	2 (5)
177*	An official pardon granted to a group of people, especially for political offences	**Amnesty (N.)**	सरकारी क्षमा	6 (1)
178*	A medicine to counteract the effect of poison	**Antidote (N.)**	विष नाशक	7
179*	Living or growing in or near water	**Aquatic (Adj.)**	जलीय	7
180	A place of refuge or safety; an institution for the mentally ill	**Asylum (N.)**	शरणस्थल, मानसिक चिकित्सालय	5 (2)
181	A place where soldiers are stationed	**Barracks (N.)**	सैनिकों के लिए बने घर	7
182*	A government run by officials in a state	**Bureaucracy (N.)**	नौकरशाहों का शासन	5 (2)

SN	Phrases	One Word (PoS)	Hindi	#R
183*	A harsh, discordant mixture of sounds	**Cacophony (N.)~**	कोलाहल, कर्कश ध्वनि	5 (2)
184	A doctor specialising in the study or treatment of heart diseases	**Cardiologist (N.)**	हृदय रोग विशेषज्ञ	5 (2)
185*	Feeding on the flesh of other animals	**Carnivorous (Adj.)**	मांसाहारी	4 (3)
186*	Gradual recovery of health and strength after illness	**Convalescence (N.)**	स्वास्थ्य लाभ (बीमारी से ठीक होने की प्रक्रिया)	6 (1)
187	A government by the people through elected representatives	**Democracy (N.)**	जनता द्वारा चुने गए प्रतिनिधियों का शासन	5 (2)
188*	A large bedroom for a number of people in a school or institution	**Dormitory (N.)**	शयनागार	5 (2)
189*	The ability to understand and share another person's feelings	**Empathy (N.)~**	सहानुभूति (दूसरे की भावना समझने की क्षमता)	3 (4)
190*	The plants and vegetation of a particular region	**Flora (N.)**	किसी क्षेत्र की वनस्पति	5 (2)
191	The killing of one's brother	**Fratricide (N.)**	भ्रातृहत्या	5 (2)
192*	A person who enjoys eating and often eats too much	**Gourmand (N.)**	अधिक खाने वाला भोजन-प्रेमी	2 (5)
193	A person who dishonestly pretends to be someone else in order to deceive	**Impostor (N.)**	ढोंगी (खुद को कोई और बताकर धोखा देने वाला)	6 (1)
194*	That which catches fire easily	**Inflammable (Adj.)**	ज्वलनशील	7
195*	Unable to be satisfied	**Insatiable (Adj.)~**	जिसकी इच्छा कभी पूरी न हो	6 (1)
196*	That which cannot be called back or reversed	**Irrevocable (Adj.)~**	जिसे बदला न जा सके	7
197	A small shelter for a dog	**Kennel (N.)**	कुत्ता-घर	4 (3)
198	Eating both plants and meat	**Omnivorous (Adj.)**	सर्वाहारी	4 (3)
199*	The art of persuasive speaking or writing	**Rhetoric (N.)**	वाक्पटुता, दिखावटी भाषा	3 (4)
200	One who helps a person in need	**Samaritan (N.)**	दूसरों की निस्वार्थ सहायता करने वाला	5 (2)

*Total **200** OWS asked **2378** times*

A2 All One Word Substitutions (OWS) (asked in SSC Exams)

SN	Phrases	One Word (PoS)	Hindi	#R
1*	To become less intense or widespread	**Abate (V.)~**	कम होना, घटना	
2	A place where animals are slaughtered for consumption as food	**Abattoir (N.)**	कसाईखाना	5 (1)
3	The head of a monastery	Abbot (N.)	मठ का प्रमुख	
4	A shortened form of a word or phrase	**Abbreviation (N.)**	संक्षिप्त रूप	4
5*	To give up one's authority or throne	**Abdicate (V.)~**	अपना पद (या दावा) छोड़ देना	7
6	The act of giving up the throne or authority	**Abdication (N.)**	अपने अधिकार अथवा पद का त्याग	3 (3)
7*	Deviation from the right course	**Aberration (N.)~**	असामान्यता, भटकाव	
8*	A state of temporary suspension or inactivity	**Abeyance (N.)~**	रुकी हुई स्थिति (अस्थायी)	1 (1)
9	The act of washing oneself, especially as a religious rite	**Ablution (N.)~**	धार्मिक कार्य के लिए शुद्धि-स्नान	
10	To renounce or give up a right or belief	**Abnegate (V.)~**	त्याग करना	
11*	To formally put an end to a system, practice, or institution	**Abolish (V.)~**	समाप्त करना	4
12*	Relating to the original inhabitants of a place	**Aboriginal (Adj.)~**	मूल निवासियों से संबंधित	
13	The original inhabitant or native of a country	**Aborigine (N.)**	मूल निवासी	4
14*	To shorten a piece of writing without losing the sense	**Abridge (V.)~**	संक्षिप्त करना	
15	A shortened version of a larger work	Abridgement (N.)	संक्षिप्त संस्करण	
16*	To cancel or do away with a law or agreement	**Abrogate (V.)~**	निरस्त या रद्द कर देना	
17	To go away suddenly and secretly in order to escape from somewhere	**Abscond (V.)~**	फरार होना	3 (1)
18	The formal forgiveness of a person's sins	Absolution (N.)	पापमुक्ति, क्षमादान	
19*	Wildly unreasonable, illogical or ridiculous	**Absurd (Adj.)~**	बेतुका	
20	A deep and seemingly bottomless pit or hole	**Abyss (N.)~**	बहुत गहरी खाई	
21*	To increase the speed	**Accelerate (V.)~**	गति बढ़ाना	2
22	An unexpected event that causes injury or death	Accident (N.)	दुर्घटना	
23*	An award, honour, or laudatory notice granted as special recognition	**Accolade (N.)~**	पुरस्कार, सम्मान	
24*	A person who helps another commit a crime; a partner in crime	**Accomplice (N.)**	सह-अपराधी	9 (3)
25*	The successful completion of a task or goal	Accomplishment (N.)	उपलब्धि; काम का पूरा होना	

[**#R** denotes repetition of word]

[E.g. in SN 24, #R- **9 (3)** denotes this word has been asked 9 times in SSC and 3 times in other exams]

SN	Phrases	One Word (PoS)	Hindi	#R
26	To be harmonious or consistent with	**Accord (V.)~**	सहमत होना	
27*	A person whose profession is to keep and inspect financial records	Accountant (N.)	मुनीम, लेखपाल	
28*	Sharp and bitter in speech or temperament	**Acerbic (Adj.)~**	कड़वा (स्वभाव या भाषा में)	1 (1)
29*	The scientific study of sound	**Acoustics (N.)**	ध्वनि-विज्ञान	9 (2)
30*	To decide and state officially in court that somebody is not guilty of a crime	**Acquit (V.)~**	बरी (दोषमुक्त) कर देना	3
31*	A judgement that a person is not guilty of the crime they were charged with	**Acquittal (N.)**	दोषमुक्त किया जाना	1 (1)
32	A person who performs difficult gymnastic feats for entertainment	**Acrobat (N.)**	कलाबाज़	4
33	A word formed from the initial letters of other words and pronounced as a word	**Acronym (N.)**	शब्दों के पहले अक्षरों से बना शब्द	5 (1)
34	An extreme fear of heights	**Acrophobia (N.)**	ऊँचाई का डर	4 (4)
35	Giving cause for legal proceedings	Actionable (Adj.)	कानूनी कार्यवाही करने योग्य	
36*	The ability to make good judgements and take quick decisions	**Acumen (N.)~**	कुशाग्र बुद्धि	2
37*	A person who is unable to stop using a harmful substance	**Addict (N.)**	नशेड़ी	2 (1)
38*	To speak formally; to deliver a speech (V.); Details of a person's location or contact place (N.)	Address (V./N.)	संबोधित करना; भाषण देना; पता	
39*	To believe in and follow a rule, belief, or plan	**Adhere (V.)~**	पालन करना	
40*	The period between the beginning of puberty and adulthood	**Adolescence (N.)**	किशोरावस्था	5 (1)
41	An extremely handsome young man	Adonis (N.)	खूबसूरत नौजवान	
42	Extremely attractive and lovable	Adorable (Adj.)	बेहद प्यारा	
43*	To make impure by adding inferior substances	**Adulterate (V.)~**	मिलावट करना	
44*	Willing to take risks and try new ideas	**Adventurous (Adj.)~**	साहसिक	
45*	A person who publicly supports or speaks in favour of a cause; a lawyer	**Advocate (N.)~**	समर्थक, वकील	
46*	Existing or living in the air	**Aerial (Adj.)**	हवाई	2
47	An irrational and intense fear of flying	Aerophobia (N.)	हवाई यात्रा से डर	
48	A person who has a strong appreciation for beauty and art	**Aesthete (N.)**	सौंदर्य-प्रेमी (व्यक्ति)	1 (1)
49*	Concerned with beauty or the appreciation of beauty	**Aesthetic (Adj.)~**	सौंदर्य संबंधी	4 (3)
50	The study of beauty and art	Aesthetics (N.)	सौंदर्यशास्त्र	
51*	A written statement confirmed by oath, for use as evidence in court	**Affidavit (N.)**	शपथ पत्र	1 (3)
52	A list of items to be discussed at a meeting	**Agenda (N.)**	कार्यसूची	5 (2)
53	To increase the importance, position or wealth	**Aggrandize (V.)~**	वृद्धि करना (शक्ति, संपत्ति या पद)	1 (1)
54*	Hostile and ready to attack or quarrel	**Aggressive (Adj.)~**	आक्रामक	2

SN* (Bold Serial no with * asterisk symbol): Word appeared as a spelling question

~ (Tilde Symbol) next to a word: It appeared as a synonym or antonym question

SN	Phrases	One Word (PoS)	Hindi	#R
55	One who is not sure about God's existence	**Agnostic (N.)~**	ईश्वर के बारे में संशयवादी व्यक्ति	3 (9)
56*	Extreme mental or physical suffering	**Agony (N.)~**	अत्यधिक पीड़ा	3
57	An extreme fear of open or public places	**Agoraphobia (N.)**	खुले या भीड़भाड़ वाले सार्वजनिक स्थानों का भय	2 (5)
58	A blank book for keeping a collection of photographs, stamps, or pictures	Album (N.)	चित्र संग्रह की किताब	
59	A medieval practice aimed at transforming base metals into gold	**Alchemy (N.)**	धातु-परिवर्तन कला, पारस विद्या	2 (2)
60	A substance for killing algae	Algaecide (N.)	शैवालनाशक	
61	An extreme fear of pain	**Algophobia (N.)**	दर्द का भय	1 (1)
62*	A person from a foreign country; a fictional being from another world	**Alien (N.)~**	विदेशी, परग्रही	4
63*	The money paid regularly to a former spouse after divorce	**Alimony (N.)**	भूतपूर्व साथी को दिया जाने वाला गुजारा भत्ता	7 (2)
64*	A story with a hidden moral or symbolic meaning	**Allegory (N.)**	छिपे नैतिक अर्थ वाली कथा	3 (1)
65*	The repetition of the same initial sound in nearby words	**Alliteration (N.)**	अनुप्रास अलंकार	4
66	A combination of two or more metals mixed together	Alloy (N.)	मिश्रधातु	
67	The soil deposited by flowing water	Alluvium (N.)	जलोढ़ मिट्टी	
68	The school or college in which one has been educated	**Alma Mater (N.)**	संस्थान जहाँ से शिक्षा प्राप्त की	2 (1)
69*	An annual calendar containing astronomical data and important dates	**Almanac (N.)**	पंचांग	2 (5)
70	The sport of climbing high mountains	Alpinism (N.)	पर्वतारोहण	
71*	A table or flat surface where offerings are made to a deity	**Altar (N.)**	पूजास्थल की वेदी	1 (1)
72	An instrument that measures altitude	Altimeter (N.)	ऊँचाई नापने का यंत्र	
73*	The height of an object or point above sea level	**Altitude (N.)**	ऊँचाई	2
74	A person who selflessly works for the welfare of others	**Altruist (N.)~**	परोपकारी	11 (4)
75*	Former students of a school, college or university	**Alumni (N.)**	भूतपूर्व छात्र	2
76*	One who engages in an activity for pleasure rather than as a profession	**Amateur (N.)~**	शौकिया व्यक्ति	12 (3)
77	An extreme fear of riding in vehicles	Amaxophobia (N.)	वाहनों का डर	
78*	A diplomatic representative of one's country in another country	**Ambassador (N.)**	राजदूत	2 (1)
79	Able to use both the left and right hands equally well	**Ambidextrous (Adj.)**	उभयहस्त (दोनों हाथों से समान रूप से काम करने वाला)	12 (3)
80	The character and atmosphere of a place	**Ambience (N.)**	वातावरण, माहौल	1 (1)

SN	Phrases	One Word (PoS)	Hindi	#R
81	A word or design that retains meaning when rotated or reflected	Ambigram (N.)	घुमाने या पलटने पर भी अर्थपूर्ण दिखने वाला शब्द-चित्र	
82*	Open to more than one interpretation	**Ambiguous (Adj.)~**	अस्पष्ट, अनेकार्थी	8 (2)
83	Having mixed or conflicting feelings about something	**Ambivalent (Adj.)~**	दुविधाग्रस्त (विरोधी भावनाओं वाला)	
84	A person who has both introverted and extroverted qualities	**Ambivert (N.)**	अंतर्मुखी और बहिर्मुखी दोनों गुणों वाला व्यक्ति	3
85	To walk slowly and in a relaxed way	**Amble (V.)~**	धीरे-धीरे टहलना	2 (2)
86	To make (something bad or unsatisfactory) better	**Ameliorate (V.)~**	बेहतर बनाना	1 (1)
87*	Readily willing to be guided or controlled	**Amenable (Adj.)**	बात या सलाह मानने को तैयार	2
88	A facility or feature that provides comfort or convenience	Amenity (N.)	सुख-सुविधा	
89*	Characterized by friendliness and absence of discord	**Amicable (Adj.)~**	मैत्रीपूर्ण, सौहार्दपूर्ण	
90	In a friendly and peaceable manner	Amicably (Adv.)	मैत्रीपूर्ण तरीके से	
91	An instrument for measuring electric current	Ammeter (N.)	विद्युत धारा मापने का यंत्र	
92*	A partial or total loss of memory	**Amnesia (N.)**	भूलने की बीमारी	6 (4)
93*	An official pardon granted to a group of people, especially for political offences	**Amnesty (N.)**	सरकारी क्षमा	6 (1)
94	Not following any moral rules and not caring about right or wrong	**Amoral (Adj.)**	नैतिकता से परे	2 (1)
95	An animal that can live both on land and in water	**Amphibian (N.)**	उभयचर जन्तु (जल और स्थल दोनों में रहने वाला जीव)	9 (5)
96	A person who has had one or more limbs removed	Amputee (N.)	जिसका हाथ या पैर काटा जा चुका हो	
97	A medical specialist who administers drugs for relieving pain during surgery	**Anaesthetist (N.)**	बेहोशी की दवा देने वाला चिकित्सक	2
98	A word or phrase formed by rearranging the letters of another word	**Anagram (N.)**	अक्षरों को पुनर्व्यवस्थित कर बना नया शब्द	2
99	A narration of past events inserted into the current storyline	Analepsis (N.)	कहानी में अतीत की घटना दिखाना	
100	A substance that relieves pain	**Analgesic (N.)**	दर्दनाशक दवा	1 (1)
101*	A comparison showing similarity between two different things	**Analogy (N.)~**	समानता के आधार पर तुलना	2
102*	A detailed examination of something complex	**Analysis (N.)**	गहन जाँच-पड़ताल	2
103	A person who believes that laws and governments are not necessary	**Anarchist (N.)**	अराजकतावादी	8 (8)
104*	A state of disorder due to absence of government or authority	**Anarchy (N.)**	अव्यवस्था, अराजकता	10 (3)

SN	Phrases	One Word (PoS)	Hindi	#R
105	The science of the bodily structure of living organisms	**Anatomy (N.)**	शरीर रचना विज्ञान	1 (1)
106*	A person who presents a radio or television programme	**Anchor (N.)**	कार्यक्रम संचालक	5 (1)
107*	Belonging to the very distant past	**Ancient (Adj.)~**	प्राचीन	2
108	An excessive or obsessive attraction towards men	Andromania (N.)	पुरुषों के प्रति अत्यधिक या असामान्य आकर्षण	
109	A short, interesting or amusing story about a real person or event	**Anecdote (N.)**	वास्तविक घटना पर आधारित छोटी कहानी	7 (1)
110	The inability to feel pleasure in normally pleasurable activities	Anhedonia (N.)	आनंद महसूस न कर पाने की स्थिति	
111	Resembling a weak old woman	**Anile (Adj.)~**	बुढ़िया के समान	
112	A strong dislike or hostility	**Animosity (N.)~**	शत्रुता	2
113*	To destroy completely	**Annihilate (V.)~**	पूर्णतः नष्ट करना	1 (1)
114*	The date on which an event happened in some previous year	**Anniversary (N.)**	सालगिरह	4
115	A note added to a text or diagram to explain or provide additional information	Annotation (N.)	टिप्पणी, व्याख्या	
116	A fixed sum paid annually	Annuity (N.)	वार्षिक भत्ता	
117*	A deviation from what is normal or expected	Anomaly (N.)	अनियमितता, असामान्यता	
118*	Having an unknown or withheld name or identity	**Anonymous (Adj.)~**	बेनाम, गुमनाम	6 (4)
119	An eating disorder marked by an obsessive desire to lose weight by refusing to eat	**Anorexia (N.)**	वजन बढ़ने के भय से खाना अत्यधिक कम करना	1 (2)
120	The main opponent or villain in a story	**Antagonist (N.)~**	विरोधी पात्र	
121*	Extremely old-fashioned	Antediluvian (Adj.)	अत्यंत प्राचीन	
122	A collection of literary works by different authors published together	**Anthology (N.)~**	साहित्यिक संग्रह	2 (2)
123	One who studies the evolution and development of human societies and cultures	**Anthropologist (N.)**	मानव-विज्ञान का अध्ययन करने वाला	4 (4)
124*	The study of human societies, cultures, and their development	**Anthropology (N.)**	मानव विज्ञान	7 (5)
125	The practice of attributing human qualities to animals or objects	Anthropomorphism (N.)	मानवीकरण (चीज़ों या जानवरों को इंसानों जैसा बताना)	
126*	To expect or look forward to	**Anticipate (V.)~**	पूर्वानुमान करना, आशा रखना	
127*	A medicine to counteract the effect of poison	**Antidote (N.)**	विष नाशक	7
128	A strong feeling of dislike or aversion	**Antipathy (N.)~**	गहरी नापसंदगी	5 (1)
129	A person who studies or collects antiques	**Antiquarian (N.)**	पुरावस्तुओं का संग्राहक या विशेषज्ञ	2 (1)
130	The exact opposite	**Antithesis (N.)~**	विपरीत	

SN	Phrases	One Word (PoS)	Hindi	#R
131	A substance in blood that neutralises toxins	Antitoxin (N.)	विषनाशक	
132*	A word opposite in meaning to another word	**Antonym (N.)~**	विलोम शब्द	1 (2)
133*	A policy of racial segregation and discrimination	**Apartheid (N.)**	नस्लीय भेदभाव	4
134*	A set of rooms forming one residence in a building	Apartment (N.)	किसी इमारत में कमरों का समूह (फ़्लैट)	
135*	Showing or feeling no interest, enthusiasm, or concern	**Apathetic (Adj.)**	उदासीन, भावहीन	2
136*	A lack of interest, enthusiasm, or concern	**Apathy (N.)~**	उदासीनता	4
137	Loss of ability to understand or express speech, due to brain damage	Aphasia (N.)	भाषाहीनता (मस्तिष्क चोट के कारण समझने या बोलने में असमर्थ)	
138*	A place where bees are kept	**Apiary (N.)**	मधुमक्खियों के पालने का स्थान	5 (6)
139	To express regret for something that one has done wrong	Apologise (V.)	क्षमा मांगना	
140	The act of abandoning one's religious or political beliefs	Apostasy (N.)	धर्म या विश्वास का त्याग	
141	A person who renounces religious or political beliefs	**Apostate (N.)**	धर्म या विश्वास को त्यागने वाला व्यक्ति	7 (4)
142	A person who is sent to spread a religious message or doctrine	Apostle (N.)	धार्मिक संदेश फैलाने के लिए भेजा गया व्यक्ति	
143*	Causing shock or dismay	**Appalling (Adj.)~**	डरावना, भयावह	
144	To belong to or be connected with something	Appertain (V.)	से संबंधित होना	
145	A person who formally requests something, especially a job	Applicant (N.)	आवेदक	
146*	An estimation of a thing's worth	Appraisal (N.)	मूल्यांकन	
147*	To rise in value	**Appreciate (V.)~**	मूल्य वृद्धि होना	
148*	A person who works for an expert to learn a trade	**Apprentice (N.)~**	शिक्षार्थी	4
149	An extreme fear of water	Aquaphobia (N.)	पानी का डर	
150*	A glass tank where fish and water plants are kept	**Aquarium (N.)**	मछलीघर	7 (2)
151*	Living or growing in or near water	**Aquatic (Adj.)**	जलीय	7
152	Suitable for growing crops	**Arable (Adj.)**	कृषि योग्य	2
153	An extreme fear of spiders	**Arachnophobia (N.)**	मकड़ियों का डर	1 (1)
154*	Based on chance rather than on reason or a plan	**Arbitrary (Adj.)~**	मनमाना	
155*	A person appointed by two parties to settle a dispute	**Arbitrator (N.)**	पंच, मध्यस्थ	6 (4)
156*	A person who studies human history through excavation of sites	**Archaeologist (N.)**	पुरातत्व विज्ञानी	1 (2)

SN	Phrases	One Word (PoS)	Hindi	#R
157*	The study of human history and prehistory through the excavation of sites	**Archaeology (N.)**	पुरातत्व शास्त्र	8 (6)
158*	Very old and no longer in use	**Archaic (Adj.)~**	अप्रचलित	1 (1)
159*	A large body of water with many islands	**Archipelago (N.)**	द्वीपसमूह	4
160	The place where public, government or historical records are kept	**Archive (N.)**	अभिलेखागार	10 (8)
161	A feeling of intense passion or enthusiasm	Ardour (N.)	जोश, उत्साह	
162	A place or scene of activity, debate, or conflict	**Arena (N.)**	अखाड़ा, रंगभूमि	5 (1)
163	A secret or disguised language used by a particular group	Argot (N.)	गुप्त भाषा या विशेष समुदाय की भाषा	
164*	A government by the nobles or the highest social class	**Aristocracy (N.)**	श्रेष्ठ जनों का शासन	6 (5)
165*	A feeling of excessive self-importance or superiority	**Arrogance (N.)~**	अहंकार	
166*	A place where weapons and military equipment are stored	**Arsenal (N.)**	शस्त्रागार	8 (8)
167	The crime of deliberately setting fire to property	**Arson (N.)**	आगजनी (अपराध)	4 (1)
168	A person who deliberately sets fire to property	**Arsonist (N.)**	आगजनी करने वाला	2 (4)
169*	Able to express ideas clearly and fluently	**Articulate (Adj.)~**	स्पष्ट बोलने वाला	3
170	The ability to speak clearly and express ideas effectively	Articulation (N.)	स्पष्ट उच्चारण	
171	An object made by humans, usually of historical or cultural significance	Artifact (N.)	मानव निर्मित ऐतिहासिक वस्तु	
172*	One who practises one of the fine arts	**Artist (N.)**	कलाकार	2
173*	One who practises severe self-discipline and abstains from bodily pleasures	**Ascetic (N.)~**	तपस्वी व्यक्ति	7 (7)
174	To attribute a cause or characteristic to something	**Ascribe (V.)**	श्रेय देना, उत्तरदायी ठहराना	3
175*	With suspicion, doubt, or disapproval	Askance (Adv.)	तिरछी दृष्टि से, संदेहपूर्वक	
176	A person who physically attacks another	Assailant (N.)	आक्रमणकारी	
177*	A person who kills somebody, especially for political reasons	Assassin (N.)	हत्यारा	
178	To agree to a request, an idea, or a suggestion	**Assent (V.)~**	स्वीकृति देना	
179	Politely firm and confident	**Assertive (Adj.)~**	आत्मविश्वासी, दृढ़	
180*	Greatly surprised or amazed	Astonished (Adj.)	अचंभित, बहुत हैरान	
181*	One who studies celestial positions to predict future events	**Astrologer (N.)**	ज्योतिषी	4 (1)
182	The study of celestial positions to predict future events	**Astrology (N.)**	ज्योतिष विद्या	1 (1)
183*	A person trained to travel in a spacecraft	**Astronaut (N.)**	अन्तरिक्ष यात्री	7 (3)
184	One who studies celestial bodies	**Astronomer (N.)**	खगोलशास्त्री	1 (4)
185	The scientific study of celestial bodies	**Astronomy (N.)**	खगोलशास्त्र	6 (2)

SN	Phrases	One Word (PoS)	Hindi	#R
186	A place of refuge or safety; an institution for the mentally ill	**Asylum (N.)**	शरणस्थल, मानसिक चिकित्सालय	5 (2)
187*	One who does not believe in the existence of God	**Atheist (N.)~**	नास्तिक	19 (7)
188	An action of making amends for a wrong or injury	**Atonement (N.)**	प्रायश्चित	1 (1)
189	A space or room just below the roof of a building	**Attic (N.)**	अटारी (छत का कमरा)	1 (1)
190*	That can be heard clearly	**Audible (Adj.)**	सुनाई देने योग्य	3 (1)
191	An official inspection of an organization's or individual's financial accounts	**Audit (N.)**	लेखा परीक्षा (हिसाब किताब की जांच)	1 (1)
192	One who officially examines financial accounts or records	**Auditor (N.)**	लेखा परीक्षक (हिसाब किताब की जांच करने वाला)	6 (2)
193*	A large hall used for public gatherings, concerts, or performances	**Auditorium (N.)**	सभागार	2 (1)
194*	Strict and plain in manner or lifestyle	**Austere (Adj.)~**	सख्त, आडंबरहीन	
195*	Something that is genuine; made in the traditional or original way	**Authentic (Adj.)~**	असली, विश्वसनीय	2 (1)
196*	A person who writes books	**Author (N.)**	लेखक	2 (1)
197	A book written by a person about their own life	**Autobiography (N.)**	आत्मकथा	11 (3)
198*	A government by one person having absolute power	**Autocracy (N.)**	तानाशाही (एक व्यक्ति का निरंकुश शासन)	9 (3)
199	A ruler who has complete power	Autocrat (N.)	तानाशाह	
200	The signature of a famous person, often given to an admirer	Autograph (N.)	हस्ताक्षर (विशेषकर प्रसिद्ध व्यक्ति का)	
201*	The right of self-governance	**Autonomy (N.)~**	स्वशासन	2 (3)
202*	An examination of a dead body to determine the cause of death	**Autopsy (N.)**	शव परीक्षण	2 (3)
203*	A mass of snow, ice and rocks falling rapidly down a mountainside	**Avalanche (N.)**	हिमस्खलन (पहाड़ से तेजी से गिरती बर्फ)	1 (1)
204	Using or showing new, experimental, or unconventional ideas; ahead of its time	**Avant-Garde (Adj.)**	अग्रगामी (समय से आगे की सोच वाला)	1 (1)
205*	Extreme greed for wealth or material gain	**Avarice (N.)~**	अत्यधिक लालच	2
206*	Having an extreme desire for wealth	**Avaricious (Adj.)~**	अत्यधिक लालची	2 (2)
207*	A place for keeping birds in a confined space	**Aviary (N.)**	पक्षीशाला, पक्षी-घर	15 (9)
208*	The operation and flying of aircraft	**Aviation (N.)**	विमानों की उड़ान का विज्ञान	1 (1)
209	The killing of birds	**Avicide (N.)**	पक्षी-हत्या	2
210	Keen interest or enthusiasm	Avidity (N.)	उत्सुकता	
211*	A statement accepted as true without proof	**Axiom (N.)~**	स्वयंसिद्ध सत्य (सिद्धांत जिसे बिना प्रमाण के सत्य माना जाता है)	2 (1)
212*	An unmarried man	**Bachelor (N.)**	अविवाहित पुरुष	2

SN	Phrases	One Word (PoS)	Hindi	#R
213	A place where bread and cakes are made	Bakery (N.)	जहाँ ब्रेड और केक बनाए जाते हैं	
214	Having no hair on the scalp	**Bald (Adj.)**	गंजा	2
215	Senseless or foolish talk or writing	Balderdash (N.)	निरर्थक बात	
216	A large bundle bound for storage or transport	**Bale (N.)**	गठरी, गट्ठा	4 (2)
217*	A poem that tells a story and has a regular rhythm and rhyme scheme	**Ballad (N.)**	गाथागीत	2
218	To pass or exchange back and forth, especially words or ideas	Bandy (V.)	विचारों का आपस में आदान-प्रदान करना	
219	One who is unable to pay his debts	**Bankrupt (N.)~**	दिवालिया	5 (3)
220	A playful and friendly exchange of teasing remarks	**Banter (N.)~**	हँसी-मज़ाक	1 (1)
221	A poet who composes and recites epic or lyrical poetry	Bard (N.)	वीरता की कहानियाँ सुनाने वाला कवि	
222	The outer protective layer of a tree (N.); To make a sharp loud sound (V.)	Bark (N./V.)	छाल; भौंकना	
223	An instrument used for measuring atmospheric pressure	**Barometer (N.)**	वायु-दाब-मापक	3 (2)
224	A place where soldiers are stationed	**Barracks (N.)**	सैनिकों के लिए बने घर	7
225*	A wooden drum in which beer or oil is stored	**Barrel (N.)**	पीपा (लकड़ी का बेलनाकार पात्र)	2
226	To revel in and make the most of something pleasing	Bask (V.)	आनंद लेना	
227*	A group of guns or missile launchers operated together at one place	**Battery (N.)**	तोपों का समूह	1 (2)
228	A short sword fixed onto the end of a gun	Bayonet (N.)	बंदूक की नोक पर लगा चाकू	
229	Something of monstrous size or power	**Behemoth (N.)~**	विशालकाय वस्तु या प्राणी	1 (1)
230	One who is fond of fighting	**Bellicose (Adj.)~**	लड़ाकू	
231*	A deep roaring sound, as made by a bull or crocodile	**Bellow (N.)**	दहाड़	1 (1)
232*	One who helps others by giving money or other aid	**Benefactor (N.)**	धन आदि से सहायता करने वाला	3 (1)
233*	A person who gains as a result of something	**Beneficiary (N.)~**	लाभार्थी	
234*	Deprived of or lacking something	**Bereft (Adj.)~**	वंचित	
235	A person who is engaged to be married	Betrothed (N.)	मंगेतर	
236*	A drink, especially one other than water	Beverage (N.)	पेय पदार्थ	
237	A large group of people or things, especially girls or birds	**Bevy (N.)**	झुंड	2 (3)
238*	A list of the books referred to in a scholarly work	**Bibliography (N.)**	संदर्भ ग्रंथसूची (संदर्भित पुस्तकों की सूची)	5
239	An obsessive desire to acquire and possess books	**Bibliomania (N.)**	किताबों के लिए पागलपन	1 (1)
240	A person who loves or collects books	**Bibliophile (N.)~**	पुस्तक प्रेमी	14 (8)
241	A 200th anniversary of an event	Bicentennial (N.)	200वीं वर्षगांठ	

SN	Phrases	One Word (PoS)	Hindi	#R
242	Happening every two years	**Biennial (Adj.)**	द्विवार्षिक	3
243	A person intolerant of different opinions, especially in religion or politics	**Bigot (N.)~**	कट्टर व्यक्ति	4
244*	Able to speak two languages	**Bilingual (Adj.)**	द्विभाषिक	5 (4)
245	Happening every two months or twice a month	Bimonthly (Adj.)	हर दो महीने में या एक महीने में दो बार होनेवाला	
246	Capable of being decomposed by natural biological processes	**Biodegradable (Adj.)**	प्राकृतिक तरीके से सड़नशील	2
247	The story of a person's life written by someone else	**Biography (N.)**	जीवनी	6 (9)
248	The study of living organisms	**Biology (N.)**	जीव विज्ञान	1 (2)
249	The removal and examination of tissue from a living body to diagnose disease	**Biopsy (N.)**	जीवित ऊतकों की जांच	1 (2)
250*	Very strange or unusual	**Bizarre (Adj.)~**	विचित्र	
251	A region of space with gravity so strong that nothing, not even light, can escape	Black hole (N.)	अत्यधिक गुरुत्व वाला अंतरिक्षीय क्षेत्र (जहाँ से प्रकाश भी नहीं निकल सकता)	
252	The act of speaking disrespectfully about sacred or religious things	**Blasphemy (N.)**	ईश्वर की निंदा	9 (1)
253	The sound made by a sheep or goat	**Bleat (N.)**	मिमियाना	3
254	A person who cannot see	Blind (Adj.)	अंधा, नेत्रहीन	
255	A spot or stain caused by a discolouring substance	Blot (N.)	दाग, धब्बा	
256*	A group of people managing or directing a company	**Board (N.)~**	निदेशक मंडल	
257	A person of South African Dutch descent	Boer (N.)	दक्षिण अफ़्रीकी डच मूल का व्यक्ति	
258	One who does not follow the usual rules of social life	**Bohemian (N.)**	परंपराविरोधी जीवन-शैली वाला	4 (2)
259	To attack with a continuous flow of questions or criticism	Bombard (V.)	बौछार करना	
260*	Using impressive-sounding words but with little meaning	**Bombastic (Adj.)~**	बड़े बड़े शब्दों वाला	2
261*	A large open-air fire, often for celebration	**Bonfire (N.)**	अलाव (अग्नि उत्सव)	3
262	Dwarf varieties of trees and shrubs grown in pots	**Bonsai (N.)**	गमले में उगाई गई छोटी झाड़ी की किस्म	2 (2)
263	A sum of money added to a person's wages as a reward for good performance	Bonus (N.)	पारितोषिक (अतिरिक्त इनाम)	
264	One who reads a lot; an avid reader	**Bookworm (N.)**	किताबी कीड़ा (पुस्तक प्रेमी)	2
265	A curved throwing weapon that returns to the thrower	Boomerang (N.)	फेंकने पर वापस लौटने वाला हथियार	
266	One who is well-versed in the knowledge of plants	**Botanist (N.)**	वनस्पति-विज्ञानी	2 (1)

SN	Phrases	One Word (PoS)	Hindi	#R
267	The scientific study of plants and their structure	**Botany (N.)**	वनस्पति विज्ञान	6 (2)
268*	A narrow point of congestion that restricts flow or progress	Bottleneck (N.)	रास्ते का संकीर्ण भाग	
269	A broad road bordered with trees	**Boulevard (N.)**	पेड़ों की कतार वाला मुख्य मार्ग	1 (1)
270*	An arrangement of flowers that is usually given as a present	**Bouquet (N.)**	गुलदस्ता	7 (1)
271*	A person belonging to the middle class	Bourgeois (N.)	मध्यम वर्ग का व्यक्ति	
272*	A small shop that sells fashionable clothes	**Boutique (N.)**	वस्त्रालय	2
273*	Affecting or relating to cows or cattle	**Bovine (Adj.)**	गाय से संबंधित	2 (2)
274	A shady place under trees	**Bower (N.)**	पेड़ों के नीचे का छायादार स्थान	2
275	To fail to observe or comply with a law or agreement	**Breach (V.)~**	नियम तोड़ना	
276	A place where beer is made	**Brewery (N.)**	बियर बनाने का कारखाना	1 (3)
277*	A set of leather straps placed around a horse's head to control it	**Bridle (N.)~**	लगाम	
278	A member of a gang of robbers	**Brigand (N.)~**	डाकू	2
279*	Hard but easily broken	**Brittle (Adj.)~**	भंगुर, आसानी से टूटने योग्य	9 (2)
280*	A family of young animals or birds produced at one time	**Brood (N.)**	एक साथ जन्मे बच्चे	2
281	A late morning meal combining breakfast and lunch	Brunch (N.)	नाश्ता+दोपहर का भोजन	
282	A woman with dark brown hair	**Brunette (N.)**	गहरे भूरे बाल वाली स्त्री	3
283*	An estimate of income and expenditure for a set period	Budget (N.)	बजट (आय-व्यय का अनुमान)	
284	A period of rising prices in financial trading	Bull market (N.)	शेयर बाज़ार में तेज़ी	
285	Gold or silver in bulk form, before being made into coins or ornaments	Bullion (N.)	सोने चाँदी की ईंट	
286	A collection of things tied or wrapped together	Bundle (N.)	गट्ठर	
287*	A large detached house with a single or double storey	Bungalow (N.)	बंगला, कोठी	
288	To carry out a task clumsily or incompetently	Bungle (V.)	गड़बड़ करना	
289	A floating marker anchored to the sea bottom to guide or warn ships	**Buoy (N.)~**	तैरता संकेतक (जहाज़ों को दिशा देने के लिए)	
290*	A government run by officials in a state	**Bureaucracy (N.)**	नौकरशाहों का शासन	5 (2)
291*	A person who breaks into buildings illegally to steal	Burglar (N.)	सेंधमार	
292	A hole or tunnel dug by an animal as a dwelling	**Burrow (N.)**	बिल	4
293	To make a low continuous humming sound like a bee	Buzz (V.)	भिनभिनाना	
294	A place where cows are sheltered	Byre (N.)	गौशाला	

SN	Phrases	One Word (PoS)	Hindi	#R
295	A hidden store of things	**Cache (N.)**	गुप्त भंडार	2 (2)
296	One who is bad at spelling	**Cacographer (N.)**	गलत वर्तनी लिखने वाला व्यक्ति	2 (2)
297	An extreme fear of ugliness or ugly things	**Cacophobia (N.)**	कुरूपता का भय	1 (2)
298*	A harsh, discordant mixture of sounds	**Cacophony (N.)~**	कोलाहल, कर्कश ध्वनि	5 (2)
299	Resembling a corpse	**Cadaverous (Adj.)~**	शव की तरह	
300	A rhythmic flow of sounds or words	**Cadence (N.)~**	लय	
301	The young one of a cow	**Calf (N.)**	बछड़ा	1 (1)
302	A person skilled in beautiful handwriting	**Calligrapher (N.)**	सुलेखक	4 (2)
303	The art of beautiful handwriting	**Calligraphy (N.)**	सुलेख	8 (7)
304*	One who is devoid of kind feeling and sympathy	**Callous (Adj.)~**	कठोर दिल वाला, संवेदनाहीन	1 (1)
305*	The act of disguising to blend with the surroundings	**Camouflage (N.)~**	छलावरण (छिपाने की तकनीक)	1 (1)
306*	A person who eats human flesh	**Cannibal (N.)**	नरभक्षक	14 (4)
307	Love for dogs	**Canophilia (N.)**	कुत्तों के प्रति प्रेम	2
308	The legal killing of someone as punishment for a crime	Capital punish-ment (N.)	मृत्युदंड (फाँसी की सज़ा)	
309*	A person who has money especially invested in business	Capitalist (N.)	पूंजीवादी	
310	A unit of weight used for measuring precious stones	Carat (N.)	रत्नों का भार मापने की इकाई	
311*	A group of travellers journeying together across a desert; a shelter of a gypsy	**Caravan (N.)**	काफिला	8 (2)
312	The dead body of an animal	**Carcass (N.)~**	पशु शव	2
313	Something which is considered to be very important	**Cardinal (Adj.)**	मुख्य, प्रधान	2
314	A doctor specialising in the study or treatment of heart diseases	**Cardiologist (N.)**	हृदय रोग विशेषज्ञ	5 (2)
315	The study of the heart and its diseases	Cardiology (N.)	हृदय विज्ञान	
316*	A picture drawn with exaggerated features for comic effect	**Caricature (N.)~**	व्यंग्य-चित्र	3 (1)
317	The ruthless killing of a large number of people	**Carnage (N.)~**	नरसंहार	
318	A person who eats meat but not seafood or fish	Carnitarian (N.)	जो मांस खाता है पर मछली या समुद्री भोजन नहीं	
319*	Feeding on the flesh of other animals	**Carnivorous (Adj.)**	मांसाहारी	4 (3)
320	A religious or joyful song, especially one sung at Christmas	Carol (N.)	क्रिसमस गीत	
321	A person who draws or makes maps	**Cartographer (N.)**	मानचित्रकार	13 (7)
322	The art or process of drawing or making maps	**Cartography (N.)**	मानचित्रकारी	5 (1)
323	A humorous drawing with exaggerated features	Cartoon (N.)	व्यंग्यचित्र	
324	A fall of water from a great height	**Cascade (N.)~**	झरना	

SN	Phrases	One Word (PoS)	Hindi	#R
325	A place where gambling games are played	**Casino (N.)**	जुआखाना	3 (3)
326	A long garment worn by clergy	Cassock (N.)	ईसाई पादरियों का लंबा वस्त्र	
327	A sudden and violent event causing great destruction	Cataclysm (N.)	प्रलय	
328*	A systematic list of items or publications	**Catalogue (N.)**	सूची	8 (2)
329	A substance that speeds up a chemical reaction without being consumed	**Catalyst (N.)~**	उत्प्रेरक	
330*	An event causing great and sudden damage or suffering	**Catastrophe (N.)~**	भारी तबाही	4
331	Causing great damage or suffering	**Catastrophic (Adj.)~**	विनाशकारी	
332*	A private meeting of members of a political party to decide policy or select candidates	**Caucus (N.)**	राजनीतिक दल की आंतरिक बैठक	1 (2)
333	A large, deep, metal pot used for cooking over open fire	Cauldron (N.)	हंडा, कड़ाही	
334	A group of soldiers who fight on horseback	**Cavalry (N.)**	घुड़सवार सेना	1 (1)
335	The sound made by a crow	Caw (N.)	कौवे की कांव-कांव	
336	A time when enemies agree to stop fighting	**Ceasefire (N.)**	युद्ध विराम	1 (1)
337	The state of being unmarried by choice	**Celibacy (N.)**	ब्रह्मचर्य	4 (2)
338	An underground place for storing wine or other provisions	**Cellar (N.)**	तहख़ाना	2
339*	A large burial ground	**Cemetery (N.)**	कब्रिस्तान	5 (1)
340	A monument erected in honour of a person whose body is buried elsewhere	Cenotaph (N.)	समाधि-स्मारक (जहाँ शव न हो)	
341*	An expression of strong disapproval or criticism	**Censure (N.)~**	फटकार	
342*	A person who is one hundred years old or more	**Centenarian (N.)**	सौ वर्ष का व्यक्ति	4
343	The 100th anniversary of an event	**Centennial (N.)**	शताब्दी	1 (1)
344	Tending to move away from the centre	Centrifugal (Adj.)	अपकेंद्री (केंद्र से दूर भागने की प्रवृत्ति)	
345*	Relating to the brain or the intellect	**Cerebral (Adj.)**	दिमागी	1 (1)
346	The art of designing or writing on wax	Cerography (N.)	मोम पर नक्काशी की कला	
347	To rub a part of the body to restore warmth or sensation	**Chafe (V.)~**	रगड़कर गरमाना	
348	The husks of corn or other grains separated by winnowing or threshing	Chaff (N.)	भूसा	
349	A feeling of annoyance or embarrassment caused by failure or disappointment	**Chagrin (N.)~**	शर्मिंदगी व निराशा की भावना	1 (1)
350	A child believed to have been secretly left in exchange for another	Changeling (N.)	बदला हुआ बच्चा	
351*	A state of utter confusion	**Chaos (N.)~**	पूर्ण अव्यवस्था	
352	A small place of Christian worship, especially within a larger institution	**Chapel (N.)**	ईसाइयों का छोटा उपासना स्थल	3
353*	Compelling attractiveness or charm that can inspire or influence others	**Charisma (N.)~**	आकर्षण	

SN	Phrases	One Word (PoS)	Hindi	#R
354*	Exercising a compelling charm which inspires devotion in others	**Charismatic (Adj.)**	आकर्षक	2
355	A person falsely claiming to have a special knowledge or skill	**Charlatan (N.)**	ढोंगी	3
356	To run after in order to catch or catch up with	**Chase (V.)**	पीछा करना	1 (1)
357*	A deep fissure in the earth's surface	Chasm (N.)	गहरी खाई	
358	The base frame of a car or other wheeled vehicle	Chassis (N.)	वाहन का ढाँचा	
359	To criticise someone severely	**Chastise (V.)~**	फटकारना	
360*	A person employed to drive a private or hired car	**Chauffeur (N.)**	मोटर-चालक	9 (6)
361*	The use of strong contrasts between light and shadow in art	**Chiaroscuro (N.)**	प्रकाश-छाया का तीव्र विरोधाभास	2
362	The use of trickery to achieve a political or financial goal	**Chicanery (N.)~**	धोखाधड़ी	
363	The art of predicting the future by examining the lines on a person's palm	Chiromancy (N.)	हस्तरेखा विद्या	
364*	A group of singers in a church	**Choir (N.)**	गायक-मंडली	3 (2)
365	A routine task, especially a household one	Chore (N.)	दैनिक काम	
366	One who plans the steps and moves for a dance	**Choreographer (N.)**	नृत्य-निर्देशक	5 (1)
367*	A disease persisting for a long time or recurring repeatedly	**Chronic (Adj.)~**	दीर्घकालिक	
368	A factual written account of events in the order of their occurrence	Chronicle (N.)	कालक्रम से अभिलेखन	
369*	Arranged in the order of time	Chronological (Adj.)	तिथिक्रम के अनुसार	
370*	An arrangement of events or dates in the order of their occurrence	**Chronology (N.)**	कालक्रम	11 (6)
371	An instrument for measuring time with extreme accuracy	**Chronometer (N.)**	अत्यधिक सटीक घड़ी	1 (1)
372	To laugh quietly without opening one's mouth	Chuckle (V.)	मुँह बंद करके हँसना	
373	Rude in a mean-spirited and surly way	**Churlish (Adj.)~**	अभद्र	
374	Extreme self-confidence or audacity	Chutzpah (N.)	ढिठाई	
375	The art of motion-picture photography	Cinematography (N.)	फ़िल्म बनाने का कार्य	
376	A secret or disguised way of writing	**Cipher (N.)**	गुप्त लिपि	2 (1)
377*	The use of many words where only a few are necessary	**Circumlocution (N.)~**	शब्द-बाहुल्य (बहुत सारे शब्दों का प्रयोग)	4
378	Based on circumstances or indirect evidence rather than direct proof	**Circumstantial (Adj.)~**	परिस्थितियों से संबंधित	
379	A fortress, typically one on high ground above a city	**Citadel (N.)~**	किला, गढ़	1 (2)
380	To climb or move with difficulty using hands and feet	Clamber (V.)	हाथ पैर के बल कठिनाई से चढ़ना	

SN	Phrases	One Word (PoS)	Hindi	#R
381	Making a loud and confused noise	**Clamorous (Adj.)~**	कोलाहलपूर्ण	
382	A loud appeal or demand	**Clamour (N.)~**	कोलाहल, शोर	
383	An extreme fear of confined or enclosed spaces	**Claustrophobia (N.)**	बंद या छोटी जगह का भय	15 (8)
384	All the customers of a business	**Clientele (N.)**	ग्राहक वर्ग	2
385	A story or situation ending at a suspenseful moment, leaving the outcome unresolved	Cliffhanger (N.)	रोमांचक स्थिति जहाँ अंत अधूरा छोड़ा जाए	
386	A small exclusive group of people with a common purpose	**Clique (N.)~**	समान विचार वाले लोगों का छोटा समूह	2 (3)
387	A room in a public building where outdoor clothes or luggage may be left	**Cloakroom (N.)**	सामान कक्ष	2 (1)
388	The sound made by a hen	Cluck (N.)	मुर्गी की आवाज	
389	Awkward in movement or manner	**Clumsy (Adj.)~**	बेढंगा	
390	The land beside or near the sea	Coast (N.)	समुद्र तट	
391	A mender or maker of shoes	**Cobbler (N.)**	मोची	1 (1)
392	A fine network of threads spun by a spider to catch its prey	Cobweb (N.)	मकड़ी का जाला	
393	A small compartment in an aircraft for the pilot	Cockpit (N.)	वायु-यान में चालक-कक्ष	
394	A drink made from a mixture of one or more alcoholic drinks	Cocktail (N.)	मिश्रित शराब	
395	An instruction added later to a will, usually to change a part of it	Codicil (N.)	वसीयतनामे के बाद का परिवर्तन पत्र	
396	To compel or force someone to do something against their will	**Coerce (V.)~**	ज़बरदस्ती करना	
397*	The use of force or threats to compel someone to act	**Coercion (N.)**	जोर जबरदस्ती	3
398*	A strongbox or small chest for holding valuables	Coffer (N.)	तिजोरी	
399	A collection of slaves	**Coffle (N.)**	गुलामों का काफिला	1 (1)
400*	A remarkable concurrence of events without apparent causal connection	**Coincidence (N.)~**	संयोग	
401*	A person with whom one works in a profession or business	**Colleague (N.)~**	सहकर्मी	5 (3)
402	A formal conversation or dialogue	**Colloquy (N.)~**	वार्तालाप	2
403	A secret agreement for a deceitful purpose	Collusion (N.)	मिलीभगत	
404	A group of animals or insects (ants) of the same kind living together	Colony (N.)	एक ही प्रजाति के जीवों का सामूहिक निवास	
405	A gigantic statue	Colossus (N.)	विशाल मूर्ति	
406*	To honour the memory of a person or event, especially with a ceremony	**Commemorate (V.)~**	स्मृति में समारोह करना	
407*	A payment to an agent, usually a percentage of sales	Commission (N.)	दलाली (बिक्री पर मिलने वाला हिस्सा)	
408	The process of making something into a product that can be bought and sold	Commodification (N.)	किसी चीज़ को बेचने योग्य बनाने की प्रक्रिया	

SN	Phrases	One Word (PoS)	Hindi	#R
409*	An act of exchanging information	**Communication (N.)~**	संचार	
410*	A feeling of deep sympathy for the suffering of others, with a desire to help	**Compassion (N.)~**	दया, अनुकम्पा	
411	A person from the same country as another	**Compatriot (N.)~**	स्वदेशवासी	
412*	A person who introduces the performers or contestants in a variety show	**Compere (N.)**	कार्यक्रम प्रस्तुतकर्ता	2 (1)
413*	Satisfied, with no desire to change or improve	**Complacent (Adj.)~**	आत्मसंतुष्ट	
414*	A thing that completes or brings to perfection	**Complement (N.)~**	पूरक	
415*	A remark that expresses approval or admiration	**Compliment (N.)~**	प्रशंसा	
416	To act in accordance with rules, requests, or wishes	**Comply (V.)~**	पालन करना	
417	A person who arranges type for printing	Compositor (N.)	प्रिंट से पहले शब्दों या वाक्यों को व्यवस्थित करने वाला	
418	A feeling of guilt or moral scruple that prevents or follows wrongdoing	**Compunction (N.)~**	अपराध-बोध, पछतावा	
419*	To hide something from view or knowledge	**Conceal (V.)~**	छिपाना	
420	Having too much pride in yourself and what you do	**Conceited (Adj.)**	अभिमानी	1 (1)
421*	Capable of being imagined or grasped mentally	Conceivable (Adj.)	कल्पनीय	
422	Having a common centre, as circles or spheres	Concentric (Adj.)	संकेन्द्री	
423	Living together of a man and woman without being married to each other	Concubinage (N.)	बिना विवाह के साथ रहना	
424*	An expression of sympathy for someone who has lost a loved one	Condolence (N.)	शोक-संवेदना (दुख प्रकट करना)	
425	An apartment building with individually owned units and shared common areas	**Condominium (N.)**	स्वामित्व वाले फ़्लैटों का सामूहिक आवास	1 (1)
426*	To accept or overlook wrongdoing without protest or censure	**Condone (V.)~**	अनदेखा करना	
427	A person who makes or sells sweets or chocolate	**Confectioner (N.)**	मिठाई बेचने वाला	2 (1)
428*	To own up to something as true	**Confess (V.)~**	कबूल करना	
429*	An arrangement of parts or elements in a particular form or figure	Configuration (N.)	एक विशेष आकृति में तत्वों की व्यवस्था	
430*	To officially take something away from somebody	**Confiscate (V.)~**	जब्त करना	
431	Actively burning	Conflagrant (Adj.)	जलता हुआ	
432*	A place where two or more rivers meet	Confluence (N.)	संगम	
433*	A person who follows accepted behaviour and established practices	Conformist (N.)	परंपरानुसार चलने वाला व्यक्ति	
434*	Belonging or pertaining to an individual from birth	**Congenital (Adj.)**	जन्मजात	2 (2)

SN	Phrases	One Word (PoS)	Hindi	#R
435*	A corporation made up of a number of different companies that operate in diversified fields	Conglomerate (N.)	कंपनियों का समूह	
436*	A group of people gathered for religious worship	**Congregation (N.)~**	धार्मिक सभा	6 (2)
437*	An opinion or conclusion formed on the basis of incomplete information	**Conjecture (N.)~**	निराधार अनुमान	
438*	A person who has expert knowledge and refined taste in a particular subject	**Connoisseur (N.)~**	किसी विषय का पारखी व्यक्ति	8 (6)
439*	An inner feeling that tells you what is right and what is wrong	**Conscience (N.)**	अन्तरात्मा	1 (3)
440*	One who does their work thoroughly and seriously	**Conscientious (Adj.)~**	कर्तव्यनिष्ठ	2 (1)
441	Compulsory enlistment for military service	Conscription (N.)	अनिवार्य सैन्य भर्ती	
442*	The preservation and protection of the environment	**Conservation (N.)~**	प्राकृतिक संरक्षण	1 (2)
443*	One who is opposed to great or sudden change	**Conservative (N.)~**	रूढ़िवादी, अपरिवर्तनवादी	2
444	To comfort someone at a time of grief or disappointment	**Console (V.)~**	सांत्वना देना	
445*	A secret plan made to do something harmful or illegal	**Conspiracy (N.)~**	षड्यंत्र	
446	A group of stars that forms a shape in the sky and has a name	**Constellation (N.)**	नक्षत्र (तारों का समूह)	8 (4)
447*	State of anxiety or dismay causing mental confusion	**Consternation (N.)~**	घबराहट	
448	Something that is restricted or limited	Constrained (Adj.)	विवश किया हुआ	
449*	Extremely skilled	**Consummate (Adj.)~**	उत्कृष्ट	1 (1)
450	The situation in which a disease is spread by touching someone or something	**Contagion (N.)~**	संक्रमण	
451*	A disease that spreads easily from one person to another through contact	**Contagious (Adj.)**	संक्रामक	5 (1)
452	Something made impure by exposure to polluting substances	**Contaminated (Adj.)~**	दूषित	
453*	Belonging to or living in the same time period as another	**Contemporary (N.)~**	समकालीन	13 (6)
454*	Feeling satisfied and happy with what one has	**Contented (Adj.)~**	संतुष्ट	
455*	Likely to cause argument or disagreement	**Contentious (Adj.)~**	झगड़ालू	
456*	Touching along the side or boundary	**Contiguous (Adj.)~**	निकटवर्ती	
457*	An event that may or may not happen; a possible future event or circumstance	Contingency (N.)	आकस्मिकता	
458	Goods illegally imported or exported	**Contraband (N.)~**	तस्करी का माल	
459	A written legal agreement (N.); To shrink or become smaller	**Contract (N./V.)~**	समझौता; सिकुड़ना	

SN	Phrases	One Word (PoS)	Hindi	#R
460*	Gradual recovery of health and strength after illness	**Convalescence (N.)**	स्वास्थ्य लाभ (बीमारी से ठीक होने की प्रक्रिया)	6 (1)
461*	A place where nuns live and work	**Convent (N.)**	ननों का मठ	3 (1)
462	A group of vehicles travelling together under escort	Convoy (N.)	काफ़िला	
463	The ceremony of crowning a king or queen	**Coronation (N.)**	राज्याभिषेक	3
464	A collection of written or spoken texts	Corpus (N.)	संग्रह, पुस्तक संग्रह	
465*	To confirm with the help of evidence	**Corroborate (V.)~**	पुष्टि करना	2 (1)
466*	A funeral procession	**Cortege (N.)**	शव-यात्रा	2 (7)
467	A person who makes maps of the universe or the world	Cosmographer (N.)	ब्रह्मांड का मानचित्र बनाने वाला	
468	The science of the general features of the universe	**Cosmography (N.)**	विश्वरचना	2
469*	A person who regards the whole world as their country	**Cosmopolitan (Adj.)**	सर्वदेशीय	7 (3)
470*	A fraudulent imitation of something genuine	**Counterfeit (N.)~**	नकली वस्तु	
471	A sudden, violent overthrow of a government by force	Coup (N.)	तख्तापलट	
472	A stanza having two lines in verse	Couplet (N.)	दो पंक्तियों का पद्य	
473	A person who takes care of cattle	Cowherd (N.)	ग्वाला	
474*	Skill in a particular craft or trade	Craftsmanship (N.)	कारीगरी	
475*	That can be believed or trusted	**Credible (Adj.)~**	विश्वसनीय	3
476*	Ready to believe things too easily	**Credulous (Adj.)~**	भोला-भाला	6 (4)
477*	A system of religious belief	Creed (N.)	आस्था-संहिता	
478	A place where a dead person's body is burnt	**Crematorium (N.)**	शवदाहगृह	2
479*	A turning point of danger or difficulty	**Crisis (N.)~**	संकट	
480*	A principle or standard by which anything is or can be judged	**Criterion (N.)**	मापदंड	1 (1)
481	A person who expresses an unfavourable opinion	**Critic (N.)~**	आलोचक	
482	The sound made by frogs	**Croak (N.)**	टर्राहट (मेंढक की आवाज़)	1 (2)
483	To break or fall apart into small fragments	**Crumble (V.)~**	चूर-चूर होना	
484	A vigorous campaign for political, social, or religious change	**Crusade (N.)~**	धर्मयुद्ध, सशक्त अभियान	2 (1)
485	Having or forming a hard outer layer	Crusted (Adj.)	पपड़ीदार	
486	A coded message or a device used for encoding or decoding secret messages	Cryptograph (N.)	गुप्त संदेश; कूटलेखन उपकरण	
487	The study or practice of writing and decoding secret messages	**Cryptography (N.)**	कूटलेखन विद्या	1 (1)
488*	A style of cooking characteristic of a particular country or region	Cuisine (N.)	भोजन, पाक शैली	
489	Deserving blame for a fault or wrongdoing	**Culpable (Adj.)~**	अपराध के लिए उत्तरदायी	1 (1)
490*	The beliefs, customs, arts, and way of life of a particular society or group	Culture (N.)	संस्कृति	

SN	Phrases	One Word (PoS)	Hindi	#R
491*	A keeper or custodian of a museum or other collection	**Curator (N.)**	संग्रहालय का संरक्षक	7 (4)
492	A regulation requiring people to remain indoors during specified hours	**Curfew (N.)**	घर से बाहर निकलने पर सरकारी रोक	2
493*	A strong desire to know or learn something	**Curiosity (N.)~**	जिज्ञासा	
494*	The system of money used in a particular country	Currency (N.)	मुद्रा	
495*	To express a wish that misfortune befall a person	**Curse (V.)~**	श्राप देना (बद्दुआ देना)	
496	The degree to which something is curved	Curvature (N.)	वक्रता; घुमाव	
497	Duty on imports or exports	Customs (N.)	सीमा शुल्क	
498*	A person who believes people act only from self-interest	**Cynic (N.)**	निंदक, संदेहवादी व्यक्ति	6 (4)
499	An extreme fear of dogs	**Cynophobia (N.)**	कुत्तों का भय	1 (2)
500*	A centre of attraction or attention	**Cynosure (N.)**	आकर्षण-बिंदु	3 (5)
501	The branch of biology dealing with the study of cells	**Cytology (N.)**	कोशिका विज्ञान	1 (1)
502	A reckless person who enjoys doing dangerous things	**Daredevil (N.)**	दुस्साहसी	1 (1)
503	A large amount of information stored in a computer system	Database (N.)	आँकड़ा-संग्रह (डेटाबेस)	
504	A state of stunned confusion	Daze (N.)	स्तब्ध अवस्था, सदमा	
505	A situation when no progress is possible	Deadlock (N.)	गतिरोध	
506	One who cannot hear	Deaf (Adj.)	बहरा	
507	A performer's first public appearance	Debut (N.)	पहला सार्वजनिक प्रदर्शन या शुरुआत	
508	A period of ten years	**Decade (N.)**	दशक	4 (2)
509	An athletic event comprising ten different events	Decathlon (N.)	दस खेलों वाली एथलेटिक प्रतियोगिता	
510	To convert secret or encrypted messages into a readable form	**Decode (V.)~**	कूट भाषा को सुलझाना	
511*	The act of injuring another's reputation by slanderous communication	**Defamation (N.)~**	मानहानि	2 (2)
512	To injure one's reputation	Defame (V.)	बदनाम करना	
513*	An open refusal to obey orders or authority	**Defiance (N.)~**	अवज्ञा	1 (1)
514*	A lack or shortage of something essential	**Deficiency (N.)~**	कमी, अभाव	
515	Loss of self-awareness and restraint in a group	Deindividuation (N.)	समूह में व्यक्तिगत पहचान खो जाना	
516	A feeling that one has experienced the present situation before	**Déjà-vu (N.)**	ऐसा अहसास कि पहले देखा या अनुभव किया है	1 (1)
517*	To give one's authority or responsibility to another	**Delegate (V.)~**	काम या जिम्मेदारी सौंपना	2 (1)
518*	The act of transferring one's authority to another	Delegation (N.)	जिम्मेदारी सौंपने की प्रक्रिया	
519*	Done consciously and intentionally	**Deliberate (Adj.)~**	जानबूझकर किया गया	

SN	Phrases	One Word (PoS)	Hindi	#R
520	Long and careful consideration or discussion	Deliberation (N.)	विचार-विमर्श	
521	Minor crime or misconduct, especially by young people	**Delinquency (N.)~**	दुराचार	
522	A young person tending to commit crimes, especially minor ones	**Delinquent (Adj.)~**	दुराचारी (युवा अपराधी)	
523	To become liquid, typically during decomposition	Deliquesce (V.)	पिघलना, गलना	
524	A disturbed state of mind caused by an illness	**Delirium (N.)**	मतिभ्रम	1 (1)
525*	A political leader who seeks support by appealing to popular desires and prejudices rather than rational argument	**Demagogue (N.)**	भड़काऊ नेता	2 (4)
526	A government by the people through elected representatives	**Democracy (N.)**	जनता द्वारा चुने गए प्रतिनिधियों का शासन	5 (2)
527*	The study of population and its dynamics	**Demography (N.)**	जनसांख्यिकी	7 (1)
528	A lion's home	Den (N.)	माँद	
529	To take away or alter the natural qualities of	Denature (V.)	विकृत करना	
530	To criticize unfairly	Denigrate (V.)	बदनाम करना, नीचा दिखाना	
531	To represent or show something in words or pictures	**Depict (V.)~**	वर्णन करना	
532	A person who gives sworn written testimony for use in court	Deponent (N.)	शपथपूर्वक बयान देने वाला	
533	One who is morally corrupt	Depraved (Adj.)	भ्रष्ट	
534*	To feel and express strong disapproval	**Deprecate (V.)~**	निंदा करना, तुच्छ बताना	1 (1)
535	To become less valuable over a period of time	Depreciate (V.)	मूल्य घटना, अवमूल्यन करना	
536	A person appointed to act on behalf of another	Deputy (N.)	उपाधिकारी	
537	Unable to think clearly because of a mental illness	Deranged (Adj.)	विक्षिप्त, पागल	
538	A person without a home, job, or property	**Derelict (N.)~**	लावारिस, बेघर व्यक्ति	2
539	Failing to discharge one's duty	Dereliction (N.)	कर्तव्य का त्याग	
540	To laugh at something in a cruel way	**Deride (V.)~**	उपहास करना	
541	A doctor who studies and treats skin diseases	**Dermatologist (N.)**	त्वचा रोग विशेषज्ञ	3 (5)
542	The scientific study of the skin and its diseases	**Dermatology (N.)**	त्वचा विज्ञान	7 (2)
543*	The misuse or violation of something considered sacred	**Desecration (N.)~**	पवित्र चीज़ का अपमान	
544	The act of leaving a duty, post, or country	Desertion (N.)	कर्तव्य-त्याग	
545	Extremely poor and lacking basic necessities	**Destitute (Adj.)~**	अत्यंत निर्धन	
546	A state of disuse or inactivity	Desuetude (N.)	अप्रचलन	
547*	One who investigates and solves crimes	**Detective (N.)**	जासूस	2

SN	Phrases	One Word (PoS)	Hindi	#R
548	The act of discouraging something by instilling fear or doubt	Deterrence (N.)	डराकर रोकने की नीति	
549*	Showing a skilful use of underhand tactics to achieve goals	**Devious (Adj.)~**	धूर्त	1 (1)
550*	Showing or having skill, especially with the hands	**Dexterous (Adj.)~**	हाथों से काम करने में निपुण	2
551*	To determine the nature of a disease	Diagnose (V.)	रोग पहचानना	
552*	The process of deciding the nature of a disease by examination	**Diagnosis (N.)**	रोग की पहचान	3 (2)
553*	A particular form of a language which is peculiar to a specific region	**Dialect (N.)**	बोली	2 (1)
554*	A method of reasoning through logical argument between opposing ideas	**Dialectic (N.)~**	तर्क-वितर्क	
555	Government by two rulers or authorities	**Diarchy (N.)**	द्वैत शासन	1 (1)
556	A bitter and violent attack in words	**Diatribe (N.)**	उग्रभाषण (कठोर निंदात्मक भाषण)	2 (2)
557*	A division into two completely opposite or contrasting parts	**Dichotomy (N.)**	दो विपरीत भागों में विभाजन	1 (1)
558*	A ruler with total power over a country, typically one who has obtained control by force	**Dictator (N.)~**	तानाशाह	3 (1)
559	Giving orders in a manner that permits no refusal	Dictatorial (Adj.)	तानाशाही रवैया वाला	
560*	A book listing words of a language with their meanings	**Dictionary (N.)**	शब्दकोश	1 (1)
561*	Modesty or shyness resulting from a lack of self-confidence	**Diffidence (N.)~**	आत्मविश्वास की कमी, झिझक	
562*	Spread over a wide area or between a large number of people	Diffuse (Adj.)	फैला हुआ	
563*	A situation requiring a choice between two equally undesirable alternatives	**Dilemma (N.)~**	दुविधा	2
564	A person with a superficial interest in art or literature	**Dilettante (N.)~**	सतही रुचि रखने वाला व्यक्ति (शौकिया)	4 (1)
565*	Careful and persistent effort in work	**Diligence (N.)~**	परिश्रम, मेहनत	
566*	Showing careful and persistent effort in one's work or duties	**Diligent (Adj.)~**	परिश्रमी, मेहनती	
567	An irresistible craving for alcoholic drinks	**Dipsomania (N.)**	शराब की लत	3 (1)
568	The person who supervises the making of a film	Director (N.)	फिल्म निर्माण का प्रमुख संचालक	
569*	A book containing names, addresses, and other information	**Directory (N.)**	नाम और पते की पुस्तक	2 (2)
570	A slow sad song sung at a funeral for a dead person	**Dirge (N.)**	मृत्यु गान, शोकगीत	2
571*	A sudden event causing great damage, destruction, or suffering	**Disaster (N.)~**	आपदा	
572	A heavy round plate of metal thrown by an athlete	Discus (N.)	चक्का (चक्का फेंक प्रतियोगिता वाला)	

SN	Phrases	One Word (PoS)	Hindi	#R
573	The state of being deprived of a right or privilege, especially the right to vote	Disenfranchisement (N.)	मताधिकार से वंचित होना	
574*	Something that is shameful and morally wrong	Disgraceful (Adj.)	शर्मनाक	
575*	Disappointed and annoyed about something	**Disgruntled (Adj.)~**	असंतुष्ट	1 (1)
576*	To change one's appearance to deceive or hide identity	**Disguise (V.)~**	भेष बदलना	2
577*	To break up into small parts as the result of impact or decay	**Disintegrate (V.)**	विघटित हो जाना	2
578	Causing a mood of gloom and depression	**Dismal (Adj.)~**	निराशापूर्ण	
579*	A feeling of distress or disappointment caused by something unexpected	**Dismay (N.)~**	निराशा, हताशा	
580*	To interrupt or disturb the normal progress of an activity or process	**Disrupt (V.)~**	बाधा डालना	
581*	A person who opposes official policy	**Dissident (N.)~**	विरोधी व्यक्ति, असहमत	
582	A range of different things	**Diversity (N.)~**	विविधता	2
583*	To reveal a secret	**Divulge (V.)~**	प्रकट करना, भेद खोलना	1 (1)
584*	A person's permanent place of residence	**Domicile (N.)~**	मूल निवास	2 (1)
585*	An area of land that is controlled by a ruler	**Dominion (N.)**	आधिपत्य (शासन क्षेत्र)	1 (1)
586	Temporarily inactive or in a state of rest	**Dormant (Adj.)~**	निष्क्रिय	2
587*	A large bedroom for a number of people in a school or institution	**Dormitory (N.)**	शयनागार	5 (2)
588	Relating to or situated on the back of an animal or plant	Dorsal (Adj.)	पीठ सम्बन्धी	
589	A state of mental weakness due to old age	**Dotage (N.)**	बुढ़ापे के कारण मानसिक कमजोरी	1 (1)
590	A heavy fall of rain that often starts suddenly	Downpour (N.)	मूसलधार बारिश	
591*	Extremely harsh or severe laws or punishments	**Draconian (Adj.)~**	अत्यंत कठोर; निर्दय	
592	A game or contest that ends with no winner	**Draw (N.)~**	अनिर्णित	6
593	The nest of a squirrel, typically in the form of a mass of twigs in a tree	**Drey (N.)**	गिलहरी का घोंसला	1 (3)
594	Light rain falling in very small drops	**Drizzle (N.)~**	हल्की बारिश	
595	An abnormal or uncontrollable urge to travel	**Dromomania (N.)**	यात्रा करने की अनियंत्रित तीव्र इच्छा	1 (1)
596	A person affected by an uncontrollable urge to travel	Dromomaniac (N.)	यात्रा करने की अनियंत्रित तीव्र इच्छा से ग्रस्त व्यक्ति	
597*	A prolonged period of abnormally low rainfall	**Drought (N.)**	सूखा	2
598	A herd or flock of animals being driven in a body	**Drove (N.)**	झुंड	2 (1)
599	Capable of being bent or pulled into different shapes	**Ductile (Adj.)**	तन्य (खींचकर तार बनाने योग्य)	2

SN	Phrases	One Word (PoS)	Hindi	#R
600	A contest between two people to settle a point of honour	Duel (N.)	द्वंद युद्ध	
601	One who cannot speak	**Dumb (Adj.)~**	गूंगा	2
602*	Something that is strong and lasts a long time without breaking or becoming weaker	**Durable (Adj.)~**	टिकाऊ	
603	The time just before night when light is fading	**Dusk (N.)~**	सांझ, सूर्यस्त का समय	1 (1)
604*	A person, animal or plant much below the usual height	**Dwarf (N.)~**	बौना	
605	A wall built to prevent the sea or a river from flooding an area	Dyke (N.)	बांध	
606	A succession of rulers belonging to one family	**Dynasty (N.)**	राजवंश	1 (1)
607	A disorder involving difficulty in reading and interpreting words, letters, and symbols	Dyslexia (N.)	पढ़ने में कठिनाई होने वाला रोग	
608	A wooden frame for holding an artist's work while it is being painted or drawn	Easel (N.)	कैनवास रखने का लकड़ी का ढाँचा	
609	One who listens secretly to private conversations	**Eavesdropper (N.)**	छिपकर बातें सुनने वाला	3
610*	Unconventional and slightly strange in behaviour or habits	**Eccentric (Adj.)~**	विचित्र	4
611*	A repetition of sound caused by reflection of sound waves	**Echo (N.)~**	प्रतिध्वनि	2
612*	Drawing ideas from many sources	**Eclectic (Adj.)~**	विविध स्रोतों से लिया हुआ	
613	A person who studies the relationships between organisms and their environment	Ecologist (N.)	पारिस्थितिकी विज्ञानी	
614*	The study of the interaction of organisms with their environment	**Ecology (N.)**	पारिस्थितिकी विज्ञान	3 (2)
615	Careful in the spending of money, time, etc.	**Economical (Adj.)~**	किफ़ायती	
616*	Feeling or expressing overwhelming happiness or joyful excitement	**Ecstatic (Adj.)~**	अत्यंत आनंदित	
617*	Fit or suitable to be eaten	**Edible (Adj.)~**	खाने योग्य	7 (1)
618	To instruct or improve someone morally or intellectually	Edify (V.)	ज्ञानवर्धन करना	
619	To prepare written material for publication by correcting or modifying it	Edit (V.)	संपादन करना	
620	To rub or wipe out	**Efface (V.)~**	मिटाना	
621*	A man behaving more like a woman than a man	**Effeminate (Adj.)~**	नारी जैसा	6 (3)
622*	Something that gives off gas bubbles	**Effervescent (Adj.)~**	बुलबुलेदार	2
623*	Achieving maximum productivity with minimum wasted effort or expense	**Efficient (Adj.)~**	कुशल	2
624	A person who believes in the equality of all people	**Egalitarian (N.)~**	समानाधिकारवादी	2 (1)

SN	Phrases	One Word (PoS)	Hindi	#R
625	One who is excessively concerned with their own advantage or welfare	**Egoist (N.)~**	स्वार्थी	4 (1)
626	A person who talks excessively about themselves and is self-admiring	**Egotist (N.)**	घमंडी	4 (1)
627*	Outrageous and disgraceful	**Egregious (Adj.)~**	बेहद खराब	
628*	The people in a country or area who are entitled to vote	**Electorate (N.)**	मतदाता समूह	2
629	A poem expressing sorrow for the dead	**Elegy (N.)**	शोकगीत	7 (4)
630	A small mischievous fairy	**Elf (N.)**	परीकथा का छोटा जादुई प्राणी	3
631*	The art of effective and persuasive public speaking	**Elocution (N.)**	वाक्पटुता, भाषण देने की कला	3
632	To run away secretly with a romantic partner	**Elope (V.)~**	प्रेमी के साथ भाग जाना	2 (1)
633*	Fluent or persuasive in speaking or writing	**Eloquent (Adj.)~**	प्रभावशाली ढंग से बोलने वाला	1 (1)
634	To make perfectly clear	**Elucidate (V.)~**	स्पष्ट करना	
635	A paradise with perfect bliss	Elysium (N.)	स्वर्ग	
636	To free from restraint	**Emancipate (V.)~**	बंधनमुक्त करना	
637*	The act of setting free from bondage of any kind	**Emancipation (N.)~**	मुक्ति	
638	An official order to stop doing business with another country	**Embargo (N.)~**	व्यापार प्रतिबंध	1 (2)
639*	Feeling ashamed and shy	Embarrassed (Adj.)	शर्मिंदा	
640	To fix an object firmly and deeply in a surrounding mass	**Embed (V.)~**	जड़ना, गाड़ना	
641	A small piece of burning or glowing coal or wood in a dying fire	Ember (N.)	अंगार	
642	To steal or misappropriate money entrusted to one's care	**Embezzle (V.)~**	गबन करना	
643*	The act of misappropriating money entrusted to one's care	**Embezzlement (N.)~**	गबन	5 (1)
644*	To give a tangible or visible form to an idea, quality, or feeling	Embody (V.)	मूर्त रूप देना, साकार करना	
645*	Having retired but retaining a title as an honour	Emeritus (Adj.)	सेवानिवृत्त होकर भी सम्मानस्वरूप पदनाम बनाए रखने वाला	
646	A medicine that causes vomiting	Emetic (N.)	वमनकारी (उल्टी लाने वाली) दवा	
647*	A person who leaves his country to live in another	**Emigrant (N.)**	देश छोड़कर जाने वाला	11 (2)
648*	A person sent on a special mission, usually diplomatic or secret	Emissary (N.)	दूत	
649*	The ability to understand and share another person's feelings	**Empathy (N.)~**	सहानुभूति (दूसरे की भावना समझने की क्षमता)	3 (4)
650	One who hires others for work	Employer (N.)	काम देनेवाला	

SN	Phrases	One Word (PoS)	Hindi	#R
651	A speech or piece of writing that praises someone highly	**Encomium (N.)~**	प्रशंसा गीत	
652*	A book or set of books giving information about all areas of knowledge	**Encyclopedia (N.)**	विश्वकोश	5 (1)
653*	To try hard to do or achieve something	**Endeavour (V.)~**	प्रयत्न करना	
654	A disease regularly found in a particular area and difficult to get rid of	**Endemic (Adj.)**	किसी विशेष क्षेत्र में प्रचलित चीज या बीमारी (स्थानीय रोग)	2
655	To sweep over something so as to surround it completely	**Engulf (V.)~**	घेर लेना	
656*	A thing or person that is mysterious or difficult to understand	**Enigma (N.)~**	पहेली, रहस्य	
657*	Difficult to interpret or understand	**Enigmatic (Adj.)~**	रहस्यमय	1 (1)
658	Doing something all together as a group	En-masse (Adv.)	समूह में, सब मिलकर	
659	A state of mental weariness from lack of occupation or interest	**Ennui (N.)~**	नीरसता से उत्पन्न मानसिक थकान	2
660*	A group of dancers, actors, or performers	Ensemble (N.)	कलाकार मंडली	
661	To preserve a right, tradition, or idea in a form that ensures it will be protected and respected	Enshrine (V.)	संरक्षित करना	
662	A scientist who studies insects	**Entomologist (N.)**	कीटविज्ञानी	3 (1)
663*	The scientific study of insects	**Entomology (N.)**	कीटविज्ञान	11 (5)
664	A group of people who travel with an important or famous person	Entourage (N.)	किसी प्रसिद्ध व्यक्ति के साथ चलने वाला दल	
665	A measure of how much disorder or randomness exists in a system	**Entropy (N.)~**	अव्यवस्था की मात्रा	
666	Likely to arouse envy	Enviable (Adj.)	ईर्षा के योग्य	
667*	Lasting for a very short time	**Ephemeral (Adj.)~**	क्षणिक, थोड़े समय के लिए	8 (5)
668	A long poem narrating heroic deeds or events of great significance	Epic (N.)	महाकाव्य	
669	One who takes great pleasure in fine food and drink	**Epicure (N.)~**	भोग-विलासप्रिय व्यक्ति	1 (3)
670	Devoted to the pursuit of pleasure, especially in food and comfort	**Epicurean (Adj.)**	भोग-विलासप्रिय	2 (1)
671	A widespread outbreak of a disease affecting many people at the same time	**Epidemic (N.)~**	महामारी	5 (4)
672	A neurological disorder causing recurring seizures and loss of consciousness	Epilepsy (N.)	मिर्गी	
673	A short speech at the end of a play	**Epilogue (N.)**	उपसंहार	6 (4)
674*	The branch of philosophy concerned with the theory of knowledge	**Epistemology (N.)**	ज्ञान का अध्ययन	1 (1)
675	A formal or literary letter; a verse letter	Epistle (N.)	काव्यपत्र	
676*	An inscription on a tombstone in memory of the person who has died	**Epitaph (N.)**	समाधि-लेख, स्मृति-लेख	19 (11)
677*	A person or thing that is a perfect example of a particular quality or type	**Epitome (N.)~**	आदर्श उदाहरण	1 (1)

SN	Phrases	One Word (PoS)	Hindi	#R
678	Marking a significant period in history	**Epochal (Adj.)~**	ऐतिहासिक रूप से बहुत महत्वपूर्ण	2
679	An imaginary line dividing Earth into northern and southern hemispheres	Equator (N.)	भूमध्य रेखा	
680*	A state of perfect balance	**Equilibrium (N.)~**	समतुल्यता	3
681	The time when day and night are of equal length	**Equinox (N.)**	जब दिन और रात समान अवधि के हो	2 (2)
682	Capable of being completely destroyed or removed	Eradicable (Adj.)	जड़ से ख़तम करने योग्य	
683*	To rub out writing	**Erase (V.)~**	मिटाना	
684	An excessive desire or compulsion to work	Ergomania (N.)	काम करने की अत्यधिक इच्छा	
685	A person who loves work	**Ergophile (N.)**	काम का प्रेमी	2
686	An error in a printed book or document	**Erratum (N.)**	मुद्रण या लेखन में अशुद्धि	1 (1)
687*	Extensive knowledge acquired through study	**Erudition (N.)**	विद्वत्ता, पांडित्य	1 (1)
688	One who accompanies another for protection, guidance, or courtesy	**Escort (N.)**	मार्गरक्षी	2
689*	Respect and admiration for someone	**Esteem (N.)~**	आदर	
690*	Lasting forever without end	**Eternal (Adj.)~**	अनंत	4 (2)
691	Endless period of time	**Eternity (N.)**	अनंतकाल	2
692*	The philosophical study of moral values and rules	Ethics (N.)	नैतिक सिद्धांत	
693	Believing one's own culture, race, or ethnic group is superior to others	Ethnocentric (Adj.)	अपनी संस्कृति को श्रेष्ठ मानने वाला	
694	The study of the characteristics and customs of different peoples and cultures	**Ethnology (N.)**	मानव जाति विज्ञान	2 (2)
695	To make pale or weak by excluding light	Etiolate (V.)	प्रकाश की कमी से पीला या कमज़ोर करना	
696*	The customary code of polite behaviour in society	**Etiquette (N.)**	शिष्टाचार	2
697	A person who studies the origin of words	**Etymologist (N.)**	शब्दों की उत्पत्ति का अध्ययन करने वाला	1 (2)
698	The study of the origin and history of words	**Etymology (N.)**	शब्दों की उत्पत्ति का अध्ययन	3 (1)
699	The study of methods to improve the genetic quality of a human population	Eugenics (N.)	मानव जाति सुधार का सिद्धांत	
700	To praise highly in speech or writing	**Eulogise (V.)~**	प्रशंसा करना	
701	A formal expression of praise for someone who has died	**Eulogy (N.)~**	प्रशंसा भाषण (अक्सर मृत्यु के बाद)	5 (5)
702*	A mild or indirect expression used in place of one considered too harsh or blunt	**Euphemism (N.)~**	कठोर बात को कोमल तरीके से कहना	4
703	Pleasant or agreeable to the ear	Euphonic (Adj.)	सुरीला	
704*	A feeling of intense happiness and excitement	**Euphoria (N.)~**	परम सुख बोध	2 (1)

SN	Phrases	One Word (PoS)	Hindi	#R
705	The practice of painlessly ending the life of a person suffering from an incurable disease	**Euthanasia (N.)**	इच्छामृत्यु	4
706*	To move people from a dangerous place to somewhere safer	**Evacuate (V.)~**	बाहर निकालना	
707	Quickly fading or disappearing like vapour	**Evanescent (Adj.)~**	क्षणिक	
708	To expel someone from a property, especially with the support of the law	Evict (V.)	बेदखल करना	
709*	Gradual development or change over time	**Evolution (N.)~**	क्रमिक विकास	
710*	To develop gradually	**Evolve (V.)~**	विकसित होना	
711*	To represent something as larger, better, or worse than it really is	**Exaggerate (V.)~**	बढ़ा-चढ़ा कर कहना	
712	A person who is examined	Examinee (N.)	परीक्षार्थी	
713	Much more than usual or expected	Exceeding (Adj.)	अत्यधिक	
714	A short piece of writing, music, or film taken from a longer whole	**Excerpt (N.)~**	भाग, अंश	1 (1)
715*	A short journey for pleasure	Excursion (N.)	भ्रमण	
716	A critical explanation or interpretation of a text, especially of scripture	Exegesis (N.)	व्याख्या	
717*	A feeling of excitement or happiness	**Exhilaration (N.)~**	हर्षोल्लास	
718	An urgent need or demand	Exigency (N.)	तत्कालिक आवश्यकता	
719	A poll taken of voters as they leave a voting place, used to predict election results	Exit Poll (N.)	मतदान के बाद का सर्वेक्षण	
720	A situation in which many people leave a place at the same time	**Exodus (N.)~**	लोगों का बड़े पैमाने पर पलायन	2
721*	To free somebody from all blame	**Exonerate (V.)~**	दोषमुक्त करना	7 (5)
722	Extremely high, especially in price or amount	**Exorbitant (Adj.)~**	अत्यधिक	
723*	A large open area of land, water or sky	Expanse (N.)	विशाल क्षेत्र	
724*	A person who lives outside his native country	**Expatriate (N.)**	विदेश में रहने वाला व्यक्ति	1 (2)
725*	A journey undertaken by a group of people for exploration or research	**Expedition (N.)**	अभियान; खोज यात्रा	1 (1)
726*	To officially make a student leave a school permanently	**Expel (V.)~**	निष्कासित करना	
727	A person who has a lot of special knowledge or skill	**Expert (N.)~**	विशेषज्ञ	
728	To make atonement for one's sins	**Expiate (V.)**	प्रायश्चित करना	2
729*	To come to an end	Expire (V.)	समाप्त होना	
730	A person who travels to unknown or new places	Explorer (N.)	खोजकर्ता	
731	To remove objectionable parts from a book	**Expurgate (V.)~**	शुद्धिकरण करना, काट छाँट करना	1 (1)
732*	A speech or presentation made without previous preparation	**Extempore (N.)**	बिना तैयारी के	15 (10)
733*	No longer in existence	**Extinct (Adj.)~**	विलुप्त	

SN	Phrases	One Word (PoS)	Hindi	#R
734*	To stop something from burning	**Extinguish (V.)~**	बुझाना	
735*	The act of obtaining something, especially money, by using force or threats	**Extortion (N.)**	जबरन वसूली	1 (1)
736	To send back a criminal or an unwanted person to the country of origin	Extradite (V.)	किसी अपराधी को उसके मूल/माँग करने वाले देश को सौंपना	
737*	A person who wastes his money on luxury	**Extravagant (Adj.)~**	फ़िज़ूल ख़र्च	4
738*	A lively and confident person who enjoys being with other people	**Extrovert (N.)~**	बहिर्मुखी व्यक्ति	5
739*	A short story with a moral, usually with animals as characters	**Fable (N.)**	नैतिक शिक्षा देने वाली छोटी कहानी	3 (2)
740	A false outer appearance used to hide the truth	**Façade (N.)~**	दिखावा	
741	Something that is achieved too easily	**Facile (Adj.)~**	सहज	
742*	An exact copy of handwriting or a picture produced by a machine	**Facsimile (N.)~**	प्रतिलिपि, हूबहू नकल	3 (1)
743	A small organised dissenting group within a larger one	Faction (N.)	गुट	
744	Something that is not genuine	**Fake (Adj.)~**	नकली	
745	A false idea or belief	**Fallacy (N.)~**	गलत धारणा	2
746*	Capable of making mistakes or being wrong	**Fallible (Adj.)~**	भूल-चूक करने योग्य	
747	Land ploughed but left unsown to restore its fertility	Fallow (Adj.)	खाली छोड़ी गई खेती की ज़मीन	
748	A complete and blatant lie	Falsehood (N.)	असत्यता	
749	A lack of food during a long period of time in a region	**Famine (N.)~**	अकाल	1 (1)
750	A person motivated by irrational enthusiasm	**Fanatic (N.)~**	कट्टरपंथी	3 (6)
751	Marked by extreme and obsessive enthusiasm for a belief or cause	**Fanatical (Adj.)~**	कट्टरतापूर्ण	
752*	A pleasant situation that one imagines but is unlikely to happen	**Fantasy (N.)**	कोरी कल्पना	2
753*	One who is difficult to please	**Fastidious (Adj.)~**	बारीकियों पर अत्यधिक ध्यान देने वाला; बहुत चुनींदा	10 (8)
754*	Causing or ending in death	**Fatal (Adj.)~**	घातक	6 (2)
755	The belief that all events are predetermined and inevitable	**Fatalism (N.)**	भाग्यवाद	3 (1)
756*	A person who believes that all events are predetermined and inevitable	**Fatalist (N.)**	भाग्यवादी	11 (4)
757	Extreme tiredness resulting from mental or physical exertion	**Fatigue (N.)~**	अत्यधिक थकान	
758*	The animals of a particular region	**Fauna (N.)**	किसी क्षेत्र के जीव-जंतु	3
759*	Possible and practical to achieve	**Feasible (Adj.)~**	संभव	3
760	A pretended attack	Feint (N.)	धोखेबाज़ी भरी चाल	

SN	Phrases	One Word (PoS)	Hindi	#R
761*	To congratulate someone in a formal manner	**Felicitate (V.)~**	बधाई देना, सम्मानित करना	1 (1)
762	Well chosen or suited to the circumstances	**Felicitous (Adj.)~**	उपयुक्त	
763	Pertaining to the cat family	**Feline (Adj.)~**	बिल्ली-प्रजाति का	
764	Relating to or involved in serious crime	Felonious (Adj.)	गंभीर अपराध से संबंधित	
765	One who advocates equal rights and opportunities for women	**Feminist (N.)**	नारीवादी	2 (2)
766	A boat that transports passengers and goods over short distances regularly	Ferry (N.)	यात्रियों को ले जाने वाली नौका	
767	Relating to a festival	**Festal (Adj.)~**	उत्सव संबंधी	
768	A bitter and prolonged quarrel between families, groups, or individuals	**Feud (N.)~**	शत्रुता	
769	Changing frequently	**Fickle (Adj.)~**	चंचल, अस्थिर	
770*	Something that is made up and does not exist in reality	**Fictitious (Adj.)~**	काल्पनिक	
771	Faithfulness or loyalty to a person, cause, or belief	**Fidelity (N.)~**	निष्ठा	
772	Something that is imagined but does not exist	Figment (N.)	मनगढ़ंत कल्पना	
773	The killing of one's own child	**Filicide (N.)**	संतान-हत्या	2
774	Having a consistency that does not easily yield to pressure	**Firm (Adj.)~**	दृढ़	
775*	An obsessive interest in something or someone	**Fixation (N.)~**	किसी से गहरा लगाव	
776*	A natural talent or aptitude for something	**Flair (N.)~**	प्रतिभा	
777*	Attracting attention with a flashy or showy style	**Flamboyant (Adj.)~**	भड़कीला	1 (1)
778	An imperfection or weakness	**Flaw (N.)~**	दोष	
779	A group of ships sailing together	**Fleet (N.)**	जहाजों का बेड़ा	3
780*	Capable of bending easily without breaking and able to be easily modified	**Flexible (Adj.)~**	लचीला	2
781	A quick, sudden movement	Flick (N.)	झटका	
782	To shine with a bright but brief or irregular light	**Flicker (V.)~**	झिलमिलाना	
783	The opposite or less desirable aspect of a situation	Flip Side (N.)	अवांछित पहलू	
784*	A group of birds of one kind	**Flock (N.)**	झुंड	2 (1)
785*	The plants and vegetation of a particular region	**Flora (N.)**	किसी क्षेत्र की वनस्पति	5 (2)
786	A person who sells and arranges cut flowers	**Florist (N.)**	फूलवाला	9 (1)
787*	To struggle clumsily or helplessly	**Flounder (V.)~**	हाथ-पाँव मारना (बुरी तरह संघर्ष करना)	2
788	An accidental stroke of good fortune	**Fluke (N.)~**	अकस्मात सफलता	2
789	Continuous movement and change	Flux (N.)	प्रवाह	

SN	Phrases	One Word (PoS)	Hindi	#R
790	The act of destroying a foetus in the womb	**Foeticide (or Feticide) (N.)**	भ्रूण हत्या	4 (1)
791	A story that is passed down from generation to generation through spoken word	Folktale (N.)	लोककथा	
792	A worker who supervises other workers	Foreman (N.)	कामगारों की निगरानी करने वाला	
793	Scientific methods and techniques used in crime investigation	**Forensics (N.)**	अपराध की जाँच में प्रयुक्त वैज्ञानिक विधियाँ	1 (1)
794	The ability to predict or plan for the future	**Foresight (N.)~**	दूरदर्शिता	
795	An introductory section of a book, typically by a person other than the author	Foreword (N.)	प्रस्तावना	
796	Deprived of property or a right as a penalty for wrongdoing	Forfeited (Adj.)	जब्त किया गया	
797	The loss or giving up of something as a penalty for wrongdoing	Forfeiture (N.)	दंडस्वरूप अधिकार/संपत्ति का खोना	
798	To make or shape metal by heating	Forge (V.)	धातु को गर्म कर ढालना	
799	The act of falsifying documents	**Forgery (N.)~**	जालसाजी	3
800	Direct and outspoken	**Forthright (Adj.)~**	स्पष्टवादी	
801*	A period of two weeks	**Fortnight (N.)**	दो सप्ताह	2
802*	Happening by chance, especially to one's advantage	Fortuitous (Adj.)	आकस्मिक	
803*	The preserved remains or impression of a prehistoric organism in rock	Fossil (N.)	जीवावशेष	
804	An abandoned child of unknown parents	Foundling (N.)	लावारिस बच्चा	
805*	An entrance hall in a building used by the public, especially a hotel or theatre	**Foyer (N.)~**	प्रवेश कक्ष (लॉबी)	3
806	Easily broken or damaged	**Fragile (Adj.)~**	नाजुक	4 (1)
807*	The condition of being weak or in poor health	**Frailty (N.)~**	कमज़ोरी	
808	The right to vote in public elections; a license to sell a company's goods or services in a particular area	**Franchise (N.)**	मताधिकार; व्यापार संचालन का अधिकार	4
809	The killing of one's brother	**Fratricide (N.)**	भ्रातृहत्या	5 (2)
810*	An act of deceiving somebody in order to make money	**Fraud (N.)**	धोखा	2 (2)
811	Causing anxiety or distress	**Fraught (Adj.)~**	चिंता या परेशानी से भरा	
812	Careful and economical with spending	**Frugal (Adj.)~**	कम खर्चीला	
813*	The feeling of being upset or annoyed as a result of being unable to change or achieve something	**Frustration (N.)~**	हताशा	
814*	A person who has escaped from captivity or is in hiding	**Fugitive (N.)~**	भगोड़ा	6 (2)
815	Doing something awkwardly or in a clumsy manner	Fumbling (Adj.)	हड़बड़ाया हुआ	
816*	A person who walks on a tightrope	**Funambulist (N.)**	रस्सी पर चलनेवाला नट	1 (3)

SN	Phrases	One Word (PoS)	Hindi	#R
817	A person or organisation that collects donations for a particular cause	Fundraiser (N.)	विशेष उद्देश्य के लिए धन-संग्रह करने वाला	
818	A simple organism without flowers or leaves that spreads quickly and can cause disease	Fungus (N.)	फफूँदी	
819	The soft, thick hair covering the body of some animals	Fur (N.)	जानवरों के शरीर का घना बाल	
820	The main body of an aircraft	Fuselage (N.)	हवाई जहाज़ का ढांचा	
821	A state of agitation especially over a trivial matter	Fuss (N.)	बेकार की चिंता	
822*	Brave, noble, and chivalrous	**Gallant (Adj.)~**	वीर	
823	Causing annoyance or resentment	Galling (Adj.)	कष्टदायक	
824	An act or remark that is calculated to gain an advantage	**Gambit (N.)**	चाल	2
825	To run or jump about playfully	**Gambol (V.)~**	उछलकूद करना	
826	Expressed in an unclear or confusing way	Garbled (Adj.)	अस्पष्ट	
827*	Excessively talkative, especially on trivial matters	**Garrulous (Adj.)~**	बातूनी	5 (5)
828	The art and practice of cooking and eating good food	**Gastronomy (N.)**	पाक कला	1 (1)
829	A person who studies and works with gemstones	Gemologist (N.)	रत्न विशेषज्ञ	
830*	A chief or commander of an army (N.); Affecting all or most people, places, or things (Adj.)	**General (N./Adj.)~**	सेनाध्यक्ष, व्यापक, सामान्य	2
831	The origin or birth of a thing	**Genesis (N.)~**	उत्पत्ति	
832*	The science of heredity	**Genetics (N.)**	आनुवंशिकी	3 (3)
833*	A person with exceptional intellectual or creative ability	**Genius (N.)~**	प्रतिभाशाली व्यक्ति	
834	The deliberate killing of a large group of people, especially of a particular nation or ethnic group	**Genocide (N.)**	नरसंहार	11 (4)
835	The category to which a film or series belongs	Genre (N.)	साहित्य/फिल्म की श्रेणी	
836*	Something that truly comes from its stated or reputed source	**Genuine (Adj.)~**	असली	
837	A belief that the Earth is the centre of the universe	Geocentrism (N.)	भू-केन्द्रीय सिद्धांत	
838	The shortest possible path between two points on a curved surface	Geodesic (N.)	वक्र सतह पर सबसे छोटा मार्ग	
839	A person who studies the Earth and the materials of which it is made	**Geologist (N.)**	भूवैज्ञानिक	2
840	The scientific study of the Earth, including its structure, rocks, and soil	**Geology (N.)**	भूगर्भशास्त्र	4 (4)
841	The branch of medical science which deals with the problems of the old	**Geriatrics (N.)**	वृद्धावस्था चिकित्सा शास्त्र	2
842	A government by old people	**Gerontocracy (N.)**	वृद्ध लोगों का शासन	1 (4)

SN	Phrases	One Word (PoS)	Hindi	#R
843	The scientific study of old age and the problems of elderly people	**Gerontology (N.)**	वृद्धावस्था का अध्ययन	2
844	To manipulate electoral boundaries for political advantage	Gerrymander (V.)	चुनावी क्षेत्रों की हेरफेर करना	
845*	A movement of part of the body to express an idea or feeling	**Gesture (N.)**	इशारा	2
846	Causing horror or shock	**Ghastly (Adj.)~**	भयावह	
847	A part of a city, especially a poor area, where people of a particular race or religion live	Ghetto (N.)	बस्ती	
848	Unintelligible or meaningless speech or writing	**Gibberish (N.)**	बेमतलब शब्द	1 (1)
849	Inflammation of the gums	Gingivitis (N.)	मसूड़े की सूजन	
850	The main point or essence of a speech, text, or matter	Gist (N.)	सार, मुख्य बात	
851*	An extremely large mass of ice which moves very slowly, often down a mountain valley	**Glacier (N.)**	हिमनदी	2
852	A pair of lenses set in a frame, worn to correct defects of vision	Glasses (N.)	चश्मा	
853	A person who fits and repairs glass in windows	Glazier (N.)	कांच का काम करनेवाला	
854*	A list of technical or special words with their meanings	**Glossary (N.)**	शब्दावली	1 (1)
855	An extreme fear of public speaking	Glossophobia (N.)	सार्वजनिक भाषण का भय	
856	To look at someone in an angry or threatening way	Glower (V.)	घूर कर देखना	
857*	One who eats excessively	**Glutton (N.)**	अत्यधिक भोजन करने वाला	11 (2)
858*	To bite like a rat	Gnaw (V.)	कुतरना	
859*	A person who enjoys eating and often eats too much	**Gourmand (N.)**	अधिक खाने वाला भोजन-प्रेमी	2 (5)
860*	A connoisseur of good food and cooking	**Gourmet (N.)~**	स्वादिष्ट भोजन का जानकार	3 (2)
861	Elegance and smoothness of movement	Grace (N.)	शालीनता	
862	Writing or drawings made on walls or public surfaces without permission	**Graffiti (N.)**	दीवार चित्रण	4 (1)
863	A piece of living tissue or plant that is transplanted surgically	Graft (N.)	प्रत्यारोपण (जीवित हिस्से को काटकर दूसरी जगह रोपना या जोड़ना)	
864*	A building where grain is stored	**Granary (N.)**	धान्यागार	4 (1)
865	A person who analyses handwriting to determine personality	**Graphologist (N.)**	हस्तलेख विशेषज्ञ	1 (1)
866	The study of handwriting to analyse personality	**Graphology (N.)**	हस्तलेख विज्ञान	2 (1)
867	Without payment	Gratis (Adv.)	निशुल्क	
868	A glass building used for growing plants that need protection from cold weather	Greenhouse (N.)	पौधा-घर	

SN	Phrases	One Word (PoS)	Hindi	#R
869*	Living in groups; tending to associate with others of one's kind	**Gregarious (Adj.)~**	झुण्ड में रहनेवाला, मिलनसार	12 (3)
870*	To reduce to powder by crushing	Grind (V.)	पीसना	
871*	The sound a bear makes	Growl (N.)	भालू के गुर्राने की आवाज	
872	A low, short guttural sound, especially as made by a pig	Grunt (N.)	घुरघुराहट (सूअर की आवाज़)	
873*	One who is easily deceived	**Gullible (Adj.)~**	भोला भाला	8 (2)
874	To eat or drink quickly and in large amounts	Gulp (V.)	निगल जाना	
875	A strong blast of wind	**Gust (N.)~**	हवा का झोंका	
876	A room filled with equipment for games and physical exercise	**Gymnasium (N.)**	व्यायामशाला	1 (1)
877	A doctor who specialises in the medical care of women's reproductive system	**Gynaecologist (N.)**	स्त्रीरोग विशेषज्ञ	2
878	The branch of medicine dealing with the study of blood and blood-forming organs	Haematology (N.)	रक्त विज्ञान	
879*	A false perception of things that do not really exist	**Hallucination (N.)~**	मतिभ्रम	4
880	A drug which makes one see things that are not really there	Hallucinogen (N.)	विभ्रामक दवा	
881	A very small village	**Hamlet (N.)**	छोटा गांव	3 (3)
882	To hinder or obstruct	**Hamper (V.)~**	रोकना	
883	An object made skillfully by hand	Handicraft (N.)	हस्तशिल्प	
884	A building in which aircraft are housed	**Hangar (N.)**	विमानशाला	9
885*	A lengthy and aggressive speech addressed to a large assembly	**Harangue (N.)**	आक्रामक भाषण	3 (2)
886*	To trouble and annoy continually	**Harass (V.)~**	परेशान करना	
887	A person or thing that signals the approach of something	**Harbinger (N.)~**	सन्देशवाहक	1 (2)
888*	A place of shelter for ships	Harbour (N.)	बंदरगाह	
889	A spear used for hunting large fish	Harpoon (N.)	मत्स्य भाला	
890	Acutely distressing	**Harrowing (Adj.)~**	खौफ़नाक	
891	Unpleasantly rough or severe, especially to the senses	**Harsh (Adj.)~**	कठोर	
892	To annoy or bother someone repeatedly	Hassle (V.)	परेशान करना	
893	A strong feeling of dislike	**Hatred (N.)~**	नफरत	
894	A large catch of fish	Haul (N.)	मछलियों की बड़ी मात्रा (पकड़)	
895	A vehicle for conveying the coffin at a funeral	**Hearse (N.)**	शव वाहन	4 (1)
896	In an enthusiastic way	Heartily (Adv.)	उत्साह से	
897	Making one feel very sad	Heart-Wrenching (Adj.)	दुखी करने वाला	
898	To interrupt a public speaker with derisive or aggressive comments	**Heckle (V.)~**	बीच-बीच में टोकना (बाधा डालना)	

SN	Phrases	One Word (PoS)	Hindi	#R
899	A person who believes that pleasure is the most important thing in life	**Hedonist (N.)**	सुखवादी	3 (6)
900*	To pay careful attention to	**Heed (V.)~**	ध्यान देना	
901	A person who is legally entitled to inherit the property or rank of another	Heir (N.)	वारिस	
902	Preferring or attracted to sunlight	**Heliophilous (Adj.)**	धूप पसंद करने वाला	2
903	Treatment using exposure to sunlight for healing	**Heliotherapy (N.)**	धूप द्वारा उपचार	1 (1)
904	A person who steers a ship	Helmsman (N.)	जहाज़ की पतवार संभालने वाला	
905	A seven-sided figure	Heptagon (N.)	सप्तभुज	
906	A systematically arranged collection of dried plants	**Herbarium (N.)**	वनस्पति संग्रहालय	2
907	An animal that feeds on plants	**Herbivorous (Adj.)**	शाकाहारी	3 (1)
908	A group of cattle or sheep	**Herd (N.)**	झुंड	3 (1)
909*	A belief or opinion that contradicts established religious doctrine; opinion contrary to accepted beliefs	**Heresy (N.)~**	किसी धर्म या स्वीकृत सिद्धांतों के विपरीत राय	3 (1)
910*	A person who holds beliefs contrary to established religious doctrine	**Heretic (N.)~**	धर्म विरोधी	1 (1)
911	A person living in solitude for religious practices	**Hermit (N.)**	संन्यासी	1 (1)
912*	To pause indecisively	**Hesitate (V.)~**	हिचकिचाना	
913*	Consisting of dissimilar elements	**Heterogeneous (Adj.)**	विविध	2 (2)
914	Enabling discovery or problem-solving through practical methods rather than theory	Heuristic (Adj.)	खोज करने में सहायक	
915	A six-sided figure	**Hexagon (N.)**	षट्भुज	1 (1)
916*	To spend winter in a dormant state	**Hibernate (V.)**	शीतनिद्रा में जाना	1 (1)
917	A condition of sleep during certain parts of the year	Hibernation (N.)	शीतनिद्रा	
918	Intellectual or cultured in taste and interests	**Highbrow (Adj.)**	बौद्धिक	1 (2)
919	To seize control of a vehicle by force, especially an aircraft	**Hijack (V.)**	अपहरण करना (विशेषतः वाहन या विमान का)	2
920*	The land lying inland from a coast or river	Hinterland (N.)	भीतरी इलाके	
921	The sound made by a snake	Hiss (N.)	साँप की फुफकारी आवाज़	
922*	Very dramatic	**Histrionic (Adj.)**	नाटकीय	1 (1)
923	A container for housing honeybees	Hive (N.)	मधुमक्खी का छत्ता	
924	To secretly store more than what is allowed	**Hoard (V.)**	गुप्त तरीके से जमा करना	1 (1)
925	Destruction or slaughter on a mass scale	Holocaust (N.)	व्यापक नरसंहार	
926	The killing of a person by another	**Homicide (N.)**	मानव हत्या	4 (2)
927*	Of the same or similar kind throughout	**Homogeneous (Adj.)~**	सजातीय	5 (1)

SN	Phrases	One Word (PoS)	Hindi	#R
928*	A word that is spelt and pronounced the same as another but has a different meaning	**Homonym (N.)**	समलिखित और समोच्चारित भिन्नार्थक शब्द	2
929	A mass of wax cells built by honey bees to store honey	Honeycomb (N.)	शहद का छत्ता	
930*	A payment given for professional services that are rendered nominally without charge	Honorarium (N.)	मानदेय, सम्मान राशि	
931*	Holding an office or position as an honour without payment	**Honorary (Adj.)**	अवैतनिक	6 (7)
932	Deserving respect or admiration for ethical and fair conduct	Honourable (Adj.)	माननीय	
933	The sound of an owl	**Hoot (N.)**	उल्लू की बोली	3 (2)
934	A large group of people	**Horde (N.)**	भीड़	5
935*	The line where the land and sky seem to meet	**Horizon (N.)**	क्षितिज	5 (1)
936	The study of time and watches	Horology (N.)	घड़ियों और समय मापन का अध्ययन	
937*	Extremely unpleasant or horrifying	**Horrendous (Adj.)~**	भयावह	
938*	The study of growing garden plants	**Horticulture (N.)**	उद्यान-विज्ञान	7 (1)
939	One who studies the art of gardening	Horticulturist (N.)	उद्यान-विज्ञान विशेषज्ञ	
940*	Friendly and welcoming to visitors	**Hospitable (Adj.)~**	सत्कार करने वाला	1 (1)
941*	The friendly reception and entertainment of guests	**Hospitality (N.)~**	अतिथि सत्कार	
942*	A person held captive for the fulfilment of demands	**Hostage (N.)**	बंधक	3
943	A woman who entertains guests	Hostess (N.)	सत्कारिणी	
944	One who loses temper very soon	Hot-headed (Adj.)	उग्र स्वभाव का	
945	Annoyed or irritated and quick to take offence at petty things	Huffy (Adj.)	झुंझलाया हुआ	
946	The organic component of soil formed by decomposed plant matter	**Humus (N.)**	जैविक मिट्टी	1 (1)
947	An assembly or parliament in which no party has a clear majority	Hung (Adj.)	बहुमत विहीन	
948*	A violent wind that has circular movement	Hurricane (N.)	चक्रवात	
949	In a quick manner	Hurriedly (Adv.)	हड़बड़ी में	
950	A box or cage for rabbits or small animals	**Hutch (N.)**	छोटे जानवरों के रहने का घर	4
951	A serpent with many heads in Greek mythology	Hydra (N.)	बहु-सिर वाला काल्पनिक सर्प	
952	The science of surveying and charting bodies of water	Hydrography (N.)	जलराशि विज्ञान	
953	An extreme or irrational fear of water, especially as a symptom of rabies	**Hydrophobia (N.)**	पानी का डर	8 (3)
954*	A song or music in praise of God	**Hymn (N.)**	स्तुति-गीत, भजन	2
955	An exaggerated statement not to be taken seriously or literally	**Hyperbole (N.)~**	अतिशयोक्ति	2 (1)
956*	Excessive preoccupation with one's health	Hypochondria (N.)	रोगभ्रम	

SN	Phrases	One Word (PoS)	Hindi	#R
957	A person who imagines illness or is abnormally anxious about health	**Hypochondriac (N.)**	रोगभ्रमी	7 (6)
958*	The practice of pretending to have virtues or beliefs one does not actually possess	**Hypocrisy (N.)~**	पाखंड	2 (2)
959*	A person who pretends to be what they are not	**Hypocrite (N.)**	पाखंडी	9 (2)
960*	A tentative theory about the natural world	**Hypothesis (N.)~**	परिकल्पना	
961*	A person who attacks or criticizes cherished beliefs or institutions	**Iconoclast (N.)~**	स्थापित मान्यताओं का विरोधी	12 (6)
962*	A person's peculiar habit or characteristic way of behaving	**Idiosyncrasy (N.)~**	विशेष स्वभाव	3 (1)
963*	A mode of behaviour or thought peculiar to an individual	Idiosyncratic (Adj.)	विशेष स्वभाव का	
964*	An image of a God used for worship	**Idol (N.)~**	प्रतिमा, मूर्ति	2
965	The practice of worshipping statues as gods	**Idolatry (N.)**	मूर्ति पूजा	2
966*	Extremely happy, peaceful, or picturesque	**Idyllic (Adj.)~**	शांत और सुखद	
967	A circular house made of blocks of hard snow	**Igloo (N.)**	बर्फ का घर	3
968*	Difficult or impossible to read	**Illegible (Adj.)**	अपठनीय	15 (8)
969*	Something that is not permitted by law	**Illicit (Adj.)~**	अवैध	3 (1)
970*	Unable to read or write	**Illiterate (Adj.)**	अनपढ़	8 (2)
971	To brighten up with lights	**Illuminate (V.)~**	प्रकाश करना	2
972*	A picture in a book used to explain or decorate the text	**Illustration (N.)**	चित्रण	2
973*	Existing only in the mind	**Imaginary (Adj.)~**	काल्पनिक	
974*	A very complex situation	**Imbroglio (N.)~**	उलझन	1 (3)
975	Something that can be copied	Imitable (Adj.)	नकल करने योग्य, अनुकरणीय	
976*	The action of using someone or something as a model	**Imitation (N.)~**	नकल, अनुकरण	
977*	A person who comes to a foreign country to settle there permanently	**Immigrant (N.)**	आप्रवासी (दूसरे देश में बसने वाला व्यक्ति)	5
978	The act of passing or coming into a new habitat or country	Immigration (N.)	किसी नए देश में बसने के लिए आना	
979	Unable to move or be moved	Immobile (Adj.)	अचल	
980	Against accepted moral standards	**Immoral (Adj.)~**	अनैतिक	1 (1)
981*	Never able to die	**Immortal (Adj.)~**	अमर	
982	Resistant to a particular infection	**Immune (Adj.)~**	प्रतिरक्षित, रोग-प्रतिरोधी	3 (1)
983	Protection or exemption from something, especially an obligation or penalty	Immunity (N.)	छूट या संरक्षण	
984	To pierce with a sharp instrument	Impale (V.)	छेदना	
985*	Not supporting any side in an argument	**Impartial (Adj.)~**	निष्पक्ष	
986	The action of formally accusing a public official of a serious offence	Impeachment (N.)	महाभियोग	
987*	The policy of extending a country's empire and influence	**Imperialism (N.)**	साम्राज्यवाद	1 (3)

SN	Phrases	One Word (PoS)	Hindi	#R
988*	Not allowing fluid to pass through; unaffected by external influence	**Impervious (Adj.)~**	अभेद्य, अप्रभावित	2 (1)
989	To harass someone persistently to do something	**Importune (V.)~**	बार-बार आग्रह करके परेशान करना	
990	A person who dishonestly pretends to be someone else in order to deceive	**Impostor (N.)**	ढोंगी (खुद को कोई और बताकर धोखा देने वाला)	6 (1)
991	Too strong to be defeated or captured	**Impregnable (Adj.)**	अभेद्य (जिसे हराना असंभव हो)	2 (2)
992	Made or done without previous preparation	**Impromptu (Adj.)~**	बिना तैयारी के	2 (1)
993	One who is too careless to plan for the future	**Improvident (Adj.)~**	अदूरदर्शी	
994	Shamelessly rude	**Impudent (Adj.)~**	ढीठ	
995*	Exemption from punishment or freedom from harmful consequences	**Impunity (N.)**	दण्ड मुक्ति	2 (1)
996	Incapable of being approached	**Inaccessible (Adj.)~**	दुर्गम	5
997	Something that is not endowed with life	**Inanimate (Adj.)~**	निर्जीव, अचेतन	2
998*	Unable to speak distinctly or express oneself clearly	**Inarticulate (Adj.)~**	व्यक्त करने में असमर्थ	2
999*	A sound that cannot be heard	**Inaudible (Adj.)**	अश्राव्य, सुनाई न देने वाला	11 (3)
1000	A deity or spirit embodied in human form	Incarnate (Adj.)	मानवरूप में अवतार	
1001*	A motive or incitement to action	**Incentive (N.)~**	प्रोत्साहन	2 (2)
1002	Continuing without pause or interruption	**Incessant (Adj.)~**	बिना रुके लगातार	1 (2)
1003	Lack of civic-mindedness or patriotism	**Incivism (N.)**	नागरिक कर्तव्यों की अवहेलना	2
1004	Travelling under a name other than one's own	**Incognito (Adj.)~**	गुप्त पहचान में	
1005*	Something that is expressed in a confusing way	**Incoherent (Adj.)~**	असंगत	
1006	Difficult or impossible to understand	**Incomprehensible (Adj.)**	समझ से बाहर	3 (1)
1007	The state of not being in agreement or harmony	Incongruence (N.)	असंगति, मेल न खाना	
1008*	Impossible to deny or disprove	**Incontrovertible (Adj.)**	अविवादित	1 (2)
1009*	Unable to be corrected or reformed	**Incorrigible (Adj.)~**	असंशोधनीय (जो कभी न सुधर सके)	15 (2)
1010*	Extraordinary or unbelievable	**Incredible (Adj.)~**	अविश्वसनीय	6 (2)
1011	Owing money to someone	**Indebted (Adj.)~**	ऋणी	
1012*	Incapable of feeling tired or exhausted	**Indefatigable (Adj.)~**	न थकने वाला	6 (2)
1013*	Something that cannot be erased or forgotten	**Indelible (Adj.)~**	स्थायी	2 (3)
1014	Too extreme or unusual to be adequately described	Indescribable (Adj.)	अवर्णनीय	

SN	Phrases	One Word (PoS)	Hindi	#R
1015*	Originating or occurring naturally in a particular place	**Indigenous (Adj.)~**	स्वदेशी	1 (3)
1016	Anger about an unfair situation or about someone's unfair behaviour	**Indignation (N.)~**	आक्रोश	3
1017*	Something that is absolutely necessary or crucial	**Indispensable (Adj.)~**	अपरिहार्य, अत्यावश्यक	3
1018	Diligent and hard-working	**Industrious (Adj.)~**	मेहनती	
1019*	Not fit to eat	**Inedible (Adj.)**	अखाद्य	4
1020*	That which cannot be expressed in words	**Ineffable (Adj.)~**	अवर्णनीय	4 (1)
1021	Someone not fit to be chosen	**Ineligible (Adj.)**	अयोग्य	2
1022	Lack of skill or ability	Ineptness (N.)	अयोग्यता	
1023	Lacking the ability to act	**Inert (Adj.)~**	अक्रिय	
1024*	Something that cannot be avoided; certain to happen	**Inevitable (Adj.)~**	अटल	13 (7)
1025*	Not to be moved by entreaty	**Inexorable (Adj.)~**	हठी, निर्दयी	1 (1)
1026*	That which cannot be put out	Inextinguishable (Adj.)	जिसे बुझाया न जा सके	
1027*	One who cannot make mistakes	**Infallible (Adj.)~**	अचूक	12 (6)
1028	The killing of an infant	**Infanticide (N.)**	शिशु हत्या	3 (2)
1029*	Without any limit or end	**Infinite (Adj.)~**	अनंत	2
1030*	A place in a large institution for the care of those who are ill	**Infirmary (N.)**	अस्पताल	2
1031*	That which catches fire easily	**Inflammable (Adj.)**	ज्वलनशील	7
1032	A cluster of flowers on a branch	Inflorescence (N.)	फूलों का गुच्छा	
1033*	Exceptionally clever or talented	**Ingenious (Adj.)~**	प्रतिभाशाली	
1034*	The money, property, etc. received from someone after their death	Inheritance (N.)	विरासत	
1035*	Not guilty of any wrongdoing and lacking knowledge or awareness of it	**Innocent (Adj.)~**	निर्दोष	
1036*	Causing no harm	**Innocuous (Adj.)~**	हानिरहित	1 (1)
1037	An indirect reference	**Innuendo (N.)~**	इशारा (गलत भावना से)	
1038*	To treat with a vaccine to promote immunity against a disease	Inoculate (V.)	टीका लगाना	
1039*	Eager to learn or know things	**Inquisitive (Adj.)~**	जिज्ञासु	
1040*	Unable to be satisfied	**Insatiable (Adj.)~**	जिसकी इच्छा कभी पूरी न हो	6 (1)
1041	To write or carve words on stone or paper	Inscribe (V.)	अंकित करना	
1042	Words carved on a stone or monument	Inscription (N.)	शिलालेख	
1043*	Harmful in a quiet and gradual way	**Insidious (Adj.)~**	धीरे-धीरे नुकसान करने वाला	
1044	One who is unable to pay debts	**Insolvent (Adj.)~**	दिवालिया	6 (11)
1045	The condition of being unable to sleep over a period of time	**Insomnia (N.)**	अनिद्रा	6 (2)

SN	Phrases	One Word (PoS)	Hindi	#R
1046	Covered with a material to stop heat, cold, electricity etc. from entering or escaping	Insulated (Adj.)	रोधक पदार्थ से ढका हुआ	
1047	A person who rebels against authority	**Insurgent (N.)~**	विद्रोही	
1048	That which cannot be perceived by touch	**Intangible (Adj.)~**	अमूर्त (स्पर्श न किए जा सकने वाला)	
1049*	To combine to form a whole	**Integrate (V.)~**	संघटित करना	
1050*	The quality of being honest and having strong moral principles	**Integrity (N.)~**	अखंडता	3
1051*	One who interferes in the affairs of others, often for selfish reasons	Interloper (N.)	दखल देने वाला व्यक्ति	
1052	An interval between two events	**Interlude (N.)**	मध्यांतर	2
1053	One who intervenes between two or more parties to settle differences	**Intermediary (Adj.)**	मध्यस्थ	2
1054	The act of burying a dead person	**Interment (N.)**	दफ़न	2 (3)
1055*	Continuing for a very long time	**Interminable (Adj.)~**	अनंतकालीन	
1056	The act of confining someone in a prison	Internment (N.)	नजरबंदी	
1057	To add something in the middle of a text or piece of music; To estimate intermediate values	Interpolate (V.)	बीच में डालना; मध्यवर्ती मान निकालना	
1058	To place or insert between one thing and another	Interpose (V.)	घुसाना	
1059	The period between two reigns	**Interregnum (N.)**	दो शासनों के बीच का काल	2
1060	To prevent or alter a result or course of events	**Intervene (V.)~**	हस्तक्षेप करना	
1061	One who dies without making a valid will	**Intestate (Adj.)**	बिन वसीयत मरा हुआ	5
1062	To force someone through fear to do or not to do something	**Intimidate (V.)**	धमकाना	2
1063	The examination or observation of one's own mental and emotional processes	**Introspection (N.)**	आत्म निरीक्षण	4
1064*	A person more focused on their own thoughts than social interaction	**Introvert (N.)~**	अन्तर्मुखी व्यक्ति	8 (5)
1065*	A person who enters without any invitation	**Intruder (N.)**	घुसपैठिया	1 (1)
1066*	To overflow or fill an area with excess water	**Inundate (V.)~**	जलमग्न कर देना, बाढ़ लाना	
1067*	A person weak and disabled by illness	Invalid (N.)	बीमारी से कमज़ोर व्यक्ति	
1068	A detailed list of things in a place	**Inventory (N.)~**	वस्तु सूची	1 (1)
1069	An animal that lacks a backbone	Invertebrate (N.)	जानवर जिसकी रीढ़ की हड्डी नहीं होती	
1070*	An official examination of the facts about a situation, crime, etc.	Investigation (N.)	जाँच पड़ताल	
1071*	A person who supervises during an examination	**Invigilator (N.)**	परीक्षा पर्यवेक्षक	7 (1)
1072	To fill someone with energy and liveliness	**Invigorate (V.)~**	स्फूर्ति देना; तरोताज़ा करना	2
1073	That which cannot be conquered	**Invincible (Adj.)~**	अजेय	6 (5)
1074	A call upon God or any other power for help or protection	Invocation (N.)	आह्वान	

SN	Phrases	One Word (PoS)	Hindi	#R
1075	A detailed list of goods dispatched with quantity and price to the purchaser	**Invoice (N.)~**	चालान	
1076	Done without conscious control or intention	Involuntary (Adj.)	अनैच्छिक	
1077*	That which cannot be harmed or wounded	Invulnerable (Adj.)	अभेद्य	
1078*	Easily provoked	**Irascible (Adj.)~**	चिड़चिड़ा	
1079	A literary device in which the opposite of what is expected occurs or is stated	**Irony (N.)**	व्यंग्य, विडंबना	2
1080*	A statement that cannot be disproved or contradicted	Irrefutable (Adj.)	अखंडनीय	
1081*	Showing a lack of proper respect for people or things held sacred	**Irreverent (Adj.)~**	अनादरपूर्ण	
1082*	That which cannot be called back or reversed	**Irrevocable (Adj.)~**	जिसे बदला न जा सके	7
1083	To supply land with water by artificial means	Irrigate (V.)	सींचना	
1084*	A piece of land entirely surrounded by water	Island (N.)	द्वीप	
1085	A small island	Islet (N.)	छोटा द्वीप	
1086	Far away from other places	**Isolated (Adj.)~**	अलग-थलग	
1087	A narrow strip of land connecting two larger land areas, with water on both sides	Isthmus (N.)	स्थलडमरूमध्य (भूमि की एक संकीर्ण पट्टी जो दो बड़े भूभागों को जोड़ती है)	
1088*	Travelling from place to place, especially to find work	**Itinerant (Adj.)**	भ्रमणकारी	4 (1)
1089*	A plan of a journey, including the route and the places to be visited	**Itinerary (N.)**	यात्रा कार्यक्रम	7 (4)
1090*	A person employed to clean and maintain a building	Janitor (N.)	चौकीदार, सफ़ाईकर्मी	
1091*	Special words and phrases used by particular groups of people, especially in their work	**Jargon (N.)~**	विशिष्ट शब्दावली	1 (2)
1092	A short journey made for pleasure	Jaunt (N.)	मनोरंजन की यात्रा	
1093	In a lively, cheerful, and self-confident manner	Jauntily (Adv.)	प्रसन्नतापूर्वक	
1094	To cross streets on foot carelessly	Jaywalk (V.)	लापरवाही से सड़क पार करना	
1095	An extreme form of patriotism	Jingoism (N.)	कट्टर राष्ट्रवाद	
1096	A person or thing believed to bring bad luck	**Jinx (N.)~**	मनहूस	2 (1)
1097	A person who rides in horse races, especially as a profession	**Jockey (N.)**	घुड़दौड़ का घुड़सवार	5
1098	The profession of collecting and writing news for media	**Journalism (N.)**	पत्रकारिता	1 (1)
1099*	A person who writes for newspapers and magazines	**Journalist (N.)**	पत्रकार	1 (1)
1100*	Cheerful and friendly in manner	**Jovial (Adj.)~**	उल्लासपूर्ण	2

SN	Phrases	One Word (PoS)	Hindi	#R
1101*	The part of a country's government responsible for its legal system	Judiciary (N.)	न्यायतंत्र	
1102	A military group that rules a country after taking power by force	**Junta (N.)**	सैन्य शासकों का समूह	2
1103*	The science or philosophy of law	**Jurisprudence (N.)**	न्यायशास्त्र	2 (2)
1104	A group of citizens who hear evidence in court and decide if someone is guilty	**Jury (N.)**	न्यायिक निर्णायक मंडल	2
1105*	Relating to young people who are not yet adults	**Juvenile (Adj.)~**	किशोर संबंधी	
1106*	To place things side by side for comparison or contrast	**Juxtapose (V.)**	समीप रखकर तुलना करना	3 (1)
1107	The philosophy that human knowledge is limited by the mind's capacity, preventing us from knowing things as they truly are	**Kantianism (N.)**	कांट के दार्शनिक विचार	2
1108	A small shelter for a dog	**Kennel (N.)**	कुत्ता-घर	4 (3)
1109*	The inner soft part of a seed, fruit, or nut	**Kernel (N.)**	गिरी, दाना	2 (1)
1110	One's relatives or family	Kin (N.)	रिश्तेदार	
1111	A small structure with one or more open sides used to sell merchandise	**Kiosk (N.)~**	छोटी दुकान, गुमटी	
1112	A government by rulers who exploit public resources for personal gain	Kleptocracy (N.)	लूट-तंत्र	
1113*	A mental condition where a person feels an uncontrollable urge to steal	**Kleptomania (N.)**	चोरी करने की मानसिक बीमारी	8 (6)
1114*	One who has a persistent neurotic impulse to steal	**Kleptomaniac (N.)**	चोरी करने की बीमारी से पीड़ित व्यक्ति	3 (1)
1115	A natural skill at doing something	**Knack (N.)~**	किसी काम में प्राकृतिक हुनर	2 (1)
1116	The sound of the funeral bell	**Knell (N.)**	शोक सूचक घंटे की ध्वनि	2 (1)
1117*	Confusingly complex and difficult to navigate	**Labyrinthine (Adj.)~**	बहुत उलझा हुआ, भूलभुलैया जैसा	
1118	A deep cut or tear in skin or flesh	Laceration (N.)	गहरा घाव	
1119	A structure with rungs used for climbing	**Ladder (N.)**	सीढ़ी	2
1120	A saltwater lake separated from the sea by rocks and sand	Lagoon (N.)	समुद्री झील	
1121	A place where wild animals live	**Lair (N.)~**	माँद	1 (2)
1122	The young one of a sheep	Lamb (N.)	मेमना	
1123*	An expression of grief	**Lament (N.)~**	शोक, विलाप	
1124	A person who cuts and polishes gems	Lapidary (N.)	रत्न तराशने वाला	
1125	The person who cuts, polishes, and engraves precious stones	Lapidist (N.)	रत्न काटने/तराशने वाला	
1126	A room or large cupboard for storing food	Larder (N.)	खाना रखने की जगह	
1127*	Denoting the second or second mentioned of two people or things	Latter (Adj.)	बाद वाला	
1128*	Worthy of high praise	**Laudable (Adj.)~**	प्रशंसनीय	
1129*	A place where clothes are washed and pressed	Laundry (N.)	धोबीघाट	

SN	Phrases	One Word (PoS)	Hindi	#R
1130*	An honour given for some achievement	Laurel (N.)	प्रतिष्ठा	
1131	Failing to give proper care or attention	**Lax (Adj.)~**	ढीला-ढाला, लापरवाह	
1132	A medicine that softens the bowels	Laxative (N.)	पेट साफ करने की दवा	
1133*	A legal agreement to use a building or land for a period of time in return for rent	Lease (N.)	पट्टा, किरायानामा	
1134	A sly, lustful look	Leer (N.)	वासनापूर्ण नज़र	
1135*	Money or property left by someone in their will	**Legacy (N.)**	विरासत	2
1136	That which is lawful	Legal (Adj.)	क़ानूनी	
1137*	Free time when one is not working or occupied	**Leisure (N.)~**	खाली समय	
1138	Resembling a lion	**Leonine (Adj.)**	सिंह जैसा	1 (1)
1139	A person who collects or studies butterflies	Lepidopterist (N.)	तितली विशेषज्ञ	
1140	A person who writes and edits dictionaries	**Lexicographer (N.)**	शब्दकोश निर्माता	12 (5)
1141	The practice of writing and compiling dictionaries	**Lexicography (N.)**	शब्दकोश निर्माण	2 (1)
1142*	A list of words in a language, arranged alphabetically	Lexicon (N.)	शब्दकोश	
1143*	Responsible according to law	**Liable (Adj.)~**	उत्तरदायी	
1144*	A person who strongly believes in personal freedom of thought and action	Libertarian (N.)	व्यक्तिगत स्वतंत्रता में विश्वास करने वाला व्यक्ति	
1145	A place where books and other materials are kept for reading or borrowing	**Library (N.)**	पुस्तकालय	1 (1)
1146	A strong band of tissue that connects bones to each other	**Ligament (N.)**	हड्डियों को जोड़ने वाले तंतु	2
1147	The centre of public attention	**Limelight (N.)~**	प्रकाश में, चर्चा में	
1148	A humorous five-line poem	Limerick (N.)	पाँच पंक्तियों वाली हास्य कविता	
1149	Eating mud	**Limivorous (Adj.)**	मिट्टी खाने वाला	2
1150	The essential part that holds everything together	Linchpin (N.)	मुख्य आधार; केंद्र बिंदु	
1151	To stay longer than necessary	**Linger (V.)~**	देर तक रुकना	
1152	A person who studies languages or knows several foreign languages well	**Linguist (N.)**	भाषाविज्ञानी, बहुभाषाविद्	1 (3)
1153*	One who can read and write	Literate (N.)	साक्षर	
1154	An understatement in which a positive idea is expressed by denying its opposite (e.g., "not bad")	Litotes (N.)	दोहरे नकारात्मक द्वारा सकारात्मक अर्थ	
1155	Farm animals raised for use or profit	Livestock (N.)	पशुधन	
1156	Very talkative	**Loquacious (Adj.)~**	बातूनी	3 (2)
1157*	Easy to understand	**Lucid (Adj.)~**	सुस्पष्ट	1 (1)
1158*	Profitable, yielding financial gain	**Lucrative (Adj.)~**	लाभकारी	
1159	A soft gentle song sung to make a child go to sleep	**Lullaby (N.)~**	लोरी	2

SN	Phrases	One Word (PoS)	Hindi	#R
1160	A unit to measure light	Lumen (N.)	प्रकाश की इकाई	
1161	A person who inspires others intellectually or morally	Luminary (N.)	महान प्रेरणास्रोत विद्वान	
1162	An amount of money that is paid at one time	Lump Sum (N.)	एकमुश्त	
1163	Related to the moon	**Lunar (Adj.)**	चन्द्र संबंधी	3
1164	One who is mentally not sound	**Lunatic (N.)**	पागल	2 (1)
1165	To make an abrupt, unsteady movement	Lurch (V.)	लड़खड़ाना	
1166	A situation of great confusion, turmoil, or chaos	Maelstrom (N.)	अत्यधिक उथल-पुथल या अराजकता की स्थिति	
1167	A person who performs tricks and illusions to entertain people	**Magician (N.)**	जादूगर	2
1168*	Kind, generous, and forgiving, especially towards an enemy	**Magnanimous (Adj.)~**	उदार चरित्र (बड़ा दिल वाला)	2 (2)
1169*	Extremely beautiful, elaborate, or impressive	**Magnificent (Adj.)~**	भव्य	
1170*	A young unmarried woman (N.); First or earliest (Adj.)	**Maiden (N./Adj.)**	अविवाहिता; पहला	1 (1)
1171	The first public speech delivered by a person	**Maiden speech (N.)~**	पहला सार्वजनिक भाषण	2
1172	The mistaken use of a word in place of a similar-sounding one	Malapropism (N.)	मिलते-जुलते शब्द की जगह गलत शब्द का प्रयोग	
1173	One who is never happy with what he has	**Malcontent (N.)**	असंतुष्ट	1 (2)
1174*	A feeling of ill will or desire to harm others	Malevolence (N.)	दुर्भावना	
1175*	Causing or wanting to cause harm to others	**Malevolent (Adj.)~**	दुर्भावनापूर्ण	
1176	A failure to function normally	Malfunction (N.)	तकनीकी खराबी	
1177*	Easy to shape in any desired form	**Malleable (Adj.)~**	आसानी से आकार लेने वाला	2
1178	Insufficient nourishment	Malnutrition (N.)	कुपोषण	
1179*	An animal that feeds its young with milk from the mother's body	**Mammal (N.)**	स्तनपायी	2
1180	In a way that is clear or obvious to the eye or mind	Manifestly (Adv.)	स्पष्ट रूप से	
1181	A written statement by a group, especially a political party, explaining their beliefs and intentions	**Manifesto (N.)**	घोषणापत्र	1 (1)
1182	A dummy used to display clothes in a shop window	Mannequin (N.)	पुतला	
1183*	A carefully planned action or movement	Manoeuvre (N.)	सोची-समझी चाल	
1184	An instrument used for measuring the pressure of liquids and gases	Manometer (N.)	दबाव नापने का यंत्र	
1185*	A large impressive house	**Mansion (N.)**	हवेली	2
1186	A document or book written by hand before being printed	**Manuscript (N.)**	हस्तलिखित (हाथ से लिखी हुई)	6 (5)
1187	Relating to the sea	Marine (Adj.)	समुद्री	
1188	Relating to soldiers or war	Martial (Adj.)	युद्ध संबंधी	

SN	Phrases	One Word (PoS)	Hindi	#R
1189*	One who demands strict conformity to rules	**Martinet (N.)**	कठोर अनुशासक	1 (2)
1190	One who is killed for the cause of religion or faith	**Martyr (N.)**	शहीद	6 (2)
1191	One who obtains pleasure from receiving pain or punishment	**Masochist (N.)**	पीड़ा में आनंद लेने वाला व्यक्ति	2
1192*	A person skilled in cutting, dressing, and laying stone in buildings	**Mason (N.)**	राजमिस्त्री	3
1193	Excessively concerned with money and possessions	**Materialistic (Adj.)**	भौतिकवादी	1 (2)
1194	A cinema show held in the afternoon	**Matinee (N.)**	दोपहर की फ़िल्म	6
1195	A woman who is the head of the family	Matriarch (N.)	मातृसत्तात्मक मुखिया	
1196	The killing of one's mother	**Matricide (N.)**	मातृहत्या	5
1197*	The state of being married	Matrimony (N.)	दाम्पत्य; विवाह-बंधन	
1198	A stately or impressive building housing a tomb or group of tombs	**Mausoleum (N.)**	मक़बरा	2
1199*	A short statement expressing a general truth or rule of conduct	**Maxim (N.)~**	कहावत, नीति-वाक्य	3 (1)
1200*	An area of grassland where animals graze	**Meadow (N.)**	चारागाह	2
1201	To move about from place to place aimlessly	**Meander (V.)~**	इधर-उधर घूमना	
1202*	A person who repairs and maintains machines	Mechanic (N.)	मशीनों की मरम्मत करने वाला	
1203	One who interferes in others' affairs	Meddler (N.)	दखल देने वाला	
1204*	To try to settle a dispute between two other parties	**Mediate (V.)**	मध्यस्थता करना	1 (1)
1205*	Belonging to the Middle Ages	Medieval (Adj.)	मध्यकालीन	
1206*	Of only average standard	**Mediocre (Adj.)~**	औसत दर्जे का	1 (1)
1207	A musical composition made up of a series of songs or short pieces	Medley (N.)	गीत समूह	
1208	Feeling or expressing pensive sadness	Melancholic (Adj.)	उदास और सोच में डूबा हुआ	
1209	A feeling of deep, lasting sadness	**Melancholy (N.)**	उदासी	3 (1)
1210*	A sound that is pleasing to hear	**Melodious (Adj.)~**	मधुर	2
1211*	A dramatic work with exaggerated emotions and sensational events	Melodrama (N.)	अतिनाटकीय नाटक	
1212	One who loves music	Melophile (N.)	संगीत प्रेमी	
1213*	An object kept as a reminder of a person or event	**Memento (N.)**	यादगार निशानी	2
1214*	A written account of personal experiences	**Memoir (N.)~**	संस्मरण	
1215*	A person or thing that is likely to cause harm; To threaten or endanger	**Menace (N./V.)~**	खतरा, डराना-धमकाना	1 (1)
1216*	A collection of wild animals kept in captivity for exhibition	**Menagerie (N.)**	पशु शाला	1 (4)
1217	One who goes from place to place, begging	**Mendicant (N.)~**	भिखारी	
1218*	A soldier who fights for any country that pays them	**Mercenary (N.)**	किराये का सैनिक	9 (7)

SN	Phrases	One Word (PoS)	Hindi	#R
1219*	A narrative technique where the line between reality and fiction is blurred, often involving self-awareness of being fictional	Metafiction (N.)	ऐसा साहित्य जो स्वयं के काल्पनिक होने का बोध कराए	
1220*	The scientific study of metals and their uses	**Metallurgy (N.)**	धातु विज्ञान	1 (1)
1221	A change in the form or nature of something	**Metamorphosis (N.)~**	कायांतरण	1 (1)
1222*	Paying careful attention to every detail	**Meticulous (Adj.)~**	बारीकी से ध्यान देने वाला	3 (1)
1223	A very small business, typically with fewer than ten employees	Microenterprise (N.)	सूक्ष्म उद्यम	
1224	An extreme fear of small things	Microphobia (N.)	छोटी चीजों से डर	
1225	An instrument for magnifying very small objects for examination	Microscope (N.)	सूक्ष्मदर्शी	
1226*	A traveller who moves from one region or country to another	**Migrant (N.)**	प्रवासी	4
1227	The movement of people or animals from one area to another	Migration (N.)	प्रवास	
1228*	A period of one thousand years	**Millennium (N.)**	हज़ार वर्ष	2 (1)
1229*	To imitate someone's actions or words in order to entertain or ridicule	Mimic (V.)	नकल उतारना	
1230*	The act of copying the behaviour or speech of other people	Mimicry (N.)	अनुकरण, नक़ल	
1231	Being conscious and attentive	Mindful (Adj.)	सचेत	
1232	A person who studies rocks and minerals	Mineralogist (N.)	खनिज विशेषज्ञ	
1233	A place where money is coined by authority of the government	**Mint (N.)**	टकसाल	11 (2)
1234*	A person who hates and avoids other people	**Misanthrope (N.)**	मानवद्वेषी	10 (8)
1235	A general contempt towards mankind	Misanthropy (N.)	मानव से घृणा	
1236	To unfairly take something belonging to another for one's use	Misappropriate (V.)	गबन करना	
1237	One who loves money and hates spending it	**Miser (N.)~**	कंजूस	3 (2)
1238	A word or name that is inappropriate for a person or thing	Misnomer (N.)	गलत नाम	
1239	One who hates the institution of marriage	**Misogamist (N.)**	विवाह से घृणा करने वाला	4 (2)
1240*	A person who hates women	**Misogynist (N.)**	स्त्री से घृणा करने वाला	7 (4)
1241	One who hates reasoning, argument, or enlightenment	**Misologist (N.)**	तर्क वितर्क से घृणा करने वाला	1 (2)
1242	One who hates new things	Misoneist (N.)	नई चीजों से घृणा करने वाला	
1243*	Helping you to remember something	Mnemonic (Adj.)	स्मृति सहायक	
1244	A large crowd of people, especially one that may become violent or cause trouble	Mob (N.)	भीड़	
1245	A particular method of working	Modus Operandi (N.)	कार्य-प्रणाली	

SN	Phrases	One Word (PoS)	Hindi	#R
1246*	Lasting for a very short time	**Momentary (Adj.)~**	क्षणिक	
1247*	Of great importance or significance	**Momentous (Adj.)~**	अत्यंत महत्वपूर्ण	2
1248*	A supreme ruler	**Monarch (N.)**	सम्राट	2
1249*	A system of government by a king or queen	**Monarchy (N.)**	राज-तंत्र	6 (3)
1250	A building where monks live as a community	**Monastery (N.)**	मठ	3 (2)
1251	A warning of impending danger	Monition (N.)	चेतावनी	
1252	A member of a religious community living in a monastery	Monk (N.)	साधु	
1253	A person who has only one spouse at a time	Monogamist (N.)	एक विवाहवादी	
1254	The practice of having only one spouse at a time	**Monogamy (N.)**	एक विवाह प्रथा	2 (1)
1255*	A detailed written study on a single subject	Monograph (N.)	विषय-विशेष पर पुस्तक	
1256*	A long speech given by one person in a play or performance	**Monologue (N.)~**	एकल संवाद	1 (2)
1257	An obsession with one particular thing	Monomania (N.)	एक ही बात की धुन	
1258*	The complete control of trade in particular goods or the supply of a particular service	**Monopoly (N.)**	एकाधिकार	2 (2)
1259	A condition of having only one copy of a chromosome	Monosomy (N.)	एक गुणसूत्र होना	
1260	One who believes in only one god	**Monotheist (N.)**	एकेश्वरवादी	1 (1)
1261*	Boring due to lack of variety	**Monotonous (Adj.)~**	नीरस, उबाऊ	2
1262	A series of shots put together sequentially to narrate something within a film	Montage (N.)	क्रमबद्ध दृश्यों का संयोजन	
1263*	A structure built to commemorate a person or event	Monument (N.)	स्मारक	
1264	To secure a boat by attaching it to an anchor	Moor (V.)	लंगर डालना	
1265	The customs and habits of a particular group	Mores (N.)	रीति रिवाज	
1266	A place where dead bodies are kept for identification	**Morgue (N.)**	मुर्दा घर	3 (5)
1267	The scientific study of the structure and form of animals and plants	Morphology (N.)	जीवों की बनावट का अध्ययन	
1268*	The state of being subject to death	**Mortality (N.)~**	नश्वरता	
1269*	A legal agreement by which a bank lends you money to buy a house	Mortgage (N.)	गिरवी	
1270	A place for keeping dead bodies before burial or cremation	**Mortuary (N.)**	शवगृह	5 (4)
1271	A picture or pattern made by arranging small pieces of coloured stone or glass	Mosaic (N.)	रंगीन पत्थर या कांच के टुकड़ों से बना कलात्मक रचना	
1272	To mark with spots or smears of colour	Mottle (V.)	धब्बेदार बनाना	

SN	Phrases	One Word (PoS)	Hindi	#R
1273	Looking or smelling extremely appetizing	**Mouth-watering (Adj.)**	मुँह में पानी ला देने वाला (अत्यंत स्वादिष्ट)	2 (1)
1274	To make a sound quieter or to wrap or cover for warmth	Muffle (V.)	आवाज़ दबाना; लपेटना	
1275	A sound that is not loud because of being obstructed	Muffled (Adj.)	दबा हुआ (आवाज़)	
1276	Proficient in speaking many languages	**Multilingual (Adj.)**	बहुभाषी	1 (2)
1277	The ability to do several things at the same time	Multitasking (N.)	एक साथ कई काम करने की क्षमता	
1278	Consisting of many things or parts	Multitudinous (Adj.)	असंख्य	
1279	A body preserved by treating it with special oils and wrapping it in cloth	Mummy (N.)	संरक्षित शव	
1280*	Ordinary and dull	**Mundane (Adj.)~**	साधारण	3 (1)
1281	A building where objects of historical, scientific, or artistic interest are kept and displayed	**Museum (N.)**	संग्रहालय	3
1282	The act of refusing to obey the orders of somebody in authority, especially by soldiers or sailors	**Mutiny (N.)**	बगावत	2
1283	Lacking foresight or intellectual insight; Short sighted	**Myopic (Adj.)~**	निकटदर्शी	2
1284*	Something that is difficult to understand or explain	Mystery (N.)	रहस्य	
1285	The compulsion to tell lies	**Mythomania (N.)**	झूठ बोलने की प्रवृत्ति	1 (1)
1286	An extreme fear of myths or lies	Mythophobia (N.)	झूठ या कल्पित कहानियों का डर	
1287	Showing a lack of experience, wisdom, or judgement	**Naive (Adj.)~**	अनुभवहीन	
1288	A person or thing that has the same name as another	**Namesake (N.)**	हमनाम	4
1289*	The habit of excessive admiration for oneself, especially one's appearance	**Narcissism (N.)**	आत्ममुग्धता (स्वयं से अत्यधिक प्रेम)	3 (1)
1290*	A person having excessive admiration for oneself, especially one's appearance	**Narcissist (N.)**	आत्ममुग्ध व्यक्ति (स्वयं से अत्यधिक प्रेम करने वाला)	11 (8)
1291	A drug that induces drowsiness, sleep, or insensibility and relieves pain	Narcotic (N.)	मादक पदार्थ	
1292*	Just beginning to exist or develop	**Nascent (Adj.)~**	नवजात	1 (1)
1293	Highly unpleasant or offensive	**Nasty (Adj.)~**	घृणित	2
1294	A person, animal or plant belonging originally to a particular place	**Native (N.)~**	स्थानीय; मूल निवासी	4 (1)
1295*	To guide the course of a ship, especially by using instruments or maps	**Navigate (V.)**	मार्ग निर्देशन करना	2
1296	A fluid secreted by flowers which is collected by bees for making honey	Nectar (N.)	पुष्प रस	
1297*	So small or unimportant as to be not worth considering	Negligible (Adj.)	नगण्य, ना के बराबर	

SN	Phrases	One Word (PoS)	Hindi	#R
1298	One who mediates in a deal or complex situation	Negotiator (N.)	समझौता कराने वाला	
1299*	The sound made by a horse	**Neigh (N.)**	हिनहिनाहट	2 (1)
1300*	A deserved and unavoidable punishment for wrongdoing	**Nemesis (N.)**	दंड जिस से बचा न जा सके	2 (1)
1301	A newly coined word, expression, or usage	**Neologism (N.)**	नवनिर्मित शब्द	3
1302	A person who has recently started an activity	**Neophyte (N.)~**	नौसिखिया	2 (1)
1303	A specialist in kidney diseases	**Nephrologist (N.)**	गुर्दा विशेषज्ञ	1 (1)
1304	The practice of giving unfair advantages to one's relatives	**Nepotism (N.)~**	भाई-भतीजावाद	8 (3)
1305	A doctor who studies the nervous system and its disorders	**Neurologist (N.)**	तंत्रिका रोग विशेषज्ञ	1 (1)
1306	The study of the nervous system and its disorders	Neurology (N.)	स्नायु विज्ञान	
1307*	The scientific study of the nervous system and brain	Neuroscience (N.)	तंत्रिका विज्ञान	
1308	A hollow space in a wall for a statue or ornament	**Niche (N.)**	आला (दीवार में बना खोखला स्थान)	1 (1)
1309	The rejection of all religious and moral principles, in the belief that life is meaningless	Nihilism (N.)	शून्यवाद	
1310*	A transcendent state in which there is neither suffering, desire, nor sense of self	**Nirvana (N.)**	मोक्ष	1 (1)
1311*	Occurring at night	**Nocturnal (Adj.)**	रात में होने वाला	1 (1)
1312	One who moves from place to place with no fixed home	**Nomad (N.)**	ख़ानाबदोश	4 (1)
1313*	A system of naming things	Nomenclature (N.)	नामकरण प्रणाली	
1314	One who is between ninety and one hundred years of age	Nonagenarian (N.)	90 से 99 वर्ष के बीच का व्यक्ति	
1315	One who does not follow accepted rules, customs, or beliefs	**Nonconformist (N.)~**	रिवाजों या नियमों को न मानने वाला	
1316	An unimportant person	Nonentity (N.)	तुच्छ व्यक्ति	
1317	A delusion of suffering from a disease	Nosomania (N.)	बीमारी से पीड़ित होने का भ्रम	
1318*	A sentimental longing for a period in the past	**Nostalgia (N.)~**	पुरानी यादों की तड़प	11 (4)
1319*	Well-known for being bad; a person of evil reputation	**Notorious (Adj.)~**	कुख्यात	10 (1)
1320	The quality of being new and original	**Novelty (N.)~**	नवीनता	
1321*	A person who is new to a profession, without training or experience	**Novice (N.)~**	नौसिखिया	5 (6)
1322	One who studies the occult meanings of numbers and their supposed influence on human life	Numerologist (N.)	अंक ज्योतिषी	
1323	The study or collection of coins	**Numismatics (N.)**	मुद्राशास्त्र	6 (5)
1324*	A person who studies or collects coins	**Numismatist (N.)**	मुद्राशास्त्री	8 (5)

SN	Phrases	One Word (PoS)	Hindi	#R
1325*	A place where young plants or trees are grown for sale or for planting elsewhere	Nursery (N.)	पेड़-पौधों को उगाने का स्थान	
1326	An extreme fear of darkness	**Nyctophobia (N.)**	अँधेरे का डर	1 (2)
1327	A big, clumsy, often slow-witted person	**Oaf (N.)~**	मूर्ख व्यक्ति	
1328	A fertile tract in a desert where the water table approaches the surface	**Oasis (N.)~**	मरुस्थल के बीच हरित भूमि	2 (1)
1329	A notice of a person's death	**Obituary (N.)**	मृत्यु सूचना	7 (2)
1330*	Not aware of or not informed about something	**Oblivious (Adj.)~**	बेखबर	
1331*	Not clearly expressed or easily understood	**Obscure (Adj.)~**	अस्पष्ट	1 (1)
1332*	A place equipped for observing celestial bodies	**Observatory (N.)**	वेधशाला	2
1333	An intense and unhealthy fixation on something	**Obsession (N.)~**	अत्यधिक लगाव	
1334*	The state of becoming outdated or no longer used	**Obsolescence (N.)~**	अप्रचलन	
1335	Becoming outdated or passing out of use	Obsolescent (Adj.)	अप्रचलित होता हुआ	
1336*	Something no longer in use	**Obsolete (Adj.)~**	अप्रचलित	19 (9)
1337	Relating to the countries of the west	**Occidental (Adj.)**	पश्चिमी देशो से संबंधीत	3
1338	A geometrical figure with eight sides	**Octagon (N.)**	अष्टभुज	4
1339	A person who is between eighty and eighty-nine years old	**Octogenarian (N.)**	80 से 89 वर्ष की आयु वाला व्यक्ति	1 (1)
1340	An eight-armed sea creature	Octopus (N.)	आठ भुजाओं वाला समुद्री जीव	
1341	A doctor who specializes in the diseases of the eye	**Oculist (N.)**	नेत्र-विशेषज्ञ	1 (1)
1342*	A long adventurous journey marked by many changes of fortune	**Odyssey (N.)**	लंबी और रोमांचक यात्रा	1 (1)
1343	An excessive or obsessive craving for wine or alcoholic drinks	**Oenomania (N.)**	शराब की लत	2
1344	Not quite coinciding with a central position	Off-Centre (Adj.)	केंद्र से हटा हुआ	
1345	A form of government by a small group of people	**Oligarchy (N.)**	अल्पतंत्र (कुछ लोगों का शासन)	8 (10)
1346*	A person who investigates and helps settle public complaints	Ombudsman (N.)	लोक शिकायत अधिकारी	
1347*	Suggesting that something unpleasant is likely to happen	**Ominous (Adj.)~**	अशुभ संकेत देने वाला	2
1348	A volume containing several books previously published separately	Omnibus (N.)	संकलन ग्रंथ	
1349	Having unlimited power	**Omnipotent (Adj.)~**	सर्वशक्तिमान	9 (6)
1350	Present everywhere	**Omnipresent (Adj.)~**	सर्वव्यापी	2 (4)
1351*	Knowing everything	**Omniscient (Adj.)~**	सर्वज्ञानी	12 (6)

SN	Phrases	One Word (PoS)	Hindi	#R
1352	An animal or person that eats both plants and meat	**Omnivore (N.)**	सर्वाहारी जीव	3
1353	Eating both plants and meat	**Omnivorous (Adj.)**	सर्वाहारी	4 (3)
1354*	That through which light cannot pass	**Opaque (Adj.)~**	अपारदर्शी	8 (1)
1355	An extreme fear of snakes	**Ophidiophobia (N.)**	साँपों का डर	3
1356	The study of snakes	**Ophiology (N.)**	सांपो का अध्ययन	2
1357*	A doctor who specializes in the diseases of the eyes	**Ophthalmologist (N.)**	नेत्र-विशेषज्ञ	4
1358	One who is stubborn about holding to one's own opinions	Opinionated (Adj.)	हठधर्मी, अपने विचारों पर दृढ़	
1359	Public disgrace arising from shameful conduct	**Opprobrium (N.)~**	सार्वजनिक निंदा	
1360*	One who sees the bright side of things	**Optimist (N.)~**	आशावादी	8 (3)
1361	A musical composition, especially one on a large scale	**Opus (N.)**	कृति, संगीत रचना	2
1362	A formal speech, especially one given on a ceremonial occasion	Oration (N.)	भाषण	
1363	A proficient public speaker	**Orator (N.)**	कुशल वक्ता	4 (1)
1364*	A piece of land or garden in which fruit trees are grown	**Orchard (N.)**	फलदार पेड़ों का बाग	8 (5)
1365*	A large body of people playing various musical instruments	Orchestra (N.)	वाद्य यंत्र बजाने वाले संगीतकारों का समूह	
1366	A very unpleasant or difficult experience	Ordeal (N.)	कठिन और कष्टदायक अनुभव	
1367	An opening or hole, particularly one in the body such as a nostril	**Orifice (N.)~**	छिद्र	
1368	A person who studies birds	**Ornithologist (N.)**	पक्षी विशेषज्ञ	4 (2)
1369	The scientific study of birds	**Ornithology (N.)**	पक्षी विज्ञान	3 (7)
1370	The branch of geography that studies mountains and their formation	Orography (N.)	पर्वतों का अध्ययन	
1371	The study of mountains	Orology (N.)	पर्वतों का अध्ययन	
1372	A child whose parents are dead	**Orphan (N.)**	अनाथ	3 (1)
1373*	A public institution for the care and protection of children without parents	**Orphanage (N.)**	अनाथालय	2
1374	Holding conventional beliefs, especially in matters of religion	**Orthodox (Adj.)~**	रूढ़िवादी	2 (1)
1375	The branch of medicine dealing with bone disorders	Orthopaedics (N.)	हड्डियों से संबंधित चिकित्सा	
1376	A doctor who treats bone disorders	**Orthopaedist (N.)**	हड्डी रोग विशेषज्ञ	5 (1)
1377	To make or become like a bone	**Ossify (V.)~**	हड्डी जैसा कठोर हो जाना	
1378	A person who looks after horses at an inn	Ostler (N.)	घोड़ों की देखभाल करने वाला	
1379*	To banish or turn out of society and fellowship	**Ostracise (V.)~**	बहिष्कृत करना	1 (1)
1380	To be more successful than someone	Outdo (V.)	किसी से बेहतर करना	

SN	Phrases	One Word (PoS)	Hindi	#R
1381	Looking or sounding bizarre, strange, or unfamiliar	**Outlandish (Adj.)~**	अजीब और अनोखा	
1382	A person who has broken the law, especially one who remains at large or is a fugitive	Outlaw (N.)	नियमविरोधी	
1383	The extent of involvement with or influence in the community	Outreach (N.)	पहुँच	
1384	The ongoing expenses of operating a business that are not directly related to production	Overhead (N.)	संचालन खर्च	
1385	To fail to notice something or to let a fault go unpunished	**Overlook (V.)~**	अनदेखी करना	
1386*	To have a strong emotional effect on someone	Overwhelm (V.)	अभिभूत करना	
1387	Pertaining to sheep	Ovine (Adj.)	भेड़ से संबंधित	
1388	The belief that war and violence are unjustified	**Pacifism (N.)**	शांतिवाद	2
1389	A person who opposes war or use of military force	**Pacifist (N.)~**	शांतिवादी	8 (2)
1390	A group of wolves; A set of 52 playing cards	**Pack (N.)**	भेड़ियों का झुंड; ताश की गड्डी	2 (2)
1391	A formal agreement between two or more nations or peoples	Pact (N.)	समझौता	
1392*	A doctor who treats children's diseases	**Paediatrician (N.)**	बच्चों का चिकित्सक	2 (1)
1393*	The study of ancient writings and scriptures	**Palaeography (N.)**	प्राचीन लिपियों का अध्ययन	1 (4)
1394	A person who studies fossils	Palaeontologist (N.)	जीवाश्मों का अध्ययन करने वाला	
1395	A word that reads the same backwards as forwards	**Palindrome (N.)**	ऐसा शब्द जो आगे और पीछे दोनों तरफ से एक जैसा हो	1 (1)
1396	Temporary relief from pain or suffering without curing the cause	Palliation (N.)	अस्थायी राहत	
1397*	Able to be felt or touched	**Palpable (Adj.)~**	स्पर्शनीय	
1398	A solution for all difficulties or diseases	**Panacea (N.)~**	रामबाण इलाज	16 (5)
1399*	A disease that spreads over a whole country or the whole world	**Pandemic (N.)**	महामारी	3 (2)
1400	A state of wild and noisy disorder	**Pandemonium (N.)~**	कोलाहल	
1401	To gratify an immoral or distasteful desire	Pander (V.)	बुरी इच्छाओं को पूरा करना	
1402	A speech or writing that praises someone excessively	**Panegyric (N.)~**	अत्यधिक प्रशंसा	1 (1)
1403*	Sudden uncontrollable fear or anxiety, often causing wildly unthinking behaviour	**Panic (N.)~**	आतंक, भगदड़	
1404	A wide, uninterrupted view	**Panorama (N.)~**	विस्तृत दृश्य	
1405	To breathe hard and with difficulty	Pant (V.)	हाँफ़ना	
1406	The belief that God is in everything, including nature	**Pantheism (N.)**	सर्वेश्वरवाद	4 (5)

SN	Phrases	One Word (PoS)	Hindi	#R
1407	A person who believes that God is present in all things in nature	**Pantheist (N.)**	सर्वेश्वरवादी	1 (3)
1408*	A temple dedicated to all the gods	Pantheon (N.)	सर्वदेवालय	
1409	A small room or cupboard for storing food, dishes, and kitchen utensils	**Pantry (N.)**	रसोई भंडार	2
1410	Photographers who aggressively pursue celebrities to take their pictures	Paparazzi (N.)	सेलेब्रिटी का पीछा करने वाले फ़ोटोग्राफ़र	
1411	A story told to illustrate a moral or spiritual truth	**Parable (N.)~**	नीति कथा	4
1412	A statement that appears self-contradictory yet may be true	**Paradox (N.)~**	विरोधाभासी परंतु सत्य कथन	2
1413	One who lives or survives on others or other lives	**Parasite (N.)**	परजीवी	5
1414	To boil food briefly or partially	Parboil (V.)	अधपका उबालना	
1415*	A person who is rejected and avoided by society	**Pariah (N.)**	समाज से बहिष्कृत व्यक्ति	1 (1)
1416	Having a limited or narrow outlook or scope	**Parochial (Adj.)~**	संकीर्ण सोच वाला	
1417*	The early release of a prisoner on condition of good behaviour	**Parole (N.)**	सशर्त रिहाई	1 (1)
1418	The crime of killing one's father, mother, or close relative	**Parricide (N.)**	माता-पिता या निकट संबंधी की हत्या	1 (1)
1419	One who has suddenly become rich but lacks social grace	**Parvenu (N.)**	नया अमीर व्यक्ति (जिसमें शिष्टाचार की कमी हो)	2 (1)
1420	The sole right to make and sell an invention	Patent (N.)	आविष्कार पर विशेष अधिकार	
1421	The scientific study of diseases	**Pathology (N.)**	रोग विज्ञान	3 (1)
1422*	A system of society or government in which men hold power and women are largely excluded from it	**Patriarchy (N.)**	पुरुष-प्रधान व्यवस्था	2
1423	The killing of one's own father	**Patricide (N.)**	पितृहत्या	3 (1)
1424	Relating to inheritance or descent through the male line	Patrilineal (Adj.)	पितृवंशीय	
1425*	Property that is given to somebody when his father dies	**Patrimony (N.)**	पैतृक संपत्ति	5
1426	A person who loves, supports and defends his country	**Patriot (N.)~**	देश-भक्त	5
1427	To go around an area to keep a watch	**Patrol (V.)~**	गश्त लगाना, पहरा करना	
1428*	One who has no money or means of livelihood	**Pauper (N.)**	कंगाल	4
1429	Concerning or consisting of money	Pecuniary (Adj.)	धन-संबंधी	
1430*	The method and practice of teaching	**Pedagogy (N.)**	शिक्षा शास्त्र	4
1431	A person who is excessively concerned with minor details or formal rules	**Pedant (N.)**	छोटी-छोटी गलतियों या नियमों पर जोर देने वाला (व्यक्ति)	4

SN	Phrases	One Word (PoS)	Hindi	#R
1432*	Excessively concerned with minor details or formalisms	**Pedantic (Adj.)**	छोटी-छोटी गलतियों या नियमों पर जोर देने वाला (स्वभाव)	2 (2)
1433*	A person who walks on foot rather than travelling in a vehicle	**Pedestrian (N.)**	पैदल यात्री	8 (4)
1434	A doctor who treats children	Pediatrician (N.)	बच्चों का डॉक्टर	
1435	The branch of medicine concerned with children and their illnesses	Pediatrics (N.)	बाल चिकित्सा	
1436*	A punishment imposed for breaking a law, rule, or contract	Penalty (N.)	जुर्माना	
1437	A special fondness or liking for something	**Penchant (N.)~**	विशेष रुचि	2
1438*	A small ornament which hangs down especially from a necklace	Pendant (N.)	गले की हार का लॉकेट	
1439*	To move into or through something	**Penetrate (V.)~**	भीतर प्रवेश करना	
1440*	A large mass of land projecting into a body of water	Peninsula (N.)	प्रायद्वीप	
1441*	The state of feeling sorry for wrongdoing	**Penitence (N.)~**	पश्चाताप	
1442*	Deep in thought	**Pensive (Adj.)~**	विचारमग्न	
1443	One who quickly understands and responds to situations	Perceptive Adj.	सूझबूझ वाला	
1444*	Lasting for an indefinitely long time	**Perennial (Adj.)~**	सदाबहार	2
1445*	A deliberate breach of faith or betrayal of trust	Perfidy (N.)	विश्वासघात	
1446*	Done as a routine but without interest	**Perfunctory (Adj.)~**	बेमन से किया गया	
1447	A structure in the garden where climbing plants can grow and people can walk under	**Pergola (N.)**	छाया करने या पौधों के चढ़ने के लिए बनाया गया ढांचा	2
1448	Continuing for a long period of time without interruption; lasting forever or indefinitely	**Perpetual (Adj.)~**	निरन्तर	3
1449*	Confused or puzzled	Perplexed (Adj.)	व्याकुल, उलझन में	
1450	An additional benefit or privilege given to an employee beyond their salary	**Perquisite (N.)~**	अतिरिक्त लाभ, विशेषाधिकार	2
1451	To subject someone to hostility or ill-treatment, especially for their beliefs	Persecute (V.)	सताना, अत्याचार करना	
1452*	Constant effort to achieve something	**Perseverance (N.)~**	निरंतर प्रयत्न	4 (1)
1453*	The people employed in an organization or engaged in a service	Personnel (N.)	कर्मचारी वर्ग	
1454	Careful reading or examination	Perusal (N.)	ध्यानपूर्वक अध्ययन	
1455*	A person who tends to see the worst aspect of situations	**Pessimist (N.)~**	निराशावादी	9 (2)
1456	A substance used for killing pests	**Pesticide (N.)**	कीटनाशक	2
1457	Morally harmful or spreading evil influence	Pestiferous (Adj.)	दुष्प्रभावकारी	
1458	A stick with a thick end used in a mortar for pounding	Pestle (N.)	मूसल	

SN	Phrases	One Word (PoS)	Hindi	#R
1459	A long wooden seat with a back for people to sit on in a church	Pew (N.)	गिरज़ाघर का बेंच	
1460*	A place where you can buy medicines	Pharmacy (N.)	दवाखाना	
1461*	An observable fact or event	Phenomenon (N.)	घटना	
1462	A person who always runs after women	Philanderer (N.)	इश्क़बाज़	
1463*	A person who loves mankind and donates money and time to help others	**Philanthropist (N.)~**	मानव प्रेमी; परोपकारी	20 (10)
1464*	Love for mankind shown by donating money and time	**Philanthropy (N.)**	मानव प्रेम; परोपकार	3 (3)
1465	A person who collects or studies stamps	**Philatelist (N.)**	डाक-टिकट संग्रहकर्ता	10 (6)
1466*	The collection and study of postage stamps	Philately (N.)	डाक-टिकट संग्रह या अध्ययन	
1467*	A person who lacks interest in art, culture, or refined ideas	**Philistine (N.)~**	कला-संस्कृति के प्रति उदासीन व्यक्ति	7 (1)
1468	A person who likes or admires women	**Philogynist (N.)**	स्त्री-प्रेमी	2
1469*	The study of languages	**Philology (N.)**	भाषाशास्त्र	3 (1)
1470*	One who loves wisdom and pursues it	Philosopher (N.)	दार्शनिक	
1471	An intense and irrational fear of something	**Phobia (N.)**	अत्यधिक और असामान्य भय	2
1472	The study and classification of sounds	**Phonetics (N.)**	ध्वनि-विज्ञान	3 (1)
1473*	A doctor who specialises in general medicine and not surgery	Physician (N.)	चिकित्सक	
1474*	The study of the functions of the human body	**Physiology (N.)**	शरीरविज्ञान	2 (2)
1475	The treatment of disease or injury through physical exercises and massage	Physiotherapy (N.)	भौतिक चिकित्सा	
1476	A place where pigs are kept	Pigsty (Sty) (N.)	सूअर रखने की जगह	
1477	A large number of things placed one on top of another	Pile (N.)	ढेर	
1478	The act of stealing something in small quantities	**Pilferage (N.)**	छोटी चोरी	1 (1)
1479*	A seat for a passenger on a bicycle or motorbike	Pillion (N.)	पीछे की सीट	
1480*	One who is among the first to explore or develop something	**Pioneer (N.)~**	नई राह दिखाने वाला	2
1481	A person who attacks and robs ships at sea	**Pirate (N.)~**	समुद्री डाकू; अवैध नकल करने वाला	2
1482	Illegally copied without the owner's permission	Pirated (Adj.)	अवैध रूप से नकल किया हुआ	
1483	Feeding on fish	Piscivorous (Adj.)	मछली खाने वाला	
1484	Playing a crucial role	**Pivotal (Adj.)~**	महत्वपूर्ण	
1485	To make someone less angry or hostile	**Placate (V.)~**	शांत करना	
1486	An inactive substance given for psychological benefit rather than medical effect	Placebo (N.)	मानसिक सुकून देने वाली नकली दवा	
1487	Not easily excited or upset	**Placid (Adj.)~**	शांत	

SN	Phrases	One Word (PoS)	Hindi	#R
1488*	To use another person's ideas or work as one's own	**Plagiarise (V.)**	साहित्यिक चोरी करना	2
1489*	The act of using another person's ideas or work as one's own	**Plagiarism (N.)**	साहित्यिक चोरी	5 (5)
1490*	One who uses another person's ideas or work as one's own	**Plagiarist (N.)**	साहित्यिक चोर	3
1491*	A person who brings a case against another in a court of law	**Plaintiff (N.)**	मुकदमा करने वाला	2 (1)
1492*	A flat metal or porcelain plate fixed on a wall as an ornament or memorial	Plaque (N.)	दीवार पर लगी सजावटी या स्मारक पट्टी	
1493*	Seeming reasonable or probable	**Plausible (Adj.)~**	विश्वसनीय लगने वाला	2
1494	A decision made by public voting	**Plebiscite (N.)~**	जनमत-संग्रह	
1495*	A solemn promise or undertaking	**Pledge (N.)~**	प्रतिज्ञा	2
1496	The state of being full or complete	Plenitude (N.)	प्रचुरता	
1497*	Capable of being bent or shaped easily without breaking	**Pliable (Adj.)~**	लचीला	
1498*	One who repairs leaking water pipes	Plumber (N.)	नल ठीक करने वाला व्यक्ति	
1499	A government by the richest people of a country	**Plutocracy (N.)**	धनी लोगों का शासन	9 (6)
1500	A speaker's platform	**Podium (N.)~**	मंच	
1501*	Evoking a keen sense of sadness or regret	**Poignant (Adj.)~**	मार्मिक	1 (1)
1502	Graceful and balanced behaviour	**Poise (N.)~**	संतुलन, शालीनता	
1503	Pertaining to controversy	Polemical (Adj.)	विवादात्मक	
1504	The science or art of governing a country or area	**Politics (N.)**	राजनीति	1 (1)
1505	The practice of having more than one husband at the same time	**Polyandry (N.)**	बहुपति प्रथा	3 (5)
1506	A person who has more than one spouse at the same time	Polygamist (N.)	बहुविवाही	
1507	The practice of having more than one spouse at the same time	**Polygamy (N.)**	बहुविवाह प्रथा	3 (3)
1508	A person who can speak several languages	**Polyglot (N.)**	बहुभाषी	10 (15)
1509	A flat shape with three or more straight sides and angles	Polygon (N.)	बहुभुज	
1510	A person who is skilled in many areas	**Polymath (N.)**	अनेक विषयों में विद्वान व्यक्ति	1 (2)
1511	One who believes in many gods	**Polytheist (N.)**	बहुदेववादी	2
1512	To think carefully and thoroughly about something	**Ponder (V.)~**	गंभीरता से विचार करना	
1513	Full of people	**Populous (Adj.)~**	घनी आबादी वाला	
1514	A place where ships load and unload goods	Port (N.)	बंदरगाह	
1515*	Something that can be carried easily	**Portable (Adj.)**	आसानी से साथ ले जाने योग्य	6
1516*	A collection of documents or works showing a person's abilities or achievements	**Portfolio (N.)**	दस्तावेज़-संग्रह	2

SN	Phrases	One Word (PoS)	Hindi	#R
1517*	Occurring, awarded, or appearing after someone's death	**Posthumous (Adj.)**	मरणोपरांत	8 (7)
1518	A medical examination of a dead body	**Postmortem (N.)**	शवपरीक्षा	4
1519*	To delay an event to a later date or time	Postpone (V.)	स्थगित करना	
1520	A note appended to a letter after the signature	**Postscript (N.)**	पत्र के अंत में हस्ताक्षर के बाद लिखा गया अतिरिक्त संदेश	2 (3)
1521*	Safe or suitable for drinking	**Potable (Adj.)**	पीने योग्य	7 (6)
1522	A liquid with healing, magical, or poisonous properties	Potion (N.)	औषधीय या जादुई तरल	
1523	A mixture of dried flowers and leaves used for making a room smell pleasant	**Potpourri (N.)**	सुगन्धित सूखे फूलों का मिश्रण; विविध वस्तुओं का संग्रह	1 (1)
1524*	The actual application of an idea, belief, or method	Practice (N.)	अमल, प्रयोग	
1525*	Dealing with things in a practical and sensible way	**Pragmatic (Adj.)~**	व्यावहारिक	
1526	One who values practicality	Pragmatist (N.)	व्यावहारिक सोच वाला	
1527*	Uncertain and risky	**Precarious (Adj.)~**	अनिश्चित और जोखिमभरा	2
1528*	A previous case that might serve as an example or guide in subsequent situations	Precedent (N.)	मिसाल, पूर्व निर्णय	
1529	A very steep or overhanging rock face or cliff on a mountain	Precipice (N.)	खड़ी चट्टान	
1530	A short version of a written text with only the main points	Precis (N.)	किसी लेख का छोटा सार	
1531	An animal that lives by killing and eating other animals	**Predator (N.)~**	शिकारी जानवर, परभक्षी	4 (1)
1532	A person who held a position before the current holder	**Predecessor (N.)~**	पूर्ववर्ती	
1533*	To say or estimate that something will happen in the future	**Predict (V.)~**	पूर्वानुमान करना	
1534*	A special liking or preference for something	**Predilection (N.)~**	विशेष लगाव या रुझान	
1535*	An introduction to a book, especially one that explains the author's aims	**Preface (N.)**	प्रस्तावना	2
1536*	Having a bias against others	Prejudiced (Adj.)	पक्षपातपूर्ण	
1537	An action or event that happens before another important one and forms an introduction to it	Prelude (N.)	प्रस्तावना, भूमिका	
1538	The first public performance of a musical or theatrical work or the first showing of a film	**Premiere (N.)**	प्रथम प्रदर्शन	2
1539	A strong feeling that something is about to happen, especially something unpleasant	**Premonition (N.)~**	पूर्वाभास	2 (1)
1540	To recommend or order a medicine or treatment	Prescribe (V.)	दवा लिखना	
1541	An assumption made without proof	**Presumption (N.)**	अनुमान (बिना प्रमाण मान लेना)	1 (1)

SN	Phrases	One Word (PoS)	Hindi	#R
1542*	Trying to appear more important or valuable than one really is	**Pretentious (Adj.)~**	दिखावटी, आडंबरपूर्ण	
1543*	To make evasive or misleading statements instead of telling the truth	**Prevaricate (V.)~**	सीधा जवाब न देकर टालना	2
1544	A group of lions	**Pride (N.)~**	शेरों का समूह	3
1545*	A right or advantage available to a person	**Privilege (N.)~**	विशेषाधिकार	
1546	A person working on a trial period	**Probationer (N.)~**	प्रशिक्षु (नया कर्मचारी)	
1547	To put off doing something, especially out of habitual carelessness or laziness	**Procrastinate (V.)~**	टालना	4 (1)
1548*	The habit of delaying things	**Procrastination (N.)~**	टालमटोल	3
1549*	Spending money freely and wastefully	**Prodigal (Adj.)~**	फिजूलखर्च करने वाला	1 (2)
1550*	A person, especially a young one, with exceptional abilities	**Prodigy (N.)~**	विलक्षण प्रतिभासंपन्न व्यक्ति	1 (1)
1551*	A high degree of skill	Proficiency (N.)	निपुणता	
1552	A general outline of a person's character or background	Profile (N.)	बाह्य रूपरेखा	
1553*	Recklessly extravagant or wasteful in the use of resources	**Profligate (Adj.)~**	अतिअपव्ययी	
1554	Working-class people regarded collectively	Proletariat (N.)	श्रमिक वर्ग	
1555*	To increase rapidly in number or spread	**Proliferate (V.)~**	तेज़ी से बढ़ना या फैलना	
1556*	A rapid increase in the number or amount of something	Proliferation (N.)	प्रसार, फैलाव	
1557*	An introduction to a literary work	**Prologue (N.)**	प्रस्तावना	4 (4)
1558*	Continuing for a long time	Prolonged (Adj.)	दीर्घकालीन	
1559	A piece of wood, metal, etc. used for supporting something or keeping it in position	**Prop (N.)**	टेक, सहारा	1 (1)
1560*	Biased or misleading information used to promote a political cause or point of view	Propaganda (N.)	राजनीतिक फायदे वाली पक्षपाती जानकारी	
1561*	A person sent by God to teach the people and give them messages from God	Prophet (N.)	पैगम्बर (ईश्वरदूत)	
1562	The force that drives or pushes something forward	Propulsion (N.)	आगे बढ़ाने वाला बल	
1563	To officially forbid something, especially by law	**Proscribe (V.)~**	प्रतिबंधित करना	1 (2)
1564	A person who has been converted to another religious or political belief	Proselyte (N.)	धर्मांतरित व्यक्ति	
1565	The central character in a story or play	**Protagonist (N.)**	नायक	3 (1)
1566*	A system of fixed rules and formal behaviour used at official meetings	**Protocol (N.)**	नियमों की प्रणाली	3 (2)
1567	The first design of something from which other forms are copied or developed	**Prototype (N.)**	नमूना	2
1568	A dry food for livestock	Provender (N.)	पशु-चारा	
1569	Narrow-mindedness or concern for one's own region at the expense of broader views	Provincialism (N.)	प्रांतीयता	

SN	Phrases	One Word (PoS)	Hindi	#R
1570	A person who moves stealthily about or loiters near a place with a view to committing a crime	Prowler (N.)	दबे पाँव घूमने वाला संदिग्ध व्यक्ति	
1571	One who studies election trends by means of opinion polls	**Psephologist (N.)**	चुनाव विश्लेषक	3 (2)
1572*	The study of elections and voting patterns	**Psephology (N.)**	चुनाव विश्लेषण	4 (1)
1573*	A false name used by an author instead of their real one	**Pseudonym (N.)**	उपनाम	7 (1)
1574*	One who studies the mind and behaviour	**Psychologist (N.)**	मनोविज्ञानी	3 (1)
1575*	The scientific study of the mind and behaviour	**Psychology (N.)**	मनोविज्ञान	9 (1)
1576*	Physical beauty, especially of a person	**Pulchritude (N.)~**	शारीरिक सुंदरता	
1577	Very careful about details and correct behaviour	**Punctilious (Adj.)~**	बारीकी से काम करने वाला	2
1578*	Having a sharply strong taste or smell	**Pungent (Adj.)~**	तीखा	2
1579	A person who gambles, places a bet, or makes a risky investment	Punter (N.)	जुआरी	
1580	To make a low continuous vibratory sound expressing contentment, as a cat does	Purr (V.)	घुरघुराना (बिल्ली की संतुष्टि की आवाज़)	
1581*	To follow or chase	**Pursue (V.)~**	पीछे लगे रहना	
1582*	Weak and cowardly	**Pusillanimous (Adj.)~**	कायर, डरपोक	
1583	To decay with a foul smell	**Putrefy (V.)~**	सड़ना	
1584	An obsessive desire to set fire to things	**Pyromania (N.)**	आग लगाने का पागलपन	1 (1)
1585	An extreme fear of fire	Pyrophobia (N.)	आग का भय	
1586	The sound made by ducks; A person who pretends to have more knowledge than he actually possesses	**Quack (N.)~**	बत्तख की आवाज; झोलाछाप डॉक्टर	2
1587*	A court or open space, usually rectangular, enclosed by a building	**Quadrangle (N.)**	चतुर्भुजाकार प्रांगण	2
1588	A creature with four feet	**Quadruped (N.)**	चौपाया	4
1589	To reject as invalid, especially by legal procedure	**Quash (V.)~**	रद्द करना	
1590*	To shake or tremble in voice	Quaver (V.)	थरथराना	
1591	A search for something	**Quest (N.)~**	खोज	2
1592	Changing quickly and unpredictably	Quicksilver (Adj.)	अस्थिर (पारे की तरह बदलने वाला)	
1593	A feather used as a pen	Quill (N.)	पंख की कलम	
1594	Occurring once every five years	**Quinquennial (Adj.)**	पंचवार्षिक	1 (1)
1595*	To the utmost or most absolute extent or degree	**Quite (Adv.)~**	पूर्ण रूप से	
1596*	Unrealistically optimistic or idealistic	**Quixotic (Adj.)~**	ख्याली, अवास्तविक	2 (1)
1597	The minimum number of people needed for a meeting	Quorum (N.)	न्यूनतम उपस्थिति	

SN	Phrases	One Word (PoS)	Hindi	#R
1598	A person who is good at telling stories in an interesting and amusing way	**Raconteur (N.)**	मज़ेदार कहानियाँ सुनाने वाला	3
1599*	The act of spreading outward from a central source	Radiation (N.)	विकिरण	
1600	A person who advocates complete political or social change	**Radical (N.)~**	उग्र सुधारवादी	
1601	A doctor who specialises in diagnosing diseases using X-rays, CT scans, and imaging	**Radiologist (N.)**	विकिरण चिकित्सा विशेषज्ञ	3
1602	The science dealing with X-rays and other high-energy waves for diagnosing and treating diseases	Radiology (N.)	विकिरण चिकित्सा विज्ञान	
1603	Speaking at length about trivial things	**Rambling (Adj.)~**	इधर-उधर की बातें करने वाला	
1604	A complex or unwanted consequence of an action	**Ramification (N.)~**	अनचाहे परिणाम	
1605	To go through an area making a lot of noise and causing damage	**Rampage (V.)~**	उत्पात मचाना	
1606	Having a stale smell or taste	**Rancid (Adj.)~**	बदबूदार, सड़ा हुआ	2 (1)
1607*	Characterized by bitterness or resentment	**Rancorous (Adj.)~**	शत्रुतापूर्ण	
1608	A sum of money demanded for the release of a prisoner	**Ransom (N.)**	फिरौती	2 (1)
1609	Greedy for money	Rapacious (Adj.)	अति लोभी	
1610*	The reasons or intentions behind a particular set of beliefs or actions	Rationale (N.)	तर्कसंगत कारण	
1611	A reduction in tax or debt	**Rebate (N.)~**	छूट	
1612*	One who opposes or takes arms against a government or ruler	Rebel (N.)	विद्रोही	
1613	To withdraw a statement or belief publicly	Recant (V.)	मुकर जाना	
1614*	A hollow object used to contain something	**Receptacle (N.)~**	पात्र	
1615*	To give and receive mutually	**Reciprocate (V.)~**	बदले में करना	
1616*	A person who lives alone and avoids other people	**Recluse (N.)~**	एकांतवासी	9 (6)
1617*	Preferring to live alone and avoid other people	Reclusive (Adj.)	एकांतप्रिय	
1618*	To set right what is wrong or inaccurate	**Rectify (V.)~**	सुधारना	2 (1)
1619	Moving in or formed by straight lines	Rectilinear (Adj.)	सीधी रेखाओं वाला	
1620*	Happening repeatedly	Recurrent (Adj.)	बारम्बार होने वाला	
1621	A process involving too much official formality	**Red-Tapism (N.)**	लाल फीताशाही (अत्यधिक औपचारिकता)	4 (2)
1622*	That which is no longer useful	**Redundant (Adj.)~**	अनावश्यक	2
1623	A direct vote by citizens on a specific political issue or policy	**Referendum (N.)**	जनमत संग्रह	2
1624	An involuntary action under a stimulus	Reflex (N.)	अनैच्छिक प्रतिक्रिया	
1625	A person who works for gradual changes to improve a system	Reformer (N.)	सुधारक	

SN	Phrases	One Word (PoS)	Hindi	#R
1626	The belief in bringing about gradual changes to improve a system	Reformism (N.)	सुधारवाद	
1627*	A person forced to leave their country due to war, persecution, or danger	**Refugee (N.)**	शरणार्थी	2 (1)
1628	The emblems and symbols of royalty; dress with medals and ribbons worn at official ceremonies	**Regalia (N.)**	राजचिह्न, पदवी चिह्न, पदक	3 (3)
1629	The killing of a king	**Regicide (N.)**	राज-हत्या	7 (6)
1630	To restore someone to health or normal life after imprisonment, addiction, or illness	**Rehabilitate (V.)~**	पूर्व दशा में लाना	
1631*	To make someone look or feel younger	**Rejuvenate (V.)~**	फिर से जवान बना देना	1 (1)
1632	To fall back into a worse state after an improvement	**Relapse (V.)~**	पूर्व दशा में आ जाना	
1633	A holy person's remains or belongings kept for reverence; something surviving from an earlier period	**Relic (N.)**	अवशेष	2
1634*	Unwilling or hesitant to do something	**Reluctant (Adj.)~**	अनिच्छुक	
1635	To send back a criminal into custody for further investigation	Remand (V.)	न्यायिक हिरासत में वापस भेजना	
1636*	The act of recalling past experiences with fondness	**Reminiscence (N.)~**	संस्मरण	1 (1)
1637*	Cancellation of a penalty or debt	**Remission (N.)~**	दंड या ऋण माफी	
1638	A deep feeling of guilt and regret	**Remorse (N.)~**	पश्चाताप	
1639*	The amount paid to a person for their work	**Remuneration (N.)~**	पारिश्रमिक	2
1640	Artistic, musical, or dramatic interpretation	Rendition (N.)	प्रस्तुतिकरण	
1641	One who deserts their principles or party	**Renegade (N.)~**	दलबदलू व्यक्ति	
1642	To restore something to a better condition	Renovate (V.)	नवीनीकरण करना	
1643	The return of someone to their own country	**Repatriation (N.)**	स्वदेश वापसी	3
1644*	The feeling of sincere regret for one's sins	Repentance (N.)	पछतावा	
1645	To fill up again	**Replenish (V.)~**	फिर से भरना	
1646	An exact or very close copy of something	Replica (N.)	नक़ल	
1647	A temporary delay or suspension of punishment, especially a death sentence	**Reprieve (N.)~**	सज़ा पर अस्थायी रोक	1 (1)
1648	A cold-blooded vertebrate animal such as a snake, lizard, or crocodile	Reptile (N.)	सरीसृप (रेंगने वाला जन्तु)	
1649*	Causing a strong dislike	**Repulsive (Adj.)~**	घिनौना	
1650	A mass held to pray for the peace of the departed soul	Requiem (N.)	मृतक के लिए प्रार्थना सभा	
1651	One who is silent or uncommunicative in speech	**Reserved (Adj.)~**	कम बोलने वाला, संकोची	
1652*	A large natural or artificial lake used as a source of water supply	**Reservoir (N.)**	जलाशय	2 (1)
1653*	The ability to deal with any kind of hardship and recover from its effects	**Resilience (N.)~**	कठिनाइयों से उबरने की क्षमता, लचीलापन	

SN	Phrases	One Word (PoS)	Hindi	#R
1654*	Able to recover quickly from difficulties or setbacks	**Resilient (Adj.)~**	विपरीत परिस्थितियों से जल्दी उबरने वाला	3 (1)
1655	The process by means of which plants and animals breathe	Respiration (N.)	श्वसन	
1656	A short period of rest or relief from penalty or obligation	**Respite (N.)~**	अस्थायी राहत, दण्डस्थगन	
1657*	To return the same sort of attack	**Retaliate (V.)~**	बदला लेना	2
1658*	Unwilling to speak about one's thoughts or feelings	**Reticent (Adj.)~**	कम बोलने वाला	6 (5)
1659	To go back over the same route that one has just taken	Retrace (V.)	उसी रास्ते पर वापस जाना	
1660	To withdraw from a forward position in battle	**Retreat (V.)~**	पीछे हटना	
1661	The action of reviewing past events in one's life	**Retrospection (N.)**	पिछली घटनाओं का पुनरावलोकन	3 (1)
1662	To renovate or improve	**Revamp (V.)~**	नया रूप देना	
1663	A tune that is played to wake soldiers in the morning	Reveille (N.)	जगाने का बिगुल	
1664	To take great pleasure in something	**Revel (V.)~**	आनंद लेना	
1665*	Feeling or showing deep and solemn respect	**Reverent (Adj.)~**	श्रद्धापूर्ण	2
1666	A state of absent-minded daydreaming	**Reverie (N.)~**	दिवास्वप्न (खयाली दुनिया)	
1667	To criticize in an abusive or angrily insulting manner	**Revile (V.)~**	गाली देना	
1668*	The art of persuasive speaking or writing	**Rhetoric (N.)**	वाक्पटुता, दिखावटी भाषा	3 (4)
1669	A specialist in diseases of the nose	Rhinologist (N.)	नाक के रोगों में विशेषज्ञ	
1670	A scale used for measuring the strength of an earthquake	Richter Scale (N.)	भूकंप की तीव्रता मापने का पैमाना	
1671	To subject to mockery or derision	**Ridicule (V.)~**	उपहास करना	
1672	Hard and difficult to bend	**Rigid (Adj.)~**	दृढ़, कठोर	3
1673	A solemn religious act	Rite (N.)	रीति-रिवाज़, धार्मिक संस्कार	
1674	A circular building or hall with a dome	Rotunda (N.)	गोल-घर	
1675	The broken remains of a building or structure	**Ruin (N.)~**	खंडहर	
1676*	The deliberate destruction of something for military or political advantage	**Sabotage (N.)~**	तोड़-फोड़	4 (1)
1677*	The violation or misuse of something regarded as sacred	**Sacrilege (N.)~**	अपवित्रीकरण	7 (2)
1678	Deriving pleasure from inflicting pain	Sadistic (Adj.)	दूसरों को पीड़ा देकर आनंद लेने वाला	
1679	A place of safety or refuge	Safe haven (N.)	सुरक्षित ठिकाना	
1680	A detailed account of a series of real or fictional events over a long period	**Saga (N.)~**	गाथा	
1681	The quality of being particularly noticeable	Salience (N.)	प्रमुखता, विशेषता	
1682	A simultaneous firing of many guns to mark an occasion	Salvo (N.)	फौजी सलामी	

SN	Phrases	One Word (PoS)	Hindi	#R
1683	One who helps a person in need	**Samaritan (N.)**	दूसरों की निस्वार्थ सहायता करने वाला	5 (2)
1684	The clandestine copying and distribution of literature banned by the state	Samizdat (N.)	प्रतिबंधित साहित्य की नकल और वितरण	
1685	A place of good climate for invalids	**Sanatorium (N.)**	आरोग्य निवास	2 (2)
1686*	The state or quality of being holy	**Sanctity (N.)**	पवित्रता	2
1687*	A protected place or nature reserve for birds and animals	**Sanctuary (N.)**	अभयारण्य	5 (2)
1688	A sacred place	**Sanctum (N.)**	पवित्र स्थल	1 (1)
1689	Involving or causing much bloodshed	Sanguinary (Adj.)	रक्तपातपूर्ण	
1690*	Optimistic in an apparently difficult situation	**Sanguine (Adj.)~**	आशावादी	1 (1)
1691*	The use of irony to mock or convey contempt	**Sarcasm (N.)~**	कटाक्षपूर्ण व्यंग्य	
1692*	The use of humour, irony, or exaggeration to criticize or mock	**Satire (N.)**	हास्य व्यंग्य	3 (2)
1693	To taste good food or drink and enjoy it to the full	**Savour (V.)~**	स्वाद लेना	
1694	A sheath for the blade of a sword	**Scabbard (N.)**	म्यान	1 (1)
1695	An event or action that brings bad reputation to somebody	Scandal (N.)	कलंकपूर्ण कृत्य	
1696	Barely sufficient or adequate	Scant (Adj.)	अपर्याप्त	
1697	A person who is blamed for the wrongdoings of others	**Scapegoat (N.)**	बलि का बकरा	4 (3)
1698*	The state of being in short supply	**Scarcity (N.)~**	अभाव	
1699	A person who is forgetful, disorganized, and unable to concentrate	Scatterbrain (N.)	अस्थिर मन वाला	
1700*	To search for and collect anything usable from discarded waste	Scavenge (V.)	कूड़े में उपयोगी चीज ढूंढना	
1701	A person who habitually doubts accepted beliefs	**Sceptic (N.)~**	संदेहवादी	2
1702*	An ornamented staff carried by rulers on ceremonial occasions as a symbol of authority	Sceptre (N.)	राजदंड (सत्ता की छड़ी)	
1703*	A plan of what is to be done and when	**Schedule (N.)**	समय सारणी	1 (1)
1704*	A formal split within a religious organization	**Schism (N.)~**	धार्मिक संगठन में फूट	
1705	A grant or payment to support a student's education	Scholarship (N.)	छात्रवृत्ति	
1706	A group of fish	**School (N.)**	मछलियों का झुंड	1 (1)
1707*	Sparkling, brilliantly lively and exciting	**Scintillating (Adj.)~**	चमकदार और अत्यंत रोचक	
1708	A set of twenty	Score (N.)	बीस का एक सेट	
1709	A loud, harsh, piercing cry	**Screech (N.)**	चीख	2
1710	A person who writes screenplays	Scriptwriter (N.)	पटकथा लेखक	
1711	A small room where dishes are washed	**Scullery (N.)**	बर्तन माँजने की जगह	2 (2)

SN	Phrases	One Word (PoS)	Hindi	#R
1712*	A person who carves or shapes figures out of stone, clay, etc.	**Sculptor (N.)**	मूर्तिकार	2 (1)
1713	Making false and damaging claims about someone to harm their reputation	**Scurrilous (Adj.)~**	अपमानजनक, अभद्र	2
1714	Not connected with religious or spiritual matters	**Secular (Adj.)**	धर्म निरपेक्ष	4 (4)
1715	A drug or other substance that induces sleep	**Sedative (N.)**	शांत करने या नींद लाने वाली दवा	3
1716	Marked by care and persistent effort	**Sedulous (Adj.)~**	परिश्रमी	
1717	A person who can foresee future events	Seer (N.)	भविष्यवक्ता	
1718	An instrument for detecting and recording earthquakes	**Seismograph (N.)**	भूकंप-सूचक यंत्र	1 (2)
1719	The scientific study of earthquakes	**Seismology (N.)**	भूकंप विज्ञान	2 (1)
1720*	To take hold of something suddenly and forcibly	**Seize (V.)~**	कब्जा करना	
1721*	A meeting for discussion or training on a specific topic	Seminar (N.)	विशेष विषय पर गोष्ठी	
1722	Showing the weaknesses or diseases of old age, especially dementia	Senile (Adj.)	बुढ़ापे के कारण सठियाया हुआ	
1723	Aware of and able to understand other people and their feelings	**Sensitive (Adj.)~**	संवेदनशील	2
1724	A person between the ages of 70 and 79	**Septuagenarian (N.)**	70 से 79 वर्ष का व्यक्ति	2
1725	A place of burial	Sepulchre (N.)	कब्र या समाधि	
1726*	The occurrence and development of events by chance in a happy or beneficial way	**Serendipity (N.)~**	आकस्मिक लाभ	3 (1)
1727*	Occurring in a sequence or order	Serial (Adj.)	अनुक्रमिक	
1728	Rearing of silkworms	**Sericulture (N.)**	रेशम कीट-पालन	3 (1)
1729	A place where snakes are kept	Serpentarium (N.)	साँप रखने की जगह	
1730*	Using very long and difficult words	Sesquipedalian (Adj.)	लंबे-लंबे शब्दों का प्रयोग करने वाला	
1731	To cut or break off from something	**Sever (V.)~**	काटकर अलग करना	
1732	A person between the ages of 60 and 69	Sexagenarian (N.)	साठ से उनहत्तर वर्ष का मनुष्य	
1733	A vertical passageway into a mine	Shaft (N.)	खदान का लंबवत मार्ग	
1734*	A close-fitting cover for the blade of a sword or knife	**Sheath (N.)~**	म्यान	6 (1)
1735*	A device used to guard and protect from danger or attack	**Shield (N.)~**	ढाल	
1736	A large number of fish swimming together	**Shoal (N.)**	मछलियों का झुंड	8 (2)
1737	Fragments scattered by an exploding bomb or shell	Shrapnel (N.)	विस्फोट से उड़े धातु के टुकड़े	
1738*	Showing astute powers of judgement; clever and judicious	**Shrewd (Adj.)~**	चतुर	
1739	To deliberately avoid someone or something	**Shun (V.)~**	जानबूझकर परहेज़ करना (टालना)	

SN	Phrases	One Word (PoS)	Hindi	#R
1740	A vehicle that travels back and forth between two places	Shuttle (N.)	आवागमन करने वाला वाहन	
1741	A short rest or sleep taken after lunch	Siesta (N.)	दोपहर का आराम	
1742*	The dark shape and outline of something visible against a bright background	**Silhouette (N.)~**	छाया-आकृति	
1743	A figure of speech comparing two unlike things using 'like' or 'as'	**Simile (N.)**	उपमा अलंकार	1 (2)
1744*	Happening at exactly the same time	**Simultaneous (Adj.)**	एक ही समय पर होने वाला	1 (2)
1745	An office with high salary but no work	**Sinecure (N.)**	आराम की नौकरी	4 (2)
1746	A large fixed container to wash hands or utensils	**Sink (N.)~**	हाथ या बर्तन धोने का पात्र	
1747	The internal or external framework of bones supporting a body	**Skeleton (N.)**	कंकाल	2
1748	To reduce or decrease in speed or intensity	**Slacken (V.)~**	धीमा पड़ जाना	
1749	False and defamatory	**Slanderous (Adj.)~**	बदनामी वाला	
1750	To have saliva dripping copiously from the mouth	Slobber (V.)	लार टपकाना	
1751	A given space, time, or position	Slot (N.)	निर्धारित स्थान, समय या पद	
1752	To kill someone by covering their nose and mouth so that they suffocate	**Smother (V.)~**	दबाना, गला घोंटना	
1753	A person who believes they are superior to others and looks down on those they consider inferior	Snob (N.)	घमंडी	
1754	Warm, comfortable, and cozy	**Snug (Adj.)~**	आरामदायक	
1755*	A person who studies human societies	Sociologist (N.)	समाजशास्त्री	
1756	The study and classification of human societies	Sociology (N.)	समाज शास्त्र	
1757*	A brief or short stay at a place	**Sojourn (N.)**	थोड़े दिन का निवास	4 (2)
1758	A room used for sunbathing or light-based therapy	Solarium (N.)	प्रकाश-चिकित्सा का कमरा	
1759	A grammatical mistake or improper use of language	Solecism (N.)	व्याकरण की गलती; शिष्टाचार का उल्लंघन	
1760	One who talks to themselves	Soliloquist (N.)	अपने आप से बातें करने वाला	
1761*	A speech in which a person talks to themselves, especially in a play	**Soliloquy (N.)**	स्वयं से बोला गया संवाद	5 (6)
1762	The state of being alone, especially when one finds it pleasant	**Solitude (N.)~**	एकांत	
1763*	Being able to pay one's debts	Solvent (Adj.)	अपने ऋण चुकाने में समर्थ	
1764*	The act or habit of walking in sleep	**Somnambulism (N.)**	नींद में चलने की आदत	2 (1)
1765*	One who walks in sleep	**Somnambulist (N.)**	नींद में चलने वाला	8 (5)
1766	One who talks in sleep	**Somniloquist (N.)**	नींद में बोलने वाला	5
1767	The act or habit of talking in one's sleep	**Somniloquy (N.)**	नींद में बोलने की आदत	1 (1)
1768	A fourteen-line poem	**Sonnet (N.)**	चौदह लाइन की कविता	2

SN	Phrases	One Word (PoS)	Hindi	#R
1769	A drug or substance that induces sleep	**Soporific (N.)~**	नींद लाने वाला (दवा)	3 (1)
1770	A type of magic in which spirits, especially evil ones, are used to make things happen	**Sorcery (N.)~**	जादू-टोना	1 (1)
1771	The killing of one's sister	**Sororicide (N.)**	बहन की हत्या	3 (1)
1772*	Something kept as a reminder of an event	**Souvenir (N.)**	निशानी	4 (3)
1773*	A person who has supreme power or authority	Sovereign (N.)	सर्वोच्च शासक	
1774	A sudden involuntary muscular contraction	Spasm (N.)	ऐंठन	
1775	A small amount of something that shows what the rest of it is like	Specimen (N.)	नमूना	
1776	The forming of a theory or conjecture without firm evidence	Speculation (N.)	अनुमान	
1777	The study of caves	**Speleology (N.)**	गुफाओं का अध्ययन	1 (1)
1778	One who spends money recklessly	**Spendthrift (N.)**	खर्चीला	3 (2)
1779	An old unmarried woman	**Spinster (N.)**	अधिक उम्र की अविवाहित महिला	1 (2)
1780	Revealing of crucial details of a film's plot	Spoiler (N.)	कहानी का रहस्य पहले बता देने वाला	
1781	One who speaks on behalf of others	**Spokesperson (N.)**	प्रवक्ता	3
1782*	Performed or occurring as a result of a sudden impulse	**Spontaneous (Adj.)~**	स्वतः होने वाला	
1783	Occurring at irregular intervals	**Sporadic (Adj.)~**	छिटपुट (कभी-कभार होने वाला)	1 (1)
1784*	Not being what it purports to be	**Spurious (Adj.)~**	जाली, नकली	
1785	A noisy argument about trivial matters	Squabble (N.)	छोटी बातों पर झगड़ा	
1786	To walk unsteadily as if about to fall	Stagger (V.)	लड़खड़ाना	
1787	Not fresh	**Stale (Adj.)~**	बासी	2
1788*	A sudden rush of a large number of frightened people or animals	Stampede (N.)	आकस्मिक भगदड़	
1789	An upright bar, post, or frame forming a support or barrier	Stanchion (N.)	स्तंभ	
1790	A formal account or record of facts	Statement (N.)	औपचारिक विवरण या घोषणा	
1791	Attractively tall, graceful, and dignified in appearance	Statuesque (Adj.)	सुडौल	
1792	The existing state of affairs at a particular time	Status quo (N.)	वर्तमान स्थिति (यथास्थिति)	
1793	A written law passed by a legislative body	**Statute (N.)**	क़ानून	2 (1)
1794	Not able to produce children	**Sterile (Adj.)~**	बाँझ	
1795	One who loads and unloads ships	**Stevedore (N.)**	जहाजी कुली	2 (1)
1796*	A person who endures pain or hardship without showing feelings or complaining	**Stoic (N.)~**	सुख-दुख में समान रहने वाला	18 (10)
1797	The quality of enduring pain or hardship without showing feelings or complaining	**Stoicism (N.)**	सुख-दुख में समान रहने का भाव	3 (1)
1798	A short stay made during a longer journey	Stopover (N.)	यात्रा में रुकना	

SN	Phrases	One Word (PoS)	Hindi	#R
1799	A room where goods are kept	Storeroom (N.)	भंडार कक्ष	
1800	One who hides on a ship to obtain a free passage	Stowaway (N.)	छिपकर यात्रा करने वाला	
1801	Left in a difficult situation without help	Stranded (Adj.)	मझधार में फँसना (असहाय छोड़ दिया जाना)	
1802	A government by the military class	**Stratocracy (N.)**	सैन्य वर्ग का शासन	3
1803*	A mental or emotional strain caused by demanding circumstances	Stress (N.)	मानसिक या भावनात्मक दबाव	
1804	Affected by an undesirable condition or unpleasant feeling	Stricken (Adj.)	पीड़ित	
1805*	Adhering closely to a particular set of rules	**Strict (Adj.)~**	नियमों के प्रति सख़्त	
1806	Angry or bitter disagreement over fundamental issues	**Strife (N.)~**	विवाद	
1807	To speak with continued involuntary repetition of sounds	Stutter (V.)	हकलाना	
1808*	A written order to attend a court of law to give evidence	**Subpoena (N.)**	न्यायालय में उपस्थिति का आदेश, समन	1 (1)
1809*	To pay money to use a product or service regularly	Subscribe (V.)	ग्राहक बनना, सदस्यता लेना	
1810*	Too willing to obey other people	**Subservient (Adj.)~**	अत्यधिक आज्ञाकारी (चापलूसीपूर्ण)	
1811*	The bare minimum needed for survival	Subsistence (N.)	जीवित रहने लायक न्यूनतम साधन	
1812*	Existing under the earth's surface	**Subterranean (Adj.)~**	भूमिगत	
1813*	So delicate or precise as to be difficult to analyse or describe	**Subtle (Adj.)~**	सूक्ष्म	
1814*	Compact and precise	**Succinct (Adj.)~**	संक्षिप्त और स्पष्ट	1 (1)
1815*	Having juicy or fleshy and thick tissues	**Succulent (Adj.)~**	रसीला	
1816	The right to vote in political elections	**Suffrage (N.)**	मताधिकार	2
1817	The action of killing oneself intentionally	**Suicide (N.)**	आत्महत्या	3
1818	A proceeding in a law court	Suit (N.)	मुकदमा	
1819	A set of rooms, especially in a hotel, for the use of one person or family	Suite (N.)	होटल में कमरों का समूह	
1820*	A brief account of a subject	**Summary (N.)~**	सारांश	1 (1)
1821*	Splendid and expensive-looking	**Sumptuous (Adj.)~**	आलीशान	
1822*	A pension paid to a retired employee	Superannuation (N.)	सेवानिवृत्ति पेंशन	
1823*	Only on the surface of something	**Superficial (Adj.)~**	ऊपरी	2 (1)
1824	Of the highest degree or quality	Superlative (Adj.)	सबसे उच्च स्तर का	
1825	Speed greater than that of sound	Supersonic (Adj.)	पराध्वनिक, ध्वनि की गति से तेज	
1826*	The belief that particular events happen in a way that cannot be explained by reason or science	**Superstition (N.)**	अंधविश्वास	2 (1)

SN	Phrases	One Word (PoS)	Hindi	#R
1827	To ask or beg for something earnestly or humbly	Supplicate (V.)	विनती करना	
1828*	The state of being the most powerful	Supremacy (N.)	सर्वोच्चता	
1829*	A sudden and powerful forward or upward movement	**Surge (N.)~**	उछाल, तेज़ी से वृद्धि	
1830	An amount of something that is more than required	**Surplus (N.)~**	अधिकता	
1831*	The act of giving up completely, especially in favour of another	**Surrender (N.)~**	आत्मसमर्पण	
1832*	Done secretly, especially because it would not be approved of	**Surreptitious (Adj.)~**	चोरी-छिपे किया गया	
1833*	A person who is believed to be involved in a crime	**Suspect (N.)**	संदिग्ध (व्यक्ति)	2
1834	A person's last performance	**Swan Song (N.)**	अंतिम प्रदर्शन	2
1835	A collection of bees	**Swarm (N.)**	मधुमक्खियों का झुंड	2 (1)
1836	A person who is fond of luxury and sensual pleasures	**Sybarite (N.)~**	विलासी व्यक्ति	
1837*	One who flatters others excessively	**Sycophant (N.)~**	चापलूस	
1838	A part of a word that can be pronounced separately	Syllable (N.)	शब्दांश	
1839	A reasoning method involving two statements from which a conclusion is reached	Syllogism (N.)	न्यायवाक्य	
1840*	A long and elaborate musical composition written for a full orchestra; a harmonious combination of sounds	**Symphony (N.)**	सामूहिक वाद्य संगीत रचना; स्वरों का मधुर सामंजस्य	2
1841*	A building where Jews meet for religious worship and teaching	**Synagogue (N.)**	यहूदियों का प्रार्थना भवन	2
1842*	A word having the same meaning as another word	**Synonym (N.)**	समानार्थक शब्द	2 (1)
1843*	Made of artificial substance or material	**Synthetic (Adj.)~**	कृत्रिम	
1844*	A forbidden or socially unacceptable practice	**Taboo (N.)~**	वर्जित	
1845	Showing poor taste and quality	Tacky (Adj.)	घटिया	
1846*	Of or connected with the sense of touch	**Tactile (Adj.)**	स्पर्श सम्बन्धी	2
1847	The young of a frog	Tadpole (N.)	मेंढक का बच्चा	
1848*	Something that can be seen and touched	**Tangible (Adj.)~**	जो देखा या छुआ जा सके	
1849	A rough, violent, troublesome person	Tartar (N.)	उग्र स्वभाव का व्यक्ति	
1850	A permanent design or mark made on the skin with ink	Tattoo (N.)	त्वचा पर गोदना	
1851	The practice of saying the same thing twice using different words	Tautology (N.)	अलग-अलग शब्दों में एक ही बात दोहराना	
1852	A person who preserves and mounts dead animals for display	**Taxidermist (N.)**	मृत जानवरों को संरक्षित व प्रदर्शित करने वाला	2
1853	The art of preserving and mounting dead animals for display	**Taxidermy (N.)**	मृत जानवरों को संरक्षित व प्रदर्शित करने की कला	3 (1)

SN	Phrases	One Word (PoS)	Hindi	#R
1854	The science of classification	Taxonomy (N.)	वर्गीकरण का विज्ञान	
1855*	A person who never takes alcoholic drinks	**Teetotaller (N.)**	शराब न पीने वाला व्यक्ति	11 (8)
1856*	The ability to communicate thoughts directly from one mind to another without speech or physical means	**Telepathy (N.)**	मन से मन की बातचीत	2 (2)
1857	An instrument for viewing distant objects in space	Telescope (N.)	दूरबीन	
1858*	A violent windstorm	**Tempest (N.)~**	तूफ़ान	2
1859*	Lasting only for a very short while	**Temporary (Adj.)~**	अस्थायी	
1860*	Holding on to something or keeping an opinion with determination	**Tenacious (Adj.)~**	दृढ़, अटल	1 (1)
1861	A violent, overbearing, quarrelsome woman	Termagant (N.)	झगड़ालू स्त्री	
1862	A station at the end of a route	Terminus (N.)	अंतिम स्टेशन	
1863*	A written statement about someone's character, usually provided by an employer	**Testimonial (N.)**	प्रशंसा पत्र	2
1864	One who believes in the existence of a god or gods	**Theist (N.)**	आस्तिक	2 (2)
1865	Government by religious leaders	**Theocracy (N.)**	धार्मिक नेताओं का शासन	2 (3)
1866	One who studies God and religious beliefs	Theologian (N.)	धर्मशास्त्री	
1867	Relating to the study of the nature of God and religious belief	Theological (Adj.)	धर्मशास्त्रीय	
1868	The study of the nature of God and religious beliefs	**Theology (N.)**	धर्मशास्त्र (धार्मिक विश्वास का अध्ययन)	6 (2)
1869	A delusion of being God or divinely chosen	Theomania (N.)	ईश्वर होने का भ्रम	
1870*	Relating to the healing of diseases	Therapeutic (Adj.)	चिकित्सा सम्बन्धी	
1871*	An instrument for measuring temperature	Thermometer (N.)	तापमापी	
1872*	Complete with regard to every detail	**Thorough (Adj.)~**	संपूर्ण	
1873*	A busy, main road for public use	Thoroughfare (N.)	सार्वजनिक मार्ग	
1874*	Showing a lack of courage or confidence	**Timid (Adj.)~**	डरपोक	
1875	A long, angry speech of criticism or accusation	**Tirade (N.)~**	गुस्से से भरा लंबा भाषण	2
1876	Existing only in name	Titular (Adj.)	नाममात्र का	
1877	A young child just beginning to walk	**Toddler (N.)~**	नन्हा बच्चा	
1878*	A strong and fast-moving stream of water	**Torrent (N.)**	पानी की तेज़ धारा	3 (3)
1879	Full of twists and turns	Tortuous (Adj.)	घुमावदार	
1880*	A system of government in which only one political party is allowed to function	**Totalitarianism (N.)**	सर्वसत्तावाद	2
1881	A natural object or symbol believed to have spiritual significance and adopted as an emblem by a clan or group	Totem (N.)	कुलचिह्न (किसी कबीले का प्रतीक)	
1882	Poisonous or harmful to health	**Toxic (Adj.)~**	विषैला	
1883	One who works against his own country	**Traitor (N.)~**	गद्दार	4 (1)
1884*	Calm, peaceful, and free from disturbance	**Tranquil (Adj.)~**	शांत	2 (2)
1885*	Beyond or above the range of normal or physical human experience	Transcendent (Adj.)	अलौकिक (उत्कृष्ट स्तर से ऊपर)	

SN	Phrases	One Word (PoS)	Hindi	#R
1886	To make a written copy of spoken or recorded material	Transcribe (V.)	लिखित रूप देना	
1887	An apparatus for reducing or increasing the voltage of an alternating current	Transformer (N.)	विद्युत परिवर्तक	
1888	One who violates a law or command	Transgressor (N.)	उल्लंघन करने वाला	
1889	Lasting for only a short time	**Transient (Adj.)~**	क्षणिक	1 (1)
1890	Lasting for only a short time	**Transitory (Adj.)~**	अस्थायी (थोड़े समय तक रहने वाला)	2
1891	To change in form, nature, or substance	Transmute (V.)	बदल देना	
1892	Relating to speeds close to the speed of sound	Transonic (Adj.)	ध्वनि के समीप गति वाला	
1893*	Allowing light to pass through so that objects can be clearly seen	**Transparent (Adj.)~**	पारदर्शी	2 (1)
1894*	To travel or move across or through a region	**Traverse (V.)**	पार जाना	2
1895	A distorted representation of something	**Travesty (N.)~**	उपहासात्मक रचना	1 (1)
1896	The crime of betraying one's country	**Treason (N.)**	देशद्रोह	1 (2)
1897	An involuntary shaking or quivering movement	Tremor (N.)	कंपन	
1898	Shaking or quivering, often because of fear or nervousness	**Tremulous (Adj.)~**	भय से काँपता हुआ	
1899	A feeling of fear or anxiety about something unpleasant that may happen	**Trepidation (N.)~**	अनहोनी की आशंका	
1900	To enter someone's land or property without permission	**Trespass (V.)**	अनधिकार प्रवेश करना	2
1901*	One who enters someone's land or property without permission	**Trespasser (N.)**	अनधिकार प्रवेश करने वाला	2
1902	A stream flowing into a larger river	Tributary (N.)	सहायक नदी	
1903	Happening every three years	**Triennial (Adj.)**	त्रैवार्षिक	3
1904	A set of three related works by the same author	**Trilogy (N.)**	तीन रचनाओं का सेट	2
1905	A stand having three legs	Tripod (N.)	तिपाई, तीन पैरों वाला	
1906	A group of three powerful people	Triumvirate (N.)	तीन शक्तिशाली व्यक्तियों का गठबंधन	
1907*	Of little importance, value, or significance	**Trivial (Adj.)~**	तुच्छ, मामूली	2
1908	An object awarded as a prize for victory or success	**Trophy (N.)**	विजय के प्रतीक के रूप में दी गई वस्तु	2
1909	A group of performers, especially dancers or acrobats	**Troupe (N.)**	मण्डली	1 (1)
1910*	The clothes, linen, and other belongings collected by a bride for her marriage	Trousseau (N.)	दुल्हन का दहेज (विवाह सामग्री)	
1911	A student who absents himself from school without permission	**Truant (N.)**	बिना अनुमति स्कूल से अनुपस्थित छात्र	4 (3)
1912	An agreement between enemies or opponents to stop fighting for a certain period	**Truce (N.)**	युद्धविराम संधि	2 (1)

SN	Phrases	One Word (PoS)	Hindi	#R
1913*	Defiantly aggressive	**Truculent (Adj.)~**	लड़ाकू	
1914*	An obviously true or hackneyed statement	Truism (N.)	सामान्य सत्य	
1915	The sound made by an elephant	**Trumpet (N.)**	हाथी की आवाज, चिंघाड़	3
1916	An extreme fear of clusters of small holes or bumps	Trypophobia (N.)	छोटे छेदों का डर	
1917*	An extremely large wave in the sea caused by an earthquake	Tsunami (N.)	भूकंप तरंग	
1918*	A sudden and violent upheaval or disturbance	**Turbulence (N.)~**	उथल-पुथल	
1919	One who switches to an opposing party	**Turncoat (N.)**	दलबदलू	4
1920	Protection of or authority over someone	Tutelage (N.)	संरक्षण	
1921	One of two children born at the same birth	Twin (N.)	जुड़वाँ	
1922	A person who is extremely rich	Tycoon (N.)	उद्योगपति	
1923*	A cruel and oppressive ruler	**Tyrant (N.)~**	तानाशाह	
1924	One who is new to a profession or activity	**Tyro (N.)~**	नौसिखिया	
1925*	In a manner fully agreed upon by all	**Unanimously (Adv.)**	सर्वसम्मति से	2
1926	A mythological animal with one horn on its forehead	Unicorn (N.)	एक सींग वाला घोड़े जैसा काल्पनिक पशु	
1927	Not having knowledge or experience of a particular subject or activity	Uninitiated (Adj.)	नौसिखिया	
1928	Found all over the world	**Universal (Adj.)~**	सार्वभौमिक	4 (1)
1929*	Something never done or known before	**Unprecedented (Adj.)~**	अभूतपूर्व (पहले कभी न हुआ)	1 (1)
1930*	Having no moral principles	**Unscrupulous (Adj.)~**	अनैतिक	
1931	Not yet used or developed	Untapped (Adj.)	अभी तक उपयोग न किया गया	
1932	Difficult to handle or manage due to size or weight	**Unwieldy (Adj.)**	संभालने में कठिन	1 (1)
1933	To improve skills to match new demands	Upskill (V.)	कौशल बढ़ाना	
1934	A rapid or sudden rise	Upsurge (N.)	अचानक वृद्धि	
1935	The upward force that a fluid exerts on a body floating in it	Upthrust (N.)	तरल में तैरते हुए शरीर पर ऊपर की ओर का बल	
1936	A large vase that usually has a pedestal or feet	Urn (N.)	कलश	
1937	A person who shows people to their seats	Usher (N.)	प्रवेश कराने वाला	
1938	One who lends money at unreasonably high interest	**Usurer (N.)**	सूदखोर	6 (2)
1939	The practice of lending money at unreasonably high interest	**Usury (N.)**	सूदखोरी	1 (1)
1940	The quality of being useful	Utility (N.)	उपयोगिता	
1941	An imagined perfect society where everything is ideal	**Utopia (N.)**	आदर्श काल्पनिक समाज	20 (2)
1942	Excessively fond of or submissive to one's wife	**Uxorious (Adj.)**	जोरू का गुलाम	1 (2)

SN	Phrases	One Word (PoS)	Hindi	#R
1943*	To waver between different opinions or actions	**Vacillate (V.)~**	निश्चय न कर पाना	
1944*	One who wanders from place to place without a settled home	**Vagabond (N.)~**	खानाबदोश	2 (1)
1945	A person who wanders from place to place without a home or job	**Vagrant (N.)~**	बेघर आवारा	
1946	Having or showing an excessively high opinion of one's appearance, abilities, or worth	**Vain (Adj.)~**	अहंकारी	
1947	A person who is unduly anxious about their health	**Valetudinarian (N.)**	बीमारी की अत्यधिक चिंता करने वाला	1 (2)
1948	A low area of land between hills	Valley (N.)	घाटी	
1949	One who deliberately damages public property	**Vandal (N.)**	तोड़-फोड़ करने वाला	2
1950	The killing of a prophet	**Vaticide (N.)**	पैगंबर की हत्या	2
1951	A person who does not eat or use any animal products	Vegan (N.)	पूर्ण शाकाहारी	
1952*	One who does not eat meat	**Vegetarian (N.)**	शाकाहारी	2 (1)
1953*	Showing strong feeling	**Vehement (Adj.)~**	उग्र	
1954*	The speed of something in a particular direction	**Velocity (N.)~**	वेग	2
1955*	A prolonged bitter quarrel with someone, especially involving murder in revenge	**Vendetta (N.)~**	प्रतिशोध	
1956*	Accorded great respect, especially because of age, wisdom, or character	**Venerable (Adj.)~**	सम्मानित	1 (1)
1957*	To regard with great respect	**Venerate (V.)~**	सम्मानित करना	
1958	Seeking to harm someone in return for a perceived injury	Vengeful (Adj.)	बदला लेने की भावना से भरा हुआ	
1959	A sin or fault that is not serious and can be forgiven	**Venial (Adj.)~**	क्षमा योग्य	2
1960	One who speaks without moving the lips, creating the illusion that the voice comes from elsewhere	**Ventriloquist (N.)**	बिना होंठ हिलाए बोलने वाला व्यक्ति	2
1961*	A new project or business activity involving some risk	**Venture (N.)~**	जोखिम भरा कार्य या व्यापार	
1962*	Conformity to facts	**Veracity (N.)~**	सच्चाई	
1963	In exactly the same words as were used originally	**Verbatim (Adj.)~**	शब्द-प्रतिशब्द हूबहू	7 (3)
1964	The use of too many words or of more difficult words than are needed to express an idea	Verbiage (N.)	शब्दाडंबर	
1965	Containing more words than necessary	**Verbose (Adj.)~**	ज़रूरत से ज़्यादा शब्दों वाला	1 (1)
1966	The quality of using more words than are needed	**Verbosity (N.)~**	शब्द-बाहुल्य	2 (2)
1967	A decision made by a jury in a court	Verdict (N.)	फ़ैसला	
1968*	Having many different skills	**Versatile (Adj.)~**	बहुमुखी (अनेक कार्यों में निपुण)	9 (7)

SN	Phrases	One Word (PoS)	Hindi	#R
1969	An animal with a spinal cord	Vertebrate (N.)	कशेरुकी जंतु (रीढ़ की हड्डी वाले जीव)	
1970	The evening prayer service in a church	**Vespers (N.)**	गिरजाघर में सायंकाल की प्रार्थना	2
1971	A trace of something that no longer exists	Vestige (N.)	अवशेष (बचा-खुचा निशान)	
1972	A person who is long experienced or practiced in an activity	**Veteran (N.)~**	अनुभवी	8 (2)
1973*	A person qualified to treat diseases and injuries in animals	**Veterinarian (N.)**	पशु चिकित्सक	1 (1)
1974*	The area near or surrounding a particular place	**Vicinity (N.)~**	आस-पास	
1975*	An evil or wicked character, especially in a story or play	**Villain (N.)~**	खलनायक	2
1976	To clear someone of blame or suspicion	**Vindicate (V.)~**	निर्दोष ठहराना	2
1977	Having or showing a strong desire for revenge	**Vindictive (Adj.)~**	प्रतिशोधी	
1978	Something of high quality belonging to a past era	**Vintage (Adj.)~**	उत्कृष्ट प्राचीन (वस्तु)	
1979	A morally good quality or behaviour	**Virtue (N.)~**	सद्गुण	
1980*	A person who possesses outstanding technical ability in a particular art or field	**Virtuoso (N.)~**	किसी कला में अत्यंत निपुण व्यक्ति	4 (1)
1981	Of a disease or poison, extremely severe or harmful in its effects	**Virulent (Adj.)~**	विषैला	
1982	In relation to or in comparison with	**Vis-à-vis (Adv.)**	के संबंध में (की तुलना में)	2
1983*	Having or showing clear ideas about what should happen in the future	**Visionary (Adj.)~**	दूरदर्शी	
1984	The cultivation of grapevines	**Viticulture (N.)**	अंगूर की खेती	2
1985*	Having a lively, attractive personality	**Vivacious (Adj.)~**	फुर्तीला, जोश पूर्ण	
1986	Easily evaporated at normal temperatures	**Volatile (Adj.)~**	वाष्पशील	1 (1)
1987	The faculty or power of using one's will	**Volition (N.)~**	इच्छा शक्ति	
1988	A simultaneous discharge or series of shots or missiles	Volley (N.)	बौछार (एक साथ प्रहार)	
1989*	Of one's own free will	**Voluntary (Adj.)~**	स्वैच्छिक	2 (1)
1990*	One who freely offers to do something	**Volunteer (N.)**	स्वयं सेवक	6 (5)
1991*	Having a very eager appetite, especially for food or reading	**Voracious (Adj.)~**	अत्यधिक लालसा वाला	1 (1)
1992*	A long sea journey	**Voyage (N.)**	समुद्री यात्रा	3 (1)
1993	One who makes long journeys, especially by sea	Voyager (N.)	यात्री	
1994*	Exposed to the possibility of being attacked or harmed, either physically or emotionally	**Vulnerable (Adj.)~**	असुरक्षित	2
1995	A jocular person who is full of amusing anecdotes	Wag (N.)	मजाकिया व्यक्ति	
1996	A homeless and helpless child	**Waif (N.)**	लावारिस	1 (1)
1997	A raised passageway in a building	Walkway (N.)	पैदल रास्ता	

SN	Phrases	One Word (PoS)	Hindi	#R
1998	To walk or move in a leisurely or aimless way	**Wander (V.)~**	भटकना	
1999*	A person responsible for the supervision of a particular place or activity	Warden (N.)	देखरेख करने वाला अधिकारी	
2000	A place where clothes are kept	**Wardrobe (N.)**	अलमारी	4
2001*	A legal document authorizing the police to make an arrest or search premises	Warrant (N.)	अधिपत्र (कानूनी आदेश)	
2002	A list of passengers and luggage	Waybill (N.)	यात्री व सामान की सूची	
2003*	Feeling or showing extreme tiredness	**Weary (Adj.)~**	थका हुआ	
2004	To take someone somewhere suddenly and quickly	Whisk (V.)	फुरती से ले जाना	
2005*	To speak in a very low tone	**Whisper (V.)~**	फुसफुसा कर बोलना	
2006	To reduce something in size by carving or cutting	Whittle (V.)	छीलना, तराशना	
2007	A woman whose husband is dead	Widow (N.)	विधवा	
2008	A man whose wife is dead	**Widower (N.)**	विधुर	3
2009	Done deliberately, knowing that it is wrong	Wilfully (Adv.)	जानबूझकर	
2010	To become limp or drooping (of plants)	**Wilt (V.)~**	मुरझाना	
2011	An unexpected piece of good fortune	**Windfall (N.)**	अप्रत्याशित लाभ	1 (2)
2012	To separate husk from the grain	Winnow (V.)	फटकना	
2013	The practice of magic	Witchery (N.)	जादू-टोना	
2014	Great sorrow or distress	**Woe (N.)~**	शोक	
2015	To dispute angrily	**Wrangle (V.)**	क्रोध से झगड़ना	1 (1)
2016	A decorative ring of flowers and leaves	**Wreath (N.)**	फूलों की माला	5 (3)
2017*	The remains of something that has been badly damaged	Wreckage (N.)	मलबा	
2018*	To move along with quick, short twisting movements	Wriggle (V.)	छटपटाना	
2019*	An extreme fear of foreigners or strangers	**Xenophobia (N.)**	विदेशी लोगों का डर	2 (4)
2020	A feeling of intense longing for something	**Yearning (N.)**	ललक	1 (1)
2021	A wooden object used for connecting animals that are pulling a vehicle	**Yoke (N.)~**	बैलगाड़ी में बैलों को जोड़ने की लकड़ी	
2022*	A person who is fanatical and uncompromising in pursuit of their religious, political, or other ideals	**Zealot (N.)**	कट्टरपंथी	3 (1)
2023*	The highest point	**Zenith (N.)~**	शीर्ष बिंदु	
2024*	A circular diagram representing the twelve astrological signs	Zodiac (N.)	राशिचक्र	
2025	A place where wild animals are kept for public display, study, or conservation	Zoo (N.)	चिड़ियाघर	
2026	A person who studies animals	Zoologist (N.)	प्राणी-विज्ञानी	
2027	The scientific study of the behaviour, structure, physiology, classification, and distribution of animals	**Zoology (N.)**	जंतुविज्ञान	1 (1)

*Total **2027** OWS asked **5757** times*

A3 One Word Substitution Practice Sets (Based on Recent SSC Papers)

Practice Set - 1

Direction (Q. 1-10): Select the option that can be used as a one word substitute for the given group of words:

1 Morbid compulsion to consume alcohol continuously.
1) Satyromania
2) Kleptomania
3) Maniac
4) Dipsomania

2 Speaking disrespectfully about sacred or religious things.
1) Biped 2) Belligerent
3) Bigamy 4) Blasphemy

3 Someone who loves and admires himself the most.
1) Recluse 2) Narcissist
3) Altruist 4) Omniscient

4 An order of law requiring people to remain indoors.
1) Curfew 2) Restriction
3) Limit 4) Check in

5 One who cannot make a mistake.
1) Impregnable
2) Inevitable
3) Inimitable
4) Infallible

6 A deal of agreement done in a company or firm.
1) Conformity
2) Acceptance
3) Concurrence
4) Contract

7 A person who likes to argue about anything.
1) Veracious
2) Reticent
3) Contentious
4) Coward

8 The person who presents and coordinates a show on stage or television.
1) Reporter 2) Anchor
3) Jockey 4) Broadcaster

9 A complete, usually alphabetical list of items, often with notes giving details.
1) Catalogue 2) Brochure
3) Pamphlet 4) Monograph

10 An unpleasant mixture of loud sounds.
1) Irony 2) Hegemony
3) Harmony 4) Cacophony

Practice Set - 2

Direction (Q. 1-10): Select the option that can be used as a one word substitute for the given group of words:

1 A sudden and violent change or upheaval.
1) Tranquility
2) Serenity
3) Equanimity
4) Turbulence

2 Not active but has the ability to be active anytime later.
1) Jubilant
2) Dormant
3) Ambiguous
4) Conscious

3 Not able to be changed or adapted.
1) Austere 2) Permissive
3) Rigid 4) Harsh

4 The act of talking to oneself, often audibly.
1) Dialogue 2) Soliloquy
3) Solitude 4) Monologue

5 Feeling of being in a place before having already experienced the present situation.
1) Spirituality
2) Illusion
3) Delusion
4) Deja-vu

6 Hospital for people with mental illnesses.
1) Asylum 2) Shelter
3) Hangar 4) Druggist

7 Lasting for a very short while.
1) Perpetual 2) Reliable
3) Eternal 4) Ephemeral

8 Departing or having departed from a country to settle elsewhere.
1) Excommunicate
2) Emigrant
3) Immigrant
4) Native

9 A room for cleaning and storing dishes and cooking utensils and for doing messy kitchen work.
1) Scullery 2) Sanatorium
3) Dormitory 4) Overlay

10 The act or process of going from the simple or basic to the complex or advanced.
1) Flourishing
2) Ennoblement
3) Wither
4) Evolution

Practice Set - 3

Direction (Q. 1-10): Select the option that can be used as a one word substitute for the given group of words:

1 Someone who walks on foot.
1) Pedestrian 2) Auditor
3) Decanter 4) Stalker

2 The state or condition of not being in agreement, accordance, or in harmony.
1) Incongruence
2) Liquidity
3) Diplomacy
4) Congeniality

3 The rules of behaviour which guide one in a formal situation.
1) Bargain 2) Affidavit
3) Protocol 4) Impropriety

4 An eloquent and skilled public speaker.
1) Elector
2) Orator
3) Spokesperson
4) Leader

5 An open space usually rectangular and enclosed in a building.
1) Quintessential

2) Quadruped
3) Quinton
4) Quadrangle

6 One who believes in the existence of God.
1) Protagonist
2) Theist
3) Atheist
4) Fatalist

7 The doctor who deals with the female reproductive system.
1) Orthodontist
2) Ophthalmologist
3) Cardiologist
4) Gynaecologist

8 A person who investigates, reports on, and helps settle complaints.
1) Spokesman
2) Bildungsroman
3) Ombudsman
4) Superhuman

9 Protect from a danger, risk, or unpleasant experience.
1) Scare 2) Sever
3) Seize 4) Shield

10 A person in charge of the old people's home or a hostel.
1) Watchman 2) Guard
3) Warder 4) Warden

Practice Set - 4

Direction (Q. 1-10): Identify the one-word substitution in the following sentence:

1 Property inherited from one's father or ancestors.
1) Patrimony 2) Manuscript
3) Forgery 4) Obsolete

2 The inability to feel pleasure in normally pleasurable activities.
1) Euphoria 2) Anhedonia
3) Dysphoria 4) Alexithymia

3 A state of stunned confusion.
1) Daze 2) Shock
3) Surprise 4) Stun

4 Water that is safe for drinking?
1) Distilled 2) Potable
3) Irrigated 4) Deionized

5 Self-punishment for wrongdoing or sin.
1) Penitence
2) Vindication
3) Exoneration
4) Redemption

6 When someone used the fictitious name instead of his own name especially in writing.
1) Pseudonym
2) Manuscript
3) Omniscient
4) Ambidextrous

7 An intense aversion or fear triggered by viewing clusters of small holes or bumps.
1) Arachnophobia
2) Trypophobia
3) Agoraphobia
4) Hydrophobia

8 The misuse or violation of something that is considered sacred.
1) Defamation
2) Desecration
3) Forgery
4) Insubordination

9 The system of government in which one person holds absolute and unrestricted power.
1) Autocracy
2) Autonomy
3) Bureaucracy
4) Democracy

10 A medicine that induces sleep.
1) Analgesic
2) Hypnotic
3) Sedative
4) Narcotic

Practice Set - 5

Direction (Q. 1-10): Identify the one-word substitution in the following sentence:

1 A short tale or narrative that illustrates a moral or spiritual lesson, often through allegorical characters and events.
1) Allegory 2) Parable
3) Fable 4) Satire

2 Unit of weight for precious stones.
1) Pure 2) Accurate
3) Reliable 4) Carat

3 A procession for a funeral.
1) Parade 2) Carousal
3) Cortege 4) Carnival

4 A person who loves or collects books.
1) Bibliophile 2) Philatelist
3) Botanist 4) Anthropologist

5 The act of a writer deliberately avoiding a resolution to a narrative, leaving it open-ended or ambiguous.
1) Denouement
2) Cliffhanger
3) Pastiche
4) Pathetic Fallacy

6 Prohibited by law or treaty from being imported or exported.
1) Restricted 2) Illegal
3) Banned 4) Contraband

7 A person who has never been married.
1) Single 2) Celibate
3) Widower 4) Bachelor

8 A person who is in charge of a museum.
1) Curator 2) Conservator
3) Director 4) Historian

9 When some people or things are existing at the same time period in the society.
1) Contemporaries
2) Periods
3) Historical events
4) History

10 A person who supports change.
1) Conservative
2) Radical
3) Reformer
4) Constitutionalist

Practice Set - 6

Direction (Q. 1-10): What does the word most nearly mean:

1 Dialectic
1) A silent observation
2) A hostile confrontation
3) A scientific measurement
4) A dialogue or interplay between opposing forces

2 Taboo
1) A law
2) A tradition
3) A forbidden or socially unacceptable practice
4) A medical procedure

3 Dismay
1) Showing admiration
2) A feeling of unhappiness
3) Horrifyingly wicked
4) Something very cumbersome

4 Gourmand
1) A person who loves and enjoys food

2) A person who avoids food
3) A type of exotic food
4) A type of cooking technique

5 Dichotomy
1) A shared understanding
2) A mutual advantage
3) A clear division between two contrasting things
4) A repeated pattern

6 Labyrinthine
1) Superficial and obvious
2) Mysterious and confusingly complex
3) Predictable and linear
4) Structured and disciplined

7 Nascent
1) Well-established
2) Primitive or newly developing
3) Deliberately hidden
4) Declining rapidly

8 Eclectic
1) Expensive
2) Carefully chosen
3) Purely traditional
4) Drawing ideas from many sources

9 Insidious
1) Open and obvious
2) Harmless and fleeting
3) Gradually harmful and subtle
4) Quickly destructive and visible

10 Microenterprises
1) Multinational corporations
2) Small Scale businesses
3) Government agencies
4) Family-owned farms

Practice Set - 7

Direction (Q. 1-10): Choose the best one-word substitute for:

1 A person who pretends to be what he is not.
1) Mimic 2) Actor
3) Impostor 4) Hypocrite

2 A strong feeling of not liking someone or something.
1) Hatred
2) Affection
3) Admiration
4) Love

3 A lover of work
1) Sluggard 2) Philologist
3) Ergophile 4) Egomaniac

4 Someone who has been forced to flee his or her country because of persecution, war or violence.
1) Shelter 2) Asylum
3) Refugee 4) Sanctuary

5 A person who questions or rejects generally accepted opinions or beliefs.
1) Heretic 2) Iconoclast
3) Dissenter 4) Apostate

6 Someone who enjoys being around people, sociable and outgoing is called?
1) Gregarious 2) Indelible
3) Famous 4) Extempore

7 One who writes traditional poems.
1) Bard 2) Lyricist
3) Dramatist 4) Essayist

8 A person who finds pleasure in their own pain or humiliation.
1) Masochist 2) Narcissist
3) Pessimist 4) Hedonist

9 The practice of helping the poor and needy, especially by donating money.
1) Misanthrope
2) Misogyny
3) Sympathy
4) Philanthropy

10 A person's peculiar habit or mannerism.
1) Idiosyncrasy
2) Illusion
3) Hypocrisy
4) Eccentricity

Practice Set - 8

Direction (Q. 1-10): What is the one-word term for:

1 Someone who dislike men is called.
1) Misandrist
2) Misogynist
3) Philanthropist
4) Manuscript

2 The killing of a whole group of people.
1) Fratricide 2) honorary
3) Genocide 4) Suicide

3 A narrative or dramatic technique in literature in which the line between reality and fiction is intentionally blurred, often involving self-referentiality or characters aware of their fictional nature.
1) Metafiction
2) Allegory
3) Surrealism
4) Parable

4 Someone who is consistently excluded or ignored by a community due to lack of trust or popularity.
1) Dissenter 2) Noble
3) Pariah 4) Loyalist

5 A speech or writing that praises someone excessively.
1) Panegyric 2) Eulogy
3) sermon 4) Editorial

6 A disease that spreads over a whole country or the world.
1) Epidemic 2) Endemic
3) Pandemic 4) pathogen

7 Dissection of a dead body to find the cause of death.
1) Autopsy 2) Biopsy
3) Surgery 4) Anatomy

8 Secret or disguised language, often used by a particular group.
1) Jargon 2) Argot
3) Dialect 4) idiom

9 A condition in which an organism has only one copy of a particular chromosome, instead of the usual two.
1) Monosomy 2) Trisomy
3) Polyploidy 4) Aneuploidy

10 A doctor who treats children.
1) Cardiologist
2) Pediatrician
3) Neurologist
4) Gynecologist

Practice Set - 9

Direction (Q. 1-10): Choose the one-word substitution for the following sentence:

1 A person who has a strong desire to travel and explore the world.
1) Philoprogenitive
2) Philopraxic
3) Dromomaniac
4) Chrematistic

2 Liable to be easily broken
1) Amateur 2) Precious
3) Tenacious 4) Brittle

3 Excessive use of words to express an idea.

1) Verbosity 2) Eloquence
3) Tautology 4) Brevity

4 The murder of a king.
1) Regicide 2) Patricide
3) Fratricide 4) Homicide

5 A person who is indifferent to or distrustful of human integrity or morality.
1) idealist 2) Cynic
3) Optimist 4) Humanitarian

6 Fear of ugliness.
1) Hydrophobia
2) Arachnophobia
3) Acrophobia
4) Cacophobia

7 A professional who prepares maps.
1) Cartographer
2) Topographer
3) Geodesist
4) Archivist

8 Showing deep respect.
1) Polite 2) Reverent
3) Courteous 4) Deferential

9 One who uses long or obscure words.
1) Sesquipedalian
2) Garrulous
3) Sophist
4) Verbose

10 A formal split within a religious organization.
1) Sedition 2) Heresy
3) Apostasy 4) Schism

Practice Set - 10

Direction (Q. 1-10): Choose the most appropriate one-word substitution for the sentence below:

1 A government ruled by the wealthy.
1) Kleptocracy
2) Plutocracy
3) Theocracy
4) Meritocracy

2 Neha approached her new hobby with enthusiasm, eager to grasp the basics as a beginner.
1) Veteran 2) Mentor
3) Apprentice 4) Expert

3 The act of imitating someone's speech, mannerisms, or actions for entertainment or ridicule.
1) satire 2) Imitation
3) Mimicry 4) Parody

4 In his extreme old age when he behaves like a fool, people often lose patience with him.
1) Superannuation
2) Dotage
3) Senescence
4) Imbecility

5 A person who believes in fate or destiny.
1) Dreamer 2) Realist
3) Idealist 4) Fatalist

6 Ravi has always been a person who vehemently opposes authority, control, or tradition, often challenging every rule set before him.
1) Conformist 2) Anarchist
3) Optimist 4) Traditionalist

7 Jennifer asked her colleague, a person who is highly educated in a specific field called?
1) Expert 2) Novice
3) Master 4) Prodigy

8 The country plunged into chaos after it was thrown into a state of political instability characterized by the removal of a leader by force.
1) Revolution 2) Insurrection
3) Coup 4) Rebellion

9 A belief or Opinion that goes against the established doctrine, especially in religion or ideology
1) Sedition
2) Heresy
3) Blasphemy
4) Schism

10 Rohit generously supported those in need, always finding joy in offering help through his thoughtful gifts and financial assistance.
1) Philanthropist
2) Benefactor
3) Sponsor
4) Donor

Practice Set - 11

Direction (Q. 1-10): Select the option that gives the most appropriate meaning of the underlined word/ phrase:

1 Rahul has done <u>a study of statistics</u> that contributed to the research.
1) Cartography
2) Choreography
3) Cinematography
4) Demography

2 Select the most appropriate meaning of the underlined phrase. Can you please stop <u>continuously complaining about</u> the student's shortcomings?
1) Crying 2) Jesting
3) Grunting 4) Whining

3 A grand function was organised to honour the <u>person who had died for a noble cause</u>.
1) prophet
2) martyr
3) philanthropist
4) volunteer

4 You can be sentenced for <u>trespassing</u> on someone else's property.
1) conspiring against others
2) leaving without permission
3) showing unselfish devotion
4) entering without permission

5 The children decorated the classroom with a <u>mellow</u> yellow paint, creating a calming atmosphere for reading time.
1) rough and textured
2) bright and sunny
3) soft and pleasant
4) dark and gloomy

6 In the makeshift <u>place of activity, debate or conflict</u>, there were hundreds of people with the queen's team of advisors and servants sitting within the ring against the wall.
1) dormitory 2) arena
3) casino 4) aviary

7 She is <u>proficient in speaking many languages.</u>
1) Heterolinguistic
2) Bilingual
3) Multilingual
4) Monolithic

8 The nation has chosen the <u>government by the people</u> over monarchy.
1) democracy 2) oligarchy
3) theocracy 4) autocracy

9 There is a lack of security and stability in his bank balance. This is indicative of a <u>hazardous and perilous</u> situation.

1) precarious 2) reliable
3) guarded 4) definite

10 Someone {who is unable to read or write} is referred to as.
1) Literate 2) Literature
3) Reader 4) illiterate

Practice Set - 12

Direction (Q. 1-5): Select the most appropriate meaning of the highlighted word:

1 He was publicly scorned due to his predilection for luxurious items.
1) observant nature
2) dreamy meditation
3) special liking
4) extreme indifference

2 Jack was given the responsibility of driving, as he was the only teetotaller.
1) Person with imagination and creative potential
2) Person who completely abstains from intoxicating drinks like alcohol
3) Person who habitually drinks to the point of losing control
4) Responsible citizen of the country with high self-esteem

3 The meeting in the conference hall has ended on a temporary agreement.
1) fight 2) agenda
3) truce 4) hot war

4 Even amidst the all-pervasive silence, the noise inside her head seemed incessant .
1) To follow an unknown course
2) To continue without any interruption
3) To impact in a strikingly negative way
4) To occur at irregular intervalsor occasionally

5 The women of this country never questioned anything. Why are they so credulous?
1) Indifferent to the basic necessities of life
2) Reluctant to face the difficulties of life with courage
3) Suspicious of everything surrounding them
4) Willing to believe promptly without adequate evidence

Direction (Q. 6-10): Choose the correct one-word substitution for the blank in the sentence below

6 Despite knowing the importance of the assignment, Rahul kept delaying it until the last minute — a clear case of ______.
1) exaggeration
2) procrastination
3) temptation
4) negotiation

7 Despite the rise of digital art, Maya chose to specialize in ______, dedicating hours to perfecting each elegant stroke by hand.
1) typography
2) cartography
3) calligraphy
4) photography

8 Despite being new to the wine club, Rachel quickly impressed everyone with her refined taste and deep knowledge, proving herself to be a true ______ of fine wines.
1) amateur 2) connoisseur
3) novice 4) spectator

9 When the two companies could not settle the dispute themselves, they agreed to appoint an independent ______ to resolve the matter.
1) arbitrator 2) dictator
3) translator 4) orator

10 Despite being wealthy, Rohan couldn't resist stealing small items from stores, suggesting he might be a ______.
1) philanthropist
2) kleptomaniac
3) pessimist
4) hypochondriac

Practice Set - 13

Direction (Q. 1-10): Choose the correct one word substitution for:

1 The study of growing fruits, vegetables, and ornamental plants.
1) Floriculture
2) Horticulture
3) Agronomy
4) Botany

2 Fear of being enclosed in small or confined spaces.
1) Agoraphobia
2) Acrophobia
3) Claustrophobia
4) Xenophobia

3 Fear of public speaking.
1) Glossophobia
2) Sociophobia
3) Anthophobia
4) Ergophobia

4 A place where wild animals are kept.
1) Aviary 2) Sanctuary
3) Menagerie 4) Park

5 A child born after the death of their father.
1) Orphan
2) Bastard
3) Posthumous
4) Ward

6 A person who pretends to have moral beliefs they don't actually possess an.
1) Hypocrite 2) Cynic
3) Pessimist 4) idealist

7 A person who eats excessively or greedily.
1) Sybarite 2) Gourmet
3) Epicure 4) Glutton

8 Something that is impossible to be read.
1) Illegible 2) Decipherable
3) Invisible 4) Unutterable

9 The sound of the funeral bell.
1) Toll 2) Ring
3) Knell 4) Echo

10 someone who believes their own culture is superior to others.
1) Ethnocentric
2) Polymathic
3) Cosmopolitan
4) Esoteric

Practice Set - 14

Direction (Q. 1-10): What is the meaning of the word:

1 Craftsmanship
1) Poor quality
2) Traditional dance
3) skill in making things
4) Imported materials

2 Obsolete
1) Modern and efficient
2) Outdated and no longer in use

3) Rare and expensive
4) Broken beyond repair

3 Storeroom
1) A building where meetings are held.
2) A room where fires are lit.
3) A room where goods are kept.
4) A place where people rest.

4 Alloys
1) Expensive stones
2) Pure gold
3) Mixtures of metals
4) Handcrafted designs

5 Superficial
1) Deep and thoughtful
2) Focusing only on surface appearance
3) Natural beauty
4) Healthy lifestyle

6 Obsession
1) A casual interest
2) A healthy habit
3) An intense and unhealthy focus
4) A harmless hobby

7 Accomplishment
1) To destroy something
2) To start or create an organization, or a system
3) The act of completing something successfully
4) Freeing someone from the control of another

8 Chiaroscuro
1) A blend of light and shadow
2) Emotional paralysis
3) A musical variation
4) A specific type of sorrow

9 Alma mater
1) A place where one works
2) A school or college that one has attended
3) A close friend
4) A foreign language

10 Obsolescence
1) Advancement
2) State of being out dated
3) Legal enforcement
4) Improvement

Practice Set - 15

Direction (Q. 1-10): What is the one-word substitute for:

1 A person who opposes official policy.
1) Activist 2) Agitator
3) Dissident 4) Atheist

2 A speech or piece of writing that praises someone highly.
1) Elegy 2) Encomium
3) Sermon 4) Soliloquy

3 An official reprimand or strong criticism.
1) Accusation
2) Denunciation
3) Censure
4) Indictment

4 One who pretends to have knowledge or skills.
1) Savante 2) Charlatan
3) Virtuoso 4) Connoisseur

5 A person who abstains from all forms of indulgence.
1) Ascetic 2) Agnostic
3) Mystic 4) Skeptic

6 A medicine to counteract the effect of another medicine.
1) Alimony
2) Antibiotic
3) Anticoagulant
4) Antidote

7 One who lives entirely for pleasure.
1) Hermit 2) Reveler
3) Glutton 4) Epicure

8 Extremely old-fashioned; belonging to a time before the biblical flood.
1) Tale
2) Obsolete
3) Antediluvian
4) Medieval

9 A state of mental weariness and lack of enthusiasm.
1) Languor 2) Ennui
3) Torpor 4) Tedium

10 A secret or disguised way of writing.
1) Cipher 2) Epistle
3) Diatribe 4) Manuscript

Practice Set - 16

Direction (Q. 1-10): What is the one-word substitute for:

1 A building where dead bodies are kept temporarily.
1) Sanctuary
2) Sepulcher
3) Crematorium
4) Mortuary

2 A person who opposes war or use of violence.
1) Pacifist 2) Terrorist
3) Militant 4) Revolutionary

3 A person who is indifferent to pain or pleasure.
1) Apathetic 2) Stoic
3) Ascetic 4) Hedonist

4 A person who loves collecting coins called?
1) Numismatist
2) Philatelist
3) Collector
4) Antiquarian

5 A group of people who have graduated from a particular school, college, or university.
1) Student 2) Visitor
3) Teacher 4) Alumni

6 A person who is excessively concerned with minor details.
1) Critic 2) Grammarian
3) Scholar 4) Pedant

7 A statement that is obviously true and needs no proof.
1) Maxim 2) Axiom
3) Proverb 4) Epigram

8 The place for ammunition and weapons.
1) Gallery 2) Library
3) Arsenal 4) Laboratory

9 A statement that appears self-contradictory yet may be true.
1) Axiom 2) Maxim
3) Paradox 4) Irony

10 Someone who does not care about rules.
1) Nonconformist
2) Illegitimate
3) Vampire
4) Tyrant

Practice Set - 17

Direction (Q. 1-10): What is the one-word substitute for:

1 A humorous poem of five lines.
1) Elegy 2) Limerick
3) Haiku 4) Sonnet

2 Despite numerous warnings and opportunities to improve her attendance, Sneha consistently failed to appear at school or work, embodying the very definition of habitual absentee-

ism.
1) Absentee 2) Truant
3) Vagabond 4) Nomad

3 A person who studies the origin and development of human societies and cultures.
1) Sociologist
2) Historian
3) Archaeologist
4) Anthropologist

4 A government or state in which those in power exploit national resources and steal.
1) Plutocracy 2) Kleptomania
3) Oligarchy 4) Kleptocracy

5 the branch of science concerned with the study of sound, its production, transmission, and effects.
1) Acoustics
2) Geology
3) Thermodynamics
4) Optics

6 The practice of deliberately expressing less than what is meant.
1) Euphemism
2) Irony
3) Hyperbole
4) Litotes

7 Too much official formality.
1) Bureaucracy
2) Etiquette
3) Red tape
4) Discipline

8 A brief note or explanation added alongside a diagram or passage to provide clarity or context.
1) Annotation 2) Footnote
3) Glossary 4) Caption

9 A speech delivered without preparation.
1) Soliloquy 2) Rebuttal
3) Monologue 4) Impromptu

10 A place where aircraft are kept.
1) Dockyard 2) Depot
3) Hangar 4) Barracks

Practice Set - 18

Direction (Q. 1-10): What is the meaning of the word:

1 Ambiguous
1) Funny and humorous
2) Clear and straightforward
3) Harsh and severe
4) Uncertain or open to interpretation

2 Epochal
1) Ancient
2) Minor
3) Highly significant or defining
4) predictable

3 Superannuation
1) A system of retirement benefits or employees
2) The act of receiving a bonus
3) A type of insurance for future health care
4) The process of becoming too old to work

4 Spendthrift
1) A person who invests money wisely
2) A person who spends money recklessly
3) A person who saves money
4) A person who borrows money

5 Chuckle
1) Laugh quietly without opening one's mouth
2) Laugh loudly
3) Laugh in a noisy, gleeful way
4) Cry like a donkey

6 Vestige
1) An expanding frontier
2) A rapidly evolving trend
3) A small surviving remnant
4) A massive innovation

7 Linchpin
1) Minor detail
2) Essential element
3) Temporary trend
4) Heavy burden

8 Entropy
1) Creative growth
2) Gradual decline into disorder
3) Vibrant energy
4) Predictable structure

9 Untapped
1) Fully used
2) Forgotten forever
3) Hidden in books
4) Not yet used or developed

10 Geodesics
1) Straightest possible paths in curved space-time
2) Gravitational waves moving through space
3) Circular orbits caused by gravitational pull
4) Fixed points of measurement in space

Practice Set - 19

Direction (Q. 1-10): Choose the most appropriate one-word substitution for the sentence below:

1 A person who hates other people or mankind.
1) Misanthrope
2) Optimist
3) Egoist
4) Misogynist

2 A short, amusing or interesting story about a real incident or person.
1) Tale 2) Allegory
3) Anecdote 4) Biography

3 A facility equipped with instruments for studying stars, planets, and other celestial bodies.
1) Laboratory
2) Observatory
3) Greenhouse
4) Archive

4 A word formed from the initial letters of a name.
1) Pseudonym
2) Homonyms
3) Acronym
4) Antonym

5 The practice of attributing human traits to non-humans.
1) Zoomorphism
2) Theomorphism
3) Anthropomorphism
4) Animism

6 An imagined perfect place or society where everything is ideal, especially in terms of laws, government, and social conditions.
1) Utopia
2) Dystopia
3) Bureaucracy
4) Aristocracy

7 A place where soldiers are stationed.
1) Barracks 2) Fortification
3) Bastion 4) Fortress

8 A speech or text that praises someone highly.
1) Epitaph 2) Eulogy
3) Sonnet 4) Lament

9 An expression of sympathy, especially on the occasion of

death.
1) Condolence
2) Consolation
3) Reassurance
4) Assurance

10 A four-footed animal.
1) Biped 2) Quadruped
3) Carnivore 4) Herbivore

Practice Set - 20

Direction (Q. 1-10): Choose the correct one word substitution for:

1 To leave suddenly and hurriedly.
1) Abscond
2) Perambulate
3) Cicumambulate
4) Loiter

2 A state of temporary disuse or suspension.
1) Intermission
2) Recess
3) Abeyance
4) Dormancy

3 A general pardon granted by a government.
1) Amnesty 2) Reprieve
3) Clemency 4) Parole

4 An act of intentionally setting fire to property.
1) Burglary 2) Vandalism
3) Arson 4) Sabotage

5 A speech made without preparation.
1) Manuscript
2) Extempore
3) Debate
4) Oration

6 A person who talks excessively.
1) Silent 2) Introvert
3) Reticent 4) Garrulous

7 The art of making maps and charts.
1) Calligraphy
2) Geography
3) Cartography
4) Topography

8 A deep and seemingly bottomless chasm.
1) Crevasse 2) Crater
3) Abyss 4) Gorge

9 A state of disuse or inactivity.
1) Hiatus
2) Oblivion
3) Interregnum
4) Desuetude

10 One who abandons his religious faith.
1) Renegade 2) Atheist
3) Heretic 4) Apostate

Answer Key Practice Set - 1:

1 - 4	2 - 4	3 - 2	4 - 1	5 - 4
6 - 4	7 - 3	8 - 2	9 - 1	10 - 4

Answer Key Practice Set - 2:

1 - 4	2 - 2	3 - 3	4 - 2	5 - 4
6 - 1	7 - 4	8 - 2	9 - 1	10 - 4

Answer Key Practice Set - 3:

1 - 1	2 - 1	3 - 3	4 - 2	5 - 4
6 - 2	7 - 4	8 - 3	9 - 4	10 - 4

Answer Key Practice Set - 4:

1 - 1	2 - 2	3 - 1	4 - 2	5 - 1
6 - 1	7 - 2	8 - 2	9 - 1	10 - 4

Answer Key Practice Set - 5:

1 - 2	2 - 4	3 - 3	4 - 1	5 - 2
6 - 4	7 - 4	8 - 1	9 - 1	10 - 3

Answer Key Practice Set - 6:

1 - 4	2 - 3	3 - 2	4 - 1	5 - 3
6 - 2	7 - 2	8 - 4	9 - 3	10 - 2

Answer Key Practice Set - 7:

1 - 3	2 - 1	3 - 3	4 - 3	5 - 2
6 - 1	7 - 1	8 - 1	9 - 4	10 - 1

Answer Key Practice Set - 8:

1 - 1	2 - 3	3 - 1	4 - 3	5 - 1
6 - 3	7 - 1	8 - 2	9 - 1	10 - 2

Answer Key Practice Set - 9:

1 - 3	2 - 4	3 - 1	4 - 1	5 - 2
6 - 4	7 - 1	8 - 2	9 - 1	10 - 4

Answer Key Practice Set - 10:

1 - 2	2 - 3	3 - 3	4 - 2	5 - 4
6 - 2	7 - 1	8 - 3	9 - 2	10 - 1

Answer Key Practice Set - 11:

1 - 4	2 - 4	3 - 2	4 - 4	5 - 3
6 - 2	7 - 3	8 - 1	9 - 1	10 - 4

Answer Key Practice Set - 12:

1 - 3	2 - 2	3 - 3	4 - 2	5 - 4
6 - 2	7 - 3	8 - 2	9 - 1	10 - 2

Answer Key Practice Set - 13:

1 - 2	2 - 3	3 - 1	4 - 3	5 - 3
6 - 1	7 - 4	8 - 1	9 - 3	10 - 1

Answer Key Practice Set - 14:

1 - 3	2 - 2	3 - 3	4 - 3	5 - 2
6 - 3	7 - 3	8 - 1	9 - 2	10 - 2

Answer Key Practice Set - 15:

1 - 3	2 - 2	3 - 3	4 - 2	5 - 1
6 - 4	7 - 4	8 - 3	9 - 2	10 - 1

Answer Key Practice Set - 16:

1 - 4	2 - 1	3 - 2	4 - 1	5 - 4
6 - 4	7 - 2	8 - 3	9 - 3	10 - 1

Answer Key Practice Set - 17:

1 - 2	2 - 2	3 - 4	4 - 4	5 - 1
6 - 4	7 - 3	8 - 1	9 - 4	10 - 3

Answer Key Practice Set - 18:

1 - 4	2 - 3	3 - 1	4 - 2	5 - 1
6 - 3	7 - 2	8 - 2	9 - 4	10 - 1

Answer Key Practice Set - 19:

1 - 1	2 - 3	3 - 2	4 - 3	5 - 3
6 - 1	7 - 1	8 - 2	9 - 1	10 - 2

Answer Key Practice Set - 20:

1 - 1	2 - 3	3 - 1	4 - 3	5 - 2
6 - 4	7 - 3	8 - 3	9 - 4	10 - 4

A4 One Word Substitutions (OWS) (asked in Other Exams)

SN	Phrases	One Word (PoS)	Hindi	#R
1	From the very beginning	Ab initio (Adv.)	शुरू से ही	
2*	Honest and straightforward	Aboveboard (Adj.)	खुला और ईमानदार	
3*	Related to education	Academic (Adj.)	शैक्षणिक	
4	An ardent follower	Acolyte (N.)	निष्ठावान अनुयायी	
5	To urge or request someone solemnly	Adjure (V.)	कसम देकर कहना	
6	To give a sketchy outline of	Adumbrate (V.)	रूपरेखा प्रस्तुत करना	
7	Involving conflict or opposition	Adversarial (Adj.)	विरोधात्मक	
8	A very long (indefinite) period of time	**Aeon (N.)**	बहुत लंबा समय	3
9	The science or practice of building or flying aircraft	Aeronautics (N.)	वायुयान विज्ञान	
10	To collect or form into a mass or group	Agglomerate (V.)	एकत्रित करना	
11	The belief that the existence of God is unknown or cannot be known	Agnosticism (N.)	ईश्वर के अस्तित्व पर अनिश्चितता	
12	A recess in the wall of a room or garden	Alcove (N.)	दीवार में बना छोटा अंदरूनी खांचा (बैठने या सजावट के लिए)	
13	A false or assumed name	Alias (N.)	उपनाम	
14	Discrimination based on the alphabetical order of names	Alphabetism (N.)	नाम के वर्णक्रम के आधार पर भेदभाव	
15	A person's alternative personality or close trusted friend	Alter ego (N.)	दूसरा व्यक्तित्व; बहुत करीबी मित्र	
16	An extreme fear of heights	Altophobia (N.)	ऊँचाई का भय	
17*	Selfless concern for the well-being of others	**Altruism (N.)~**	परोपकार	
18	Able to live on both land and water	Amphibious (Adj.)	उभयचर (जल-थल दोनों में रहने वाला)	
19	The surgical removal of a limb or body part	Amputation (N.)	अंग काटने की क्रिया	
20*	A person, thing, or idea placed in the wrong time period	Anachronism (N.)	समय से बाहर (काल-विसंगति)	
21	A drug that makes the body unable to feel pain	Anaesthetic (N.)	बेहोशी की दवा	
22*	A thing or an event that exists or comes prior to another	**Antecedent (N.)~**	पूर्ववर्ती (पहले की घटना)	
23	An obsessive love for flowers	Anthomania (N.)	फूलों का अत्यधिक शौक	
24	A relic or monument of ancient times	Antiquity (N.)	प्राचीन वस्तुएं	
25	Relating to or predicting a disaster	**Apocalyptic (Adj.)~**	प्रलय संबंधी	2
26	The highest point in the development of something; a climax or culmination	**Apogee (N.)~**	उच्चतम बिंदु	
27	A person who prepares and sells medicines (old term for pharmacist)	Apothecary (N.)	औषध बनाने या बेचने वाला (पुराने समय का)	

[**#R** denotes repetition of word]

[E.g. in SN 25, #R- **2** denotes this word has been asked 2 times in other exams]

SN	Phrases	One Word (PoS)	Hindi	#R
28	The settlement of disputes by a neutral party	**Arbitration (N.)~**	मध्यस्थता	
29	Living or often found in trees	Arboreal (Adj.)	वृक्षों पर रहने वाला	
30	A person who studies or cares for trees	Arborist (N.)	वृक्ष विशेषज्ञ	
31	A person who is skilled in the use of the bow and arrow	Archer (N.)	धनुर्धर	
32	A fleet of warships	Armada (N.)	युद्धपोतों का बेड़ा	
33	The formal stating of charges in a court of law	Arraignment (N.)	न्यायालय में आरोपों की औपचारिक प्रस्तुति	
34*	A worker skilled in making things by hand	Artisan (N.)	शिल्पकार	
35	A person who physically or verbally attacks another	Assaulter (N.)	हमलावर	
36	To test or analyse the content or quality of something	Assay (V.)	परीक्षण करना	
37*	The process by which a person, group, or thing is absorbed into a larger entity or culture	**Assimilation (N.)~**	आत्मसात	
38	The belief that God does not exist	**Atheism (N.)**	नास्तिकता	2
39	Until we meet again	Au revoir (Ph.)	अलविदा (फिर मिलेंगे)	
40*	Willing to take risks or do something shocking	**Audacious (Adj.)~**	साहसी	
41*	A group of people who listen to or watch a performance or speech	**Audience (N.)**	श्रोता, दर्शक	3
42	An extreme fear of being alone or isolated	Autophobia (N.)	एकांत का भय	
43	An imaginary line about which a body rotates	**Axis (N.)**	धुरी, अक्ष	2
44	A popular activity or trend that attracts many followers	Bandwagon (N.)	लोकप्रिय चलन	
45	A large shed for storing grain, straw or keeping animals	Barn (N.)	खलिहान	
46*	Fond of battling and fighting; hostile and aggressive	**Belligerent (Adj.)~**	लड़ाकू	
47	Confused or puzzled, often in a surprised way	Bemused (Adj.)	हक्का-बक्का; भौचक्का	
48*	To surround a place with the intention of capturing it	**Besiege (V.)~**	घेराबंदी करना	
49	An obsessive love of books	Bibliophilia (N.)	पुस्तक-प्रेम	
50	An extreme fear of books	Bibliophobia (N.)	पुस्तकों का भय	
51*	A period of excessive indulgence in an activity, especially drinking alcohol or eating	Binge (N.)	अत्यधिक सेवन	
52	A person who writes the account of another person's life	Biographer (N.)	जीवनी लेखक	
53*	Done openly and without any shame	**Blatant (Adj.)~**	खुलेआम और बेशर्म	
54*	A severe snowstorm with high winds and low visibility	Blizzard (N.)	बर्फीला तूफान	
55	Relating to workers who do manual labour	Blue-collar (Adj.)	श्रमिक वर्ग से जुड़ा	
56	An intellectual or literary woman (historically used, sometimes derogatorily)	Bluestocking (N.)	बुद्धिजीवी स्त्री	
57	Language that sounds impressive but has little meaning	Bombast (N.)	शब्दाडंबर; खोखली भाषा	
58	A thing that is helpful or beneficial	**Boon (N.)~**	वरदान	

SN* (Bold Serial no with * asterisk symbol): Word appeared as a spelling question

~ (Tilde Symbol) next to a word: It appeared as a synonym or antonym question

SN	Phrases	One Word (PoS)	Hindi	#R
59	An idea or invention considered to be a particular person's creation	Brainchild (N.)	दिमाग़ की उपज	
60*	A light, gentle wind	Breeze (N.)	हल्की हवा	
61	A rich fabric woven with a raised pattern, typically with gold or silver thread	Brocade (N.)	जरी वस्त्र	
62*	To think deeply and unhappily about something	Brood (V.)	चिंता में डूबे रहना	
63	A small stream	Brook (N.)	छोटी जलधारा	
64	To intimidate someone with stern or abusive words	**Browbeat (V.)~**	डराना-धमकाना	
65	To mix up someone's mind or ideas, or to make something difficult to understand	Bumfuzzle (V.)	उलझन में डालना	
66*	An illegal entry into a building with intent to commit a crime, especially theft	Burglary (N.)	सेंधमारी	
67*	An organized series of activities to achieve a particular goal	Campaign (N.)	अभियान	
68	Relating to or resembling a dog or dogs	Canine (Adj.)	कुत्ता संबंधी	
69	The practice of eating the flesh of one's own species	Cannibalism (N.)	नरभक्षण	
70	A military station or camp	Cantonment (N.)	सैनिक छावनी	
71	A valley with steep sides of rock	Canyon (N.)	गहरी घाटी	
72*	To surrender to an enemy on agreed terms	**Capitulate (V.)~**	शर्तों पर आत्मसमर्पण करना	
73	Relating to the heart	Cardiac (Adj.)	हृदय संबंधी	
74	A public merrymaking and procession	**Carnival (N.)~**	मेला, उत्सव	
75*	An association of independent businesses formed to control prices or limit competition	Cartel (N.)	उत्पादक संघ (जो कीमतें या प्रतिस्पर्धा नियंत्रित करे)	
76*	A person who does not marry, typically for religious reasons	**Celibate (N.)**	ब्रह्मचारी	2
77	To examine and remove or suppress objectionable content	Censor (V.)	आपत्तिजनक सामग्री हटाना	
78	A person who makes or sells candles	**Chandler (N.)**	मोमबत्ती बनाने या बेचने वाला	2
79*	A person who is blindly devoted to an idea	**Chauvinist (N.)**	पक्षपाती व्यक्ति	2
80	The treatment of disease by the use of chemical substances	Chemotherapy (N.)	रसायन चिकित्सा	
81	The sound made by cricket or cicada	**Chirp (N.)**	झींगुरों की आवाज़	3
82	The science of colours and their properties	Chromatics (N.)	रंग विज्ञान	
83	The study of biological rhythms and cycles in living organisms	Chronobiology (N.)	जैविक लय का अध्ययन	
84	The quality of being rude and bad-tempered	**Churlishness (N.)~**	असभ्यता, अशिष्टता	
85	To sail or travel completely around something	Circumnavigate (V.)	परिक्रमा करना	
86	Polite and reasonable	Civilized (Adj.)	सभ्य	
87	A group of followers hired to applaud at a performance	**Claque (N.)**	किराए पर रखे गए प्रशंसक	4

SN	Phrases	One Word (PoS)	Hindi #R
88*	Information that is very confidential and protected	Classified (Adj.)	गोपनीय
89	The action of retrieving money that has already been paid or distributed	Clawback (N.)	पहले दिए गए धन को पुनः प्राप्त करना
90*	Kindness shown to somebody when they are being punished	**Clemency (N.)~**	क्षमाशीलता, कृपालुता
91*	To come together to form one mass or whole	**Coalesce (V.)~**	संगठित होना
92	An ancient text	Codex (N.)	प्राचीन ग्रंथ
93	A person of the same age	Coeval (N.)	समान आयु का व्यक्ति
94	Relating to or in a state of coma	Comatose (Adj.)	बेहोशी की स्थिति में
95	A person who provides analysis and commentary on events, especially in sports or news	Commentator (N.)	टिप्पणीकार, समीक्षक
96*	Dedicated to a cause or activity	**Committed (Adj.)~**	समर्पित, निष्ठावान
97	A person who writes music, especially classical music	Composer (N.)	संगीतकार
98*	Including all or nearly all elements or aspects	**Comprehensive (Adj.)~**	व्यापक
99	A mixture of various ingredients or elements	Concoction (N.)	विभिन्न वस्तुओं का मिश्रण
100	A trusted advisor or counsellor of a mafia or political family	Consigliere (N.)	विश्वसनीय सलाहकार
101	Happening or existing at the same time	Contemporaneous (Adj.)	समकालीन
102	A deep feeling of regret or guilt for one's wrongdoing	Contrition (N.)	पछतावा
103	A confusing and difficult problem	**Conundrum (N.)~**	पहेली
104	A secret religious meeting	Conventicle (N.)	गुप्त धार्मिक सभा
105	The organization of different things or people so that they work together	**Coordination (N.)~**	सामंजस्य
106*	Something that is the natural and direct result of another one	Corollary (N.)	स्वाभाविक परिणाम
107*	A correction issued after the publication of a document	Corrigendum (N.)	शुद्धिपत्र, संशोधन
108	The science of the origin and development of the universe	Cosmology (N.)	ब्रह्माण्ड विज्ञान
109	A four-wheeled closed horse-drawn carriage (often for two passengers)	Coupe (N.)	बंद घोड़ागाड़ी
110*	The design and production of high-fashion, custom-made clothing	Couture (N.)	उच्च-फ़ैशन परिधान कला
111	Having or showing a great desire to possess something belonging to someone else	**Covetous (Adj.)~**	दूसरे की वस्तुओं की लालसा रखने वाला
112	To have a strong desire for something	**Crave (V.)~**	तीव्र इच्छा करना
113	A nursery where children are cared for while their parents are at work	**Creche (N.)**	पालना-घर, शिशु सदन 3
114	To express disapproval or find fault	**Criticise (V.)~**	आलोचना करना

SN	Phrases	One Word (PoS)	Hindi	#R
115	The science dealing with extremely low temperatures	Cryogenics (N.)	अत्यधिक ठंडे तापमान का विज्ञान	
116	A lover of dogs	Cynophilist (N.)	कुत्तों का प्रेमी	
117	The use of the fingers and hands to communicate and convey ideas; finger spelling	**Dactylology (N.)**	हाथों व उँगलियों से संवाद की पद्धति	2
118*	A place where milk and milk products are processed	Dairy (N.)	डेयरी (दुग्ध-उत्पाद की जगह)	
119	Starting again; from the beginning	De novo (Adv./ Adj.)	नए सिरे से	
120	Charming, confident and stylish	**Debonair (Adj.)~**	आकर्षक व शालीन	
121	A stoppered glass container for holding alcoholic drinks, especially wine	**Decanter (N.)**	मादक पेय रखने का पात्र	8
122*	Occurring every ten years	Decennial (Adj.)	दशवार्षिक	
123	Shedding leaves annually	Deciduous (Adj.)	पर्णपाती	
124*	To convert a text written in code into normal language	**Decipher (V.)~**	गूढ़ लिपि समझना	
125	The act of throwing someone out of a window	Defenestration (N.)	खिड़की से बाहर फेंकने की क्रिया	
126	The killing of a god	Deicide (N.)	देवहत्या	
127	To do something that one considers to be beneath one's dignity	Deign (V.)	कृपा करके करना	
128	A mental condition causing memory loss and decline in thinking ability	Dementia (N.)	याददाश्त व मानसिक क्षमता कमजोर होने की बीमारी	
129	A person who loves trees	Dendrophile (N.)	वृक्ष प्रेमी	
130*	To declare to be morally wrong or evil	**Denounce (V.)~**	निंदा करना	
131	A person who treats diseases and conditions of the teeth	Dentist (N.)	दंत चिकित्सक	
132*	A public expression of strong criticism	Denunciation (N.)	सार्वजनिक निंदा	
133	A ruler who exercises absolute and oppressive power	**Despot (N.)~**	तानाशाह	2
134	To cause something to seem less valuable	Detract (V.)	महत्वे कम करना	
135	The state of being harmed or damaged	**Detriment (N.)~**	नुकसान	
136	The transfer of power from higher to lower levels of government	Devolution (N.)	सत्ता हस्तांतरण	
137	Slow or tending to cause delay	**Dilatory (Adj.)~**	विलंब करने वाला	
138	A person having excessive craving for alcohol	**Dipsomaniac (N.)**	शराब की तीव्र लत वाला व्यक्ति	2
139	To take a machine or structure into separate pieces	**Dismantle (V.)~**	अलग-अलग हिस्सों में खोलना	
140	To make doubts, fears, or beliefs disappear	**Dispel (V.)~**	दूर करना, मिटा देना	
141	The action of moving something from its place or position, especially people from their homes	Displacement (N.)	विस्थापन	
142	To twist or change the shape, meaning, or truth of something	**Distort (V.)~**	विकृत करना, गलत रूप में प्रस्तुत करना	
143	A field of activity or knowledge	Domain (N.)	क्षेत्र; दायरा	

SN	Phrases	One Word (PoS)	Hindi	#R
144	The exercise of power or control over others	Domination (N.)	किसी पर नियंत्रण	
145	A collection of documents on someone or something	**Dossier (N.)~**	दस्तावेज़ संग्रह	
146	A phrase with two meanings	Double entendre (N.)	दोहरे अर्थ वाला वाक्य	
147	A short hymn or song praising God	Doxology (N.)	स्तुति-गान	
148	To cheat someone by lying or tricking	**Dupe (V.)~**	धोखा देना	
149	Relating to an imagined society in which there is suffering and injustice	**Dystopian (Adj.)**	काल्पनिक दुःखद समाज संबंधी	2
150*	With great interest or excitement	**Eagerly (Adv.)~**	उत्सुकता से	
151	Designated for a specific purpose	Earmarked (Adj.)	निर्धारित	
152	An official order issued by authority	Edict (N.)	शासकीय आदेश	
153	A magical or medicinal potion	**Elixir (N.)~**	औषधीय या चमत्कारी पेय	
154*	Fluent and persuasive in speaking or writing	**Eloquence (N.)~**	वाक्पटुता	2
155	Able to understand and share another person's feelings	Empathetic (Adj.)	सहानुभूति रखने वाला	
156*	Based on observation or experience rather than theory	**Empirical (Adj.)~**	अनुभव आधारित	
157	All together; as a group	En bloc (Adv.)	सामूहिक रूप से	
158	The process of changing information into secret code	Encryption (N.)	कूटलेखन (गुप्त कोड में बदलना)	
159	The custom of marrying within one's own tribe or community	**Endogamy (N.)**	अंतर्विवाह	2
160*	Having an internal cause or origin	Endogenous (Adj.)	आंतरिक	
161*	To happen as a result	**Ensue (V.)~**	परिणामस्वरूप होना	
162	Involved in difficulties or complicated circumstances	Entangled (Adj.)	जटिल परिस्थितियों में फंसा हुआ	
163	The practice of eating insects by humans	Entomophagy (N.)	कीट खाने की प्रथा	
164	A person who studies the spread and control of diseases	**Epidemiologist (N.)**	महामारी विज्ञानी	2
165	The study of the spread and control of diseases	Epidemiology (N.)	महामारी विज्ञान	
166	An inscription on a building, statue, or coin	Epigraph (N.)	शिलालेख	
167*	Written in the form of letters or documents	Epistolary (Adj.)	पत्रात्मक	
168*	A word or phrase used to describe a characteristic of a person or thing	**Epithet (N.)~**	उपाधि (किसी गुण के आधार पर दिया गया नाम)	
169*	A period of time that is very important in history	**Epoch (N.)~**	इतिहास का विशिष्ट युग	
170	Giving one's name to something, or named after a particular person	Eponymous (Adj.)	जिसके नाम पर कुछ रखा गया हो	
171*	A calm and balanced state of mind, especially in trouble	**Equanimity (N.)~**	मानसिक संतुलन	
172	A person who is skilled in horsemanship	**Equestrian (N.)~**	घुड़सवार	3
173*	Having or showing great knowledge or learning	**Erudite (Adj.)~**	विद्वान	
174	The guiding beliefs of a person, group, or organization	Ethos (N.)	मूल भावना	
175	To assess the value or quality of something	**Evaluate (V.)~**	मूल्यांकन करना	

SN	Phrases	One Word (PoS)	Hindi	#R
176	By virtue of one's job, rank, or position	Ex Officio (Adj.)	पद के कारण (स्वतः सदस्य)	
177	A person who carries out a sentence of death on a condemned person	Executioner (N.)	जल्लाद (फाँसी देने वाला)	
178*	Related to human existence	**Existential (Adj.)~**	अस्तित्व संबंधी	2
179*	To remove completely or erase officially from a record	**Expunge (V.)~**	पूरी तरह मिटाना	
180*	To remove completely	**Extirpate (V.)~**	जड़ से उखाड़ना	
181	To praise enthusiastically	**Extol (V.)~**	प्रशंसा करना	
182*	Not relevant to the matter at hand	**Extraneous (Adj.)~**	असंबंधित	
183	An elaborate and spectacular entertainment	**Extravaganza (N.)**	भव्य प्रदर्शन	2
184*	The farthest point	Extremity (N.)	अंतिम छोर	
185	That which can be freed	Extricable (Adj.)	निकालने योग्य	
186	The practice of deceiving someone into believing something that is not true	**Fabrication (N.)~**	मनगढ़ंत कहानी या झूठी रचना	
187	The development of events outside a person's control	Fate (N.)	भाग्य	
188	To understand a difficult problem or situation after much thought (V.); A unit used to measure the depth of water (N.)	**Fathom (V./N.)**	गहराई से समझना; गहराई नापने की इकाई	2
189	A socially awkward or embarrassing mistake	Faux pas (N.)	शर्मनाक गलती	
190	An achievement requiring great courage	**Feat (N.)~**	वीरतापूर्ण कार्य	
191	Relating to a system of government in which states unite but retain internal independence	Federal (Adj.)	संघीय	
192	Lacking physical or mental strength; weak	**Feeble (Adj.)~**	कमज़ोर	
193*	To pretend or give a false appearance of something	**Feign (V.)~**	दिखावा करना	
194	A serious crime	Felony (N.)	गंभीर अपराध	
195	To move restlessly with small repeated movements	Fidget (V.)	बेचैनी से हिलना-डुलना	
196	Involving trust between a trustee and beneficiary	Fiduciary (Adj.)	विश्वास पर आधारित	
197	To refuse to obey or accept something	**Flout (V.)~**	अवहेलना करना	
198	A young horse	Foal (N.)	घोड़े का बच्चा	
199	A member of a family or group who lived in the past; an ancestor	Forefather (N.)	पूर्वज	
200*	Difficult to overcome	**Formidable (Adj.)~**	अत्यंत कठिन	
201	A thing at which someone excels	**Forte (N.)~**	विशेष योग्यता	
202	In a very loud manner	Fortissimo (Adv.)	बहुत ऊँची आवाज़ में	
203	The quality of being easily broken or damaged	**Fragility (N.)~**	नाज़ुकता	
204*	Having a pleasant smell	Fragrant (Adj.)	सुगंधित	
205	A poem composed without any particular metrical pattern	Free Verse (N.)	मुक्त छंद	
206*	A mass of small bubbles on the top of a liquid	Froth (N.)	झाग	
207	To express vehement protest	Fulminate (V.)	कड़ी निंदा करना	

SN	Phrases	One Word (PoS)	Hindi	#R
208	To talk a lot about unimportant things	Gab (V.)	बेकार की बातें करना	
209	A device used for strangling, typically a wire or cord	Garrotte (N.)	गला घोंटने का यंत्र	
210*	Willing to give more than usual or expected	**Generous (Adj.)~**	उदार	
211	Relating to or involving old people	Geriatric (Adj.)	वृद्धावस्था संबंधी	
212	An agent that destroys germs	Germicide (N.)	रोगाणुनाशक	
213	To speak quickly in a way that cannot be understood	Gibber (V.)	जल्दी-जल्दी बड़बड़ाना	
214*	Extremely large	**Gigantic (Adj.)~**	विशालकाय	
215	A person who travels widely around the world	Globetrotter (N.)	घुमक्कड़; विश्व यात्री	
216*	To engage in casual conversation or rumors about others	Gossip (V.)	गपशप करना	
217*	The act of speaking or writing in an exaggerated, bombastic, or pompous manner to impress others	Grandiloquence (N.)	आडंबरपूर्ण भाषा	
218	An informal way of spreading information or rumours through conversation	Grapevine (N.)	अफ़वाह का माध्यम	
219	A place where the remains of dead people are buried	Graveyard (N.)	कब्रिस्तान	
220	A small growth of trees without underbrush	Grove (N.)	उपवन	
221	Tiring and demanding	**Gruelling (Adj.)~**	थकाऊ	
222	Rough and low in pitch	**Gruff (Adj.)~**	कर्कश	
223	Foolish talk or ideas	Guff (N.)	बकवास	
224	A loud and boisterous laugh, often one that is unrestrained or hearty	Guffaw (N.)	जोरदार हँसी	
225*	An artful or simulated semblance	Guise (N.)	वेश	
226	To deceive or trick someone	Gull (V.)	धोखा देना	
227	Happy and carefree	**Halcyon (Adj.)~**	सुखद और तनाव-मुक्त	
228	A book that gives instructions about a particular tool or machine	Handbook (N.)	विवरण पुस्तिका	
229	Extremely strong, strict, or intense	Hard-core (Adj.)	कट्टर; बेहद कठोर	
230	An opening or door in a floor, roof, or aircraft	Hatch (N.)	ढक्कननुमा द्वार	
231*	Arrogantly superior and disdainful	**Haughty (Adj.)~**	घमंडी	
232	A place that provides refuge	Haven (N.)	आश्रय स्थल	
233*	An untidy pile of something	Heap (N.)	ढेर	
234	The belief that pleasure is the most important thing in life	Hedonism (N.)	सुखवाद	
235	Controlled or dominated by one's wife	**Henpecked (Adj.)**	जोरू का गुलाम	3
236*	Property that descends to an heir	**Heritage (N.)~**	विरासत	2
237	The study of tissues	Histology (N.)	ऊतक विज्ञान	
238	A person who studies and writes about the past	Historian (N.)	इतिहासकार	
239	Inclined to kill a person	Homicidal (Adj.)	हत्या की प्रवृत्ति वाला	
240	A form of government by the military	Hoplarchy (N.)	सैनिकों द्वारा शासन	
241	The central part of a wheel	Hub (N.)	पहिये का मध्य भाग	
242	A person with an abnormally curved spine causing a rounded upper back	Hunchback (N.)	कुबड़ा	

SN	Phrases	One Word (PoS)	Hindi	#R
243	The branch of science dealing with liquids in motion and their mechanical applications	**Hydraulics (N.)**	द्रव-यांत्रिकी	3
244	The condition of being overly sensitive to sounds	Hyperacusis (N.)	ध्वनि अतिसंवेदनशीलता	
245	Using exaggerated statements or claims not meant to be taken literally	Hyperbolic (Adj.)	अतिशयोक्तिपूर्ण	
246	The practice of marrying someone of higher social status	Hypergamy (N.)	उच्च वर्ग में विवाह	
247	An abnormally low body temperature	Hypothermia (N.)	अल्प तपावस्था	
248	In the same source as previously mentioned	Ibid. (Adv.)	उसी स्रोत में	
249	To set on fire	**Ignite (V.)~**	जलाना	
250	Public shame and loss of honour	**Ignominy (N.)~**	बदनामी	
251	The quality of being impossible or hard to read	Illegibility (N.)	अपठनीयता	
252	The practice of referring to oneself in the third person	Illeism (N.)	अपने आप को तीसरे व्यक्ति के रूप में पुकारना	
253	Existing from a time beyond memory; very ancient	Immemorial (Adj.)	अत्यंत प्राचीन	
254*	Having very little or no money	**Impecunious (Adj.)~**	निर्धन	
255	That which cannot be noticed	**Imperceptible (Adj.)**	अतिसूक्ष्म	2
256*	Rude and not showing respect	**Impertinent (Adj.)~**	अशिष्ट	
257*	Acting quickly without thought	**Impetuous (Adj.)~**	उतावला	
258*	Unable to be appeased	**Implacable (Adj.)~**	जिसे मनाया न जा सके	
259	An advance of money given for a specific purpose, to be accounted for later	Imprest (N.)	अग्रिम राशि	
260	To question or challenge the truth or validity of something	**Impugn (V.)~**	सत्यता पर सवाल उठाना	
261	Lack of skill, ability, or competence	**Ineptitude (N.)~**	अयोग्यता	
262*	Impossible to explain	Inexplicable (Adj.)	जिसे समझाया ना जा सके	
263	In a way that is unable to be separated	Inextricably (Adv.)	अटूट रूप से	
264	An inappropriate remark	Infelicity (N.)	अनुचित टिप्पणी	
265	To bring oneself into favour with someone by flattering or trying to please them	Ingratiate (V.)	चापलूसी करके प्रसन्न करना	
266*	A substance that forms part of a mixture or dish	Ingredient (N.)	सामग्री, घटक	
267	To prohibit someone from doing something	**Inhibit (V.)~**	रोकना	
268*	Impossible to copy or imitate	Inimitable (Adj.)	जिसकी नकल न की जा सके	
269	A person who introduces new ideas or methods	Innovator (N.)	नए विचार लाने वाला व्यक्ति	
270	Not attended by enough people to make it valid	Inquorate (Adj.)	अपर्याप्त सदस्य (बैठक के लिए)	
271*	To impart or suggest in an artful or indirect way	**Insinuate (V.)~**	घुमा-फिरा कर कहना	
272*	A person with highly developed intellect	**Intellectual (N.)~**	बौद्धिक व्यक्ति	

SN	Phrases	One Word (PoS)	Hindi	#R
273	Lacking moderation or sobriety	Intemperate (Adj.)	संयमहीन	
274	Planned or meant for a particular purpose	Intended (Adj.)	इच्छित	
275	Relating to or causing mutually destructive conflict within a group	Internecine (Adj.)	आपसी हिंसक संघर्ष	
276	Great fearlessness, especially in dangerous situations	Intrepidity (N.)	निडरता	
277*	Overwhelmed with things or people	Inundated (Adj.)	अत्यधिक भरा हुआ	
278	Having a habit that is firmly established and unlikely to change	Inveterate (Adj.)	पुरानी आदत	
279*	That which cannot be seen	**Invisible (Adj.)**	अदृश्य	2
280*	Impossible to repair or make right	Irreparable (Adj.)	जिस क्षति की पूर्ति ना हो सके	
281	A person who has been in jail many times	Jailbird (N.)	जेल का अभ्यस्त अपराधी	
282	Having two contrasting or opposite sides	Janus-faced (Adj.)	दोहरा चरित्र वाला	
283	An overwhelming force	Juggernaut (N.)	अत्यंत शक्तिशाली शक्ति	
284*	A person who performs tricks with their hands to amuse people	Juggler (N.)	कलाबाज़	
285*	An untidy collection of things	Jumble (N.)	अव्यवस्थित ढेर	
286	The official power to make legal decisions	**Jurisdiction (N.)~**	अधिकार क्षेत्र	
287	A government by the least qualified or most unprincipled citizens	**Kakistocracy (N.)**	अयोग्य लोगों का शासन	2
288	A person who spoils others' enjoyment	Killjoy (N.)	मज़ा किरकिरा करने वाला	
289	An instrument for measuring the quality of milk	Lactometer (N.)	दूध की शुद्धता मापने का यंत्र	
290	To publicly criticize someone using satire	Lampoon (V.)	व्यंग्य में आलोचना करना	
291	Sumptuously rich or elaborate	**Lavish (Adj.)~**	भव्य	
292*	A person who represents others in a court of law	Lawyer (N.)	वकील	
293	An act of ending the employment of a worker or group of workers	**Layoff (N.)~**	कर्मचारियों की छंटनी	
294*	A direct descent from an ancestor	Lineage (N.)	वंश	
295	Lacking energy or enthusiasm	**Listless (Adj.)~**	थका और सुस्त	
296	A printing process using a flat stone or metal plate	Lithography (N.)	शिलाचित्रण	
297	A feeling of intense dislike or disgust	Loathing (N.)	तीव्र घृणा	
298	An extreme fear of words or talking	Logophobia (N.)	शब्दों से डर	
299	Bringing light or insight	Luciferous (Adj.)	प्रकाश देने वाला	
300	A distinguished conductor or performer of classical music	**Maestro (N.)~**	संगीत उस्ताद	
301	A wealthy and influential business person	Magnate (N.)	उद्योगपति	
302	A great work of art	Magnum Opus (N.)	सर्वश्रेष्ठ कृति	
303*	Illegal or dishonest conduct by a public official	Malfeasance (N.)	पद का दुरुपयोग	
304	Corrupt behaviour by a public official	Malversation (N.)	भ्रष्टाचार (पैसों का)	
305	The killing of a husband by his wife	Mariticide (N.)	पति की हत्या	

SN	Phrases	One Word (PoS)	Hindi	#R
306*	A form of society in which the mother or female is head of the family	Matriarchy (N.)	स्त्री-प्रधान व्यवस्था	
307	A person who is independent in thought or action	**Maverick (N.)~**	स्वतंत्र विचारों वाला व्यक्ति	
308*	To interfere in others' affairs	**Meddle (V.)~**	दखल देना	
309	A mental condition marked by an exaggerated sense of power or importance	**Megalomania (N.)**	अत्यधिक आत्ममहत्त्व की बीमारी	5
310	A person who has an obsessive love for music	Melomaniac (N.)	संगीत के प्रति जुनूनी व्यक्ति	
311	Of low status and requiring little skill; lacking respect	Menial (Adj.)	निम्न स्तरीय	
312	A government by people selected on the basis of ability and merit	Meritocracy (N.)	योग्यता आधारित शासन	
313	A person who studies the earth's atmosphere and conditions and predicts the weather condition	Meteorologist (N.)	मौसम वैज्ञानिक	
314	An apparatus that measures and records quantity, degree, or rate	Meter (N.)	मापक यंत्र	
315	The quality of paying careful attention to every detail	Meticulousness (N.)	बारीकी से ध्यान देने का गुण	
316	A word or expression used as a substitute for something else with which it is closely associated	Metonym (N.)	संबंधित नाम का प्रयोग	
317*	A person who makes or sells women's hats	Milliner (N.)	महिलाओं की टोपियाँ बनाने-बेचने वाला	
318	A person who extracts ore, coal or other mineral	Miner (N.)	खदान में काम करने वाला	
319	A person who hates men	**Misandrist (N.)**	पुरुष द्वेषी	2
320	A hatred for marriage	Misogamy (N.)	विवाह द्वेषी	
321	An extreme fear of memories (especially bad ones)	Mnemophobia (N.)	स्मृति भय	
322	A small portion or limited quantity	**Modicum (N.)~**	अल्प मात्रा	
323	A unit of a spacecraft that can function independent of the other	Module (N.)	स्वतंत्र इकाई	
324	A person who works for an organisation but secretly gives information to its competitor or enemy	Mole (N.)	जासूस, गुप्तचर	
325	A doctrine or belief that there is only one God	**Monotheism (N.)**	एकेश्वरवाद	3
326	The sound made by a cow	Moo (N.)	गाय की आवाज	
327*	An area of muddy or marshy ground	Morass (N.)	दलदली भूमि	
328	To extract money as a fine or tax	Mulct (V.)	जुर्माना वसूलना	
329*	Shared by two or more parties	**Mutual (Adj.)~**	पारस्परिक	
330	The lowest point of something	**Nadir (N.)~**	निम्नतम बिंदु	
331	To successfully achieve or accomplish something	Nail (V.)	सफल होना	
332	A short sleep, especially during the day	**Nap (N.)~**	झपकी	
333*	An account that tells the particulars of an act or event	Narrative (N.)	कथा	

SN	Phrases	One Word (PoS)	Hindi	#R
334	Not willing to accept new ideas	Narrow-minded (Adj.)	संकीर्ण सोच वाला	
335*	The process of planning and directing a route	Navigation (N.)	मार्ग-निर्देशन	
336	An extreme fear of death or dead bodies	Necrophobia (N.)	मृत्यु या मृत शरीर का भय	
337	A government by new or inexperienced rulers	**Neocracy (N.)**	नए लोगों का शासन	3
338	An extreme fear of clouds	Nephophobia (N.)	बादलों का डर	
339	A user of the internet	Netizen (N.)	इंटरनेट उपयोगकर्ता	
340	An extreme fear of being without a mobile phone	**Nomophobia (N.)**	मोबाइल से दूर रहने का डर	4
341	The small amount of toothpaste that is shown in advertisements	Nurdle (N.)	टूथपेस्ट की थोड़ी मात्रा	
342*	The act of doing what one is told by someone in authority	Obedience (N.)	आज्ञापालन	
343	The act of watching something carefully	Observation (N.)	निरीक्षण	
344	The branch of medicine dealing with pregnancy and childbirth	Obstetrics (N.)	प्रसूति विज्ञान	
345	A government by the mob	**Ochlocracy (N.)**	भीड़ का शासन	2
346	General hatred, disgust, or strong disapproval	Odium (N.)	घृणा	
347	The study and description of the structure and characteristics of teeth	Odontography (N.)	दाँतों का वर्णनात्मक अध्ययन	
348	The scientific study of the structure and disease of teeth	Odontology (N.)	दंत विज्ञान	
349	The cultivation or growing of vegetables	Olericulture (N.)	सब्जी की खेती	
350	The branch of medicine that deals with the prevention, diagnosis, and treatment of cancer	**Oncology (N.)**	कैंसर विज्ञान	2
351	The philosophical study of the nature of being, reality, and existence	Ontology (N.)	अस्तित्व का अध्ययन	
352	Strongly against something	**Opposed (Adj.)~**	विरोधी	
353	A person whose job is to test eyes, sell glasses, etc.	**Optician (N.)**	चश्मा बनाने वाला	3
354	An ability to express oneself well in speech	**Oracy (N.)**	वाक् कौशल (बोलने की कला)	2
355	The art of skilful and effective public speaking	**Oratory (N.)~**	भाषण कला	3
356	The curved path followed by a planet or object around another body	**Orbit (N.)**	परिक्रमा पथ	2
357	To arrange carefully for desired result	Orchestrate (V.)	योजना बनाकर करना	
358	Military supplies including weapons, ammunition, combat vehicles, and maintenance tools and equipment	Ordnance (N.)	सैन्य हथियार	
359	A dentist who specialises in the alignment of teeth	Orthodontist (N.)	टेढ़े-मेढ़े दांत ठीक करने वाला दंत-विशेषज्ञ	
360	The study of correct spellings of words	Orthography (N.)	वर्तनी विज्ञान	
361	The science that deals with human skeleton recovery and interpretation	**Osteology (N.)**	हड्डियों का वैज्ञानिक अध्ययन	2
362	A figure of speech in which apparently contradictory terms appear in conjunction	**Oxymoron (N.)**	परस्पर विरोधी शब्दों का एक साथ प्रयोग	2

SN	Phrases	One Word (PoS)	Hindi	#R
363	The study of fossils	Palaeontology (N.)	जीवाश्म विज्ञान	
364	A government by people having equal power and responsibility	Pantisocracy (N.)	समान अधिकार वाले लोगों का शासन	
365*	The expression of stories through face, movement, and gestures	**Pantomime (N.)**	मूक अभिनय	2
366*	A standard or typical example	**Paradigm (N.)~**	आदर्श उदाहरण	
367	The addition of a letter or syllable to a word in particular contexts as the language develops	Paragoge (N.)	शब्द के अंत में अक्षर जोड़ना	
368	A person who is perfect or who is a perfect example of a particular good quality	**Paragon (N.)~**	आदर्श व्यक्ति	
369	A mental condition characterized by delusions	**Paranoia (N.)~**	संदेह रोग	
370	Language used by a particular group of people	Parlance (N.)	किसी समूह की भाषा	
371*	Unwilling to spend money	**Parsimonious (Adj.)~**	बहुत कंजूस	
372	An extreme unwillingness to spend money	**Parsimony (N.)~**	कंजूसी	
373	The office or position of a pastor	Pastorate (N.)	पादरी का पद	
374	The record of descent of an animal	**Pedigree (N.)~**	वंशावली	
375	An enclosure for keeping animals (especially sheep, pigs, or cattle)	Pen (N.)	पशुओं को रखने का बाड़ा	
376	A regular payment to retired persons for their past service	Pension (N.)	सेवानिवृत्ति वेतन	
377	A five-sided polygon	Pentagon (N.)	पंचभुज	
378	Second from last	Penultimate (Adj.)	अंतिम से पहले	
379	By itself; in itself	Per se (Adv.)	अपने आप में	
380	To travel through a place or area	Perambulate (V.)	टहलना, भ्रमण करना	
381	A baby carriage	Perambulator (N.)	शिशु गाड़ी	
382*	Unable to be trusted	**Perfidious (Adj.)~**	विश्वासघाती	
383	A doctor who specializes in treating gums	Periodontist (N.)	मसूड़ों का चिकित्सक	
384	An apparatus used by submerged submarines to see above water	Periscope (N.)	पनडुब्बी से बाहर देखने का यंत्र	
385*	The criminal offense of knowingly making false statements under oath in judicial proceedings	**Perjury (N.)~**	झूठी गवाही	
386	To commit a harmful, illegal or immoral action	**Perpetrate (V.)~**	अपराध करना	
387*	Continuing or occurring again and again for a long time	**Persistent (Adj.)~**	लगातार	
388*	Quick in noticing, understanding or judging things accurately	**Perspicacious (Adj.)~**	तेज़ दिमाग वाला	
389*	Very determined and refusing to be defeated by problems	**Pertinacious (Adj.)~**	अड़ियल	
390	The branch of science concerned with the origin, structure, and composition of rocks	Petrology (N.)	शिला विज्ञान (चट्टानों का अध्ययन)	
391	An extreme fear of swallowing	Phagophobia (N.)	निगलने का डर	
392*	A person who goes on a journey to a holy place	**Pilgrim (N.)**	तीर्थयात्री	2
393	The act of robbing ships at sea; or illegally copying copyrighted material	Piracy (N.)	समुद्री डकैती; अवैध नकल	
394	A very small amount of money	Pittance (N.)	बहुत कम पैसा	

SN	Phrases	One Word (PoS)	Hindi	#R
395	A building or theatre designed for showing the positions and movements of planets and stars	Planetarium (N.)	तारामंडल	
396	An overused statement lacking originality	**Platitude (N.)**	घिसी-पिटी बातें	3
397	The quality of seeming reasonable or probable	Plausibility (N.)	विश्वसनीयता	
398	An excessive desire for wealth or money	Plutomania (N.)	धन की अत्यधिक इच्छा	
399	A person who is extremely fond of the rains	Pluviophile (N.)	बारिश प्रेमी	
400	A person who writes poetry	Poet (N.)	कवि	
401	A strong verbal or written attack on someone or something	Polemic (N.)	विवादात्मक लेख या भाषण	
402	The ability to speak several languages	Polyglotism (N.)	बहुभाषिता	
403	A belief in the worship of more than one God	**Polytheism (N.)**	बहुदेववाद	2
404*	A painting, photograph, or drawing of a person, especially of the face	Portrait (N.)	चित्र, तस्वीर	
405	A temporary police force	Posse (N.)	अस्थायी पुलिस दल	
406	A book of low quality produced quickly to get money	Potboiler (N.)	पैसे कमाने के लिए जल्दबाज़ी में बनाई गई कृति	
407	The quality of being easy to predict	Predictability (N.)	पूर्वानुमान योग्यता	
408	A sign or warning of something to come	Presage (N.)	पूर्वाभास	
409	Able to foretell what will happen in future	Prescient (Adj.)	दूरदर्शी	
410	Based on an assumption without proof	**Presumably (Adv.)~**	अनुमानतः	
411	The act of speaking or acting in an evasive way	**Prevarication (N.)**	बहानेबाजी या टालमटोल	2
412	The right of succession to the first born	Primogeniture (N.)	बड़े बेटे को विरासत मिलने का अधिकार	
413	An official statement	Proclamation (N.)	घोषणा	
414	A person whose job is to supervise students during examinations	Proctor (N.)	परीक्षा निरीक्षक	
415	The habit of spending money wastefully	Prodigality (N.)	फिज़ूलखर्ची	
416	A descendant of a person, animal, or plant; offspring	Progeny (N.)	वंशज, संतान	
417	An explosive for firing a bullet or a rocket	Propellant (N.)	गोली या रॉकेट में आगे धकेलने वाला पदार्थ (ईंधन)	
418	Relating to or accurately predicting the future	Prophetic (Adj.)	भविष्यसूचक	
419*	Ordinary and not especially interesting or unusual	**Prosaic (Adj.)~**	साधारण, नीरस	
420	The act of officially forbidding something	Proscription (N.)	निषेध, प्रतिबंध	
421*	To cut away dead parts of a plant	Prune (V.)	छांटना	
422	Relating to physical illness or symptoms that are caused by the mind	Psychosomatic (Adj.)	मानसिक कारणों से उत्पन्न शारीरिक बीमारी	
423*	Inclined to argue or fight readily	**Pugnacious (Adj.)~**	झगड़ालू	
424	To strike repeatedly with the fists	Pummel (V.)	लगातार मुक्का मारना	
425	To remove people or things from an organization or place in a sudden and violent way	**Purge (V.)~**	निकाल फेंकना	

SN	Phrases	One Word (PoS)	Hindi	#R
426	The scope or range of authority, influence, or understanding	**Purview (N.)~**	अधिकार या समझ का दायरा	2
427	The art of making fireworks and showing them in public	**Pyrotechnics (N.)**	आतिशबाजी बनाने की कला	2
428*	A situation in which you are confused about what to do	**Quandary (N.)~**	दुविधा	
429	A stanza or poem of four lines	Quatrain (N.)	चौपाई	
430	The 500th anniversary of something	Quincentenary (N.)	500वीं वर्षगांठ	
431	Violent and uncontrolled anger	Rage (N.)	क्रोध	
432	The establishment of harmonious relations between countries or groups previously in conflict	Rapprochement (N.)	संबंध-सुधार	
433	A person who accepts facts and is practical	Realist (N.)	यथार्थवादी व्यक्ति	
434	The act of withdrawing a statement or belief publicly	Recantation (N.)	बयान वापस लेना	
435	A preliminary survey or inspection	Recce (N.)	जांच-पड़ताल	
436*	Without thinking of the consequences	**Reckless (Adj.)~**	लापरवाह	
437	An activity done for enjoyment	Recreation (N.)	मनोरंजन	
438	An institution to which young offenders are sent as an alternative to prison	Reformatory (N.)	सुधार गृह	
439	At uniform intervals of time	Regularly (Adv.)	नियमित रूप से	
440*	The belief that people are born again with a different body after death	Reincarnation (N.)	पुनर्जन्म	
441	To voluntarily give up or surrender something	**Relinquish (V.)~**	त्यागना	
442	The action of correcting a fault or deficiency	Remediation (N.)	सुधार	
443	To recall past experiences with fondness	**Reminisce (V.)~**	पुरानी बातें याद करना	2
444	Showing no regret or guilt for wrongdoing	Remorseless (Adj.)	जिसे पछतावा न हो	
445	The act of giving up something	Renunciation (N.)	त्याग	
446	An official order to supply or use something	**Requisition (N.)**	आधिकारिक मांग	3
447*	Able to find clever ways to solve problems	**Resourceful (Adj.)~**	सूझ-बूझ वाला	
448	The return of lost or stolen property, or compensation for damage	Restitution (N.)	वापसी, भरपाई	
449	A person or business that sells goods to the public	Retailer (N.)	खुदरा विक्रेता	
450	A small handbag carried by women	Reticule (N.)	महिलाओं का छोटा बैग	
451	To reduce costs or spending	**Retrench (V.)~**	कटौती करना	
452*	A severe deserved punishment	Retribution (N.)	दंड, उचित सज़ा	
453	Return to earlier state	Retrogression (N.)	पतन (पीछे की ओर जाना)	
454*	The act of hurting someone in return	Revenge (N.)	बदला	
455	To officially cancel or withdraw an agreement, decision, or promise	**Revoke (V.)~**	रद्द करना	
456*	A person who engages in revolution	Revolutionary (N.)	क्रांतिकारी व्यक्ति	
457*	An expression of great enthusiasm or praise	Rhapsody (N.)	अत्यधिक प्रशंसा	

SN	Phrases	One Word (PoS)	Hindi #R
458	The branch of medical science that deals with the study and treatment of the nose	Rhinology (N.)	नासिका विज्ञान
459	A luxurious hotel or establishment; symbol of elegance	Ritz (N.)	आलीशान जगह
460	A small raised platform on a stage	**Rostrum (N.)~**	मंच
461	A request to reply to an invitation	RSVP (N.)	आमंत्रण का उत्तर देने का अनुरोध
462	A person who deliberately tries to destroy or damage something, specially public property	**Saboteur (N.)~**	तोड़फोड़ करने वाला
463	Enjoyments that someone gets from being violent or cruel or from causing pain	Sadism (N.)	पीड़ा से आनंद पाने की प्रवृत्ति
464	The ability to stay calm in a difficult situation	Sangfroid (N.)	धैर्य
465*	An object orbiting a planet	Satellite (N.)	उपग्रह
466	To walk in a slow relaxed manner	**Saunter (V.)~**	इत्मीनान से चलना, टहलना
467	A person who is very knowledgeable and is an expert in a particular subject	**Savant (N.)~**	विद्वान
468	To put an end to something	Scotch (V.)	समाप्त करना
469	A person or thing that causes suffering	Scourge (N.)	आफत
470	A board game in which players buildup words from small size lettered tiles	Scrabble (N.)	शब्द बनाने का खेल
471*	To move or climb quickly but with difficulty, often using your hands to help you	**Scramble (V.)~**	जल्दबाजी में चढ़ना
472	A person who writes or copies documents	Scribe (N.)	लिखने वाला व्यक्ति
473	An apparatus used for breathing underwater	Scuba (N.)	पानी के अंदर सांस लेने का उपकरण (स्कूबा)
474	To move hurriedly with short quick steps	Scurry (V.)	तेजी से भागना
475	The scientific study of the moon	Selenology (N.)	चंद्र विज्ञान
476	The scientific study of meaning in language	Semantics (N.)	शब्दार्थ विज्ञान
477*	Similarity of appearance	**Semblance (N.)~**	समानता का आभास
478	A training college for priests	Seminary (N.)	धर्मशिक्षा का संस्थान
479	A family of languages that includes Hebrew	Semitic (Adj.)	सेमिटिक जाति/भाषा से संबंधित
480	A religious discourse	Sermon (N.)	उपदेश
481	The 150th anniversary of something	Sesquicentennial (N.)	150वीं वर्षगांठ
482	A large area of land where sheep are kept for grazing	Sheep run (N.)	भेड़-चारागाह
483	A bad-tempered or aggressively assertive woman	Shrew (N.)	झगड़ालू महिला
484	A partner in a business who takes no active part in its management	Sleeping Partner (N.)	निष्क्रिय साझेदार
485*	A lazy and inactive person	Sluggard (N.)	आलसी
486	To sleep lightly or peacefully	Slumber (V.)	हल्की नींद सोना
487	Having or showing an excessive pride in oneself or one's achievements	**Smug (Adj.)~**	आत्मसंतुष्ट (घमंड से)
488	An explosive sound made through the nose	Snort (N.)	नाक से फुफकारना

SN	Phrases	One Word (PoS)	Hindi	#R
489	The state of being serious and calm	**Sobriety (N.)~**	संयम	
490	Something that gives feeling of comfort	**Solace (N.)~**	सांत्वना	
491	Being the only one	**Sole (Adj.)~**	एकमात्र	
492	False but seemingly plausible	**Specious (Adj.)~**	भ्रामक	
493	To flow out quickly or to make something flow out quickly, in large amounts	Spew (V.)	जोर से निकलना	
494	Occasionally; at irregular intervals	Sporadically (Adv.)	कभी-कभी	
495	Active and lively	**Spry (Adj.)~**	फुर्तीला	
496	To make a loud, harsh cry	**Squawk (V.)~**	कर्कश आवाज़ निकालना	
497	A fully grown male horse kept for breeding	**Stallion (N.)**	नर घोड़ा	2
498*	A plan of action to achieve a goal	Strategy (N.)	रणनीति	
499	A leisurely walk	**Stroll (N.)~**	सैर	
500*	A trick or a dishonest way of achieving something	**Subterfuge (N.)~**	छल	
501	The highest point of a mountain	**Summit (N.)~**	शिखर	
502*	To order someone to appear	**Summon (V.)~**	बुलाना	
503*	The close observation of a person or place, especially to detect illegal activity	**Surveillance (N.)~**	निगरानी	
504*	A group of individuals or organizations combined to promote a common interest	Syndicate (N.)	संघ	
505*	A brief summary of something	**Synopsis (N.)~**	सारांश	
506*	Reserved and not talkative	**Taciturn (Adj.)~**	कम बोलने वाला	
507	One behind another; together	Tandem (Adv.)	एक के पीछे एक, क्रम में	
508	A place where animal hides are treated	Tannery (N.)	चमड़ा कारख़ाना	
509	The quality of being determined	**Tenacity (N.)~**	दृढ़ता	
510*	The period of holding a position	**Tenure (N.)~**	कार्यकाल	
511	A written declaration of beliefs or final wishes, especially a will	**Testament (N.)~**	वसीयत; प्रमाण	
512	An extreme fear of death	**Thanatophobia (N.)**	मृत्यु भय	2
513	A political system based on the government of men by God	**Thearchy (N.)**	ईश्वर का शासन	3
514	A marriage between gods or between a god and a mortal	Theogamy (N.)	देवविवाह	
515	An extreme fear of becoming pregnant	Tokophobia (N.)	गर्भधारण का डर	
516	An outstanding or impressive achievement	Tour de force (N.)	शानदार प्रदर्शन (असाधारण उपलब्धि)	
517*	A person who travels to a foreign country for pleasure or cultural exchange	Tourist (N.)	पर्यटक	
518	Movement of something from one place to another	Translocation (N.)	स्थानांतरण	
519	A formal piece of writing that considers and examines a particular subject	Treatise (N.)	किसी विषय पर औपचारिक लेख	
520	A playing card of the suit chosen to rank above others; a decisive advantage	Trump (N.)	तुरुप का पत्ता, निर्णायक लाभ	
521	Swollen or distended	**Turgid (Adj.)~**	सूज़ा हुआ, फूला हुआ	

SN	Phrases	One Word (PoS)	Hindi	#R
522	The art of arranging printed text in an attractive and readable form	Typography (N.)	मुद्रण कला	
523*	Existing or being everywhere at the same time	**Ubiquitous (Adj.)~**	एक ही समय में हर जगह मौजूद	
524	Beyond one's legal power or authority (Adj.); Acting beyond legal authority (Adv.)	Ultra vires (Adj./ Adv.)	अधिकार क्षेत्र से बाहर	
525*	Fully agreed upon by all	**Unanimous (Adj.)~**	सर्वसम्मत	
526	Working in a job that does not fully use one's skills or abilities	Underemployed (Adj.)	अल्प-रोज़गार	
527	Not capable of being proved false	Unfalsifiable (Adj.)	गलत सिद्ध न किया जा सकने वाला	
528	Impossible to understand	Unintelligible (Adj.)	समझ में न आने वाला	
529	Poorly educated or illiterate	Unlettered (Adj.)	अनपढ़	
530*	A major change or disturbance, especially one causing confusion	Upheaval (N.)	उथल-पुथल	
531	The killing of one's wife	**Uxoricide (N.)**	पत्नी की हत्या	2
532*	Not exact or clear	**Vague (Adj.)~**	अस्पष्ट	
533*	Great courage in battle	**Valour (N.)~**	वीरता	
534*	The native language or dialect of a region	Vernacular (N.)	स्थानीय भाषा	
535*	Experienced through another person	**Vicarious (Adj.)~**	परोक्ष (दूसरे के अनुभव से)	
536	In a manner experienced through another person	Vicariously (Adv.)	परोक्ष रूप से	
537	A short descriptive piece of writing or acting about a person, place or event	**Vignette (N.)**	लघु वर्णन, संक्षिप्त चित्रण	3
538	Physical strength and energy	**Vigour (N.)~**	जोश	
539	Doing something out of free will	Voluntarily (Adv.)	स्वेच्छापूर्वक	
540	The opinions or beliefs of the majority; public opinion	Vox Populi (N.)	जनमत	
541	Amusing and strange	Wacky (Adj.)	मज़ेदार और अजीब	
542	A place with circular currents of water, which can pull objects down into it	Whirlpool (N.)	भँवर	
543	An extreme fear of arid or dry places	Xerophobia (N.)	शुष्क स्थानों का भय	
544	The general intellectual, moral, and cultural climate of an era	Zeitgeist (N.)	किसी समय की सोच और संस्कृति	
545*	A soft, gentle breeze (named after the Greek god of the west wind)	Zephyr (N.)	मंद हवा (ग्रीक देवता के नाम पर)	

*Total **545** OWS asked **629** times*

A5 One Word Substitution Practice Sets (Based on Recent Other Exam Papers)

Practice Set - 1

Direction (Q. 1-10): Select the option that can be used as a one-word substitute for the given group of words.

1 An official order to appear in court.
1) Mandate
2) Warrant
3) Summons
4) Decree

2 A person who completely abstains from consuming alcoholic drinks.
1) Tippler 2) Heretic
3) Sot 4) Teetotaller

3 A brief summary or outline.
1) Synopsis 2) Spontaneity
3) Solidarity 4) Semantics

4 A person who does not follow the usual rules.
1) Heretic 2) Maverick
3) Renegade 4) Anarchist

5 A person who has a tendency to commit murder.
1) Suicidal 2) Pensive
3) Regretful 4) Homicidal

6 An individual that is inordinately and abnormally affected by musical or other tones in certain ranges of sound.
1) Philomath
2) Bibliophile
3) Melomaniac
4) Autophile

7 A person who believes that their own gender is superior to the other.
1) chauvinist
2) bigamist
3) feminist
4) ableist

8 A handwriting expert.
1) Graphologist
2) Philatelist
3) Genealogist
4) Numismatist

9 A person who loves trees.
1) Arctophile
2) Audiophile
3) Pluviophile
4) Dendrophile

10 A loud and boisterous laugh, often one that is unrestrained or hearty.
1) Snicker 2) Giggle
3) Guffaw 4) Chuckle

Practice Set - 2

Direction (Q. 1-10): Select the option that can be used as a one-word substitute for the given group of words.

1 The act of giving up one's citizenship.
1) Deportation
2) Exile
3) Immigration
4) Renunciation

2 One who is fond of battling and fighting.
1) Belligerent
2) Philanthropist
3) Pacifist
4) Benevolent

3 Someone who is inclined to quarrel or fight readily.
1) Theist 2) Pugnacious
3) Veteran 4) Ligature

4 The act of taking back something previously said or written.
1) Revision
2) Reversal
3) Reiteration
4) Recantation

5 Relating to or involving old people.
1) Juvenile
2) Geriatric
3) Adolescent
4) Archaic

6 Great courage in the face of danger, especially in battle.
1) Valour 2) Indolence
3) Treachery 4) Cowardice

7 Mass of small bubbles on the top of a liquid.
1) Cream 2) Mist
3) Froth 4) Dew

8 Public shame and loss of honour.
1) Ignominy
2) Epidemic
3) Ineligible
4) Contemporary

9 A west wind breeze personified on the name of a Greek God.
1) Calais 2) Zeus
3) Zephyr 4) Boreas

10 Take a machine or structure into separate pieces.
1) Disillusion
2) Dismantle
3) Dissuade
4) Dissipate

Practice Set - 3

Direction (Q. 1-10): Select the option that can be used as a one-word substitute for the given group of words.

1 The official power to make legal decisions and judgments.
1) Adjuration
2) Prosecution
3) Jurisdiction
4) Recitation

2 The process of converting information into a code to prevent unauthorised access.
1) Encryption
2) Accreditation
3) Synchronization

4) Demonetisation

3 The practice of deceiving someone into believing something that is not true.
1) Ambiguity
2) Fabrication
3) Obfuscate
4) Fallacy

4 To cut off a part of the body.
1) Amputation
2) Euthanasia
3) Emasculation
4) Exorcism

5 To examine or analyse something (such as a metal or an idea) to determine its quality, nature, or components.
1) Argue 2) Assay
3) Assert 4) Assist

6 A place for published materials like books and periodicals, emphasising accessibility and circulation for a wider audience.
1) Museum 2) Library
3) Bookstore4) Archives

7 The condition of being overly sensitive to sounds.
1) Melomaniac
2) Earshot
3) Melophile
4) Hyperacusis

8 The process by which people visit a place frequently to find information about it.
1) Survey 2) Decree
3) Recce 4) Patrol

9 The quality of being easily broken or damaged.
1) Longevity 2) Legibility
3) Fragility 4) Agility

10 To move hurriedly with short quick steps.
1) Crawl 2) Scurry
3) Loiter 4) Squid

Practice Set - 4

Direction (Q. 1-10): Select the option that can be used as a one-word substitute for the given group of words.

1 A trick or a dishonest way of achieving something.
1) Espionage
2) Sabotage
3) Subterfuge
4) Persistence

2 Used to convey that what is asserted is very likely though not known for certain.
1) Pejoratively
2) Prescriptively
3) Pertinently
4) Presumably

3 Careful plans or methods for achieving a particular goal, usually over a long period of time.
1) Tactic 2) Strategy
3) Scheme 4) Experiment

4 To prohibit someone from doing something.
1) Provoke 2) Beside
3) Incite 4) Inhibit

5 A way of speaking or writing that makes something sound bigger and better than they are.
1) Euphemistic
2) Rhetorical
3) Hyperbolic
4) Diabolical

6 A person who specialises in the alignment of teeth.
1) Paediatrician
2) Podiatrist
3) Optometrist
4) Orthodontist

7 Agreed to by everyone.
1) Unanimous
2) Optional
3) Mandatory
4) Controversial

8 To remove fears, doubts and false ideas, usually by proving them wrong or unnecessary.
1) Rebut 2) Dispel
3) Impede 4) Quell

9 Marriage within one's tribe.
1) Autogamy
2) Bigamy
3) Endogamy
4) Exogamy

10 An act of punishing or harming somebody in return for what they have done to you, your family, or your friends.
1) Mercy
2) Justice
3) Forgiveness
4) Revenge

Practice Set - 5

Direction (Q. 1-10): Select the option that can be used as a one-word substitute for the given group of words.

1 A place where soldiers are quartered.
1) Cantonment
2) Factory
3) Camp
4) Tent

2 The main features which are considered to be outstanding universal value and are still relevant.
1) Architecture
2) Society
3) Estate
4) Heritage

3 Businessman or businesswoman who is very wealthy and influential.
1) Artisan 2) Magnate
3) Diplomat 4) Peasant

4 A belief that pleasure or happiness is the highest good in life.
1) Nihilism
2) Epicureanism
3) Hedonism
4) Egotism

5 A space with a specific address.
1) Treaty 2) Destination
3) Domain 4) Proletariat

6 A person who deliberately tries to destroy or damage something, especially public property.
1) Altruist
2) Saboteur
3) Self-absorbed
4) Terrorist

7 A person who makes or sells

women's hats.
1) Designer 2) Seamstress
3) Draper 4) Milliner

8 Animals that can live on both land and water.
1) Terrestrial
2) Aquatic
3) Amphibious
4) Arboreal

9 A person who studies the earth's atmosphere and conditions and predicts the weather condition.
1) Meteorologist
2) Biologist
3) Geologist
4) Astronomer

10 Object which moves around its planet.
1) Constellation
2) Satellite
3) Galaxy
4) Star

Practice Set - 6

Direction (Q. 1-10): Select the option that can be used as a one-word substitute for the highlighted group of words in the given sentence.

1 She was praised for her ability to speak many languages fluently.
1) linguistics
2) translation
3) bilingualism
4) polyglotism

2 In business, it is important to weigh the pros and cons of a proposal before taking a decision.
1) evacuate 2) eradicate
3) evaluate 4) evaporate

3 Hari is a driver who is heedless of danger and has sometimes met with accidents.
1) reckless 2) amiable
3) cautious 4) independent

4 The people who were listening enjoyed the music played by the famous maestro.
1) congregation
2) revolutionaries
3) spectators
4) audience

5 The professor's period of service or official position at the university is highly respected by colleagues.
1) Term 2) Tenure
3) Service 4) Appointment

6 The criminal was sentenced to ten years in prison for committing a serious crime such as murder .
1) misdemeanour
2) felony
3) offense
4) indictment

7 Sadly, there are still many poorly educated or lacking in education gained from books people in the world.
1) rude 2) scholarly
3) silly 4) unlettered

8 Despite it all, Gandhi remained firm in his beliefs and never gave up.
1) diffident
2) poised
3) indisposed
4) committed

9 The company filed a lawsuit against the website for illegally copying and selling its software without permission.
1) Plagiarism
2) Piracy
3) Theft
4) Fraud

10 His idea was dismissed as something that cannot be proved or disproved.
1) unfalsifiable
2) speculative
3) hypothetical
4) ambiguous

Practice Set - 7

Direction (Q. 1-10): Select the option that can be used as a one-word substitute for the underlined group of words in the given sentence.

1 The company decided to cut away unnecessary parts in order to improve efficiency or appearance, streamlining its operations and reducing overhead costs.
1) expand 2) accumulate
3) prune 4) complicate

2 Cinnamon was known in Biblical times, as a/an part of the mixture or compound that was mixed with oils for anointing people's bodies.
1) additive 2) iceberg
3) appetizer 4) ingredient

3 People who thought that the person who wrote the music was a computer tended to dislike the piece more than those who believed it was human.
1) quixotic 2) ventriloquist
3) vocalist 4) composer

4 After weeks of bland meals, he began to ask for earnestly something spicy and flavourful.
1) float 2) snub
3) crave 4) reckon

5 Her novel was criticised for a style of speaking or writing that is pompous and inflated in expression.
1) Bombast
2) Oratory
3) Hyperbole
4) Rhetoric

6 The designer studied the science of colours and their properties to enhance the visual appeal of her work.
1) graphics 2) chromatics
3) aesthetics4) optics

7 The company reduced staff to cut down expenses.
1) deflect 2) curtail
3) revoke 4) retrench

8 The meeting was postponed because it was not attended by enough people to make it valid.
1) inquorate 2) dissolved
3) treason 4) tyranny

9 The scholar's favourite pursuit was immersing himself in one or another formal piece of writing that considers and examines a particular subject.
1) exegesis 2) annotation
3) treatise 4) manuscript

10 The new policy was introduced to put an end to corruption and prevent future abuses of power.
1) invoke 2) concede
3) scotch 4) prolong

Practice Set - 8

Direction (Q. 1-10): Select the option that can be used as a one-word substitute for the underlined group of words in the given sentence.

1 She is known for her habit of spending money carelessly.
1) prodigality
2) generosity
3) hospitality
4) frugality

2 Ten thousand dollars of this year's budget is to be kept or intended for the renovation of the building.
1) impeded
2) obscured
3) submerged
4) earmarked

3 he was accused of the criminal offense of knowingly making false statements under oath in judicial proceedings.
1) slander 2) collusion
3) libel 4) perjury

4 She tried to hide her violent and uncontrolled anger, but her clenched fists gave her away.
1) stasis 2) cordiality
3) rage 4) consortium

5 The couple reminisced about their happy and carefree days spent travelling the world.
1) halcyon
2) vintage
3) serendipitous
4) bygone

6 He argued that the act of doing what one is told by someone in authority must be rooted in truth and conscience.
1) orientation
2) obeisance
3) obedience
4) obsession

7 During our visit to the coastline, we saw a seabird commonly found near the coast, gliding effortlessly over the waves.
1) Penguin 2) Gull
3) Hawk 4) Ostrich

8 His unwillingness to spend money unnecessarily sometimes made him unpopular at social gatherings.
1) traditionality
2) conservatism
3) austerity
4) parsimony

9 In the digital age, smartphones have become existing or being everywhere at the same time in our daily lives.
1) evanescent
2) fugacious
3) ubiquitous
4) recondite

10 The stern gaze of the person whose job is to watch people taking exams in order to check that they do not cheat kept the testing room in order, maintaining an atmosphere of integrity.
1) ambassador
2) delegate
3) custodian
4) proctor

Practice Set - 9

Direction (Q. 1-10): Select the option that can be used as a one-word substitute for the underlined group of words in the given sentence.

1 As a legal expert, Jaya's range of outlook or understanding extends beyond mere courtroom proceedings to encompass a broad understanding of legal principles and precedents.
1) proviso 2) purlieu
3) purview 4) purvey

2 The new mobile service company became an overwhelming force in the industry.
1) exhaustion
2) juggernaut
3) incapacity
4) fragility

3 She was about sixty-five, active and able to move quickly, thin spinster, who had spent all her life looking after an ailing mother.
1) graceful 2) clumsy
3) spry 4) tenacious

4 The new policy was declared void because it was beyond the legal power or authority of the legislature.
1) Ultra Vires
2) Codification
3) Legislation
4) Amendment

5 Sheldon is not accepted by a social group because he is not liked and is excluded from every group outing.
1) a minimalist
2) an apostle
3) a pariah
4) a fatalist

6 Due to health concerns, the company's president had to step away from his position.
1) claim 2) hold
3) approve 4) relinquish

7 The practice of giving the right of succession to the first born was considered to be the strongest reason for the prevalence of polygamy from one generation to another.

1) uxoricide
2) primogeniture
3) adverse possession
4) plutocracy

8 After retirement, he received a <u>regular payment from the company for his past service</u>.
1) Stipend 2) Fee
3) Salary 4) Pension

9 Why don't we <u>walk around</u> through the night and see where we reach.
1) rest 2) gush
3) stroll 4) stay

10 The umpteen requests for product samples ended up making the marketing team feel <u>overwhelmed with a rush</u>.
1) whimsical
2) flummoxed
3) nonchalant
4) inundated

Practice Set - 10

Direction (Q. 1-10): Which of the following is the most suitable meaning of the word.

1 Implacable
1) Peaceful
2) Unable to be appeased
3) Easily calmed
4) Optimistic

2 Zeitgeist
1) The digital age and public opinion
2) Marginalised communities and their voice
3) Content quickly replicated and shared across the internet
4) The general intellectual, moral, and cultural climate of an era

3 Trump
1) To trumpet loudly, to blare or drown out
2) To trample
3) To devise a fraud, to employ trickle
4) To get the better of by using a key or hidden resource

4 Vague
1) free from deception
2) not exact or clear
3) circumstantial
4) easily understood

5 Feeble
1) someone who is selfish
2) someone who is weak
3) someone who is brave
4) someone who has strong feelings

6 Predictability
1) The complexity of math
2) The random nature of something
3) The ability to be consistently expected
4) The difficulty of solving problems

7 Inextricably
1) In a harmful way
2) In a loosely connected manner
3) In a convincing fashion
4) In a way that is unable to be separated

8 Netizen
1) Viral memes or reels
2) People who do not use internet
3) Posts on internet
4) Users of internet

9 Slumber
1) Deep thinking
2) Sound sleep
3) Sleep deprivation
4) Lack of enthusiasm

10 Specious
1) Believable and compelling
2) False but seemingly plausible
3) Too technical to understand
4) Harsh and accusatory

Answer Key Practice Set - 1:

1 - 3	2 - 4	3 - 1	4 - 2	5 - 4
6 - 3	7 - 1	8 - 1	9 - 4	10 - 3

Answer Key Practice Set - 2:

1 - 4	2 - 1	3 - 2	4 - 4	5 - 2
6 - 1	7 - 3	8 - 1	9 - 3	10 - 2

Answer Key Practice Set - 3:

1 - 3	2 - 1	3 - 2	4 - 1	5 - 2
6 - 2	7 - 4	8 - 3	9 - 3	10 - 2

Answer Key Practice Set - 4:

1 - 3	2 - 4	3 - 2	4 - 4	5 - 3
6 - 4	7 - 1	8 - 2	9 - 3	10 - 4

Answer Key Practice Set - 5:

1 - 1	2 - 4	3 - 2	4 - 3	5 - 3
6 - 2	7 - 4	8 - 3	9 - 1	10 - 2

Answer Key Practice Set - 6:

1 - 4	2 - 3	3 - 1	4 - 4	5 - 2
6 - 2	7 - 4	8 - 4	9 - 2	10 - 1

Answer Key Practice Set - 7:

1 - 3	2 - 4	3 - 4	4 - 3	5 - 1
6 - 2	7 - 4	8 - 1	9 - 3	10 - 3

Answer Key Practice Set - 8:

1 - 1	2 - 4	3 - 4	4 - 3	5 - 1
6 - 3	7 - 2	8 - 4	9 - 3	10 - 4

Answer Key Practice Set - 9:

1 - 3	2 - 2	3 - 3	4 - 1	5 - 3
6 - 4	7 - 2	8 - 4	9 - 3	10 - 4

Answer Key Practice Set - 10:

1 - 2	2 - 4	3 - 4	4 - 2	5 - 2
6 - 3	7 - 4	8 - 4	9 - 2	10 - 2

PART - B
(IDIOMS / PHRASES)

__Contents__:-

** Additional non-PYQ Phrasal Verbs are included in Chapter F1.*

__Updated and Additional Content__: -

1. **New SSC Idioms**: Added new Idioms from **417 sets** asked by SSC after the publication of the last edition (May 2024).
2. **Expanded Idioms Coverage**: Added new Idioms from 470 sets of other competitive exams. The 2026 edition now covers a total of 1,277 additional sets (470 + 807) from other exams since the 2023 edition.

__Additional Symbols for smarter and efficient preparation__: -

1. **#R (Repetition Count)**: The #R tag, used to show how many times an Idiom has been asked in competitive exams. The number **outside** the bracket shows SSC repetitions; the number **inside** the bracket shows repetitions across the additional 1,277 sets.

Blackbook's Proven Coverage:

Since the May 2024 edition, SSC and other exams asked approx. 1975 Idioms in exams, out of which approx. 1679 were already present in Blackbook and only 296 were new. That's an impressive **85.01% coverage rate**, powered not just by SSC PYQs but also by our inclusion of other competitive exam vocabulary.

IDIOMS, PROVERBS & PHRASAL VERBS

Introduction

An Idiom is a fixed phrase with a figurative meaning. "**Burn the midnight oil**" does not mean setting oil on fire. It means to study or work late into the night.

A Proverb is a short saying that gives practical advice or a general truth. "**A stitch in time saves nine**" means fixing a small problem early prevents it from becoming bigger.

A Phrasal Verb is a verb combined with a preposition or adverb that creates a new meaning. "**Break down**" does not mean breaking something downward. It means to stop working or to lose emotional control.

How Exams Test IDIOMS

The question format is straightforward. You are given an idiom, proverb, or phrasal verb and asked to pick its correct meaning from four options. Sometimes, a sentence is given with a highlighted expression, and you must identify what it means. Here are some real questions from recent SSC papers:

- "Select the most appropriate meaning of the idiom: Beat around the bush" Options: to accomplish a task, to avoid the main topic, to work very hard, to celebrate success. Answer: To avoid the main topic
- "She was on cloud nine after getting the promotion." Options: confused, extremely happy, nervous, exhausted. Answer: Extremely happy

How to Use This Chapter

Most books give you only the English meaning. Blackbook goes a step further. Wherever an exact Hindi idiom exists, we have included it along with its explanation in brackets. This makes it easier to remember because you already know the Hindi equivalent. For example:

- **Add fuel to the fire** = आग में घी डालना (विवाद को और अधिक बढ़ा देना)
- **All bark and no bite** = जो गरजते हैं वो बरसते नहीं (खोखली धमकी)

When you read "आग में घी डालना", you instantly connect it with "Add fuel to the fire" because the meaning clicks in your own language. That is the advantage of having precise Hindi idioms, not just translations.

#R (Repetition Count): The number in the last column (#R) shows how many times that idiom has been asked in SSC exams. The number in brackets shows how many times it appeared in other exams like DSSSB, CDS, AFCAT etc. For example, if an idiom shows **8 (2)**, it means it was asked **8 times in SSC** and **2 times in other exams**. Higher the #R, more important the idiom.

To give you an idea, here are some of the most repeated idioms across SSC papers:

- **Beat around the bush** 23 (27) – asked 23 times in SSC exams and 27 times in other exams
- **Spill the beans** 27 (20) – asked 27 times in SSC and 20 exams times in other exams
- **Bite the bullet** 19 (25) – asked 19 times in SSC and 25 exams times in other exams

Idioms with high repetition count should be your top priority. They keep coming back in different shifts, different years, and sometimes even across different exams. Idioms are **scoring questions** because if you know the idiom, you get the mark in seconds. No calculation, no analysis.

B1 Top 200 Idioms & Phrases (asked in SSC Exams)

SN	Idioms/Phrases	English Meaning	Hindi Meaning	#R
1	**Beat about (or around) the bush**	To avoid talking about the main topic	घुमा-फिराकर बात करना (मुख्य बात पर न आना)	23 (27)
2	**Hit the nail on the head**	To say or do something exactly right	सटीक जवाब देना, बिल्कुल सही होना	18 (29)
3	**Spill the beans**	To tell a secret, often by accident	राज़ उगल देना (भेद खोलना)	27 (20)
4	**Bite the bullet**	To accept a difficult situation and deal with it bravely	कड़वा घूँट पीना (मज़बूरी में स्वीकार करना)	19 (25)
5	**Under the weather**	Not feeling well; slightly ill	तबीयत ठीक न होना (थोड़ा बीमार)	24 (18)
6	**Cost an arm and a leg**	To cost a lot of money	भारी कीमत चुकाना (बहुत महँगा पड़ना)	24 (15)
7	**Once in a blue moon**	Very rarely; almost never	ईद का चाँद होना (कभी-कभार)	21 (18)
8	**A piece of cake**	Something that is very easy to do	बाएँ हाथ का खेल (बहुत आसान काम)	20 (16)
9	**Call it a day**	To decide to stop working for the day	इतिश्री करना (आज का काम समाप्त करना)	19 (17)
10	**Hit the sack (or hay)**	To go to bed; to sleep	बिस्तर पर जाना (सोने जाना)	17 (19)
11	**Let the cat out of the bag**	To reveal a secret by mistake	ग़लती से राज़ उजागर करना (भेद खोल देना)	14 (22)
12	**Break the ice**	To make people feel more relaxed in a social situation	बातचीत शुरू करना	13 (22)
13	**A blessing (or boon) in disguise**	Something that seems bad at first but turns out to be good	छुपा हुआ वरदान (बुरा लगने वाला पर फ़ायदेमंद)	23 (11)
14	**A bolt from the blue**	A sudden and unexpected event	आकस्मिक घटना	15 (19)
15	**Bury the hatchet**	To stop fighting or arguing and become friendly	झगड़ा खत्म करना	18 (15)
16	**Burn the midnight oil**	To work or study late into the night	देर रात तक काम करना	16 (16)
17	**Wild goose chase**	A search for something that is impossible to find	भूसे में सुई ढूँढना (व्यर्थ की खोज)	18 (13)
18	**Face the music**	To accept consequences	किये का फल भुगतना (परिणाम का सामना करना)	23 (7)
19	**On cloud nine**	Extremely happy; in a state of bliss	ख़ुशी से फूले न समाना (बेहद ख़ुश)	16 (14)
20	**Sit on the fence**	To avoid taking sides or making a decision	तटस्थ रहना (किसी का पक्ष न लेना)	20 (10)
21	**Bite off more than one can chew**	To take on more responsibility than one can manage	हैसियत से बाहर (अपनी क्षमता से ज़्यादा काम उठाना)	14 (15)

[**#R** denotes repetition of word]

[E.g. in SN 19, #R- **16 (14)** denotes this word has been asked 16 times in SSC and 14 times in other exams]

SN	Idioms/Phrases	English Meaning	Hindi Meaning	#R
22	**A fish out of water**	A person in an unfamiliar environment where they feel awkward	असहज परिस्थिति (जहाँ व्यक्ति अजनबी महसूस करे)	18 (9)
23	**Blow one's own trumpet (or horn)**	To talk proudly about one's achievements	अपने मुँह मियाँ मिट्ठू बनना (अपनी प्रशंसा स्वयं करना)	19 (8)
24	**At the drop of a hat (or dime)**	Immediately; without hesitation	फ़ौरन (बिना पल गँवाए)	12 (14)
25	**Cry over spilt milk**	To waste time being upset about something that has already happened	अब पछताए होत क्या जब चिड़िया चुग गई खेत (बीती बातों पर व्यर्थ पछताना)	13 (13)
26	**Flog (or beat) a dead horse**	To waste effort on something that cannot succeed	व्यर्थ प्रयास करना	16 (10)
27	**Gift of the gab**	Ability to speak persuasively and eloquently	वाक्पटुता (बोलने की कला में माहिर होना)	22 (4)
28	**Take with a pinch (or grain) of salt**	To be skeptical about something; to not fully believe it	आँख मूँदकर विश्वास न करना (संदेह के साथ मानना)	16 (10)
29	**Break a leg**	Used to wish someone good luck, especially before a performance	शुभकामनाएँ (मंच पर जाने से पहले दी जाने वाली बधाई)	13 (12)
30	**Cut corners**	To do something in the easiest or cheapest way	सस्ता जुगाड़ करना (गुणवत्ता से समझौता करना)	9 (16)
31	**Eleventh hour**	At the last possible moment	अंतिम क्षण में	15 (9)
32	**Have an axe to grind**	Have a hidden selfish motive	अपना उल्लू सीधा करना (स्वार्थ सिद्ध करना)	12 (12)
33	**Smell a rat**	To suspect that something is wrong or dishonest	दाल में कुछ काला होना (शक होना)	15 (9)
34	**In hot water**	In a situation where you are likely to be punished or criticized	मुसीबत में फँसना (ग़लती की वजह से परेशानी में)	13 (10)
35	**Read between the lines**	To understand the real or hidden meaning behind what is said	छिपा हुआ अर्थ समझना (इशारों को समझना)	16 (7)
36	**See eye to eye**	To agree completely with someone about something	पूरी तरह सहमत होना (एक राय होना)	13 (10)
37	**Through thick and thin**	In all circumstances, both good and bad	सुख-दुख में (हर हाल में साथ)	17 (6)
38	**Throw in the towel OR Throw up the sponge**	To accept that you have been beaten	हथियार डाल देना (हार मान लेना)	11 (12)
39	**Leave no stone unturned**	To do everything possible to find something or achieve something	आकाश-पाताल एक करना (कोई कसर न छोड़ना)	15 (7)
40	**A dime a dozen**	Very common and of little value	कौड़ियों के भाव (बहुत सस्ता)	12 (9)
41	**Add fuel to the fire (or flame)**	To make a bad situation worse	आग में घी डालना (स्थिति और बिगाड़ना)	14 (7)
42	**Back to the drawing board**	Time to start planning again after a failure	नए सिरे से सोचना (फिर से योजना बनाना)	10 (11)
43	**Storm in a teacup**	A lot of unnecessary anger about something small	बात का बतंगड़ (छोटी बात पर हंगामा)	15 (6)

SN	Idioms/Phrases	English Meaning	Hindi Meaning	#R
44	**A hard nut to crack**	A difficult problem or person	लोहे के चने चबाना (मुश्किल काम या व्यक्ति)	17 (3)
45	**All at sea**	Confused and uncertain	असमंजस में (भ्रमित और अनिश्चित)	15 (5)
46	**Miss the boat (or bus)**	To fail to take advantage of an opportunity	मौक़ा हाथ से निकल जाना (अवसर खो देना)	13 (7)
47	**Take the bull by the horns**	To face a difficult situation directly and with courage	मुसीबत का डटकर सामना करना (साहस से निपटना)	10 (10)
48	**Turn a deaf ear**	To deliberately ignore what someone is saying	अनसुना करना (ध्यान न देना)	14 (6)
49	**Bark up the wrong tree**	To make a wrong assumption or pursue a mistaken course	गलत दिशा में प्रयास करना; गलत व्यक्ति को दोष देना	13 (6)
50	**Give someone the cold shoulder**	To deliberately ignore or be unfriendly to someone	नजरअंदाज करना	11 (8)
51	**Hold one's horses**	To wait and be patient; to slow down	धैर्य रखना (रुको, जल्दबाज़ी मत करो)	12 (7)
52	**In the same boat**	In the same difficult or unpleasant situation as someone else	एक ही नाव में सवार होना (समान मुसीबत में होना)	12 (7)
53	**Jump the gun**	To start something before the right time; to act prematurely	जल्दबाज़ी करना (वक़्त से पहले क़दम उठाना)	7 (12)
54	**Rain cats and dogs**	To rain very heavily	मूसलाधार बारिश (जमकर पानी बरसना)	13 (6)
55	**A dark horse**	An unexpectedly successful person or competitor	छुपा रुस्तम (अप्रत्याशित विजेता)	9 (9)
56	**On thin ice**	In a risky or dangerous situation	ख़तरे में होना (जोख़िम भरी स्थिति में)	15 (3)
57	**Red letter day**	A day that is very important or special	महत्वपूर्ण दिन (यादगार दिन)	14 (4)
58	**Snake in the grass**	A treacherous person who pretends to be a friend	आस्तीन का साँप (छिपा हुआ दुश्मन)	13 (5)
59	**Throw caution to the wind**	To take a risk without worrying about the consequences	जोख़िम उठाना (लापरवाही से काम करना)	11 (7)
60	**As fit as a fiddle**	In excellent physical health	चंगा-भला (पूरी तरह स्वस्थ)	11 (6)
61	**Burn one's bridges (or boats)**	To do something that makes it impossible to go back	पीछे हटने के सारे रास्ते खत्म करना	7 (10)
62	**By leaps and bounds**	Very quickly and in large amounts	दिन दूनी रात चौगुनी (बहुत तेज़ी से)	15 (2)
63	**Go the extra mile**	To make more effort than expected	आवश्यकता से अधिक प्रयास करना	8 (9)
64	**Go up in smoke**	To be destroyed or ruined completely; to fail	धुआँ हो जाना (बर्बाद हो जाना)	8 (9)
65	**Play devil's advocate**	To argue against something even if you agree with it, to test the strength of the argument	विपरीत पक्ष रखना (बहस के लिए उल्टा तर्क देना)	9 (8)
66	**White elephant**	Something that costs a lot to keep but is useless	महँगी लेकिन बेकार चीज़ (ख़र्चीला बोझ)	11 (6)

SN	Idioms/Phrases	English Meaning	Hindi Meaning	#R
67	**Black sheep**	A person who is considered a disgrace to a family or group	अपनी बुरी हरकतों से परिवार का नाम खराब करने वाला	7 (9)
68	**Eat humble pie**	To apologize and admit being wrong	माफ़ी माँगना (अपनी ग़लती मानकर शर्मिंदा होना)	13 (3)
69	**In a nutshell**	In a very few words; briefly	निचोड़ बताना (संक्षेप में)	13 (3)
70	**Jump on the bandwagon**	To join an activity, trend, or opinion that has become popular	बहती गंगा में हाथ धोना (लोकप्रिय चलन का हिस्सा बनना)	9 (7)
71	**Leave someone in the lurch**	To leave someone alone when they need help; to abandon someone in a difficult situation	मँझधार में छोड़ देना (मुसीबत में अकेला छोड़ना)	11 (5)
72	**Pull someone's leg**	To joke with someone by saying something untrue	टाँग खींचना (मज़ाक करना)	14 (2)
73	**The ball is in your court**	It is now your turn to act or make a decision	अब गेंद तुम्हारे पाले में है (अब फ़ैसला आपका है)	8 (8)
74	**The lion's share**	The largest or best portion of something	शेर का हिस्सा (सबसे बड़ा हिस्सा)	9 (7)
75	**Turn over a new leaf**	To start behaving in a better way	नई शुरुआत करना (सुधर जाना)	8 (8)
76	**A cock and bull story**	An absurd and untrue story	बेसिर-पैर की कहानी (झूठी और बेतुकी बात)	10 (5)
77	**Be all ears**	Listening with full attention; very eager to hear	कान लगाए बैठना (पूरे ध्यान से सुनना)	11 (4)
78	**By fits and starts**	In an irregular way; intermittently	रुक-रुककर (अनियमित रूप से)	11 (4)
79	**By the skin of one's teeth**	By a very small margin; only just	बाल-बाल (बहुत कम अंतर से)	10 (5)
80	**Fight tooth and nail**	To fight with all one's strength and determination	जी-जान से लड़ना (पूरी ताक़त लगा देना)	9 (6)
81	**Nip in the bud**	To stop something bad before it has a chance to develop	शुरुआत में ही रोक देना (कली में ही तोड़ देना)	9 (6)
82	**Turn a blind eye**	To pretend not to notice something	अनदेखा करना (जानबूझकर नज़रअंदाज़ करना)	7 (8)
83	**A chip off the old block**	A person who resembles their parent in character	जैसा बाप वैसा बेटा (माँ-बाप जैसी संतान)	8 (6)
84	**A feather in one's cap**	An achievement to be proud of	गर्व करने योग्य उपलब्धि	8 (6)
85	**At one's wits' end**	Completely frustrated and not knowing what to do	बुद्धि चकराना (पूरी तरह से उलझन में)	10 (4)
86	**Best of both worlds**	The benefits of two different situations enjoyed together	दोनों हाथों में लड्डू (दोनों तरफ से फायदा)	10 (4)
87	**Cold feet**	A loss of nerve or confidence	हाथ-पाँव ठंडे पड़ना (घबराहट होना)	10 (4)
88	**Get out of hand**	To become uncontrollable or difficult to manage	हाथ से निकलना (नियंत्रण से बाहर होना)	11 (3)
89	**Grease someone's palm**	To bribe someone	हथेली गरम करना (रिश्वत देना)	12 (2)

SN	Idioms/Phrases	English Meaning	Hindi Meaning	#R
90	**Hit below the belt**	To attack unfairly or dishonestly	अनुचित प्रहार करना (नियमों के विरुद्ध)	7 (7)
91	**It's all Greek to me (or Latin and Greek)**	Something that is completely incomprehensible	सर के ऊपर से जाना (समझ से बिल्कुल परे)	8 (6)
92	**Kick the bucket**	To die	दम तोड़ना (मर जाना)	7 (7)
93	**Last straw**	The last in a series of problems that finally causes a reaction	सब्र का आख़िरी प्याला (बर्दाश्त की सीमा)	9 (5)
94	**Pull oneself together**	To become calm and behave normally after being upset	ख़ुद को संभालना (भावुक स्थिति से उबरना)	10 (4)
95	**Under a cloud**	In a state of suspicion or disfavour	संदेह के घेरे में (बदनामी की स्थिति में)	10 (4)
96	**Up in arms**	Angry and ready to fight or argue	विरोध में उठ खड़ा होना (नाराज़गी में)	7 (7)
97	**A fair-weather friend**	A friend only in good times	सुख के साथी (स्वार्थी मित्र)	13
98	**A stone's throw**	A very short distance	बहुत कम दूरी	11 (2)
99	**Catch someone red-handed**	To catch someone in the act of doing something wrong	रंगे हाथों पकड़ना (अपराध करते हुए पकड़ना)	9 (4)
100	**Elephant in the room**	An obvious problem that everyone ignores	अनदेखी की गई बड़ी समस्या	5 (8)
101	**Hand in (or and) glove**	Working closely together, often for dishonest purposes	मिलीभगत (घनिष्ठ संबंध)	9 (4)
102	**Keep at arm's length**	To avoid becoming too friendly or close with someone	दूर से सलाम करना (दूरी बनाए रखना)	11 (2)
103	**Sell like hotcakes**	To sell very quickly and in large quantities	हाथों-हाथ बिकना (तेज़ी से बिकना)	7 (6)
104	**A bed of roses**	A pleasant, comfortable, or easy situation	फूलों की सेज (आसान और सुखद स्थिति)	5 (7)
105	**Apple of one's eye**	A person who is greatly cherished and loved	आँखों का तारा (बेहद प्रिय व्यक्ति)	10 (2)
106	**Bad blood**	Feelings of hatred or hostility between people	आपसी दुश्मनी (पुरानी रंजिश)	10 (2)
107	**By hook or by crook**	By any means necessary	हर हाल में (किसी भी तरीक़े से)	6 (6)
108	**Call a spade a spade**	To speak honestly and directly	साफ-साफ कहना (बिना लाग-लपेट के कड़वा सच बोलना)	5 (7)
109	**Go (or run) around in circles**	To waste time without making progress	व्यर्थ भाग-दौड़ करना (समय बर्बाद करना)	10 (2)
110	**In the nick of time**	At the last possible moment; just in time	ठीक समय पर (बिल्कुल आख़िरी मौक़े पर)	7 (5)
111	**Ins and outs**	All the details and complications of something	पूरा विवरण (भीतर की सारी बातें)	8 (4)
112	**Out of the blue**	Completely unexpectedly; with no prior warning	अचानक / बिना किसी पूर्व सूचना के (अप्रत्याशित रूप से)	10 (2)

SN	Idioms/Phrases	English Meaning	Hindi Meaning	#R
113	**Steal someone's thunder**	To take someone else's attention or credit	दूसरे का श्रेय छीनना (किसी की तारीफ़ लूटना)	6 (6)
114	**Strain every nerve**	To try as hard as possible	एड़ी-चोटी का ज़ोर लगाना (जी-तोड़ मेहनत)	6 (6)
115	**Take to one's heels**	To flee; to run away in fear	रफ़ूचक्कर होना (भाग खड़ा होना)	8 (4)
116	**Wear one's heart on one's sleeve**	To make your feelings obvious to everyone	खुले दिल से भाव दिखाना (भावनाएँ न छिपाना)	8 (4)
117	**A bird's-eye view**	A view from a high position; a general overview	ऊपर से देखा गया विस्तृत दृश्य	7 (4)
118	**Add insult to injury**	To make a bad situation worse by adding humiliation	जले पर नमक छिड़कना (बुरी स्थिति को और बुरा बनाना)	7 (4)
119	**Back to square one**	Back to the very beginning; having to start again	फिर से शुरू (जहाँ से चले थे वहीं वापस)	5 (6)
120	**Bigger (or other) fish to fry**	More important matters to deal with	ज़्यादा ज़रूरी काम (और बड़े मसले)	7 (4)
121	**Blow hot and cold**	To keep changing one's attitude	कभी हाँ कभी ना (रवैये में अस्थिरता)	4 (7)
122	**Build castles in the air**	To have dreams or plans that are unlikely to happen	हवाई क़िले बनाना (असंभव सपने देखना)	8 (3)
123	**Drop in a bucket (or ocean)**	A very small amount compared to what is needed	ऊँट के मुँह में जीरा (ज़रूरत के मुक़ाबले नगण्य मात्रा)	6 (5)
124	**Eat like a horse**	To eat a lot	बहुत अधिक खाना	8 (3)
125	**Fair and square**	Completely honest and straightforward	ईमानदार और साफ़	6 (5)
126	**Full of beans**	Very energetic and lively	जोश और ऊर्जा से भरपूर	10 (1)
127	**In black and white**	In writing; in a form that provides clear proof	लिखित रूप में (काले-सफ़ेद में)	10 (1)
128	**In high (or good) spirits**	Very cheerful and happy	उत्साह से भरा (ख़ुशनुमा मिज़ाज में)	7 (4)
129	**Kill two birds with one stone**	To accomplish two goals with one effort or action	एक तीर से दो शिकार (एक ही प्रयास में दो लक्ष्य हासिल करना)	9 (2)
130	**Man of letters**	A person who is very knowledgeable about literature; a writer	विद्वान व्यक्ति (साहित्यकार)	6 (5)
131	**Man of straw**	A person who has no real power or importance	कमज़ोर व्यक्ति (कठपुतली)	7 (4)
132	**Play it by ear**	To decide what to do as a situation develops rather than planning in advance	परिस्थिति के अनुसार काम करना (बिना तैयारी के)	5 (6)
133	**Spick and span**	Very clean and neat	एकदम चकाचक (साफ़-सुथरा)	10 (1)
134	**Wolf in sheep's clothing**	Someone who seems friendly but is actually dangerous	भेड़ की खाल में भेड़िया (छिपा हुआ ख़तरनाक व्यक्ति)	5 (6)
135	**A bee in one's bonnet**	An obsessive idea or preoccupation	सनक सवार होना (किसी बात की धुन)	3 (7)

SN	Idioms/Phrases	English Meaning	Hindi Meaning	#R
136	**A bitter pill to swallow**	An unpleasant fact that one must accept	कड़वा घूँट पीना (एक अप्रिय स्थिति जिसे मजबूरी में स्वीकार करना पड़े)	4 (6)
137	**A close shave**	A situation where you only just avoid an accident or disaster	बाल-बाल बचना (नज़दीकी बचाव)	7 (3)
138	**A flash in the pan**	Short-lived success	क्षणिक सफलता	3 (7)
139	**Above board**	Honest and transparent	पारदर्शी और ईमानदार	3 (7)
140	**Against the clock**	In a great hurry to finish before a deadline	समय से दौड़ (समय की कमी में तेजी से काम करना)	8 (2)
141	**As cool as a cucumber**	Very calm and composed, especially under pressure	शांत और संयमित (दबाव में भी स्थिर)	8 (2)
142	**At sixes and sevens**	In a state of confusion or disarray	अस्त-व्यस्त (अव्यवस्थित या असमंजस में)	6 (4)
143	**Bell the cat**	To take on a risky or dangerous task that others are afraid to do	बिल्ली के गले में घंटी बाँधना (जोखिम भरा काम करना)	7 (3)
144	**Between a rock and a hard place**	In a difficult situation where both options are bad	आगे कुआँ पीछे खाई (दो कठिन विकल्पों के बीच फँस जाना)	3 (7)
145	**Bite the dust**	To die or be destroyed; to fail	धूल चाटना (हार जाना या मारा जाना)	6 (4)
146	**Crocodile tears**	Tears or sadness that are not sincere	मगरमच्छ के आँसू (दिखावटी या झूठा दुःख)	7 (3)
147	**Cut the mustard**	To meet expectations or perform satisfactorily	मापदंड पर खरा उतरना	2 (8)
148	**Cut to the chase**	To get to the main point without delay	सीधे मुद्दे पर आना	7 (3)
149	**Get a taste of one's own medicine**	To experience the same treatment that one has given to others	जैसे को तैसा (दूसरों के साथ किए व्यवहार का अनुभव करना)	5 (5)
150	**Get one's act together**	To organize oneself and start behaving more effectively	ख़ुद को व्यवस्थित करना (अपने काम सुधारना)	6 (4)
151	**Keep an eye on**	To watch or monitor someone or something carefully	नज़र रखना (निगरानी करना)	6 (4)
152	**Keep the wolf from the door**	To have just enough money to buy food and other essentials; to avoid poverty	गरीबी या भुखमरी से बचना (किसी तरह गुज़ारा करना)	10
153	**Learn (or know) the ropes**	To learn how a particular job or activity is done	काम के तौर-तरीक़े सीखना (अनुभव प्राप्त करना)	6 (4)
154	**On tenterhooks**	Very anxious or excited while waiting for something to happen	बेचैनी से इंतज़ार में (चिंता में होना)	8 (2)
155	**Pour (or throw) cold water on**	To discourage or criticize an idea or plan	उम्मीदों पर पानी फेर देना (हतोत्साहित करना)	8 (2)
156	**Red herring**	Something that draws attention away from the main issue	भ्रामक संकेत (असली मुद्दे से ध्यान भटकाने वाली बात)	6 (4)
157	**Run out of steam**	To lose energy, enthusiasm, or motivation	जोश ठंडा पड़ना (ऊर्जा ख़त्म होना)	4 (6)

SN	Idioms/Phrases	English Meaning	Hindi Meaning	#R
158	**Shot in the dark**	A wild guess; an attempt that is unlikely to succeed	अंधेरे में तीर चलाना (अंदाज़ा लगाना)	4 (6)
159	**Straight from the horse's mouth**	Heard from the person directly involved	पहले हाथ की जानकारी (सीधे संबंधित व्यक्ति से सुनी बात)	9 (1)
160	**A bone of contention**	A subject that causes disagreement	झगड़े की जड़ (विवाद का कारण)	8 (1)
161	**A bull in a China shop**	A clumsy person in a situation requiring care	नाज़ुक जगह पर लापरवाह व्यक्ति	5 (4)
162	**A cakewalk**	An easy task	बच्चों का खेल (बेहद आसान काम)	8 (1)
163	**A chip on one's shoulder**	A persistent feeling of resentment	दिल में मलाल रखना (पुरानी घटना पर अभी तक गुस्सा रहना)	6 (3)
164	**A damp squib**	Something that fails to meet expectations	ऊँची दुकान फीका पकवान (निराशाजनक परिणाम)	3 (6)
165	**Apple of discord**	Something that causes conflict or disagreement	फ़साद की जड़ (झगड़े का कारण)	6 (3)
166	**Burn the candle at both ends**	To exhaust oneself by working too hard or staying up late	दिन-रात एक करना (अत्यधिक काम करना)	1 (8)
167	**Chicken-hearted**	Lacking courage; cowardly	दिल का कमजोर (कायर)	6 (3)
168	**Child's play**	Something very easy to do	बच्चों का खेल (बहुत आसान)	8 (1)
169	**Cry wolf**	To raise false alarms or ask for help when it is not needed	बार-बार झूठी चेतावनी देना	5 (4)
170	**Feather one's nest**	To make money, often dishonestly, for oneself	अपना घर भरना (पद का लाभ उठाकर बेईमानी से धनी बनना)	8 (1)
171	**For good**	Permanently or forever	हमेशा के लिए	5 (4)
172	**Forty winks**	A short sleep or nap	झपकी लेना (थोड़ी देर की नींद)	8 (1)
173	**Have one's back to the wall (or against the wall)**	Be in a difficult situation with limited options	मुश्किल में फँसना	4 (5)
174	**Icing on the cake**	Something extra that makes a good thing even better	सोने पे सुहागा (अतिरिक्त ख़ुशी या लाभ)	5 (4)
175	**In seventh heaven**	Extremely happy; in a state of great joy	सातवें आसमान पर (बेहद ख़ुश)	5 (4)
176	**Make up one's mind**	To decide; to come to a firm decision	फ़ैसला करना (दृढ़ निश्चय करना)	7 (2)
177	**Move heaven and earth**	To try extremely hard to do something; to do everything possible	आकाश-पाताल एक कर देना (हर संभव प्रयास करना)	5 (4)
178	**On the ball**	Very alert and quick to understand and react to things	मुस्तैद रहना (चौकन्ना होना)	7 (2)
179	**Play second fiddle**	To be less important or in a weaker position than someone else	किसी के नीचे काम करना (दूसरी भूमिका में होना)	3 (6)
180	**Put one's foot down**	To firmly insist on something or refuse to allow something	सख़्ती से मना करना (दृढ़ता से विरोध करना)	6 (3)
181	**Slap on the wrist**	A gentle punishment that is not severe	बहुत हल्की सज़ा (नाममात्र का दंड)	6 (3)

SN	Idioms/Phrases	English Meaning	Hindi Meaning	#R
182	**When pigs fly**	Something that will never happen	जब सूरज पश्चिम से उगेगा (असंभव बात)	5 (4)
183	**A backseat driver**	A person who gives unwanted advice, especially about driving	अनचाही सलाह देने वाला (दख़ल देने वाला)	6 (2)
184	**A fool's paradise**	A state of happiness based on false beliefs	खयाली पुलाव पकाना (भ्रम में खुश रहना)	6 (2)
185	**A green thumb**	A natural skill for growing plants	बागवानी में निपुणता	4 (4)
186	**A greenhorn**	An inexperienced person	अनुभवहीन व्यक्ति (नौसिखिया)	6 (2)
187	**A Herculean task**	A very difficult task requiring great strength or effort	बहुत कठिन काम	7 (1)
188	**A mare's nest**	A false discovery; A messy, chaotic situation	खोदा पहाड़, निकली चुहिया (जो महत्वपूर्ण लगे पर बेकार हो)	6 (2)
189	**All and sundry**	Everyone, without exception	हर कोई बिना किसी भेदभाव के	5 (3)
190	**An Achilles' heel**	A fatal weakness in someone or something otherwise strong	कमज़ोर नस (सबसे कमज़ोर पहलू)	8
191	**At daggers drawn**	In a state of bitter enmity or conflict	जानी दुश्मनी (कट्टर विरोध में)	5 (3)
192	**At loggerheads**	In strong disagreement or dispute	कड़ी असहमति में	5 (3)
193	**Bend over backwards**	To make great efforts to help or please someone	किसी की मदद के लिए पूरी कोशिश करना	4 (4)
194	**Blaze a trail**	To be the first to do something new; to pioneer	मिसाल कायम करना (अग्रणी होना)	5 (3)
195	**Bring to light**	To reveal or make known something that was hidden	प्रकाश में लाना (छुपी बात उजागर करना)	7 (1)
196	**Burn one's fingers**	To suffer bad results from something risky	अपने पैरों पर कुल्हाड़ी मारना (जोखिम के कारण नुकसान उठाना)	5 (3)
197	**Die in harness**	To die while still working or in service	सेवाकाल में मृत्यु (काम करते हुए मरना)	5 (3)
198	**Draw the line**	To set a limit on what one will do or accept	सीमा तय करना (हद बाँधना)	5 (3)
199	**Easier said than done**	More difficult to do than to talk about	कहना आसान है करना मुश्किल	6 (2)
200	**Eat like a bird**	To eat very little	चिड़िया की तरह चुगना (बहुत कम खाना)	3 (5)

*Total **200** Idioms asked **3211** times*

B2 All Idioms & Phrases (asked in SSC Exams)

SN	Idioms/Phrases	English Meaning	Hindi Meaning	#R
1	A babe in the woods	An inexperienced and naive person	अनुभवहीन व्यक्ति (भोला-भाला और असहाय)	
2	**A backseat driver**	A person who gives unwanted advice, especially about driving	अनचाही सलाह देने वाला (दख़ल देने वाला)	6 (2)
3	**A bad egg**	A dishonest or unreliable person	बेईमान व्यक्ति (भरोसे के लायक़ नहीं)	4
4	A bad hair day	A day when everything seems to go wrong	बुरा दिन (जब सब कुछ ग़लत हो जाए)	
5	A bad hat	A person of bad character	बदमाश (बुरे चरित्र वाला)	
6	**A bad patch**	A difficult or unhappy period of time	मुश्किल दौर (अस्थायी)	3
7	**A baker's dozen**	A group of thirteen	दर्जन में तेरह (12 की जगह 13)	3 (4)
8	A ball of fire	A very energetic and enthusiastic person	ऊर्जावान व्यक्ति (जोशीला और सक्रिय)	
9	A ballpark figure	A rough estimate or approximation	मोटा-मोटी हिसाब (अनुमानित आँकड़ा)	
10	A baptism of fire	A difficult first experience of something	पहली ही बार में बड़ी चुनौती (कठिन अनुभव)	
11	A bear garden	A noisy and chaotic scene or place	शोरगुल वाली जगह (अफ़रा-तफ़री का माहौल)	
12	A beast of burden	An animal used for carrying heavy loads	बोझ ढोने वाला पशु (भारवाहक जानवर)	
13	A bed of nails	A very difficult or unpleasant situation	काँटों की सेज (बेहद कठिन स्थिति)	
14	**A bed of roses**	A pleasant, comfortable, or easy situation	फूलों की सेज (आसान और सुखद स्थिति)	5 (7)
15	**A bee in one's bonnet**	An obsessive idea or preoccupation	सनक सवार होना (किसी बात की धुन)	3 (7)
16	A beehive of activity	A place full of busy activity	अत्यधिक व्यस्त जगह (चहल-पहल वाली जगह)	
17	A belly laugh	A loud, deep, hearty laugh	ठहाका (खुलकर और ज़ोर से हँसना)	
18	**A bird's-eye view**	A view from a high position; a general overview	ऊपर से देखा गया विस्तृत दृश्य	7 (4)
19	A bite at the cherry	An attempt or opportunity to do something	एक और मौका मिलना	
20	**A bitter pill to swallow**	An unpleasant fact that one must accept	कड़वा घूँट पीना (एक अप्रिय स्थिति जिसे मजबूरी में स्वीकार करना पड़े)	4 (6)
21	**A blessing (or boon) in disguise**	Something that seems bad at first but turns out to be good	छुपा हुआ वरदान (बुरा लगने वाला पर फ़ायदेमंद)	23 (11)

[**#R** denotes repetition of word]

[E.g. in SN 18, #R- **7 (4)** denotes this word has been asked 7 times in SSC and 4 times in other exams]

SN	Idioms/Phrases	English Meaning	Hindi Meaning	#R
22	**A blind alley**	A course of action that leads nowhere	बंद गली (ऐसी स्थिति जहाँ आगे बढ़ने का कोई रास्ता न हो)	2 (1)
23	A blind spot	A portion of a field that cannot be seen	दृष्टि का वह क्षेत्र जो स्पष्ट रूप से दिखाई नहीं देता	
24	**A bolt from the blue**	A sudden and unexpected event	आकस्मिक घटना	15 (19)
25	**A bone of contention**	A subject that causes disagreement	झगड़े की जड़ (विवाद का कारण)	8 (1)
26	**A bone to pick**	A matter of complaint or disagreement that one wants to discuss	शिकायत का मुद्दा (हिसाब चुकता करना या स्पष्टीकरण मांगना)	4
27	A bosom friend	A very close and dear friend	घनिष्ठ मित्र	
28	A bowl of cherries	A very pleasant or enjoyable situation	सुखद स्थिति (मज़े की ज़िंदगी)	
29	A breach of confidence	The breaking of trust by revealing confidential information	विश्वासघात (गोपनीयता तोड़ना)	
30	A breath of fresh air	A refreshing or welcome change	नई और ताजगी भरी चीज	
31	**A broken reed**	A weak or unreliable person	अविश्वसनीय व्यक्ति	1 (2)
32	**A brown study**	A state of deep thought or daydreaming	गहन विचार में डूबना	2
33	**A bull in a China shop**	A clumsy person in a situation requiring care	नाज़ुक जगह पर लापरवाह व्यक्ति	5 (4)
34	A bun in the oven	Pregnant	पेट से होना (गर्भवती होना)	
35	**A burning question**	An important question that needs to be answered urgently	ज्वलंत सवाल (अति महत्वपूर्ण मुद्दा)	2
36	**A cakewalk**	An easy task	बच्चों का खेल (बेहद आसान काम)	8 (1)
37	**A can of worms**	A complex situation that causes problems	मुसीबत का पिटारा (जटिल और पेचीदा समस्या)	2 (2)
38	A cash cow	A business or product that provides a steady source of income	कामधेनु (लगातार आय देने वाला जरिया)	
39	**A catnap**	A short sleep, especially during the day	झपकी (हल्की और छोटी नींद)	2
40	A cat's paw	A person used by another to do unpleasant work	दूसरे के हाथों का खिलौना (जिसे कोई अपने फायदे के लिए इस्तेमाल करे)	
41	**A change of heart**	A change in one's attitude or feelings	हृदय परिवर्तन (विचार या भावना में बदलाव)	3
42	**A charley horse**	A painful muscle cramp	माँसपेशियों में ऐंठन	2
43	**A chink in someone's armour**	A weakness that can be exploited	कवच में दरार (कमजोरी)	1 (2)
44	**A chip off the old block**	A person who resembles their parent in character	जैसा बाप वैसा बेटा (माँ-बाप जैसी संतान)	8 (6)
45	**A chip on one's shoulder**	A persistent feeling of resentment	दिल में मलाल रखना (पुरानी घटना पर अभी तक गुस्सा रहना)	6 (3)
46	**A clarion call**	A strong and clear call to action	बिगुल फूंकना (कार्यवाही के लिए स्पष्ट आह्वान)	2 (1)
47	A clean slate	A situation where past mistakes are forgotten	नई शुरुआत (पुराने रिकॉर्ड को मिटाकर शून्य से शुरू करना)	

SN	Idioms/Phrases	English Meaning	Hindi Meaning	#R
48	**A close shave**	A situation where you only just avoid an accident or disaster	बाल-बाल बचना (नज़दीकी बचाव)	7 (3)
49	A closed book	Something or someone completely unknown or not understood at all	रहस्यमय या अनजान	
50	**A cock and bull story**	An absurd and untrue story	बेसिर-पैर की कहानी (झूठी और बेतुकी बात)	10 (5)
51	A cog in the machine	A small or unimportant part of a larger system	बड़े तंत्र में मामूली व्यक्ति	
52	**A cold fish**	A person who seems unfriendly and unemotional	भावनाहीन व्यक्ति	3
53	A copycat	A person who copies another's behaviour or work	नक़लची (नक़ल करने वाला)	
54	**A couch potato**	A lazy person who watches a lot of TV	आलसी व्यक्ति (दिन भर टीवी देखने वाला)	5
55	A creature of habit	A person who always does the same things	नियम और दिनचर्या का पक्का	
56	A cuckoo in the nest	An unwanted person in a group or place	बिन बुलाया मेहमान (अवांछित व्यक्ति)	
57	**A cut above**	Better than other similar things or people	औरों से बेहतर	2
58	A dab hand at something	Very skilled at something	किसी काम में माहिर होना	
59	**A damp squib**	Something that fails to meet expectations	ऊँची दुकान फीका पकवान (निराशाजनक परिणाम)	3 (6)
60	A damsel in distress	A young woman in need of rescue	संकट में फँसी नारी (मदद की ज़रूरत वाली महिला)	
61	**A daredevil**	A reckless person who enjoys taking risks	जोखिम उठाने वाला (ख़तरों से खेलने वाला)	2
62	**A dark horse**	An unexpectedly successful person or competitor	छुपा रुस्तम (अप्रत्याशित विजेता)	9 (9)
63	**A dead duck**	Someone or something destined to fail	असफल होने वाला	1 (2)
64	A dead heat	A race or competition ending in a tie	बराबरी का मुकाबला	
65	**A dead letter**	A law or rule no longer followed or enforced	निष्क्रिय क़ानून (ऐसा नियम जो काग़ज़ों तक सीमित हो)	2
66	A dead loss	A person or thing that is completely useless	बिल्कुल बेकार (पूरी तरह निरर्थक)	
67	**A dead ringer**	A person or thing that looks exactly like another	हूबहू शक्ल मिलना (हमशक्ल)	2 (1)
68	**A diamond in the rough**	A person with good qualities despite rough exterior	कोरा हीरा (छिपे गुणों वाला व्यक्ति)	3
69	**A dime a dozen**	Very common and of little value	कौड़ियों के भाव (बहुत सस्ता)	12 (9)
70	A dish fit for the gods	Extremely delicious food	अत्यंत स्वादिष्ट भोजन (देवताओं के योग्य)	
71	A dog and pony show	An elaborate but superficial presentation	दिखावटी प्रदर्शन (भड़कीला लेकिन खोखला)	
72	**A dog in the manger**	A selfish person who prevents others from using something	न ख़ुद उपयोग करना, न दूसरों को करने देना	2 (1)

SN	Idioms/Phrases	English Meaning	Hindi Meaning	#R
73	**A dog-eat-dog**	A fiercely competitive situation	गलाकाट प्रतिस्पर्धा (जहाँ कोई किसी का नहीं)	2
74	A dog's breakfast	A messy or badly done thing	अव्यवस्थित काम (बुरी तरह किया गया)	
75	**A dog's life**	A miserable and difficult existence	दयनीय जीवन (कष्टपूर्ण जीवन जीना)	2
76	A dressing-down	A severe scolding	फटकार (कड़ी डाँट)	
77	**A dry run**	A practice or rehearsal	पूर्वाभ्यास (असली काम से पहले अभ्यास)	2 (1)
78	**A dying duck in a thunderstorm**	Looking extremely unhappy or dejected	बुझा हुआ चेहरा (अत्यंत निराश)	2
79	**A fair-weather friend**	A friend only in good times	सुख के साथी (स्वार्थी मित्र)	13
80	**A far cry from**	Very different from	ज़मीन-आसमान का अंतर (बहुत अलग)	2 (1)
81	A fate worse than death	A very unpleasant or terrible experience or situation	मौत से भी बदतर स्थिति	
82	**A feather in one's cap**	An achievement to be proud of	गर्व करने योग्य उपलब्धि	8 (6)
83	**A fifth wheel**	An unnecessary or unwanted person	अनावश्यक व्यक्ति (जो समूह में फ़ालतू हो)	2
84	A fighting chance	A small but real possibility of success	जीतने की थोड़ी संभावना	
85	A fine state of affairs	An unpleasant or unsatisfactory situation	बुरी हालत	
86	**A fire in one's belly**	A strong sense of ambition, energy, or determination	सीने में आग होना (कुछ हासिल करने का अत्यधिक जोश)	2 (1)
87	**A fish out of water**	A person in an unfamiliar environment where they feel awkward	असहज परिस्थिति (जहाँ व्यक्ति अजनबी महसूस करे)	18 (9)
88	A five-finger discount	The act of stealing or shoplifting	हाथ साफ करना (दुकान से चोरी करना)	
89	**A flash in the pan**	Short-lived success	क्षणिक सफलता	3 (7)
90	A flea in one's ear	A sharp rebuke or scolding	कड़ी फटकार (तीखी डाँट)	
91	A flea market	A market selling second-hand goods	पुराने सामान का बाज़ार	
92	**A fly in the ointment**	A small problem that spoils something otherwise good	दूध में मक्खी पड़ना (छोटी कमी जो वस्तु का मजा या मूल्य घटा दे)	1 (2)
93	**A fly on the wall**	An unnoticed observer	चोरी-छिपे देखने वाला (अनजान दर्शक)	3
94	A fly on the wheel	Someone who overestimates their own influence or power in a situation	अपने को अत्यधिक महत्वपूर्ण समझने वाला	
95	**A flying visit**	A very brief visit	संक्षिप्त मुलाक़ात (बहुत कम समय के लिए मिलना)	2
96	**A fool's paradise**	A state of happiness based on false beliefs	खयाली पुलाव पकाना (भ्रम में खुश रहना)	6 (2)
97	A frog in a well	A person with limited experience or narrow view	कुएँ का मेंढक (सीमित ज्ञान वाला व्यक्ति)	

SN	Idioms/Phrases	English Meaning	Hindi Meaning	#R
98	A game-changer	Something that significantly alters the situation	स्थिति बदलने वाला	
99	A gatecrasher	An uninvited guest at an event	बिन बुलाया मेहमान (बिना निमंत्रण के घुसने वाला)	
100	A good Samaritan	A helpful and compassionate person	परोपकारी (निस्वार्थ मदद करने वाला)	
101	**A green thumb**	A natural skill for growing plants	बागवानी में निपुणता	4 (4)
102	**A greenhorn**	An inexperienced person	अनुभवहीन व्यक्ति (नौसिखिया)	6 (2)
103	**A grey area**	An unclear or ambiguous situation or topic	अस्पष्ट क्षेत्र	3
104	**A hair's breadth**	By a very small margin	रत्ती भर अंतर (बहुत छोटा फ़ासला)	4 (1)
105	**A hard nut to crack**	A difficult problem or person	लोहे के चने चबाना (मुश्किल काम या व्यक्ति)	17 (3)
106	**A heart-to-heart**	An honest and open conversation	दिल खोलकर बात करना	2
107	A henpecked husband	A husband who is dominated by his wife	जोरू का ग़ुलाम (पत्नी के नियंत्रण में रहने वाला)	
108	**A Herculean task**	A very difficult task requiring great strength or effort	बहुत कठिन काम	7 (1)
109	A Himalayan blunder	A very serious mistake	बहुत बड़ी ग़लती	
110	**A hornet's nest**	A situation that causes serious trouble	ततैया का छत्ता (विवादास्पद स्थिति)	6
111	A Judas kiss	An act that appears friendly but is actually intended to harm or betray	पीठ में छुरा घोंपना (विश्वासघात)	
112	**A kick in the teeth**	A sudden and unexpected rejection, setback, or insult	आशाओं पर पानी फिरना (बड़ी निराशा या धोखा)	2 (1)
113	A king's ransom	An extremely large amount of money	बहुत बड़ी रकम, भारी धनराशि	
114	**A laughing stock**	A person open to ridicule	हँसी का पात्र (मज़ाक बन जाना)	3 (1)
115	A lean patch	A period of poor performance	असफलता का दौर (ख़राब समय)	
116	**A left-handed (or backhanded) compliment**	A remark that sounds like praise but is actually an insult	दोहरे अर्थ वाली तारीफ (प्रशंसा के रूप में अपमानजनक टिप्पणी)	3
117	**A lemon**	A product, especially a car, that is faulty	ख़राब सामान (ख़ासकर गाड़ी)	2
118	**A little bird told me**	Used to say that you know something but will not reveal how you found out	उड़ती-उड़ती ख़बर मिली है (गुप्त सूत्र से पता चलना)	1 (2)
119	A loudmouth	A person who talks too much or too loudly	बड़बोला (ज़्यादा बोलने वाला)	
120	**A lump in one's throat**	A tight feeling in the throat caused by strong emotion, making it difficult to speak	गला भर आना (भावुकता के कारण बोल न पाना)	2
121	**A mare's nest**	A false discovery; A messy, chaotic situation	खोदा पहाड़, निकली चुहिया (जो महत्वपूर्ण लगे पर बेकार हो)	6 (2)
122	A mincing walk	A walk with short, delicate steps	नाज़ुक अंदाज़ में चलना	
123	A month of Sundays	A very long time	बहुत लंबा समय (बरसों)	
124	A one-trick pony	A person or thing with only one special skill or talent	एक ही हुनर वाला (सीमित क्षमता)	

SN	Idioms/Phrases	English Meaning	Hindi Meaning	#R
125	**A penny for your thoughts**	Used to ask someone what they are thinking about	कोई क्या सोच रहा है यह पूछने का तरीका (क्या सोच रहे हो?)	2 (5)
126	**A piece of cake**	Something that is very easy to do	बाएँ हाथ का खेल (बहुत आसान काम)	20 (16)
127	A rift in the lute	A small problem that threatens to destroy a relationship	छोटी दरार जो बड़ी हो सकती है (संबंधों में खटास)	
128	A sight for sore eyes	A person or thing that you are happy to see	आँखों की ठंडक (सुखद दृश्य)	
129	A slice of the pie	A share of the available money, profits, or benefits	लाभ में हिस्सेदारी (अपना हिस्सा)	
130	**A smash hit**	A great success, especially in entertainment	शानदार सफलता	1 (2)
131	**A stone's throw**	A very short distance	बहुत कम दूरी	11 (2)
132	**A stumbling block**	Something that makes it difficult to achieve something	अड़चन (रास्ते में रुकावट)	2
133	A tough row to hoe	A very difficult task or situation	कठिन काम, मुश्किल राह	
134	**A voice crying in the wilderness**	A warning that no one pays attention to	अनसुनी चेतावनी	3
135	About-turn	A complete change in opinion or direction	पूर्ण बदलाव (राय या दिशा में पलटाव)	
136	**Above board**	Honest and transparent	पारदर्शी और ईमानदार	3 (7)
137	**Acid test**	A decisive test that proves the truth or value of something	अग्नि परीक्षा (निर्णायक जाँच)	2 (1)
138	**Adam's ale**	Plain water	पानी (सादा पानी)	2
139	**Add fuel to the fire (or flame)**	To make a bad situation worse	आग में घी डालना (स्थिति और बिगाड़ना)	14 (7)
140	**Add insult to injury**	To make a bad situation worse by adding humiliation	जले पर नमक छिड़कना (बुरी स्थिति को और बुरा बनाना)	7 (4)
141	After a fashion	In a way that is barely acceptable	जैसे-तैसे (कामचलाऊ तरीक़े से)	
142	**After one's own heart**	A person who shares one's tastes and preferences	अपने मन का व्यक्ति (समान पसंद वाला)	2
143	**Against the clock**	In a great hurry to finish before a deadline	समय से दौड़ (समय की कमी में तेजी से काम करना)	8 (2)
144	Aid and abet	To help and encourage someone to do something wrong, especially to commit a crime	अपराध में मदद करना	
145	**Air (or wash) dirty linen in public**	To talk about personal or private matters in front of others	घर की बातें बाहर करना (निजी विवाद सार्वजनिक करना)	2 (4)
146	Alarums and excursions	Chaotic activity and confusion	अव्यवस्था और उथल-पुथल	
147	**Alive and kicking**	Active, healthy, and full of energy	सही-सलामत (स्वस्थ और चुस्त)	4
148	**All agog**	Very eager and excited	बेहद उत्सुक और उत्साहित	1 (1)
149	All along	From the beginning	शुरू से ही (हमेशा से)	
150	**All and sundry**	Everyone, without exception	हर कोई बिना किसी भेदभाव के	5 (3)
151	**All at sea**	Confused and uncertain	असमंजस में (भ्रमित और अनिश्चित)	15 (5)
152	**All bark and no bite**	Threatening but not willing to act	जो गरजते हैं वो बरसते नहीं (ख़ाली धमकी)	1 (1)

SN	Idioms/Phrases	English Meaning	Hindi Meaning	#R
153	**All eyes and ears**	Fully attentive; alert to everything	आँख-कान खुले रखना (पूरी तरह सतर्क)	3
154	**All fingers and thumbs (all thumbs)**	Clumsy or awkward with one's hands	अनाड़ी (हाथ के काम में अकुशल)	3 (2)
155	**All hands on deck**	A situation requiring everyone's help	सबकी मदद की ज़रूरत	2
156	All hat and no cattle	Full of boastful talk but lacking action or substance	बड़ी-बड़ी बातें करने वाला (दिखावा ज़्यादा, काम कम)	
157	All in	Completely exhausted	पूरी तरह थका हुआ	
158	**All in a day's work**	Part of one's normal routine	रोज़मर्रा का काम (सामान्य काम)	1 (2)
159	**All in all**	Considering everything; on the whole	कुल मिलाकर (सब कुछ देखते हुए)	1 (2)
160	**All moonshine**	Complete nonsense; false or unrealistic ideas	वास्तविकता से दूर (झूठी या काल्पनिक बातें)	4 (1)
161	All of a sudden	Suddenly; unexpectedly	अचानक (बिना किसी चेतावनी के)	
162	All over hell's half acre	Everywhere; scattered over a wide area	हर जगह (इधर-उधर फैला हुआ)	
163	**All wet**	Completely wrong or mistaken	पूरी तरह ग़लत (ग़लतफ़हमी में)	2
164	Alma mater	The school, college, or university one attended	वह संस्था जहाँ से शिक्षा प्राप्त की	
165	**Alphabet soup**	An excessive or confusing use of abbreviations or acronyms	संक्षिप्त रूपों की भरमार	2
166	**An ace in the hole**	A hidden advantage kept for the right moment	तुरुप का इक्का (आपात स्थिति के लिए छिपा हुआ दाँव)	2
167	**An ace up one's sleeve**	A secret resource or advantage kept in reserve	तुरुप का इक्का (गुप्त योजना या चौंकाने वाला दाँव)	3 (4)
168	**An Achilles' heel**	A fatal weakness in someone or something otherwise strong	कमज़ोर नस (सबसे कमज़ोर पहलू)	8
169	An Aladdin's cave	A place full of valuable or interesting things	ख़ज़ाने से भरी जगह	
170	An albatross around one's neck	A heavy burden or guilt that hinders one's progress	गले का बोझ (पीछा न छोड़ने वाली मुसीबत)	
171	An armchair critic	A person who criticizes without practical experience	बिना अनुभव के आलोचना करने वाला	
172	An armchair expert	A person who gives advice without practical experience	बिना अनुभव के सलाह देने वाला	
173	An arrow in one's quiver	An available resource, option, or strategy	तरकश का तीर (उपलब्ध विकल्प)	
174	An article of faith	A firmly held belief or fundamental principle	अटूट विश्वास	
175	An eager beaver	An enthusiastic and hard-working person	अति उत्साही व्यक्ति (बहुत मेहनती)	
176	**An eagle eye**	Sharp, keen observation	चील जैसी नज़र (तेज़ नज़र)	2
177	**An eye-opener**	Something surprising that reveals the truth	आँखें खोलने वाला अनुभव (हक़ीक़त से रूबरू कराने वाली बात)	1 (2)
178	An eyesore	Something ugly or unpleasant to look at	देखने में बुरी लगने वाली चीज़	
179	**An old head on young shoulders**	A young person who is wise and mature beyond their age	उम्र से ज़्यादा समझदार (कम उम्र में बुद्धिमान)	3 (1)

SN	Idioms/Phrases	English Meaning	Hindi Meaning	#R
180	**An open book**	A person who is easy to know and understand; having no secrets	खुली किताब (पूरी तरह स्पष्ट व्यक्तित्व)	5
181	**An uphill battle**	A task that is very difficult to achieve	कठिन संघर्ष (मुश्किल लड़ाई)	1 (1)
182	**An uphill task**	A difficult or demanding task	कठिन कार्य	1 (1)
183	Angle for	To try to get something in a clever, indirect way	घुमा-फिराकर हासिल करना (चतुराई से पाना)	
184	Any port in a storm	A place of refuge or shelter during difficulty	मुसीबत में सहारा	
185	Appeal to Caesar	To appeal to the highest authority	सर्वोच्च अधिकारी से अपील	
186	**Apple of discord**	Something that causes conflict or disagreement	फ़साद की जड़ (झगड़े का कारण)	6 (3)
187	**Apple of one's eye**	A person who is greatly cherished and loved	आँखों का तारा (बेहद प्रिय व्यक्ति)	10 (2)
188	**Apples and oranges**	Two completely different things that cannot be compared	दो बिल्कुल अलग चीजें (जिनकी तुलना न हो सके)	5 (1)
189	Apropos of nothing	Without any connection to what was being discussed	बिना किसी संदर्भ के (बेवजह)	
190	**Argus-eyed**	Extremely vigilant and watchful	पैनी नज़र वाला (अत्यंत सतर्क)	3
191	**Armed to the teeth**	Heavily or fully armed	हथियारों से लैस (पूरी तरह सशस्त्र)	3
192	**Around the clock**	Continuously; all day and night	चौबीसों घंटे (दिन-रात लगातार)	3
193	**Around the corner**	About to happen very soon	बहुत नज़दीक (जल्द होने वाला)	2 (1)
194	As a matter of fact	In reality; actually	वास्तव में (सच तो यह है कि)	
195	As bald as a cue ball	Completely bald	पूरी तरह गंजा	
196	**As clean as a whistle**	Extremely clean or completely free from guilt	बिलकुल साफ़ (पूरी तरह निर्दोष)	2
197	As clear as a bell	Very clear and easy to understand	बिल्कुल स्पष्ट	
198	**As clear as mud**	Not clear at all; very confusing	बिलकुल अस्पष्ट (समझ से बाहर)	2
199	**As cool as a cucumber**	Very calm and composed, especially under pressure	शांत और संयमित (दबाव में भी स्थिर)	8 (2)
200	**As daft as a brush**	Extremely silly or foolish	निहायत बेवक़ूफ़ (बहुत मूर्ख)	2
201	As dead as a doornail	Completely dead; no longer functioning	पूरी तरह मृत (बिलकुल ख़त्म)	
202	**As easy as pie**	Very easy to do	बाएँ हाथ का खेल (बहुत आसान)	2
203	**As fit as a fiddle**	In excellent physical health	चंगा-भला (पूरी तरह स्वस्थ)	11 (6)
204	As good as gold	Well-behaved and obedient	आज्ञाकारी और शिष्ट	
205	**As hard as nails**	Very tough or emotionally cold and unsympathetic	पत्थर दिल (कठोर और निर्दयी)	4
206	As high as a kite	Intoxicated by drugs or alcohol	नशे में धुत (पूरी तरह मदहोश)	
207	As keen as mustard	Extremely enthusiastic and eager	अत्यधिक उत्साही (बहुत जोशीला)	
208	**As phony as a three-dollar bill**	Completely fake or fraudulent	पूरी तरह नक़ली (एकदम फ़र्ज़ी)	2
209	**As right as rain**	Perfectly fine or in good health	एकदम दुरुस्त (बिल्कुल ठीक)	1 (2)
210	As sly as a fox	Very cunning and clever	लोमड़ी जैसा चालाक (चतुर और धूर्त)	
211	**As the crow flies**	Measured by the shortest straight-line distance	नाक की सीध में (सीधी रेखा में)	2 (1)

SN	Idioms/Phrases	English Meaning	Hindi Meaning	#R
212	**As thick as thieves**	Very friendly and sharing secrets	घनिष्ठ मित्र (एकदम पक्के दोस्त)	2 (1)
213	As thick as two short planks	Extremely stupid	महामूर्ख (बेहद बेवक़ूफ़)	
214	As tight as the bark on a tree	Extremely stingy; very miserly	मक्खीचूस (बेहद कंजूस)	
215	Ascend (or mount) the throne	To become king or queen; to begin to rule	राजगद्दी पर बैठना (सिंहासन ग्रहण करना)	
216	Ask for trouble	To behave in a way that is likely to cause problems	आ बैल मुझे मार (ख़ुद मुसीबत मोल लेना)	
217	Asleep at the wheel	Not paying attention to one's duties or responsibilities	लापरवाह (अपने काम में असावधान)	
218	**At a crossroads**	At a critical point where an important decision must be made	दोराहे पर (निर्णायक मोड़ पर)	3 (2)
219	**At a loose end (or At loose ends)**	Having nothing to do; restless or unsettled	खाली (बेकार और बेचैन)	2
220	At a loss	Uncertain what to think, say, or do	असमंजस में (क्या करें समझ न आए)	
221	**At a loss for words**	Unable to think of anything to say	हक्का-बक्का (बोलती बंद)	1 (1)
222	At a low ebb	In a weak state or at a low point	गिरावट की स्थिति में (बदहाली में)	
223	**At a snail's pace**	Very slowly	कछुआ चाल (बहुत धीमी गति से)	6 (1)
224	**At a stretch**	Continuously; without stopping	एक साँस में (बिना रुके)	3 (1)
225	**At all costs**	No matter what sacrifice or effort is required	किसी भी क़ीमत पर (हर हाल में)	2
226	At any cost	No matter what sacrifice or effort is required	किसी भी क़ीमत पर (हर हाल में)	
227	At any rate	In any case; whatever happens	बहरहाल (चाहे जो भी हो)	
228	**At cross purposes**	Having different or conflicting intentions without realizing it	विपरीत उद्देश्य से काम करना	2 (2)
229	**At daggers drawn**	In a state of bitter enmity or conflict	जानी दुश्मनी (कट्टर विरोध में)	5 (3)
230	At each other's throats	Fighting or arguing bitterly	एक-दूसरे के ख़ून के प्यासे (आपस में लड़ते हुए)	
231	**At face value**	As it appears; without questioning	ऊपरी तौर पर मान लेना (बिना अधिक सोचे-विचारे स्वीकारना)	2
232	**At large**	Free; not captured or confined	फ़रार (अभी तक पकड़ा नहीं गया)	2 (1)
233	**At loggerheads**	In strong disagreement or dispute	कड़ी असहमति में	5 (3)
234	At one's disposal	Available for one's use	सेवा में हाज़िर (उपलब्ध)	
235	**At one's fingertips**	Readily available or easily accessible	उंगलियों पर होना (पूरी तरह रटा हुआ या सहज उपलब्ध)	2
236	**At one's wits' end**	Completely frustrated and not knowing what to do	बुद्धि चकराना (पूरी तरह से उलझन में)	10 (4)
237	At random	Without any definite plan or pattern	बेतरतीब (बिना किसी क्रम के)	
238	At short notice	With very little warning or time to prepare	कम समय में (अचानक सूचना पर)	
239	**At sixes and sevens**	In a state of confusion or disarray	अस्त-व्यस्त (अव्यवस्थित या असमंजस में)	6 (4)
240	**At someone's beck and call**	Always ready to do whatever someone asks	इशारे पर नाचना (हर हुक्म मानने को तैयार)	5 (1)

SN	Idioms/Phrases	English Meaning	Hindi Meaning	#R
241	**At someone's elbow**	Very close to someone	बिल्कुल पास में	1 (1)
242	At someone's expense	In a way that harms or disadvantages someone; benefiting oneself while causing loss to another	किसी और के खर्चे पर; किसी का नुकसान करके अपना फ़ायदा उठाना	
243	At stake	At risk; in a position to be lost or won	दाँव पर (जोखिम में)	
244	**At the drop of a hat (or dime)**	Immediately; without hesitation	फ़ौरन (बिना पल गँवाए)	12 (14)
245	**At the end of one's rope (or tether)**	Having no more patience or strength left	धैर्य की सीमा पर (हिम्मत जवाब दे जाना)	1 (3)
246	At the top of one's lungs	As loudly as possible	गला फाड़कर (पूरी ताक़त से चिल्लाना)	
247	**At variance with**	In disagreement or conflict with	विरोध में या असहमत	2
248	Back in the saddle	Back in control or working again after a break	फिर से काम पर (छुट्टी के बाद वापसी)	
249	Back on one's feet	Recovered and healthy or financially stable again	फिर से संभलना (तंदुरुस्त या स्थिर होना)	
250	Back to basics	A return to fundamental principles	बुनियादी बातों पर लौटना (मूल सिद्धांतों पर ध्यान)	
251	**Back to square one**	Back to the very beginning; having to start again	फिर से शुरू (जहाँ से चले थे वहीं वापस)	5 (6)
252	**Back to the drawing board**	Time to start planning again after a failure	नए सिरे से सोचना (फिर से योजना बनाना)	10 (11)
253	Back-to-back	Happening one after another without a break	एक के बाद एक (लगातार बिना रुके)	
254	**Bad (or rotten) apple**	A person who has a bad influence on others in a group	एक गंदी मछली सारे तालाब को गंदा करती है (बुरी संगत)	1 (1)
255	**Bad blood**	Feelings of hatred or hostility between people	आपसी दुश्मनी (पुरानी रंजिश)	10 (2)
256	**Bag and baggage**	With all one's belongings	बोरिया-बिस्तर (सारा सामान)	4 (1)
257	Bag of tricks	All the methods or resources available	सारे हथकंडे (सभी संसाधन और तरीक़े)	
258	Banana oil	Nonsense; insincere flattery	बकवास (झूठी चापलूसी)	
259	**Bang for the buck**	Good value for money	पैसा वसूल (पैसे की पूरी क़ीमत)	2
260	**Bark up the wrong tree**	To make a wrong assumption or pursue a mistaken course	गलत दिशा में प्रयास करना; गलत व्यक्ति को दोष देना	13 (6)
261	Batten down the hatches	To prepare for a difficult or dangerous situation	कमर कस लेना (मुश्किल के लिए तैयार होना)	
262	Be afraid of one's own shadow	To be extremely timid or easily frightened	अपनी परछाईं से डरना (बेहद डरपोक)	
263	**Be all ears**	Listening with full attention; very eager to hear	कान लगाए बैठना (पूरे ध्यान से सुनना)	11 (4)
264	**Be all eyes**	Watching with full attention; very attentive	आँखें गड़ाए (पूरे ध्यान से देखना)	1 (1)

SN	Idioms/Phrases	English Meaning	Hindi Meaning	#R
265	**Be all one to someone**	Of no importance; making no difference	कोई फ़र्क़ न पड़ना (कोई मायने न रखना)	2
266	Be floored	To be extremely surprised or shocked	हक्का-बक्का रह जाना (बेहद हैरान होना)	
267	Be gifted with	To be naturally endowed with a talent or quality	जन्मजात प्रतिभा (किसी विशेष गुण से युक्त होना)	
268	**Be glad to see the back of**	To be happy when someone leaves	पीछा छूटने पर ख़ुश होना (किसी के जाने से राहत महसूस करना)	4 (1)
269	**Be going places**	To be on the path to success	सफलता की सीढ़ियां चढ़ना	2
270	Be in troubled waters	To be in a difficult or problematic situation	मुसीबत में होना (कठिन परिस्थिति में फँसना)	
271	Be my guest	Used to give permission or invite someone to do something	आपकी मर्ज़ी (बेशक कीजिए)	
272	Be tied to someone's apron strings	Excessively dependent on someone	किसी पर अत्यधिक निर्भर होना	
273	Be under no illusion	To understand the true situation clearly	भ्रम में न होना (हक़ीक़त से वाक़िफ़)	
274	**Bear a grudge**	To continue to feel angry or bitter about something	मन में मैल रखना (पुरानी रंजिश रखना)	2 (1)
275	**Bear fruit**	To produce positive results	फल देना (सफलता मिलना)	3 (2)
276	**Bear the brunt of**	To suffer the main force or worst part of something	सबसे ज़्यादा तकलीफ़ झेलना (मार सहना)	3 (2)
277	**Bear the palm**	To win; to be victorious	जीत का सेहरा लेना (विजयी होना)	5 (1)
278	Beard the lion in his den	To confront a powerful or dangerous person on their own ground	शेर की माँद में घुसना (ताक़तवर को उसके घर में चुनौती देना)	
279	**Beat a retreat**	To withdraw or run away, especially to avoid trouble	दुम दबाकर भागना (ख़तरे से पीछे हटना)	3 (2)
280	**Beat about (or around) the bush**	To avoid talking about the main topic	घुमा-फिराकर बात करना (मुख्य बात पर न आना)	23 (27)
281	**Beat one's brains out**	To try very hard to think of or remember something	सिर खपाना (दिमाग़ पर ज़ोर डालना)	2
282	**Beat the air**	To make futile efforts; to struggle in vain	हवा में मुक्के मारना (व्यर्थ प्रयास)	2
283	Beat the band	To an extreme degree; exceedingly	चरम सीमा तक (बेहद तेज़ी से)	
284	**Beat the clock**	To finish something before a deadline	समय सीमा में पूरा करना (वक़्त से पहले ख़त्म करना)	1 (1)
285	Beat the drum for	To speak enthusiastically in support of something	ढोल पीटना (ज़ोर-शोर से प्रचार करना)	
286	**Beat the rap**	To escape punishment or blame	सज़ा से बच निकलना (क़ानूनी कार्यवाही से बरी होना)	2
287	**Beggars description**	Too extreme or remarkable to describe	वर्णन से परे (शब्दों में बयान न हो सके)	2
288	Beginner's luck	Good luck experienced by a beginner	शुरुआती क़िस्मत (नए व्यक्ति को मिली सफलता)	

SN	Idioms/Phrases	English Meaning	Hindi Meaning	#R
289	**Behind closed doors**	In private; secretly	बंद दरवाज़ों के पीछे (गुप्त रूप से)	3 (1)
290	Behind schedule	Later than planned; not on time	समय से पीछे चलना (देरी होना)	
291	**Behind someone's back**	Without someone's knowledge; secretly	पीठ पीछे (बिना बताए या छुपकर)	1 (2)
292	**Behind the eight ball**	In a difficult or disadvantageous situation	मुश्किल स्थिति में (फँसा हुआ)	2
293	**Behind the scenes**	Out of public view; in secret	पर्दे के पीछे (जनता की नज़रों से दूर)	2 (1)
294	**Behind the times**	Old-fashioned; out of date	समय से पीछे (पुराने ख़यालात का)	2
295	**Bell the cat**	To take on a risky or dangerous task that others are afraid to do	बिल्ली के गले में घंटी बाँधना (जोखिम भरा काम करना)	7 (3)
296	Belle of the ball	The most admired or attractive woman at an event	महफिल की जान (सबसे आकर्षक महिला)	
297	Bells and whistles	Attractive but unnecessary extra features	अनावश्यक तामझाम (आकर्षक पर गैर-जरूरी सुविधाएँ)	
298	**Bend over backwards**	To make great efforts to help or please someone	किसी की मदद के लिए पूरी कोशिश करना	4 (4)
299	Bend someone's ear	To talk to someone at tedious length, especially about a problem	कान पकाना (बहुत बातें करके बोर करना)	
300	**Bent out of shape**	Upset or angry, especially about something minor	बात का बतंगड़ बनाना (छोटी बात पर भड़क जाना)	1 (1)
301	**Beside oneself**	Overwhelmed with emotion; unable to control oneself	आपे से बाहर होना (अत्यधिक भावुक या व्याकुल होना)	2 (1)
302	**Beside the mark**	Irrelevant; not to the point	असंगत या विषय से हटकर	3 (1)
303	**Best of both worlds**	The benefits of two different situations enjoyed together	दोनों हाथों में लड्डू (दोनों तरफ से फायदा)	10 (4)
304	**Best thing since sliced bread**	A very good invention or innovation	बेहद उपयोगी आविष्कार	3 (2)
305	**Between a rock and a hard place**	In a difficult situation where both options are bad	आगे कुआँ पीछे खाई (दो कठिन विकल्पों के बीच फँस जाना)	3 (7)
306	**Between Scylla and Charybdis**	Having to choose between two equally dangerous alternatives	आगे कुआँ पीछे खाई (दो कठिन विकल्पों के बीच फँस जाना)	4 (1)
307	**Between the devil and the deep blue sea**	In a difficult situation with two equally bad choices	आगे कुआँ पीछे खाई (दो कठिन विकल्पों के बीच फँस जाना)	2 (2)
308	**Beyond the pale**	Outside the bounds of acceptable behaviour	सीमा से बाहर (बिलकुल अस्वीकार्य)	2
309	Beyond the shadow of a doubt	Without any doubt; completely certain	निश्चित रूप से (बिना किसी संदेह के)	
310	**Bid defiance**	To openly resist or challenge	खुलेआम विरोध करना (खुली चुनौती देना)	2 (1)
311	Bid fair	To seem likely to succeed or happen	अच्छे आसार होना (सफल होने के लक्षण दिखना)	
312	**Bide one's time**	To wait patiently for the right moment to act	सही समय का इंतज़ार करना (मौक़े की तलाश में रहना)	1 (1)

SN	Idioms/Phrases	English Meaning	Hindi Meaning	#R
313	Big bucks	A large amount of money	मोटा पैसा (बहुत बड़ी रकम)	
314	Big draw	A person or thing that attracts a lot of attention	बड़ा आकर्षण (लोकप्रिय व्यक्ति या वस्तु)	
315	Big fish	An important or powerful person	बड़ी हस्ती (प्रभावशाली व्यक्ति)	
316	**Bigger (or other) fish to fry**	More important matters to deal with	ज़्यादा ज़रूरी काम (और बड़े मसले)	7 (4)
317	**Bite off more than one can chew**	To take on more responsibility than one can manage	हैसियत से बाहर (अपनी क्षमता से ज़्यादा काम उठाना)	14 (15)
318	Bite one's thumb at someone	To show scorn or disrespect to someone	अंगूठा दिखाकर चिढ़ाना (अपमान करना)	
319	**Bite one's tongue**	To stop oneself from saying something	ज़ुबान पर लगाम लगाना (बोलने से ख़ुद को रोकना)	2 (3)
320	**Bite someone's head off**	To respond to someone angrily without good reason	बेवजह ग़ुस्सा करना (तुनकमिज़ाजी दिखाना)	2
321	**Bite the bullet**	To accept a difficult situation and deal with it bravely	कड़वा घूँट पीना (मज़बूरी में स्वीकार करना)	19 (25)
322	**Bite the dust**	To die or be destroyed; to fail	धूल चाटना (हार जाना या मारा जाना)	6 (4)
323	**Black and blue**	Badly bruised due to beating or injury	नीला-पीला पड़ना (मारपीट या चोट के कारण शरीर पर गहरे निशान होना)	2 (1)
324	Black ox	Bad luck or misfortune	दुर्भाग्य	
325	**Black sheep**	A person who is considered a disgrace to a family or group	अपनी बुरी हरकतों से परिवार का नाम खराब करने वाला	7 (9)
326	**Blaze a trail**	To be the first to do something new; to pioneer	मिसाल कायम करना (अग्रणी होना)	5 (3)
327	Blood, sweat and tears	Extremely hard work and effort	ख़ून-पसीना एक करना (जी-तोड़ मेहनत)	
328	Blow a fuse	To suddenly become very angry	आपा खोना (अचानक बहुत ज्यादा गुस्सा हो जाना)	
329	**Blow hot and cold**	To keep changing one's attitude	कभी हाँ कभी ना (रवैये में अस्थिरता)	4 (7)
330	Blow it out your ear	A rude dismissal; an expression of contempt or disbelief	भाड़ में जाओ (अपनी सलाह अपने पास रखो)	
331	**Blow one's own trumpet (or horn)**	To talk proudly about one's achievements	अपने मुँह मियाँ मिट्ठू बनना (अपनी प्रशंसा स्वयं करना)	19 (8)
332	Blow one's top	To become extremely angry	पारा चढ़ना (गुस्से से आगबबूला होना)	
333	Blow smoke	To deceive or mislead someone	धूल झोंकना (गुमराह करना); हवाई बातें करना	
334	Blow something out of proportion	To make something seem more important than it really is	बात का बतंगड़ बनाना (बढ़ा-चढ़ाकर बताना)	
335	**Blue blood**	Noble or aristocratic ancestry	कुलीन, ऊँचे खानदान का	4 (2)
336	**Blue in the face**	Exhausted from repeated but futile attempts	थककर चूर (बहुत बोलने या समझाने से)	1 (1)

SN	Idioms/Phrases	English Meaning	Hindi Meaning	#R
337	**Blue-eyed boy**	A person treated with special favour	आँखों का तारा (अत्यधिक चहेता या पसंदीदा व्यक्ति)	4
338	Bob's your uncle	Used to say that something will be done easily	काम आसानी से पूरा हो जाना	
339	**Body and soul**	With all one's energy and effort	तन-मन से (पूरी निष्ठा और शक्ति के साथ)	3
340	**Boil the ocean**	To attempt something impossibly difficult	पानी में आग लगाना (असंभव काम करने की कोशिश करना)	2 (2)
341	Bold move	A daring or courageous action	साहसिक कदम (जोखिम भरा फैसला)	
342	**Born with a silver spoon in one's mouth**	Born into a rich family	अमीर घराने में जन्म	5 (1)
343	Bottom line	The most important fact or consideration	कुल मिलाकर (सबसे महत्वपूर्ण बिंदु या अंतिम निष्कर्ष)	
344	Box someone's ear	To slap someone on the ear	कान के नीचे जड़ देना (थप्पड़ मारना)	
345	**Bread and butter (or cheese)**	One's main source of income	रोजी-रोटी (जीविका का मुख्य साधन)	4 (2)
346	Break a lance with	To engage in an argument or contest with someone	मुक़ाबला करना (बहस या प्रतियोगिता में उतरना)	
347	**Break a leg**	Used to wish someone good luck, especially before a performance	शुभकामनाएँ (मंच पर जाने से पहले दी जाने वाली बधाई)	13 (12)
348	Break a sweat	To exert physical effort	पसीना बहाना (मेहनत करना)	
349	Break loose	To escape from control or restraint	बंधन तोड़कर भागना (आज़ाद हो जाना)	
350	**Break new (or fresh) ground**	To do something new and innovative	नई पहल करना (किसी क्षेत्र में कुछ नया करना)	5
351	Break one's duck	To score for the first time or achieve one's first success	खाता खोलना (पहली सफलता पाना)	
352	Break Priscian's head	To violate the rules of grammar	व्याकरण की ग़लतियाँ करना	
353	**Break the bank**	To cost too much money	बहुत महँगा	2 (2)
354	**Break the ice**	To make people feel more relaxed in a social situation	बातचीत शुरू करना	13 (22)
355	Breast the tape	To win a race by crossing the finish line first	दौड़ जीतना	
356	**Breathe down one's neck**	To watch someone too closely in a way that annoys them	सिर पर सवार होना (नज़दीक से निगरानी करना)	2 (4)
357	**Breathe one's last**	To die	अंतिम साँस लेना (मर जाना)	2
358	**Bridge the gap**	To reduce differences between two things or groups	अंतर कम करना	2
359	**Bring home the bacon**	To earn money for one's family; to succeed	रोज़ी-रोटी कमाना (परिवार का पेट पालना); सफलता प्राप्त करना	1 (1)
360	**Bring someone to book**	To punish someone or make them explain their behaviour	जवाबदेह ठहराना, दण्डित करना	4 (1)
361	Bring someone to their knees	To defeat someone completely; to force to submit	घुटनों पर लाना (हार मनवाना)	

SN	Idioms/Phrases	English Meaning	Hindi Meaning	#R
362	**Bring the house down**	To make an audience laugh or applaud enthusiastically	महफिल लूट लेना (जोरदार तालियां और वाहवाही बटोरना)	3 (2)
363	**Bring to light**	To reveal or make known something that was hidden	प्रकाश में लाना (छुपी बात उजागर करना)	7 (1)
364	Broth of a boy	A lively and high-spirited young man	जोशीला नौजवान	
365	Buck the system	To resist or fight against established rules or authority	व्यवस्था के ख़िलाफ़ जाना (नियमों का विरोध करना)	
366	Buck the trend (or tide)	To resist or go against the prevailing trend or popular opinion	धारा के विपरीत चलना (प्रचलित रुझान के विरुद्ध जाना)	
367	Bug someone	To annoy or irritate someone	परेशान करना (नाक में दम करना या चिढ़ाना)	
368	**Build castles in the air**	To have dreams or plans that are unlikely to happen	हवाई क़िले बनाना (असंभव सपने देखना)	8 (3)
369	**Bull's-eye**	The centre of a target; a perfect hit	निशाने का केंद्र (सटीक निशाना)	1 (2)
370	**Burn a hole in one's pocket**	Money that someone is tempted to spend quickly	जेब में छेद करना (पैसा ख़र्च करने को बेताब)	1 (3)
371	**Burn one's bridges (or boats)**	To do something that makes it impossible to go back	पीछे हटने के सारे रास्ते खत्म करना	7 (10)
372	**Burn one's fingers**	To suffer bad results from something risky	अपने पैरों पर कुल्हाड़ी मारना (जोखिम के कारण नुकसान उठाना)	5 (3)
373	**Burn the candle at both ends**	To exhaust oneself by working too hard or staying up late	दिन-रात एक करना (अत्यधिक काम करना)	1 (8)
374	**Burn the midnight oil**	To work or study late into the night	देर रात तक काम करना	16 (16)
375	Burst into tears	To suddenly start crying	फफक कर रो पड़ना (अचानक रोने लगना)	
376	Burst someone's bubble	To destroy someone's illusions or hopes	उम्मीदों पर पानी फेरना (भ्रम तोड़ना)	
377	**Bury one's head in the sand**	To refuse to think about or deal with a problem	समस्या से मुँह मोड़ना	1 (2)
378	**Bury the hatchet**	To stop fighting or arguing and become friendly	झगड़ा खत्म करना	18 (15)
379	Butterfingers	A clumsy person who drops things	अनाड़ी व्यक्ति (चीजें गिराने वाला)	
380	**Butterflies in the stomach**	A nervous feeling in the stomach	घबराहट महसूस करना	4 (3)
381	**Button one's lip**	To stop talking; to keep quiet	होंठ सिलना (चुप रहना)	2
382	**Buy a pig in a poke**	Something bought without being examined or seen first	बिना जाँच-परख के चीज़ ख़रीदना (अंधेरे में सौदा करना)	1 (2)
383	Buy the farm	To die	परलोक सिधारना (मृत्यु हो जाना)	
384	By a whisker	By a very small amount	बहुत कम अन्तर से	
385	**By and by**	Before long; eventually	थोड़ी देर बाद, जल्द ही	3
386	**By and large**	On the whole; in general	कुल मिलाकर (मोटे तौर पर)	3
387	**By courtesy of**	With the help or permission of	की अनुमति से; की कृपा से	1 (1)
388	**By fair means or foul**	By any means, whether honest or not	साम-दाम-दंड-भेद से (किसी भी तरीके से, चाहे सही हो या गलत)	4

SN	Idioms/Phrases	English Meaning	Hindi Meaning	#R
389	By far	By a great amount	काफी हद तक (सबसे अधिक)	
390	**By fits and starts**	In an irregular way; intermittently	रुक-रुककर (अनियमित रूप से)	11 (4)
391	**By hook or by crook**	By any means necessary	हर हाल में (किसी भी तरीक़े से)	6 (6)
392	**By leaps and bounds**	Very quickly and in large amounts	दिन दूनी रात चौगुनी (बहुत तेज़ी से)	15 (2)
393	By the same token	Similarly; for the same reason	उसी तरह से	
394	**By the skin of one's teeth**	By a very small margin; only just	बाल-बाल (बहुत कम अंतर से)	10 (5)
395	By the sweat of one's brow	By one's own hard work and effort	पसीने की कमाई से (कड़ी मेहनत से)	
396	**By word of mouth**	Told from person to person verbally	मौखिक रूप से (ज़बानी)	2
397	**Call a spade a spade**	To speak honestly and directly	साफ-साफ कहना (बिना लाग-लपेट के कड़वा सच बोलना)	5 (7)
398	**Call into question**	To cause doubt about something	सवाल उठाना (संदेह करना)	2 (1)
399	**Call it a day**	To decide to stop working for the day	इतिश्री करना (आज का काम समाप्त करना)	19 (17)
400	Call of nature	The need to urinate or defecate	शौचालय जाने की ज़रूरत	
401	**Call the shots**	To be in control and make decisions	निर्णय लेने वाला होना	5
402	Cannot make head or tail of	To be completely unable to understand something	सिर-पैर समझ न आना (बिल्कुल पल्ले न पड़ना)	
403	**Can't cut the mustard**	To be unable to deal with difficulties or meet standards	काम के लायक न होना	1 (1)
404	**Can't hold a candle to**	To be not nearly as good as someone or something	पाँव की धूल होना (तुलना में बहुत पीछे होना)	4 (1)
405	Can't think straight	To be unable to think clearly	दिमाग़ काम न करना (सोच न पाना)	
406	Cap in hand	In a humble and respectful manner	विनम्रतापूर्वक या गिड़गिड़ाते हुए	
407	Cards are stacked against someone	To be in a situation where success is very unlikely	किस्मत साथ न देना (परिस्थितियाँ प्रतिकूल होना)	
408	**Carrot and stick**	A combination of rewards and punishments used to encourage behaviour	इनाम और दंड की नीति	3 (2)
409	Carry coals to Newcastle	To supply something that is already plentiful	तेली को तेल बेचना (व्यर्थ का काम)	
410	Carry the ball	To be in charge and take responsibility	जिम्मेदारी संभालना	
411	Carry the can	To take the blame, especially for something one did not do	बलि का बकरा बनना (दूसरों की गलती का दोष अपने सिर लेना)	
412	**Carry the day**	To win or succeed	जीत हासिल करना	6 (1)
413	Carry weight	To have influence or importance	महत्व रखना	
414	**Carve out a niche**	To create a special position for oneself	अपनी अलग पहचान बनाना (विशेष स्थान बनाना)	2
415	Cash-strapped	Short of money	पैसों की तंगी (आर्थिक कमी)	
416	Cast a slur on	To make unfair or damaging remarks about someone	कलंक लगाना (बदनामी करना या कीचड़ उछालना)	

SN	Idioms/Phrases	English Meaning	Hindi Meaning	#R
417	**Cast pearls before swine**	To give valuable things to people who do not appreciate them	भैंस के आगे बीन बजाना (मूर्ख को क़ीमती चीज़ देना)	3 (3)
418	Cast someone adrift	To leave someone without help or support	बीच मझधार में छोड़ना (बेसहारा छोड़ देना)	
419	**Cast the first stone**	To be the first to criticize or blame someone	ख़ुद दोषी होते हुए दूसरों पर पहले दोष लगाना	2
420	**Catch a Tartar**	To find oneself dealing with someone unexpectedly powerful or formidable	अपने से ज्यादा ताकतवर से भिड़ना	4 (3)
421	Catch a weasel asleep	To surprise someone who is normally very alert or shrewd	चालाक को भी चकमा दे देना	
422	**Catch off guard**	To surprise someone when they are not prepared	किसी को बिना तैयारी के अचानक चौंका देना	1 (1)
423	**Catch someone red-handed**	To catch someone in the act of doing something wrong	रंगे हाथों पकड़ना (अपराध करते हुए पकड़ना)	9 (4)
424	Catch someone's fancy	To attract or appeal to someone	मन को भा जाना (पसंद आना या आकर्षित करना)	
425	**Catch-22**	A dilemma from which there is no escape	ऐसी फँसी हुई स्थिति जिसका कोई उपाय न हो	3
426	Catch-all	Something that covers a wide range of things	जिसमें सब कुछ शामिल हो	
427	Cat's in the cradle	A parent being too busy for their child, leading to distant relations	काम में उलझकर परिवार को नज़रअंदाज़ करने की स्थिति	
428	**Cat's whiskers (or pajamas)**	An excellent person or thing	सर्वश्रेष्ठ	2
429	**Chalk and cheese**	Completely different from each other	ज़मीन-आसमान का फ़र्क़ (बिलकुल अलग)	4 (1)
430	Change colour	To become pale or blush from emotion	चेहरे का रंग बदलना (शर्म या डर से)	
431	Change for the better	An improvement in a situation	सुधार होना	
432	**Change hands**	To pass to a different owner	मालिक बदलना (स्वामित्व बदलना)	2 (1)
433	Change horses in midstream	To change plans or leaders in the middle of an activity	बीच मझधार में नाव बदलना (गलत समय पर बदलाव करना)	
434	**Change one's tune**	To change one's attitude or opinion	सुर बदलना (परिस्थितियों के अनुसार रवैया बदलना)	1 (6)
435	**Chapter and verse**	Exact details or sources	सटीक जानकारी (पूरा ब्यौरा)	3 (1)
436	**Chase rainbows**	To pursue unrealistic or impossible dreams	हवाई किले बनाना (असंभव सपनों के पीछे भागना)	2
437	**Cheek by jowl**	Very close together	बिल्कुल पास-पास	3
438	Cheek to cheek	Dancing or standing very close together, face to face	गाल से गाल लगाकर (बहुत करीब)	
439	**Chew the cud**	To think carefully about something	सोच-विचार करना	4 (2)
440	**Chew the fat**	To have a long friendly conversation	गप्पें मारना (लंबी बातचीत करना)	3 (1)
441	**Chew the scenery**	To act in an exaggerated or overly dramatic way	ज़रूरत से ज़्यादा नाटक करना	1 (2)
442	Chicken feed	A very small amount of money	बहुत कम पैसा	

SN	Idioms/Phrases	English Meaning	Hindi Meaning	#R
443	**Chicken out**	To decide not to do something because of fear	डर कर पीछे हटना	2
444	**Chicken-hearted**	Lacking courage; cowardly	दिल का कमजोर (कायर)	6 (3)
445	**Child's play**	Something very easy to do	बच्चों का खेल (बहुत आसान)	8 (1)
446	Clean hands	Free from guilt or dishonesty	निर्दोष (किसी गलत काम में शामिल न होना)	
447	Clear the air	To get rid of bad feelings or misunderstandings	गलतफहमी दूर करना	
448	**Clear the decks**	To prepare for an activity by dealing with anything in the way	बाधाएँ हटाना (मैदान साफ़ करना)	2
449	**Clip someone's wings**	To limit someone's freedom or power	पंख काटना (स्वतंत्रता को सीमित करना)	2 (1)
450	**Cloak and dagger**	Involving secrecy and intrigue	गुप्त और रहस्यमय	3 (1)
451	Close the book on	To stop doing something or dealing with something finally	किसी बात को पूरी तरह समाप्त कर देना	
452	Close to someone's heart	Very important or meaningful to someone	दिल के करीब होना (अत्यंत प्रिय या महत्वपूर्ण)	
453	**Close-fisted**	Unwilling to spend money	कंजूस व्यक्ति	4 (2)
454	Cloven hoof	A sign of evil or devilish character	बुरी प्रकृति का संकेत	
455	**Clutch (or grasp) at straws**	To try anything in desperation with little hope of success	सफलता के लिए हाथ पैर मारना	4 (1)
456	Cock of the walk	A person who dominates others in a group	दादागिरी दिखाने वाला	
457	**Cold comfort**	Something that offers little comfort in a bad situation	नाममात्र की तसल्ली	2
458	**Cold feet**	A loss of nerve or confidence	हाथ-पाँव ठंडे पड़ना (घबराहट होना)	10 (4)
459	**Come (or get) to the point**	To talk about the most important thing	मुद्दे पर आना (सीधी बात करना)	2
460	Come (or spring) to mind	To suddenly come into one's thoughts	अचानक याद आना (ध्यान में आना)	
461	Come between the bark and the tree	To interfere in a close relationship, especially a family matter	निजी मामलों में दखल देना	
462	Come clean	To tell the truth about something	सच उगल देना (ईमानदारी से सब कुछ बता देना)	
463	**Come hell or high water**	Whatever difficulties may occur	चाहे जो हो जाए (हर परिस्थिति का सामना करने की जिद)	2
464	Come high	To cost a lot of money	जेब पर भारी पड़ना (महँगा होना)	
465	**Come in handy**	To be useful	जरूरत के समय उपयोगी साबित होना	2
466	**Come of age**	To reach the age when one is legally an adult	वयस्क होना	2 (1)
467	**Come out into the open**	To become known to everyone	खुलकर सामने आना	2
468	**Come out of one's shell**	To become less shy and more sociable	झिझक छोड़ना (घुलना-मिलना शुरू करना)	1 (1)
469	**Come rain or shine**	Whatever happens; no matter what	चाहे बारिश हो या धूप (हर हाल में)	4 (1)
470	Come to a standstill	To stop completely	ठप्प पड़ जाना (पूरी तरह रुक जाना)	

SN	Idioms/Phrases	English Meaning	Hindi Meaning	#R
471	**Come to blows**	To start fighting	मारपीट पर उतर आना	2
472	**Come to grief**	To suffer serious trouble, failure, or disaster	मुसीबत में पड़ना	2
473	**Come to light**	To become known	प्रकाश में आना (पता चलना)	3
474	Come to terms with	To accept or deal with a difficult situation	स्वीकार करना (हालात से समझौता कर लेना)	
475	Come true	To happen as expected or hoped	सच होना (उम्मीद के मुताबिक़ घटित होना)	
476	**Come what may**	Whatever happens	चाहे जो हो जाए (हर हाल में)	2
477	**Cook someone's goose**	To ruin someone's plans or chances	खेल बिगाड़ना (किसी की योजना चौपट करना)	2 (4)
478	**Cook the books**	To change financial records dishonestly	खातों में हेरफेर करना (धोखाधड़ी करना)	2 (1)
479	Cool it	To become calm or stop being angry	शांत हो जाना (ठंडा पड़ना)	
480	**Cool one's heels**	To be kept waiting	इंतज़ार में बैठा रहना (मजबूरी में प्रतीक्षा करना)	2 (1)
481	**Cost an arm and a leg**	To cost a lot of money	भारी कीमत चुकाना (बहुत महँगा पड़ना)	24 (15)
482	Cost someone dearly	To cause someone a lot of problems or loss	भारी पड़ना (बड़ा नुक़सान होना)	
483	Count down the days	To wait eagerly for something	दिन गिनना (बेसब्री से इंतज़ार करना)	
484	**Count one's blessings**	To be grateful for what one has	जो है उसके लिए शुक्रगुज़ार होना	1 (1)
485	Cover all bases	To deal with every part of a situation	सभी पहलुओं पर ध्यान देना (हर बात का ख़याल रखना)	
486	Crash and burn	To fail completely	औंधे मुँह गिरना (बुरी तरह असफल होना)	
487	Creature comforts	Things that make life comfortable and pleasant	भौतिक सुख-सुविधाएँ (आराम की चीज़ें)	
488	**Crocodile tears**	Tears or sadness that are not sincere	मगरमच्छ के आँसू (दिखावटी या झूठा दुःख)	7 (3)
489	**Cross one's fingers**	To hope that something will happen the way you want	अच्छे परिणाम की कामना करना	1 (5)
490	**Cross someone's mind**	To come into someone's thoughts	मन में आना (ख़्याल आना)	1 (2)
491	Cross someone's palm with silver	To pay someone for a service; to bribe	किसी को पैसे देना; रिश्वत देना	
492	**Cross swords**	To compete or fight against someone	दो-दो हाथ करना (प्रतियोगिता या मुक़ाबला करना)	4
493	Cross the finish line	To complete a race or task	किसी काम को पूरा करना	
494	**Cross the Rubicon**	To do something that cannot be undone	ऐसा निर्णय लेना जिससे वापस न लौटा जा सके	2
495	**Crux of the matter**	The most important part of an issue	मुद्दे की बात (मामले का सबसे महत्वपूर्ण पहलू)	3 (1)

SN	Idioms/Phrases	English Meaning	Hindi Meaning	#R
496	**Cry (or ask) for the moon**	To ask for something that is impossible to get	चाँद माँगना (असंभव चीज़ की इच्छा करना)	2 (5)
497	**Cry over spilt milk**	To waste time being upset about something that has already happened	अब पछताए होत क्या जब चिड़िया चुग गई खेत (बीती बातों पर व्यर्थ पछताना)	13 (13)
498	**Cry stinking fish**	To say bad things about one's own products or work	अपनी ही चीज़ की बुराई करना	1 (3)
499	**Cry wolf**	To raise false alarms or ask for help when it is not needed	बार-बार झूठी चेतावनी देना	5 (4)
500	**Cudgel one's brains**	To think very hard about something	दिमाग़ पर ज़ोर डालना (बहुत सोचना)	2 (1)
501	**Curry favour with**	To try to gain someone's approval by flattering them	चापलूसी करना (जी-हुज़ूरी करना)	3
502	**Cut a long story short**	To get to the point without unnecessary details	संक्षेप में कहना	2
503	**Cut a sorry (or poor) figure**	To make a bad impression	ख़राब छवि बनाना (कमज़ोर या नाकाम दिखना)	4 (1)
504	**Cut and dried**	Decided and unlikely to change	पहले से तय (स्पष्ट और अंतिम)	2
505	Cut both ways	To have both positive and negative effects	फायदे और नुकसान दोनों होना	
506	**Cut corners**	To do something in the easiest or cheapest way	सस्ता जुगाड़ करना (गुणवत्ता से समझौता करना)	9 (16)
507	**Cut from the same cloth**	Very similar in character	एक ही थाली के चट्टे-बट्टे (स्वभाव में बिल्कुल एक जैसा होना)	2
508	Cut it out	To stop doing something annoying	परेशान करना बंद करना	
509	**Cut no ice (with someone)**	To have no influence or effect on someone	प्रभावित न कर पाना (असरहीन होना)	4 (1)
510	Cut one's teeth on	To get one's first experience of something	अनुभव प्राप्त करना (शुरुआत करना या बुनियादी हुनर सीखना)	
511	Cut someone dead	To deliberately ignore someone	मुँह फेर लेना (जानबूझकर अनदेखा करना)	
512	Cut someone off without a shilling (or a penny)	To disinherit someone completely	वसीयत से बेदखल करना	
513	**Cut someone short**	To interrupt someone while they are speaking	बीच में टोकना (बोलते हुए रोक देना)	3
514	**Cut someone some slack**	To be lenient with someone	नरमी बरतना (छूट देना या ढील देना)	1 (1)
515	**Cut the cackle**	To stop talking nonsense and get to the point	बकवास बंद करना (सीधे काम की बात पर आना)	2
516	**Cut the Gordian knot**	To solve a difficult problem decisively	जटिल समस्या का समाधान निकालना	4
517	**Cut the mustard**	To meet expectations or perform satisfactorily	मापदंड पर खरा उतरना	2 (8)
518	**Cut to the chase**	To get to the main point without delay	सीधे मुद्दे पर आना	7 (3)
519	**Cut to the quick**	To hurt someone's feelings deeply	दिल पर चोट पहुँचाना (गहरा मानसिक दुःख पहुँचाना)	2 (2)

SN	Idioms/Phrases	English Meaning	Hindi Meaning	#R
520	Dance attendance on someone	To serve someone with excessive attentiveness	जी-हुज़ूरी करना (अत्यधिक सेवा करना)	
521	**Dance to someone's tune**	To do exactly what someone else wants	किसी के इशारों पर नाचना (कठपुतली बनना)	2
522	Day and night	Continuously; all the time	दिन-रात एक करना (निरंतर या हर समय)	
523	Dead in the water	Unable to make progress; failing	पूरी तरह रुका हुआ (योजना का विफल होना)	
524	**Dead meat**	A person who is in serious trouble	गंभीर मुसीबत में होना	1 (1)
525	Dead men's shoes	A position available only after someone's departure	किसी के हटने/मरने पर मिलने वाला पद	
526	Dead set against	Strongly opposed to something	पूरी तरह ख़िलाफ़ होना (सख़्त विरोध करना)	
527	Deep pockets	Having a lot of money or financial resources	मोटा पैसा होना (धनी होना)	
528	Dice with death	To put one's life at risk	मौत से खेलना (जान जोख़िम में डालना)	
529	Die a dog's death	To die in a shameful or miserable way	कुत्ते की मौत मरना (शर्मनाक मृत्यु)	
530	**Die in harness**	To die while still working or in service	सेवाकाल में मृत्यु (काम करते हुए मरना)	5 (3)
531	Diehard	A person unwilling to change; stubbornly persistent	दृढ़ या न झुकनेवाला	
532	**Dig up dirt on someone**	To discover damaging information about someone	पोल खोलना (भेद पता करना)	2
533	Dine with Duke Humphrey	To go without food; remain hungry	भूखे पेट रहना (ख़ाना न मिलना)	
534	**Do a good turn**	To do something helpful or kind for someone	नेकी करना (किसी की सहायता करना)	5
535	Do a roaring trade	To sell a large amount of goods very quickly	ज़बरदस्त व्यापार करना (अत्यधिक मुनाफा कमाना)	
536	Do or die	A situation requiring extreme effort with no middle ground	करो या मरो (अंतिम प्रयास करना)	
537	Do something on autopilot	To do something automatically without thinking	बिना सोचे-समझे करना (आदत वश स्वचालित रूप से करना)	
538	**Doctor the accounts**	To falsify or manipulate financial records	ख़ातों में हेरफ़ेर करना (धोखाधड़ी करना)	2
539	Dodge a bullet	To narrowly avoid a dangerous situation	बाल-बाल बचना (बड़ी मुसीबत से सुरक्षित निकलना)	
540	**Donkey's years**	A very long time	बहुत लंबा समय	5 (1)
541	**Don't buy it**	To not believe something	विश्वास न करना (बातों में न आना)	1 (1)
542	Don't care a hang	To not care at all about something	रत्ती भर भी परवाह न करना (कोई मतलब न होना)	
543	**Dot the i's and cross the t's**	Pay attention to every small detail	बारीकी से काम करना (हर छोटी बात का ध्यान रखना)	2 (1)
544	Down and out	Completely without money, resources, or hope	कंगाल और बेबस	

SN	Idioms/Phrases	English Meaning	Hindi Meaning	#R
545	**Down for the count**	Defeated, unconscious, or unable to continue	पस्त हो जाना (हार मान लेना)	1 (1)
546	**Down in the dumps**	Feeling sad and depressed	हताश (उदास और निराश)	2
547	Down in the mouth	Unhappy or dejected	मुँह लटकाना (मायूस दिखना)	
548	**Down the road**	In the future; at a later time	आगे चलकर (भविष्य में)	1 (1)
549	**Down to earth**	Practical, realistic, and unpretentious	व्यावहारिक और सरल (ज़मीन से जुड़ा इंसान)	4 (1)
550	Down with	To be opposed to something; to be ill with	किसी के ख़िलाफ़; बीमार	
551	**Drag one's feet**	To be deliberately slow or reluctant to act	टालमटोल करना (जानबूझकर देरी करना)	4
552	**Draw a blank**	To fail to get an answer or remember something	हाथ ख़ाली रहना (याद न आना)	6
553	Draw first blood	To be the first to gain an advantage	शुरुआती बढ़त हासिल करना (पहला वार करना)	
554	**Draw on one's fancy**	To use one's imagination	कल्पना का उपयोग करना	2 (1)
555	**Draw the line**	To set a limit on what one will do or accept	सीमा तय करना (हद बाँधना)	5 (3)
556	**Draw the long bow**	To exaggerate or overstate	बढ़ा-चढ़ाकर बोलना	2 (1)
557	Dressed to kill	Dressed very attractively to impress	शानदार कपड़ों में सजना (आकर्षक दिखना)	
558	**Dressed to the nines**	Dressed very elegantly or formally	बेहद सलीक़े से तैयार होना	1 (3)
559	Drill something into someone	To teach through constant, forceful repetition	बार-बार समझाकर दिमाग़ में बिठाना	
560	**Drive home**	To emphasize a point clearly and forcefully	पूरी तरह स्पष्ट करना (ज़ोर देकर समझाना)	2
561	**Drive someone up the wall**	Make someone extremely annoyed	नाक में दम करना (बहुत परेशान कर देना)	3 (4)
562	Drop a line	To send a short, informal message	संक्षिप्त संदेश भेजना	
563	**Drop in a bucket (or ocean)**	A very small amount compared to what is needed	ऊँट के मुँह में जीरा (ज़रूरत के मुक़ाबले नगण्य मात्रा)	6 (5)
564	**Drop like flies**	To fall ill or die in large numbers	बड़ी संख्या में गिरना या मरना	1 (1)
565	**Drop names (or name-dropping)**	Mentioning famous people to impress others	बड़े लोगों का नाम लेना (रौब जमाने के लिए)	2
566	Drop off the radar	To stop being noticed or monitored; to disappear from attention	नज़रों से ओझल होना (ध्यान से हट जाना)	
567	Dust and ashes	Something utterly disappointing or worthless	निराशाजनक (व्यर्थ और बेकार)	
568	Ease someone's mind	To alleviate someone's anxiety	चिंता दूर करना (मन हल्का करना)	
569	**Easier said than done**	More difficult to do than to talk about	कहना आसान है करना मुश्किल	6 (2)
570	**Easy does it**	Do something carefully and slowly	आराम से (सावधानी और धैर्य से काम करना)	1 (1)
571	Easy money	Money obtained without much effort	बिना मेहनत की कमाई	

SN	Idioms/Phrases	English Meaning	Hindi Meaning	#R
572	Easy on the ears	Pleasant to listen to	कानों को भाने वाला (सुनने में अच्छा)	
573	**Eat crow**	To admit that you were wrong	अपनी ग़लती मानना (शर्मिंदा होना)	2
574	**Eat humble pie**	To apologize and admit being wrong	माफ़ी माँगना (अपनी ग़लती मानकर शर्मिंदा होना)	13 (3)
575	**Eat like a bird**	To eat very little	चिड़िया की तरह चुगना (बहुत कम खाना)	3 (5)
576	**Eat like a horse**	To eat a lot	बहुत अधिक खाना	8 (3)
577	**Eat one's words**	To retract something one has said	थूक कर चाटना (अपनी गलती मानना)	2
578	**Eat someone's salt**	To be someone's guest or under obligation	नमक खाना (किसी का मेहमान या कृतज्ञ होना)	2
579	Eat the leek	To be forced to take back one's words humiliatingly	अपनी बात निगलना (अपमान सहकर ग़लती मानना)	
580	**Elbow grease**	Hard physical effort	कड़ी मेहनत	2
581	**Elbow room**	Enough space to move or work in	पर्याप्त जगह (काम करने की स्वतंत्रता)	2 (3)
582	**Elephant in the room**	An obvious problem that everyone ignores	अनदेखी की गई बड़ी समस्या	5 (8)
583	**Eleventh hour**	At the last possible moment	अंतिम क्षण में	15 (9)
584	**End in a fiasco**	To result in complete failure	पूर्ण असफलता	2
585	Even the score	To retaliate against someone who has wronged you	हिसाब बराबर करना (बदला लेना)	
586	Evening of life	Old age	बुढ़ापा (जीवन की संध्या)	
587	Every inch	Completely; in every way	पूर्णतः (हर तरह से)	
588	**Every nook and cranny**	Every part of a place	कोना-कोना (हर जगह)	1 (1)
589	Evil twin	A bad or opposite version of someone	दुष्ट प्रतिरूप (विपरीत स्वभाव का जुड़वा)	
590	**Explore every avenue**	To try all possible opportunities	हर संभव रास्ता आज़माना	3
591	**Eyewash**	Deception or false appearance	आँखों में धूल झोंकना (धोखा)	6 (2)
592	**Face the music**	To accept consequences	किये का फल भुगतना (परिणाम का सामना करना)	23 (7)
593	Face to face	In person	आमने-सामने	
594	Faint-hearted	Those lacking courage or determination	कमज़ोर दिल वाले (डरपोक या हिचकिचाने वाले)	
595	**Fair and square**	Completely honest and straightforward	ईमानदार और साफ़	6 (5)
596	Fair's fair	Used to say that treatment should be fair and equal	न्यायपूर्ण व्यवहार होना चाहिए	
597	Fall between two stools	To fail due to inability to choose	दो नावों पर सवार होना (दुविधा के कारण असफल होना)	
598	**Fall flat**	To fail to achieve the intended effect	बेअसर होना (पूरी तरह विफल होना)	7 (1)
599	**Fall foul of**	To get into trouble or conflict with	मुसीबत में फँसना	3 (1)
600	Fall into line	To follow rules or conform	नियमों का पालन करना	

SN	Idioms/Phrases	English Meaning	Hindi Meaning	#R
601	**Fall off the radar**	To no longer be noticed or monitored	नज़रों से ओझल होना	2
602	**Fall short**	To fail to meet a standard or requirement	उम्मीदों पर खरा न उतरना (अपेक्षा से कम रह जाना)	2
603	Fan the flames	To worsen a situation	आग में घी डालना (स्थिति बिगाड़ना)	
604	**Far and wide**	Over a large area or everywhere	दूर-दूर तक (हर जगह)	3 (1)
605	Feast one's eyes on	To gaze at something with great pleasure	आँख भरकर देखना (प्रसन्नता से निहारना)	
606	**Feather one's nest**	To make money, often dishonestly, for oneself	अपना घर भरना (पद का लाभ उठाकर बेईमानी से धनी बनना)	8 (1)
607	**Feel at home**	To feel comfortable and relaxed	सहज महसूस करना (घर जैसा आरामदायक अनुभव होना)	2 (1)
608	**Feel blue**	To feel sad or depressed	उदास महसूस करना (मन भारी होना)	2
609	Feel someone's pulse	To try to discover someone's opinions or intentions	नब्ज टटोलना (दूसरों के विचार या रुख जानना)	
610	**Feel the pinch**	To experience financial hardship	पैसों की तंगी महसूस करना	5 (1)
611	**Few and far between**	Rare and scarce	दुर्लभ (बहुत कम मिलने वाला)	2 (1)
612	Fiddle while Rome burns	To do trivial things while ignoring a serious crisis	संकट के समय ग़ैर-ज़रूरी काम करना	
613	**Fight fire with fire**	To respond to an attack using the same methods	लोहे से लोहा काटना (शत्रु के तरीके से उसे जवाब देना)	2
614	Fight one's own battles	To deal with one's own problems independently	अपनी लड़ाई ख़ुद लड़ना	
615	**Fight shy of**	To be unwilling to do or become involved in something	बचकर निकलना (कतराना या झिझकना)	4 (1)
616	**Fight to the bitter end**	To continue to fight until the very end	अंतिम दम तक लड़ना (परिणाम की चिंता किये बिना डटे रहना)	1 (1)
617	**Fight tooth and nail**	To fight with all one's strength and determination	जी-जान से लड़ना (पूरी ताक़त लगा देना)	9 (6)
618	**Find one's feet**	To become familiar and confident in a new situation	पैर जमाना (नई जगह पर सहज होना)	1 (1)
619	Fire the imagination	To make someone feel very interested in something	कल्पना को पंख लगाना (प्रेरित करना)	
620	**First and foremost**	Most importantly, above all else	सबसे पहले (सबसे महत्वपूर्ण बात यह है कि...)	2
621	**Fish in troubled waters**	To take advantage of a chaotic situation	बहती गंगा में हाथ धोना (दूसरों की मुसीबत का फ़ायदा उठाना)	3 (1)
622	Fit like a glove	To fit perfectly	बिलकुल सटीक बैठना	
623	Flex one's muscles	To display one's power or strength	शक्ति प्रदर्शन करना	
624	**Flog (or beat) a dead horse**	To waste effort on something that cannot succeed	व्यर्थ प्रयास करना	16 (10)
625	Fly by the seat of one's pants	To act on instinct without planning	अंदाज़े से चलना (बिना योजना के काम करना)	
626	Fly high	To be very successful	ऊँची उड़ान भरना (सफलता के शिखर पर होना)	

SN	Idioms/Phrases	English Meaning	Hindi Meaning	#R
627	**Fly into a rage (or passion)**	To become very angry suddenly	आग बबूला होना (अति क्रोधित होना)	3
628	**Fly off the handle**	To lose one's temper suddenly	गुस्सा होना	3 (4)
629	Fly the nest	To leave one's parents' home	घर छोड़कर आत्मनिर्भर होना	
630	**Fly under the radar**	To avoid being detected or noticed	नज़रों से बचकर (बिना ध्यान आकर्षित किए)	2 (2)
631	**Foam at the mouth**	To be extremely angry and agitated	बहुत ग़ुस्सा होना (आग-बबूला होना)	3 (2)
632	Follow one's nose	To go straight ahead; to act on instinct	नाक की सीध में चलना	
633	**Follow suit**	To do the same as others have done	देखा-देखी करना	2 (1)
634	**Food for thought**	Something to think about seriously	सोचने पर मजबूर करने वाली बात	2
635	**Foot the bill**	To pay the cost of something	ख़र्च उठाना (बिल का भुगतान करना)	3
636	Footloose and fancy-free	Free from responsibilities or romantic commitments	बेफ़िक्र और आज़ाद; बंधन-मुक्त	
637	**For better or worse**	Whether the results are good or bad	चाहे अच्छा हो या बुरा (हर हाल में)	2
638	**For good**	Permanently or forever	हमेशा के लिए	5 (4)
639	For keeps	To keep permanently; not to return	सदा के लिए पास रखना	
640	For old times' sake	For sentimental reasons	पुरानी यादों के लिए (भावुकता के कारण)	
641	**Forty winks**	A short sleep or nap	झपकी लेना (थोड़ी देर की नींद)	8 (1)
642	**Foul play**	Unfair or dishonest behaviour	बेईमानी	2
643	Four corners of the earth	All parts of the world	दुनिया के कोने-कोने से (विश्व भर से)	
644	Fringe benefits	Extra benefits beyond salary	अतिरिक्त सुविधाएँ (वेतन के अलावा मिलने वाले लाभ)	
645	**From cradle to grave**	Throughout one's entire life	जन्म से मृत्यु तक (जीवन भर)	1 (1)
646	From far and wide	From all directions	दूर-दूर से (हर तरफ़ से)	
647	**From pillar to post**	From one place to another without achieving	दर-दर की ठोकरें खाना (इधर से उधर भटकना)	1 (1)
648	**From rags to riches**	To rise from poverty to wealth	शून्य से शिखर तक (ग़रीबी से अमीरी का सफ़र)	4 (4)
649	**From scratch**	From the very beginning	शुरुआत से (बिल्कुल नए सिरे से)	3
650	From stem to stern	Completely; from one end to the other	पूरी तरह से	
651	**From the bottom of one's heart**	With complete sincerity	तहे दिल से (सच्चे मन से)	1 (1)
652	**Full of beans**	Very energetic and lively	जोश और ऊर्जा से भरपूर	10 (1)
653	**Full of hot air**	Full of empty, boastful talk	बड़बोला (खोखली बातों से भरा)	3
654	**Full of sound and fury**	Loud but meaningless or ineffective	दिखावा ज़्यादा, काम कम	2
655	Full steam ahead	To proceed with full energy and determination	पूरे जोश के साथ आगे बढ़ना	
656	**Gain ground**	To make progress or advance	आगे बढ़ना (प्रगति करना)	2

SN	Idioms/Phrases	English Meaning	Hindi Meaning	#R
657	**Gall and wormwood**	Something extremely bitter or irritating	घृणास्पद (अत्यंत कड़वा अनुभव)	2 (2)
658	Gather rosebuds	To enjoy life's pleasures while one can	अवसर का लाभ उठाना (जब तक समय है जीवन के सुख लेना)	
659	**Gentleman at large**	A man of independent means with no fixed job	स्वतंत्र साधनों वाला (बिना तय काम का व्यक्ति)	2 (1)
660	**Get a foot in the door**	To gain an initial opportunity or access	मौक़ा मिलना (पहली बार अवसर पाना)	1 (1)
661	Get a gold star	To receive recognition or praise for good work	प्रशंसा या शाबाशी पाना (उत्कृष्ट कार्य के लिए सम्मान)	
662	**Get a second wind**	To experience renewed energy after being tired	नई ऊर्जा मिलना	3
663	**Get a taste of one's own medicine**	To experience the same treatment that one has given to others	जैसे को तैसा (दूसरों के साथ किए व्यवहार का अनुभव करना)	5 (5)
664	Get away scot-free	To escape punishment or consequences entirely	बिना सज़ा के बच निकलना (साफ़ छूट जाना)	
665	Get cracking	To start doing something immediately	फटाफट शुरू करना	
666	**Get down to brass tacks**	To focus on the essential facts or practical details	मुद्दे की बात करना	4 (2)
667	Get down to business	To start dealing with the important matters	गंभीरता से काम शुरू करना	
668	**Get in someone's hair**	To annoy someone, especially by being constantly near them	किसी के सिर पर सवार रहना (लगातार परेशान करना)	2
669	Get into a scrape	To find oneself in a difficult or embarrassing situation	मुसीबत में फँसना	
670	Get into hot water	To be in serious trouble	कठिनाई में होना	
671	Get it in the neck	To be severely criticized or punished	भारी फटकार खाना, सज़ा मिलना	
672	Get mixed up	To become confused; or to become involved in something bad	उलझन में पड़ना / ग़लत संगत में पड़ना	
673	Get more kicks than halfpence	To receive more criticism or punishment than reward	इनाम कम सज़ा ज़्यादा	
674	**Get off on the wrong foot**	To start a relationship or an activity badly	किसी रिश्ते या काम की ख़राब शुरुआत करना	1 (2)
675	**Get on like a house on fire**	To become very good friends quickly	जल्दी दोस्त बनना	2
676	**Get on someone's nerves**	To annoy or irritate someone continuously	नाक में दम करना (दिमाग़ ख़राब करना)	7
677	**Get one's act together**	To organize oneself and start behaving more effectively	ख़ुद को व्यवस्थित करना (अपने काम सुधारना)	6 (4)
678	Get one's dander up	To become very angry or lose one's temper	ग़ुस्सा होना (आग बबूला होना)	
679	**Get one's ducks in a row**	To get everything organized and prepared	व्यवस्थित करना	2 (1)
680	**Get one's head around**	To comprehend or understand something difficult	समझने की कोशिश करना (जटिल बात समझना)	2
681	Get one's money's worth	To receive good value for the money spent	पैसा वसूल होना (पूरा लाभ उठाना)	
682	Get one's own back	To take revenge on someone	हिसाब बराबर करना (बदला लेना)	

SN	Idioms/Phrases	English Meaning	Hindi Meaning	#R
683	Get one's own way	To get what one wants, often despite opposition	अपनी बात मनवाना	
684	**Get one's walking papers**	To be officially dismissed or fired from a job	नौकरी से हाथ धोना (नौकरी से निकाला जाना)	1 (1)
685	Get oneself into a mess	To create problems for oneself	ख़ुद को मुसीबत में डालना	
686	**Get out of hand**	To become uncontrollable or difficult to manage	हाथ से निकलना (नियंत्रण से बाहर होना)	11 (3)
687	Get rid of	To dispose of something unwanted	छुटकारा पाना	
688	**Get someone's goat**	To irritate or annoy someone	चिढ़ाना	2 (1)
689	**Get something off one's chest**	To express something that has been worrying or troubling you	दिल का बोझ हल्का करना (खुलकर बात कह देना)	4
690	Get something out of one's system	To do something you have wanted to do so you no longer feel the need	मन की भड़ास निकालना (इच्छा पूरी करके मन हल्का करना)	
691	**Get the axe**	To lose one's job; to be dismissed	नौकरी खो देना	1 (2)
692	**Get the green light**	To get permission or approval to proceed	हरी झंडी मिलना (अनुमति प्राप्त करना)	2
693	**Get the hang of**	To learn how to do or use something	समझ आ जाना (काम करने का तरीक़ा सीखना)	1 (2)
694	Get the message	To understand what someone is trying to tell you, especially indirectly	इशारा समझना (बात की गहराई समझना)	
695	Get the picture	To understand the situation or what is being explained	स्थिति समझना	
696	**Get the sack**	To be dismissed from one's job	नौकरी से निकाला जाना	4
697	**Get under someone's skin**	To irritate or annoy someone intensely	नाक में दम करना (बहुत परेशान करना)	1 (2)
698	**Get up on the wrong side of the bed**	To start the day in a bad mood	दिन की ख़राब शुरुआत	3
699	**Get wind of**	To learn about something, especially a secret, indirectly	भनक लग जाना	4 (1)
700	**Gift of the gab**	Ability to speak persuasively and eloquently	वाक्पटुता (बोलने की कला में माहिर होना)	22 (4)
701	**Gird up one's loins**	To prepare oneself for something difficult or challenging	कमर कसना (कठिनाई के लिए तैयार होना)	2 (2)
702	Give a false alarm	To signal a danger or problem that does not actually exist	झूठी चेतावनी देना (अफ़वाह फैलाना)	
703	**Give a free hand**	To give someone complete freedom to act	खुली छूट देना (पूरा अधिकार सौंपना)	2
704	**Give a piece of one's mind**	To tell someone exactly what you think, especially when angry	डाँटना (खरी-खोटी सुनाना)	6
705	**Give a wide berth**	To stay away from someone or something	दूर रहना	1 (3)
706	**Give and take**	Mutual concession and compromise	आपसी समझौता	4
707	**Give it a shot (or whirl)**	To attempt or try something	हाथ आज़माना (कोशिश करना)	3 (2)

SN	Idioms/Phrases	English Meaning	Hindi Meaning	#R
708	**Give oneself airs**	To act in a superior or pretentious manner	घमंड दिखाना (शान बघारना या इतराना)	2 (1)
709	**Give someone a hand**	To help someone with a task	हाथ बँटाना (मदद करना)	2
710	Give someone a ring	To call someone on the telephone	फ़ोन करना	
711	Give someone enough rope	To give someone freedom to act, often so they make mistakes	किसी को इतनी छूट देना कि वह खुद गलती कर बैठे	
712	**Give someone the cold shoulder**	To deliberately ignore or be unfriendly to someone	नजरअंदाज करना	11 (8)
713	**Give someone the slip**	To escape from someone who is following or looking for you	चकमा देकर भागना	1 (1)
714	**Give the benefit of the doubt**	To believe someone's statement without proof, even if you are suspicious	संदेह का लाभ देना (ईमानदार मान लेना)	2 (1)
715	**Give the devil his due**	To acknowledge the merit of someone you dislike	दुश्मन की भी अच्छाई मानना (बुरे की भी सही बात स्वीकार करना)	2 (1)
716	**Give the game away**	To reveal a secret or spoil a surprise	भांडा फोड़ना (राज़ खोल देना)	2
717	**Give up the ghost**	To die; or (of a machine) to stop working completely	दम तोड़ना / काम करना बंद करना	3
718	**Give vent to**	To express strong feelings forcefully	भड़ास निकालना (भावनाओं को ज़ोरदार ढंग से व्यक्त करना)	3
719	**Gnash one's teeth**	To grind one's teeth together, especially in anger or frustration	दाँत पीसना (अत्यधिक क्रोध या लाचारी जताना)	2
720	**Go (or run) around in circles**	To waste time without making progress	व्यर्थ भाग-दौड़ करना (समय बर्बाद करना)	10 (2)
721	**Go (or start) with a bang**	To be very successful or start impressively	धमाकेदार शुरुआत या शानदार सफलता	1 (1)
722	**Go a long way**	To be very helpful or successful; to last for a long time	बहुत काम आना (महत्वपूर्ण योगदान देना)	2
723	**Go against the grain**	To do something contrary to one's nature or principles	स्वभाव के विरुद्ध होना (सिद्धांतों के विपरीत काम करना)	4
724	**Go bananas**	To become very angry or excited	बहुत ज़्यादा उत्तेजित या गुस्सा हो जाना	5 (1)
725	**Go belly up**	To go bankrupt or fail completely	दिवालिया होना (धंधा पूरी तरह बंद होना)	1 (1)
726	Go blank	To suddenly be unable to remember something	दिमाग़ ख़ाली हो जाना (अचानक कुछ याद न आना)	
727	Go bonkers	To become crazy or act wildly	पागल हो जाना (सठिया जाना)	
728	Go bust	To become bankrupt	दिवालिया हो जाना	
729	**Go by the book**	To follow rules or procedures exactly	क़ायदे-क़ानून से चलना (नियमों का सख़्ती से पालन करना)	1 (1)
730	**Go cold turkey**	To stop an addictive habit suddenly and completely	एक झटके में छोड़ना (बिना धीरे-धीरे कम किए आदत त्यागना)	2 (2)
731	Go down a storm	To be received with great enthusiasm; to be very successful	धूम मचा देना (बहुत सफल होना)	
732	**Go down in flames**	To fail spectacularly and completely	बुरी तरह असफल होना	4 (1)

SN	Idioms/Phrases	English Meaning	Hindi Meaning	#R
733	**Go down like a lead balloon**	To be received very badly; to fail to impress	दर्शकों को बिल्कुल पसंद न आना	4 (3)
734	**Go down the drain**	To be wasted or lost	पूरी तरह बर्बाद हो जाना	2 (2)
735	Go down the tubes	To be ruined, or fail	पूरी तरह नाकाम हो जाना	
736	Go downhill	To deteriorate or decline	गिरावट आना	
737	Go Dutch	To share the cost of something equally	अपना-अपना बिल चुकाना (ख़र्च बराबर बाँटना)	
738	Go easy on	To use something sparingly; or to treat someone leniently	कम इस्तेमाल करना / नरमी बरतना	
739	**Go for a song**	To be sold very cheaply	मिट्टी के मोल बिकना (सस्ते में बिकना)	5 (1)
740	**Go for the jugular**	To attack someone's weakest point	किसी की सबसे कमज़ोर नस पर वार करना	1 (1)
741	Go hard with	To be difficult or unpleasant for someone	किसी के लिए स्थिति मुश्किल होना	
742	Go haywire	To stop working correctly and become out of control	बेक़ाबू होना (गड़बड़ा जाना)	
743	Go nuts	To become crazy or very excited	पागल-सा हो जाना	
744	**Go off on a tangent**	To change subject suddenly	मुद्दे से भटकना	2
745	Go off the air	To stop broadcasting a radio or tv programme	प्रसारण बंद करना	
746	Go over one's head	To be too difficult for someone to understand	सिर के ऊपर से जाना (समझ से बाहर होना)	
747	**Go pear-shaped**	To go badly wrong	काम बिगड़ जाना	2
748	Go red in the face	To become embarrassed or angry	शर्म या ग़ुस्से से चेहरा लाल हो जाना	
749	**Go scot-free**	To escape without punishment or injury	सज़ा से बचना	2
750	Go suck a lemon	A rude expression telling someone to go away	दफ़ा हो जाओ	
751	**Go the extra mile**	To make more effort than expected	आवश्यकता से अधिक प्रयास करना	8 (9)
752	**Go the whole hog**	To do something completely and thoroughly	किसी काम को पूरा करना	1 (1)
753	**Go through a rough (or sticky) patch**	To experience a difficult period	मुश्किल दौर से गुज़रना	2
754	Go through a sticky patch	To be in a difficult or awkward situation	कठिन या उलझी हुई स्थिति में होना	
755	**Go through fire and water**	To face any danger or difficulty for someone	किसी के लिए हर ख़तरा उठाना	5
756	Go through the roof	To rise very high; to become very angry	बहुत बढ़ जाना; बहुत ग़ुस्सा होना	
757	Go through with a fine-tooth comb	Examining every small detail	बारीकी से जाँच करना	
758	**Go to hell in a handbasket**	To deteriorate rapidly and uncontrollably	तेज़ी से बिगड़ना	1 (2)
759	**Go to rack and ruin**	To be destroyed or fall into disrepair	बर्बाद होना	2

SN	Idioms/Phrases	English Meaning	Hindi Meaning	#R
760	**Go to someone's head**	To make someone arrogant or overconfident	सिर पर चढ़ना (सफलता का घमंड होना)	2
761	Go to the devil	An angry dismissal telling someone to go away	भाड़ में जाओ	
762	**Go to the dogs**	To deteriorate or decline in quality or standards	हालत बदतर होना (पतन होना)	6
763	**Go to the wall**	To fail completely or be ruined financially	दिवालिया हो जाना (पूरी तरह तबाह होना)	1 (1)
764	**Go to the winds**	To be scattered, lost, or disregarded	हवा हो जाना (बर्बाद हो जाना)	2
765	**Go up in smoke**	To be destroyed or ruined completely; to fail	धुआँ हो जाना (बर्बाद हो जाना)	8 (9)
766	Go with the flow	To accept things as they happen without trying to change them	धारा के साथ बहना (हालात के अनुसार ढलना)	
767	God's acre	A churchyard or burial ground	चर्च का क़ब्रिस्तान	
768	**God's ape**	A person who is naturally foolish	पैदाइशी मूर्ख	2 (1)
769	**Go-getter**	An ambitious and determined person	महत्वाकांक्षी व्यक्ति	1 (2)
770	**Golden mean**	A moderate middle course	मध्यम मार्ग (संतुलन का रास्ता)	2
771	**Grease someone's palm**	To bribe someone	हथेली गरम करना (रिश्वत देना)	12 (2)
772	Grease the skids	To clear the way for something	रास्ता साफ करना, काम जल्दी करवाना	
773	Grease the wheels	To make a process or situation run more smoothly	काम आसान बनाना	
774	Greener pastures	A new place or situation that offers better opportunities	बेहतर अवसर	
775	**Green-eyed**	jealous	ईर्ष्या करने वाला	2 (1)
776	**Grin (or beam) from ear to ear**	To smile very widely, showing great happiness	बत्तीसी दिखाना (बहुत बड़ी मुस्कान)	2
777	**Grist to the mill**	Something useful or advantageous	अपने काम की चीज़	1 (1)
778	**Hail from**	To come from or originate from a place	का निवासी होना / से आना	2
779	Hair in the butter	A challenging, delicate, or difficult situation	नाज़ुक परिस्थिति	
780	**Halcyon days**	A very happy and peaceful period in the past	शांति और खुशहाली के दिन	1 (2)
781	**Hale and hearty**	Healthy and strong	तंदुरुस्त	2
782	Half the battle	A major part of the work required to achieve success	आधी जीत	
783	**Hand in (or and) glove**	Working closely together, often for dishonest purposes	मिलीभगत (घनिष्ठ संबंध)	9 (4)
784	**Hand in hand**	Together or in cooperation	साथ-साथ	2
785	**Hand over fist**	Very quickly, especially when making or losing money	बहुत तेज़ी से (ख़ासकर पैसा कमाना या गँवाना)	1 (1)
786	Handle with kid gloves	To treat someone or something very carefully and gently	सावधानी से पेश आना (नाज़ुकी से संभालना)	
787	**Hands down**	Definitely; easily; without a doubt	बिना किसी शक के / आसानी से	2
788	**Hang by a thread (or hair)**	To be in a very precarious or dangerous situation	अधर में लटकना (ख़तरे में होना)	3

SN	Idioms/Phrases	English Meaning	Hindi Meaning	#R
789	Hang fire	To delay making a decision or taking action	मामला लटकाए रखना (देरी करना)	
790	Hang in the balance	To be uncertain or undecided	अनिश्चित स्थिति में होना	
791	Hang in there	To persevere during difficult times	हिम्मत न हारना	
792	Hang on every word	To listen very carefully to everything someone says	एक-एक शब्द ध्यान से सुनना	
793	Hang one's head	To feel or show great shame or embarrassment	सिर झुकना (शर्मिंदा होना)	
794	**Hang up one's boots**	To retire from a sport or a career	संन्यास लेना (काम या खेल से सेवानिवृत्त होना)	3
795	**Hard and fast**	Fixed and strict; not to be changed	सख़्त और अपरिवर्तनीय	5
796	Hard cash	Physical currency; actual money	नक़द पैसा	
797	Hard hit	To be severely affected by something negative	बुरी तरह प्रभावित होना	
798	**Hard of hearing**	Unable to hear well; partially deaf	ऊँचा सुनना (कम सुनाई देना)	2 (1)
799	Hard to come by	Difficult to find or obtain	मुश्किल से मिलना	
800	Hard to swallow	Difficult to believe or accept	गले न उतरना (विश्वास करना कठिन होना)	
801	**Hard up**	To have very little money	तंगी में होना	1 (1)
802	**Harp on**	To talk repeatedly about something in a boring way	एक ही राग अलापना (एक ही बात दोहराते रहना)	1 (1)
803	**Haul over the coals**	To scold or reprimand severely	खरी-खोटी सुना देना (डाँटना)	1 (1)
804	Have a bash	To make an attempt; to try	हाथ आज़माना / कोशिश करना	
805	**Have a blast**	To have a great time; to enjoy very much	मौज-मस्ती करना	2
806	**Have a face like thunder**	To look very angry	चेहरा तमतमाना / ग़ुस्से में होना	2 (1)
807	**Have a finger in every pie**	To be involved in many activities or affairs	कई कामों में शामिल होना	6 (1)
808	Have a good run	To experience a period of success or good fortune	अच्छा समय बीतना	
809	**Have a gut feeling**	To have a strong intuition about something	अंतरात्मा की आवाज़	4
810	Have a heart of stone	To be cruel and unsympathetic	पत्थर दिल होना (निर्दयी होना)	
811	Have a long face	To look unhappy or disappointed	मुँह लटका होना (उदास दिखना)	
812	**Have a lot on one's plate**	To have a lot of things to deal with or worry about	सिर पर बोझ (बहुत सारी ज़िम्मेदारियाँ होना)	3
813	Have a narrow escape	To barely avoid a serious danger or trouble	बाल-बाल बचना	
814	Have a nodding acquaintance	To know someone or something slightly	किसी को हल्का फुल्का जानना	
815	**Have a soft spot for**	To have special affection or fondness for someone	विशेष लगाव होना	2
816	**Have a whale of a time**	To have great fun; to enjoy very much	बहुत मज़ा करना	3 (1)
817	Have a yen for	To have a strong desire or longing for something	तीव्र इच्छा होना	

SN	Idioms/Phrases	English Meaning	Hindi Meaning	#R
818	**Have an axe to grind**	Have a hidden selfish motive	अपना उल्लू सीधा करना (स्वार्थ सिद्ध करना)	12 (12)
819	**Have an iron will**	To have very strong determination	लोहे जैसी इच्छाशक्ति (दृढ़ संकल्प)	4
820	Have an itching palm	To be greedy for money or bribes	हथेली में खुजली होना (रिश्वत का लालची होना)	
821	Have an ox on one's tongue	To be unable to speak freely due to fear or bribery	मुँह न खोल पाना (रिश्वत या डर के कारण चुप रहना)	
822	**Have ants in one's pants**	To be extremely restless or impatient	बहुत बेचैन होना	2
823	Have egg on one's face	To be embarrassed because of something one has done	पानी-पानी हो जाना (अपनी हरकत से शर्मिंदा होना)	
824	Have green fingers	To be skilled at growing plants	बागवानी में निपुण होना	
825	**Have hollow legs**	To be able to eat or drink a lot without showing effects	खाने-पीने की क्षमता बहुत ज़्यादा होना	1 (1)
826	**Have itchy feet**	A strong desire to travel or move to a new place	पाँव में खुजली (घूमने की तीव्र इच्छा होना)	1 (1)
827	**Have one foot in the grave**	Be very old or near death	क़ब्र में पाँव लटके होना (मौत के क़रीब होना)	2 (1)
828	**Have one's back to the wall (or against the wall)**	Be in a difficult situation with limited options	मुश्किल में फँसना	4 (5)
829	**Have one's hands full**	To be very busy with many tasks	बहुत व्यस्त होना	4
830	**Have one's head in the clouds**	To be unrealistic or lost in daydreams	ख़याली पुलाव पकाना (हक़ीक़त से दूर होना)	5 (1)
831	Have one's heart set on	To want something very much	दिल से चाहना	
832	**Have second thoughts**	To reconsider a decision or plan	पुनर्विचार करना (हिचकिचाहट होना)	2 (1)
833	Have someone rolling in the aisles	To make people laugh uncontrollably	हँसा-हँसा कर लोटपोट कर देना	
834	Have someone's back	To be ready to support or defend someone	पीठ थामना (समर्थन करना)	
835	Have something on the brain	To be obsessed with something	धुन सवार होना / जुनून होना	
836	Have something under one's belt	To have already done or experienced something	झोली में होना (अनुभव या उपलब्धि हासिल करना)	
837	Have the ball at one's feet	To be in the best position to succeed	मौक़ा हाथ में होना	
838	**Have the blues**	To feel sad or depressed	मायूस होना (उदासी महसूस करना)	2 (2)
839	**Have the last laugh**	To be ultimately victorious after setbacks	अंत में जीत हासिल करना	3
840	**Have the upper hand**	To have more power or control than someone else	पलड़ा भारी होना (बढ़त में होना)	2 (1)
841	Have two strings to one's bow	Have alternative plans or resources	एक से अधिक विकल्प होना	
842	Have words with	To argue with someone	किसी से बहस करना	
843	**Head and shoulders above**	Significantly better or superior to others	औरों से कहीं बेहतर	2 (5)

SN	Idioms/Phrases	English Meaning	Hindi Meaning	#R
844	**Head over heels**	To fall deeply and completely in love	पूरी तरह प्यार में डूब जाना	4 (3)
845	**Heads will roll**	People will be dismissed or punished	कड़ी सज़ा या बर्ख़ास्तगी होना	2
846	Heap coals of fire on someone's head	Shame someone by being kind after being wronged	दुश्मन को शर्मिंदा करना (बुराई का जवाब भलाई से देना)	
847	**Hear it on the grapevine**	To learn something through gossip or rumour	उड़ती-उड़ती ख़बर सुनना (अफ़वाहों के ज़रिए पता चलना)	1 (1)
848	**Heart and soul**	With complete dedication and commitment	जी-जान से / पूरे मन से	4
849	**Heart in one's mouth**	To be extremely nervous or anxious	कलेजा मुँह को आना (बहुत डरना)	2 (2)
850	**Heart is in the right place**	To have good intentions	दिल का साफ़ होना (नीयत अच्छी होना)	2
851	Hearts go out to	To feel sympathy or compassion for someone	सहानुभूति होना (किसी के दुख में दुखी होना)	
852	**Heave a sigh of relief**	To feel relieved after stress or worry ends	चैन की साँस लेना (राहत महसूस करना)	2
853	**Helter-skelter**	In a disorderly and confused manner	अव्यवस्थित	1 (4)
854	**High and dry**	To abandon someone in a difficult situation	अधर में छोड़ देना (मुसीबत में अकेला या असहाय छोड़ देना)	6 (2)
855	High and low	To search everywhere thoroughly; to look in every possible place	चप्पा-चप्पा छान मारना (हर जगह खोजना)	
856	**High and mighty**	Arrogant, acting superior	घमंडी	2
857	**High time**	The appropriate time, often overdue	सही समय	1 (2)
858	**High-handed**	In an arrogant or domineering manner	घमंड से (दबंगई से)	1 (1)
859	**Hit a bad patch**	To begin experiencing a temporary difficult period	मुश्किल दौर में पड़ना (अस्थायी)	2 (2)
860	**Hit a brick wall**	To encounter an obstacle that is impossible to overcome	किसी बाधा के कारण काम रुक जाना	2
861	Hit a dead end	To reach a point where no further progress is possible	आगे न बढ़ने की स्थिति	
862	**Hit below the belt**	To attack unfairly or dishonestly	अनुचित प्रहार करना (नियमों के विरुद्ध)	7 (7)
863	Hit the big time	To become very successful or famous	बड़े मुक़ाम पर पहुँचना (सफल होना)	
864	**Hit the books**	To study intensively	कड़ी मेहनत से पढ़ाई करना	4 (4)
865	**Hit the ceiling (or roof)**	To become extremely angry	आग-बबूला हो जाना (बहुत अधिक गुस्सा होना)	3 (2)
866	**Hit the ground running**	To start doing something and proceed quickly and successfully	जोश के साथ शुरुआत करना (बिना समय गँवाए काम में जुटना)	2 (3)
867	**Hit the jackpot**	To win a lot of money or have great success	किस्मत का तारा चमकना (अचानक बड़ी कामयाबी या धन मिलना)	4
868	Hit the mark	To achieve the desired result; to be accurate	निशाना सही बैठना (सफल होना)	
869	**Hit the nail on the head**	To say or do something exactly right	सटीक जवाब देना, बिल्कुल सही होना	18 (29)

SN	Idioms/Phrases	English Meaning	Hindi Meaning	#R
870	**Hit the road**	To leave; to start a journey	रवाना होना (यात्रा शुरू करना)	1 (1)
871	**Hit the sack (or hay)**	To go to bed; to sleep	बिस्तर पर जाना (सोने जाना)	17 (19)
872	**Hobson's choice**	A situation in which there appears to be a choice but there is really only one option	मजबूरी का सौदा (विकल्प न होना)	5 (3)
873	Hocus pocus	Words or tricks used to deceive someone; nonsense intended to confuse	जादू-टोना जैसी बातें (धोखा देने वाली बातें)	
874	**Hoist by one's own petard**	To be harmed by something that was intended to harm someone else	अपने ही जाल में फँसना (ख़ुद की खोदी खाई में गिरना)	2
875	**Hold (or stand) one's ground**	To refuse to change your opinion or give way	अपनी बात पर अड़े रहना (पीछे न हटना)	5
876	**Hold a brief for**	To speak in support of someone or something; to advocate for	समर्थन करना (वकालत करना)	2 (1)
877	**Hold good**	To remain true, valid, or applicable	सही साबित होना, मान्य रहना (लागू होना)	2
878	Hold one's head high	To feel proud and confident; to not be ashamed	सिर ऊँचा करके चलना (गर्व महसूस करना)	
879	**Hold one's horses**	To wait and be patient; to slow down	धैर्य रखना (रुको, जल्दबाज़ी मत करो)	12 (7)
880	**Hold one's tongue**	To stay silent; to not say anything even when one wants to	ज़ुबान पर लगाम देना (चुप रहना)	4 (2)
881	**Hold out an olive branch**	To make an offer of peace or reconciliation	शांति का प्रस्ताव (सुलह की पहल)	3 (1)
882	Hold someone's feet to the fire	To pressure someone to fulfil their obligations or commitments	दबाव डालना (ज़िम्मेदारी निभाने को मजबूर करना)	
883	**Hold the fort**	To take care of a place or job temporarily while someone is away	ज़िम्मेदारी सँभालना (अनुपस्थिति में देखभाल करना)	1 (1)
884	Hold the key	To be the crucial factor in achieving something or solving a problem	चाबी हाथ में होना (नियंत्रण या समाधान होना)	
885	**Hold water**	To be sound and valid when examined or tested; to be reasonable	तर्कसंगत होना (बात में दम होना)	4
886	**Hope against hope**	To continue to hope for something even when success seems very unlikely	नाउम्मीदी में भी उम्मीद रखना (असंभव उम्मीद)	2
887	Horse sense	Basic common sense and practical judgment	व्यावहारिक ज्ञान (सामान्य बुद्धि)	
888	**Horses for courses**	The idea that different people or things are suitable for different situations	योग्यता के अनुसार काम (विशेषज्ञता की क़द्र)	2
889	**Hot potato**	A subject or problem that is difficult and controversial to deal with	ज्वलंत मुद्दा (पेचीदा मामला जिससे लोग बचना चाहें)	3 (3)
890	Hot under the collar	Feeling angry or annoyed	गुस्से में (नाराज़)	
891	**House of cards**	An organization or plan that is very weak and can easily be destroyed	ताश का महल (अत्यंत अस्थिर ढाँचा)	3 (1)
892	**Hue and cry**	A loud noise or expression of anger or protest from a group of people	शोर-गुल (विरोध में)	4 (3)
893	Huff and puff	To breathe heavily or show anger	हाँफना; गुस्सा दिखाना	

SN	Idioms/Phrases	English Meaning	Hindi Meaning	#R
894	Husband one's resources	To use money, time, or resources carefully and economically	संसाधनों की बचत करना (किफ़ायत से इस्तेमाल करना)	
895	**Icing on the cake**	Something extra that makes a good thing even better	सोने पे सुहागा (अतिरिक्त ख़ुशी या लाभ)	5 (4)
896	If it's not one thing, it's another	Used to say that there is always something going wrong	एक मुसीबत ख़त्म नहीं हुई कि दूसरी शुरू (परेशानियों का सिलसिला)	
897	**Ill at ease**	Feeling anxious or embarrassed; not comfortable	असहज महसूस करना (बेचैनी होना)	4 (2)
898	I'll eat my hat	Expression of certainty something won't happen	अविश्वास दिखाना (चुनौती देना कि ऐसा नहीं होगा)	
899	**In a fix**	In a difficult situation that is hard to escape from	मुश्किल में फँसा होना	3 (2)
900	In a flutter	In a state of nervous excitement or agitation	घबराहट में (उत्तेजित अवस्था)	
901	In a fog	In a state of confusion; unable to think clearly	दिमाग़ सुन्न होना (भ्रम में होना)	
902	**In a jiffy**	Very quickly; in a very short time	पलक झपकते ही / फ़ौरन	1 (4)
903	**In a nutshell**	In a very few words; briefly	निचोड़ बताना (संक्षेप में)	13 (3)
904	**In a pickle**	In a difficult or confusing situation	मुसीबत में फँसना (पेचीदा स्थिति)	4
905	In a quandary	In a state of uncertainty or confusion about what to do	दुविधा में होना (असमंजस में)	
906	**In a tight corner (or spot)**	In a difficult situation that is hard to escape from	मुश्किल हालात में फँसा होना (कोने में दबा होना)	5 (1)
907	In a time warp	In a state where things have not changed from the past	समय के साथ न बदलना	
908	**In apple-pie order**	In perfect order; very neat and tidy	पूरी तरह व्यवस्थित (एकदम सुव्यवस्थित)	5 (3)
909	In bad taste	Offensive; likely to upset or annoy people	अपमानजनक (बुरा लगने वाला)	
910	In bits and pieces	In many small parts; not complete	टुकड़ों में (थोड़ा-थोड़ा करके)	
911	**In black and white**	In writing; in a form that provides clear proof	लिखित रूप में (काले-सफ़ेद में)	10 (1)
912	**In cahoots with**	Working together secretly, often for dishonest purposes	साँठ-गाँठ में (मिलीभगत में)	2
913	In character	Typical of someone's usual way of behaving	स्वभाव के अनुसार (उम्मीद के मुताबिक़)	
914	**In cold blood**	In a planned way and without showing any emotion	ठंडे दिमाग़ से (सोच-समझकर किया गया)	5
915	**In deep water**	In serious trouble or difficulty	बड़ी मुश्किल में (गहरे संकट में)	4 (1)
916	**In dire straits**	In a very bad or difficult situation, especially financial	अत्यंत कठिन स्थिति में (भयंकर संकट में)	4 (1)
917	In dribs and drabs	In small amounts over a period of time	थोड़ा-थोड़ा करके (रिसते हुए)	
918	In Dutch with	In trouble or disfavour with someone	किसी की नज़रों में गिरा होना (किसी की नाराज़गी या मुसीबत में होना)	

SN	Idioms/Phrases	English Meaning	Hindi Meaning	#R
919	In force	Currently valid or operating; or in large numbers	लागू; बड़ी संख्या में (प्रभावी)	
920	**In full swing**	At the most active or busiest stage	पूरे ज़ोरों से (चरम पर)	3
921	In harmony with	In agreement with; in a way that combines well with	तालमेल में होना (सहमति में)	
922	In harness	Doing one's regular work; or working together with someone	काम में जुटना (अपनी दिनचर्या या ड्यूटी पर होना)	
923	**In high (or good) spirits**	Very cheerful and happy	उत्साह से भरा (ख़ुशनुमा मिज़ाज में)	7 (4)
924	In high dudgeon	In a state of strong anger or resentment	भारी गुस्से में (नाराज़गी में)	
925	**In hot water**	In a situation where you are likely to be punished or criticized	मुसीबत में फँसना (ग़लती की वजह से परेशानी में)	13 (10)
926	In lieu of	Instead of; in place of	के स्थान पर (के बदले में)	
927	In light of	Considering; because of; taking into account	के मद्देनज़र (को ध्यान में रखते हुए)	
928	In limbo	In an uncertain or undecided state	अधर में लटकना (अनिश्चितता की स्थिति)	
929	In line with	In agreement with; similar to	के अनुरूप (के अनुसार)	
930	In love with the sound of one's own voice	To enjoy talking too much, often boring others	बस अपनी ही सुनाना (बहुत बोलने वाला)	
931	**In low spirits**	Feeling sad or depressed; not cheerful	उत्साहहीन (उदास या निराश)	2 (1)
932	In ones and twos	In small groups of one or two people at a time	एक-दो करके (धीरे-धीरे थोड़े-थोड़े)	
933	In one's birthday suit	Wearing no clothes; naked	नग्न (जन्मदिन की पोशाक में = बिल्कुल नंगा)	
934	In queer street	In financial difficulty or debt	क़र्ज़ के बोझ तले (तंगहाली में)	
935	In raptures	Feeling extreme pleasure or enthusiasm	गदगद होना (अत्यधिक प्रसन्न)	
936	**In seventh heaven**	Extremely happy; in a state of great joy	सातवें आसमान पर (बेहद ख़ुश)	5 (4)
937	**In someone's good books**	In favour with someone; approved of by someone	किसी की नज़रों में अच्छा होना (पक्ष में होना)	3 (1)
938	In someone's shoes	In another person's situation, experiencing what they experience	किसी की जगह होना (दूसरे की परिस्थिति को समझना)	
939	**In stitches**	Laughing a lot; very amused	हँसते-हँसते लोटपोट होना (बहुत हँसना)	1 (1)
940	**In the air**	Felt by people to be happening or about to happen	हवा में होना (चर्चा या अनुभूति)	4
941	In the ascendant	Becoming more powerful or popular	सितारा बुलंद होना (शक्ति या प्रसिद्धि में वृद्धि)	
942	**In the blink (or twinkling) of an eye**	Very quickly; almost instantly	पलक झपकते ही (क्षण भर में)	3 (1)
943	**In the dark**	Not knowing about something that other people know	अंधेरे में होना (अनजान रहना)	3 (2)
944	**In the doldrums**	In a state of inactivity, stagnation, or depression	उदास अवस्था में (निष्क्रियता की स्थिति)	5 (1)

SN	Idioms/Phrases	English Meaning	Hindi Meaning	#R
945	**In the driver's seat**	In control of a situation	बागडोर हाथ में होना (पूरी तरह नियंत्रण में)	2 (2)
946	In the egg	At a very early stage of development	प्रारंभिक अवस्था में (शुरुआती दौर)	
947	**In the eye of the storm**	At the centre of a difficult, controversial, or violent situation	मुसीबत के घेरे में (विवादों के बीच होना)	4
948	In the flesh	Physically present; in person	व्यक्तिगत रूप से उपस्थित (सामने होना)	
949	In the fullness of time	Eventually; when the appropriate time comes	समय आने पर; उचित समय पर	
950	**In the groove**	Performing well and with confidence; in a good rhythm	सामंजस्य में होना (लय में होना)	2 (1)
951	**In the heat of the moment**	While feeling very angry or excited, without thinking clearly	आवेश में आकर (बिना सोचे-समझे)	4 (4)
952	**In the limelight**	Receiving a lot of public attention	सुर्ख़ियों में होना (चर्चा का केंद्र)	3
953	**In the long run**	Over a long period of time in the future; eventually	अंततः (लंबे समय में)	7 (1)
954	In the long term	Over a long period of time; relating to the distant future	लंबे समय में (भविष्य में)	
955	**In the nick of time**	At the last possible moment; just in time	ठीक समय पर (बिल्कुल आख़िरी मौक़े पर)	7 (5)
956	In the offing	Likely to happen or appear soon	संभावित (निकट भविष्य में होने वाला)	
957	**In the pink (of health)**	In excellent health condition	तंदुरुस्त (एकदम स्वस्थ)	2 (2)
958	**In the red**	In debt; owing money; operating at a loss	लाल स्याही में होना (घाटे या कर्ज में होना)	5 (3)
959	In the running	Having a chance of winning or being successful	प्रतियोगिता में शामिल (दौड़ में होना)	
960	**In the same boat**	In the same difficult or unpleasant situation as someone else	एक ही नाव में सवार होना (समान मुसीबत में होना)	12 (7)
961	**In the same breath**	To say two contradictory things at the same time	एक ही समय में दो विरोधी बातें कहना (एक साँस में)	2
962	**In the soup**	In trouble or difficulty	मुसीबत में (फँसा हुआ)	3 (1)
963	In the strictest confidence	In complete secrecy	पूर्ण गोपनीयता से	
964	In the swim	Involved in and aware of what is happening	मुख्यधारा में होना (पूरी तरह सूचित रहना)	
965	**In the teeth of**	In spite of; directly against	कड़े विरोध के बावजूद (सामना करते हुए)	3
966	**In two minds**	Unable to decide between two choices; uncertain	दोराहे पर होना (तय न कर पाना)	5
967	**In vogue**	Currently popular or fashionable	प्रचलन में (फ़ैशन में)	3
968	**Ins and outs**	All the details and complications of something	पूरा विवरण (भीतर की सारी बातें)	8 (4)
969	**Iron fist**	Harsh or ruthless control	सख़्त नियंत्रण	4
970	It goes without saying	Something is so obvious that it does not need to be mentioned	कहने की ज़रूरत नहीं (स्वतः स्पष्ट होना)	

SN	Idioms/Phrases	English Meaning	Hindi Meaning	#R
971	**It's a small world**	Used to express surprise when you meet someone you know in an unexpected place	दुनिया बहुत छोटी है (अचानक मुलाक़ात होने पर)	3
972	**It's all Greek to me (or Latin and Greek)**	Something that is completely incomprehensible	सर के ऊपर से जाना (समझ से बिल्कुल परे)	8 (6)
973	It's all in one's head	Something exists only in one's imagination; not real	मन का वहम होना (केवल कल्पना में मौजूद)	
974	**It's not rocket science**	Something that is not very difficult to do or understand	कोई बहुत बड़ी बात नहीं (आसान काम होना)	1 (1)
975	**Ivory tower**	A place or situation where someone is protected from ordinary life and problems	वास्तविकता से कोसों दूर (हक़ीक़त से अनजान रहना)	3 (3)
976	Jack up the rates	To increase prices or rates suddenly and significantly	दाम बढ़ा देना	
977	**Jaundiced eye**	A critical or negative way of looking at something, often due to bitterness	पक्षपाती नज़रिया (कड़वाहट भरी दृष्टि)	3
978	Jockey for position	To compete for a favourable position	बेहतर स्थिति के लिए प्रतिस्पर्धा करना	
979	Jog someone's memory	To remind someone of something they may have forgotten	याद ताज़ा करना (स्मृति जगाना)	
980	Jump at the opportunity (or chance)	To eagerly accept an opportunity when it is offered	मौक़े पर चौका मारना (अवसर को तुरंत पकड़ना)	
981	Jump down someone's throat	To react to someone in a very angry and critical way	फटकारना (बिना बात ग़ुस्सा करना)	
982	Jump in with both feet	To become completely involved in something without hesitation	पूरे जोश से कूद पड़ना (बिना हिचक पूरी तरह शामिल होना)	
983	**Jump on the bandwagon**	To join an activity, trend, or opinion that has become popular	बहती गंगा में हाथ धोना (लोकप्रिय चलन का हिस्सा बनना)	9 (7)
984	Jump out of one's skin	To be extremely surprised or frightened	उछल पड़ना (बहुत चौंकना)	
985	**Jump the gun**	To start something before the right time; to act prematurely	जल्दबाज़ी करना (वक़्त से पहले क़दम उठाना)	7 (12)
986	**Jump the shark**	To reach a point where the quality of something begins to decline, often noticeably	चरम के बाद गिरावट (लोकप्रियता घटना)	1 (1)
987	**Jump through hoops**	To do many difficult things in order to get what you want	बहुत पापड़ बेलना (जी-तोड़ कोशिश करना)	2 (1)
988	Jury is out	It is not yet decided; opinions are divided	अभी फ़ैसला होना बाकी है (अनिर्णीत)	
989	Kangaroo court	An unofficial court that makes unfair judgments without proper legal procedure	अवैध या फ़र्ज़ी अदालत (न्याय का मज़ाक़)	
990	**Keep (or hold) at bay**	To prevent something or someone from coming too near or becoming a problem	दूर रखना (रोके रखना)	4 (2)
991	**Keep (or put) one's nose to the grindstone**	To continue to work hard, especially at something difficult or boring	कोल्हू का बैल बनना (कड़ी मेहनत में जुटे रहना)	2

SN	Idioms/Phrases	English Meaning	Hindi Meaning	#R
992	Keep a civil tongue in one's head	To speak politely, especially when angry or upset	ज़ुबान पर लगाम रखना (शालीनता से बात करना)	
993	**Keep a good table**	To provide good food regularly, especially when entertaining guests	अच्छा भोजन परोसना (मेहमानों को बढ़िया खाना खिलाना)	2 (1)
994	**Keep a level head**	To stay calm and make sensible decisions in a difficult situation	ठंडा दिमाग़ रखना (समझदारी और धैर्य दिखाना)	2
995	**Keep a low profile**	To avoid attracting attention; to behave quietly	ध्यान आकर्षित न करना (चुपचाप रहना)	2
996	**Keep a stiff upper lip**	To not show emotion or complain when facing difficulty	भावनाओं पर क़ाबू रखना (दुख प्रकट न करना)	2
997	**Keep a straight face**	To not laugh or smile when you want to	गंभीर बने रहना (हँसी रोककर चेहरा सीधा रखना)	3 (1)
998	Keep a weather eye open (or out)	To stay alert or watchful	चौकन्ना रहना, सतर्क रहना	
999	Keep abreast of	To stay informed about the latest developments	ताज़ा जानकारी से अवगत रहना (जानकारी रखना)	
1000	**Keep an ear to the ground**	To stay alert and well-informed about what is happening around	कान खुले रखना (हर गतिविधि पर नज़र रखना)	4 (3)
1001	**Keep an eye on**	To watch or monitor someone or something carefully	नज़र रखना (निगरानी करना)	6 (4)
1002	Keep an open house	To be ready to welcome visitors at any time	सबका स्वागत करना (खुले दिल का होना)	
1003	**Keep at arm's length**	To avoid becoming too friendly or close with someone	दूर से सलाम करना (दूरी बनाए रखना)	11 (2)
1004	**Keep body and soul together**	To have just enough money to survive; to stay alive	पेट पालना (किसी तरह गुज़ारा करना)	4
1005	Keep count of	To remember or record the total number of something	हिसाब रखना (गिनती याद रखना)	
1006	**Keep in abeyance**	To delay or suspend something temporarily	ठंडे बस्ते में रखना (टालना)	1 (1)
1007	Keep in check	To control something and prevent it from increasing or spreading	नियंत्रण में रखना (क़ाबू में रखना)	
1008	**Keep in touch**	To continue to communicate with someone, especially by phone, letter, or email	संपर्क में रहना (मेल-जोल बनाए रखना)	2
1009	**Keep on a leash**	To control something tightly	नियंत्रण में रखना	1 (1)
1010	**Keep one's cards close to one's chest**	To keep one's plans or ideas secret	पत्ते न खोलना (अपनी योजना गुप्त रखना)	1 (3)
1011	**Keep one's chin up**	To stay positive and hopeful in a difficult time	हिम्मत न हारना (हौसला बनाए रखना)	4 (3)
1012	**Keep one's head**	To remain calm and act sensibly in a difficult situation	धीरज न खोना (शांत दिमाग़ से सोचना)	4
1013	Keep one's head above water	To just manage to survive or continue, especially financially	डूबने से बचना (किसी तरह गुज़ारा करना)	
1014	Keep one's shirt on	To stay calm and not become angry or impatient	धैर्य रखना (उत्तेजित न होना)	

SN	Idioms/Phrases	English Meaning	Hindi Meaning	#R
1015	**Keep one's temper**	To manage not to become angry despite being provoked	ग़ुस्से पर क़ाबू पाना (आपा न खोना)	1 (1)
1016	Keep one's wig on	To remain calm and not get angry or impatient	शांत होना (ग़ुस्सा न करना)	
1017	Keep one's word	To do what you promised or said you would do	वादा निभाना (ज़ुबान का पक्का होना)	
1018	Keep pace	To move at the same speed	कदम से कदम मिलाना (बराबर चलना)	
1019	**Keep someone in the loop**	Aware of and involved in what is happening	सूचित रखना (जानकारी साझा करना)	2
1020	Keep someone on a string	To control someone while keeping them uncertain	किसी को अधर में लटकाए रखना	
1021	Keep someone posted	To continue to give someone the latest information about something	ताज़ा जानकारी देते रहना (ख़बर देते रहना)	
1022	**Keep something under one's hat**	To keep something secret; to not tell anyone about something	मुँह में ताला लगाना (राज़ अपने तक रखना)	2 (1)
1023	**Keep the ball rolling**	To maintain the momentum of an activity; to keep something going	काम जारी रखना (सिलसिला चलाए रखना)	3
1024	**Keep the wolf from the door**	To have just enough money to buy food and other essentials; to avoid poverty	गरीबी या भुखमरी से बचना (किसी तरह गुज़ारा करना)	10
1025	**Keep up appearances**	To hide problems and seem successful or fine to others	दिखावा करना (ऊपरी बनावट रखना)	3
1026	**Keep up with the Joneses**	To try to match others in wealth, lifestyle, or status	दूसरों की बराबरी करना (पड़ोसियों जैसा बनने की कोशिश)	2
1027	Keep your pants (or shirt) on	To be patient and not become anxious or angry; used to tell someone to calm down	धीरज रखो (जल्दबाज़ी मत करो)	
1028	Kick one's heels	To wait somewhere with nothing to do; to be kept waiting	हाथ पर हाथ धरे बैठना (इंतज़ार में समय गँवाना)	
1029	Kick someone when they are down	To make things worse for someone who is already having problems	गिरते को लात मारना (मुसीबत में और परेशान करना)	
1030	**Kick the bucket**	To die	दम तोड़ना (मर जाना)	7 (7)
1031	**Kick up a fuss (or make a fuss)**	To complain loudly or cause a disturbance about something	हंगामा खड़ा करना (बवाल करना)	7
1032	**Kill two birds with one stone**	To accomplish two goals with one effort or action	एक तीर से दो शिकार (एक ही प्रयास में दो लक्ष्य हासिल करना)	9 (2)
1033	**Kith and kin**	One's friends and relatives	सगे-संबंधी (नाते-रिश्तेदार)	2 (1)
1034	Kitty-corner	Positioned diagonally across from something	तिरछा / कोने के सामने	
1035	**Knock on wood (or touch wood)**	Said when you hope for good luck or to avoid jinxing yourself	नज़र न लगे कहकर अपशकुन टालना (लकड़ी को छूना)	1 (1)
1036	Know how many beans make five	To be sensible and have good practical judgment; to not be easily deceived	अक्लमंद होना (दुनियादारी की समझ होना)	
1037	**Know something inside out**	To know something very thoroughly; to be completely familiar with something	रग-रग से वाकिफ़ होना (पूरी जानकारी होना)	2

SN	Idioms/Phrases	English Meaning	Hindi Meaning	#R
1038	Know something like the back of one's hand	To know a place or subject very well	चप्पे-चप्पे से वाकिफ़ होना (पूरी तरह परिचित होना)	
1039	Know what's what	To have good judgment and understanding of things; to know what is important	असली स्थिति को समझना (भले-बुरे की पहचान होना)	
1040	**Know where the shoe pinches**	The cause of difficulty that only the affected person knows	जहाँ जूता काटता है (समस्या की जड़)	3
1041	**Know which way the wind blows**	To understand how a situation is likely to develop or what people are likely to do	हवा का रुख पहचानना (परिस्थिति को समझना)	2 (1)
1042	**Lame excuse**	An excuse that is not convincing or believable	कमज़ोर बहाना (झूठा या अविश्वसनीय बहाना)	2
1043	Land a job	To succeed in getting a job, especially a good one	नौकरी मिलना (नौकरी हासिल करना)	
1044	Large-hearted	Generous, kind, and forgiving	दरियादिल (बड़े दिल वाला)	
1045	Last but not least	Last in order but not in importance	क्रम में अंतिम, पर कम महत्वपूर्ण नहीं	
1046	**Last resort**	The final option when all other plans fail	आख़िरी उपाय	2
1047	**Last straw**	The last in a series of problems that finally causes a reaction	सब्र का आख़िरी प्याला (बर्दाश्त की सीमा)	9 (5)
1048	Late in the day	Too late to be useful or to change a situation	बहुत देर हो जाना (जब सुधार की गुंजाइश न बचे)	
1049	Laugh like a drain	To laugh loudly and uninhibitedly	ज़ोर से हंसना	
1050	Lay down one's arms	To surrender; to stop fighting	हथियार डाल देना (आत्मसमर्पण करना)	
1051	Lay hands on	To find, catch, or touch someone	हाथ लगाना	
1052	Lay it on thick	To exaggerate greatly	नमक-मिर्च लगाकर बोलना (बढ़ा-चढ़ाकर कहना)	
1053	Lay one's cards on the table	To be honest and open about your intentions or feelings	खुलकर बात करना (ईमानदार होना)	
1054	Lay someone by the heels	To capture or imprison someone	क़ैद करना / पकड़ लेना	
1055	Lead astray	To guide someone into bad behaviour	गुमराह करना (ग़लत रास्ते पर ले जाना)	
1056	**Lead someone by the nose**	To control someone completely	नकेल हाथ में होना (पूरी तरह नियंत्रित करना)	3 (1)
1057	Lean and mean	Efficient, competitive, and ready for action	फुर्तीला और असरदार	
1058	**Learn (or know) the ropes**	To learn how a particular job or activity is done	काम के तौर-तरीक़े सीखना (अनुभव प्राप्त करना)	6 (4)
1059	Learn by heart	To memorize something so that you can remember it exactly	मुँह ज़बानी याद करना (कंठस्थ करना)	
1060	**Leave no stone unturned**	To do everything possible to find something or achieve something	आकाश-पाताल एक करना (कोई कसर न छोड़ना)	15 (7)

SN	Idioms/Phrases	English Meaning	Hindi Meaning	#R
1061	**Leave someone in the lurch**	To leave someone alone when they need help; to abandon someone in a difficult situation	मँझधार में छोड़ देना (मुसीबत में अकेला छोड़ना)	11 (5)
1062	**Leave someone out in the cold**	To ignore someone or exclude them from a group or activity	नज़रअंदाज़ करना (अलग-थलग कर देना)	4 (3)
1063	Left, right and centre	Everywhere; in all directions; on all sides	हर जगह (चारों ओर)	
1064	**Lend a hand**	To help someone do something	हाथ बँटाना (मदद करना)	1 (1)
1065	**Lend an ear**	To listen carefully to what someone is saying	कान लगाकर सुनना (ध्यान से सुनना)	5 (1)
1066	Lesser of two evils	The less harmful of two unpleasant choices	दो बुराइयों में छोटी बुराई (तुलनात्मक रूप से बेहतर विकल्प)	
1067	**Let (or blow) off steam**	To release built-up energy, emotions, or frustration	भड़ास निकालना (ग़ुस्सा या तनाव कम करना)	1 (3)
1068	Let fly at	To attack or criticize harshly	ज़ोरदार हमला या आलोचना करना	
1069	**Let off the hook**	No longer in trouble or no longer having to deal with a problem	झंझट से छुटकारा (मुसीबत से बचना)	3 (1)
1070	**Let one's hair down**	To relax and behave in an informal or uninhibited way	बेफ़िक्र होकर मौज करना (खुलकर मज़े करना)	3
1071	**Let something slip through one's fingers**	To fail to take advantage of an opportunity; to lose something carelessly	हाथ आया मौक़ा गँवाना (अवसर खो देना)	1 (1)
1072	**Let the cat out of the bag**	To reveal a secret by mistake	ग़लती से राज़ उजागर करना (भेद खोल देना)	14 (22)
1073	**Let the chips fall where they may**	To allow events to happen without trying to control the outcome	राम भरोसे छोड़ना (जो होगा देखा जाएगा)	1 (1)
1074	Let the dust settle	To wait for a situation to become calmer or clearer before taking action	स्थितियों के सामान्य होने का इंतज़ार करना (शांति लौटने देना)	
1075	**Let the grass grow under one's feet**	To delay taking action; to waste time instead of acting	हाथ पर हाथ धरकर बैठना (निष्क्रिय रहना)	3
1076	**Level playing field**	A situation where everyone has an equal chance of succeeding	समान अवसर की स्थिति (बराबरी का मुक़ाबला)	3 (1)
1077	Lick into shape	To bring into proper condition	ठीक हालत में लाना	
1078	Lick one's wounds	To spend time recovering after a defeat or disappointment	घाव चाटना (हार से उबरना)	
1079	Lie low	To hide or stay somewhere quietly to avoid being found or noticed	छिपे रहना (नज़रों से दूर रहना)	
1080	**Life and soul of the party**	The most lively and entertaining person at a social event	महफ़िल की जान (पार्टी को रंगीन बनाने वाला)	1 (1)
1081	**Life in the fast lane**	An exciting but often stressful lifestyle full of activity	भागदौड़ और रोमांच भरा जीवन (तेज़ रफ़्तार ज़िंदगी)	3 (1)
1082	Life is a bowl of cherries	Life is pleasant and enjoyable	ज़िंदगी बड़ी आसान है (व्यंग्य में)	
1083	**Light at the end of the tunnel**	A sign that a difficult or unpleasant situation is about to end	आशा की किरण (मुश्किल के बाद उम्मीद)	2 (2)
1084	**Light years away**	Very far away in distance, time, or progress	बहुत दूर होना (कोसों दूर)	1 (1)

SN	Idioms/Phrases	English Meaning	Hindi Meaning	#R
1085	Like a bat out of hell	Extremely fast; at great speed	बहुत तेज़ी से (बेतहाशा भागना)	
1086	**Like a cat on a hot tin roof (or bricks)**	Very nervous or restless	बहुत बेचैन	2 (2)
1087	**Like a red rag to a bull**	Something that makes someone very angry	साँड को लाल कपड़ा दिखाना (मुसीबत को न्योता देना)	2 (1)
1088	**Like a shag on a rock**	Completely alone and without help	बिल्कुल अकेला (असहाय स्थिति में)	1 (1)
1089	Like nailing jelly to a wall	Trying to do something that is practically impossible	असंभव काम की कोशिश (बेकार का प्रयास)	
1090	**Like oil and water**	Two things or people that do not go well together	तेल और पानी की तरह (असंगत होना)	1 (1)
1091	Like pulling teeth	Very difficult and requiring a lot of effort	नाकों चने चबाना (बेहद मुश्किल काम)	
1092	Like shooting fish in a barrel	To do something that is very easy	बच्चों का खेल (बेहद आसान काम)	
1093	Like talking to a brick wall	Speaking to someone who ignores everything you say	दीवार से बात करना (जो सुने ही नहीं)	
1094	**Like two peas in a pod**	Very similar to each other	एक ही थाली के चट्टे-बट्टे (एक जैसे)	4 (4)
1095	**Lily-livered**	Cowardly; lacking courage	कायर (डरपोक, बुज़दिल)	1 (1)
1096	**Lion's den**	A very dangerous or risky situation	मौत के मुँह में जाना (ख़तरनाक स्थिति में पड़ना)	1 (1)
1097	Little by little	Gradually; in small steps or amounts	धीरे-धीरे (क्रमशः)	
1098	**Live hand to mouth**	To have only just enough money to live on and nothing extra	मुश्किल से गुज़ारा करना (जितना कमाना उतना खाना)	6 (2)
1099	Live high on the hog	To live in luxury or extravagance	ऐश-ओ-आराम से रहना (विलासितापूर्ण जीवन)	
1100	**Live wire**	A lively, energetic, and enthusiastic person	ज़िंदादिल व्यक्ति (चुस्त-फुर्तीला इंसान)	3 (1)
1101	Loaded language	Language deliberately used to provoke strong feelings	भावनाएँ भड़काने वाली भाषा	
1102	**Loaves and fishes**	Personal material gain or benefits	भौतिक लाभ (स्वार्थ की पूर्ति)	2 (2)
1103	**Lock horns**	To have an argument or fight with someone	सींग फँसाना (झगड़ा करना या भिड़ जाना)	1 (1)
1104	**Lock, stock and barrel**	Including everything; entirely	पूरी तरह से (सब कुछ मिलाकर)	1 (2)
1105	**Long in the tooth**	Getting old	उम्रदराज़ होना (बूढ़ा होना)	2 (1)
1106	Long shot	An attempt or guess that is unlikely to succeed but worth trying	सफलता की कम संभावना (दूर की कौड़ी)	
1107	Look black	To appear threatening or gloomy; when the situation looks bad	संकट के बादल दिखना (स्थितियाँ चिंताजनक होना)	
1108	Look blue	To appear sad or unhappy	उदास दिखना (मायूस लगना)	
1109	Look down one's nose	To regard someone or something as inferior; to show contempt	नाक-भौं सिकोड़ना (तुच्छ या निम्न समझना)	

SN	Idioms/Phrases	English Meaning	Hindi Meaning	#R
1110	Look forward to	To feel excited and pleased about something that is going to happen	बेसब्री से इंतज़ार करना (खुशी के साथ प्रतीक्षा करना)	
1111	**Look sharp**	To hurry up; to be quick and alert	मुस्तैद रहना (सतर्क रहना)	2
1112	**Loose cannon**	A person who behaves unpredictably and may cause problems	बेक़ाबू व्यक्ति (खतरनाक और अनियंत्रित व्यक्ति)	1 (2)
1113	Loosen the apron strings	To give someone more freedom	नियंत्रण ढीला करना (आज़ादी देना)	
1114	**Loosen the purse strings**	To become more willing to spend money or give money	जेब ढीली करना (ख़र्च बढ़ाना)	3
1115	Lose by a neck	To lose by a very small margin	बहुत कम अंतर से हारना	
1116	Lose count of	To fail to remember the total number of something	गिनती भूलना (याद न रहना कितने थे)	
1117	**Lose face**	To be less respected or look stupid because of something you have done	नज़रों से गिरना (शर्मिंदा होना)	1 (2)
1118	**Lose ground**	To become less successful or powerful; to lose an advantage	पिछड़ जाना / अपनी स्थिति खोना	4
1119	**Lose heart**	To stop believing that you can succeed	हिम्मत हारना (निराश हो जाना)	1 (1)
1120	**Lose one's head**	To become unable to think clearly or act sensibly	आपा खोना (समझ-बूझ खो बैठना)	4 (2)
1121	**Lose one's marbles**	To become crazy or act very strangely	पागल होना (दिमाग़ ख़राब होना)	4 (3)
1122	**Lose one's temper**	To become very angry	आपा खोना (ग़ुस्सा होना)	2
1123	Lose one's touch	To lose the ability or skill to do something well	पहले जैसी कुशलता न रहना (हाथ का हुनर जाता रहना)	
1124	**Mad as a hatter**	Completely crazy or eccentric	पूरी तरह सनकी या पागल (पूर्णतः पागल)	3
1125	Made out of whole cloth	Completely invented or made up; not based on fact	मनगढ़ंत (पूरी तरह झूठा और काल्पनिक)	
1126	Magic (or silver) bullet	A simple solution to a complicated problem	रामबाण इलाज (जटिल समस्या का सरल समाधान)	
1127	**Maiden speech**	The first speech made by someone	पहला भाषण	6
1128	**Make a beeline for**	To go quickly and directly toward something or someone	बिना रुके किसी चीज़ की ओर जाना (सीधे पहुँचना)	6 (1)
1129	**Make a clean breast of**	To confess everything honestly	अपराध स्वीकार करना (साफ़-साफ़ इक़रार करना)	5 (1)
1130	Make a comeback	To return to a successful position after a period of being unsuccessful	वापसी करना (फिर से सफल होना)	
1131	Make a dent in	To make progress in something; to reduce an amount noticeably	कुछ असर डालना; कमी लाना	
1132	Make a fool of oneself	To do something that makes you look silly or stupid	हँसी का पात्र बनना (बेवकूफ़ी भरी हरकत करना)	
1133	Make a fortune	To earn a very large amount of money	मालामाल होना (बहुत धन कमाना)	
1134	**Make a hash of**	To do something very badly; to ruin something	कबाड़ा करना (काम बिगाड़ देना)	2 (1)
1135	Make a living	To earn enough money to support yourself	रोज़ी-रोटी कमाना (जीविका चलाना)	

SN	Idioms/Phrases	English Meaning	Hindi Meaning	#R
1136	Make a mockery of	To make something appear ridiculous or worthless	मज़ाक़ बना देना (उपहास करना)	
1137	**Make a mountain out of a molehill**	To make a small problem seem much bigger than it actually is	राई का पहाड़ बनाना (छोटी सी बात को बड़ा बनाना)	4
1138	**Make a pig's ear of something**	To do something very badly	बुरी तरह बिगाड़ देना (गड़बड़ कर देना)	1 (1)
1139	Make a pile	To earn a large amount of money	मालामाल होना (ढेर सारा पैसा कमाना)	
1140	**Make a quick buck**	To earn money quickly, often in a dishonest or careless way	दो नंबर से या जल्दी पैसा कमाना (आसान पैसा)	2
1141	**Make a scapegoat of**	To blame someone unfairly for something that is not their fault	बलि का बकरा बनाना (दूसरों के दोष के लिए किसी को दंडित करना)	3
1142	Make a scene	To cause a public disturbance by expressing strong emotion, especially anger	तमाशा खड़ा करना (सार्वजनिक स्थान पर चिल्लाना या हंगामा करना)	
1143	Make a splash	To attract a lot of attention, especially by being successful	धूम मचाना (सबका ध्यान आकर्षित करना)	
1144	Make a wry face	To twist your face to show disappointment, disgust, or amusement	मुँह बनाना (असंतोष प्रकट करना)	
1145	**Make amends**	To do something to correct a mistake that you have made or bad behaviour	प्रायश्चित करना (भरपाई करना)	3
1146	Make an ass of oneself	To behave stupidly and make yourself look foolish	मूर्खता करना (बेवकूफ़ बनना)	
1147	**Make both ends meet**	To have just enough money to pay for basic needs	किसी तरह से गुज़ारा करना (आमदनी में ख़र्च पूरा करना)	6 (1)
1148	**Make bricks without straw**	To try to do something without the necessary resources	बिना संसाधन काम करना (असंभव प्रयास करना)	1 (1)
1149	Make fun of	To mock or ridicule	मज़ाक उड़ाना	
1150	**Make head or tail of**	To understand something	समझना	3 (1)
1151	Make it big	To become very successful or famous	बड़ा आदमी बनना (बड़ी कामयाबी पाना)	
1152	**Make light of**	To treat something as if it is not important or serious	हल्के में लेना (गंभीरता से न लेना)	2 (1)
1153	Make matters worse	To make a bad situation even worse	मामला और बिगाड़ना (स्थिति और ख़राब करना)	
1154	Make merry	To enjoy yourself by eating, drinking, and having fun	मौज-मस्ती करना (जश्न मनाना)	
1155	**Make no bones about**	To say or do something openly without hesitation	साफ़-साफ़ कहना (बिना झिझक स्पष्ट बोलना)	5 (3)
1156	Make no headway	To fail to make any progress toward a goal	प्रगति न करना (आगे न बढ़ना)	
1157	**Make one's flesh crawl (or creep)**	To make someone feel very frightened or disgusted	रोंगटे खड़े कर देना (घृणा या डर से सिहर उठना)	3
1158	**Make one's blood boil**	To make someone extremely angry	ख़ून खौलना (बहुत गुस्सा आना)	4 (1)

SN	Idioms/Phrases	English Meaning	Hindi Meaning	#R
1159	**Make one's blood run cold**	To feel very frightened or horrified	हाथ-पैर ठंडे पड़ना (भयभीत होना)	1 (1)
1160	**Make one's mark**	To become successful or famous in a particular area	नाम कमाना (अपनी पहचान बनाना)	4 (1)
1161	**Make one's mouth water**	To make someone want to eat something because it looks or smells delicious	मुँह में पानी लाना (ललचाना)	3
1162	Make one's toes curl	To cause embarrassment, disgust, or discomfort	शर्म, घिन या असहजता से सिकुड़ जाना	
1163	Make room	To move so that there is space for someone or something else	जगह बनाना (स्थान देना)	
1164	Make short work of	To finish or deal with something very quickly	चुटकी में निपटा देना (जल्द ख़त्म करना)	
1165	Make the most of	To use something to its best advantage	अधिकतम लाभ उठाना	
1166	**Make up one's mind**	To decide; to come to a firm decision	फ़ैसला करना (दृढ़ निश्चय करना)	7 (2)
1167	**Make waves**	To cause trouble or controversy; to create a significant impression	हंगामा खड़ा करना / विवाद पैदा करना	1 (1)
1168	Make-believe	To pretend or imagine that something is true or real	दिखावा करना / कल्पना करना (बहाना बनाना)	
1169	**Man in the street**	An average person; typical member of the public	आम आदमी (साधारण व्यक्ति)	3
1170	**Man of letters**	A person who is very knowledgeable about literature; a writer	विद्वान व्यक्ति (साहित्यकार)	6 (5)
1171	Man of means	A person who has a lot of money; a rich person	धनी व्यक्ति (संपन्न आदमी)	
1172	Man of spirit	A person with courage, energy, and determination	साहसी व्यक्ति (हिम्मतवाला)	
1173	**Man of straw**	A person who has no real power or importance	कमज़ोर व्यक्ति (कठपुतली)	7 (4)
1174	**Man of the world**	A man with a lot of experience of life and other people	अनुभवी और व्यावहारिक व्यक्ति (दुनियादार)	1 (1)
1175	**Mealy-mouthed**	Unwilling to say what you really mean, especially to avoid causing offense	दबी ज़ुबान से बोलने वाला (साफ़ बात न करने वाला)	2
1176	Meet one's eyes	To look directly at someone, especially when you are being honest	आँखों में आँखें डालना (नज़र मिलाना)	
1177	**Meet one's Waterloo**	To suffer a final defeat; to be completely defeated	अंतिम और निर्णायक हार का सामना करना	2 (3)
1178	Meet someone halfway	To agree to do part of what someone wants in order to reach an agreement	बीच का रास्ता निकालना (समझौता करना)	
1179	Melting pot	A place where people of different races, cultures, and ideas mix together	संस्कृतियों का मिश्रण (विविधता का केंद्र)	
1180	Memory like a sieve	A very poor memory; the tendency to forget things easily	कमज़ोर याददाश्त (छलनी जैसी याद)	
1181	Mend one's ways	To start behaving better; to stop doing bad things	चाल-चलन सुधारना (अपनी बुराइयाँ छोड़ना)	

SN	Idioms/Phrases	English Meaning	Hindi Meaning	#R
1182	**Method in one's madness**	A sensible reason for what seems like crazy behaviour	पागलपन या बेतुके कार्यों के पीछे कारण होना	2
1183	**Midas touch**	The ability to make a lot of money or be successful in everything	पारस जैसा स्पर्श (जिस काम में हाथ डालें वही सफल हो जाना)	2
1184	Might as well (do something)	Doing something is equally reasonable	चलो यही सही	
1185	**Milk and water**	Weak and lacking determination or strong opinions	कमज़ोर और प्रभावहीन	1 (1)
1186	Milk of human kindness	The natural tendency to be kind and sympathetic	मानवीय दया (स्वाभाविक करुणा)	
1187	**Mince matters (or words)**	To speak carefully or vaguely to avoid offending	घुमा-फिराकर बात करना (साफ़ न बोलना)	5
1188	Mind one's language	To be careful not to say anything rude or offensive	ज़ुबान सँभालकर बात करना (शिष्ट भाषा का प्रयोग)	
1189	**Mind one's p's and q's**	To be very careful about what you say or do; to behave properly	शिष्टाचार का पूरा ध्यान रखना (हरकतों पर ध्यान)	2
1190	**Miss the boat (or bus)**	To fail to take advantage of an opportunity	मौक़ा हाथ से निकल जाना (अवसर खो देना)	13 (7)
1191	**Monkey business**	Dishonest, silly, or mischievous behaviour	हेराफ़ेरी (धोखाधड़ी वाली हरकत)	1 (1)
1192	Months on end	For several months continuously	लगातार कई महीनों तक (बिना रुके)	
1193	Moot point	A subject that people disagree about or that has no clear answer	विवादास्पद विषय (बहस का मुद्दा)	
1194	More or less	Approximately; to some extent	लगभग / कम-बेसी (थोड़ा-बहुत)	
1195	**Move heaven and earth**	To try extremely hard to do something; to do everything possible	आकाश-पाताल एक कर देना (हर संभव प्रयास करना)	5 (4)
1196	Move the goalposts	To change the rules or requirements unfairly	खेल के बीच में नियम बदल देना (बेईमानी करना)	
1197	Moved to tears	Feeling such strong emotion that you start crying	आँखें भर आना (भावुक होकर रो पड़ना)	
1198	**Much ado about nothing**	A lot of fuss or excitement about something unimportant	बात का बतंगड़ (बिना बात का शोर-शराबा)	1 (3)
1199	**Mum's the word**	Used to tell someone to keep a secret	मुँह बंद रखना (राज़ न खोलना)	1 (1)
1200	Nail it	To do something perfectly	कुछ बिल्कुल सही करना	
1201	**Nail one's colours to the mast**	To state publicly what you believe and refuse to change your position	अपना पक्ष स्पष्ट रूप से रखना (डटे रहना)	1 (1)
1202	Nail-biting	Very exciting or tense because the outcome is uncertain	रोमांचक (जिसमें अंत तक उत्सुकता बनी रहे)	
1203	Neck and crop	Completely; entirely	पूरी तरह से (एकदम से)	
1204	**Neck of the woods**	A particular area or region	आस-पास का इलाक़ा (पड़ोस)	2 (1)
1205	Neck or nothing	Taking a risk where you either succeed completely or fail completely	सब कुछ दाँव पर लगा देना (आर या पार का जोख़िम)	
1206	**Needle in a haystack**	Something that is almost impossible to find	घास के ढेर में सुई ढूँढना (नामुमकिन तलाश)	5 (2)

SN	Idioms/Phrases	English Meaning	Hindi Meaning	#R
1207	**Neither fish nor fowl**	Something that does not fit into any category; neither one thing nor another	न इधर का न उधर का (अस्पष्ट श्रेणी का)	3
1208	Nerves of steel	The ability to remain calm and brave in difficult situations	लोहे के दिल वाला (फ़ौलादी इरादे)	
1209	Never-never land	An imaginary ideal place; an unrealistic fantasy world	ख़याली जगह (काल्पनिक आदर्श दुनिया)	
1210	**New kid on the block**	A person who has recently joined a group, organization, or place	नया खिलाड़ी / नया सदस्य (नवागंतुक)	2
1211	**New lease of life**	A chance to be happy, healthy, or successful again after a difficult time	नया जीवन मिलना (नई उमंग)	3 (4)
1212	**New York minute**	A very short period of time	पल भर (बहुत कम समय)	1 (1)
1213	Night owl	A person who prefers to be active at night and goes to bed late	देर रात तक जागने वाला व्यक्ति (रात्रिचर)	
1214	Nig-nog	A foolish person	मूर्ख व्यक्ति (बेवक़ूफ़)	
1215	**Nine days' wonder**	Something that attracts a lot of attention but is soon forgotten	चार दिन की चाँदनी फिर अँधेरी रात (जो केवल थोड़े समय के लिए हो)	4
1216	Nine times out of ten	Almost always; in most cases	अधिकतर (लगभग हमेशा)	
1217	**Nip in the bud**	To stop something bad before it has a chance to develop	शुरुआत में ही रोक देना (कली में ही तोड़ देना)	9 (6)
1218	No dice	Used to refuse a request or to say something is not possible	कोई गुंजाइश नहीं (साफ़ इनकार)	
1219	No ifs and buts	No excuses or objections allowed	कोई अगर-मगर नहीं (कोई बहाना नहीं)	
1220	**No love lost between**	Two people who have strong mutual dislike for each other	आपसी नफ़रत (एक-दूसरे को पसंद न करना)	4 (1)
1221	No spring chicken	No longer young	जवानी ख़त्म होना (उम्रदराज़ होना)	
1222	**No strings attached**	Without any special conditions or restrictions	बिना किसी शर्त के (पूरी तरह स्वतंत्र)	2
1223	Nobody's fool	Someone who is too intelligent or experienced to be deceived	चतुर व्यक्ति (समझदार)	
1224	Not breathe a word	To not tell anyone about a secret	मुँह न खोलना (किसी बात को गुप्त रखना)	
1225	Not have a clue	To know nothing about something; to not understand something at all	अता-पता न होना (बिल्कुल जानकारी न होना)	
1226	**Not have a leg to stand on**	To have no facts or evidence to support an argument or claim	कोई ठोस आधार न होना (बात में दम न होना)	2
1227	**Not hold water**	To be illogical or not able to be supported by facts	तर्कसंगत न होना (बात खोखली होना)	2
1228	**Not mince words (or matters)**	To say what you mean clearly and directly, even if it upsets people	बिना घुमाए-फिराए साफ़-साफ़ बोलना	6
1229	**Not one's cup of tea**	Something that one does not like or is not good at	बस की बात न होना / पसंद न होना	5
1230	**Not play with a full deck**	To be mentally deficient or lacking intelligence	दिमाग़ ढीला होना (मूर्खतापूर्ण व्यवहार)	1 (3)
1231	Not see eye to eye	To not agree with someone about something	सहमत न होना (विचार न मिलना)	

SN	Idioms/Phrases	English Meaning	Hindi Meaning	#R
1232	Not someone's line	Not within one's area of knowledge or interest	मेरे क्षेत्र का नहीं (मेरी महारत का विषय नहीं)	
1233	Not turn a hair	To show no emotion or reaction at all	पत्थर का दिल होना (अविचलित या अप्रभावित रहना)	
1234	**Not worth one's salt**	Not good at one's job; not deserving the money one earns	नमक हराम (काम के लायक़ न होना)	1 (3)
1235	Nothing doing	Used to say that you will not do something or that something is not possible	सवाल ही पैदा नहीं होता (बिल्कुल नामुमकिन)	
1236	Nothing to sneeze at	Something that is important and should not be ignored	मामूली बात न होना (महत्वपूर्ण होना)	
1237	Now and again (or then)	Sometimes, but not often	कभी-कभार (यदा-कदा)	
1238	**Null and void**	Having no legal power; not valid	शून्य (क़ानूनी रूप से बेकार)	2
1239	Nurse back to health	To care for someone until they recover	किसी की देखभाल करके स्वस्थ बनाना	
1240	Odd man (one) out	A person or thing that is different from the others in a group	असंगत व्यक्ति (जो समूह से अलग दिखे)	
1241	Odds and ends	Small things of various types that are not very important or valuable	इधर-उधर की छोटी-मोटी चीज़ें (फुटकर सामान)	
1242	Of (or to) no avail	Without success; ineffective	व्यर्थ (किसी काम का नहीं)	
1243	**Of the first water**	Of the highest quality or degree	अव्वल दर्जे का (सबसे अच्छी गुणवत्ता वाला)	2
1244	Of the old school	Having traditional beliefs or values	पुराने ज़माने की सोच वाला (परंपरावादी)	
1245	Off base	Completely wrong about something	पूरी तरह ग़लत (ग़लतफ़हमी में होना)	
1246	Off one's food	Having no desire to eat; not hungry	भूख न होना (खाने का मन न करना)	
1247	Off one's rocker	Crazy; behaving in a very strange way	सिर फिरा हुआ (पागल होना)	
1248	Off the beaten track (or path)	In a place where not many people go	दूर-दराज़ (आम राह से हटकर)	
1249	Off the cuff	Said or done without any preparation	बिना तैयारी के (तुरंत बोला या किया हुआ)	
1250	Off the record	Not intended to be made public or published	अनौपचारिक रूप से (ग़ैर-आधिकारिक)	
1251	Off the wall	Strange or unusual in an amusing way	अजीबोग़रीब (असामान्य)	
1252	**Off-colour**	Feeling slightly ill	तबियत ठीक न होना (हल्का बीमार)	2
1253	Oily tongue	Someone who speaks in an insincere flattering way	चिकनी-चुपड़ी बातें करना (चापलूसी)	
1254	Old hand	A person who is very experienced at something	पुराना खिलाड़ी (अनुभवी व्यक्ति)	
1255	**Old hat**	Old-fashioned; no longer interesting or exciting	पुराना या दक़ियानूसी (अप्रचलित)	1 (1)

SN	Idioms/Phrases	English Meaning	Hindi Meaning	#R
1256	On (or at) the double	Very quickly; immediately	पलक झपकते ही (बहुत तेज़ी से)	
1257	**On (or in) the cards**	Likely to happen	संभावित (होने के आसार होना)	3 (1)
1258	On a collision course	Moving toward a situation in which a disagreement or fight is likely	टकराव की ओर बढ़ना (संघर्ष की दिशा में)	
1259	**On a roll**	Experiencing a period of success or good luck	लगातार सफलता की लय में होना	2 (1)
1260	**On a shoestring**	With very little money; on a very small budget	बहुत कम पैसों में (अल्प बजट में)	1 (1)
1261	On a wing and a prayer	With only a slight chance of success; hoping for luck	बस उम्मीद के सहारे (बहुत कम संभावना के साथ)	
1262	**On account of**	Because of; due to	की वजह से (के कारण)	2
1263	On all hands	From all directions	हर तरफ़ से (सब ओर से)	
1264	**On and off (or off and on)**	Intermittently; sometimes happening and sometimes not	कभी-कभार / रुक-रुक कर (अनियमित रूप से)	6
1265	**On cloud nine**	Extremely happy; in a state of bliss	ख़ुशी से फूले न समाना (बेहद ख़ुश)	16 (14)
1266	**On edge**	Nervous, anxious, or unable to relax	बेचैन या तनावग्रस्त (घबराया हुआ)	2 (2)
1267	On good terms	Having a friendly relationship with someone	अच्छे संबंध होना (मैत्रीपूर्ण रिश्ता)	
1268	On high alert	In a state of maximum readiness for danger or an emergency	पूरी तरह सतर्क (चौकन्ना)	
1269	On merit	Judged according to quality or worth rather than other factors	योग्यता के आधार पर (गुणवत्ता से)	
1270	On one's guard	Being watchful and careful to avoid danger or problems	सावधान रहना (चौकन्ना रहना)	
1271	**On one's high horse**	Acting as if one is better or more important than others	अकड़ दिखाना (घमंड में होना)	2 (1)
1272	**On one's last legs**	Very tired, weak, or about to fail or die	ख़त्म होने की कगार पर (बहुत ख़राब स्थिति में)	3
1273	**On pins and needles**	Very nervous or anxious about something that is going to happen	काँटों पर होना (बेचैनी और घबराहट में होना)	2 (3)
1274	**On purpose**	Intentionally; not by accident or mistake	जानबूझकर (सोच-समझकर किया गया)	2
1275	**On shank's mare (or pony)**	Walking; traveling by foot	पैदल चलना (अपने पैरों से जाना)	2
1276	On someone's radar	Being noticed, monitored, or under consideration	नज़र में होना (ध्यान में होना)	
1277	**On tenterhooks**	Very anxious or excited while waiting for something to happen	बेचैनी से इंतज़ार में (चिंता में होना)	8 (2)
1278	On the air	Being broadcast on radio or television	प्रसारित होना (रेडियो/टीवी पर आना)	
1279	On the attack	Acting aggressively against an opponent	आक्रामक रवैया (हमलावर रुख़)	
1280	On the back foot	In a difficult situation where one is forced to react rather than act	बचाव की मुद्रा में (कमज़ोर स्थिति में होना)	
1281	**On the ball**	Very alert and quick to understand and react to things	मुस्तैद रहना (चौकन्ना होना)	7 (2)

SN	Idioms/Phrases	English Meaning	Hindi Meaning	#R
1282	**On the breadline**	Very poor; having barely enough money to live	अत्यंत ग़रीब (भुखमरी की हालत में)	2
1283	**On the brink (or verge) of**	Very close to something, especially something important or dangerous	कगार पर (बिल्कुल क़रीब)	4
1284	On the contrary	Used to show that the opposite of what was said is true	इसके विपरीत (उल्टा)	
1285	On the cuff	On credit; without paying immediately	उधार पर	
1286	**On the face of it**	Judging by how something first appears; apparently	पहली नज़र में (ऊपरी तौर पर देखने पर)	1 (1)
1287	**On the horizon**	Likely to happen soon; approaching	जल्द ही होने वाला (निकट भविष्य में)	1 (1)
1288	**On the horns of a dilemma**	Having to choose between two equally unpleasant options	आगे कुआँ पीछे खाई (दो कठिन विकल्पों के बीच फँस जाना)	2 (1)
1289	On the job	While doing one's work; at work	काम करते समय (कार्यरत)	
1290	On the level	Honest and truthful; legitimate	ईमानदार (सच्चा)	
1291	On the rocks	In difficulty; likely to fail	टूटने की कगार पर होना (डगमगाती स्थिति में होना)	
1292	**On the same page**	Having the same understanding or opinion about something	एक मत होना (सहमत होना)	4 (2)
1293	**On the same wavelength**	Thinking in a similar way; having a good understanding of each other	एक जैसी सोच (आपसी तालमेल और समझ होना)	1 (1)
1294	**On the spur of the moment**	Done suddenly without planning; impulsively	बिना सोचे-समझे (तुरंत; अचानक)	2 (1)
1295	On the square	Honest and fair; trustworthy	ईमानदारी से काम करना (सच्चाई से)	
1296	**On the straight and narrow**	Following a morally correct way of life	सही रास्ते पर (नेकी की राह पर)	1 (1)
1297	On the stroke of (time)	Exactly at the specified time	बिल्कुल निर्धारित समय पर	
1298	On the tip of one's tongue	Almost able to remember or say something but not quite	ज़ुबान पर होना (याद आते-आते न आना)	
1299	**On the wane**	Becoming less strong, important, or popular; declining	घटता हुआ / पतन की ओर (कमज़ोर होना)	3
1300	On the warpath	Very angry and ready to argue or fight	तलवार खींच लेना (गुस्से में होना)	
1301	On the wrong side of sixty	Older than sixty	साठ के पार होना (किसी उम्र से ऊपर होना)	
1302	**On thin ice**	In a risky or dangerous situation	ख़तरे में होना (जोख़िम भरी स्थिति में)	15 (3)
1303	On top of the world	Feeling extremely happy; elated	सातवें आसमान पर (बेहद ख़ुश और सफ़ल)	
1304	**Once and for all**	Completely and finally; in a way that will not change	हमेशा-हमेशा के लिए (अंतिम रूप से)	5
1305	**Once in a blue moon**	Very rarely; almost never	ईद का चाँद होना (कभी-कभार)	21 (18)
1306	One step at a time	Progressing slowly and carefully; taking things gradually	एक-एक कदम बढ़ाना (धीरे-धीरे और संभलकर चलना)	

SN	Idioms/Phrases	English Meaning	Hindi Meaning	#R
1307	**One's cup of tea**	Something that one enjoys or does well	पसंदीदा काम	4
1308	One's number is up	The time has come when something bad will happen to someone	वक़्त आ गया है (मौत या मुसीबत क़रीब है)	
1309	One-track mind	Thinking only about one subject or idea and nothing else	एक ही धुन सवार होना (एक ही दिशा में सोचना)	
1310	Open one's heart	To reveal one's innermost thoughts and feelings	दिल खोलकर रख देना (मन की बात कहना)	
1311	**Open Pandora's box**	A process that creates many complicated problems	मुसीबतों का पिटारा (समस्याओं का स्रोत)	1 (2)
1312	Open-ended	Without a fixed ending or limit	असीमित (बिना किसी निश्चित सीमा के)	
1313	Out and about	Going out and doing things, especially after being ill or inactive	बाहर घूमना-फिरना (सक्रिय रहना)	
1314	**Out and out**	Complete; total	पूरी तरह से (बिल्कुल)	1 (1)
1315	Out at the elbows	Poor and shabbily dressed; showing signs of poverty	फ़टेहाल होना (अत्यंत निर्धन)	
1316	**Out for the count**	Unconscious or sleeping very deeply	घोड़े बेचकर सोना (गहरी नींद में); ढेर हो जाना (बेहोश होना)	1 (1)
1317	Out of bounds	Beyond the permitted area; not allowed	सीमा से बाहर (प्रतिबंधित; जहाँ जाने की अनुमति न हो)	
1318	Out of context	Separated from the original meaning or situation and therefore misunderstood	संदर्भ से बाहर (ग़लत अर्थ में लिया गया)	
1319	**Out of date**	No longer current or in fashion; obsolete	पुराना (अप्रचलित)	2
1320	Out of favour	No longer liked or approved of by someone	किसी की नज़रों से गिरना (अप्रिय होना)	
1321	Out of gear	Not working correctly; out of order	ठीक से काम न करना (गड़बड़ होना)	
1322	Out of one's wits	Extremely worried, frightened, or confused	हक्का-बक्का रह जाना (घबराहट में बुद्धि काम न करना)	
1323	**Out of order**	Not working correctly; behaving in an unacceptable way	ख़राब; अनुचित व्यवहार (बेकार)	2
1324	Out of print	No longer being published and therefore unavailable to buy	छपाई बंद होना (अनुपलब्ध पुस्तक)	
1325	**Out of sorts**	Feeling slightly unwell or in a bad mood	तबीयत ठीक न होना (अस्वस्थ या चिड़चिड़ापन)	2
1326	**Out of the blue**	Completely unexpectedly; with no prior warning	अचानक / बिना किसी पूर्व सूचना के (अप्रत्याशित रूप से)	10 (2)
1327	Out of the frying pan into the fire	Going from a bad situation to an even worse one	आसमान से गिरा, खजूर में अटका (एक मुसीबत से दूसरी बड़ी मुसीबत में)	
1328	**Out of the question**	Not possible; completely impractical	सवाल ही नहीं उठता (असंभव)	3 (1)
1329	**Out of the woods**	No longer in danger or difficulty	खतरे से बाहर (मुश्किल दौर से निकलना)	4 (1)

SN	Idioms/Phrases	English Meaning	Hindi Meaning	#R
1330	Out of thin air	From or into nothing; appearing or disappearing suddenly	अचानक प्रकट या गायब होना	
1331	Out of this world	Extremely good or impressive; wonderful	इस दुनिया से परे (असाधारण, लाजवाब)	
1332	Out on one's ear	To be dismissed or thrown out abruptly, especially in disgrace	बेइज़्ज़ती से निकाला जाना (धक्के मारकर बाहर करना)	
1333	**Over (or above) one's head**	Too difficult for someone to understand	सिर के ऊपर से गुज़रना (समझ से परे)	2
1334	**Over and above**	In addition to; besides	के अतिरिक्त (के अलावा)	2
1335	Over and over again	Many times; repeatedly	बार-बार (लगातार)	
1336	**Over head and ears**	Deeply or completely involved (in love or debt)	प्यार या कर्ज में पूरी तरह डूबा हुआ	4
1337	**Over one's dead body**	Used to say that you will not allow something to happen	मेरी लाश से होकर (कड़ा विरोध करना)	2 (1)
1338	**Over the moon**	Extremely happy; delighted	फूले न समाना (बहुत ख़ुश होना)	2 (4)
1339	Over-egg the pudding	To spoil something by trying too hard to improve it	अति से अनर्थ होना (ज़्यादा करके बिगाड़ना)	
1340	Pacing up and down	Walking nervously back and forth in a small area	चहलकदमी करना (बेचैनी में इधर-उधर टहलना)	
1341	**Paddle one's own canoe**	To be independent and manage one's own affairs	अपने पैरों पर खड़ा होना (आत्मनिर्भर होना)	2 (2)
1342	**Pain in the neck**	A person or thing that is very annoying	जी का जंजाल (परेशान करने वाला व्यक्ति या चीज़)	3 (1)
1343	Pale into insignificance	To seem much less important when compared with something else	फीका पड़ जाना (कम महत्वपूर्ण लगना)	
1344	Paper over the cracks	To hide problems or disagreements without really solving them	लीपापोती करना (कमियों पर पर्दा डालना)	
1345	**Pardon (or excuse) my French**	Apology for using bad language	अशिष्ट भाषा के लिए माफ़ी	1 (1)
1346	**Part and parcel**	An essential or fundamental part of something	अनिवार्य अंग (अभिन्न हिस्सा)	6 (1)
1347	Parthian (or parting) shot	A critical remark made when leaving	विदाई की चोट (जाते-जाते किया गया तीखा प्रहार)	
1348	Pass muster	To be accepted as satisfactory	कसौटी पर खरा उतरना (मानक पूरा करना)	
1349	Pass the baton	To hand over responsibility or control to someone else	ज़िम्मेदारी सौंपना (बागडोर थमाना)	
1350	**Pass the buck**	To blame someone else or make them responsible for a problem	दूसरों पर पल्ला झाड़ना (दोष मढ़ना)	5 (3)
1351	**Pass the hat around**	To collect money from a group of people, usually for a particular purpose	चंदा इकट्ठा करना (पैसे जमा करना)	2
1352	**Pass with flying colours**	Very successfully	झंडे गाड़कर (शानदार सफलता के साथ)	1 (1)
1353	**Pat on the back**	Praise or recognition for something done well	पीठ थपथपाना (शाबाशी देना)	2 (1)
1354	Pay heed to	To pay attention to something; to consider something carefully	ध्यान देना (गौर करना)	

SN	Idioms/Phrases	English Meaning	Hindi Meaning	#R
1355	**Pay lip service**	To say you support something without actually doing anything to help	खोखला वादा (दिखावटी समर्थन)	5 (1)
1356	**Pay off (or settle) old scores**	To take revenge for past wrongs or injuries	पुराना हिसाब चुकाना (बदला लेना)	2
1357	Pay on the nail	To pay immediately and in full	नक़द और तुरंत भुगतान करना (फ़ौरन देना)	
1358	**Pay through the nose**	To pay much more than something is worth	भारी क़ीमत देना (बहुत ज़्यादा पैसे देना)	6 (1)
1359	Pell-mell	In a confused or disorderly way; hastily	अस्त-व्यस्त (अव्यवस्थित तरीके से)	
1360	**Penelope's web**	A task that is never completed; something that must be done again and again	अंतहीन कार्य (कभी न ख़त्म होने वाला काम)	3 (1)
1361	**Perfect storm**	A situation where several bad things happen at once, creating a very difficult situation	अत्यंत प्रतिकूल परिस्थिति (मुसीबतों का एक साथ आना)	2
1362	Pick (or tear) to pieces	To criticize something or someone very severely	धज्जियाँ उड़ाना (कड़ी आलोचना करना)	
1363	Pick a quarrel	To deliberately start an argument with someone	झगड़ा मोल लेना (जानबूझकर बहस शुरू करना)	
1364	Pick and choose	To select only the things you want from a larger group	चुन-चुनकर लेना (अपनी पसंद के अनुसार छाँटना)	
1365	**Pick holes in**	To find faults or weaknesses in something, especially in an argument or plan	बाल की खाल निकालना (कमियाँ निकालना, आलोचना करना)	4 (3)
1366	Pick someone's pocket	To steal from someone's pocket without them noticing	जेब काटना (चोरी करना)	
1367	Pick up the threads	To continue something after it has been interrupted	सूत्र संभालना (फिर से शुरू करना)	
1368	**Pie in the sky**	An idea or plan that is not practical and unlikely to happen	हवाई क़िला (असंभव योजना)	2 (1)
1369	Pigeon-hole	To put someone or something into a category that is too narrow or simple	ठप्पा लगा देना (सीमित श्रेणी में बाँध देना)	
1370	**Pin money**	A small amount of money for personal use	जेब ख़र्च (छोटी-मोटी राशि)	2 (1)
1371	**Pipe dream**	A hope or plan that is impossible to achieve	ख्याली पुलाव पकाना (असंभव सपना)	4 (1)
1372	Pitch and toss	A simple gambling game where coins are thrown	चित-पट का खेल (सिक्के उछालने का जुआ)	
1373	Plain (or clear) as day	Very obvious and easy to see or understand	दिन की तरह साफ़ (बिल्कुल स्पष्ट)	
1374	Play a joke (or trick)	To trick someone or do something funny to amuse yourself	मज़ाक करना, शरारत करना (ठिठोली करना)	
1375	**Play devil's advocate**	To argue against something even if you agree with it, to test the strength of the argument	विपरीत पक्ष रखना (बहस के लिए उल्टा तर्क देना)	9 (8)
1376	**Play ducks and drakes**	To waste money or resources carelessly	पैसा पानी की तरह बहाना (लापरवाही से ख़र्च करना)	3 (3)

SN	Idioms/Phrases	English Meaning	Hindi Meaning	#R
1377	**Play fast and loose**	To behave in a careless, deceitful or irresponsible way often by ignoring rules	बेईमानी और लापरवाही से काम करना (नियमों की परवाह न करना)	1 (2)
1378	Play for time	To deliberately delay in order to gain more time	टाल-मटोल करना (समय खींचना)	
1379	Play gooseberry	To be an unwanted third person with a couple who want to be alone	कबाब में हड्डी (दो प्रेमियों के बीच तीसरा व्यक्ति)	
1380	Play havoc (or wreak havoc)	To cause a lot of damage or problems	तबाही मचाना (तहस-नहस करना)	
1381	**Play it by ear**	To decide what to do as a situation develops rather than planning in advance	परिस्थिति के अनुसार काम करना (बिना तैयारी के)	5 (6)
1382	Play it safe	To be careful and avoid taking risks	सुरक्षित रास्ता चुनना (कोई जोख़िम न लेना)	
1383	**Play one's ace**	To use one's best advantage at the right moment	अपना तुरुप का इक्का खेलना (सबसे बड़ा दाँव लगाना)	2
1384	**Play one's cards right**	To deal with a situation cleverly to get the result you want	सही चाल चलना (चतुराई से काम करना)	2
1385	**Play second fiddle**	To be less important or in a weaker position than someone else	किसी के नीचे काम करना (दूसरी भूमिका में होना)	3 (6)
1386	**Play to the gallery**	To act in an exaggerated way to impress people	वाहवाही लूटना (लोकप्रियता के लिए काम करना)	2 (1)
1387	Play truant	To stay away without permission	बिना बताए ग़ायब रहना (काम से अनुपस्थित रहना)	
1388	**Play with fire**	To do something that is dangerous or could cause problems	आग से खेलना (ख़तरा मोल लेना)	6
1389	**Plenty more fish in the sea**	Many other opportunities or alternatives exist	और भी कई विकल्प मौजूद हैं	1 (1)
1390	**Plum job**	A very good, desirable, and well-paid job	बढ़िया और अच्छी तनख़्वाह वाली नौकरी	1 (1)
1391	**Pocket (or swallow) an insult**	To accept an insult without reacting or protesting	अपमान का घूँट पी लेना (बेइज़्ज़ती सहना)	2
1392	**Point-blank**	Very directly; or from a very close distance	सीधे तौर पर (बहुत क़रीब से)	2
1393	**Poke (or stick) one's nose in**	To interfere in other people's business	टाँग अड़ाना (दूसरों के मामले में दख़ल देना)	3 (1)
1394	Poles apart	Completely different in views, opinions, or situations	ज़मीन आसमान का फ़र्क़ (बिल्कुल विपरीत होना)	
1395	Pop the question	To ask someone to marry you	हाथ माँगना (शादी का प्रस्ताव रखना)	
1396	Potluck dinner	A meal where each guest brings food to share	सामूहिक भोजन (जहाँ सब अपनी पसंद का खाना लाते हैं)	
1397	Pound of flesh	Something that is legally owed but is cruel or excessive to demand	क़ानूनी पर नैतिक रूप से ग़लत (जायज़ लेकिन बेरहम माँग)	
1398	**Pour (or throw) cold water on**	To discourage or criticize an idea or plan	उम्मीदों पर पानी फेर देना (हतोत्साहित करना)	8 (2)

SN	Idioms/Phrases	English Meaning	Hindi Meaning	#R
1399	**Pour oil on troubled waters**	To try to calm a disagreement or difficult situation	झगड़ा शांत करना (मामला ठंडा करना)	2 (4)
1400	**Pour out one's heart**	To tell someone your deepest feelings and thoughts	दिल की बात कहना (मन खोलकर बताना)	2
1401	Press into service	To make someone or something start being used for a purpose	जबरन काम पर लगाना (सेवा में लेना)	
1402	**Prime the pump**	To encourage economic activity by investing money	विकास को गति देना (शुरुआती निवेश से)	1 (1)
1403	Promise the earth (or moon)	To promise much more than you can actually give	चाँद-तारे तोड़ लाने की बात करना (असंभव वादे करना)	
1404	Provide a blueprint	To provide a detailed plan or model for something	खाका पेश करना (विस्तृत योजना देना)	
1405	Public enemy number one	A person or thing considered the most dangerous or harmful	जनता का सबसे बड़ा दुश्मन (सबसे ख़तरनाक व्यक्ति)	
1406	Pull (or make) a face	To make an expression of dislike, disgust, or disapproval	मुँह बनाना (असंतोष या नापसंदगी व्यक्त करना)	
1407	**Pull a fast one**	To trick or deceive someone, often suddenly or cleverly	आँखों में धूल झोंकना (धोखा दैना)	4
1408	**Pull a long face**	To look unhappy or disappointed	मुँह लटकाना (जानबूझकर उदास दिखना)	6
1409	Pull a rabbit out of a hat	To do something surprising or unexpected, especially to solve a problem	अचानक कोई चमत्कार करना (हैरतअंगेज़ काम करना)	
1410	Pull no punches	To speak or write honestly and directly, without trying to soften criticism	दो टूक कहना (साफ़-साफ़ बोलना)	
1411	**Pull one's socks up**	To make a determined effort to improve	कमर कसना (अधिक मेहनत करना)	3 (1)
1412	Pull one's weight	To do your fair share of work in a group	अपना पूरा योगदान देना (अपनी ज़िम्मेदारी निभाना)	
1413	**Pull oneself together**	To become calm and behave normally after being upset	ख़ुद को संभालना (भावुक स्थिति से उबरना)	10 (4)
1414	**Pull out all the stops**	To do everything possible to achieve something	एड़ी-चोटी का ज़ोर लगाना (पूरी कोशिश करना)	2 (2)
1415	**Pull someone's chestnuts out of the fire**	To rescue someone from a difficult situation, often taking risks yourself	दूसरों की ख़ातिर मुसीबत मोल लेना (दूसरे की मदद में ख़तरा उठाना)	1 (1)
1416	**Pull someone's leg**	To joke with someone by saying something untrue	टाँग खींचना (मज़ाक करना)	14 (2)
1417	**Pull strings**	To use your influence or connections to get an advantage	जुगाड़ लगाना / सिफ़ारिश करना (पहुँच का इस्तेमाल करना)	5 (3)
1418	**Pull the plug**	To stop something, especially by withdrawing financial support	काम रोक देना / समर्थन वापस लेना (अचानक बंद करना)	3 (2)
1419	Pull the rug out from under	To suddenly remove support or help from someone	पैरों तले ज़मीन खिसका देना (अचानक सहारा छीनना)	
1420	Pull the trigger	To make a final decision to do something	अंतिम निर्णय लेना (फ़ैसला करना)	

SN	Idioms/Phrases	English Meaning	Hindi Meaning	#R
1421	**Pull the wool over someone's eyes**	To deceive someone by hiding the truth	आँखों में धूल झोंकना (धोखा देना)	2 (1)
1422	**Put a spoke in someone's wheel**	To prevent someone from carrying out a plan	रोड़ा अटकाना (काम में बाधा डालना)	4 (4)
1423	Put an end to	To cause something to stop or finish	समाप्त करना (रोक देना)	
1424	**Put heads together**	To discuss something together to find a solution	मिलकर काम करना (सोच-विचार करना)	2
1425	Put into action	To start doing something that has been planned or discussed	अमल में लाना (लागू करना)	
1426	Put on airs	To act in an arrogant or affected manner	अकड़ दिखाना (बड़ा बनने का नाटक)	
1427	Put on hold	To delay something until a later time	स्थगित करना (कुछ समय के लिए रोकना)	
1428	**Put on ice**	To delay something, often for a long time or indefinitely	ठंडे बस्ते में डाल देना (लंबे समय के लिए टालना)	2
1429	**Put on the back burner**	Given less attention; temporarily not being dealt with	ठंडे बस्ते में डालना (फ़िलहाल के लिए टाल देना)	1 (1)
1430	**Put one's best foot forward**	To try to make a good impression; to make the best effort	पूरी कोशिश करना (अच्छा प्रभाव डालना)	1 (1)
1431	**Put one's foot down**	To firmly insist on something or refuse to allow something	सख़्ती से मना करना (दृढ़ता से विरोध करना)	6 (3)
1432	**Put one's foot in one's mouth**	To say something that embarrasses you or upsets someone	ग़लती से किसी को शर्मिंदा करना (बोलते समय भूल करना)	1 (3)
1433	**Put one's hand to the plough (or plow)**	To begin a difficult task with determination	कठिन काम शुरू करना (जुट जाना)	2 (1)
1434	Put someone in mind of	To remind someone of something or someone	याद दिलाना (किसी चीज़ की याद ताज़ा करना)	
1435	Put someone out of countenance	To make someone feel embarrassed or uncomfortable	शर्मिंदा करना (बेचैन कर देना)	
1436	Put someone's back up	To make someone annoyed or angry	चिढ़ाना (भड़काना)	
1437	**Put the cart before the horse**	To do things in the wrong order	गाड़ी को घोड़े के आगे रखना (काम उलटे क्रम में करना)	3 (5)
1438	Put the color (or roses) back in someone's cheeks	To make someone look healthy and vigorous	गालों पर लाली लाना (स्वस्थ और ताज़ा दिखाना)	
1439	**Put the pedal to the metal**	To drive very fast; to do something with maximum speed or effort	एड़ी-चोटी का ज़ोर लगाना (पूरी रफ़्तार से काम करना)	3
1440	Put the touch on	To ask someone for money, especially as a loan or bribe	किसी से पैसे माँगना (उधार या रिश्वत माँगना)	
1441	Put to the sword	To kill people, especially in war	मौत के घाट उतारना (तलवार से मारना)	
1442	**Put two and two together**	To work out the truth from the facts available	परिस्थितियों से निष्कर्ष निकालना (अंदाज़ा लगाना)	3
1443	Put up the shutters	To stop doing business, permanently or temporarily	कारोबार बंद करना (दुकान बंद करना)	

SN	Idioms/Phrases	English Meaning	Hindi Meaning	#R
1444	**Quake (or shake) in one's boots**	To be very frightened	डर से थर-थर काँपना (भयभीत होना)	3
1445	**Queer (or odd) fish**	A strange or unusual person	अजीबोग़रीब इंसान (सनकी व्यक्ति)	2 (2)
1446	**Queer the pitch**	To spoil someone's plans or chances of success	खेल बिगाड़ देना (किसी का मौक़ा ख़राब करना)	3 (1)
1447	Quicken the pulse	To make someone feel excited or interested	धड़कनें बढ़ा देना (रोमांचित करना)	
1448	Quit on someone	To abandon or stop supporting someone	किसी का साथ छोड़ देना	
1449	**Rain cats and dogs**	To rain very heavily	मूसलाधार बारिश (जमकर पानी बरसना)	13 (6)
1450	**Rain on someone's parade**	To spoil someone's enjoyment or plans	रंग में भंग डालना (मज़ा किरकिरा करना)	1 (5)
1451	**Raise a dust (or stink)**	To cause a commotion or protest	हंगामा खड़ा करना (बवाल मचाना)	1 (1)
1452	**Raise eyebrows**	To cause surprise or mild disapproval	भौहें चढ़ाना (आश्चर्यचकित करना या आपत्ति जताना)	3
1453	Raise the alarm	To warn people of danger	खतरे की घंटी बजाना (चेतावनी देना)	
1454	Raise the bar	To set higher standards or expectations	स्तर ऊँचा करना (मानक बढ़ाना)	
1455	Raise the wind	To get the money needed for something	धन का इंतज़ाम करना (पूँजी जुटाना)	
1456	**Rank and file**	The ordinary members of an organization rather than the leaders	साधारण कर्मचारी (निचले स्तर के कर्मचारी)	2 (1)
1457	**Rare bird**	A very unusual person or thing	दुर्लभ व्यक्ति या वस्तु (अनोखा इंसान)	2
1458	**Rat race**	A way of life in which people compete aggressively for wealth or power	अंधी दौड़ (भागदौड़ भरी ज़िंदगी)	2
1459	Ray of hope	A small reason to feel hopeful in a bad situation	आशा की किरण (उम्मीद की एक झलक)	
1460	Reach a deadlock	To come to a complete standstill with no agreement possible	मामला अटक जाना (सहमति न बन पाना)	
1461	Reach a milestone	To achieve an important point in development or progress	मील का पत्थर (महत्वपूर्ण उपलब्धि)	
1462	Reach for the stars	To have very high ambitions	आकाश छूने की चाह (बहुत ऊँचा लक्ष्य रखना)	
1463	**Read between the lines**	To understand the real or hidden meaning behind what is said	छिपा हुआ अर्थ समझना (इशारों को समझना)	16 (7)
1464	Receive a kickback	To receive an illegal payment, especially as a bribe	कमीशन या रिश्वत लेना (ग़ैर-क़ानूनी भुगतान लेना)	
1465	**Red herring**	Something that draws attention away from the main issue	भ्रामक संकेत (असली मुद्दे से ध्यान भटकाने वाली बात)	6 (4)
1466	**Red letter day**	A day that is very important or special	महत्वपूर्ण दिन (यादगार दिन)	14 (4)
1467	**Red tape**	Official rules and procedures that seem unnecessary and cause delay	लालफ़ीताशाही (बेवजह की सरकारी औपचारिकताएँ)	2 (1)

SN	Idioms/Phrases	English Meaning	Hindi Meaning	#R
1468	Reinvent the wheel	To waste time trying to create something that already exists	पहले से मौजूद चीज़ फिर से बनाना	
1469	**Rest on one's laurels**	To be satisfied with past achievements and not try to do more	पुरानी उपलब्धियों पर संतुष्ट रहना (आगे प्रयास न करना)	5 (1)
1470	Riding high	Very successful and popular at the moment	सफलता के शिखर पर (लोकप्रिय और कामयाब होना)	
1471	**Ring a bell**	To sound familiar; to remind someone of something	जाना-पहचाना लगना (याद आना)	1 (2)
1472	Ring-fence	To protect or reserve something for a specific purpose	किसी चीज़ को अलग रख देना (विशेष उद्देश्य के लिए)	
1473	Rip up old sores (or reopen old wounds)	To remind someone of unpleasant events from the past	पुराने घाव कुरेदना (पुरानी कड़वाहट याद दिलाना)	
1474	**Rise like a phoenix**	To recover and become successful again after failure	फिर से सफल होना (राख से उठना)	3
1475	**Rise to the occasion**	To deal successfully with a difficult situation	मौक़े पर खरा उतरना (चुनौती स्वीकार करना)	2 (1)
1476	Rise with the lark	To get up very early in the morning	मुर्गे की बाँग पर उठना (सूर्योदय से पहले जागना)	
1477	Risk life and limb	To put yourself in danger of death or serious injury	जान जोख़िम में डालना (ख़तरा उठाना)	
1478	Risk one's neck	To do something dangerous or risky	जान जोख़िम में डालना (बड़ा ख़तरा मोल लेना)	
1479	**Rock the boat**	To do something that upsets a settled situation	स्थिति बिगाड़ना (अशांति फैलाना)	2 (1)
1480	Roll out the red carpet	To give someone a very special welcome	लाल कालीन बिछाना (भव्य स्वागत करना)	
1481	**Roll up one's sleeves**	To prepare to work hard on something	कमर कसना (मेहनत के लिए तैयार होना)	3 (1)
1482	Roll with the punches	To adapt to difficult situations and accept problems calmly	हालात के अनुसार ढल जाना	
1483	Rolling in cash	Very rich	पैसों में लोटना (बहुत अमीर होना)	
1484	**Root and branch**	Completely and thoroughly	जड़ से उखाड़ फेंकना (पूरी तरह से)	2
1485	Rose-coloured glasses	A cheerful way of looking at things that ignores negative aspects	गुलाबी चश्मे से देखना (सिर्फ अच्छा पक्ष देखना)	
1486	Royal road	An easy way to achieve something	आसान रास्ता (सरल उपाय)	
1487	Rub salt into the wound	To make someone's pain or embarrassment worse	जले पर नमक छिड़कना (दुख को और बढ़ाना)	
1488	**Rub someone the wrong way**	To irritate or annoy someone	चिढ़ाना या परेशान करना (ग़लत तरीके से पेश आना)	3
1489	**Ruffle someone's feathers**	To upset or annoy someone	नाराज़ करना (परेशान करना)	2 (1)
1490	**Rule the roost**	To be the person who makes decisions and controls others	हुकुम चलाना (घर का मुखिया होना)	6 (1)
1491	**Run amok**	To behave in a wild or uncontrolled way	बेक़ाबू होना (अनियंत्रित हो जाना)	2
1492	Run around like a headless chicken	To act in a frantic or disorganized way	अव्यवस्थित तरीके से काम करना (भागदौड़ करना)	

SN	Idioms/Phrases	English Meaning	Hindi Meaning	#R
1493	Run errands	To do small tasks, usually involving going somewhere	छोटे-मोटे काम करना (इधर-उधर के काम निपटाना)	
1494	Run into rough weather	To experience problems or difficulties	काले बादल छाना (मुश्किल समय आना)	
1495	**Run out of steam**	To lose energy, enthusiasm, or motivation	जोश ठंडा पड़ना (ऊर्जा ख़त्म होना)	4 (6)
1496	**Run riot**	To behave in an uncontrolled way; to spread quickly	बेलगाम हो जाना (अनियंत्रित व्यवहार)	2
1497	**Run short of**	To have insufficient supply	कम पड़ जाना	2
1498	Run wild	To behave in an uncontrolled manner	बेलगाम होना (नियंत्रण से बाहर हो जाना)	
1499	Run-of-the-mill	Ordinary; not special in any way	औसत दर्जे का (साधारण)	
1500	Rust bucket	An old car or other vehicle that is rusty and in poor condition	खटारा गाड़ी (जंग खाई गाड़ी)	
1501	**Sacred cow**	Something beyond criticism	अनिंदनीय (जिसकी आलोचना न की जा सके)	2
1502	**Safe pair of hands**	A person who can be trusted to do something well	भरोसेमंद हाथ (विश्वसनीय व्यक्ति)	2
1503	**Sail close to the wind**	To take risks by doing something that is almost illegal or dishonest	जोख़िम भरा काम करना (ख़तरनाक रास्ता अपनाना)	2 (2)
1504	**Salad days**	The time when you are young and inexperienced	जवानी के दिन (अनुभवहीनता का समय)	2
1505	**Salt of the earth**	A very good and honest person who can be trusted	धरती का रत्न (नेक और सच्चा इंसान)	4
1506	**Save for a rainy day**	To save money for when it might be needed in the future	मुसीबत के समय के लिए बचत (बुरे दिनों के लिए पैसे जोड़ना)	2 (3)
1507	Save one's breath	To not waste time saying something that will not be listened to	व्यर्थ की बहस न करना (अपनी ऊर्जा बचाना)	
1508	**Saved by the bell**	Rescued from a difficult situation at the last moment	बाल-बाल बचना (आख़िरी वक़्त पर बच जाना)	2
1509	School someone in something	Train or instruct thoroughly	किसी को अच्छी तरह सिखाना	
1510	**Scrape the bottom of the barrel**	To use the worst people or things because there is nothing better left	मजबूरी में घटिया या अंतिम विकल्प अपनाना	2 (2)
1511	**Scratch one's head**	To be confused or unable to understand something	सिर खुजलाना (असमंजस में पड़ना)	2
1512	**Sea change**	A complete and dramatic change	कायापलट होना (बड़ा बदलाव)	4 (2)
1513	Second banana	A person in a secondary role	दूसरे नंबर का (सहायक भूमिका)	
1514	Second to none	The best; better than anyone or anything else	सर्वश्रेष्ठ (जिसके जैसा कोई दूसरा न हो)	
1515	**See eye to eye**	To agree completely with someone about something	पूरी तरह सहमत होना (एक राय होना)	13 (10)
1516	See pink elephants	To hallucinate, especially due to intoxication	नशे में भ्रम होना (काल्पनिक चीज़ें दिखना)	
1517	**See the light of day**	To be published or made known to people; to be born	सामने आना (नज़र में आना)	3

SN	Idioms/Phrases	English Meaning	Hindi Meaning	#R
1518	**Sell like hotcakes**	To sell very quickly and in large quantities	हाथों-हाथ बिकना (तेज़ी से बिकना)	7 (6)
1519	Send someone packing	To make someone leave quickly, often angrily	दरवाज़ा दिखाना (नौकरी या जगह से निकाल देना)	
1520	**Send to Coventry**	To refuse to speak to someone as a punishment	अनदेखा करना (बातचीत बंद कर देना)	2
1521	**Separate the wheat from the chaff**	To separate the good from the bad	गेहूँ और भूसे को अलग करना (अच्छे-बुरे की पहचान)	2 (1)
1522	Set at liberty	To free someone; to release	आज़ाद करना (मुक्त करना)	
1523	**Set in one's ways**	Not willing to change habits or opinions	अपनी आदतों में अड़ियल (जिद्दी)	1 (1)
1524	Set one's face against	To be determined to oppose something	डटकर विरोध करना (सख़्त आपत्ति जताना)	
1525	Set one's sights on	To decide to achieve a particular thing	लक्ष्य निर्धारित करना (निशाना बनाना)	
1526	**Set the record straight**	To give the true facts about something that has been wrongly reported	सच्चाई सामने लाना (गलतफहमी दूर करना)	1 (2)
1527	**Set the Thames on fire**	To do something remarkable	आश्चर्यजनक कार्य करना (कमाल कर देना)	2 (1)
1528	Set the wheels in motion	To begin a process or course of action	प्रक्रिया शुरू करना (कार्यवाही आरंभ करना)	
1529	**Sharp as a tack**	Very intelligent and quick to understand things	तेज़-तर्रार (बहुत बुद्धिमान)	1 (1)
1530	Sharp practices	Clever but dishonest business methods	बेईमानी के तौर-तरीके	
1531	Shed light on	To make something clearer and easier to understand	प्रकाश डालना (स्पष्ट करना)	
1532	**Shoot the breeze**	To talk in a relaxed, informal way	गपशप करना (इधर-उधर की बातें करना)	1 (1)
1533	**Shot in the arm**	Something that gives encouragement or new energy	नई जान डाल देना (हौसला बढ़ाना)	3 (3)
1534	**Shot in the dark**	A wild guess; an attempt that is unlikely to succeed	अंधेरे में तीर चलाना (अंदाज़ा लगाना)	4 (6)
1535	**Show a clean pair of heels**	To run away quickly	नौ दो ग्यारह हो जाना (भाग जाना)	6 (2)
1536	Show a leg	To get out of bed; to hurry up and get going	बिस्तर छोड़ो, जल्दी करो	
1537	Show of hands	A way of voting by raising hands	हाथ उठाकर मतदान (खुला वोट)	
1538	**Show the white feather**	To act in a cowardly way	कायरता दिखाना (डरपोक होना)	2 (3)
1539	Show the white flag	To show that you accept defeat and want to stop fighting	आत्मसमर्पण करना (हार मान लेना)	
1540	Silver tongue	The ability to speak in a way that makes people do what you want	वाक्पटुता (मीठी और प्रभावशाली बोली)	
1541	Sing a different tune (or change one's tune)	To change your opinion or behaviour, especially when you were wrong	राग बदलना (अपना रवैया बदल लेना)	

SN	Idioms/Phrases	English Meaning	Hindi Meaning	#R
1542	Sit at the feet of	To be taught by someone as their student	शिष्य बनना (किसी के मार्गदर्शन में सीखना)	
1543	Sit in judgment	To criticize or judge others	फ़ैसला या आलोचना करना	
1544	Sit on a gold mine	To own something that is worth a lot of money	ख़ज़ाने पर बैठे होना (अनमोल चीज़ पास होना)	
1545	**Sit on the fence**	To avoid taking sides or making a decision	तटस्थ रहना (किसी का पक्ष न लेना)	20 (10)
1546	Sit tight	To wait and not take any action	धैर्य रखना (जमे रहना)	
1547	**Sitting duck**	An easy target; someone who is easy to attack or criticize	आसान निशाना (असुरक्षित व्यक्ति)	1 (1)
1548	**Skeleton in the cupboard (or closet)**	An embarrassing secret from someone's past	पुराना शर्मनाक राज़ (छिपा हुआ भेद)	3 (2)
1549	**Slap on the wrist**	A gentle punishment that is not severe	बहुत हल्की सज़ा (नाममात्र का दंड)	6 (3)
1550	**Sleep like a log (or baby)**	To sleep very deeply and soundly	घोड़े बेचकर सोना (गहरी नींद)	1 (1)
1551	**Sleep on it**	To wait until the next day before making a decision	सोच-विचार के लिए समय लेना (रात भर सोचना)	1 (1)
1552	**Slip of the tongue**	An accidental error when speaking	ज़बान फिसलना (बोलते समय ग़लती)	2 (1)
1553	**Slip one's mind**	To forget something temporarily	दिमाग़ से निकल जाना (भूल जाना)	2
1554	**Slow and steady wins the race**	Being careful and consistent leads to success	धीरे-धीरे और स्थिर रहकर सफलता मिलती है (निरंतर प्रयास)	1 (1)
1555	Small potatoes (or beer)	Something or someone that is not important	तुच्छ या महत्वहीन (छोटी बात)	
1556	**Smell a rat**	To suspect that something is wrong or dishonest	दाल में कुछ काला होना (शक होना)	15 (9)
1557	Smell blood	To recognize that someone is in a weak position and can be defeated	कमज़ोरी भाँपना (प्रतिद्वंद्वी की दुर्बलता समझना)	
1558	**Smoke and mirrors**	Something that deceives or confuses people	आँखों में धूल झोंकना (सच छुपाने की चाल)	2
1559	**Smooth (or plain) sailing**	Making good progress without difficulties	आसान सफ़र (बिना रुकावट के)	2
1560	Smooth someone's ruffled feathers	To make someone less angry or upset	नाराज़गी दूर करना (किसी को शांत करना)	
1561	**Snake in the grass**	A treacherous person who pretends to be a friend	आस्तीन का साँप (छिपा हुआ दुश्मन)	13 (5)
1562	**Snowball effect**	A situation that becomes more significant as it continues	बढ़ता हुआ प्रभाव (तेज़ी से फैलना)	2
1563	**Snowed under**	Having too much work to deal with	काम के बोझ तले दबा हुआ (बहुत व्यस्त)	2 (1)
1564	So far so good	Everything has been satisfactory up to this point	अब तक सब ठीक है (फ़िलहाल कोई समस्या नहीं)	
1565	**Soft option**	A choice that is easier but may not be best	आसान विकल्प (मुश्किल से बचने का रास्ता)	3
1566	Sore point	A subject that makes someone upset when mentioned	दुखती रग (संवेदनशील मुद्दा)	

SN	Idioms/Phrases	English Meaning	Hindi Meaning	#R
1567	**Sought after**	Wanted by many people; in high demand	बहुत माँग वाला (लोकप्रिय)	1 (1)
1568	Sound a red alert	To issue a warning about an emergency	ख़तरे की घंटी बजाना (चेतावनी देना)	
1569	Sound as a bell	In perfect condition; completely healthy or functional	एकदम ठीक-ठाक, पूरी तरह स्वस्थ	
1570	Sour grapes	Criticizing something you cannot have	खट्टे अंगूर (अप्राप्य चीज़ को बुरा कहना)	
1571	Sow dragon's teeth	To do something that creates problems for the future	मुसीबत बुलाना (भविष्य में झगड़े के बीज बोना)	
1572	**Sow one's wild oats**	To do foolish or wild things when young	जवानी में मौज-मस्ती करना (लापरवाह जीवन)	3
1573	**Speak of the devil**	Said when someone you were just talking about appears	शैतान का नाम लिया, शैतान हाज़िर (बात करते ही सामने आ जाना)	2 (1)
1574	**Speak one's mind**	To express your opinions honestly and directly	मन की बात कहना (खुलकर बोलना)	5
1575	**Speak volumes**	To show something very clearly without needing words	बहुत कुछ कह जाना (स्पष्ट संकेत देना)	1 (1)
1576	**Spick and span**	Very clean and neat	एकदम चकाचक (साफ़-सुथरा)	10 (1)
1577	**Spill the beans**	To tell a secret, often by accident	राज़ उगल देना (भेद खोलना)	27 (20)
1578	**Spin one's wheels**	To use energy without making any progress	बेकार की मेहनत करना (प्रगति के बिना ऊर्जा खर्च करना)	3
1579	**Split hairs**	To make unnecessary distinctions about small details	बाल की खाल निकालना (छोटी बातों पर बहस)	2 (2)
1580	**Split one's sides**	To laugh uncontrollably	लोटपोट होना (जोर से हँसना)	2 (1)
1581	**Spread like wildfire**	To become known very fast over a large area	जंगल की आग की तरह फैलना (तेज़ी से फैलना)	2 (3)
1582	**Square deal**	Fair and honest treatment	ईमानदारी का सौदा (न्यायसंगत व्यवहार)	2 (1)
1583	**Square meal**	A large, satisfying, and nutritious meal	भरपेट भोजन (पौष्टिक खाना)	1 (1)
1584	**Square peg in a round hole**	A person who is not suited to their environment	बेमेल व्यक्ति (अनुपयुक्त स्थिति में)	4 (2)
1585	**Stab (someone) in the back**	To harm someone who trusts you	पीठ में छुरा घोंपना (विश्वासघात करना)	5
1586	Stand a chance	To have a possibility of achieving something	संभावना होना (सफलता की गुंजाइश)	
1587	**Stand in one's own light**	To act in a way that damages your own prospects	अपने ही पैर पर कुल्हाड़ी मारना (ख़ुद को नुक़सान)	2
1588	**Stand on one's own two feet**	To be able to support oneself without help	अपने पैरों पर खड़ा होना (आत्मनिर्भर होना)	1 (2)
1589	Stand-offish	Cold and unfriendly in manner	रूखा और दूरी बनाए रखने वाला (अलग-थलग)	
1590	Star-crossed lovers	Lovers destined to have an unhappy relationship	दुर्भाग्यशाली प्रेमी (जिनका मिलन किस्मत में न हो)	

SN	Idioms/Phrases	English Meaning	Hindi Meaning	#R
1591	**Start (or set or get) the ball rolling**	To begin a process or activity	शुरुआत करना (कार्य आरंभ करना)	2
1592	**Steal a march on**	To secretly gain an advantage over someone	बाज़ी मार लेना (चुपके से आगे निकल जाना)	4
1593	**Steal someone's thunder**	To take someone else's attention or credit	दूसरे का श्रेय छीनना (किसी की तारीफ़ लूटना)	6 (6)
1594	Steal the show	To be the most impressive or popular in a performance	महफ़िल लूट लेना (सबका ध्यान आकर्षित करना)	
1595	**Steer clear of**	To take care to avoid something or someone	किनारा करना (दूर रहना)	3 (1)
1596	**Step (or tread) on someone's toes**	To offend someone by getting involved in their responsibilities	किसी के काम में टांग अड़ाना (किसी के काम में दखल देना)	2 (1)
1597	Step up to the plate	To take action and accept responsibility	ज़िम्मेदारी उठाना (आगे बढ़कर काम संभालना)	
1598	Stepping stone	A means of advancement to something better	सफलता की सीढ़ी (आगे बढ़ने का ज़रिया)	
1599	Stew in one's own juices	To suffer the consequences of one's own actions	अपनी करनी का फल भोगना	
1600	**Stick one's neck out**	To take a risk by doing or saying something bold	गर्दन फँसाना (जोख़िम मोल लेना)	2 (2)
1601	**Stick to one's guns**	To refuse to change your opinions or plans	अपनी बात पर अडिग रहना (अड़े रहना)	5 (3)
1602	Stick-in-the-mud	A person who is unwilling to try new things	रूढ़िवादी व्यक्ति (बदलाव में अनिच्छुक)	
1603	**Sticky fingers**	A habit of stealing things	हाथ साफ करना (चोरी की आदत होना)	2 (1)
1604	Stiff-necked	Refusing to change or obey; arrogantly stubborn	अड़ियल (ज़िद्दी और घमंडी)	
1605	Sting in the tail	An unpleasant surprise at the end of something	अंत में अप्रिय आश्चर्य (अंतिम झटका)	
1606	**Stir up a hornet's nest**	To do something that causes serious trouble	ततैया के छत्ते में हाथ डालना (मुसीबत खड़ी करना)	5 (1)
1607	**Storm in a teacup**	A lot of unnecessary anger about something small	बात का बतंगड़ (छोटी बात पर हंगामा)	15 (6)
1608	**Straight from the horse's mouth**	Heard from the person directly involved	पहले हाथ की जानकारी (सीधे संबंधित व्यक्ति से सुनी बात)	9 (1)
1609	Straight shooter	Someone who is honest and says what they think	ईमानदार और सीधा व्यक्ति (खरा बोलने वाला)	
1610	Straighten up and fly right	To start behaving well or responsibly	सीधे रास्ते पर आना (सुधर जाना)	
1611	**Strain every nerve**	To try as hard as possible	एड़ी-चोटी का ज़ोर लगाना (जी-तोड़ मेहनत)	6 (6)
1612	Straw in the wind	A small hint or indication of future events	हवा का रुख़ (भविष्य का संकेत)	
1613	Stretch one's legs	To take a walk, especially after sitting	टाँगें सीधी करना (टहलना)	
1614	Strike (or touch) a chord	To evoke an emotional response	दिल को छू लेना	

SN	Idioms/Phrases	English Meaning	Hindi Meaning	#R
1615	Strike a bargain	To make a deal that both sides agree to	सौदा तय करना (सहमति पर पहुँचना)	
1616	Strike a chill into someone's heart	To make someone feel suddenly frightened	कलेजा मुँह को आना (डर से काँपना)	
1617	**Strike the colours**	To admit defeat; to lower the flag in surrender	हथियार डाल देना (हार मानना)	1 (1)
1618	Stuffed shirt	A person who behaves in a very formal and self-important way	घमंडी व्यक्ति (अकड़ू और दिखावेबाज़)	
1619	Suffer in silence	To endure hardship without expressing grief or complaint	चुपचाप सहना (बिना शिकायत झेलना)	
1620	**Suit someone to a T**	To be exactly right for someone	बिल्कुल सही होना (एकदम उपयुक्त)	2
1621	Sum and substance	The main or essential part of something	सार (मुख्य बात)	
1622	**Swan song**	The last piece of work by an artist before death or retirement	अंतिम प्रदर्शन (विदाई की प्रस्तुति)	2
1623	**Sweep under the carpet (or rug)**	To try to hide a problem or keep it secret	बात दबा देना (समस्या छिपाना)	2 (6)
1624	Sweeping statement	A statement that is too general and ignores important facts	ढालू बयान (बारीकियों को नज़रअंदाज़ करने वाला)	
1625	**Swim with the tide (or go with the flow)**	To behave like others rather than act independently	धारा के साथ बहना (भीड़ का अनुसरण करना)	2
1626	**Swollen-headed**	Too proud of yourself; having an exaggerated sense of your own importance	घमंडी (अहंकारी)	2
1627	**Sword of Damocles**	A bad thing that might happen to you at any time	सिर पर लटकती तलवार (मँडराता ख़तरा)	4
1628	**Take a back seat**	To become less active; to allow others to take control	पीछे हटना (कम सक्रिय भूमिका लेना)	3 (1)
1629	Take a chill pill	To relax and stop being angry or upset	शांत हो जाना (आराम करना)	
1630	Take a dim view of	To regard something with disapproval	अनुचित समझना (नापसंद करना)	
1631	Take a fancy to	To start to like someone or something	पसंद आना (आकर्षित होना)	
1632	Take a leaf out of someone's book	To copy what someone else does because they are successful	किसी का अनुकरण करना (पदचिह्नों पर चलना)	
1633	**Take a leap in the dark**	To do something without knowing what will happen	अंधेरे में छलांग लगाना (अनजान जोख़िम लेना)	1 (2)
1634	**Take a rain check**	To refuse an offer but suggest accepting it at a later time	अभी नहीं, बाद में (प्रस्ताव टालना)	2 (6)
1635	Take a shortcut	To use a faster route or method	छोटा रास्ता अपनाना (जल्दी का तरीक़ा)	
1636	**Take a toll on**	To cause damage or suffering gradually	धीरे-धीरे नुकसान पहुँचाना (बुरा असर डालना)	2
1637	Take care of	To look after someone or something	देखभाल करना	
1638	**Take exception to**	To strongly disagree with or be upset by something	आपत्ति जताना (बुरा मानना)	5

SN	Idioms/Phrases	English Meaning	Hindi Meaning	#R
1639	**Take for granted**	To not appreciate something; to assume something is true	क़द्र न करना; मान लेना (महत्व न समझना)	3
1640	**Take French leave**	To leave without asking permission or saying goodbye	बिना अनुमति के अनुपस्थित रहना (चुपके से चले जाना)	4 (1)
1641	**Take heart**	To start to feel more hopeful and confident	हिम्मत जुटाना (उत्साहित होना)	4 (1)
1642	**Take in one's stride**	To handle something difficult without becoming upset	सहजता से स्वीकारना (शांत रहकर निपटना)	2
1643	**Take into account (or take account of)**	To consider something when making a decision	ध्यान में रखना (विचार करना)	2
1644	Take it easy	To relax and not work too hard; to stay calm	आराम करना; धीरज रखना (चिंता न करना)	
1645	Take notice	To give attention to something important	ध्यान देना (संज्ञान लेना)	
1646	**Take off one's hat to**	To express admiration for someone	सम्मान व्यक्त करना (प्रशंसा करना)	5 (1)
1647	Take one's breath away	To make someone feel extremely surprised or impressed	दाँतों तले उँगली दबाना (आश्चर्यचकित करना)	
1648	**Take one's cue from**	To use someone's actions as a signal for what to do	संकेत लेना (अनुसरण करना)	2
1649	Take one's eye off the ball	To stop giving attention to what is important	ध्यान हटाना (मुख्य बात से चूकना)	
1650	**Take pains**	To try very hard to do something well	मेहनत करना (बड़ी सावधानी से काम करना)	4 (1)
1651	Take someone at their word	To believe what someone says without question	किसी की बात मान लेना (बिना सबूत विश्वास करना)	
1652	**Take someone for a ride**	To trick or deceive someone	उल्लू बनाना (धोखा देना)	2 (2)
1653	**Take stock of**	To think carefully about a situation before making a decision	जायज़ा लेना (आकलन करना)	5
1654	**Take the bull by the horns**	To face a difficult situation directly and with courage	मुसीबत का डटकर सामना करना (साहस से निपटना)	10 (10)
1655	Take the heat	To accept criticism, pressure, or responsibility	आलोचना झेलना (दबाव सहना)	
1656	Take the veil	To become a nun; to join a religious order	संन्यासिन बनना	
1657	Take the wind out of one's sails	To suddenly take away someone's confidence or enthusiasm	हवा निकाल देना (उत्साह कम करना)	
1658	**Take time by the forelock**	To seize an opportunity promptly; to act quickly	मौके पर चौका मारना (अवसर का तुरंत लाभ उठाना)	1 (1)
1659	**Take to heart**	To think about something seriously and let it affect you	दिल पर लेना (गहराई से प्रभावित होना)	4 (1)
1660	**Take to one's heels**	To flee; to run away in fear	रफ़ूचक्कर होना (भाग खड़ा होना)	8 (4)
1661	**Take to task**	To criticize someone strongly for a mistake	फटकारना (डाँटना)	7 (1)
1662	**Take up (or pick or accept) the gauntlet**	To accept a challenge	चुनौती स्वीकार करना (मुक़ाबले के लिए तैयार होना)	3 (1)

SN	Idioms/Phrases	English Meaning	Hindi Meaning	#R
1663	Take up space (or room)	To fill or use a certain amount of space	जगह घेरना (स्थान लेना)	
1664	Take up the gauntlet	To accept a challenge or invitation to fight	चुनौती स्वीकार करना (ललकार उठाना)	
1665	Take up the hatchet	To start a fight or conflict	युद्ध की तैयारी करना (लड़ाई छेड़ना)	
1666	**Take with a pinch (or grain) of salt**	To be skeptical about something; to not fully believe it	आँख मूँदकर विश्वास न करना (संदेह के साथ मानना)	16 (10)
1667	**Taken aback**	Surprised and slightly upset	हक्का-बक्का रह जाना (अचंभित होना)	4
1668	**Talk through one's hat**	To talk about something without knowing the facts	बकवास करना (बिना जाने बोलना)	3 (4)
1669	Tall tale	An unlikely and exaggerated story	बढ़ा-चढ़ाकर कही गई कहानी (डींग)	
1670	**Teething problems**	Problems that happen in the early stages	प्रारंभिक कठिनाइयाँ (शुरुआती समस्याएँ)	2
1671	Tell tales out of school	To reveal private or confidential information to outsiders	भेद खोलना (गोपनीय बात बाहर बताना)	
1672	**That ship has sailed**	It is too late to do something; the chance is gone	मौक़ा निकल जाना (अब बहुत देर हो गई)	1 (1)
1673	That's all she wrote	The end of the story; nothing more to add	बस इतना ही (कहानी ख़त्म)	
1674	**The ABC of something**	The most basic or fundamental aspects of something	किसी चीज़ की बुनियादी बातें	2
1675	**The alpha and omega**	The beginning and the end; the most essential part	आदि और अंत (सबसे महत्वपूर्ण हिस्सा)	2 (2)
1676	The ayes have it	Most people have voted yes	हाँ की जीत (बहुमत पक्ष में है)	
1677	**The ball is in your court**	It is now your turn to act or make a decision	अब गेंद तुम्हारे पाले में है (अब फ़ैसला आपका है)	8 (8)
1678	The beauty of it	The most pleasing feature of something	सबसे अच्छी बात (आकर्षक पहलू)	
1679	The bee's knees	An outstanding person or thing	कमाल की चीज़ (बेहतरीन)	
1680	The calm before the storm	A quiet period before a period of activity or trouble	तूफ़ान से पहले की शांति (मुसीबत से पहले का सुकून)	
1681	The devil is beating his wife	Rain while the sun is shining	धूप में बारिश होना	
1682	The elixir of life	A magical potion believed to grant eternal life or cure all diseases	अमृत, संजीवनी	
1683	The fur flies	A fierce argument or fight breaks out	बवाल मचना (तू-तू मैं-मैं होना)	
1684	The game is up	The deception or scheme is exposed	भांडा फूट जाना (भेद खुलना)	
1685	The gnomes of Zurich	Powerful international bankers	बड़े अंतर्राष्ट्रीय बैंकर	
1686	The graveyard shift	A work shift during the night, typically midnight to 8am	रात की पाली (देर रात का काम)	
1687	**The green-eyed monster**	Jealousy	ईर्ष्या (जलन की भावना)	2 (1)
1688	**The lion's share**	The largest or best portion of something	शेर का हिस्सा (सबसे बड़ा हिस्सा)	9 (7)

SN	Idioms/Phrases	English Meaning	Hindi Meaning	#R
1689	The movers and shakers	People who have influence and make important things happen	प्रभावशाली लोग (निर्णय लेने वाले)	
1690	The nitty-gritty	The practical or essential aspects of something	मूल बातें (महत्वपूर्ण विवरण)	
1691	The old Adam	The tendency to be sinful; original sin	मानव प्रकृति का बुरा पक्ष (पाप की प्रवृत्ति)	
1692	The passing bell	A church bell rung to announce someone's death	मृत्यु की घंटी (शोक सूचक)	
1693	The penny drops (or dropped)	Suddenly understands or realises something	अचानक बात समझ में आना	
1694	**The pros and cons**	The arguments for and against something	पक्ष और विपक्ष (नफ़ा-नुक़सान)	5 (2)
1695	**The seamy side**	The unattractive or sordid aspects of life	परदे के पीछे की सच्चाई (अप्रिय पहलू)	2
1696	The smallest room in the house	A euphemism for the toilet or bathroom	शौचालय (विनम्र रूप में)	
1697	The sound of leather on willow	The characteristic sound of a cricket match (ball hitting bat)	बल्ले पर गेंद लगने की ध्वनि	
1698	The Straw that broke the camel's back	The last in a series of problems that finally causes a reaction	सब्र का बाँध टूट जाना (बर्दाश्त की सीमा पार)	
1699	**The tail wagging the dog**	A situation where a minor element controls a major one	उलटी गंगा बहना (छोटी चीज़ द्वारा बड़ी को नियंत्रित करना)	1 (1)
1700	**The thin end of the wedge**	A small change that leads to bigger, often unwanted changes	छोटी चिंगारी (बड़ी मुसीबत की शुरुआत)	1 (1)
1701	**The tip of the iceberg**	A small part of a much larger, hidden problem	हिमखंड की नोक (बड़ी समस्या की छोटी सी झलक)	3 (1)
1702	The university of life	Practical wisdom gained through real-life experience	ज़िंदगी का तजुर्बा ही असली पाठशाला	
1703	The wheels came off	A situation has failed or collapsed	पटरी से उतरना (योजना का बिखर जाना)	
1704	The whole ball of wax	Everything; the entire thing	सब कुछ (पूरा मामला)	
1705	**The whys and wherefores**	The detailed reasons for something	कारण और स्पष्टीकरण (तर्क-वितर्क)	2
1706	**The world is one's oyster**	One can achieve anything they want	दुनिया अवसरों से भरी है (जो चाहो पा सकते हो)	2
1707	There is no gainsaying	Something that cannot be disputed or denied	अकाट्य (इनकार नही किया जा सकता)	
1708	**Think on one's feet**	To react and think quickly in difficult situations	तुरंत निर्णय लेना (फ़ौरन सोचना)	2
1709	**Think outside the box**	To think in an original or creative way	नई और अलग सोच (रचनात्मक विचार)	3
1710	**Thorn in the flesh**	Something or someone that continually causes problems	आँख का काँटा (लगातार परेशानी)	2 (1)
1711	Through and through	Completely; to the fullest extent	पूरी तरह से (हर तरह से)	
1712	**Through thick and thin**	In all circumstances, both good and bad	सुख-दुख में (हर हाल में साथ)	17 (6)

SN	Idioms/Phrases	English Meaning	Hindi Meaning	#R
1713	Throw (or put) out of gear	To disrupt the normal functioning of something	व्यवस्था बिगाड़ देना (काम में बाधा डालना)	
1714	Throw a fit	To become extremely angry or upset	आपा खो देना (गुस्से में भड़कना)	
1715	Throw a hissy fit	To have a childish outburst of temper	बच्चों जैसा गुस्सैल नखरा दिखाना	
1716	**Throw a spanner (or wrench) in the works**	To do something that prevents a plan from succeeding	काम में रोड़ा अटकाना (योजना बिगाड़ना)	2 (4)
1717	**Throw caution to the wind**	To take a risk without worrying about the consequences	जोखिम उठाना (लापरवाही से काम करना)	11 (7)
1718	**Throw down the gauntlet**	To challenge someone to a contest or fight	ललकारना (चुनौती देना)	3 (1)
1719	**Throw dust in one's eyes**	To try to confuse or deceive someone	आँखों में धूल झोंकना (धोखा देना)	5 (3)
1720	**Throw in the towel OR Throw up the sponge**	To accept that you have been beaten	हथियार डाल देना (हार मान लेना)	11 (12)
1721	**Throw one's cap over the windmill**	To act without thinking of consequences	बिना सोचे-समझे जोख़िम लेना	2
1722	**Throw one's hat in the ring**	To announce that you are going to compete in a contest	मैदान में उतरना (प्रतियोगिता में शामिल होना)	2 (1)
1723	Throw someone a curveball	To surprise someone with something unexpected or difficult	अचानक चौंका देना	
1724	Throw spaghetti at the wall	To try many different approaches hoping something will work	बहुत सी कोशिशें करना यह देखने के लिए कि क्या काम आता है	
1725	**Throw the baby out with the bathwater**	To get rid of something valuable while getting rid of something unwanted	अंधी काट-छाँट (बुरे के साथ अच्छे को भी हानि पहुँचाना)	1 (1)
1726	Throw up one's cards	To admit defeat and stop trying	हार स्वीकार करना (योजना छोड़ना)	
1727	Thrown in at the deep end	To be forced to deal with something difficult without help	बिना तैयारी के बड़ी चुनौती में डालना (सीधे गहरे में)	
1728	**Thumb one's nose**	To show contempt or defiance towards someone	अपमान करना (तिरस्कार दिखाना)	1 (1)
1729	**Tick (or check) all the boxes**	To satisfy all the necessary criteria	सभी मापदंडों पर खरा उतरना (ज़रूरी शर्तें पूरी करना)	2
1730	**Tickled pink**	Very happy and pleased	बाग़-बाग़ होना (बहुत ख़ुश होना)	2 (1)
1731	Tide someone over	To help someone through a difficult time	कठिन समय में सहारा देना	
1732	Tie oneself in knots	To become very confused or worried	उलझन में पड़ना (भ्रमित होना)	
1733	**Tie the knot**	To get married	शादी करना (विवाह बंधन में बँधना)	1 (3)
1734	**Tighten one's belt**	To reduce spending because there is less money available	ख़र्च में कटौती करना (मितव्ययता बरतना)	2
1735	Tight-lipped	Unwilling to talk about something	मुँह बंद रखना (बात ना बताना)	
1736	**Till the cows come home**	For an extremely long time	अनिश्चित काल तक (बहुत लंबे समय तक)	2 (1)
1737	**Tilt at windmills**	To fight against imaginary enemies or problems	हवा में तलवार चलाना (काल्पनिक दुश्मनों से लड़ना)	1 (1)
1738	Time after time	Many times over a period of time	बार-बार (हर बार)	

SN	Idioms/Phrases	English Meaning	Hindi Meaning	#R
1739	**Time and again**	Very often over a period of time	बार-बार (अक्सर)	2
1740	Time flies	Used to say that time seems to pass quickly	समय पलक झपकते निकल जाता है (वक़्त कैसे उड़ता है)	
1741	Tip one's hand	To accidentally reveal your intentions	भेद खोल देना (योजना बता देना)	
1742	**Tit for tat**	An action done in return for something done to you	जैसे को तैसा (बदले में वही व्यवहार)	2
1743	**To and fro**	In one direction and then the other	आगे-पीछे (इधर-उधर)	2
1744	To oil the hinges of silence	to bribe someone to remain quiet	चुप रहने के लिए रिश्वत देना	
1745	**To one's heart's content**	As much or as long as one wants	जी भरकर (मन चाहे जितना)	1 (1)
1746	**To the best of one's ability**	As well as one is able to	अपनी पूरी क्षमता से (जितना हो सके)	2
1747	To the letter	Doing exactly what is required, with no changes	अक्षरशः (पूरी तरह नियम मानना)	
1748	**To the manner born**	Naturally able to do something because of background or training	जन्मजात प्रतिभा (स्वाभाविक रूप से कुशल)	1 (1)
1749	To the point	Dealing only with what is important; direct	सटीक (मुद्दे की बात)	
1750	**Toe the line**	To obey rules and accept authority	नियम मानना (अनुशासन में रहना)	4
1751	**Toffee-nosed**	Acting in a superior way; snobbish	नकचढ़ा (घमंडी)	2
1752	**Token strike**	A short strike intended as a symbolic protest	सांकेतिक हड़ताल (प्रतीकात्मक विरोध)	2
1753	**Tongue in cheek**	Said or done humorously, not meant to be taken seriously	मज़ाक में कहना (व्यंग्यात्मक)	3 (2)
1754	Too close for comfort	So close that it causes worry or discomfort	असहज होने जितना करीब (ख़तरनाक निकटता)	
1755	Too close to call	So close that the outcome cannot be predicted	काँटे की टक्कर (बहुत करीबी मुक़ाबला)	
1756	**Too many irons in the fire**	To be trying to do too many things at once	एक साथ बहुत सारे कामों में उलझना (बहुत व्यस्त)	4 (3)
1757	Touch a sore spot	To mention something that upsets or bothers someone	दुखती रग पर हाथ रखना	
1758	Touch and go	Uncertain and risky; possibly failing	अनिश्चित (जोख़िम भरा)	
1759	Touch base with someone	To briefly contact someone to exchange updates	किसी से संक्षेप में संपर्क करना (हालचाल लेना)	
1760	Tough cheese	Used to show lack of sympathy	तुम्हारी किस्मत ख़राब (मुझे कोई हमदर्दी नहीं)	
1761	Tough cookie	A strong, resilient person not easily beaten	मज़बूत इरादे वाला (आसानी से न टूटने वाला)	
1762	Tough sledding	Difficult work or progress; a situation hard to advance through	कठिन परिस्थिति, मुश्किल दौर	
1763	Tout de suite	Immediately, at once	तुरंत, फ़ौरन	
1764	Tread carefully	To act carefully to avoid making mistakes	फूँक-फूँक कर कदम रखना (सावधानी बरतना)	
1765	**Tricks of the trade**	Methods and skills known only by experienced people	विशेष व्यावसायिक कौशल (पेशे की बारीकियाँ)	1 (2)

SN	Idioms/Phrases	English Meaning	Hindi Meaning	#R
1766	Trip off the tongue	To be easy and pleasant to say	ज़ुबान पर आसानी से चढ़ना (सहज बोला जा सकना)	
1767	Trip over one's tongue	To make a mistake while speaking; to stumble over words	बोलते-बोलते ग़लती करना (ज़ुबान लड़खड़ाना)	
1768	Trip the light fantastic	To dance gracefully	थिरकना, ख़ूबसूरती से नाचना	
1769	**True colours**	One's real personality or beliefs	असली चेहरा (वास्तविक स्वभाव)	2
1770	True-blue	Extremely loyal and unwavering in support	पक्का वफ़ादार	
1771	Trump card	An advantage that you keep until needed	तुरुप का पत्ता (अचूक हथियार)	
1772	**Turn (or earn) an honest penny**	To make money in an honest way	ईमानदारी से कमाना (सच्ची मेहनत)	2
1773	**Turn a blind eye**	To pretend not to notice something	अनदेखा करना (जानबूझकर नज़रअंदाज़ करना)	7 (8)
1774	**Turn a deaf ear**	To deliberately ignore what someone is saying	अनसुना करना (ध्यान न देना)	14 (6)
1775	Turn back the clock (or hands of time)	To go back to an earlier time	समय को पीछे मोड़ना (बीते हुए पल को वापस लाना)	
1776	**Turn one's coat**	To change your beliefs or loyalty	दलबदलू होना (पक्ष बदलना)	2
1777	Turn one's hand to	To try to do something that you have not done before	हाथ आज़माना (कोई नया काम करना)	
1778	**Turn over a new leaf**	To start behaving in a better way	नई शुरुआत करना (सुधर जाना)	8 (8)
1779	Turn purple with rage	To become very angry	गुस्से से तमतमाना (क्रोध से लाल होना)	
1780	**Turn someone's head**	To make someone too proud because of praise or success	घमंड चढ़ जाना (सफलता से अहंकारी होना)	2
1781	**Turn the corner**	To start to improve after a difficult period	मुश्किल दिन पार करना (सुधार की ओर मुड़ना)	1 (3)
1782	**Turn the tables**	To change a situation so that you now have an advantage	पासा पलटना (स्थिति अपने पक्ष में करना)	1 (5)
1783	Turn the tide	To reverse the course of events in one's favour	हालात का रुख़ पलट देना	
1784	**Turn turtle**	To overturn completely, especially of a boat	उलट जाना (पलट जाना)	1 (2)
1785	**Turn up one's nose at**	To refuse something because you think it is not good enough	नाक-भौं सिकोड़ना (नापसंदगी दिखाना)	3 (1)
1786	**Turning point**	A time when an important change happens	निर्णायक मोड़ (महत्वपूर्ण परिवर्तन)	2
1787	Twiddle one's thumbs	To do nothing while waiting for something	ख़ाली बैठना (बेकार में वक़्त गँवाना)	
1788	**Twist someone's arm**	To persuade someone to do something they don't want to do	जबरन राज़ी करना (दबाव डालना)	3 (1)
1789	Uncharted waters	A new and unfamiliar situation with unknown risks or dangers	अनजानी राह (अज्ञात क्षेत्र में क़दम रखना)	
1790	**Under a cloud**	In a state of suspicion or disfavour	संदेह के घेरे में (बदनामी की स्थिति में)	10 (4)

SN	Idioms/Phrases	English Meaning	Hindi Meaning	#R
1791	**Under duress**	Forced to do something by threats	दबाव में (ज़बरदस्ती की स्थिति में)	1 (1)
1792	Under fire	Being attacked or strongly criticized	आलोचना या हमले का शिकार (निशाने पर)	
1793	**Under someone's nose**	Very close to someone but not noticed	नाक के नीचे (बिल्कुल सामने)	2 (1)
1794	**Under someone's thumb**	Completely under someone's control	इशारों पर नाचना (किसी के नियंत्रण में)	4
1795	Under the gun	Under great pressure to do something	दबाव में (जल्दी करने के लिए मजबूर)	
1796	Under the sun	Anywhere in the world	इस दुनिया में (कहीं भी)	
1797	**Under the weather**	Not feeling well; slightly ill	तबीयत ठीक न होना (थोड़ा बीमार)	24 (18)
1798	Under the wire	To just barely complete something within a deadline	ऐन वक़्त पर काम पूरा करना	
1799	**Under wraps**	To keep something secret or hidden until a later time	गुप्त रखना (छुपाकर रखना)	4
1800	**Up against the wall**	In serious difficulty with no escape	कोई चारा न होना (मुश्किल में फँसा हुआ)	2
1801	**Up in arms**	Angry and ready to fight or argue	विरोध में उठ खड़ा होना (नाराज़गी में)	7 (7)
1802	**Up in the air**	Not yet settled or decided	अधर में लटका हुआ (अनिश्चित)	2
1803	Up the ante	To increase the level of something, especially demands	दाँव बढ़ाना (शर्तें कठिन करना)	
1804	**Up the creek**	In a difficult situation with no easy solution	मुसीबत में फँसा हुआ (बिना सहारे के)	3
1805	**Up to the mark**	Good enough; meeting expectations	मानक के अनुरूप (उम्मीद के मुताबिक)	3 (1)
1806	Up to the minute	Completely current; having the very latest information	एकदम ताज़ा जानकारी	
1807	Ups and downs	Good and bad experiences; periods of success and failure	उतार-चढ़ाव (अच्छे-बुरे दिन)	
1808	**Upset the apple cart**	To spoil someone's plans or arrangements	काम में खलल डालना (बनी-बनाई योजना बिगाड़ देना)	4 (2)
1809	**Vanish (or disappear) into thin air**	To disappear suddenly and completely	हवा में ग़ायब हो जाना (चंपत होना)	4 (1)
1810	Vent one's spleen	To express anger or frustration	भड़ास निकालना (गुस्सा उतारना)	
1811	**Vexed question**	A difficult question that has been discussed a lot without resolution	विवादास्पद मुद्दा (जटिल सवाल)	2
1812	**Vicious cycle (or circle)**	A situation where problems cause more problems	दुश्चक्र में फँसना (समस्याओं का सिलसिला)	4
1813	**Vote with one's feet**	To show that you disapprove by leaving	पैरों से मतदान (असहमति जताते हुए जाना)	2 (1)
1814	Vote with one's pocketbook (or wallet)	To express preferences through spending or financial decisions	अपने पैसे खर्च करके अपनी राय जताना	
1815	Wag school	To play truant; to skip school without permission	स्कूल से गैरहाज़िर रहना	

SN	Idioms/Phrases	English Meaning	Hindi Meaning	#R
1816	**Wait in the wings**	To be ready to take action or appear when needed	तैयार रहना	1 (1)
1817	**Walk a tightrope**	To be in a difficult situation requiring careful balance	रस्सी पर चलना (नाज़ुक स्थिति में सावधानी)	3 (2)
1818	**Walk of life**	A particular area of work or way of living	जीवन का क्षेत्र (पेशा या सामाजिक स्तर)	2
1819	**Walk on air**	To feel very happy and excited	सातवें आसमान पर होना (अत्यधिक खुश)	5
1820	**Walk on eggshells**	To be very careful not to offend or upset someone	फूँक-फूँक कर कदम रखना	1 (5)
1821	Walk the talk	To do what one says one will do	कथनी और करनी में एकता (वचन निभाना)	
1822	**Want to curl up and die**	To feel so embarrassed that you want to hide	शर्म से पानी-पानी होना (बेहद लज्जित)	2
1823	**Wash one's hands of**	To refuse to be responsible for something anymore	पल्ला झाड़ना (ज़िम्मेदारी से मुक्त होना)	2 (1)
1824	Watch grass grow	To be very bored or do something very boring	अत्यंत उबाऊ काम करना (बेहद बोरियत)	
1825	**Water under the bridge**	Past events that cannot be changed and should be forgotten	रात गई बात गई (जो हो गया सो हो गया)	5 (1)
1826	**Wax and wane**	To grow stronger then weaker in alternating phases	उतार-चढ़ाव होना (घटना-बढ़ना)	1 (1)
1827	We must do lunch sometime	A polite but often insincere suggestion to meet for a meal	कभी मिलते हैं खाने पर (औपचारिक निमंत्रण)	
1828	**Weal and woe**	Good fortune and misfortune	सुख और दुख (अच्छा और बुरा समय)	5 (1)
1829	**Wear and tear**	Damage that happens to something from normal use	घिसाव (सामान्य उपयोग से होने वाली टूट-फूट)	3
1830	**Wear one's heart on one's sleeve**	To make your feelings obvious to everyone	खुले दिल से भाव दिखाना (भावनाएँ न छिपाना)	8 (4)
1831	Wear out one's welcome	To stay so long that the host no longer wants you	इतना ठहरना कि मेज़बान तंग हो जाए	
1832	Wear the green willow	To mourn for lost love	प्रेम-वियोग में शोक मनाना	
1833	Weasel words	Deliberately misleading, vague, or evasive language	गोलमोल वाली बातें	
1834	**Weather the storm**	To successfully deal with a difficult situation	तूफ़ान का सामना करना (कठिन दौर से गुजरना)	3 (3)
1835	Wee (or small) hours	The very early hours after midnight	आधी रात के बाद का समय (रात 12 से 4 का समय)	
1836	**Wet behind the ears**	Too young and inexperienced to be reliable	अनुभवहीन (कच्चा और नया)	7 (1)
1837	**Wet blanket**	A person who discourages enjoyment or enthusiasm	कबाब में हड्डी (मज़ा किरकिरा करने वाला)	4 (3)
1838	Wet one's whistle	To have an alcoholic drink	गला तर करना (पीना)	
1839	Whatever floats your boat	Whatever suits you or makes you happy	जो तुम्हें ठीक लगे (अपनी पसंद के अनुसार)	

SN	Idioms/Phrases	English Meaning	Hindi Meaning	#R
1840	Wheels within wheels	A complex situation with many interconnected parts	जटिल स्थिति (परदे के पीछे की उलझन)	
1841	**When pigs fly**	Something that will never happen	जब सूरज पश्चिम से उगेगा (असंभव बात)	5 (4)
1842	When the balloon goes up	When a crisis or action begins	जब मुसीबत शुरू हो (संकट आने पर)	
1843	**When the crunch comes**	At the moment of decision or crisis	निर्णायक क्षण पर (जब फ़ैसला लेना हो)	2
1844	Whet one's appetite	To make someone want something more	उत्सुकता या इच्छा जगाना (भूख बढ़ाना)	
1845	**Whistle in the dark**	To try to stay cheerful in a frightening situation	डर छिपाने के लिए साहस दिखाना (बहादुरी का दिखावा)	3
1846	**White elephant**	Something that costs a lot to keep but is useless	महँगी लेकिन बेकार चीज़ (ख़र्चीला बोझ)	11 (6)
1847	**White lie**	A harmless lie told to be polite	मासूम झूठ (जो दिल न दुखाए)	2
1848	**Whole nine yards**	Everything; the whole thing	सब कुछ (पूरा-पूरा)	5 (2)
1849	Whoop it up	To celebrate or enjoy yourself in a noisy way	शोर-शराबे से जश्न मनाना (धूमधाम से)	
1850	Wide of the mark	Not accurate or correct at all	निशाने से दूर (ग़लत)	
1851	Wild and woolly	Rough, uncultivated, and uncivilized	असभ्य और बेतरतीब (जंगली)	
1852	**Wild goose chase**	A search for something that is impossible to find	भूसे में सुई ढूँढना (व्यर्थ की खोज)	18 (13)
1853	Wildcat strike	A strike organized without official union authorization	अनाधिकृत हड़ताल (बिना यूनियन की मंज़ूरी)	
1854	**Will-o'-the-wisp**	Something that is impossible to get or achieve	मृगतृष्णा (भ्रामक लक्ष्य)	3
1855	Win by a nose	To win by a very narrow margin	बहुत कम अंतर से जीतना	
1856	**Win laurels**	To earn praise and honour	कीर्ति प्राप्त करना (सम्मान पाना)	3 (1)
1857	Win on points	To win by accumulating points rather than a knockout	अंकों के आधार पर जीतना	
1858	Wine and dine	To entertain someone generously with food and drink	भव्य आतिथ्य (शानदार खाने-पीने की मेहमानी)	
1859	Wipe someone's nose	To defeat or humiliate someone decisively	किसी को चालाकी से बुरी तरह मात देना	
1860	Wipe the floor with	To defeat someone very easily and completely	धूल चटा देना (बुरी तरह हराना)	
1861	With a vengeance	With much greater force than expected	ज़ोर-शोर से (पूरी ताक़त से)	
1862	With bated breath	In a worried, anxious, or excited way	साँस रोककर (उत्सुकता से इंतज़ार)	
1863	With bells on	Eagerly; with great enthusiasm and readiness	पूरे जोश और उत्साह से	
1864	**With might and main**	With all one's strength and energy	एड़ी-चोटी का ज़ोर लगाना (पूरी ताक़त से)	3
1865	With one voice	Speaking or acting together as one group	एक स्वर में (एकमत से)	

SN	Idioms/Phrases	English Meaning	Hindi Meaning	#R
1866	With one's tail between one's legs	Looking ashamed because of defeat	दुम दबाकर (शर्मिंदा होकर)	
1867	**With open arms**	In a very welcoming way	खुले दिल से (गर्मजोशी से स्वागत)	4 (4)
1868	Without question	Definitely; certainly	निस्संदेह (बेशक)	
1869	**Without rhyme or reason**	Without any sensible reason or purpose	बिना सिर-पैर के (बिना किसी तर्क)	1 (1)
1870	**Wolf in sheep's clothing**	Someone who seems friendly but is actually dangerous	भेड़ की खाल में भेड़िया (छिपा हुआ ख़तरनाक व्यक्ति)	5 (6)
1871	Work like a charm	To be very effective and successful	जादू की तरह काम करना (बेहतरीन नतीजा)	
1872	Work like a dog	To work extremely hard	कोल्हू के बैल की तरह काम करना (कड़ी मेहनत करना)	
1873	Work like a dream	To function very well and smoothly	मक्खन की तरह चलना (शानदार काम करना)	
1874	**Work one's fingers to the bone**	To work very hard over a long period	जी-तोड़ मेहनत करना (कठिन परिश्रम करना)	2
1875	Work one's way through school	To earn money to pay for one's education while studying	पढ़ाई के साथ काम करके ख़र्च उठाना	
1876	Work the system	To exploit rules or procedures for personal advantage	व्यवस्था का फायदा उठाना	
1877	Worlds apart	Very different in opinion or nature	ज़मीन-आसमान का अंतर (बिल्कुल भिन्न)	
1878	**Worth one's weight in gold**	Very valuable or helpful	सोने में तौले जाने लायक़ (अत्यंत मूल्यवान)	2
1879	**Wrangle over an ass's shadow**	To quarrel over something unimportant	बेकार की बात पर झगड़ा (तुच्छ विषय पर बहस)	3
1880	Wrap someone in cotton wool	To be excessively protective towards someone	रुई के फाहों में रखना (ज़रूरत से ज़्यादा सुरक्षा देना)	
1881	**Writing on the wall**	A clear warning sign that something bad is going to happen	आने वाली मुसीबत का संकेत (भविष्य की चेतावनी)	2 (1)
1882	Yellow-bellied	Cowardly; lacking courage	कायर (डरपोक)	
1883	**Yeoman service**	Very good, useful, and loyal service	उत्कृष्ट और निस्वार्थ सेवा (बढ़िया सेवा)	4 (1)
1884	You can say that again	Used to show you strongly agree with what someone said	बिल्कुल सही कहा (पूरी तरह सहमत हूँ)	
1885	**Your guess is as good as mine**	Used to say that you do not know the answer to a question	मुझे भी उतना ही पता है जितना आपको (मुझे भी नहीं पता)	2 (1)
1886	**Zero tolerance**	A policy of refusing to accept any violation of rules	कठोर अनुशासन (कोई छूट नहीं)	2 (1)
1887	**Zip your lip**	To stop talking or keep a secret	मुँह पर ताला लगाना (चुप रहना)	1 (3)

*Total **1887** Idioms asked **6981** times*

B3 Idioms & Phrases Practice Sets (Based on Recent SSC Papers)

Practice Set - 1

Direction (Q. 1-10): Choose the correct meaning of the given idiom from the options:

1 Bury the hatchet
1) To reconcile after a conflict
2) To deepen hostility
3) To run away
4) To forget someone's name

2 Make one's toes curl
1) To be and remain active, alert, and focused
2) To insult, offend, or upset someone, especially by involving oneself in that which is someone else's responsibility
3) To tentatively begin or get involved in a new experience
4) To cause one an acute feeling of disgust, shame, embarrassment, or anguish

3 Sit on the fence
1) Take a risk
2) Remain silent
3) Stay neutral
4) Join both sides

4 By the skin of one's teeth
1) With deceptive appearance
2) With the barest possible margin
3) Through inherited privilege
4) With false humility

5 Back to the drawing board
1) To start over after a failure
2) To complete a task successfully
3) To take a short break from work
4) To finalize a project

6 Carry coals to Newcastle
1) Seek advice from experts
2) Provide something where it is already abundant
3) Complain without cause
4) Travel without direction

7 Blow hot and cold
1) To change one's mood or opinion frequently
2) To talk boastfully
3) To enjoy both success and failure
4) To remain consistent in behaviour

8 Came of age
1) Reached adulthood legally or socially
2) Understood morality for the first time
3) Abandoned earlier beliefs
4) Inherited property

9 Break one's duck
1) Abandon a hobby
2) Spoil a good start
3) Achieve a first success after previous failures
4) Undergo bankruptcy

10 Chapter and Verse
1) With half-formed reasoning
2) Incomplete explanation
3) With precise reference and detail
4) Through analogy or example

Practice Set - 2

Direction (Q. 1-10): Choose the correct meaning of the given idiom from the options:

1 Cut me dead
1) Ignored me deliberately
2) Insulted me openly
3) Misunderstood me accidentally
4) Praised me sarcastically

2 Wear out one's welcome
1) To welcome one with an extensive or elaborate display of friendliness and hospitality
2) An expression of glib commiseration used when one shares some unpleasant condition or situation with one or more other people
3) To remain a guest in a place, especially someone's home, for too long, to the point where the host no longer wishes one to stay
4) To greet someone very happily and eagerly; to give someone a very warm, enthusiastic welcome

3 Wear out one's welcome
1) To tie up loose ends
2) To delay resolution
3) To create a new problem
4) To solve a complex problem decisively

4 Eat crow
1) Enjoy luxurious food
2) Give lavish charity
3) Suffer physical punishment
4) Admit one's error and endure humiliation

5 Currying favour
1) Seeking emotional validation
2) Seeking approval through flattery
3) Avoiding direct confrontation
4) Asking for forgiveness subtly

6 Fly off the handle
1) To escape quietly
2) To disappear quickly
3) To become suddenly angry
4) To handle a situation smartly

7 Cook someone's goose
1) Help someone succeed
2) Ruin someone's plans or prospects
3) Save someone from trouble
4) Make fun of someone

8 Coals of fire upon his head
1) To punish someone for hypocrisy
2) To provoke guilt through accusation
3) To offer false forgiveness
4) To shame an enemy through kindness

9 Fiddle while Rome burns
1) To play music at night
2) To waste time in trivialities during a crisis

3) To seek artistic approval
4) To incite rebellion

10 Flash in the pan
1) A bright idea
2) A sudden success that fails to last
3) A criminal plan
4) A methodical worker

Practice Set - 3

Direction (Q. 1-10): Choose the correct meaning of the given idiom from the options:

1 Hang fire
1) Delay taking action or making a decision
2) Create urgency
3) Withdraw support
4) Complete a task early

2 Jump the shark
1) To take unnecessary risk
2) To betray someone close
3) To reach a peak and begin to decline
4) To grow rapidly

3 Know which way the wind blows
1) Determine compass directions
2) Predict literal weather
3) Sense how events or opinion are trending before acting
4) Forget instructions

4 Keeps a good table
1) Serves generous and high-quality meals
2) Maintains a disciplined home
3) Follows religious rule strictly
4) Provides food to the poor regularly

5 Harp on the same string
1) To play a strategic game
2) To be fickle in opinion
3) To remain emotionally distant
4) To repeat a single idea endlessly

6 In the doldrums
1) Sailing in high winds
2) In a state of depression or inactivity
3) On the verge of success
4) Working with great energy

7 King's ransom
1) To demand something or some action from someone by threatening them with a harmful consequence if they do not comply
2) An exorbitant sum of money
3) An opening speech at the Parliament
4) Budget session

8 Has two strings in his bow
1) He is indecisive in crucial matters.
2) He has two romantic interests simultaneously.
3) He has an additional skill or option to rely on.
4) He uses deception to achieve goals.

9 Hobson's choice
1) A dilemma between two evils
2) A free and fair decision
3) No real choice at all
4) A selection made under duress

10 In the bud
1) In the early or developing stage
2) On the verge of destruction
3) During a time of celebration
4) In the final phase of execution

Practice Set - 4

Direction (Q. 1-10): Choose the correct meaning of the given idiom from the options:

1 Play gooseberry
1) Act as mediator in a dispute
2) Be an unwanted third person with a courting couple
3) Tell jokes badly
4) Refuse commitment

2 Make no bones about it
1) To hesitate before speaking
2) To remain neutral
3) To be direct and honest
4) To confuse the listener

3 Not fit to hold a candle to
1) Excellent in comparison
2) Similar in ability
3) Greatly inferior to
4) Superior to in some aspects

4 Make a clean breast of it
1) To admit something honestly
2) To run away quickly
3) To change sides
4) To start a new job

5 Not in my line
1) Beyond my authority
2) Not related to my area of expertise
3) Not aligned with my values
4) Below my status

6 Not worth his salt
1) Lacking in courage
2) Unable to learn
3) too proud to work
4) Undeserving of the pay/ respect he gets

7 Not to mince matters
1) To speak delicately
2) To speak without hesitation or euphemism
3) To revise opinions often
4) To avoid detail intentionally

8 Wrap someone in cotton wool
1) To fold, coil, or bend completely around someone or something
2) Be over-protective towards someone
3) Bring cotton wool and cover a person to hide him
4) Try to hide the sin committed by someone
1) In a state of painful suspense
2) Physically restrained
3) Emotionally numb
4) Confused by contradictions

10 Move heaven and earth
1) To relocate frequently
2) To work tirelessly to achieve something
3) To stay silent in protest
4) To follow blindly

Practice Set - 5

Direction (Q. 1-10): Choose the correct meaning of the given idiom from the options:

1 To dine with Duke Humphrey
1) To remain hungry or skip a meal
2) To negotiate with royalty
3) To act with vanity
4) To lose social standing

2 Will not pass muster
1) will not meet required standards
2) will not bring any excitement
3) will not escape attention

4) will not create any disturbance

3 Rest on his laurels
1) To withdraw from success
2) To bask in past glory and avoid current effort
3) To criticize one's own success
4) To challenge past achievements

4 The green-eyed monster
1) Anger 2) Sloth
3) Jealousy 4) Pride

5 Rising to the occasion
1) Performing exceptionally under pressure
2) Evading failure with excuses
3) Taking advantage of a mistake
4) Over-preparing for a situation

6 Where the shoe pinches
1) The turning point in fortune
2) The hidden benefit in hardship
3) The point of real difficulty or discomfort
4) The weakest member in a team

7 Hornet's nest
1) A confusing situation
2) A source of controversy and trouble
3) A peaceful debate
4) A place of retreat

8 True-blue
1) Completely unexpectedly
2) Loyal and steadfast
3) A long, albeit vague, period of time
4) A police car

9 To send someone to Coventry
1) To award someone symbolic punishment
2) To exile someone to a faraway place
3) To ignore someone deliberately
4) To mock someone publicly

10 A bitter pill to swallow
1) A spicy food
2) A difficult truth to accept
3) A cure for disease
4) A happy surprise

Practice Set - 6

Direction (Q. 1-10): Choose the correct meaning of the given idiom from the options:

1 Throw cold water on something
1) To discourage
2) To cool down
3) To wash something
4) To celebrate

2 To be off base
1) To be on the right track
2) To be confused
3) To be wrong or mistaken
4) To change your mind

3 A slap on the wrist
1) A painful injury
2) A mild warning or light punishment
3) A friendly gesture
4) A public compliment

4 Give someone the cold shoulder
1) To treat someone warmly
2) To ignore someone
3) To scold someone
4) To make someone comfortable

5 Smell a rat
1) To be very clean
2) To suspect something
3) To follow orders
4) To be afraid

6 Cry wolf
1) Be truthful
2) Lie unnecessarily
3) Help others
4) Raise a false alarm

7 Go against the grain
1) To move in the wrong direction
2) To oppose the norm
3) To feel uncomfortable
4) To cut something

8 Get your walking papers
1) Go on vacation
2) Receive a promotion
3) Be given permission to retire
4) Be fired or dismissed from a job

9 Jump through hoops
1) To go through many difficulties
2) To be very happy
3) To perform tricks
4) To escape quickly

10 In the same boat
1) Facing the same situation
2) Being very wealthy
3) Traveling together
4) Owning a boat

Practice Set - 7

Direction (Q. 1-10): Choose the correct meaning of the given idiom from the options:

1 Break the bank
1) To save money
2) To rob a bank
3) To spend too much money
4) To invest wisely

2 The lion's share
1) A fair portion
2) A small contribution
3) The largest part
4) An equal distribution

3 Let sleeping dogs lie
1) Avoid bringing up past conflicts
2) Wake someone up
3) Be very careful
4) Hide from danger

4 Wear your heart on your sleeve
1) Keep your feelings private
2) Pretend to have emotions
3) Express emotions openly
4) Be dishonest about your intentions

5 Hit below the belt
1) A clever move
2) A fair insult
3) An unfair or unethical remark
4) A surprising compliment

6 Pull the wool over someone's eyes
1) To keep someone warm
2) To deceive someone
3) To make a mistake
4) To give advice

7 Eat humble pie
1) To be very happy
2) To eat something bitter
3) To celebrate a victory
4) To admit a mistake

8 Burned the midnight oil
1) Worked late at night
2) Slept well
3) Celebrated
4) Lit candles

9 Toe the line
1) To win a race
2) To cross boundaries
3) To take a shortcut
4) To follow rules

10 Cast the first stone

1) To accuse someone first
2) To start a fight
3) To throw a rock
4) To give up

Practice Set 8

Direction (Q. 1-10): Select the most appropriate meaning of the following idiom.

1 All in the same boat
1) When everybody is travelling in the same vehicle
2) When everyone is dealing with the same situation
3) When everyone has to start all over again
4) When a task can be accomplished together

2 A bitter pill
1) Facing a distressing situation
2) Talking nonsense
3) Arguing unnecessarily
4) Getting furious easily

3 At sixes and sevens
1) Heavy rains
2) In happy mood
3) In disorder
4) Having dispute

4 Till the cows come home
1) Immediately
2) Not for a long time
3) At dusk
4) For a very long, indefinite amount of time

5 Call it a day
1) Stop working on something
2) Begin with an assignment
3) Name a particular day
4) Involve many people for a simple job

6 A piece of cake
1) Easy to do or achieve
2) A cake that broke into pieces
3) A cake which is sold as a piece
4) A slice of cake for eating

7 A blue-eyed boy
1) an unwelcome intruder
2) a miser
3) an unperceived observer
4) one who is favourite

8 To bring to light
1) To engage in conversation
2) To disengage
3) To lighten
4) To disclose

9 A snake in the grass
1) A worthless person
2) A secret or hidden enemy
3) A man of ability
4) A man with a straightforward attitude

10 An axe to grind
1) To have a selfish reason that influences the actions
2) To make a supreme effort
3) To tackle a problem in a bold and direct fashion
4) Bitterly hostile

Practice Set 9

Direction (Q. 1-10): Select the most appropriate meaning of the following idiom.

1 An open book
1) someone who gives advice based on theory not practice
2) a person of whom her mother is extremely proud
3) a helpful person
4) a person or thing that is easy to learn about and understand

2 Be in apple-pie order
1) Be in a happy mood
2) Be in chronological order
3) Be perfectly arranged and tidy
4) Be extra sweet to people

3 Cut from the same cloth
1) To share resources
2) To have very similar qualities
3) To belong to the same family
4) To have the same origin

4 Apple of one's eye
1) Very precious
2) Very docile
3) Very stubborn
4) Very strong

5 Cross swords
1) To stop fighting or arguing
2) To do something very quickly
3) To have an argument with someone
4) To begin taking part in a new activity

6 Baker's Dozen
1) A pile of bread
2) One unit extra with one dozen
3) Choosing quality over quantity
4) When shopkeepers put something extra

7 Cloak and dagger
1) Suffer harm or damage because of conflict
2) Having a complaint that needs to be discussed
3) A situations involving secrecy, spying and mystery
4) Saying or doing something that can lead to a serious fight or disagreement

8 Beginner's luck
1) To get unusual or unexpected success in one's first attempt in doing something
2) To be successful all the time
3) To work hard to achieve success
4) To be lucky in achieving one's goals

9 Be on the same page
1) Having the same understanding
2) Doing things with a partner
3) Staying in the same place
4) Reading something together

10 Not one's cup of tea
1) Impossible task
2) Very easy
3) Something disliked
4) Something enjoyable

Practice Set 10

Direction (Q. 1-10): Select the most appropriate meaning of the following idiom.

1 To flog a dead horse
1) To waste one's energy on a lost cause
2) To remain valid
3) To escape from the situation
4) To achieve something easily

2 Be up to the minute.
1) At the last possible instant or opportunity
2) To wait or pause
3) To be as current as is possible
4) At a very rapid pace

3 Your guess is as good as mine
1) To have no idea of the answer
2) To predict a disaster
3) To guess an incredible idea
4) To be superstitious

4 Weal and woe
1) Early and late
2) Hot and cold
3) Simplicity and complexity
4) Joy and sorrow

5 To have sticky fingers
1) To be suspicious
2) To punish for a crime
3) To remain joyful in a difficult situation
4) To have a tendency to steal

6 Split one's sides
1) To roar with laughter
2) To overeat
3) To undergo surgery
4) To scream in agony

7 The Midas touch
1) Financial hardship
2) The ability to turn anything into gold
3) A bad reputation
4) A lucky streak

8 To get someone's goat
1) To have affection for somebody
2) To steal something
3) To make one feel good
4) To irritate someone

9 A dime a dozen
1) To be in a difficult situation
2) Very rare
3) Very common
4) To take revenge

10 Last resort
1) Last ride
2) Last friend remaining
3) Last hotel on the way
4) Last course of action

Practice Set - 11

Direction (Q. 1-10): Select the most appropriate meaning of the following idiom.

1 In black and white
1) Officially in writing
2) In verbal form
3) In secret
4) Unclear terms

2 Cry over spilt milk
1) Be indifferent
2) Ignore problems
3) Regret a past loss
4) Work harder

3 To keep the wolf away from the door
1) To avoid financial hardship
2) To escape from a dangerous situation
3) To protect oneself from enemies
4) To stay away from risky opportunities

4 Make a clean breast of
1) Argue 2) Confess
3) Whisper 4) Accuse

5 Ace in the hole
1) A lot to do
2) A second chance to do something
3) On the point of
4) A hidden advantage

6 Barking up the wrong tree
1) Apologizing
2) praising someone
3) Accusing wrongly
4) Succeeding quickly

7 Cut no ice
1) Have no effect
2) Create trouble
3) Be sharp
4) Stop something

8 Clutching at straws
1) Laughing loudly
2) Hoping without reason
3) Boasting unnecessarily
4) Winning easily

9 Blow one's own horn
1) To praise oneself excessively
2) To play a musical instrument
3) To help others in need
4) To remain silent in a conversation

10 Get to the point
1) Speak directly
2) Interrupt
3) Avoid the matter
4) Speak indirectly

Practice Set - 12

Direction (Q. 1-10): Select the most appropriate meaning of the following idiom.

1 Keep one on a tight leash
1) To keep one's plans, intentions, or information secret from everyone else
2) To continue to inform someone about something so that they have current information
3) To not allow one very much independence or autonomy
4) To maintain a significant degree of physical separation from someone or something

2 Steal someone's thunder
1) Mock them
2) Take credit for their work
3) Help them
4) Ignore them

3 Go the extra mile
1) Work half- heartedly
2) Stay idle
3) Work harder than expected
4) Leave midway

4 Jump the gun
1) Succeed quickly
2) Act prematurely
3) Wait patiently
4) Fire a gun

5 Jack up the rates
1) Increase prices
2) Drop prices
3) Stay unchanged
4) Sell everything

6 On cloud nine
1) Lazy
2) Extremely happy
3) very angry
4) confused

7 Give someone a cold shoulder
1) Treat warmly
2) Praise someone
3) Ignore someone
4) Invite for dinner

8 Speak your mind
1) Express frankly
2) Stay Silent
3) Lie
4) Gossip

9 Pull someone's leg
1) Joke with them
2) Praise them
3) Annoy them
4) Criticize them

10 A white elephant
1) Lucky charm
2) Valuable Item
3) Costly burden
4) Rare animal

Practice Set - 13

Direction (Q. 1-10): Select the most appropriate idiom that can substitute the underlined segment in the given sentence.

1 We took it slowly and carefully and got it done in no time.
1) one step at a time
2) one step closer
3) one step ahead
4) one step fix

2 He has a knack for ignoring problems intentionally in his department, hoping they will just go away.
1) turning point
2) turning a blind eye
3) turning a corner
4) turning a leaf

3 Our Principal looked disappointed when no one expressed the willingness to join the trip.
1) Pulled a long face
2) Made a comeback
3) High and dry
4) Gave a single shot

4 Don't assume that everyone but you is happy. The grass is always redder on one side.
1) sky is red in the evening
2) grass is always greener on the other side
3) plant is always greener on all sides
4) fruit is yellow on the other side

5 His old car has become a financial burden on him now.
1) An eyesore
2) A rare bird
3) A white elephant
4) An apple of one's eye

6 A false and selfish friend will never be by your side in times of difficulty.
1) fair weather friend
2) great hand
3) past master
4) good samaritan

7 You will get the truth given by somebody who is directly involved and therefore likely to be accurate.
1) shooting off the cuff
2) with kid gloves
3) calling a spade a spade
4) straight from the horse's mouth

8 Despite the initial setbacks, the team remained optimistic and pushed through to achieve their goals.
1) kept a close eye
2) kept a bay
3) kept a stiff upper lip
4) kept their chin up

9 After suffering for a long time, Roy finally passed away this month.
1) burnt his boats
2) brought down the house
3) breathed his last
4) blazed the trail

10 Due to her impoverished state, most of her relatives treated her with contempt.
1) Gave a wide space to her
2) Turned up their nose at her
3) Turned the corner at her
4) Came in handy

Practice Set - 14

Direction (Q. 1-10): Select the most appropriate idiom that can substitute the underlined segment in the given sentence.

1 Delivering that furniture to the tenth floor without the lift and an incline is incredibly foolish and next to impossible.
1) like a tree known by its fruits
2) as tight as the bark of the tree
3) like going between the bark and the tree
4) like nailing jelly to the tree

2 Roshan, it's time for you to give your speech to the whole school, wishing you luck to do well.
1) break a leg
2) hands down
3) high five
4) down in the dumps

3 The politicians had always been an easy target for the media.
1) fishes out of water
2) dark horses
3) sitting ducks
4) the Achilles' heel

4 We need to make sure that criminals like these get more from the authorities than a very mild punishment.
1) a taste of their own medicine
2) a blessing in disguise
3) an axe to grind
4) a slap on the wrist

5 The players like the coach because he is honest, realistic and practical in dealing with them.
1) by and large
2) sick and tired
3) down to earth
4) far and wide

6 Reena decided not to go to work today because she was feeling sick.
1) fit as a fiddle
2) going down in flames
3) sitting on the fence
4) under the weather

7 I know Covid has made you terribly ill, but the good thing is that you have developed immunity against it for further infections.
1) crossing palms with silver
2) being in the quicksilver
3) the silver spoon
4) the silver lining in the cloud

8 The internal conflicts within the party were dismissed as an insignificant exaggeration.
1) the cherry on the cake
2) a storm in a teacup
3) rain cats and dogs
4) a frog in the well

9 Popular cosmetics brands in India are very expensive.
1) cost an arm and a leg
2) up in arms
3) flog a dead horse

4) take it with a pinch of salt

10 Read the books of APJ Abdul Kalam, who was a scholar.

1) a man of straw
2) a man of letters
3) a queer fish
4) a dare devil

Practice Set - 15

Direction (Q. 1-10): Select the most appropriate idiom that can substitute the underlined segment in the given sentence.

1 He is very strict with his students but good-natured.

1) his eyes are bigger than his stomach
2) his heart misses a beat
3) he has a big mouth
4) his heart is in the right place

2 He wanted to be a professional basketball player but given his height, luck was against him.

1) the cards were stacked against him
2) his health was not in his favour
3) his principles were against him
4) the ball was against him

3 I have been living without a lot of money since I lost my job.

1) keeping my chin up
2) as genuine as a three-dollar bill
3) receiving a kickback
4) living hand to mouth

4 We were asked to vote for the candidates by raising our hands to indicate voting for or against a proposition.

1) getting out of hand
2) changing hands
3) a show of hands
4) tipping our hands

5 He thinks his new plan will undoubtedly produce the desired result.

1) sour grapes
2) go pear-shaped
3) go suck a lemon
4) bear fruit

6 I know you're blaming me for all that has happened but I wasn't at fault alone.

1) it is always darkest before the dawn
2) it takes two to tango
3) leave no stone unturned
4) make hay while the sun shines

7 I know you have been really busy with your work, but can you just give me a few minutes?

1) snowed under
2) through thick and thin
3) jumped on the bandwagon
4) on cloud nine

8 It makes me believe that life is wonderful and pleasant.

1) I'm up in the air
2) I'm facing the music
3) I'm changing my tune
4) life is a bowl of cherries

9 Sharon doing the work all by herself? Seems like it is possible, but is very unlikely to happen.

1) pie in the sky
2) a piece of cake
3) a bad egg
4) bent out of shape

10 The poor chef did not believe that his simple recipe would be sold quickly and in large quantities and he could earn such a profit.

1) Piece of cake
2) Up in arms
3) Sell like hot cakes
4) Run around in circles

Practice Set - 16

Direction (Q. 1-10): Select the most appropriate meaning of the underlined idiom.

1 If you want to participate in the Olympics, you need to hit the ground running.

1) Started working energetically
2) took a break
3) Made a mistake
4) Fell down

2 He gave his heart and soul to make the entire show a success.

1) offer of peace and harmony
2) practical experience
3) partially useful knowledge
4) entire energy and effort

3 The resort manager planned to welcome the guests with open arms when they arrived.

1) in a secretive way
2) in a melancholy spirit
3) in a cordial manner
4) without any delay

4 He goes hard with one and all.

1) To be busy over trifles
2) To be difficult
3) To remain neutral
4) To be unreliable

5 Our neighbour told my brother to keep an eye on their pet dog in their absence.

1) To look after something or someone
2) To accomplish something too ambitious
3) To wait for something that is disturbing
4) To ignore something or someone

6 It was just an action in the nick of time that prepared all of us for further arrangements.

1) Just in time
2) Delayed as expected
3) Unnatural happenings
4) Forceful labour

7 The winner's performance was head and shoulders above all other participants' in the dance competition.

1) Well informed of current trends
2) Caught between two alternatives
3) Much better than others
4) Worse than others

8 The sergeant ordered the soldiers to be armed to the teeth as he expected it to be a tough fight.

1) Separated from the worthless
2) Active without any goals
3) Working in a great hurry
4) Well-equipped or prepared

9 Ron always blows his own trumpet by mentioning his academic achievements.

1) To blow air into an instrument
2) To talk proudly about one's success

3) To ignore someone in the presence of others
4) To save one's money with great effort using different means

10 Meera wanted to prove to those around her that she was not a fair-weather friend.
1) Friend for all situations
2) Helping and caring companion
3) Reliable friend in tough times
4) Unreliable friend in difficult times

Practice Set - 17

Direction (Q. 1-10): Select the most appropriate idiom to fill in the blank.

1 The politician's speech was full of vague promises but ultimately it was just _____ .
1) pulling strings
2) a red herring
3) smoke and mirrors
4) the last straw

2 The manager's refusal to adapt to modern methods proved to be his _____.
1) achilles' heel
2) baptism by fire
3) swan song
4) stepping stone

3 She took the criticism _____ and used it to improve her performance.
1) at face value
2) with a grain of salt
3) in stride
4) out of context

4 The CEO resigned, citing personal reasons, but insiders knew it was just a _____.
1) can of worms
2) slip of the tongue
3) red herring
4) feather in the cap

5 His sudden resignation caught everyone _____.
1) red-handed
2) off guard
3) in limbo
4) on thin ice

6 After months of subtle manipulation, she finally showed her true colours and _____.
1) stabbed him in the back
2) played her cards right
3) took the bull by the horns
4) burned the midnight oil

7 The board's decision to withdraw the bid came completely _____ for the stakeholders.
1) off the wall
2) out of the blue
3) behind closed doors
4) under fire

8 His inability to nurse his ailing mother was the _____ that stopped him from focusing on his duty.
1) sparrow around his neck
2) eagle around his neck
3) pigeon around his neck
4) albatross around his neck

9 Despite numerous setbacks, she remained optimistic and continued to _____.
1) turn over a new leaf
2) keep her nose to the grindstone
3) throw caution to the wind
4) pull the plug

10 During the debate, he was clearly uncomfortable and kept trying to _____.
1) bite the bullet
2) face the music
3) beat around the bush
4) let the cat out of the bag

Practice Set - 18

Direction (Q. 1-10): Select the most appropriate idiom to fill in the blank.

1 The renowned publisher decided to withdraw a book from the market. No one was interested in the book as the arguments presented were _____.
1) high and mighty
2) beside the mark
3) out of the woods
4) under the rose

2 I'm _____ about whether to accept the job offer or continue freelancing. Both options have their advantages.
1) on the fence
2) up in arms
3) left out in cold
4) cutting corners

3 I finally completed the marathon. I can really _____ for this accomplishment.
1) up a creek without a paddle
2) eat like a horse
3) pat myself on the back
4) blow hot and cold

4 We hear the judges from their _____ that only CNG buses should run in Delhi.
1) ivory tower
2) square meal
3) melting pot
4) look sharp

5 Rakesh was worthy to get accolades from his colleagues as he had worked _____.
1) his heart to the spleen
2) his bone out of his cage
3) his eyes out of sockets
4) his fingers to the bone

6 Taking the summer job proved to be _____ for Anand's visa applications.
1) on thecontrary
2) ablessing in disguise
3) come up
4) come in high

7 I'm _____until my family arrives from their holiday. I cannot wait to see them.
1) bearing the gift of the gab
2) losing ground
3) counting down the days
4) getting myself into a mess

8 After a day long trek, we were so tired that we were ready to _____.
1) face the music
2) get into deep water
3) go from rags to riches
4) hit the sack

9 Mala _____ by cheating on the exam to win her bet with Priya.
1) get the sack
2) look down upon
3) hit below the belt

4) fell out

10 John was always _____ about becoming a millionaire without doing any hard work.
1) a storm in a tea cup
2) eating like a horse
3) having an ace up his sleeve
4) building castles in the air

Practice Set - 19

Direction (Q. 1-10): Identify the meaning of the idiom highlighted in bold.

1 The boss called the employees together for a meeting. He said he didn't know who was stealing from the company, but that he would leave no stone unturned until he found out who it was.
1) Search everywhere and do everything possible to find the answer
2) Punish all employees for the theft
3) Ignore the situation and hope it resolves itself
4) Ask only a few employees about the issue

2 Talking about her current book and her previous best seller is like comparing apples and oranges.
1) The two books are very similar
2) The two books are completely different
3) The two books are both about fruits
4) The two books are equally successful

3 Lucy's conceited conduct with her colleagues has left her high and dry.
1) Impoverished
2) Superseding
3) Helpless
4) Surrounded by people

4 Mr. smith: There's a little time before lunch. I think I'm going to lie down for a while and catch forty winks. What does the idiom catch forty winks mean in this context?
1) Eat a quick snack.
2) Take a short nap.
3) Go for a walk.
4) Daydream while lying down.

5 I know you are ready. Go break a leg now.
1) say Good Luck to someone
2) ask someone not to go for a task
3) say Bad Luck to someone
4) not saying anything to someone

6 Rina pulled a long face since her husband had not bought her a diamond necklace on their anniversary.
1) To be electrified
2) To be ecstatic
3) To be euphoric
4) To look saddened

7 The builder hired several carpenters and electricians to work on the building, but he left them in the lurch when it came time to pay them.
1) Abandoned them in a difficult situation without help
2) Gave them extra money for their hard work
3) Praised them for their excellent craftsmanship
4) Provided them with new jobs after the work was done

8 He decided to bite the bullet by finally agreeing to surgery as it was the only option left for him to survive.
1) to avoid getting into something at all
2) to get something over with because it is inevitable
3) to keep the past hanging with you always
4) to not get over with anything in life at all

9 The mode of payment is cash is a pain in the neck for those who have no habit of carrying cash around them.
1) When something is not up to the mark
2) When something is unacceptable
3) When someone/something is very funny
4) When someone/something is very annoying

10 Looking at the situation, the best plan of action would be to throw caution to the wind.
1) Take risks
2) Ignore the situation
3) Playing safe
4) Take a meeting and ask for everyone's input

Practice Set - 20

Direction (Q. 1-10): Based on the situation in the sentence, select the most appropriate idiom to fill in the blank.

1 Spill the _____.
1) beads 2) beans
3) tea 4) milk

2 Although Greta Thunberg gave a moving speech at the UN about environmental damage, it could _____.
1) break the ice
2) cut no ice
3) walk on thin ice
4) be the icing on the cake

3 It was all _____. He did not really mean what he said.
1) blue in the face
2) tuck in
3) tongue in cheek
4) a storm in a tea cup

4 Hit the _____.
1) bag 2) head
3) bay 4) sack

5 After many years of rivalry, the two schools decided to _____ and participate in a National Event together.
1) be in the doldrums
2) go cold turkey
3) bell the cat
4) bury the hatchet

6 With the increasing market prices and stagnant salaries, he is _____.
1) beating the rap
2) feeling the pinch
3) getting it off his chest
4) taking a break

7 Despite the criticism, the artist took it in stride and considered it _____.
1) a chip on their shoulder
2) a piece of cake
3) break a leg
4) as water under the bridge

8 Sitting on the _____.
1) boundary 2) wall
3) tree 4) fence

9 I thought Sadhna would always stick by me, but when I got into trouble, she turned out to be a/an _____
1) white elephant
2) fair-weather friend
3) hard nut to crack
4) open secret

10 It is not everybody's _____.
1) mug of ice
2) cup of coffee
3) cup of milk
4) cup of tea

Answer Key Practice Set - 1:

1 - 1	2 - 4	3 - 3	4 - 2	5 - 1
6 - 2	7 - 1	8 - 1	9 - 3	10 - 3

Answer Key Practice Set - 2:

1 - 1	2 - 3	3 - 4	4 - 4	5 - 2
6 - 3	7 - 2	8 - 4	9 - 2	10 - 2

Answer Key Practice Set - 3:

1 - 1	2 - 3	3 - 3	4 - 1	5 - 4
6 - 2	7 - 2	8 - 3	9 - 3	10 - 1

Answer Key Practice Set - 4:

1 - 2	2 - 3	3 - 3	4 - 1	5 - 2
6 - 4	7 - 2	8 - 2	9 - 1	10 - 2

Answer Key Practice Set - 5:

1 - 1	2 - 1	3 - 2	4 - 3	5 - 1
6 - 3	7 - 2	8 - 2	9 - 3	10 - 2

Answer Key Practice Set - 6:

1 - 1	2 - 3	3 - 2	4 - 2	5 - 2
6 - 4	7 - 2	8 - 4	9 - 1	10 - 1

Answer Key Practice Set - 7:

1 - 3	2 - 3	3 - 1	4 - 3	5 - 3
6 - 2	7 - 4	8 - 1	9 - 4	10 - 1

Answer Key Practice Set - 8:

1 - 2	2 - 1	3 - 3	4 - 4	5 - 1
6 - 1	7 - 4	8 - 4	9 - 2	10 - 1

Answer Key Practice Set - 9:

1 - 4	2 - 3	3 - 2	4 - 1	5 - 3
6 - 2	7 - 3	8 - 1	9 - 1	10 - 3

Answer Key Practice Set - 10:

1 - 1	2 - 3	3 - 1	4 - 4	5 - 4
6 - 1	7 - 2	8 - 4	9 - 3	10 - 4

Answer Key Practice Set - 11:

1 - 1	2 - 3	3 - 1	4 - 2	5 - 4
6 - 3	7 - 1	8 - 2	9 - 1	10 - 1

Answer Key Practice Set - 12:

1 - 3	2 - 2	3 - 3	4 - 2	5 - 1
6 - 2	7 - 3	8 - 1	9 - 1	10 - 3

Answer Key Practice Set - 13:

1 - 1	2 - 2	3 - 1	4 - 2	5 - 3
6 - 1	7 - 4	8 - 4	9 - 3	10 - 2

Answer Key Practice Set - 14:

1 - 4	2 - 1	3 - 3	4 - 4	5 - 3
6 - 4	7 - 4	8 - 2	9 - 1	10 - 2

Answer Key Practice Set - 15:

1 - 4	2 - 1	3 - 4	4 - 3	5 - 4
6 - 2	7 - 1	8 - 4	9 - 1	10 - 3

Answer Key Practice Set - 16:

1 - 1	2 - 4	3 - 3	4 - 2	5 - 1
6 - 1	7 - 3	8 - 4	9 - 2	10 - 4

Answer Key Practice Set - 17:

1 - 3	2 - 1	3 - 3	4 - 3	5 - 2
6 - 1	7 - 2	8 - 4	9 - 2	10 - 3

Answer Key Practice Set - 18:

1 - 2	2 - 1	3 - 3	4 - 1	5 - 4
6 - 2	7 - 3	8 - 4	9 - 3	10 - 4

Answer Key Practice Set - 19:

1 - 1	2 - 2	3 - 3	4 - 2	5 - 1
6 - 4	7 - 1	8 - 2	9 - 4	10 - 1

Answer Key Practice Set - 20:

1 - 2	2 - 2	3 - 3	4 - 4	5 - 4
6 - 2	7 - 4	8 - 4	9 - 2	10 - 4

B4 Idioms & Phrases (Asked in other than SSC Exams)

SN	Idioms/Phrases	English Meaning	Hindi Meaning	#R
1	A cold day in hell	Used to say that something is extremely unlikely to happen	कभी न होने वाली बात	
2	A fair crack of the whip	A fair opportunity to do something	बराबरी का मौका (सामान अवसर)	
3	**A fine kettle of fish**	An awkward or difficult situation	उलझन भरी या मुश्किल स्थिति	2
4	A fool's errand	A task or activity that has no chance of success	व्यर्थ का काम (असफल होने वाला प्रयास)	
5	A foregone conclusion	A result that is certain or inevitable before it happens	पहले से तय नतीजा (निश्चित परिणाम)	
6	A heart of gold	A very kind and generous nature	सोने जैसा दिल (बहुत दयालु स्वभाव)	
7	A man of his word	A person who keeps their promises	ज़ुबान का पक्का (जो अपनी बात निभाए)	
8	A match made in heaven	A perfect marriage, especially of two people who are ideally suited to each other	रब ने बना दी जोड़ी (आदर्श जोड़ी)	
9	A matter of life and death	An extremely urgent or critical situation	जीवन-मरण का प्रश्न (बहुत महत्वपूर्ण या गंभीर मामला)	
10	A mile a minute	Very fast	बहुत तेज़ गति से	
11	A mile off	Very easily noticeable or recognizable from far away	दूर से ही पहचाना जा सकने वाला; स्पष्ट	
12	A millstone around one's neck	A heavy burden that makes progress difficult or impossible	गले का पत्थर (भारी बोझ या जिम्मेदारी)	
13	A notch above	Slightly better than others	औरों से थोड़ा बेहतर	
14	A passing resemblance	A slight or superficial similarity that is not very noticeable	हल्की-सी समानता	
15	A purple patch	A period of exceptional success or good luck	सुनहरा समय (सफलता का दौर)	
16	A ray of sunshine	Source of happiness	ख़ुशी कि किरण (खुशी लाने वाला)	
17	A roaring success	A great and impressive success	जबरदस्त सफलता	
18	A shrinking violet	A very shy, timid, or modest person	अत्यंत शर्मीला या संकोची व्यक्ति	
19	A snowball's chance in hell	No chance at all or impossible	बिल्कुल भी संभावना न होना	
20	**A stalking horse**	A person or thing that is used to conceal someone's real intentions	असली मकसद को छुपाने के लिए मुखौटा	3
21	**A stroke of luck**	An unexpected piece of good fortune	किस्मत चमकना (अप्रत्याशित भाग्य)	2
22	**A tall order**	A difficult or demanding task that is hard to accomplish	मुश्किल काम (असंभव-सी माँग)	3
23	A turn of the screw	An additional action that worsens an already bad situation	बद से बदतर (खराब स्थिति को और बिगाड़ना)	
24	Across the board	Affecting everyone or everything equally	सभी पर समान रूप से लागू होना	
25	Against all (or long) odds	To struggle in spite of great difficulty or unfavourable chances	विपरीत परिस्थितियों में संघर्ष करना	

[**#R** denotes repetition of word]

[E.g. in SN 22, #R- **3** denotes this word has been asked 3 times in other exams]

SN	Idioms/Phrases	English Meaning	Hindi Meaning	#R
26	Airy-fairy	Impractical, vague, or unrealistic; not based on solid facts	हवा-हवाई (अवास्तविक या काल्पनिक)	
27	**All in one's head**	Imaginary or not real	सिर्फ दिमाग की उपज (काल्पनिक)	3
28	All of a doodah	In a state of excitement or panic	घबराहट या हड़बड़ी में होना	
29	**All the better**	Even more desirable or advantageous	सोने पे सुहागा (और भी बेहतर)	2
30	All the rage	Very popular or fashionable at the present time	चलन में होना (बहुत लोकप्रिय)	
31	Anything but	Not at all; the complete opposite of something	बिल्कुल नहीं (इसके अलावा कुछ भी)	
32	As busy as a bee	Very busy and hardworking	बहुत व्यस्त	
33	As cute as a button	Very cute or attractive	बहुत प्यारा	
34	As happy as Larry	Extremely happy and content	बहुत खुश	
35	As ugly as sin	Extremely unattractive or ugly	अत्यंत बदसूरत (भद्दा)	
36	At a rate of knots	Extremely fast or quickly	बहुत तेज गति से	
37	At odds	In disagreement or conflict	असहमत (विवाद में)	
38	At the bottom of the ladder	At the lowest position or rank	सबसे निचले पायदान पर	
39	**Backstairs influence**	A secret or underhand influence, typically through unofficial channels	गुप्त सिफारिश या अनुचित दबाव	2
40	**Bag of bones**	An extremely thin person	हड्डियों का ढाँचा (अत्यधिक दुबला)	2
41	Banana republic	A small country with a weak economy and political instability	राजनीतिक रूप से अस्थिर और आर्थिक रूप से कमज़ोर देश	
42	Bare one's teeth	To show aggression or anger	दाँत पीसना (गुस्सा दिखाना)	
43	Be a law unto oneself	To behave independently and not follow accepted rules or conventions	अपने मन का राजा होना (नियमों की परवाह न करना)	
44	Be as good as one's word	To keep one's promise; to do what one has promised	जुबान का पक्का होना (वादा निभाना)	
45	Be bad news	To be a person or thing that causes trouble or problems	मुसीबत की जड़ (संकट का कारण बनना)	
46	Be in eclipse	To be less successful or popular than before	ग्रहण लग जाना (महत्त्व कम होना)	
47	Be in the mire	To be in a difficult or unpleasant situation	दलदल में फँसा होना (मुश्किल में होना)	
48	Be in the running	To have a chance of winning or being successful; to be a contender	दौड़ में होना (जीतने की संभावना में होना)	
49	Be left holding the baby	To be left with an unwanted responsibility, often unfairly	जिम्मेदारी सिर पर आ जाना	
50	Be no slouch	To be very good or capable at something	किसी काम में माहिर होना	
51	Be out of action	To be unable to function or work, typically due to injury or breakdown	काम करने में असमर्थ होना	
52	Beam in one's eye	A fault that is greater in oneself than in the person one is criticizing	अपनी बड़ी कमी को भूलकर दूसरों की छोटी कमी देखना	
53	Bed of thorns	A very difficult or uncomfortable situation	काँटों की सेज (बहुत ही असहज स्थिति)	
54	Bend the elbow	To drink alcohol excessively	अत्यधिक शराब पीना	
55	Between whiles	During intervals; now and then; occasionally	बीच-बीच में; कभी-कभी	

SN	Idioms/Phrases	English Meaning	Hindi Meaning	#R
56	Bid someone welcome	To greet someone warmly	स्वागत करना	
57	Big cheese	An important or influential person	बड़ा आदमी (प्रभावशाली व्यक्ति)	
58	Big-ticket	Very expensive	बहुत महंगा	
59	Bigwig	An important or influential person	बड़ा आदमी (प्रभावशाली व्यक्ति)	
60	**Bite the hand that feeds you**	To act ungratefully or harmfully toward someone who has helped you	जिस थाली में खाना उसी में छेद करना (एहसान फरामोशी)	3
61	Black spot	A place where accidents or crimes frequently occur	दुर्घटनाओं या अपराध की जगह	
62	Blow one's brains out	To commit suicide by shooting oneself in the head	सिर में गोली मारकर आत्महत्या करना	
63	Blow one's money	To spend money recklessly	पैसे उड़ाना (फिजूलखर्ची करना)	
64	Blow one's stack	To suddenly become very angry	आपा खोना (बहुत गुस्सा होना)	
65	**Blow the gaff**	To reveal a secret or expose a scheme	राज़ खोलना; भेद उजागर करना	2
66	Blow-by-blow	Describing every detail of an event in the order it happened	विस्तृत विवरण	
67	Blue devils	A state of depression or low spirits	उदासी या अवसाद की स्थिति	
68	**Blue-sky thinking**	A creative, imaginative thinking without practical constraints	रचनात्मक सोच	2
69	**Bluestocking**	An educated, intellectual, or literary woman	अत्यधिक पढ़ी-लिखी महिला	4
70	Bookworm	A person who loves reading and spends a lot of time reading	किताबी कीड़ा (पढ़ने का शौकीन)	
71	Bounce off the walls	To be extremely excited, energetic, or hyperactive	अत्यधिक उत्साहित होना	
72	Brain drain	The emigration of highly skilled or educated people from a country	प्रतिभा पलायन	
73	Brass monkey weather	Extremely cold weather	बहुत ठंडा मौसम	
74	Break cover	To come out of hiding; to reveal oneself	छिपने की जगह से बाहर आना	
75	**Break ground**	To start construction; to be innovative or pioneering	शिलान्यास करना; नई खोज करना	2
76	Break the back of	To complete the most difficult or largest part of a task	काम का सबसे कठिन हिस्सा पूरा करना	
77	Bring owls to Athens	To do something unnecessary; to bring something to where it already exists in abundance	तेली के घर तेल ले जाना (व्यर्थ के काम करना)	
78	Broken-hearted	Overwhelmed by grief, sorrow, or disappointment	दिल टूटा हुआ (बेहद दुखी)	
79	Build bridges	To improve relationships between people or groups	संबंध सुधारना; मेल-मिलाप करना	
80	Burn oneself out	To exhaust oneself through overwork	खुद को पूरी तरह थका देना	
81	Butter someone up	Flatter someone to gain favour or advantage	मक्खन लगाना (चापलूसी करना)	
82	By dint of	By means of; because of	के बल पर (की वजह से)	
83	By long odds	By a great difference; most certainly	बड़े अंतर से; निश्चित रूप से	
84	Call it a night	To stop what you are doing, especially in the evening	आज के लिए काम बंद करना	
85	**Call to the colours**	Summon to military service	सेना में बुलावा	2

SN	Idioms/Phrases	English Meaning	Hindi Meaning	#R
86	Can't see the forest for the trees	To fail to understand the main point because of focusing on details	बारीकियों में उलझकर मुख्य बात भूलना	
87	Carry a torch for	To have unrequited love for someone; to champion a cause	एकतरफा प्यार करना; किसी मुद्दे का समर्थन करना	
88	Cast aspersions	To make damaging remarks about someone	कीचड़ उछालना (बदनाम करना)	
89	Cast one's bread upon the waters	To do good without expecting anything in return	नेकी कर दरिया में डाल (बिना स्वार्थ के भलाई करना)	
90	Cast-iron stomach	The ability to eat anything without digestive problems; strong digestion	मजबूत पाचन शक्ति	
91	Cat got your tongue	Used to ask someone why they are not speaking (usually out of shyness or guilt)	मुँह में दही जमना (बोल न पाना)	
92	Catch one's breath	To pause to rest and recover normal breathing; to take a break	साँस लेना (थोड़ा आराम करना)	
93	**Catch someone's eye**	To attract someone's attention	ध्यान आकर्षित करना	2
94	Chewed and digested	Fully understood or thoroughly thought over	अच्छी तरह समझा हुआ	
95	Child in the cradle	An innocent or inexperienced person	भोला या अनुभवहीन व्यक्ति	
96	Chock-a-block	Completely full	खचाखच भरा हुआ	
97	Clear-cut	Definite and easy to understand	साफ-साफ (स्पष्ट)	
98	**Close, but no cigar**	Used when someone almost succeeds but ultimately fails	बहुत करीब होकर भी सफल न होना	2
99	**Clouds on the horizon**	Signs of future trouble or difficulties	संकट के बादल (आने वाली मुसीबत के संकेत)	4
100	Cock a snook	To show disrespect or contempt, especially by a rude gesture	नाक-भौं चढ़ाना (खुलेआम अपमान करना)	
101	Conspicuous by one's absence	Noticeably absent from a place where one would be expected to be	अनुपस्थिति स्पष्ट होना	
102	Cost a bomb	To be very expensive	बहुत महँगा होना	
103	Country mile	A very long distance	कोसो दूर (बहुत लम्बी दूरी)	
104	**Crack a book**	To open a book to study	किताब खोलना (पढ़ाई करना)	2
105	Cry halves	To demand an equal share	आधा हिस्सा माँगना	
106	Culture vulture	A person who is very interested in art and culture	कला-संस्कृति का शौकीन	
107	Cup of joe	A cup of coffee	एक कप कॉफी	
108	Cupboard love	An affection shown in order to get something	स्वार्थी प्रेम (फायदे के लिए दिखावटी स्नेह)	
109	**Curtain lecture**	A private scolding given by a wife to her husband	पत्नी द्वारा पति को एकांत में दी गई फटकार	2
110	Cut and run	To make a quick escape; to leave hurriedly to avoid trouble	नौ दो ग्यारह होना (भाग जाना)	
111	Cut the cord	To become independent; to break ties with someone or something	अपने पैरों पर खड़ा होना (आत्मनिर्भर बनना)	
112	**Cutting edge**	The most advanced or innovative stage of development	अत्याधुनिक	2
113	Daylight robbery	A blatant overcharging; charging far too much for something	दिनदहाड़े लूट (बहुत महँगा)	

SN	Idioms/Phrases	English Meaning	Hindi Meaning	#R
114	Death blow	An action or event that causes the end or failure of something	घातक प्रहार (अंतिम आघात जो किसी चीज़ को समाप्त कर दे)	
115	Die in the last ditch	To fight until the very end; to never surrender	अंतिम साँस तक लड़ना	
116	Dig in one's heels	To refuse to change one's mind or give in; to be stubbornly determined	जिद पर अड़े रहना	
117	Dirt cheap	Very cheap	कौड़ियों के दाम (बहुत सस्ता)	
118	**Dog days**	The hottest period of summer	गर्मी के सबसे गर्म दिन	4
119	**Dog-tired**	Extremely tired	बुरी तरह थका हुआ	2
120	Dollars to doughnuts	Almost certain	लगभग निश्चित	
121	Don't give up the day job	A way of telling someone that they are not very good at a new activity	तुम्हारे बस की बात नहीं	
122	Double-talk	A deliberately confusing or misleading speech	गोलमोल बातें (भ्रामक भाषा)	
123	**Doubting Thomas**	A person who refuses to believe something without direct personal evidence	संदेहशील व्यक्ति (बिना प्रमाण के न मानने वाला)	2
124	Down the hatch	Used as a toast (phrase) before drinking	शराब पीने से पहले की अभिव्यक्ति	
125	Down to the wire	Until the last possible moment; to the very end	अंतिम क्षण तक	
126	Drink like a fish	To drink alcohol excessively	बहुत अधिक शराब पीना	
127	Drive a hard bargain	To negotiate aggressively for a favourable deal	सख्ती से मोलभाव करना	
128	Drop the ball	To make a mistake or fail at something	गलती कर देना	
129	Dyed-in-the-wool	Firmly fixed in beliefs or habits	कट्टर	
130	**Early bird**	A person who gets up or arrives early	सुबह जल्दी उठने वाला; समय से पहले आने वाला	2
131	Ebb and flow	A recurring pattern of coming and going; rising and falling; fluctuation	उतार-चढ़ाव (बदलाव की प्रक्रिया)	
132	Elvis has left the building	A phrase used to signal that an event has completely finished and it's time to go	खेल खत्म (जाने का वक्त हो गया)	
133	Ever and anon	Now and then; occasionally	कभी-कभार	
134	Every man and his dog	A very large number of people; almost everyone	बड़ी तादाद में लोग या लगभग सभी	
135	Every trick in the book	Every possible method or technique	हर हथकंडा अपनाना (हर संभव तरीका)	
136	Everyone and his brother	A very large number of people; almost everyone	बड़ी तादाद में लोग या लगभग सभी	
137	Excess baggage	Something or someone unwanted and burdensome	अनावश्यक बोझ	
138	Fabian policy	A strategy of delay to weaken opposition	विलंब की नीति	
139	Fair play	A just and honest treatment; equal opportunity for all	निष्पक्ष व्यवहार; ईमानदारी	
140	Fall by the wayside	To fail to continue or be abandoned before completion	बीच में छूट जाना; असफल हो जाना	
141	Fall in a heap	To collapse suddenly; to fail completely	भावनात्मक रूप से टूटना	
142	Fall on deaf ears	To be ignored or not taken into account	अनसुना कर दिया जाना	

SN	Idioms/Phrases	English Meaning	Hindi Meaning	#R
143	Feel free	Used to give permission; you are welcome to	बेझिझक करे; अनुमति देना	
144	Feel like a million dollars	To feel extremely good, attractive, or healthy	बहुत अच्छा महसूस करना	
145	**Feet of clay**	A hidden weakness in someone otherwise admired	मिट्टी के पाँव होना (छिपी हुई कमजोरी)	2
146	Field day	An opportunity for great enjoyment or activity; a time of unusual success	मौज-मस्ती या आनंद का दिन	
147	Find common ground	To find shared interests or beliefs that enable agreement	समान मत ढूँढ़ना	
148	**Fire and brimstone**	Angry speech threatening punishment, especially religious	धार्मिक दंड की चेतावनी	2
149	Fit and trim	In good physical condition	सुडौल और स्वस्थ	
150	Fit to be tied	Extremely angry	गुस्से से आग-बबूला	
151	Flesh and blood	Human nature with its weaknesses; one's family or relatives	मानवीय कमजोरी; सगा संबंधी	
152	**Fool's gold**	Something that appears valuable but is actually worthless	नकली मूल्यवान चीज	2
153	For all intents and purposes	In every practical sense	व्यावहारिक रूप से	
154	Fuddy-duddy	An old-fashioned, conservative, or fussy person	पुराने खयालों वाला या रूढ़िवादी व्यक्ति	
155	**Get a buzz**	To get a feeling of excitement or pleasure	उत्साहित महसूस करना	2
156	Get even	To take revenge	हिसाब बराबर करना (बदला लेना)	
157	Get into a huddle	To gather closely together to discuss something privately	गुपचुप बातचीत के लिए इकट्ठा होना	
158	Get one's feet wet	To begin to do something new; to gain initial experience	किसी चीज़ में हाथ आजमाना (शुरुआती अनुभव लेना)	
159	Get the jitters	To feel extremely nervous or anxious	हाथ-पाँव फूलना (घबराहट होना)	
160	Give currency to	To spread or popularize (an idea, rumour, etc.)	बढ़ावा देना (अफवाह आदि को)	
161	Give free rein	To allow complete freedom to act or decide	बेलगाम छोड़ देना (पूरी आज़ादी देना)	
162	Give someone a big hand	To applaud enthusiastically	जोरदार तालियाँ बजाना	
163	Give someone a leg up	To help someone get started or advance	किसी को आगे बढ़ने में मदद करना	
164	Glass ceiling	An invisible barrier preventing advancement, especially for women	अदृश्य रुकावट (तरक्की में बाधा)	
165	Go for the throat	To attack aggressively at the weakest point	कमजोरी पर वार करना	
166	Go great guns	To proceed with great speed, energy, or success	धुआंधार प्रगति करना	
167	Go like a bomb	To go very fast; to be very successful	बहुत सफल होना	
168	Go out of one's way	To make a special effort to do something, especially to help someone	विशेष प्रयास करना (खासकर किसी की मदद के लिए)	
169	**Go under the knife**	To undergo a medical operation or surgery	सर्जरी या ऑपरेशन करवाना	2
170	Go without saying	To be obvious; to be taken for granted	कहने की जरूरत नहीं (स्पष्ट होना)	

SN	Idioms/Phrases	English Meaning	Hindi Meaning	#R
171	Golden handshake	A generous payment given when someone leaves a job	सेवानिवृत्ति पर मिलने वाला बड़ा भुगतान	
172	**Golden opportunity**	An excellent chance that should not be missed	सुनहरा अवसर (बेहतरीन मौका)	2
173	Gordian knot	An extremely difficult problem	जटिल समस्या	
174	Gravy train	An easy way to earn money with little effort	आसान पैसा कमाने का रास्ता	
175	Green with envy	Extremely envious	ईर्ष्या से जलना	
176	Grin and bear it	To accept a difficult situation without complaining	मुस्कुराकर सह लेना (बिना शिकायत सहना)	
177	Hammer and tongs	With great energy and enthusiasm	पूरी ताकत से	
178	Hard on the eyes	Unpleasant or ugly to look at	आँखों को चुभना (देखने में अच्छा न लगना)	
179	Have a brush with	To have a brief encounter or conflict with something	हलकी मुठभेड़ होना	
180	Have a conniption	To become very angry, upset, or hysterical over something	गुस्से या घबराहट का दौरा पड़ना	
181	Have a lot to answer for	To be responsible for many problems	बहुत सी समस्याओं का ज़िम्मेदार होना	
182	Have a meltdown	To have an emotional breakdown	भावनात्मक रूप से टूट जाना	
183	Have a mind like a steel trap	To have a sharp and quick mind	तेज दिमाग होना	
184	Have a screw loose	To be slightly crazy or eccentric	दिमाग का पेंच ढीला होना (सनकी या पागल सा)	
185	Have a sweet tooth	To love eating sweet things	मीठा खाने का शौकीन	
186	**Have nine lives**	To be able to survive many difficult or dangerous situations	बार-बार ख़तरे से बच निकलना	2
187	**Have one's cake and eat it too**	To want two incompatible or mutually exclusive things at the same time	एक ही समय में दो विरोधाभासी फायदे चाहना (दोनों हाथों में लड्डू चाहना)	8
188	Have one's heart in one's boots	To feel very sad, depressed, or discouraged	बहुत निराश महसूस करना	
189	Have the time of one's life	To have an extremely enjoyable experience	जीवन का सबसे सुखद समय बिताना	
190	Heart skips a beat	To feel sudden excitement or fear	धड़कन रुक जाना (उत्तेजना/डर से)	
191	Heath Robinson	An absurdly complicated or impractical device	बेहद जटिल और अव्यावहारिक व्यवस्था	
192	Hidden depths	Surprising qualities not immediately obvious	छिपे हुए गुण (अप्रत्याशित क्षमताएं)	
193	Hit a nerve	To upset someone by mentioning a sensitive topic	दुखती रग पर हाथ रखना (संवेदनशील मुद्दे को छेड़ना)	
194	**Hit a snag**	To encounter an unexpected or hidden obstacle or problem	अड़चन आना	2
195	Hither and thither	In various directions	इधर-उधर	
196	Hold all the aces	To have all the advantages; to be in a winning position	सारे पत्ते हाथ में होना (अनुकूल स्थिति)	
197	**Hole-and-corner**	Done secretly, often dishonestly	छिपकर किया गया (अक्सर बेईमानी से)	3
198	Hook, line, and sinker	Completely and without doubt	पूरी तरह से; बिना शक	

SN	Idioms/Phrases	English Meaning	Hindi Meaning	#R
199	Hunky-dory	Everything is fine or satisfactory	सब ठीक-ठाक है	
200	Hustle and bustle	A busy, noisy activity	भाग-दौड़ (चहल-पहल)	
201	In a body	All together as a group	सामूहिक रूप से	
202	In a lather	In a state of agitation or nervous excitement	घबराहट में (परेशान)	
203	In a sweat	Become anxious or worried	पसीने छूटना (घबराना)	
204	In bad shape	In poor condition	खराब हालत में	
205	In no time	Very quickly	झट से (फौरन)	
206	In one's absence	When someone is not present	गैरहाजिरी में	
207	In poor taste	Offensive, inappropriate, or lacking good judgment	अशोभनीय (बेतुका)	
208	In spades	To a great degree; very much; abundantly	बहुत ज़्यादा; भरपूर तरीके से	
209	In the bag	Certain to be achieved	मुट्ठी में होना (सुनिश्चित सफलता)	
210	In the prime of life	At the time of greatest health, strength, or success	जीवन के सर्वोत्तम दौर में	
211	In the zone	Fully focused and performing at one's best	पूर्ण एकाग्रता में	
212	In tune with the times	Up to date with current trends	समय के साथ चलना	
213	It beats me	Used to say that you do not understand something or do not know the answer	समझ से बाहर	
214	Jump ship	To leave an organization or project, especially in difficult times	डूबते जहाज को छोड़ना (मुश्किल में साथ छोड़ना)	
215	Jump the queue	To move ahead of others unfairly; to skip the queue	कतार तोड़कर आगे निकलना	
216	Keep in the dark	To not tell someone about something	अंधेरे में रखना (छुपाना)	
217	Keep one's cool	To remain calm under pressure	दिमाग ठंडा रखना (शांत रहना)	
218	Keep one's eyes peeled	To watch carefully	आँखें खुली रखना (सतर्क रहना)	
219	Keep someone on their toes	To keep someone alert and ready	चौकन्ना रखना	
220	Keep tabs on	To monitor closely	नजर रखना	
221	**Keep your finger on the pulse**	To be aware of the latest trends or developments	नब्ज टटोलते रहना (जागरूक रहना)	2
222	**Kick the can down the road**	To postpone dealing with a problem	समस्या टालना	2
223	Kick up one's heels	To enjoy oneself in a lively or uninhibited way	बेफिक्र होकर मौज-मस्ती करना	
224	Knee-jerk reaction	A quick response that is made without any thought or consideration	बिना सोचे-समझे दी गई प्रतिक्रिया	
225	Knit one's brows	To frown in concentration, puzzlement, or displeasure	भौहें सिकोड़ना (गहरी सोच या नाराज़गी में)	
226	Knock someone over	To push someone down; to shock or astonish greatly	गिरा देना; हैरान कर देना	
227	Knock someone's socks off	To greatly impress or astonish someone	बहुत प्रभावित करना	
228	Lame duck	A person or thing that is ineffective, unsuccessful, or powerless	निष्प्रभावी या शक्तिहीन व्यक्ति	

SN	Idioms/Phrases	English Meaning	Hindi Meaning	#R
229	**Land on one's feet**	To be lucky and successful after a difficult situation	कठिनाइयों के बावजूद ठीक स्थिति में पहुँच जाना	2
230	Larger than life	Having an exaggerated or impressive personality	असाधारण व्यक्तित्व	
231	Leave someone to their own devices	To allow someone to do as they wish without supervision	अपने हाल पर छोड़ देना (बिना रोक-टोक अपनी मर्जी से काम करने देना)	
232	Let someone off the hook	To free someone from an obligation or difficult situation	किसी को मुसीबत या जिम्मेदारी से बचाना	
233	Life in the raw	Life as it really is, without pretense	असल जिंदगी (बिना दिखावे की जिंदगी)	
234	Like a bear with a sore head	To be very irritable and bad-tempered	बहुत चिड़चिड़ा या गुस्सैल होना	
235	Like a kid in a candy store	Very excited and enthusiastic	बहुत उत्साहित	
236	**Like a ton of bricks**	To have a sudden and overwhelming impact	गाज गिरना (अचानक भारी झटका लगना)	2
237	Like water off a duck's back	Having no effect on someone	कोई असर न होना	
238	Lily-white	Pure white; innocent; morally pure	बेदाग (अत्यंत शुद्ध)	
239	Listen with half an ear	To listen without giving full attention	अनमने ढंग से सुनना (ध्यान न देना)	
240	Loaded for bear	Fully prepared for any challenge	पूरी तरह तैयार	
241	Lone wolf	A person who prefers to work or be alone	अकेला काम करने वाला	
242	Look like a dog's dinner	To be very messy, untidy, or badly organized	बेढंगा या अजीब दिखना	
243	**Look to one's laurels**	To be careful not to lose one's position of superiority	अपनी श्रेष्ठता बनाए रखने की चिंता करना	2
244	Loose talk	Careless or indiscreet conversation; gossip	लापरवाह बातचीत	
245	Lose the plot	To become confused or lose focus	भटक जाना (समझ न पाना)	
246	Lost in translation	Meaning changed or lost when converting between languages	अनुवाद में अर्थ खो जाना	
247	Lynch law	The practice of punishing someone without a proper trial	भीड़ का न्याय (बिना कानूनी प्रक्रिया के सज़ा)	
248	Make a clean sweep	Win with a large margin	बड़े अंतर से जीतना	
249	Make all the difference	To have a significant effect	बड़ा फर्क पड़ना	
250	Make heavy weather of	To make something seem more difficult than it is	आसान काम को मुश्किल बनाना	
251	Make like a tree and leave	Go away	चले जाओ	
252	**Make no odds**	To make no significant difference	कोई अंतर या प्रभाव न डालना	2
253	Man of few words	A person who speaks briefly and to the point	कम बोलने वाला	
254	Man of honour	A man who is honest and has strong moral principles	इज़्ज़तदार आदमी (सिद्धांतवादी और वचनबद्ध)	
255	Man of weight	An influential or important person	प्रभावशाली व्यक्ति	

SN	Idioms/Phrases	English Meaning	Hindi Meaning	#R
256	Matters of the head and heart	Issues involving both logic and emotions	दिमाग और दिल के मामले (तर्क और भावना)	
257	Mean business	To be serious about what one says or intends to do	गंभीर होना	
258	Meat and potatoes	The basic, fundamental, or essential part of something	किसी चीज का मुख्य या बुनियादी हिस्सा	
259	Meet with indifference	To be ignored or receive no reaction	ठंडी प्रतिक्रिया मिलना (उदासीनता)	
260	Mend fences	To repair a damaged relationship	रिश्ते सुधारना	
261	Money to burn	More money than one needs	ज़रूरत से ज़्यादा पैसा	
262	Muddy the waters	To make a situation more confusing or unclear	स्थिति को और अधिक उलझा देना	
263	Muster in force	To gather in large numbers	बड़ी संख्या में इकट्ठा होना	
264	My way or the highway	Accept my terms or leave	मेरी बात मानो या चलते बनो	
265	Nail in the coffin	A final factor leading to failure or end	असफलता का अंतिम कारण	
266	Next to nothing	Very little; almost nothing	नाममात्र (बहुत कम)	
267	Not have a ghost of a chance	To have no chance at all	ज़रा भी संभावना न होना	
268	Not keep one's word	To fail to keep a promise	वादा न निभाना	
269	Not know someone from Adam	To not know someone at all; to have never met them	अनजान होना	
270	Nuts and bolts	The basic practical details of a subject or activity	किसी चीज़ की बुनियादी कार्यप्रणाली या बारीकियां	
271	Nutty as a fruitcake	Completely crazy	पूरा पागल	
272	Old wives' tale	A traditional belief that is untrue or unscientific	दादी-नानी की कहानी (अंधविश्वास)	
273	On hand	Available and ready	उपलब्ध	
274	**On the bench**	To be a presiding judge; to be temporarily not involved in an activity	न्यायाधीश के पद पर होना; अस्थायी रूप से किसी प्रक्रिया में शामिल न होना	2
275	On the blink	Not functioning properly; out of order	खराब (ठीक से काम न करना)	
276	On the button	Exactly right	सटीक (एकदम सही)	
277	On the dot	At the exact time specified	बिल्कुल सही समय पर	
278	On the fly	While in motion; without preparation	चलते-फिरते बिना तैयारी के	
279	On the hook	To be responsible for something	जिम्मेदार होना	
280	On the other side	From a different perspective	किसी बात का दूसरा पहलू या उल्टा पक्ष	
281	**On the trot**	One after another without pause; continuously	लगातार (एक के बाद एक)	2
282	On the up and up	Honest and legitimate; improving	ईमानदार और साफ़-सुथरा; तरक्की की राह पर	
283	Out of nowhere	Unexpectedly; suddenly	अचानक (कहीं से भी)	
284	Out of the way	Remote, far from main places	दूर स्थित	
285	**Out on a limb**	In a risky, isolated, or vulnerable position	जोखिम भरी या अकेली स्थिति में	2
286	Over the hill	To be past one's prime; too old to be effective or attractive	उम्र दराज होना (बूढ़ा होना)	

SN	Idioms/Phrases	English Meaning	Hindi Meaning	#R
287	Over the top	To do something excessively; to exceed limits	हद पार करना (ज़रूरत से ज़्यादा करना)	
288	Overstep the mark	To go beyond acceptable limits; to behave inappropriately	हद पार करना (मर्यादा का उल्लंघन करना)	
289	Paint the town red	Go out to celebrate wildly	खूब मौज-मस्ती करना	
290	Palmy days	A time of prosperity and success	सुनहरे दिन (अच्छे दिन)	
291	**Palsy-walsy (or pally-wally)**	Very friendly, often in a way that seems insincere	बहुत दोस्ताना (अक्सर दिखावटी)	2
292	**Paper tiger**	A person or thing that appears threatening or powerful but is actually weak	कागजी शेर (दिखने में मजबूत लेकिन कमजोर)	2
293	Pass oneself off as	To pretend to be someone or something else	फर्जी पहचान देना	
294	Pay over the odds	To pay more than something is worth	अधिक कीमत चुकाना	
295	**Pearls of wisdom**	A wise or supposedly wise remark (often used ironically)	ज्ञान की बात (प्रायः व्यंग्यात्मक प्रयोग में)	3
296	Pick a fight	To deliberately start an argument or confrontation	पंगा लेना (जानबूझकर झगड़ा करना)	
297	Pick up the pace	To start doing something faster; to increase speed	रफ्तार तेज़ करना (गति बढ़ाना)	
298	Pillar of the society (or community)	A respected and important member of society	समाज का स्तंभ (सम्मानित व्यक्ति)	
299	Pin back one's ears	To listen very carefully or to pay close attention	कान लगाकर सुनना (ध्यान देना)	
300	Pinch pennies	To be very careful with money; to be frugal	कंजूसी करना (पैसा बचाना)	
301	Play hell with	To cause damage or confusion to something	भारी नुकसान पहुँचाना	
302	Point the finger at	To blame or accuse someone	उँगली उठाना (दोष लगाना)	
303	Pull oneself up by one's bootstraps	To improve one's situation through one's own efforts	अपने बल पर उठना	
304	Punching bag	A person who is repeatedly criticized, attacked, or bullied	अनुचित आलोचना का शिकार व्यक्ति	
305	Push one's luck	To take a risk by asking for or doing too much	किस्मत को जरुरत से ज्यादा आजमाना (जोखिम उठाना)	
306	Push someone's buttons	To deliberately annoy someone	किसी को उकसाना (चिढ़ाना)	
307	**Push the boat out**	To spend money freely, especially to celebrate	खूब खर्च करना (जश्न मनाना)	2
308	Push the envelope	To go beyond established limits; to innovate or try something new and risky	सीमाओं को तोड़ना	
309	Put a sock in it	Tell someone to stop talking or be quiet	चुप रहने को कहना	
310	Put one's oar in	To give unwanted advice or interfere in something	बिना माँगे सलाह देना; दखल देना	
311	Put one's shoulder to the wheel	To work hard at something	जी-जान लगाकर काम करना	
312	Put out to pasture	To force to retire or stop working, often due to age	जबरन सेवानिवृत्त करना	
313	Put the screws on	To pressure or coerce someone strongly	दबाव डालना	

SN	Idioms/Phrases	English Meaning	Hindi Meaning	#R
314	Pyrrhic victory	A victory that comes at such great cost it is not worth winning	ऐसी जीत जिसमें बहुत कुछ खोना पड़े	
315	**Raise someone's hackles**	To make someone angry	किसी को गुस्सा दिलाना	2
316	Raring to go	Very eager and enthusiastic to start	शुरू करने को बेताब	
317	Reach an accord	To achieve agreement	समझौता करना	
318	Reap the harvest	To receive the results or consequences of one's actions	मेहनत का फल पाना	
319	Return the favour	To do something nice for someone who has done something nice for you	एहसान का बदला चुकाना	
320	Ride the gravy train	To earn money easily without much effort	मुफ्त की मलाई खाना (बिना मेहनत लाभ उठाना)	
321	Rob Peter to pay Paul	To take from one to give to another, solving nothing	एक की जेब से निकालकर दूसरे को देना	
322	Rub shoulders with	To associate with important people	बड़े लोगों के साथ उठना-बैठना	
323	Rule of thumb	A practical guideline based on experience rather than exact measurement	व्यावहारिक अनुभव के आधार पर	
324	Run for the hills	To flee or escape quickly from a dangerous situation	खतरे से बचने के लिए भागना	
325	Run like the wind	To run very fast	बहुत तेज दौड़ना	
326	**Run the gauntlet**	To go through a dangerous or hostile situation	कठिनाइयों या खतरों से गुजरना	2
327	**Save face**	To avoid humiliation or embarrassment	इज़्ज़त बचाना; मान रखना	3
328	Save someone's bacon	To rescue someone from a difficult situation	किसी को मुसीबत से बचाना	
329	Say one's piece	To express one's opinion	अपनी बात कहना	
330	Screw up one's courage	To force oneself to be brave	हिम्मत जुटाना	
331	**See red**	To become very angry	गुस्से से लाल होना	2
332	Separate the sheep from the goats	To distinguish between good and bad people or things	अच्छे और बुरे में अंतर करना	
333	Set by the ears	To cause people to quarrel or fight	कान भरना (झगड़ा भड़काना)	
334	Set in stone	To be fixed and unchangeable; not able to be altered	पत्थर कि लकीर (जो बदला न जा सके)	
335	**Sheet anchor**	A reliable or principal support	मुख्य सहारा	3
336	Shoot from the hip	To speak or act without careful thought or consideration	बिना सोचे बोलना	
337	Short fuse	A tendency to get angry very quickly	तुनक मिज़ाज (जल्दी गुस्सा होना)	
338	Shoulder to shoulder	Side by side; working together in unity	कंधे से कंधा मिलाकर (एकजुट होकर)	
339	**Show one's hand**	To reveal one's intentions or plans	पत्ते खोल देना (योजना प्रकट करना)	2
340	Show-stopper	A performance or act that is so impressive it receives overwhelming applause	शानदार और प्रभावशाली प्रदर्शन	
341	Sick at heart	Very unhappy or disappointed; deeply troubled	दिल से दुखी; बहुत निराश	
342	Sing from the same hymn sheet	To express the same opinion or give the same information publicly	एक ही राग अलापना (समान बात कहना)	

SN	Idioms/Phrases	English Meaning	Hindi Meaning #R
343	Sink or swim	To fail or succeed by one's own efforts alone	अपने दम पर आर या पार
344	Sixth sense	An intuitive ability to perceive things beyond the five senses	छठी इंद्री (पूर्वाभास)
345	Smell something fishy	To sense something suspicious	दाल में कुछ काला लगना (संदेह होना)
346	Someone's ears are burning	A feeling that someone is talking about you in your absence	पीठ पीछे चर्चा होना (याद किया जाना)
347	Someone's ears are flapping	A feeling that someone is listening intently to a private conversation	छिपकर सुनना
348	Spare no expense	To spend as much money as necessary without limiting costs	खर्च की परवाह न करना
349	Square the circle	To attempt an impossible task	असंभव काम करने की कोशिश
350	Stuff and nonsense	Used to express that something is ridiculous or untrue	बेकार की बातें
351	Swim with sharks	To associate or compete with dangerous people	खतरनाक लोगों के बीच रहना
352	Take a stand	To publicly express and defend an opinion or position	अपना रुख स्पष्ट करना
353	Take as gospel	To believe something without question	आँख मूँदकर विश्वास करना
354	Take it up a notch	To increase the level or intensity of something	अधिक प्रयास करना
355	Take no prisoners	To be ruthless or uncompromising	निर्दयता से काम करना
356	Take someone/ something by storm	To quickly gain popularity or success	तूफान की तरह छा जाना (अचानक ज़बरदस्त सफलता पाना)
357	Take the biscuit	To be the most surprising, annoying, or extreme example of something	सबसे बुरा उदाहरण होना
358	Take the law into one's own hands	To punish someone without legal authority	कानून अपने हाथ में लेना
359	Take the plunge	To decide to do something risky	कूद पड़ना (जोखिम उठाना)
360	Talk big	To boast; to speak with exaggerated self-importance	डींग हांकना (बड़ी-बड़ी बातें करना)
361	Talk nineteen to the dozen	To talk very quickly and continuously	बहुत तेज और लगातार बोलना
362	Talk someone's head off	To talk to someone for a very long time, often boringly	किसी का सिर खा जाना (बहुत बातें करना)
363	Tall talk	Boastful or exaggerated speech	लंबी-चौड़ी हांकना
364	Ten out of ten	A perfect score; used to express that something is excellent	दस में से दस (पूर्ण अंक या बिल्कुल सही)
365	The bare bones	The basic facts or essential elements without details	मुख्य बिंदु
366	The coast is clear	There is no danger or obstacle	रास्ता साफ है
367	The curtain falls	The end of an event or performance	पर्दा गिरना (समाप्ति होना)
368	The feathers fly	A heated argument or fight breaks out	गरमागरम बहस
369	The jewel in the crown	The most valuable possession or achievement	सबसे मूल्यवान हिस्सा
370	The onus is on	The responsibility is entirely yours	जिम्मेदारी आपके कंधों पर है
371	**The order of the day**	The prevailing state of things; what is usual, popular, or currently accepted	वर्तमान प्रचलन 2
372	The primrose path	A life of pleasure that leads to ruin	सुखद लेकिन विनाशकारी रास्ता

SN	Idioms/Phrases	English Meaning	Hindi Meaning	#R
373	The school of hard knocks	Learning through difficult life experiences rather than formal education	ठोकर खाकर सीखना (जीवन के कड़वे अनुभवों से सीखना)	
374	The ugly duckling	Someone unpromising who later becomes successful	जो शुरुआत में साधारण या कमजोर लगे, लेकिन आगे चलकर श्रेष्ठ निकले	
375	Thick in the head	To be slow to understand; stupid or dull	मोटा दिमाग होना (मूर्ख या मंदबुद्धि)	
376	Throw into a tailspin	To cause someone or something to lose control or become chaotic	अफरा-तफरी मचाना	
377	Throw one's weight around	To act in a domineering or bullying manner	रुतबा दिखाना (धौंस जमाना)	
378	**Throw someone under the bus**	To betray or sacrifice someone for personal gain	बलि का बकरा बनाना (अपने फायदे के लिए किसी को फँसा देना)	2
379	Tie someone's hands	To prevent someone from acting freely	हाथ बाँध देना (कुछ करने से रोकना)	
380	To the backbone	Through and through; completely and thoroughly	पूरी तरह से	
381	To the bitter end	Until something is completely finished, however unpleasant	मरते दम तक (अंत तक)	
382	To the hilt	Completely; to the maximum extent	पूरी तरह से	
383	Toil and moil	To work very hard	कठिन परिश्रम	
384	Top-notch	Of the highest possible quality	अव्वल दर्जे का	
385	Topsy-turvy	In a state of complete disorder or confusion	उलटा-पुलटा (अस्त-व्यस्त)	
386	Toss and turn	To move restlessly in bed, unable to sleep	करवटें बदलना (बेचैनी में रात काटना)	
387	Try one's hand at	To attempt or try doing something for the first time	हाथ आज़माना (पहली बार कोशिश करना)	
388	Turn one's stomach	To make someone feel disgusted or nauseous	जी मिचलाना (घृणा होना)	
389	Turn to account	To use something to one's advantage	परिस्थिति का फायदा लेना	
390	Turn up the heat	To increase pressure	दबाव बढ़ाना	
391	Turn upside down	To search thoroughly; to create disorder	अच्छी तरह खोजना; उलट-पुलट करना	
392	Twenty-three skidoo	Hasty departure	जल्दी निकलना	
393	Twist the knife	To make a bad situation even worse	जले पर नमक छिड़कना (दुख बढ़ाना)	
394	**Under lock and key**	Kept securely locked or guarded	सुरक्षित रखना	2
395	Under the table	Done secretly, especially involving illegal payment	मेज के नीचे (गुप्त रूप से)	
396	Up for grabs	Available to anyone who wants it	उपलब्ध	
397	Use a sledgehammer to crack a nut	To use excessive force or resources for a simple task	चींटी मारने के लिए तोप चलाना (ज़रूरत से ज़्यादा ताकत लगाना)	
398	Van Gogh's ear for music	To be tone-deaf or have no musical ability at all	संगीत की बिल्कुल समझ न होना	
399	Verbal diarrhoea	The tendency to talk too much, often without substance	अत्यधिक बातचीत	
400	Walk a mile in someone's shoes	To try to understand someone else's experiences or perspective	किसी की जगह खुद को रखकर देखना	
401	Ways and means	Methods and resources for achieving something	उद्देश्य प्राप्ति के तरीके	
402	Wear a long face	To look unhappy or disappointed	मुँह लटकाना (उदास दिखना)	

SN	Idioms/Phrases	English Meaning	Hindi Meaning #R
403	Weigh one's words	To choose what one says carefully	तौलकर बोलना (सोच-समझकर बोलना)
404	Wipe the smile off someone's face	To cause someone to lose their happiness or confidence suddenly	किसी की मुस्कान गायब कर देना
405	Wish upon a star	To hope for something unlikely or dream of something	किसी असंभव इच्छा की कामना करना
406	With a heavy heart	With great sadness or reluctance	भरी मन से (बहुत दुःख के साथ)
407	With all guns blazing	With maximum force and effort	पूरी ताकत के साथ
408	Within an ace of	Very close to achieving something	लगभग हासिल कर लेना
409	Without a doubt	Certainly; definitely	निस्संदेह
410	Wrestle with one's demons	To struggle with personal problems, inner conflicts, past trauma, bad habits, or emotional issues	आंतरिक द्वंद्व (अपनी कमज़ोरियों या बुरी आदतों से लड़ना)
411	Wring someone's neck	To be very angry with someone	गर्दन मरोड़ना (बहुत गुस्सा होना)
412	X marks the spot	Used to indicate the exact location of something	सटीक स्थान
413	Yellow journalism	Sensationalist journalism that exaggerates news for readership	सनसनीखेज़ और भ्रामक पत्रकारिता

*Total **413** Idioms asked **489** times*

B5 Idioms & Phrases Practice Sets (Based on Recent Other Exam Papers)

Practice Set - 1

Direction (Q. 1-10): Select the most appropriate meaning of the given idiom.

1 Tilt at windmills
1) To be young and inexperienced
2) To waste time dealing with enemies and problems that do not exist
3) To blow hot air
4) To celebrate good news

2 Don't give up the day job
1) What you're trying to do is irrelevant
2) Don't treat them they way you want to be treated
3) Don't look for a new job when you have one
4) Don't try doing it, you are likely to fail

3 Be bad news
1) feelings of hate
2) someone who behaves in a dishonest way
3) someone who is considered undesirable
4) to be ill

4 Like a kid in a candy store
1) Very annoying
2) Very stubborn
3) Very clumsy
4) Very excited

5 Hit a nerve
1) To ignore someone
2) To successfully complete a difficult task without any problems
3) To provoke a reaction by referring to a sensitive topic
4) To physically injure someone

6 Blow the gaff
1) Divulge a secret
2) Keep a secret
3) Create confusion
4) Argue loudly

7 Nutty as a fruitcake
1) Crazy or strange in behaviour
2) Something that is not likely to ever happen
3) To become tied up
4) To be naughty

8 Carrying the torch
1) Holding an actual torch
2) Running a race
3) Leading a protest
4) Continuing a cause or tradition

9 Be full of beans
1) Be full of energy
2) Feel exhausted
3) Be in a bad mood
4) Be hungry

10 Up for grabs
1) The complete or full extent of something
2) Available for anyone to take or win
3) Help each other mutually
4) A point in the distance where something disappears from view

Practice Set - 2

Direction (Q. 1-10): Select the most appropriate meaning of the given idiom.

1 The coast is clear
1) Life is pleasant and comfortable
2) To be free of responsibilities and liabilities
3) There is no danger of being caught
4) Free of threat by sea

2 Fly off the handle
1) To handle something carefully
2) To ignore somebody
3) To fly an airplane
4) To get angry quickly

3 Sell Like hot cakes
1) No profit at all
2) Unable to sellout anything
3) Quick sellout
4) No sellout at all

4 In the fast lane
1) A thrilled and fast paced lane on the road
2) A life filled with excitement
3) A life filled with sorrowness
4) A dull and boring life which needs excitement

5 Feather one's nest
1) To make one's lodgings comfortable
2) To make money for oneself by way of dishonest means
3) To look at something with a lot of pleasure
4) To make something more important than it really is

6 See eye to eye
1) Agree or have the same opinion as someone else
2) The feeling of success or accomplishment
3) Happening consistently or repeatedly every year
4) Changes and new experiences make life more enjoyable

7 Add insult to injury
1) To make a bad situation worse
2) Wish good luck
3) Very calm and composed
4) Focus closely on

8 Bite the dust
1) To behave weirdly
2) To stop living
3) To recall old memories
4) To abuse

9 Want to curl up and die
1) Feel terribly ashamed and embarrassed
2) Feel overjoyed
3) Feel excited
4) Feel indifferent

10 Be a killjoy
1) Something that is contrary to someone's natural feelings, beliefs, or habits.
2) A difficult problem or a person who is hard to understand or deal with.
3) A positive aspect or hope in an otherwise bad situation.
4) Someone who spoils the fun

or dampens others' enthusiasm.

Practice Set - 3

Direction (Q. 1-10): Select the most appropriate meaning of the given idiom.

1 Call it a night
1) To stay up all night working or partying
2) To decide to stop an activity for the rest of the night
3) To predict that it will be a long and tiring night
4) To make a phone call late at night

2 Hook, line and sinker
1) Being creative and happy
2) Helping others benevolently
3) Having an advantage
4) Accepting without hesitation or reservation

3 Make like a tree and leave
1) To be at ease
2) To prepare immediately
3) To leave quickly
4) To run fast

4 Above board
1) Across
2) Invincible
3) Honest
4) Imperious

5 Give it a shot
1) Try to do something
2) Shoot someone
3) Give a chance to someone
4) Give orders

6 In hot water
1) To be in a heated or angry argument
2) To be in liquid or fluid situation
3) To be in a warm or comfortable situation
4) To be in a difficult or troublesome situation

7 Neither fish nor fowl
1) Difficult to describe or classify
2) Neither this or that
3) Strict rules and regulations
4) Feel awkward because of unfamiliarity

8 Butterflies in the stomach
1) To be jealous
2) To be unwell
3) To be nervous
4) To be happy

9 At the end of your tether
1) Feel unable to deal with something
2) Feel at peace
3) Be full of energy
4) Be highly motivated

10 All roads lead to Rome
1) All roads to Rome are very good
2) In a city, there are many paths
3) Different paths take one to the same goal
4) In Rome, All roads are well-connected

Practice Set - 4

Direction (Q. 1-10): In the following items an idiom is given. Select the response that correctly describes the meaning of the idiom.

1 To bear the brunt of
1) To enjoy pleasant consequences
2) To create a disturbance
3) To suffer unpleasant consequences
4) To work very hard

2 Call to the colours
1) To join the army
2) To join the rebels
3) To refuse to help
4) To reveal true intentions

3 Make heavy weather
1) Cloud seeding
2) To pollute the air
3) To complain about wet and rainy conditions
4) Unnecessarily create difficulty in dealing with a task

4 With a grain of salt
1) Completely believed it
2) Accepted it but with doubt
3) Ignored it altogether
4) Was surprised by it

5 The world is your oyster
1) You have all the opportunity to obtain what you wish from life
2) Life is a precious gift
3) Life is a puzzle you cannot ever unravel
4) The world will dazzle you if you are not careful

6 To pull someone's chestnuts out of the fire
1) Try hard as one can to do something
2) To make someone pause abruptly
3) Over a brief period of time
4) To rescue someone from a difficulty

7 Take a rain check
1) To politely decline an offer, with the implication that one may take it up at a later date
2) To continuously improve by practising
3) Something that happens very rarely
4) To achieve two things by doing a single action

8 Get under someone's skin
1) To fall intensely in love with someone
2) To cause intense liking in someone
3) To understand someone completely
4) To annoy or irritate someone intensely

9 To put one's oar in
1) To interfere with
2) To give respect
3) To manipulate someone
4) To surrender oneself

10 Straight and narrow
1) Be excessively careful
2) Honest and morally acceptable way of being
3) Follow the straight path defined by society
4) To not deviate from one's goal

Practice Set - 5

Direction (Q. 1-10): In the following items an idiom or a proverb is given. Select the response that correctly describes the meaning of the idiom or proverb.

1 A purple patch
1) A beautiful valley of flowers
2) The final bloom of the season
3) A great run of luck or success or form
4) A bodily discolouration related heredity to

2 Someone's ears are burning
1) The feeling when someone thinks others are talking about them
2) Being excessively jealous of

others
3) Being angry due to unfair criticism
4) Itching to enter into an argument

3 Listen with half an ear
1) Not pay full attention
2) Being impartial
3) Being imperious
4) Listening with ironic distaste

4 Dyed in the wool
1) Changing notions because of a fluffy mind
2) Assuming a different colour
3) Adapting to conditions
4) Unchanging and firm in belief and conviction

5 At the drop of a hat
1) Rarely
2) Immediately
3) Slowly
4) Carefully

6 Put out to pasture
1) To retire or render redundant
2) To feed someone
3) To diminish importance
4) To incubate

7 Fight fire with fire
1) Use the same force or strategy of one's opponent to counter them
2) Use incendiary tactics to destroy by fire
3) Add fuel to further escalate a fiery situation
4) Scorch one's opponent with a barrage of firing

8 Turn one's stomach
1) Being nauseated by something or someone
2) Being plagued by a stomach upset
3) Unable to cope with the changes
4) Switch sides while asleep

9 Someone's ears are flapping
1) Someone in a state of intense agitation
2) Someone in a state of heightened excitement
3) Someone desperate to eavesdrop on a conversation
4) Someone embarrassed at being caught in the act of lying

10 Throw down the gauntlet
1) To accept
2) To challenge
3) To write
4) To speak

Practice Set - 6

Direction (Q. 1-10): Select the most appropriate meaning of the underlined idiom/proverb/phrase in the given sentence.

1 After losing the match, the coach told the team to <u>keep their chin up</u>.
1) Stay proud and arrogant
2) Be ready to fight
3) Remain cheerful in a difficult situation
4) Stay focused on winning

2 The manager hired more people for the upcoming project as <u>two heads are better than one</u>.
1) It's better to have more people for a task
2) One man is enough for a task
3) Good things will happen if you wait patiently
4) Don't pass judgement on others

3 He always believes in <u>making hay while the sun shines</u>.
1) helping those who help him
2) making the best use of a favourable situation
3) seeking advice from everyone
4) using crooked methods to succeed

4 She <u>rained on his parade</u> by telling him the bad news.
1) joined his celebration
2) spoiled his plans
3) showered him with praise
4) gave him an umbrella

5 He just tends <u>to put his foot in his mouth</u> when he is forced to speak for too long,
1) to brag about himself
2) to stammer
3) to say something embarrassing
4) to become nervous

6 He <u>broke the ice</u> by telling a funny joke at the start of the meeting.
1) Made everyone laugh
2) Caused a problem
3) Started a conversation
4) Cooled the atmosphere

7 Meera and her friend are always <u>at odds</u> over which movie to watch.
1) Unaware 2) In conflict
3) Confused 4) In agreement

8 When making decisions, note that <u>a stitch in time saves nine</u>.
1) Immediate action can prevent more work in the future.
2) Practice makes perfect.
3) Collaboration is preferable to individual effort.
4) Minor accomplishments often go unnoticed.

9 The new policy is just a <u>flash in the pan</u>; it won't last long.
1) A permanent solution
2) A sudden failure
3) A brief success
4) A long-term achievement

10 After agreeing to help her friend with an ambitious startup, she realised she was <u>in for a penny, in for a pound</u>, and decided to give it her all.
1) suffering losses and was under huge debt
2) saving money through small investments
3) out of all the pennies and pounds
4) committed to the course of action, even though expensive

Practice Set - 7

Direction (Q. 1-10): In the following question, out of the four given options, select the one which best expresses the meaning of the idiom/phrase.

1 Wrestle with the devil
1) To confront a deep-seated fea
2) To deceive someone for persona gain
3) To struggle with a moral dilemm or temptation
4) To waste time on unimportar matters

2 Right on the button
1) To get an electric current
2) To get dressed elegantly
3) Exactly correct
4) To make a wrong move

3 To steal someone's thunder
1) To do it all over again from tl beginning
2) To refuse to acknowledge som thing you know is real
3) To take credit for somethi

someone else did
4) To openly express one's feelings and thoughts

4 The ship has sailed
1) The matter is carried over
2) The matter is decided
3) The opportunity has passed
4) Seeking new opportunities

5 Hang in there
1) Telling someone not to give up
2) Telling someone to go to sleep
3) Telling someone to calm down
4) Telling someone to start over

6 throw a wrench in the works
1) To improve a plan
2) To cause a disruption or problem in a plan or process
3) To successfully fix a problem
4) To finish a project

7 To put one's shoulder to the wheel
1) To start something vigorously
2) To display a wrong act
3) To learn the procedures
4) To try every possible way

8 Play second fiddle
1) To take unnecessary risks
2) To disrupt an ongoing event
3) To perform exceptionally well
4) To be in a subordinate position

9 Gall and wormwood
1) To develop righteousness and virtue through adversity
2) To harbor intense feelings of animosity and resentment
3) To experience refreshing clarity and ease
4) To be positioned at the most basic place within a company

10 To save one's bacon
1) To save one's food
2) To prevent somebody from falling, losing being harmed
3) To save someone from embarrassment
4) To mollify

Practice Set - 8

Direction (Q. 1-10): Select the most appropriate idiom/phrase that can be used as a substitute for the underlined group of words in the given sentence.

1 The news of the celebrity's secret wedding became known very quickly to a lot of people .
1) hit the nail on the head
2) jumped the gun
3) spread like wildfire
4) went over the top

2 Even though he made a mistake in the meeting, Arjun apologised quickly to avoid embarrassment and maintain his dignity.
1) to bark up the wrong tree
2) to keep the ball in his court
3) to save his face
4) at the drop of a hat

3 Despite their differences, they managed to agree on the basic issues .
1) Play devil's advocate
2) Find common ground
3) Hit the books
4) Go the extra mile

4 Parent pay an extremely high price for children education.
1) Give through their hands
2) Pay through their nose
3) Feel the burden of paying
4) Pay through their hurt and lungs

5 Despite his excuses, his actions were made known publicly.
1) brought to light
2) kept at bay
3) swept under the carpet
4) called it a day

6 I can't believe she didn't show up for the meeting; she made a mistake.
1) called it a day
2) dropped the ball
3) spilled the beans
4) added insult to injury

7 Completing the project in just one day was a task that was very difficult to accomplish.
1) to turn over a new leaf
2) to read between the lines
3) a tall order
4) to take the bull by the horns

8 During the party, Rohit was very clumsy and careless, causing accidental damage everywhere.
1) a bull in a china shop
2) reading between the lines
3) taking the bull by the horns
4) turning over a new leaf

9 Everyone who knows Vikram knows that he is someone who always speaks in a very direct and honest way.
1) shoots from the hip
2) hits the nail on its head
3) cuts corners
4) jumps through hoops

10 My father takes a resolute stand where honesty is concerned.
1) Turns to account
2) puts his foot down
3) gains ground
4) is hand and glove

Practice Set - 9

Direction (Q. 1-10): A statement has been given with highlighted text. You are required to replace the text with correct idiom from the given options.

1 Ashok kept quiet at the board meeting, who knew he had an advantage that was currently being withheld for future purposes the whole time.
1) A black sheep
2) Missed the boat
3) An ace hidden up his sleeve
4) Light at the end of the tunnel

2 The job done was lousy, it was evident they were trying to save money.
1) on a wild goose chase
2) cutting corners
3) getting out of hand
4) biting the bullet

3 I had more important things to do than just sit at a dinner table.
1) to play devil's advocate
2) to take a rain check
3) to throw caution to the wind
4) bigger fish to fry

4 When they heard about the surprise quiz, the students were not at all excited.
1) (on) cloud nine
2) beating around the bush
3) Anything but
4) all ears

5 Winning the lottery just when he was about to go bankrupt was an unexpected and lucky event.
1) a blessing in disguise

2) a shot in the arm
3) a black sheep
4) a stroke of luck

6 The unconventional artist decided to <u>try new things that have not been tried before</u> with his new exhibition.
1) push the envelope
2) push his luck
3) push the buttons
4) play it by ear

7 Our new neighbour <u>seizes every occasion to start a quarrel</u>.
1) Pick a fight
2) A bolt from the blue
3) Waiting in the wings
4) A new lease of life

8 The deadline of the task was approaching, so we decided to <u>accelerate our efforts</u>.
1) put the pedal to the floor
2) step on the grass
3) pick up the pace
4) hit the ground running

9 They are using <u>advanced and innovative technology</u> in their new gadgets.
1) Crack a book
2) Smash hit
3) Dead meat
4) Cutting edge

10 The politician made tall promises but later <u>failed to act on them</u>.
1) paid lip service
2) turned a deaf ear
3) hit below the belt
4) threw in the towel

Practice Set - 10

Direction (Q. 1-10): In the following questions, four alternatives are given for the idioms / phrase underlined in the sentence. Choose the alternative which best expresses the meaning of the idioms / phrase.

1 He tried to <u>throw his weight around</u> to get the team to follow his orders.
1) Use influence or authority in an overbearing way
2) Carry heavy objects
3) Loss weight through Exercise
4) Act generously and kindly

2 As a leading political figure, he is used to being <u>in the limelight</u>.
1) giving speeches
2) being criticised
3) the centre of attraction
4) wielding power

3 Since discussions on the marriage proposal were not to her liking, Savita <u>put her foot down</u>.
1) stood up 2) got out
3) was firm 4) walked fast

4 Helen's business has been <u>in the red</u> for quite some time.
1) best in the market
2) Popular
3) Making profit
4) Making loss

5 He was a superstar but his popularity is <u>on the wane</u>.
1) at its peak 2) growing less
3) increasing 4) spiralling

6 The plan worked, but it was a <u>Pyrrhic victory</u> for the company.
1) A loss disguised as a win
2) A victory achieved at great cost, almost to the point of being a loss
3) A symbolic and irrelevant success
4) A flawless and effortless win

7 He was determined to <u>hit the ground running</u> on the new project.
1) Start something with enthusiasm and energy
2) Take a slow and cautious approach
3) Abandon a project Midway
4) Avoid hard work altogether

8 The manager's promises turned out to be a <u>red herring</u>.
1) A deliberate distraction from the main issue
2) A symbol of good luck
3) A factual and important point
4) A type of fish

9 <u>It is an uphill task</u>, but you will have to do it.
1) the work is above the hill
2) it is a very easy task
3) it is a very difficult task
4) It is almost impossible for others

10 The CEO's sudden resignation <u>threw the board into a tailspin</u>.
1) Made them very successful
2) Caused extreme confusion and panic
3) Motivated them to act
4) Made them feel hopeful

Answer Key Practice Set - 1:

1 - 2	2 - 4	3 - 3	4 - 4	5 - 3
6 - 1	7 - 1	8 - 4	9 - 1	10 - 2

Answer Key Practice Set - 2:

1 - 3	2 - 4	3 - 3	4 - 2	5 - 2
6 - 1	7 - 1	8 - 2	9 - 1	10 - 4

Answer Key Practice Set - 3:

1 - 2	2 - 4	3 - 3	4 - 3	5 - 1
6 - 4	7 - 1	8 - 3	9 - 1	10 - 3

Answer Key Practice Set - 4:

1 - 3	2 - 1	3 - 4	4 - 2	5 - 1
6 - 4	7 - 1	8 - 4	9 - 1	10 - 2

Answer Key Practice Set - 5:

1 - 3	2 - 1	3 - 1	4 - 4	5 - 2
6 - 1	7 - 1	8 - 1	9 - 3	10 - 2

Answer Key Practice Set - 6:

1 - 3	2 - 1	3 - 2	4 - 2	5 - 3
6 - 3	7 - 2	8 - 1	9 - 3	10 - 4

Answer Key Practice Set - 7:

1 - 3	2 - 3	3 - 3	4 - 3	5 - 1
6 - 2	7 - 1	8 - 4	9 - 2	10 - 2

Answer Key Practice Set - 8:

1 - 3	2 - 3	3 - 2	4 - 2	5 - 1
6 - 2	7 - 3	8 - 1	9 - 1	10 - 2

Answer Key Practice Set - 9:

1 - 3	2 - 2	3 - 4	4 - 3	5 - 4
6 - 1	7 - 1	8 - 3	9 - 4	10 - 1

Answer Key Practice Set - 10:

1 - 1	2 - 3	3 - 3	4 - 4	5 - 2
6 - 2	7 - 1	8 - 1	9 - 3	10 - 2

B6 Proverbs (Asked in SSC and other Exams)

SN	Proverbs	English Meaning	Hindi Meaning	#R
1	**A bad workman blames his tools**	An unskilled person blames their equipment rather than their own lack of ability	नाच न जाने आंगन टेढ़ा (अपनी अयोग्यता छिपाने के लिए साधनों को दोष देना)	(2)
2	**A bird in the hand is worth two in the bush**	It is better to keep what you have than to risk losing it by trying to get something better	नौ नकद न तेरह उधार (जो पास है वह अनिश्चित से बेहतर है)	2 (18)
3	A blind man is no judge of colours	A person who lacks knowledge or experience in a field cannot offer a valid opinion	अंधा क्या जाने बसंत की बहार (अनुभवहीन व्यक्ति विषय की परख नहीं कर सकता)	
4	A chain is only as strong as its weakest link	The overall strength of a group depends on its weakest member	पूरी व्यवस्था की ताकत उसके सबसे कमज़ोर हिस्से पर निर्भर करती है	
5	A closed mouth catches no flies	Avoiding unnecessary talk prevents trouble	चुप रहने में भलाई है (कम बोलो तो फायदा)	
6	A door must either be open or shut	One must make a clear decision between two options	दो नावों पर पैर नहीं रख सकते (स्पष्ट निर्णय ज़रूरी है)	
7	**A drowning man will clutch at a straw**	A desperate person will try anything to save themselves	डूबते को तिनके का सहारा (संकट में मामूली सी मदद भी बड़ी लगती है)	(2)
8	A fair exchange is no robbery	If both parties agree to an equal trade, no one is cheated	बराबर का सौदा, कोई धोखा नहीं (समान मूल्य का आदान-प्रदान न्यायसंगत है)	
9	A fish rots from the head down	Problems in an organization originate from its leadership; failure starts at the top	मछली सिर से सड़ती है (नेतृत्व खराब तो पूरा संगठन खराब)	
10	**A fool and his money are soon parted**	Foolish people quickly lose their wealth	मूर्ख के हाथ में पैसा नहीं टिकता	(6)
11	**A friend in need is a friend indeed**	A true friend helps during difficult times	मुसीबत में काम आए वही सच्चा दोस्त (संकट के समय साथ देने वाला ही असली दोस्त है)	(2)
12	A friend to all is a friend to none	A person who is friends with everyone is not truly loyal to anyone.	जो सबका मित्र है वह किसी का सच्चा मित्र नहीं	
13	A golden key can open any door	Money can achieve or obtain anything	धन से सब कुछ संभव है	
14	A good listener is a silent flatterer	Listening attentively makes others feel valued	ध्यान से सुनना भी एक तरह की प्रशंसा है	
15	A good mind possesses a kingdom within itself	Inner peace and wisdom are more valuable than material wealth	अच्छा मन ही सच्चा साम्राज्य है	
16	A goose quill is more dangerous than a lion's claw	The written word can cause more damage than physical force	कलम की धार तलवार से तेज़ होती है	
17	A happy heart is better than a full purse	Happiness is more valuable than wealth	खुशी धन से बेहतर है	

[**#R** denotes repetition of word]

[E.g. in SN 2, #R- **2 (18)** denotes this word has been asked 2 times in SSC and 18 times in other exams]

SN	Proverbs	English Meaning	Hindi Meaning	#R
18	**A house divided against itself cannot stand**	Unity is essential for survival; internal conflict leads to failure	आपसी फूट से पतन होता है	2 (1)
19	A hungry belly has no ears	A hungry person cannot pay attention to reason or advice	भूखे भजन न होय गोपाला (भूखा पेट किसी की नहीं सुनता)	
20	A journey of a thousand miles begins with a single step	Every great achievement starts with taking the first step	हज़ार मील की यात्रा एक कदम से शुरू होती है	
21	**A leopard can't change its spots**	People cannot change their fundamental nature or character	कुत्ते की पूंछ टेढ़ी की टेढ़ी (मूल स्वभाव नहीं बदलता)	3 (12)
22	A man is known by the company he keeps	People are judged by their friends and associates	व्यक्ति की पहचान उसकी संगत से होती है	
23	A nod is as good as a wink to a blind horse	Only a small hint is needed for someone who already understands	समझदार को इशारा काफी है	
24	**A penny saved is a penny earned**	Money saved is as valuable as money earned	बचत भी कमाई है	(2)
25	**A picture is worth a thousand words**	An image can convey a complex idea more effectively than words	एक तस्वीर हजार शब्दों के बराबर होती है	3 (2)
26	A rising tide lifts all boats	General prosperity benefits everyone in a society	प्रगति से सबको लाभ होता है	
27	**A rolling stone gathers no moss**	A person who keeps moving and changing will not accumulate wealth, status, or responsibilities	लुढ़कते पत्थर पर काई नहीं जमती (जो घूमता रहे वह धन-सम्पत्ति नहीं जोड़ पाता)	1 (5)
28	A ship in harbor is safe, but that is not what ships are built for	Taking risks is necessary to achieve meaningful success	बंदरगाह में जहाज सुरक्षित है, पर वह उसके लिए नहीं बना (जोखिम उठाए बिना बड़ी सफलता नहीं मिलती)	
29	A smooth sea never made a skilled sailor (or mariner)	Adversity and challenges develop competence and character	तप कर ही सोना खरा होता है (कठिनाइयाँ ही इंसान को मजबूत और कुशल बनाती हैं)	
30	**A soft answer turns away wrath**	A gentle, calm reply can defuse anger	मीठी वाणी से क्रोध शांत होता है	(2)
31	**A stitch in time saves nine**	It is better to deal with a problem early before it becomes worse	समय पर किया गया छोटा सुधार बड़ी मुसीबत टालता है	3 (12)
32	A stumble may prevent a fall	A small mistake can help avoid a bigger one	छोटी गलती बड़ी गलती से बचा सकती है	
33	**A tree is known by its fruit**	A person is judged by their actions and results, not words	इंसान अपने कर्मों से पहचाना जाता है	1 (1)
34	A volunteer is worth twenty pressed men	Willing workers are more effective than forced ones	स्वेच्छा से किया काम अधिक प्रभावी होता है	
35	**A watched pot never boils**	Time appears to pass slowly when you are anxiously waiting for something	बेसब्री से इंतजार करने पर समय धीरे बीतता है	(3)
36	A wonder lasts but nine days	Something attracts attention for only a short time	चार दिन की चाँदनी, फिर अंधेरी रात (नया आकर्षण जल्दी खत्म हो जाता है)	
37	**Absence makes the heart grow fonder**	Being away from someone increases affection for them	दूरी से प्रेम बढ़ता है	(3)

SN	Proverbs	English Meaning	Hindi Meaning	#R
38	**Actions speak louder than words**	What people do is more important than what they say	कथनी से करनी ज़्यादा असरदार होती है	3 (20)
39	Adversity and loss make a man wise	People gain wisdom through hardship and loss	इंसान ठोकर खाकर संभलता है (विपत्ति इंसान को समझदार बनाती है)	
40	After a storm comes a calm	Peaceful times follow difficult ones	अँधेरे के बाद उजाला आता है (कठिन समय के बाद शांति और सुख आता है)	
41	**After victory, tighten your helmet strap**	Stay cautious even after success	जीत के बाद भी सतर्क रहना जरूरी है	(2)
42	All good things must come to an end	Pleasant situations do not last forever	अच्छा वक्त हमेशा नहीं रहता	
43	**All roads lead to Rome**	There are many different ways to reach the same goal	मंजिल तक पहुंचने के कई रास्ते होते हैं	(3)
44	**All that glitters is not gold**	Appearances can be deceiving; not everything attractive is valuable	हर चमकने वाली चीज सोना नहीं होती (दिखावा हमेशा सच नहीं होता)	(4)
45	All work and no play makes Jack a dull boy	Constant work without leisure makes a person dull and uninteresting	काम के साथ मनोरंजन जरूरी है	
46	**All's fair in love and war**	In certain extreme situations, any behaviour is acceptable	प्यार और जंग (मुश्किल परिस्थिति) में सब जायज है	1 (1)
47	All's well that ends well	A successful outcome makes up for earlier difficulties	अंत भला तो सब भला	
48	**Always a bridesmaid, never a bride**	Always close to success but never achieving it	हमेशा दूसरे स्थान पर (हमेशा क़रीब पहुँचकर भी सफलता न मिलना)	1 (1)
49	An apple a day keeps the doctor away	Eating nutritious food regularly helps maintain good health	स्वस्थ आहार बीमारी से बचाता है	
50	**An idle mind is the devil's workshop**	People who have nothing to do are likely to get into mischief	खाली दिमाग शैतान का घर (निठल्लापन बुरे विचार लाता है)	(4)
51	An ounce of prevention is worth a pound of cure	It's easier to prevent a problem than to fix it	रोकथाम इलाज से बेहतर है	
52	Appearances can be deceiving	Things may not be as they seem on the surface	हाथी के दाँत खाने के और दिखाने के और (चीजें हमेशा वैसी नहीं होती जैसी वे दिखती हैं)	
53	As you sow, so shall you reap	Your actions determine your results	जैसा बोओगे वैसा काटोगे	
54	**Barking dogs seldom bite**	Those who make the most threats rarely act on them	जो गरजते हैं, वो बरसते नहीं	(2)
55	Beauty and honesty seldom agree	Beautiful and honest qualities rarely coexist	सुंदरता और ईमानदारी कम ही साथ होती हैं	
56	Beauty is in the eye of the beholder	Beauty is subjective to each person	सुंदरता देखने वाले की नजर में होती है	
57	**Beauty is only skin deep**	Physical beauty is superficial and does not reflect inner character	भीतरी गुण बाहरी सुंदरता से बढ़कर होते हैं	2 (1)
58	Beggars bleed and rich men feed	The poor suffer while the rich prosper	गरीब पिसता है, अमीर खाता है	
59	**Beggars can't be choosers**	People in need must accept what's offered	जरूरतमंद को पसंद-नापसंद का अधिकार नहीं	(4)

SN	Proverbs	English Meaning	Hindi Meaning	#R
60	Better bend than break	It is better to be flexible and adapt than to be stubborn and fail	झुकना टूटने से बेहतर है	
61	**Better late than never**	It is better to do something late than not at all	देर आए दुरुस्त आए (देर से आना अच्छा है, ना आने से)	2 (5)
62	Better safe than sorry	It is wiser to be cautious than to take risks and regret it later	दुर्घटना से देर भली (सावधानी में ही बुद्धिमानी है)	
63	**Better the devil you know than the devil you don't**	It is safer to deal with a familiar problem than risk an unknown one	अनजाना खतरा लेने से जाना-पहचाना मुसीबत बेहतर है	1 (1)
64	**Birds of a feather (flock together)**	People with similar interests or characteristics tend to associate with each other	चोर-चोर मौसेरे भाई (एक जैसे स्वभाव के लोग साथ रहते हैं)	6 (8)
65	**Blood is thicker than water**	Family bonds are stronger than other relationships	खून का रिश्ता सबसे मजबूत होता है	(5)
66	Bloom where you are planted	Accept your circumstances and make the best of them	जहाँ हो वहीं विकसित होना सीखो (परिस्थिति में ढलना)	
67	**Charity begins at home**	One should help family and close ones first	भलाई की शुरुआत अपने घर से होती है	(2)
68	**Children should be seen and not heard**	Children should behave quietly and not speak unless spoken to	बच्चों को चुप रहना चाहिए (जब तक बोलने को न कहा जाए)	1 (1)
69	Cleanliness is next to godliness	Being clean is a sign of spiritual purity	स्वच्छता ईश्वर भक्ति के समान है	
70	**Cross the stream where it is shallowest**	Choose the easiest way to accomplish something	सबसे आसान रास्ता अपनाना	(2)
71	**Curiosity killed the cat**	Being too curious can lead to trouble	अत्यधिक जिज्ञासा हानिकारक हो सकती है	(2)
72	**Cut one's coat according to one's cloth**	Live within your means; adapt to your circumstances	जितनी लंबी चादर, उतने पैर पसारना (आय के अनुसार खर्च करना)	3 (2)
73	**Dead men tell no tales**	Dead people cannot reveal secrets	मुर्दे राज नहीं खोलते	(2)
74	**Desperate times call for desperate measures**	In extreme situations, extreme actions may be necessary	विपत्ति में कठोर निर्णय लेने पड़ते हैं	2 (1)
75	Discretion is the better part of valour	It's wise to avoid unnecessary risks	जान है तो जहान है (सावधानी बहादुरी का श्रेष्ठ हिस्सा है)	
76	Do good and good will come to you	Good deeds bring good results	कर भला तो हो भला	
77	**Don't count your chickens before they hatch**	Don't assume success before it happens	सफलता मिलने से पहले जश्न नहीं मनाना चाहिए	3 (16)
78	**Don't cross the bridge until you come to it**	Don't worry about a problem until it actually happens	जब आएगी तब देखी जाएगी (समस्या उत्पन्न होने पर ही उसे निपटाना)	4 (6)
79	**Don't judge a book by its cover**	Don't form an opinion based on outward appearance alone	केवल बाहरी दिखावे से पूर्वानुमान नहीं लगाना चाहिए	11 (3)
80	**Don't look a gift horse in the mouth**	Don't be critical of a gift or favour	दान के घोड़े के दाँत नहीं गिनते (उपहारों में कमियां नहीं निकालनी चाहिए)	1 (3)

SN	Proverbs	English Meaning	Hindi Meaning	#R
81	Don't pay for the promise, pay for the performance	Judge by results not promises	वादे पर नहीं, काम पर भरोसा करें	
82	**Don't put all your eggs in one basket**	Don't risk everything on a single venture; diversify	सब कुछ दांव पर न लगाना (अलग-अलग विकल्प रखना)	4 (11)
83	Empty bags cannot stand upright	A poor or hungry person cannot function properly	खाली पेट इंसान ठीक से काम नहीं कर सकता	
84	**Empty vessels make the most noise**	Those with little knowledge talk the most	थोथा चना बाजे घना (कम ज्ञान वाले ज्यादा बोलते हैं)	(8)
85	Even a worm will turn	Even the meekest will retaliate if pushed too far	अत्याचार सहने की भी एक सीमा होती है	
86	Even Homer sometimes nods	Even the best make mistakes sometimes	बड़े-बड़ों से भी चूक होती है	
87	**Every cloud has a silver lining**	There is something positive in every bad situation	मुसीबत में भी उम्मीद की किरण (दुःख के बाद सुख आता है)	8 (14)
88	Every day is not Sunday	Good times don't last forever	हर दिन अच्छा नहीं होता	
89	**Every dog has his day**	Everyone gets a chance or a moment of success eventually	हर कुत्ते का दिन आता है (सबका भाग्य कभी न कभी चमकता है)	3
90	Every little helps	Even small contributions are valuable	बूँद-बूँद से घड़ा भरता है (छोटी-छोटी मदद भी काम आती है)	
91	Example is better than precept	Actions teach more effectively than advice	कथनी से करनी भली (उपदेश से बेहतर उदाहरण होता है)	
92	Faint heart never won fair lady	Timidity prevents success, especially in love	डरपोक कभी सफल नहीं होता	
93	**Familiarity breeds contempt**	Knowing someone or something too well leads to a loss of respect	घर की मुर्गी दाल बराबर (अत्यधिक निकटता से सम्मान कम होता है)	2 (2)
94	**Fools rush in where angels fear to tread**	Ignorant people act without thinking in situations where wise people are cautious	मूर्ख वहाँ हाथ डालते हैं जहाँ बुद्धिमान कतराते हैं	(3)
95	**Forbidden fruit is the sweetest**	What's prohibited is most desirable	मना की हुई चीज ज्यादा लुभाती है	(2)
96	Forewarned is forearmed	Prior knowledge helps one prepare	पहले से चेतावनी मिलना तैयारी का मौका देता है	
97	**Fortune favours the bold**	Success comes to those who take risks	भाग्य साहसी का साथ देता है	(4)
98	Fortune knocks once at every man's door	Everyone gets at least one opportunity in life	किस्मत हर किसी का दरवाजा एक बार खटखटाती ही है	
99	Give a dog a bad name and hang him	Once someone is falsely labeled, they are easily punished	बदनाम कर दो, फिर सज़ा देना आसान हो जाता है	
100	Give someone an inch and they'll take a mile	If you give a little, they'll want much more	किसी को उंगली पकड़ाओ तो वो पूरा हाथ पकड़ लेता है	
101	Great boast, small roast	When someone talks big or boasts a lot, but their actual results are very small	ऊँची दुकान फीके पकवान (बड़ी-बड़ी बातें, काम छोटा)	
102	**Great minds think alike**	Intelligent people often have the same ideas or opinions	बुद्धिमानों की सोच एक जैसी होती है	1 (2)

SN	Proverbs	English Meaning	Hindi Meaning	#R
103	**Half a loaf is better than no bread**	Having something, even if less than desired, is better than nothing	कुछ न होने से कुछ होना भला	1 (1)
104	Harm watch, harm catch	If you look for ways to harm others, you will eventually be harmed yourself	जो दूसरों के लिए गड्ढा खोदता है, खुद उसमें गिरता है	
105	**Haste makes waste**	Acting too quickly often leads to mistakes and wasted effort	जल्दी का काम शैतान का (जल्दबाजी में काम बिगड़ता है)	2 (7)
106	**He who laughs last laughs longest**	Final success is more satisfying than early triumph	अंत भला तो सब भला (अंतिम विजय ही असली विजय है)	1 (1)
107	He who pays the piper calls the tune	The person who provides money controls decisions	पैसा देने वाला ही फ़ैसला करता है	
108	He who rides a tiger is afraid to dismount	Once involved in danger, it is hard to withdraw	शेर की सवारी, उतरना भारी (ख़तरे में पड़ने के बाद पीछे हटना मुश्किल होता है)	
109	**Health is better than wealth (or health is wealth)**	Good health is more valuable than money	पहला सुख निरोगी काया (स्वास्थ्य धन से अधिक मूल्यवान है)	(2)
110	**Honesty is the best policy**	Being truthful is the best approach	ईमानदारी सबसे अच्छी नीति है	(2)
111	Hope lies in united efforts	Success is possible only when people work together	एकता में बल है (सामूहिक प्रयासों में ही आशा होती है)	
112	If at first you don't succeed, try, try again	Keep trying after failure	करत करत अभ्यास के जड़मति होत सुजान (कोशिश करते रहो, सफलता मिलेगी)	
113	If it ain't broke, don't fix it	Don't change something that works well	जो ठीक चल रहा हो, उसे बदलना नहीं चाहिए	
114	If you pay peanuts, you get monkeys	Low pay attracts low-quality workers	कम दाम, घटिया काम	
115	**Ignorance is bliss**	Not knowing about something unpleasant can make one happier	अज्ञानता परमानंद है (अनजान रहना कभी कभी अच्छा होता है)	2 (1)
116	In for a penny, in for a pound	Once involved, go all the way	जब शुरू किया है, तो पूरा निभाओ	
117	In the land of the blind, the one-eyed man is king	Among the incompetent, even someone with slight ability seems exceptional	अंधों में काना राजा (मूर्खों में थोड़ा समझदार)	
118	It is always darkest before the dawn	Things are at their worst just before they improve	सुबह होने से पहले अंधेरा सबसे गहरा होता है (मुसीबत के बाद राहत)	
119	It is the part of a good shepherd to shear his flock, not to skin it	A leader should take fairly from those they lead, not exploit them	अच्छा रखवाला भेड़ों की ऊन उतारता है, उनकी खाल नहीं	
120	**It never rains but it pours**	When problems come they come in abundance	मुसीबत कभी अकेले नहीं आती	1 (2)
121	**It takes two to tango**	Both parties involved in a situation are responsible for it	एक हाथ से ताली नहीं बजती (किसी गतिविधि के लिए दोनों पक्ष जिम्मेदार हैं)	3 (3)
122	**Jack of all trades, master of none**	A person who can do many things but is not expert in any	कई काम करने में सक्षम पर किसी में भी माहिर नहीं	2 (6)

SN	Proverbs	English Meaning	Hindi Meaning	#R
123	Keep your friends close and your enemies closer	Know your enemies well to protect yourself	दोस्त से ज्यादा दुश्मन पर नज़र रखो	
124	Kill the goose that lays the golden egg	Destroy a source of ongoing benefit for short-term gain	सोने के अंडे देने वाली मुर्गी को मारना (अपने लाभ के स्रोत को नष्ट करना)	
125	**Knowledge is power**	Having knowledge gives strength and advantage	ज्ञान ही शक्ति है	(3)
126	**Let bygones be bygones**	Forget past disagreements and move on	पुरानी बातों पर मिट्टी डालना (बीती बातों को भूल जाना)	3 (1)
127	**Let sleeping dogs lie**	Don't interfere with a situation if it might cause trouble	गड़े मुर्दे न उखाड़ना (पुरानी विवादित बात न छेड़ना)	7 (5)
128	**Look before you leap**	Consider the consequences before taking action	सोच-समझकर काम करना	2 (5)
129	**Make hay while the sun shines**	Take advantage of favourable conditions while they last	मौके पर चौका मारना (अनुकूल अवसर का लाभ उठाना)	3 (7)
130	**Make one's bed and lie in it**	Accept the consequences of one's own actions	जैसी करनी, वैसी भरनी (अपने कर्मों का फल भुगतना)	1 (1)
131	Make yourself all honey and the flies will devour you	Being too nice leads to exploitation	ज़्यादा नरमी शोषण को बुलावा देती है	
132	Man proposes, God disposes	Humans plan but outcomes are in God's hands	आदमी लाख करें वही होता है, जो मंज़ूर-ए-खुदा होता है	
133	Many a mickle makes a muckle	Small amounts accumulate to large totals	बूँद-बूँद से घड़ा भरता है	
134	**Many hands make light work**	A job is easier with more people helping	मिलकर काम करने से काम आसान हो जाता है	(3)
135	Might as well be hanged for a sheep as a lamb	If punishment is inevitable, commit the bigger act	जब सज़ा मिलनी ही है तो बड़ा काम क्यों न करें	
136	Might makes right	Those with power can impose their will as justice	जिसकी लाठी उसकी भैंस (ताक़तवर की बात ही कानून)	
137	Misery loves company	Unhappy people want others to be unhappy too	दुखी लोग दूसरों को भी दुखी देखना चाहते हैं	
138	**Money doesn't grow on trees**	Money is not easily obtained and should be spent wisely	पैसे पेड़ पर नहीं उगते (मेहनत से कमाते हैं)	2 (1)
139	Money talks	Money gives power and influence	पैसा बोलता है (पैसे की ताकत)	
140	**Necessity is the mother of invention**	Difficult situations inspire creative solutions	आवश्यकता आविष्कार की जननी है	(4)
141	**Never put off till tomorrow what you can do today**	Don't delay tasks unnecessarily	आज का काम कल पर मत टालो	(2)
142	Night brings counsel	Sleep on a problem before deciding; morning brings clearer thinking	रात भर सोचकर लिया गया फैसला बेहतर होता है	
143	**No man is an island**	Everyone depends on others; no one is self-sufficient	इंसान अकेला नहीं रह सकता	(2)
144	No news is good news	The absence of news is a sign that nothing bad has happened	कोई खबर न आना ही अच्छी खबर है	

SN	Proverbs	English Meaning	Hindi Meaning	#R
145	**No pain, no gain**	Success requires effort and sacrifice	बिना परिश्रम सफलता नहीं मिलती	1 (2)
146	**Nothing ventured, nothing gained**	You cannot achieve anything worthwhile without taking risks	बिना जोखिम उठाए कुछ नहीं मिलता	1 (1)
147	Old habits die hard	Difficult to change long-standing behaviour	पुरानी आदतें मुश्किल से छूटती हैं	
148	**Once bitten, twice shy**	A bad experience makes one cautious about the same situation	दूध का जला छाछ भी फूँक-फूँक कर पीता है (अपनी गलती से सीख लेना)	4 (4)
149	One good turn deserves another	Kindness should be repaid with kindness	नेकी के बदले नेकी (भलाई का बदला भलाई)	
150	One man's trash is another man's treasure	What is worthless to one person may be valuable to another	एक का कचरा दूसरे का खजाना	
151	**One swallow does not make a summer**	One single positive event does not mean everything is fine	एक फूल से बहार नहीं आती (एक सफलता से स्थायी सफलता तय नहीं होती)	(2)
152	**One's bark is worse than one's bite**	Someone seems threatening but is actually harmless	गरजने वाले बादल बरसते नहीं (डांट ज्यादा, नुकसान कम)	1 (1)
153	Opportunity makes the thief	Circumstances can tempt people to do wrong	मौका इंसान को चोर बना देता है	
154	**Penny wise and pound foolish**	Being careful with small amounts but wasteful with large ones	छोटे खर्च में सतर्क लेकिन बड़े खर्च में लापरवाह	2 (1)
155	Possession is nine-tenths of the law	Having something in your possession is a strong claim to ownership	जिसके पास कब्जा होता है, वही मालिक माना जाता है	
156	Practice makes perfect	Regular practice leads to mastery	करत करत अभ्यास के जड़मति होत सुजान (निरंतर अभ्यास से ही कुशलता आती है)	
157	Pride comes before a fall	Arrogance leads to downfall	अहंकार इंसान के विनाश का कारण बनता है	
158	**Rome wasn't built in a day**	Great things take time to accomplish	महान कार्य में समय लगता है	(12)
159	Shallow brooks are noisy	Those with little knowledge often talk the most	अधजल गगरी छलकत जाए (कम ज्ञान वाले ज़्यादा बोलते हैं)	
160	**Silence is golden**	Sometimes it's better to say nothing	मौन रहना कई बार बुद्धिमानी होती है	(2)
161	Slow and steady wins the race	Consistency and patience are more important than speed	धीरे और स्थिर चलने वाला ही जीतता है (धैर्य और निरंतरता से सफलता मिलती है)	
162	**Sow the wind and reap the whirlwind**	Suffer severe consequences from foolish actions	अपना बोया काटना (किये का परिणाम भुगतना)	1 (1)
163	**Still waters run deep**	Quiet people often have strong emotions or deep thoughts	शांत चित्त वाले गहरे होते हैं	2 (2)
164	**Strike while the iron is hot**	Take advantage of an opportunity immediately	मौके पर चौका मारना (अवसर का लाभ उठाना)	3 (3)
165	**Sup with the devil**	Be very cautious when dealing with dangerous people	दुष्ट संगति में सावधानी जरूरी है	1 (1)

SN	Proverbs	English Meaning	Hindi Meaning	#R
166	That which is not sought is lost	If you do not actively look or try, you will fail to gain or keep something	जो ढूंढा नहीं, वो मिला नहीं	
167	The age of miracles is past	Miracles or extraordinary events no longer happen; such things are no longer believed in	चमत्कार का समय बीत गया	
168	**The apple doesn't fall far from the tree**	Children resemble their parents in character	संतान के गुण अपने माता-पिता से मिलते-जुलते होते हैं	(3)
169	The best wine comes out of an old bottle	Experience and age bring refinement and quality	पुराने लोग या चीज़ें अनुभव के कारण बेहतर होते हैं	
170	The bigger they are, the harder they fall	Powerful people have more to lose when they fail	जितना अधिक शक्तिशाली, पतन या हार से उबरना उतना ही मुश्किल	
171	The cobbler's children have no shoes	Experts often fail to apply their skills to benefit their own family	कारीगर के घर ही कमी रह जाती है	
172	The darkest hour has only sixty minutes	Even the worst times will pass	बुरा वक्त भी बीत जाता है	
173	The devil makes work for idle hands	If people have nothing to do, they are more likely to get into trouble	खाली दिमाग शैतान का घर (खाली रहने से बुरे विचार आते हैं)	
174	**The die is cast**	A decision has been made and cannot be changed	तीर कमान से निकल जाना (फैसला हो जाना)	1 (1)
175	**The early bird catches the worm**	Those who start early have the best chance of success	जो जागत है सो पावत है (जागरूक और सक्रिय व्यक्ति को फायदा होता है)	1 (8)
176	**The end justifies the means**	A good result excuses any method used to achieve it	अच्छा परिणाम गलत साधनों को भी जायज़ ठहराता है	1 (1)
177	The face is the index of the mind	Facial expressions reveal inner feelings	चेहरा मन का दर्पण होता है	
178	**The grass is always greener on the other side**	Other people's situations always seem better than your own	दूसरे की थाली में घी ज़्यादा नज़र आता है (दूसरों की चीज़ें अपनी तुलना में बेहतर लगती है)	2 (3)
179	**The pen is mightier than the sword**	The written or spoken word is more powerful than violence	तलवार से ज्यादा ताकत कलम में होती है	(8)
180	**The pot calling the kettle black**	Criticizing someone for a fault you have yourself	उल्टा चोर कोतवाल को डांटे	2 (2)
181	**The proof of the pudding is in the eating**	Something's true value is only known by trying it	असली परख अनुभव से होती है	1 (3)
182	**The road to hell is paved with good intentions**	Good intentions without proper action can still lead to harmful results	केवल अच्छे इरादों से काम नहीं चलता	(2)
183	The second mouse gets the cheese	Sometimes it's safer to wait and learn from others' mistakes instead of rushing in first	दूसरों की गलती से सीखना (जो सब्र करता है, वही लाभ पाता है)	
184	**The squeaky wheel gets the grease**	Those who complain most get attention	शिकायत करने वाले की सुनवाई पहले होती है	1 (3)
185	There but for the grace of God go I	I could have been in the same bad situation if not for luck or mercy	भगवान की कृपा न होती तो मेरी भी वही हालत होती	

SN	Proverbs	English Meaning	Hindi Meaning	#R
186	**There's many a slip between the cup and the lip**	Things can go wrong at the last moment; nothing is certain	हाथ आया मुँह न लगा (काम पूरा होने से पहले भी बिगड़ सकता है)	1 (1)
187	**There's no smoke without fire**	rumours usually have some basis in truth	बिना आग के धुआँ नहीं उठता (अफ़वाह में कुछ न कुछ सच्चाई होती है)	1 (1)
188	**There's no such thing as a free lunch**	Everything has a price; nothing is truly free	मुफ्त में कुछ नहीं मिलता (हर चीज़ की कीमत होती है)	1 (3)
189	Third time's a charm	After failing twice, the third attempt is likely to succeed	तीसरी बार में काम बनता है	
190	Those who live in glass houses should not throw stones	Don't criticize others if you have similar faults	जिनके घर शीशे के होते हैं, वे दूसरों पर पत्थर नहीं फ़ेंका करते	
191	**Time and tide wait for no man**	Opportunities don't wait; time passes regardless	समय किसी का इंतज़ार नहीं करता	(2)
192	Time is money	Time is valuable and shouldn't be wasted	समय ही धन है	
193	To strain at a gnat and swallow a camel	To worry about small matters while ignoring important issues	छोटी बातों में उलझना और बड़े मुद्दों को नज़रअंदाज़ करना	
194	**Too many chiefs and not enough Indians**	Too many people want to lead and not enough want to work	ज्यादा मालिक कम कर्मचारी (अकुशल स्थिति)	1 (1)
195	**Too many cooks spoil the broth**	Too many people involved make things worse	ज़्यादा लोग मिलकर काम बिगाड़ देते हैं	(4)
196	Too much of a good thing	Even beneficial things can become harmful in excess	अति सर्वत्र वर्जयेत (किसी भी चीज़ की अधिकता बुरी है)	
197	Trees that are slow to grow bear the best fruit	Good things take time to develop	सब्र का फल मीठा होता है	
198	**Two heads are better than one**	Working together produces better results than alone	एक से भले दो (सहयोग से काम आसान होता है)	1 (4)
199	**Two wrongs don't make a right**	Responding to wrongdoing with wrongdoing is not justified	बुराई का जवाब बुराई से देने पर सब ठीक नहीं होता	(6)
200	**United we stand, divided we fall**	People are stronger together than apart	एकता में बल है	1 (1)
201	**Variety is the spice of life**	New and different experiences make life interesting	जीवन में बदलाव और विविधता ही उसे मज़ेदार बनाती है	(3)
202	**Virtue is its own reward**	Doing good is rewarding in itself	अच्छा काम अपने आप में ही एक इनाम है (नेकी कर दरिया में डाल)	(2)
203	Vows made in storms are forgotten in calms	Promises made in crisis are often forgotten when times improve	बुरे समय में किया गया वादा अच्छे समय में भुला दिया जाता है	
204	Walls have ears	Be careful, someone might be listening	दीवारों के भी कान होते हैं (सावधान रहो)	
205	Waste not, want not	If you use resources wisely, you will not face scarcity	अगर आप आज चीज़ों को बर्बाद नहीं करेंगे, तो भविष्य में उनकी कमी नहीं होगी	
206	Well begun is half done	A good start makes success easier	अच्छी शुरुआत से सफलता की संभावना अच्छी होती है	
207	**What goes around comes around**	Your actions eventually return to you	जैसा करोगे, वैसा भरोगे	1 (1)

SN	Proverbs	English Meaning	Hindi Meaning	#R
208	What you lose on the swings, you gain on the roundabouts	Losses in one area are balanced by gains in another	एक जगह का नुकसान दूसरी जगह पूरा हो जाता है	
209	**When in Rome, do as the Romans do**	Adapt to local customs wherever you are	जैसा देश, वैसा भेष	(3)
210	When life gives you lemons, make lemonade	Make the best of a bad situation; turn adversity into opportunity	आपदा में अवसर ढूंढना (मुसीबत का सकारात्मक उपयोग)	
211	**When the cat's away, the mice will play**	People misbehave when authority is absent	बिल्ली के न रहने पर चूहे उछलते हैं (निगरानी न हो तो लोग मनमानी करते हैं)	(3)
212	**Where there's a will, there's a way**	Determination and perseverance can overcome any obstacle	जहाँ चाह, वहाँ राह (दृढ़ निश्चय से रास्ता निकल ही आता है)	1 (3)
213	You are what you eat	Your health depends on what you consume	जैसा खाओ अन्न, वैसा बने मन	
214	**You can catch more flies with honey than with vinegar**	Kindness is more effective than harshness	नम्रता और मिठास से काम जल्दी बनता है	(3)
215	**You can lead a horse to water, but you can't make it drink**	You can offer opportunities but can't force acceptance	आप किसी को अवसर दे सकते हैं, पर उसे अपनाने के लिए मजबूर नहीं कर सकते	(3)
216	**You can't make an omelette without breaking eggs**	Success requires sacrifice or tough actions	कुछ पाने के लिए कुछ खोना (या सहना) पड़ता है	(3)
217	You can't teach an old dog new tricks	Older people resist change or learning new things	बूढ़े व्यक्ति की आदतें बदलना मुश्किल होता है	
218	You can't unscramble an egg	Some actions cannot be undone	बीती बात को सुधारा नहीं जा सकता	
219	**You snooze, you lose**	If you are not alert, you will miss an opportunity	जो सोता है, वो खोता है	1 (1)

*Total **219** Proverbs asked **640** times*

B7 Proverb Practice Sets
(Based on Recent SSC & Other Exam Papers)

Practice Set - 1

Direction (Q. 1-10): Select the most appropriate meaning of the given proverb.

1 A cat has nine lives.
1) Cats have a long life.
2) A cat can survive disastrous events.
3) A cat can live for nine years.
4) A cat is a healthy animal.

2 Beauty is only skin deep.
1) External beauty does not reflect a person's inner qualities.
2) A person's true worth lies in their appearance.
3) Beauty is permanent and never fades.
4) Beautiful people are always kind and wise.

3 The forbidden fruit is the sweetest.
1) To be drawn to things that one is prohibited from doing or having.
2) To crave for the food which is bad for health.
3) To be drawn to do things which are of no use.
4) To choose something contrary to the choice of others.

4 A rolling stone gathers no moss.
1) Movement makes you free from responsibilities.
2) An active life keeps you healthy and fit.
3) Constant movement prevents a person from establishing roots or long-term stability.
4) One must not be lazy and laid back to be successful in life.

5 A hungry belly has no ears.
1) A well-fed person ignores all opinions freely.
2) A starving person ignores advice or reasoning.
3) A starving person listens to advice carefully.
4) A hungry person listens more than usual.

6 A fool and his money are soon parted.
1) A careless person quickly loses their money
2) Money is never lost if handled properly
3) Only foolish people should handle money
4) A wise person always saves all their money

7 A drowning man will clutch at a straw.
1) A sinking man will use even a straw to breathe.
2) Someone who is in a very difficult situation will take any available opportunity to improve it.
3) One who learns swimming uses tubes to swim.
4) One who swims in a river will possibly drown easily.

8 A picture is worth a thousand words.
1) It is easier to explain something through pictures than words.
2) Thousand words make a picture.
3) It is is easier to paint than to write.
4) Audio visual learning is the best for teaching.

9 Bury your head in the sand.
1) Refuse to confront or acknowledge a problem.
2) Refuse to forget about the past.
3) Be ashamed of something.
4) To work hard to reach somewhere.

10 A stitch in time saves nine.
1) Tailoring is a valuable skill.
2) Timely action prevents more work.
3) Saving money for the future.
4) Drunk or intoxicated.

Practice Set - 2

Direction (Q. 1-10): Select the most appropriate meaning of the given proverb.

1 The proof of the pudding is in the eating.
1) Don't assume success before it actually happens.
2) The most noticeable or loudest problems get attention.
3) The quality of something can be judged after you have tried it.
4) Time feels longer when you're waiting for something to happen.

2 When the cat's away, the mice will play.
1) Too many people trying to manage something can ruin it.
2) There is something positive in every negative situation.
3) You can't achieve something important without some sacrifices.
4) People will naturally take advantage of the absence of someone in authority to do as they like.

3 Beggars can't be choosers.
1) You should aspire to have the best

2) You can't make your own decisions
3) If you rely on others, then you should be content with what you get
4) You should take what you get

4 Beauty lies in the eye of the beholder.
1) Beauty is confined to the eye only
2) Beauty is to be seen everywhere
3) Beauty is only for those who hold on to it
4) Perception of beauty is subjective

5 Don't put too many irons in the fire.
1) When you make money quickly, it's very easy to lose it quickly as well.
2) Don't depend on someone else to do a good job; do it yourself.
3) If you can do something today, do it as soon as possible.
4) Don't try to do too many things at the same time; focus on one thing at a time.

6 Don't count your chickens before they hatch.
1) Planning for the future guarantees results
2) Avoid making assumptions about future
3) Focus on small goals before aiming higher
4) Prepare in advance for better results

7 Better late than never.
1) It's better not to do something at all.
2) Doing something late is better than not doing it at all.
3) Never try to be late.
4) It's better to be on time.

8 Don't put all your eggs in one basket.
1) Diversify your risks to avoid complete loss
2) Save your resources for future use
3) Simplicity leads to better decisions
4) Avoid multitasking to achieve better results

9 Blood is thicker than water.
1) Family relationships are negatively affected by friendships
2) Water flows more freely than blood
3) Family relationships are the strongest of all
4) Friendship is the strongest of all relationships

10 The age of miracles is past.
1) The people should completely rely on miracles.
2) The people should not rely on miracles.
3) The people should not rely on practical solutions.
4) The people may rely on supernatural things.

Practice Set - 3

Direction (Q. 1-10): Select the most appropriate meaning of the given proverb.

1 Jack of all trades, master of none.
1) Someone who gains multiple skills to succeed
2) Someone who dabbles in many things but is not skilled in any
3) Someone who is uninterested in learning new skills
4) A person skilled in many areas and is often the best at everything

2 Fortune favours the brave.
1) Courageous actions are often rewarded amply.
2) Fortune is erratic and has nothing to do with courage.
3) Courageous people do not depend on good fortune.
4) Smart people know that fortune is often arbitrary.

3 Familiarity breeds contempt.
1) The feeling of strong disrespect towards some people
2) When one pursues goals without any thought or experience
3) When people are below dignity that they do not deserve any respect
4) The more we are close to someone, the more likely we know their flaws

4 He who plays the piper calls the tune.
1) Money is the source of all power.
2) A person who pays for something has the right to decide how it is done.
3) A person's success is determined by their connections.
4) Never tell people about your plans.

5 Even a worm will turn.
1) Even the most patient person will resist if pushed too far.
2) Even the happiest person will cry if treated too kindly.
3) Even the strongest person will agree if praised too much.
4) Even the laziest person will work if rewarded with sweet gifts.

6 Still waters run deep.
1) A busy person will not become stagnant.
2) A placid exterior hides a passionate or subtle nature.
3) A person is unable to change things or render help in a given situation.
4) Things that are prohibited seem very desirable.

7 To strain at a gnat and swallow a camel.
1) To fuss over trifles while ignoring big issues.
2) To be extremely physically weak.
3) To have a very large appetite.
4) To be meticulous in

everything.

8 Let sleeping dogs lie.
1) Avoid disturbing a situation that may cause trouble
2) Sleeping dogs must always be woken
3) Always confront problems immediately
4) Trouble should be created to teach a lesson

9 Example is better than precept.
1) Always preach with different examples.
2) A good reputation precedes a wise man's words.
3) Give a lot of examples.
4) One's actions can teach more effectively than a lecture.

10 Make hay while the sun shines.
1) Don't work in the heat
2) Use opportunities while they last
3) Work hard only in good weather
4) Save resources for rainy days

Practice Set - 4

Direction (Q. 1-10): Select the most appropriate proverb that can substitute the underlined segment in the given sentence.

1 The diplomat attempted to resolve the conflict through backchannel negotiations, but his efforts failed because the parties involved were too rigid and unwilling to compromise.
1) Old habits die hard
2) You can lead a horse to water, but you can't make it drink
3) You can't teach an old dog new tricks
4) What goes around comes around

2 I just feel like he can't focus on the small details on this project, since he keeps getting hung up on the most mundane details at the expense of our overall productivity.
1) People who live in glass houses shouldn't throw stones
2) If you want something done right, you have to do it yourself
3) The early bird gets the worm
4) One shouldn't miss the forest for the trees

3 Despite facing many challenges during her training, she became confident because difficult situations teach a person to become capable and skilled.
1) Rome was not built in a day
2) Actions speak louder than words
3) Every cloud has a silver lining
4) A smooth sea never made a skilled mariner

4 Just because he won one match, Raj didn't celebrate, knowing that one success does not indicate overall achievement.
1) Haste makes waste
2) Every cloud has a silver lining
3) A swallow does not make the summer
4) Rome was not built in a day

5 Saniya invited her best friends to her house and they had a blast till the wee hours of the night.
1) The early bird catches the worm.
2) One good turn deserves another.
3) The best wine comes out of an old bottle.
4) When the cat is away, the mice will play.

6 Although the competition was tough, Nikhil decided to take the risk and present his bold idea to the judges, knowing that one has to make a lot of effort to achieve something difficult.
1) The squeaky wheel gets the grease
2) Faint heart never won fair maiden
3) One swallow doesn't make a summer
4) One good turn deserves another

7 Caught unprepared by the sudden inspection, he exemplified that being informed equips one against unforeseen challenges.
1) Many hands make light work
2) Out of sight, out of mind
3) Let sleeping dogs lie
4) Forewarned is forearmed

8 During the review meeting, everyone noticed a few unexpected errors in the final draft, and the senior editor just shrugged, saying that even the most skilled people can occasionally make mistakes.
1) Homer sometimes nods
2) He who sups with the devil should have a long spoon
3) A nod is as good as a wink
4) The cobbler's children have no shoes

9 Despite tripping over the loose stone, Ravi continued carefully, because a minor setback can help avoid a bigger disaster.
1) Haste makes waste
2) A stumble may prevent a fall
3) Rome was not built in a day
4) One should look before they leap

10 Rohan's talent for painting and his meticulous attention

to detail mirror his mother's skills perfectly, showing that a child often inherits the character and abilities of their parents.
1) A leopard can't change its spots
2) What you lose on the swings, you gain on the roundabouts
3) Blood is thicker than water
4) The apple doesn't fall far from the tree

Practice Set - 5

Direction (Q. 1-10): Select the proverb that conveys the same meaning as the underlined segment in the given sentence.

1 She endeavoured to reform his ingrained habits, but it's impossible to alter one's inherent nature.
1) Every cloud has a silver lining
2) Time and tide wait for no man
3) A leopard can't change its spots
4) Better late than never

2 Rohit, remember, being rude to your junior because your boss was rude to you is not fair.
1) Every dog has his day
2) Let sleeping dogs lie
3) Two wrongs do not make a right
4) As you sow, so shall you reap

3 He always finds faults in others but fails to notice his own mistakes. He criticises people for things he is also guilty of.
1) Honesty is the best policy.
2) A bird in the hand is worth two in the bush.
3) Rome wasn't built in a day.
4) The pot calls the kettle black.

4 She helped her classmates with genuine concern, proving that helping others brings help in return.
1) Actions speak louder than words
2) Every cloud has a silver lining
3) Charity begins at home
4) Do good and good will come to you

5 My brother wanted to do a part-time job along with his studies, which became too much for him to handle.
1) Haste makes waste
2) Bite off more than one can chew
3) No pain, no gain
4) Beggars can't be choosers

6 Margaret never complained despite the hardships and betrayals she faced; she carried on with quiet strength, choosing to endure life's hardships with patience and resilience.
1) Be a camel in the desert of life
2) Grin and bear it
3) Make hay while the sun shines
4) Rome wasn't built in a day

7 Sanjay was nervous about starting his new business, but he finally registered the company, believing that taking the first step, no matter how small, is the key to achieving something big.
1) A journey of a thousand miles begins with a single step
2) One should not put all one's eggs in one basket
3) Where there's a will, there's a way
4) Practice makes perfect

8 Even when tempted to lie, she remembered that being truthful is always the right choice.
1) Honesty is the best policy.
2) Practice makes perfect
3) Too many cooks spoil the broth
4) Actions speak louder than words

9 The teacher always reminded the students that maintaining cleanliness is almost as important as being virtuous.
1) A person is known by the company he keeps
2) Health is wealth
3) A soft answer turns away wrath
4) Cleanliness is next to godliness

10 I think they killed him because he knew too much. People who are dead cannot reveal secrets .
1) A burnt child dreads the fire
2) Dead men tell no tales
3) A wolf in sheep's clothing
4) One lie draws ten after it

Answer Key Practice Set - 1:

1 - 2	2 - 1	3 - 1	4 - 3	5 - 2
6 - 1	7 - 2	8 - 1	9 - 1	10 - 2

Answer Key Practice Set - 2:

1 - 3	2 - 4	3 - 3	4 - 4	5 - 4
6 - 2	7 - 2	8 - 1	9 - 3	10 - 2

Answer Key Practice Set - 3:

1 - 2	2 - 1	3 - 4	4 - 2	5 - 1
6 - 2	7 - 1	8 - 1	9 - 4	10 - 2

Answer Key Practice Set - 4:

1 - 2	2 - 4	3 - 4	4 - 3	5 - 4
6 - 2	7 - 4	8 - 1	9 - 2	10 - 4

Answer Key Practice Set - 5:

1 - 3	2 - 3	3 - 4	4 - 4	5 - 2
6 - 2	7 - 1	8 - 1	9 - 4	10 - 2

B8 Phrasal Verbs (asked in SSC and Other Exams)

1 **Arrive at** - To reach a decision or conclusion after thinking (निष्कर्ष पर पहुँचना) *[#R-2]*

2 **Ask after** - To enquire about someone's health or welfare (हाल-चाल पूछना) *[#R-3]*

3 **Ask for** - To request something (माँगना) *[#R-3]*

4 **Ask out** - To invite someone on a date (डेट पर बुलाना) *[#R-3]*

5 **Ask over** - To invite someone to your home (अपने घर पर बुलाना) *[#R-3]*

6 **Ask round (or around)** - To ask several people for information (कई लोगों से पूछना) *[#R-3]*

7 **Average out** - To result in a balanced amount over time (औसत पर आना)

8 **Back out** - To withdraw from a commitment or agreement (वादे से पीछे हटना) *[#R-3]*

9 **Back up** - i) To support someone (समर्थन करना)
ii) To make a copy of data (बैकअप लेना)
iii) To move in reverse (पीछे जाना) *[#R-4]*

10 **Be down** - i) To be depressed or sad (उदास होना)
ii) To be reduced or lower (कम होना)

11 **Be off** - i) To leave or depart (रवाना होना)
ii) To be cancelled (रद्द होना)
iii) To have a holiday from work (छुट्टी पर होना)

12 **Bear down** - i) To press down with force (ज़ोर से दबाना)
ii) To approach in a threatening way (धमकाते हुए आना)

13 **Bear in mind** - To remember or consider something (ध्यान में रखना)

14 **Bear out** - To confirm or support something as true (पुष्टि करना)

15 **Bear up** - To remain strong in difficult times (हिम्मत बनाए रखना) *[#R-2]*

16 **Bear with** - To be patient with someone (धैर्य रखना)

17 **Black out** - i) To lose consciousness (बेहोश होना)
ii) To have a power failure (बिजली गुल होना)

18 **Blow out** - i) To extinguish by blowing (फूँक मार कर बुझाना)
ii) To burst (tyre) (फटना) *[#R-4]*

19 **Blow over** - To pass or end without serious harm (टाल जाना; शांत हो जाना)

20 **Blow up** - i) To explode (विस्फोट होना)
ii) To inflate (फुलाना)
iii) To lose one's temper (गुस्सा होना)

21 **Boil down** - i) To reduce a liquid by boiling (उबालकर कम करना)
ii) To simplify or condense (संक्षेप में करना) *[#R-2]*

22 **Bounce off** - To discuss ideas with someone for feedback (विचार साझा करना (प्रतिक्रिया के लिए))

23 **Break away** - i) To escape from captivity (भागना)
ii) To separate from a group (अलग होना) *[#R-2]*

24 **Break down** - i) To stop functioning (machine) (खराब होना)
ii) To fail (negotiations) (विफल होना)
iii) To lose emotional control (रो पड़ना) *[#R-4]*

25 **Break in** - i) To enter by force (ज़बरदस्ती घुसना)
ii) To make new shoes comfortable (जूते सहज करना)
iii) To interrupt (बीच में बोलना) *[#R-3]*

26 **Break into** - i) To enter illegally (ज़बरदस्ती घुस जाना)
ii) To suddenly start (laughing, crying) (अचानक शुरू होना) *[#R-4]*

27 **Break off** - i) To detach (तोड़ना)
ii) To end a relationship or engagement (रिश्ता तोड़ना)

28 **Break out** - i) To escape (भागना)
ii) To start suddenly (war, fire, disease) (अचानक शुरू होना)

29 **Break up** - i) To end a relationship (संबंध तोड़ना)
ii) To disperse (तितर-बितर होना)
iii) To divide into pieces (टुकड़े करना) *[#R-2]*

30 **Break with** - To end a connection with tradition or person (परंपरा तोड़ना) *[#R-2]*

[**#R** denotes repetition of word]

[E.g. in SN 26, #R- **4** denotes this word has been asked 4 times in SSC and other exams]

31 **Bring about** - To cause something to happen (घटित करना) *[#R-2]*

32 **Bring forward** - i) To reschedule to an earlier time (समय पहले करना)
ii) To present or propose an idea or plan (प्रस्तुत करना) *[#R-2]*

33 **Bring out** - i) To publish (प्रकाशित करना)
ii) To reveal qualities (गुण उजागर करना)

34 **Bring up** - i) To raise a child (पालन-पोषण करना)
ii) To mention a topic (विषय उठाना)
iii) To vomit (उल्टी करना) *[#R-2]*

35 **Brush off** - To dismiss someone rudely (रूखेपन से टालना)

36 **Buckle down** - To start working seriously (गंभीरता से काम करना) *[#R-3]*

37 **Butt in** - To interrupt rudely (बीच में टांग अड़ाना)

38 **Call at** - To visit a place briefly (किसी जगह जाना) *[#R-3]*

39 **Call down** - i) To invoke or summon (criticism, blessing) (आह्वान करना)
ii) To criticize or scold someone (डाँटना)

40 **Call for** - i) To demand (माँग करना)
ii) To require (ज़रूरत होना)
iii) To collect someone (लेने आना) *[#R-2]*

41 **Call off** - To cancel an event (रद्द करना) *[#R-6]*

42 **Call on (or upon)** - i) To visit someone (मिलने जाना)
ii) To formally request someone to do something (आह्वान करना) *[#R-3]*

43 **Call out** - i) To shout (पुकारना)
ii) To challenge someone (चुनौती देना)
iii) To summon for duty (ड्यूटी पर बुलाना)

44 **Carry on** - i) To continue (जारी रखना)
ii) To behave excitedly / make a fuss (हंगामा करना) *[#R-3]*

45 **Carry out** - To perform or complete a task (पूरा करना) *[#R-3]*

46 **Cast aside** - To reject or discard (त्याग देना)

47 **Catch up** - i) To reach the same level or position as others (बराबरी करना)
ii) To do something that you missed or delayed (पिछड़ा काम पूरा करना)
iii) To update oneself on recent events (जानकारी लेना)

48 **Check someone over** - To examine someone thoroughly, especially medically (किसी की अच्छी तरह जाँच करना)

49 **Chew out** - To scold severely (डाँटना)

50 **Chew over** - To think about carefully (सोच-विचार करना)

51 **Chill out** - To relax (आराम करना) *[#R-2]*

52 **Chuck down** - To throw down carelessly (लापरवाही से फेंकना)
ii) To Rain heavily (ज़ोरों से बारिश होना)

53 **Clam up** - To suddenly stop talking (चुप हो जाना)

54 **Comb through** - To search thoroughly (बारीकी से खोजना)

55 **Come about** - To happen (घटित होना)

56 **Come across** - i) To find by chance (संयोग से मिलना)
ii) To appear or seem to others (प्रतीत होना)
iii) To communicate or be understood (समझ में आना) *[#R-4]*

57 **Come by** - i) To obtain something (often with difficulty) (हासिल करना)
ii) To visit someone (मिलने जाना) *[#R-2]*

58 **Come into** - i) To inherit (विरासत में पाना)
ii) To enter a place (प्रवेश करना) *[#R-3]*

59 **Come off** - i) To succeed (सफल होना)
ii) To become detached (अलग होना / निकलना)

60 **Come out** - i) To become known or public (सामने आना)
ii) To be released or published (प्रकाशित होना)
iii) To emerge or appear (निकलना / बाहर आना)

61 **Come over** - i) To visit casually (मिलने आना)
ii) (Feeling) To affect suddenly (महसूस होना) *[#R-3]*

62 **Come round (or around)** - i) To regain consciousness (होश आना)
ii) To change one's opinion (राय बदलना)
iii) To visit informally (मिलने आना) *[#R-2]*

63 **Come through** - i) To survive a difficult situation (बच निकलना)
ii) To be received (message, result) (प्राप्त होना)
iii) To provide help when needed (काम आना) *[#R-3]*

64 **Come up** - i) To arise or occur (उत्पन्न होना / सामने आना)
ii) To be mentioned or discussed (चर्चा में आना)
iii) To approach someone (पास आना) *[#R-3]*

65 **Cordon off** - To close off an area with barriers (घेराबंदी करना)

66 **Cover up** - To hide or conceal (esp. wrongdoing) (छिपाना)

67 **Crack down** - To take strict measures or action (कड़ी कार्रवाई करना)

68 **Crack up** - i) To burst out laughing (हँसी छूटना)
ii) To have a mental breakdown (टूट जाना / पागल होना) *[#R-4]*

69 **Cross out** - To draw a line through something written (काट देना)

70 **Crow about (or over)** - To boast about a victory (डींग मारना)

71 **Cry down** - To criticize or belittle (आलोचना करना)

72 **Cut down** - i) To reduce the amount or quantity of something (कम करना)
ii) To chop down a tree (पेड़ काटना / गिराना)
iii) To kill or critically undermine someone (मार गिराना) *[#R-2]*

73 **Cut in** - i) To interrupt (बीच में बोलना)
ii) To move in front suddenly (traffic) (बीच में आ जाना)

74 **Dig around** - To search for information (खोजबीन करना)

75 **Do away with** - To abolish or eliminate (समाप्त करना)

76 **Dole out** - To distribute in small amounts (बाँटना)

77 **Double down** - i) To strengthen one's commitment or effort despite risk (अपनी बात पर और ज़ोर देना)
ii) To intensify one's actions or stance (दोगुनी मेहनत / ज़ोर लगाना)
iii) To refuse to back off from a position (पीछे न हटना)

78 **Doze off** - To fall asleep unintentionally (झपकी आ जाना) *[#R-3]*

79 **Draw up** - i) To prepare a document (तैयार करना)
ii) To stop (vehicle) (रुकना)

80 **Drop in** - i) To visit casually or unexpectedly (बिना बताए मिलने आना)
ii) To decrease suddenly (अचानक गिरना / कम होना)
iii) To stop by a place briefly (कहीं थोड़ी देर के लिए जाना)

81 **Egg on** - To encourage someone to do something (often bad) (उकसाना) *[#R-3]*

82 **Expand on (or upon)** - To give more details about (विस्तार से बताना)

83 **Face up** - To confront or accept a difficult reality (सच्चाई स्वीकार करना / सामना करना)

84 **Fall about** - To laugh uncontrollably (लोट-पोट होना) *[#R-2]*

85 **Fall back** - i) To retreat or withdraw (पीछे हटना)
ii) To move to a less advanced position (पीछे लौटना) *[#R-3]*

86 **Fall down** - i) To collapse (गिरना)
ii) To fail (plan, argument) (असफल होना)

87 **Fall for** - i) To fall in love with (प्यार हो जाना)
ii) To be deceived by (धोखा खाना) *[#R-3]*

88 **Fall off** - i) To decrease (कम होना)
ii) To become detached and drop to the ground (अलग होकर नीचे गिरना) *[#R-2]*

89 **Fall on (or upon)** - i) To attack (हमला करना)
ii) To be the responsibility of (ज़िम्मेदारी होना) *[#R-2]*

90 **Fall out** - i) To quarrel or have a disagreement (झगड़ा होना)
ii) To drop out or become displaced (गिरना / निकलना)
iii) (Military) To leave a formation (कतार तोड़ना) *[#R-5]*

91 **Fall through** - To fail to happen (विफल होना)

92 **Figure out** - To understand or solve (समझना)

93 **Follow up** - i) To take further action after an initial step (आगे कार्रवाई करना)
ii) To check on the progress or outcome of something (जाँच-पड़ताल करना)
iii) To add something supplementary (अनुवर्ती कदम उठाना)

94 **Frown on (or upon)** - To disapprove of (अस्वीकृत करना)

95 **Gear up** - i) To prepare or get ready (तैयारी करना)
ii) To equip oneself with necessary tools or gear (साज-सज्जा करना)
iii) To increase production or activity (उत्पादन / गतिविधि बढ़ाना)

96 **Get along** - i) To manage or survive (गुज़ारा करना)
ii) To make progress (आगे बढ़ना / प्रगति करना)
iii) To have a friendly relationship (अच्छे संबंध रखना) *[#R-4]*

97 **Get away** - i) To escape from a place or person (भाग जाना, बच निकलना)
ii) To go on a holiday (छुट्टी पर जाना) *[#R-5]*

98 **Get back** - i) To return (वापस आना)
ii) To recover something (वापस पाना)
iii) To retaliate (बदला लेना)

99 **Get off** - i) To disembark / leave a vehicle (उतरना)
ii) To escape severe punishment (कम सज़ा पाना)
iii) To finish work for the day (काम से छुट्टी पाना) *[#R-3]*

100 **Get on** - i) To board a vehicle (चढ़ना, सवार होना)
ii) To make progress (तरक्की करना)
iii) To grow old (बूढ़ा होना) *[#R-4]*

101 **Get over** - i) To recover from illness or shock (से उबरना)
ii) To overcome a difficulty (पर काबू पाना)
iii) To communicate effectively (समझा पाना) *[#R-2]*

102 **Get through** - i) To complete or finish something difficult (पूरा करना)
ii) To successfully contact by phone (फोन पर संपर्क होना)
iii) To pass an examination (परीक्षा पास करना)
iv) To survive a difficult period (कठिन समय से गुज़रना) *[#R-2]*

103 **Give away** - i) To give something free of cost (मुफ्त में देना)
ii) To reveal a secret unintentionally (राज़ खोलना)
iii) To present the bride to groom in wedding (कन्यादान करना) *[#R-3]*

104 **Give in** - i) To surrender or yield (हार मानना)
ii) To submit something formally (जमा करना) *[#R-2]*

105 **Give off** - To emit or release smell, heat, light, etc. (निकालना, छोड़ना) *[#R-4]*

106 **Give out** - i) To distribute to many people (बाँटना, वितरित करना)
ii) To stop working or functioning (काम करना बंद करना)
iii) To announce publicly (घोषणा करना) *[#R-5]*

107 **Give over** - i) To stop doing something annoying (बंद करो)
ii) To dedicate for a specific purpose (समर्पित करना) *[#R-3]*

108 **Give up** - i) To stop trying or doing something (हार मानना, छोड़ देना)
ii) To quit a habit (आदत छोड़ना)
iii) To surrender oneself (समर्पण करना) *[#R-5]*

109 **Give way** - i) To collapse or break (टूट जाना)
ii) To yield or allow something to pass (रास्ता देना)

110 **Go about** - i) To approach or deal with a task (किसी काम को करना)
ii) To continue doing usual activities (रोज़मर्रा के काम करना)

111 **Go along** - i) To proceed or continue (आगे बढ़ना)
ii) To cooperate (साथ चलना) *[#R-2]*

112 **Go down** - i) To decrease or fall (गिरना, कम होना)
ii) To be remembered or recorded (याद किया जाना)
iii) To be received by audience (स्वीकार किया जाना) *[#R-2]*

113 **Go in** - i) To enter a place (अंदर जाना)
ii) To become involved (शामिल होना)
iii) To be hidden by clouds — of sun (बादलों में छिपना) *[#R-2]*

114 **Go off** - i) To explode or fire (फटना, बजना);
ii) To go bad or spoil (खराब होना);
iii) To leave suddenly (चले जाना)
iv) Suddenly react strongly in anger (अचानक गुस्सा करना) *[#R-4]*

115 **Go over** - i) To review or examine carefully (जाँचना, दोहराना)
ii) To be received in a particular way (प्रभाव पड़ना)

116 **Go through** - i) To experience something difficult (कठिन अनुभव से गुज़रना)
ii) To examine carefully (ध्यान से जाँचना)
iii) To use up or consume (खर्च करना, उपयोग करना)
iv) To be officially approved (मंज़ूर होना) *[#R-5]*

117 **Hammer out** - To reach an agreement after lengthy discussion (मुश्किल से समझौता करना) *[#R-2]*

118 **Hand down** - i) To pass from one generation

to another (पीढ़ी-दर-पीढ़ी देना)
ii) To announce an official decision (फैसला सुनाना)

119 **Hand in** - To submit work to authority (जमा करना) *[#R-2]*

120 **Hand off** - To transfer responsibility to someone (जिम्मेदारी सौंपना) *[#R-2]*

121 **Hand out** - To distribute to a group of people (बाँटना) *[#R-2]*

122 **Hand over** - To give control or possession to someone (सौंपना, हवाले करना) *[#R-2]*

123 **Hang about (or around)** - To wait or spend time idly in a place (इधर-उधर घूमना, वक्त बिताना)

124 **Hang in** - To persist despite difficulties (डटे रहना) *[#R-7]*

125 **Hang together** - i) To remain united (एकजुट रहना)
ii) (Of argument) To be consistent and logical (तर्कसंगत होना)

126 **Hear out** - To listen to someone until they finish (पूरी बात सुनना)

127 **Hold on** - i) To wait (रुकना, ठहरना)
ii) To grip tightly (कसकर पकड़ना)
iii) To persist (डटे रहना)

128 **Hold out** - i) To resist or endure (टिके रहना)
ii) To extend or offer (बढ़ाना, पेश करना)
iii) To last or survive (चलना, बचा रहना)

129 **Hold up** - i) To delay (देर करना, रोकना)
ii) To rob at gunpoint (बंदूक की नोक पर लूटना)
iii) To remain strong or valid (टिकना, मज़बूत रहना)

130 **Horse around** - To play in a rough or silly way (मस्ती करना)

131 **Keep up** - i) To continue at the same rate (जारी रखना)
ii) To maintain in good condition (बनाए रखना)
iii) To prevent from sleeping (सोने न देना)
iv) To stay informed or updated (जानकारी रखना)

132 **Knock down** - i) To demolish a structure (गिराना, तोड़ना)
ii) To reduce a price (दाम कम करना)

133 **Knuckle down** - To start working hard (गंभीरता से काम करना)

134 **Lag behind** - To fail to keep up with others (पीछे रह जाना)

135 **Lap up** - i) To accept eagerly (उत्साह से स्वीकारना)
ii) To drink quickly (जल्दी पी जाना)

136 **Latch on** - i) To understand an idea (समझना)
ii) To attach oneself to someone (किसी से चिपकना)

137 **Lay off** - i) To dismiss workers temporarily or permanently (नौकरी से निकालना)
ii) To stop doing something annoying (बंद करो)

138 **Lay out** - i) To arrange or spread out (फैलाना, सजाना)
ii) To explain clearly (स्पष्ट रूप से समझाना)
iii) To spend money (खर्च करना)
iv) To knock someone down (मार गिराना) *[#R-2]*

139 **Laze away** - To spend time doing nothing (आराम में बिताना)

140 **Let down** - i) To disappoint someone (निराश करना)
ii) To lower something (नीचे करना)
iii) To make clothing longer (कपड़े की लंबाई बढ़ाना)

141 **Let off** - i) To not punish or punish lightly (बख्श देना)
ii) To release gas or pressure (छोड़ना) *[#R-2]*

142 **Level with** - To be honest with someone (ईमानदारी से बात करना)

143 **Live down** - To overcome shame of past event (कलंक मिटाना)

144 **Live through** - To experience and survive (से गुज़रना)

145 **Live up** - To enjoy life to the fullest (जी भर कर जीना)

146 **Look after** - To take care of (देखभाल करना) *[#R-3]*

147 **Look down on (or upon)** - To consider inferior (किसी को तुच्छ समझना) *[#R-7]*

148 **Look into** - To investigate (जाँच करना)

149 **Look out** - i) To be careful or vigilant (सावधान रहना)
ii) To watch from a window or opening (बाहर देखना)

150 **Look over** - To examine quickly (जल्दी से जाँचना)

151 **Look through** - i) To examine or read something quickly (देखना, जाँचना)
ii) To ignore someone deliberately (नज़रअंदाज़ करना) *[#R-3]*

152 **Look to** - To rely on for help (उम्मीद रखना)

153 **Look up** - i) To search for information (खोजना, देखना)
ii) To improve or get better (सुधरना)
iii) To raise one's eyes (ऊपर देखना) *[#R-2]*

154 **Look upon** - To regard in a particular way (के रूप में देखना) *[#R-3]*

155 **Make away** - To escape or flee (भाग जाना)

156 **Make do** - To manage with limited resources (काम चलाना)

157 **Make off** - To leave hurriedly or escape (जल्दी से भागना) *[#R-2]*

158 **Make out** - i) To see or understand with difficulty (समझना, देखना)
ii) To write out (a cheque / document) (लिखना)
iii) To claim or pretend (दावा करना)

159 **Make over** - i) To transfer ownership officially (हस्तांतरित करना)
ii) To transform appearance (रूप बदलना)

160 **Make up** - i) To fabricate or invent (बनाना, गढ़ना)
ii) To reconcile (सुलह करना)
iii) To apply cosmetics (श्रृंगार करना) *[#R-3]*

161 **Mark up** - To increase the price (दाम बढ़ाना)

162 **Measure up** - i) To be good enough or adequate (खरा उतरना)
ii) To meet expectations or required standards (मानकों पर खरा होना)
iii) To assess the size or dimensions of something (नाप लेना)

163 **Mellow out** - To become more relaxed (शांत होना)

164 **Mull over** - To think about carefully (गहराई से सोचना)

165 **Nose out** - i) To discover by searching (खोज निकालना)
ii) To win narrowly (थोड़े अंतर से जीतना)

166 **Palm off** - To deceive into accepting something worthless (धोखे से थमाना) *[#R-2]*

167 **Pass away** - To die (euphemism) (गुज़र जाना) *[#R-2]*

168 **Pass off** - i) To happen successfully (सफलतापूर्वक होना)
ii) To present falsely (धोखे से पेश करना)
iii) To ignore or treat something lightly (टाल देना)

169 **Pass out** - i) To lose consciousness (बेहोश होना)
ii) To graduate from training (प्रशिक्षण पूरा करना)
iii) To distribute (बांटना)

170 **Phase out** - To discontinue gradually (धीरे-धीरे बंद करना)

171 **Pick on** - To single out for criticism or bullying (तंग करना)

172 **Play down** - To minimize importance of (कम महत्व देना)

173 **Play on** - To exploit someone's emotions (का फायदा उठाना)

174 **Point out** - To draw attention to (ध्यान दिलाना)

175 **Pore over** - To study or examine intently (ध्यान से पढ़ना) *[#R-2]*

176 **Potter around** - To do small tasks in a leisurely way (इधर-उधर काम करना)

177 **Pull off** - To succeed in something difficult (मुश्किल काम करना)

178 **Pull together** - To work as a team (मिलकर काम करना)

179 **Pull up** - i) To stop a vehicle (रुकना)
ii) To reprimand or criticize (डाँटना)
iii) To improve performance or progress (सुधार करना) *[#R-2]*

180 **Put across** - To communicate effectively (प्रभावी ढंग से समझाना) *[#R-3]*

181 **Put by** - To save for future (बचत करना)

182 **Put down** - i) To place on surface (नीचे रखना)
ii) To suppress forcefully (कुचलना)
iii) To criticize or humiliate (अपमानित करना)
iv) To kill a sick animal (दया मृत्यु देना) *[#R-3]*

183 **Put in** - i) To spend time or effort (समय देना)
ii) To submit a formal request (आवेदन करना)
iii) To insert or place something (डालना / रखना) *[#R-4]*

184 **Put off** - i) To postpone (टालना)
ii) To discourage or disgust (हतोत्साहित करना) *[#R-5]*

185 **Put on** - i) To wear clothing (पहनना)
ii) To gain weight (वज़न बढ़ना)
iii) To pretend or fake (दिखावा करना)
iv) To switch on (चालू करना) *[#R-3]*

186 **Put out** - i) To extinguish (बुझाना)
ii) To cause inconvenience (असुविधा होना)
iii) To produce or publish (निकालना, प्रकाशित

करना) [#R-5]

187 **Put up** - i) To erect or build (खड़ा करना)
ii) To provide accommodation (ठहराना)
iii) To increase price (बढ़ाना)
iv) To offer resistance or fight back (प्रतिरोध करना) [#R-9]

188 **Roll back** - To reduce to previous level (पहले के स्तर पर लाना)

189 **Run across** - To meet by chance (अचानक मिलना)

190 **Run away** - i) To flee or escape (भाग जाना)
ii) To leave home secretly (घर छोड़कर भागना) [#R-5]

191 **Run down** - i) To criticize unfairly (बुराई करना)
ii) To knock down with vehicle (कुचलना)
iii) To gradually lose power (धीरे-धीरे खत्म होना) [#R-2]

192 **Run into** - i) To meet unexpectedly (अचानक मिलना)
ii) To collide with (टकराना)
iii) To encounter problems (समस्या आना) [#R-3]

193 **Run out** - i) To be exhausted or used up (खत्म होना)
ii) To expire (समाप्त होना)
iii) To leave quickly (भाग जाना) [#R-3]

194 **Run over** - i) To hit with a vehicle (वाहन से कुचलना)
ii) To review quickly (जल्दी से दोहराना)
iii) To overflow (उबलकर बहना) [#R-3]

195 **Scale up** - To increase in size (बढ़ाना)

196 **See through** - i) To detect the true nature of (असलियत समझना)
ii) To persist until completion (पूरा करना) [#R-2]

197 **Send off** - i) To dispatch by post (भेजना)
ii) To order off the field (sports) (मैदान से बाहर करना)

198 **Set about** - To begin doing with determination (शुरू करना) [#R-3]

199 **Set aside** - i) To reserve for special purpose (अलग रखना)
ii) To declare invalid (रद्द करना)
iii) To ignore temporarily (नज़रअंदाज़ करना)[#R-2]

200 **Set down** - i) To put in writing officially (लिखित में रखना)
ii) To land (aircraft) (उतरना)

201 **Set forth** - i) To present or explain (प्रस्तुत करना)
ii) To begin a journey (यात्रा शुरू करना)

202 **Set in** - To begin and continue (bad weather / situation) (शुरू होना) [#R-5]

203 **Set off** - i) To begin a journey (रवाना होना)
ii) To trigger or cause to start (शुरू करना)
iii) To detonate (विस्फोट करना) [#R-3]

204 **Set on** - To attack (हमला करना)

205 **Set out** - i) To begin a journey (यात्रा शुरू करना)
ii) To intend or aim (का इरादा करना)
iii) To present, explain, or arrange clearly (व्यवस्थित करना) [#R-3]

206 **Set up** - i) To establish or start (स्थापित करना)
ii) To arrange or organize (व्यवस्था करना)
iii) To frame someone falsely (फँसाना) [#R-4]

207 **Shake off** - To get rid of (से छुटकारा पाना) [#R-4]

208 **Slack off** - To work less hard (ढील देना)

209 **Slip off** - To remove quickly; to leave quietly (उतारना)

210 **Stand against** - To oppose or resist (के विरुद्ध खड़ा होना) [#R-2]

211 **Stand by** - i) To wait in readiness (तैयार रहना)
ii) To support loyally (साथ देना) [#R-2]

212 **Stand for** - i) To represent or mean (का मतलब होना)
ii) To tolerate (बर्दाश्त करना)
iii) To be a candidate (चुनाव लड़ना)

213 **Stand out** - To be conspicuous or superior (अलग दिखना) [#R-2]

214 **Stand up** - i) To rise to a standing position (खड़ा होना)
ii) To remain valid or convincing (टिकना)
iii) To fail to keep a date with someone (धोखा देकर न आना)

215 **Stave off** - To prevent or delay something bad (टालना)

216 **Stir up** - To cause trouble or strong emotions (भड़काना)

217 **Take after** - To resemble a parent or relative (पर जाना) [#R-8]

218 **Take apart** - i) To disassemble (अलग-अलग करना)
ii) To criticize harshly (कड़ी आलोचना करना) [#R-3]

219 **Take back** - i) To return (वापस करना)
ii) To retract statement (वापस लेना) *[#R-3]*

220 **Take in** - i) To understand (समझना)
ii) To deceive (धोखा देना)
iii) To make clothing smaller (कपड़ा छोटा करना)
iv) To provide accommodation (शरण देना) *[#R-4]*

221 **Take off** - i) (Of aircraft) To leave ground (उड़ान भरना)
ii) To remove clothing (उतारना)
iii) To become successful suddenly (अचानक सफल होना)
iv) To have time off work (छुट्टी लेना) *[#R-5]*

222 **Take out** - i) To remove from a place (निकालना)
ii) To go out socially with someone (बाहर ले जाना)
iii) To obtain officially, e.g. insurance / loan (प्राप्त करना) *[#R-3]*

223 **Take over** - To assume control (नियंत्रण लेना) *[#R-2]*

224 **Take up** - i) To begin a hobby or activity (शुरू करना)
ii) To occupy space or time (घेरना)
iii) To accept an offer (स्वीकार करना)
iv) To shorten clothing (छोटा करना) *[#R-4]*

225 **Talk over** - To discuss thoroughly (विस्तार से चर्चा करना) *[#R-4]*

226 **Throw over** - To abandon or reject (छोड़ देना)

227 **Tide over** - To help through difficult period (कठिन समय में मदद करना) *[#R-3]*

228 **Tone down** - To make less strong (कम करना)

229 **Touch on** - To mention briefly (संक्षेप में बताना)

230 **Trip over** - To stumble on something (से ठोकर खाना)

231 **Tuck in (or into)** - To eat heartily (मज़े से खाना)

232 **Tuck up** - To make comfortable in bed (कंबल ओढ़ाना)

233 **Turn against** - To become hostile to (के खिलाफ हो जाना) *[#R-2]*

234 **Turn around (or round)** - i) To reverse direction (पलटना)
ii) To improve a situation (स्थिति सुधारना)

235 **Turn down** - i) To refuse or reject (ठुकराना)
ii) To reduce volume or intensity (कम करना) *[#R-3]*

236 **Turn in** - i) To go to bed (सोने जाना)
ii) To hand over to authorities (पुलिस के हवाले करना)

237 **Turn out** - i) To prove to be (साबित होना)
ii) To attend an event (उपस्थित होना)
iii) To produce (बनाना)
iv) To force someone to leave (निकाल देना) *[#R-3]*

238 **Turn over** - i) To flip (पलटना)
ii) To hand over (सौंपना) *[#R-2]*

239 **Turn up** - i) To arrive unexpectedly (आ जाना)
ii) To increase volume (तेज़ करना)
iii) To be found (मिलना) *[#R-2]*

240 **Wear out** - i) To become unusable through use (घिस जाना)
ii) To exhaust (थका देना)

241 **Win out** - To succeed eventually (अंत में जीतना)

242 **Wind down** - i) To relax after stress (आराम करना)
ii) To gradually reduce or end (धीरे-धीरे बंद करना)

243 **Work out** - i) To exercise (कसरत करना)
ii) To calculate (हिसाब करना)
iii) To develop successfully (सफल होना)

244 **Write off** - i) To cancel a debt (माफ करना)
ii) To dismiss as worthless (खारिज करना)
iii) To damage beyond repair (पूरी तरह बरबाद करना) *[#R-2]*

245 **Zero in** - i) To aim or direct precisely (निशाना साधना)
ii) To focus or concentrate closely (ध्यान केंद्रित करना)

*Total **245** Phrasal Verbs asked **496** times*

B9 Phrasal Verb Practice Sets

(Based on Recent SSC & Other Exam Papers)

Practice Set - 1

Direction (Q. 1-10): Select the most appropriate option that can substitute the underlined segment in the given sentence.

1 The most effective way to enhance your vocabulary is to look to unknown words in a dictionary.
1) write off
2) set by
3) stand against
4) look up

2 Once the seminar was over, the host gave up the certificates to the active participants.
1) brought about
2) put across
3) gave away
4) came by

3 Do not later about the street.
1) latter about
2) litter about
3) litre about
4) loiter around

4 The demonstration passed away peacefully.
1) passed out
2) passed off
3) passed
4) No improvement required

5 If we want to promote national integrity in our country, then we must desist our tendency of taking up with others.
1) coming round
2) setting out
3) looking down upon
4) bringing forward

6 As there was no one to look thorough the orphan, he had to take refuge in the orphanage.
1) look upon
2) look down upon
3) look through
4) look after

7 If you give away smoking, your health will improve.
1) give off
2) give out
3) No substitution required
4) give up

8 If there is no need to substitute it, select 'No substitution required'. Manisha set apart with her friends to explore the countryside.
1) set aside 2) set in
3) set out 4) No substitution required

9 I opened the box beneath the table and took of a book, the Materia Medica.
1) No substitution required
2) take off
3) took in
4) took out

10 We set up on the journey early in the morning.
1) set about
2) No improvement required
3) set off
4) set in

Practice Set - 2

Direction (Q. 1-10): Select the most appropriate option that can substitute the underlined segment in the given sentence.

1 The wedding was put on until January.
1) put up 2) put in
3) put down 4) put off

2 The recent cloudburst completely dismantled the village and its people.
1) tookup 2) took back
3) tookafter 4) took apart

3 The firefighters tried their best to extinguish the fire.
1) put in 2) put out
3) put off 4) put on

4 Samita asked out a favour of going early today.
1) asked over
2) asked around
3) asked after
4) asked for

5 Her thinning grey hair was hanging on her bony forehead.
1) urging ahead
2) straggling over
3) sinking from
4) falling about

6 The walls of the marriage hall were covered by beautiful purple curtains.
1) covered of
2) covered with
3) covered on
4) covered upon

7 The new chief is gifted at the power of eloquence.
1) gifted of 2) gifted among
3) gifted for 4) gifted with

8 Thousands of people were killed by the train accident that took place last Wednesday.
1) killed in
2) killed to
3) killed from
4) killed of

9 The teacher called up the class due to the sudden snowstorm.
1) called on the class
2) called out the class
3) called off the class

4) called in the class

10 I am <u>down with</u> her complaints.
1) looked down with
2) passed out with
3) held down with
4) fed up with

Practice Set - 3

Direction (Q. 1-10): Fill in the blank with most appropriate phrasal verb:.

1 When the scandal broke, the minister tried to _____ responsibility and blame his aides.
1) frown upon
2) brush off
3) pass the buck
4) touch on

2 Radium _______ rays that can damage the eyes.
1) gives away
2) gives up
3) gives over
4) gives off

3 He finally _____ to the pressure and resigned.
1) gave in 2) gave up
3) gave out 4) gave over

4 The goons _____ the unsuspecting victims when the latter walked into the dark alley.
1) set up 2) set upon
3) set along 4) set down

5 The spokesperson tried to _____ the media frenzy by issuing a calm, factual statement.
1) tone down
2) carry out
3) take off
4) crack down

6 The boisterous crowd _____ with its merry-making even amidst pouring rain.
1) played on
2) flowed on
3) carried on
4) carried out

7 The team reported that they had _____ the contract with tooth and comb before forwarding its recommendation.
1) pored over
2) plied over
3) poured over
4) ruh over

8 The investigation team will _____ every detail before concluding the report.
1) look over 2) go through
3) call off 4) fall back

9 The startup failed to _____ the expectations it had generated among investors.
1) live down 2) live through
3) live up to 4) live over

10 We need to _____ a solution to this problem before it gets worse.
1) cut down on
2) break down
3) come up with
4) break up

Practice Set - 4

Direction (Q. 1-10): Fill in the blank with most appropriate phrasal verb:

1 She was so overwhelmed with tasks that she had to _____ some responsibilities to her assistant.
1) hand out 2) hand down
3) hand in 4) hand over

2 The elder child takes _____ his father. They look like siblings.
1) up 2) after
3) in 4) before

3 The deal fell through because the parties couldn't _____ on the terms.
1) take over
2) put across
3) see eye to eye
4) carry on

4 He could not _____ his habitual irregularity at work and was ultimately suspended.
1) get on with
2) get away with
3) get on
4) get off

5 After months of negotiation, the two sides finally _____ an agreement acceptable to both parties.
1) arrived to
2) arrived at
3) arrived on
4) arrived with

6 Her speech was so moving that it _____ strong emotions in the audience.
1) put up
2) brought out
3) stirred up
4) gave off

7 The scientist was unable to _____ a definitive conclusion from the data.
1) draw out
2) bring up
3) make over
4) arrive at

8 The fire was so intense that the firefighters struggled to_____it_____.
1) put - off 2) set - in
3) put - out 4) take - over

9 The teacher asked the students to_____ their assignments.
1) hand in
2) hand out
3) hand over
4) hand off

10 The professor asked the student to _____ on her thesis argument.
1) follow up 2) expand on
3) point out 4) call for

Practice Set - 5

Direction (Q. 1-5): The following sentence has been split into four segments. Identify the segment that contains an error in phrasal verb.

1 Gita got onto / the book / she was reading / this morning.
1) she was reading
2) the book
3) Gita got onto
4) this morning

2 Mrs. Premlatha asked / Malini to hand down / all the / payment slips.
1) all the
2) payment slips
3) Mrs. Premlatha asked
4) Malini to hand down

3 Bindu asked Arya to fill out for / her so that she could / take care of / her sick father.
1) take care of
2) her so that he could
3) her sick father
4) Bindu asked Arya to fill out for

4 Tina dropped behind of / college and / went straight / into a good job.
1) into a good job
2) Tina dropped behind of
3) college and
4) went straight

5 Tara was late for the meeting / but somehow managed / to catch out with / everything she had missed.
1) everything she had missed
2) Tara was late for the meeting
3) to catch out with
4) but somehow managed

Direction (Q. 6-10): Which of the following sentences contains an error in the use of a phrasal verb?

6 1) Clean out the backyard this weekend.
2) The old lady broke down when she heard her son lost his job.
3) Make over the bed daily. It is a good habit.
4) Try your level best before you decide to give up.

7 1) Clean up the mess in the kitchen. It is unhygienic.
2) We look forward to seeing you during the event.
3) To earn a significant profit, you are advised to deal in electronic items.
4) Why does she break out with all her near and dear ones?

8 1) Pushpa came across an old photo in the album and asked me to recognise the face in it.
2) Please suggest me some tips to get out nervousness.
3) Back up your essential files. Technology is only sometimes reliable.
4) Please turn up the heater. The weather is too cold today.

9 1) Can you please take care for my belongings for some time?
2) While visiting the library, I came across an interesting book.
3) Let's call off the picnic as there is a possibility of heavy rain.
4) It is wise to put up with one's quarrelsome neighbours.

10 1) All the workers have called between the strike.
2) All the workers have called through the strike.
3) All the workers have called at the strike.
4) All the workers have called off the strike.

Answer Key Practice Set - 1:

1 - 4	2 - 3	3 - 4	4 - 2	5 - 3
6 - 4	7 - 4	8 - 3	9 - 4	10 - 3

Answer Key Practice Set - 2:

1 - 4	2 - 4	3 - 2	4 - 4	5 - 2
6 - 2	7 - 4	8 - 1	9 - 3	10 - 4

Answer Key Practice Set - 3:

1 - 3	2 - 4	3 - 1	4 - 2	5 - 1
6 - 3	7 - 1	8 - 2	9 - 3	10 - 3

Answer Key Practice Set - 4:

1 - 4	2 - 2	3 - 3	4 - 2	5 - 2
6 - 3	7 - 4	8 - 3	9 - 1	10 - 2

Answer Key Practice Set - 5:

1 - 3	2 - 4	3 - 4	4 - 2	5 - 3
6 - 3	7 - 4	8 - 2	9 - 1	10 - 4

PART - C
(SYNONYMS & ANTONYMS)

***Contents*:-**

***Updated and Additional Content*: -**

1. **New SSC Syno-Anto:** Added new words from **417 sets** asked by SSC after the publication of the last edition (May 2024).
2. **Expanded Idioms Coverage:** Added new words from 470 sets of other competitive exams. The 2026 edition now covers a total of 1,277 additional sets (470 + 807) from other exams since the 2023 edition.
3. **Hindi meaning to every Synonyms & Antonyms** asked in SSC or other exams.

***Additional Symbols for smarter and efficient preparation*: -**

1. Blackbook readers already know we provide **#R** to show how many times a word has been asked in SSC exams till now. In this edition we have improved it further to show more information in #R.
2. The number shown outside the bracket ( ), as usual shows **the number of times a word has been asked** by SSC. The no. inside bracket indicates the number of times it has been asked in those additional 1,277 sets and is important for preparation of SSC and other exams.
3. **Bold** SN. present in some SN. signifies that this word has also been asked as a spelling question in SSC exams.
4. The **tilde symbol (~)** present in some Synonyms & Antonyms signifies that this word has also been asked as OWS question in SSC exams.
5. Provided Additional Synonyms & Antonyms from List 2 in **Curly Bracket { }**.

SYNONYMS & ANTONYMS

Introduction

A synonym is a word with a similar meaning (Happy = Joyful), and an antonym is a word with the opposite meaning (Happy = Sad). In competitive exams, the options are designed to confuse you. The difference between the right and wrong answer often comes down to a set of rules that most students never learn.

How Exams Test SYNO-ANTO *(Special tricks to Eliminate Wrong Options)*

Trick	Questions (PYQ)	Explanation	Rule
1. Same PoS	Synonym of RESPECT (Noun): (A) Deference (Noun) (B) Vigorous (Adj) (C) Blame (Verb) (D) Criticize (Verb) Ans: A	3 out of 4 options have wrong PoS. Vigorous is Adjective, Blame and Criticize are Verbs. Only Deference is a Noun like the question word.	Noun = Noun Verb = Verb Adj. = Adj.
2. Same Scale	Synonym of SUMPTUOUS: (A) Humble (B) Lavish (C) Minuscule (D) Mammoth Ans: B	Sumptuous means luxurious/grand (luxury scale). Minuscule and Mammoth measure size, which is a completely different scale. Only Lavish matches the luxury scale.	Synonyms must measure the same feature as the word.
3. Match Intensity	Synonym of ANGER: (A) Frenzy (B) Fury (C) Delight (D) Dismay Ans: B	Anger is moderate intensity. Frenzy means wild, uncontrolled madness, which is far too extreme. Fury is strong anger and sits closest to Anger on the intensity scale: < Anger < Fury < Frenzy Always match the level.	Strong = Strong Mild = Mild Match the degree.
4. Person vs Quality	Synonym of ANTAGONIST: (A) Nerd (B) Adversary (C) Amiable (D) Evil Ans: B	Antagonist is a person. Amiable and Evil are qualities/adjectives, not persons. Antagonist is evil, but 'evil' is not a synonym for a person. Only Adversary (person) fits.	Person = Person Quality = Quality Never mix the two.
5. Opposite Traps	Synonym of THRIFTY: (A) Prudent (B) Extravagant (C) Generous (D) Wasteful Ans: A	1-3 out of 4 options are antonyms placed as traps. Students who vaguely know the meaning may confuse the direction and pick an opposite word.	Always check: does the Q ask Synonym or Antonym?
6. Same Domain	Synonym of BOGUS: (A) Criticize (B) Humane (C) False (D) Strong Ans: C	Bogus = fake (authenticity domain). Criticize is judgment, Humane is morality, Strong is physical power. All 3 wrong options are from completely unrelated domains. Only False fits.	Synonyms must come from the same semantic field.

A Word of Caution

These rules work in most cases, but competitive exams are not always textbook-perfect. Sometimes the exam body asks direct questions, sometimes contextual ones. Sometimes none of the options are a perfect match, but one fits better than the rest. Sometimes a weaker synonym is marked correctly because all other options are antonyms or completely unrelated. For example, in a real SSC exam, the synonym of DESPISE (extreme hatred) was asked and the correct answer was Dislike, which is far weaker in intensity, simply because no stronger option like Detest or Loathe was available.

If a question has a genuinely incorrect answer key, it can be challenged during the objection window, and if accepted, it may be treated as a bonus question. In most cases, the question is testing whether you can pick the best option, not the perfect one.

Golden Rule: Your job is to find the best answer among the given options. Use these tricks to eliminate 2-3 wrong options quickly, then choose the most fitting one from what remains. Be judicious, not rigid.

How to Use This Chapter

This is not just a dictionary or a list of words. Every entry in this chapter has been carefully included based on real exam data, so you know exactly what to focus on and how much attention each word deserves. Here is how to read the symbols:

1. **Candid** (Adj.) - Truthful and straightforward (निष्कपट, स्पष्ट) **[#R-25 (10)]**

   Syno: Frank (स्पष्टवादी), Honest (ईमानदार), Forthright (निष्कपट)

   Anto: Devious (कपटी), Deceitful (धोखेबाज), Dishonest (बेईमान)

2. **Feeble** (Adj.) - Lacking physical strength due to age or illness (कमज़ोर) ~ **[#R-16 (11)]**

   Syno: Weak (दुर्बल), Wimpy (निर्बल), Decrepit (जर्जर)

   Anto: Strong (मजबूत), Sturdy (सुदृढ़), Robust (हृष्टपुष्ट)

3. **Abundant** (Adj.) - Existing or available in large quantities (प्रचुर) [**#R-23 (10)]**

   Syno: Plentiful (प्रचुर), Ample (काफ़ी), Copious (अधिक)

   Anto: Scarce (कम), Meagre (अल्प), Sparse (छिटपुट)

#R (Repetition Count): The number in the last column shows how many times that word has been asked in SSC exams. The number in brackets shows how many times it appeared in other exams like DSSSB, CDS, AFCAT etc. For example, if a word shows **[#R-8 (2)]**, it means it was asked 8 times in SSC and 2 times in other exams. Higher the **#R**, more important the word. Words with high repetition count should be your top priority.

~ (Tilde Symbol): If you see a ~ next to the word, it means that word has also been asked as a One Word Substitution question in previous exams. The detailed OWS coverage is present in the OWS chapter, but this marker is here to alert you that this word carries extra weight. Do not take it lightly.

(Bold Serial Number**):** Serial numbers written in **bold** indicate that the word has also been asked as a spelling question in SSC exams. Since the word is already covered here, it has been removed from the Spelling chapter to avoid repetition. Pay special attention to the spelling of these words.

C1 Top 100 Syno + Anto (Common List) (asked in SSC Exams)

1 **Abandon** (V./N.) - (छोड़ देना; नियंत्रणहीनता) *[#R-26 (9)]*
To leave or give up completely (V.); A complete lack of restraint (N.)

Syno: Desert (छोड़ देना), Forsake (त्यागना), Relinquish (परित्याग करना), Leave (छोड़ना); Dereliction (उपेक्षा) {Discontinue (बंद करना); Unrestraint (अनियंत्रण)}

Anto: Retain (बनाए रखना), Continue (जारी रखना), Keep (रखना), Adopt (अपनाना); Constraint (नियंत्रण)

2 **Candid** (Adj.) - (निष्कपट, स्पष्ट) *[#R-25 (10)]*
Truthful and straightforward

Syno: Frank (स्पष्टवादी), Honest (ईमानदार), Forthright (निष्कपट), Blunt (स्पष्टवादी), Direct (सीधा) {Outspoken (मुखर), Straightforward (सीधा)}

Anto: Devious (कपटी), Cunning (चालाक), Artful (धूर्त), Deceitful (धोखेबाज), Tactful (व्यवहारकुशल), Dishonest (बेईमान), Evasive (टालमटोल करने वाला), Biased (पक्षपाती), Guarded (सतर्क) {Diplomatic (कूटनीतिक)}

3 **Abundant** (Adj.) - (प्रचुर) *[#R-23 (10)]*
Existing or available in large quantities

Syno: Plentiful (प्रचुर), Ample (काफ़ी) {Copious (अधिक), Plenty (प्रचुर)}

Anto: Meagre (अल्प), Insufficient (अपर्याप्त), Deficient (अपर्याप्त), Sparse (छिटपुट), Scarce (कम) {Scant (अपर्याप्त)}

4 **Benevolent** (Adj.) - (परोपकारी, दयालु) *[#R-18 (14)]*
Kind and wishing good for others

Syno: Kind (दयालु), Generous (उदार), Gracious (कृपालु), Compassionate (करुणामय) {Kind-Hearted (नेकदिल)}

Anto: Malevolent (दुर्भावनापूर्ण), Merciless (निर्दयी), Stingy (कंजूस), Cruel (क्रूर), Unkind (दयाहीन) {Selfish (स्वार्थी), Miserly (कंजूस), Malignant (घातक), Malicious (द्वेषपूर्ण)}

5 **Diligent** (Adj.) - (परिश्रमी)~ *[#R-20 (10)]*
Having or showing care and conscientiousness in work

Syno: Industrious (परिश्रमी), Hardworking (मेहनती), Assiduous (परिश्रमी), Untiring (न थकने वाला), Careful (सावधान) {Conscientious (कर्तव्यनिष्ठ), Meticulous (बारीकी से काम करने वाला)}

Anto: Lazy (आलसी), Idle (निष्क्रिय), Inactive (सुस्त) {Careless (लापरवाह)}

6 **Generous** (Adj.) - (उदार)~ *[#R-13 (17)]*
Showing readiness to give, especially money

Syno: Kind (दयालु), Lavish (फिजूलखर्च) {Benevolent (परोपकारी), Magnanimous (उदारमना), Bountiful (भरपूर)}

Anto: Stingy (कंजूस), Miserly (कंजूस), Selfish (स्वार्थी), Mean (कंजूस), Greedy (लालची) {Uncharitable (कृपाहीन), Frugal (मितव्ययी), Niggardly (कंजूस)}

7 **Timid** (Adj.) - (डरपोक)~ *[#R-14 (15)]*
Showing a lack of courage or confidence; easily frightened

Syno: Cowardly (कायर), Shy (शर्मीला), Fearful (भयभीत), Nervous (घबराया हुआ), Humble (विनम्र) {Meek (विनम्र)}

Anto: Brave (साहसी), Bold (साहसिक), Courageous (वीर), Daring (साहसी), Audacious (बेधड़क) {Venturesome (साहसिक), Confident (आत्मविश्वासी)}

8 **Barren** (Adj.) - (बंजर, बांझ) *[#R-20 (7)]*
Unable to produce vegetation; not productive; unable to have offspring

Syno: Unproductive (अनुत्पादक), Infertile (बंजर), Desolate (उजड़ा हुआ) {Unfruitful (फलहीन), Fruitless (निष्फल)}

Anto: Fertile (उपजाऊ)

9 **Feeble** (Adj.) - (कमज़ोर)~ *[#R-16 (11)]*
Lacking physical strength due to age or illness

Syno: Weak (दुर्बल), Wimpy (निर्बल), Decrepit (जर्जर)

Anto: Strong (मजबूत), Effective (प्रभावी), Sturdy (सुदृढ़), Powerful (शक्तिशाली), Robust (हृष्टपुष्ट) {Competent (सक्षम), Durable (टिकाऊ)}

[**#R** denotes repetition of word]

[E.g. in SN 9, #R- **16 (11)** denotes this word has been asked 16 times in SSC and 11 times in other exams]

10 Meticulous (Adj.) - (सावधान)~ *[#R-13 (12)]*
Showing great attention to detail; very careful and precise

Syno: Careful (सावधान), Precise (सटीक), Methodical (नियमित), Perfect (पूर्ण), Perfectionist (पूर्णतावादी) {Scrupulous (नैतिकतापूर्ण), Conscientious (अंतरात्मा के अनुसार), Mindful (ध्यानशील), Thorough (गहन)}

Anto: Careless (लापरवाह), Chaotic (अराजक), Sloppy (असावधान), Negligent (असावधान), Regardless (बेपरवाह) {Slovenly (गंदा), Haphazard (अव्यवस्थित)}

11 Trivial (Adj.) - (तुच्छ)~ *[#R-13 (12)]*
Of little value or importance

Syno: Small (छोटा), Minor (छोटा), Insignificant (महत्वहीन), Superficial (सतही) {Unimportant (महत्वहीन)}

Anto: Significant (महत्वपूर्ण), Essential (अनिवार्य), Important (महत्वपूर्ण), Serious (गंभीर), Profound (गहन)

12 Boisterous (Adj.) - (शोरगुल वाला, उपद्रवी) *[#R-16 (8)]*
Very noisy, energetic, and hard to control

Syno: Noisy (शोरगुल वाला), Clamorous (कोलाहलपूर्ण) {Rowdy (उपद्रवी), Cheerful (प्रसन्न)}

Anto: Calm (शांत), Peaceful (शांतिपूर्ण), Placid (स्थिर), Quiet (चुप) {Restrained (संयमित), Silent (मौन), Solemn (गंभीर), Phlegmatic (अप्रभावित)}

13 Hostile (Adj.) - (शत्रुतापूर्ण) *[#R-19 (5)]*
Showing opposition or dislike; unfriendly

Syno: Belligerent (झगड़ालू), Warlike (लड़ाकू) {Adverse (विरोधी), Aggressive (आक्रामक)}

Anto: Amiable (सौम्य), Friendly (मित्रवत), Sympathetic (सहानुभूतिपूर्ण), Hospitable (मेहमाननवाज़), Gentle (कोमल), Favourable (अनुकूल) {Amicable (सौहार्दपूर्ण)}

14 Mitigate (V.) - (कम करना) *[#R-15 (9)]*
To make less severe, serious, or painful

Syno: Allay (शांत करना), Lessen (कम करना), Reduce (घटाना) {Alleviate (हल्का करना), Relieve (राहत देना), Diminish (घटाना)}

Anto: Aggravate (बिगाड़ना), Intensify (तीव्र करना), Increase (बढ़ाना) {Exacerbate (खराब करना), Worsen (बिगड़ जाना)}

15 Absurd (Adj.) - (बेतुका)~ *[#R-15 (8)]*
Wildly unreasonable or illogical

Syno: Ridiculous (हास्यास्पद), Irrational (अतर्कसंगत), Silly (मूर्ख) {Foolish (मूर्ख), Senseless (निरर्थक), Unreasonable (अतार्किक)}

Anto: Sensible (समझदार), Reasonable (उचित), Realistic (वास्तविक) {Rational (तर्कसंगत)}

16 Amiable (Adj.) - (मिलनसार) *[#R-9 (14)]*
Having or displaying a friendly and pleasant manner

Syno: Friendly (मित्रवत) {Good-Natured (अच्छे स्वभाव वाला), Pleasant (सुखद), Harmonious (सामंजस्यपूर्ण), Cordial (हार्दिक)}

Anto: Hostile (शत्रुतापूर्ण), Unfriendly (अमित्रवत) {Disagreeable (अप्रिय)}

17 Erudite (Adj.) - (विद्वान)~ *[#R-14 (9)]*
Having great knowledge or learning

Syno: Scholarly (विद्वतापूर्ण), Learned (ज्ञानी), Knowledgeable (जानकार), Educated (शिक्षित)

Anto: Unscholarly (अविद्वान), Ignorant (अज्ञानी), Uninformed (बेख़बर)

18 **Baffle** (V.) - (भ्रमित करना) *[#R-20 (2)]*
To confuse or puzzle someone; to hinder or prevent from achieving a goal

Syno: Puzzle (उलझाना), Perplex (उलझन में डालना), Confuse (भ्रमित करना)

Anto: {Enlighten (स्पष्ट करना), Facilitate (सुगम बनाना)}

19 Eccentric (Adj.) - (विचित्र, सनकी)~ *[#R-11 (11)]*
Unconventional and slightly strange

Syno: Queer (अजीब), Peculiar (अलग प्रकार का), Bizarre (विचित्र), Idiosyncratic (विशिष्ट स्वभाव वाला) {Unconventional (अपरंपरागत), Abnormal (असामान्य), Strange (अजीबोगरीब)}

Anto: Customary (पारंपरिक), Normal (सामान्य) {Conventional (परंपरागत)}

20 Alleviate (V.) - (कम करना, राहत देना) *[#R-9 (12)]*
To reduce or ease pain, suffering, or difficulty

Syno: Mitigate (कम करना), Relieve (राहत देना), Diminish (घटना), Reduce (घटाना) {Mollify (शांत करना), Ameliorate (सुधारना), Lighten (हल्का करना), Soothe (सांत्वना देना), Lessen (न्यून करना)}

Anto: Aggravate (बढ़ाना) {Intensify (तीव्र करना), Escalate (तीव्र करना)}

21 Colossal (Adj.) - (विशाल) *[#R-13 (8)]*
Extremely large or great

Syno: Enormous (विराट), Gigantic (विशालकाय),

Immense (अपार), Huge (बहुत बड़ा), Massive (विशाल)

Anto: Small (छोटा), Tiny (बहुत छोटा), Teeny (बहुत ही छोटा), Minimal (न्यूनतम) {Petite (नन्हा), Negligible (महत्वहीन), Short (नाटा)}

22 Dubious (Adj.) - (संदिग्ध) *[#R-10 (11)]*
Hesitating or doubting

Syno: Doubtful (संदेहपूर्ण), Fishy (संदेहजनक) {Uncertain (अनिश्चित), Unclear (अस्पष्ट)}

Anto: Likely (संभवतः), Certain (निश्चित), Indisputable (अविवादित) {Incontestable (निस्संदेह), Trustworthy (विश्वसनीय)}

23 Spurious (Adj.) - (जाली)~ *[#R-11 (10)]*
False or not what it claims to be

Syno: Fake (नकली), Fraudulent (धोखाधड़ी) {Feigned (बनावटी)}

Anto: Authentic (वास्तविक), Genuine (असली)

24 Harmony (N.) - (सामंजस्य) *[#R-13 (7)]*
Agreement or concord; pleasant arrangement of parts

Syno: Consensus (सहमति), Peace (शांति) {Unity (एकता), Accord (समझौता)}

Anto: Strife (संघर्ष), Conflict (विवाद), Hatred (घृणा), Discord (कलह) {Incoherence (असंगति)}

25 Insipid (Adj.) - (फीका) *[#R-9 (11)]*
Lacking taste, flavour, or interest

Syno: Bland (बेस्वाद), Tasteless (फीका) {Plain (सादा), Flat (फीका), Dull (नीरस), Prosaic (सामान्य)}

Anto: Tasty (स्वादिष्ट), Appetizing (भूख बढ़ाने वाला) {Delicious (स्वादिष्ट), Piquant (तीखा), Interesting (रोचक), Flavourful (स्वादयुक्त), Zesty (चटपटा), Lively (जीवंत)}

26 Lucid (Adj.) - (स्पष्ट)~ *[#R-16 (4)]*
Expressed clearly; easy to understand. Also, bright or luminous

Syno: Clear (स्पष्ट) {Explicit (साफ़-साफ़)}

Anto: Vague (अस्पष्ट), Dark (अंधेरा), Ambiguous (अस्पष्ट), Confusing (भ्रामक) {Obscure (अस्पष्ट)}

27 Obstinate (Adj.) - (जिद्दी) *[#R-13 (7)]*
Refusing stubbornly to change one's opinion or action

Syno: Stubborn (ज़िद्दी), Adamant (अडिग) {Tenacious (हठी), Headstrong (अपनी ज़िद पर चलने वाला)}

Anto: Flexible (लचीला), Docile (विनम्र), Obedient (आज्ञाकारी), Pliable (लचीला) {Amenable (सहमत)}

28 Vigilant (Adj.) - (सावधान) *[#R-12 (8)]*
Keeping careful watch for possible danger

Syno: Watchful (चौकस), Cautious (सजग), Alert (सतर्क) {Aware (जागरूक)}

Anto: Careless (लापरवाह), Negligent (बेपरवाह), Rash (अविवेकी) {Inattentive (असावधान), Distracted (ध्यान भटका हुआ)}

29 **Brave** (Adj.) - (साहसी) *[#R-15 (4)]*
Showing courage or ready to face danger

Syno: Daring (साहसी), Fearless (निडर), Courageous (बहादुर)

Anto: Cowardly (कायर), Timid (डरपोक) {Fearful (डरपोक)}

30 Clandestine (Adj.) - (गुप्त) *[#R-8 (11)]*
Kept secret or done secretively

Syno: Secret (गोपनीय) {Covert (छिपा हुआ)}

Anto: Open (खुला), Overt (प्रत्यक्ष), Known (ज्ञात), Honest (निष्कपट) {Public (सार्वजनिक), Conspicuous (स्पष्ट), Legal (कानूनी)}

31 Genuine (Adj.) - (असली)~ *[#R-13 (6)]*
Truly what something is said to be; authentic

Syno: Original (मूल), Authentic (प्रामाणिक), Real (वास्तविक) {True (सच), Sincere (ईमानदार)}

Anto: Fake (नकली), Spurious (जाली), False (असत्य), Dubious (संदिग्ध) {Fictitious (काल्पनिक)}

32 **Sporadic** (Adj.) - (छिटपुट)~ *[#R-7 (12)]*
Occurring at irregular intervals or only in a few places

Syno: Scattered (बिखरे हुए), Occasional (कभी-कभार), Infrequent (दुर्लभ) {Intermittent (अंतरायिक)}

Anto: Systematic (व्यवस्थित), Regular (नियमित), Frequent (बार-बार) {Constant (स्थिर), Persistent (दृढ़)}

33 **Transient** (Adj.) - (क्षणिक)~ *[#R-12 (7)]*
Lasting a short time

Syno: Transitory (अस्थायी), Fleeting (क्षणिक), Temporary (अस्थायी)

Anto: Permanent (स्थायी) {Lasting (स्थायी), Eternal (अनन्त), Perpetual (निरंतर)}

34 Affluent (Adj.) - (धनी) *[#R-11 (7)]*
Having a great deal of money; wealthy

Syno: Prosperous (समृद्ध), Wealthy (धनवान)

Anto: Poor (गरीब), Destitute (अत्यंत गरीब) {Deprived (वंचित), Impoverished (दरिद्र)}

35 **Bleak** (Adj.) - (उदास, निराशाजनक) *[#R-10 (8)]*
Cold, empty, or without hope

Syno: Depressing (निराशाजनक), Grim (भयानक), Gloomy (उदास)

Anto: Bright (प्रफुल्लित), Cheerful (आनन्दित), Cordial (सौहार्दपूर्ण) {Verdant (हरा-भरा), Lush (घना)}

36 **Callous** (Adj.) - (कठोर, संवेदनाहीन)~ *[#R-13 (5)]*
Showing no sympathy or cruel disregard for others

Syno: Brutal (निर्दयी), Insensitive (संवेदनहीन), Cruel (क्रूर) {Unfeeling (असंवेदनशील)}

Anto: Sensitive (संवेदनशील), Sympathetic (सहानुभूतिपूर्ण), Merciful (दयालु), Tender (कोमल), Caring (देखभाल करने वाला), Concerned (ध्यान देने वाला) {Kind (दयालु), Considerate (विचारशील)}

37 **Coarse** (Adj.) - (खुरदुरा; असभ्य) *[#R-9 (9)]*
Rough or loose in texture or grain; Vulgar or crude in speech or manner

Syno: Rough (रूखा), Crude (भद्दा) {Scratchy (खरोंचदार)}

Anto: Smooth (चिकना), Gentle (कोमल), Refined (परिष्कृत), Buttery (मक्खन जैसा) {Soft (मुलायम), Delicate (नाजुक), Fine (बारीक), Chaste (शालीन)}

38 **Dismal** (Adj.) - (निराशाजनक; अत्यंत खराब)~ *[#R-9 (9)]*
Very depressing or gloomy; extremely poor in quality

Syno: Gloomy (उदास) {Dejected (निराश), Dreary (नीरस), Bleak (निराशाजनक)}

Anto: Cheerful (प्रसन्न), Lively (जीवंत), Luminous (उज्ज्वल) {Bright (उज्ज्वल), Pleasant (सुखद), Cordial (गर्मजोशी वाला), Cheery (हर्षित), Animated (सजीव), Positive (सकारात्मक)}

39 **Ephemeral** (Adj.) - (अल्पकालिक)~ *[#R-8 (10)]*
Lasting for a very short time

Syno: Transient (क्षणिक), Fleeting (पल भर का), Short-lived (अल्पकालिक) {Transitory (अस्थायी), Brief (संक्षिप्त)}

Anto: Eternal (अनन्त), Permanent (स्थायी) {Enduring (टिकाऊ), Long-Lasting (दीर्घकालिक)}

40 **Frugal** (Adj.) - (मितव्ययी)~ *[#R-13 (5)]*
Economical with money or food

Syno: Economical (अल्पव्ययी), Thrifty (किफायती)

Anto: Wasteful (बर्बाद करने वाला), Spendthrift (फिजूलखर्च व्यक्ति), Profligate (अपव्ययी), Prodigal (फिजूलखर्च), Extravagant (फिजूलखर्च)

41 **Morose** (Adj.) - (उदास) *[#R-11 (7)]*
Very sad, quiet, and unwilling to talk to others

Syno: Gloomy (उदास), Sullen (बदमिजाज), Mournful (शोकपूर्ण) {Ill-Tempered (बदमिजाज)}

Anto: Cheerful (खुश), Jovial (हंसमुख), Uplifted (उत्साहित)

42 **Obscure** (Adj.) - (अस्पष्ट)~ *[#R-7 (11)]*
Unclear or not well known

Syno: Confusing (भ्रामक), Unknown (अज्ञात)

Anto: Clear (स्पष्ट), Prominent (प्रमुख), Distinct (सुस्पष्ट) {Famous (प्रसिद्ध)}

43 **Reluctant** (Adj.) - (अनिच्छुक)~ *[#R-11 (7)]*
Not willing or eager; hesitant to act

Syno: Hesitant (हिचकिचाता हुआ), Unwilling (अनिच्छुक) {Averse (विरुद्ध), Disinclined (अनिच्छुक)}

Anto: Eager (उत्सुक), Willing (इच्छुक), Inclined (इच्छुक), Enthusiastic (उत्साही)

44 **Taciturn** (Adj.) - (अल्पभाषी)~ *[#R-10 (8)]*
Reserved in speech; saying very little

Syno: Silent (मौन), Reticent (संकोची), Reserved (संकोची) {Uncommunicative (असंवादी), Unresponsive (प्रतिक्रियाहीन)}

Anto: Talkative (बातूनी), Loquacious (अत्यधिक बोलने वाला) {Garrulous (बातूनी)}

45 **Abolish** (V.) - (समाप्त करना)~ *[#R-12 (5)]*
To formally put an end to something

Syno: Eliminate (हटाना), Cancel (रद्द करना) {Eradicate (उन्मूलन करना), Destroy (नष्ट करना)}

Anto: Build (बनाना), Construct (निर्माण करना), Establish (स्थापित करना), Continue (जारी रखना) {Create (सृजन करना), Restore (पुनर्स्थापित करना)}

46 **Authentic** (Adj.) - (विश्वसनीय, असली)~ *[#R-9 (8)]*
Genuine; real; true in origin; not fake or copied

Syno: Genuine (वास्तविक)

Anto: False (असत्य), Fake (नकली) {Spurious (नकली), Falsified (जाली)}

47 **Conceal** (V.) - (छिपाना)~ *[#R-9 (8)]*
To keep something hidden from sight

Syno: Hide (छुपाना), Disguise (भेष बदलना)

Anto: Reveal (दिखाना) {Unwrap (खोलना), Illuminate (उजागर करना)}

48 **Gloomy** (Adj.) - (उदास) *[#R-13 (4)]*
Dark or poorly lit, appearing depressing or

frightening

Syno: Murky (गहरा), Dull (धुंधला), Unhappy (उदास), Cloudy (बादल छाये), Dismal (निराशाजनक) {Depressed (निराश)}

Anto: Bright (उज्ज्वल), Radiant (चमकदार), Buoyant (प्रसन्न), Cheerful (खुश), Lively (ऊर्जावान)

49 Judicious (Adj.) - (विवेकपूर्ण) *[#R-13 (4)]*
Having, showing, or done with good judgment or sense

Syno: Wise (बुद्धिमान), Cautious (सतर्क), Prudent (चतुर), Sensible (समझदार), Thoughtful (विचारशील) {Reasonable (तर्कसंगत)}

Anto: Rash (उतावला), Unwise (मूर्ख) {Indiscreet (अविवेकी)}

50 Modest (Adj.) - (विनम्र) *[#R-9 (8)]*
Unassuming in estimation of one's abilities

Syno: Humble (नम्र), Shy (शर्मीला), Demure (संकोची)

Anto: Vain (अहंकारी), Conceited (घमंडी), Arrogant (अकड़बाज) {Immodest (अशिष्ट), Luxurious (भव्य)}

51 Perilous (Adj.) - (खतरनाक) *[#R-13 (4)]*
Full of danger or risk

Syno: Hazardous (खतरनाक), Dangerous (खतरनाक) {Risky (जोखिम भरा)}

Anto: Safe (सुरक्षित)

52 Prudent (Adj.) - (विवेकी) *[#R-15 (2)]*
Showing careful judgment and planning for the future

Syno: Cautious (सावधान), Wise (बुद्धिमान), Frugal (अल्पव्ययी), Judicious (विवेकपूर्ण) {Careful (सावधान)}

Anto: Unwise (अविवेकी), Careless (लापरवाह), Indiscreet (असावधान), Stupid (मूर्ख), Thoughtless (विचारहीन), Wasteful (अपव्ययी)

53 Transparent (Adj.) - (पारदर्शी)~ *[#R-10 (7)]*
Easy to see through; clear or open

Syno: Lucid (स्पष्ट), Clear (साफ)

Anto: Opaque (अपारदर्शी)

54 Admonish (V.) - (डाँटना; चेतावनी देना) *[#R-9 (7)]*
To warn or scold someone firmly

Syno: Chide (फटकारना), Reprimand (डाँटना), Warn (चेतावनी देना), Counsel (सलाह देना) {Censure (निंदा करना)}

Anto: Praise (प्रशंसा करना), Applaud (तालियाँ बजाना) {Compliment (तारीफ़ करना)}

55 Apparent (Adj.) - (स्पष्ट) *[#R-9 (7)]*
Clearly visible; or seeming to be true but not necessarily so

Syno: Obvious (प्रत्यक्ष), Manifest (स्पष्ट), Seeming (जाहिर) {Evident (सुस्पष्ट), Presumed (अनुमानित)}

Anto: Ambiguous (अस्पष्ट), Hidden (छिपा हुआ) {Vague (अनिश्चित)}

56 Arrogant (Adj.) - (अभिमानी) *[#R-11 (5)]*
Showing too much pride

Syno: Haughty (घमंडी)

Anto: Modest (विनम्र), Humble (विनम्र)

57 **Calm** (Adj./N.) - (शांत; स्थिरता) *[#R-12 (4)]*
Peaceful and not excited (Adj.); A state of peace (N.)

Syno: Peaceful (शांतिपूर्ण), Relaxed (तनाव मुक्त), Quiet (शांत), Placid (शांत, स्थिर) {Unruffled (अविचलित)}

Anto: Excited (उत्तेजित), Turbulent (अशांत), Upset (व्याकुल); Frenzy (उन्माद), Agitation (उत्तेजना) {Stormy (तूफानी)}

58 Extravagant (Adj.) - (फ़िज़ूलख़र्च)~ *[#R-7 (9)]*
Spending too much money or using resources without control

Syno: Expensive (महंगा) {Excessive (अत्यधिक)}

Anto: Economical (किफायती), Thrifty (कमखर्च), Frugal (कम खर्च वाला), Restrained (नियंत्रित) {Miserly (कंजूस), Reasonable (तर्कसंगत), Meagre (अल्प)}

59 **Fragile** (Adj.) - (नाजुक)~ *[#R-12 (4)]*
Easily broken or damaged

Syno: Brittle (भुरभुरा), Delicate (कोमल), Frail (कमज़ोर) {Flimsy (कमज़ोर)}

Anto: Tough (कठोर), Strong (मजबूत), Robust (मज़बूत), Healthy (स्वस्थ) {Sturdy (मज़बूत), Durable (टिकाऊ)}

60 Futile (Adj.) - (व्यर्थ) *[#R-11 (5)]*
Incapable of producing result

Syno: Unsuccessful (असफल), Useless (बेकार), Fruitless (निष्फल) {Pointless (निरर्थक)}

Anto: Effective (कारगर), Fruitful (फलदायक), Productive (उत्पादक), Worthy (योग्य), Useful (उपयोगी) {Valuable (मूल्यवान)}

61 Garrulous (Adj.) - (बातूनी)~ *[#R-9 (7)]*
Excessively talkative, especially on trivial matters

Syno: Talkative (बातूनी), Voluble (वाचाल), Loquacious (बातूनी)

Anto: Taciturn (मौन), Quiet (शांत), Reserved (कम बोलने वाला) {Reticent (अल्पभाषी)}

62 **Malice** (N.) - (द्वेष) *[#R-10 (6)]*
The intention or desire to do evil; ill will

Syno: Bitterness (कड़वाहट) {Ill Will (दुर्भावना), Grudge (मनमुटाव), Hatred (घृणा)}

Anto: Goodwill (सद्भावना), Kindness (दयालुता), Sympathy (सहानुभूति) {Cordiality (आत्मीयता)}

63 **Meagre** (Adj.) - (अपर्याप्त) *[#R-12 (4)]*
Lacking in quantity or quality

Syno: Inadequate (अपर्याप्त) {Scanty (कम), Insufficient (अपर्याप्त), Scarce (दुर्लभ)}

Anto: Plentiful (प्रचुर), Sufficient (पर्याप्त), Adequate (पर्याप्त) {Abundant (प्रचुर)}

64 **Monotonous** (Adj.) - (नीरस, एकसमान)~ *[#R-9 (7)]*
Dull and boring due to lack of variety

Syno: Dull (नीरस), Boring (उबाऊ) {Dreary (नीरस), Tiresome (थकाऊ), Tedious (उबाऊ), Repetitive (दोहराव वाला)}

Anto: Interesting (दिलचस्प), Engrossing (रोचक), Varied (विविध) {Exciting (रोमांचक)}

65 **Mundane** (Adj.) - (साधारण, नीरस)~ *[#R-11 (5)]*
Lacking interest or excitement; dull

Syno: Ordinary (साधारण), Everyday (रोजमर्रा का), Commonplace (सामान्य), Banal (नीरस) {Worldly (सांसारिक), Common (सामान्य), Tedious (उबाऊ)}

Anto: Extraordinary (असाधारण), Exceptional (विशेष) {Unique (अनोखा), Exciting (रोमांचक)}

66 **Pernicious** (Adj.) - (हानिकारक) *[#R-10 (6)]*
Causing serious harm, often gradually

Syno: Injurious (हानिकारक), Dangerous (खतरनाक), Malicious (दुर्भावनापूर्ण), Spiteful (द्वेषपूर्ण) {Harmful (नुकसानदेह), Destructive (विनाशकारी)}

Anto: Beneficial (लाभकारी), Innocuous (अहानिकर), Kind (दयालु)

67 **Persuade** (V.) - (राज़ी करना) *[#R-13 (3)]*
To make someone do something by reasoning

Syno: Coax (फुसलाना), Convince (समझाना), Impress (प्रभावित करना)

Anto: Dissuade (मना करना), Deter (हतोत्साहित करना) {Discourage (हतोत्साहित करना)}

68 **Tedious** (Adj.) - (उबाऊ) *[#R-11 (5)]*
Too long, slow, or dull; tiresome or monotonous

Syno: Dull (नीरस), Tiresome (थकाऊ), Dreary (निराशाजनक), Boring (उबाऊ)

Anto: Interesting (रोचक), Exciting (रोमांचक), Delightful (आनंददायक)

69 **Tranquil** (Adj.) - (शांत)~ *[#R-11 (5)]*
Free from disturbance; calm

Syno: Peaceful (शांतिपूर्ण), Calm (शांत), Sober (शांत)

Anto: Stormy (तूफानी), Disturbed (परेशान), Violent (हिंसक), Unquiet (अशांत) {Excited (उत्साहित), Noisy (शोरगुल वाला)}

70 **Abundance** (N.) - (प्रचुरता) *[#R-8 (7)]*
A very large quantity of something

Syno: {Plethora (अधिकता), Plenty (भरपूर)}

Anto: Scarcity (अभाव), Dearth (कमी), Scantiness (अपर्याप्तता), Meagreness (अल्पता) {Shortage (तंगी), Handful (मुट्ठी भर)}

71 **Adamant** (Adj.) - (अटल) *[#R-6 (9)]*
Refusing to be persuaded or to change one's mind; firm and unyielding

Syno: Stubborn (जिद्दी)

Anto: Yielding (झुकनेवाला), Flexible (लचीला) {Lenient (नरम), Unsure (अनिश्चित)}

72 **Ameliorate** (V.) - (सुधारना)~ *[#R-7 (8)]*
To make something bad or unsatisfactory better

Syno: Improve (बेहतर करना)

Anto: Worsen (बदतर बनाना), Exacerbate (और बिगाड़ना) {Deteriorate (और खराब होना), Aggravate (बिगाड़ना)}

73 **Blunt** (Adj.) - (कम धार वाला; मुँहफट) *[#R-10 (5)]*
Not sharp; rude and very direct in speech

Syno: Dull (कम तेज़), Insensitive (असंवेदनशील) {Snippy (रूखा)}

Anto: Sharp (तेज़), Polite (विनम्र) {Pointed (नुकीला), Edgy (नुकीला)}

74 **Concise** (Adj.) - (संक्षिप्त) *[#R-9 (6)]*
Giving information clearly in few words

Syno: Brief (संक्षिप्त) {Capsule (निचोड़)}

Anto: Lengthy (लंबा) {Wordy (अधिक शब्दों वाला), Elaborate (विस्तृत), Unabridged (असंक्षिप्त)}

75 **Condemn** (V.) - (निंदा करना; दंड देना) *[#R-9 (6)]*
To express complete disapproval; to sentence to punishment

Syno: Criticize (आलोचना करना), Punish (सजा

देना), Denounce (दोषी ठहराना), Censure (फटकार लगाना) {Blame (दोष लगाना)}

Anto: Praise (प्रशंसा करना), Applaud (सराहना करना) {Approve (स्वीकृति देना)}

76 **Disdain** (N./V.) - (तिरस्कार; तुच्छ समझना) *[#R-4 (11)]*
Contempt or strong dislike (N.); To consider unworthy of respect (V.)

Syno: Contempt (अवमानना) {Scorn (तिरस्कार); Hate (घृणा), Disregard (अवहेलना)}

Anto: Admiration (प्रशंसा), Respect (सम्मान), Favour (अनुकूलता) {Approval (सहमति); Praise (प्रशंसा)}

77 **Jovial** (Adj.) - (प्रसन्नचित्त)~ *[#R-9 (6)]*
Cheerful and friendly

Syno: Joyous (खुश) {Mirthful (हँसमुख), Merry (खुशमिजाज)}

Anto: Gloomy (उदास), Sorrowful (दुखी), Morose (उदास), Petulant (चिड़चिड़ा) {Cheerless (उदास)}

78 **Rectify** (V.) - (सुधारना)~ *[#R-11 (4)]*
To put something right

Syno: Correct (सही करना), Amend (संशोधन करना)

Anto: Worsen (बदतर करना), Falsify (झूठा बनाना), Corrupt (भ्रष्ट करना)

79 **Turbulent** (Adj.) - (अशांत) *[#R-11 (4)]*
Characterized by disorder, conflict, or lack of control

Syno: Violent (हिंसक), Agitated (उत्तेजित), Disordered (अव्यवस्थित) {Stormy (तूफानी)}

Anto: Placid (शांत), Calm (शांत), Peaceful (शांतिपूर्ण), Settled (स्थिर) {Tranquil (शांत)}

80 **Zenith** (N.) - (शीर्ष बिंदु)~ *[#R-7 (8)]*
The highest point reached; point directly overhead

Syno: Summit (शिखर), Pinnacle (चरम) {Apex (शीर्ष)}

Anto: Nadir (निम्नतम बिंदु), Bottom (तल) {Base (आधार), Depth (गहराई)}

81 **Adversity** (N.) - (विपत्ति) *[#R-10 (4)]*
A difficult or unpleasant situation

Syno: Misfortune (दुर्भाग्य), Hardship (कठिनाई), Misery (दुःख)

Anto: Prosperity (समृद्धि)

82 **Attract** (V.) - (आकर्षित करना) *[#R-11 (3)]*
To draw someone by appealing qualities

Syno: Fascinate (मोहित करना), Entice (लुभाना) {Engage (आकर्षित करना)}

Anto: Repel (पीछे हटाना), Deter (रोकना), Repulse (विकर्षित करना)

83 **Audacity** (N.) - (दुस्साहस) *[#R-9 (5)]*
Bold behavior that can seem rude

Syno: Nerve (हिम्मत), Boldness (साहस)

Anto: Cowardice (कायरता), Timidity (डरपोकपन), Modesty (विनम्रता) {Gentility (शिष्टता), Politeness (शालीनता)}

84 **Awkward** (Adj.) - (बेढंगा) *[#R-10 (4)]*
Clumsy or ungraceful; or causing difficulty

Syno: Clumsy (अनाड़ी), Unskilful (अकुशल)

Anto: Convenient (सुविधाजनक), Graceful (गरिमापूर्ण) {Clever (चतुर)}

85 **Cacophony** (N.) - (कोलाहल, कर्कश ध्वनि)~ *[#R-10 (4)]*
A harsh, jarring, or discordant mixture of sounds

Syno: Noise (शोर), Discord (कलह)

Anto: Harmony (सुरों का मेल), Symphony (मधुर संगीत)

86 **Eager** (Adj.) - (उत्सुक) *[#R-13 (1)]*
Very interested and excited to do or get something

Syno: Keen (तत्पर), Avid (उत्सुक), Enthusiastic (उत्साहित)

Anto: Disinterested (अनिच्छुक), Indifferent (उदासीन) {Apathetic (भावहीन)}

87 **Eloquent** (Adj.) - (वाक्पटु)~ *[#R-8 (6)]*
Fluent or persuasive in speaking or writing

Syno: Fluent (धाराप्रवाह), Articulate (स्पष्ट बोलने वाला), Expressive (भावपूर्ण)

Anto: Inarticulate (अस्पष्ट), Inexpressive (भावहीन) {Ineffective (अप्रभावी)}

88 **Exaggerate** (V.) - (बढ़ा-चढ़ाकर कहना)~ *[#R-11 (3)]*
To present something as more than it really is

Syno: Magnify (बड़ा करना), Amplify (बढ़ाना) {Overstate (बढ़ा-चढ़ाकर कहना)}

Anto: Unembellish (सरलता से कहना), Understate (कम करके कहना)

89 **Fastidious** (Adj.) - (सूक्ष्मदर्शी)~ *[#R-11 (3)]*
Very attentive to accuracy and detail

Syno: Careful (सावधान), Meticulous (अत्यंत सावधान) {Particular (चुनिंदा)}

Anto: Lax (ढीला), Lackadaisical (लापरवाह), Sloppy (अव्यवस्थित), Easy-going (बेपरवाह), Indifferent (उदासीन) {Careless (लापरवाह)}

90 **Humble** (Adj.) - (विनम्र) *[#R-12 (2)]*
Having a modest view of one's importance

Syno: Meek (सहनशील), Modest (शालीन) {Unassuming (सादा)}

Anto: Arrogant (अभिमानी), Assertive (आत्मविश्वासी), Pompous (दिखावटी), Proud (गर्वित)

91 **Industrious** (Adj.) - (परिश्रमी)~ *[#R-9 (5)]*
Showing steady effort and hard work

Syno: Diligent (मेहनती)

Anto: Lethargic (सुस्त), Indolent (आलसी), Lazy (आलसी)

92 **Insolent** (Adj.) - (बदतमीज़) *[#R-11 (3)]*
Showing a rude and arrogant lack of respect

Syno: Disrespectful (असम्मानजनक), Bold (साहसी), Rude (अशिष्ट) {Insulting (अपमानजनक)}

Anto: Humble (विनम्र), Submissive (आज्ञाकारी), Mannerly (शिष्ट), Courteous (विनम्र) {Affable (मिलनसार)}

93 **Laconic** (Adj.) - (संक्षिप्त) *[#R-7 (7)]*
Using very few words

Syno: Concise (संक्षिप्त), Crisp (सटीक), Brief (संक्षिप्त)

Anto: Verbose (शब्दाडंबरपूर्ण), Wordy (शब्दों से भरा) {Loquacious (बातूनी), Voluble (बातूनी), Longwinded (लंबा)}

94 **Lament** (V./N.) - (विलाप; रोना-पीटना)~ *[#R-9 (5)]*
To mourn a person's loss or death (V); An expression of grief or sorrow (N.)

Syno: Mourn (शोक मनाना) {Wail (विलाप करना)}

Anto: Rejoice (खुश होना), Celebrate (जश्न मनाना), Applaud (तालियाँ बजाना); Applause (तालियाँ) {Exultation (उल्लास), Delight (आनंद)}

95 **Melancholy** (Adj./N.) - (उदासी)~ *[#R-11 (3)]*
Feeling thoughtful sadness (Adj.); Deep sadness or gloom (N.)

Syno: Sorrowful (दुखी), Sad (दुखी), Gloomy (उदास); Sadness (निराशा) {Despondency (निराशा)}

Anto: Cheerful (प्रसन्न), Pleasant (सुखद); Ecstasy (परमानंद) {Cheery (खुशमिज़ाज)}

96 **Naive** (Adj.) - (अनुभवहीन)~ *[#R-10 (4)]*
Showing a lack of experience, wisdom, or judgment

Syno: Ingenuous (निष्कपट), Gullible (सीधा), Simple (सरल)

Anto: Artful (चालाक), Experienced (अनुभवी), Sophisticated (परिष्कृत), Cynical (निंदक) {Wise (बुद्धिमान)}

97 **Opaque** (Adj.) - (अपारदर्शी)~ *[#R-8 (6)]*
Not able to be seen through or unclear

Syno: Arcane (गूढ़)

Anto: Transparent (पारदर्शी), Clear (स्पष्ट), Pellucid (स्वच्छ), Intelligible (समझ में आने योग्य) {Obvious (स्पष्ट)}

98 **Peculiar** (Adj.) - (विचित्र) *[#R-12 (2)]*
Strange or unusual in nature

Syno: Strange (अजीब), Unusual (असामान्य) {Abnormal (असामान्य)}

Anto: Usual (सामान्य), Normal (सामान्य), Ordinary (साधारण), Familiar (जाना-पहचाना) {Common (सामान्य)}

99 **Serene** (Adj.) - (शांत) *[#R-8 (6)]*
Calm, peaceful, and untroubled; tranquil

Syno: Calm (शांत) {Peaceful (शांतिपूर्ण)}

Anto: Turbulent (अशांत), Ruffled (उत्तेजित), Stressed (तनावपूर्ण), Chaotic (अराजक) {Agitated (व्याकुल)}

100 **Triumph** (N.) - (विजय) *[#R-9 (5)]*
A great victory or success

Syno: Victory (विजय)

Anto: Defeat (हार), Failure (असफलता), Sorrow (दुःख)

*Total **100** Syno+Anto asked **1844** times*

C2 Synonyms + Antonyms (Common) List (asked in SSC Exams)

1 **Abandon** (V./N.) - (छोड़ देना; नियंत्रणहीनता) *[#R-26 (9)]*
To leave or give up completely (V.); A complete lack of restraint (N.)
Syno: Desert (छोड़ देना), Forsake (त्यागना), Relinquish (परित्याग करना), Leave (छोड़ना); Dereliction (उपेक्षा) {Discontinue (बंद करना); Unrestraint (अनियंत्रण)}
Anto: Retain (बनाए रखना), Continue (जारी रखना), Keep (रखना), Adopt (अपनाना); Constraint (नियंत्रण)

2 **Abate** (V.) - (कम करना)~ *[#R-5 (7)]*
To become less intense or to reduce
Syno: Moderate (नियंत्रित करना) {Subside (घटना), Decrease (घटाना), Diminish (क्षीण करना), Reduce (कम करना), Lessen (कम होना)}
Anto: Increase (वृद्धि करना), Intensify (तीव्र करना), Aggravate (बढ़ाना) {Grow (बढ़ना), Extend (विस्तार करना)}

3 **Abbreviate** (V.) - (संक्षिप्त करना) *[#R-2 (1)]*
To shorten a word or phrase
Syno: Shorten (छोटा करना) {Compress (संकुचित करना)}
Anto: Expand (विस्तार करना)

4 **Abdicate** (V.) - (त्यागना)~ *[#R-3 (2)]*
To formally give up a position or power
Syno: Abandon (छोड़ देना) {Renounce (त्यागना)}
Anto: Assume (ग्रहण करना) {Claim (दावा करना)}

5 **Abduct** (V.) - (अपहरण करना) *[#R-1 (2)]*
To take someone away illegally by force
Syno: {Kidnap (अपहरण करना)}
Anto: Release (मुक्त करना)

6 **Aberration** (N.) - (असामान्यता)~ *[#R-2]*
A departure from what is normal
Syno: Deviation (विचलन)
Anto: Normality (सामान्यता)

7 **Abeyance** (N.) - (निलंबन)~ *[#R-4 (2)]*
A temporary stopping or suspension
Syno: Suspension (निलंबन), Inactivity (निष्क्रियता) {Dormancy (सुप्तावस्था)}
Anto: Continuation (निरंतरता)

8 **Abide** (V.) - (पालन करना, निवास करना) *[#R-2 (1)]*
To accept or act in accordance with; To live or reside
Syno: Dwell (निवास करना)
Anto: Reject (अस्वीकार करना) {Shun (दूर रहना)}

9 **Ability** (N.) - (योग्यता) *[#R-2 (3)]*
The means or skill to do something
Syno: Capacity (क्षमता), Skill (कौशल) {Competence (काबिलियत)}
Anto: {Weakness (कमज़ोरी), Incapacity (अयोग्यता)}

10 **Abjure** (V.) - (त्यागना) *[#R-2 (5)]*
To solemnly renounce a belief or claim
Syno: Renounce (त्यागना) {Recant (मुकरना), Withdraw (वापस लेना)}
Anto: Acquire (प्राप्त करना) {Accept (स्वीकार करना)}

11 **Abolish** (V.) - (समाप्त करना)~ *[#R-12 (5)]*
To formally put an end to something
Syno: Eliminate (हटाना), Cancel (रद्द करना) {Eradicate (उन्मूलन करना), Destroy (नष्ट करना)}
Anto: Build (बनाना), Construct (निर्माण करना), Establish (स्थापित करना), Continue (जारी रखना) {Create (सृजन करना), Restore (पुनर्स्थापित करना)}

12 **Abominable** (Adj.) - (घृणित) *[#R-3 (1)]*
Causing moral revulsion; very bad or unpleasant
Syno: Obnoxious (अप्रिय) {Repugnant (घृणास्पद)}
Anto: Delightful (मनोहर), Admirable (प्रशंसनीय)

13 **Aboriginal** (Adj./N.) - (मूल निवासी; आदिवासी)~ *[#R-1 (1)]*
Relating to original inhabitants (Adj.); An original native person (N.)
Syno: {Native (स्थानीय)}
Anto: Immigrant (आप्रवासी)

14 **Abort** (V.) - (बंद कर देना) *[#R-2]*
To terminate prematurely
Syno: End (समाप्त करना)
Anto: Commence (आरंभ करना)

15 **Abortive** (Adj.) - (असफल) *[#R-1 (2)]*
Failing to produce the intended result
Syno: Unsuccessful (विफल) {Ineffective

(प्रभावहीन)}

Anto: {Successful (सफल)}

16 **Abound** (V.) - (प्रचुर मात्रा में होना) *[#R-1 (2)]*
To exist in large numbers or amounts

Syno: Flourish (फलना-फूलना)

Anto: {Lack (कमी होना)}

17 **Abridge** (V.) - (संक्षेप करना)~ *[#R-4 (2)]*
To shorten without losing sense

Syno: Shorten (छोटा करना)

Anto: Stretch (खींचना), Elongate (लम्बा करना) {Enlarge (बढ़ाना)}

18 **Abrogate** (V.) - (रद्द करना)~ *[#R-9 (2)]*
To repeal or do away with a law or agreement

Syno: Repeal (रद्द करना), Abolish (समाप्त करना) {Annul (निरस्त करना)}

Anto: Establish (स्थापित करना), Uphold (कायम रखना)

19 **Abrupt** (Adj.) - (अचानक) *[#R-5 (1)]*
Sudden and unexpected

Syno: Sudden (अचानक)

Anto: Gradual (क्रमिक), Smooth (बिना रुकावट)

20 **Abscond** (V.) - (फरार होना)~ *[#R-6 (1)]*
To escape or run away secretly

Syno: Flee (भाग जाना)

Anto: Remain (बने रहना), Appear (उपस्थित होना), Endure (टिके रहना)

21 **Absolute** (Adj.) - (पूर्ण) *[#R-6 (1)]*
Total and not restricted; certain

Syno: Complete (पूरा), Definite (निश्चित)

Anto: Limited (सीमित), Incomplete (अधूरा)

22 **Absolve** (V.) - (दोषमुक्त करना) *[#R-9 (3)]*
To declare free from blame or guilt

Syno: Acquit (दोषमुक्त करना), Pardon (क्षमा करना)

Anto: Condemn (निंदा करना), Accuse (दोष लगाना), Blame (दोष देना)

23 **Absorb** (V.) - (सोख लेना) *[#R-5 (1)]*
To take in or soak up

Syno: Soak (सोखना) {Consume (उपभोग करना)}

Anto: Dismiss (खारिज करना), Eject (बाहर फेंकना), Emit (निकालना)

24 **Abstain** (V.) - (परहेज करना) *[#R-5 (6)]*
To restrain oneself from doing something

Syno: Refrain (बचना) {Resist (प्रतिरोध करना)}

Anto: Indulge (लिप्त होना), Pursue (अनुसरण करना) {Partake (सहभागी होना)}

25 **Abstruse** (Adj.) - (जटिल) *[#R-3 (3)]*
Difficult to understand; obscure

Syno: Complicated (पेचीदा), Difficult (कठिन)

Anto: Clear (स्पष्ट) {Comprehensible (समझने योग्य), Obvious (प्रत्यक्ष)}

26 **Absurd** (Adj.) - (बेतुका)~ *[#R-15 (8)]*
Wildly unreasonable or illogical

Syno: Ridiculous (हास्यास्पद), Irrational (अतर्कसंगत), Silly (मूर्ख) {Foolish (मूर्ख), Senseless (निरर्थक), Unreasonable (अतार्किक)}

Anto: Sensible (समझदार), Reasonable (उचित), Realistic (वास्तविक) {Rational (तर्कसंगत)}

27 **Abundance** (N.) - (प्रचुरता) *[#R-8 (7)]*
A very large quantity of something

Syno: {Plethora (अधिकता), Plenty (भरपूर)}

Anto: Scarcity (अभाव), Dearth (कमी), Scantiness (अपर्याप्तता), Meagreness (अल्पता) {Shortage (तंगी), Handful (मुट्ठी भर)}

28 **Abundant** (Adj.) - (प्रचुर) *[#R-23 (10)]*
Existing or available in large quantities

Syno: Plentiful (प्रचुर), Ample (काफ़ी) {Copious (अधिक), Plenty (प्रचुर)}

Anto: Meagre (अल्प), Insufficient (अपर्याप्त), Deficient (अपर्याप्त), Sparse (छिटपुट), Scarce (कम) {Scant (अपर्याप्त)}

29 **Abusive** (Adj.) - (अपमानजनक, क्रूर) *[#R-4 (1)]*
Involving or characterised by cruel treatment

Syno: Scornful (तिरस्कारी), Harmful (हानिकारक)

Anto: Laudatory (प्रशंसात्मक) {Praiseful (प्रशंसापूर्ण)}

30 **Accede** (V.) - (सहमत होना) *[#R-6 (3)]*
To agree to a demand or request

Syno: Consent (सहमति देना), Comply (पालन करना) {Endorse (समर्थन करना)}

Anto: Deny (इनकार करना), Refuse (मना करना) {Disapprove (अस्वीकार करना)}

31 **Accentuate** (V.) - (जोर देना, प्रमुख बनाना) *[#R-2 (1)]*
To make more noticeable or prominent

Syno: {Emphasise (जोर देना)}

Anto: Disparage (नीचा दिखाना), Obscure (अस्पष्ट करना)

32 **Accept** (V.) - (स्वीकार करना) *[#R-10]*
To agree to receive or take

Syno: Agree (सहमत होना)

Anto: Reject (अस्वीकार करना), Deny (इनकार करना)

33 **Access** (N.) - (पहुँच) *[#R-3]*

[Bold SN, indicates that it has been asked in Spelling]

[In Word, ~ indicates that it has been asked in OWS]

The right or ability to use

Syno: Avenue (मार्ग)

Anto: Denial (अस्वीकृति)

34 Accessory (N.) - (सहायक उपकरण) *[#R-2]*
An extra item added for usefulness

Syno: Attachment (संलग्न वस्तु)

Anto: Essential (आवश्यक वस्तु)

35 Accolade (N.) - (सम्मान)~ *[#R-4 (4)]*
An honor or award

Syno: Praise (प्रशंसा) {Award (पुरस्कार), Laurels (गौरव)}

Anto: Blame (दोष), Criticism (आलोचना)

36 Accomplish (V.) - (सफल होना, पूरा करना) *[#R-6 (6)]*
To achieve or complete successfully

Syno: Achieve (प्राप्त करना) {Attain (हासिल करना)}

Anto: Fail (असफल होना), Miss (छूट जाना)

37 **Accord** (N./V.) - (समझौता; प्रदान करना)~ *[#R-2 (1)]*
Agreement or harmony (N.); To grant or give (V.)

Syno: Confer (प्रदान करना)

Anto: Disagreement (असहमति)

38 Accountable (Adj.) - (जवाबदेह) *[#R-2 (2)]*
Required to justify actions or decisions

Syno: Answerable (उत्तरदायी)

Anto: Irresponsible (गैर ज़िम्मेदार) {Exempt (मुक्त, रहित)}

39 Accumulate (V.) - (संचय करना) *[#R-4 (8)]*
To gather or collect something gradually over time

Syno: {Amass (इकट्ठा करना), Gather (जमा करना), Acquire (अर्जित करना), Store (संग्रह करना)}

Anto: Disperse (छितराना), Scatter (बिखेरना), Squander (बर्बाद करना)

40 Accurate (Adj.) - (सटीक) *[#R-12]*
Free from error; exact and correct in all details

Syno: Precise (सटीक), Correct (सही), Exact (सटीक)

Anto: Inexact (गलत), Faulty (दोषपूर्ण), Unreliable (अविश्वसनीय)

41 Accuse (V.) - (आरोप लगाना) *[#R-5 (1)]*
To charge someone with an offense or crime

Syno: Indict (आरोपित करना)

Anto: Exculpate (दोषमुक्त करना), Defend (बचाव करना)

42 Accustomed (Adj.) - (आदी) *[#R-2 (1)]*
Usual or familiar due to habit

Syno: Habituated (अभ्यस्त)

Anto: Unusual (असामान्य)

43 Acknowledge (V.) - (स्वीकार करना) *[#R-3 (1)]*
To accept or admit the existence or truth of something

Syno: Confirm (स्वीकार करना)

Anto: Deny (इनकार करना), Decline (अस्वीकार करना)

44 Acquiesce (V.) - (मान लेना) *[#R-1 (7)]*
To accept something reluctantly but without protest

Syno: Concur (सहमत होना) {Accede (स्वीकार करना), Submit (समर्पण करना)}

Anto: {Resist (विरोध करना)}

45 Acquire (V.) - (हासिल करना) *[#R-4 (1)]*
To get or gain possession of something

Syno: Procure (प्राप्त करना), Obtain (अभिप्राप्त करना) {Develop (विकसित करना)}

Anto: Lose (खोना), Discard (त्यागना)

46 Acquisition (N.) - (अधिग्रहण) *[#R-1 (2)]*
Something bought or obtained

Syno: {Recovery (पुनःप्राप्ति)}

Anto: Loss (हानि)

47 **Acquisitive** (Adj.) - (लाभ का इच्छुक) *[#R-1 (1)]*
Eager to acquire and possess material things or ideas

Syno: Greedy (लालची)

Anto: {Unsparing (उदार)}

48 Acquit (V.) - (दोषमुक्त करना)~ *[#R-7 (3)]*
To declare someone free from a charge of wrongdoing

Syno: {Absolve (मुक्त करना)}

Anto: Convict (दोषी ठहराना), Condemn (दोषी ठहराना), Blame (दोष लगाना) {Accuse (आरोप लगाना)}

49 Acrimonious (Adj.) - (कटु) *[#R-5 (8)]*
Angry and bitter, typically in speech or discussion

Syno: Bitter (कड़वा)

Anto: {Harmonious (मेलजोल वाला), Pleasant (सुखद), Warm-hearted (गर्मजोशी वाला)}

50 **Active** (Adj.) - (सक्रिय) *[#R-5 (3)]*
Doing things energetically; not idle or passive

Syno: Busy (व्यस्त) {Energetic (ऊर्जावान)}

Anto: Inert (जड़), Abeyant (निलंबित), Passive (निष्क्रिय) {Dormant (सुप्त)}

51 Acumen (N.) - (कुशाग्र बुद्धि)~ *[#R-3 (5)]*
The ability to judge situations quickly and accurately

Syno: Brilliance (प्रतिभा) {Sharpness (कुशाग्रता), Acuity (तेज बुद्धि), Ingenuity (चतुराई)}

Anto: Stupidity (मूर्खता)

52 **Acute** (Adj.) - (तीव्र) *[#R-5 (2)]*
Severe or intense in effect

Syno: Sharp (तेज) {Severe (गंभीर)}

Anto: Blunt (कम धार वाला) {Dull (मंद)}

53 Adamant (Adj.) - (अटल) *[#R-6 (9)]*
Refusing to be persuaded or to change one's mind; firm and unyielding

Syno: Stubborn (जिद्दी)

Anto: Yielding (झुकनेवाला), Flexible (लचीला) {Lenient (नरम), Unsure (अनिश्चित)}

54 Adept (Adj.) - (कुशल) *[#R-4 (2)]*
Very skilled or proficient at something

Syno: Skilled (निपुण) {Dexterous (दक्ष)}

Anto: Inept (अकुशल) {Crude (अपरिष्कृत)}

55 Adequate (Adj.) - (पर्याप्त) *[#R-7 (1)]*
Enough or satisfactory

Syno: Sufficient (पर्याप्त), Enough (काफी)

Anto: Wanting (अपर्याप्त)

56 Adhere (V.) - (पालन करना)~ *[#R-7 (5)]*
To stick firmly or follow closely

Syno: Comply (अनुपालन करना)

Anto: Flout (अवहेलना करना) {Disobey (अवज्ञा करना)}

57 Adjust (V.) - (अनुकूल बनाना) *[#R-2 (1)]*
To change something slightly to get the desired result

Syno: Adapt (तालमेल बिठाना) {Accommodate (समायोजित करना)}

Anto: Disorganise (अव्यवस्थित करना)

58 **Admire** (V.) - (प्रशंसा करना) *[#R-8]*
To regard with respect or warm approval

Syno: Appreciate (सराहना करना)

Anto: Dislike (नापसंद करना), Despise (घृणा करना), Ridicule (उपहास करना)

59 Admonish (V.) - (डाँटना; चेतावनी देना) *[#R-9 (7)]*
To warn or scold someone firmly

Syno: Chide (फटकारना), Reprimand (डाँटना), Warn (चेतावनी देना), Counsel (सलाह देना) {Censure (निंदा करना)}

Anto: Praise (प्रशंसा करना), Applaud (तालियाँ बजाना) {Compliment (तारीफ़ करना)}

60 Adore (V.) - (बहुत ही पसंद करना) *[#R-2 (1)]*
To love and respect deeply

Syno: Admire (प्रशंसा करना)

Anto: Despise (घृणा करना) {Condemn (निंदा करना)}

61 Adorn (V.) - (सजाना) *[#R-2 (1)]*
To make more beautiful or attractive

Syno: Beautify (सुंदर बनाना)

Anto: Disfigure (विकृत करना)

62 Adroit (Adj.) - (कुशल) *[#R-1 (3)]*
Clever or skilful

Syno: Skilful (निपुण) {Capable (सक्षम)}

Anto: {Incompetent (अक्षम), Clumsy (अनाड़ी)}

63 Adulation (N.) - (चापलूसी) *[#R-5 (2)]*
Excessive admiration or praise

Syno: Flattery (खुशामद), Adoration (अत्यधिक प्रेम)

Anto: Abuse (गाली)

64 Adulterate (V.) - (मिलावट करना)~ *[#R-3]*
To make weaker or impure by adding another substance

Syno: Contaminate (दूषित करना), Taint (मिलावट करना)

Anto: Purify (शुद्ध करना)

65 Advance (V.) - (आगे बढ़ना) *[#R-9 (1)]*
To move forwards in a purposeful way

Syno: Progress (प्रगति करना), Proceed (आगे बढ़ना)

Anto: Retreat (पीछे हटना), Retard (धीमा करना), Linger (ठहरा रहना)

66 **Advanced** (Adj.) - (प्रगतिशील; आधुनिक) *[#R-3]*
Modern and well developed

Syno: Progressive (उन्नतिशील)

Anto: Rudimentary (प्रारंभिक), Elementary (प्राथमिक)

67 Advantage (N.) - (लाभ) *[#R-2]*
A favorable or superior position

Syno: Boon (वरदान)

Anto: Minus (नुकसान)

68 **Advent** (N.) - (आगमन) *[#R-2]*
The arrival of a notable person or event

Syno: Arrival (आगमन)

Anto: Departure (प्रस्थान)

69 Adversary (N.) - (विरोधी) *[#R-5 (1)]*
An opponent in a contest or dispute

Syno: Rival (प्रतिद्वंद्वी), Opponent (प्रतिपक्षी)

Anto: Ally (मित्र), Helper (सहायक) {Comrade (साथी)}

70 Adverse (Adj.) - (विपरीत) *[#R-4 (4)]*
Harmful or unfavourable

Syno: Negative (नकारात्मक), Unfavourable (प्रतिकूल)

Anto: Propitious (अनुकूल) {Beneficial (लाभकारी)}

71 Adversity (N.) - (विपत्ति) *[#R-10 (4)]*
A difficult or unpleasant situation

Syno: Misfortune (दुर्भाग्य), Hardship (कठिनाई), Misery (दुःख)

Anto: Prosperity (समृद्धि)

72 **Advocacy** (N.) - (समर्थन) *[#R-1 (2)]*
Public support for a cause or policy

Syno: {Promotion (बढ़ावा)}

Anto: Discouragement (हतोत्साहन) {Opposition (विरोध)}

73 Advocate (V.) - (समर्थन करना)~ *[#R-2 (2)]*
To publicly support or recommend

Syno: Support (समर्थन करना)

Anto: {Oppose (विरोध करना)}

74 **Affable** (Adj.) - (मिलनसार) *[#R-2 (2)]*
Easy to approach and talk to

Syno: {Friendly (मित्रवत)}

Anto: Surly (चिड़चिड़ा), Hostile (शत्रुतापूर्ण) {Reserved (संकोची)}

75 **Affinity** (N.) - (लगाव) *[#R-4 (3)]*
A natural liking or sympathy for something

Syno: Empathy (सहानुभूति) {Rapport (संबंध), Intimacy (करीबी रिश्ता)}

Anto: Aversion (घृणा), Dislike (नापसंद)

76 Affirm (V.) - (पुष्टि करना) *[#R-7]*
To state as a fact; assert publicly

Syno: Confirm (सुनिश्चित करना)

Anto: Refuse (इनकार करना), Disagree (असहमत होना)

77 **Affirmative** (Adj.) - (सकारात्मक) *[#R-2]*
Expressing agreement or consent

Syno: Positive (सकारात्मक)

Anto: Negative (नकारात्मक)

78 Affliction (N.) - (पीड़ा) *[#R-3 (1)]*
Something that causes pain or suffering

Syno: Bane (अभिशाप) {Distress (परेशानी)}

Anto: Pleasure (आनंद), Consolation (सांत्वना)

79 Affluence (N.) - (धन-वैभव) *[#R-5 (7)]*
The state of having great wealth

Syno: Wealth (धन), Richness (संपन्नता)

Anto: Poverty (गरीबी) {Indigence (दरिद्रता), Destitution (निर्धनता)}

80 Affluent (Adj.) - (धनी) *[#R-11 (7)]*
Having a great deal of money; wealthy

Syno: Prosperous (समृद्ध), Wealthy (धनवान)

Anto: Poor (गरीब), Destitute (अत्यंत गरीब) {Deprived (वंचित), Impoverished (दरिद्र)}

81 **Aggrandize** (V.) - (शक्ति बढ़ाना)~ *[#R-1 (1)]*
To increase the power, status, or wealth

Syno: {Augment (वृद्धि करना)}

Anto: Belittle (महत्व घटाना)

82 Aggravate (V.) - (बिगाड़ना, चिढ़ाना) *[#R-9 (3)]*
To make worse; to irritate or annoy

Syno: Irritate (चिढ़ाना), Intensify (तेज़ करना), Annoy (परेशान करना)

Anto: Alleviate (शांत करना), Soothe (सांत्वना देना) {Conciliate (मेल-मिलाप करना)}

83 **Agile** (Adj.) - (फुर्तीला) *[#R-7 (1)]*
Able to move quickly and easily

Syno: Nimble (चुस्त), Active (सक्रिय), Quick (तेज) {Energetic (ऊर्जावान)}

Anto: Lethargic (सुस्त), Sluggish (धीमा)

84 Agitate (V.) - (उत्तेजित करना; भड़काना) *[#R-4]*
To make someone nervous or upset; To stir up public feeling or movement

Syno: Upset (अशांत करना)

Anto: Pacify (शांत करना), Calm (शांति देना), Soothe (सांत्वना देना)

85 Agony (N.) - (कष्ट)~ *[#R-7 (1)]*
Extreme physical or mental suffering

Syno: Pain (दर्द)

Anto: Pleasure (आनंद), Delight (ख़ुशी), Comfort (आराम), Ecstasy (परमानंद)

86 Agreement (N.) - (समझौता) *[#R-2 (1)]*
A situation in which people have the same opinion or a formal arrangement

Syno: Consent (सहमति)

Anto: Discord (असहमति)

87 **Alacrity** (N.) - (तत्परता) *[#R-3 (4)]*
Brisk and cheerful readiness

Syno: Willingness (इच्छा), Eagerness (उत्सुकता) {Cheerfulness (प्रसन्नता)}

Anto: Indifference (उदासीनता) {Apathy (उदासीनता), Lethargy (सुस्ती)}

88 Alert (Adj.) - (सतर्क) *[#R-5 (3)]*

Quick to notice and react to danger or problems

Syno: Watchful (सावधान), Vigilant (निगरानी रखने वाला)

Anto: Careless (बेपरवाह), Distracted (विचलित) {Inattentive (अनमना)}

89 Alien (N.) - (विदेशी व्यक्ति)~ *[#R-2 (2)]*
A person from another place

Syno: {Foreigner (विदेशी)}

Anto: Native (स्थानीय)

90 Alienate (V.) - (दूर कर देना) *[#R-2 (1)]*
To cause someone to feel isolated or estranged

Syno: Estrange (अलग करना)

Anto: Reconcile (मेल-मिलाप करना)

91 **Alight** (V.) - (उतरना) *[#R-2]*
To descend from a train, bus, or other form of transport

Syno: Descend (उतरना)

Anto: Embark (चढ़ना)

92 **Allay** (V.) - (शांत करना) *[#R-5 (2)]*
To diminish or put at rest fear, suspicion, or worry

Syno: Relieve (राहत देना), Pacify (शांत करना) {Assuage (तसल्ली देना)}

Anto: Aggravate (बढ़ाना, भड़काना)

93 **Allege** (V.) - (आरोप लगाना) *[#R-2]*
To claim that someone has done something illegal or wrong, typically without proof

Syno: Charge (आरोप लगाना)

Anto: Deny (इनकार करना)

94 Alleviate (V.) - (कम करना, राहत देना) *[#R-9 (12)]*
To reduce or ease pain, suffering, or difficulty

Syno: Mitigate (कम करना), Relieve (राहत देना), Diminish (घटना), Reduce (घटाना) {Mollify (शांत करना), Ameliorate (सुधारना), Lighten (हल्का करना), Soothe (सांत्वना देना), Lessen (न्यून करना)}

Anto: Aggravate (बढ़ाना) {Intensify (तीव्र करना), Escalate (तीव्र करना)}

95 **Allow** (V.) - (अनुमति देना) *[#R-1 (3)]*
To give someone permission to do something

Syno: Permit (अनुमति देना)

Anto: {Forbid (मना करना), Prohibit (प्रतिबंध लगाना)}

96 Allure (N./V.) - (मोह; आकर्षित करना) *[#R-7 (1)]*
The power to attract (N.); To attract or tempt (V.)

Syno: Appeal (आकर्षण); Tempt (प्रलोभित करना), Attract (आकर्षित करना)

Anto: Repulse (विकर्षित करना)

97 **Ally** (N.) - (मित्र) *[#R-4 (2)]*
A person or group united for a common purpose

Syno: {Supporter (समर्थक), Associate (सहयोगी)}

Anto: Enemy (शत्रु)

98 **Aloof** (Adj.) - (अलग-थलग) *[#R-2 (1)]*
Not friendly or forthcoming; cool and distant

Syno: Detached (अलग) {Unfriendly (अमित्र)}

Anto: Friendly (मित्रवत)

99 **Alter** (V.) - (बदलना) *[#R-3]*
To change in form, nature, or character

Syno: Transform (परिवर्तित करना)

Anto: Preserve (संरक्षित रखना)

100 **Alteration** (N.) - (परिवर्तन, बदलाव) *[#R-1 (3)]*
The act or process of changing

Syno: Modification (संशोधन) {Amendment (संशोधन)}

Anto: {Fixation (स्थिरता), Stagnation (ठहराव)}

101 Altruistic (Adj.) - (परोपकारी) *[#R-2 (2)]*
Showing selfless concern for the well-being of others

Syno: Philanthropic (परहितकारी) {Generous (उदार)}

Anto: Selfish (स्वार्थी) {Egoistic (स्वार्थी)}

102 Amass (V.) - (जमा करना) *[#R-2 (2)]*
To gather or collect a large amount over time

Syno: Gather (एकत्र करना)

Anto: Distribute (वितरित करना) {Scatter (बिखेरना)}

103 Amateur (Adj./N.) - (गैर-पेशेवर; नौसिखिया)~ *[#R-10 (1)]*
Not professional (Adj.); A person who does an activity as a hobby (N.)

Syno: Beginner (नौसिखिया)

Anto: Professional (पेशेवर); Expert (विशेषज्ञ)

104 **Amazing** (Adj.) - (अद्भुत) *[#R-2]*
Causing great surprise or wonder

Syno: Astonishing (हैरान करने वाला)

Anto: Ordinary (साधारण)

105 Ambiguous (Adj.) - (अस्पष्ट)~ *[#R-7 (5)]*
Having more than one possible meaning; not clear

Syno: Vague (अस्पष्ट)

Anto: Clear (स्पष्ट), Certain (निश्चित), Precise

(सटीक) {Definite (सुनिश्चित), Unequivocal (असंदिग्ध)}

106 Ambition (N.) - (महत्वाकांक्षा) *[#R-2]*
A strong desire or determination to achieve something

Syno: Eagerness (उत्सुकता)

Anto: Laziness (आलस्य)

107 Ambitious (Adj.) - (महत्वाकांक्षी) *[#R-3 (1)]*
Having or showing a strong desire to achieve success, power, or a goal

Syno: Aspiring (आकांक्षी)

Anto: Unenthusiastic (उत्साहहीन), Lazy (आलसी)

108 **Ameliorate** (V.) - (सुधारना)~ *[#R-7 (8)]*
To make something bad or unsatisfactory better

Syno: Improve (बेहतर करना)

Anto: Worsen (बदतर बनाना), Exacerbate (और बिगाड़ना) {Deteriorate (और खराब होना), Aggravate (बिगाड़ना)}

109 **Amend** (V.) - (संशोधित करना) *[#R-4 (3)]*
To change or correct something to make it better or more accurate

Syno: Alter (बदलना), Rectify (सही करना) {Change (परिवर्तन करना)}

Anto: {Worsen (खराब करना)}

110 Amiable (Adj.) - (मिलनसार) *[#R-9 (14)]*
Having or displaying a friendly and pleasant manner

Syno: Friendly (मित्रवत) {Good-Natured (अच्छे स्वभाव वाला), Pleasant (सुखद), Harmonious (सामंजस्यपूर्ण), Cordial (हार्दिक)}

Anto: Hostile (शत्रुतापूर्ण), Unfriendly (अमित्रवत) {Disagreeable (अप्रिय)}

111 Amicable (Adj.) - (मैत्रीपूर्ण (समझौते के लिए))~ *[#R-3 (2)]*
Showing a spirit of friendliness and goodwill, especially in settling disagreements

Syno: Friendly (मित्रतापूर्ण)

Anto: Unfriendly (अमित्रतापूर्ण), Hostile (शत्रुतापूर्ण)

112 Amorphous (Adj.) - (आकारहीन) *[#R-1 (2)]*
Without a clearly defined shape or form

Syno: {Nebulous (धुंधला)}

Anto: Definite (निश्चित)

113 **Ample** (Adj.) - (प्रचुर) *[#R-9 (4)]*
Enough or more than enough; plentiful

Syno: Sufficient (पर्याप्त), Abundant (प्रचुर मात्रा में) {Plentiful (भरपूर)}

Anto: Scarce (दुर्लभ), Meagre (अल्प) {Insufficient (अपर्याप्त)}

114 Amplify (V.) - (बढ़ाना) *[#R-8 (2)]*
To make something stronger, larger, louder, or more intense

Syno: Magnify (विस्तारित करना), Boost (बढ़ावा देना) {Increase (वृद्धि करना)}

Anto: Reduce (कम करना), Contract (संकुचित करना), Lessen (घटाना)

115 **Amusing** (Adj.) - (मनोरंजक) *[#R-2]*
Causing laughter, fun, or enjoyment

Syno: Laughable (हँसी योग्य)

Anto: Boring (उबाऊ)

116 Anachronistic (Adj.) - (पुराने ज़माने का) *[#R-1 (2)]*
Belonging to a different time; old-fashioned or out of date

Syno: Outdated (अप्रचलित)

Anto: {Contemporary (समकालीन)}

117 **Analogous** (Adj.) - (समान) *[#R-2 (2)]*
Similar or comparable in certain respects

Syno: {Similar (सदृश)}

Anto: Dissimilar (असमान), Disagreeing (विपरीत) {Different (भिन्न)}

118 Ancestor (N.) - (पूर्वज) *[#R-2 (1)]*
A person from whom one is descended

Syno: Forefather (पितामह) {Forerunner (अग्रदूत)}

Anto: Descendant (वंशज)

119 Ancient (Adj.) - (प्राचीन)~ *[#R-3 (1)]*
Belonging to the very distant past and no longer in existence

Syno: Antique (पुरातन)

Anto: Modern (आधुनिक)

120 **Angry** (Adj.) - (क्रोधित) *[#R-2]*
Feeling strong anger or rage

Syno: Furious (क्रोधित)

Anto: Serene (शांत)

121 Annihilate (V.) - (नष्ट करना)~ *[#R-4 (2)]*
To destroy completely

Syno: Destroy (विनाश करना)

Anto: {Fabricate (बनाना), Create (निर्माण करना)}

122 **Annoy** (V.) - (परेशान करना) *[#R-10 (1)]*
To irritate someone or make them slightly angry

Syno: Offend (नाराज़ करना), Irritate (चिढ़ाना),

Anger (क्रोधित करना), Disturb (परेशान करना)

Anto: Satisfy (संतुष्ट करना), Comfort (सांत्वना देना), Gratify (तृप्त करना), Delight (आनन्दित करना) {Please (प्रसन्न करना)}

123 **Anodyne** (Adj.) - (सौम्य) *[#R-1 (1)]*
Soothing and not offensive

Syno: Benign (हानिरहित)

Anto: {Painful (पीड़ादायक)}

124 **Anomalous** (Adj.) - (असामान्य) *[#R-4]*
Deviating from what is standard, normal, or expected

Syno: Peculiar (विचित्र)

Anto: Customary (परंपरागत), Regular (नियमित), Conforming (अनुरूप)

125 **Antipathy** (N.) - (घृणा)~ *[#R-5 (3)]*
A strong feeling of dislike or hostility

Syno: Enmity (शत्रुता), Dislike (नापसंद)

Anto: Love (प्रेम) {Appreciation (प्रशंसा), Rapport (मेल-जोल)}

126 Antique (Adj.) - (प्राचीन) *[#R-10]*
Belonging to ancient times; very old

Syno: Ancient (पुरातन), Outdated (पुराना)

Anto: Recent (हाल का), Modern (आधुनिक)

127 Anxiety (N.) - (चिंता; बेचैनी) *[#R-7]*
A feeling of worry, nervousness, or unease

Syno: Worry (फ़िक्र), Distress (परेशानी)

Anto: Placidity (प्रशांतता), Calmness (शांति), Certainty (निश्चितता)

128 Anxious (Adj.) - (चिंतित) *[#R-7 (5)]*
Feeling or showing worry or nervousness

Syno: Nervous (बेचैन), Apprehensive (आशंकित) {Eager (उत्सुक), Worried (परेशान), Scared (डरा हुआ)}

Anto: Calm (शांत), Unconcerned (बेपरवाह) {Composed (संयत)}

129 Apathy (N.) - (उदासीनता)~ *[#R-6 (2)]*
Lack of interest, enthusiasm, or concern

Syno: Indifference (निरपेक्षता), Disinterest (उदासी) {Lethargy (सुस्ती)}

Anto: Interest (दिलचस्पी), Enthusiasm (उत्साह) {Sensibility (संवेदनशीलता)}

130 **Apex** (N.) - (शिखर) *[#R-5 (1)]*
The top or highest part of something

Syno: Pinnacle (चोटी), Top (शीर्ष)

Anto: Base (आधार), Bottom (तल) {Abyss (गहराई)}

131 **Aplomb** (N.) - (आत्मविश्वास) *[#R-1 (1)]*
Self-confidence in difficult situations

Syno: Self-Assurance (आत्मविश्वास)

Anto: {Diffidence (आत्मविश्वास की कमी)}

132 **Apologetic** (Adj.) - (क्षमाप्रार्थी) *[#R-1 (1)]*
Showing regret for an offense or mistake

Syno: Contrite (पश्चातापी)

Anto: {Impenitent (बिना पछतावे का)}

133 Appalling (Adj.) - (डरावना; भयावह)~ *[#R-7 (2)]*
Causing great shock or horror

Syno: Shocking (चौंकाने वाला) {Terrifying (भयानक), Harrowing (दिल दहलाने वाला)}

Anto: Consoling (सांत्वना देने वाला), Appealing (मनभावन)

134 Apparent (Adj.) - (स्पष्ट) *[#R-9 (7)]*
Clearly visible; or seeming to be true but not necessarily so

Syno: Obvious (प्रत्यक्ष), Manifest (स्पष्ट), Seeming (जाहिर) {Evident (सुस्पष्ट), Presumed (अनुमानित)}

Anto: Ambiguous (अस्पष्ट), Hidden (छिपा हुआ) {Vague (अनिश्चित)}

135 **Apparition** (N.) - (भूत-प्रेत) *[#R-2]*
A ghost or ghostlike image of a person

Syno: Spirit (आत्मा)

Anto: Reality (वास्तविकता)

136 Appease (V.) - (शांत करना) *[#R-6 (2)]*
To pacify or calm someone by giving in to demands

Syno: Pacify (शांत करना)

Anto: Inflame (भड़काना) {Incense (क्रोधित करना), Frighten (डराना)}

137 **Applaud** (V.) - (सराहना करना) *[#R-7 (6)]*
To show approval by clapping or praising

Syno: Approve (अनुमोदन करना) {Praise (प्रशंसा करना)}

Anto: Denounce (निंदा करना), Criticize (आलोचना करना), Censure (निन्दा करना), Taunt (ताना मारना) {Castigate (डांटना)}

138 **Apportion** (V.) - (बाँटना) *[#R-1 (2)]*
To divide and distribute

Syno: Allocate (आवंटित करना)

Anto: {Assemble (इकट्ठा करना)}

139 Apposite (Adj.) - (उपयुक्त) *[#R-5 (2)]*
Apt or suitable for a particular situation

Syno: Appropriate (उचित), Relevant (संबंधित), Suitable (उपयुक्त)

Anto: Inappropriate (अनुपयुक्त)

140 **Appraise** (V.) - (मूल्यांकन करना) *[#R-2 (1)]*
To assess the value or quality of something

Syno: Judge (आंकना), Assess (आकलन करना)

Anto: {Neglect (उपेक्षा करना)}

141 Appreciation (N.) - (प्रशंसा) *[#R-2 (2)]*
Recognition and enjoyment of the good qualities of someone or something

Syno: {Gratitude (आभार), Admiration (सराहना)}

Anto: Antipathy (घृणा), Disregard (अनादर)

142 Apprehend (V.) - (गिरफ्तार करना; समझना) *[#R-1 (4)]*
To arrest someone for a crime; to understand or perceive

Syno: Arrest (गिरफ्तार करना) {Seize (पकड़ना), Fear (डरना)}

Anto: {Emancipate (मुक्त करना)}

143 **Apprehension** (N.) - (भय) *[#R-2 (2)]*
Anxiety or fear that something bad or unpleasant will happen

Syno: Fear (डर) {Anxiety (चिंता)}

Anto: Excitement (उत्साह) {Confidence (विश्वास)}

144 **Apprise** (V.) - (सूचित करना) *[#R-2 (5)]*
To inform or tell someone

Syno: Inform (जानकारी देना)

Anto: Hide (छिपाना) {Mislead (गुमराह करना)}

145 Appropriate (Adj.) - (उपयुक्त) *[#R-5 (3)]*
Suitable or proper for a situation

Syno: Fitting (उचित) {Suitable (उपयुक्त)}

Anto: Unsuitable (अनुचित), Irrelevant (असंगत), Improper (अनुचित) {Inapposite (अनुपयुक्त)}

146 Arbitrary (Adj.) - (मनमाना)~ *[#R-1 (3)]*
Based on personal choice rather than reason or rule

Syno: Random (अनियमित)

Anto: {Lawful (कानूनी), Regular (नियमित)}

147 **Arcane** (Adj.) - (गुप्त) *[#R-3 (2)]*
Understood by few; mysterious or secret

Syno: Mysterious (रहस्यमय), Hidden (छिपा हुआ) {Abstruse (समझने में कठिन)}

Anto: Public (सार्वजनिक) {Common (सामान्य)}

148 **Ardent** (Adj.) - (उत्साही) *[#R-5 (3)]*
Showing strong enthusiasm or passion

Syno: Passionate (जोशीला), Committed (प्रतिबद्ध) {Intense (तीव्र), Devoted (समर्पित)}

Anto: Apathetic (उदासीन)

149 Arduous (Adj.) - (कठिन) *[#R-2 (10)]*
Requiring great effort; difficult and tiring

Syno: Difficult (मुश्किल), Strenuous (श्रमसाध्य) {Challenging (चुनौतीपूर्ण)}

Anto: {Facile (सरल), Effortless (सहज), Easy (आसान), Doable (संभव), Smooth (सुगम), Trivial (मामूली)}

150 Argument (N.) - (तर्क-वितर्क; बहस) *[#R-3]*
A strong disagreement; or a reason or set of reasons given to support an idea

Syno: Explanation (स्पष्टीकरण)

Anto: Agreement (सहमति)

151 **Arid** (Adj.) - (शुष्क) *[#R-3 (1)]*
Having little or no rain; too dry to support vegetation

Syno: Dry (सूखा)

Anto: Wet (गीला), Fertile (उपजाऊ)

152 Aroma (N.) - (सुगंध) *[#R-4]*
A distinctive, typically pleasant smell

Syno: Scent (खुशबू), Fragrance (खुशबू)

Anto: Stink (दुर्गंध)

153 Arraign (V.) - (दोष लगाना) *[#R-5 (3)]*
To call someone before a court to answer a criminal charge

Syno: Prosecute (मुकदमा चलाना)

Anto: Free (मुक्त करना), Justify (सही ठहराना) {Exculpate (दोषमुक्त करना), Acquit (बरी करना), Pardon (क्षमा करना)}

154 Array (N.) - (समूह) *[#R-1 (2)]*
An impressive display or range of things

Syno: {Collection (संग्रह)}

Anto: Unit (इकाई)

155 Arrogance (N.) - (अहंकार)~ *[#R-2 (2)]*
The quality of being arrogant; overbearing pride

Syno: Haughtiness (घमंड) {Conceit (घमंड)}

Anto: Humility (विनम्रता) {Submissiveness (आज्ञाकारिता)}

156 Arrogant (Adj.) - (अभिमानी) *[#R-11 (5)]*
Showing too much pride

Syno: Haughty (घमंडी)

Anto: Modest (विनम्र), Humble (विनम्र)

157 Articulate (Adj.) - (स्पष्ट)~ *[#R-3 (2)]*
Expressing oneself readily, clearly, and effectively

Syno: Distinct (सुस्पष्ट)

Anto: Unclear (अस्पष्ट) {Ineloquent (अनाड़ी), Halting (अटक-अटक कर बोलने वाला)}

158 Ascend (V.) - (ऊपर उठना) *[#R-6 (2)]*
To move upward or go higher

Syno: Climb (चढ़ना)

Anto: Descend (नीचे उतरना) {Plunge (नीचे गिरना)}

159 Ascertain (V.) - (सुनिश्चित करना) *[#R-3 (2)]*
To find something out for certain; to make sure of

Syno: Discover (खोजना) {Verify (सत्यापित करना)}

Anto: Overlook (अनदेखी करना), Disprove (खंडन करना)

160 **Asperity** (N.) - (कठोरता) *[#R-3]*
Harshness of tone or manner

Syno: Harshness (सख्ती)

Anto: Civility (शिष्टाचार)

161 **Assault** (V.) - (आक्रमण करना) *[#R-5 (1)]*
To make a physical attack

Syno: Attack (हमला करना)

Anto: Defend (बचाव करना), Guard (सुरक्षा करना), Retreat (पीछे हटना)

162 **Assemble** (V.) - (इकट्ठा करना) *[#R-6 (1)]*
To gather together in one place for a common purpose

Syno: Amass (जमा करना) {Gather (एकत्र होना)}

Anto: Disperse (छितराना), Scatter (बिखेरना)

163 **Assent** (N.) - (सहमति)~ *[#R-1 (5)]*
The expression of approval or agreement

Syno: {Agreement (समझौता)}

Anto: Dissent (असहमति) {Disagreement (मतभेद)}

164 Assert (V.) - (जोर देकर कहना) *[#R-4]*
To state a fact or belief confidently and forcefully

Syno: Declare (घोषणा करना), Emphasize (जोर देना)

Anto: Abandon (त्यागना), Deny (इनकार करना)

165 Assertion (N.) - (घोषणा) *[#R-1 (1)]*
A confident and forceful statement of fact or belief

Syno: Declaration (घोषणा)

Anto: {Denial (इनकार)}

166 **Assertive** (Adj.) - (आत्मविश्वासी)~ *[#R-2 (2)]*
Having or showing a confident and forceful personality

Syno: Confident (आत्मविश्वासी), Domineering (दबंग)

Anto: {Retiring (संकोची)}

167 Assiduous (Adj.) - (परिश्रमी) *[#R-6 (4)]*
Showing great care and perseverance

Syno: Diligent (मेहनती) {Laborious (श्रमसाध्य), Meticulous (सूक्ष्मदर्शी)}

Anto: Idle (निष्क्रिय), Neglectful (लापरवाह) {Unoccupied (खाली)}

168 **Assist** (V.) - (सहायता करना) *[#R-4 (2)]*
To help someone, typically by doing a share of the work

Syno: Help (मदद करना), Facilitate (सुविधाजनक बनाना), Aid (सहायता करना)

Anto: Obstruct (बाधा डालना) {Counteract (विरोध करना)}

169 Assuage (V.) - (शांत करना) *[#R-2 (5)]*
To make a feeling less intense

Syno: Mollify (सांत्वना देना) {Alleviate (कम करना), Mitigate (शमन करना), Calm (शांत करना), Relieve (राहत देना)}

Anto: Provoke (उकसाना) {Traumatise (चोट पहुँचाना)}

170 **Astonishment** (N.) - (आश्चर्य) *[#R-4 (2)]*
Great surprise; sudden wonder or amazement

Syno: Surprise (आश्चर्य), Wonderment (हैरानी)

Anto: Calmness (शांति), Composure (संयम)

171 Astute (Adj.) - (चालाक) *[#R-6 (3)]*
Having sharp judgment or keen insight

Syno: Shrewd (चतुर) {Canny (चतुर)}

Anto: Gullible (भोला), Idiotic (मूर्खतापूर्ण), Stupid (मूर्ख) {Naive (भोला)}

172 Attack (N./V.) - (आक्रमण; हमला करना) *[#R-6 (2)]*
An act of violence (N.); To use violence to harm (V.)

Syno: Assault (हमला)

Anto: Defence (रक्षा) {Defend (रक्षा करना)}

173 **Attenuate** (V.) - (कमजोर करना) *[#R-2]*
To reduce force or effect

Syno: Weaken (कमजोर करना)

Anto: Strengthen (मजबूत करना)

174 Attract (V.) - (आकर्षित करना) *[#R-11 (3)]*
To draw someone by appealing qualities

Syno: Fascinate (मोहित करना), Entice (लुभाना) {Engage (आकर्षित करना)}

Anto: Repel (पीछे हटाना), Deter (रोकना), Repulse (विकर्षित करना)

175 Audacious (Adj.) - (साहसी)~ *[#R-5 (7)]*
Showing willingness to take bold risks

Syno: Bold (निर्भीक) {Daring (निडर), Brave (वीर), Courageous (साहसी), Cheeky (मुँहफट)}

Anto: Cowardly (कायर), Timid (डरपोक) {Timorous (डरा हुआ)}

176 Audacity (N.) - (दुस्साहस) *[#R-9 (5)]*
Bold behavior that can seem rude

Syno: Nerve (हिम्मत), Boldness (साहस)

Anto: Cowardice (कायरता), Timidity (डरपोकपन), Modesty (विनम्रता) {Gentility (शिष्टता), Politeness (शालीनता)}

177 Augment (V.) - (वृद्धि करना) *[#R-3 (2)]*
To make something greater by adding to it

Syno: {Enhance (बेहतर बनाना)}

Anto: Decrease (घटाना), Diminish (कम करना), Degrade (खराब करना)

178 **August** (Adj.) - (प्रतिष्ठित) *[#R-3 (2)]*
Respected and impressive

Syno: Majestic (शानदार), Dignified (गरिमामय), Eminent (प्रसिद्ध)

Anto: {Humble (विनम्र)}

179 Auspicious (Adj.) - (शुभ) *[#R-4 (2)]*
Showing signs of success or good fortune

Syno: Fortunate (भाग्यशाली), Favourable (अनुकूल)

Anto: Ominous (अशुभ), Unlucky (बदकिस्मत)

180 Austere (Adj.) - (सादा; सख्त)~ *[#R-7 (5)]*
Very simple; plain; strict in manner or lifestyle; without luxury or decoration

Syno: Strict (कठोर), Unadorned (सादा), Stern (कड़क) {Sombre (गंभीर)}

Anto: Genial (मिलनसार) {Luxurious (विलासितापूर्ण), Flexible (लचीला)}

181 Authentic (Adj.) - (विश्वसनीय, असली)~ *[#R-9 (8)]*
Genuine; real; true in origin; not fake or copied

Syno: Genuine (वास्तविक)

Anto: False (असत्य), Fake (नकली) {Spurious (नकली), Falsified (जाली)}

182 Autonomy (N.) - (स्वराज्य)~ *[#R-9 (1)]*
The right or condition of self-government

Syno: Independence (स्वतंत्रता)

Anto: Dependence (निर्भरता)

183 Avarice (N.) - (लालच)~ *[#R-1 (2)]*
Extreme greed for wealth or material gain

Syno: Greed (लोभ)

Anto: {Charity (दान)}

184 Aversion (N.) - (घृणा) *[#R-1 (7)]*
A strong dislike or disinclination

Syno: Dislike (नापसंद) {Hostility (शत्रुता)}

Anto: {Liking (पसंद), Attraction (आकर्षण)}

185 **Avert** (V.) - (रोकना) *[#R-2 (1)]*
To turn away or prevent something undesirable

Syno: Prevent (रोकना)

Anto: Aid (सहायता करना)

186 **Avoid** (V.) - (बचना; टालना) *[#R-4 (2)]*
To keep away from or stop oneself from doing something

Syno: Evade (टालना)

Anto: Meet (मिलना) {Seek (खोजना)}

187 Awful (Adj.) - (ख़राब) *[#R-2 (1)]*
Very bad or unpleasant

Syno: Terrible (बहुत बुरा)

Anto: Wonderful (अद्भुत)

188 Awkward (Adj.) - (बेढंगा) *[#R-10 (4)]*
Clumsy or ungraceful; or causing difficulty

Syno: Clumsy (अनाड़ी), Unskilful (अकुशल)

Anto: Convenient (सुविधाजनक), Graceful (गरिमापूर्ण) {Clever (चतुर)}

189 **Babble** (V.) - (बड़बड़ाना) *[#R-3]*
To talk foolishly or rapidly

Syno: Blabber (बकवास करना)

Anto: Quieten (शांत होना)

190 **Baffle** (V.) - (भ्रमित करना) *[#R-20 (2)]*
To confuse or puzzle someone; to hinder or prevent from achieving a goal

Syno: Puzzle (उलझाना), Perplex (उलझन में डालना), Confuse (भ्रमित करना)

Anto: {Enlighten (स्पष्ट करना), Facilitate (सुगम बनाना)}

191 **Banal** (Adj.) - (तुच्छ, साधारण) *[#R-2 (3)]*
So lacking in originality as to be obvious and boring

Syno: Commonplace (सामान्य) {Mundane (साधारण)}

Anto: Novel (नवीन) {Ingenious (सृजनशील)}

192 **Bane** (N.) - (अभिशाप) *[#R-2 (2)]*

A cause of great distress or annoyance

Syno: Curse (शाप)

Anto: Boon (वरदान)

193 Barbaric (Adj.) - (अत्यंत क्रूर) *[#R-7 (6)]*
Extremely cruel, primitive, or uncivilized

Syno: Uncivilized (असभ्य), Crude (अशिष्ट) {Brutal (निर्दयी)}

Anto: Civilized (सभ्य)

194 **Barbarous** (Adj.) - (बहुत क्रूर, असभ्य) *[#R-2 (1)]*
Showing savage cruelty and lack of civilization

Syno: Brutal (क्रूर)

Anto: Civilized (सभ्य) {Polite (विनम्र)}

195 **Bare** (Adj.) - (नंगा, बहुत साधारण) *[#R-3]*
Without covering, exposed or simple, minimal

Syno: Basic (मूलभूत)

Anto: Covered (ढका हुआ)

196 Barren (Adj.) - (बंजर, बांझ) *[#R-20 (7)]*
Unable to produce vegetation; not productive; unable to have offspring

Syno: Unproductive (अनुत्पादक), Infertile (बंजर), Desolate (उजड़ा हुआ) {Unfruitful (फलहीन), Fruitless (निष्फल)}

Anto: Fertile (उपजाऊ)

197 Barrier (N.) - (बाधा, रुकावट) *[#R-3 (2)]*
A fence or other obstacle that prevents movement or access

Syno: Bound (सीमा)

Anto: Opening (खुला रास्ता)

198 Beautiful (Adj.) - (सुंदर) *[#R-6 (1)]*
Pleasing the senses or mind aesthetically

Syno: Handsome (आकर्षक), Pretty (मनोहर)

Anto: Ugly (कुरूप), Blemished (विकृत) {Hideous (भयानक)}

199 Beguile (V.) - (छल करना, धोखे से मोहित करना) *[#R-2 (2)]*
To charm or enchant someone, sometimes in a deceptive way

Syno: Deceive (छल करना) {Delude (भ्रम में डालना)}

Anto: {Repel (विकर्षित करना)}

200 **Bellicose** (Adj.) - (झगड़ालू)~ *[#R-1 (1)]*
Showing a desire to fight or argue

Syno: Warlike (युद्ध जैसा)

Anto: {Peaceful (शांतिपूर्ण)}

201 Belligerent (Adj.) - (लड़ाकू)~ *[#R-4 (5)]*
Hostile and aggressive

Syno: Hostile (शत्रुतापूर्ण), Antagonistic (विरोधी), Contentious (विवादास्पद)

Anto: Peaceful (शांतिपूर्ण) {Pacifist (शांतिवादी), Amiable (मिलनसार), Acquiescent (मौन सहमत)}

202 Benediction (N.) - (आशीर्वाद) *[#R-1 (1)]*
The utterance of a blessing

Syno: {Blessings (आशीर्वाद)}

Anto: Criticism (आलोचना)

203 Beneficial (Adj.) - (लाभदायक) *[#R-3]*
Favourable or advantageous; resulting in good

Syno: Advantageous (लाभकारी), Helpful (सहायक)

Anto: Harmful (हानिकारक)

204 Benevolence (N.) - (परोपकार) *[#R-6 (1)]*
The quality of being kind and well-meaning

Syno: Kindness (दयालुता), Compassion (करुणा)

Anto: Cruelty (क्रूरता) {Acrimony (कटुता)}

205 Benevolent (Adj.) - (परोपकारी, दयालु) *[#R-18 (14)]*
Kind and wishing good for others

Syno: Kind (दयालु), Generous (उदार), Gracious (कृपालु), Compassionate (करुणामय) {Kind-Hearted (नेकदिल)}

Anto: Malevolent (दुर्भावनापूर्ण), Merciless (निर्दयी), Stingy (कंजूस), Cruel (क्रूर), Unkind (दयाहीन) {Selfish (स्वार्थी), Miserly (कंजूस), Malignant (घातक), Malicious (द्वेषपूर्ण)}

206 Benign (Adj.) - (दयालु, हानिरहित) *[#R-9 (1)]*
Gentle, kind, and not harmful

Syno: Favourable (हितकारी)

Anto: Malignant (घातक), Wicked (दुष्ट)

207 Bereavement (N.) - (शोक, मृत्यु-जनित वियोग) *[#R-3]*
The state of suffering loss, especially the death of a loved one

Syno: Deprivation (अभाव), Grief (दुःख)

Anto: Joy (आनंद)

208 **Beseech** (V.) - (विनती करना) *[#R-5 (3)]*
To ask someone urgently and emotionally

Syno: Beg (भीख माँगना), Implore (गुहार लगाना) {Ask (पूछना), Request (निवेदन करना)}

Anto: Command (आज्ञा देना)

209 Betrayal (N.) - (धोखा) *[#R-5 (1)]*
The act of being disloyal to someone who trusts you

Syno: {Treachery (विश्वासघात)}

Anto: Protection (सुरक्षा), Loyalty (निष्ठा)

210 Bewilder (V.) - (चकित करना) *[#R-1 (1)]*
To cause someone to become perplexed and confused

Syno: {Baffle (हैरान करना)}

Anto: Enlighten (प्रबुद्ध करना)

211 Bifurcate (V.) - (दो भागों में विभाजित करना) *[#R-5]*
To divide into two branches or parts

Syno: Split (विभाजित करना), Divide (विभाजित करना)

Anto: Combine (जोड़ना)

212 Bizarre (Adj.) - (विचित्र)~ *[#R-5 (2)]*
Very strange or unusual

Syno: Grotesque (विकृत), Odd (अनोखा), Weird (अजीब) {Unusual (असामान्य)}

Anto: Usual (सामान्य), Ordinary (साधारण)

213 Blame (V.) - (दोष लगाना) *[#R-2 (1)]*
To assign responsibility for a fault

Syno: {Accuse (आरोप लगाना)}

Anto: Praise (प्रशंसा करना), Compliment (तारीफ करना)

214 **Blasphemous** (Adj.) - (धर्मनिंदक) *[#R-2]*
Sacrilegious against God or sacred things

Syno: Profane (अपवित्र)

Anto: Pious (धार्मिक)

215 Blatant (Adj.) - (स्पष्ट, खुल्लम-खुल्ला)~ *[#R-1 (3)]*
Very obvious or done openly without shame

Syno: Obvious (प्रत्यक्ष)

Anto: {Concealed (छिपा हुआ), Subtle (सूक्ष्म)}

216 Bleak (Adj.) - (उदास, निराशाजनक) *[#R-10 (8)]*
Cold, empty, or without hope

Syno: Depressing (निराशाजनक), Grim (भयानक), Gloomy (उदास)

Anto: Bright (प्रफुल्लित), Cheerful (आनन्दित), Cordial (सौहार्दपूर्ण) {Verdant (हरा-भरा), Lush (घना)}

217 **Blend** (V.) - (मिलाना) *[#R-5 (1)]*
To mix or combine things smoothly

Syno: Merge (विलय करना), Fuse (मिलना), Mix (मिलाना), Combine (जोड़ना)

Anto: {Separate (अलग करना)}

218 Bliss (N.) - (पूर्ण आनंद) *[#R-8]*
Perfect happiness or great joy

Syno: Happiness (खुशी), Joy (आनंद), Pleasure (सुख), Euphoria (अत्यधिक आनंद)

Anto: Sorrow (दुःख), Misery (दुर्दशा)

219 **Blissful** (Adj.) - (अत्यंत आनंदित) *[#R-3]*
Extremely happy and full of joy

Syno: Joyful (आनंदित)

Anto: Miserable (दुखी)

220 **Blistering** (Adj.) - (अत्यधिक गर्म) *[#R-4 (2)]*
Very hot and burning strongly

Syno: {Scorching (बहुत गर्म)}

Anto: Chilly (ठंडा)

221 Block (V.) - (रोकना) *[#R-1 (1)]*
To stop or prevent movement

Syno: {Obstruct (रोकना)}

Anto: Clear (साफ़ करना)

222 Bloom (N./V.) - (फूल; विकसित होना) *[#R-3]*
A flower (N.); To produce flowers or flourish (V.)

Syno: Flower (फूल)

Anto: Wither (मुरझाना)

223 **Blunt** (Adj.) - (कम धार वाला; मुँहफट) *[#R-10 (5)]*
Not sharp; rude and very direct in speech

Syno: Dull (कम तेज़), Insensitive (असंवेदनशील) {Snippy (रूखा)}

Anto: Sharp (तेज़), Polite (विनम्र) {Pointed (नुकीला), Edgy (नुकीला)}

224 Boast (N./V.) - (शेखी; डिंग हाँकना) *[#R-1 (2)]*
A thing to be proud of (N.); To speak with excessive pride (V.)

Syno: Pride (गर्व) {Brag (डींग हाँकना)}

Anto: {Deprecate (निंदा करना)}

225 Bogus (Adj.) - (जाली) *[#R-2 (1)]*
Not genuine or true

Syno: Fake (नकली), False (झूठा)

Anto: {Authentic (प्रामाणिक)}

226 Boisterous (Adj.) - (शोरगुल वाला, उपद्रवी) *[#R-16 (8)]*
Very noisy, energetic, and hard to control

Syno: Noisy (शोरगुल वाला), Clamorous (कोलाहलपूर्ण) {Rowdy (उपद्रवी), Cheerful (प्रसन्न)}

Anto: Calm (शांत), Peaceful (शांतिपूर्ण), Placid (स्थिर), Quiet (चुप) {Restrained (संयमित), Silent (मौन), Solemn (गंभीर), Phlegmatic (अप्रभावित)}

227 **Boldness** (N.) - (साहस) *[#R-3]*
Confidence and courage; willingness to take risks

Syno: Bravery (वीरता)

Anto: Timidity (डरपोकपन)

228 Bombastic (Adj.) - (बड़े-बड़े शब्दों वाला, आडंबरपूर्ण)~ *[#R-5]*
Using big, showy, or exaggerated words
Syno: Pretentious (दिखावटी)
Anto: Plain (सरल), Simple (सहज)

229 **Bossy** (Adj.) - (हुक्म चलाने वाला) *[#R-3]*
Fond of giving people orders; domineering
Syno: Controlling (नियंत्रणकारी)
Anto: Submissive (आज्ञाकारी)

230 **Bountiful** (Adj.) - (उदार, प्रचुर) *[#R-2]*
Large in quantity and generous in giving
Syno: Generous (दानशील)
Anto: Meagre (अल्प)

231 **Brave** (Adj.) - (साहसी) *[#R-15 (4)]*
Showing courage or ready to face danger
Syno: Daring (साहसी), Fearless (निडर), Courageous (बहादुर)
Anto: Cowardly (कायर), Timid (डरपोक) {Fearful (डरपोक)}

232 Brazen (Adj.) - (बेशर्म) *[#R-6 (1)]*
Showing boldness or shameless behaviour
Syno: Bold (साहसी), Unashamed (निर्लज्ज)
Anto: Modest (विनम्र), Timid (डरपोक) {Shy (संकोची)}

233 **Breach** (N.) - (उल्लंघन)~ *[#R-1 (2)]*
An act of breaking a rule or gap
Syno: Violation (उल्लंघन)
Anto: {Abidance (पालन)}

234 Brevity (N.) - (संक्षिप्तता) *[#R-1 (3)]*
Concise use of words; shortness of time
Syno: Crispness (सुस्पष्टता) {Concision (संक्षिप्तता)}
Anto: {Verbosity (शब्दाडंबर)}

235 Brief (Adj.) - (संक्षिप्त) *[#R-2 (3)]*
Short in time or length; concise
Syno: {Concise (संक्षिप्त), Short (छोटा)}
Anto: Elaborate (विस्तृत), Lengthy (लंबा)

236 **Bright** (Adj.) - (चमकदार) *[#R-6 (2)]*
Giving out or reflecting much light; shining
Syno: Radiant (चमकीला)
Anto: Bleak (धुंधला), Dusky (कम रोशनी वाला), Dull (बेरौनक) {Dark (अंधेरा)}

237 Brisk (Adj.) - (तेज़) *[#R-6 (3)]*
Active, fast, and energetic
Syno: Quick (फुर्तीला), Energetic (ऊर्जावान) {Hurried (जल्दबाज़)}
Anto: Slow (धीमा) {Lazy (आलसी), Idle (निष्क्रिय)}

238 Brittle (Adj.) - (भंगुर)~ *[#R-11 (2)]*
Hard but liable to break easily
Syno: Fragile (नाज़ुक)
Anto: Strong (मजबूत), Resilient (लचीला), Robust (तंदुरुस्त) {Unbreakable (अटूट)}

239 Broad (Adj.) - (चौड़ा) *[#R-3]*
Having a larger distance from side to side; wide
Syno: Wide (विस्तृत)
Anto: Narrow (संकीर्ण)

240 Brusque (Adj.) - (रूखा) *[#R-1 (1)]*
Abrupt or offhand in speech or manner
Syno: Abrupt (रूखा)
Anto: {Courteous (विनम्र)}

241 Brutal (Adj.) - (निर्दयी) *[#R-6 (1)]*
Extremely cruel, violent, or harsh
Syno: Savage (बर्बर), Cruel (क्रूर), Ruthless (निर्दय)
Anto: Humane (मानवीय)

242 Bucolic (Adj.) - (ग्रामीण) *[#R-1 (3)]*
Relating to the pleasant aspects of the countryside and country life
Syno: {Pastoral (ग्राम्य), Rural (ग्रामीण)}
Anto: Urban (शहरी)

243 Buoyant (Adj.) - (तैरता हुआ, खुशमिज़ाज) *[#R-4 (3)]*
Able to float or rise; Cheerful, positive, and lively in mood
Syno: Cheerful (खुशमिज़ाज) {Upbeat (उत्साहित), Floating (तैरता हुआ)}
Anto: Gloomy (उदास), Weighted (भारी किया हुआ) {Heavy (भारी)}

244 **Bustle** (N.) - (हड़बड़ी) *[#R-2 (1)]*
Busy excited activity
Syno: Haste (जल्दबाज़ी), Rush (जल्दी)
Anto: {Stillness (स्थिरता)}

245 Cacophony (N.) - (कोलाहल, कर्कश ध्वनि)~ *[#R-10 (4)]*
A harsh, jarring, or discordant mixture of sounds
Syno: Noise (शोर), Discord (कलह)
Anto: Harmony (सुरों का मेल), Symphony (मधुर संगीत)

246 **Cajole** (V.) - (फुसलाना) *[#R-5 (4)]*
To persuade someone by sustained coaxing or flattery

Syno: Flatter (चापलूसी करना), Entice (लुभाना), Persuade (मनाना) {Deceive (धोखा देना)}

Anto: Bully (धमकाना), Repulse (विकर्षित करना)

247 Calamity (N.) - (आपदा) *[#R-4 (4)]*
An event causing great damage or distress

Syno: Catastrophe (महाविपत्ति), Disaster (विपत्ति), Debacle (पराजय) {Adversity (प्रतिकूलता)}

Anto: Happiness (खुशी) {Blessing (आशीर्वाद)}

248 Callous (Adj.) - (कठोर, संवेदनाहीन)~ *[#R-13 (5)]*
Showing no sympathy or cruel disregard for others

Syno: Brutal (निर्दयी), Insensitive (संवेदनहीन), Cruel (क्रूर) {Unfeeling (असंवेदनशील)}

Anto: Sensitive (संवेदनशील), Sympathetic (सहानुभूतिपूर्ण), Merciful (दयालु), Tender (कोमल), Caring (देखभाल करने वाला), Concerned (ध्यान देने वाला) {Kind (दयालु), Considerate (विचारशील)}

249 **Callow** (Adj.) - (अनुभवहीन) *[#R-4]*
Inexperienced and immature, especially due to youth

Syno: Inexperienced (अनुभवहीन)

Anto: Sophisticated (परिष्कृत)

250 **Calm** (Adj./N.) - (शांत; स्थिरता) *[#R-12 (4)]*
Peaceful and not excited (Adj.); A state of peace (N.)

Syno: Peaceful (शांतिपूर्ण), Relaxed (तनाव मुक्त), Quiet (शांत), Placid (शांत, स्थिर) {Unruffled (अविचलित)}

Anto: Excited (उत्तेजित), Turbulent (अशांत), Upset (व्याकुल); Frenzy (उन्माद), Agitation (उत्तेजना) {Stormy (तूफानी)}

251 Camouflage (N./V.) - (छलावरण; छिपाना)~ *[#R-9 (1)]*
A disguise to hide (N.); To conceal or hide (V.)

Syno: Disguise (भेष बदलना, छिपाना)

Anto: Reveal (प्रकट करना), Exhibit (प्रदर्शित करना)

252 **Candid** (Adj.) - (निष्कपट, स्पष्ट) *[#R-25 (10)]*
Truthful and straightforward

Syno: Frank (स्पष्टवादी), Honest (ईमानदार), Forthright (निष्कपट), Blunt (स्पष्टवादी), Direct (सीधा) {Outspoken (मुखर), Straightforward (सीधा)}

Anto: Devious (कपटी), Cunning (चालाक), Artful (धूर्त), Deceitful (धोखेबाज), Tactful (व्यवहारकुशल), Dishonest (बेईमान), Evasive (टालमटोल करने वाला), Biased (पक्षपाती), Guarded (सतर्क) {Diplomatic (कूटनीतिक)}

253 Candour (N.) - (स्पष्टवादिता) *[#R-1 (2)]*
The quality of being open and honest

Syno: Honesty (ईमानदारी)

Anto: {Deceit (छल)}

254 **Cantankerous** (Adj.) - (झगड़ालू) *[#R-3 (5)]*
Bad-tempered, argumentative, and uncooperative

Syno: Quarrelsome (झगड़ालू) {Grouchy (चिड़चिड़ा), Ill-Tempered (बदमिजाज)}

Anto: {Convivial (आनंददायक)}

255 Capable (Adj.) - (सक्षम) *[#R-6 (1)]*
Having the ability or quality necessary to achieve something

Syno: Competent (योग्य)

Anto: Inept (अकुशल), Incompetent (अयोग्य)

256 Capricious (Adj.) - (मनमौजी) *[#R-8 (4)]*
Changing mood or behavior suddenly and unpredictably

Syno: Whimsical (सनकी), Arbitrary (मनमाना) {Moody (मिज़ाजी), Fluctuating (बदलता हुआ)}

Anto: Firm (दृढ़), Reasonable (उचित), Stable (स्थिर) {Steady (टिकाऊ)}

257 Captivate (V.) - (आकर्षित करना) *[#R-4 (3)]*
To attract and hold interest and attention; to charm

Syno: Allure (लुभाना) {Charm (मोहित करना), Fascinate (मोह लेना)}

Anto: Disillusion (मोहभंग करना), Distract (विचलित करना) {Offend (नाराज़ करना)}

258 **Captivating** (Adj.) - (आकर्षक) *[#R-4 (2)]*
Extremely attractive and holding attention completely

Syno: {Fascinating (मोहक)}

Anto: Boring (उबाऊ), Repugnant (घिनौना)

259 Capture (V./N.) - (पकड़ना; कब्जा) *[#R-5]*
To catch or seize (V.); The act of catching or taking control (N.)

Syno: Arrest (गिरफ्तार करना)

Anto: Release (रिहा करना), Liberate (मुक्त करना)

260 **Carnal** (Adj.) - (शारीरिक) *[#R-3 (1)]*
Relating to physical, especially sexual, needs

Syno: Earthly (सांसारिक)

Anto: Spiritual (आध्यात्मिक)

261 Casual (Adj.) - (अनौपचारिक) *[#R-4 (1)]*
Relaxed and informal; not planned

Syno: Occasional (यदाकदा)

Anto: Formal (औपचारिक), Planned (आयोजित)

262 Catastrophe (N.) - (आपदा)~ *[#R-5 (2)]*
An event causing great damage or suffering

Syno: Calamity (विपत्ति), Tragedy (त्रासदी), Disaster (विनाश)

Anto: Success (सफलता) {Blessing (आशीर्वाद)}

263 Catch (V.) - (पकड़ना) *[#R-1 (1)]*
To take hold or capture

Syno: {Grab (थामना)}

Anto: Drop (गिराना)

264 Caustic (Adj.) - (तीखा, कटु) *[#R-3 (1)]*
Able to burn tissue; sarcastically biting

Syno: Acidic (अम्लीय), Sarcastic (ताना मारने वाला)

Anto: Kind (दयालु) {Flattering (चापलूसीपूर्ण)}

265 Cautious (Adj.) - (सतर्क) *[#R-6 (6)]*
Careful to avoid potential problems or dangers

Syno: Careful (सावधान) {Vigilant (चौकन्ना), Alert (चौकस), Prudent (विवेकी)}

Anto: Negligent (लापरवाह), Reckless (असावधान) {Careless (बेपरवाह)}

266 Cavalier (Adj.) - (बेपरवाह) *[#R-3]*
Showing lack of concern; dismissive

Syno: Curt (रूखा)

Anto: Humble (विनम्र), Considerate (विचारशील)

267 Cease (V.) - (रोकना) *[#R-9 (3)]*
To bring or come to an end

Syno: Stop (रोकना), Conclude (समाप्त करना), Terminate (समाप्त करना) {Discontinue (बंद करना)}

Anto: Continue (जारी रखना), Initiate (आरंभ करना), Start (शुरू करना), Commence (प्रारंभ करना)

268 Celebrate (V.) - (उत्सव मनाना) *[#R-3]*
To mark a happy event with enjoyment

Syno: Honour (सम्मान करना), Rejoice (आनंद मनाना)

Anto: Disgrace (अपमान करना)

269 **Celerity** (N.) - (शीघ्रता) *[#R-3 (4)]*
Swiftness of movement

Syno: {Speed (गति)}

Anto: Slowness (धीमापन) {Sluggishness (सुस्ती)}

270 Celestial (Adj.) - (स्वर्गीय, आकाशीय) *[#R-2 (4)]*
Positioned in or relating to the sky

Syno: {Heavenly (स्वर्गीय)}

Anto: Hellish (नरक समान), Terrestrial (स्थलीय) {Earthly (धरातलीय)}

271 Censure (N./V.) - (आलोचना; निंदा करना)~ *[#R-4 (6)]*
Severe disapproval (N.); To criticise officially (V.)

Syno: Criticise (आलोचना करना) {Reprimand (फटकार), Condemn (निंदा करना), Rebuke (डाँट)}

Anto: Praise (प्रशंसा), Applause (तालियाँ) {Approve (मंजूरी देना)}

272 Certain (Adj.) - (निश्चित) *[#R-4 (1)]*
Known for sure; beyond doubt

Syno: Sure (पक्का), Definite (सुनिश्चित)

Anto: Doubtful (संदेहपूर्ण)

273 **Chagrin** (N.) - (शर्मिंदगी)~ *[#R-2]*
Distress or embarrassment at failure

Syno: Embarrassment (लज्जा)

Anto: Pleasure (आनंद)

274 Challenge (N./V.) - (समस्या; चुनौती देना) *[#R-5 (1)]*
A difficult task (N.); To question or dare (V.)

Syno: Objection (आपत्ति); Object (आपत्ति करना), Question (प्रश्न करना), Dare (चुनौती देना) {Confront (सामना करना)}

Anto: Solution (समाधान)

275 Change (V.) - (बदलना) *[#R-2 (1)]*
To make or become different

Syno: Alter (परिवर्तन करना)

Anto: {Stabilize (स्थिर करना)}

276 Chaos (N.) - (अव्यवस्था, अफरातफरी)~ *[#R-9 (2)]*
Complete disorder and confusion

Syno: Disorder (गड़बड़ी), Confusion (भ्रम), Disarray (अव्यवस्थित स्थिति)

Anto: Orderliness (क्रमबद्धता) {Order (क्रम), Arrangement (व्यवस्था)}

277 **Chaotic** (Adj.) - (अव्यवस्थित) *[#R-2 (3)]*
In complete confusion and disorder

Syno: {Confused (भ्रमित)}

Anto: Systematic (सुनियोजित), Organised (व्यवस्थित) {Orderly (क्रमबद्ध), Calm (शांत)}

278 Charming (Adj.) - (मनमोहक) *[#R-3]*
Pleasant or attractive

Syno: Delightful (आनंददायक)

Anto: Repulsive (घृणित)

279 **Chaste** (Adj.) - (पवित्र) *[#R-5 (2)]*
Not having any sexual nature or intention

Syno: Pure (शुद्ध) {Virtuous (चरित्रवान)}

Anto: Corrupt (भ्रष्ट) {Dirty (अपवित्र)}

280 **Chastise** (V.) - (सज़ा देना)~ *[#R-7 (2)]*
To rebuke or reprimand severely

Syno: Upbraid (फटकारना), Reprimand (डांटना), Discipline (अनुशासित करना), Flog (कोड़े मारना) {Punish (दंडित करना)}

Anto: Praise (प्रशंसा करना), Extol (बड़ाई करना) {Compliment (तारीफ करना)}

281 Chauvinism (N.) - (कट्टरता) *[#R-1 (2)]*
Excessive or prejudiced loyalty to one's own group

Syno: Zealotry (अतिउत्साह) {Jingoism (उग्र देशभक्ति)}

Anto: {Unbiasedness (निष्पक्षता)}

282 Cherish (V.) - (संजोना) *[#R-6 (3)]*
To protect and care for lovingly

Syno: Nurture (पालन-पोषण करना), Admire (प्रशंसा करना)

Anto: Abandon (त्याग देना), Despise (तिरस्कार करना) {Deprecate (निंदा करना), Discard (त्यागना), Detest (घृणा करना)}

283 **Chicanery** (N.) - (छल)~ *[#R-2]*
The use of tricks to deceive

Syno: Deception (धोखा)

Anto: Honesty (ईमानदारी)

284 **Chide** (V.) - (डाँटना) *[#R-3 (1)]*
To speak angrily to someone for a fault

Syno: Rebuke (फटकारना), Scold (डाँटना)

Anto: Applaud (सराहना करना)

285 Chivalrous (Adj.) - (शिष्ट, शौर्यवान) *[#R-4 (1)]*
Courteous and gallant, especially towards women

Syno: Heroic (वीरतापूर्ण) {Gallant (बहादुर)}

Anto: Cowardly (कायरतापूर्ण), Ungallant (अशिष्ट)

286 Chronic (Adj.) - (दीर्घकालिक)~ *[#R-4 (3)]*
Persisting for a long time or constantly recurring

Syno: Persistent (निरंतर)

Anto: Infrequent (कभी-कभार) {Temporary (अस्थायी), Acute (अल्पकालिक)}

287 **Churlish** (Adj.) - (असभ्य)~ *[#R-1 (3)]*
Rude in a mean-spirited and surly way

Syno: {Rude (अशिष्ट), Sullen (चिड़चिड़ा)}

Anto: Courteous (विनम्र) {Accommodating (सहयोगी)}

288 Circuitous (Adj.) - (घुमावदार) *[#R-2 (1)]*
Longer than the most direct way

Syno: Roundabout (चक्करदार)

Anto: Direct (सीधा)

289 Circumspect (Adj.) - (सावधान) *[#R-1 (3)]*
Wary and unwilling to take risks

Syno: Cautious (सतर्क) {Careful (सावधानीपूर्ण)}

Anto: {Careless (लापरवाह), Incautious (असावधान)}

290 **Clamorous** (Adj.) - (कोलाहलपूर्ण)~ *[#R-1 (1)]*
Making a loud and confused noise

Syno: {Boisterous (शोरगुल वाला)}

Anto: Quiet (शांत)

291 **Clamour** (N.) - (कोलाहल)~ *[#R-3]*
Loud and confused noise

Syno: Uproar (हंगामा)

Anto: Quiet (शांति)

292 Clandestine (Adj.) - (गुप्त) *[#R-8 (11)]*
Kept secret or done secretively

Syno: Secret (गोपनीय) {Covert (छिपा हुआ)}

Anto: Open (खुला), Overt (प्रत्यक्ष), Known (ज्ञात), Honest (निष्कपट) {Public (सार्वजनिक), Conspicuous (स्पष्ट), Legal (कानूनी)}

293 **Clarity** (N.) - (स्पष्टता) *[#R-1 (2)]*
The quality of being clear

Syno: Lucidity (सुबोधता)

Anto: {Confusion (उलझन)}

294 **Clash** (N.) - (टकराव) *[#R-2]*
A violent confrontation

Syno: Conflict (संघर्ष)

Anto: Harmony (सामंजस्य)

295 **Clumsy** (Adj.) - (अनाड़ी)~ *[#R-3]*
Awkward in movement or in handling things

Syno: Unskilful (अकुशल)

Anto: Graceful (सलीकेदार)

296 **Cluster** (N.) - (समूह) *[#R-2]*
A group of similar things or people positioned close together

Syno: Assemblage (जमावड़ा)

Anto: Individual (व्यक्ति)

297 Coarse (Adj.) - (खुरदुरा; असभ्य) *[#R-9 (9)]*
Rough or loose in texture or grain; Vulgar or crude in speech or manner

Syno: Rough (रूखा), Crude (भद्दा) {Scratchy (खरोंचदार)}

Anto: Smooth (चिकना), Gentle (कोमल), Refined

(परिष्कृत), Buttery (मक्खन जैसा) {Soft (मुलायम), Delicate (नाजुक), Fine (बारीक), Chaste (शालीन)}

298 **Coerce** (V.) - (दबाव डालना)~ *[#R-2 (1)]*
To persuade an unwilling person to do something by using force or threats

Syno: Pressurize (दबाव डालना) {Compel (मजबूर करना)}

Anto: Allow (अनुमति देना)

299 **Cogent** (Adj.) - (ठोस, युक्तिसंगत, प्रबल) *[#R-7 (4)]*
Clear, logical, and convincing

Syno: Effective (प्रभावी), Convincing (विश्वसनीय), Persuasive (मनाने वाला), Rational (तार्किक)

Anto: Unconvincing (अविश्वसनीय) {Ineffective (अप्रभावी)}

300 Collapse (V.) - (गिर जाना) *[#R-3]*
To fall down or fail suddenly

Syno: Fall (गिरना)

Anto: Flourish (फलना-फूलना), Mend (मरम्मत करना)

301 Colloquial (Adj.) - (बोलचाल संबंधी) *[#R-3 (2)]*
Used in ordinary conversation; not formal or literary

Syno: Familiar (परिचित), Conversational (वार्तालापिक)

Anto: Formal (औपचारिक) {Literary (साहित्यिक)}

302 Colossal (Adj.) - (विशाल) *[#R-13 (8)]*
Extremely large or great

Syno: Enormous (विराट), Gigantic (विशालकाय), Immense (अपार), Huge (बहुत बड़ा), Massive (विशाल)

Anto: Small (छोटा), Tiny (बहुत छोटा), Teeny (बहुत ही छोटा), Minimal (न्यूनतम) {Petite (नन्हा), Negligible (महत्वहीन), Short (नाटा)}

303 **Comely** (Adj.) - (सुहावना) *[#R-4]*
Pleasant to look at; attractive

Syno: Pretty (सुंदर)

Anto: Grotesque (बेढंगा)

304 **Comic** (Adj.) - (हास्यजनक) *[#R-4 (1)]*
Causing or meant to cause laughter

Syno: Funny (मजाकिया)

Anto: Tragic (दुखद)

305 **Command** (N.) - (आदेश) *[#R-3]*
An authoritative order

Syno: Instruction (निर्देश)

Anto: Request (निवेदन)

306 **Commence** (V.) - (शुरू करना) *[#R-10 (1)]*
To begin or start something

Syno: Start (आरंभ करना), Launch (शुरू करना), Initiate (प्रारंभ करना), Begin (शुरू करना)

Anto: Conclude (समाप्त करना), Close (बंद करना), Terminate (समाप्त करना), End (अंत करना)

307 Commendable (Adj.) - (प्रशंसनीय) *[#R-2]*
Deserving praise

Syno: Praiseworthy (प्रशंसा के योग्य)

Anto: Blameworthy (निंदनीय)

308 Commitment (N.) - (वचनबद्धता, प्रतिज्ञा) *[#R-1 (1)]*
The state of being dedicated to a cause or activity; A promise or pledge to do something

Syno: {Guarantee (गारंटी)}

Anto: Breach (उल्लंघन)

309 Committed (Adj.) - (प्रतिबद्ध)~ *[#R-4 (1)]*
Feeling dedication and loyalty; wholeheartedly dedicated

Syno: Engaged (व्यस्त), Devoted (समर्पित), Dedicated (कर्तव्यनिष्ठ)

Anto: Uncertain (अनिश्चित) {Unmotivated (अप्रेरित)}

310 Common (Adj.) - (सामान्य) *[#R-3 (1)]*
Occurring, found, or done often; prevalent

Syno: Usual (आम)

Anto: Rare (दुर्लभ)

311 Commotion (N.) - (हल्ला गुल्ला) *[#R-3 (3)]*
A state of confused and noisy disturbance

Syno: Disturbance (व्यवधान), Fuss (हंगामा), Bustle (हलचल) {Uproar (शोरगुल), Turmoil (उथल-पुथल)}

Anto: {Quietude (शांति)}

312 Compact (Adj.) - (सघन) *[#R-3 (2)]*
Closely packed and dense

Syno: Dense (घना) {Condensed (संघनित)}

Anto: Loose (ढीला), Expandable (विस्तारयोग्य) {Scattered (बिखरा हुआ)}

313 Compassion (N.) - (दया)~ *[#R-3 (2)]*
Sympathetic pity and concern for the sufferings of others

Syno: Pity (करुणा), Kindness (दयालुता)

Anto: Meanness (नीचता) {Indifference (उदासीनता), Animosity (शत्रुता)}

314 Compassionate (Adj.) - (सहानुभूतिपूर्ण) *[#R-4 (1)]*
Feeling or showing sympathy and concern for

others

Syno: Sympathetic (सहानुभूतिशील) {Kind (दयालु)}

Anto: Heartless (निर्दयी), Cruel (बेरहम)

315 Compel (V.) - (मजबूर करना) *[#R-5 (1)]*
To force or oblige someone to act

Syno: Obligate (बाध्य करना), Coerce (विवश करना), Induce (प्रेरित करना) {Force (बल प्रयोग करना)}

Anto: Dissuade (समझाकर रोकना)

316 Competence (N.) - (योग्यता) *[#R-2 (1)]*
The ability to do something successfully

Syno: Ability (योग्यता) {Capability (क्षमता)}

Anto: Incompetence (अक्षमता)

317 Competent (Adj.) - (सक्षम) *[#R-7 (3)]*
Having necessary ability or skill to do something successfully

Syno: Capable (सक्षम), Qualified (योग्य), Skilled (कुशल)

Anto: {Inept (अयोग्य), Ignorant (अज्ञानी)}

318 Complacent (Adj.) - (आत्मसंतुष्ट)~ *[#R-4 (5)]*
Showing smug satisfaction with oneself or one's achievements

Syno: Smug (आत्मसंतुष्ट), Satisfied (संतुष्ट) {Contented (तृप्त)}

Anto: Concerned (चिंतित) {Dissatisfied (असंतुष्ट), Discontented (अतृप्त)}

319 **Complex** (Adj.) - (जटिल) *[#R-2 (3)]*
Consisting of many different and connected parts

Syno: Convoluted (पेचीदा) {Intricate (उलझा हुआ)}

Anto: Simple (सरल)

320 **Compliant** (Adj.) - (आज्ञाकारी) *[#R-2 (3)]*
Inclined to agree with others or obey rules

Syno: Submissive (अधीन), Yielding (झुकने वाला) {Meek (नम्र)}

Anto: {Unyielding (अटल), Defiant (अवज्ञाकारी)}

321 Complicated (Adj.) - (जटिल) *[#R-3]*
Difficult to understand or deal with

Syno: Complex (पेचीदा)

Anto: Simple (सरल)

322 **Comply** (V.) - (आज्ञापालन करना)~ *[#R-4 (2)]*
To act in accordance with a wish or command

Syno: Obey (आज्ञा मानना)

Anto: Oppose (विरोध करना), Challenge (चुनौती देना), Deny (इनकार करना) {Disobey (अवज्ञा करना), Resist (प्रतिरोध करना)}

323 **Compose** (V./Adj.) - (रचना करना; शांत) *[#R-2 (2)]*
To write or create a work of art; to calm oneself

Syno: Collect (संग्रह करना) {Create (रचना करना)}

Anto: Agitated (व्याकुल) {Raze (ध्वस्त करना)}

324 Comprehensive (Adj.) - (विस्तृत)~ *[#R-3 (3)]*
Including all or nearly all elements of something

Syno: Complete (पूर्ण)

Anto: Restricted (सीमित), Superficial (ऊपरी) {Incomplete (अधूरा), Shallow (सतही)}

325 Conceal (V.) - (छिपाना)~ *[#R-9 (8)]*
To keep something hidden from sight

Syno: Hide (छुपाना), Disguise (भेष बदलना)

Anto: Reveal (दिखाना) {Unwrap (खोलना), Illuminate (उजागर करना)}

326 Concede (V.) - (स्वीकार करना) *[#R-3 (3)]*
To admit or yield

Syno: Capitulate (हार मानना) {Admit (मानना), Affirm (पुष्टि करना)}

Anto: Deny (इनकार करना)

327 Conceit (N.) - (अहंकार) *[#R-10 (1)]*
Excessive pride in oneself

Syno: Vanity (दंभ), Egotism (अभिमान), Pride (गर्व), Smugness (अहंकार), Arrogance (घमंड) {Pomposity (दिखावा)}

Anto: Modesty (विनम्रता), Humility (नम्रता)

328 Concise (Adj.) - (संक्षिप्त) *[#R-9 (6)]*
Giving information clearly in few words

Syno: Brief (संक्षिप्त) {Capsule (निचोड़)}

Anto: Lengthy (लंबा) {Wordy (अधिक शब्दों वाला), Elaborate (विस्तृत), Unabridged (असंक्षिप्त)}

329 Condemn (V.) - (निंदा करना; दंड देना) *[#R-9 (6)]*
To express complete disapproval; to sentence to punishment

Syno: Criticize (आलोचना करना), Punish (सजा देना), Denounce (दोषी ठहराना), Censure (फटकार लगाना) {Blame (दोष लगाना)}

Anto: Praise (प्रशंसा करना), Applaud (सराहना करना) {Approve (स्वीकृति देना)}

330 Condone (V.) - (माफ कर देना)~ *[#R-4 (2)]*
To accept and allow morally wrong behavior to continue

Syno: Overlook (अनदेखा करना), Forgive (माफ करना), Pardon (क्षमा करना) {Excuse (क्षमा करना)}

Anto: {Condemn (निंदा करना)}

331 Conducive (Adj.) - (अनुकूल) *[#R-2 (1)]*
Making a certain situation or outcome likely or possible

Syno: Helpful (उपयोगी) {Facilitative (सुविधाजनक)}

Anto: Unfavourable (प्रतिकूल)

332 **Confederate** (Adj./V.) - (संघीय; संघ बनाना) *[#R-1 (1)]*
Joined by agreement (Adj.); To form or enter into an alliance (V.)

Syno: Combined (संयुक्त)

Anto: {Disband (भंग करना)}

333 Confess (V.) - (कबूल करना)~ *[#R-4 (1)]*
To admit or state that one has committed a crime

Syno: Admit (स्वीकार करना), Acknowledge (मानना)

Anto: Deny (इनकार करना), Disavow (नकार देना) {Conceal (छिपाना)}

334 Confident (Adj.) - (आत्मविश्वासी) *[#R-2 (5)]*
Feeling or showing confidence in oneself

Syno: {Bold (निडर)}

Anto: Diffident (संकोची) {Unsure (अनिश्चित), Hesitant (झिझकने वाला), Wavering (अस्थिर)}

335 Confidential (Adj.) - (गोपनीय) *[#R-4 (1)]*
Meant to be kept secret

Syno: Secret (गुप्त)

Anto: Revealed (उजागर किया हुआ) {Public (सार्वजनिक)}

336 **Confine** (V.) - (सीमित करना) *[#R-4 (1)]*
To keep or restrict someone or something within certain limits

Syno: Restrict (प्रतिबंधित करना), Limit (सीमित करना) {Imprison (कैद करना)}

Anto: Liberate (मुक्त करना)

337 Confirm (V.) - (पुष्टि करना) *[#R-3]*
To establish the truth or correctness of something

Syno: Corroborate (समर्थन करना)

Anto: Reject (अस्वीकार करना), Contradict (खंडन करना)

338 Conflict (N./V.) - (विवाद; टकराना) *[#R-4 (2)]*
Serious disagreement or fight (N.); To clash or be opposed (V.)

Syno: Clash (टकराव), Battle (युद्ध)

Anto: Accord (समझौता) {Harmonise (तालमेल करना)}

339 **Confront** (V.) - (सामना करना) *[#R-5 (1)]*
To meet someone face to face with hostile intent

Syno: Challenge (चुनौती देना), Accost (टोकना)

Anto: Avoid (टालना)

340 **Confuse** (V.) - (भ्रमित करना) *[#R-3]*
To make someone unable to think clearly

Syno: Puzzle (उलझाना)

Anto: Clarify (स्पष्ट करना)

341 Confusion (N.) - (भ्रम) *[#R-3]*
The state of being bewildered or unclear in one's mind

Syno: Muddle (गड़बड़), Commotion (हंगामा)

Anto: Clarity (स्पष्टता)

342 **Congenial** (Adj.) - (अनुकूल) *[#R-6 (1)]*
Pleasant because of similar personality, qualities, or interests

Syno: Cordial (हार्दिक), Compatible (संगत), Pleasant (सुखद), Favourable (अनुकूल)

Anto: Unpleasant (अप्रिय) {Unsympathetic (असहानुभूतिपूर्ण)}

343 Conjecture (N.) - (अनुमान)~ *[#R-2]*
A guess without proof

Syno: Guess (अंदाज़ा)

Anto: Certainty (निश्चितता)

344 Conscientious (Adj.) - (कर्तव्यनिष्ठ)~ *[#R-3 (1)]*
Wishing to do what is right, especially to do one's work or duty well and thoroughly

Syno: Dutiful (कर्तव्यनिष्ठ), Sedulous (परिश्रमी), Honest (ईमानदार)

Anto: {Irresponsible (गैर जिम्मेदार)}

345 Conscious (Adj.) - (सचेत) *[#R-4 (4)]*
Aware of and responding to one's surroundings; awake

Syno: Mindful (सावधान) {Cognisant (सचेत)}

Anto: Unaware (अनजान) {Ignorant (अज्ञानी)}

346 Consensus (N.) - (आम सहमति) *[#R-5 (2)]*
A general agreement

Syno: Unanimity (सर्वसम्मति), Agreement (सहमति)

Anto: Disagreement (असहमति), Discord (अनबन)

347 Consent (N./V.) - (स्वीकृति; सहमती देना) *[#R-6 (4)]*
Permission or agreement (N.); To agree or comply (V.)

Syno: Assent (सहमति) {Permission (अनुमति);

Agree (सहमत होना)}

Anto: Dissent (असहमति), Interdiction (प्रतिबंध), Refusal (इनकार) {Conflict (संघर्ष)}

348 **Conserve** (V.) - (संरक्षित करना) *[#R-1 (2)]*
To protect from harm or waste

Syno: {Preserve (सुरक्षित रखना)}

Anto: Destroy (नष्ट करना) {Deplete (घटाना)}

349 Considerable (Adj.) - (काफ़ी) *[#R-1 (1)]*
Notably large in size or amount

Syno: Significant (महत्वपूर्ण)

Anto: {Trifling (तुच्छ)}

350 Considerate (Adj.) - (ध्यान रखनेवाला) *[#R-1 (1)]*
Careful not to cause inconvenience or hurt to others

Syno: Thoughtful (विचारशील)

Anto: {Insensitive (असंवेदनशील)}

351 Consistent (Adj.) - (एकसमान) *[#R-2 (2)]*
Acting or done in the same way over time

Syno: Constant (स्थिर) {Steady (सुस्थिर)}

Anto: Unpredictable (अनिश्चित) {Varying (अस्थिर)}

352 **Console** (V.) - (सांत्वना देना)~ *[#R-2 (2)]*
To comfort someone in grief or disappointment

Syno: Solace (तसल्ली देना) {Comfort (सांत्वना देना)}

Anto: Agitate (उत्तेजित करना) {Aggravate (बिगाड़ना)}

353 Conspicuous (Adj.) - (सुस्पष्ट) *[#R-4 (4)]*
Standing out so as to be clearly visible

Syno: Evident (प्रत्यक्ष), Obvious (स्पष्ट), Noticeable (ध्यान देने योग्य) {Prominent (प्रमुख)}

Anto: Obscure (अस्पष्ट) {Unnoticeable (अप्रत्यक्ष), Veiled (ढका हुआ)}

354 Constant (Adj.) - (स्थिर) *[#R-4]*
Occurring continuously over a period of time

Syno: Steady (अटल)

Anto: Varying (परिवर्तनीय), Fluctuating (अस्थिर), Changing (परिवर्तनशील)

355 Consternation (N.) - (घबराहट)~ *[#R-2 (1)]*
Feelings of anxiety or dismay at something unexpected

Syno: Dismay (हताशा)

Anto: {Satisfaction (संतोष)}

356 **Constrain** (V.) - (प्रतिबंधित करना) *[#R-1 (1)]*
To compel or force someone to follow a particular course of action

Syno: Restrict (प्रतिबंध लगाना)

Anto: {Support (समर्थन करना)}

357 **Construct** (V.) - (निर्माण करना) *[#R-3 (4)]*
To build or erect something

Syno: {Create (सृजन करना)}

Anto: Demolish (ध्वस्त करना) {Dismantle (खंडित करना)}

358 **Construe** (V.) - (व्याख्या करना) *[#R-2 (1)]*
To interpret in a particular way

Syno: {Interpret (व्याख्या करना)}

Anto: Obscure (अस्पष्ट करना), Misunderstand (गलत समझना)

359 Contaminate (V.) - (दूषित करना) *[#R-7 (3)]*
To make impure by adding pollutants

Syno: Pollute (प्रदूषित करना)

Anto: Cleanse (साफ करना), Purify (शुद्ध करना)

360 Contemplate (V.) - (विचार करना) *[#R-3 (3)]*
To think about thoughtfully

Syno: {Consider (विचार करना), Envisage (कल्पना करना)}

Anto: Ignore (अनसुनी करना), Disregard (उपेक्षा करना), Overlook (नज़रअंदाज़ करना)

361 Contempt (N.) - (घृणा) *[#R-4 (3)]*
A strong feeling of scorn

Syno: Hatred (घृणा) {Disregard (अनदेखी), Disrespect (अपमान)}

Anto: Regard (सम्मान), Admiration (प्रशंसा), Approbation (सराहना) {Respect (आदर)}

362 Contentious (Adj.) - (विवादास्पद)~ *[#R-1 (1)]*
Causing or likely to cause argument

Syno: {Controversial (विवादग्रस्त)}

Anto: Agreeable (सहमत)

363 Continue (V.) - (जारी रखना) *[#R-3]*
To persist in an activity or process

Syno: Maintain (बनाए रखना)

Anto: Halt (रुकना), Stop (रोकना)

364 Contradict (V.) - (विरुद्ध बात करना) *[#R-5 (3)]*
To state the opposite or deny

Syno: Refute (खंडन करना), Contravene (उल्लंघन करना) {Gainsay (खंडन करना), Oppose (विरोध करना)}

Anto: Agree (स्वीकार करना), Concur (सहमत होना) {Corroborate (पुष्टि करना)}

365 Contrary (Adj.) - (विपरीत) *[#R-4 (1)]*
Opposite in nature, direction, or meaning

Syno: Opposite (विरोधी)

Anto: Agreeable (सहमत), Similar (समान) {Compatible (संगत)}

366 **Control** (V./N.) - (काबू करना; नियंत्रण) *[#R-4]*
To regulate behaviour (V.); The power to influence (N.)

Syno: Regulate (नियंत्रित करना); Grip (पकड़)

Anto: Chaos (अराजकता)

367 **Convalesce** (V.) - (स्वास्थ्य अच्छा होना) *[#R-3]*
To recover health and strength after illness or operation

Syno: Recover (स्वस्थ होना)

Anto: Collapse (अचानक कमजोर पड़ना)

368 **Conventional** (Adj.) - (परंपरागत) *[#R-1 (3)]*
Based on or in accordance with what is generally done

Syno: Customary (रिवाजी) {Usual (सामान्य)}

Anto: {Uncommon (असामान्य), Unusual (असाधारण)}

369 Convict (V./N.) - (दोषी ठहराना; अपराधी) *[#R-5 (1)]*
To declare someone guilty of an offense (V.); A person found guilty of a crime (N.)

Syno: Criminal (अपराधी), Culprit (दोषी)

Anto: Acquit (दोषमुक्त करना)

370 Conviction (N.) - (दृढ़ विश्वास) *[#R-1 (3)]*
A firmly held belief or opinion; also, a formal declaration of guilt

Syno: Belief (विश्वास)

Anto: {Doubt (संदेह)}

371 Convince (V.) - (मनाना) *[#R-4 (1)]*
To make someone firmly believe something is true

Syno: Persuade (मनाना), Assure (आश्वस्त करना)

Anto: Doubt (संदेह करना), Dissuade (मना करना) {Disbelieve (अविश्वास करना)}

372 Convoluted (Adj.) - (जटिल) *[#R-2 (5)]*
Extremely complex and difficult to follow

Syno: Complex (उलझा हुआ) {Complicated (पेचीदा)}

Anto: Simple (सरल) {Straightforward (सीधा)}

373 Cooperative (Adj.) - (सहकारी) *[#R-1 (1)]*
Involving mutual assistance toward a common goal

Syno: {Complaisant (अनुकूल)}

Anto: Unsupportive (असहायक)

374 Copious (Adj.) - (प्रचुर) *[#R-7 (6)]*
Abundant in supply or quantity

Syno: Plentiful (भरपूर), Profuse (अत्यधिक) {Extensive (व्यापक)}

Anto: Scarce (दुर्लभ), Meagre (अल्प) {Scanty (अल्प)}

375 **Cordial** (Adj.) - (दोस्ताना) *[#R-11 (1)]*
Warm and friendly

Syno: Friendly (मैत्रीपूर्ण), Amicable (सौहार्दपूर्ण), Warm (गर्मजोशी भरा)

Anto: Hostile (शत्रुतापूर्ण)

376 **Corpulent** (Adj.) - (मोटा) *[#R-2 (3)]*
Fat or overweight

Syno: Rotund (गोल-मटोल) {Fleshy (मांसल), Obese (अत्यधिक मोटा)}

Anto: Slim (पतला) {Slight (दुबला)}

377 Corroborate (V.) - (समर्थन करना)~ *[#R-5 (2)]*
To confirm or give support to a statement or finding

Syno: Confirm (पुष्टि करना), Support (समर्थन करना), Affirm (पुष्टि से कहना)

Anto: Contradict (खंडन करना), Oppose (विरोध करना)

378 Corrupt (Adj.) - (भ्रष्ट) *[#R-2]*
Dishonest or morally wrong

Syno: Depraved (दुराचारी)

Anto: Honest (ईमानदार)

379 Counterfeit (Adj./V.) - (नकली; जालसाज़ी करना)~ *[#R-2 (6)]*
Not genuine or fake (Adj.); To imitate fraudulently (V.)

Syno: Fake (जाली)

Anto: Authentic (प्रामाणिक) {Genuine (वास्तविक), Valid (मान्य)}

380 **Courage** (N.) - (साहस) *[#R-4 (1)]*
The ability to do something that frightens one

Syno: Valour (वीरता)

Anto: Cowardice (कायरता) {Timidity (डरपोकपन)}

381 Courageous (Adj.) - (साहसी) *[#R-6]*
Not deterred by danger or pain

Syno: Valiant (वीरतापूर्ण), Gutsy (हिम्मती), Bold (साहसी, निडर)

Anto: Diffident (संकोची), Cowardly (कायर)

382 Courteous (Adj.) - (विनम्र) *[#R-5 (3)]*
Polite, respectful, or considerate in manner

Syno: Polite (शिष्ट)

Anto: Rude (असभ्य), Discourteous (अशिष्ट), Impolite (अभद्र)

383 **Crafty** (Adj.) - (चालाक) *[#R-2]*
Clever at achieving aims by indirect methods

Syno: Cunning (कुटिल)

Anto: Artless (सीधा-सादा)

384 Creative (Adj.) - (रचनात्मक) *[#R-1 (2)]*
Having or involving imagination to create something

Syno: Innovative (नवीन)

Anto: {Unimaginative (अकल्पनाशील)}

385 Credible (Adj.) - (विश्वसनीय)~ *[#R-4 (2)]*
Able to be believed; convincing

Syno: Believable (विश्वास योग्य), Dependable (भरोसेमंद)

Anto: Unlikely (अविश्वसनीय), Unreliable (अभरोसेमंद)

386 Credulous (Adj.) - (भोला)~ *[#R-2]*
Having too great a readiness to believe things

Syno: Gullible (आसानी से विश्वास करने वाला)

Anto: Skeptical (संदेहशील)

387 **Creep** (V.) - (रेंगना) *[#R-1 (1)]*
To move slowly and carefully to avoid being noticed

Syno: Tiptoe (दबे पाँव चलना)

Anto: {Rush (जल्दी करना)}

388 Crisis (N.) - (संकट)~ *[#R-1 (1)]*
A time of intense difficulty or danger

Syno: Catastrophe (विपत्ति)

Anto: {Blessing (आशीर्वाद)}

389 **Criticise** (V.) - (आलोचना करना)~ *[#R-6 (1)]*
To indicate the faults in a disapproving way

Syno: Censure (निंदा करना)

Anto: Commend (प्रशंसा करना), Approve (मंजूर करना), Praise (सराहना करना)

390 **Crooked** (Adj.) - (मुड़ा हुआ) *[#R-4 (4)]*
Bent or twisted; dishonest or illegal

Syno: Twisted (ऐंठा हुआ) {Dishonest (बेईमान)}

Anto: Straight (सीधा) {Straightforward (स्पष्टवादी)}

391 Crucial (Adj.) - (अत्यंत महत्वपूर्ण) *[#R-5 (5)]*
Decisive or critical in success or failure

Syno: Vital (आवश्यक), Important (महत्वपूर्ण) {Pivotal (निर्णायक), Momentous (अतिमहत्वपूर्ण)}

Anto: Trivial (तुच्छ) {Unimportant (महत्वहीन)}

392 **Crude** (Adj.) - (कच्चा, अशिष्ट) *[#R-3 (2)]*
In a natural or raw state; Rude or unpolished in manner

Syno: Unrefined (अशोधित) {Boorish (अशिष्ट)}

Anto: Ripe (पका हुआ), Refined (परिष्कृत)

393 Cruel (Adj.) - (क्रूर) *[#R-5 (1)]*
Wilfully causing pain or suffering to others

Syno: Brutal (निर्दयी)

Anto: Kind (दयालु), Sympathetic (सहानुभूतिपूर्ण)

394 **Crusade** (N.) - (अभियान, धर्मयुद्ध)~ *[#R-1 (1)]*
A vigorous campaign for political, social, or religious change

Syno: Campaign (अभियान)

Anto: {Stoppage (रोक)}

395 Cryptic (Adj.) - (गुप्त) *[#R-2 (1)]*
Mysterious or obscure in meaning

Syno: Mysterious (रहस्यमय) {Enigmatic (पहेली जैसा)}

Anto: Definite (निश्चित)

396 **Culmination** (N.) - (चरम बिंदु, अंतिम चरण) *[#R-3 (1)]*
The highest or climactic point of something

Syno: Climax (चरम सीमा)

Anto: Beginning (शुरुआत), Commencement (प्रारंभ)

397 **Culpable** (Adj.) - (दोषी)~ *[#R-6 (2)]*
Deserving blame or responsibility

Syno: Guilty (दोषी) {Accountable (जवाबदेह)}

Anto: Innocent (निर्दोष), Blameless (बेकसूर)

398 Cumbersome (Adj.) - (भारी) *[#R-4]*
Large or heavy and difficult to carry or use

Syno: Heavy (भारी)

Anto: Convenient (सुविधाजनक)

399 **Cunning** (Adj.) - (चतुर) *[#R-3 (2)]*
Skilled in achieving one's ends by deceit

Syno: Shrewd (होशियार), Slick (चालाक) {Dodgy (संदिग्ध), Sly (धूर्त)}

Anto: Simple (सरल)

400 **Cupidity** (N.) - (लोभ) *[#R-2]*
Greed for money or possessions

Syno: Greed (लालच)

Anto: Largesse (उदारता)

401 **Curb** (V.) - (नियंत्रण करना) *[#R-2 (2)]*
To restrain or keep in check

Syno: {Suppress (दबाना)}

Anto: Allow (अनुमति देना), Free (मुक्त करना)

402 Curious (Adj.) - (उत्सुक) *[#R-5 (2)]*
Eager to know or learn something

Syno: Inquisitive (उत्सुकतापूर्ण), Interested (रुचि रखनेवाला)

Anto: Uninterested (उदासीन)

403 **Current** (Adj.) - (वर्तमान) *[#R-2]*
Happening now or up-to-date

Syno: Present (वर्तमान)

Anto: Past (अतीत)

404 Cursory (Adj.) - (शीघ्रता या असावधानी से किया हुआ) *[#R-2 (4)]*
Hasty and not thorough or detailed

Syno: {Quick (त्वरित)}

Anto: Thorough (व्यापक) {Calculated (सोचा-समझा), Intensive (गहन)}

405 Curtail (V.) - (घटाना) *[#R-8 (3)]*
To reduce in extent or quantity

Syno: Downsize (कम करना) {Shorten (छोटा करना)}

Anto: Enlarge (बड़ा करना), Lengthen (लंबा करना), Amplify (बढ़ाना), Increase (वृद्धि करना) {Elongate (विस्तारित करना)}

406 **Cynical** (Adj.) - (निंदक, दोषदर्शी) *[#R-3 (1)]*
Believing that people act only for self-interest

Syno: Pessimistic (निराशावादी)

Anto: Optimistic (आशावादी), Credulous (विश्वासी) {Trusting (विश्वास करने वाला)}

407 **Dainty** (Adj.) - (नाजुक, मनोहर) *[#R-6 (4)]*
Delicately small and pretty

Syno: Elegant (आकर्षक) {Graceful (सुंदर)}

Anto: Crude (भद्दा), Clumsy (अनाड़ी), Inelegant (भद्दा) {Coarse (खुरदुरा), Vigorous (जोरदार), Ugly (बदसूरत)}

408 **Damage** (N./V.) - (नुकसान; क्षति करना) *[#R-5 (2)]*
Physical harm reducing value (N); To cause harm or injury (V)

Syno: Destruction (विनाश); Afflict (पीड़ित करना), Mar (खराब करना)

Anto: Mend (मरम्मत करना), Flawlessness (त्रुटिहीनता, बेदाग अवस्था) {Repair (मरम्मत करना)}

409 Damp (Adj./N.) - (नम; सीलन) *[#R-3 (1)]*
Slightly wet or humid (Adj); Moisture in the air (N)

Syno: Wet (गीला) {Humid (नमी वाला)}

Anto: Dry (सूखा), Arid (शुष्क)

410 Dangerous (Adj.) - (खतरनाक) *[#R-2 (1)]*
Able or likely to cause harm or injury

Syno: Hazardous (जोखिमपूर्ण), Risky (जोखिम भरा)

Anto: {Innocuous (हानिरहित)}

411 **Dank** (Adj.) - (नम) *[#R-1 (1)]*
Unpleasantly wet, cold, and slightly musty

Syno: {Damp (सीलनयुक्त)}

Anto: Dry (सूखा)

412 **Daring** (Adj.) - (साहसी) *[#R-3 (1)]*
Showing boldness and willingness to take risks

Syno: Courageous (वीर), Fearless (निडर)

Anto: Cautious (सतर्क)

413 **Daunt** (V.) - (भयभीत करना) *[#R-3 (1)]*
To make someone feel intimidated or lose confidence

Syno: Discourage (हतोत्साहित करना) {Demoralize (मनोबल तोड़ना)}

Anto: Encourage (प्रोत्साहित करना), Cheer (उत्साहित करना)

414 **Dauntless** (Adj.) - (निडर) *[#R-1 (2)]*
Showing fearlessness and strong determination

Syno: Brave (बहादुर) {Intrepid (निडर)}

Anto: {Cowardly (कायर)}

415 **Dazzling** (Adj.) - (बहुत चमकीला) *[#R-2 (2)]*
Extremely bright, especially blinding the eyes temporarily

Syno: Brilliant (चमकीला)

Anto: Lacklustre (फीका) {Murky (अंधेरा)}

416 Dearth (N.) - (कमी) *[#R-5 (7)]*
A scarcity or lack of something

Syno: Scarcity (दुर्लभता), Shortage (कमी) {Lack (अभाव), Paucity (अल्पता), Deficit (घाटा)}

Anto: Abundance (प्रचुरता)

417 Debacle (N.) - (पतन) *[#R-3 (1)]*
A sudden and complete failure

Syno: Downfall (गिरावट)

Anto: Success (सफलता)

418 Debilitate (V.) - (कमजोर करना) *[#R-1 (6)]*
To make someone weak and infirm

Syno: Weaken (दुर्बल करना) {Incapacitate (अक्षम बनाना), Attenuate (कमज़ोर करना)}

Anto: {Strengthen (मजबूत करना)}

419 **Debilitating** (Adj.) - (दुर्बल करने वाला) *[#R-1 (2)]*
Making someone very weak and infirm

Syno: {Crippling (अपंग करने वाला), Enfeebling (कमजोर बना देने वाला)}

Anto: Invigorating (बलवर्धक)

420 **Debonair** (Adj.) - (आकर्षक, शिष्ट)~ *[#R-3 (2)]*
Confident, stylish, and charming in manner

Syno: Elegant (सुन्दर), Charming (मोहक)

Anto: {Clumsy (भद्दा)}

421 **Decadent** (Adj.) - (अनैतिक; विलासी) *[#R-1 (3)]*
Characterized by moral or cultural decline; excessively luxurious or self-indulgent

Syno: {Luxurious (विलासी)}

Anto: Virtuous (सदाचारी) {Moral (नैतिक)}

422 **Decamp** (V.) - (भाग जाना) *[#R-2]*
To leave suddenly or secretly

Syno: Flee (भागना)

Anto: Remain (बने रहना)

423 **Decay** (N./V.) - (क्षय; सड़ना) *[#R-4 (4)]*
A process of rotting or deterioration (N.); To rot or deteriorate gradually (V.)

Syno: Decompose (सड़ना) {Fade (फीका पड़ना)}

Anto: Growth (वृद्धि) {Regeneration (पुनर्जनन), Survival (जीवित रहना); Flourish (फलना-फूलना)}

424 Deceit (N.) - (छल) *[#R-2 (2)]*
The act of deceiving by hiding the truth

Syno: {Dishonesty (बेईमानी)}

Anto: Honesty (ईमानदारी), Plainness (स्पष्टता)

425 Deceive (V.) - (धोखा देना) *[#R-5 (1)]*
To deliberately make someone believe something untrue

Syno: Cheat (ठगना), Trick (चाल चलना), Mislead (भ्रमित करना), Betray (विश्वासघात करना)

Anto: Enlighten (सच्चाई बताना)

426 Deception (N.) - (धोखा) *[#R-1 (2)]*
The action of deceiving someone

Syno: Trickery (छलकपट) {Fraud (कपट)}

Anto: {Honesty (ईमानदारी)}

427 **Deceptive** (Adj.) - (कपटी) *[#R-2 (3)]*
Giving an appearance different from the true one; misleading

Syno: Cheating (धोखेबाज़) {Misleading (गुमराह करने वाला)}

Anto: Honest (ईमानदार)

428 Decimate (V.) - (बरबाद करना) *[#R-4 (1)]*
To destroy or reduce something greatly

Syno: Wreck (नष्ट कर देना), Destroy (नष्ट करना)

Anto: Preserve (रक्षा करना)

429 Decipher (V.) - (अर्थ निकालना)~ *[#R-4 (6)]*
To succeed in understanding or interpreting something

Syno: Decode (संकेत समझना), Interpret (व्याख्या करना)

Anto: Garble (गलत व्याख्या करना)

430 Decline (N./V.) - (गिरावट; अस्वीकार करना) *[#R-2 (7)]*
A gradual decrease in strength or quality (N.); To decrease or politely refuse (V.)

Syno: {Descent (गिरावट); Refuse (मना करना)}

Anto: Ascend (चढ़ना), Increase (वृद्धि) {Growth (विकास); Accept (स्वीकार करना)}

431 **Decry** (V.) - (आलोचना करना) *[#R-1 (1)]*
To openly criticize or condemn

Syno: {Denounce (निंदा करना)}

Anto: Praise (प्रशंसा करना)

432 Dedication (N.) - (समर्पण) *[#R-1 (1)]*
The quality of being committed

Syno: Commitment (प्रतिबद्धता)

Anto: {Apathy (उदासीनता)}

433 **Deface** (V.) - (बिगाड़ना) *[#R-1 (1)]*
To spoil the surface or appearance

Syno: {Deform (रूप बिगाड़ना)}

Anto: Build (निर्माण करना)

434 **Defeat** (N.) - (हार) *[#R-2 (1)]*
A loss or failure

Syno: Setback (असफलता)

Anto: Victory (विजय)

435 **Defend** (V.) - (बचाव करना) *[#R-3 (1)]*
To protect someone or something from attack

Syno: Protect (सुरक्षित करना)

Anto: Surrender (समर्पण करना), Abandon (त्यागना) {Attack (हमला करना)}

436 Defer (V.) - (स्थगित करना) *[#R-6 (6)]*
To postpone something to a later time

Syno: Postpone (टालना), Delay (देरी करना)

Anto: {Expedite (शीघ्र करना), Prepone (पहले करना), Hasten (जल्दी करना)}

437 Defiance (N.) - (अवज्ञा)~ *[#R-1 (2)]*
Open refusal to obey rules or authority

Syno: Resistance (प्रतिरोध) {Disobedience (अनाज्ञाकारिता)}

Anto: {Obedience (आज्ञापालन)}

438 **Defiant** (Adj.) - (विद्रोही) *[#R-1 (1)]*
Showing resistance or refusal to obey

Syno: Rebellious (बागी)

Anto: {Obedient (आज्ञाकारी)}

439 Deficiency (N.) - (कमी, अभाव)~ *[#R-3]*
A lack or shortage of something necessary

Syno: Inadequacy (अपर्याप्तता), Shortage (अभाव)

Anto: Excess (अधिकता)

440 Deficient (Adj.) - (कमी वाला, अपूर्ण) *[#R-4]*
Lacking in something

Syno: Lacking (अभाव), Incomplete (अधूरा), Insufficient (अपर्याप्त)

Anto: Ample (पर्याप्त)

441 **Deficit** (N.) - (अभाव) *[#R-2 (5)]*
The amount by which something is too small

Syno: {Loss (हानि)}

Anto: Abundance (प्रचुरता), Surplus (अधिशेष)

442 **Defile** (V.) - (अपवित्र करना) *[#R-6 (5)]*
To make something impure or spoil its purity

Syno: Corrupt (भ्रष्ट करना) {Pollute (प्रदूषित करना)}

Anto: Purify (शुद्ध करना), Honour (सम्मानित करना), Elevate (उन्नति करना) {Cleanse (स्वच्छ करना), Upgrade (उन्नत करना)}

443 Definite (Adj.) - (निश्चित) *[#R-3 (2)]*
Clearly stated; not vague or doubtful

Syno: Precise (सटीक)

Anto: Vague (अस्पष्ट) {Uncertain (अनिश्चित), Unsure (संदिग्ध)}

444 **Defunct** (Adj.) - (अप्रचलित) *[#R-2]*
No longer existing or functioning

Syno: Obsolete (पुराना)

Anto: Extant (वर्तमान में मौजूद)

445 **Defy** (V.) - (अवज्ञा करना) *[#R-3]*
To openly resist or refuse to obey

Syno: Repel (प्रतिकार करना), Disobey (आज्ञा न मानना)

Anto: Yield (समर्पण करना)

446 Degradation (N.) - (पतन) *[#R-2]*
The process of decline or deterioration

Syno: Degeneration (पतन)

Anto: Development (विकास)

447 **Dejected** (Adj.) - (उदास) *[#R-2 (1)]*
Sad or low in spirits

Syno: Depressed (निराश)

Anto: Cheerful (आनन्दित) {Elated (प्रफुल्लित)}

448 Delegate (N./V.) - (प्रतिनिधि; सौंपना)~ *[#R-3 (1)]*
A person chosen to represent others (N.); To assign authority or task (V.)

Syno: Representative (प्रतिनिधि); Nominate (नामांकन करना)

Anto: Retain (बनाये रखना)

449 Deleterious (Adj.) - (हानिकारक) *[#R-4 (2)]*
Causing harm or damage

Syno: Harmful (नुकसानदेह) {Damaging (हानिप्रद)}

Anto: Harmless (हानिरहित)

450 Deliberate (Adj.) - (जानबूझकर)~ *[#R-7 (2)]*
Done consciously and intentionally

Syno: Intentional (इरादतन), Intended (उद्देश्यपूर्ण), Planned (योजनाबद्ध)

Anto: Spontaneous (स्वाभाविक), Unintentional (अनैच्छिक), Rash (उतावला) {Casual (लापरवाह)}

451 Deliberately (Adv.) - (जानबूझकर) *[#R-2]*
Done on purpose, not by accident

Syno: Intentionally (इरादतन)

Anto: Unintentionally (अनजाने में)

452 Delicate (Adj.) - (नाज़ुक) *[#R-4 (4)]*
Easily damaged or requiring careful handling; fine or subtle in quality

Syno: Fragile (भंगुर), Frail (कमज़ोर) {Enjoyment (आनंद)}

Anto: Firm (दृढ़), Crude (खुरदुरा) {Strong (मजबूत), Tough (सख्त), Coarse (खुरदरा)}

453 Delicious (Adj.) - (स्वादिष्ट) *[#R-3 (1)]*
Highly pleasant to the taste

Syno: {Tasty (ज़ायकेदार)}

Anto: Insipid (बेस्वाद), Distasteful (अरुचिकर)

454 Delight (N.) - (आनंद) *[#R-6 (3)]*
Great pleasure

Syno: Joy (ख़ुशी), Enchantment (प्रसन्नता) {Happiness (प्रसन्नता), Amusement (मनोरंजन)}

Anto: Sorrow (शोक), Displeasure (अप्रसन्नता) {Disgust (घृणा)}

455 **Delineate** (V.) - (वर्णन करना) *[#R-2 (1)]*
To describe or show something clearly

Syno: Depict (चित्रित करना), Explain (समझाना)

Anto: {Obscure (अस्पष्ट करना)}

456 Deluge (N.) - (बाढ़) *[#R-2 (1)]*
A severe flood

Syno: Flood (जलप्रलय), Overflow (उफान)

Anto: {Drought (सूखा)}

457 Delusion (N.) - (भ्रम) *[#R-3 (1)]*
A false belief maintained despite reality

Syno: Illusion (माया)

Anto: Reality (वास्तविकता)

458 **Demented** (Adj.) - (पागल) *[#R-2]*
Mentally unsound or irrational

Syno: Idiotic (मूर्खतापूर्ण)

Anto: Sensible (समझदार)

459 Demolish (V.) - (ध्वस्त करना) *[#R-9 (2)]*
To completely destroy or knock down

Syno: Dismantle (तोड़ना) {Destroy (नष्ट करना), Wreck (बर्बाद करना)}

Anto: Build (बनाना), Establish (स्थापित करना), Construct (निर्माण करना), Fabricate (गढ़ना)

460 Demonstrate (V.) - (प्रदर्शित करना) *[#R-2]*
To clearly show or prove something

Syno: Show (दिखाना)

Anto: Hide (छिपाना)

461 **Demure** (Adj.) - (संकोची) *[#R-3]*
Reserved, modest, and shy in behavior

Syno: Sober (सादा)

Anto: Bold (साहसी)

462 Denial (N.) - (इनकार) *[#R-2]*
The action of declaring something to be untrue

Syno: Dismissal (अस्वीकार)

Anto: Affirmation (पुष्टि)

463 **Dense** (Adj.) - (घना) *[#R-8]*
Closely compacted in substance

Syno: Thick (सघन)

Anto: Sparse (छिटपुट)

464 **Deny** (V.) - (इंकार करना) *[#R-3 (4)]*
To state that one refuses to admit the truth

Syno: Refuse (मना करना)

Anto: Agree (सहमत होना), Accept (स्वीकार करना)

465 **Departure** (N.) - (प्रस्थान) *[#R-2]*
The act of leaving a place

Syno: Exodus (पलायन)

Anto: Advent (आगमन)

466 **Depict** (V.) - (वर्णन करना)~ *[#R-2]*
To show or represent by drawing or other art form

Syno: Characterize (विशेषता बताना)

Anto: Hide (छिपाना)

467 **Deplete** (V.) - (कम करना) *[#R-3]*
To use up the supply or resources of

Syno: Reduce (घटाना)

Anto: Restore (पुनर्स्थापित करना), Expand (विस्तार करना)

468 Deplorable (Adj.) - (निंदनीय) *[#R-4 (5)]*
Deserving strong condemnation; shockingly bad

Syno: Despicable (घृणित) {Undesirable (अप्रिय)}

Anto: Commendable (सराहनीय)

469 **Deplore** (V.) - (खेद प्रकट करना) *[#R-3 (3)]*
To strongly disapprove or feel deep regret

Syno: Regret (खेद करना)

Anto: Praise (प्रशंसा करना), Relish (आनंद लेना) {Applaud (ताली बजाना)}

470 Depressed (Adj.) - (उदास) *[#R-2 (1)]*
In a state of general unhappiness or despondency

Syno: Doleful (दुखी)

Anto: Cheerful (प्रसन्न) {Elated (प्रफुल्लित)}

471 **Deprive** (V.) - (वंचित करना) *[#R-1 (2)]*
To deny a person or place the possession or use of something

Syno: Divest (छीन लेना)

Anto: {Give (देना)}

472 Derision (N.) - (उपहास) *[#R-3 (3)]*
Contemptuous ridicule or mockery

Syno: Ridicule (उपहास)

Anto: Admiration (प्रशंसा), Adulation (चापलूसी)

473 **Derisive** (Adj.) - (तिरस्कारपूर्ण) *[#R-1 (1)]*
Expressing or causing contemptuous ridicule or scorn

Syno: {Mocking (उपहासपूर्ण)}

Anto: Respectful (सम्मानजनक)

474 Derogatory (Adj.) - (अपमानजनक) *[#R-6 (5)]*
Showing disrespect or lack of regard

Syno: Disparaging (निंदात्मक), Insulting (अपमानजनक), Sarcastic (व्यंग्यात्मक)

Anto: Complimentary (प्रशंसात्मक), Appreciative (सराहनात्मक), Laudatory (प्रशंसात्मक) {Praising (प्रशंसात्मक)}

475 **Desecrate** (V.) - (अपवित्र करना) *[#R-2 (1)]*
To show disrespect to something sacred

Syno: {Violate (उल्लंघन करना)}

Anto: Sanctify (पवित्र करना)

476 Desert (V.) - (परित्याग करना) *[#R-2]*
To abandon someone or something

Syno: Abandon (त्याग देना)

Anto: Populate (आबाद करना)

477 **Desiccated** (Adj.) - (शुष्क) *[#R-1 (1)]*
Dried out; having had moisture removed

Syno: Dry (सूखा)

Anto: {Moistened (गीला)}

478 Desire (N.) - (इच्छा) *[#R-2]*
A strong feeling of wanting

Syno: Longing (लालसा)

Anto: Apathy (उदासीनता)

479 **Desolate** (Adj.) - (उजड़ा हुआ) *[#R-4 (4)]*
Deserted of people and in a state of bleak emptiness

Syno: Bleak (सुनसान), Barren (बंजर), Lonely (अकेला) {Melancholic (उदासीन)}

Anto: Festive (उत्सवपूर्ण) {Fertile (उपजाऊ), Cheerful (आनंदित), Thriving (फलता-फूलता)}

480 Despair (N./V.) - (हताशा; निराश होना) *[#R-9 (4)]*
A complete loss of hope (N.); To lose or be without hope (V.)

Syno: Misery (दुर्दशा), Hopelessness (निराशा) {Sorrow (दुःख)}

Anto: Hope (आशा), Optimism (आशावाद), Faith (विश्वास) {Elation (उत्साह)}

481 Despicable (Adj.) - (घिनौना) *[#R-3 (2)]*
Deserving hatred and contempt

Syno: Hateful (घृणित), Contemptible (तिरस्कार्य)

Anto: Admirable (प्रशंसनीय) {Reputable (सम्मानित)}

482 Despise (V.) - (घृणा करना) *[#R-6 (1)]*
To feel contempt or deep repugnance for something

Syno: Abhor (घृणा करना), Hate (नफरत करना), Undervalue (कम महत्व देना), Dislike (नापसंद करना)

Anto: Admire (प्रशंसा करना) {Accept (स्वीकार करना)}

483 Despondent (Adj.) - (हताश) *[#R-3 (1)]*
In low spirits from loss of hope or courage

Syno: Dejected (उदास), Depressed (निराश)

Anto: Hopeful (आशापूर्ण) {Elated (प्रफुल्लित)}

484 **Destitute** (Adj.) - (निर्धन)~ *[#R-4 (8)]*
Without the basic necessities of life

Syno: Indigent (दरिद्र), Impoverished (गरीब), Broke (कंगाल)

Anto: Affluent (समृद्ध) {Wealthy (धनी), Prosperous (सम्पन्न), Opulent (भव्य)}

485 Destroy (V.) - (नष्ट करना) *[#R-6 (1)]*
To put an end to something by damaging it

Syno: Ruin (बर्बाद करना), Demolish (ध्वस्त करना)

Anto: Preserve (रक्षा करना), Restore (मरम्मत करना) {Establish (स्थापना करना)}

486 Desultory (Adj.) - (असंगठित) *[#R-2]*
Lacking a plan, purpose, or enthusiasm

Syno: Haphazard (बेतरतीब)

Anto: Methodical (क्रमबद्ध)

487 Deter (V.) - (रोकना) *[#R-4]*
To prevent or discourage someone from doing something

Syno: Hinder (बाधा डालना)

Anto: Encourage (प्रोत्साहित करना), Incite (उत्तेजित करना)

488 Detest (V.) - (घृणा करना) *[#R-5 (2)]*
To dislike intensely

Syno: Loathe (घृणा करना) {Abhor (घृणा करना)}

Anto: Like (पसंद करना), Adore (पूजना)

489 Detrimental (Adj.) - (हानिकारक) *[#R-7 (4)]*
Tending to cause harm

Syno: Damaging (नुकसानदेह), Harmful (हानिकारक) {Injurious (घातक)}

Anto: Harmless (हानिरहित), Benign (हितकारी), Beneficial (लाभकारी), Advantageous (लाभकारी)

490 Deviate (V.) - (भटकना) *[#R-2 (3)]*
To depart from an established course

Syno: Veer (दिशा बदलना) {Differ (भिन्न होना), Divert (मोड़ना)}

Anto: Concentrate (केंद्रित करना) {Follow (अनुसरण करना)}

491 Devious (Adj.) - (चालाक)~ *[#R-4 (3)]*
Showing a skilful use of underhanded tactics to achieve goals

Syno: {Dishonest (बेईमान)}

Anto: Straight (सीधा), Sincere (ईमानदार), Outspoken (स्पष्टवादी) {Forthright (निष्कपट), Innocent (भोला)}

492 **Devoid** (Adj.) - (ख़ाली) *[#R-3 (2)]*
Entirely lacking or free from

Syno: Empty (खाली)

Anto: Full (भरा हुआ) {Loaded (लदा हुआ)}

493 Devout (Adj.) - (धार्मिक, निष्ठावान) *[#R-5]*
Having or showing deep religious feeling or commitment

Syno: Pious (धार्मिक)

Anto: Irreverent (अश्रद्धालु)

494 **Dexterity** (N.) - (कुशलता) *[#R-2 (2)]*
The skill in performing tasks, especially with hands

Syno: Adroitness (निपुणता) {Finesse (कुशलता)}

Anto: {Clumsiness (अनाड़ीपन)}

495 Diabolical (Adj.) - (दुष्ट) *[#R-2]*
Belonging to or so evil as to recall the Devil

Syno: Malicious (दुर्भावनापूर्ण)

Anto: Moral (नैतिक)

496 Diffidence (N.) - (संकोच)~ *[#R-3 (4)]*
The modesty or shyness from lack of self-confidence

Syno: Meekness (विनम्रता) {Shyness (शर्म)}

Anto: Self-Assurance (आत्मविश्वास) {Confidence (आत्मविश्वास)}

497 **Diffident** (Adj.) - (संकोची) *[#R-4 (4)]*
Modest or shy because of lack of self-confidence

Syno: Timid (संकोची) {Bashful (शर्मीला), Hesitant (संकोची)}

Anto: Confident (आत्मविश्वासी), Aggressive (आक्रामक)

498 **Digress** (V.) - (विषय से भटकना) *[#R-1 (1)]*
To leave the main subject temporarily in speech or writing

Syno: {Deviate (भटकना)}

Anto: Stay (ठहरना)

499 **Dilate** (V.) - (फैलाना) *[#R-3]*
To make or become wider, larger, or more open

Syno: Widen (चौड़ा करना)

Anto: Contract (सिकुड़ना), Compress (दबाना)

500 Dilemma (N.) - (दुविधा)~ *[#R-4 (3)]*
A situation requiring choice between equally undesirable alternatives

Syno: Predicament (कठिन स्थिति), Quandary (असमंजस), Plight (संकट) {Confusion (भ्रम)}

Anto: Solution (समाधान) {Confidence (आत्मविश्वास)}

501 Diligent (Adj.) - (परिश्रमी)~ *[#R-20 (10)]*
Having or showing care and conscientiousness in work

Syno: Industrious (परिश्रमी), Hardworking (मेहनती), Assiduous (परिश्रमी), Untiring (न थकने वाला), Careful (सावधान) {Conscientious (कर्तव्यनिष्ठ), Meticulous (बारीकी से काम करने वाला)}

Anto: Lazy (आलसी), Idle (निष्क्रिय), Inactive (सुस्त) {Careless (लापरवाह)}

502 Diminish (V.) - (घटाना) *[#R-6 (6)]*
To make or become less

Syno: Reduce (कम करना), Weaken (कमजोर करना) {Decline (गिरना)}

Anto: Increase (बढ़ाना), Grow (बढ़ना)

503 Disaster (N.) - (आपदा)~ *[#R-3 (1)]*
A sudden event that causes great damage or loss of life

Syno: Misfortune (दुर्भाग्य)

Anto: Success (सफलता) {Prosperity (समृद्धि)}

504 Discard (V.) - (त्यागना) *[#R-2 (2)]*
To get rid of something unwanted

Syno: {Abandon (त्याग देना)}

Anto: Adopt (अपनाना), Accept (स्वीकार करना)

505 **Disclose** (V.) - (प्रकट करना) *[#R-3 (1)]*
To make secret or new information known

Syno: Reveal (प्रकट करना)

Anto: Conceal (छिपाना) {Withhold (रोकना)}

506 Disconsolate (Adj.) - (अत्यंत दुखी) *[#R-2]*
Without consolation or comfort; unhappy

Syno: Unhappy (उदास)

Anto: Joyous (प्रसन्न)

507 **Discontent** (N.) - (असंतोष) *[#R-2]*
A lack of satisfaction with one's situation

Syno: Dissatisfaction (असंतुष्टि)

Anto: Satisfaction (संतोष)

508 **Discord** (N.) - (मनमुटाव) *[#R-2 (1)]*
Disagreement between people

Syno: {Tumult (हंगामा)}

Anto: Harmony (सामंजस्य)

509 Discourage (V.) - (मनोबल तोड़ना; रोकना) *[#R-1 (1)]*
To reduce confidence or enthusiasm; To try to prevent someone from doing something

Syno: {Prevent (रोकना)}

Anto: Persuade (राज़ी करना)

510 Discreet (Adj.) - (सावधान, संकोची) *[#R-5 (2)]*
Careful and prudent in speech or actions

Syno: Careful (सावधान), Reserved (संकोची)

Anto: Heedless (बेपरवाह), Tactless (अविवेकी), Open (स्पष्ट) {Careless (लापरवाह), Unwise (अविवेकी)}

511 Discretion (N.) - (समझदारी) *[#R-2 (2)]*
The quality of being careful and prudent

Syno: {Prudence (विवेक)}

Anto: Indiscretion (अविवेक), Inattention (लापरवाही)

512 **Discriminate** (V.) - (भेदभाव करना) *[#R-3]*
To recognize or make distinctions between things

Syno: Distinguish (भेद करना), Differentiate (अलग करना)

Anto: Equalize (बराबर करना)

513 Disdain (N./V.) - (तिरस्कार; तुच्छ समझना) *[#R-4 (11)]*
Contempt or strong dislike (N.); To consider unworthy of respect (V.)

Syno: Contempt (अवमानना) {Scorn (तिरस्कार); Hate (घृणा), Disregard (अवहेलना)}

Anto: Admiration (प्रशंसा), Respect (सम्मान), Favour (अनुकूलता) {Approval (सहमति); Praise (प्रशंसा)}

514 **Disgrace** (N.) - (कलंक; बदनामी) *[#R-4]*
Loss of respect or reputation

Syno: Dishonour (अपमान)

Anto: Honour (सम्मान)

515 Disgruntled (Adj.) - (असंतुष्ट)~ *[#R-2 (4)]*
Angry or dissatisfied

Syno: Annoyed (नाराज़) {Doleful (उदास)}

Anto: Pleased (प्रसन्न) {Contented (संतुष्ट)}

516 Disgust (N.) - (घृणा) *[#R-2]*
Strong dislike or revulsion

Syno: Dislike (नापसंद)

Anto: Delight (आनंद)

517 **Dishearten** (V.) - (हतोत्साह करना) *[#R-3]*
To cause loss of confidence or determination

Syno: Depress (निराश करना)

Anto: Encourage (हौसला देना)

518 **Dishevel** (V./Adj.) - (बिखेरना; अस्त-व्यस्त) *[#R-7]*
To make hair or clothes untidy (V.); Messy, disordered (Adj.)

Syno: Clutter (अव्यवस्थित करना); Untidy (अस्त-व्यस्त)

Anto: Tidy (साफ-सुथरा), Ordered (व्यवस्थित)

519 Disillusioned (Adj.) - (मोहभंग) *[#R-2]*
Disappointed after discovering something is less good than believed

Syno: Disenchanted (मोहभंग)

Anto: Enthusiastic (उत्साही)

520 **Dismal** (Adj.) - (निराशाजनक; अत्यंत खराब)~ *[#R-9 (9)]*
Very depressing or gloomy; extremely poor in quality

Syno: Gloomy (उदास) {Dejected (निराश), Dreary (नीरस), Bleak (निराशाजनक)}

Anto: Cheerful (प्रसन्न), Lively (जीवंत), Luminous (उज्ज्वल) {Bright (उज्ज्वल), Pleasant (सुखद), Cordial (गर्मजोशी वाला), Cheery (हर्षित), Animated (सजीव), Positive (सकारात्मक)}

521 Disparate (Adj.) - (भिन्न) *[#R-4 (1)]*
Essentially different in kind; not allowing comparison

Syno: Different (विभिन्न)

Anto: Similar (समान), Alike (एक जैसा)

522 **Dispel** (V.) - (दूर करना)~ *[#R-1 (1)]*
To make something disappear

Syno: {Disperse (तितर-बितर करना)}

Anto: Accumulate (इकट्ठा करना)

523 **Disperse** (V.) - (तितर-बितर करना) *[#R-2]*
To distribute or spread over a wide area

Syno: Scatter (बिखेरना)

Anto: Gather (एकत्रित करना)

524 **Display** (V.) - (प्रदर्शित करना) *[#R-1 (1)]*
To show something clearly so that it can be seen

Syno: {Exhibit (प्रदर्शित करना)}

Anto: Hide (छिपाना)

525 **Dispute** (N./V.) - (झगड़ा; विवाद करना) *[#R-4]*
A disagreement or debate (N.); To argue or question (V.)

Syno: Quarrel (झगड़ा)

Anto: Agreement (सहमति); Concede (स्वीकार करना)

526 **Dissemble** (V.) - (छिपाना) *[#R-1 (2)]*
To conceal one's true motives, feelings, or beliefs

Syno: {Conceal (छिपाना)}

Anto: Reveal (प्रकट करना)

527 Disseminate (V.) - (प्रसारित करना) *[#R-3 (1)]*
To spread information or ideas widely

Syno: Disperse (फैलाना), Circulate (प्रसारित करना) {Spread (फैलाना)}

Anto: Conceal (छिपाना)

528 Dissident (Adj./N.) - (असहमत; विरोधी)~ *[#R-1 (2)]*

Disagreeing or dissenting (Adj.); A person who opposes official policy (N.)

Syno: {Rebellious (विद्रोही)}

Anto: Orthodox (पारंपरिक) {Conformist (परंपरा मानने वाला)}

529 **Dissolve** (V.) - (विलीन होना) *[#R-2]*
To gradually disappear or fade away

Syno: Fade (फीका पड़ना)

Anto: Appear (सामने आना)

530 Dissuade (V.) - (मना करना) *[#R-3 (1)]*
To persuade someone not to take an action

Syno: Discourage (हतोत्साहित करना)

Anto: Persuade (राजी करना), Encourage (प्रोत्साहित करना)

531 **Distant** (Adj.) - (दूर) *[#R-3 (3)]*
Far away in space or time

Syno: Faraway (बहुत दूर) {Far (दूर)}

Anto: Close (निकट), Near (नज़दीक) {Adjoining (सटा हुआ)}

532 **Distasteful** (Adj.) - (अरुचिकर, नापसंद) *[#R-2]*
Causing dislike or disgust

Syno: Unpleasant (अप्रिय)

Anto: Pleasant (सुखद)

533 Distinct (Adj.) - (भिन्न; स्पष्ट) *[#R-1 (2)]*
Recognizably different; clearly defined or noticeable

Syno: {Unique (विशिष्ट)}

Anto: Vague (अस्पष्ट) {Similar (समान)}

534 Diverse (Adj.) - (भिन्न) *[#R-2 (5)]*
Showing a great deal of variety; very different

Syno: Distinctive (विशिष्ट) {Varied (विविध)}

Anto: Identical (समान) {Similar (समान), Uniform (एकरूप)}

535 Divine (Adj.) - (दैवीय) *[#R-2]*
Of, from, or like God or a god

Syno: Celestial (दिव्य)

Anto: Lowly (मामूली)

536 Divulge (V.) - (भेद खोलना)~ *[#R-5 (1)]*
To make known private or sensitive information

Syno: Reveal (प्रकट करना)

Anto: Conceal (छिपाना), Hide (छुपाना)

537 **Divulgence** (N.) - (पर्दाफाश) *[#R-3]*
The act of divulging; disclosure

Syno: Revelation (प्रकटीकरण)

Anto: Concealment (गोपनीयता)

538 Docile (Adj.) - (आज्ञाकारी) *[#R-6 (2)]*
Easily controlled or willing to obey instructions

Syno: Submissive (आज्ञाकारी), Pliable (लचीला)

Anto: Headstrong (जिद्दी), Opposing (विरोधी), Unwilling (अनिच्छुक) {Obstinate (हठी), Wilful (स्वेच्छाचारी)}

539 **Dogmatic** (Adj.) - (कट्टर) *[#R-4 (1)]*
Asserting beliefs as absolutely true without openness to discussion

Syno: {Rigid (कठोर)}

Anto: Liberal (उदार), Flexible (लचीला), Amenable (सहमत होने वाला)

540 **Doleful** (Adj.) - (दुख भरा) *[#R-3 (2)]*
Expressing sorrow

Syno: Mournful (शोकमय)

Anto: Cheerful (खुश), Joyous (खुशी से भरा)

541 **Doomed** (Adj.) - (बर्बाद) *[#R-1 (1)]*
Likely to have an unfortunate and inescapable outcome

Syno: {Ruined (नष्ट)}

Anto: Blessed (भाग्यशाली)

542 **Dormant** (Adj.) - (निष्क्रिय)~ *[#R-5 (4)]*
Temporarily inactive or inoperative

Syno: {Inactive (अक्रिय)}

Anto: Active (सक्रिय)

543 Doubtful (Adj.) - (अनिश्चित) *[#R-2 (2)]*
Feeling uncertain about something

Syno: Uncertain (अनिश्चित) {Sceptical (संदेहशील)}

Anto: Decisive (निर्णायक) {Confident (आत्मविश्वासी)}

544 Dreadful (Adj.) - (भयानक) *[#R-1 (1)]*
Extremely bad, serious, or causing great fear

Syno: Terrible (भयंकर)

Anto: {Pleasant (सुखद)}

545 Dreary (Adj.) - (उदास) *[#R-1 (4)]*
Dull, bleak, and lifeless; depressing

Syno: Dull (उबाऊ)

Anto: {Bright (उज्ज्वल), Cheerful (खुश)}

546 Dubious (Adj.) - (संदिग्ध) *[#R-10 (11)]*
Hesitating or doubting

Syno: Doubtful (संदेहपूर्ण), Fishy (संदेहजनक) {Uncertain (अनिश्चित), Unclear (अस्पष्ट)}

Anto: Likely (संभवतः), Certain (निश्चित), Indisputable (अविवादित) {Incontestable (निस्संदेह), Trustworthy (विश्वसनीय)}

547 **Dulcet** (Adj.) - (मधुर) *[#R-2]*
Pleasantly sweet or soothing, especially in sound

Syno: Sweet (मधुर)

Anto: Harsh (कठोर)

548 Dwindle (V.) - (घटना) *[#R-5 (3)]*
To diminish gradually in size, amount, or strength

Syno: Decrease (कम करना) {Abate (कम होना)}

Anto: Increase (बढ़ना), Grow (विकसित होना)

549 **Dynamic** (Adj.) - (गतिशील) *[#R-3 (1)]*
Showing constant change, energy, or progress

Syno: Energetic (ऊर्जावान)

Anto: Static (स्थिर)

550 Eager (Adj.) - (उत्सुक) *[#R-13 (1)]*
Very interested and excited to do or get something

Syno: Keen (तत्पर), Avid (उत्सुक), Enthusiastic (उत्साहित)

Anto: Disinterested (अनिच्छुक), Indifferent (उदासीन) {Apathetic (भावहीन)}

551 **Ebb** (V.) - (कम होना) *[#R-2]*
To recede or decline

Syno: Sink (डूबना)

Anto: Flow (बहना)

552 Ebullient (Adj.) - (जोशीला) *[#R-8 (1)]*
Cheerful and full of energy

Syno: Enthusiastic (उत्साहित), Joyful (आनंदित)

Anto: Dejected (निराश), Depressed (उदास), Weary (थका हुआ)

553 Eccentric (Adj.) - (विचित्र, सनकी)~ *[#R-11 (11)]*
Unconventional and slightly strange

Syno: Queer (अजीब), Peculiar (अलग प्रकार का), Bizarre (विचित्र), Idiosyncratic (विशिष्ट स्वभाव वाला) {Unconventional (अपरंपरागत), Abnormal (असामान्य), Strange (अजीबोगरीब)}

Anto: Customary (पारंपरिक), Normal (सामान्य) {Conventional (परंपरागत)}

554 Eccentricity (N.) - (विचित्रता) *[#R-2]*
The quality of being eccentric

Syno: Mannerism (विशिष्ट व्यवहार)

Anto: Normalcy (सामान्यता)

555 Eclectic (Adj.) - (विभिन्न स्रोतों से चुना हुआ)~ *[#R-1 (1)]*
Drawing ideas or style from many different sources

Syno: Diverse (विभिन्न)

Anto: {Uniform (एकरूप)}

556 Ecstasy (N.) - (परमानंद) *[#R-6 (4)]*
An overwhelming feeling of great happiness or joyful excitement

Syno: Joy (आनंद), Happiness (खुशी), Bliss (परम सुख) {Delight (प्रसन्नता)}

Anto: Despair (निराशा), Depression (अवसाद), Agony (यातना)

557 **Efface** (V.) - (मिटाना)~ *[#R-3 (2)]*
To erase or remove a mark

Syno: Abolish (समाप्त करना), Destroy (नष्ट करना)

Anto: {Preserve (संरक्षित करना), Maintain (बनाए रखना)}

558 **Efficacious** (Adj.) - (कारगर) *[#R-3]*
Successful in producing a desired result; effective

Syno: Effective (प्रभावशाली)

Anto: Ineffective (अप्रभावी), Useless (बेकार)

559 Efficacy (N.) - (क्षमता) *[#R-3 (1)]*
The ability to produce a desired or intended result

Syno: Efficiency (कुशलता) {Potency (शक्ति)}

Anto: Inadequacy (अयोग्यता)

560 Efficient (Adj.) - (कुशल)~ *[#R-4 (1)]*
Achieving maximum output with minimum effort or waste

Syno: Capable (सक्षम), Competent (योग्य) {Proficient (निपुण)}

Anto: Incompetent (अक्षम), Idle (निष्क्रिय)

561 Egregious (Adj.) - (बेहद खराब)~ *[#R-2 (1)]*
Extremely bad or shocking

Syno: Shocking (अत्यंत बुरा) {Atrocious (घटिया)}

Anto: Mild (हल्का)

562 Elaborate (Adj.) - (विस्तृत) *[#R-4]*
Intricate and rich in detail

Syno: Detailed (विस्तृत), Intricate (जटिल), Complex (पेचीदा)

Anto: Minimal (न्यूनतम)

563 **Elated** (Adj.) - (प्रफुल्लित) *[#R-5 (5)]*
Extremely happy and excited

Syno: Exalted (अत्यंत प्रसन्न) {Ecstatic (अति प्रसन्न), Joyful (आनंदित)}

Anto: Disheartened (निराश), Depressed (उदास), Discouraged (हतोत्साहित) {Dejected (निराश), Sad (दुखी)}

564 Elegant (Adj.) - (सुरुचिपूर्ण) *[#R-6 (2)]*
Graceful and stylish in appearance or manner

Syno: Graceful (आकर्षक)

Anto: Crude (अशिष्ट), Awkward (अजीब), Undignified (अभद्र) {Uncouth (असभ्य), Unrefined (अपरिष्कृत)}

565 Eliminate (V.) - (हटाना) *[#R-3 (1)]*
To completely remove or get rid of something

Syno: Exclude (बाहर करना), Remove (निकालना)

Anto: Add (जोड़ना)

566 Eloquent (Adj.) - (वाक्पटु)~ *[#R-8 (6)]*
Fluent or persuasive in speaking or writing

Syno: Fluent (धाराप्रवाह), Articulate (स्पष्ट बोलने वाला), Expressive (भावपूर्ण)

Anto: Inarticulate (अस्पष्ट), Inexpressive (भावहीन) {Ineffective (अप्रभावी)}

567 **Elucidate** (V.) - (स्पष्ट करना)~ *[#R-4 (3)]*
To make something clear or explain

Syno: Explicate (व्याख्या करना), Clarify (स्पष्ट करना) {Explain (समझाना)}

Anto: Obfuscate (अस्पष्ट करना), Obscure (धुंधला करना) {Confuse (भ्रमित करना)}

568 **Elude** (V.) - (बचना) *[#R-1 (2)]*
To evade or escape skilfully from danger or pursuit

Syno: Escape (भागना)

Anto: {Encounter (सामना करना)}

569 **Elusive** (Adj.) - (पकड़ में न आने वाला) *[#R-5 (3)]*
Difficult to find, catch, or achieve

Syno: Evasive (बचने वाला), Slippery (फिसलन भरा), Intangible (अस्पर्शी), Baffling (चकित करने वाला) {Mysterious (रहस्यमय), Ambiguous (अस्पष्ट)}

Anto: Definite (निश्चित)

570 **Emaciated** (Adj.) - (कृशकाय (दुबला-पतला)) *[#R-2 (2)]*
Abnormally thin or weak due to illness or lack of food

Syno: {Gaunt (दुबला)}

Anto: Fat (मोटा), Healthy (स्वस्थ) {Hefty (तगड़ा)}

571 **Emancipate** (V.) - (मुक्त करना)~ *[#R-3 (4)]*
To set free from legal, social, or political control

Syno: Liberate (आजाद करना) {Free (मुक्त करना)}

Anto: {Enslave (दास बनाना), Detain (हिरासत में लेना)}

572 Emancipation (N.) - (मुक्ति)~ *[#R-3 (1)]*
The process of being set free from legal, social, or political restrictions

Syno: Freedom (स्वतंत्रता) {Liberation (मुक्ति)}

Anto: Bondage (बंधन)

573 **Embezzle** (V.) - (गबन करना)~ *[#R-1 (5)]*
To steal money that one is trusted to manage

Syno: Misappropriate (दुरुपयोग करना) {Abstract (चुराना, निकालना)}

Anto: {Compensate (मुआवज़ा देना)}

574 Embrace (V.) - (स्वीकार करना) *[#R-2 (3)]*
To hold closely; accept enthusiastically

Syno: Accept (मान लेना) {Hug (गले लगाना)}

Anto: Reject (अस्वीकार करना) {Exclude (बाहर करना)}

575 **Emerge** (V.) - (प्रकट होना) *[#R-9 (3)]*
To come out or come into view

Syno: Appear (दिखाई देना) {Arise (उठना)}

Anto: Vanish (गायब होना), Disappear (लुप्त होना)

576 Eminent (Adj.) - (प्रसिद्ध) *[#R-6 (3)]*
Famous and highly respected in a field or profession

Syno: Famous (प्रसिद्ध), Prominent (प्रमुख), Renowned (विख्यात) {Distinguished (प्रतिष्ठित)}

Anto: Obscure (अज्ञात), Ordinary (साधारण), Inconspicuous (छिपा हुआ) {Insignificant (महत्वहीन), Unknown (अपरिचित)}

577 Empathy (N.) - (समानुभूति)~ *[#R-3 (2)]*
The ability to understand and share the feelings of another

Syno: Affinity (संबंध)

Anto: Apathy (उदासीनता), Mercilessness (निर्दयता) {Disdain (तिरस्कार)}

578 **Empty** (Adj.) - (खाली) *[#R-3]*
Containing nothing; not filled or occupied

Syno: Vacant (रिक्त)

Anto: Full (भरा हुआ)

579 **Emulate** (V.) - (अनुकरण करना) *[#R-3 (2)]*
To try to match or surpass by imitation

Syno: Imitate (नकल करना)

Anto: Neglect (ध्यान न देना)

580 Enchanting (Adj.) - (मनमोहक) *[#R-2 (6)]*
Having an often mysterious or magical power to attract or delight

Syno: Appealing (आकर्षक), Alluring (लुभावना) {Attractive (आकर्षक), Pleasant (सुखद)}

Anto: {Repellent (अरुचिकर), Boring (उबाऊ)}

581 **Encomium** (N.) - (प्रशंसा)~ *[#R-1 (3)]*
A speech or writing that gives high praise

Syno: {Praise (प्रशंसा)}

Anto: Castigation (फटकार) {Hypercriticism (अत्यधिक आलोचना)}

582 Encounter (V.) - (सामना करना) *[#R-4 (2)]*
To unexpectedly face or experience something difficult

Syno: Face (सामना करना), Experience (अनुभव करना)

Anto: Avoid (टालना)

583 Encourage (V.) - (प्रोत्साहित करना) *[#R-7 (3)]*
To give support, confidence, or hope to someone

Syno: Stimulate (उत्तेजित करना) {Urge (आग्रह करना), Motivate (प्रेरित करना)}

Anto: Dishearten (निराश करना), Discourage (हतोत्साहित करना), Oppose (विरोध करना) {Deter (रोकना)}

584 **Encumbrance** (N.) - (बाधा) *[#R-4]*
Something that makes an action difficult

Syno: Obstacle (बाधा), Hurdle (अड़चन)

Anto: Asset (संपत्ति)

585 Endeavour (N./V.) - (प्रयास; कोशिश करना)~ *[#R-7 (3)]*
An attempt or effort to achieve something (N.); To try hard to achieve something (V.)

Syno: Attempt (कोशिश), Aim (लक्ष्य), Effort (प्रयास) {Strive (प्रयास करना), Aspire (आकांक्षा रखना), Venture (साहसिक कार्य)}

Anto: Laziness (आलस), Inactivity (निष्क्रियता)

586 **Endorse** (V.) - (समर्थन करना) *[#R-3 (3)]*
To publicly approve or support something

Syno: Approve (मंजूरी देना) {Certify (प्रमाणित करना)}

Anto: Renounce (त्यागना), Disapprove (अस्वीकार करना)

587 Endurance (N.) - (सहनशीलता) *[#R-2 (2)]*
The ability to endure hardship or difficulty without giving up

Syno: {Patience (सहनशीलता), Stamina (सहनशक्ति)}

Anto: Indolence (आलस्य)

588 Energetic (Adj.) - (ऊर्जावान) *[#R-1 (1)]*
Showing or involving great activity or vitality

Syno: Vibrant (जीवंत)

Anto: {Lethargic (सुस्त)}

589 Enervate (V.) - (निर्बल करना) *[#R-5 (2)]*
To cause someone to lose energy or strength

Syno: Devitalize (शक्तिहीन करना), Weaken (कमजोर करना), Exhaust (थका देना)

Anto: {Strengthen (मजबूत करना), Invigorate (सबल बनाना)}

590 Enhance (V.) - (सुधारना) *[#R-3]*
To increase or improve the quality or value of something

Syno: Improve (बेहतर करना)

Anto: Impair (नुकसान पहुँचाना), Diminish (कम करना)

591 Enigma (N.) - (पहेली)~ *[#R-4 (1)]*
A mysterious or puzzling person or thing

Syno: Puzzle (पहेली), Riddle (पहेली) {Mystery (रहस्य)}

Anto: Clarity (स्पष्टता)

592 Enigmatic (Adj.) - (रहस्यमय)~ *[#R-4 (3)]*
Difficult to understand

Syno: Mysterious (रहस्यमय)

Anto: Obvious (स्पष्ट), Clear (साफ़), Straightforward (सीधा)

593 **Enlarge** (V.) - (बड़ा करना) *[#R-2 (2)]*
To make or become larger or more extensive

Syno: {Increase (बढ़ाना)}

Anto: Condense (गाढ़ा करना), Curtail (घटाना) {Abridge (संक्षिप्त करना)}

594 **Enliven** (V.) - (जीवंत करना) *[#R-2]*
To make something more lively or interesting

Syno: Cheer (उत्साहित करना)

Anto: Dishearten (निराश करना)

595 Enmity (N.) - (शत्रुता) *[#R-3 (2)]*
The state of active opposition or hostility

Syno: Hostility (दुश्मनी)

Anto: Amicability (मैत्री), Friendship (मित्रता) {Amity (सौहार्द)}

596 **Ennui** (N.) - (ऊब)~ *[#R-2 (1)]*
A feeling of boredom due to lack of interest or excitement

Syno: Boredom (बोरियत)

Anto: Excitement (उत्साह)

597 Enormous (Adj.) - (विशाल) *[#R-9 (4)]*
Extremely large in size, amount, or degree

Syno: Immense (अपार), Huge (विशाल), Massive (वृहद), Large (बड़ा)

Anto: Tiny (छोटा), Minute (सूक्ष्म), Negligible (महत्वहीन) {Petite (छोटे कद का)}

598 **Enrage** (V./Adj.) - (गुस्सा भड़काना; क्रोधित) *[#R-4 (1)]*
To make someone very angry (V.); Very angry (Adj.)

Syno: Infuriate (क्रोधित करना); Furious (गुस्से में) {Anger (क्रोधित करना)}

Anto: Pleased (प्रसन्न)

599 **Enrich** (V.) - (समृद्ध करना) *[#R-3 (2)]*
To improve or increase the quality or value of something

Syno: {Enhance (बढ़ाना)}

Anto: Reduce (घटाना), Deplete (खाली करना) {Impoverish (निर्धन बनाना)}

600 **Ensconce** (V.) - (छिपाना) *[#R-2 (1)]*
To settle or hide someone in a safe or secret place

Syno: Conceal (छुपाना)

Anto: Unveil (अनावरण करना)

601 **Entangle** (V.) - (उलझाना) *[#R-2 (1)]*
To cause to become twisted together or caught in

Syno: Implicate (फंसाना), Trap (फँसाना)

Anto: {Untwist (सुलझाना)}

602 **Enthralled** (Adj.) - (मंत्रमुग्ध) *[#R-2]*
Completely interested or charmed

Syno: Fascinated (मोहित)

Anto: Bored (ऊबा हुआ)

603 Enthusiasm (N.) - (उत्साह) *[#R-5 (2)]*
An intense and eager interest or enjoyment

Syno: Zeal (जोश) {Passion (जुनून)}

Anto: Lethargy (सुस्ती), Apathy (उदासीनता)

604 Enthusiastic (Adj.) - (उत्साही) *[#R-2 (1)]*
Showing strong interest, excitement, or approval

Syno: {Eager (उत्सुक)}

Anto: Casual (लापरवाह), Apathetic (उदासीन)

605 **Entice** (V.) - (लुभाना) *[#R-6 (1)]*
To attract or tempt by offering pleasure or advantage

Syno: Lure (आकर्षित करना), Entrap (फंसाना), Beguile (मोहित करना), Allure (प्रलोभन देना)

Anto: Repulse (विकर्षित करना)

606 Entire (Adj.) - (पूरा) *[#R-2 (2)]*
With no part left out; whole

Syno: {Whole (संपूर्ण)}

Anto: Partial (आंशिक), Incomplete (अपूर्ण)

607 **Enumerate** (V.) - (गिनती करना) *[#R-2]*
To mention a number of things one by one

Syno: List (सूचीबद्ध करना)

Anto: Guess (अनुमान लगाना)

608 **Enunciate** (V.) - (स्पष्ट उच्चारण करना) *[#R-2]*
To say or pronounce clearly

Syno: Articulate (स्पष्ट बोलना)

Anto: Mispronounce (गलत उच्चारण करना)

609 Envious (Adj.) - (ईर्ष्यालु) *[#R-1 (3)]*
Feeling jealous of someone's possessions or advantages

Syno: {Resentful (आक्रोशित), Jealous (जलनशील)}

Anto: Generous (उदार)

610 Ephemeral (Adj.) - (अल्पकालिक)~ *[#R-8 (10)]*
Lasting for a very short time

Syno: Transient (क्षणिक), Fleeting (पल भर का), Short-lived (अल्पकालिक) {Transitory (अस्थायी), Brief (संक्षिप्त)}

Anto: Eternal (अनन्त), Permanent (स्थायी) {Enduring (टिकाऊ), Long-Lasting (दीर्घकालिक)}

611 Epitome (N.) - (उत्तम रूप; सारांश)~ *[#R-5]*
A perfect example; A summary

Syno: Example (उदाहरण), Type (प्रकार)

Anto: Expansion (विस्तार)

612 Equanimity (N.) - (समभाव)~ *[#R-2 (4)]*
Mental calmness, especially in difficulty

Syno: Calm (शांति) {Patience (धैर्य)}

Anto: Agitation (उत्तेजना)

613 Equivocal (Adj.) - (अनेकार्थी; अनिश्चित) *[#R-7 (2)]*
Open to multiple meanings; unclear

Syno: Ambiguous (अस्पष्ट)

Anto: Explicit (स्पष्ट) {Obvious (प्रत्यक्ष), Clear (साफ़)}

614 Eradicate (V.) - (जड़ से उखाड़ना) *[#R-7 (4)]*
To destroy completely or remove from roots

Syno: Abolish (अन्त करना), Destroy (नष्ट करना), Uproot (उखाड़ना) {Remove (हटाना), Eliminate (समाप्त करना)}

Anto: Preserve (संरक्षित करना), Conserve (संरक्षण करना)

615 Erode (V.) - (भूमि कटाव होना) *[#R-2 (1)]*
To gradually wear away soil or rock

Syno: Disintegrate (विघटित होना)

Anto: Fix (ठीक करना)

616 Erudite (Adj.) - (विद्वान)~ *[#R-14 (9)]*
Having great knowledge or learning

Syno: Scholarly (विद्वतापूर्ण), Learned (ज्ञानी), Knowledgeable (जानकार), Educated (शिक्षित)

Anto: Unscholarly (अविद्वान), Ignorant (अज्ञानी), Uninformed (बेख़बर)

617 **Escalate** (V.) - (बढ़ाना) *[#R-3 (3)]*
To increase rapidly or grow more intense

Syno: {Increase (बढ़ाना)}

Anto: Reduce (कम करना), Plunge (गिरना), Diminish (घटाना) {Shrink (सिकुड़ना), Fall (गिरना)}

618 **Eschew** (V.) - (परहेज करना) *[#R-1 (6)]*
To deliberately avoid or stay away from something.

Syno: Avoid (बचना) {Dodge (चकमा देना)}

Anto: {Embrace (अपनाना), Use (उपयोग करना)}

619 Esoteric (Adj.) - (गूढ़) *[#R-6 (2)]*
Understood by a small group; obscure.

Syno: Abstruse (जटिल), Mysterious (रहस्यमय)

Anto: Straightforward (स्पष्ट), Common (सामान्य), Familiar (परिचित)

620 Essential (Adj.) - (अत्यावश्यक) *[#R-2 (2)]*
Absolutely necessary or very important.

Syno: Vital (महत्वपूर्ण), Crucial (आवश्यक)

Anto: {Unimportant (महत्वहीन), Unnecessary (अनावश्यक)}

621 Establish (V.) - (स्थापित करना) *[#R-4 (2)]*
To set up on permanent basis; to prove or show to be true

Syno: {Create (सृजन करना)}

Anto: Destroy (नष्ट करना), Demolish (ध्वस्त करना), Displace (स्थानांतरित करना) {Disprove (खंडन करना)}

622 Esteem (N.) - (सम्मान)~ *[#R-4 (2)]*
Respect or admiration.

Syno: Regard (आदर), Respect (सम्मान)

Anto: Disregard (अवहेलना), Condemnation (निंदा) {Contempt (अवमानना), Disdain (तिरस्कार)}

623 Estimate (N.) - (अनुमान) *[#R-4 (2)]*
A rough judgment or calculation of amount or value.

Syno: Assessment (मूल्यांकन), Evaluation (आकलन)

Anto: Actuality (वास्तविकता)

624 Eternal (Adj.) - (शाश्वत (सदैव रहने वाला))~ *[#R-7 (2)]*
Lasting forever; without end.

Syno: Perpetual (शाश्वत), Everlasting (चिरस्थायी), Infinite (अनंत)

Anto: Temporary (अस्थायी), Transient (क्षणिक) {Ephemeral (क्षणभंगुर)}

625 Ethical (Adj.) - (नैतिक) *[#R-2 (1)]*
Relating to moral principles and right behavior.

Syno: Equitable (न्यायसंगत)

Anto: Immoral (अनैतिक) {Underhanded (बेईमान)}

626 Euphoria (N.) - (परमानंद)~ *[#R-1 (1)]*
A feeling of intense excitement and happiness

Syno: {Rapture (अत्यधिक आनंद)}

Anto: Depression (अवसाद)

627 **Evade** (V.) - (टालना) *[#R-3 (2)]*
To avoid by cleverness

Syno: Avoid (बचना), Bypass (बचकर निकलना)

Anto: Confront (सामना करना)

628 **Evanescent** (Adj.) - (क्षणिक)~ *[#R-4 (1)]*
Quickly fading or disappearing.

Syno: Fleeting (पल भर का)

Anto: Permanent (स्थायी), Enduring (टिकाऊ) {Lasting (चिरस्थायी)}

629 **Evasive** (Adj.) - (चकमा देने वाला) *[#R-6 (3)]*
Not direct or clear

Syno: Devious (कपटी)

Anto: Frank (स्पष्टवादी), Truthful (सच्चा) {Straightforward (सीधा), Forthright (स्पष्टवादी), Clear (साफ़)}

630 **Eventual** (Adj.) - (अंतिम) *[#R-2]*
Occurring at the end; ultimate

Syno: Ultimate (चरम)

Anto: Initial (प्रारंभिक)

631 Evidence (N.) - (प्रमाण) *[#R-2]*
Facts or information showing truth

Syno: Proof (प्रमाण)

Anto: Concealment (छिपाव)

632 **Evident** (Adj.) - (स्पष्ट) *[#R-6 (4)]*
Plain or obvious; clearly seen or understood

Syno: Clear (साफ़) {Obvious (प्रत्यक्ष), Apparent (स्पष्ट)}

Anto: Indistinct (अस्पष्ट), Hidden (छिपा हुआ), Obscure (धुंधला), Doubtful (संदिग्ध)

633 Evince (V.) - (प्रकट करना) *[#R-3]*
To reveal or indicate clearly

Syno: Show (दिखाना)

Anto: Conceal (छिपाना)

634 **Evoke** (V.) - (आह्वान करना) *[#R-3 (3)]*
To bring or recall to the conscious mind

Syno: Induce (प्रेरित करना) {Elicit (उत्पन्न करना), Call (बुलाना)}

Anto: Forget (भूलना), Stop (रोकना) {Disregard (अनदेखा करना)}

635 Exacerbate (V.) - (बढ़ाना) *[#R-3 (6)]*
To make a problem, bad situation, or negative feeling worse

Syno: Worsen (बिगाड़ना), Aggravate (और बिगाड़ना) {Complicate (जटिल बनाना)}

Anto: Alleviate (कम करना) {Soothe (शांत करना)}

636 Exaggerate (V.) - (बढ़ा-चढ़ाकर कहना)~ *[#R-11 (3)]*
To present something as more than it really is

Syno: Magnify (बड़ा करना), Amplify (बढ़ाना) {Overstate (बढ़ा-चढ़ाकर कहना)}

Anto: Unembellish (सरलता से कहना), Understate (कम करके कहना)

637 **Exalt** (V.) - (प्रशंसा करना) *[#R-1 (2)]*
To hold in very high regard or praise highly

Syno: Praise (प्रशंसा करना)

Anto: {Disgrace (अपमानित करना)}

638 **Exasperate** (V.) - (क्रोधित करना) *[#R-5 (1)]*
To irritate or annoy extremely

Syno: Infuriate (उत्तेजित करना), Annoy (परेशान करना), Frustrate (निराश करना)

Anto: Soothe (सांत्वना देना) {Pacify (शांत करना)}

639 Exasperation (N.) - (झुंझलाहट) *[#R-1 (1)]*
A feeling of intense irritation or annoyance

Syno: {Irritation (चिड़चिड़ापन)}

Anto: Enjoyment (आनंद)

640 Exceptional (Adj.) - (असाधारण) *[#R-6 (1)]*
Unusually good; outstanding

Syno: Extraordinary (असाधारण), Outstanding (उत्कृष्ट)

Anto: Common (सामान्य), Ordinary (साधारण), Unremarkable (महत्वहीन)

641 Excessive (Adj.) - (अत्यधिक) *[#R-3 (3)]*
More than normal or desirable

Syno: Exorbitant (बहुत ज़्यादा) {Inordinate (असामान्य)}

Anto: Moderate (सीमित)

642 **Excited** (Adj.) - (उत्तेजित) *[#R-2]*
Very enthusiastic and eager

Syno: Eager (उत्सुक)

Anto: Bored (ऊबा हुआ)

643 **Exclusion** (N.) - (बहिष्करण) *[#R-2]*
The act of keeping out

Syno: Prohibition (निषेध)

Anto: Admittance (प्रवेश)

644 Exclusive (Adj.) - (विशेष) *[#R-1 (1)]*
Only for certain people; not shared

Syno: {Specific (विशेष)}

Anto: Inclusive (समावेशी)

645 Excruciating (Adj.) - (असहनीय) *[#R-4 (2)]*
Intensely painful

Syno: Piercing (तीव्र), Painful (कष्टदायी)

Anto: Mild (हल्का)

646 **Exculpate** (V.) - (दोषमुक्त करना) *[#R-2]*
To free from blame; prove not guilty

Syno: Exonerate (निर्दोष ठहराना)

Anto: Condemn (दोषी ठहराना)

647 Exemplary (Adj.) - (आदर्श) *[#R-3 (6)]*
Serving as a perfect model; extremely good

Syno: Impeccable (त्रुटिरहित), Excellent (उत्कृष्ट) {Exceptional (असाधारण), Commendable (प्रशंसनीय), Honourable (सम्मानजनक)}

Anto: Unsatisfactory (असंतोषजनक) {Reprehensible (निंदनीय)}

648 Exhale (V.) - (साँस छोड़ना) *[#R-2]*
To breathe out in a deliberate manner

Syno: Emit (उत्सर्जन करना)

Anto: Inhale (साँस लेना)

649 **Exhaustion** (N.) - (थकावट) *[#R-1 (1)]*
A state of being very tired

Syno: {Fatigue (थकान)}

Anto: Replenishment (पुनः पूर्ति)

650 Exhaustive (Adj.) - (संपूर्ण) *[#R-2 (1)]*
Covering all parts completely

Syno: {Thorough (विस्तृत)}

Anto: Incomplete (अधूरा)

651 **Exigent** (Adj.) - (अत्यावश्यक) *[#R-1 (1)]*
Pressing or demanding

Syno: {Imperative (अनिवार्य)}

Anto: Undemanding (सरल)

652 **Exiguous** (Adj.) - (अल्प) *[#R-2]*
Very small in amount

Syno: Scanty (कम)

Anto: Plentiful (प्रचुर)

653 **Exodus** (N.) - (पलायन)~ *[#R-2 (5)]*
A mass departure of people, especially emigrants

Syno: {Exit (निकास), Evacuation (निकासी)}

Anto: Arrival (आगमन), Influx (प्रवाह) {Entry (प्रवेश)}

654 **Exorbitant** (Adj.) - (अत्यधिक)~ *[#R-3 (3)]*
Unreasonably high in amount or price

Syno: Excessive (अधिक), High (ऊंचा)

Anto: Modest (मामूली) {Cheap (सस्ता), Moderate (मध्यम)}

655 **Exotic** (Adj.) - (विदेशी, असामान्य) *[#R-2 (2)]*
Coming from a foreign place or strikingly unusual and attractive

Syno: Strange (अजीब)

Anto: Ordinary (सामान्य) {Common (आम)}

656 **Expedite** (V.) - (शीघ्रता से पूरा करना) *[#R-1 (3)]*
To make something happen faster

Syno: {Accelerate (तेज करना), Hasten (जल्दी करना)}

Anto: Hinder (बाधा डालना)

657 Expensive (Adj.) - (महंगा) *[#R-3 (2)]*
Costing a lot of money

Syno: Dear (महंगा)

Anto: Cheap (सस्ता) {Affordable (किफ़ायती)}

658 Explicit (Adj.) - (स्पष्ट) *[#R-6 (4)]*
Stated clearly and in detail

Syno: Clear (स्पष्ट), Lucid (सुस्पष्ट), Specific (विशिष्ट), Obvious (ज़ाहिर) {Definitive (निश्चित)}

Anto: Ambiguous (अस्पष्ट) {Implicit (अप्रत्यक्ष), Hidden (छिपा हुआ)}

659 Exquisite (Adj.) - (उत्कृष्ट, अति सुंदर) *[#R-5 (4)]*
Extremely beautiful or delicate

Syno: Delicate (कोमल), Beautiful (सुंदर) {Elegant (सुरुचिपूर्ण), Refined (परिष्कृत)}

Anto: Rough (खुरदरा), Coarse (भद्दा) {Ordinary (साधारण), Tactless (अभद्र)}

660 Extinct (Adj.) - (विलुप्त)~ *[#R-4 (2)]*
No longer in existence

Syno: Vanished (लुप्त), Dead (मृत) {Non-Existent (अस्तित्वहीन)}

Anto: Alive (जीवित), Living (जीवित) {Prevailing (प्रचलित)}

661 Extirpate (V.) - (उखाड़ फेंकना)~ *[#R-1 (2)]*
To root out and destroy completely

Syno: {Annihilate (नष्ट करना)}

Anto: Establish (स्थापित करना)

662 **Extol** (V.) - (प्रशंसा करना)~ *[#R-2 (3)]*
To praise enthusiastically

Syno: Praise (प्रशंसा करना) {Acclaim (सराहना करना)}

Anto: Censure (निंदा करना) {Criticise (आलोचना करना)}

663 Extract (V.) - (निकालना) *[#R-2]*
To remove or take out

Syno: Withdraw (वापस लेना)

Anto: Insert (डालना)

664 **Extravagance** (N.) - (फ़िज़ूलखर्ची) *[#R-2]*
The lack of restraint in spending money or use of resources

Syno: Self-Indulgence (मनमर्जी खर्च)

Anto: Parsimony (कंजूसी)

665 Extravagant (Adj.) - (फ़िज़ूलख़र्च)~ *[#R-7 (9)]*
Spending too much money or using resources without control

Syno: Expensive (महंगा) {Excessive (अत्यधिक)}

Anto: Economical (किफायती), Thrifty (कमखर्च), Frugal (कम खर्च वाला), Restrained (नियंत्रित) {Miserly (कंजूस), Reasonable (तर्कसंगत), Meagre (अल्प)}

666 Extricate (V.) - (मुक्त करना) *[#R-2 (1)]*
To free from difficulty or entanglement

Syno: Free (मुक्त करना), Remove (हटाना)

Anto: {Entangle (उलझाना)}

667 Exuberance (N.) - (उल्लास) *[#R-2 (3)]*
The quality of being full of energy and excitement

Syno: Vibrancy (जीवंतता), Excitement (उत्सुकता) {Exhilaration (उत्साह)}

Anto: {Apathy (उदासीनता), Disinterest (निष्क्रियता)}

668 Exuberant (Adj.) - (उत्साही) *[#R-2 (1)]*
Full of lively energy and excitement

Syno: Eager (उत्सुक)

Anto: Repressed (नियंत्रित) {Lethargic (सुस्त)}

669 Exultation (N.) - (उल्लास) *[#R-3 (1)]*
A feeling of great joy after success

Syno: Jubilation (जश्न)

Anto: Agony (पीड़ा)

670 **Fabricate** (V.) - (बनाना, जालसाजी करना) *[#R-4 (6)]*
To invent or make something, often dishonestly

Syno: Concoct (गढ़ना), Construct (निर्माण करना), Forge (जालसाज़ी करना) {Assemble (इकट्ठा करना)}

Anto: Break (तोड़ना) {Destroy (नष्ट करना), Demolish (ध्वस्त करना), Dismantle (विघटित करना)}

671 **Fabulous** (Adj.) - (शानदार) *[#R-2 (2)]*
Extraordinary or very impressive

Syno: Remarkable (उल्लेखनीय), Marvellous (अद्भुत) {Staggering (चौंकाने वाला)}

Anto: {Ordinary (सामान्य)}

672 **Façade** (N.) - (मुखौटा)~ *[#R-2]*
The front face of a building; false outward appearance

Syno: Frontage (सामने का भाग)

Anto: Truth (सत्य)

673 **Facilitate** (V.) - (सुगम बनाना) *[#R-5 (1)]*
To make an action or process easy or easier

Syno: Ease (सुविधाजनक बनाना), Enable (सक्षम करना)

Anto: Hinder (बाधा डालना) {Block (रोकना)}

674 **Fair** (Adj.) - (निष्पक्ष) *[#R-4]*
Following rules; just and reasonable

Syno: Unbiased (पक्षपातरहित), Reasonable (उचित)

Anto: Unjust (अन्यायी)

675 **Fake** (Adj.) - (नकली)~ *[#R-3 (1)]*
Not real

Syno: False (झूठा) {Imitation (नक़ली)}

Anto: Real (असली), Genuine (वास्तविक)

676 **Fallacy** (N.) - (भ्रांति)~ *[#R-4 (1)]*
A false belief based on wrong reasoning

Syno: Error (त्रुटि) {Delusion (भ्रम)}

Anto: Truth (सत्य)

677 **False** (Adj.) - (झूठा) *[#R-2 (2)]*
Not true

Syno: Untrue (असत्य)

Anto: {Genuine (असली)}

678 **Famous** (Adj.) - (प्रसिद्ध) *[#R-6 (3)]*
Known about by many people

Syno: Renowned (विख्यात) {Celebrated (विख्यात)}

Anto: Obscure (अज्ञात), Unknown (अज्ञात) {Ordinary (साधारण)}

679 **Fanatic** (N.) - (कट्टरपंथी)~ *[#R-4]*
A person with excessive zeal for extreme causes

Syno: Enthusiast (उत्साही)

Anto: Moderate (संयमी), Tolerant (सहिष्णु)

680 **Fanatical** (Adj.) - (कट्टर)~ *[#R-2 (4)]*
Having extreme and one-sided zeal

Syno: {Extremist (उग्रवादी)}

Anto: Liberal (उदार), Moderate (संयमी) {Open-Minded (खुले विचारों वाला), Tolerant (सहनशील)}

681 **Fascinating** (Adj.) - (मनमोहक) *[#R-4 (1)]*
Extremely interesting

Syno: Appealing (आकर्षक), Interesting (रोचक), Captivating (मोहित करने वाला) {Enchanting (मनोहर)}

Anto: Repulsive (घृणित)

682 **Fascination** (N.) - (आकर्षण) *[#R-2]*
A strong attraction or interest

Syno: Appeal (अपील)

Anto: Repulsion (घृणा)

683 **Fasten** (V.) - (बांधना) *[#R-5]*
To close or join securely

Syno: Affix (संलग्न करना), Bolt (कसकर बंद करना)

Anto: Release (मुक्त करना)

684 **Fastidious** (Adj.) - (सूक्ष्मदर्शी)~ *[#R-11 (3)]*
Very attentive to accuracy and detail

Syno: Careful (सावधान), Meticulous (अत्यंत सावधान) {Particular (चुनिंदा)}

Anto: Lax (ढीला), Lackadaisical (लापरवाह), Sloppy (अव्यवस्थित), Easy-going (बेपरवाह), Indifferent (उदासीन) {Careless (लापरवाह)}

685 **Fatigue** (N./Adj.) - (थकान; थका देना)~ *[#R-9 (1)]*
Extreme physical or mental tiredness (N.); Exhausted, worn out (Adj.)

Syno: Tiredness (थकावट), Weariness (थकान), Exhaustion (थकान)

Anto: Strength (शक्ति), Energy (ऊर्जा)

686 **Fatigued** (Adj.) - (थका हुआ) *[#R-1 (1)]*
Extremely tired

Syno: Tired (थका)

Anto: {Energetic (ऊर्जावान)}

687 **Fatuous** (Adj.) - (मूर्ख) *[#R-4]*
Silly and pointless

Syno: Silly (बेवकूफ़), Irrational (तर्कहीन)

Anto: Sensible (समझदार), Brilliant (बुद्धिमान)

688 Feasible (Adj.) - (व्यावहारिक, संभव)~ *[#R-3 (1)]*
Possible to do easily or conveniently

Syno: Practical (वास्तविक) {Practicable (कार्यसाध्य)}

Anto: Implausible (अविश्वसनीय), Impractical (अव्यावहारिक)

689 **Fecund** (Adj.) - (उपजाऊ) *[#R-4]*
Able to produce much growth or offspring

Syno: Fertile (उर्वर)

Anto: Barren (बंजर), Sterile (बाँझ), Sparse (विरल)

690 **Feeble** (Adj.) - (कमज़ोर)~ *[#R-16 (11)]*
Lacking physical strength due to age or illness

Syno: Weak (दुर्बल), Wimpy (निर्बल), Decrepit (जर्जर)

Anto: Strong (मजबूत), Effective (प्रभावी), Sturdy (सुदृढ़), Powerful (शक्तिशाली), Robust (हृष्टपुष्ट) {Competent (सक्षम), Durable (टिकाऊ)}

691 **Felicitous** (Adj.) - (उपयुक्त; सुखद)~ *[#R-2]*
Well-chosen or appropriate; Relating to happiness or good fortune

Syno: Appropriate (उचित)

Anto: Unfortunate (दुर्भाग्यपूर्ण)

692 **Felicity** (N.) - (परम सुख) *[#R-5 (5)]*
A state of great happiness

Syno: Bliss (आनंद), Happiness (खुशी) {Joyfulness (हर्ष)}

Anto: Sorrow (दुःख), Misery (कष्ट)

693 Ferocious (Adj.) - (क्रूर) *[#R-5 (2)]*
Savagely fierce, cruel, or violent

Syno: Fierce (उग्र), Frightful (भयानक)

Anto: Mild (सौम्य), Gentle (कोमल) {Docile (आज्ञाकारी)}

694 Fertile (Adj.) - (उपजाऊ) *[#R-7 (5)]*
Capable of becoming pregnant or producing many ideas

Syno: Productive (फलदायी)

Anto: Barren (बंजर) {Desolate (उजाड़)}

695 **Fervour** (N.) - (जोश) *[#R-2]*
Intense and passionate feeling

Syno: Enthusiasm (उत्साह)

Anto: Apathy (उदासीनता)

696 **Fetish** (N.) - (आकर्षण) *[#R-2]*
An unusual attachment to an object or idea

Syno: Desire (इच्छा)

Anto: Indifference (उदासीनता)

697 **Feud** (N.) - (झगड़ा)~ *[#R-3 (2)]*
A long bitter conflict

Syno: {Strife (संघर्ष)}

Anto: Harmony (सौहार्द)

698 **Fickle** (Adj.) - (चंचल)~ *[#R-5 (8)]*
Changing frequently, especially regarding loyalties

Syno: Unstable (अस्थिर), Unpredictable (अनिश्चित) {Inconsistent (असंगत), Vacillating (डांवाडोल)}

Anto: Constant (स्थायी), Stable (स्थिर), Firm (मजबूत) {Certain (निश्चित)}

699 Fictitious (Adj.) - (काल्पनिक)~ *[#R-5 (2)]*
Not real or true, being imaginary or fabricated

Syno: Imaginary (कल्पित), False (झूठा)

Anto: Real (वास्तविक), Factual (तथ्यात्मक)

700 **Fidelity** (N.) - (निष्ठा)~ *[#R-2 (1)]*
Faithfulness to a person, cause, or belief

Syno: Loyalty (वफादारी)

Anto: Treachery (विश्वासघात)

701 **Fiendish** (Adj.) - (दुष्ट) *[#R-2]*
Extremely cruel or unpleasant

Syno: Cruel (क्रूर)

Anto: Friendly (मित्रतापूर्ण)

702 Fierce (Adj.) - (उग्र) *[#R-3 (1)]*
Intensely aggressive or ferocious

Syno: Aggressive (आक्रामक), Furious (क्रोधित)

Anto: Gentle (कोमल) {Weak (कमजोर)}

703 **Figurative** (Adj.) - (अलंकारिक) *[#R-1 (5)]*
Metaphorical; not literal

Syno: {Flowery (अलंकारपूर्ण)}

Anto: Literal (शाब्दिक)

704 **Filthy** (Adj./Adv.) - (गंदा; बेहद) *[#R-5]*
Disgustingly dirty; To a great degree

Syno: Dirty (मैला), Foul (गंदा); Extremely (अत्यंत)

Anto: Clean (स्वच्छ)

705 **Flagitious** (Adj.) - (कुकर्मी) *[#R-2 (1)]*
Criminal; villainous

Syno: Criminal (अपराधी)

Anto: Virtuous (सदाचारी) {Innocent (निर्दोष)}

706 **Flaunt** (V.) - (दिखावा करना) *[#R-4]*
To display ostentatiously to provoke envy or

admiration

Syno: Exhibit (प्रदर्शित करना)

Anto: Cover (ढकना), Hide (छिपाना)

707 **Flaw** (N.) - (त्रुटि)~ *[#R-2]*
A mark, fault, or imperfection that mars a substance or object

Syno: Defect (दोष)

Anto: Perfection (पूर्णता)

708 Flawless (Adj.) - (निर्दोष) *[#R-1 (1)]*
Without any blemishes or imperfections

Syno: {Faultless (त्रुटिहीन)}

Anto: Defective (दोषयुक्त)

709 **Fleeting** (Adj.) - (क्षणिक) *[#R-4 (2)]*
Lasting for a very short time

Syno: Momentary (क्षणभंगुर), Brief (संक्षिप्त) {Ephemeral (अल्पकालिक)}

Anto: Lasting (स्थायी) {Eternal (शाश्वत)}

710 Flimsy (Adj.) - (कमजोर) *[#R-4 (2)]*
Light and insubstantial; easily damaged

Syno: Feeble (निर्बल), Weak (दुर्बल) {Thin (पतला)}

Anto: Sturdy (मजबूत), Strong (शक्तिशाली)

711 Flippant (Adj.) - (चुलबुला) *[#R-2 (3)]*
Not showing a serious or respectful attitude

Syno: {Disrespectful (असम्मानजनक)}

Anto: Serious (गंभीर), Earnest (गंभीर)

712 Flourish (V.) - (पनपना) *[#R-3 (1)]*
To grow well or develop rapidly

Syno: Thrive (फलना-फूलना)

Anto: Degenerate (पतन होना)

713 **Foe** (N.) - (शत्रु) *[#R-2 (1)]*
An enemy or opponent

Syno: Enemy (शत्रु)

Anto: Friend (मित्र)

714 **Follow** (V.) - (अनुसरण करना) *[#R-4]*
To go or come after someone or something

Syno: Obey (पालन करना), Emulate (अनुकरण करना)

Anto: Predate (पूर्ववर्ती होना), Lead (नेतृत्व करना)

715 **Foment** (V.) - (उत्तेजित करना) *[#R-5]*
To instigate or stir up undesirable sentiment

Syno: Incite (भड़काना)

Anto: Quell (दबाना), Quash (दबाना), Regulate (नियंत्रित करना), Dampen (शांत करना)

716 **Foolish** (Adj.) - (मूर्खतापूर्ण) *[#R-1 (2)]*
Lacking good sense or judgment

Syno: {Fatuous (मूर्खतापूर्ण)}

Anto: {Wise (बुद्धिमान)}

717 **Forbid** (V.) - (मना करना) *[#R-6 (6)]*
To refuse to allow something

Syno: Ban (प्रतिबंधित करना), Preclude (रोकना), Prohibit (निषेध करना) {Outlaw (गैरकानूनी घोषित करना)}

Anto: Allow (अनुमति देना) {Permit (अनुमति देना), Admit (स्वीकार करना)}

718 **Forgive** (V.) - (क्षमा करना) *[#R-3]*
To stop feeling angry toward someone

Syno: Pardon (माफ़ करना)

Anto: Loathe (घृणा करना), Condemn (निंदा करना)

719 **Former** (Adj.) - (भूतपूर्व) *[#R-5]*
Having previously filled a particular role

Syno: Previous (पिछला)

Anto: Latter (बाद का), Current (वर्तमान)

720 Formidable (Adj.) - (विकट, भयंकर)~ *[#R-1 (3)]*
Inspiring fear or respect

Syno: {Scary (भयावह), Powerful (शक्तिशाली)}

Anto: Trivial (मामूली) {Surmountable (जीतने योग्य)}

721 **Forthright** (Adj.) - (स्पष्टवादी)~ *[#R-4]*
Direct and honest; straightforward

Syno: Outspoken (मुखर)

Anto: Devious (कपटी), Uncandid (अस्पष्ट)

722 Fortify (V.) - (मजबूत करना) *[#R-4 (3)]*
To strengthen with defensive works against attack

Syno: Strengthen (सुदृढ़ करना), Secure (सुरक्षित करना) {Toughen (कठोर बनाना)}

Anto: Undermine (कमजोर करना) {Weaken (कमजोर करना)}

723 **Fortitude** (N.) - (साहस) *[#R-2 (3)]*
Courage in pain or adversity

Syno: Bravery (वीरता), Grit (दृढ़ता) {Forbearance (धैर्य)}

Anto: {Cowardice (डरपोकपन)}

724 Fortunate (Adj.) - (भाग्यशाली) *[#R-1 (2)]*
Favoured by or involving good luck

Syno: {Lucky (भाग्यशाली)}

Anto: Unfortunate (दुर्भाग्यशाली)

725 **Fragile** (Adj.) - (नाजुक)~ *[#R-12 (4)]*
Easily broken or damaged

Syno: Brittle (भुरभुरा), Delicate (कोमल), Frail

(कमज़ोर) {Flimsy (कमज़ोर)}

Anto: Tough (कठोर), Strong (मजबूत), Robust (मज़बूत), Healthy (स्वस्थ) {Sturdy (मज़बूत), Durable (टिकाऊ)}

726 Fragrance (N.) - (सुगंध) *[#R-2 (1)]*
A pleasant sweet smell

Syno: Aroma (खुशबू)

Anto: Stench (दुर्गंध) {Stink (बदबू)}

727 **Frail** (Adj.) - (कमजोर) *[#R-6 (4)]*
Weak and delicate

Syno: Feeble (दुर्बल), Fragile (नाजुक) {Weak (कमजोर)}

Anto: Robust (हृष्ट-पुष्ट), Strong (मजबूत) {Sturdy (हट्टा-कट्टा)}

728 Fraudulent (Adj.) - (कपटपूर्ण) *[#R-2 (1)]*
Obtained or done by deception or criminal fraud

Syno: Deceitful (बेईमान), Counterfeit (नकली)

Anto: {Genuine (वास्तविक)}

729 Freedom (N.) - (स्वतंत्रता) *[#R-3 (1)]*
The power to act, speak, or think without restraint

Syno: {Liberty (आज़ादी)}

Anto: Captivity (कैद), Bondage (गुलामी)

730 **Frenzy** (N.) - (उन्माद) *[#R-3 (2)]*
A state of uncontrolled excitement or wild behavior

Syno: {Hysteria (उन्माद), Fury (क्रोध)}

Anto: Calmness (शांति)

731 Frequent (Adj.) - (बारंबार) *[#R-4 (4)]*
Happening often

Syno: Constant (निरंतर)

Anto: Rare (दुर्लभ), Intermittent (रुक रुक कर होने वाला), Seldom (कभी कभार) {Irregular (अनियमित)}

732 **Fresh** (Adj.) - (ताजा) *[#R-1 (4)]*
Recently made or obtained; not stale

Syno: {New (नया), Modern (आधुनिक)}

Anto: {Stale (बासी)}

733 Fright (N.) - (डर) *[#R-3 (1)]*
A sudden intense fear

Syno: Dread (भय)

Anto: Reassurance (आश्वासन)

734 Frigid (Adj.) - (अत्यंत ठंडा) *[#R-3 (2)]*
Very cold in temperature

Syno: Freezing (जमा देने वाला)

Anto: Warm (गर्म) {Tropical (उष्णकटिबंधीय)}

735 Frivolous (Adj.) - (गैर-गंभीर) *[#R-6 (6)]*
Not having any serious purpose or value

Syno: Puerile (बचकाना), Trivial (महत्वहीन), Flippant (छिछोरा), Worthless (बेकार)

Anto: {Serious (गंभीर), Solemn (संजीदा)}

736 **Frugal** (Adj.) - (मितव्ययी)~ *[#R-13 (5)]*
Economical with money or food

Syno: Economical (अल्पव्ययी), Thrifty (किफायती)

Anto: Wasteful (बर्बाद करने वाला), Spendthrift (फिजूलखर्च व्यक्ति), Profligate (अपव्ययी), Prodigal (फिजूलखर्च), Extravagant (फिजूलखर्च)

737 **Frustrate** (V.) - (निराश करना) *[#R-1 (1)]*
To prevent a plan from succeeding or being fulfilled

Syno: {Thwart (विफल करना)}

Anto: Foster (प्रोत्साहन देना)

738 **Fuel** (V.) - (उकसाना) *[#R-1 (1)]*
To stimulate or provoke

Syno: {Fire (आग लगाना)}

Anto: Deter (हतोत्साहित करना)

739 Fundamental (Adj.) - (मौलिक) *[#R-2 (1)]*
Forming a necessary base; of central importance

Syno: Basic (आधारभूत)

Anto: {Unimportant (महत्वहीन)}

740 Furious (Adj.) - (क्रोधित) *[#R-1 (3)]*
Extremely angry

Syno: {Angry (गुस्सैल), Inflamed (भड़का हुआ), Livid (अत्यंत क्रोधित)}

Anto: Unperturbed (शांत)

741 Furtive (Adj.) - (गुप्त) *[#R-4]*
Attempting to avoid notice; sly or stealthy

Syno: Secretive (गोपनीय)

Anto: Open (खुला), Straight (सीधा)

742 **Fusion** (N.) - (संलयन) *[#R-3 (4)]*
The process of joining into one

Syno: Blend (मिश्रण)

Anto: {Separation (अलगाव)}

743 Futile (Adj.) - (व्यर्थ) *[#R-11 (5)]*
Incapable of producing result

Syno: Unsuccessful (असफल), Useless (बेकार), Fruitless (निष्फल) {Pointless (निरर्थक)}

Anto: Effective (कारगर), Fruitful (फलदायक), Productive (उत्पादक), Worthy (योग्य), Useful

(उपयोगी) {Valuable (मूल्यवान)}

744 Gallant (Adj.) - (पराक्रमी)~ *[#R-4 (2)]*
Brave and noble

Syno: Courageous (साहसी), Brave (बहादुर)

Anto: Cowardly (कायरतापूर्ण), Craven (डरपोक) {Timid (डरपोक)}

745 **Gap** (N.) - (अंतर) *[#R-1 (1)]*
A noticeable difference or disparity; an opening or space

Syno: {Difference (अंतर)}

Anto: Continuity (निरंतरता)

746 Garrulous (Adj.) - (बातूनी)~ *[#R-9 (7)]*
Excessively talkative, especially on trivial matters

Syno: Talkative (बातूनी), Voluble (वाचाल), Loquacious (बातूनी)

Anto: Taciturn (मौन), Quiet (शांत), Reserved (कम बोलने वाला) {Reticent (अल्पभाषी)}

747 **Gather** (V.) - (एकत्र करना) *[#R-4]*
To come together or assemble

Syno: Congregate (एकत्रित होना)

Anto: Divide (विभाजित करना), Disperse (फैलाना), Spread (बिखेरना)

748 **Gaudy** (Adj.) - (भड़कीला) *[#R-2]*
Extravagantly bright or showy, typically tasteless

Syno: Flashy (चमकदार)

Anto: Sober (सादा)

749 Generous (Adj.) - (उदार)~ *[#R-13 (17)]*
Showing readiness to give, especially money

Syno: Kind (दयालु), Lavish (फिजूलखर्च) {Benevolent (परोपकारी), Magnanimous (उदारमना), Bountiful (भरपूर)}

Anto: Stingy (कंजूस), Miserly (कंजूस), Selfish (स्वार्थी), Mean (कंजूस), Greedy (लालची) {Uncharitable (कृपाहीन), Frugal (मितव्ययी), Niggardly (कंजूस)}

750 **Genial** (Adj.) - (मिलनसार) *[#R-5 (4)]*
Friendly and cheerful

Syno: Cordial (मैत्रीपूर्ण), Convivial (मिलनसार), Cheerful (खुशमिजाज) {Friendly (मित्रवत)}

Anto: Boorish (असभ्य), Hostile (शत्रुतापूर्ण) {Sullen (उदास)}

751 Genius (N.) - (प्रतिभाशाली व्यक्ति)~ *[#R-2 (1)]*
Exceptional intellectual or creative power; a person with such ability

Syno: {Wizard (प्रतिभाशाली व्यक्ति)}

Anto: Fool (मूर्ख व्यक्ति)

752 Gentle (Adj.) - (सौम्य) *[#R-1 (2)]*
Mild in temperament or behaviour; kind or tender

Syno: Sympathetic (सहानुभूतिपूर्ण) {Amiable (मिलनसार)}

Anto: {Ferocious (क्रूर)}

753 Genuine (Adj.) - (असली)~ *[#R-13 (6)]*
Truly what something is said to be; authentic

Syno: Original (मूल), Authentic (प्रामाणिक), Real (वास्तविक) {True (सच), Sincere (ईमानदार)}

Anto: Fake (नकली), Spurious (जाली), False (असत्य), Dubious (संदिग्ध) {Fictitious (काल्पनिक)}

754 **Ghastly** (Adj.) - (भयानक)~ *[#R-3]*
Extremely unpleasant

Syno: Horrible (डरावना), Gruesome (भयावह)

Anto: Pleasant (सुखद)

755 Gigantic (Adj.) - (विशाल)~ *[#R-4 (6)]*
Of very great size or extent; huge or enormous

Syno: Huge (बहुत बड़ा) {Enormous (अत्यधिक बड़ा), Monstrous (राक्षसी)}

Anto: Tiny (छोटा), Microscopic (सूक्ष्म) {Puny (बहुत छोटा)}

756 **Give up** (V.) - (त्यागना) *[#R-2 (1)]*
To stop trying; to surrender

Syno: {Abandon (छोड़ देना)}

Anto: Persist (दृढ़ रहना)

757 **Glance** (V.) - (एक नज़र देखना; सरसरी नज़र) *[#R-1 (1)]*
To look briefly

Syno: {Glimpse (झलक देखना)}

Anto: Stare (घूरना)

758 **Glee** (N.) - (खुशी) *[#R-6]*
Great delight; exuberant joy

Syno: Mirth (उल्लास), Happiness (प्रसन्नता)

Anto: Woe (दुःख)

759 Gloomy (Adj.) - (उदास) *[#R-13 (4)]*
Dark or poorly lit, appearing depressing or frightening

Syno: Murky (गहरा), Dull (धुंधला), Unhappy (उदास), Cloudy (बादल छाये), Dismal (निराशाजनक) {Depressed (निराश)}

Anto: Bright (उज्ज्वल), Radiant (चमकदार), Buoyant (प्रसन्न), Cheerful (खुश), Lively (ऊर्जावान)

760 **Glorify** (V.) - (बड़ाई करना) *[#R-2 (1)]*
To praise and worship; acknowledge the majesty of God

Syno: Celebrate (गुणगान करना), Praise (प्रशंसा करना)

Anto: {Vilify (बदनाम करना)}

761 **Glut** (N./V.) - (भरमार; अधिकता में देना) *[#R-3 (5)]*
An excessive supply (N.); To supply to excess (V.)

Syno: {Surplus (अधिशेष); Satiate (तृप्त करना)}

Anto: Starve (भूखा रखना) {Diet (संतुलित आहार)}

762 Gorgeous (Adj.) - (भव्य) *[#R-1 (1)]*
Very beautiful or attractive

Syno: {Ravishing (आकर्षक)}

Anto: Ordinary (सामान्य)

763 Grab (V.) - (पकड़ना) *[#R-3]*
To grasp or seize suddenly and roughly

Syno: Catch (पकड़ना), Seize (जब्त करना)

Anto: Release (मुक्त करना)

764 Graceful (Adj.) - (गरिमापूर्ण) *[#R-4 (2)]*
Having grace or elegance

Syno: Elegant (शिष्ट)

Anto: Awkward (अजीब) {Coarse (असभ्य)}

765 Gracious (Adj.) - (शालीन) *[#R-4 (1)]*
Courteous, kind, and pleasant

Syno: Polite (विनम्र)

Anto: Rude (असभ्य)

766 Gradual (Adj.) - (क्रमिक) *[#R-4 (2)]*
Taking place slowly or by degrees

Syno: Continuous (निरंतर)

Anto: Abrupt (अचानक), Rapid (तेज) {Volatile (अस्थिर)}

767 Grandeur (N.) - (भव्यता) *[#R-4 (1)]*
Splendour and impressiveness of appearance

Syno: Magnificence (वैभव)

Anto: Insignificance (महत्वहीनता) {Simplicity (सादगी)}

768 **Grant** (V.) - (अनुमति देना; अनुदान देना) *[#R-1 (2)]*
To give or allow something requested

Syno: {Allow (अनुमति देना)}

Anto: Refuse (मना करना)

769 Graphic (Adj.) - (चित्रात्मक, सजीव) *[#R-1 (1)]*
Relating to visual art or representation; giving a vivid or detailed description

Syno: Vivid (जीवंत)

Anto: {Sketchy (अधूरा)}

770 **Grapple** (V.) - (संघर्ष करना) *[#R-1 (2)]*
To engage in a close fight or struggle

Syno: {Grasp (पकड़ना)}

Anto: Release (मुक्त करना)

771 Gratification (N.) - (संतोष) *[#R-3 (2)]*
The pleasure from satisfying a desire

Syno: Satisfaction (संतुष्टि), Contentment (तृप्ति)

Anto: Dissatisfaction (असंतोष)

772 **Gratify** (V.) - (संतुष्ट करना) *[#R-3 (1)]*
To give pleasure or satisfaction

Syno: Satisfy (तृप्त करना)

Anto: Annoy (परेशान करना), Disappoint (निराश करना)

773 **Gratitude** (N.) - (आभार) *[#R-1 (2)]*
The quality of being thankful

Syno: {Thankfulness (कृतज्ञता)}

Anto: Thanklessness (कृतघ्नता)

774 Gratuitous (Adj.) - (अकारण; निःशुल्क) *[#R-2 (1)]*
Uncalled for or lacking good reason; given free of charge

Syno: Unwarranted (अकारण), Unjustified (अनुचित)

Anto: {Warranted (जायज़)}

775 Grave (Adj.) - (गंभीर) *[#R-4 (1)]*
Serious or solemn in manner

Syno: Serious (संजीदा)

Anto: Frivolous (तुच्छ), Trivial (मामूली), Humorous (हास्यपूर्ण)

776 Gregarious (Adj.) - (मिलनसार)~ *[#R-6 (4)]*
Fond of company or sociable

Syno: Sociable (मिलनसार)

Anto: Unsociable (असामाजिक), Introverted (अंतर्मुखी), Solitary (एकांतप्रिय) {Antisocial (समाजविरोधी)}

777 Grief (N./V.) - (शोक; दुःखी होना) *[#R-5 (1)]*
Deep sorrow (N.); To feel deep sorrow (V.)

Syno: Anguish (पीड़ा), Pain (दर्द), Sorrow (शोक)

Anto: Joy (आनंद)

778 **Grim** (Adj.) - (कठोर) *[#R-3 (3)]*
Forbidding or stern in appearance

Syno: Stern (कठोर), Serious (गंभीर) {Gloomy (विषादपूर्ण)}

Anto: Pleasant (सुखद)

779 **Grisly** (Adj.) - (भयानक) *[#R-5 (1)]*

Causing horror or disgust

Syno: Gruesome (भयावह), Atrocious (घृणित)

Anto: Attractive (आकर्षक), Pleasant (सुखद), Comforting (आरामदायक)

780 Grotesque (Adj.) - (विचित्र) *[#R-4]*
Comically or repulsively ugly

Syno: Ugly (बदसूरत)

Anto: Attractive (आकर्षक), Beautiful (सुंदर), Natural (प्राकृतिक)

781 Grudge (N.) - (मनमुटाव) *[#R-3 (4)]*
A persistent feeling of resentment from a past insult

Syno: Envy (ईर्ष्या) {Malice (द्वेष), Aversion (घृणा)}

Anto: Goodwill (सद्भाव), Benevolence (परोपकार) {Friendship (मित्रता)}

782 **Gruelling** (Adj.) - (थकानेवाला)~ *[#R-1 (2)]*
Extremely tiring and demanding

Syno: Challenging (चुनौतीपूर्ण)

Anto: {Relaxing (आरामदायक)}

783 Gruesome (Adj.) - (भयानक) *[#R-2]*
Causing repulsion or horror; grisly

Syno: Hideous (घृणित)

Anto: Gracious (शालीन)

784 Grumble (V.) - (बड़बड़ाना) *[#R-4 (1)]*
To complain in a bad-tempered way

Syno: Complain (शिकायत करना), Murmur (बुड़बुड़ाना), Groan (कराहना)

Anto: Praise (प्रशंसा करना) {Compliment (तारीफ़ करना)}

785 **Grumpy** (Adj.) - (चिड़चिड़ा) *[#R-4]*
Bad-tempered and easily annoyed

Syno: Irritable (झुंझलाहट भरा)

Anto: Pleasant (सुखद), Amiable (मिलनसार)

786 **Guile** (N.) - (चालाकी) *[#R-6 (3)]*
Sly or cunning intelligence

Syno: Cunning (चतुराई), Deceit (धोखा), Slyness (चालाकी)

Anto: Honesty (ईमानदारी) {Candour (स्पष्टवादिता)}

787 Guilt (N.) - (अपराधबोध) *[#R-3]*
The fact of having committed an offense

Syno: Remorse (पश्चाताप), Contrition (पछतावा)

Anto: Innocence (निर्दोषता)

788 **Gullibility** (N.) - (भोलापन) *[#R-2]*
A tendency to be easily deceived

Syno: Simplicity (सादगी)

Anto: Skepticism (संदेहवाद)

789 Gullible (Adj.) - (भोला)~ *[#R-6 (2)]*
Easily deceived or tricked

Syno: Innocent (भोला-भाला), Naïve (सीधा-सादा)

Anto: Cynical (संशयवादी), Suspicious (संदेही), Wise (बुद्धिमान)

790 **Gumption** (N.) - (सहज बुद्धि) *[#R-3]*
The ability to deal with situations wisely

Syno: Acumen (कुशाग्रता)

Anto: Stupidity (मूर्खता), Inanity (निरर्थकता)

791 Guzzle (V.) - (बहुत खाना पीना) *[#R-3]*
To drink or eat greedily

Syno: Imbibe (अवशोषित करना, पीना)

Anto: Starve (भूखा रहना)

792 Habitual (Adj.) - (नियमित) *[#R-2]*
Done regularly; usual or customary

Syno: Continuous (लगातार)

Anto: Occasional (यदाकदा)

793 **Haggard** (Adj.) - (थका-हारा) *[#R-4 (1)]*
Looking exhausted and unwell from fatigue or worry

Syno: Emaciated (दुर्बल), Exhausted (थका हुआ)

Anto: Fresh (ताज़ा) {Exuberant (उल्लसित)}

794 **Hamper** (V./N.) - (बाधा डालना; टोकरी)~ *[#R-7 (5)]*
To hinder or impede progress (V.); A basket with a lid (N.)

Syno: Hinder (बाधित करना), Block (रोकना), Restrict (प्रतिबंधित करना) {Retard (धीमा करना); Basket (टोकरी, पात्र)}

Anto: Promote (बढ़ावा देना), Help (मदद करना) {Assist (सहायता करना)}

795 **Hamstrung** (V.) - (अपंग करना) *[#R-1 (1)]*
To cripple or disable

Syno: Cripple (लंगड़ा करना)

Anto: {Empower (सशक्त करना)}

796 **Handy** (Adj.) - (सुविधाजनक) *[#R-4 (1)]*
Convenient to handle or use

Syno: Convenient (सुविधाजनक), Useful (उपयोगी) {Accessible (सुलभ)}

Anto: Inconvenient (असुविधाजनक)

797 Haphazard (Adj.) - (अव्यवस्थित) *[#R-2 (3)]*
Lacking any obvious principle of organization

Syno: Random (बेतरतीब) {Unsystematic (अव्यवस्थित)}

Anto: {Deliberate (जानबूझकर), Systematic

(योजनाबद्ध)}

798 **Hapless** (Adj.) - (दुर्भाग्यशाली) *[#R-5 (2)]*
Having bad luck

Syno: Unlucky (भाग्यहीन), Ill-Fated (दुर्भाग्यपूर्ण), Unfortunate (अभागा)

Anto: {Fortunate (भाग्यशाली)}

799 Happiness (N.) - (खुशी) *[#R-1 (1)]*
The state of being happy

Syno: Bliss (आनंद)

Anto: {Misery (दुख)}

800 **Happy** (Adj.) - (प्रसन्न) *[#R-2]*
Feeling or showing pleasure or contentment

Syno: Blissful (आनंदित)

Anto: Sad (उदास)

801 Harass (V.) - (परेशान करना)~ *[#R-5 (1)]*
To subject to aggressive pressure or intimidation

Syno: Bother (तंग करना), Molest (सताना), Intimidate (डराना) {Irritate (चिढ़ाना)}

Anto: Comfort (दिलासा देना), Relieve (राहत देना)

802 **Hard** (Adj.) - (कठिन; कठोर) *[#R-2]*
Solid or firm; difficult; lacking sympathy

Syno: Difficult (मुश्किल)

Anto: Charitable (दयालु)

803 **Hardship** (N.) - (कष्ट) *[#R-2 (1)]*
Severe suffering or privation

Syno: Tribulation (पीड़ा), Misery (दुख)

Anto: {Opportunity (अवसर)}

804 **Harmonious** (Adj.) - (मैत्रीपूर्ण) *[#R-2 (1)]*
Forming a pleasing or consistent whole

Syno: {Peaceful (शांतिपूर्ण)}

Anto: Discordant (कलहपूर्ण)

805 Harmony (N.) - (सामंजस्य) *[#R-13 (7)]*
Agreement or concord; pleasant arrangement of parts

Syno: Consensus (सहमति), Peace (शांति) {Unity (एकता), Accord (समझौता)}

Anto: Strife (संघर्ष), Conflict (विवाद), Hatred (घृणा), Discord (कलह) {Incoherence (असंगति)}

806 **Harrowing** (Adj.) - (पीड़ादायक)~ *[#R-2]*
Causing great distress or suffering

Syno: Excruciating (तीव्र पीड़ादायक)

Anto: Pleasant (सुखद)

807 **Harsh** (Adj.) - (कठोर)~ *[#R-5 (1)]*
Unpleasantly rough or jarring to the senses

Syno: Brutal (निर्दयी) {Severe (कठोर)}

Anto: Gentle (कोमल), Lenient (नरम)

808 **Haste** (N.) - (शीघ्रता) *[#R-6 (2)]*
Excessive speed or urgency of movement or action

Syno: Hurry (जल्दी)

Anto: Delay (देरी)

809 Hasty (Adj.) - (जल्दबाजी) *[#R-4 (3)]*
Done or acting with excessive speed or urgency

Syno: Quick (तेज़) {Abrupt (अचानक)}

Anto: Cautious (सावधान)

810 Haughty (Adj.) - (अहंकारी)~ *[#R-6 (4)]*
Arrogantly superior and disdainful

Syno: Conceited (घमंडी), Arrogant (अभिमानी)

Anto: Humble (विनम्र), Modest (संयमी)

811 Hazard (N.) - (खतरा) *[#R-4]*
A danger or risk

Syno: Danger (खतरा), Risk (जोखिम)

Anto: Protection (रक्षा), Safety (सुरक्षा)

812 Hazardous (Adj.) - (खतरनाक) *[#R-5 (5)]*
Involving risk or danger

Syno: Dangerous (जोखिम भरा), Risky (जोखिमपूर्ण)

Anto: Secure (सुरक्षित) {Safe (निरापद)}

813 **Hefty** (Adj.) - (भारी) *[#R-1 (1)]*
Large in size or weight; strong

Syno: {Massive (विशाल)}

Anto: Slight (हल्का)

814 Hegemony (N.) - (प्रभुत्व) *[#R-2 (2)]*
The leadership or dominance by one group over others

Syno: {Dominance (प्रभुता)}

Anto: Subordination (अधीनता)

815 **Hesitant** (Adj.) - (हिचकिचाने वाला) *[#R-1 (2)]*
Tentative, unsure, or slow in acting or speaking

Syno: Reluctant (अनिच्छुक) {Undecided (अनिश्चित)}

Anto: {Firm (दृढ़)}

816 Hesitate (V.) - (संकोच करना)~ *[#R-5]*
To pause before saying or doing something, especially through uncertainty

Syno: Pause (रुकना), Dither (हिचकिचाना), Falter (लड़खड़ाना)

Anto: Advance (आगे बढ़ना), Resolve (संकल्प करना)

817 Hideous (Adj.) - (घिनौना) *[#R-5 (3)]*

Ugly or disgusting to look at

Syno: {Unpleasant (अप्रिय), Repulsive (विकर्षक)}

Anto: Beautiful (सुंदर), Charming (मोहक), Attractive (आकर्षक) {Alluring (लुभावना)}

818 Hilarious (Adj.) - (हास्यप्रद) *[#R-3 (5)]*
Extremely amusing

Syno: {Uproarious (अत्यंत हास्यप्रद), Comical (हास्यास्पद)}

Anto: Sad (दुखी), Serious (गंभीर), Humourless (हास्यरहित) {Tragic (दुखद), Grim (गंभीर)}

819 Hinder (V.) - (बाधा डालना) *[#R-9 (3)]*
To create difficulty or cause delay

Syno: Impede (रोकना), Obstruct (रास्ता रोकना)

Anto: Aid (सहायता करना), Help (मदद करना), Facilitate (सुविधा देना) {Assist (सहायता देना)}

820 Holistic (Adj.) - (समग्र) *[#R-1 (2)]*
Viewing something as a whole with interconnected parts

Syno: Comprehensive (पूर्ण)

Anto: {Partial (आंशिक)}

821 Honest (Adj.) - (ईमानदार) *[#R-6 (1)]*
Free of deceit; truthful and sincere

Syno: Upright (सच्चा), Sincere (निष्कपट)

Anto: Corrupt (भ्रष्ट) {Deceptive (धोखेबाज)}

822 **Hope** (N./V.) - (आशा; उम्मीद रखना) *[#R-5 (1)]*
A feeling of expectation and desire (N.); To want something to happen (V.)

Syno: Wish (इच्छा)

Anto: Doubt (संदेह), Despair (निराशा) {Anguish (पीड़ा)}

823 Horrendous (Adj.) - (भयानक)~ *[#R-2 (1)]*
Extremely unpleasant, horrifying, or terrible

Syno: {Dreadful (डरावना)}

Anto: Pleasant (सुखद)

824 Hospitable (Adj.) - (मेहमाननवाज़)~ *[#R-3 (4)]*
Friendly and welcoming to guests

Syno: Congenial (सुखद) {Cordial (हार्दिक), Welcoming (स्वागत करने वाला)}

Anto: Rude (असभ्य)

825 Hostile (Adj.) - (शत्रुतापूर्ण) *[#R-19 (5)]*
Showing opposition or dislike; unfriendly

Syno: Belligerent (झगड़ालू), Warlike (लड़ाकू) {Adverse (विरोधी), Aggressive (आक्रामक)}

Anto: Amiable (सौम्य), Friendly (मित्रवत), Sympathetic (सहानुभूतिपूर्ण), Hospitable (मेहमाननवाज़), Gentle (कोमल), Favourable (अनुकूल) {Amicable (सौहार्दपूर्ण)}

826 Hostility (N.) - (दुश्मनी) *[#R-4 (5)]*
An unfriendly or aggressive attitude

Syno: Enmity (शत्रुता)

Anto: Friendship (मित्रता) {Friendliness (मैत्रीभाव), Hospitality (मेहमाननवाज़ी)}

827 Huge (Adj.) - (विशाल) *[#R-2 (3)]*
Extremely large in size; enormous

Syno: Big (बड़ा) {Gigantic (विराट)}

Anto: Minute (सूक्ष्म) {Tiny (छोटा), Small (लघु)}

828 Humane (Adj.) - (दयालु) *[#R-6 (2)]*
Having or showing compassion or benevolence

Syno: Sympathetic (सहानुभूतिपूर्ण)

Anto: Cruel (क्रूर), Unkind (निर्दयी)

829 **Humble** (Adj.) - (विनम्र) *[#R-12 (2)]*
Having a modest view of one's importance

Syno: Meek (सहनशील), Modest (शालीन) {Unassuming (सादा)}

Anto: Arrogant (अभिमानी), Assertive (आत्मविश्वासी), Pompous (दिखावटी), Proud (गर्वित)

830 **Humility** (N.) - (नम्रता) *[#R-8 (2)]*
A modest view of one's own importance

Syno: {Modesty (विनम्रता)}

Anto: Pride (गर्व), Arrogance (अहंकार), Vanity (अभिमान)

831 **Hummock** (N.) - (टीला) *[#R-1 (1)]*
A small rounded hill or mound

Syno: {Knoll (छोटी पहाड़ी)}

Anto: Ditch (खाई)

832 Humorous (Adj.) - (हास्यजनक) *[#R-1 (2)]*
Causing laughter and amusement; comic

Syno: Witty (हाज़िरजवाब) {Funny (मज़ेदार)}

Anto: {Tragic (दुखद)}

833 Hypocrisy (N.) - (पाखंड)~ *[#R-1 (1)]*
The practice of claiming beliefs one does not have

Syno: Deceit (छल)

Anto: {Honesty (ईमानदारी)}

834 **Hysteria** (N.) - (उन्माद) *[#R-1 (1)]*
A state of extreme, uncontrolled emotion

Syno: Madness (पागलपन)

Anto: {Serenity (शांति)}

835 **Hysterical** (Adj.) - (भावनाओं से अभिभूत; अत्यधिक मजेदार) *[#R-2]*

Affected by uncontrolled extreme emotion; Extremely funny

Syno: Funny (हास्यास्पद)

Anto: Controlled (नियंत्रित)

836 Ideal (Adj.) - (आदर्श) *[#R-3]*
Perfect or most suitable

Syno: Excellent (उत्कृष्ट)

Anto: Flawed (त्रुटिपूर्ण), Faulty (दोषपूर्ण)

837 **Identical** (Adj.) - (समान) *[#R-4 (2)]*
Exactly alike in every detail

Syno: Same (एक जैसा), Similar (सदृश)

Anto: Different (अलग) {Distinct (विशिष्ट), Diverse (विविध)}

838 Idiosyncrasy (N.) - (अनोखापन)~ *[#R-2 (1)]*
A behaviour peculiar to an individual

Syno: Peculiarity (विचित्रता)

Anto: Generality (सामान्यता)

839 **Idle** (Adj.) - (निष्क्रिय; आलसी) *[#R-3 (1)]*
Avoiding work; not active or engaged

Syno: Unoccupied (बेकार)

Anto: Diligent (परिश्रमी), Active (कार्यरत) {Occupied (व्यस्त)}

840 **Ignoble** (Adj.) - (असम्मानजनक) *[#R-2 (1)]*
Not honourable in character or purpose

Syno: Unworthy (अयोग्य) {Shameful (शर्मनाक)}

Anto: Dignified (सम्मानपूर्ण)

841 Ignominious (Adj.) - (शर्मनाक) *[#R-1 (3)]*
Deserving or causing public disgrace

Syno: Disgraceful (अपमानजनक) {Shameful (लज्जाजनक), Dishonourable (अनादरपूर्ण)}

Anto: {Glorious (गौरवशाली)}

842 Ignominy (N.) - (अपमान)~ *[#R-4 (2)]*
Public shame or disgrace

Syno: Disgrace (कलंक), Dishonour (बदनामी)

Anto: Glory (गौरव), Esteem (प्रतिष्ठा) {Honour (सम्मान)}

843 Illicit (Adj.) - (अवैध)~ *[#R-9 (1)]*
Forbidden by law, rules, or custom

Syno: Illegal (गैरकानूनी), Unlawful (विधिविरुद्ध)

Anto: Lawful (कानूनी), Legal (वैध), Ethical (नैतिक)

844 **Illuminate** (V.) - (प्रकाशित करना)~ *[#R-4]*
To light up; make clear or understandable

Syno: Brighten (उज्वल करना), Explain (समझाना), Elucidate (स्पष्ट करना)

Anto: Darken (अंधेरा करना)

845 Imaginary (Adj.) - (काल्पनिक)~ *[#R-1 (1)]*
Existing only in the imagination

Syno: Fictitious (मनगढ़ंत)

Anto: {Real (वास्तविक)}

846 **Imbecile** (N./Adj.) - (मूर्ख; मूर्खतापूर्ण) *[#R-4 (1)]*
A person lacking intelligence (N.); Lacking intelligence (Adj.)

Syno: Idiot (बेवकूफ), Dunce (बेवक़ूफ़); Foolish (मूर्खतापूर्ण) {Stupid (मूर्ख)}

Anto: Intelligent (बुद्धिमान)

847 Imitate (V.) - (नकल करना) *[#R-5]*
To take or follow as a model

Syno: Copy (प्रतिलिपि करना), Ape (अनुकरण करना), Mimic (नकल उतारना)

Anto: Innovate (नवाचार करना)

848 Imitation (N./Adj.) - (नकल; नकली)~ *[#R-2 (2)]*
A copy of something (N.); Made to resemble something else, not genuine (Adj.)

Syno: Artificial (बनावटी), Fake (नकली) {Facsimile (प्रतिलिपि)}

Anto: {Original (असली)}

849 Immaculate (Adj.) - (बेदाग) *[#R-4]*
Perfectly clean, neat, or tidy

Syno: Impeccable (निर्दोष)

Anto: Filthy (गंदा), Messy (अव्यवस्थित), Foul (बदबूदार)

850 Immense (Adj.) - (विशाल) *[#R-4 (1)]*
Extremely large or great in scale or degree

Syno: Massive (भारी), Huge (बहुत बड़ा)

Anto: Tiny (छोटा)

851 Imminent (Adj.) - (शीघ्र घटित होने वाला) *[#R-6 (2)]*
About to happen very soon

Syno: Forthcoming (आगामी), Impending (निकट), Approaching (नजदीक आता हुआ) {Threatening (धमकीपूर्ण)}

Anto: Distant (दूर) {Remote (दूरदराज)}

852 Immortal (Adj.) - (अमर)~ *[#R-1 (1)]*
Living forever; never dying or decaying

Syno: {Undying (अमर)}

Anto: Temporary (नश्वर)

853 **Immune** (Adj.) - (सुरक्षित)~ *[#R-5 (1)]*
Resistant to a particular infection or toxin; not affected by something

Syno: Resistant (प्रतिरोधी)

Anto: Vulnerable (असुरक्षित), Susceptible

(प्रभावित होने योग्य), Sensitive (संवेदनशील)

854 **Immutable** (Adj.) - (अपरिवर्तनीय) *[#R-3]*
Unable to be changed

Syno: Unchanging (स्थिर)

Anto: Alterable (परिवर्तनीय)

855 Impartial (Adj.) - (निष्पक्ष)~ *[#R-5 (4)]*
Treating all sides equally without favour

Syno: Fair (न्यायपूर्ण), Neutral (पक्षरहित) {Unbiased (तटस्थ)}

Anto: Biased (पक्षपाती)

856 Impeccable (Adj.) - (त्रुटिहीन) *[#R-10 (3)]*
Completely free from faults or errors

Syno: Perfect (परिपूर्ण), Flawless (दोषरहित), Faultless (निर्दोष)

Anto: Inexact (असटीक), Imperfect (अपूर्ण), Flawed (त्रुटिपूर्ण), Faulty (दोषपूर्ण)

857 Impecunious (Adj.) - (निर्धन)~ *[#R-1 (4)]*
Having little or no money

Syno: {Penurious (कंगाल)}

Anto: Wealthy (धनी)

858 **Impede** (V.) - (बाधा डालना) *[#R-5 (5)]*
To delay or stop progress by creating an obstacle

Syno: Hinder (रोकना), Thwart (विफल करना) {Obstruct (अवरोध करना)}

Anto: Advance (आगे बढ़ाना), Facilitate (सुगम बनाना), Expedite (शीघ्रता करना)

859 Imperious (Adj.) - (हुक्म चलाने वाला) *[#R-2 (3)]*
Arrogant and domineering; acting with unjustified authority

Syno: {Commanding (प्रभावशाली)}

Anto: Meek (आज्ञाकारी) {Submissive (आज्ञाकारी), Modest (नम्र)}

860 Impertinent (Adj.) - (अशिष्ट)~ *[#R-3 (4)]*
Not showing proper respect

Syno: Impolite (अभद्र) {Rude (असभ्य)}

Anto: Respectful (आदरपूर्वक), Polite (शिष्ट) {Courteous (विनम्र)}

861 Impervious (Adj.) - (अभेद्य)~ *[#R-3 (3)]*
Not allowing fluid to pass through

Syno: Impenetrable (अनुप्रवेश्य) {Impermeable (अपारगम्य), Unaffected (अप्रभावित)}

Anto: Permeable (रिसने योग्य) {Penetrable (भेद्य)}

862 Impetuous (Adj.) - (जल्दबाज)~ *[#R-4 (6)]*
Acting or done quickly and without thought or care

Syno: Hasty (जल्दबाज़ी) {Impulsive (असंयमी)}

Anto: Cautious (सावधान) {Careful (सतर्क), Deliberate (सोच-विचार कर किया हुआ), Poised (संतुलित)}

863 Impious (Adj.) - (अधार्मिक) *[#R-2 (1)]*
Not showing respect or reverence, especially for a god

Syno: Irreverent (अश्रद्धालु), Irreligious (अधार्मिक)

Anto: {Reverent (श्रद्धालु)}

864 Implore (V.) - (विनती करना) *[#R-2 (1)]*
To beg someone earnestly or desperately to do something

Syno: Plead (गुहार लगाना)

Anto: {Demand (मांगना)}

865 **Impolite** (Adj.) - (असभ्य) *[#R-2 (1)]*
Not having or showing good manners; rude

Syno: Rude (रूखा)

Anto: Courteous (विनम्र)

866 Important (Adj.) - (महत्वपूर्ण) *[#R-3 (1)]*
Of great significance or value

Syno: Significant (अर्थपूर्ण)

Anto: Trivial (तुच्छ)

867 **Impoverished** (Adj.) - (गरीब) *[#R-4 (1)]*
Made poor

Syno: Penniless (धनहीन)

Anto: Affluent (समृद्ध), Rich (अमीर) {Flourishing (समृद्ध)}

868 **Impromptu** (Adj.) - (तात्कालिक)~ *[#R-3 (4)]*
Done without preparation; improvisational

Syno: {Offhand (बिना सोचे), Improvised (तात्कालिक), Unprepared (बिना तैयारी के)}

Anto: Premeditated (पूर्वनियोजित), Prepared (तैयार), Planned (योजनाबद्ध)

869 **Improvident** (Adj.) - (फिजूलखर्च)~ *[#R-1 (1)]*
Careless about future needs; wasteful

Syno: {Spendthrift (खर्चीला)}

Anto: Thrifty (किफ़ायती)

870 **Impudent** (Adj.) - (निर्लज्ज)~ *[#R-4 (2)]*
Not showing due respect for another person; impertinent

Syno: {Rude (अशिष्ट)}

Anto: Polite (विनम्र), Modest (नम्र), Respectful (सम्मानजनक)

871 Impulsive (Adj.) - (आवेगी) *[#R-2 (2)]*
Acting or done without forethought

Syno: {Rash (उतावला)}

Anto: Thoughtful (विचारशील), Cautious (सतर्क)

872 **Impute** (V.) - (आरोप लगाना) *[#R-3 (2)]*
To say that someone is responsible for something

Syno: Attribute (उत्तरदायी ठहराना)

Anto: Defend (बचाव करना), Support (समर्थन करना)

873 Inadvertent (Adj.) - (अनजाना) *[#R-4 (4)]*
Done without intention; accidental

Syno: Unintentional (अनिच्छापूर्ण)

Anto: Deliberate (सोचा-समझा) {Purposeful (उद्देश्यपूर्ण)}

874 **Incapacitate** (V.) - (अक्षम बनाना) *[#R-2]*
To prevent from functioning normally

Syno: Cripple (विकलांग करना)

Anto: Facilitate (सुगम बनाना)

875 Incentive (N.) - (प्रोत्साहन)~ *[#R-1 (1)]*
A thing that motivates or encourages someone

Syno: {Motivator (प्रेरक)}

Anto: Hindrance (बाधा)

876 **Inception** (N.) - (शुरुआत) *[#R-3 (1)]*
The beginning or start of something

Syno: Beginning (प्रारंभ)

Anto: Conclusion (निष्कर्ष), Termination (समाप्ति) {End (अंत)}

877 **Incessant** (Adj.) - (निरंतर)~ *[#R-7 (1)]*
Continuing without stopping or interruption

Syno: Persistent (लगातार), Continuous (निरंतर), Ceaseless (बिना रुके) {Continual (निरंतर)}

Anto: Intermittent (अनियमित), Sporadic (छिटपुट)

878 Incite (V.) - (उकसाना) *[#R-4 (2)]*
To encourage or stir up action, often violent

Syno: Inflame (भड़काना)

Anto: Discourage (हतोत्साहित करना), Restrain (रोकना), Prohibit (निषेध करना) {Calm (शांत करना)}

879 **Inclement** (Adj.) - (खराब) *[#R-4 (1)]*
Harsh, unpleasant, or severe, especially weather

Syno: Stormy (उथल-पुथल भरा), Unfavourable (प्रतिकूल)

Anto: Mild (हल्का)

880 Incorporate (V.) - (शामिल करना) *[#R-2]*
To take in or contain as part of a whole

Syno: Integrate (मिलाना)

Anto: Exclude (बाहर करना)

881 Incorrigible (Adj.) - (असुधार्य)~ *[#R-4]*
Incapable of being corrected or improved

Syno: Unalterable (अपरिवर्तनीय)

Anto: Reformable (सुधार योग्य), Reclaimable (सुधारने योग्य)

882 Incredible (Adj.) - (अविश्वसनीय)~ *[#R-8 (4)]*
Impossible to believe

Syno: Unbelievable (अविश्वसनीय), Unimaginable (अकल्पनीय) {Shocking (चौंकाने वाला)}

Anto: Possible (संभव), Believable (विश्वसनीय), Ordinary (साधारण) {Credible (विश्वसनीय)}

883 Indelible (Adj.) - (अमिट)~ *[#R-3 (3)]*
Making marks that cannot be removed or erased

Syno: Inerasable (न मिटने योग्य) {Everlasting (सदा रहने वाला), Permanent (स्थायी)}

Anto: Temporary (अस्थायी)

884 Indict (V.) - (आरोप लगाना) *[#R-4]*
To formally accuse of or charge with a crime

Syno: Charge (आरोप लगाना)

Anto: Exonerate (दोषमुक्त करना), Release (रिहा करना)

885 **Indifferent** (Adj.) - (उदासीन) *[#R-1 (6)]*
Having no particular interest or sympathy

Syno: {Unconcerned (उदासीन), Apathetic (उदासीन), Uncaring (बेपरवाह)}

Anto: Attentive (सचेत) {Curious (जिज्ञासु), Compassionate (दयालु)}

886 Indigenous (Adj.) - (स्वदेशी)~ *[#R-2 (8)]*
Originating or occurring naturally in a particular place

Syno: Aboriginal (आदिवासी) {Native (स्वदेशी), Home-Grown (देशी)}

Anto: Alien (विदेशी) {Foreign (विदेशी)}

887 **Indigent** (Adj.) - (निर्धन) *[#R-1 (9)]*
Very poor and lacking basic necessities

Syno: Impoverished (निर्धन) {Poor (गरीब)}

Anto: {Affluent (समृद्ध)}

888 **Indignant** (Adj.) - (क्रोधित) *[#R-1 (1)]*
Feeling or showing anger at unfair treatment

Syno: {Resentful (रोषपूर्ण)}

Anto: Pleased (खुश)

889 Indispensable (Adj.) - (अनिवार्य)~ *[#R-6 (3)]*
Absolutely necessary

Syno: Essential (आवश्यक)

Anto: Superfluous (अनावश्यक), Inessential

(गैरज़रूरी) {Unimportant (महत्वहीन)}

890 Indolent (Adj.) - (आलसी) *[#R-6 (6)]*
Wanting to avoid activity or exertion

Syno: Lazy (सुस्त) {Languid (सुस्त)}

Anto: Diligent (परिश्रमी), Lively (जीवंत), Active (सक्रिय), Energetic (ऊर्जावान)

891 Indomitable (Adj.) - (अजेय) *[#R-4 (3)]*
Not able to be defeated or controlled

Syno: Unconquerable (अजेय), Invincible (अपराजेय) {Unyielding (अडिग)}

Anto: Submissive (जो आसानी से झुक जाए)

892 **Industrious** (Adj.) - (परिश्रमी)~ *[#R-9 (5)]*
Showing steady effort and hard work

Syno: Diligent (मेहनती)

Anto: Lethargic (सुस्त), Indolent (आलसी), Lazy (आलसी)

893 Ineffable (Adj.) - (अवर्णनीय)~ *[#R-2 (1)]*
Too great or extreme to be expressed or described in words

Syno: Inexpressible (अव्यक्त) {Unutterable (अवर्णनीय)}

Anto: Expressible (अभिव्यक्त)

894 Ineluctable (Adj.) - (अनिवार्य) *[#R-2]*
Impossible to avoid or escape

Syno: Inevitable (अनिवार्य)

Anto: Preventable (रोके जाने योग्य)

895 Inept (Adj.) - (अयोग्य) *[#R-7 (1)]*
Lacking skill or ability

Syno: Clumsy (अनाड़ी)

Anto: Talented (प्रतिभाशाली), Competent (सक्षम), Skilful (कुशल)

896 Inertia (N.) - (निष्क्रियता) *[#R-4 (1)]*
A tendency to do nothing or to remain unchanged

Syno: Inactivity (सुस्ती)

Anto: Energy (ऊर्जा), Vigour (जोश) {Activity (गतिविधि)}

897 Inevitable (Adj.) - (अपरिहार्य)~ *[#R-6 (3)]*
That cannot be avoided or prevented from happening

Syno: Unavoidable (अपरिहार्य) {Certain (निश्चित)}

Anto: Avoidable (टालने योग्य) {Preventable (रोकने योग्य), Evadable (टालने योग्य)}

898 **Inevitably** (Adv.) - (निश्चित रूप से) *[#R-1 (1)]*
As is certain to happen; unavoidably

Syno: Certainly (अवश्य)

Anto: {Unexpectedly (अचानक)}

899 **Inexpensive** (Adj.) - (सस्ता) *[#R-2]*
Not costing a lot of money

Syno: Cheap (सस्ता)

Anto: Dear (महंगा)

900 Infamous (Adj.) - (बदनाम) *[#R-1 (1)]*
Well-known for bad reasons

Syno: Notorious (कुख्यात)

Anto: {Noble (महान)}

901 **Infernal** (Adj.) - (नरक-संबंधी) *[#R-1 (3)]*
Relating to hell or the underworld

Syno: {Hellish (भयावह)}

Anto: Heavenly (स्वर्गीय) {Paradisiac (स्वर्गिक)}

902 **Infirm** (Adj.) - (दुर्बल) *[#R-4 (1)]*
Not physically or mentally strong, especially through age or illness

Syno: Weak (कमजोर)

Anto: Strong (मजबूत), Robust (स्वस्थ)

903 **Infirmity** (N.) - (दुर्बलता) *[#R-1 (1)]*
A physical or mental weakness

Syno: {Feebleness (कमजोरी)}

Anto: Strength (शक्ति)

904 Ingenuous (Adj.) - (निष्कपट) *[#R-2 (5)]*
Innocent and unsuspecting

Syno: Innocent (निर्दोष), Candid (खुले दिल का) {Honest (ईमानदार)}

Anto: {Deceitful (धोखेबाज), Devious (कपटी), Calculating (चालाक)}

905 Inherent (Adj.) - (अन्तर्निहित, स्वाभाविक) *[#R-5 (2)]*
Existing as a permanent or essential part

Syno: Inborn (जन्मजात), Natural (प्राकृतिक) {Inbuilt (अंतर्निहित)}

Anto: Extraneous (बाहरी)

906 Inimical (Adj.) - (शत्रुतापूर्ण) *[#R-3 (1)]*
Tending to obstruct or harm

Syno: Harmful (हानिकारक), Hostile (दुश्मनीपूर्ण)

Anto: {Supportive (सहायक)}

907 Initiate (V.) - (आरंभ करना) *[#R-4 (2)]*
To cause a process or action to begin

Syno: Start (शुरू करना) {Begin (शुरू करना), Commence (आरंभ करना)}

Anto: Finish (समाप्त करना), Conclude (समाप्त करना)

908 **Innate** (Adj.) - (जन्मजात) *[#R-3 (2)]*

Existing naturally from birth

Syno: Inherent (अंतर्निहित) {Intrinsic (अंतर्निहित)}

Anto: Acquired (अर्जित), Learned (सीखा हुआ)

909 Innocuous (Adj.) - (हानिरहित)~ *[#R-6 (5)]*
Not harmful or offensive

Syno: Harmless (हानिरहित), Inoffensive (अहानिकर) {Benign (सौम्य)}

Anto: Pernicious (हानिकारक), Harmful (घातक)

910 **Inordinate** (Adj.) - (अत्यधिक) *[#R-2 (3)]*
Excessively large or beyond normal limits

Syno: {Exorbitant (अत्यधिक)}

Anto: Reasonable (उचित) {Moderate (मध्यम)}

911 Inquisitive (Adj.) - (जिज्ञासु)~ *[#R-10 (1)]*
Eager to ask questions or gain knowledge

Syno: Curious (जिज्ञासु) {Agog (उत्सुक)}

Anto: Indifferent (उदासीन), Unconcerned (बेपरवाह), Uninterested (अरुचिपूर्ण), Disinterested (उदासीन), Ignorant (बेख़बर)

912 **Insane** (Adj.) - (पागल) *[#R-4]*
Mentally ill; Extremely foolish

Syno: Crazy (सनकी), Mad (पागल)

Anto: Wise (बुद्धिमान)

913 Inscrutable (Adj.) - (रहस्यमय) *[#R-4 (1)]*
Impossible to understand or interpret

Syno: Inexplicable (समझ से बाहर) {Mysterious (रहस्यमय)}

Anto: Comprehensible (स्पष्ट)

914 **Insert** (V.) - (डालना) *[#R-3]*
To place, fit, or thrust something into another thing

Syno: Enter (प्रवेश करना)

Anto: Extract (निकालना), Remove (हटाना)

915 Insidious (Adj.) - (घातक)~ *[#R-4 (3)]*
Proceeding in a gradual, subtle way, but with harmful effects

Syno: Crafty (चालाक), Deceptive (छलपूर्ण), Harmful (नुकसानदेह) {Cunning (चालाक), Deceitful (छली), False (झूठा)}

Anto: Sincere (ईमानदार)

916 Insipid (Adj.) - (फीका) *[#R-9 (11)]*
Lacking taste, flavour, or interest

Syno: Bland (बेस्वाद), Tasteless (फीका) {Plain (सादा), Flat (फीका), Dull (नीरस), Prosaic (सामान्य)}

Anto: Tasty (स्वादिष्ट), Appetizing (भूख बढ़ाने वाला) {Delicious (स्वादिष्ट), Piquant (तीखा), Interesting (रोचक), Flavourful (स्वादयुक्त), Zesty (चटपटा), Lively (जीवंत)}

917 Insolent (Adj.) - (बदतमीज़) *[#R-11 (3)]*
Showing a rude and arrogant lack of respect

Syno: Disrespectful (असम्मानजनक), Bold (साहसी), Rude (अशिष्ट) {Insulting (अपमानजनक)}

Anto: Humble (विनम्र), Submissive (आज्ञाकारी), Mannerly (शिष्ट), Courteous (विनम्र) {Affable (मिलनसार)}

918 **Insolvent** (Adj.) - (दिवालिया)~ *[#R-1 (1)]*
Unable to pay debts owed

Syno: {Bankrupt (दिवालिया)}

Anto: Affluent (धनी)

919 Inspire (V.) - (प्रेरित करना) *[#R-3 (3)]*
To fill someone with the urge or ability to act or create

Syno: Animate (सजीव बनाना), Stimulate (उत्तेजित करना), Motivate (प्रोत्साहित करना) {Encourage (प्रोत्साहित करना)}

Anto: {Daunt (हिम्मत तोड़ना), Dissuade (मना करना)}

920 Instant (Adj.) - (तात्कालिक) *[#R-4]*
Happening immediately without delay

Syno: Immediate (तुरंत)

Anto: Delayed (विलम्बित), Gradual (धीरे-धीरे)

921 **Insular** (Adj.) - (संकीर्ण सोच वाला) *[#R-1 (2)]*
Ignorant of or uninterested in cultures, ideas, or peoples outside one's own experience

Syno: {Detached (अलग)}

Anto: Cosmopolitan (सर्वदेशीय) {Unbiased (निष्पक्ष)}

922 **Insuperable** (Adj.) - (अजेय) *[#R-1 (1)]*
Impossible to overcome or defeat

Syno: Insurmountable (अजेय)

Anto: {Surmountable (जीतने योग्य)}

923 Integral (Adj.) - (अनिवार्य) *[#R-2 (2)]*
Forming an essential and necessary part of a whole

Syno: Essential (आवश्यक) {Fundamental (आधारभूत)}

Anto: Extra (अतिरिक्त)

924 Integrate (V.) - (एकीकृत करना)~ *[#R-3 (1)]*
To combine separate parts into a whole

Syno: Unite (एकजुट करना), Assimilate (अपनाना)

Anto: Separate (अलग करना) {Disengage (अलग करना)}

925 **Integration** (N.) - (एकीकरण) *[#R-4]*
The process of combining parts into a whole
Syno: Unification (संघटन), Unity (एकता)
Anto: Fragmentation (विखंडन)

926 Intelligible (Adj.) - (समझ में आने योग्य) *[#R-4]*
Able to be understood clearly
Syno: Comprehensible (समझ में आने योग्य), Lucid (स्पष्ट)
Anto: Incoherent (असंगत)

927 Intense (Adj.) - (प्रबल) *[#R-4 (2)]*
Of extreme force, degree, or strength
Syno: Powerful (शक्तिशाली), Strong (मजबूत)
Anto: Moderate (मध्यम), Faint (मंद) {Calm (शांत), Low (निम्न)}

928 Interfere (V.) - (हस्तक्षेप करना) *[#R-3 (1)]*
To get involved so as to hinder or disrupt an activity
Syno: Obstruct (बाधित करना), Restrict (प्रतिबंधित करना) {Meddle (हस्तक्षेप करना)}
Anto: Advance (प्रगति करना)

929 Interrogate (V.) - (पूछताछ करना) *[#R-2]*
To question someone formally or intensively
Syno: Investigate (जांच पड़ताल करना)
Anto: Reply (उत्तर देना)

930 **Intervene** (V.) - (हस्तक्षेप करना)~ *[#R-3]*
To come between events to prevent or change an outcome
Syno: Arbitrate (सुलह कराना), Meddle (दखल देना)
Anto: Abstain) (दूर रहना)

931 Intransigent (Adj.) - (अडिग) *[#R-6 (4)]*
Unwilling or refusing to change one's views or to agree about something
Syno: Stubborn (जिद्दी), Unyielding (न झुकने वाला) {Unbending (कठोर)}
Anto: Subservient (आज्ञाकारी), Compromising (समझौता करने वाला) {Yielding (मान लेने वाला), Flexible (लचीला)}

932 Intrepid (Adj.) - (निडर) *[#R-5 (5)]*
Fearless and adventurous
Syno: Fearless (निडर), Gallant (वीर) {Brave (साहसी)}
Anto: Cowardly (कायर), Meek (डरपोक)

933 Intricate (Adj.) - (जटिल) *[#R-5 (6)]*
Very complicated or detailed
Syno: Complex (पेचीदा), Complicated (जटिल)
Anto: Simple (सरल) {Ordinary (साधारण)}

934 Intriguing (Adj.) - (दिलचस्प) *[#R-3 (3)]*
Making someone curious or eager to know more
Syno: Gripping (रोमांचक), Interesting (रुचिकर)
Anto: Boring (उबाऊ)

935 Intrinsic (Adj.) - (स्वाभाविक) *[#R-2 (2)]*
Belonging naturally; essential
Syno: {Inherent (अंतर्निहित)}
Anto: Extrinsic (बाह्य), Extraneous (अतिरिक्त) {Acquired (अर्जित)}

936 Introvert (N.) - (अंतर्मुखी)~ *[#R-2 (1)]*
A quiet, reserved person who prefers solitude
Syno: Reserved (संकोची)
Anto: {Extrovert (बहिर्मुखी)}

937 Inundate (V.) - (भरमार कर देना)~ *[#R-3]*
To flood or overwhelm with too much of something
Syno: Overwhelm (दबा देना)
Anto: Drain (निकालना)

938 **Invade** (V.) - (आक्रमण करना) *[#R-2 (1)]*
To enter forcefully or in large numbers
Syno: Intrude (घुसपैठ करना)
Anto: Surrender (समर्पण करना)

939 **Invective** (N.) - (अपमानजनक भाषा) *[#R-2 (1)]*
Insulting, abusive, or highly critical language
Syno: Abuse (गाली), Tirade (कटु भाषण)
Anto: {Politeness (विनम्रता)}

940 **Invigorate** (V.) - (ऊर्जा भरना)~ *[#R-1 (1)]*
To give energy, strength, or enthusiasm
Syno: {Arouse (जगाना)}
Anto: Tire (थकाना)

941 **Invigorating** (Adj.) - (ताज़गी भरा) *[#R-2 (1)]*
Making one feel strong, healthy, and full of energy
Syno: Refreshing (ताज़गी भरा)
Anto: Dull (नीरस) {Exhausting (थकाने वाला)}

942 **Invincible** (Adj.) - (अजेय (जिसे हराया ना जा सके))~ *[#R-7 (2)]*
Too powerful to be defeated or overcome
Syno: Unassailable (अभेद्य), Unbeatable (अपराजेय) {Inviolable (अलंघनीय)}
Anto: Vulnerable (असुरक्षित, कमज़ोर), Powerless (शक्तिहीन)

943 Irascible (Adj.) - (चिड़चिड़ा)~ *[#R-2]*
Having or showing a tendency to be easily angered

Syno: Irritable (जल्दी क्रोधित होने वाला)

Anto: Amiable (मिलनसार)

944 **Irreproachable** (Adj.) - (निर्दोष) *[#R-1 (1)]*
Beyond criticism or blame

Syno: Faultless (दोषरहित)

Anto: {Impeachable (आरोप लगाने योग्य)}

945 **Irresolute** (Adj.) - (अनिश्चित) *[#R-2]*
Unable to make a firm decision

Syno: Undecided (असमंजस में)

Anto: Decisive (निर्णायक)

946 Irritate (V.) - (परेशान करना) *[#R-5]*
To make someone feel annoyed or irritated

Syno: Displease (नाराज़ करना), Annoy (परेशान करना)

Anto: Delight (खुशी देना), Pacify (शांत करना)

947 **Isolate** (V.) - (अलग करना) *[#R-4]*
To cause a person or place to be or remain alone or apart from others

Syno: Detach (अलग करना), Seclude (अलग करना), Separate (अलग करना)

Anto: Associate (जोड़ना)

948 **Jaded** (Adj.) - (थका हुआ) *[#R-5 (1)]*
Tired, bored, or lacking enthusiasm after having too much of something

Syno: Tired (थका हुआ), Fatigued (थकान से चूर) {Exhausted (थका हुआ)}

Anto: Refreshed (तरोताज़ा), Renewed (पुनर्जीवित), Cheerful (प्रसन्न)

949 Jeopardy (N.) - (खतरा) *[#R-6 (2)]*
Danger of loss, harm, or failure

Syno: Risk (जोखिम), Peril (खतरा)

Anto: Safety (सुरक्षा), Protection (संरक्षण) {Assurance (आश्वासन)}

950 **Jettison** (V.) - (फेंक देना) *[#R-3]*
To throw away or discard forcibly

Syno: Discard (फेंक देना), Eject (निकाल देना)

Anto: Accept (स्वीकार करना)

951 **Jolly** (Adj.) - (खुशमिजाज) *[#R-3]*
Happy and cheerful

Syno: Amused (प्रसन्न)

Anto: Morose (उदास), Serious (गंभीर)

952 Jovial (Adj.) - (प्रसन्नचित्त)~ *[#R-9 (6)]*
Cheerful and friendly

Syno: Joyous (खुश) {Mirthful (हँसमुख), Merry (खुशमिजाज)}

Anto: Gloomy (उदास), Sorrowful (दुखी), Morose (उदास), Petulant (चिड़चिड़ा) {Cheerless (उदास)}

953 Jubilant (Adj.) - (उल्लासित) *[#R-9 (2)]*
Feeling or expressing great happiness and triumph

Syno: Ecstatic (अत्यंत खुश), Rejoicing (जश्न मनाने वाला), Happy (खुश), Overjoyed (अति प्रसन्न) {Triumphant (विजयी), Joyful (आनंदित)}

Anto: Depressed (अवसादग्रस्त), Gloomy (उदास), Despondent (निराश), Sorrowful (दुखी)

954 Jubilation (N.) - (उल्लास) *[#R-1 (1)]*
A feeling of great happiness and triumph

Syno: Rejoicing (जश्न)

Anto: {Sorrow (दुख)}

955 Judicious (Adj.) - (विवेकपूर्ण) *[#R-13 (4)]*
Having, showing, or done with good judgment or sense

Syno: Wise (बुद्धिमान), Cautious (सतर्क), Prudent (चतुर), Sensible (समझदार), Thoughtful (विचारशील) {Reasonable (तर्कसंगत)}

Anto: Rash (उतावला), Unwise (मूर्ख) {Indiscreet (अविवेकी)}

956 **Just** (Adj.) - (न्यायसंगत) *[#R-4]*
Based on or behaving according to what is morally right and fair

Syno: Fair (उचित)

Anto: Corrupt (भ्रष्ट), Unfair (अनुचित)

957 Juvenile (Adj./N.) - (नाबालिग; किशोर व्यक्ति)~ *[#R-5 (3)]*
Relating to young people (Adj.); A young person (N.)

Syno: Childish (बचकाना), Young (युवा) {Youthful (युवा)}

Anto: Adult (वयस्क)

958 Keen (Adj.) - (उत्सुक; तीक्ष्ण) *[#R-8 (1)]*
Having or showing eagerness or enthusiasm; (of a blade) sharp

Syno: Enthusiastic (उत्साही), Eager (लालायित)

Anto: Indifferent (उदासीन), Blunt (धार रहित), Dull (मंद)

959 **Key** (Adj.) - (मुख्य) *[#R-1 (1)]*
Of crucial importance

Syno: {Important (महत्वपूर्ण)}

Anto: Negligible (तुच्छ)

960 **Knack** (N.) - (कौशल)~ *[#R-4]*
An acquired or natural skill at performing a task

Syno: Dexterity (निपुणता)

Anto: Inability (अक्षमता), Dullness (मंदता)

961 **Knave** (N.) - (दुष्ट) *[#R-3 (2)]*
A dishonest or unscrupulous man

Syno: Scoundrel (बदमाश), Rogue (धूर्त) {Villain (खलनायक)}

Anto: Paragon (आदर्श व्यक्ति) {Gentleman (सज्जन)}

962 Knowledge (N.) - (ज्ञान) *[#R-2]*
Facts, information, and skills acquired through experience or education

Syno: Wisdom (बुद्धिमत्ता)

Anto: Ignorance (अज्ञान)

963 Laborious (Adj.) - (श्रमसाध्य, परिश्रमी) *[#R-3 (1)]*
Requiring considerable effort and time; Hardworking

Syno: Assiduous (कठिन परिश्रमी)

Anto: Facile (सहज) {Lazy (आलसी)}

964 Lackadaisical (Adj.) - (उदासीन) *[#R-3 (1)]*
Lacking enthusiasm and determination; carelessly lazy

Syno: Careless (लापरवाह) {Listless (उदासीन)}

Anto: Enthusiastic (उत्साही)

965 **Lack-Lustre** (Adj.) - (बिना चमक का) *[#R-2]*
Lacking energy, interest, or excitement; dull

Syno: Humdrum (नीरस)

Anto: Radiant (चमकीला)

966 Laconic (Adj.) - (संक्षिप्त) *[#R-7 (7)]*
Using very few words

Syno: Concise (संक्षिप्त), Crisp (सटीक), Brief (संक्षिप्त)

Anto: Verbose (शब्दाडंबरपूर्ण), Wordy (शब्दों से भरा) {Loquacious (बातूनी), Voluble (बातूनी), Longwinded (लंबा)}

967 Lacuna (N.) - (अभाव) *[#R-1 (5)]*
An unfilled space or interval; a gap

Syno: Hiatus (विराम) {Shortcoming (कमी)}

Anto: {Abundance (प्रचुरता)}

968 **Laid-Back** (Adj.) - (आरामतलब) *[#R-1 (1)]*
Relaxed and easy-going

Syno: {Easygoing (सहज)}

Anto: Ambitious (महत्वाकांक्षी)

969 Lament (V./N.) - (विलाप; रोना-पीटना)~ *[#R-9 (5)]*
To mourn a person's loss or death (V); An expression of grief or sorrow (N.)

Syno: Mourn (शोक मनाना) {Wail (विलाप करना)}

Anto: Rejoice (खुश होना), Celebrate (जश्न मनाना), Applaud (तालियाँ बजाना); Applause (तालियाँ) {Exultation (उल्लास), Delight (आनंद)}

970 Languid (Adj.) - (सुस्त) *[#R-6 (5)]*
Displaying or having a disinclination for physical exertion or effort; slow and relaxed

Syno: Sluggish (सुस्त) {Lazy (आलसी), Lethargic (निष्क्रिय), Indifferent (उदासीन)}

Anto: Energetic (ऊर्जावान), Animated (सजीव), Vigorous (बलवान) {Dynamic (सक्रिय)}

971 **Lassitude** (N.) - (थकान) *[#R-4]*
A state of physical or mental weariness; lack of energy

Syno: Sluggishness (सुस्ती), Weariness (थकान)

Anto: Enthusiasm (उत्साह), Vigor (जोश)

972 **Latent** (Adj.) - (छुपा हुआ) *[#R-7 (1)]*
Existing but not yet developed or manifest; concealed

Syno: Hidden (छिपा हुआ)

Anto: Obvious (स्पष्ट), Evident (प्रत्यक्ष), Manifest (प्रकट) {Active (सक्रिय)}

973 Laudable (Adj.) - (प्रशंसनीय)~ *[#R-2 (3)]*
Deserving praise and commendation

Syno: {Praiseworthy (प्रशंसनीय)}

Anto: Deplorable (शर्मनाक) {Condemnable (निंदनीय)}

974 **Launch** (V.) - (प्रारंभ करना) *[#R-2]*
To start or set in motion

Syno: Introduce (शुरू करना)

Anto: Withdraw (वापस लेना)

975 **Lavish** (Adj.) - (विलासितापूर्ण)~ *[#R-9 (4)]*
Sumptuously rich or grand; given or spent in generous abundance

Syno: Expensive (महंगा), Bountiful (उदार/दानशील), Opulent (वैभवशाली), Excessive (अत्यधिक), Generous (उदार) {Luxurious (विलासी), Grand (भव्य)}

Anto: Scarce (दुर्लभ), Frugal (मितव्ययी), Moderate (संयमित) {Modest (साधारण)}

976 **Lax** (Adj.) - (ढीला-ढाला, लापरवाह)~ *[#R-2 (1)]*
Not strict or careful; showing lack of discipline

Syno: Negligent (लापरवाह)

Anto: Reliable (विश्वसनीय) {Concerned (चिंतित)}

977 Leisure (N.) - (फुर्सत; इत्मीनान)~ *[#R-6 (1)]*
Free time; Unhurried pace or manner
Syno: Relaxation (आराम), Recreation (मनोरंजन)
Anto: Work (कार्य) {Hurry (जल्दी)}

978 Lenient (Adj.) - (सहनशील) *[#R-4 (4)]*
Permissive, merciful, or tolerant
Syno: Easy-going (सहनशील)
Anto: Strict (सख्त) {Harsh (कठोर)}

979 **Lethal** (Adj.) - (घातक) *[#R-6 (1)]*
Sufficient to cause death
Syno: Deadly (जानलेवा), Fatal (घातक)
Anto: Harmless (हानिरहित)

980 **Lethargic** (Adj.) - (सुस्त) *[#R-7 (6)]*
Sluggish and apathetic
Syno: Inactive (निष्क्रिय), Lazy (आलसी)
Anto: Lively (जीवंत), Dynamic (गतिशील), Active (सक्रिय) {Energetic (ऊर्जावान), Keen (उत्सुक)}

981 Lethargy (N.) - (सुस्ती) *[#R-4 (2)]*
A lack of energy and enthusiasm
Syno: Hebetude (निष्क्रियता), Drowsiness (नींद से भरा हुआ)
Anto: Energy (ऊर्जा), Vigour (उत्साह) {Vitality (स्फूर्ति), Persistence (दृढ़ता)}

982 **Levity** (N.) - (हल्कापन) *[#R-2 (2)]*
The lack of seriousness; lightness of manner or speech
Syno: Funniness (मजाकियापन) {Frivolity (तुच्छता)}
Anto: Gravity (गंभीरता)

983 **Liability** (N.) - (देनदारी) *[#R-2 (2)]*
The state of being legally responsible for something
Syno: Debt (कर्ज)
Anto: Asset (संपत्ति) {Advantage (लाभ)}

984 **Liberate** (V.) - (मुक्त करना) *[#R-1 (1)]*
To set free from bondage or oppression
Syno: Free (स्वतंत्र करना)
Anto: {Bind (बांधना)}

985 **Liberty** (N.) - (स्वतंत्रता) *[#R-9 (2)]*
The condition of being free from captivity or oppression
Syno: Freedom (आजादी) {Autonomy (स्वायत्तता)}
Anto: Dependence (निर्भरता), Bondage (बंधन), Slavery (गुलामी)

986 **Listless** (Adj.) - (उदासीन)~ *[#R-1 (6)]*
Lacking energy or enthusiasm
Syno: Exhausted (थका हुआ) {Lethargic (सुस्त)}
Anto: {Active (सक्रिय), Agile (चुस्त)}

987 **Loathe** (V.) - (घृणा करना) *[#R-8]*
To feel intense dislike or disgust for
Syno: Abhor (घृणा करना), Hate (नफ़रत करना)
Anto: Like (पसंद करना), Love (प्यार करना), Admire (प्रशंसा करना)

988 **Lofty** (Adj.) - (उच्च) *[#R-5 (2)]*
Of imposing height; noble in character or spirit
Syno: Noble (महान), Towering (ऊँचा)
Anto: Low (नीचा) {Mean (नीच), Stunted (अविकसित)}

989 Logical (Adj.) - (तार्किक) *[#R-3]*
According to rules of logic
Syno: Rational (तर्कसंगत)
Anto: Illogical (अतार्किक), Contradictory (विरोधाभासी)

990 Lonely (Adj.) - (अकेला) *[#R-2]*
Sad due to lack of company
Syno: Alone (अकेला)
Anto: Crowded (भीड़भाड़)

991 **Loquacious** (Adj.) - (बातूनी)~ *[#R-3 (5)]*
Tending to talk a great deal
Syno: Talkative (बातूनी)
Anto: Taciturn (अल्पभाषी) {Silent (चुप), Reticent (अल्पभाषी), Subdued (दबा हुआ)}

992 **Loyal** (Adj.) - (वफादार) *[#R-3 (2)]*
Showing firm and constant support
Syno: Devoted (समर्पित)
Anto: Fickle (चंचल), Treacherous (विश्वासघाती) {Disloyal (गद्दार)}

993 Loyalty (N.) - (निष्ठा) *[#R-2]*
A strong feeling of support or allegiance
Syno: Faithfulness (वफादारी)
Anto: Treason (देशद्रोह)

994 Lucid (Adj.) - (स्पष्ट)~ *[#R-16 (4)]*
Expressed clearly; easy to understand. Also, bright or luminous
Syno: Clear (स्पष्ट) {Explicit (साफ़-साफ़)}
Anto: Vague (अस्पष्ट), Dark (अंधेरा), Ambiguous (अस्पष्ट), Confusing (भ्रामक) {Obscure (अस्पष्ट)}

995 **Lucidity** (N.) - (स्पष्टता) *[#R-1 (2)]*

Clarity of expression; intelligibility. Also, brightness; luminosity

Syno: Clarity (स्पष्टता)

Anto: {Confusion (भ्रम, अस्पष्टता)}

996 Lucrative (Adj.) - (लाभदायक)~ *[#R-1 (7)]*
Producing a great deal of profit

Syno: Worthwhile (सार्थक) {Profitable (लाभदायक), Fruitful (फलदायक)}

Anto: {Unprofitable (नुकसानदायक)}

997 Ludicrous (Adj.) - (हास्यास्पद) *[#R-2 (6)]*
So foolish, unreasonable, or out of place as to be amusing; ridiculous

Syno: Crazy (बेतुका) {Humorous (हास्यप्रद), Ridiculous (हास्यास्पद), Bizarre (विचित्र)}

Anto: Wise (बुद्धिमान) {Reasonable (वाजिब), Solemn (गंभीर), Sensible (समझदार)}

998 Lugubrious (Adj.) - (उदास) *[#R-2 (4)]*
Looking or sounding sad and dismal

Syno: {Melancholy (उदास), Unhappy (दुखी)}

Anto: Optimistic (आशावादी), Joyous (आनंदमय) {Happy (खुश), Joyful (आनंदित)}

999 Luminous (Adj.) - (प्रकाशमान) *[#R-5 (1)]*
Full of or shedding light; bright or shining, especially in the dark

Syno: Radiant (उज्ज्वल), Resplendent (चमकीला)

Anto: Dim (मंद), Gloomy (अंधकारमय)

1000 Lunacy (N.) - (पागलपन) *[#R-2 (1)]*
A state of insanity or extreme foolish behaviour

Syno: {Insanity (पागलपन)}

Anto: Sanity (विवेक)

1001 Luscious (Adj.) - (रसीला) *[#R-1 (5)]*
(Of food or wine) having a pleasingly rich, sweet taste. Also, richly verdant or opulent

Syno: Juicy (रसीला) {Delicious (स्वादिष्ट), Sumptuous (शानदार)}

Anto: {Insipid (बेस्वाद), Acrid (तीखा)}

1002 **Lustre** (N.) - (चमक) *[#R-2]*
A gentle shine or soft glow on a surface

Syno: Shine (चमक)

Anto: Matte (चमकरहित)

1003 **Maestro** (N.) - (उस्ताद)~ *[#R-3]*
A distinguished musician, especially a conductor of classical music

Syno: Expert (विशेषज्ञ)

Anto: Amateur (शौकिया व्यक्ति)

1004 **Magnanimity** (N.) - (उदारता) *[#R-1 (2)]*
The fact or condition of being magnanimous; generosity

Syno: Altruism (परोपकार) {Charitableness (दानशीलता)}

Anto: {Meanness (नीचता)}

1005 Magnanimous (Adj.) - (उदार)~ *[#R-7 (6)]*
Very generous or forgiving, especially toward a rival or less powerful person

Syno: Chivalrous (उदार), Noble (महान), Charitable (दानशील), Generous (दरियादिल) {Bighearted (विशाल हृदय वाला)}

Anto: Vindictive (प्रतिशोधी), Petty (तुच्छ) {Spiteful (द्वेषपूर्ण), Miserly (कंजूस)}

1006 Magnificent (Adj.) - (भव्य)~ *[#R-8 (2)]*
Impressively beautiful, elaborate, or extravagant; striking

Syno: Splendid (शानदार), Grand (विशाल), Glorious (गौरवशाली)

Anto: Modest (साधारण) {Dreadful (भयानक)}

1007 Maintain (V.) - (बनाए रखना) *[#R-2]*
To keep something in good condition or at a certain level

Syno: Care (परवाह करना)

Anto: Abandon (त्यागना)

1008 **Maleficent** (Adj.) - (नुकसान पहुंचाने वाला) *[#R-1 (2)]*
Doing evil or harm

Syno: {Malicious (द्वेषपूर्ण)}

Anto: Benevolent (परोपकारी)

1009 Malevolent (Adj.) - (दुर्भावनापूर्ण, बुरा चाहने वाला)~ *[#R-2 (2)]*
Having or showing a wish to do evil to others

Syno: Despiteful (द्वेषपूर्ण)

Anto: Kind (दयालु) {Benign (सौम्य)}

1010 **Malice** (N.) - (द्वेष) *[#R-10 (6)]*
The intention or desire to do evil; ill will

Syno: Bitterness (कड़वाहट) {Ill Will (दुर्भावना), Grudge (मनमुटाव), Hatred (घृणा)}

Anto: Goodwill (सद्भावना), Kindness (दयालुता), Sympathy (सहानुभूति) {Cordiality (आत्मीयता)}

1011 Malicious (Adj.) - (दुर्भावनापूर्ण) *[#R-2 (6)]*
Characterized by malice; intending or intended to do harm

Syno: {Spiteful (द्वेषपूर्ण), Nasty (बुरा), Wicked (दुष्ट)}

Anto: Benign (सौम्य), Decent (शालीन) {Benevolent (परोपकारी), Kindly (दयालु)}

1012 Malign (V./Adj.) - (बदनाम करना; हानिकारक) *[#R-4 (3)]*
To speak about someone in a spitefully critical manner (V.); Wishing or causing harm (Adj.)

Syno: Besmirch (कलंकित करना); Baleful (हानिकारक), Evil (दुष्ट) {Slander (बदनाम करना)}

Anto: Praise (प्रशंसा करना) {Benign (सौम्य)}

1013 Malignant (Adj.) - (घातक) *[#R-3]*
Very dangerous or showing harmful intent

Syno: Vicious (दुष्ट), Harmful (हानिकारक)

Anto: Benign (अहानिकारक)

1014 Malleable (Adj.) - (लचीला)~ *[#R-2 (2)]*
Easily influenced; pliable; able to be hammered or pressed

Syno: {Moldable (ढलने योग्य)}

Anto: Intractable (अडिग), Stiff (कठोर) {Hard (कठिन)}

1015 **Mammoth** (Adj.) - (विशाल) *[#R-3 (8)]*
Huge; of enormous size or amount

Syno: Gigantic (विशालकाय), Enormous (विशाल) {Huge (बहुत बड़ा)}

Anto: Infinitesimal (अति सूक्ष्म) {Tiny (छोटा), Small (छोटा)}

1016 Manage (V.) - (प्रबंधन करना) *[#R-1 (2)]*
To administer; run; succeed in doing or achieving something

Syno: {Handle (संभालना), Afford (सक्षम होना)}

Anto: Fail (विफल होना)

1017 Mandatory (Adj.) - (अनिवार्य) *[#R-5 (2)]*
Required by law or rules; compulsory

Syno: Compulsory (अनिवार्य), Essential (आवश्यक), Imperative (अनिवार्य)

Anto: Optional (वैकल्पिक) {Voluntary (स्वैच्छिक)}

1018 **Manifest** (Adj.) - (स्पष्ट) *[#R-5 (1)]*
Clear or obvious to the eye or mind

Syno: Obvious (स्पष्ट), Apparent (प्रत्यक्ष)

Anto: Hidden (छिपा हुआ), Concealed (छुपा हुआ)

1019 Manufacture (N./V.) - (उत्पादन; निर्माण करना) *[#R-1 (1)]*
The production of goods (N.); To make on a large scale or fabricate (V.)

Syno: {Produce (उत्पादित करना)}

Anto: Destroy (नष्ट करना)

1020 Marvellous (Adj.) - (अद्भुत) *[#R-5 (2)]*
Causing great wonder; extraordinary

Syno: Wonderful (शानदार)

Anto: Terrible (भयानक) {Awful (भयानक), Ordinary (साधारण)}

1021 Massive (Adj.) - (विशाल) *[#R-4 (4)]*
Large and heavy or solid

Syno: Huge (विशाल) {Enormous (विशाल), Gigantic (विशाल)}

Anto: Tiny (छोटा)

1022 **Maverick** (Adj./N.) - (गैर-पारंपरिक; स्वतंत्र विचारक)~ *[#R-4 (4)]*
Independent and unorthodox (Adj.); An independent, unconventional person (N.)

Syno: Bohemian (परंपरा-विरोधी) {Non-Conformist (अपरंपरावादी)}

Anto: Conventional (परंपरागत); Conformist (परंपरावादी) {Conservative (रूढ़िवादी)}

1023 Meagre (Adj.) - (अपर्याप्त) *[#R-12 (4)]*
Lacking in quantity or quality

Syno: Inadequate (अपर्याप्त) {Scanty (कम), Insufficient (अपर्याप्त), Scarce (दुर्लभ)}

Anto: Plentiful (प्रचुर), Sufficient (पर्याप्त), Adequate (पर्याप्त) {Abundant (प्रचुर)}

1024 **Mean** (Adj./V.) - (नीच; संकेत करना) *[#R-3 (4)]*
Unkind, spiteful, or unfair; To intend to convey or refer to (a particular thing); signify

Syno: Unkind (निर्दयी) {Average (औसत), Malicious (दुर्भावनापूर्ण); Imply (संकेत करना)}

Anto: Noble (महान) {Generous (उदार)}

1025 **Meandering** (Adj.) - (घुमावदार; अनिश्चित) *[#R-6 (2)]*
Following a winding path; Aimless or lacking direction

Syno: Wandering (भटकता हुआ), Curved (वक्र) {Winding (घुमावदार)}

Anto: Direct (सीधा), Straight (सीधा), Determined (निर्धारित)

1026 Meddle (V.) - (हस्तक्षेप करना)~ *[#R-3 (2)]*
To interfere unnecessarily in matters that are not one's concern

Syno: Interfere (दखल देना)

Anto: Ignore (नजरअंदाज करना)

1027 Mediocre (Adj.) - (साधारण)~ *[#R-1 (4)]*
Of only moderate quality; not very good

Syno: {Satisfactory (संतोषजनक), Average

(औसत)}

Anto: Exceptional (असाधारण) {Superlative (श्रेष्ठ)}

1028 **Meek** (Adj.) - (विनम्र) *[#R-2 (2)]*
Quiet, gentle, and easily imposed on

Syno: Submissive (आज्ञाकारी) {Modest (विनम्र)}

Anto: Assertive (हठी) {Bold (साहसी)}

1029 Melancholy (Adj./N.) - (उदासी)~ *[#R-11 (3)]*
Feeling thoughtful sadness (Adj.); Deep sadness or gloom (N.)

Syno: Sorrowful (दुखी), Sad (दुखी), Gloomy (उदास); Sadness (निराशा) {Despondency (निराशा)}

Anto: Cheerful (प्रसन्न), Pleasant (सुखद); Ecstasy (परमानंद) {Cheery (खुशमिज़ाज)}

1030 **Mellow** (Adj.) - (नरम या सौम्य) *[#R-4 (1)]*
Pleasantly smooth or soft; free from harshness

Syno: Genial (सौम्य) {Ripe (पका हुआ)}

Anto: Hard (कठोर), Harsh (सख्त)

1031 Melodious (Adj.) - (सुरीला)~ *[#R-3]*
Producing or having a pleasant tune

Syno: Tuneful (धुनी), Harmonious (मधुर)

Anto: Tuneless (बेसुरा)

1032 Menace (N.) - (खतरा)~ *[#R-4 (2)]*
A threat or danger

Syno: Threat (धमकी), Nuisance (परेशानी)

Anto: Comfort (आराम), Help (सहायता) {Felicity (परम सुख) }

1033 Mendacious (Adj.) - (झूठा) *[#R-4 (4)]*
Not telling the truth; lying

Syno: Dishonest (बेईमान) {False (झूठा)}

Anto: Truthful (सत्यवादी) {Veracious (सत्यवादी)}

1034 **Mercurial** (Adj.) - (चंचल) *[#R-3 (3)]*
Subject to sudden or unpredictable changes of mood or mind

Syno: Volatile (परिवर्तनशील) {Capricious (मनमौजी), Quick-Changing (त्वरित परिवर्तनशील)}

Anto: Invariable (अपरिवर्तनीय), Tranquil (शांत)

1035 **Mercy** (N.) - (दया) *[#R-3]*
Kindness or forgiveness shown to someone under one's power

Syno: Sympathy (सहानुभूति), Clemency (कृपा)

Anto: Sternness (कठोरता)

1036 **Merge** (V.) - (विलीन करना) *[#R-1 (1)]*
To combine or cause to combine to form a single entity

Syno: Blend (मिश्रण करना)

Anto: {Divide (विभाजित करना)}

1037 **Merit** (N.) - (गुण) *[#R-2 (1)]*
A good or admirable quality

Syno: Virtue (सद्गुण)

Anto: Fault (दोष)

1038 **Merry** (Adj.) - (प्रसन्न) *[#R-1 (1)]*
Cheerful and lively

Syno: Happy (खुश)

Anto: {Glum (उदास)}

1039 Meticulous (Adj.) - (सावधान)~ *[#R-13 (12)]*
Showing great attention to detail; very careful and precise

Syno: Careful (सावधान), Precise (सटीक), Methodical (नियमित), Perfect (पूर्ण), Perfectionist (पूर्णतावादी) {Scrupulous (नैतिकतापूर्ण), Conscientious (अंतरात्मा के अनुसार), Mindful (ध्यानशील), Thorough (गहन)}

Anto: Careless (लापरवाह), Chaotic (अराजक), Sloppy (असावधान), Negligent (असावधान), Regardless (बेपरवाह) {Slovenly (गंदा), Haphazard (अव्यवस्थित)}

1040 Meticulously (Adv.) - (सावधानीपूर्वक) *[#R-4]*
In a way that shows great attention to detail; very thoroughly

Syno: Carefully (ध्यान से), Methodically (क्रमबद्ध तरीके से)

Anto: Carelessly (लापरवाही से), Chaotically (अव्यवस्थित ढंग से)

1041 **Mettle** (N.) - (साहस) *[#R-1 (1)]*
A person's ability to face difficulties bravely

Syno: {Courage (साहस)}

Anto: Cowardice (कायरता)

1042 **Mild** (Adj.) - (हल्का) *[#R-1 (1)]*
Not severe, serious, or harsh

Syno: Gentle (नरम)

Anto: {Rough (कठोर)}

1043 Miniature (Adj.) - (लघु) *[#R-3 (2)]*
Very small

Syno: Diminutive (नन्हा) {Small (छोटा), Tiny (बहुत छोटा)}

Anto: Large (बड़ा)

1044 Minute (Adj.) - (सूक्ष्म; अत्यंत बारीकी से किया गया) *[#R-1 (4)]*
Extremely small; or showing very careful

and detailed attention

Syno: {Detailed (विस्तृत), Exact (सटीक)}

Anto: Enormous (अत्यधिक बड़ा)

1045 Mirage (N.) - (दृष्टि भ्रम, मृगतृष्णा) *[#R-2 (1)]*
An optical illusion; something illusory

Syno: Illusion (भ्रम), Fantasy (कल्पना)

Anto: {Reality (वास्तविकता)}

1046 **Misanthropic** (Adj.) - (मानव द्वेषी) *[#R-2 (2)]*
Disliking humankind and avoiding human society

Syno: Antisocial (असामाजिक)

Anto: Sociable (सामाजिक) {Philanthropic (परोपकारी)}

1047 Miscellaneous (Adj.) - (विविध) *[#R-1 (1)]*
Of various types or from different sources

Syno: Various (विभिन्न)

Anto: {Pure (शुद्ध)}

1048 **Miser** (N.) - (कंजूस)~ *[#R-1 (2)]*
A person who hoards money and spends very little

Syno: {Skinflint (कंजूस)}

Anto: Spendthrift (फिजूलखर्च)

1049 Miserable (Adj.) - (दुखी) *[#R-6 (4)]*
Very unhappy or uncomfortable

Syno: {Dejected (निराश), Dismal (उदास)}

Anto: Happy (खुश), Cheerful (प्रसन्न), Joyful (आनंदित)

1050 Misery (N.) - (दुख) *[#R-3 (3)]*
A state of great mental or physical distress

Syno: Torture (यातना) {Anguish (वेदना)}

Anto: Bliss (परमानंद) {Pleasure (आनंद)}

1051 **Misfortune** (N.) - (दुर्भाग्य) *[#R-2 (2)]*
Bad luck

Syno: Calamity (विपत्ति) {Mishap (दुर्घटना)}

Anto: Blessing (आशीर्वाद) {Prosperity (समृद्धि)}

1052 Mitigate (V.) - (कम करना) *[#R-15 (9)]*
To make less severe, serious, or painful

Syno: Allay (शांत करना), Lessen (कम करना), Reduce (घटाना) {Alleviate (हल्का करना), Relieve (राहत देना), Diminish (घटाना)}

Anto: Aggravate (बिगाड़ना), Intensify (तीव्र करना), Increase (बढ़ाना) {Exacerbate (खराब करना), Worsen (बिगड़ जाना)}

1053 Modern (Adj.) - (आधुनिक) *[#R-4 (1)]*
Relating to the present or recent times

Syno: New (नया) {Current (वर्तमान)}

Anto: Ancient (प्राचीन)

1054 Modest (Adj.) - (विनम्र) *[#R-9 (8)]*
Unassuming in estimation of one's abilities

Syno: Humble (नम्र), Shy (शर्मीला), Demure (संकोची)

Anto: Vain (अहंकारी), Conceited (घमंडी), Arrogant (अकड़बाज) {Immodest (अशिष्ट), Luxurious (भव्य)}

1055 Mollify (V.) - (शांत करना) *[#R-1 (2)]*
To appease the anger or anxiety of someone

Syno: Pacify (शांत करना) {Allay (शांत करना)}

Anto: {Aggravate (बिगाड़ना)}

1056 Momentous (Adj.) - (महत्वपूर्ण)~ *[#R-2 (2)]*
Of great importance, especially affecting future events

Syno: Important (जरूरी), Significant (महत्त्वपूर्ण)

Anto: {Trivial (तुच्छ)}

1057 Monotonous (Adj.) - (नीरस, एकसमान)~ *[#R-9 (7)]*
Dull and boring due to lack of variety

Syno: Dull (नीरस), Boring (उबाऊ) {Dreary (नीरस), Tiresome (थकाऊ), Tedious (उबाऊ), Repetitive (दोहराव वाला)}

Anto: Interesting (दिलचस्प), Engrossing (रोचक), Varied (विविध) {Exciting (रोमांचक)}

1058 **Morbid** (Adj.) - (अप्रिय वस्तुओं (जैसे रोग, मृत्यु) में रुचि रखने वाला) *[#R-10]*
Having an unhealthy interest in disturbing subjects

Syno: Depressed (उदास), Gloomy (निराशाजनक), Ghastly (भयानक), Nasty (घिनौना)

Anto: Cheerful (प्रसन्न), Cordial (हार्दिक), Healthy (स्वस्थ)

1059 **Moribund** (Adj.) - (अन्त के करीब) *[#R-2 (1)]*
At the point of death or stagnant

Syno: Dying (मरता हुआ)

Anto: {Thriving (फलता-फूलता)}

1060 Morose (Adj.) - (उदास) *[#R-11 (7)]*
Very sad, quiet, and unwilling to talk to others

Syno: Gloomy (उदास), Sullen (बदमिजाज), Mournful (शोकपूर्ण) {Ill-Tempered (बदमिजाज)}

Anto: Cheerful (खुश), Jovial (हंसमुख), Uplifted (उत्साहित)

1061 Mortal (Adj.) - (मरणशील) *[#R-2 (2)]*

Subject to death; also, causing death

Syno: Deadly (घातक), Lethal (प्राणघातक) {Temporary (अस्थायी)}

Anto: {Immortal (अमर)}

1062 Muddle (N.) - (उलझन) *[#R-3 (1)]*
An untidy or disorganized state

Syno: Confusion (उलझन) {Disorder (अव्यवस्था)}

Anto: Order (व्यवस्था)

1063 **Muddy** (Adj.) - (कीचड़ युक्त, मटमैला) *[#R-1 (1)]*
Covered with mud or dirty; Dull in color or tone

Syno: Filthy (गंदा)

Anto: {Vivid (चमकीला)}

1064 Mundane (Adj.) - (साधारण, नीरस)~ *[#R-11 (5)]*
Lacking interest or excitement; dull

Syno: Ordinary (साधारण), Everyday (रोजमर्रा का), Commonplace (सामान्य), Banal (नीरस) {Worldly (सांसारिक), Common (सामान्य), Tedious (उबाऊ)}

Anto: Extraordinary (असाधारण), Exceptional (विशेष) {Unique (अनोखा), Exciting (रोमांचक)}

1065 **Munificence** (N.) - (उदारता) *[#R-2]*
The quality of great generosity in giving

Syno: Generousness (दानशीलता)

Anto: Stinginess (कंजूसी)

1066 Munificent (Adj.) - (उदार) *[#R-4 (5)]*
More generous than usual in giving money or gifts

Syno: Generous (दानशील), Magnanimous (उदार) {Liberal (उदार)}

Anto: Stingy (कंजूस), Miserly (कंजूस) {Parsimonious (कंजूस), Frugal (किफायती)}

1067 **Murky** (Adj.) - (धुंधला) *[#R-1 (4)]*
Dark, gloomy, dirty, or unclear; difficult to understand

Syno: {Dirty (गंदा)}

Anto: Bright (उज्ज्वल) {Apparent (स्पष्ट)}

1068 **Muster** (V.) - (इकट्ठा करना) *[#R-1 (1)]*
To assemble or collect together

Syno: {Gather (इकट्ठा करना)}

Anto: Disperse (तितर-बितर करना)

1069 **Nadir** (N.) - (निम्नतम बिंदु)~ *[#R-6 (1)]*
The lowest point in the fortunes of a person or organization

Syno: Bottom (तल), Base (निम्न स्तर)

Anto: Zenith (चरम सीमा), Climax (चरमोत्कर्ष)

1070 **Naive** (Adj.) - (अनुभवहीन)~ *[#R-10 (4)]*
Showing a lack of experience, wisdom, or judgment

Syno: Ingenuous (निष्कपट), Gullible (सीधा), Simple (सरल)

Anto: Artful (चालाक), Experienced (अनुभवी), Sophisticated (परिष्कृत), Cynical (निंदक) {Wise (बुद्धिमान)}

1071 **Narrow** (Adj.) - (संकीर्ण) *[#R-4]*
Small in width or extent; limited

Syno: Cramped (संकीर्ण), Slender (पतला)

Anto: Wide (चौड़ा), Broad (चौड़ा)

1072 Nascent (Adj.) - (आरम्भिक)~ *[#R-4 (2)]*
Just beginning to exist or develop

Syno: Budding (उभरता हुआ), Primitive (प्रारंभिक) {Emerging (उभरता हुआ)}

Anto: Withering (मुरझाता हुआ) {Mature (परिपक्व)}

1073 **Nasty** (Adj.) - (घृणित)~ *[#R-3 (3)]*
Highly unpleasant; causing strong dislike

Syno: Despicable (घृणित) {Awful (भयानक), Foul (घिनौना)}

Anto: Pleasant (सुखद) {Benevolent (परोपकारी)}

1074 **Native** (Adj./N.) - (स्थानीय; मूल निवासी)~ *[#R-7 (1)]*
Born in a place; indigenous; A person born in a place

Syno: Indigenous (मूल निवासी)

Anto: Alien (विदेशी), Foreign (विदेशी), Exotic (विदेशी)

1075 Nebulous (Adj.) - (अस्पष्ट) *[#R-4 (6)]*
Unclear or vague; cloud-like

Syno: Vague (अस्पष्ट) {Ambiguous (भ्रम पैदा करने वाला)}

Anto: Clear (स्पष्ट), Definite (निश्चित)

1076 Nefarious (Adj.) - (दुष्ट) *[#R-5 (5)]*
Extremely wicked or criminal

Syno: Wicked (दुष्ट), Iniquitous (अन्यायपूर्ण) {Pernicious (हानिकारक), Heinous (जघन्य)}

Anto: Virtuous (सदाचारी), Pious (धार्मिक) {Noble (श्रेष्ठ), Respectable (सम्मानजनक), Admirable (प्रशंसनीय)}

1077 Neglect (N./V.) - (अनदेखी, नज़रअंदाज़ करना) *[#R-6 (4)]*
The lack of proper care (N.); To fail to care for or pay attention to (V.)

Syno: Disregard (उपेक्षा करना), Ignore (अनदेखा

करना) {Avoid (टालना)}

Anto: Care (देखभाल); Remember (याद रखना), Attend (ध्यान देना) {Regard (सम्मान), Concern (चिंता); Appreciate (सराहना)}

1078 Negligent (Adj.) - (लापरवाह) *[#R-5 (3)]*
Failing to take proper care

Syno: Careless (लापरवाह) {Inattentive (असावधान)}

Anto: Careful (सावधान), Attentive (ध्यान देने वाला)

1079 **Nepotism** (N.) - (भाई-भतीजावाद)~ *[#R-2 (2)]*
The practice of favoring relatives or friends unfairly

Syno: Favouritism (पक्षपात) {Patronage (संरक्षण)}

Anto: Impartiality (निष्पक्षता)

1080 **Nimble** (Adj.) - (फुर्तीला) *[#R-1 (7)]*
Quick and light in movement or action; agile

Syno: Agile (चुस्त) {Prompt (तत्पर)}

Anto: {Slow (धीमा), Dull (मंद), Languid (सुस्त), Tardy (विलंबी)}

1081 Noble (Adj.) - (महान) *[#R-4 (1)]*
Having high moral qualities and honor

Syno: Dignified (गरिमामय) {Aristocratic (उच्च वर्ग से संबंधित)}

Anto: Common (मामूली), Servile (दासतापूर्ण)

1082 **Nominal** (Adj.) - (बहुत मामूली, नाममात्र का) *[#R-3]*
Existing in name only; very small

Syno: Supposed (माना जाता है)

Anto: Significant (महत्वपूर्ण), Excessive (अत्यधिक)

1083 Nonchalant (Adj.) - (उदासीन) *[#R-3 (4)]*
Calm and relaxed; showing little concern

Syno: Carefree (निश्चिंत) {Casual (लापरवाह), Apathetic (उदासीन)}

Anto: Caring (देखभाल करने वाला), Considerate (विचारशील) {Anxious (चिंतित), Involved (शामिल)}

1084 **Notion** (N.) - (धारणा) *[#R-3 (4)]*
An idea or belief about something

Syno: Belief (विश्वास) {Impression (प्रभाव), Concept (अवधारणा), Perception (धारणा)}

Anto: Reality (वास्तविकता) {Misunderstanding (गलतफहमी)}

1085 Notorious (Adj.) - (कुख्यात)~ *[#R-6 (1)]*
Well known for bad qualities or deeds

Syno: Disreputable (बदनाम), Infamous (कुख्यात) {Disgraceful (शर्मनाक)}

Anto: Reputed (प्रतिष्ठित), Unknown (अज्ञात), Inconspicuous (आसानी से न दिखने वाला)

1086 Nourish (V.) - (पालन पोषण करना) *[#R-1 (3)]*
To provide food for growth and health

Syno: {Nurture (पालन-पोषण करना)}

Anto: Starve (भूखा रहना) {Famish (भूखा रखना)}

1087 **Novel** (Adj.) - (नया) *[#R-6 (1)]*
New or original

Syno: Unique (अनूठा) {Modern (आधुनिक)}

Anto: Traditional (पारंपरिक), Old (पुराना), Banal (घिसा-पिटा)

1088 Novice (N.) - (नौसिखिया)~ *[#R-3 (3)]*
A person new to or inexperienced in a field or situation

Syno: Beginner (शुरुआती), Amateur (अनुभवहीन) {Entrant (किसी क्षेत्र में नया व्यक्ति)}

Anto: Expert (विशेषज्ञ)

1089 Noxious (Adj.) - (हानिकारक) *[#R-2]*
Harmful, poisonous, or very unpleasant

Syno: Harmful (हानिकारक)

Anto: Beneficial (लाभकारी)

1090 **Nugatory** (Adj.) - (निरर्थक) *[#R-3 (2)]*
Of no value or importance; Useless

Syno: Futile (व्यर्थ) {Ineffectual (अप्रभावी)}

Anto: Significant (महत्वपूर्ण), Productive (उत्पादक) {Valid (मान्य)}

1091 Nuisance (N.) - (कष्ट) *[#R-3]*
A cause of annoyance or inconvenience

Syno: Bother (परेशानी)

Anto: Pleasure (आनंद), Delight (प्रसन्नता)

1092 Numerous (Adj.) - (प्रचुर) *[#R-3 (3)]*
Existing in large numbers; Many

Syno: Many (बहुत से), Several (कई)

Anto: Scarce (दुर्लभ) {Few (थोड़े)}

1093 Obdurate (Adj.) - (हठी) *[#R-5 (5)]*
Stubbornly refusing to change

Syno: Stubborn (जिद्दी), Obstinate (हठी) {Intractable (अडिग), Adamant (अटल)}

Anto: Amenable (अनुकूल), Compassionate (दयालु), Yielding (मान जाने वाला) {Flexible (लचीला), Compliant (आज्ञाकारी)}

1094 Obedient (Adj.) - (आज्ञाकारी) *[#R-5]*
Willing to follow orders or requests

Syno: Devoted (समर्पित)

Anto: Disobedient (अवज्ञाकारी), Resistant

(विरोधी)

1095 **Objection** (N.) - (आपत्ति) *[#R-3 (1)]*
An expression of opposition

Syno: Disapproval (नापसंदगी)

Anto: Assent (सहमति), Approval (समर्थन) {Acceptance (स्वीकृति)}

1096 Objective (Adj./N.) - (उद्देश्य; तटस्थ भाव से) *[#R-3]*
A goal to achieve (N.); Based on facts, not feelings (Adj.)

Syno: Unbiased (निष्पक्ष); Purpose (उद्देश्य)

Anto: Prejudiced (पक्षपाती)

1097 **Obligatory** (Adj.) - (अनिवार्य) *[#R-3 (6)]*
Required by a legal, moral, or other rule

Syno: Necessary (आवश्यक), Mandatory (अनिवार्य), Compulsory (अनिवार्य) {Essential (आवश्यक)}

Anto: {Voluntary (स्वैच्छिक)}

1098 **Obliged** (Adj.) - (आभारी) *[#R-1 (1)]*
Feeling grateful or thankful

Syno: {Thankful (आभारी)}

Anto: Thankless (एहसान न मानने वाला)

1099 Oblivious (Adj.) - (अनजान)~ *[#R-3 (2)]*
Not aware of what is happening around

Syno: Ignorant (अज्ञानी) {Unaware (अनभिज्ञ)}

Anto: Conscious (चेतन) {Concerned (चिंतित)}

1100 **Obloquy** (N.) - (निंदा) *[#R-1 (3)]*
Strong public criticism or verbal abuse

Syno: {Abuse (गाली-गलौज)}

Anto: Praise (प्रशंसा)

1101 Obscene (Adj.) - (अश्लील) *[#R-12]*
Offensive to moral standards

Syno: Indecent (भद्दा), Dirty (अश्लील)

Anto: Decent (शालीन)

1102 Obscure (Adj.) - (अस्पष्ट)~ *[#R-7 (11)]*
Unclear or not well known

Syno: Confusing (भ्रामक), Unknown (अज्ञात)

Anto: Clear (स्पष्ट), Prominent (प्रमुख), Distinct (सुस्पष्ट) {Famous (प्रसिद्ध)}

1103 Obsequious (Adj.) - (चापलूस) *[#R-7 (4)]*
Obedient or attentive to an excessive or servile degree

Syno: Servile (दासतापूर्ण), Submissive (विनम्र), Fawning (चापलूसी करने वाला)

Anto: Assertive (स्पष्ट बोलने वाला), Domineering (हावी), Obstinate (अडिग) {Dignified (गरिमामय), Insolent (बदतमीज़)}

1104 **Obsession** (N.) - (जुनून)~ *[#R-3 (1)]*
A thought or idea that constantly occupies the mind

Syno: Fascination (मोह) {Fetish (विशष प्रेम)}

Anto: Dislike (नापसंद)

1105 Obsolete (Adj.) - (अप्रचलित)~ *[#R-4 (6)]*
No longer produced or used

Syno: Outdated (पुराना)

Anto: Current (वर्तमान), Recent (हाल का) {Modern (आधुनिक), Renovated (नवीनीकृत), Useful (उपयोगी)}

1106 Obstinate (Adj.) - (जिद्दी) *[#R-13 (7)]*
Refusing stubbornly to change one's opinion or action

Syno: Stubborn (ज़िद्दी), Adamant (अडिग) {Tenacious (हठी), Headstrong (अपनी ज़िद पर चलने वाला)}

Anto: Flexible (लचीला), Docile (विनम्र), Obedient (आज्ञाकारी), Pliable (लचीला) {Amenable (सहमत)}

1107 Obstreperous (Adj.) - (कोलाहलपूर्ण) *[#R-2 (3)]*
Noisy and difficult to control

Syno: Noisy (शोरगुल भरा), Unruly (अनियंत्रित) {Disruptive (बाधाकारी)}

Anto: {Submissive (आज्ञाकारी)}

1108 **Obstruct** (V.) - (रोक लगाना) *[#R-9 (1)]*
To block or slow movement or progress

Syno: Block (रोकना), Curb (नियंत्रित करना) {Prevent (रोकना)}

Anto: Assist (सहायता करना), Allow (अनुमति देना), Clear (साफ करना)

1109 **Obtuse** (Adj.) - (मंदबुद्धि) *[#R-2 (1)]*
Slow to understand; insensitive

Syno: {Dull (समझ में धीमा)}

Anto: Sharp-Witted (तेज़-बुद्धि), Astute (चालाक)

1110 Obvious (Adj.) - (स्पष्ट) *[#R-6 (4)]*
Easy to see or understand

Syno: Evident (प्रत्यक्ष), Clear (साफ)

Anto: Hidden (छिपा हुआ), Ambiguous (अस्पष्ट), Cryptic (गूढ़) {Obscure (अस्पष्ट)}

1111 **Occlude** (V.) - (रुकावट डालना) *[#R-1 (1)]*
To stop, close, or block a passage or opening

Syno: Obstruct (अवरुद्ध करना)

Anto: {Facilitate (सुविधाजनक बनाना)}

1112 **Occult** (Adj.) - (गुप्त; अलौकिक) *[#R-2 (4)]*
Hidden or secret; Relating to supernatural

Syno: Supernatural (अलौकिक)

Anto: Intelligible (समझने योग्य) {Transparent (पारदर्शी), Natural (प्राकृतिक)}

1113 **Occupy** (V.) - (कब्जा करना) *[#R-2]*
To fill, use, or take possession of a place or time

Syno: Fill (भर देना)

Anto: Free (मुक्त करना)

1114 **Odious** (Adj.) - (घृणित) *[#R-2 (3)]*
Extremely unpleasant

Syno: Hateful (नफरत भरा), Repugnant (नापसंद करने योग्य) {Repulsive (घिनौना)}

Anto: {Desirable (पसंदीदा)}

1115 **Offend** (V.) - (नाराज करना) *[#R-1 (1)]*
To cause someone to feel upset or annoyed

Syno: Annoy (परेशान करना)

Anto: {Please (आनंदित करना)}

1116 **Old** (Adj.) - (पुराना) *[#R-3]*
Having lived long; not young

Syno: Aged (वृद्ध)

Anto: New (नया)

1117 Ominous (Adj.) - (अमंगल)~ *[#R-7 (1)]*
Giving a sign that something bad may happen

Syno: Threatening (धमकी भरा), Inauspicious (अशुभ)

Anto: Auspicious (शुभ) {Propitious (शुभ)}

1118 Onerous (Adj.) - (कठिन) *[#R-1 (2)]*
Involving great effort or difficulty

Syno: Arduous (कठिन) {Wearying (थकाने वाला)}

Anto: {Easy (आसान)}

1119 Opaque (Adj.) - (अपारदर्शी)~ *[#R-8 (6)]*
Not able to be seen through or unclear

Syno: Arcane (गूढ़)

Anto: Transparent (पारदर्शी), Clear (स्पष्ट), Pellucid (स्वच्छ), Intelligible (समझ में आने योग्य) {Obvious (स्पष्ट)}

1120 **Oppose** (V.) - (विरोध करना) *[#R-3 (1)]*
To disagree with and attempt to prevent

Syno: Resist (विरोध करना)

Anto: Encourage (प्रोत्साहित करना), Favour (समर्थन करना)

1121 Optimal (Adj.) - (उत्तम) *[#R-1 (1)]*
Best or most favorable

Syno: Best (सर्वश्रेष्ठ)

Anto: {Poor (खराब)}

1122 Optimist (N.) - (आशावादी)~ *[#R-2 (3)]*
A person who is hopeful about the future

Syno: Idealist (आदर्शवादी)

Anto: Pessimist (निराशावादी) {Cynic (निंदक)}

1123 Optimistic (Adj.) - (आशावादी) *[#R-4 (6)]*
Hopeful and confident about the future

Syno: {Hopeful (आशावादी), Bright (उज्ज्वल), Sanguine (आशावादी)}

Anto: Pessimistic (निराशावादी), Hopeless (निराश), Doubtful (संदेहपूर्ण), Gloomy (निराशावादी)

1124 Opulence (N.) - (समृद्धि) *[#R-2 (2)]*
Great wealth or luxury

Syno: Prosperity (समृद्धि) {Wealth (संपत्ति)}

Anto: Poverty (गरीबी) {Frugality (मितव्ययिता)}

1125 Opulent (Adj.) - (धनी) *[#R-10 (2)]*
Very rich, costly and luxurious

Syno: Rich (अमीर), Luxurious (विलासितापूर्ण), Sumptuous (भव्य) {Wealthy (धनी)}

Anto: Poor (गरीब), Economical (किफायती), Destitute (निर्धन) {Sparse (विरल)}

1126 **Oracular** (Adj.) - (रहस्यमयी) *[#R-2 (1)]*
Mysterious and hard to understand, yet wise

Syno: Cryptic (गूढ़)

Anto: Lucid (स्पष्ट)

1127 Ordinary (Adj.) - (साधारण) *[#R-1 (2)]*
With no special or distinctive features; normal

Syno: Usual (सामान्य)

Anto: {Exceptional (असाधारण)}

1128 **Orthodox** (Adj.) - (पारंपरिक)~ *[#R-3 (1)]*
Following traditional beliefs or practices

Syno: Traditional (पारंपरिक)

Anto: Unconventional (अपरंपरागत), Heretical (परंपरा-विरोधी) {Heterodox (विधर्मी)}

1129 Ostentation (N.) - (दिखावट; आडंबर) *[#R-2 (3)]*
An act of showing off

Syno: Pomp (दिखावा) {Pretension (दिखावा)}

Anto: Modesty (विनम्रता) {Simplicity (सादगी)}

1130 Ostentatious (Adj.) - (दिखावटी) *[#R-4 (4)]*
Showing off in a way meant to attract attention

Syno: Flashy (भड़कीला), Showy (दिखावटी)

Anto: Restrained (संयमित), Modest (बिना दिखावे का) {Plain (सादा)}

1131 Ostracise (V.) - (निष्कासित करना)~ *[#R-5 (1)]*
To exclude someone from a society or group

Syno: Expel (निकाल देना), Banish (निर्वासित करना)

Anto: Welcome (स्वागत करना), Embrace (गले लगाना)

1132 **Outlandish** (Adj.) - (विचित्र)~ *[#R-1 (2)]*
Bizarre or unfamiliar in appearance or sound

Syno: {Absurd (बेतुका)}

Anto: Ordinary (साधारण) {Conventional (पारंपरिक)}

1133 Outrageous (Adj.) - (शर्मनाक) *[#R-2 (1)]*
Shockingly bad or excessive

Syno: Shocking (चौंकाने वाला)

Anto: Reasonable (उचित) {Pleasing (मनभावन)}

1134 **Overlook** (V.) - (नज़रअंदाज़ करना)~ *[#R-3 (4)]*
To fail to notice something

Syno: Neglect (अनदेखा करना) {Disregard (उपेक्षा करना)}

Anto: Notice (ध्यान देना), Consider (विचार करना)

1135 **Overstrung** (Adj.) - (तनावग्रस्त) *[#R-1 (1)]*
Extremely nervous

Syno: Nervous (घबराया हुआ)

Anto: {Calm (शांत)}

1136 **Pacify** (V.) - (शांत करना) *[#R-7 (4)]*
To make someone calm or less angry

Syno: Soothe (शांत करना), Calm Down (शांत हो जाना)

Anto: Enrage (क्रोधित करना), Aggravate (भड़काना) {Antagonize (विरोध करना), Irritate (चिढ़ाना), Provoke (उकसाना)}

1137 Palatable (Adj.) - (स्वादिष्ट; स्वीकार्य) *[#R-3 (4)]*
Pleasant to taste; acceptable or agreeable

Syno: Tempting (ललचाने वाला) {Satisfactory (संतोषजनक)}

Anto: {Unacceptable (अस्वीकार्य)}

1138 Palatial (Adj.) - (आलीशान) *[#R-1 (1)]*
Like a palace, very large and grand

Syno: {Magnificent (भव्य)}

Anto: Poor (मामूली)

1139 **Pale** (Adj.) - (रंगहीन) *[#R-2 (1)]*
Light in colour or having little colour

Syno: Colourless (रंगहीन) {Sallow (पीलापन लिए हुआ)}

Anto: Bright (उज्ज्वल)

1140 **Palliate** (V.) - (शांत करना; बहाना बनाना) *[#R-2 (2)]*
To reduce pain or severity without curing; to make an offence seem less serious

Syno: Relieve (राहत देना)

Anto: Worsen (बिगाड़ना) {Reprehend (निंदा करना)}

1141 **Pandemonium** (N.) - (कोलाहल)~ *[#R-2 (3)]*
A state of wild noise and confusion

Syno: Chaos (अव्यवस्था) {Anarchy (अराजकता)}

Anto: Harmony (सामंजस्य) {Peace (शांति)}

1142 **Panegyric** (N.) - (प्रशंसा)~ *[#R-1 (1)]*
A formal speech or writing praising someone

Syno: {Applause (प्रशंसा)}

Anto: Criticism (आलोचना)

1143 **Paradox** (N.) - (विरोधाभास)~ *[#R-2 (3)]*
A statement or situation that seems self-contradictory

Syno: Puzzle (उलझन) {Anomaly (विसंगति)}

Anto: {Certainty (निश्चितता), Truth (सत्य)}

1144 **Parched** (Adj.) - (सूखा) *[#R-1 (2)]*
Extremely dry or very thirsty

Syno: Arid (शुष्क)

Anto: {Wet (गीला), Humid (नमी वाला)}

1145 **Pardon** (N./V.) - (माफी; क्षमा करना) *[#R-3 (2)]*
The forgiveness or cancellation of punishment (N.); To forgive or cancel punishment (V.)

Syno: Remission (छूट) {Excuse (माफ करना)}

Anto: Punish (दंडित करना), Condemn (दोषी ठहराना)

1146 Parity (N.) - (समानता) *[#R-1 (1)]*
The state of being equal in status, value, or pay

Syno: Equality (समानता)

Anto: {Inequality (असमानता)}

1147 **Parochial** (Adj.) - (सीमित दृष्टि वाला)~ *[#R-2 (2)]*
Having a limited or narrow outlook or scope

Syno: Narrow (छोटा सोचने वाला) {Conventional (परंपरागत)}

Anto: Global (वैश्विक) {Open-Minded (खुले विचारों वाला)}

1148 Parsimonious (Adj.) - (कम खर्च करने वाला)~ *[#R-4 (4)]*
Unwilling to spend money or resources

Syno: {Stingy (कंजूस)}

Anto: Extravagant (फिजूलखर्च), Lavish (खर्चीला), Generous (दानी), Profuse (प्रचुर) {Charitable (परोपकारी)}

1149 Particularly (Adv.) - (विशेष रूप से) *[#R-2]*
To a higher degree than is usual or average, especially

Syno: Especially (विशेष रूप से)

Anto: Generally (सामान्यतः)

1150 Paucity (N.) - (अभाव) *[#R-4 (5)]*
The state of having too little of something

Syno: Shortage (कमी) {Scarcity (अभाव)}

Anto: Plethora (बहुतायत), Surplus (अधिकता) {Plenty (भरपूर), Abundance (बहुतायत)}

1151 Peculiar (Adj.) - (विचित्र) *[#R-12 (2)]*
Strange or unusual in nature

Syno: Strange (अजीब), Unusual (असामान्य) {Abnormal (असामान्य)}

Anto: Usual (सामान्य), Normal (सामान्य), Ordinary (साधारण), Familiar (जाना-पहचाना) {Common (सामान्य)}

1152 **Peevish** (Adj.) - (चिड़चिड़ा) *[#R-2 (1)]*
Easily irritated by small things

Syno: Irritable (चिड़चिड़ा)

Anto: Good-Natured (अच्छे स्वभाव वाला) {Affable (मिलनसार)}

1153 **Pellucid** (Adj.) - (पारदर्शक, स्पष्ट) *[#R-2]*
Very clear; easy to understand

Syno: Clear (साफ़)

Anto: Murky (धुंधला)

1154 **Penchant** (N.) - (रुचि)~ *[#R-5 (4)]*
A strong or habitual liking for something

Syno: Liking (पसंद), Fondness (लगाव) {Tendency (प्रवृत्ति)}

Anto: Dislike (नापसंद), Hatred (घृणा) {Aversion (अरुचि)}

1155 Penitence (N.) - (पश्चाताप)~ *[#R-3 (1)]*
The feeling of sorrow and regret for wrongdoing

Syno: Repentance (पश्चाताप) {Contrition (गहरा पछतावा)}

Anto: Brazenness (बेशर्मी)

1156 Penitent (Adj.) - (पश्चातापी) *[#R-1 (1)]*
Feeling regret for wrongdoing

Syno: {Remorseful (पछतावे से भरा)}

Anto: Unrepentant (बिना पश्चाताप वाला)

1157 **Penniless** (Adj.) - (कंगाल) *[#R-5]*
Having no money; very poor

Syno: Broke (दिवालिया)

Anto: Rich (अमीर)

1158 Pensive (Adj.) - (विचारमग्न)~ *[#R-4 (1)]*
Engaged in deep or serious thought

Syno: Thoughtful (विचारशील)

Anto: Thoughtless (विचारहीन) {Flippant (लापरवाह)}

1159 Penury (N.) - (दरिद्रता) *[#R-4 (4)]*
Extreme poverty or destitution

Syno: Poverty (गरीबी)

Anto: Wealth (धन), Opulence (समृद्धि) {Luxury (विलासिता)}

1160 Perceive (V.) - (समझना) *[#R-4]*
To become aware or understand something

Syno: Notice (ध्यान देना), Recognise (पहचानना)

Anto: Neglect (उपेक्षा करना)

1161 Perennial (Adj.) - (बारहमासी)~ *[#R-3 (1)]*
Lasting for a long time

Syno: Lasting (टिकाऊ)

Anto: Temporary (अस्थायी) {Seasonal (मौसमी)}

1162 Perfidious (Adj.) - (विश्वासघाती)~ *[#R-3 (2)]*
Deceitful and untrustworthy

Syno: Disloyal (विश्वासघाती), Treacherous (धोखेबाज़)

Anto: Loyal (वफादार)

1163 Perfunctory (Adj.) - (लापरवाही से किया गया)~ *[#R-4 (3)]*
Done with little effort or care

Syno: Careless (लापरवाह), Cursory (जल्दी-जल्दी किया गया)

Anto: Careful (सावधान) {Assiduous (मेहनती), Sincere (निष्ठापूर्ण)}

1164 **Peril** (N.) - (खतरा) *[#R-6 (1)]*
Serious and immediate danger

Syno: Danger (खतरा), Hazard (जोखिम)

Anto: Safety (सुरक्षा) {Security (सुरक्षा)}

1165 Perilous (Adj.) - (खतरनाक) *[#R-13 (4)]*
Full of danger or risk

Syno: Hazardous (खतरनाक), Dangerous (खतरनाक) {Risky (जोखिम भरा)}

Anto: Safe (सुरक्षित)

1166 **Periodic** (Adj.) - (नियमित) *[#R-2]*
Occurring at fixed intervals

Syno: Regular (नियमित)

Anto: Irregular (अनियमित)

1167 **Perish** (V.) - (मरना) *[#R-4]*
To die, especially suddenly or violently

Syno: Die (मरना), Decease (मृत्यु होना)

Anto: Thrive (फलना-फूलना), Grow (बढ़ना)

1168 Permit (V.) - (अनुमति देना) *[#R-3 (5)]*
To allow something to happen

Syno: Grant (मंजूर करना), Approve (सहमति देना) {Sanction (मंजूरी देना), Concede (स्वीकार करना)}

Anto: Forbid (मना करना) {Prohibit (निषेध करना)}

1169 Pernicious (Adj.) - (हानिकारक) *[#R-10 (6)]*
Causing serious harm, often gradually

Syno: Injurious (हानिकारक), Dangerous (खतरनाक), Malicious (दुर्भावनापूर्ण), Spiteful (द्वेषपूर्ण) {Harmful (नुकसानदेह), Destructive (विनाशकारी)}

Anto: Beneficial (लाभकारी), Innocuous (अहानिकर), Kind (दयालु)

1170 **Perpetual** (Adj.) - (लगातार)~ *[#R-4 (4)]*
Never ending or changing

Syno: Permanent (स्थायी) {Continuous (निरंतर), Constant (निरंतर), Unceasing (लगातार), Everlasting (सदाबहार)}

Anto: Intermittent (अनियमित), Transitory (क्षणिक)

1171 Perpetuate (V.) - (स्थायी बनाना) *[#R-1 (2)]*
To make something continue for a long time

Syno: Preserve (संरक्षित करना)

Anto: {Destroy (बर्बाद करना), Cease (रोकना)}

1172 **Perplex** (V.) - (उलझन में डालना) *[#R-3 (1)]*
To confuse someone completely

Syno: Bewilder (भ्रमित करना), Confuse (भ्रमित करना) {Baffle (चकित करना)}

Anto: Simplify (सरल बनाना)

1173 Perseverance (N.) - (निरंतर प्रयास)~ *[#R-5 (3)]*
The continued effort despite difficulties

Syno: Endurance (सहनशीलता), Steadfastness (स्थिरता)

Anto: Irresolution (दुविधा), Indifference (उदासीनता), Instability (अस्थिरता) {Hesitation (हिचकिचाहट), Doubt (संदेह)}

1174 Persevere (V.) - (दृढ़ रहना) *[#R-2 (1)]*
To continue despite difficulties

Syno: Persist (लगातार प्रयास करना)

Anto: Discontinue (बंद करना) {Give Up (हार मान लेना)}

1175 Persist (V.) - (दृढ़ रहना) *[#R-5 (1)]*
To continue firmly despite difficulty

Syno: Continue (जारी रखना), Insist (जोर देना)

Anto: Cease (रोकना), Discontinue (बंद करना)

1176 **Perspicuity** (N.) - (स्पष्टता) *[#R-1 (2)]*
The quality of being clear and easy to understand

Syno: {Clarity (स्पष्टता)}

Anto: Vagueness (अस्पष्टता)

1177 Persuade (V.) - (राज़ी करना) *[#R-13 (3)]*
To make someone do something by reasoning

Syno: Coax (फुसलाना), Convince (समझाना), Impress (प्रभावित करना)

Anto: Dissuade (मना करना), Deter (हतोत्साहित करना) {Discourage (हतोत्साहित करना)}

1178 Pertinent (Adj.) - (प्रासंगिक) *[#R-2 (3)]*
Directly related to the matter

Syno: Relevant (संबंधित) {Suitable (उपयुक्त)}

Anto: Irrelevant (अप्रासंगिक)

1179 Perturb (V.) - (परेशान करना) *[#R-1 (1)]*
To make someone anxious or disturbed

Syno: {Worry (चिंता करना)}

Anto: Soothe (शांत करना)

1180 **Perturbed** (Adj.) - (व्याकुल) *[#R-2 (1)]*
Feeling anxious or unsettled

Syno: Disturbed (परेशान) {Anxious (चिंतित)}

Anto: Calm (शांत)

1181 Peruse (V.) - (जांचना) *[#R-3 (1)]*
To read or examine carefully

Syno: Read (पढ़ना), Examine (परीक्षण करना), Check (जांचना)

Anto: {Neglect (ध्यान न देना)}

1182 Pervasive (Adj.) - (व्यापक) *[#R-3 (2)]*
Spreading widely throughout

Syno: Widespread (व्यापक), Extensive (विस्तृत) {Ubiquitous (सर्वव्यापी)}

Anto: Limited (सीमित)

1183 **Pessimistic** (Adj.) - (निराशावादी) *[#R-2 (2)]*
Expecting the worst to happen

Syno: Cynical (निराशावादी) {Despondent (निराश)}

Anto: Bright (आशाजनक) {Optimistic (आशावादी)}

1184 **Petty** (Adj.) - (तुच्छ) *[#R-2]*
Of little importance; trivial

Syno: Small (तुच्छ)

Anto: Big (महत्वपूर्ण)

1185 Philanthropist (N.) - (परोपकारी)~ *[#R-5]*
A person who helps others, especially by donating money

Syno: Benefactor (हितैषी), Humanitarian (मानवतावादी)

Anto: Miser (कंजूस), Misanthrope (मानवद्वेषी)

1186 Phlegmatic (Adj.) - (भावहीन) *[#R-2 (2)]*
Unemotional and calmly steady

Syno: Calm (शांत) {Apathetic (उदासीन), Even-Tempered (संतुलित स्वभाव वाला)}

Anto: Ardent (उत्साही)

1187 **Pinnacle** (N.) - (शिखर) *[#R-4 (2)]*
The highest or most successful point

Syno: Summit (शिखर), Culmination (चरम बिंदु), Peak (उच्चतम बिंदु) {Apex (शीर्ष)}

Anto: Base (आधार) {Nadir (निम्नतम बिंदु)}

1188 Pious (Adj.) - (धार्मिक) *[#R-6]*
Deeply religious or devout

Syno: Religious (धार्मिक), Devout (भक्तिपूर्ण)

Anto: Sinful (पापी)

1189 **Piquant** (Adj.) - (चटपटा) *[#R-6 (4)]*
Having a pleasantly sharp taste or appetizing flavour

Syno: Spicy (मसालेदार), Appealing (मनभावन) {Exciting (रोमांचक)}

Anto: Bland (फीका)

1190 Pithy (Adj.) - (संक्षिप्त) *[#R-2 (1)]*
Short but full of meaning

Syno: Brief (संक्षिप्त), Concise (संक्षिप्त)

Anto: {Verbose (बहुत शब्दों वाला)}

1191 **Placate** (V.) - (शांत करना)~ *[#R-2 (2)]*
To reduce anger or hostility

Syno: Appease (मनाना) {Pacify (शांत करना), Reconcile (मेल-मिलाप करना)}

Anto: Enrage (क्रोधित करना)

1192 **Placid** (Adj.) - (शांत)~ *[#R-3 (6)]*
Not easily upset or excited; calm and peaceful

Syno: {Calm (शांत), Tranquil (शांत)}

Anto: Stormy (तूफानी), Angry (क्रोधी), Turbulent (अशांत)

1193 **Plain** (Adj.) - (सरल) *[#R-2]*
Simple; not decorated or elaborate

Syno: Simple (साधारण)

Anto: Fancy (सजावटी)

1194 Plausible (Adj.) - (विश्वसनीय)~ *[#R-7 (4)]*
Seeming reasonable or probable

Syno: Credible (विश्वसनीय), Believable (भरोसेमंद) {Probable (संभावित)}

Anto: Inconceivable (अकल्पनीय), Implausible (अविश्वसनीय), Unlikely (असंभावित) {Unthinkable (अकल्पनीय)}

1195 Pleasure (N.) - (आनंद) *[#R-3 (1)]*
A feeling of happy satisfaction and enjoyment

Syno: Happiness (खुशी)

Anto: Pain (दर्द) {Displeasure (अप्रसन्नता)}

1196 Plentiful (Adj.) - (प्रचुर) *[#R-2 (3)]*
Existing in large quantities; abundant

Syno: Ample (पर्याप्त), Abundant (प्रचुर)

Anto: {Scanty (कम)}

1197 **Plethora** (N.) - (अधिकता) *[#R-2 (7)]*
A large or excessive amount of something

Syno: Excess (अधिकता), Abundance (बहुतायत) {Overabundance (अत्यधिक मात्रा)}

Anto: {Dearth (अभाव), Rarity (दुर्लभता)}

1198 Pliable (Adj.) - (लचीला)~ *[#R-4 (4)]*
Easily bent or easily influenced

Syno: Malleable (आसानी से ढलने योग्य) {Flexible (लचीला)}

Anto: Rigid (कठोर) {Stiff (कठोर), Stubborn (जिद्दी)}

1199 Plight (N.) - (दुर्दशा) *[#R-3]*
A difficult or unfortunate situation

Syno: Difficulty (कठिनाई)

Anto: Advantage (लाभ), Benefit (फायदा)

1200 Plunge (V.) - (कूदना) *[#R-3]*
To jump or dive quickly and forcefully

Syno: Dive (गोता लगाना)

Anto: Ascend (ऊपर चढ़ना), Rise (उठना)

1201 **Poach** (V.) - (अवैध शिकार करना) *[#R-1 (1)]*
To hunt or take game or fish illegally

Syno: Hunt (शिकार करना)

Anto: {Give (देना)}

1202 Poignant (Adj.) - (मार्मिक)~ *[#R-3 (4)]*
Deeply moving; causing sadness or emotional pain

Syno: Emotional (भावनात्मक), Touching (मर्मस्पर्शी), Sad (उदास) {Painful (पीड़ादायक), Disturbing (परेशान करने वाला)}

Anto: {Insipid (भावहीन)}

1203 **Polarize** (V.) - (दो गुटों में बाँटना) *[#R-2]*
To cause division into two opposing groups

Syno: Segregate (अलग करना)

Anto: Combine (मिलाना)

1204 **Polite** (Adj.) - (विनम्र) *[#R-4 (1)]*
Showing good manners or respect

Syno: Humble (नम्र)

Anto: Rude (असभ्य)

1205 Pompous (Adj.) - (घमंडी, दिखावटी) *[#R-8 (2)]*
Showing exaggerated importance or dignity

Syno: Boastful (डींग मारने वाला), Pretentious (दिखावटी) {Grandiose (भव्य)}

Anto: Humble (विनम्र), Modest (नम्र), Submissive (आज्ञाकारी)

1206 **Ponderous** (Adj.) - (नीरस, भारी) *[#R-3 (2)]*
Slow and clumsy; dull or overly serious

Syno: Heavy (भारी) {Awkward (अजीब), Laboured (कठिन)}

Anto: Light (हल्का), Graceful (सुंदर)

1207 **Porous** (Adj.) - (छेददार) *[#R-2]*
Having small holes that let air or liquid pass

Syno: Permeable (भेद्य)

Anto: Impermeable (अभेद्य)

1208 **Potent** (Adj.) - (प्रबल) *[#R-2 (2)]*
Having great power, influence, or effect

Syno: Powerful (शक्तिशाली)

Anto: Weak (कमज़ोर) {Feeble (दुर्बल)}

1209 Potential (Adj./N.) - (संभावित; क्षमता) *[#R-4 (2)]*
Capable of developing in the future (Adj.); hidden ability or capacity (N.)

Syno: Capability (योग्यता) {Possible (संभव)}

Anto: Lacking (अभाव); Certainty (निश्चितता) {Unlikely (असंभावित)}

1210 Pragmatic (Adj.) - (व्यावहारिक)~ *[#R-4 (6)]*
Dealing with things realistically in a way that is based on practical considerations

Syno: Realistic (वास्तविक) {Practical (व्यावहारिक)}

Anto: Impractical (अव्यावहारिक), Idealistic (आदर्शवादी) {Theoretical (सैद्धांतिक)}

1211 **Praise** (N./V.) - (प्रशंसा; प्रशंसा करना) *[#R-6 (3)]*
Expression of approval or worship (N.); to express approval or admiration (V.)

Syno: Compliment (तारीफ) {Accolade (सम्मान)}

Anto: Rebuke (डांटना), Condemn (निंदा करना) {Criticize (आलोचना करना)}

1212 Precarious (Adj.) - (अस्थिर)~ *[#R-7 (3)]*
Not secure; likely to fall, fail, or collapse

Syno: Perilous (खतरनाक), Dangerous (खतरनाक), Insecure (असुरक्षित)

Anto: Safe (सुरक्षित), Stable (स्थिर), Reliable (भरोसेमंद) {Secure (सुरक्षित)}

1213 Precious (Adj.) - (मूल्यवान; प्रिय; उत्कृष्ट) *[#R-5 (1)]*
Very valuable or important; Cherished or beloved; Of high quality, flawless

Syno: {Valuable (कीमती)}

Anto: Worthless (बेकार), Cheap (सस्ता), Defective (दोषपूर्ण)

1214 Precise (Adj.) - (सटीक) *[#R-6 (2)]*
Marked by exactness and accuracy of expression or detail

Syno: Accurate (सटीक) {Exact (सटीक)}

Anto: Vague (अस्पष्ट)

1215 **Precocious** (Adj.) - (समय से पहले समझदार) *[#R-1 (2)]*
Developing abilities earlier than usual

Syno: {Advanced (उन्नत), Intelligent (बुद्धिमान)}

Anto: Backward (पिछड़ा)

1216 **Predicament** (N.) - (दुविधा) *[#R-6 (1)]*
A difficult, unpleasant, or embarrassing situation

Syno: Plight (संकट), Dilemma (दुविधा) {Quandary (उलझन)}

Anto: Solution (समाधान)

1217 Predilection (N.) - (पसंद)~ *[#R-4 (2)]*
A preference or special liking for something

Syno: Preference (प्राथमिकता)

Anto: Dislike (नापसंद), Aversion (घृणा) {Antipathy (नफरत)}

1218 Prefer (V.) - (पसंद करना) *[#R-1 (1)]*
To like better

Syno: {Favour (पसंद करना)}

Anto: Dislike (नापसंद करना)

1219 Prejudice (N.) - (पक्षपात) *[#R-7]*
An unfair opinion without reason

Syno: Bias (पक्षपात), Intolerance (असहनीयता)

Anto: Impartiality (निष्पक्षता), Fairness (न्याय)

1220 Preposterous (Adj.) - (बेतुका) *[#R-2 (5)]*
Completely unreasonable or absurd

Syno: Outrageous (बेतुका) {Ridiculous (ऊटपटाँग), Absurd (बेतुका), Incredible (अविश्वसनीय)}

Anto: Reasonable (उचित)

1221 Preserve (V.) - (संरक्षण करना) *[#R-2 (1)]*
To maintain (something) in its original or existing state

Syno: Maintain (बनाए रखना)

Anto: Neglect (ध्यान न देना)

1222 Prevent (V.) - (रोकना) *[#R-3 (2)]*
To stop something from happening

Syno: Avert (टालना), Block (अवरोध करना)

Anto: Induce (प्रेरित करना) {Promote (बढ़ावा देना)}

1223 Primary (Adj.) - (प्राथमिक) *[#R-2 (1)]*
Most important or earliest

Syno: Dominant (प्रमुख)

Anto: Secondary (द्वितीयक)

1224 Primitive (Adj.) - (प्राचीन) *[#R-3 (1)]*
Relating to an early stage of development

Syno: Basic (मूलभूत), Ancient (प्राचीन)

Anto: Sophisticated (परिष्कृत)

1225 Priority (N.) - (प्राथमिकता) *[#R-4 (1)]*
The condition of being regarded as more important

Syno: Precedence (प्राधान्य), Preference (पसंद)

Anto: Triviality (तुच्छता)

1226 **Pristine** (Adj.) - (अछूता) *[#R-2 (9)]*
In original condition; pure and not spoiled

Syno: Immaculate (निर्दोष) {Fresh (ताज़ा), Unspoiled (अछूता)}

Anto: Sullied (कलंकित) {Dirty (गंदा), Tarnished (दाग़दार)}

1227 Privilege (N.) - (विशेषाधिकार)~ *[#R-2 (2)]*
A special right or advantage

Syno: Honour (सम्मान) {Prerogative (विशेषाधिकार), Opportunity (अवसर)}

Anto: Disadvantage (नुकसान)

1228 **Proactive** (Adj.) - (सक्रिय) *[#R-3 (1)]*
Taking action in advance; acting before problems arise

Syno: Anticipatory (पूर्वानुमानी)

Anto: Careless (लापरवाह), Reactive (घटना के बाद प्रतिक्रिया करने वाला)

1229 Probably (Adv.) - (संभवतः) *[#R-2]*
Almost certainly; likely to happen

Syno: Likely (संभवतः)

Anto: Improbably (असंभाव्य रूप से)

1230 **Probity** (N.) - (ईमानदारी) *[#R-1 (4)]*
The quality of being honest and morally upright

Syno: {Uprightness (सच्चाई), Integrity (ईमानदारी)}

Anto: Deceit (छल) {Dishonesty (बेईमानी)}

1231 Proclaim (V.) - (घोषणा करना) *[#R-2 (1)]*
To announce officially or publicly

Syno: Declare (घोषित करना) {Announce (घोषणा करना)}

Anto: Conceal (छिपाना)

1232 **Procrastinate** (V.) - (देर करना)~ *[#R-5 (2)]*
To delay or postpone action; put off doing something

Syno: Delay (देरी करना)

Anto: Expedite (शीघ्रता करना) {Hasten (जल्दी करना)}

1233 Procrastination (N.) - (देरी)~ *[#R-2]*
The act of delaying action

Syno: Delay (विलंब)

Anto: Eagerness (उत्सुकता)

1234 Procure (V.) - (प्राप्त करना) *[#R-3 (1)]*
To obtain (something), especially with care or effort

Syno: Obtain (प्राप्त करना) {Secure (सुनिश्चित करना)}

Anto: Forfeit (गँवाना)

1235 Prodigal (Adj.) - (खर्चीला)~ *[#R-5 (3)]*
Wastefully extravagant

Syno: Wasteful (व्यर्थ), Lavish (खर्चीला), Extravagant (फ़िज़ूलख़र्च)

Anto: {Thrifty (कमखर्च), Parsimonious (कंजूस)}

1236 Prodigious (Adj.) - (विशाल) *[#R-2 (2)]*
Extremely large, great, or impressive

Syno: Immense (बहुत बड़ा) {Colossal (विशाल)}

Anto: Meagre (बहुत कम) {Minuscule (अत्यंत छोटा)}

1237 Productive (Adj.) - (उत्पादक) *[#R-1 (1)]*
Producing or able to produce large amounts of goods, crops, or other commodities

Syno: {Fruitful (फलदायक)}

Anto: Futile (व्यर्थ)

1238 Profane (Adj.) - (अपवित्र) *[#R-2 (5)]*
Not sacred; vulgar or disrespectful

Syno: Coarse (अशिष्ट)

Anto: Divine (दिव्य) {Sacred (पवित्र), Pure (शुद्ध), Pious (धार्मिक)}

1239 Proficient (Adj.) - (कुशल) *[#R-6 (1)]*
Skilled and competent at doing something

Syno: Adept (निपुण), Accomplished (निपुण), Skilful (कुशल)

Anto: Clumsy (अनाड़ी) {Incompetent (अयोग्य)}

1240 **Profit** (N./V.) - (मुनाफा, लाभ उठाना) *[#R-3]*
A financial gain or advantage (N.); To gain benefit (V.)

Syno: Benefit (लाभ)

Anto: Loss (हानि), Expense (व्यय)

1241 Profligate (Adj.) - (फ़िज़ूलख़र्च)~ *[#R-4 (3)]*
Wasteful and immoral

Syno: Wasteful (खर्चालू), Extravagant (अत्यधिक खर्चीला), Immoral (अनैतिक)

Anto: Thrifty (मितव्ययी) {Frugal (मितव्ययी), Virtuous (सदाचारी)}

1242 Profound (Adj.) - (गहरा, गहन ज्ञान वाला) *[#R-7 (6)]*
Very great or intense; Having deep insight or understanding

Syno: Deep (गहरा) {Extreme (अत्यधिक)}

Anto: Superficial (ऊपरी), Shallow (कम गहरा), Ignorant (अज्ञानी)

1243 Profuse (Adj.) - (प्रचुर) *[#R-8 (5)]*
Existing in very large quantity

Syno: Abundant (प्रचुर), Aplenty (बहुत) {Extravagant (फिजूलखर्च)}

Anto: Sparse (अल्प), Scant (कम), Scarce (कम), Meagre (अल्प)

1244 Progress (N./V.) - (प्रगति; प्रगति करना) *[#R-7 (2)]*
Movement or change toward improvement (N.); To advance (V.)

Syno: Development (विकास), Betterment (सुधार) {Breakthrough (महत्वपूर्ण प्रगति)}

Anto: Decline (पतन), Retreat (पीछे हटना)

1245 **Prohibit** (V.) - (प्रतिबंधित करना) *[#R-4 (3)]*
To officially forbid by authority

Syno: Ban (प्रतिबंध लगाना), Exclude (बहिष्कृत करना) {Forbid (निषेध करना), Prevent (रोकना)}

Anto: Permit (अनुमति देना)

1246 Prolific (Adj.) - (फलदायक) *[#R-3 (4)]*
Producing many results, works, or offspring

Syno: Productive (उत्पादक) {Profuse (प्रचुर)}

Anto: Unproductive (अनुत्पादक) {Barren (अनुपजाऊ)}

1247 Promote (V.) - (बढ़ावा देना) *[#R-3 (3)]*
To actively support or help something grow or succeed

Syno: Boost (बढ़ावा देना) {Encourage (प्रोत्साहित करना)}

Anto: Obstruct (बाधा डालना) {Oppose (विरोध करना)}

1248 Prompt (Adj.) - (शीघ्र) *[#R-4 (1)]*
Done without delay

Syno: Immediate (तत्काल), Quick (तेज)

Anto: Sluggish (सुस्त), Delayed (विलंबित)

1249 Propagate (V.) - (प्रसार करना; बढ़ाना) *[#R-3]*
To promote an idea or knowledge widely; To increase or multiply

Syno: Spread (फैलाना)

Anto: Suppress (दबाना), Deplete (कम करना)

1250 Propitiate (V.) - (शांत करना) *[#R-3 (1)]*
To win back favor by pleasing actions

Syno: Appease (संतुष्ट करना)

Anto: Enrage (क्रोधित करना)

1251 **Propitious** (Adj.) - (अनुकूल) *[#R-4 (2)]*
Giving a good chance of success

Syno: Hopeful (आशाजनक), Auspicious (शुभ), Favourable (सहायक)

Anto: Inauspicious (अशुभ) {Unfavourable (नुकसानदेह)}

1252 **Proscribe** (V.) - (प्रतिबंध लगाना)~ *[#R-2 (3)]*
To forbid, especially by law

Syno: Ban (प्रतिबंधित करना), Prohibit (निषेध करना)

Anto: {Legalise (अनुमति देना)}

1253 Prosperity (N.) - (समृद्धि) *[#R-8 (2)]*
The state of being prosperous

Syno: Wealth (धन), Richness (समृद्धि)

Anto: Adversity (विपत्ति), Failure (असफलता) {Poorness (गरीबी)}

1254 Protect (V.) - (सुरक्षित रखना) *[#R-2 (1)]*
To keep safe from harm or injury

Syno: Guard (रक्षा करना)

Anto: Harm (हानि पहुंचाना) {Ravage (नष्ट करना)}

1255 Protest (N./V.) - (विरोध; आपत्ति जताना) *[#R-4]*

An expression of opposition (N.); To express strong disagreement (V.)

Syno: Object (आपत्ति), Resist (प्रतिरोध), Oppose (विरोध करना)

Anto: Support (समर्थन)

1256 **Protract** (V.) - (लंबा करना, स्थगित करना) *[#R-3 (3)]*

To extend the time or duration of something

Syno: Prolong (अवधि बढ़ाना) {Stretch (खींचना)}

Anto: Shorten (छोटा करना), Curtail (कम करना) {Cut Short (छोटा करना)}

1257 **Proud** (Adj.) - (गर्वित) *[#R-1 (4)]*

Feeling satisfaction because of achievement or status

Syno: Haughty (अहंकारी) {Conceited (अभिमानी)}

Anto: {Humble (विनम्र)}

1258 Provoke (V.) - (उत्तेजित करना) *[#R-5 (4)]*

To cause a strong or unwanted reaction

Syno: Arouse (उकसाना), Enrage (क्रोधित करना) {Irritate (चिढ़ाना), Incite (उकसाना), Agitate (उत्तेजित करना)}

Anto: Soothe (शांत करना), Appease (संतुष्ट करना), Pacify (सुलह कराना) {Deter (रोकना)}

1259 **Proximity** (N.) - (निकटता) *[#R-1 (3)]*

Nearness in space, time, or relationship

Syno: Closeness (समीपता) {Nearness (निकटता)}

Anto: {Remoteness (दूरी)}

1260 Prudent (Adj.) - (विवेकी) *[#R-15 (2)]*

Showing careful judgment and planning for the future

Syno: Cautious (सावधान), Wise (बुद्धिमान), Frugal (अल्पव्ययी), Judicious (विवेकपूर्ण) {Careful (सावधान)}

Anto: Unwise (अविवेकी), Careless (लापरवाह), Indiscreet (असावधान), Stupid (मूर्ख), Thoughtless (विचारहीन), Wasteful (अपव्ययी)

1261 **Pseudo** (Adj.) - (नकली) *[#R-1 (1)]*

Not genuine; sham

Syno: {False (झूठा)}

Anto: Genuine (असली)

1262 **Punctilious** (Adj.) - (सटीक, अति-सावधान)~ *[#R-1 (2)]*

Showing great attention to detail or correct behaviour

Syno: {Scrupulous (नैतिक)}

Anto: Easy-Going (लापरवाह) {Lax (लापरवाह)}

1263 Pusillanimous (Adj.) - (कायर)~ *[#R-1 (1)]*

Showing a lack of courage or determination; timid

Syno: {Timorous (कायर)}

Anto: Brave (बहादुर)

1264 Quaint (Adj.) - (अजीब) *[#R-4 (1)]*

Attractively unusual or old-fashioned

Syno: Queer (विचित्र) {Old-Fashioned (पुराना ढंग का)}

Anto: Common (सामान्य), Ordinary (साधारण)

1265 Quarantine (N./V.) - (अलगाव; अलग करना) *[#R-1 (2)]*

The isolation to prevent the spread of disease; place of such isolation; To isolate to prevent spread

Syno: Isolation (अलगाव) {Restrain (रोकना)}

Anto: {Assimilate (मिलाना)}

1266 Quarrel (N.) - (झगड़ा) *[#R-2 (2)]*

An angry disagreement

Syno: Feud (दुश्मनी)

Anto: Harmony (सामंजस्य) {Accord (समझौता), Reconciliation (सुलह)}

1267 **Quash** (V.) - (खारिज करना)~ *[#R-3]*

To reject or void, especially by legal procedure

Syno: Reject (अस्वीकार करना), Crush (कुचलना)

Anto: Support (समर्थन करना)

1268 Queer (Adj.) - (अजीब) *[#R-2 (2)]*

Odd or strange

Syno: Strange (विचित्र)

Anto: Ordinary (साधारण) {Typical (सामान्य)}

1269 **Quell** (V.) - (शांत करना) *[#R-4 (4)]*

To stop unrest or disorder forcefully

Syno: Suppress (दबाना) {Subdue (वश में करना), Reduce (कम करना)}

Anto: Agitate (भड़काना), Provoke (उकसाना) {Incite (उकसाना)}

1270 Querulous (Adj.) - (शिकायती) *[#R-4 (2)]*

Complaining in a petulant or whining manner

Syno: Grouchy (चिड़चिड़ा), Complaining (शिकायत करने वाला)

Anto: Uncomplaining (जो शिकायत न करे) {Cheerful (प्रसन्न), Content (संतुष्ट)}

1271 Quiescent (Adj.) - (शांत) *[#R-5 (2)]*

Being inactive or at rest

Syno: Dull (मंद), Dormant (सोया हुआ) {Inactive

(निष्क्रिय)}

Anto: Active (सक्रिय), Animated (जीवंत)

1272 Quixotic (Adj.) - (कल्पनात्मक)~ *[#R-3]*
Unrealistically idealistic

Syno: Idealistic (आदर्शवादी)

Anto: Pragmatic (यथार्थवादी)

1273 Rabble (N.) - (भीड़) *[#R-1 (4)]*
A noisy, disorderly crowd of people

Syno: {Mob (भीड़), Assemblage (जमावड़ा)}

Anto: Elite (विशिष्ट समूह) {Nobility (उच्च वर्ग)}

1274 **Radiance** (N.) - (चमक) *[#R-2]*
The light or brightness given off by something

Syno: Sparkle (चमक)

Anto: Dullness (मंदता)

1275 Radiant (Adj.) - (चमकदार) *[#R-1 (2)]*
Shining brightly or giving off light

Syno: Glowing (चमकीला) {Luminous (प्रकाशमान)}

Anto: {Dull (फीका)}

1276 **Radical** (Adj.) - (मौलिक)~ *[#R-4 (2)]*
Very great or fundamental

Syno: Fanatical (कट्टरपंथी), Absolute (पूर्ण), Profound (गहरा) {Revolutionary (परिवर्तनकारी)}

Anto: Conservative (रूढ़िवादी) {Moderate (मध्यम)}

1277 **Rambling** (Adj.) - (दूर तक फैला हुआ, बहुत लंबा)~ *[#R-3]*
Lengthy and confused or inconsequential

Syno: Long-Winded (लंबा)

Anto: Coherent (समझने में सरल), Direct (सीधा)

1278 Random (Adj.) - (अनियमित) *[#R-4 (4)]*
Made or chosen without method or plan

Syno: Arbitrary (मनमाना), Chance (अचानक) {Haphazard (अव्यवस्थित), Casual (आकस्मिक)}

Anto: Systematic (व्यवस्थित), Specific (विशेष) {Deliberate (जानबूझकर), Planned (योजनाबद्ध)}

1279 **Rapaciousness** (N.) - (लोभ) *[#R-1 (1)]*
Aggressive greed

Syno: {Voraciousness (लालच)}

Anto: Generosity (दानशीलता)

1280 **Rapid** (Adj.) - (तेज़) *[#R-9 (2)]*
Happening very fast or in a short time

Syno: Quick (जल्दी), Prompt (तुरंत), Hasty (जल्दबाज़), Swift (तेज़)

Anto: Slow (धीमा)

1281 **Rapture** (N.) - (आनंद) *[#R-3]*
A feeling of intense pleasure or joy

Syno: Delight (प्रसन्नता), Ecstasy (परमानंद)

Anto: Misery (दुःख)

1282 **Rare** (Adj.) - (कम मिलने वाला) *[#R-4 (1)]*
Not common or not often found

Syno: Scarce (दुर्लभ) {Precious (अनमोल)}

Anto: Usual (सामान्य), Familiar (परिचित), Common (आम/सर्वसामान्य)

1283 **Rarely** (Adv.) - (कभी-कभार) *[#R-2 (1)]*
Not often; infrequently

Syno: Seldom (शायद ही कभी)

Anto: Frequently (अक्सर)

1284 Rational (Adj.) - (तार्किक) *[#R-3]*
Based on reason or logical thinking

Syno: Logical (तर्कसंगत)

Anto: Illogical (अतार्किक)

1285 Raucous (Adj.) - (तीखी आवाज़ वाला) *[#R-2 (2)]*
Harsh, loud, and disturbing in sound

Syno: {Boisterous (हंगामेदार)}

Anto: Subdued (धीमा), Dulcet (मधुर) {Soft (नरम)}

1286 **Ravage** (V.) - (बर्बाद करना) *[#R-4 (2)]*
To cause severe and extensive damage

Syno: Demolish (ध्वस्त करना), Damage (नुकसान करना) {Destroy (नष्ट करना)}

Anto: Restore (पुनः स्थापित करना) {Renovate (मरम्मत करना)}

1287 **Ravish** (V.) - (मोहित करना) *[#R-2]*
To delight intensely

Syno: Enthral (मंत्रमुग्ध करना)

Anto: Repel (पीछे हटाना)

1288 **Ready** (Adj.) - (तैयार) *[#R-2]*
Fully prepared and suitable for action

Syno: Prepared (तैयार)

Anto: Unprepared (अतैयार)

1289 Rebuke (N./V.) - (फटकार; फटकारना) *[#R-1 (2)]*
Sharp criticism (N.); To scold or criticize severely (V.)

Syno: {Scold (डाँटना)}

Anto: Flattery (चापलूसी) {Commend (प्रशंसा करना)}

1290 Recalcitrant (Adj.) - (जिद्दी) *[#R-3 (2)]*
Stubbornly disobedient or uncooperative

Syno: Rebellious (विद्रोही), Disobedient (अवज्ञाकारी) {Unruly (अनियंत्रित)}

Anto: Amenable (सहयोगी) {Obedient (आज्ञाकारी)}

1291 Recede (V.) - (पीछे हटना) *[#R-5 (1)]*
To go or move back from a position
Syno: Wane (कम होना)
Anto: Advance (आगे बढ़ना), Extend (विस्तार करना) {Proceed (आगे बढ़ना)}

1292 Receive (V.) - (प्राप्त करना; स्वागत करना) *[#R-3]*
To get or accept; To welcome or admit
Syno: Get (पाना)
Anto: Give (देना)

1293 Reckless (Adj.) - (लापरवाह)~ *[#R-8 (1)]*
Acting without thinking about consequences
Syno: Careless (बेपरवाह), Thoughtless (बिना सोचे), Rash (उतावला)
Anto: Cautious (सावधान) {Careful (सतर्क)}

1294 Recluse (Adj./N.) - (एकांतप्रिय; संन्यासी)~ *[#R-2 (2)]*
Living in seclusion (Adj.); A person who lives a solitary life and avoids others (N.)
Syno: Solitary (एकांतप्रिय)
Anto: Extrovert (बहिर्मुखी) {Gregarious (मिलनसार); Socialite (सामाजिक व्यक्ति)}

1295 Recondite (Adj.) - (जटिल) *[#R-3 (2)]*
Difficult to understand or known by very few people
Syno: {Concealed (छिपा हुआ)}
Anto: Straightforward (सरल), Simple (साधारण), Clear (स्पष्ट)

1296 **Recover** (V.) - (ठीक होना) *[#R-2]*
To return to a normal state of health, mind, or strength
Syno: Regain (पुनः प्राप्त करना)
Anto: Lose (खोना)

1297 Rectify (V.) - (सुधारना)~ *[#R-11 (4)]*
To put something right
Syno: Correct (सही करना), Amend (संशोधन करना)
Anto: Worsen (बदतर करना), Falsify (झूठा बनाना), Corrupt (भ्रष्ट करना)

1298 **Redeem** (V.) - (मुक्त करना) *[#R-3]*
To save or make up for past faults or loss
Syno: Save (बचाना)
Anto: Violate (उल्लंघन करना), Forfeit (ज़ब्त करना)

1299 **Redemption** (N.) - (मुक्ति) *[#R-2 (2)]*
The act of being saved from sin, error, or evil
Syno: Atonement (प्रायश्चित) {Retrieval (पुनः प्राप्ति)}
Anto: {Violation (उल्लंघन)}

1300 Redolent (Adj.) - (सुगंधित) *[#R-1 (1)]*
Having a strong smell or strongly suggestive of something
Syno: {Pungent (तेज़ गंध वाला)}
Anto: Unscented (बिना गंध का)

1301 Redundancy (N.) - (अनावश्यकता) *[#R-7]*
The state of being more than needed
Syno: Excess (अधिकता)
Anto: Requirement (आवश्यकता)

1302 Redundant (Adj.) - (अनावश्यक)~ *[#R-5 (2)]*
More than needed
Syno: Superfluous (अनावश्यक), Unnecessary (फालतू)
Anto: Concise (संक्षिप्त), Essential (आवश्यक), Required (आवश्यक)

1303 **Refined** (Adj.) - (परिष्कृत, शुद्ध किया हुआ) *[#R-3 (2)]*
Made pure or polished by removing impurities
Syno: {Elegant (सलीके वाला)}
Anto: Crude (अशुद्ध) {Rough (खुरदरा)}

1304 **Regret** (N./V.) - (पछतावा; पछताना) *[#R-3 (2)]*
A feeling of sorrow or remorse (N.); To feel sad over something (V.)
Syno: Sadness (उदासी); Repent (पश्चाताप करना)
Anto: Contentment (संतोष) {Rejoice (खुशी मनाना)}

1305 Regular (Adj.) - (नियमित) *[#R-2 (2)]*
Happening at fixed intervals; usual or according to rule
Syno: Usual (सामान्य) {Common (आम), Uniform (समान)}
Anto: Abnormal (असामान्य)

1306 Reiterate (V.) - (दोहराना) *[#R-1 (1)]*
To say or state something again for emphasis or clarity
Syno: Repeat (पुनरावृत्ति करना)
Anto: {Retract (वापस लेना)}

1307 **Rejoice** (V.) - (आनन्दित होना) *[#R-1 (1)]*
To feel or show great joy or delight
Syno: Exult (बहुत खुश होना)
Anto: {Lament (विलाप करना)}

1308 Rejuvenate (V.) - (नया करना)~ *[#R-4 (1)]*
To make someone or something feel young,

fresh, or lively again

Syno: Update (नवीनतम करना), Refresh (ताज़ा करना)

Anto: {Ruin (बर्बाद करना)}

1309 **Relay** (V.) - (आगे भेजना) *[#R-1 (2)]*
To receive and pass on information

Syno: {Convey (पहुँचाना)}

Anto: Hold (पकड़ना)

1310 **Release** (V.) - (मुक्त करना) *[#R-3 (1)]*
To let something go or set free

Syno: Free (मुक्त करना), Acquit (दोषमुक्त करना)

Anto: Confine (सीमित करना) {Restrain (बाँधना)}

1311 **Relevant** (Adj.) - (प्रासंगिक) *[#R-8 (2)]*
Closely connected with or appropriate to the subject

Syno: Applicable (लागू होने योग्य) {Apt (उचित)}

Anto: Inapplicable (लागू नहीं), Insignificant (महत्वहीन), Inappropriate (अनुचित) {Unrelated (असंबंधित)}

1312 **Reliable** (Adj.) - (विश्वसनीय) *[#R-8 (1)]*
Able to be trusted because of consistent quality or performance

Syno: Dependable (भरोसेमंद), Stable (स्थिर), Trustworthy (विश्वसनीय)

Anto: Untrustworthy (अविश्वसनीय) {Questionable (संदेहास्पद)}

1313 **Relinquish** (V.) - (त्यागना)~ *[#R-5 (8)]*
To voluntarily give up possession, control, or claim

Syno: Discard (त्यागना), Surrender (समर्पित करना), Abandon (त्याग देना) {Abdicate (त्यागना), Give Up (छोड़ देना)}

Anto: Retain (रखना), Continue (जारी रखना) {Possess (रखना)}

1314 **Reluctant** (Adj.) - (अनिच्छुक)~ *[#R-11 (7)]*
Not willing or eager; hesitant to act

Syno: Hesitant (हिचकिचाता हुआ), Unwilling (अनिच्छुक) {Averse (विरुद्ध), Disinclined (अनिच्छुक)}

Anto: Eager (उत्सुक), Willing (इच्छुक), Inclined (इच्छुक), Enthusiastic (उत्साही)

1315 **Rely** (V.) - (निर्भर करना) *[#R-2 (1)]*
To depend on with full trust or confidence

Syno: Depend (निर्भर करना)

Anto: Distrust (अविश्वास करना)

1316 **Remarkable** (Adj.) - (उल्लेखनीय) *[#R-3 (2)]*
Worthy of attention; striking

Syno: Astounding (आश्चर्यजनक) {Noticeable (ध्यान देने योग्य)}

Anto: Normal (सामान्य) {Modest (कम दिखावटी)}

1317 **Remember** (V.) - (याद करना) *[#R-2]*
To bring something from the past back into the mind

Syno: Recall (पुनः स्मरण करना)

Anto: Forget (भूल जाना)

1318 **Remission** (N.) - (माफी, छूट)~ *[#R-1 (1)]*
A temporary lessening of disease or pain; forgiveness of penalty or debt

Syno: Pardon (क्षमा)

Anto: {Censure (आलोचना)}

1319 **Remorse** (N.) - (पश्चाताप)~ *[#R-6 (6)]*
Deep regret or guilt for a wrong committed

Syno: Regret (खेद) {Repentance (पश्चाताप)}

Anto: Indifference (लापरवाही), Satisfaction (संतोष) {Impenitence (कठोरता)}

1320 **Remote** (Adj.) - (दूरस्थ) *[#R-3]*
Far away from people, places, or main centers

Syno: Isolated (एकांत), Aloof (दूर)

Anto: Close (निकट)

1321 **Renaissance** (N.) - (पुनर्जागरण) *[#R-1 (1)]*
A period or act of renewed interest and growth in art, culture, or learning

Syno: {Revival (पुनरुत्थान)}

Anto: Decadence (पतन)

1322 **Renegade** (N.) - (देशद्रोही)~ *[#R-1 (1)]*
A person who abandons a religion, cause, or party

Syno: {Traitor (गद्दार)}

Anto: Follower (अनुयायी)

1323 **Renowned** (Adj.) - (प्रसिद्ध) *[#R-3 (3)]*
Known or talked about by many people

Syno: Famous (प्रसिद्ध) {Illustrious (प्रतिष्ठित), Well-Known (प्रसिद्ध)}

Anto: Unknown (अज्ञात), Obscure (अस्पष्ट)

1324 **Repeal** (N./V.) - (रद्दीकरण; रद्द करना) *[#R-2 (1)]*
The act of officially cancelling a law (N.); To cancel formally (V.)

Syno: Cancellation (रद्दीकरण) {Cancel (रद्द करना)}

Anto: Approval (अनुमोदन)

1325 **Repel** (V.) - (पीछे हटाना) *[#R-5]*
To force back, keep away, or resist

Syno: Rebuff (ठुकराना), Resist (विरोध करना)

Anto: Attract (आकर्षित करना)

1326 **Replenish** (V.) - (फिर से भरना)~ *[#R-1 (4)]*
To fill something up again

Syno: Restore (पुनर्स्थापित करना) {Refill (फिर से भरना)}

Anto: {Deplete (खाली करना)}

1327 Replete (Adj.) - (भरा हुआ) *[#R-1 (1)]*
Filled or well-supplied with something

Syno: Full (पूर्ण)

Anto: {Empty (खाली)}

1328 Reprimand (N./V.) - (डांट; फटकारना) *[#R-8 (5)]*
An official expression of disapproval (N.); To officially scold or rebuke (V.)

Syno: Condemnation (निंदा), Reproach (निन्दा); Rebuke (फटकार) {Admonish (धिक्कारना), Scold (डांटना)}

Anto: Praise (प्रशंसा), Reward (पुरस्कार), Forgiveness (क्षमा), Compliment (तारीफ)

1329 **Reproach** (N./V.) - (निंदा; उलाहना देना) *[#R-5 (3)]*
An act of blaming or criticizing (N.); To express blame or disappointment (V.)

Syno: Rebuke (निंदा), Condemnation (निंदा); Berate (फटकारना), Admonish (चेतावनी देना) {Disgrace (कलंक); Disapprove (अस्वीकृति)}

Anto: Praise (प्रशंसा)

1330 **Reprobate** (Adj.) - (दुराचारी) *[#R-3 (2)]*
Without moral principles

Syno: Degenerate (पतित), Wicked (दुष्ट) {Immoral (अनैतिक)}

Anto: Virtuous (नैतिक)

1331 Reprove (V.) - (डांटना) *[#R-3]*
To officially or formally scold or criticize

Syno: Scold (डांटना), Rebuke (फटकार लगाना)

Anto: Eulogize (प्रशंसा करना)

1332 **Repudiate** (V.) - (अस्वीकार करना) *[#R-2 (2)]*
To refuse to accept; reject

Syno: Renounce (त्यागना)

Anto: Accept (स्वीकार करना)

1333 Repugnant (Adj.) - (अस्वीकार्य) *[#R-1 (5)]*
Extremely distasteful; unacceptable

Syno: {Offensive (आक्रामक), Abhorrent (घृणित), Abominable (घिनौना)}

Anto: Pleasant (सुखद) {Amiable (मिलनसार), Glorious (गौरवशाली)}

1334 Repulsive (Adj.) - (घिनौना)~ *[#R-8 (2)]*
Causing strong disgust or dislike

Syno: Disgusting (घृणास्पद)

Anto: Pleasant (सुखद), Attractive (आकर्षक)

1335 Rescind (V.) - (रद्द करना) *[#R-2 (4)]*
To officially cancel or withdraw a law

Syno: Revoke (निरस्त करना) {Repeal (निरस्त करना), Abrogate (समाप्त करना)}

Anto: Reinstate (पुनः स्थापित करना) {Sanction (मंजूरी देना)}

1336 **Resign** (V.) - (त्यागपत्र देना) *[#R-2 (1)]*
To voluntarily leave a job or other position

Syno: Surrender (आत्मसमर्पण करना) {Renounce (त्यागना)}

Anto: Join (जुड़ना)

1337 Resilience (N.) - (लचीलापन)~ *[#R-1 (7)]*
The capacity to recover quickly from difficulties

Syno: {Tenacity (सहनशक्ति), Strength (मजबूती)}

Anto: Rigidity (कठोरता) {Vulnerability (कमजोरी), Fragility (नाज़ुकपन)}

1338 Resilient (Adj.) - (सहनशील)~ *[#R-4 (5)]*
Able to recover quickly from stress, damage, or difficulties

Syno: Supple (नरम), Strong (मजबूत) {Flexible (लचीला), Tough (कठोर)}

Anto: Fragile (नाज़ुक), Weak (कमजोर) {Stiff (सख़्त)}

1339 Resistance (N.) - (विरोध) *[#R-1 (1)]*
The act of opposing, refusing, or fighting against something

Syno: {Refusal (इंकार)}

Anto: Tolerance (सहनशीलता)

1340 **Resistant** (Adj.) - (प्रतिरोधी) *[#R-1 (1)]*
Able or tending to resist something

Syno: Opposing (विरोधी)

Anto: {Vulnerable (असुरक्षित)}

1341 Resolute (Adj.) - (दृढ़ संकल्पित) *[#R-11 (2)]*
Showing firm determination and purpose

Syno: Determined (निश्चयी), Strong (मजबूत)

Anto: Indecisive (दुविधाग्रस्त), Wavering (अस्थिर), Complacent (लापरवाह)

1342 **Resolve** (N.) - (संकल्प) *[#R-3]*
Firm determination

Syno: Decision (निर्णय)

Anto: Indecision (अनिश्चितता)

1343 Respectful (Adj.) - (आदरपूर्ण) *[#R-1 (1)]*
Feeling or showing deference and respect

Syno: Dutiful (आज्ञाकारी)

Anto: {Discourteous (असभ्य)}

1344 **Restive** (Adj.) - (बेचैन) *[#R-1 (4)]*
Showing impatience, uneasiness, or resistance to control

Syno: Restless (अस्थिर) {Impatient (व्याकुल), Discontented (असंतुष्ट)}

Anto: {Cooperative (सहयोगी)}

1345 Resurgence (N.) - (पुनरुत्थान) *[#R-2]*
A renewed rise or return after a period of decline

Syno: Renewal (नवीनीकरण)

Anto: Decline (पतन)

1346 Retain (V.) - (बनाए रखना) *[#R-3]*
To continue to have something; to keep possession of

Syno: Maintain (बनाए रखना)

Anto: Release (मुक्त करना), Forget (भूलना)

1347 Retaliate (V.) - (बदला लेना)~ *[#R-4 (2)]*
To make an attack or assault in return for a similar attack

Syno: Avenge (बदला लेना), React (प्रतिक्रिया करना)

Anto: {Forgive (माफ करना)}

1348 Reticent (Adj.) - (अल्पभाषी)~ *[#R-5 (6)]*
Not revealing one's thoughts or feelings readily

Syno: Silent (मौन) {Restrained (संयमित)}

Anto: Communicative (संवादी), Talkative (बातूनी) {Garrulous (बातूनी), Outgoing (बहिर्मुखी), Voluble (वाचाल)}

1349 **Retired** (Adj.) - (सेवानिवृत्त) *[#R-1 (2)]*
Having left one's job and ceased to work

Syno: {Former (भूतपूर्व)}

Anto: Active (सक्रिय)

1350 **Retract** (V.) - (वापस लेना) *[#R-1 (1)]*
To take back

Syno: Revoke (रद्द करना)

Anto: {Proclaim (घोषित करना)}

1351 **Retreat** (N./V.) - (आश्रय स्थल; पीछे हटना)~ *[#R-4 (4)]*
A place of refuge (N.); To move back or withdraw (V.)

Syno: Withdrawal (वापसी)

Anto: Advance (आगे बढ़ना)

1352 Retrieve (V.) - (वापस पाना) *[#R-2 (1)]*
To get or bring something back; to regain possession of

Syno: Recover (पुनः प्राप्त करना)

Anto: {Lose (खोना)}

1353 **Revamp** (V.) - (पुनर्गठन करना)~ *[#R-2 (2)]*
To give new and improved form, structure, or appearance to

Syno: Restructure (पुनर्गठन करना) {Reconstruct (पुनर्निर्माण करना), Renovate (नवीनीकरण करना)}

Anto: Damage (क्षति पहुँचाना)

1354 Reveal (V.) - (प्रकट करना) *[#R-5 (3)]*
To make previously unknown or secret information known to others

Syno: Disclose (खोलना)

Anto: Hide (छिपाना), Conceal (गुप्त रखना)

1355 **Revel** (V.) - (जश्न मनाना)~ *[#R-2 (1)]*
To get great pleasure from a situation or experience

Syno: Make Merry (खुशी मनाना) {Rejoice (खुश होना)}

Anto: Mourn (शोक मनाना)

1356 Revelation (N.) - (अनावरण) *[#R-1 (2)]*
A surprising, previously unknown fact made known dramatically

Syno: Disclosure (प्रकटीकरण) {Unveiling (अनावरण)}

Anto: {Concealment (छिपाव)}

1357 Revere (V.) - (सम्मान करना) *[#R-3]*
To feel deep respect or admiration for something

Syno: Respect (सम्मान करना)

Anto: Despise (तिरस्कार करना)

1358 Reverence (N.) - (श्रद्धा) *[#R-4 (3)]*
Deep respect for someone or something

Syno: Respect (सम्मान करना)

Anto: Contempt (घृणा), Disrespect (अनादर) {Scorn (तिरस्कार)}

1359 Reverent (Adj.) - (श्रद्धालु)~ *[#R-1 (1)]*
Showing deep respect

Syno: Respectful (आदरपूर्ण)

Anto: {Disrespectful (अनादरपूर्ण)}

1360 **Reverie** (N.) - (स्वप्न-लोक)~ *[#R-2 (1)]*
A state of being pleasantly lost in one's thoughts

Syno: Day-Dream (सुखद कल्पना)

Anto: Reality (वास्तविकता)

1361 **Revive** (V.) - (पुनर्जीवित करना) *[#R-5]*
To restore to life or consciousness; regain life, consciousness, or strength

Syno: Restore (पुनः स्थापित करना), Recover (पुनः प्राप्त करना)

Anto: Ruin (बर्बाद करना), Damage (क्षति पहुंचाना)

1362 **Revoke** (V.) - (निरस्त करना)~ *[#R-3]*
To cancel the validity of a decision or law

Syno: Repeal (रद्द करना)

Anto: Proclaim (घोषित करना), Implement (लागू करना)

1363 **Ridicule** (N./V.) - (उपहास; मज़ाक उड़ाना)~ *[#R-3]*
Unkind mockery (N.); To mock or make fun of (V.)

Syno: Derision (उपहास)

Anto: Flattery (चापलूसी); Commend (प्रशंसा करना)

1364 Ridiculous (Adj.) - (बेतुका) *[#R-1 (1)]*
Deserving or inviting derision or mockery; absurd

Syno: {Funny (मजेदार)}

Anto: Reasonable (तर्कसंगत)

1365 **Rife** (Adj.) - (प्रचुर) *[#R-1 (2)]*
Very common, especially of something undesirable

Syno: {Widespread (व्यापक)}

Anto: Scarce (दुर्लभ)

1366 Rift (N.) - (दरार) *[#R-1 (1)]*
A crack, split, or break in something

Syno: Break (टूट)

Anto: {Joint (जोड़)}

1367 **Rigid** (Adj.) - (कठोर)~ *[#R-5 (1)]*
Unable to bend or be forced out of shape; not flexible

Syno: Inflexible (दृढ़), Stiff (सख्त)

Anto: Flexible (लचीला)

1368 Rigorous (Adj.) - (कठिन) *[#R-1 (2)]*
Extremely thorough, exhaustive, or accurate

Syno: {Rigid (कठोर)}

Anto: Lenient (नरम)

1369 Rival (N./V.) - (प्रतिद्वंद्वी; प्रतिस्पर्धा करना) *[#R-2 (1)]*
A competing person or thing (N.); To compete with (V.)

Syno: Compete (प्रतिस्पर्धा करना)

Anto: Comrade (साथी) {Accomplice (सहयोगी)}

1370 Robust (Adj.) - (मजबूत) *[#R-6 (1)]*
Strong and healthy; vigorous

Syno: Healthy (स्वस्थ), Sturdy (मजबूत)

Anto: Feeble (दुर्बल) {Frail (कमज़ोर)}

1371 **Rotund** (Adj.) - (गोल) *[#R-2]*
Plump (of a person)

Syno: Round (गोलाकार)

Anto: Slim (पतला)

1372 **Rough** (Adj.) - (खुरदुरा) *[#R-4 (1)]*
Having an uneven or irregular surface; not smooth or level

Syno: Coarse (खुरदुरा)

Anto: Smooth (चिकना)

1373 **Rowdy** (Adj.) - (हुड़दंगी) *[#R-2]*
Noisy and disorderly

Syno: Boisterous (कोलाहलपूर्ण)

Anto: Compliant (आज्ञाकारी)

1374 Rudimentary (Adj.) - (बुनियादी) *[#R-2 (1)]*
Basic or elementary

Syno: Primitive (प्राथमिक), Elementary (मूलभूत)

Anto: {Advanced (उच्च स्तर का)}

1375 Ruin (V.) - (बर्बाद करना)~ *[#R-2 (2)]*
To destroy or cause downfall

Syno: Despoil (लूटना) {Devastate (उजाड़ना)}

Anto: Mend (मरम्मत करना) {Repair (ठीक करना)}

1376 **Rustic** (Adj.) - (देहाती) *[#R-2 (2)]*
Rural or countryside-related

Syno: {Artless (सरल)}

Anto: Urban (शहरी), Urbane (सभ्य) {Fancy (दिखावटी)}

1377 Ruthless (Adj.) - (निर्दयी) *[#R-8 (2)]*
Having or showing no pity or compassion for others

Syno: Merciless (निर्मम), Inhumane (अमानवीय) {Brutal (क्रूर)}

Anto: Kind (दयालु), Compassionate (करुणामय), Lenient (उदार)

1378 **Saboteur** (N.) - (तोड़-फोड़ करने वाला)~ *[#R-1 (1)]*
A person who engages in sabotage

Syno: Vandal (विध्वंसक)

Anto: {Ally (सहयोगी)}

1379 Sacred (Adj.) - (पवित्र) *[#R-9 (2)]*
Connected with God or religion and deserving respect

Syno: Holy (पवित्र), Consecrated (अभिषिक्त)

Anto: Profane (अपवित्र)

1380 Sagacious (Adj.) - (बुद्धिमान) *[#R-8 (4)]*
Having keen mental discernment and good judgment

Syno: Insightful (सूझबूझ वाला), Judicious (न्यायसंगत) {Astute (चतुर), Wise (बुद्धिमान)}

Anto: Dull (मंद), Obtuse (मंदबुद्धि), Foolish (मूर्ख), Ignorant (अज्ञानी) {Unwise (अविवेकी)}

1381 Salient (Adj.) - (महत्वपूर्ण) *[#R-7 (2)]*
Most noticeable or important

Syno: Prominent (प्रमुख), Noticeable (ध्यान देने योग्य) {Notable (उल्लेखनीय)}

Anto: Insignificant (महत्वहीन), Negligible (नगण्य), Inconspicuous (अदृश्य सा, अप्रकट)

1382 **Salubrious** (Adj.) - (सेहतमंद) *[#R-2 (4)]*
Health-giving

Syno: Wholesome (पौष्टिक), Beneficial (लाभकारी) {Healthy (स्वस्थ), Salutary (हितकारी), Pleasant (सुखद)}

Anto: {Unhealthy (अस्वस्थ)}

1383 **Salvage** (V.) - (बचाना) *[#R-4 (1)]*
To save goods from damage or destruction

Syno: Save (बचाना)

Anto: Damage (क्षति करना), Forfeit (गँवा देना) {Lose (हारना)}

1384 **Sane** (Adj.) - (समझदार) *[#R-5]*
Of sound mind; not mad or mentally ill

Syno: Sensible (विवेकी)

Anto: Crazy (पागल), Paranoid (वहमी)

1385 Sanguine (Adj.) - (आशावादी)~ *[#R-4 (6)]*
Optimistic or positive, especially in difficulty

Syno: Buoyant (प्रफुल्लित) {Optimistic (आशावादी)}

Anto: Hopeless (निराश), Melancholic (उदास), Pessimistic (निराशावादी) {Depressed (अवसादग्रस्त), Morose (रूखा)}

1386 Sarcastic (Adj.) - (व्यंग्यात्मक) *[#R-5]*
Marked by using irony to mock or convey contempt

Syno: Sardonic (व्यंग्यपूर्ण), Caustic (कटु)

Anto: Gracious (कृपालु), Courteous (विनम्र)

1387 Sardonic (Adj.) - (व्यंग्यपूर्ण) *[#R-1 (3)]*
Grimly mocking or cynical

Syno: {Mocking (उपहास पूर्ण)}

Anto: Gracious (अनुग्रह पूर्ण) {Sincere (निष्कपट)}

1388 Satiate (V.) - (तृप्त करना) *[#R-2 (1)]*
To satisfy fully; to provide more than enough

Syno: Satisfy (संतुष्ट करना)

Anto: {Deprive (वंचित करना)}

1389 Satisfaction (N.) - (संतोष) *[#R-3]*
The fulfilment of needs or desires; pleasure from fulfilment

Syno: Contentment (तृप्ति), Delight (प्रसन्नता)

Anto: Dissatisfaction (असंतोष)

1390 Savage (Adj./N.) - (बर्बर; बर्बर व्यक्ति) *[#R-7 (4)]*
Fierce, violent, uncivilized (Adj.); A cruel or primitive person (N.)

Syno: Brutal (निर्दयी) {Feral (जंगली); Barbarian (बर्बर)}

Anto: Civilized (सभ्य), Tame (वश में), Cultured (संस्कारी) {Refined (सुसंस्कृत)}

1391 Savoury (Adj.) - (नमकीन) *[#R-3]*
Salty or non-sweet; morally acceptable

Syno: Salty (नमकीन)

Anto: Sweet (मीठा)

1392 Scanty (Adj.) - (अल्प) *[#R-6 (5)]*
Small or insufficient in quantity or amount

Syno: Deficient (अपर्याप्त), Limited (सीमित), Meagre (कम) {Scarce (दुर्लभ), Insufficient (अपर्याप्त), Sparse (विरल)}

Anto: Profuse (प्रचुर), Abundant (प्रचुर) {Plentiful (प्रचुर)}

1393 Scarce (Adj.) - (दुर्लभ) *[#R-5 (2)]*
Insufficient for the demand; in short supply

Syno: Limited (सीमित)

Anto: Ample (पर्याप्त), Plentiful (प्रचुर) {Copious (बहुतायत), Abundant (प्रचुर)}

1394 Scarcity (N.) - (कमी)~ *[#R-3 (3)]*
The state of being scarce or in short supply; shortage

Syno: {Insufficiency (कमी), Dearth (अभाव)}

Anto: Plenty (बहुतायत), Excess (अति)

1395 **Scared** (Adj.) - (डरा हुआ) *[#R-4]*
Feeling fear or anxiety

Syno: Afraid (भयभीत), Frightened (डरा हुआ)

Anto: Brave (साहसी)

1396 Scatter (V.) - (बिखेरना) *[#R-4]*
To throw in various random directions

Syno: Disperse (फैलाना)

Anto: Gather (इकट्ठा करना)

1397 **Sceptic** (N.) - (संदेहवादी)~ *[#R-1 (3)]*
A person inclined to question or doubt accepted opinions

Syno: {Disbeliever (नास्तिक), Cynic (निंदक)}

Anto: Believer (विश्वासी)

1398 **Sceptical** (Adj.) - (संदेहवादी) *[#R-1 (7)]*
Not easily convinced; having doubts or reservations

Syno: Incredulous (अविश्वासी) {Doubtful (संदेहपूर्ण)}

Anto: {Convinced (आश्वस्त), Certain (निश्चित), Trusting (विश्वासी)}

1399 Scintillating (Adj.) - (चमकीला)~ *[#R-4 (2)]*
Sparkling or shining brightly

Syno: Glittering (चमकदार) {Sparkling (चमकदार)}

Anto: Dark (अंधेरा), Lacklustre (फीका)

1400 **Scold** (V.) - (डांटना) *[#R-3]*
To rebuke angrily

Syno: Chide (डांटना)

Anto: Praise (प्रशंसा करना)

1401 Scorn (V.) - (अपमान करना) *[#R-4]*
To treat with disrespect

Syno: Despise (तिरस्कार करना), Condemn (निंदा करना)

Anto: Praise (प्रशंसा करना)

1402 **Scrap** (V.) - (फेंक देना) *[#R-1 (2)]*
To discard or remove; to fight or quarrel

Syno: Reject (अस्वीकार करना)

Anto: {Reinstate (पुनः स्थापित करना)}

1403 **Scrawny** (Adj.) - (दुबला) *[#R-1 (1)]*
Unattractively thin and bony

Syno: Skinny (पतला)

Anto: {Plump (मोटा)}

1404 Secure (Adj./V.) - (निश्चिंत; सुरक्षित करना) *[#R-4 (2)]*
Fixed or protected and not likely to fail (Adj.); To protect or make safe (V.)

Syno: Safe (सुरक्षित); Protect (सुरक्षित करना)

Anto: Attackable (आक्रमण योग्य); Endanger (संकट में) {Precarious (अनिश्चित)}

1405 Segregate (V.) - (अलग करना) *[#R-2]*
To set apart from the rest or from each other

Syno: Isolate (पृथक करना)

Anto: Integrate (एकीकृत करना)

1406 Seize (V.) - (पकड़ना, ज़ब्त करना)~ *[#R-4]*
To take hold of suddenly and forcibly

Syno: Catch (पकड़ना)

Anto: Loosen (ढीला करना), Release (रिहाई करना), Clear (मुक्त करना)

1407 **Sensitive** (Adj.) - (संवेदनशील)~ *[#R-2 (1)]*
Quick to detect or respond to slight changes; easily offended; kept secret

Syno: {Vulnerable (नाज़ुक)}

Anto: Numb (सुन्न), Strong (सहनशील)

1408 Serendipity (N.) - (आकस्मिक लाभ)~ *[#R-2 (3)]*
The occurrence of events by chance in a happy or beneficial way

Syno: Godsend (ईश्वरीय उपहार) {Chance (अवसर), Coincidence (संयोग)}

Anto: Misfortune (दुर्भाग्य)

1409 Serene (Adj.) - (शांत) *[#R-8 (6)]*
Calm, peaceful, and untroubled; tranquil

Syno: Calm (शांत) {Peaceful (शांतिपूर्ण)}

Anto: Turbulent (अशांत), Ruffled (उत्तेजित), Stressed (तनावपूर्ण), Chaotic (अराजक) {Agitated (व्याकुल)}

1410 Serious (Adj.) - (गंभीर) *[#R-2 (3)]*
Solemn or thoughtful in character or manner

Syno: Earnest (तत्पर), Severe (कठोर) {Solemn (गंभीरतापूर्ण)}

Anto: {Trivial (तुच्छ), Half-Hearted (अर्ध-उत्साहित)}

1411 **Sever** (V.) - (अलग करना)~ *[#R-2 (2)]*
To divide by cutting or slicing, especially suddenly and forcibly

Syno: {Cut Off (काट देना)}

Anto: Unite (एकजुट करना)

1412 **Severe** (Adj.) - (गंभीर, कठोर, तीव्र) *[#R-6 (6)]*
Very great or intense in degree

Syno: {Harsh (कठोर), Difficult (मुश्किल), Strong (तीव्र)}

Anto: Mild (हल्का), Gentle (कोमल), Tolerant (सहिष्णु)

1413 Shrewd (Adj.) - (चालाक)~ *[#R-3 (3)]*
Having sharp powers of judgment; astute

Syno: Smart (बुद्धिमान), Judicious (विवेकी)

{Cunning (धूर्त)}
Anto: Naive (भोला-भाला) {Stupid (मूर्ख)}

1414 **Shriek** (V.) - (चीखना) *[#R-2 (2)]*
To utter a piercing sound
Syno: Yell (चिल्लाना)
Anto: {Whisper (फुसफुसाना)}

1415 **Shrink** (V.) - (सिकुड़ना) *[#R-2 (1)]*
To become or make smaller in size or amount
Syno: Diminish (घटाना) {Contract (सिकुड़ना)}
Anto: Expand (फैलाना)

1416 **Shy** (Adj.) - (शर्मीला) *[#R-1 (1)]*
Nervous or timid in the company of other people
Syno: Timid (डरपोक)
Anto: {Impudent (बेशर्म)}

1417 **Significant** (Adj.) - (महत्वपूर्ण) *[#R-2 (3)]*
Sufficiently great or important to be worthy of attention; noteworthy
Syno: {Important (महत्वपूर्ण)}
Anto: Paltry (तुच्छ), Inconsequential (महत्वहीन) {Unimportant (महत्वहीन), Meaningless (निरर्थक)}

1418 **Silent** (Adj.) - (चुप) *[#R-1 (1)]*
Not making or accompanied by any sound
Syno: {Reticent (मौन)}
Anto: Noisy (कोलाहलपूर्ण)

1419 **Similar** (Adj.) - (समान) *[#R-2 (2)]*
Resembling without being identical
Syno: Alike (समान)
Anto: Unlike (असमान) {Dissimilar (भिन्न), Different (अलग)}

1420 **Simple** (Adj.) - (सरल) *[#R-2 (1)]*
Easily understood or done; presenting no difficulty
Syno: Elementary (प्राथमिक)
Anto: Complex (जटिल)

1421 **Sincere** (Adj.) - (ईमानदार) *[#R-1 (2)]*
Free from pretence or deceit; genuinely felt
Syno: Serious (गंभीर) {Heartfelt (हृदय से)}
Anto: {False (असत्य)}

1422 **Sinister** (Adj.) - (अमंगलकारी) *[#R-2 (1)]*
Giving the impression of harm or evil
Syno: Evil (दुष्ट) {Threatening (धमकी भरा)}
Anto: Propitious (अनुकूल)

1423 **Slack** (Adj.) - (ढीला) *[#R-4 (1)]*
Loose or not tight
Syno: Careless (लापरवाह), Feeble (कमजोर), Inactive (निष्क्रिय)
Anto: {Tight (कसा हुआ)}

1424 **Slacken** (V.) - (कम करना)~ *[#R-2 (1)]*
To make or become less tight or less active
Syno: {Decrease (कम होना)}
Anto: Increase (बढ़ाना), Intensify (तेज करना)

1425 **Slander** (V.) - (कलंक लगाना) *[#R-3]*
To spread false statements to harm reputation
Syno: Defame (बदनाम करना)
Anto: Admire (प्रशंसा करना), Praise (सराहना करना)

1426 **Slender** (Adj.) - (पतला) *[#R-5 (1)]*
Gracefully thin
Syno: Slim (दुबला-पतला), Frail (नाज़ुक) {Thin (बहुत पतला)}
Anto: Stout (मजबूत)

1427 **Slothful** (Adj.) - (आलसी) *[#R-1 (2)]*
Unwilling to make an effort to work
Syno: {Lazy (आलसी)}
Anto: Lively (जीवंत) {Sprightly (फुर्तीला)}

1428 **Sluggish** (Adj.) - (सुस्त) *[#R-7 (1)]*
Slow-moving or inactive
Syno: {Inactive (निष्क्रिय)}
Anto: Active (सक्रिय), Alert (सतर्क), Swift (तेज़), Prompt (तुरंत), Rapid (तीव्र)

1429 **Smooth** (Adj.) - (चिकना) *[#R-1 (2)]*
Having an even and regular surface
Syno: Flat (सपाट)
Anto: {Rough (खुरदुरा), Rutted (खाईदार)}

1430 **Sneer** (V.) - (उपहास करना) *[#R-5]*
To mock with contempt
Syno: Mock (मज़ाक उड़ाना)
Anto: Praise (प्रशंसा करना), Laud (प्रशंसा करना)

1431 **Solace** (N.) - (सांत्वना)~ *[#R-2]*
Comfort in sadness or distress
Syno: Comfort (दिलासा देना)
Anto: Distress (पीड़ा)

1432 **Solemn** (Adj.) - (गंभीर) *[#R-3 (3)]*
Formal and dignified; not cheerful or smiling
Syno: Serious (गंभीर), Dignified (गरिमापूर्ण), Pensive (विचारमग्न) {Sober (गंभीर)}
Anto: {Frivolous (हल्का-फुल्का)}

1433 **Solicit** (V.) - (अनुरोध करना) *[#R-2 (1)]*

To ask for or try to obtain something from someone

Syno: Request (अनुरोध करना)

Anto: Refuse (मना करना) {Oppose (विरोध करना)}

1434 Solitary (Adj.) - (एकांत) *[#R-6 (1)]*
Done or existing alone

Syno: Lonely (अकेला), Singular (एकवचन), Single (एकल)

Anto: Gregarious (मिलनसार) {Populous (घना आबाद)}

1435 **Solitude** (N.) - (एकांतवास)~ *[#R-2]*
The state or situation of being alone

Syno: Seclusion (एकांत)

Anto: Company (संगति)

1436 **Sombre** (Adj.) - (उदास) *[#R-6]*
Dark, dull, or serious in mood or colour

Syno: Gloomy (उदास), Doleful (शोकाकुल), Drab (फीका)

Anto: Cheerful (प्रसन्न)

1437 **Somnolent** (Adj.) - (निद्रालु) *[#R-2 (1)]*
Of a kind likely to induce sleep

Syno: Drowsy (नींद में)

Anto: Awake (जागा हुआ)

1438 **Soothe** (V.) - (शांत करना) *[#R-2 (3)]*
To gently calm feelings or emotions

Syno: Mollify (मनाना), Pacify (शांत करना)

Anto: {Excite (उत्तेजित करना), Aggravate (बिगाड़ना)}

1439 Sophisticated (Adj.) - (परिष्कृत, उन्नत) *[#R-2 (3)]*
Having worldly experience and knowledge of culture

Syno: Refined (सुसंस्कृत) {Experienced (अनुभवी)}

Anto: Primitive (आदिम) {Unrefined (अशिष्ट), Naive (भोला-भाला)}

1440 **Soporific** (Adj.) - (नींद लाने वाला)~ *[#R-2]*
Causing sleep or drowsiness

Syno: Sleep-Inducing (नींद लाने वाला)

Anto: Stimulating (उत्तेजक)

1441 **Sordid** (Adj.) - (घटिया) *[#R-7 (1)]*
Involving ignoble actions and motives; arousing moral distaste and contempt

Syno: Dirty (गंदा), Unpleasant (अप्रिय) {Dishonourable (अपमानजनक)}

Anto: Reputable (प्रतिष्ठित), Honourable (सम्माननीय)

1442 Spacious (Adj.) - (विशाल) *[#R-2]*
Having ample space

Syno: Roomy (विशाल)

Anto: Cramped (संकीर्ण)

1443 **Sparse** (Adj.) - (विरल) *[#R-4 (1)]*
Thinly dispersed or scattered

Syno: {Infrequent (दुर्लभ)}

Anto: Abundant (प्रचुर), Dense (घना)

1444 Specific (Adj.) - (विशिष्ट) *[#R-2 (3)]*
Clearly defined or identified

Syno: {Precise (सटीक), Exact (यथार्थ)}

Anto: General (सामान्य), Random (अनियमित)

1445 **Speculate** (V.) - (अनुमान लगाना) *[#R-2 (1)]*
To form an idea without firm evidence

Syno: Guess (अनुमान लगाना) {Contemplate (विचार करना)}

Anto: Dismiss (खारिज करना)

1446 **Spellbound** (Adj.) - (मंत्रमुग्ध) *[#R-2]*
Held completely by something, as if by magic

Syno: Enthralled (मोहित)

Anto: Disenchanted (मोहभंग)

1447 Split (N./V.) - (विभाजन; विभाजित करना) *[#R-3]*
A division (N.); To break into parts or disunite (V.)

Syno: Division (विभाजन); Divide (विभाजित करना)

Anto: Join (जोड़ना)

1448 Spontaneous (Adj.) - (आकस्मिक)~ *[#R-4 (5)]*
Occurring suddenly without planning

Syno: Impulsive (आवेगशील), Instinctive (सहज) {Unplanned (अनियोजित), Extempore (तत्काल)}

Anto: Deliberate (जानबूझकर) {Conscious (सोच-समझकर), Contrived (बनावटी)}

1449 **Sporadic** (Adj.) - (छिटपुट)~ *[#R-7 (12)]*
Occurring at irregular intervals or only in a few places

Syno: Scattered (बिखरे हुए), Occasional (कभी-कभार), Infrequent (दुर्लभ) {Intermittent (अंतरायिक)}

Anto: Systematic (व्यवस्थित), Regular (नियमित), Frequent (बार-बार) {Constant (स्थिर), Persistent (दृढ़)}

1450 **Spruce** (Adj.) - (साफ-सुथरा) *[#R-2 (2)]*
Neat and tidy in appearance

Syno: Smart (सुसज्जित), Natty (सजीला)

Anto: {Unkempt (अस्त-व्यस्त), Tacky (बेढंगा)}

1451 Spurious (Adj.) - (जाली)~ *[#R-11 (10)]*
False or not what it claims to be

Syno: Fake (नकली), Fraudulent (धोखाधड़ी) {Feigned (बनावटी)}

Anto: Authentic (वास्तविक), Genuine (असली)

1452 **Squalid** (Adj.) - (गंदा) *[#R-3 (3)]*
Extremely dirty and unpleasant, especially as a result of poverty or neglect

Syno: {Dirty (गंदा)}

Anto: Clean (स्वच्छ) {Attractive (आकर्षक), Immaculate (बिल्कुल साफ़)}

1453 **Squander** (V.) - (बर्बाद करना) *[#R-4 (7)]*
To waste money, time, or resources foolishly

Syno: Frivol (बेकार करना) {Waste (बर्बाद करना), Expend (खर्च करना)}

Anto: Skimp (कंजूसी करना), Hoard (जमा करना), Save (बचाना) {Preserve (संरक्षित करना), Conserve (संरक्षित करना)}

1454 **Stability** (N.) - (स्थिरता) *[#R-2 (2)]*
The state of being stable

Syno: {Strength (शक्ति)}

Anto: Inconsistency (असंगति), Volatility (अस्थिरता)

1455 **Stable** (Adj.) - (स्थिर) *[#R-5 (2)]*
Not likely to change or fail; firm and steady

Syno: Anchored (मजबूती से जुड़ा हुआ) {Steady (स्थिर)}

Anto: Shaky (डगमगाता हुआ), Mutable (परिवर्तनशील) {Unstable (अस्थिर)}

1456 Stagnant (Adj.) - (स्थिर) *[#R-1 (2)]*
Showing no activity; dull and sluggish

Syno: Motionless (गतिहीन)

Anto: {Active (सक्रिय), Advancing (प्रगति पर)}

1457 **Startle** (V.) - (चौंका देना) *[#R-4]*
To cause sudden shock or alarm

Syno: Surprise (आश्चर्यचकित करना), Amaze (चकित करना), Frighten (डराना)

Anto: Soothe (शांत करना)

1458 **Static** (Adj.) - (स्थिर) *[#R-1 (1)]*
Lacking movement or change

Syno: Inert (अक्रिय)

Anto: {Dynamic (गतिशील)}

1459 Stationary (Adj.) - (स्थिर) *[#R-8 (1)]*
Not moving or not intended to be moved

Syno: Fixed (स्थिर), Still (स्थिर)

Anto: Moving (चलता हुआ), Unsteady (अस्थिर), Shifting (बदलता हुआ)

1460 **Staunch** (Adj.) - (निष्ठावान) *[#R-1 (1)]*
Loyal and committed in attitude

Syno: {Loyal (वफादार)}

Anto: Unsteady (अस्थिर)

1461 Steadfast (Adj.) - (दृढ़) *[#R-1 (2)]*
Resolutely or dutifully firm and unwavering

Syno: {Stubborn (जिद्दी)}

Anto: Wavering (डगमगाने वाला) {Unreliable (अविश्वसनीय)}

1462 **Steady** (Adj.) - (स्थिर) *[#R-4]*
Firm, balanced, not shaking

Syno: Stable (स्थिर), Abiding (स्थायी)

Anto: Shaky (कांपता हुआ), Wavering (हिचकिचाता हुआ)

1463 **Sterile** (Adj.) - (बाँझ)~ *[#R-2 (1)]*
Not able to produce children or young; free from bacteria or other living microorganisms; totally clean

Syno: Barren (बंजर)

Anto: Fertile (उपजाऊ)

1464 **Stern** (Adj.) - (कठोर) *[#R-9 (1)]*
Serious and strict in discipline or authority

Syno: Strict (कठोर)

Anto: Lenient (नरम), Light (हल्का) {Forgiving (क्षमाशील)}

1465 Stimulate (V.) - (उत्तेजित करना) *[#R-3 (2)]*
To raise levels of physiological or nervous activity in the body or any biological system

Syno: Energize (ऊर्जा प्रदान करना), Provoke (उकसाना) {Encourage (प्रोत्साहित करना)}

Anto: Subdue (दबाना)

1466 Stingy (Adj.) - (कंजूस) *[#R-8 (2)]*
Unwilling to give or spend; ungenerous

Syno: {Miserly (कंजूस)}

Anto: Generous (उदार), Extravagant (फिजूलखर्ची) {Liberal (उदार)}

1467 **Stoical** (Adj.) - (सहनशील) *[#R-1 (1)]*
Enduring pain and hardship without showing feelings or complaining

Syno: Apathetic (भावहीन)

Anto: {Emotional (भावनात्मक)}

1468 Stormy (Adj.) - (तूफानी) *[#R-1 (1)]*
Marked by storms or violent disturbance

Syno: {Turbulent (अशांत)}

Anto: Serene (शांत)

1469 **Strange** (Adj.) - (अजीब) *[#R-6 (1)]*
Unusual or surprising in a way that is unsettling or hard to understand

Syno: Abnormal (असामान्य), Odd (अजीब) {Surreal (अवास्तविक)}

Anto: Familiar (परिचित), Mundane (साधारण)

1470 **Strength** (N.) - (शक्ति) *[#R-2 (2)]*
The quality or state of being physically strong

Syno: Power (शक्ति)

Anto: Debilitation (कमजोरी) {Frailty (दुर्बलता), Weakness (कमज़ोरी)}

1471 **Strenuous** (Adj.) - (कठिन) *[#R-4]*
Requiring or using great effort or exertion

Syno: Difficult (मुश्किल), Formidable (अत्यंत कठिन)

Anto: Effortless (सरल), Easy (आसान)

1472 **Stretch** (V.) - (खींचना) *[#R-3]*
To extend or pull tight; exaggerate

Syno: Extend (विस्तार करना)

Anto: Lessen (कम करना), Compress (संकुचित करना)

1473 **Strict** (Adj.) - (सख्त)~ *[#R-1 (1)]*
Demanding obedience to rules

Syno: Austere (कठोर)

Anto: {Lenient (उदार)}

1474 **Stringent** (Adj.) - (कठोर) *[#R-6 (5)]*
Strict, precise, and exacting regulations or conditions

Syno: Tough (कठिन), Strict (सख्त), Rigorous (सख्त)

Anto: Lenient (नरम)

1475 **Strive** (V.) - (प्रयास करना) *[#R-1 (3)]*
To make great efforts to achieve or obtain something

Syno: Attempt (प्रयास करना) {Struggle (संघर्ष करना)}

Anto: {Rest (आराम करना)}

1476 **Strong** (Adj.) - (मजबूत) *[#R-2 (1)]*
Having great physical power or strength

Syno: {Powerful (शक्तिशाली)}

Anto: Delicate (नाज़ुक), Weak (कमजोर)

1477 **Stubborn** (Adj.) - (जिद्दी) *[#R-2 (2)]*
Unreasonably obstinate; difficult to move or treat

Syno: Adamant (अटल), Obstinate (हठी)

Anto: {Pliable (लचीला)}

1478 **Stunning** (Adj.) - (चकाचौंध कर देने वाला) *[#R-3]*
Extremely impressive or attractive

Syno: Gorgeous (मनमोहक)

Anto: Unattractive (अनाकर्षक), Mundane (साधारण)

1479 **Stupendous** (Adj.) - (अद्भुत) *[#R-5]*
Extremely impressive

Syno: Stunning (चकाचौंध कर देने वाला)

Anto: Unimpressive (प्रभावहीन)

1480 **Stupor** (N.) - (अर्धचेतना) *[#R-3]*
A state of near-unconsciousness or insensibility

Syno: Slumber (नींद)

Anto: Consciousness (चेतना)

1481 **Sturdy** (Adj.) - (मजबूत) *[#R-4 (1)]*
Strongly and solidly built

Syno: Tough (मज़बूत)

Anto: Feeble (कमजोर), Delicate (नाजुक), Fragile (नाज़ुक) {Tender (नाज़ुक)}

1482 **Suave** (Adj.) - (सौम्य) *[#R-1 (2)]*
Charming, confident, and elegant

Syno: {Polished (शिष्ट)}

Anto: Rude (असभ्य) {Awkward (अजीब)}

1483 **Subdued** (Adj.) - (दबा हुआ) *[#R-1 (2)]*
Quieter or less intense than usual; oppressed

Syno: {Gentle (कोमल)}

Anto: Excited (उत्साहित) {Uncontrolled (अनियंत्रित)}

1484 **Subjugate** (V.) - (वश में करना) *[#R-3 (2)]*
To bring under domination or control

Syno: Conquer (जीतना)

Anto: Liberate (मुक्त करना)

1485 **Sublime** (Adj.) - (उत्कृष्ट) *[#R-5 (1)]*
Inspiring great admiration or awe

Syno: {Noble (महान)}

Anto: Ludicrous (बेतुका), Inferior (घटिया), Mediocre (साधारण)

1486 **Submissive** (Adj.) - (आज्ञाकारी) *[#R-2 (2)]*
Ready to obey or accept the will of others

Syno: Obedient (आज्ञाकारी)

Anto: Stubborn (जिद्दी) {Obstinate (हठी),

Domineering (हावी)}

1487 Subsequent (Adj.) - (आगामी) *[#R-4 (1)]*
Coming after something in time; following
Syno: Later (बाद का), Consecutive (लगातार)
Anto: Prior (पूर्व), Preceding (पूर्ववर्ती)

1488 Subside (V.) - (कम होना) *[#R-2 (2)]*
To become less intense, violent, or severe
Syno: Descend (उतरना)
Anto: Enlarge (बढ़ाना) {Stand (खड़ा रहना), Ascend (चढ़ना)}

1489 Substantial (Adj.) - (महत्वपूर्ण, पर्याप्त) *[#R-4 (6)]*
Of considerable importance, size, or worth
Syno: Significant (महत्वपूर्ण) {Considerable (काफी), Sizeable (पर्याप्त)}
Anto: Flimsy (कमजोर), Worthless (बेकार) {Insignificant (महत्वहीन)}

1490 Subterfuge (N.) - (छल)~ *[#R-2 (2)]*
Deceit used in order to achieve one's goal
Syno: {Deception (छल)}
Anto: Candor (स्पष्टवादिता), Honesty (ईमानदारी)

1491 Subtle (Adj.) - (सूक्ष्म)~ *[#R-4 (5)]*
Delicate or precise and hard to notice or describe
Syno: Nuanced (सूक्ष्म), Understated (शालीन) {Indirect (अप्रत्यक्ष)}
Anto: Harsh (कठोर) {Evident (स्पष्ट), Obvious (स्पष्ट), Gross (सकल)}

1492 Succinct (Adj.) - (संक्षिप्त)~ *[#R-4 (1)]*
Briefly and clearly expressed
Syno: Brief (संक्षिप्त)
Anto: Long-Winded (बहुत लंबा बोलने वाला), Lengthy (लंबा)

1493 Succulent (Adj.) - (रसीला)~ *[#R-2 (1)]*
(Of food) tender, juicy, and tasty
Syno: Juicy (रसदार)
Anto: {Unappetising (बेस्वाद)}

1494 Sufficient (Adj.) - (पर्याप्त) *[#R-8 (1)]*
Enough to meet a need or requirement
Syno: Enough (पर्याप्त) {Adequate (पर्याप्त)}
Anto: Meagre (अल्प), Inadequate (अपर्याप्त)

1495 Suitable (Adj.) - (उपयुक्त; पर्याप्त; योग्य) *[#R-2 (2)]*
Right or proper; Enough for a need; Qualified
Syno: Appropriate (उचित)
Anto: {Inept (अयोग्य), Insufficient (अपर्याप्त)}

1496 **Sullen** (Adj.) - (उदास; चिड़चिड़ा) *[#R-3 (1)]*
Bad-tempered and sulky; gloomy
Syno: Grim (उदास)
Anto: Cheerful (प्रसन्न), Agreeable (सुखद) {Genial (खुशमिज़ाज)}

1497 Summon (V.) - (बुलवाना)~ *[#R-2 (1)]*
To authoritatively or urgently call on someone to be present
Syno: Call (बुलाना)
Anto: Dismiss (बर्खास्त करना)

1498 Sumptuous (Adj.) - (भव्य)~ *[#R-3 (2)]*
Splendid and expensive-looking
Syno: Opulent (ऐश्वर्यपूर्ण), Lavish (भव्य)
Anto: Inexpensive (सस्ता) {Economical (किफ़ायती)}

1499 Supercilious (Adj.) - (घमंडी) *[#R-1 (3)]*
Behaving as if superior to others
Syno: Arrogant (अहंकारी)
Anto: {Unassertive (विनम्र), Respectful (सम्मानजनक)}

1500 Superficial (Adj.) - (ऊपरी, दिखावटी)~ *[#R-6 (5)]*
Existing or occurring only on the surface, lacking depth; Not genuine or authentic
Syno: Shallow (उथला)
Anto: Profound (गहरा), Deep (गहरा), Genuine (वास्तविक) {Comprehensive (पूर्ण), Substantial (पर्याप्त)}

1501 Superfluous (Adj.) - (अनावश्यक) *[#R-4 (1)]*
More than needed; unnecessary
Syno: Extra (अतिरिक्त) {Surplus (अधिशेष)}
Anto: Necessary (आवश्यक), Essential (जरूरी)

1502 **Supernatural** (Adj.) - (अलौकिक) *[#R-3]*
Beyond natural laws or scientific explanation
Syno: Mystical (रहस्यमय), Occult (रहस्यपूर्ण)
Anto: Natural (प्राकृतिक)

1503 Support (V.) - (समर्थन करना) *[#R-4 (2)]*
To give help or hold up
Syno: Bolster (मजबूत करना), Agree (सहमत होना) {Aid (सहायता करना)}
Anto: Oppose (विरोध करना), Refute (गलत सिद्ध करना) {Restrain (रोकना)}

1504 Supreme (Adj.) - (सर्वोच्च, प्रमुख) *[#R-5]*
Highest in rank, power, or quality; Chief or principal
Syno: Head (प्रमुख), Matchless (बेजोड़),

Paramount (सर्वोपरि)

Anto: Inferior (हीन)

1505 Surge (N.) - (तेज़ उछाल)~ *[#R-2 (1)]*
A sudden strong rise or movement

Syno: Rise (उठान), Rush (दौड़)

Anto: {Decrease (कमी)}

1506 Surrender (V.) - (हार मानना)~ *[#R-3]*
To stop resisting and submit

Syno: Yield (आत्मसमर्पण करना)

Anto: Withstand (सामना करना)

1507 Surreptitious (Adj.) - (गुप्त)~ *[#R-4 (3)]*
Done secretly to avoid notice or approval

Syno: Secretive (गुप्त) {Clandestine (छिपा हुआ)}

Anto: Open (खुला), Overt (प्रकट)

1508 Surveillance (N.) - (निगरानी)~ *[#R-1 (1)]*
The close and careful watching of a person or place

Syno: {Observation (निगरानी)}

Anto: Neglect (अनदेखी)

1509 Susceptible (Adj.) - (संवेदनशील) *[#R-3 (3)]*
Likely to be influenced or harmed by something

Syno: Impressionable (प्रभावित करने योग्य) {Vulnerable (अतिसंवेदनशील)}

Anto: Immune (अप्रभावित)

1510 Sustain (V.) - (बनाए रखना) *[#R-4 (1)]*
To support or keep something going

Syno: Support (समर्थन करना), Continue (जारी रखना)

Anto: Obstruct (बाधा डालना)

1511 **Sustainable** (Adj.) - (टिकाऊ) *[#R-2 (4)]*
Able to be maintained at a certain rate or level

Syno: Maintainable (बनाए रखने योग्य), Viable (व्यवहार्य) {Endurable (सहनीय)}

Anto: {Temporary (अस्थायी)}

1512 **Sustenance** (N.) - (पोषण) *[#R-2 (1)]*
The food or support that gives strength and nourishment

Syno: Nourishment (पोषण) {Food (भोजन)}

Anto: Starvation (भुखमरी)

1513 **Swift** (Adj.) - (तीव्र) *[#R-2 (1)]*
Happening quickly or promptly

Syno: Quick (जल्दी)

Anto: Slow (धीमा)

1514 Swindle (N.) - (धोखा) *[#R-2]*
An act of cheating

Syno: Fraud (धोखा)

Anto: Honesty (ईमानदारी)

1515 Sympathy (N.) - (सहानुभूति) *[#R-1 (2)]*
The feelings of pity or concern for others' suffering

Syno: {Compassion (दया), Condolence (शोक संवेदना)}

Anto: Cruelty (निर्दयता)

1516 Synthetic (Adj.) - (कृत्रिम)~ *[#R-3]*
Made by chemical synthesis to imitate a natural product

Syno: Fake (नकली)

Anto: Natural (प्राकृतिक)

1517 Systematically (Adv.) - (व्यवस्थित रूप से) *[#R-2]*
In an orderly and planned manner

Syno: Methodically (क्रमबद्ध तरीके से)

Anto: Haphazardly (लापरवाही से)

1518 Taboo (Adj.) - (वर्जित)~ *[#R-2]*
Socially prohibited

Syno: Unacceptable (अस्वीकार्य)

Anto: Acceptable (स्वीकार्य)

1519 **Tacit** (Adj.) - (अनकहा) *[#R-2 (2)]*
Understood without being spoken openly

Syno: {Implied (संकेतित), Insinuated (इशारा किया)}

Anto: Explicit (स्पष्ट)

1520 Taciturn (Adj.) - (अल्पभाषी)~ *[#R-10 (8)]*
Reserved in speech; saying very little

Syno: Silent (मौन), Reticent (संकोची), Reserved (संकोची) {Uncommunicative (असंवादी), Unresponsive (प्रतिक्रियाहीन)}

Anto: Talkative (बातूनी), Loquacious (अत्यधिक बोलने वाला) {Garrulous (बातूनी)}

1521 Tactful (Adj.) - (विवेकी) *[#R-3 (2)]*
Showing sensitivity in dealing with difficult situations

Syno: {Diplomatic (कूटनीतिक)}

Anto: Undiplomatic (अकूटनीतिक), Ungracious (अशिष्ट), Careless (लापरवाह)

1522 **Tame** (Adj.) - (पालतू; शांत) *[#R-3 (4)]*
Gentle and not wild

Syno: Domesticated (पालतू)

Anto: {Wild (जंगली), Savage (क्रूर)}

1523 **Tangled** (Adj.) - (उलझा हुआ) *[#R-2]*
Twisted together in a confused way

Syno: Knotted (गांठदार)

Anto: Simple (सरल)

1524 **Tarnish** (V.) - (कलंकित करना) *[#R-3 (4)]*
To lose shine or damage reputation

Syno: Blot (कलंक); Damage (क्षति करना) {Stain (दाग लगाना); Spoil (खराब करना)}

Anto: {Brighten (चमकाना)}

1525 **Taut** (Adj.) - (सख्त) *[#R-2]*
Stretched or pulled tight; not slack

Syno: Tight (कसा हुआ)

Anto: Slack (ढीला)

1526 Tedious (Adj.) - (उबाऊ) *[#R-11 (5)]*
Too long, slow, or dull; tiresome or monotonous

Syno: Dull (नीरस), Tiresome (थकाऊ), Dreary (निराशाजनक), Boring (उबाऊ)

Anto: Interesting (रोचक), Exciting (रोमांचक), Delightful (आनंददायक)

1527 **Temerity** (N.) - (गुस्ताख़ी) *[#R-4 (4)]*
Excessive confidence or boldness

Syno: Audacity (साहस), Impudence (गुस्ताखी), Boldness (निडरता)

Anto: Diffidence (संकोच) {Timidity (डरपोकपन)}

1528 Temperate (Adj.) - (संयमी) *[#R-3 (2)]*
Showing moderation or self-restraint; mild in temperature

Syno: Moderate (मध्यम)

Anto: {Excessive (अत्यधिक)}

1529 Tempest (N.) - (तूफान)~ *[#R-2 (1)]*
A violent windy storm

Syno: Storm (आंधी)

Anto: {Tranquillity (शांति)}

1530 **Temporal** (Adj.) - (लौकिक) *[#R-1 (2)]*
Relating to worldly affairs, not spiritual; secular

Syno: {Worldly (सांसारिक)}

Anto: Spiritual (आध्यात्मिक) {Eternal (शाश्वत)}

1531 Tenacious (Adj.) - (दृढ़)~ *[#R-5 (4)]*
Holding firmly; not giving up easily

Syno: Persistent (डटा हुआ), Stubborn (जिद्दी)

Anto: Yielding (समर्पित) {Irresolute (अनिश्चित), Docile (विनम्र)}

1532 Tender (Adj.) - (कोमल) *[#R-1 (1)]*
Gentle and soft

Syno: {Delicate (नाज़ुक)}

Anto: Rough (खुरदरा)

1533 **Tense** (Adj.) - (तनावपूर्ण) *[#R-1 (1)]*
Tight or nervous

Syno: {Taut (तना हुआ)}

Anto: Relaxed (आरामदायक)

1534 Tentative (Adj.) - (संभावित) *[#R-2]*
Not certain or fixed; provisional

Syno: Provisional (अस्थायी)

Anto: Definite (निश्चित)

1535 **Tenuous** (Adj.) - (पतला) *[#R-1 (3)]*
Very weak or slight; very slender or fine; insubstantial

Syno: Thin (दुबला) {Insubstantial (कमज़ोर), Slender (पतला)}

Anto: {Substantial (मज़बूत)}

1536 **Terse** (Adj.) - (संक्षिप्त) *[#R-5 (8)]*
Using very few words, often sounding rude or unfriendly

Syno: Brief (लघु), Short (छोटा) {Compact (संक्षिप्त), Brusque (रुखा), Laconic (संक्षिप्त), Incisive (सटीक)}

Anto: Wordy (शब्दाडंबरपूर्ण), Verbose (बहुत बोलने वाला) {Detailed (विस्तृत)}

1537 Threaten (V.) - (धमकाना) *[#R-2]*
To state an intention to cause harm

Syno: Intimidate (भयभीत करना)

Anto: Reassure (आश्वस्त करना)

1538 **Thrifty** (Adj.) - (किफ़ायती) *[#R-4 (3)]*
Using money and other resources carefully and not wastefully

Syno: Economical (किफ़ायती), Frugal (किफ़ायती), Prudent (विवेकी)

Anto: Extravagant (फिजूलखर्च)

1539 Thrive (V.) - (उन्नति करना) *[#R-6 (5)]*
To grow or develop well and vigorously

Syno: Flourish (फलना-फूलना), Prosper (समृद्ध होना), Grow (बढ़ना)

Anto: Fail (विफल होना), Shrink (सिकुड़ना) {Struggle (संघर्ष करना), Decline (पतन होना)}

1540 Thwart (V.) - (विफल करना) *[#R-6 (3)]*
To prevent someone from accomplishing something

Syno: Impede (बाधित करना), Curb (नियंत्रित करना)

Anto: Assist (सहायता करना), Allow (अनुमति देना) {Encourage (प्रोत्साहित करना), Abet (सहायता करना)}

1541 Timid (Adj.) - (डरपोक)~ *[#R-14 (15)]*
Showing a lack of courage or confidence; easily frightened

Syno: Cowardly (कायर), Shy (शर्मीला), Fearful (भयभीत), Nervous (घबराया हुआ), Humble (विनम्र) {Meek (विनम्र)}

Anto: Brave (साहसी), Bold (साहसिक), Courageous (वीर), Daring (साहसी), Audacious (बेधड़क) {Venturesome (साहसिक), Confident (आत्मविश्वासी)}

1542 Timorous (Adj.) - (भयभीत) *[#R-3 (1)]*
Showing fear, nervousness, or lack of confidence

Syno: {Apprehensive (चिंतित)}

Anto: Bold (साहसिक), Brazen (निर्लज्ज)

1543 **Toil** (N./V.) - (कठोर श्रम; मेहनत करना) *[#R-2 (2)]*
Exhausting labour (N.); To work extremely hard (V.)

Syno: Sweat (पसीना), Labour (परिश्रम करना) {Effort (प्रयास)}

Anto: {Sloth (आलस्य)}

1544 **Torpid** (Adj.) - (सुस्त) *[#R-3]*
Mentally or physically inactive

Syno: Inactive (निष्क्रिय)

Anto: Dynamic (गतिशील), Active (सक्रिय)

1545 **Toxic** (Adj.) - (विषैला)~ *[#R-3]*
Containing poisonous substances

Syno: Poisonous (जहरीला), Lethal (घातक)

Anto: Healthy (स्वस्थ)

1546 Traditional (Adj.) - (पारंपरिक) *[#R-5 (1)]*
Existing as part of a long-established tradition

Syno: {Conventional (परंपरागत)}

Anto: Unusual (असामान्य), Modern (आधुनिक), Contemporary (समकालीन)

1547 **Traitor** (N.) - (गद्दार)~ *[#R-3]*
A person who betrays a friend, cause, or country

Syno: Deceiver (धोखेबाज)

Anto: Patriot (देशभक्त), Loyalist (वफादार व्यक्ति)

1548 **Tramp** (N./V.) - (घुमक्कड़; पैदल घूमना) *[#R-2 (1)]*
A vagrant or wanderer (N.); To walk heavily or travel on foot (V.)

Syno: Wanderer (भटकने वाला)

Anto: {Hover (मंडराना)}

1549 Tranquil (Adj.) - (शांत)~ *[#R-11 (5)]*
Free from disturbance; calm

Syno: Peaceful (शांतिपूर्ण), Calm (शांत), Sober (शांत)

Anto: Stormy (तूफानी), Disturbed (परेशान), Violent (हिंसक), Unquiet (अशांत) {Excited (उत्साहित), Noisy (शोरगुल वाला)}

1550 **Transient** (Adj.) - (क्षणिक)~ *[#R-12 (7)]*
Lasting a short time

Syno: Transitory (अस्थायी), Fleeting (क्षणिक), Temporary (अस्थायी)

Anto: Permanent (स्थायी) {Lasting (स्थायी), Eternal (अनन्त), Perpetual (निरंतर)}

1551 Transparent (Adj.) - (पारदर्शी)~ *[#R-10 (7)]*
Easy to see through; clear or open

Syno: Lucid (स्पष्ट), Clear (साफ)

Anto: Opaque (अपारदर्शी)

1552 Treacherous (Adj.) - (विश्वासघाती) *[#R-7 (2)]*
Involving betrayal, deception, or lack of trust

Syno: Unfaithful (अविश्वासी), Disloyal (विश्वासघाती) {Deceitful (धोखेबाज़)}

Anto: Faithful (वफादार)

1553 Tremendous (Adj.) - (अद्भुत, असीम) *[#R-2 (3)]*
Very great in amount, scale, or intensity

Syno: Huge (विशाल), Remarkable (उल्लेखनीय) {Excellent (उत्कृष्ट)}

Anto: {Minuscule (अत्यंत छोटा), Tiny (नन्हा)}

1554 **Trenchant** (Adj.) - (तीखा, प्रभावशाली) *[#R-3 (1)]*
Sharp, forceful, and effective in expression

Syno: Incisive (सटीक)

Anto: Dull (प्रभावहीन), Feeble (कमज़ोर) {Blunt (भोथरा)}

1555 **Trepidation** (N.) - (भय)~ *[#R-2 (1)]*
A feeling of fear or anxiety about something

Syno: Nervousness (घबराहट)

Anto: Calm (शांति) {Composure (संयम)}

1556 Trigger (N./V.) - (चालक यंत्र; प्रेरित करना) *[#R-2 (1)]*
A device that sets a mechanism in motion (N.); To cause or start something (V.)

Syno: Initiator (आरंभकर्ता)

Anto: Halt (रोकना)

1557 **Trite** (Adj.) - (घिसा-पिटा) *[#R-1 (1)]*
Overused and lacking originality or freshness

Syno: Commonplace (सामान्य)

Anto: {Novel (नया)}

1558 **Triumph** (N.) - (विजय) *[#R-9 (5)]*
A great victory or success

Syno: Victory (विजय)

Anto: Defeat (हार), Failure (असफलता), Sorrow (दुःख)

1559 **Triumphant** (Adj.) - (विजयी) *[#R-2 (2)]*
Having achieved victory or success

Syno: Victorious (विजयी)

Anto: Unsuccessful (असफल) {Defeated (पराजित), Depressed (निराश)}

1560 **Trivial** (Adj.) - (तुच्छ)~ *[#R-13 (12)]*
Of little value or importance

Syno: Small (छोटा), Minor (छोटा), Insignificant (महत्वहीन), Superficial (सतही) {Unimportant (महत्वहीन)}

Anto: Significant (महत्वपूर्ण), Essential (अनिवार्य), Important (महत्वपूर्ण), Serious (गंभीर), Profound (गहन)

1561 **Truculent** (Adj.) - (उग्र)~ *[#R-2]*
Eager or quick to argue or fight; aggressively defiant

Syno: Ferocious (क्रूर)

Anto: Amiable (मिलनसार)

1562 **Tryst** (N.) - (गुप्त मुलाक़ात) *[#R-2]*
A private or secret romantic meeting

Syno: Meeting (मुलाकात)

Anto: Separation (विभाजन)

1563 **Tumult** (N.) - (कोलाहल) *[#R-2 (1)]*
A loud, confused noise or disturbance

Syno: Uproar (हंगामा)

Anto: Calmness (शांति) {Tranquility (शांति)}

1564 **Turbid** (Adj.) - (मटमैला) *[#R-1 (1)]*
(Of a liquid) cloudy or thick with suspended matter

Syno: {Muddy (कीचड़ युक्त)}

Anto: Clear (साफ़)

1565 **Turbulent** (Adj.) - (अशांत) *[#R-11 (4)]*
Characterized by disorder, conflict, or lack of control

Syno: Violent (हिंसक), Agitated (उत्तेजित), Disordered (अव्यवस्थित) {Stormy (तूफानी)}

Anto: Placid (शांत), Calm (शांत), Peaceful (शांतिपूर्ण), Settled (स्थिर) {Tranquil (शांत)}

1566 **Turgid** (Adj.) - (सूजा हुआ)~ *[#R-2]*
Swollen or congested; overly pompous in style

Syno: Inflated (फुला हुआ)

Anto: Humble (विनम्र)

1567 **Turpitude** (N.) - (नीचता) *[#R-1 (2)]*
Moral depravity or wickedness

Syno: {Corruption (भ्रष्टाचार)}

Anto: Morality (नैतिकता)

1568 **Tyranny** (N.) - (अत्याचार) *[#R-2 (1)]*
Cruel and oppressive government or rule

Syno: Autocracy (तानाशाही) {Cruelty (क्रूरता)}

Anto: Autonomy (आत्म-शासन)

1569 **Ubiquitous** (Adj.) - (सर्वव्यापी)~ *[#R-2 (7)]*
Present or found everywhere

Syno: Omnipresent (सर्वव्यापी), Pervasive (सर्वव्यापी) {Common (सामान्य), Everywhere (हर जगह)}

Anto: {Rare (दुर्लभ), Scarce (अपर्याप्त)}

1570 **Ulterior** (Adj.) - (गुप्त) *[#R-2]*
Existing beyond what is obvious; intentionally hidden

Syno: Hidden (छिपा हुआ)

Anto: Overt (प्रकट)

1571 **Unbiased** (Adj.) - (निष्पक्ष) *[#R-3]*
Showing no prejudice; impartial

Syno: Objective (तटस्थ)

Anto: Prejudiced (पक्षपात पूर्ण)

1572 **Uncanny** (Adj.) - (रहस्यमय) *[#R-4]*
Strange or mysterious, especially in an unsettling way

Syno: Mysterious (रहस्यमय), Spooky (डरावना)

Anto: Ordinary (साधारण)

1573 **Uncouth** (Adj.) - (असभ्य) *[#R-1 (3)]*
Lacking good manners or social grace

Syno: {Graceless (अनाकर्षक), Awkward (अजीब)}

Anto: Refined (शिष्ट) {Elegant (सलीकेदार)}

1574 **Undermine** (V.) - (कमजोर करना) *[#R-1 (2)]*
To damage the base or reduce strength, power, or effectiveness

Syno: {Defeat (हराना)}

Anto: Enhance (बढ़ाना) {Strengthen (मजबूत करना)}

1575 **Unequivocal** (Adj.) - (स्पष्ट) *[#R-1 (1)]*
Leaving no doubt; clear and definite

Syno: Unambiguous (असंदिग्ध)

Anto: {Ambiguous (अस्पष्ट)}

1576 Unique (Adj.) - (अद्वितीय) *[#R-3 (2)]*
Being the only one of its kind; unlike anything else

Syno: Distinctive (विशेष), Exclusive (विशिष्ट) {Exceptional (असाधारण)}

Anto: {Common (सामान्य)}

1577 **Unitary** (Adj.) - (एकात्मक) *[#R-3 (1)]*
Forming a single or uniform entity

Syno: {Undivided (अविभाजित)}

Anto: Multiple (अनेक), Divided (विभाजित)

1578 Unprecedented (Adj.) - (अनोखा)~ *[#R-2 (4)]*
Never done or known before

Syno: {Unrivalled (अद्वितीय)}

Anto: Familiar (परिचित), Known (ज्ञात) {Conventional (परंपरागत), Usual (सामान्य)}

1579 Unruly (Adj.) - (अनियंत्रित) *[#R-3 (1)]*
Disorderly and difficult to control or discipline

Syno: Lawless (बेकानून), Disobedient (अवज्ञाकारी)

Anto: Orderly (व्यवस्थित) {Tractable (आज्ञाकारी)}

1580 Unscrupulous (Adj.) - (अनैतिक)~ *[#R-2 (1)]*
Having or showing no moral principles; not honest or fair

Syno: Dishonest (बेईमान)

Anto: Conscientious (नैतिक) {Honest (ईमानदार)}

1581 **Unsullied** (Adj.) - (निष्कलंक) *[#R-2 (1)]*
Not spoiled or made impure

Syno: Impeccable (निर्दोष)

Anto: Tarnished (कलंकित) {Defiled (अपवित्र)}

1582 **Urbane** (Adj.) - (सभ्य) *[#R-1 (4)]*
Polite, refined, and courteous in manner

Syno: {Suave (शिष्ट)}

Anto: Crude (असभ्य) {Discourteous (अशिष्ट), Rude (असभ्य)}

1583 **Urge** (N./V.) - (तीव्र इच्छा; प्रेरित करना) *[#R-4 (1)]*
A strong desire or impulse (N.); to persuade or encourage persistently (V.)

Syno: Impulse (प्रेरणा); Appeal (अनुरोध)

Anto: Deter (निवारण करना) {Reluctance (अनिच्छा)}

1584 Utilitarian (Adj.) - (उपयोगी) *[#R-3 (1)]*
Designed to be useful or practical rather than attractive

Syno: Useful (उपयोगी), Functional (कार्यात्मक)

Anto: Decorative (सजावटी) {Stylish (सजावटी)}

1585 Vacant (Adj.) - (खाली) *[#R-4 (1)]*
Not occupied; having no people or contents

Syno: Bare (नंगा), Uninhabited (अनावासित), Empty (खाली) {Desolate (सुनसान)}

Anto: Occupied (अधिकृत)

1586 **Vacate** (V.) - (खाली करना) *[#R-3]*
To leave a place previously occupied

Syno: Depart (प्रस्थान करना)

Anto: Occupy (कब्जा करना)

1587 Vacillate (V.) - (निश्चय न कर पाना)~ *[#R-6 (4)]*
To waver between choices; be unable to decide

Syno: Waver (डगमगाना), Hesitate (हिचकिचाना) {Dither (संदेह करना)}

Anto: Decide (निर्णय लेना) {Persist (दृढ़ रहना)}

1588 Vacillation (N.) - (अनिश्चितता) *[#R-2 (2)]*
The inability to decide between different choices

Syno: Irresolution (अनिर्णय) {Hesitancy (संकोच)}

Anto: Steadfastness (दृढ़ता) {Decisiveness (निर्णायकता)}

1589 **Vagrant** (N./Adj.) - (भटकने वाला)~ *[#R-3 (2)]*
A homeless wanderer (N); Wandering without settled home (Adj.)

Syno: Drifter (भटकने वाला) {Nomad (खानाबदोश)}

Anto: Settled (बसा हुआ) {Steady (स्थिर)}

1590 Vague (Adj.) - (अस्पष्ट)~ *[#R-5 (8)]*
Not clear, definite, or exact in meaning

Syno: Unclear (अस्पष्ट), Indefinite (अनिश्चित), Hazy (धुंधला) {Inexplicit (अस्पष्ट)}

Anto: Clear (स्पष्ट), Definite (निर्धारित) {Precise (सटीक)}

1591 **Vain** (Adj.) - (व्यर्थ; अहंकारी)~ *[#R-6 (2)]*
Excessively proud of oneself; also futile or without result

Syno: Useless (बेकार), Futile (निरर्थक)

Anto: Modest (विनम्र), Productive (परिणाम देने वाला), Humble (विनम्र)

1592 Valiant (Adj.) - (वीर) *[#R-2 (3)]*
Showing courage or determination

Syno: Courageous (साहसी) {Brave (निडर)}

Anto: Cowardly (कायरतापूर्ण)

1593 **Valid** (Adj.) - (मान्य) *[#R-1 (2)]*
Based on sound logic or fact; acceptable

Syno: Logical (तार्किक)

Anto: {Invalid (अमान्य), False (गलत)}

1594 **Validate** (V.) - (मान्य करना) *[#R-1 (3)]*
To confirm or prove something as legitimate or correct

Syno: Confirm (निश्चित करना) {Authenticate (प्रमाणित करना), Substantiate (सिद्ध करना)}

Anto: {Refute (खंडन करना)}

1595 Valuable (Adj.) - (मूल्यवान) *[#R-1 (1)]*
Having high worth or importance

Syno: Precious (अनमोल)

Anto: {Inexpensive (सस्ता)}

1596 **Vanish** (V.) - (गायब होना) *[#R-5]*
To disappear suddenly and completely

Syno: Disappear (लुप्त होना)

Anto: Emerge (प्रकट होना)

1597 **Vanity** (N.) - (अहंकार) *[#R-3]*
Excessive pride in one's appearance or achievements

Syno: Conceit (घमंड)

Anto: Modesty (नम्रता), Humility (विनम्रता)

1598 Vanquish (V.) - (हराना; जीतना) *[#R-6 (1)]*
To defeat completely or thoroughly; To conquer or subjugate

Syno: Defeat (पराजित करना), Conquer (जीतना)

Anto: Liberate (मुक्त करना), Surrender (आत्मसमर्पण करना)

1599 Variety (N.) - (विविधता) *[#R-1 (1)]*
The state of being different or diverse; lack of sameness

Syno: {Diversity (भिन्नता)}

Anto: Similarity (समानता)

1600 **Vast** (Adj.) - (विशाल) *[#R-2 (2)]*
Of very great extent or size; enormous

Syno: Extensive (व्यापक) {Huge (बहुत बड़ा)}

Anto: Small (छोटा)

1601 Vendetta (N.) - (दुश्मनी)~ *[#R-2]*
A prolonged bitter quarrel or hostile campaign

Syno: Disagreement (असहमति)

Anto: Harmony (सामंजस्य)

1602 Venerable (Adj.) - (पूजनीय)~ *[#R-2 (4)]*
Highly respected because of age, wisdom, or character

Syno: Esteemed (प्रतिष्ठित) {Respectable (आदरणीय), Celebrated (प्रसिद्ध)}

Anto: Immature (अपरिपक्व)

1603 Venerate (V.) - (सम्मान करना)~ *[#R-3 (4)]*
To regard with deep respect or reverence

Syno: Revere (इज्जत करना), Respect (सम्मान करना)

Anto: Despise (घृणा करना)

1604 **Venial** (Adj.) - (क्षमा योग्य)~ *[#R-3 (1)]*
Slight in nature and deserving forgiveness

Syno: Pardonable (माफ़ करने योग्य)

Anto: Unpardonable (अक्षम्य)

1605 **Venom** (N.) - (ज़हर) *[#R-2 (1)]*
Poison produced by a snake or insect

Syno: Poison (विष)

Anto: {Antidote (विषनाशक)}

1606 Veracity (N.) - (सत्यता)~ *[#R-5 (7)]*
Conformity to facts; accuracy or truth

Syno: Truth (सत्य) {Accuracy (शुद्धता), Truthfulness (सत्यता), Credibility (विश्वसनीयता)}

Anto: Deceit (छल), Falsehood (झूठ), Myth (मिथक) {Falsity (असत्यता)}

1607 **Verbose** (Adj.) - (शब्दाडंबरपूर्ण; अधिक बोलने वाला)~ *[#R-4 (4)]*
Using more words than necessary

Syno: Talkative (बातूनी) {Diffuse (विस्तारित), Babbling (बड़बड़ाने वाला)}

Anto: Brief (संक्षिप्त) {Concise (संक्षिप्त)}

1608 **Verity** (N.) - (सत्यता) *[#R-2 (1)]*
A true principle or belief of fundamental importance

Syno: Truth (सत्य)

Anto: Falsehood (असत्य)

1609 Versatile (Adj.) - (बहुमुखी; परिवर्तनशील)~ *[#R-4]*
Able to adapt or be adapted to many different functions or activities

Syno: Flexible (परिवर्तनीय)

Anto: Limited (सीमित), Amateur (शौकिया), Inflexible (अपरिवर्तनीय)

1610 **Vexed** (Adj.) - (परेशान) *[#R-1 (3)]*
Difficult, problematic, or causing annoyance

Syno: Annoyed (परेशान) {Displeased (अप्रसन्न)}

Anto: {Resolved (सुलझा हुआ)}

1611 **Viable** (Adj.) - (करने योग्य) *[#R-3 (4)]*
Capable of working successfully; feasible

Syno: Workable (चलने योग्य) {Conceivable

(कल्पनीय), Feasible (संभव)}

Anto: Impracticable (अव्यावहारिक)

1612 **Vice** (N.) - (बुराई) *[#R-4 (1)]*
Immoral or wicked behaviour

Syno: Immorality (अनैतिकता)

Anto: Virtue (गुण)

1613 Vicinity (N.) - (आसपास)~ *[#R-2]*
The area near or surrounding a particular place

Syno: Proximity (निकटता)

Anto: Remoteness (सुदूरता)

1614 Vicious (Adj.) - (क्रूर) *[#R-4 (2)]*
Deliberately cruel or violent

Syno: Cruel (निर्दयी) {Wicked (दुष्ट)}

Anto: Virtuous (नेक), Gentle (विनम्र)

1615 Victorious (Adj.) - (विजयी) *[#R-1 (1)]*
Having won a victory; triumphant

Syno: Champion (विजयी)

Anto: {Defeated (पराजित)}

1616 **Vigilance** (N.) - (सतर्कता) *[#R-1 (1)]*
The state of keeping careful watch for danger

Syno: {Alertness (सतर्कता)}

Anto: Indifference (उदासीनता)

1617 Vigilant (Adj.) - (सावधान) *[#R-12 (8)]*
Keeping careful watch for possible danger

Syno: Watchful (चौकस), Cautious (सजग), Alert (सतर्क) {Aware (जागरूक)}

Anto: Careless (लापरवाह), Negligent (बेपरवाह), Rash (अविवेकी) {Inattentive (असावधान), Distracted (ध्यान भटका हुआ)}

1618 Vigorous (Adj.) - (जोरदार) *[#R-5]*
Strong, healthy, and full of energy

Syno: Strenuous (ज़ोरदार), Energetic (ऊर्जावान)

Anto: Spiritless (निर्जीव), Frail (नाजुक)

1619 **Vindicate** (V.) - (दोषमुक्त करना)~ *[#R-4 (1)]*
To clear someone of blame or suspicion

Syno: Exonerate (दोषमुक्त करना), Justify (सही ठहराना)

Anto: Accuse (आरोप लगाना) {Incriminate (दोषी ठहराना)}

1620 **Vindictive** (Adj.) - (प्रतिशोधी)~ *[#R-4 (6)]*
Having a strong or unreasonable desire for revenge

Syno: Spiteful (द्वेषपूर्ण), Revengeful (बदला लेने वाला) {Malicious (दुर्भावनापूर्ण)}

Anto: {Forgiving (क्षमाशील)}

1621 **Vintage** (Adj.) - (प्राचीन)~ *[#R-2]*
Of high quality from the past

Syno: Classic (उत्कृष्ट)

Anto: Modern (आधुनिक)

1622 Violent (Adj.) - (हिंसक, उग्र) *[#R-3 (3)]*
Using physical force to hurt, damage, or kill

Syno: Aggressive (आक्रामक) {Wild (बेकाबू), Tumultuous (अशांत)}

Anto: Gentle (कोमल)

1623 Virtual (Adj.) - (लगभग वास्तविक) *[#R-1 (1)]*
Almost as described but not completely real

Syno: {Simulated (नकली)}

Anto: Authentic (प्रामाणिक)

1624 **Virtue** (N.) - (सद्गुण)~ *[#R-7 (2)]*
Behaviour showing high moral standards

Syno: {Probity (ईमानदारी)}

Anto: Vice (अवगुण), Wickedness (दुष्टता), Demerit (अवगुण)

1625 **Virulent** (Adj.) - (घातक)~ *[#R-2]*
Extremely harmful or severe; bitterly hostile

Syno: Deadly (जानलेवा)

Anto: Amicable (मैत्रीपूर्ण)

1626 **Vital** (Adj.) - (महत्वपूर्ण) *[#R-4 (6)]*
Absolutely necessary or extremely important

Syno: Essential (आवश्यक), Crucial (निर्णायक)

Anto: Trivial (तुच्छ), Superfluous (अनावश्यक) {Dispensable (परित्याज्य), Unnecessary (अनावश्यक)}

1627 **Vitiate** (V.) - (बिगाड़ना) *[#R-2]*
To spoil or reduce the quality or effectiveness of something

Syno: Impair (क्षीण करना)

Anto: Improve (सुधारना)

1628 **Vituperate** (V.) - (निंदा करना) *[#R-2]*
To blame or insult someone using harsh language

Syno: Abuse (गाली देना)

Anto: Praise (प्रशंसा करना)

1629 Vivacious (Adj.) - (ज़िंदादिल)~ *[#R-6 (3)]*
Attractively lively, animated, and full of energy

Syno: Lively (जीवंत), Energetic (ऊर्जावान)

Anto: Apathetic (उदासीन) {Weary (थका हुआ), Languid (सुस्त)}

1630 **Vivid** (Adj.) - (जीवंत) *[#R-6 (3)]*
Producing strong, clear images or feelings

Syno: Evocative (स्मरणात्मक), Bright (उज्ज्वल), Lucid (स्पष्ट) {Clear (स्पष्ट), Lively (जीवंत)}

Anto: Murky (धुंधला), Vague (अस्पष्ट)

1631 Vociferous (Adj.) - (कोलाहलपूर्ण) *[#R-3 (2)]*
Expressing opinions loudly and forcefully

Syno: {Loud (शोरगुल करने वाला)}

Anto: Silent (मौन), Mild (संयमित) {Quiet (शांत)}

1632 **Volatile** (Adj.) - (परिवर्तनशील, उड़नशील)~ *[#R-1 (3)]*
Changing rapidly and unpredictably; easily evaporating

Syno: {Unstable (अस्थिर)}

Anto: Certain (निश्चित) {Immutable (अपरिवर्तनीय)}

1633 **Volition** (N.) - (इच्छा)~ *[#R-2 (1)]*
The power or act of making a conscious choice

Syno: Choice (विकल्प)

Anto: Compulsion (विवशता) {Unwillingness (अनिच्छा)}

1634 **Voluble** (Adj.) - (वाचाल, बहुत बोलने वाला) *[#R-2 (1)]*
Speaking a lot, easily and fluently

Syno: {Garrulous (बातूनी)}

Anto: Reserved (संकोची), Reticent (अल्पभाषी)

1635 Voracious (Adj.) - (भुक्खड़; अतृप्त)~ *[#R-4 (4)]*
Eating very much; Having insatiable desire, never fully satisfied

Syno: Greedy (लालची), Insatiable (अतृप्त) {Hungry (भूखा), Gluttonous (पेटू)}

Anto: {Contented (संतुष्ट)}

1636 **Vulgar** (Adj.) - (अश्लील) *[#R-4]*
Lacking good taste or refinement

Syno: Abusive (गाली-गलौच)

Anto: Refined (सभ्य), Decorous (शिष्ट)

1637 Vulnerable (Adj.) - (असुरक्षित, अतिसंवेदनशील)~ *[#R-6 (7)]*
Easily harmed physically or emotionally

Syno: Exposed (असुरक्षित), At Risk (जोखिम में), Defenseless (रक्षाहीन) {Susceptible (संवेदनशील), Prone (संवेदनशील), Defenceless (रक्षाहीन)}

Anto: Secure (सुरक्षित) {Invulnerable (अभेद्य), Impervious (अप्रभावित)}

1638 **Wan** (Adj.) - (पीला, फीका) *[#R-3]*
Pale or weak in appearance or health

Syno: Pallid (निस्तेज, फीका)

Anto: Healthy (स्वस्थ)

1639 **Wane** (V.) - (कम होना, घटना) *[#R-5 (5)]*
To decrease in strength, amount, or intensity

Syno: Decline (गिरना)

Anto: Increase (बढ़ना), Intensify (तीव्र होना), Grow (बढ़ना) {Swell (सूजना), Rise (उठना)}

1640 **Wanton** (Adj.) - (उद्दंड; निरंकुश) *[#R-1 (2)]*
Deliberate and unprovoked; cruel or reckless

Syno: Obscene (भद्दा)

Anto: {Wholesome (नैतिक)}

1641 **Warm** (Adj.) - (गर्म; स्नेही) *[#R-2]*
Having a comfortably high temperature; friendly in manner

Syno: Amicable (मैत्रीपूर्ण)

Anto: Cool (ठंडा)

1642 **Warn** (V.) - (चेतावनी देना) *[#R-3]*
To inform in advance about a possible danger or problem

Syno: Alert (सचेत करना)

Anto: Imperil (खतरे में डालना)

1643 **Wary** (Adj.) - (सतर्क) *[#R-3]*
Cautious about possible dangers or problems

Syno: Alert (चौकन्ना)

Anto: Rash (उतावला), Careless (लापरवाह)

1644 **Wavering** (Adj.) - (अस्थिर) *[#R-2 (1)]*
Hesitating or indecisive

Syno: Fluctuating (उतार-चढ़ाव वाला)

Anto: Unchanging (अपरिवर्तनीय)

1645 Weary (Adj.) - (थका हुआ)~ *[#R-3 (1)]*
Tired due to effort or lack of rest

Syno: Exhausted (थका माँदा), Tired (थका हुआ) {Fatigued (थका हुआ)}

Anto: Refreshed (तरोताजा)

1646 Weird (Adj.) - (अजीब) *[#R-3 (1)]*
Strange or uncanny

Syno: Strange (विचित्र) {Unnatural (अप्राकृतिक)}

Anto: Usual (प्रचलित), Normal (सामान्य)

1647 Whimsical (Adj.) - (मनमौजी) *[#R-3 (3)]*
Playfully unusual or fanciful

Syno: Funny (मजेदार), Weird (अजीब) {Fanciful (मनमाना)}

Anto: Practical (व्यावहारिक) {Common (सामान्य)}

1648 Wholesome (Adj.) - (स्वास्थ्यप्रद) *[#R-3 (3)]*
Good for health or moral well-being

Syno: Sound (स्वस्थ) {Nourishing (पौष्टिक), Healthy (स्वस्थ)}

Anto: Impure (अशुद्ध) {Unhealthy (अस्वस्थ)}

1649 **Wily** (Adj.) - (चालाक; धूर्त) *[#R-5 (1)]*
Skilled at gaining an advantage, especially deceitfully

Syno: Cunning (कपटी), Crafty (कुटिल) {Sly (चालाक)}

Anto: Honest (ईमानदार)

1650 Winsome (Adj.) - (आकर्षक) *[#R-2 (1)]*
Attractive or pleasing in appearance or character

Syno: Charming (मनमोहक)

Anto: Repelling (घिनौना) {Unamiable (अप्रिय)}

1651 Wisdom (N.) - (बुद्धिमत्ता) *[#R-6 (2)]*
The quality of having experience, knowledge, and good judgment

Syno: Insight (अंतर्दृष्टि), Knowledge (ज्ञान) {Sagacity (विवेकशीलता)}

Anto: Stupidity (मूर्खता), Imbecility (पागलपन), 3Folly (मूर्खता)

1652 **Withdraw** (V.) - (पीछे हटना) *[#R-2]*
To remove or take away something from a particular place

Syno: Retreat (पीछे हटना)

Anto: Advance (आगे बढ़ना)

1653 **Wrathful** (Adj.) - (क्रोधित) *[#R-1 (2)]*
Full of intense anger

Syno: Furious (उग्र) {Enraged (क्रोधित)}

Anto: {Calm (शांत)}

1654 **Yell** (V.) - (चिल्लाना) *[#R-4]*
To shout very loudly

Syno: Shout (चिल्लाना)

Anto: Whisper (फुसफुसाना)

1655 Yield (V./N.) - (स्वीकार करना; उपज) *[#R-6 (3)]*
To give way to arguments or demands (V.); The amount produced (N.)

Syno: Submit (समर्पण करना), Concede (स्वीकार करना); Produce (उत्पादन), Harvest (पैदावार)

Anto: Resist (विरोध करना) {Confront (सामना करना)}

1656 **Yoke** (N./V.) - (गुलामी; बाँधना)~ *[#R-3]*
A wooden bar used to join animals (N.); To join together (V.)

Syno: Harness (जोतना)

Anto: Liberty (स्वतंत्रता)

1657 **Zeal** (N.) - (उत्साह) *[#R-2 (3)]*
Great energy or enthusiasm for a goal

Syno: {Zest (उत्साह), Passion (जुनून)}

Anto: Apathy (उदासीनता)

1658 Zealous (Adj.) - (उत्साही) *[#R-2 (1)]*
Showing strong enthusiasm or eagerness

Syno: Enthusiastic (उत्साहपूर्ण)

Anto: Indifferent (उदासीन)

1659 Zenith (N.) - (शीर्ष बिंदु)~ *[#R-7 (8)]*
The highest point reached; point directly overhead

Syno: Summit (शिखर), Pinnacle (चरम) {Apex (शीर्ष)}

Anto: Nadir (निम्नतम बिंदु), Bottom (तल) {Base (आधार), Depth (गहराई)}

1660 **Zest** (N.) - (उत्साह) *[#R-3]*
Great enthusiasm and energy

Syno: Enthusiasm (उत्साहपूर्णता)

Anto: Monotonousness (नीरसता), Dullness (उबाऊपन)

*Total **1660** Syno+Anto asked **9812** times*

C3 Top 100 Synonyms (asked in SSC Exams)

1 **Forbear** (V.) - (संयम बरतना) *[#R-6 (6)]*
To restrain oneself from doing something
Syno: Refrain (परहेज करना)

2 **Contemptuous** (Adj.) - (अनादरपूर्ण) *[#R-1 (9)]*
Showing strong dislike or disrespect
Syno: Derisive (मज़ाक उड़ाने वाला) {Disrespectful (अनादरयुक्त), Disdainful (तिरस्कारपूर्ण)}

3 **Banish** (V.) - (निर्वासित करना) *[#R-7 (2)]*
To send someone away from a country as punishment
Syno: Expel (निकाल देना), Exile (देश-निकाला देना), Deport (देश से निकालना), Relegate (नीचे स्तर पर भेजना) {Dispel (दूर करना)}

4 **Erroneous** (Adj.) - (गलत) *[#R-6 (2)]*
Containing or characterized by error
Syno: False (झूठा), Invalid (अमान्य), Wrong (गलत), Inaccurate (अशुद्ध), Fallacious (भ्रांतिपूर्ण) {Mistaken (भ्रांत)}

5 **Forsake** (V.) - (त्यागना) *[#R-5 (3)]*
To abandon or give up
Syno: Abandon (छोड़ देना), Desert (छोड़कर भाग जाना) {Discard (त्याग देना)}

6 **Impart** (V.) - (प्रसारित करना) *[#R-4 (4)]*
To make information known; communicate
Syno: Transmit (संचारित करना)

7 **Obliterate** (V.) - (मिटाना) *[#R-3 (5)]*
To destroy completely; wipe out
Syno: Annihilate (नष्ट करना), Abolish (हटाना), Erase (मिटाना) {Demolish (ध्वस्त करना), Eradicate (मिटा देना), Destroy (नष्ट करना)}

8 **Frantic** (Adj.) - (घबराया हुआ) *[#R-4 (3)]*
Wild or distraught with fear or anxiety
Syno: Agitated (व्याकुल), Distraught (घबराया हुआ), Violent (उग्र) {Berserk (उन्मादी), Panicky (आतंकित), Desperate (बेताब)}

9 **Hurdle** (N.) - (बाधा) *[#R-6 (1)]*
A difficulty or obstacle
Syno: Obstacle (रुकावट), Impediment (अड़चन)

10 **Obligation** (N.) - (दायित्व) *[#R-4 (3)]*
A moral or legal duty or commitment
Syno: Commitment (प्रतिबद्धता), Duty (कर्तव्य), Responsibility (जिम्मेदारी) {Binding (बंधन)}

11 **Sycophant** (N.) - (चापलूस)~ *[#R-3 (4)]*
A person who flatters someone powerful for gain
Syno: Fawner (खुशामदी), Flatterer (चापलूस) {Adulator (चाटुकार)}

12 **Anticipate** (V.) - (पूर्वानुमान करना)~ *[#R-5 (1)]*
To expect or prepare for something in advance
Syno: Expect (उम्मीद करना), Predict (भविष्यवाणी करना)

13 **Companion** (N.) - (साथी) *[#R-1 (5)]*
A person or animal with whom one spends time or travels
Syno: Mate (संगी) {Comrade (सहचर)}

14 **Deteriorate** (V.) - (ख़राब होना) *[#R-4 (2)]*
To become progressively worse
Syno: Worsen (बिगड़ना), Dilapidate (खंडहर बनना), Retrogress (पतन होना) {Decline (गिरना)}

15 **Foster** (V.) - (बढ़ावा देना) *[#R-2 (4)]*
To encourage or help develop
Syno: Promote (प्रोत्साहित करना), Nurture (पालन-पोषण करना)

16 **Impediment** (N.) - (बाधा) *[#R-3 (3)]*
A hindrance or obstruction in doing something
Syno: Obstruction (अवरोध), Obstacle (रुकावट), Barrier (रोक) {Hurdle (अड़चन), Restriction (प्रतिबंध)}

17 **Luxuriant** (Adj.) - (प्रचुर) *[#R-4 (2)]*
Rich and profuse in growth
Syno: Abundant (बहुतायत), Lush (भरपूर), Flourishing (फलता-फूलता)

18 **Precedence** (N.) - (प्राथमिकता) *[#R-6]*
The condition of having higher importance or priority
Syno: Priority (प्राथमिकता)

19 **Wander** (V.) - (भटकना)~ *[#R-5 (1)]*
To move about aimlessly or casually
Syno: Roam (घूमना), Deviate (विचलित होना)

[**#R** denotes repetition of word]

[E.g. in SN 17, #R- **4 (2)** denotes this word has been asked 4 times in SSC and 2 times in other exams]

20 **Achieve** (V.) - (हासिल करना) *[#R-4 (1)]*
To complete something by hard work and skill
Syno: Accomplish (पूरा करना), Succeed (सफल होना) {Attain (प्राप्त करना)}

21 **Amaze** (V.) - (चकित करना) *[#R-4 (1)]*
To surprise greatly
Syno: Astonish (आश्चर्यचकित करना)

22 **Dedicate** (V.) - (समर्पित करना) *[#R-3 (2)]*
To devote to a task or purpose
Syno: Devote (समर्पण करना), Commit (प्रतिबद्ध होना)

23 **Deride** (V.) - (मज़ाक उड़ाना)~ *[#R-3 (2)]*
To express contempt for; to ridicule
Syno: Mock (मज़ाक उड़ाना), Ridicule (उपहास करना), Taunt (ताना मारना) {Disdain (तिरस्कार करना)}

24 **Envisage** (V.) - (कल्पना करना) *[#R-1 (4)]*
To consider or imagine a future possibility
Syno: Imagine (परिकल्पना करना) {Contemplate (विचार करना)}

25 **Fling** (V.) - (फेंकना) *[#R-2 (3)]*
To throw or hurl forcefully
Syno: Throw (फेंकना), Propel (धकेलना)

26 **Flout** (V.) - (अवहेलना करना)~ *[#R-4 (1)]*
To openly disregard a rule, law, or convention
Syno: Mock (अवज्ञा करना), Defy (अवहेलना करना) {Disregard (अनदेखा करना)}

27 **Garnish** (V.) - (सजावट करना) *[#R-4 (1)]*
To decorate or embellish something, especially food
Syno: Adorn (सजाना), Embellish (सुशोभित करना), Decorate (सजावट करना)

28 **Innuendo** (N.) - (इशारा)~ *[#R-2 (3)]*
An allusive or oblique remark or hint
Syno: Insinuation (इशारा), Implication (संकेत) {Hint (इशारा), Allusion (संकेत)}

29 **Jealous** (Adj.) - (ईर्ष्यालु) *[#R-3 (2)]*
Feeling or showing envy of someone or their achievements and advantages
Syno: Envious (ईर्ष्यालु)

30 **Sanction** (N.) - (अनुमति) *[#R-4 (1)]*
The official approval or authorization
Syno: Permission (अनुमति), Approval (स्वीकृति); Permit (अनुमति)

31 **Stroll** (V.) - (टहलना)~ *[#R-2 (3)]*
To walk in a leisurely way
Syno: Walk (चलना), Saunter (आराम से चलना) {Roam (घूमना)}

32 **Tepid** (Adj.) - (गुनगुना) *[#R-1 (4)]*
Slightly warm; not hot or cold
Syno: Warm (हल्का गर्म) {Dull (नीरस), Lukewarm (गुनगुना), Moderate (मध्यम)}

33 **Yearn** (V.) - (तीव्र इच्छा करना) *[#R-2 (3)]*
To feel a deep longing for something
Syno: Desire (इच्छा करना), Crave (लालसा करना)

34 **Adapt** (V.) - (ढालना) *[#R-4]*
To make something suitable for a new use or purpose
Syno: Adjust (तालमेल बिठाना)

35 **Anger** (N.) - (क्रोध) *[#R-4]*
A strong feeling of annoyance or hostility
Syno: Fury (प्रकोप), Rage (प्रकोप), Displeasure (असंतोष)

36 **Anguish** (N.) - (पीड़ा) *[#R-4]*
Severe mental or physical pain or suffering
Syno: Agony (यातना), Ache (दर्द), Sorrow (दुख), Pain (वेदना)

37 **Bashful** (Adj.) - (शर्मीला) *[#R-4]*
Reluctant to draw attention to oneself; shy
Syno: Shy (लजीला), Introverted (अंतर्मुखी)

38 **Bind** (V.) - (बाँधना) *[#R-4]*
To tie or fasten something tightly
Syno: Fasten (कसना), Secure (सुरक्षित करना), Unite (एकजुट करना)

39 **Contrite** (Adj.) - (पश्चातापी) *[#R-4]*
Feeling or expressing remorse; affected by guilt
Syno: Regretful (खेदपूर्ण), Remorseful (पश्चातापपूर्ण)

40 **Conundrum** (N.) - (पहेली)~ *[#R-2 (2)]*
A confusing and difficult problem or question
Syno: Problem (समस्या) {Confusion (भ्रम)}

41 **Crux** (N.) - (सार) *[#R-3 (1)]*
The decisive or most important point at issue
Syno: Essence (मूल), Gist (सार) {Core (केंद्र)}

42 **Deadly** (Adj.) - (जानलेवा) *[#R-2 (2)]*
Causing or able to cause death
Syno: Fatal (प्राणघातक) {Lethal (घातक)}

43 **Deft** (Adj.) - (निपुण) *[#R-1 (3)]*
Showing skill and quickness
Syno: Skilful (कुशल)

44 **Determined** (Adj.) - (दृढ़निश्चयी) *[#R-4]*

[Bold SN, indicates that it has been asked in Spelling]

[In Word, ~ indicates that it has been asked in OWS]

Having made a firm decision and being resolved not to change it

Syno: Resolved (संकल्पित), Resolute (दृढ़निश्चयी), Decisive (निर्णायक)

45 **Devastate** (V.) - (नष्ट करना) *[#R-2 (2)]*
To cause complete destruction or ruin

Syno: Destroy (नष्ट करना), Destruct (नष्ट करना) {Ruin (बर्बाद करना)}

46 **Discern** (V.) - (पहचानना) *[#R-3 (1)]*
To perceive or recognize clearly

Syno: Discriminate (भेद करना), Perceive (जानना) {Determine (निर्धारित करना)}

47 **Disparity** (N.) - (असमानता) *[#R-2 (2)]*
A great difference

Syno: Difference (अंतर), Diversity (विविधता) {Inequality (असमानता)}

48 **Disrupt** (V.) - (भंग करना)~ *[#R-3 (1)]*
To interrupt by causing disorder or trouble

Syno: Break (तोड़ना), Disturb (परेशान करना)

49 **Distinguished** (Adj.) - (प्रतिष्ठित) *[#R-3 (1)]*
Very successful and highly respected

Syno: Dignified (गरिमामय), Acclaimed (प्रशंसित), Honoured (सम्मानित) {Esteemed (प्रतिष्ठित)}

50 **Dodge** (V.) - (चकमा देना) *[#R-4]*
To avoid or evade by quick or clever action

Syno: Avoid (टालना), Evade (बचना), Sidestep (बचकर निकलना)

51 **Estrange** (V.) - (पराया कर देना) *[#R-2 (2)]*
To cause people to become distant or unfriendly.

Syno: Separate (अलग होना) {Alienate (दूर कर देना)}

52 **Execute** (V.) - (पालन करना, पूरा करना) *[#R-3 (1)]*
To carry out or put into effect

Syno: Implement (लागू करना), Accomplish (पूरा करना)

53 **Fatal** (Adj.) - (घातक)~ *[#R-3 (1)]*
Causing death

Syno: Deadly (जानलेवा) {Disastrous (विनाशकारी)}

54 **Feign** (V.) - (दिखावा करना)~ *[#R-3 (1)]*
To pretend to be affected by a feeling or state

Syno: Pretend (नाटक करना)

55 **Fury** (N.) - (क्रोध) *[#R-3 (1)]*
Wild or violent anger

Syno: Anger (गुस्सा) {Rage (रोष)}

56 **Glib** (Adj.) - (चिकनी-चुपड़ी बातें करने वाला) *[#R-4]*
Fluent and voluble but insincere and shallow

Syno: Artful (चालाक), Slick (चालाक)

57 **Hoodwink** (V.) - (आँख में धूल झोंकना) *[#R-4]*
To deceive or trick someone

Syno: Deceive (धोखा देना), Cheat (बेईमानी करना), Defraud (ठगना)

58 **Impetus** (N.) - (प्रेरणा) *[#R-2 (2)]*
Force or motivation that makes something happen

Syno: Encouragement (प्रोत्साहन), Incitement (उकसावा) {Momentum (गति), Stimulant (उत्तेजक)}

59 **Incognito** (Adj./Adv.) - (गुमनाम; गुप्त रूप से)~ *[#R-1 (3)]*
Having one's identity hidden (Adj.); with identity hidden (Adv.)

Syno: Anonymous (अज्ञात) {Concealed (छिपा हुआ); Secretly (गुप्त रूप से)}

60 **Labour** (N.) - (श्रम) *[#R-1 (3)]*
Physical or mental work

Syno: Toil (कड़ी मेहनत) {Drudge (कठिन परिश्रम)}

61 **Labyrinth** (N.) - (भूलभुलैया) *[#R-3 (1)]*
A complex network of passages; a maze

Syno: Meander (घुमाव), Maze (भूलभुलैया) {Complexity (जटिलता)}

62 **Lurid** (Adj.) - (भड़कीला) *[#R-2 (2)]*
Unpleasantly vivid; ghastly; sensational; gruesome; terrible or distorted

Syno: Shocking (चौंकाने वाला), Over-Bright (अत्यधिक चमकीला) {Violent (हिंसक)}

63 **Onus** (N.) - (भार) *[#R-2 (2)]*
A duty or responsibility placed on someone

Syno: Responsibility (ज़िम्मेदारी), Burden (बोझ)

64 **Palpable** (Adj.) - (स्पष्ट)~ *[#R-2 (2)]*
Easily felt or clearly noticeable

Syno: Detectable (पता लगाने योग्य), Tangible (स्पर्शनीय) {Obvious (स्पष्ट)}

65 **Panacea** (N.) - (रामबाण)~ *[#R-4]*
A remedy for all problems or diseases

Syno: Cure-All (सर्वरोग निवारण), Remedy (इलाज)

66 **Paramount** (Adj.) - (सर्वोपरि) *[#R-2 (2)]*
More important than anything else

Syno: Central (केंद्रीय), Supreme (सर्वोच्च)

67 **Pester** (V.) - (सताना) *[#R-2 (2)]*
To annoy someone repeatedly

Syno: Annoy (परेशान करना) {Bother (कष्ट देना)}

68 **Pleasant** (Adj.) - (सुखद) *[#R-3 (1)]*

Giving a sense of happy satisfaction or enjoyment

Syno: Amusing (मनोरंजक), Delightful (आनंददायक), Refreshing (ताज़गी भरा) {Enjoyable (आनंद देने वाला)}

69 **Ponder** (V.) - (चिंतन करना)~ *[#R-2 (2)]*
To think carefully and seriously about something

Syno: Meditate (ध्यान लगाना), Contemplate (विचार करना) {Think (सोचना)}

70 **Pugnacious** (Adj.) - (लड़ाकू)~ *[#R-3 (1)]*
Quick to argue or ready to fight

Syno: Truculent (आक्रामक), Belligerent (झगड़ालू), Waspish (चिड़चिड़ा) {Quarrelsome (झगड़ालू)}

71 **Quandary** (N.) - (दुविधा)~ *[#R-3 (1)]*
A state of uncertainty in a difficult situation

Syno: Dilemma (कठिन चुनाव), Impasse (अटकाव)

72 **Rampart** (N.) - (किलेबंदी) *[#R-4]*
A defensive wall built for protection

Syno: Bulwark (किलेबंदी), Parapet (सुरक्षा-दीवार)

73 **Requisite** (Adj./N.) - (अनिवार्य; आवश्यक वस्तु) *[#R-3 (1)]*
Necessary for a purpose (Adj.); Something that is required (N.)

Syno: Obligatory (अनिवार्य), Essential (आवश्यक); Precondition (पूर्व शर्त) {Necessity (आवश्यकता)}

74 **Respect** (N.) - (आदर) *[#R-3 (1)]*
A feeling of esteem or admiration

Syno: Deference (सम्मान), Honour (गौरव) {Regard (सम्मान)}

75 **Tendency** (N.) - (प्रवृत्ति) *[#R-2 (2)]*
An inclination towards a particular behaviour or characteristic

Syno: Propensity (प्रवृत्ति), Proneness (झुकाव) {Predisposition (पूर्व-प्रवृत्ति)}

76 **Transcend** (V.) - (पार करना) *[#R-1 (3)]*
To go beyond or rise above a limit or level

Syno: Eclipse (पीछे छोड़ देना) {Surpass (पीछे छोड़ना), Cross (पार करना)}

77 **Ablaze** (Adj.) - (जलता हुआ) *[#R-3]*
Burning fiercely or filled with anger

Syno: Burning (जलता हुआ), Furious (क्रोधित)

78 **Abysmal** (Adj.) - (बहुत खराब) *[#R-1 (2)]*
Extremely bad or shocking in quality

Syno: Terrible (भयानक) {Deplorable (दयनीय), Appalling (भयावह)}

79 **Acclaim** (N.) - (सार्वजनिक सराहना) *[#R-1 (2)]*
Enthusiastic public praise

Syno: Praise (प्रशंसा)

80 **Accrue** (V.) - (जमा होना) *[#R-3]*
To accumulate or receive payments or benefits over time

Syno: Accumulate (इकट्ठा होना), Collect (जमा होना), Gather (एकत्र होना)

81 **Adjourn** (V.) - (स्थगित करना) *[#R-2 (1)]*
To stop something temporarily and continue later

Syno: Postpone (टालना)

82 **Admit** (V.) - (स्वीकार करना) *[#R-1 (2)]*
To confess to be true or to be the case

Syno: Acknowledge (स्वीकार करना)

83 **Amity** (N.) - (मैत्री, सौहार्द) *[#R-1 (2)]*
A friendly relationship

Syno: Goodwill (सद्भाव) {Friendship (मित्रता)}

84 **Appalled** (Adj.) - (स्तब्ध) *[#R-1 (2)]*
Greatly shocked or horrified

Syno: Disgusted (घृणा से भरा हुआ) {Alarmed (घबराया हुआ)}

85 **Artful** (Adj.) - (चालाक) *[#R-3]*
Clever or skilful, typically in a crafty or cunning way

Syno: Cunning (चतुर), Crafty (कपटी)

86 **Attain** (V.) - (प्राप्त करना) *[#R-2 (1)]*
To succeed in achieving something desired

Syno: Achieve (हासिल करना)

87 **Awry** (Adj.) - (तिरछा) *[#R-3]*
Out of correct position

Syno: Crooked (टेढ़ा), Askew (एक तरफ झुका हुआ)

88 **Bibliophile** (N.) - (पुस्तक प्रेमी)~ *[#R-3]*
A person who loves or collects books

Syno: Booklover (किताबों का शौकीन)

89 **Bonhomie** (N.) - (खुशमिज़ाजी) *[#R-3]*
Cheerful friendliness and easy sociability

Syno: Companionship (साथ), Friendliness (मिलनसारिता), Geniality (सौहार्दपूर्णता)

90 **Calibrate** (V.) - (मानकीकृत करना) *[#R-2 (1)]*
To mark a gauge with a standard scale

Syno: Gauge (मापना), Adjust (समायोजित करना) {Regulate (नियंत्रित करना)}

91 **Calumny** (N.) - (बदनामी, झूठा आरोप) *[#R-1 (2)]*
False statements meant to damage reputation

Syno: Slander (मानहानि)

92 **Capitulate** (V.) - (हथियार डालना)~ *[#R-3]*
To stop resisting and surrender; to accept defeat

Syno: Surrender (आत्मसमर्पण करना)

93 **Castigate** (V.) - (कड़ी निंदा करना) *[#R-1 (2)]*
To criticize or punish someone severely

Syno: Condemn (निंदा करना)

94 **Cavil** (V.) - (कमी निकालना) *[#R-1 (2)]*
To raise petty objections

Syno: Quibble (तर्क-वितर्क करना) {Complain (शिकायत करना)}

95 **Coddle** (V.) - (लाड़ प्यार करना) *[#R-2 (1)]*
To treat in an indulgent or overprotective way

Syno: Pamper (लाड़ करना), Indulge (लाड़-प्यार करना)

96 **Comprehend** (V.) - (समझना) *[#R-3]*
To understand something mentally

Syno: Understand (समझना), Assimilate (पूरी तरह से समझ लेना), Grasp (बूझना)

97 **Consequence** (N.) - (परिणाम) *[#R-2 (1)]*
A result or effect of an action or condition

Syno: Outcome (नतीजा) {Result (परिणाम)}

98 **Contemplation** (N.) - (चिंतन) *[#R-2 (1)]*
The action of thinking deeply

Syno: Meditation (ध्यान), Reflection (चिंतन) {Introspection (आत्मचिंतन)}

99 **Craven** (Adj.) - (डरपोक) *[#R-1 (2)]*
Contemptibly lacking in courage

Syno: Cowardly (कायर)

100 **Crescendo** (N.) - (उत्कर्ष) *[#R-2 (1)]*
The loudest point in a gradually increasing sound

Syno: Climax (चरम बिंदु), Escalation (वृद्धि) {Upsurge (उछाल)}

*Total **100** Synonyms asked **453** times*

C4

Synonyms
(asked in SSC Exams)

1 **Abettor** (N.) - (अपराध में सहयोगी)
A person who encourages or helps in a crime
Syno: Accomplice (सहअपराधी)

2 **Ablaze** (Adj.) - (जलता हुआ) *[#R-3]*
Burning fiercely or filled with anger
Syno: Burning (जलता हुआ), Furious (क्रोधित)

3 **Ablution** (N.) - (स्नान)~
The act of washing, especially for religious purification
Syno: Washing (धुलाई)

4 **Abnegate** (V.) - (त्यागना)~ *[#R-2]*
To deny or give up something
Syno: Renounce (त्यागना), Deny (अस्वीकार करना)

5 **Abnormal** (Adj.) - (असामान्य) *[#R-1 (1)]*
Deviating from what is normal or usual
Syno: Unnatural (अस्वाभाविक) {Strange (अजीब)}

6 **Abode** (N.) - (निवास) *[#R-1 (1)]*
A place of residence; a house or home
Syno: Dwelling (आवास)

7 **Absorbing** (Adj.) - (रोचक)
Extremely interesting and attention-holding
Syno: Engrossing (आकर्षक)

8 **Abysmal** (Adj.) - (बहुत खराब) *[#R-1 (2)]*
Extremely bad or shocking in quality
Syno: Terrible (भयानक) {Deplorable (दयनीय), Appalling (भयावह)}

9 **Acclaim** (N.) - (सार्वजनिक सराहना) *[#R-1 (2)]*
Enthusiastic public praise
Syno: Praise (प्रशंसा)

10 **Accoutrement** (N.) - (साज-सामान)
Additional items of dress or equipment
Syno: Equipment (उपकरण)

11 **Accredit** (V.) - (मान्यता देना)
To officially recognize, accept, or approve
Syno: Certify (प्रमाणित करना)

12 **Accrue** (V.) - (जमा होना) *[#R-3]*
To accumulate or receive payments or benefits over time
Syno: Accumulate (इकट्ठा होना), Collect (जमा होना), Gather (एकत्र होना)

13 **Achieve** (V.) - (हासिल करना) *[#R-4 (1)]*
To complete something by hard work and skill
Syno: Accomplish (पूरा करना), Succeed (सफल होना) {Attain (प्राप्त करना)}

14 **Acknowledgement** (N.) - (स्वीकृति)
Recognition of the importance or quality of something
Syno: Confirmation (पुष्टि)

15 **Acne** (N.) - (मुँहासे)
A skin condition with pimples
Syno: Pimples (फुंसियाँ)

16 **Acquaint** (V.) - (परिचित कराना) *[#R-2]*
To make someone aware of or familiar with something
Syno: Introduce (परिचय कराना), Familiarise (परिचित कराना)

17 **Acquiescent** (Adj.) - (आज्ञाकारी)
Ready to accept something without protest
Syno: Tractable (आज्ञाकारी)

18 **Actuate** (V.) - (चालू करना)
To cause a machine or device to operate
Syno: Move (चलाना)

19 **Adapt** (V.) - (ढालना) *[#R-4]*
To make something suitable for a new use or purpose
Syno: Adjust (तालमेल बिठाना)

20 **Addicted** (Adj.) - (आदी)
Physically or mentally dependent on a substance or activity
Syno: Dependent (निर्भर)

21 **Adjourn** (V.) - (स्थगित करना) *[#R-2 (1)]*
To stop something temporarily and continue later
Syno: Postpone (टालना)

22 **Adjustment** (N.) - (तालमेल)
A small change made to achieve a desired result
Syno: Modification (संशोधन)

23 **Admit** (V.) - (स्वीकार करना) *[#R-1 (2)]*

[**#R** denotes repetition of word]

[E.g. in SN 13, #R- **4 (1)** denotes this word has been asked 4 times in SSC and 1 time in other exams]

To confess to be true or to be the case

Syno: Acknowledge (स्वीकार करना)

24 Advantageous (Adj.) - (लाभदायक)
Giving an advantage; helpful or beneficial

Syno: Favourable (अनुकूल)

25 **Adversely** (Adv.) - (प्रतिकूल रूप से)
In a harmful or negative way

Syno: Detrimentally (हानिकारक रूप से)

26 Advise (V.) - (सलाह देना)
To give advice or consultation

Syno: Prescribe (निर्देश देना)

27 **Aegis** (N.) - (संरक्षण)
The protection, backing, or support of an organization

Syno: Protection (सुरक्षा)

28 Affectionate (Adj.) - (स्नेही)
Readily showing fondness or tenderness

Syno: Sympathetic (सहानुभूतिपूर्ण)

29 **Affiliated** (Adj.) - (संबद्ध)
Connected or associated with

Syno: Allied (संबंधित)

30 **Afflict** (V.) - (सताना) *[#R-1 (1)]*
To cause pain or suffering

Syno: Torment (यातना देना)

31 **Affront** (N.) - (अपमान)
An action or remark causing outrage or offense

Syno: Insult (बेइज़्ज़ती)

32 **Afraid** (Adj.) - (डरा हुआ) *[#R-2]*
Feeling fear or anxiety; frightened

Syno: Scared (भयभीत)

33 Aggregate (N.) - (कुल) *[#R-1 (1)]*
A whole formed by combining elements

Syno: Total (कुल) {Accumulation (संग्रह)}

34 **Aghast** (Adj.) - (भयभीत) *[#R-1 (1)]*
Filled with horror or shock

Syno: Horrified (आतंकित) {Shocked (हैरान)}

35 **Agnostic** (N.) - (ईश्वर के बारे में संशयवादी व्यक्ति)~
A person who is unsure about God

Syno: Sceptic (संदेहवादी)

36 **Agonizingly** (Adv.) - (कष्टदायक रूप से)
In an extremely painful, distressing, or difficult manner

Syno: Painfully (दर्दनाक रूप से)

37 **Agreed** (Adj.) - (सहमत)
Having the same opinion

Syno: Supported (समर्थित)

38 **Aim** (N.) - (लक्ष्य)
A purpose or intention

Syno: Purpose (उद्देश्य)

39 Aisle (N.) - (गलियारा)
A passage between rows of seats

Syno: Passage (रास्ता)

40 **Alarm** (N.) - (घबराहट)
A feeling of fear or anxiety

Syno: Panic (भय)

41 **Allude** (V.) - (संकेत करना) *[#R-1 (1)]*
To refer to indirectly

Syno: Mention Indirectly (अप्रत्यक्ष रूप से उल्लेख करना)

42 Altruism (N.) - (परोपकार)~ *[#R-1 (1)]*
The belief or practice of selfless concern for the well-being of others

Syno: Benevolence (परोपकारिता) {Selflessness (निस्वार्थता)}

43 **Altruist** (N.) - (परोपकारी)~ *[#R-1 (1)]*
A person who shows concern for the welfare of others

Syno: Philanthropist (परोपकारी) {Humanitarian (मानवतावादी)}

44 **Amalgam** (N.) - (मिश्रण)
A mixture or blend

Syno: Mixture (मिश्रण)

45 **Amaze** (V.) - (चकित करना) *[#R-4 (1)]*
To surprise greatly

Syno: Astonish (आश्चर्यचकित करना)

46 **Amble** (V.) - (टहलना)~
To walk or move at a slow, relaxed pace

Syno: Wander (इधर-उधर घूमना)

47 **Amity** (N.) - (मैत्री, सौहार्द) *[#R-1 (2)]*
A friendly relationship

Syno: Goodwill (सद्भाव) {Friendship (मित्रता)}

48 **Amorous** (Adj.) - (कामुक)
Showing, feeling, or relating to sexual desire

Syno: Erotic (कामोत्तेजक)

49 **Amputate** (V.) - (अंग काटना)
To cut off a limb, typically by surgical operation

Syno: Sever (अलग करना)

50 Amusement (N.) - (मनोरंजन) *[#R-2]*
The state or experience of finding something funny or enjoyable

[Bold SN, indicates that it has been asked in Spelling]

 [In Word, ~ indicates that it has been asked in OWS]

Syno: Pleasure (आनंद), Entertainment (मनोरंजन)

51 Analogy (N.) - (समरूपता)~
Comparison between two different things that highlights their similarities
Syno: Comparison (तुलना)

52 **Analytical** (Adj.) - (विश्लेषणात्मक)
Relating to or using analysis or logical reasoning
Syno: Logical (तार्किक)

53 **Anchorite** (N.) - (तपस्वी)
A person who lives alone for religious reasons
Syno: Hermit (संन्यासी)

54 **Anger** (N.) - (क्रोध) *[#R-4]*
A strong feeling of annoyance or hostility
Syno: Fury (प्रकोप), Rage (प्रकोप), Displeasure (असंतोष)

55 Anguish (N.) - (पीड़ा) *[#R-4]*
Severe mental or physical pain or suffering
Syno: Agony (यातना), Ache (दर्द), Sorrow (दुःख), Pain (वेदना)

56 Animation (N.) - (उत्साह)
The state of being lively or full of energy
Syno: Ebullience (प्रफुल्लता)

57 Announce (V.) - (घोषणा करना) *[#R-2]*
To make a public or formal declaration
Syno: Advertise (विज्ञापन करना), Declare (घोषित करना)

58 Annul (V.) - (रद्द करना) *[#R-1 (1)]*
To declare invalid (an official agreement, decision, or result)
Syno: Invalidate (अमान्य करना) {Terminate (समाप्त करना)}

59 **Answer** (N.) - (जवाब)
A reply or solution
Syno: Reply (उत्तर)

60 **Antagonist** (N.) - (विरोधी)~ *[#R-2]*
A person who opposes or is hostile to another
Syno: Opponent (प्रतिद्वंद्वी), Adversary (विपक्षी)

61 **Anthology** (N.) - (साहित्यिक संग्रह)~
A collection of poems, stories, etc. written by different people
Syno: Collection (संकलन)

62 Anticipate (V.) - (पूर्वानुमान करना)~ *[#R-5 (1)]*
To expect or prepare for something in advance
Syno: Expect (उम्मीद करना), Predict (भविष्यवाणी करना)

63 **Apogee** (N.) - (उच्चतम बिंदु)~
The highest point
Syno: Peak (शिखर)

64 **Aporetic** (Adj.) - (उलझन में)
Full of doubt or confusion
Syno: Conflicted (दुविधाग्रस्त)

65 **Appalled** (Adj.) - (स्तब्ध) *[#R-1 (2)]*
Greatly shocked or horrified
Syno: Disgusted (घृणा से भरा हुआ) {Alarmed (घबराया हुआ)}

66 Appeal (N.) - (आकर्षण)
The quality that makes someone or something attractive
Syno: Charm (मनोहरता)

67 Appear (V.) - (दिखाई देना)
To come into sight or become noticeable
Syno: Seem (प्रतीत होना)

68 Application (N.) - (प्रयोग)
The act of putting something into use
Syno: Implementation (अमल)

69 Aptitude (N.) - (योग्यता)
A natural ability to do something
Syno: Talent (प्रतिभा)

70 **Artful** (Adj.) - (चालाक) *[#R-3]*
Clever or skilful, typically in a crafty or cunning way
Syno: Cunning (चतुर), Crafty (कपटी)

71 **Ascription** (N.) - (आरोपण)
Giving credit or blame to someone
Syno: Attribution (आरोपण)

72 Asleep (Adj.) - (सोया हुआ)
In a state of sleep
Syno: Dormant (सुप्त)

73 **Asphyxiating** (Adj.) - (दम घुटने वाला)
Causing unconsciousness or death by preventing access to air
Syno: Smothering (दमघोंटू)

74 **Assail** (V.) - (हमला करना)
To make a concerted or violent attack on
Syno: Attack (आक्रमण करना)

75 Assess (V.) - (मूल्यांकन करना)
To evaluate or estimate the nature, ability, or quality of
Syno: Measure (मापना)

76 Assimilation (N.) - (आत्मसात)~

The process of taking in and fully understanding

Syno: Absorption (अवशोषण)

77 **Assume** (V.) - (मान लेना)
To suppose something without proof

Syno: Think (सोचना)

78 **Astonish** (V.) - (आश्चर्यचकित करना)
To surprise someone greatly

Syno: Stun (चकित करना)

79 **Astound** (V.) - (हैरान कर देना) *[#R-2]*
To shock or surprise someone very much

Syno: Bewilder (हक्का-बक्का कर देना)

80 **Atrocity** (N.) - (अत्याचार) *[#R-2]*
An extremely cruel or violent act

Syno: Barbarity (क्रूरता), Violence (हिंसा)

81 **Attain** (V.) - (प्राप्त करना) *[#R-2 (1)]*
To succeed in achieving something desired

Syno: Achieve (हासिल करना)

82 **Attire** (N.) - (पोशाक)
Clothing or garments worn

Syno: Dress (कपड़े)

83 **Attribute** (N.) - (गुण) *[#R-2]*
A quality or feature

Syno: Characteristic (विशेषता), Quality (गुणवत्ता)

84 **Attune** (V.) - (अनुकूल करना)
To make something in harmony

Syno: Assimilate (अपनाना)

85 **Aura** (N.) - (प्रभामंडल)
A distinctive atmosphere surrounding someone or something

Syno: Halo (तेजोमंडल)

86 **Autocratic** (Adj.) - (एकतंत्रीय)
Relating to a ruler who has absolute power

Syno: Dictatorial (तानाशाही)

87 **Avaricious** (Adj.) - (लालची)~
Having extreme greed

Syno: Greedy (लोभी)

88 **Avenge** (V.) - (बदला लेना)
To inflict harm in return for an injury

Syno: Punish (दंडित करना)

89 **Awe** (N.) - (आदर; भय मिश्रित श्रद्धा)
A feeling of wonder mixed with respect and fear

Syno: Admiration (प्रशंसा)

90 **Awry** (Adj.) - (तिरछा) *[#R-3]*
Out of correct position

Syno: Crooked (टेढ़ा), Askew (एक तरफ झुका हुआ)

91 **Backfire** (V.) - (उल्टा पड़ जाना) *[#R-1 (1)]*
To have the opposite effect and cause failure

Syno: Collapse (विफल होना) {Rebound (पलटना)}

92 **Backstab** (V.) - (धोखा देना)
To secretly harm or betray someone who trusts you

Syno: Betray (विश्वासघात करना)

93 **Bait** (N.) - (चारा)
Food used to entice fish or animals as prey

Syno: Allurement (प्रलोभन)

94 **Ban** (V.) - (प्रतिबंध लगाना)
To officially or legally prohibit something

Syno: Prohibit (रोकना)

95 **Banality** (N.) - (साधारणता)
The lack of originality or interest

Syno: Triviality (महत्वहीनता)

96 **Bang** (V.) - (ज़ोर से मारना)
To strike or put down forcefully and noisily

Syno: Beat (पीटना)

97 **Banish** (V.) - (निर्वासित करना) *[#R-7 (2)]*
To send someone away from a country as punishment

Syno: Expel (निकाल देना), Exile (देश-निकाला देना), Deport (देश से निकालना), Relegate (नीचे स्तर पर भेजना) {Dispel (दूर करना)}

98 **Bankrupt** (Adj.) - (दिवालिया)~
Unable to pay debts

Syno: Insolvent (कर्ज़ में डूबा हुआ)

99 **Banner** (N.) - (पताका)
A long strip of cloth bearing a slogan or design

Syno: Poster (विज्ञापन-पत्र)

100 **Banter** (N.) - (हंसी-ठिठोली)~ *[#R-2]*
Playful teasing talk

Syno: Repartee (हाजिर जवाबी)

101 **Barbed** (Adj.) - (काँटेदार, चुभने वाला (शब्द/वाक्य))
Having sharp points; using unkind or critical words

Syno: Spiteful (द्वेषपूर्ण)

102 **Bargain** (N.) - (सस्ता सौदा) *[#R-2]*
A good deal; something bought at a low price

Syno: Deal (सौदा)

103 **Bashful** (Adj.) - (शर्मीला) *[#R-4]*
Reluctant to draw attention to oneself; shy

Syno: Shy (लजीला), Introverted (अंतर्मुखी)

104 **Batter** (V.) - (बार-बार मारना)
To hit repeatedly and violently
Syno: Beat (पीटना)

105 Battle (N.) - (युद्ध)
A long fight between large armed groups
Syno: Combat (संघर्ष)

106 **Bawdy** (Adj.) - (अश्लील, भद्दा)
Showing rude or sexual humour in an offensive way
Syno: Coarse (अशिष्ट)

107 **Beckon** (V.) - (इशारे से बुलाना)
To make a gesture with the hand, arm, or head to encourage someone to come nearer or follow
Syno: Call (बुलाना)

108 Behaviour (N.) - (व्यवहार)
The way in which one acts or conducts oneself, especially towards others
Syno: Conduct (आचरण)

109 Behold (V.) - (देखना)
To see or observe someone or something, especially of remarkable or impressive nature
Syno: Look (नज़र डालना)

110 **Behoove** (V.) - (उचित होना)
To be appropriate or necessary for someone
Syno: Befit (उपयुक्त होना)

111 Belief (N.) - (विश्वास)
An acceptance that something exists or is true
Syno: Faith (आस्था)

112 Beneficiary (N.) - (लाभार्थी)~
A person who derives advantage from something
Syno: Recipient (प्राप्तकर्ता)

113 Benefit (N.) - (फायदा)
An advantage or profit
Syno: Advantage (फायदा)

114 Bereft (Adj.) - (वंचित)~ *[#R-1 (1)]*
Deprived of or lacking something
Syno: Deprived (वंचित)

115 **Berserk** (Adj.) - (पागल)
Out of control with anger
Syno: Demented (विक्षिप्त)

116 **Bestial** (Adj.) - (जानवरों जैसा, असभ्य)
Like an animal; brutal or savage
Syno: Brutish (पाशविक, निर्दयी)

117 Bewilderment (N.) - (भौचक्कापन)
A state of being confused and puzzled
Syno: Confusion (उलझन)

118 **Bewitch** (V.) - (मोहित करना) *[#R-2]*
To cast a spell over someone or gain control by magic
Syno: Captivate (मोहित करना), Allure (लुभाना)

119 **Bibliophile** (N.) - (पुस्तक प्रेमी)~ *[#R-3]*
A person who loves or collects books
Syno: Booklover (किताबों का शौकीन)

120 **Bind** (V.) - (बाँधना) *[#R-4]*
To tie or fasten something tightly
Syno: Fasten (कसना), Secure (सुरक्षित करना), Unite (एकजुट करना)

121 **Bitterness** (N.) - (कड़वाहट)
An angry or resentful feeling due to bad experiences
Syno: Rancour (द्वेष)

122 **Blabber** (V.) - (बकवास करना)
To talk foolishly or too much
Syno: Prattle (बड़बड़ाना)

123 Blast (V.) - (विस्फोट करना)
To explode or release something with great force
Syno: Blow Up (उड़ा देना)

124 Blink (V.) - (पलक झपकाना)
To shut and open the eyes quickly
Syno: Flicker (झिलमिलाना)

125 Blister (N.) - (फफ़ोला, छाला) *[#R-2]*
A small bubble on the skin filled with fluid
Syno: Bubble (बुलबुला)

126 **Blitz** (N.) - (तेज़ हमला) *[#R-1 (1)]*
A sudden, intense military attack
Syno: Assault (हमला) {Attack (आक्रमण)}

127 **Blunder** (N./V.) - (भूल; गलती करना) *[#R-1 (1)]*
A careless or stupid mistake (N.); To make such a mistake (V.)
Syno: Mistake (गलती) {Fumble (गड़बड़ करना)}

128 Board (N.) - (खानपान)~
Meals provided
Syno: Food (भोजन)

129 **Bolster** (V.) - (मजबूत करना)
To support or make stronger

Syno: Strengthen (सशक्त करना)

130 **Bonanza** (N.) - (अप्रत्याशित लाभ)
A sudden increase in wealth or good fortune
Syno: Bonus (अतिरिक्त लाभ)

131 **Bonhomie** (N.) - (खुशमिज़ाजी) *[#R-3]*
Cheerful friendliness and easy sociability
Syno: Companionship (साथ), Friendliness (मिलनसारिता), Geniality (सौहार्दपूर्णता)

132 **Brace** (V.) - (मजबूत करना)
To stiffen, support, or prepare for difficulty
Syno: Fortify (सशक्त करना)

133 **Brat** (N.) - (बिगड़ैल बच्चा)
A child, typically a badly behaved one
Syno: Rascal (शरारती)

134 **Breakthrough** (N.) - (महत्वपूर्ण खोज)
A sudden, important discovery or development
Syno: Discovery (खोज)

135 **Breezy** (Adj.) - (हवादार)
Pleasantly windy and fresh
Syno: Airy (हवादार)

136 **Broken** (Adj.) - (टूटा हुआ)
Damaged and not in one piece or working
Syno: Fragmented (खंडित)

137 **Brutalize** (V.) - (अत्याचार करना)
To treat in a savage and violent way
Syno: Ill-Treat (बुरा व्यवहार करना)

138 **Buddy** (N.) - (साथी)
A close friend
Syno: Associate (सहयोगी)

139 **Bulky** (Adj.) - (भारी) *[#R-1 (1)]*
Taking up much space, typically inconveniently; large and unwieldy
Syno: Massive (विशाल) {Enormous (अत्यधिक बड़ा)}

140 **Bull-Headed** (Adj.) - (जिद्दी)
Stubborn or obstinate
Syno: Headstrong (हठी)

141 **Bully** (N.) - (डराने-धमकाने वाला)
A person who intimidates, threatens, or mistreats someone weaker
Syno: Oppressor (दबाने वाला)

142 Bumptious (Adj.) - (अहंकारी)
Self-assertive or proud to an irritating degree
Syno: Conceited (घमंडी)

143 **Burden** (N.) - (बोझ)
A heavy load or responsibility
Syno: Load (भार)

144 **Burgle** (V.) - (सेंधमारी करना)
To enter illegally with intent to commit a crime, especially theft
Syno: Rob (चोरी करना)

145 **Cadaverous** (Adj.) - (मुर्दे जैसा, अत्यधिक कमजोर और पीला)~
Looking pale and thin, corpse-like
Syno: Pale (पीला-सा)

146 **Cadence** (N.) - (लय)~
A rhythmic flow of sounds or words
Syno: Rhythm (ताल)

147 **Caginess** (N.) - (चालाकी, जानकारी छिपाना)
A reluctance to give information owing to caution
Syno: Guilefulness (चतुराई)

148 **Calculating** (Adj.) - (चालाक)
Acting in a planned, often selfish way
Syno: Manipulative (छल करने वाला)

149 Calculation (N.) - (गणना)
A mathematical determination of size or number
Syno: Counting (गिनती)

150 **Caliber** (N.) - (क्षमता)
The quality of someone's character or ability level
Syno: Capacity (सामर्थ्य)

151 Calibrate (V.) - (मानकीकृत करना) *[#R-2 (1)]*
To mark a gauge with a standard scale
Syno: Gauge (मापना), Adjust (समायोजित करना) {Regulate (नियंत्रित करना)}

152 Calumny (N.) - (बदनामी, झूठा आरोप) *[#R-1 (2)]*
False statements meant to damage reputation
Syno: Slander (मानहानि)

153 Cancel (V.) - (रद्द करना)
To decide that a planned event will not occur
Syno: Abolish (निरस्त करना)

154 **Canny** (Adj.) - (चालाक)
Showing shrewdness and good judgment
Syno: Clever (होशियार)

155 Capitulate (V.) - (हथियार डालना)~ *[#R-3]*
To stop resisting and surrender; to accept defeat
Syno: Surrender (आत्मसमर्पण करना)

156 **Caprice** (N.) - (सनक)
A sudden and unpredictable change in mood or behavior
Syno: Impulse (अचानक आई इच्छा)

157 **Carcass** (N.) - (शव)~
The dead body of an animal
Syno: Corpse (मृत शरीर)

158 Careful (Adj.) - (सावधान)
Using attention to avoid mistakes or danger; showing caution
Syno: Cautious (सतर्क)

159 **Caress** (V.) - (प्यार से छूना)
To touch lovingly
Syno: Embrace (गले लगाना)

160 Caricature (N.) - (व्यंग्यात्मक चित्रण)~
An exaggerated representation for comic effect
Syno: Exaggeration (अतिशयोक्ति)

161 **Carnage** (N.) - (नरसंहार)~
A large-scale slaughter or loss of life
Syno: Slaughter (हत्याकांड)

162 **Carnival** (N.) - (उत्सव)~
A public festival featuring music and dancing
Syno: Fest (उत्सव)

163 **Carouse** (V.) - (शराब पीकर मौज-मस्ती करना) *[#R-2]*
To drink alcohol and enjoy oneself noisily
Syno: Frolic (उल्लास मनाना), Quaff (उत्साह से पीना)

164 **Cascade** (N.) - (झरना)~
A waterfall
Syno: Waterfall (जलप्रपात)

165 **Castigate** (V.) - (कड़ी निंदा करना) *[#R-1 (2)]*
To criticize or punish someone severely
Syno: Condemn (निंदा करना)

166 **Catalyst** (N.) - (उत्प्रेरक)~
A substance or person that speeds up change
Syno: Activator (सक्रियक)

167 **Catalyze** (V.) - (प्रेरित करना) *[#R-2]*
To cause or speed up a reaction
Syno: Initiate (शुरू करना), Accelerate (तेज़ करना)

168 **Cavil** (V.) - (कमी निकालना) *[#R-1 (2)]*
To raise petty objections
Syno: Quibble (तर्क-वितर्क करना) {Complain (शिकायत करना)}

169 **Cavity** (N.) - (गड्ढा)
A hollow space or hole
Syno: Hole (छेद)

170 **Cavort** (V.) - (कूदना)
To jump or dance around excitedly
Syno: Jump (उछलना)

171 Ceremonial (Adj.) - (औपचारिक) *[#R-1 (1)]*
Relating to formal public events
Syno: Formal (औपचारिक)

172 **Chafe** (V.) - (चिढ़ना, चिढ़ाना)~
To feel or cause irritation
Syno: Irritate (चिढ़ाना)

173 Character (N.) - (चरित्र)
The mental and moral qualities of a person
Syno: Trait (विशेषता)

174 **Characterize** (V.) - (वर्णन करना)
To describe the distinctive qualities of
Syno: Delineate (चित्रित करना)

175 Charisma (N.) - (आकर्षण)~ *[#R-2]*
A compelling personal charm that inspires devotion
Syno: Charm (मोहकता)

176 **Chary** (Adj.) - (सतर्क)
Cautiously or suspiciously reluctant to do something
Syno: Cautious (सावधान)

177 **Cheer** (V.) - (उत्साहित करना)
To give comfort or support to
Syno: Encourage (प्रोत्साहित करना)

178 **Cheerless** (Adj.) - (उदास)
Lacking cheerful enthusiasm or brightness
Syno: Gloomy (मायूस)

179 **Choke** (V.) - (गला घोंटना)
To prevent someone from breathing
Syno: Block (अवरोधित करना)

180 **Choosy** (Adj.) - (नकचढ़ा) *[#R-2]*
Excessively picky or hard to please
Syno: Selective (चयनशील), Picky (नखरेबाज़)

181 **Chorus** (N.) - (सामूहिक गायन)
A large organized group of singers
Syno: Choir (गायक मंडली)

182 **Circumstantial** (Adj.) - (परिस्थितिजन्य)~
Based on indirect evidence or surrounding circumstances, not on direct proof
Syno: Indirect (अप्रत्यक्ष)

183 **Circumvent** (V.) - (चकमा देना)
To find a way around an obstacle

Syno: Escape (बच निकलना)

184 **Citadel** (N.) - (किला)~
A fortress protecting or dominating a city
Syno: Fortress (गढ़)

185 Clairvoyant (Adj.) - (भविष्यदर्शी)
Having psychic powers
Syno: Prophetic (भविष्यसूचक)

186 Clarify (V.) - (स्पष्ट करना)
To make clear
Syno: Illustrate (समझाना)

187 **Clasp** (N.) - (पकड़)
A fastening device
Syno: Catch (पकड़)

188 **Clean** (Adj.) - (साफ़)
Free from dirt or moral corruption
Syno: Honest (ईमानदार)

189 **Clement** (Adj.) - (सौम्य)
Mild, especially of weather
Syno: Mild (नरम)

190 Clever (Adj.) - (चतुर) *[#R-2]*
Quick to understand
Syno: Intelligent (बुद्धिमान)

191 Client (N.) - (ग्राहक)
A person who uses professional services
Syno: Customer (खरीदार)

192 **Climax** (N.) - (शिखर)
The most intense, exciting, or important point
Syno: Culmination (चरम)

193 **Clinch** (V.) - (पक्का करना)
To confirm or settle a contract or bargain
Syno: Finalize (अंतिम रूप देना)

194 Cloistered (Adj.) - (एकान्तवासी)
Kept away from the outside world; sheltered
Syno: Isolated (अलग-थलग)

195 **Cloudburst** (N.) - (बादल फटना)
A sudden and very heavy rainfall
Syno: Rainstorm (बारिश का तूफान)

196 **Clout** (N.) - (प्रभाव)
Power or influence, especially social or political
Syno: Power (शक्ति)

197 **Cocoon** (N.) - (सुरक्षा कवच)
A protective case or shelter
Syno: Encasement (आवरण)

198 Coddle (V.) - (लाड़ प्यार करना) *[#R-2 (1)]*
To treat in an indulgent or overprotective way
Syno: Pamper (लाड़ करना), Indulge (लाड़-प्यार करना)

199 Cognitive (Adj.) - (बौद्धिक)
Related to thinking, knowing, and understanding
Syno: Mental (मानसिक)

200 Coincidence (N.) - (संयोग)~
A remarkable concurrence of events without apparent causal connection
Syno: Chance (संयोग)

201 Collaborate (V.) - (मिलकर काम करना)
To work jointly on an activity or project
Syno: Collude (मिलीभगत करना)

202 **Collate** (V.) - (एकत्र करना) *[#R-1 (1)]*
To collect and combine texts, information, or data
Syno: Assemble (इकट्ठा करना)

203 Colleague (N.) - (सहकर्मी)~ *[#R-1 (1)]*
A person with whom one works in a profession or business
Syno: Co-Worker (सहयोगी)

204 Combustible (Adj.) - (ज्वलनशील) *[#R-1 (1)]*
Able to catch fire and burn easily
Syno: Inflammable (ज्वलनशील)

205 Commemorate (V.) - (पुण्यस्मरण करना)~
To recall and show respect in a ceremony
Syno: Celebrate (उत्सव मनाना)

206 **Commerce** (N.) - (व्यापार)
The activity of buying and selling, especially on a large scale
Syno: Trade (व्यवसाय)

207 **Commute** (V.) - (परिवर्तित करना)
To travel between home and work; to change one thing into another
Syno: Convert (बदलना)

208 Companion (N.) - (साथी) *[#R-1 (5)]*
A person or animal with whom one spends time or travels
Syno: Mate (संगी) {Comrade (सहचर)}

209 Compensate (V.) - (मुआवजा देना) *[#R-1 (1)]*
To give money or benefit as reparation for loss
Syno: Reimburse (क्षतिपूर्ति करना)

210 Complaisant (Adj.) - (विनम्र)
Eager to please
Syno: Submissive (आज्ञाकारी)

211 Compliance (N.) - (अनुपालन)
The act of obeying or agreeing to a rule
Syno: Consent (सहमति)

212 Comprehend (V.) - (समझना) *[#R-3]*
To understand something mentally
Syno: Understand (समझना), Assimilate (पूरी तरह से समझ लेना), Grasp (बूझना)

213 **Compulsion** (N.) - (बाध्यता) *[#R-2]*
The action of forcing or being forced to do something
Syno: Obligation (दायित्व, बंधन)

214 **Compunction** (N.) - (पश्चाताप)~ *[#R-2]*
A feeling of guilt or moral scruple
Syno: Scruple (नैतिक संकोच), Remorse (पछतावा)

215 Concession (N.) - (रियायत) *[#R-2]*
A thing granted in response to demands
Syno: Allowance (छूट, भत्ता)

216 Conclude (V.) - (समाप्त करना) *[#R-1 (1)]*
To bring something to an end
Syno: End (अंत करना) {Terminate (समाप्त करना)}

217 **Concoct** (V.) - (कहानी बनाना)
To invent or create a story or plan
Syno: Fabricate (मनगढ़ंत करना)

218 **Concordant** (Adj.) - (सुसंगत)
In agreement
Syno: Harmonious (सामंजस्यपूर्ण)

219 Concurrence (N.) - (सहमति)
The fact of having the same opinion
Syno: Agreement (सहमति)

220 **Condescending** (Adj.) - (दूसरों को नीचा जताने वाला)
Having or showing patronizing superiority
Syno: Patronising (नीचा दिखाने वाला)

221 Condescension (N.) - (श्रेष्ठता का दिखावा)
An attitude of patronizing superiority
Syno: Disdain (तिरस्कार)

222 Confiscate (V.) - (जब्त करना)~ *[#R-2]*
To take or seize someone's property with authority
Syno: Seize (जब्त करना)

223 Conflagration (N.) - (भीषण आग) *[#R-2]*
An extensive fire that destroys a great deal of property
Syno: Fire (आग)

224 Congestion (N.) - (भीड़भाड़)
The state of being very full of people or traffic
Syno: Gridlock (ट्रैफिक जाम)

225 Congregation (N.) - (समूह)~ *[#R-2]*
A group of people assembled for religious worship
Syno: Assembly (सभा), Meeting (बैठक)

226 **Congruent** (Adj.) - (समरूप) *[#R-1 (1)]*
In agreement or harmony
Syno: Identical (समान) {Coinciding (मेल खाता हुआ)}

227 **Congruous** (Adj.) - (संगत) *[#R-1 (1)]*
In agreement or harmony
Syno: Balanced (संतुलित) {Harmonious (सामंजस्यपूर्ण)}

228 Conjure (V.) - (जादू करना) *[#R-2]*
To make something appear unexpectedly or seemingly from nowhere as if by magic
Syno: Invoke (आह्वान करना), Appeal (आकर्षित करना)

229 **Conjurer** (N.) - (जादूगर)
A person who performs magic tricks to amuse an audience
Syno: Magician (बाज़ीगर)

230 Connoisseur (N.) - (विशेषज्ञ)~
An expert judge in matters of taste
Syno: Judge (परखने वाला)

231 **Connote** (V.) - (अतिरिक्त अर्थ सूचित करना) *[#R-2]*
To imply or suggest an idea or feeling in addition to the literal meaning
Syno: Convey (सूचित करना)

232 Consciousness (N.) - (चेतना) *[#R-2]*
The state of being awake and aware of one's surroundings
Syno: Awareness (जागरूकता)

233 **Conscript** (N.) - (जबरन भर्ती किया गया व्यक्ति)
A person forced into military service
Syno: Draftee (सेना में भर्ती किया गया व्यक्ति)

234 **Consecutive** (Adj.) - (लगातार)
Following continuously
Syno: Successive (क्रमागत)

235 Consequence (N.) - (परिणाम) *[#R-2 (1)]*
A result or effect of an action or condition
Syno: Outcome (नतीजा) {Result (परिणाम)}

236 Consequent (Adj.) - (परिणामस्वरूप)
Following as a result or effect
Syno: Ensuing (परिणामी)

237 Conservation (N.) - (संरक्षण)~
The action of conserving something
Syno: Preservation (संरक्षण)

238 **Consignee** (N.) - (प्राप्तकर्ता)
The person to whom something is shipped
Syno: Recipient (प्राप्तकर्ता)

239 **Consort** (N.) - (साथी) *[#R-2]*
Companion or spouse, especially of a king or queen
Syno: Partner (साथी)

240 Conspiracy (N.) - (षड्यंत्र)~
A secret plan to do harm
Syno: Plot (साजिश)

241 Constraint (N.) - (प्रतिबंध) *[#R-2]*
A limitation or restriction
Syno: Control (नियंत्रण), Restrictions (रोक)

242 Consult (V.) - (राय लेना)
To seek information or advice
Syno: Discuss (चर्चा करना)

243 **Contagion** (N.) - (संक्रमण)~
The spread of disease by contact
Syno: Transmission (प्रसारण)

244 **Contemplation** (N.) - (चिंतन) *[#R-2 (1)]*
The action of thinking deeply
Syno: Meditation (ध्यान), Reflection (चिंतन) {Introspection (आत्मचिंतन)}

245 Contemptible (Adj.) - (घृणास्पद)
Deserving contempt; despicable
Syno: Abhorrent (घृणित)

246 Contemptuous (Adj.) - (अनादरपूर्ण) *[#R-1 (9)]*
Showing strong dislike or disrespect
Syno: Derisive (मज़ाक उड़ाने वाला) {Disrespectful (अनादरयुक्त), Disdainful (तिरस्कारपूर्ण)}

247 **Contingent** (Adj.) - (आकस्मिक) *[#R-1 (1)]*
Occurring by chance; not certain
Syno: Accidental (आकस्मिक)

248 **Contraband** (Adj.) - (अवैध, प्रतिबंधित)~
Illegally traded
Syno: Smuggled (तस्करी किया हुआ)

249 **Contravene** (V.) - (उल्लंघन करना)
To violate the prohibition or order of a law or treaty
Syno: Breach (भंग करना)

250 **Contrite** (Adj.) - (पश्चातापी) *[#R-4]*
Feeling or expressing remorse; affected by guilt
Syno: Regretful (खेदपूर्ण), Remorseful (पश्चातापपूर्ण)

251 **Controvert** (V.) - (अस्वीकार करना)
To deny the truth of something
Syno: Contradict (खंडन करना)

252 **Conundrum** (N.) - (पहेली)~ *[#R-2 (2)]*
A confusing and difficult problem or question
Syno: Problem (समस्या) {Confusion (भ्रम)}

253 **Converge** (V.) - (मिलना) *[#R-1 (1)]*
To come together from different directions to meet
Syno: Coincide (संयोग से मिलना) {Merge (विलीन होना)}

254 Converse (V.) - (बातचीत करना)
To engage in conversation
Syno: Talk (वार्तालाप करना)

255 Convert (V.) - (परिवर्तित करना)
To cause to change in form, character, or function
Syno: Transform (रूपांतरित करना)

256 **Cornucopia** (N.) - (प्रचुरता) *[#R-2]*
A symbol of abundance and nourishment
Syno: Abundance (बाहुल्य), Profusion (बहुतायत)

257 **Corrective** (Adj.) - (सुधारात्मक)
Designed to correct or counteract something harmful
Syno: Restorative (पुनर्स्थापनकारी)

258 **Corridor** (N.) - (गलियारा)
A long passage in a building with doors to rooms
Syno: Passage (मार्ग)

259 **Coruscate** (V.) - (चमकना)
To sparkle or flash with light
Syno: Sparkle (जगमगाना)

260 Counsel (N.) - (सलाह)
Formal advice
Syno: Advice (परामर्श)

261 **Cove** (N.) - (खाड़ी)
A small sheltered bay
Syno: Bay (खाड़ी)

262 Covenant (N.) - (संविदा) *[#R-2]*
An agreement

Syno: Contract (अनुबंध), Bond (बंधपत्र)

263 Coveted (Adj.) - (इच्छित)
Greatly desired or envied
Syno: Desired (चाहा हुआ)

264 **Craven** (Adj.) - (डरपोक) *[#R-1 (2)]*
Contemptibly lacking in courage
Syno: Cowardly (कायर)

265 **Crescendo** (N.) - (उत्कर्ष) *[#R-2 (1)]*
The loudest point in a gradually increasing sound
Syno: Climax (चरम बिंदु), Escalation (वृद्धि) {Upsurge (उछाल)}

266 **Critically** (Adv.) - (आलोचनात्मक रूप से)
In a way that expresses disapproval or judgment
Syno: Severely (कठोरता से)

267 **Cruddy** (Adj.) - (गंदा)
Dirty, unpleasant, or of poor quality
Syno: Dirty (मैला)

268 **Cruise** (N.) - (समुद्री यात्रा)
A leisure journey by ship
Syno: Voyage (समुद्र यात्रा)

269 Crust (N.) - (परत)
The tough outer part of a loaf of bread
Syno: Shell (खोल)

270 **Crux** (N.) - (सार) *[#R-3 (1)]*
The decisive or most important point at issue
Syno: Essence (मूल), Gist (सार) {Core (केंद्र)}

271 **Curative** (Adj.) - (रोगनिवारक)
Able to cure disease
Syno: Healing (उपचारात्मक)

272 Custom (N.) - (रीति-रिवाज)
A traditional practice
Syno: Habit (आदत)

273 **Customise** (V.) - (अनुकूलित करना)
To modify according to individual needs
Syno: Personalise (व्यक्तिगत बनाना)

274 **Cute** (Adj.) - (प्यारा)
Attractive in a pretty or endearing way
Syno: Charming (आकर्षक)

275 **Dame** (N.) - (प्रतिष्ठित महिला)
A woman awarded a British title equivalent to knight
Syno: Lady (स्त्री)

276 **Damsel** (N.) - (अविवाहित युवती)
A young unmarried woman
Syno: Maiden (कुँवारी)

277 **Dandy** (Adj.) - (बहुत आकर्षक)
Very good or stylish
Syno: Beautiful (सुंदर)

278 **Danger** (N.) - (खतरा) *[#R-1 (2)]*
The possibility of suffering harm or injury
Syno: Hazard (जोखिम) {Peril (संकट)}

279 **Dapper** (Adj.) - (सजा-धजा)
Neat and trim in dress or appearance
Syno: Stylish (बना-ठना)

280 **Deadly** (Adj.) - (जानलेवा) *[#R-2 (2)]*
Causing or able to cause death
Syno: Fatal (प्राणघातक) {Lethal (घातक)}

281 **Debased** (Adj.) - (भ्रष्ट)
Reduced in quality, value, or dignity
Syno: Corrupted (भ्रष्ट)

282 Decadence (N.) - (पतन) *[#R-1 (1)]*
Moral or cultural decline characterized by excessive indulgence
Syno: Decline (गिरावट) {Degeneration (क्षय)}

283 **Decapitate** (V.) - (सिर काट देना) *[#R-2]*
Cut off the head of (a person or animal)
Syno: Behead (सिर काटना)

284 Decency (N.) - (शिष्टता)
The quality of being proper and morally acceptable
Syno: Courtesy (शिष्टाचार)

285 Declension (N.) - (पतन)
Deviation from moral standards
Syno: Decay (क्षय)

286 **Declining** (Adj.) - (घटते हुए)
Becoming less in strength or quality
Syno: Decreasing (घटता हुआ)

287 Decrease (N.) - (कमी)
A reduction in amount or size
Syno: Decline (गिरावट)

288 **Decree** (N.) - (अदालती हुक्म)
An official legal order
Syno: Verdict (निर्णय)

289 **Decrepit** (Adj.) - (निर्बल) *[#R-2]*
Worn out, weak, or in a ruined condition
Syno: Feeble (दुर्बल), Wrecked (बुरी हालत में)

290 **Decrepitude** (N.) - (जर्जरता)
A state of extreme weakness or decay

Syno: Feebleness (कमज़ोरी)

291 **Dedicate** (V.) - (समर्पित करना) *[#R-3 (2)]*
To devote to a task or purpose
Syno: Devote (समर्पण करना), Commit (प्रतिबद्ध होना)

292 **Deepen** (V.) - (गहरा करना)
To make something deeper or stronger
Syno: Intensify (तीव्र करना)

293 **Defect** (N.) - (दोष) *[#R-1 (1)]*
A fault or imperfection in something
Syno: Flaw (त्रुटि) {Shortcoming (कमी)}

294 Deference (N.) - (आदर) *[#R-3]*
Polite respect shown to someone due to status
Syno: Respect (सम्मान), Obeisance (अभिवादन)

295 **Deft** (Adj.) - (निपुण) *[#R-1 (3)]*
Showing skill and quickness
Syno: Skilful (कुशल)

296 **Dehydrated** (Adj.) - (निर्जलित)
Suffering from excessive loss of water
Syno: Drained (सूखा हुआ)

297 **Delectable** (Adj.) - (स्वादिष्ट) *[#R-1 (2)]*
Very pleasant to taste or enjoy
Syno: Luscious (रसीला) {Delicious (लज़ीज़), Pleasant (सुखद)}

298 **Delinquent** (Adj.) - (कर्तव्यहीन)~
Failing in duty or law
Syno: Offending (उल्लंघनकारी)

299 Deliver (V.) - (वितरित करना) *[#R-1 (1)]*
To take and give to the right person or place
Syno: Deposit (सौंपना)

300 **Demise** (N.) - (मृत्यु) *[#R-1 (2)]*
A person's death
Syno: Death (मौत)

301 **Denizen** (N.) - (निवासी)
An inhabitant or occupant of a particular place
Syno: Inhabitant (निवासी)

302 **Denouement** (N.) - (अंतिम परिणाम) *[#R-2]*
The concluding resolution of a narrative
Syno: Conclusion (उपसंहार), Resolution (समाधान)

303 **Deposition** (N.) - (शपथपूर्वक बयान)
The process of giving sworn evidence
Syno: Testimony (गवाही)

304 **Deride** (V.) - (मज़ाक उड़ाना)~ *[#R-3 (2)]*
To express contempt for; to ridicule
Syno: Mock (मज़ाक उड़ाना), Ridicule (उपहास करना), Taunt (ताना मारना) {Disdain (तिरस्कार करना)}

305 **Derive** (V.) - (प्राप्त करना)
To get or obtain something from a source
Syno: Obtain (हासिल करना)

306 Description (N.) - (वर्णन)
A spoken or written account of a person, object, or event
Syno: Definition (परिभाषा)

307 Design (V.) - (रूपरेखा तैयार करना) *[#R-1 (1)]*
To plan or create something
Syno: Fabricate (निर्माण करना)

308 Desperation (N.) - (निराशा)
A state of despair resulting in rash behavior
Syno: Hopelessness (आशाहीनता)

309 **Desynchronize** (V.) - (तालमेल बिगाड़ना)
To disrupt timing or coordination
Syno: Disrupt (बाधित करना)

310 **Detain** (V.) - (रोकना) *[#R-1 (1)]*
To hold back or keep under custody
Syno: Delay (विलंब करना)

311 Detect (V.) - (पता लगाना) *[#R-1 (1)]*
To discover or identify the presence or existence of
Syno: Discover (खोज निकालना)

312 Deteriorate (V.) - (ख़राब होना) *[#R-4 (2)]*
To become progressively worse
Syno: Worsen (बिगड़ना), Dilapidate (खंडहर बनना), Retrogress (पतन होना) {Decline (गिरना)}

313 Determined (Adj.) - (दृढ़निश्चयी) *[#R-4]*
Having made a firm decision and being resolved not to change it
Syno: Resolved (संकल्पित), Resolute (दृढ़निश्चयी), Decisive (निर्णायक)

314 **Detractor** (N.) - (आलोचक)
A person who criticizes something or someone, often unfairly
Syno: Critic (निंदक)

315 **Devastate** (V.) - (नष्ट करना) *[#R-2 (2)]*
To cause complete destruction or ruin
Syno: Destroy (नष्ट करना), Destruct (नष्ट करना) {Ruin (बर्बाद करना)}

316 Devote (V.) - (समर्पित करना) *[#R-2]*
To give time or attention to
Syno: Dedicate (समर्पित करना)

317 Devour (V.) - (निगलना)
To eat eagerly or greedily
Syno: Consume (खाना)

318 Dialectic (N.) - (तर्क-वितर्क)~
The logical reasoning through discussion and arguments
Syno: Argumentation (बहस)

319 **Dicey** (Adj.) - (अनिश्चित)
Unpredictable and potentially dangerous
Syno: Uncertain (अनिश्चित)

320 Dictator (N.) - (तानाशाह)~
A ruler with total power over a country, typically obtained by force
Syno: Tyrant (अत्याचारी)

321 **Dignity** (N.) - (गौरव) *[#R-1 (1)]*
The state or quality of being worthy of honour or respect
Syno: Grace (गरिमा) {Honour (सम्मान)}

322 **Dilatory** (Adj.) - (सुस्त)~
Slow or tending to delay
Syno: Tardy (देर से आने वाला)

323 **Dilettante** (N.) - (शौकिया)~
A person who pursues an activity casually rather than seriously
Syno: Amateur (नौसिखिया)

324 Diligence (N.) - (परिश्रम)~
Careful and persistent effort
Syno: Effort (प्रयास)

325 Diminutive (Adj.) - (बहुत छोटा) *[#R-2 (1)]*
Extremely or unusually small
Syno: Miniature (छोटा रूप), Petite (छोटा सा) {Small (छोटा)}

326 **Dingy** (Adj.) - (धुंधला) *[#R-1 (2)]*
Dark and dirty looking
Syno: Dreary (फीका) {Dirty (गंदा), Dark (अंधेरा)}

327 **Disarray** (N.) - (अव्यवस्था)
A state of disorder or confusion
Syno: Disorder (अव्यवस्था)

328 Disastrous (Adj.) - (विनाशकारी)
Causing great damage
Syno: Calamitous (आपदाजनक)

329 Discern (V.) - (पहचानना) *[#R-3 (1)]*
To perceive or recognize clearly
Syno: Discriminate (भेद करना), Perceive (जानना) {Determine (निर्धारित करना)}

330 **Disclaimer** (N.) - (अस्वीकरण)
A statement denying responsibility
Syno: Denial (इनकार)

331 **Discover** (V.) - (खोजना) *[#R-2]*
To find something or someone unexpectedly
Syno: Find (खोज निकालना)

332 Disease (N.) - (बीमारी)
A sickness or harmful condition affecting the body
Syno: Illness (रोग)

333 Disguise (V.) - (भेष बदलना; पहचान छिपाना)~ *[#R-2]*
To hide identity or appearance
Syno: Camouflage (भेष बदलना), Concealment (गोपनीयता)

334 Disparaging (Adj.) - (निंदात्मक) *[#R-1 (2)]*
Expressing a low or critical opinion
Syno: Belittling (छोटा दिखाने वाला)

335 Disparity (N.) - (असमानता) *[#R-2 (2)]*
A great difference
Syno: Difference (अंतर), Diversity (विविधता) {Inequality (असमानता)}

336 **Disproportionately** (Adv.) - (असमान रूप से)
To an unequal or improper extent
Syno: Unreasonably (अतार्किक रूप से)

337 Disrupt (V.) - (भंग करना)~ *[#R-3 (1)]*
To interrupt by causing disorder or trouble
Syno: Break (तोड़ना), Disturb (परेशान करना)

338 **Dissipate** (V.) - (बर्बाद करना)
To waste, scatter, or gradually disappear
Syno: Spend (व्यय करना)

339 **Dissipated** (Adj.) - (बिखरा हुआ)
Scattered or no longer concentrated
Syno: Disappeared (गायब)

340 **Distaste** (N.) - (अरुचि)
A dislike or aversion
Syno: Loathing (नफ़रत)

341 Distinguished (Adj.) - (प्रतिष्ठित) *[#R-3 (1)]*
Very successful and highly respected
Syno: Dignified (गरिमामय), Acclaimed (प्रशंसित), Honoured (सम्मानित) {Esteemed (प्रतिष्ठित)}

342 Distraction (N.) - (ध्यान भंग)
Something that diverts attention
Syno: Confusion (भ्रम)

343 Distribute (V.) - (वितरित करना) *[#R-1 (1)]*
To give shares of something; deal out

Syno: Circulate (फैलाना)

344 Division (N.) - (विभाजन)
The act or process of separating into parts
Syno: Demarcation (सीमा-निर्धारण)

345 **Divisive** (Adj.) - (मतभेद बढ़ाने वाला)
Tending to cause disagreement or hostility between people
Syno: Conflicting (विरोधी)

346 Dodge (V.) - (चकमा देना) *[#R-4]*
To avoid or evade by quick or clever action
Syno: Avoid (टालना), Evade (बचना), Sidestep (बचकर निकलना)

347 **Doggedness** (N.) - (दृढ़ता)
Persistent determination despite difficulties
Syno: Perseverance (लगन)

348 Domicile (N.) - (निवास स्थान)~
A person's permanent residence
Syno: Home (घर)

349 **Dour** (Adj.) - (उदास)
Relentlessly severe, stern, or gloomy in manner or appearance
Syno: Morose (गमगीन)

350 **Drag** (V.) - (खींचना) *[#R-3]*
To pull with effort or force
Syno: Pull (खींचना)

351 **Dread** (N.) - (डर)
Great fear
Syno: Fear (भय)

352 Dreaded (Adj.) - (भयानक)
Regarded with great fear or apprehension
Syno: Feared (डरावना)

353 **Drivel** (N.) - (बकवास)
Silly or meaningless talk
Syno: Blather (बकबक)

354 **Drizzle** (N.) - (बूंदाबांदी)~
Very light rain
Syno: Sprinkle (छिड़काव)

355 Drowsy (Adj.) - (नींद से भरा हुआ) *[#R-2]*
Sleepy and lethargic; half asleep
Syno: Sleepy (नींद भरा)

356 **Dubiously** (Adv.) - (संदेहपूर्वक)
In a way that shows doubt or uncertainty
Syno: Sceptically (अविश्वास के साथ)

357 **Duct** (N.) - (नलिका) *[#R-2]*
A tube or passage for flow
Syno: Canal (नहर, नलिका)

358 **Duo** (N.) - (जोड़ी) *[#R-2]*
Two people or things together
Syno: Pair (जोड़ा)

359 **Dupe** (V.) - (धोखा देना)~
To deceive someone
Syno: Deceive (छल करना)

360 **Duplication** (N.) - (नकल)
The act or process of making a copy
Syno: Copying (नकल करना)

361 **Dust** (V.) - (धूल झाड़ना)
To remove dust from a surface by wiping or brushing
Syno: Clean (सफ़ाई करना)

362 Early (Adv.) - (जल्दी, अपेक्षा से पहले)
Sooner than expected
Syno: Beforehand (पहले से)

363 Earn (V.) - (कमाना) *[#R-3]*
To receive money or benefit as a result of work or effort
Syno: Achieve (हासिल करना), Gain (लाभ पाना), Receive (प्राप्त करना)

364 **Earnestly** (Adv.) - (ईमानदारी से) *[#R-1 (1)]*
In a sincere, serious, and honest manner
Syno: Sincerely (पूरी निष्ठा से) {Artlessly (बिना दिखावे के)}

365 **Easiness** (N.) - (सहजता)
The quality of being easy or uncomplicated
Syno: Simplicity (सरलता)

366 Ecclesial (Adj.) - (चर्च से संबंधित)
Relating to the Christian Church or its clergy
Syno: Churchly (चर्च का)

367 Echelon (N.) - (श्रेणी)
A level or rank in an organization, profession, or society
Syno: Rank (पद)

368 Echo (V.) - (गूंजना)~
To repeat or reflect sound
Syno: Reverberate (प्रतिध्वनित होना)

369 **Economical** (Adj.) - (किफ़ायती)~
Using money or resources carefully
Syno: Thrifty (मितव्ययी)

370 Ecstatic (Adj.) - (अति प्रसन्न)~
Extremely happy
Syno: Happy (खुश)

371 **Edacious** (Adj.) - (भुक्खड़)
Having an insatiable appetite for food or consumption
Syno: Gluttonous (बहुत खाने वाला)

372 Education (N.) - (शिक्षा)
The process of systematic teaching and learning
Syno: Pedagogy (शिक्षा शास्त्र)

373 Eerie (Adj.) - (भयानक) *[#R-1 (2)]*
Strange and frightening
Syno: Mysterious (रहस्यमय) {Creepy (डरावना)}

374 Effect (N.) - (प्रभाव) *[#R-1 (2)]*
A change that is the result of a cause or action
Syno: Result (परिणाम) {Impact (असर)}

375 Efficiency (N.) - (दक्षता) *[#R-2]*
The state or quality of being efficient
Syno: Capability (सामर्थ्य), Effectiveness (प्रभावशीलता)

376 Effigy (N.) - (पुतला) *[#R-1 (1)]*
A sculpture or model of a person
Syno: Dummy (प्रतिकृति)

377 **Effrontery** (N.) - (निर्लज्जता) *[#R-1 (2)]*
Shameless or rude boldness
Syno: Audacity (बेहयाई)

378 **Elapse** (V.) - (बीतना)
To pass or go by (of time)
Syno: Cease (समाप्त होना)

379 Elastic (Adj.) - (लचीला) *[#R-2]*
Able to return to normal shape after being stretched or bent
Syno: Flexible (लचीला)

380 Eligible (Adj.) - (योग्य) *[#R-1 (1)]*
Meeting conditions to do or obtain something
Syno: Qualified (योग्य)

381 **Elixir** (N.) - (अमृत)~ *[#R-1 (1)]*
A magical potion or remedy
Syno: Potion (औषधि)

382 **Elope** (V.) - (भाग जाना)~
To run away secretly to get married
Syno: Abscond (फरार होना)

383 **Embargo** (N.) - (निषेध)~ *[#R-1 (1)]*
An official ban on trade or commercial activity
Syno: Barrier (बाधा) {Ban (प्रतिबंध)}

384 **Embed** (V.) - (गाड़ना)~ *[#R-1 (1)]*
To fix an object firmly and deeply in a surrounding mass
Syno: Bury (दफनाना) {Insert (डालना)}

385 Embellish (V.) - (सजाना) *[#R-1 (2)]*
To make something more attractive by adding details
Syno: Decorate (सजाना)

386 Embezzlement (N.) - (गबन)~
The theft of funds
Syno: Misappropriation (दुरुपयोग)

387 **Emblem** (N.) - (प्रतीक)
A symbol or object representing a group or idea
Syno: Symbol (चिह्न)

388 **Embroil** (V.) - (उलझाना) *[#R-1 (1)]*
To involve someone deeply in conflict or trouble
Syno: Confuse (उलझाना)

389 Emit (V.) - (उत्सर्जन करना) *[#R-1 (2)]*
To produce and send out something
Syno: Discharge (निकालना) {Release (मुक्त करना)}

390 Emphasis (N.) - (महत्व) *[#R-2 (1)]*
Special importance or attention given to something
Syno: Attention (ध्यान), Importance (महत्व) {Stress (ज़ोर)}

391 Emphasize (V.) - (ज़ोर देना) *[#R-2]*
To give special importance to something
Syno: Stress (बल देना), Highlight (रेखांकित करना)

392 Emphatic (Adj.) - (दृढ़) *[#R-2]*
Expressed forcefully and clearly
Syno: Vigorous (जोरदार), Firm (मजबूत)

393 Empirical (Adj.) - (अनुभवसिद्ध)~
Based on observation or experience rather than theory
Syno: Practical (व्यावहारिक)

394 Encroach (V.) - (अतिक्रमण करना) *[#R-2 (1)]*
To gradually enter into another's area, rights, or property
Syno: Intrude (घुसपैठ करना)

395 Energy (N.) - (ऊर्जा)
Strength and vitality
Syno: Power (शक्ति)

396 **Enforced** (Adj.) - (लागू)
Made compulsory by authority or force
Syno: Imposed (थोपा हुआ)

397 Engage (V.) - (व्यस्त रखना) *[#R-1 (1)]*
To occupy, attract, or involve someone's interest or attention
Syno: Occupy (व्यस्त रखना)

398 Engaging (Adj.) - (आकर्षक)
Charming and attractive
Syno: Captivating (मोहक)

399 **Engender** (V.) - (उत्पन्न करना) *[#R-1 (1)]*
To cause or produce; to bring something into existence
Syno: Generate (उत्पन्न करना)

400 **Engross** (V.) - (ध्यान खींचना)
To absorb all the attention or interest of
Syno: Absorb (खींच लेना)

401 **Engrossing** (Adj.) - (रोचक)
Holding attention completely
Syno: Involving (संलग्न करने वाला)

402 **Engulf** (V.) - (निगल जाना)~ *[#R-2 (1)]*
To sweep over and cover something completely
Syno: Inundate (डुबोना), Envelop (ढाँक लेना)

403 **Enjoyable** (Adj.) - (आनंददायक)
Giving pleasure or delight
Syno: Delightful (मनोहर)

404 Enlightening (Adj.) - (ज्ञानवर्धक)
Giving knowledge or insight
Syno: Illuminating (ज्ञानप्रद)

405 Enough (Adj.) - (पर्याप्त)
As much or as many as required; sufficient
Syno: Sufficient (पर्याप्त)

406 **Enraged** (Adj.) - (क्रोधित) *[#R-2]*
Very angry
Syno: Furious (प्रचंड क्रोधी), Angered (गुस्साया हुआ)

407 **Entail** (V.) - (आवश्यक बनाना)
To involve something as a necessary part or result
Syno: Necessitate (ज़रूरी बनाना)

408 **Enthrall** (V.) - (मंत्रमुग्ध करना) *[#R-3]*
To keep someone completely interested or charmed
Syno: Mesmerize (मोहित करना), Enchant (सम्मोहित करना), Captivate (आकर्षित करना)

409 **Entropy** (N.) - (अव्यवस्था का माप)~
A lack of order or gradual fall into disorder
Syno: Decay (पतन)

410 Envisage (V.) - (कल्पना करना) *[#R-1 (4)]*
To consider or imagine a future possibility
Syno: Imagine (परिकल्पना करना) {Contemplate (विचार करना)}

411 Envoy (N.) - (दूत)
A diplomatic messenger or representative
Syno: Ambassador (राजदूत)

412 **Envy** (N.) - (ईर्ष्या)
A jealous feeling toward someone's advantages
Syno: Jealousy (जलन)

413 **Epistemic** (Adj.) - (ज्ञान से जुड़ा)
Relating to knowledge or knowing
Syno: Knowledge-Related (ज्ञान-संबंधी)

414 Epoch (N.) - (युग)~
A distinct or important period in history
Syno: Era (युग)

415 **Epochal** (Adj.) - (ऐतिहासिक)~ *[#R-2]*
Extremely significant
Syno: Momentous (महत्वपूर्ण), Defining (निर्णायक)

416 **Erect** (V.) - (खड़ा करना)
To build or stand something upright
Syno: Raise (उठाना)

417 **Errand** (N.) - (किसी काम के लिए की गई छोटी यात्रा)
A short trip to deliver or collect something
Syno: Assignment (सौंपा गया काम)

418 **Erring** (Adj.) - (गलती करने वाला)
Being mistaken or wrong in judgment
Syno: Blundering (भूल करने वाला)

419 Erroneous (Adj.) - (गलत) *[#R-6 (2)]*
Containing or characterized by error
Syno: False (झूठा), Invalid (अमान्य), Wrong (गलत), Inaccurate (अशुद्ध), Fallacious (भ्रांतिपूर्ण) {Mistaken (भ्रांत)}

420 **Erstwhile** (Adj.) - (पूर्व)
Belonging to an earlier time
Syno: Former (पूर्व)

421 Escapade (N.) - (रोमांचक कार्य)
An exciting or daring adventure or incident.
Syno: Adventure (साहसिक कार्य)

422 **Espionage** (N.) - (जासूसी) *[#R-2]*
The secret activity of spying to get information.
Syno: Spying (जासूसी)

423 **Esteemed** (Adj.) - (सम्मानित)
Highly respected.
Syno: Prominent (प्रतिष्ठित)

424 **Estrange** (V.) - (पराया कर देना) *[#R-2 (2)]*

To cause people to become distant or unfriendly.

Syno: Separate (अलग होना) {Alienate (दूर कर देना)}

425 **Eulogy** (N.) - (स्तुति)~
Speech or writing of high praise

Syno: Tribute (सम्मान)

426 **Evaluate** (V.) - (मूल्यांकन करना)~
To judge or assess.

Syno: Assess (आकलन करना)

427 **Evangelise** (V.) - (धर्मप्रचार करना)
To preach or spread religious beliefs.

Syno: Preachify (उपदेश देना)

428 Eventually (Adv.) - (आखिरकार) *[#R-2 (1)]*
In the end after time or delay

Syno: Finally (अंत में), Ultimately (अंततः)

429 Evolution (N.) - (विकास)~
The gradual development or growth

Syno: Development (विकास)

430 Evolve (V.) - (विकसित होना)~
To develop gradually

Syno: Develop (विकसित होना)

431 **Exactly** (Adv.) - (बिल्कुल सही)
In an accurate or correct manner

Syno: Precisely (सटीक रूप से)

432 Exaggeration (N.) - (अतिशयोक्ति) *[#R-1 (1)]*
A statement that overstates reality

Syno: Amplification (विस्तार)

433 **Exaltation** (N.) - (प्रशंसा)
The state of being praised highly

Syno: Ecstasy (परमानंद)

434 **Examine** (V.) - (निरीक्षण करना)
To inspect or investigate thoroughly

Syno: Inspect (जाँच करना)

435 Exceed (V.) - (पार करना)
To be greater than in number or size

Syno: Surpass (आगे निकल जाना)

436 **Excerpt** (N.) - (अंश)~
A short part taken from a larger work

Syno: Extract (अंश)

437 Excitement (N.) - (उत्तेजना) *[#R-1 (2)]*
A feeling of great enthusiasm and eagerness

Syno: Enthusiasm (उत्साह) {Keenness (उत्सुकता)}

438 **Exciting** (Adj.) - (रोमांचक)
Causing great enthusiasm and eagerness

Syno: Electrifying (रोमांचकारी)

439 **Excogitate** (V.) - (गहराई से सोचकर कुछ नया निकालना)
To think out or devise carefully

Syno: Invent (ईजाद करना)

440 **Execrate** (V.) - (कोसना)
To feel or express great hatred

Syno: Curse (अभिशाप देना)

441 **Execute** (V.) - (पालन करना, पूरा करना) *[#R-3 (1)]*
To carry out or put into effect

Syno: Implement (लागू करना), Accomplish (पूरा करना)

442 Exempt (Adj./V.) - (मुक्त; छूट देना) *[#R-3]*
Free from obligation (Adj.); To free from duty (V.)

Syno: Immune (अप्रभावित); Exclude (बाहर रखना)

443 Exhibit (V.) - (प्रदर्शित करना)
To publicly display or show

Syno: Display (दिखाना)

444 Exhilaration (N.) - (उल्लास)~
A feeling of excitement and happiness

Syno: Excitement (उत्साह)

445 **Exhort** (V.) - (उकसाना) *[#R-1 (1)]*
To strongly encourage or urge someone to do something

Syno: Pressure (दबाव डालना) {Coax (फुसलाना)}

446 **Exorcise** (V.) - (भूत उतारना)
To drive out an evil spirit

Syno: Expel (निष्कासित करना)

447 **Expandable** (Adj.) - (विस्तार योग्य)
Capable of being expanded

Syno: Extensible (विस्तार योग्य)

448 Expectation (N.) - (अपेक्षा)
Belief that something will happen

Syno: Hope (आशा, उम्मीद)

449 **Expended** (Adj.) - (लगभग समाप्त) *[#R-2]*
Already used or consumed

Syno: Exhausted (समाप्त)

450 **Experienced** (Adj.) - (अनुभवी)
Having knowledge from practice

Syno: Seasoned (माहिर)

451 Expertise (N.) - (विशेषज्ञता)
An expert skill or knowledge

Syno: Proficiency (दक्षता)

452 **Expiation** (N.) - (प्रायश्चित)

The act of making amends for wrongdoing
Syno: Atonement (प्रायश्चित)

453 Explain (V.) - (समझाना)
To make something clear or give reasons
Syno: Elaborate (विस्तार से बताना)

454 Exponent (N.) - (समर्थक)
A person who promotes an idea
Syno: Proponent (प्रस्तावक)

455 Expose (V.) - (बेनकाब करना)
To make something visible by uncovering
Syno: Reveal (खुलासा करना)

456 **Expository** (Adj.) - (व्याख्यात्मक)
Intended to explain or describe something
Syno: Illustrative (उदाहरणात्मक)

457 **Expound** (V.) - (विस्तार से समझाना)
To explain an idea systematically and in detail
Syno: Expatiate (विस्तार से बताना)

458 **Extenuate** (V.) - (कम करना) *[#R-1 (1)]*
To make guilt or an offense seem less serious
Syno: Diminish (कम करना) {Mitigate (घटाना)}

459 **Exterminate** (V.) - (जड़ से मिटाना)
To destroy completely
Syno: Eradicate (उखाड़ फेंकना)

460 **Extortionate** (Adj.) - (अत्यधिक महंगा)
Unreasonably high or unfair in cost
Syno: Exorbitant (अत्यधिक)

461 **Extraordinarily** (Adv.) - (असाधारण रूप से)
To a remarkable degree
Syno: Incredibly (अविश्वसनीय रूप से)

462 Extrinsic (Adj.) - (बाहरी) *[#R-2]*
Coming from outside
Syno: Outward (बाह्य), Acquired (अर्जित)

463 Extrovert (Adj.) - (बहिर्मुखी)~
Outgoing, socially confident
Syno: Talkative (बातूनी)

464 **Exude** (V.) - (रिसना)
To flow out slowly, especially liquid or smell
Syno: Ooze (टपकना)

465 **Fabulously** (Adv.) - (अद्भुत रूप से)
In an extremely good or desirable manner
Syno: Fantastically (आश्चर्यजनक रूप से)

466 **Facile** (Adj.) - (सरल)~ *[#R-2 (1)]*
Seeming simple but lacking deep thought
Syno: Shallow (उथला), Simplistic (अति सरलीकृत) {Superficial (सतही)}

467 **Facility** (N.) - (कौशल)
Ease or skill in doing something
Syno: Skill (कुशलता)

468 Facsimile (N.) - (प्रतिलिपि)~
An exact copy, especially of written or printed material
Syno: Replica (नकल)

469 **Factual** (Adj.) - (तथ्यात्मक)
Based on facts, not opinions
Syno: Empirical (अनुभवसिद्ध)

470 **Fad** (N.) - (जुनून, सनक)
Something very popular for a short time
Syno: Sensation (सनसनी)

471 **Faddish** (Adj.) - (फैशनपरस्त)
Following a fashion or fad; trendy
Syno: Fashionable (चलन में, प्रचलित)

472 Faithful (Adj.) - (वफादार) *[#R-2]*
Remaining true to a person, promise, or duty
Syno: Devoted (समर्पित), Loyal (निष्ठावान)

473 **Fall Guy** (N.) - (बलि का बकरा)
A person blamed or punished for others' wrong actions
Syno: Scapegoat (बलि का बकरा)

474 Fantastic (Adj.) - (शानदार) *[#R-1 (2)]*
Extraordinarily good or attractive
Syno: Fanciful (कल्पनात्मक) {Superb (उत्कृष्ट)}

475 **Fantastically** (Adv.) - (अद्भुत रूप से)
In a manner that is imaginative or improbable
Syno: Fabulously (असाधारण रूप से)

476 **Farcical** (Adj.) - (हास्यास्पद)
Extremely silly and ridiculous
Syno: Absurd (बेतुका)

477 **Fare** (V.) - (प्रगति करना)
to perform or succeed
Syno: Progress (प्रगति करना)

478 Fascinate (V.) - (मंत्रमुग्ध करना) *[#R-2 (1)]*
To draw irresistibly the attention of someone
Syno: Captivate (मोहित करना), Entice (लुभाना) {Charm (आकर्षित करना)}

479 **Fast** (Adj./Adv.) - (तेज़; शीघ्रता से) *[#R-1 (1)]*
Moving quickly (Adj.); at high speed (Adv.)
Syno: Quick (शीघ्र) {Rapid (तीव्र)}

480 Fatal (Adj.) - (घातक)~ *[#R-3 (1)]*

Causing death
Syno: Deadly (जानलेवा) {Disastrous (विनाशकारी)}

481 **Favoured** (Adj.) - (पसंदीदा)
Liked or given preference
Syno: Preferred (प्राथमिक)

482 **Feasibility** (N.) - (संभाव्यता)
The state of being easily or conveniently done
Syno: Probability (संभावना)

483 **Feat** (N.) - (उपलब्धि)~
An achievement requiring courage, skill, or strength
Syno: Accomplishment (सफलता)

484 Feign (V.) - (दिखावा करना)~ *[#R-3 (1)]*
To pretend to be affected by a feeling or state
Syno: Pretend (नाटक करना)

485 Felicitate (V.) - (बधाई देना)~
To offer congratulations to
Syno: Congratulate (अभिनंदन करना)

486 **Festivity** (N.) - (उत्सव) *[#R-2]*
The celebration of something in a joyful way
Syno: Celebration (जश्न)

487 **Fetch** (V.) - (जाकर लाना)
To go for and then bring back someone or something
Syno: Bring (लाना)

488 **Fiction** (N.) - (कल्पना)
Literature describing imaginary events and people
Syno: Fantasy (परिकल्पना)

489 **Fillip** (N.) - (प्रोत्साहन)
A stimulus or boost to an activity
Syno: Boost (बढ़ावा)

490 **Final** (Adj.) - (अंतिम)
Coming at the end
Syno: Concluding (समापनकारी)

491 **Firewall** (N.) - (सुरक्षा दीवार)
A wall preventing fire spread; computer security system
Syno: Bulwark (रक्षा-कवच)

492 Firm (Adj.) - (दृढ़)~ *[#R-1 (1)]*
Strong and steady
Syno: Determined (निश्चित) {Steadfast (अटल)}

493 **Firmly** (Adv.) - (मजबूती से)
With little possibility of movement; securely
Syno: Stiffly (कड़ाई से)

494 **Fissure** (N.) - (दरार)
A long narrow crack
Syno: Cleavage (विभाजन)

495 Flabbergasted (Adj.) - (चकित) *[#R-2 (1)]*
Greatly surprised or astonished
Syno: Dumbfounded (स्तब्ध), Astonished (आश्चर्यचकित) {Surprised (हैरान)}

496 **Flagrant** (Adj.) - (निंदनीय) *[#R-1 (1)]*
Conspicuously or obviously offensive
Syno: Atrocious (अत्यंत बुरा) {Scandalous (बदनामी भरा)}

497 Flair (N.) - (प्रतिभा)~ *[#R-2]*
A special aptitude for doing something well
Syno: Talent (कौशल)

498 **Flash** (N.) - (चमक)
A sudden bright light
Syno: Blink (टिमटिमाना)

499 **Flattery** (N.) - (चापलूसी)
Excessive or insincere praise
Syno: Adulation (बढ़ा-चढ़ाकर तारीफ़)

500 **Fleck** (N.) - (धब्बा) *[#R-2]*
A very small spot or mark
Syno: Spot (धब्बा)

501 **Fledgling** (N.) - (नौसिखिया)
A young bird or beginner
Syno: Apprentice (प्रशिक्षु)

502 **Fling** (V.) - (फेंकना) *[#R-2 (3)]*
To throw or hurl forcefully
Syno: Throw (फेंकना), Propel (धकेलना)

503 **Float** (V.) - (तैरना)
To rest or move on liquid surface
Syno: Drift (बहना)

504 Flounder (V.) - (जूझना)~ *[#R-1 (1)]*
To struggle or have difficulty
Syno: Struggle (संघर्ष करना)

505 **Flout** (V.) - (अवहेलना करना)~ *[#R-4 (1)]*
To openly disregard a rule, law, or convention
Syno: Mock (अवज्ञा करना), Defy (अवहेलना करना) {Disregard (अनदेखा करना)}

506 **Fluke** (N.) - (संयोग)~
An unlikely chance occurrence
Syno: Chance (मौका)

507 Fluorescent (Adj.) - (चमकीला)
Vividly bright; appearing to glow
Syno: Glowing (चमकता हुआ)

508 **Flutter** (N.) - (फड़फड़ाहट)
A quick irregular movement
Syno: Flicker (झिलमिलाहट)

509 Foliage (N.) - (पत्तियाँ)
Plant leaves, collectively
Syno: Greenery (हरियाली)

510 **Fondness** (N.) - (स्नेह)
Affection or liking
Syno: Liking (पसंद)

511 **Forbear** (V.) - (संयम बरतना) *[#R-6 (6)]*
To restrain oneself from doing something
Syno: Refrain (परहेज करना)

512 **Foreboding** (N.) - (आशंका)
A fearful feeling
Syno: Alarm (भय)

513 **Forego** (V.) - (त्यागना) *[#R-2]*
To omit or decline to take something
Syno: Leave (छोड़ना), Give Up (त्यागना)

514 **Forgery** (N.) - (जालसाज़ी)~
The act of making fake documents
Syno: Counterfeiting (नकली बनाना)

515 **Forsake** (V.) - (त्यागना) *[#R-5 (3)]*
To abandon or give up
Syno: Abandon (छोड़ देना), Desert (छोड़कर भाग जाना) {Discard (त्याग देना)}

516 **Forswear** (V.) - (शपथपूर्वक त्यागना)
To agree to give up something
Syno: Forsake (त्यागना)

517 **Fossilize** (V.) - (जीवाश्म बनाना)
To preserve an organism as a fossil
Syno: Petrify (पत्थर बनाना)

518 Foster (V.) - (बढ़ावा देना) *[#R-2 (4)]*
To encourage or help develop
Syno: Promote (प्रोत्साहित करना), Nurture (पालन-पोषण करना)

519 **Foundation** (N.) - (नींव)
The basis or groundwork of something; the lowest part of a building
Syno: Base (आधार)

520 **Fowl** (N.) - (पालतू पक्षी)
A bird, especially one bred for eating
Syno: Bird (पक्षी)

521 Foyer (N.) - (प्रवेश कक्ष)~
An entrance hall in a building used by public
Syno: Lobby (भवन का मुख्य प्रवेश स्थल)

522 **Fragmented** (Adj.) - (खंडित)
Broken into parts
Syno: Broken (टूटा हुआ)

523 Frantic (Adj.) - (घबराया हुआ) *[#R-4 (3)]*
Wild or distraught with fear or anxiety
Syno: Agitated (व्याकुल), Distraught (घबराया हुआ), Violent (उग्र) {Berserk (उन्मादी), Panicky (आतंकित), Desperate (बेताब)}

524 **Fraternise** (V.) - (मिलना-जुलना)
To associate or form a friendship with someone
Syno: Associate (मिलना-जुलना)

525 **Freelance** (Adj.) - (स्वतंत्र)
Working independently
Syno: Self-Employed (स्व-रोजगार)

526 **Frisky** (Adj.) - (चंचल)
Playful and lively
Syno: Playful (शरारती)

527 **Frivolity** (N.) - (हल्कापन)
The lack of seriousness
Syno: Levity (हल्कापन)

528 **Frontier** (N.) - (सरहद)
A line or border separating two countries
Syno: Boundary (सीमा)

529 Frozen (Adj.) - (जमा हुआ)
Turned into ice or solid due to extreme cold
Syno: Icy (बर्फीला)

530 Fruitful (Adj.) - (लाभदायक)
Producing good or helpful results
Syno: Productive (लाभकारी)

531 Fruition (N.) - (सफलता)
The point at which a plan is realized
Syno: Accomplishment (उपलब्धि)

532 Funny (Adj.) - (मजेदार) *[#R-2]*
Causing laughter or amusement; humorous
Syno: Humorous (हास्यपूर्ण)

533 **Furbish** (V.) - (चमकाना)
To polish or clean to make bright
Syno: Shine (चमकना)

534 **Fury** (N.) - (क्रोध) *[#R-3 (1)]*
Wild or violent anger
Syno: Anger (गुस्सा) {Rage (रोष)}

535 Fuse (V.) - (मिला कर एक करना)
To join or blend into one
Syno: Combine (मिलाना)

536 **Fustian** (Adj.) - (आत्मप्रशंसा से भरा)
Pompous or pretentious in speech or writing
Syno: Bombastic (आडम्बरपूर्ण)

537 **Gaff** (N.) - (चाल)
A trick or deception
Syno: Trick (तरकीब)

538 **Gala** (N.) - (उत्सव)
A social occasion with special entertainments
Syno: Carnival (मेला)

539 **Gallivant** (V.) - (मौज-मस्ती में घूमना)
To go around in pursuit of pleasure
Syno: Meander (इधर-उधर घूमना)

540 **Gambol** (V.) - (उछल-कूद करना)~
To jump or skip about playfully
Syno: Frisk (उछलना)

541 **Garble** (V.) - (तोड़ना-मरोड़ना)
To distort or confuse a message or account
Syno: Confuse (भ्रमित करना)

542 **Garnish** (V.) - (सजावट करना) *[#R-4 (1)]*
To decorate or embellish something, especially food
Syno: Adorn (सजाना), Embellish (सुशोभित करना), Decorate (सजावट करना)

543 **Gasp** (V.) - (हांफना)
To breathe laboriously
Syno: Pant (हांफना)

544 Gauge (N.) - (मापक यंत्र)
An instrument for measuring
Syno: Measure (माप)

545 **Generic** (Adj.) - (सामान्य; व्यापक) *[#R-2 (1)]*
Relating to a class or group; applicable to all
Syno: Universal (विश्वव्यापी), General (सामान्य) {Broad (व्यापक)}

546 **Genesis** (N.) - (उत्पत्ति)~ *[#R-1 (1)]*
The beginning or origin of something
Syno: Inception (शुरुआत) {Origin (आरंभ)}

547 **Genre** (N.) - (शैली) *[#R-1 (1)]*
A category of artistic composition
Syno: Category (श्रेणी)

548 **Glare** (N.) - (तेज चमक)
A harsh bright light
Syno: Dazzle (चकाचौंध)

549 Gleam (N./V.) - (झलक; चमकना) *[#R-2]*
A brief or soft shine (N.); To shine lightly or briefly (V.)
Syno: Sheen (चमक), Shine (चमकना)

550 **Glib** (Adj.) - (चिकनी-चुपड़ी बातें करने वाला) *[#R-4]*
Fluent and voluble but insincere and shallow
Syno: Artful (चालाक), Slick (चालाक)

551 Glimpse (N.) - (झलक) *[#R-2]*
A brief or partial view
Syno: Glance (एक नज़र)

552 Glorious (Adj.) - (शानदार) *[#R-2]*
Having, worthy of, or bringing fame or admiration
Syno: Splendid (भव्य)

553 Glowing (Adj.) - (चमकदार)
Giving out light or heat; expressing great praise
Syno: Dazzling (दमकता हुआ)

554 **Glum** (Adj.) - (उदास)
Dejected or morose
Syno: Dismal (निराशाजनक)

555 **Gnome** (N.) - (बौना)
A small mythical creature resembling a tiny old man
Syno: Dwarf (बौना)

556 **Golden** (Adj.) - (सुनहरा)
Made of or resembling gold
Syno: Shining (चमकता हुआ)

557 **Gorge** (N.) - (घाटी)
A deep narrow valley
Syno: Canyon (गहरी घाटी)

558 **Gospel** (N.) - (ईसा चरित, सत्य)
The teaching and revelation of Christ; Complete truth
Syno: Faith (आस्था)

559 Gourmet (N.) - (खाने पीने का शौक़ीन व्यक्ति)~ *[#R-2]*
A lover or expert of good food
Syno: Gastronome (खाद्य प्रेमी), Epicure (भोजन का आनंद लेने वाला)

560 **Graciously** (Adv.) - (शालीनतापूर्वक)
In a kind manner
Syno: Nicely (अच्छे से)

561 **Grasp** (V.) - (पकड़ना, समझना) *[#R-2 (1)]*
To seize or hold firmly; to understand
Syno: Clinch (मजबूती से पकड़ना), Understand (समझना)

562 Grateful (Adj.) - (कृतज्ञ)
Feeling or showing thankfulness

Syno: Thankful (आभारी)

563 Gravity (N.) - (गंभीरता)
The extreme importance or seriousness
Syno: Depth (गहराई)

564 Greed (N.) - (लालच) *[#R-1 (1)]*
The intense and selfish desire for wealth or power
Syno: Cupidity (लोभ) {Avarice (लालच)}

565 **Greet** (V.) - (अभिवादन करना)
To address with kind wishes upon meeting
Syno: Welcome (स्वागत करना)

566 Grievous (Adj.) - (गंभीर) *[#R-2]*
Very severe or serious
Syno: Painful (पीड़ादायक), Serious (गंभीर)

567 **Grin** (N.) - (मुस्कुराहट)
A wide, happy smile
Syno: Smile (मुस्कान)

568 **Grit** (N.) - (साहस) *[#R-2]*
The courage and resolve
Syno: Courage (हिम्मत)

569 Groan (N.) - (कराहट)
A deep sound of pain
Syno: Grumble (बड़बड़ाना)

570 **Gruff** (Adj.) - (रूखा)~
Rough and low in pitch
Syno: Rough (खुरदुरा)

571 Guard (V.) - (सुरक्षा करना)
To protect from harm or danger
Syno: Defend (बचाव करना)

572 Gullet (N.) - (गला)
The throat or passage for food
Syno: Throat (कंठ)

573 **Gust** (N.) - (तेज़ झोंका)~
A sudden strong rush of wind
Syno: Blow (झोंका)

574 **Habitant** (N.) - (निवासी)
A resident; dweller
Syno: Denizen (निवासी)

575 Habitat (N.) - (आवास)
The natural home of an organism
Syno: Niche (विशेष स्थान)

576 Hackneyed (Adj.) - (घिसा-पिटा) *[#R-2 (1)]*
Overused and no longer original
Syno: Tired (थका हुआ, घिसा-पिटा) {Stale (बासी)}

577 Hallucination (N.) - (मायाजाल)~
The apparent perception of something not present
Syno: Delusion (भ्रम)

578 **Hallway** (N.) - (गलियारा)
A corridor or passageway in a building
Syno: Aisle (रास्ता)

579 **Hardly** (Adv.) - (मुश्किल से)
Only just; almost not
Syno: Barely (मुश्किल से)

580 **Hate** (V.) - (घृणा करना) *[#R-2]*
To dislike intensely
Syno: Detest (नफरत करना), Loathe (घृणा करना)

581 **Hearsay** (N.) - (अफवाह)
Information heard from others, not personally verified
Syno: Buzz (चर्चा)

582 **Hearth** (N.) - (चूल्हा)
The floor of a fireplace
Syno: Fireside (अग्निकुंड के पास)

583 **Heartless** (Adj.) - (निर्दयी)
Lacking compassion or feeling
Syno: Cruel (कठोर)

584 **Heckle** (V.) - (उपहास करना)~
To interrupt a speaker with derisive or aggressive comments
Syno: Taunt (ताना मारना)

585 **Hegemonic** (Adj.) - (वर्चस्ववादी)
Dominant, especially by one group over others
Syno: Supreme (सर्वोच्च)

586 **Herald** (N./V.) - (दूत; घोषणा करना) *[#R-3]*
A sign or messenger of something (N.); To announce or signal (V.)
Syno: Messenger (संदेशवाहक); Announce (घोषणा करना)

587 Herculean (Adj.) - (अत्यंत कठिन) *[#R-2]*
Requiring great strength or effort
Syno: Strong (मजबूत, कठिन)

588 Heretic (N.) - (परंपरा-विरोधी)~ *[#R-1 (2)]*
A person who holds beliefs contrary to accepted doctrine
Syno: Dissenter (असहमतिवादी)

589 **Hermetic** (Adj.) - (गुप्त)
Completely sealed or kept secret

Syno: Esoteric (रहस्यमय)

590 **Hesitation** (N.) - (हिचकिचाहट)
The action of pausing before saying or doing something
Syno: Reluctance (अनिच्छा)

591 **Heyday** (N.) - (स्वर्णिम काल)
The period of greatest success or strength
Syno: Prime (उत्कृष्ट अवस्था)

592 **Hide** (V.) - (छिपाना) *[#R-1 (1)]*
To put or keep out of sight or secret
Syno: Conceal (छिपाना) {Harbour (छिपाकर रखना)}

593 **Hind** (Adj.) - (पिछला) *[#R-2]*
Situated at the back; posterior
Syno: Rear (पिछला)

594 **Hire** (V.) - (नियुक्त करना)
To employ someone
Syno: Engage (नियोजित करना)

595 **Hoax** (N./V.) - (झूठी चाल; धोखा देना) *[#R-1 (1)]*
A false trick or fraud (N.); To deceive someone (V.)
Syno: Trick (चाल) {Humbug (धोखा)}

596 **Homilies** (N.) - (उपदेश)
Religious talks or moral speeches
Syno: Sermons (प्रवचन)

597 **Honour** (N.) - (सम्मान) *[#R-1 (1)]*
High respect or esteem
Syno: Respect (आदर)

598 **Hoodwink** (V.) - (आँख में धूल झोंकना) *[#R-4]*
To deceive or trick someone
Syno: Deceive (धोखा देना), Cheat (बेईमानी करना), Defraud (ठगना)

599 **Horrid** (Adj.) - (भयंकर)
Causing strong fear
Syno: Offensive (आपत्तिजनक)

600 **Hound** (V./N.) - (परेशान करना; शिकारी कुत्ता) *[#R-2]*
To pursue or harass continuously (V.); A dog used for hunting (N.)
Syno: Chase (पीछा करना); Beagle (शिकारी कुत्ता)

601 **Howl** (N.) - (चीख)
A long, sad cry
Syno: Wail (विलाप)

602 **Huddle** (N.) - (भीड़) *[#R-1 (1)]*
A small close group
Syno: Gathering (जमावड़ा) {Cluster (समूह)}

603 **Humdrum** (Adj.) - (नीरस) *[#R-2 (1)]*
Lacking excitement; boringly monotonous
Syno: Monotonous (एकरस), Boring (उबाऊ) {Mundane (साधारण)}

604 **Humiliation** (N.) - (अपमान) *[#R-1 (1)]*
A feeling of deep shame or loss of dignity
Syno: Dishonour (अनादर) {Ignominy (तिरस्कार)}

605 **Hurdle** (N.) - (बाधा) *[#R-6 (1)]*
A difficulty or obstacle
Syno: Obstacle (रुकावट), Impediment (अड़चन)

606 **Hybrid** (Adj.) - (मिश्रित)
Made by combining two elements
Syno: Composite (संयुक्त)

607 **Hyperbole** (N.) - (अतिशयोक्ति)~
An exaggerated statement not meant literally
Syno: Overstatement (बढ़ा-चढ़ाकर कहना)

608 **Hypothesis** (N.) - (परिकल्पना)~
A proposed explanation for testing
Syno: Speculation (अनुमान)

609 **Iconic** (Adj.) - (प्रतिष्ठित) *[#R-2]*
Widely recognized and well-established
Syno: Legendary (विख्यात), Exemplary (आदर्श)

610 **Ideology** (N.) - (विचारधारा)
A system of ideas forming a theory
Syno: Belief (विश्वास)

611 **Idleness** (N.) - (आलस्य) *[#R-2]*
The state of being idle or inactive
Syno: Lethargy (सुस्ती)

612 **Ignoramus** (N.) - (मूर्ख) *[#R-2]*
An ignorant or uneducated person
Syno: Dunce (मूर्ख), Fool (मूर्ख)

613 **Ill-Bred** (Adj.) - (असभ्य)
Badly brought up or rude
Syno: Uncouth (अशिष्ट)

614 **Illness** (N.) - (बीमारी)
A condition of poor physical or mental health
Syno: Sickness (अस्वस्थता)

615 **Illogical** (Adj.) - (तर्कहीन)
Lacking sense or clear, sound reasoning
Syno: Absurd (बेतुका)

616 **Imbue** (V.) - (प्रेरित करना) *[#R-3]*
To fill or inspire with a feeling or quality
Syno: Fill (भरना), Infuse (भरना), Instil (मन में बिठा देना)

617 **Immerse** (V.) - (डुबोना) *[#R-3]*
To involve oneself deeply in an activity

Syno: Submerge (जलमग्न करना), Involve (शामिल करना)

618 **Impair** (V.) - (हानि पहुँचाना)
To damage or reduce strength or effectiveness
Syno: Weaken (कमजोर करना)

619 **Impart** (V.) - (प्रसारित करना) *[#R-4 (4)]*
To make information known; communicate
Syno: Transmit (संचारित करना)

620 **Impasse** (N.) - (गतिरोध, बंद रास्ता)
A deadlocked situation with no possible progress
Syno: Deadlock (गतिरोध)

621 **Impediment** (N.) - (बाधा) *[#R-3 (3)]*
A hindrance or obstruction in doing something
Syno: Obstruction (अवरोध), Obstacle (रुकावट), Barrier (रोक) {Hurdle (अड़चन), Restriction (प्रतिबंध)}

622 **Imperial** (Adj.) - (साम्राज्यवादी)
Relating to an empire
Syno: Sovereign (सर्वोच्च)

623 **Impetus** (N.) - (प्रेरणा) *[#R-2 (2)]*
Force or motivation that makes something happen
Syno: Encouragement (प्रोत्साहन), Incitement (उकसावा) {Momentum (गति), Stimulant (उत्तेजक)}

624 **Implacable** (Adj.) - (अटल)~ *[#R-2 (1)]*
Unable to be appeased
Syno: Relentless (निरंतर), Unyielding (अडिग)

625 **Implausible** (Adj.) - (अविश्वसनीय)
Not seeming reasonable or believable
Syno: Improbable (असंभाव्य)

626 **Implicate** (V.) - (फंसाना)
To show involvement
Syno: Accuse (आरोप लगाना)

627 **Implicit** (Adj.) - (निहित) *[#R-2]*
Implied though not plainly expressed
Syno: Tacit (मौन), Unspoken (अनकहा)

628 **Importune** (V.) - (विनती करना)~
To ask someone repeatedly and persistently
Syno: Appeal (निवेदन करना)

629 **Impost** (N.) - (कर) *[#R-1 (1)]*
A tax or similar compulsory payment
Syno: Tax (कर) {Levy (शुल्क)}

630 **Impress** (V.) - (प्रभावित करना)
To make a strong effect on someone
Syno: Impact (प्रभावित करना)

631 **Imprisonment** (N.) - (कारावास) *[#R-2]*
The state of being imprisoned
Syno: Incarceration (कैद), Confinement (नजरबंदी)

632 **Imprudent** (Adj.) - (बेपरवाह) *[#R-1 (1)]*
Not showing care for the consequences of an action; rash
Syno: Careless (लापरवाह) {Unwise (नासमझ)}

633 **Impurity** (N.) - (अशुद्धि)
A contaminating substance
Syno: Scum (गंदगी)

634 **Inactive** (Adj.) - (निष्क्रिय)
Not engaging in much physical activity
Syno: Lethargic (सुस्त)

635 **Inanimate** (Adj.) - (निर्जीव)~
Not alive
Syno: Lifeless (प्राणहीन)

636 **Inanition** (N.) - (भोजन की कमी की वजह से सुस्ती, दुर्बलता)
Exhaustion caused by lack of food
Syno: Lethargy (सुस्ती)

637 **Inarticulate** (Adj.) - (अस्पष्ट)~
Unable to express ideas clearly
Syno: Incoherent (असंगत)

638 **Incapable** (Adj.) - (अक्षम)
Lacking ability or capacity
Syno: Incompetent (अयोग्य)

639 **Incense** (V.) - (क्रोधित करना)
To make very angry
Syno: Exasperate (उत्तेजित करना)

640 **Incessantly** (Adv.) - (लगातार) *[#R-2]*
Without interruption; constantly
Syno: Continuously (निरंतर), Steadily (लगातार)

641 **Incident** (N.) - (घटना)
An event or occurrence
Syno: Event (घटना)

642 **Incognito** (Adj./Adv.) - (गुमनाम; गुप्त रूप से)~ *[#R-1 (3)]*
Having one's identity hidden (Adj.); with identity hidden (Adv.)
Syno: Anonymous (अज्ञात) {Concealed (छिपा हुआ); Secretly (गुप्त रूप से)}

643 **Inconsistency** (N.) - (विसंगति)

Lack of agreement or uniformity
Syno: Anomaly (असामान्यता)

644 **Incumbent** (Adj./N.) - (आवश्यक; पदधारी) *[#R-2 (1)]*
Necessary as a duty (Adj.); A person holding an official position (N.)
Syno: Required (आवश्यक); Occupant (पदधारी) {Present (उपस्थित)}

645 **Indebted** (Adj.) - (ऋणी)~
Owing gratitude for service or favour
Syno: Thankful (आभारी)

646 **Indemnity** (N.) - (भरपाई)
Compensation for loss or damage
Syno: Restitution (भरपाई)

647 **Index** (N.) - (सूची)
An alphabetical list of names or subjects
Syno: Guide (मार्गदर्शक)

648 **Indictment** (N.) - (अभियोग) *[#R-1 (1)]*
A formal charge or accusation of a serious crime
Syno: Accusation (आरोप) {Arraignment (अभियोग)}

649 **Indignation** (N.) - (रोष)~ *[#R-2]*
Strong anger or annoyance at injustice
Syno: Anger (क्रोध), Offense (नाराज़गी)

650 **Indiscreet** (Adj.) - (असावधान)
Lacking prudence, circumspection, or caution
Syno: Careless (लापरवाह)

651 **Indissoluble** (Adj.) - (अविनाशी)
Unable to be destroyed; lasting
Syno: Permanent (स्थायी)

652 Indistinguishable (Adj.) - (समरूप)
Not able to be identified as different or distinct
Syno: Equivalent (समान)

653 **Indolently** (Adv.) - (आलस्यपूर्वक)
In a lazy or idle manner
Syno: Languidly (सुस्ती से)

654 **Induction** (N.) - (प्रवेश, समावेशन)
Formal entry into a position or group
Syno: Inauguration (उद्घाटन)

655 **Indulgence** (N.) - (क्षमाशीलता; ढील देना)
An occasion when you allow or do not mind someone's failure or bad behaviour
Syno: Leniency (नरमी)

656 **Infamy** (N.) - (कुख्याति) *[#R-1 (1)]*
The state of being famous for something bad
Syno: Notoriety (बदनामी)

657 Infatuation (N.) - (सम्मोह, मुग्धता)
A strong but brief feeling of admiration or love
Syno: Passion (जुनून)

658 **Inference** (N.) - (निष्कर्ष)
A conclusion reached on the basis of evidence and reasoning
Syno: Conclusion (निष्कर्ष)

659 **Infructuous** (Adj.) - (निष्फल)
Not producing any useful result; futile
Syno: Fruitless (व्यर्थ)

660 **Infuriate** (V.) - (क्रोधित करना)
To make someone extremely angry and impatient
Syno: Enrage (क्रोधित करना)

661 **Infuse** (V.) - (भर देना)
To fill or spread through something
Syno: Fill (भरना)

662 **Inhibitor** (N.) - (निरोधक)
Something that slows down or prevents a process
Syno: Deterrent (बाधा)

663 **Injustice** (N.) - (अन्याय)
Unfair treatment
Syno: Discrimination (भेदभाव)

664 **Innuendo** (N.) - (इशारा)~ *[#R-2 (3)]*
An allusive or oblique remark or hint
Syno: Insinuation (इशारा), Implication (संकेत) {Hint (इशारा), Allusion (संकेत)}

665 **Insensitive** (Adj.) - (असंवेदनशील)
Showing no concern for others' feelings
Syno: Callous (निर्दयी)

666 **Insignia** (N.) - (प्रतीक)
A distinguishing mark showing rank, office, or membership
Syno: Symbol (चिन्ह)

667 **Insist** (V.) - (जोर देना) *[#R-2]*
To demand something forcefully, not accepting refusal
Syno: Persist (दृढ़ रहना), Urge (प्रेरित करना)

668 Instigate (V.) - (उकसाना) *[#R-2]*
To incite someone to do something, especially

something bad

Syno: Kindle (भड़काना), Raise (उठाना)

669 **Instill** (V.) - (मन में बिठाना)
To gradually but firmly establish an idea or attitude in a person's mind

Syno: Inculcate (सिखाना)

670 Insufficient (Adj.) - (अपर्याप्त)
Not enough; inadequate

Syno: Lacking (अपर्याप्त)

671 Insult (V.) - (अपमान करना)
To treat or speak to with disrespect

Syno: Offend (अपमानित करना)

672 **Integrant** (N.) - (अविभाज्य अंग)
An essential part of a whole

Syno: Item (अंश)

673 Integrity (N.) - (ईमानदारी)~
The quality of being honest and having strong moral principles

Syno: Honesty (ईमानदारी)

674 Intensify (V.) - (सशक्त करना)
To make something stronger or more intense

Syno: Strengthen (मजबूत करना)

675 **Intently** (Adv.) - (ध्यानपूर्वक)
In a way that shows close attention or concentration

Syno: Closely (सावधानीपूर्वक)

676 **Interdiction** (N.) - (प्रतिबंध) *[#R-2]*
The action of prohibiting or forbidding something

Syno: Decree (फरमान, आज्ञा)

677 Interference (N.) - (हस्तक्षेप) *[#R-2]*
The action of interfering or the process of being interfered with

Syno: Obstruction (अवरोध), Meddling (हस्तक्षेप)

678 **Interlinked** (Adj.) - (आपस में जुड़े हुए)
Connected or linked with each other

Syno: Interlaced (जुड़ा हुआ)

679 **Interpret** (V.) - (व्याख्या करना) *[#R-1 (2)]*
To explain the meaning of information, words, or actions

Syno: Clarify (स्पष्ट करना) {Decipher (गुप्त अर्थ समझना)}

680 **Intersperse** (V.) - (बिखेरना)
To scatter or place here and there

Syno: Scatter (बिखेरना)

681 **Intractable** (Adj.) - (जिद्दी)
Hard to control or deal with

Syno: Defiant (विद्रोही)

682 **Intuitive** (Adj.) - (सहज)
Based on instinct

Syno: Instinctive (स्वाभाविक)

683 **Invariable** (Adj.) - (अपरिवर्तनीय)
Never changing

Syno: Constant (स्थिर)

684 **Inventory** (N.) - (सूची)~
A complete list of items or goods

Syno: Catalogue (सूचीपत्र)

685 Investigate (V.) - (जांच करना) *[#R-2]*
To carry out a formal inquiry or examine something carefully

Syno: Examine (परीक्षण करना), Search (खोजना)

686 **Invidious** (Adj.) - (ईर्ष्याजनक)
Likely to cause resentment or hostility

Syno: Hateful (घृणित)

687 **Invoice** (N.) - (बिल, भुगतान सूची)~
A list of goods or services with amount due

Syno: Statement (विवरण)

688 **Iota** (N.) - (थोड़ा सा)
An extremely small amount

Syno: Bit (थोड़ा)

689 Irregular (Adj.) - (अनियमित)
Not even or balanced in shape or arrangement

Syno: Uneven (असमान)

690 Irrepressible (Adj.) - (अनियंत्रित)
Unable to be controlled

Syno: Uncontrollable (बेकाबू)

691 **Irreverence** (N.) - (अनादर) *[#R-2]*
A lack of respect for people or things that are generally taken seriously

Syno: Disrespect (अनादर)

692 Irrevocable (Adj.) - (अटल)~ *[#R-3]*
Not able to be changed, reversed, or recovered; final

Syno: Irreversible (वापस न होने वाला), Unalterable (अपरिवर्तनीय), Final (अंतिम)

693 **Irritated** (Adj.) - (खिन्न)
Feeling slightly angry or annoyed

Syno: Annoyed (परेशान)

694 **Isolated** (Adj.) - (अलग-थलग)~ *[#R-2]*
Separated from others; alone

Syno: Lonely (अकेला), Deserted (सुनसान)

695 **Jabber** (V.) - (बकबक करना)
To talk rapidly without sense
Syno: Chatter (गपशप करना)

696 **Jangle** (V.) - (खनखनाना)
To make a sharp ringing metallic sound
Syno: Clang (खनखनाना)

697 **Jape** (N.) - (मजाक)
A joke or jest
Syno: Quip (चुटकुला)

698 **Jar** (V.) - (तर्क-वितर्क करना; झगड़ना) *[#R-2]*
to argue or quarrel angrily
Syno: Altercate (तर्क-वितर्क करना)

699 Jargon (N.) - (विशेष शब्दावली)~ *[#R-2]*
Special words or expressions used by a profession or group
Syno: Slang (विशिष्ट बोली), Terminology (तकनीकी शब्दावली)

700 Jealous (Adj.) - (ईर्ष्यालु) *[#R-3 (2)]*
Feeling or showing envy of someone or their achievements and advantages
Syno: Envious (ईर्ष्यालु)

701 Jejune (Adj.) - (नीरस) *[#R-1 (1)]*
Naive, simplistic, and superficial; dry and uninteresting
Syno: Drab (फीका) {Boring (उबाऊ)}

702 **Jinx** (N.) - (अशकुन)~
A person or thing that brings bad luck
Syno: Spell (जादू)

703 Jostle (V.) - (धक्का-मुक्की करना)
To push, elbow, or bump against someone roughly
Syno: Shove (धक्का देना)

704 Judge (V.) - (निर्णय करना)
To form an opinion or decide
Syno: Decide (निर्णय लेना)

705 **Junk** (N.) - (कबाड़) *[#R-1 (2)]*
Old or discarded items of little or no value
Syno: Waste (कचरा) {Discard (त्यागी हुई वस्तु), Scrap (रद्दी)}

706 **Jurisdiction** (N.) - (न्यायक्षेत्र)~
The legal authority to make decisions and judgments
Syno: Governance (शासन)

707 Justifiable (Adj.) - (तर्कसंगत)
Able to be shown to be right or reasonable; defensible
Syno: Reasonable (उचित)

708 **Justify** (V.) - (उचित ठहराना)
To show or prove to be right or reasonable
Syno: Explain (समझाना)

709 Keep (V.) - (रखना)
To hold or retain in one's possession
Syno: Hold (पकड़ना)

710 **Kid** (V.) - (मजाक करना)
To joke or deceive lightly for fun
Syno: Joke (मजाक करना)

711 **Kilter** (N.) - (संतुलन)
Good condition or working order
Syno: Order (क्रम)

712 **Kinship** (N.) - (संबंध)
A blood relationship or family connection
Syno: Relationship (रिश्ता)

713 **Kiosk** (N.) - (गुमटी, छोटी दुकान)~
A small open-fronted booth used for selling things or displaying information
Syno: Store (स्टोर)

714 **Kit** (N.) - (उपकरण)
A set of articles or equipment needed for a specific purpose
Syno: Equipment (उपकरण)

715 **Knavery** (N.) - (धूर्तता)
Dishonest behavior
Syno: Deceit (छल)

716 **Knavish** (Adj.) - (कपटी, बेईमान)
Dishonest or unscrupulous
Syno: Unscrupulous (बेईमान)

717 **Kudos** (N.) - (प्रशंसा)
Praise for achievement
Syno: Praise (तारीफ़)

718 Labour (N.) - (श्रम) *[#R-1 (3)]*
Physical or mental work
Syno: Toil (कड़ी मेहनत) {Drudge (कठिन परिश्रम)}

719 Labyrinth (N.) - (भूलभुलैया) *[#R-3 (1)]*
A complex network of passages; a maze
Syno: Meander (घुमाव), Maze (भूलभुलैया) {Complexity (जटिलता)}

720 Labyrinthine (Adj.) - (भूलभुलैया जैसा)~
Extremely complicated
Syno: Complex (जटिल)

721 **Laden** (Adj.) - (भरा हुआ)
Heavily loaded or weighed down
Syno: Full (पूर्ण)

722 Laggard (Adj.) - (सुस्त)
Sluggish; slow-moving
Syno: Dawdling (सुस्त)

723 **Laud** (V.) - (प्रशंसा करना)
To praise highly, especially in a public context
Syno: Acknowledge (सराहना करना)

724 **Layout** (N.) - (रूपरेखा, नक़्शा)
The way in which the parts of something are arranged or laid out
Syno: Arrangement (व्यवस्था)

725 **Lean** (Adj.) - (दुबला) *[#R-1 (1)]*
Thin, particularly due to an absence of fat
Syno: Thin (पतला) {Slender (पतला/सुडौल)}

726 Leap (V.) - (कूदना)
To jump suddenly or move quickly
Syno: Hop (कूदना)

727 Leave (V.) - (छोड़ना)
To depart
Syno: Exit (निकास)

728 Legend (N.) - (पौराणिक कथा)
A traditional story popularly regarded as historical but unauthenticated
Syno: Tradition (परंपरा)

729 Legitimate (Adj.) - (वैध) *[#R-1 (1)]*
Legal or genuine
Syno: Genuine (असली)

730 **Level** (Adj.) - (समतल)
Flat or even
Syno: Flat (सपाट)

731 Leverage (N.) - (प्रभाव)
Influence or power to affect outcomes
Syno: Influence (प्रभाव)

732 **Levitate** (V.) - (तैरना (हवा में))
To rise and hover in the air by supposed magical powers
Syno: Float (तैरना)

733 **Light Up** (V.) - (प्रकाशित करना)
To illuminate or become illuminated
Syno: Illuminate (रोशनी देना)

734 **Limpid** (Adj.) - (स्पष्ट) *[#R-2]*
Completely clear and free of anything that darkens
Syno: Clear (साफ), Lucid (सुस्पष्ट)

735 **Linked** (Adj.) - (जुड़ा हुआ)
Connected or joined with something
Syno: Associated (संबंधित)

736 **Lint** (N.) - (रोआँ, रूई के छोटे रेशे)
Fine fibers that separate from cloth or yarn surface
Syno: Fur (रोआँ)

737 **Lithe** (Adj.) - (लचीला)
Thin, supple, and graceful
Syno: Flexible (लचीला)

738 **Litter** (N.) - (कचरा)
Rubbish or debris scattered untidily
Syno: Trash (कूड़ा)

739 **Little** (Adj.) - (थोड़ा)
Small in size, amount, or degree
Syno: Trivial (तुच्छ)

740 **Livid** (Adj.) - (बहुत क्रोधित) *[#R-2]*
Furiously angry
Syno: Furious (उग्र)

741 **Lock** (V.) - (बंद करना)
To fasten with a key
Syno: Shut (बंद करना)

742 Longevity (N.) - (दीर्घायु)
A long life
Syno: Durability (टिकाऊपन)

743 **Longing** (N.) - (लालसा) *[#R-2]*
A yearning desire
Syno: Yearning (तड़प)

744 **Look** (V.) - (देखना)
To turn eyes to see
Syno: See (देखना)

745 **Lousy** (Adj.) - (खराब) *[#R-3]*
Very poor or bad
Syno: Awful (भयंकर), Terrible (भयानक), Pitiful (दयनीय)

746 Loving (Adj.) - (प्रेमपूर्ण)
Showing love
Syno: Affectionate (स्नेही)

747 **Lucky** (Adj.) - (भाग्यशाली)
Having, bringing, or resulting from good luck
Syno: Auspicious (शुभ)

748 **Lull** (N.) - (शांति) *[#R-2]*
A period of calm or diminished activity
Syno: Calm (शांति)

749 **Lullaby** (N.) - (लोरी)~
A song used to help a child sleep
Syno: Song (गीत)

750 **Lure** (V.) - (लुभाना) *[#R-3]*
To tempt or attract
Syno: Attract (आकर्षित करना)

751 **Lurid** (Adj.) - (भड़कीला) *[#R-2 (2)]*
Unpleasantly vivid; ghastly; sensational; gruesome; terrible or distorted
Syno: Shocking (चौंकाने वाला), Over-Bright (अत्यधिक चमकीला) {Violent (हिंसक)}

752 **Lurk** (V.) - (घात में रहना, छिपकर रहना) *[#R-2]*
To be or remain hidden so as to wait in ambush
Syno: Sneak (चुपके से चलना), Prowl (दबे पाँव घूमना)

753 Luxuriant (Adj.) - (प्रचुर) *[#R-4 (2)]*
Rich and profuse in growth
Syno: Abundant (बहुतायत), Lush (भरपूर), Flourishing (फलता-फूलता)

754 Lying (Adj.) - (झूठा)
Deliberately false
Syno: Misleading (भ्रामक)

755 **Lyrical** (Adj.) - (संगीतमय)
Expressing the writer's emotions in an imaginative and beautiful way
Syno: Musical (संगीतपूर्ण)

756 **Madness** (N.) - (पागलपन) *[#R-1 (1)]*
The state of being mentally ill, especially severely. Also, extremely foolish behaviour
Syno: Insanity (पागलपन)

757 **Magical** (Adj.) - (जादुई)
Relating to, using, or resembling magic
Syno: Enchanting (मोहक)

758 Magnificence (N.) - (भव्यता)
Great beauty or impressive splendor
Syno: Grandeur (शानदारपन)

759 **Magnify** (V.) - (बढ़ाना) *[#R-2]*
To make something appear larger; to exaggerate or increase size
Syno: Enlarge (बड़ा करना), Expand (विस्तार करना)

760 Major (Adj.) - (महत्वपूर्ण)
Important or serious
Syno: Considerable (उल्लेखनीय)

761 **Makeshift** (Adj.) - (अस्थायी)
Serving as a temporary substitute
Syno: Provisional (अस्थायी)

762 **Malady** (N.) - (रोग) *[#R-1 (1)]*
A disease or ailment
Syno: Illness (बीमारी)

763 **Malediction** (N.) - (अभिशाप)
A spoken wish of evil or harm on someone
Syno: Curse (शाप)

764 **Manacle** (V.) - (हथकड़ी लगाना)
To restrain with metal chains or handcuffs
Syno: Fetter (बेड़ी लगाना)

765 Mandate (N./V.) - (आदेश; अनिवार्य करना) *[#R-2 (1)]*
An official order or authority (N.); To officially order or authorize (V.)
Syno: Decree (राजाज्ञा), Command (आज्ञा) {Injunction (आदेश)}

766 **Mandible** (N.) - (जबड़ा)
The jaw or jawbone, especially the lower jawbone
Syno: Jaw (जबड़ा)

767 **Mania** (N.) - (सनक, पागलपन) *[#R-2]*
Excessive enthusiasm or desire; an obsession
Syno: Madness (जुनून)

768 Manual (N.) - (नियमावली)
A handbook of instructions
Syno: Handbook (विवरण पुस्तिका)

769 **Mask** (V.) - (छिपाना) *[#R-1 (1)]*
To hide or cover something
Syno: Conceal (ढकना)

770 Masquerade (V.) - (ढोंग करना)
To pretend or appear falsely as something else
Syno: Act (अभिनय करना)

771 Mastery (N.) - (प्रवीणता, आधिपत्य)
Complete control or skill in something
Syno: Authority (अधिकार)

772 **Masticate** (V.) - (चबाना) *[#R-1 (1)]*
To chew food
Syno: Chew (चबाना) {Munch (चबाना)}

773 **Matching** (Adj.) - (मेल खाता हुआ)
Corresponding or identical in type or details
Syno: Resembling (समान)

774 **Materiel** (N.) - (सैन्य सामग्री)
Military materials and equipment
Syno: Military Supplies (सैन्य आपूर्ति)

775 Maxim (N.) - (कहावत)~
A short, pithy statement expressing a general truth or rule of conduct
Syno: Proverb (कहावत)

776 **Mayhem** (N.) - (अव्यवस्था)
Violent or damaging disorder
Syno: Chaos (अराजकता)

777 Measure (N./V.) - (आकलन; मापना) *[#R-1 (2)]*
A standard unit or method of assessment (N.); To calculate or estimate size or amount (V.)
Syno: Gauge (नापना) {Steps (कदम)}

778 Mediation (N.) - (मध्यस्थता)
Intervention in a dispute in order to resolve it; arbitration
Syno: Intervention (हस्तक्षेप)

779 Mellifluous (Adj.) - (मधुर) *[#R-2]*
(Of a voice or words) sweet or musical; pleasant to hear
Syno: Dulcet (मधुर), Musical (संगीतमय)

780 Memoir (N.) - (संस्मरण)~
A historical account or biography written from personal knowledge
Syno: Diary (डायरी)

781 Mentor (N.) - (मार्गदर्शक) *[#R-2]*
An experienced and trusted adviser
Syno: Guide (मार्गदर्शक)

782 **Mesmerise** (V.) - (मंत्रमुग्ध करना)
To hold attention completely
Syno: Fascinate (मोहित करना)

783 **Metamorphosis** (N.) - (रूपांतरण)~
A complete change in form or nature
Syno: Change (परिवर्तन)

784 Mince (V.) - (छोटे-छोटे टुकड़े करना)
To cut into very small pieces; to walk with short, affected steps
Syno: Chop (काटना)

785 **Mindfulness** (N.) - (सजगता)
The state of being conscious and aware of the present moment
Syno: Awareness (जागरूकता)

786 Miraculous (Adj.) - (चमत्कारी) *[#R-1 (1)]*
Extraordinary
Syno: Incredible (अविश्वसनीय) {Extraordinary (असाधारण)}

787 Mirth (N.) - (आनंद)
Amusement, especially shown by laughter
Syno: Delight (प्रसन्नता)

788 **Misdeed** (N.) - (कुकर्म)
A wrong or immoral action
Syno: Transgression (अपराध)

789 **Misleading** (Adj.) - (भ्रामक)
Giving a wrong impression
Syno: Mendacious (झूठा)

790 **Missive** (N.) - (लंबा कार्यालयी पत्र)
A letter, especially a long or official one
Syno: Letter (पत्र)

791 **Mistake** (N.) - (गलती)
An action or judgment that is misguided or wrong
Syno: Error (त्रुटि)

792 **Mitigation** (N.) - (गम्भीरता कम कर देना) *[#R-1 (1)]*
The action of reducing severity or seriousness
Syno: Reduction (कमी) {Alleviation (राहत)}

793 **Mock** (V.) - (मजाक उड़ाना)
To tease or laugh at scornfully
Syno: Taunt (ताना मारना)

794 **Moderation** (N.) - (संयम)
The practice of using something in a limited and balanced way
Syno: Temperance (संयम)

795 **Monolithic** (Adj.) - (विशालकाय)
Very large and solid
Syno: Huge (विशाल)

796 **Moral** (Adj.) - (नैतिक)
Concerned with right and wrong
Syno: Ethical (नीतिपरक)

797 **Morale** (N.) - (मनोबल) *[#R-2]*
The confidence and enthusiasm of a person or group
Syno: Self-Confidence (आत्मविश्वास)

798 **Mordant** (Adj.) - (तीखा, व्यंग्यात्मक) *[#R-2]*
Sharply sarcastic or cutting in a hurtful way
Syno: Bitter (तीखा), Sarcastic (व्यंग्यात्मक)

799 Motif (N.) - (रूपांकन, योजना)
A decorative pattern or recurring theme
Syno: Design (रचना)

800 Motive (N.) - (प्रेरणा) *[#R-2]*
A reason for doing something
Syno: Reason (कारण), Intention (इरादा)

801 **Mourn** (V.) - (शोक मनाना)
To feel sadness for loss
Syno: Grieve (दुख मनाना)

802 **Multitude** (N.) - (झुंड) *[#R-1 (1)]*
A large number of people or things
Syno: Mass (समूह) {Horde (भीड़)}

803 **Munch** (V.) - (चबाना)
To eat by chewing continuously and often noisily
Syno: Chew (चबाना)

804 **Mutant** (Adj.) - (उत्परिवर्तित)
Changed from the normal type due to mutation
Syno: Deviant (विचलित)

805 **Mutate** (V.) - (उत्परिवर्तित होना)
To change or cause to change in form or nature
Syno: Change (बदलना)

806 **Nacreous** (Adj.) - (मोती जैसा)
Having a pearly, nacre-like shine
Syno: Iridescent (चमकदार)

807 **Nap** (N.) - (झपकी)~
A short daytime sleep
Syno: Siesta (दोपहर की नींद)

808 **Nark** (V.) - (चिढ़ाना)
To irritate or annoy someone
Syno: Irritate (परेशान करना)

809 **Nascence** (N.) - (उत्पत्ति)
The process of coming into being; the beginning or early stage
Syno: Incipience (प्रारंभ)

810 Naughty (Adj.) - (शरारती) *[#R-1 (1)]*
Badly behaved or disobedient; mischievous
Syno: Impish (नटखट) {Mischievous (शरारती)}

811 Nauseous (Adj.) - (घृणाजनक)
Causing or feeling sickness and urge to vomit
Syno: Loathsome (घिनौना)

812 Necessary (Adj.) - (आवश्यक)
Required or needed
Syno: Essential (ज़रूरी)

813 Negotiation (N.) - (सौदेबाजी)
A discussion to reach an agreement
Syno: Bargaining (मोलभाव)

814 **Neophyte** (N.) - (नवशिक्षु)~
A person who is new to an activity or field
Syno: Beginner (नया सीखने वाला)

815 **Nexus** (N.) - (संबंध) *[#R-1 (1)]*
A connection linking things together
Syno: Link (संपर्क) {Connection (संबंध)}

816 **Niggard** (N.) - (कंजूस)
A stingy or ungenerous person
Syno: Miser (कंजूस)

817 **Nihilistic** (Adj.) - (शून्यवादी)
Rejecting religious and moral principles
Syno: Cynical (संशयवादी)

818 **Nincompoop** (N.) - (मूर्ख) *[#R-2 (1)]*
A foolish or stupid person
Syno: Fool (मूर्ख)

819 **Nomadic** (Adj.) - (खानाबदोश) *[#R-2]*
Moving from place to place
Syno: Roving (घूमन्तू), Wandering (भटकने वाला)

820 **Nonplussed** (Adj.) - (चकित)
So surprised and confused that one cannot react
Syno: Puzzled (उलझन में)

821 Nostalgia (N.) - (अतीत की याद)~
A sentimental longing for the past
Syno: Longing (गहरी इच्छा)

822 Nostalgic (Adj.) - (बीते वक्त की याद दिलाने वाला)
Feeling longing for the past
Syno: Dreamy (सपनों में खोये रहना)

823 **Nudge** (V.) - (हलके धक्के से ध्यान आकर्षित करना)
To push or touch gently
Syno: Poke (कोंचना)

824 Nurture (V.) - (पालन-पोषण करना)
To care for and encourage growth
Syno: Grow (बढ़ाना)

825 **Oasis** (N.) - (मरुस्थल में हराभरा स्थान)~ *[#R-1 (1)]*
A fertile place in a desert with water
Syno: Spring (झरना)

826 Obfuscation (N.) - (भ्रम) *[#R-2]*
The act of making something unclear
Syno: Confusion (उलझन)

827 **Oblate** (N.) - (मठ में रहने वाला बाहरी आदमी)
A lay person living in a monastery without vows
Syno: Devotee (भक्त)

828 Obligation (N.) - (दायित्व) *[#R-4 (3)]*
A moral or legal duty or commitment
Syno: Commitment (प्रतिबद्धता), Duty (कर्तव्य),

Responsibility (जिम्मेदारी) {Binding (बंधन)}

829 Obliterate (V.) - (मिटाना) *[#R-3 (5)]*
To destroy completely; wipe out
Syno: Annihilate (नष्ट करना), Abolish (हटाना), Erase (मिटाना) {Demolish (ध्वस्त करना), Eradicate (मिटा देना), Destroy (नष्ट करना)}

830 Obnoxious (Adj.) - (घृणित) *[#R-1 (2)]*
Extremely unpleasant or offensive
Syno: Disgusting (घिनौना) {Awful (भयानक), Abhorrent (अत्यंत बुरा)}

831 Observe (V.) - (अवलोकन करना)
To notice or see carefully
Syno: Watch (ध्यान से देखना)

832 Obstacle (N.) - (बाधा) *[#R-1 (1)]*
Something that blocks or hinders progress
Syno: Barrier (अवरोध) {Hindrance (बाधा)}

833 **Obstruction** (N.) - (बाधा)
The act or state of blocking or being blocked
Syno: Hindrance (अवरोध)

834 Obtain (V.) - (प्राप्त करना)
To get, acquire, or secure something
Syno: Achieve (हासिल करना)

835 **Obtainable** (Adj.) - (मिलने योग्य)
Easy to get or acquire
Syno: Accessible (सुलभ)

836 **Obtrusive** (Adj.) - (अनचाहे रूप से स्पष्ट)
Too noticeable in an unwelcome way
Syno: Prominent (प्रमुख)

837 Occur (V.) - (घटित होना)
To happen or take place
Syno: Happen (होना)

838 **Offensive** (Adj.) - (आपत्तिजनक)
Causing hurt, anger, or strong displeasure
Syno: Upsetting (परेशान करने वाला)

839 Omission (N.) - (चूक)
The act of leaving out something
Syno: Deletion (हटाना)

840 **Omnipresent** (Adj.) - (सर्वव्यापी)~
Present everywhere; found in all places
Syno: Universal (सभी जगह पाया जाने वाला)

841 Omniscient (Adj.) - (सर्वज्ञ)~
Knowing everything
Syno: All-Knowing (सर्वज्ञ)

842 **Onus** (N.) - (भार) *[#R-2 (2)]*
A duty or responsibility placed on someone
Syno: Responsibility (ज़िम्मेदारी), Burden (बोझ)

843 **Operational** (Adj.) - (कार्यशील)
Ready to function or in working condition
Syno: Effective (प्रभावी)

844 Opinion (N.) - (राय) *[#R-2]*
A personal view or judgment
Syno: View (दृष्टिकोण), Idea (विचार)

845 **Opportune** (Adj.) - (अनुकूल) *[#R-1 (1)]*
Done or occurring at a favorable or useful time
Syno: Timely (समय पर) {Appropriate (उपयुक्त)}

846 **Opposite** (Adj.) - (विपरीत)
Totally different
Syno: Antagonistic (विरोधी)

847 **Ordain** (V.) - (घोषित करना) *[#R-1 (1)]*
To officially order or decree something
Syno: Proclaim (घोषित करना)

848 **Organise** (V.) - (व्यवस्थित करना) *[#R-2]*
To arrange systematically
Syno: Arrange (व्यवस्थित करना), Coordinate (तालमेल बिठाना)

849 **Orifice** (N.) - (छिद्र)~
An opening in a body or object
Syno: Opening (खुला भाग)

850 **Ossified** (Adj.) - (कठोर)
Rigid and unchanging
Syno: Rigid (कठोर)

851 **Ossify** (V.) - (हड्डी बन जाना, सख्त हो जाना)~ *[#R-2]*
To turn into bone or become rigid
Syno: Harden (कठोर हो जाना)

852 **Ostensibly** (Adv.) - (प्रकट रूप से) *[#R-2]*
According to what appears to be true
Syno: Supposedly (कथित रूप से), Apparently (प्रकट रूप से)

853 **Outraged** (Adj.) - (बेहद नाराज)
Feeling strong anger or shock
Syno: Angry (क्रोधित)

854 **Ovation** (N.) - (अभिनंदन)
Loud and enthusiastic public applause
Syno: Applause (तालियाँ)

855 **Over** (Adj.) - (समाप्त)
Finished or completed
Syno: Bygone (बीता हुआ)

856 **Oversee** (V.) - (निरीक्षण करना)
To supervise work or people officially

Syno: Supervise (निगरानी करना)

857 **Overture** (N.) - (प्रस्तावना)
An introduction to something more important
Syno: Preamble (आरंभिक कथन)

858 **Overwhelmed** (Adj.) - (अभिभूत) *[#R-2]*
Feeling sudden strong emotion
Syno: Surprised (आश्चर्यचकित)

859 **Pace** (N.) - (रफ़्तार) *[#R-1 (1)]*
The speed or rate
Syno: Speed (गति) {Rate (दर)}

860 **Pacific** (Adj.) - (शांतिपूर्ण) *[#R-2]*
Peaceful in character or intent
Syno: Peaceful (शांत), Mollifying (शांत करने वाला)

861 **Pail** (N.) - (बाल्टी) *[#R-1 (1)]*
A container used to hold liquids
Syno: Bucket (बाल्टी)

862 **Palimpsestic** (Adj.) - (परतदार)
Having layers from different times
Syno: Layered (कई स्तरों वाला)

863 **Pallid** (Adj.) - (पीला)
Unnaturally pale, often due to illness
Syno: Pale (पीला)

864 Palpable (Adj.) - (स्पष्ट)~ *[#R-2 (2)]*
Easily felt or clearly noticeable
Syno: Detectable (पता लगाने योग्य), Tangible (स्पर्शनीय) {Obvious (स्पष्ट)}

865 **Pamper** (V.) - (लाड़ प्यार करना) *[#R-2]*
To treat with excessive care or attention
Syno: Coddle (लाड़ प्यार से पालना), Mollycoddle (अत्यधिक लाड़ करना)

866 **Panacea** (N.) - (रामबाण)~ *[#R-4]*
A remedy for all problems or diseases
Syno: Cure-All (सर्वरोग निवारण), Remedy (इलाज)

867 Panache (N.) - (शान)
Showy confidence of style or manner
Syno: Flamboyance (भड़कीलापन)

868 Panic (N.) - (घबराहट)~ *[#R-2]*
Sudden uncontrollable fear or anxiety
Syno: Fright (डर), Frenzy (उन्माद)

869 **Panorama** (N.) - (विस्तृत दृश्य)~
A wide, unbroken view of a large area
Syno: Scene (दृश्य)

870 **Parade** (N.) - (जुलूस)
A public procession of people or vehicles
Syno: Procession (शोभायात्रा)

871 **Paradise** (N.) - (स्वर्ग) *[#R-1 (1)]*
A perfectly happy or ideal place
Syno: Bliss (आनंद) {Heaven (स्वर्ग)}

872 **Paragon** (N.) - (आदर्श)~
A perfect example of a quality
Syno: Epitome (उत्कृष्ट उदाहरण)

873 **Paramount** (Adj.) - (सर्वोपरि) *[#R-2 (2)]*
More important than anything else
Syno: Central (केंद्रीय), Supreme (सर्वोच्च)

874 **Paranoia** (N.) - (पागलपन भरा संदेह)~
A mental state of extreme suspicion or delusion
Syno: Anxiety (चिंता)

875 **Paranoid** (Adj.) - (संदेहग्रस्त) *[#R-2 (1)]*
Showing extreme or irrational suspicion
Syno: Suspicious (संदेहशील), Distrustful (अविश्वासी) {Sceptical (शक करने वाला)}

876 Parlour (N.) - (बैठक)
A room used for sitting or receiving guests
Syno: Room (कमरा)

877 **Parsimony** (N.) - (कंजूसी)~ *[#R-2]*
The extreme unwillingness to spend money or use resources
Syno: Miserliness (कंजूसी), Frugality (कम खर्च करने की आदत)

878 Partisan (Adj.) - (पक्षपाती)
Strongly biased
Syno: Biased (एकतरफ़ा)

879 Passion (N.) - (जुनून)
A strong and barely controllable emotion
Syno: Desire (इच्छा)

880 Pathetic (Adj.) - (दयनीय) *[#R-2]*
Arousing pity due to weakness or sadness
Syno: Pitiful (दयनीय)

881 **Pathos** (N.) - (करुणा)
A quality that evokes pity or sadness
Syno: Sorrow (दुःख)

882 Patience (N.) - (धैर्य)
The ability to wait calmly
Syno: Endurance (सहनशीलता)

883 **Patrol** (V.) - (गश्त लगाना)~ *[#R-1 (1)]*
To keep watch by moving around
Syno: Inspect (निरीक्षण करना) {Monitor (निगरानी करना)}

884 Patron (N.) - (संरक्षक) *[#R-1 (1)]*

A person who gives financial or other support
Syno: Sponsor (प्रायोजक) {Backer (समर्थक)}

885 **Pawn** (V.) - (गिरवी रखना)
To give as security for a loan
Syno: Pledge (गिरवी रखना)

886 **Peak** (N.) - (चरम) *[#R-1 (1)]*
The highest or most extreme point
Syno: Zenith (चरम बिन्दु)

887 **Pedigree** (N.) - (वंश)~
The record of descent or ancestry; lineage
Syno: Lineage (वंशावली)

888 Pejorative (Adj.) - (अपमानजनक)
Expressing contempt or disapproval
Syno: Derogatory (अपमानजनक)

889 **Penalise** (V.) - (दंडित करना)
To subject to some form of punishment
Syno: Punish (सजा देना)

890 Perception (N.) - (धारणा) *[#R-1 (1)]*
The ability to become aware through the senses
Syno: Awareness (जागरूकता)

891 **Perceptive** (Adj.) - (सूक्ष्मदर्शी)
Showing deep understanding or insight
Syno: Astute (कुशाग्र)

892 **Perdurable** (Adj.) - (स्थायी)
Lasting for a very long time
Syno: Long-Lasting (लंबे समय तक चलने वाला)

893 Perforate (V.) - (छिद्र करना) *[#R-1 (1)]*
To make one or more holes in something
Syno: Pierce (भेदना) {Puncture (छेद करना)}

894 Perjury (N.) - (झूठी शपथ)~
The crime of lying under oath in court
Syno: Falsehood (असत्य)

895 **Perky** (Adj.) - (प्रफुल्लित)
Cheerful and lively
Syno: Cheerful (खुश)

896 **Permeate** (V.) - (फैल जाना)
To spread through something
Syno: Diffuse (फैलना)

897 **Perquisite** (N.) - (अतिरिक्त लाभ)~
A benefit received because of a job or position
Syno: Privilege (विशेषाधिकार)

898 Persecution (N.) - (अत्याचार)
The cruel treatment because of beliefs or identity
Syno: Oppression (अत्याचार)

899 Persiflage (N.) - (हँसी-मज़ाक)
Light joking or teasing
Syno: Banter (मज़ाक)

900 **Persistently** (Adv.) - (लगातार)
In a firm and continuing manner
Syno: Continuously (निरंतर)

901 Perspicacious (Adj.) - (चतुर)~ *[#R-1 (2)]*
Having sharp understanding and insight
Syno: Shrewd (चतुर) {Insightful (सूझ-बूझ वाला)}

902 Perspicuous (Adj.) - (स्पष्ट) *[#R-2 (1)]*
Clearly expressed and easy to understand
Syno: Clear (साफ़), Precise (सटीक) {Lucid (स्पष्ट)}

903 **Pert** (Adj.) - (चुलबुला)
Attractively lively or cheeky
Syno: Lively (उत्साहपूर्ण)

904 **Perverse** (Adj.) - (दुष्ट)
Deliberately behaving in an unacceptable way
Syno: Nefarious (कुटिल)

905 Pester (V.) - (सताना) *[#R-2 (2)]*
To annoy someone repeatedly
Syno: Annoy (परेशान करना) {Bother (कष्ट देना)}

906 Petite (Adj.) - (नाजुक)
Small and delicate
Syno: Small (छोटा)

907 **Petition** (N.) - (याचिका)
A formal written request
Syno: Appeal (निवेदन)

908 **Petrify** (V.) - (पत्थर बनाना, भयभीत करना)
To frighten completely; or turn into stone
Syno: Harden (कठोर बनाना)

909 **Phonetic** (Adj.) - (उच्चारण-संबंधी)
Relating to speech sounds
Syno: Spoken (उच्चरित)

910 **Pillage** (V.) - (लूटना)
To rob a place using violence, especially in wartime
Syno: Plunder (लूटना)

911 Pioneer (Adj.) - (पथप्रदर्शक)~
Introducing something new
Syno: Primary (पहला)

912 **Piquancy** (N.) - (चटपटापन)
A pleasantly sharp or appetizing taste
Syno: Zest (चटपटापन)

913 **Pitfall** (N.) - (जोखिम)
A hidden or unsuspected danger or difficulty
Syno: Hazard (खतरा)

914 **Pity** (N.) - (दया)
A feeling of sorrow for others
Syno: Mercy (कृपा)

915 **Plaudit** (N.) - (प्रशंसा) *[#R-1 (1)]*
Praise or applause given by an audience
Syno: Praise (प्रशंसा) {Applause (तालियाँ)}

916 **Plea** (N.) - (याचना) *[#R-2]*
An urgent and emotional request
Syno: Appeal (अनुरोध)

917 Plead (V.) - (निवेदन करना) *[#R-2]*
To make an emotional appeal; argue for a claim
Syno: Request (अनुरोध करना), Beseech (विनती करना)

918 Pleasant (Adj.) - (सुखद) *[#R-3 (1)]*
Giving a sense of happy satisfaction or enjoyment
Syno: Amusing (मनोरंजक), Delightful (आनंददायक), Refreshing (ताज़गी भरा) {Enjoyable (आनंद देने वाला)}

919 **Pleasing** (Adj.) - (प्रसन्नतादायक) *[#R-1 (1)]*
Attractive or agreeable
Syno: Gratifying (संतोषजनक) {Appetizing (ललचाने वाला)}

920 **Plebiscite** (N.) - (जनमत संग्रह)~ *[#R-2]*
A direct public vote on an important issue
Syno: Referendum (सार्वजनिक मतदान)

921 Pledge (V.) - (प्रतिज्ञा करना)~ *[#R-1 (1)]*
To commit by a serious or formal promise
Syno: Promise (वादा करना)

922 **Plenteous** (Adj.) - (भरपूर)
Existing in large quantity
Syno: Profuse (अत्यधिक)

923 **Plod** (V.) - (थके क़दमों से चलना) *[#R-1 (1)]*
To walk slowly with heavy steps
Syno: Drag (घसीटते हुए चलना)

924 Plough (V.) - (जोतना)
To turn up the earth for cultivation
Syno: Cultivate (खेती करना)

925 Plump (Adj.) - (गोल-मटोल)
Pleasantly fat or rounded in shape
Syno: Fat (मोटा)

926 **Podium** (N.) - (मंच)~
A small raised platform for standing or speaking
Syno: Dais (मंच)

927 **Polished** (Adj.) - (सभ्य)
Shiny by rubbing; refined and elegant
Syno: Cultured (सुसंस्कृत)

928 **Pollute** (V.) - (प्रदूषित करना)
To make water, air, or place dirty or harmful
Syno: Contaminate (दूषित करना)

929 Pollution (N.) - (प्रदूषण)
The presence of harmful substances in the environment
Syno: Contamination (दूषण)

930 **Ponder** (V.) - (चिंतन करना)~ *[#R-2 (2)]*
To think carefully and seriously about something
Syno: Meditate (ध्यान लगाना), Contemplate (विचार करना) {Think (सोचना)}

931 **Populace** (N.) - (जनता)
The people living in a particular country or area
Syno: People (लोग)

932 Popular (Adj.) - (लोकप्रिय) *[#R-1 (1)]*
Liked or admired by many people
Syno: Favourite (पसंदीदा)

933 **Populous** (Adj.) - (घनी आबादी वाला)~
Having a large population; densely populated
Syno: Crowded (भीड़-भाड़ वाला)

934 Portray (V.) - (चित्रित करना)
To depict someone or something in a work of art or literature
Syno: Depict (वर्णन करना)

935 **Posterior** (Adj.) - (पिछला)
Coming after or situated behind
Syno: Dorsal (पीठ का)

936 Practical (Adj.) - (व्यावहारिक) *[#R-1 (1)]*
Related to real use or action, not theory
Syno: Sensible (समझदार) {Useful (उपयोगी)}

937 Preamble (N.) - (प्रस्तावना)
An introductory or opening statement
Syno: Introduction (परिचय)

938 **Precedence** (N.) - (प्राथमिकता) *[#R-6]*
The condition of having higher importance or priority

Syno: Priority (प्राथमिकता)

939 Precision (N.) - (सटीकता)
The quality of being exact and accurate
Syno: Accuracy (शुद्धता)

940 Preference (N.) - (प्राथमिकता)
A greater liking for one option over others
Syno: Tendency (रूझान)

941 **Premonition** (N.) - (पूर्वाभास)~ *[#R-1 (1)]*
A strong feeling that something is about to happen, especially something unpleasant
Syno: Forewarning (पूर्व सूचना) {Warning (चेतावनी)}

942 Preponderance (N.) - (प्रमुखता)
The quality or fact of being greater in number, quantity, or importance
Syno: Dominance (वर्चस्व)

943 Prerogative (N.) - (विशेषाधिकार) *[#R-2 (1)]*
A special right belonging to a person or group
Syno: Privilege (सुविधा)

944 Presumptuous (Adj.) - (अभिमानी) *[#R-1 (2)]*
Acting beyond what is proper or allowed
Syno: Arrogant (अभिमानी) {Bold (धृष्ट), Overconfident (अति आत्मविश्वासी)}

945 **Pretend** (V.) - (बहाना बनाना) *[#R-2]*
To act as if something false is true
Syno: Feign (बहाना करना)

946 Prevalent (Adj.) - (प्रचलित)
Widely existing at a particular time or place
Syno: Common (सामान्य)

947 **Preventive** (Adj.) - (निवारक)
Designed to prevent something
Syno: Protective (सुरक्षात्मक)

948 Principal (Adj.) - (मुख्य)
Most important
Syno: Major (प्रमुख)

949 Principle (N.) - (सिद्धांत)
A fundamental rule or belief that guides actions
Syno: Axiom (स्वयंसिद्ध)

950 **Probe** (V.) - (छानबीन करना) *[#R-2]*
To examine or search deeply
Syno: Investigate (जांच पड़ताल करना), Search (खोजना)

951 Proclivity (N.) - (प्रवृत्ति) *[#R-1 (2)]*
A natural or habitual inclination
Syno: Tendency (प्रवृत्ति)

952 Prodigy (N.) - (प्रतिभाशाली व्यक्ति)~ *[#R-1 (1)]*
A person, especially a young one, endowed with exceptional qualities or abilities
Syno: Genius (प्रतिभाशाली व्यक्ति) {Whiz (प्रतिभावान)}

953 **Profess** (V.) - (घोषित करना) *[#R-2]*
To claim openly but often falsely that one has (a quality or feeling)
Syno: Declare (घोषणा करना), Admit (स्वीकार करना)

954 **Prognosis** (N.) - (भविष्यवाणी) *[#R-1 (1)]*
A judgment or prediction about future outcome, especially medical
Syno: Forecast (पूर्वानुमान)

955 Proliferate (V.) - (तेजी से बढ़ना)~ *[#R-1 (1)]*
To increase rapidly in numbers; multiply
Syno: Reproduce (पैदा करना) {Escalate (बढ़ाना)}

956 Promiscuous (Adj.) - (असंयमी)
Showing lack of careful choice or selectiveness, especially in relationships
Syno: Indiscriminate (बिना सोचे-समझे)

957 **Promising** (Adj.) - (आशाजनक)
Showing signs of future success or good results
Syno: Bright (उज्वल)

958 Promotion (N.) - (पदोन्नति)
The act of supporting something or raising someone to a higher position
Syno: Elevation (उन्नति)

959 **Prone** (Adj.) - (झुकाव वाला) *[#R-1 (2)]*
Having a tendency or inclination; being likely
Syno: Inclined (झुकाव वाला)

960 **Proof** (N.) - (सबूत)
Evidence that shows a fact or truth
Syno: Evidence (साक्ष्य)

961 Propel (V.) - (धकेलना)
To push or drive something forward
Syno: Move (हिलाना)

962 Prophecy (N.) - (भविष्यवाणी)
A statement about future events
Syno: Prediction (पूर्वानुमान)

963 **Prophylactic** (Adj.) - (निवारक)
Intended to prevent disease
Syno: Preventive (निवारक)

964 **Propinquity** (N.) - (निकटता)
The state of being close

Syno: Nearness (समीपता)

965 Proposal (N.) - (प्रस्ताव) *[#R-1 (1)]*
An idea or plan for approval
Syno: Scheme (योजना) {Proffer (प्रस्ताव)}

966 **Proposition** (N.) - (प्रस्ताव)
A plan or suggestion for consideration
Syno: Proposal (प्रस्ताव)

967 Protrude (V.) - (बाहर निकलना)
To stick out or extend beyond a surface
Syno: Bulge (उभरना)

968 **Provenance** (N.) - (उत्पत्ति) *[#R-2]*
The origin or source of something
Syno: Origin (मूल स्थान)

969 Pugnacious (Adj.) - (लड़ाकू)~ *[#R-3 (1)]*
Quick to argue or ready to fight
Syno: Truculent (आक्रामक), Belligerent (झगड़ालू), Waspish (चिड़चिड़ा) {Quarrelsome (झगड़ालू)}

970 **Pull** (V.) - (खींचना)
To draw something towards oneself
Syno: Drag (घसीटना)

971 Pupil (N.) - (विद्यार्थी)
A student in a school
Syno: Student (छात्र)

972 **Purge** (V.) - (शुद्ध करना)~
To cleanse or clear out
Syno: Evacuate (खाली करना)

973 Pursue (V.) - (पीछा करना)~ *[#R-1 (1)]*
To follow or chase
Syno: Chase (पीछा करना) {Follow (पीछे चलना)}

974 **Purview** (N.) - (क्षेत्राधिकार)~
The scope or range of authority or concern
Syno: Domain (क्षेत्राधिकार)

975 Puzzled (Adj.) - (असमंजस में)
Unable to understand clearly
Syno: Confused (उलझन में)

976 **Quack** (N.) - (धोखेबाज़)~
A dishonest person pretending to have expert knowledge
Syno: Fake (नकली)

977 **Quail** (V.) - (सहम जाना)
To feel or show fear or nervousness
Syno: Cringe (घबरा जाना)

978 **Quake** (V.) - (काँपना)
to shake or tremble
Syno: Tremble (कांपना)

979 Quandary (N.) - (दुविधा)~ *[#R-3 (1)]*
A state of uncertainty in a difficult situation
Syno: Dilemma (कठिन चुनाव), Impasse (अटकाव)

980 Quarrelsome (Adj.) - (झगड़ालू)
Inclined to argue or fight
Syno: Querulous (चिड़चिड़ा)

981 Quarry (N.) - (शिकार)
A person or animal that is hunted or searched for
Syno: Victim (पीड़ित)

982 **Quest** (N.) - (खोज)~ *[#R-2]*
A long or difficult search
Syno: Search (तलाश)

983 **Quicken** (V.) - (तेज़ करना)
To make or become faster or quicker
Syno: Accelerate (गति बढ़ाना)

984 Quintessential (Adj.) - (सर्वोत्तम) *[#R-1 (2)]*
Representing the most perfect or typical example of a quality or class
Syno: Typical (विशिष्ट) {Exemplary (आदर्श)}

985 Quite (Adv.) - (काफ़ी)~
To a certain or fairly significant extent
Syno: Noticeably (ध्यान देने योग्य रूप से)

986 **Quiver** (V.) - (काँपना) *[#R-2]*
To shake gently
Syno: Tremble (कांपना), Shake (हिलना)

987 **Rabid** (Adj.) - (कट्टर)
Having extreme or fanatical beliefs or feelings
Syno: Extreme (चरम)

988 **Ragged** (Adj.) - (फटे हुए)
Wearing tattered clothes; jagged or uneven
Syno: Torn (फटा हुआ)

989 **Ramification** (N.) - (जटिल अनपेक्षित परिणाम)~
A complex or unwelcome result of an action
Syno: Consequence (परिणाम)

990 Rampant (Adj.) - (अनियंत्रित) *[#R-1 (2)]*
Spreading or growing without control
Syno: Excessive (अत्यधिक) {Uncontrolled (अनियंत्रित), Regnant (प्रभावशाली)}

991 **Rampart** (N.) - (किलेबंदी) *[#R-4]*
A defensive wall built for protection
Syno: Bulwark (किलेबंदी), Parapet (सुरक्षा-दीवार)

992 **Rancor** (N.) - (गहरी दुश्मनी)
Deep, bitter hostility or resentment
Syno: Animosity (शत्रुता)

993 **Ravenous** (Adj.) - (भूखा) *[#R-2]*
Extremely hungry
Syno: Esurient (अत्यधिक भूखा), Starved (भूखा)

994 Ravine (N.) - (खाई)
A deep, narrow gorge with steep sides
Syno: Abyss (गहराई)

995 Ravishing (Adj.) - (मोहक)
Extremely attractive or delightful
Syno: Stunning (अत्यंत सुंदर)

996 Realm (N.) - (क्षेत्र) *[#R-3]*
A kingdom or a particular field or domain
Syno: Field (क्षेत्र), Dimension (आयाम)

997 Rebellious (Adj.) - (विद्रोही) *[#R-2]*
Showing a desire to resist authority, control, or convention
Syno: Unruly (उपद्रवी), Disobedient (अवज्ञाकारी)

998 Recapitulate (V.) - (सार बताना)
To summarize and state again the main points
Syno: Summarize (सारांश देना)

999 **Recapitulation** (N.) - (सारांश; पुनः स्मरण) *[#R-2]*
A brief summary or restatement of main points; The act of recalling something
Syno: Summary (सारांश), Recall (याद करना)

1000 Recently (Adv.) - (हाल ही में)
Not long ago
Syno: Lately (हाल ही में)

1001 Receptacle (N.) - (पात्र)~
An object used to hold or contain something
Syno: Container (पात्र)

1002 Recipient (N.) - (प्राप्तकर्ता)
A person or thing that receives something
Syno: Receiver (प्राप्तकर्ता)

1003 Reckon (V.) - (सोचना) *[#R-2 (1)]*
To establish by counting or calculation
Syno: Think (सोचना), Count (गिनना) {Imagine (कल्पना करना)}

1004 Recollect (V.) - (याद करना) *[#R-1 (1)]*
To call something back to mind
Syno: Remember (याद करना) {Recall (याद करना)}

1005 Reconcile (V.) - (मेल-मिलाप करना) *[#R-1 (2)]*
To restore harmony or make things compatible
Syno: Resolve (सुलझाना)

1006 **Reconnoitre** (V.) - (खोज करना)
To examine an area, especially for military purposes
Syno: Inspect (निरीक्षण करना)

1007 **Recreant** (N.) - (कायर)
A cowardly or disloyal person
Syno: Coward (डरपोक)

1008 **Recumbent** (Adj.) - (लेटा हुआ)
Lying down
Syno: Prostrate (गिरा हुआ)

1009 **Refuge** (N.) - (शरण) *[#R-2]*
A place or state of safety from danger or trouble
Syno: Shelter (आश्रय)

1010 **Regal** (Adj.) - (शाही)
Royal or magnificent
Syno: Majestic (शानदार)

1011 **Regard** (N.) - (सम्मान) *[#R-2]*
Respect or consideration
Syno: Respect (आदर)

1012 Regime (N.) - (शासन) *[#R-2]*
A system or method of government or rule
Syno: Authority (अधिकार), Rule (नियम)

1013 **Regress** (V.) - (पतन होना)
To return to a less developed or earlier state
Syno: Backslide (पीछे हटना)

1014 **Rehabilitate** (V.) - (पुनर्स्थापित करना)~
To restore to health, normal life, or proper condition
Syno: Restore (पुनर्स्थापित करना)

1015 Relief (N.) - (राहत)
Alleviation of pain, distress, or anxiety; aid in time of danger
Syno: Aid (सहायता)

1016 Relish (V.) - (आनंद लेना) *[#R-3]*
To enjoy something greatly
Syno: Enjoy (आनंद लेना), Adore (प्यार करना)

1017 **Relocation** (N.) - (स्थानांतरण)
The act of moving to a new place to live or work
Syno: Migration (प्रवास)

1018 **Remedial** (Adj.) - (उपचारात्मक) *[#R-1 (1)]*
Given or intended as a remedy or cure
Syno: Corrective (सुधारात्मक)

1019 **Remedy** (N.) - (उपचार) *[#R-3]*
A means of curing a problem

Syno: Cure (इलाज), Panacea (रामबाण इलाज)

1020 Remind (V.) - (याद दिलाना)
To cause someone to remember
Syno: Recall (स्मरण करना)

1021 **Reminisce** (V.) - (पुरानी यादों में खो जाना)~
To think or talk with pleasure about past experiences
Syno: Remember (याद करना)

1022 Reminiscence (N.) - (याद)~
A memory or story about a past event
Syno: Remembrance (स्मरण)

1023 Rendezvous (N.) - (नियोजित बैठक) *[#R-2]*
A planned meeting
Syno: Appointment (मुलाकात)

1024 Renounce (V.) - (त्यागना) *[#R-3]*
To formally give up or declare abandonment of something
Syno: Forsake (परित्याग करना), Abjure (शपथपूर्वक त्यागना), Reject (ठुकराना)

1025 **Repartee** (N.) - (हाजिर जवाबी) *[#R-2 (1)]*
Conversation marked by quick, witty replies
Syno: Response (प्रतिउत्तर)

1026 **Repeated** (Adj.) - (बार-बार होने वाला)
Done or happening many times
Syno: Reiterated (पुनरावृत्ति)

1027 Repercussion (N.) - (प्रतिक्रिया) *[#R-2 (1)]*
An indirect or unexpected result, usually negative
Syno: Consequence (परिणाम), Reaction (प्रतिक्रिया)

1028 **Replace** (V.) - (प्रतिस्थापित करना) *[#R-2]*
To take the place of another
Syno: Substitute (प्रतिस्थापित करना)

1029 **Repose** (N.) - (विश्राम)
A state of rest or calm
Syno: Rest (विश्राम)

1030 Representative (Adj.) - (प्रतिनिधिक)
Serving as a typical example
Syno: Typical (प्रतिनिधिक)

1031 Reproduce (V.) - (नकल बनाना)
To produce a copy or representation
Syno: Replicate (हूबहू नकल करना)

1032 **Reproof** (N.) - (फटकार)
An expression of blame or disapproval
Syno: Rebuke (फटकार)

1033 Repugnance (N.) - (घृणा)
A strong feeling of disgust or dislike
Syno: Aversion (अरुचि)

1034 Repulse (V.) - (पीछे हटाना) *[#R-2 (1)]*
To drive back or force away
Syno: Repel (प्रतिकर्षित करना, पीछे हटाना)

1035 Reputation (N.) - (प्रतिष्ठा) *[#R-1 (2)]*
The general opinion or image of someone
Syno: Prestige (सम्मान) {Character (चरित्र), Fame (प्रसिद्धि)}

1036 Request (N./V.) - (निवेदन; अनुरोध करना) *[#R-3]*
A polite or formal act of asking (N.); To ask politely (V.)
Syno: Plea (निवेदन); Ask (पूछना)

1037 Requirement (N.) - (आवश्यकता) *[#R-1 (1)]*
Something that is necessary or needed
Syno: Essential (आवश्यक) {Necessity (आवश्यकता)}

1038 Requisite (Adj./N.) - (अनिवार्य; आवश्यक वस्तु) *[#R-3 (1)]*
Necessary for a purpose (Adj.); Something that is required (N.)
Syno: Obligatory (अनिवार्य), Essential (आवश्यक); Precondition (पूर्व शर्त) {Necessity (आवश्यकता)}

1039 Resentment (N.) - (रंजिश, मन में बैठा हुआ रोष) *[#R-1 (1)]*
Bitter indignation at unfair treatment
Syno: Anger (गुस्सा)

1040 **Resignation** (N.) - (त्यागपत्र) *[#R-2]*
The act of formally giving up a job or position
Syno: Acceptance (स्वीकृति), Surrender (छोड़ देना)

1041 Resolution (N.) - (संकल्प) *[#R-2]*
A firm and determined decision
Syno: Decision (निर्णय)

1042 **Respect** (N.) - (आदर) *[#R-3 (1)]*
A feeling of esteem or admiration
Syno: Deference (सम्मान), Honour (गौरव) {Regard (सम्मान)}

1043 **Respite** (N.) - (विराम)~ *[#R-2]*
A short period of rest or relief from something difficult
Syno: Break (ठहराव), Hiatus (अंतराल)

1044 Resplendent (Adj.) - (चमकीला) *[#R-2 (1)]*
Very bright, colorful, and impressive to look at

Syno: Dazzling (चकाचौंध), Magnificent (शानदार)

1045 **Restrain** (V.) - (नियंत्रित करना) *[#R-2]*
To prevent or hold back; to keep under control or within limits

Syno: Control (नियंत्रण करना), Constrain (सीमित करना)

1046 **Restraint** (N.) - (संयम) *[#R-2]*
Self-control; the act of holding back

Syno: Self-control (आत्म-नियंत्रण), Control (नियंत्रण)

1047 **Restrict** (V.) - (सीमित करना) *[#R-3]*
To put a limit on; to keep under control

Syno: Prohibit (मना करना)

1048 **Result** (N.) - (परिणाम) *[#R-1 (2)]*
The outcome of an action

Syno: Outcome (नतीजा)

1049 **Reticence** (N.) - (अल्पभाषिता)
The habit of speaking very little

Syno: Reserve (संकोच)

1050 Retort (V.) - (तीखा जवाब देना)
To reply quickly and angrily

Syno: Reply (उत्तर देना)

1051 Revenue (N.) - (आय)
Income, especially when of an organization and of a substantial nature

Syno: Income (प्राप्ति)

1052 **Revile** (V.) - (गाली देना)~ *[#R-3]*
To criticize in an abusive or angrily insulting manner

Syno: Abuse (दुर्व्यवहार करना)

1053 **Revolt** (N.) - (विद्रोह) *[#R-2]*
A violent action in opposition to a government or law

Syno: Riot (दंगा)

1054 **Revolution** (N.) - (परिक्रमा)
The act of moving in a circular path

Syno: Gyration (घूर्णन)

1055 Rhythm (N.) - (ताल) *[#R-1 (1)]*
A strong, regular repeated pattern of movement or sound

Syno: Tempo (गति) {Cadence (लय)}

1056 **Riddle** (N.) - (पहेली) *[#R-2]*
A puzzling question

Syno: Puzzle (पहेली)

1057 Right (Adj.) - (सही)
Morally good or correct

Syno: Correct (सही)

1058 **Rind** (N.) - (छिलका)
The tough outer skin of certain fruit, especially citrus fruit

Syno: Peel (छिलका)

1059 **Rip** (V.) - (फाड़ना)
To tear or pull quickly or forcibly away

Syno: Tear (चीरना)

1060 **Ripeness** (N.) - (परिपक्वता)
The quality of being fully grown or developed

Syno: Maturity (परिपक्वता)

1061 **Rivet** (V.) - (ध्यान खींचना)
To completely capture and hold someone's attention

Syno: Engage (व्यस्त रखना)

1062 **Rob** (V.) - (लूटना)
To take property unlawfully by force or threat

Syno: Plunder (लूटना)

1063 **Robe** (N.) - (पोशाक) *[#R-2]*
A long, loose outer garment

Syno: Cloak (चोगा, ओढ़नी)

1064 Rogue (N.) - (दुष्ट)
A dishonest or unprincipled person

Syno: Ruffian (गुंडा)

1065 Rotate (V.) - (घूमना)
To move or cause to move in a circle around an axis

Syno: Revolve (परिक्रमण करना)

1066 **Rout** (N.) - (पराजय)
A disorderly retreat of defeated troops

Syno: Defeat (पराजय)

1067 **Royal** (Adj.) - (राजसी)
Relating to a king, queen, or other sovereign

Syno: Kingly (राजा जैसा)

1068 **Ruck** (N.) - (भीड़)
A dense mass of people or things

Syno: Mass (जनसमूह)

1069 **Rumour** (N.) - (अफवाह)
A currently circulating story or report of uncertain truth

Syno: Hearsay (सुनी-सुनाई बात)

1070 **Ruse** (N.) - (चाल)
An action intended to deceive someone

Syno: Trick (तरकीब)

1071 **Rushed** (Adj.) - (जल्दी में)
Done or acting with great speed; hurried
Syno: Pressed (दबाव में)

1072 Sacrilege (N.) - (पवित्रता का हनन)~ *[#R-1 (1)]*
The violation or misuse of what is regarded as sacred
Syno: Blasphemy (ईश्वर निन्दा)

1073 **Saga** (N.) - (गाथा)~
A long story of heroic achievement
Syno: Narrative (कथा)

1074 **Sailor** (N.) - (नाविक)
A person who works on a ship or boat
Syno: Mariner (समुद्री यात्री)

1075 **Salacious** (Adj.) - (कामुक) *[#R-1 (1)]*
Showing improper or excessive sexual interest
Syno: Lustful (कामुक) {Obscene (अश्लील)}

1076 **Salty** (Adj.) - (नमकीन)
Tasting of or containing salt
Syno: Saline (लवणीय)

1077 **Sanction** (N.) - (अनुमति) *[#R-4 (1)]*
The official approval or authorization
Syno: Permission (अनुमति), Approval (स्वीकृति); Permit (अनुमति)

1078 Sanguinity (N.) - (आशावाद)
The optimism or positive outlook, especially in difficulty
Syno: Optimism (आशावाद)

1079 Satisfy (V.) - (संतुष्ट करना)
To meet the expectations, needs, or desires of someone
Syno: Delight (प्रसन्न करना)

1080 **Sauciness** (N.) - (ढीठता)
The quality of being bold and lively; impertinence
Syno: Impudence (बेशर्मी)

1081 **Saucy** (Adj.) - (धृष्ट, ढीठ)
Boldly rude or disrespectful in a playful, teasing way
Syno: Cheeky (धृष्ट)

1082 **Savour** (N.) - (स्वाद)~ *[#R-2]*
Taste or smell, especially with pleasure
Syno: Taste (स्वाद, चखना)

1083 Scale (N.) - (पैमाना)
The relative size or extent of something
Syno: Magnitude (मात्रा)

1084 Scam (N.) - (धोखाधड़ी) *[#R-2]*
A dishonest scheme
Syno: Swindle (ठगी, ठगना)

1085 **Scandalized** (Adj.) - (स्तब्ध)
Shocked or horrified by something considered immoral or improper
Syno: Shocked (आश्चर्यचकित)

1086 **Scion** (N.) - (वारिस)
A descendant of a notable family
Syno: Heir (उत्तराधिकारी)

1087 **Scour** (V.) - (रगड़ना, मांजना)
To clean or brighten surface by rubbing hard
Syno: Scrub (साफ़ करना)

1088 **Scowl** (V.) - (तिरछी नज़र से देखना)
To look angrily
Syno: Frown (नाराज़गी से देखना)

1089 Scramble (N.) - (हाथापाई; हड़बड़ी)~
A confused struggle or fight
Syno: Melee (हाथापाई)

1090 **Scream** (V.) - (चिल्लाना)
To cry out loudly
Syno: Cry (चिल्लाना)

1091 Scrumptious (Adj.) - (स्वादिष्ट) *[#R-2]*
Extremely appetizing or delicious
Syno: Tasty (स्वादिष्ट), Delicious (लज़ीज़)

1092 Scrutiny (N.) - (जांच)
Critical observation or examination
Syno: Analysis (विश्लेषण)

1093 **Scurrility** (N.) - (अभद्रता)
Vulgar or abusive language; indecent behavior
Syno: Vulgarity (अश्लीलता)

1094 **Scuttle** (V.) - (जल्दी-बाज़ी में भागना) *[#R-1 (1)]*
To run hurriedly or furtively with short quick steps
Syno: Scamper (भागना)

1095 **Seclusion** (N.) - (एकांत) *[#R-1 (2)]*
The state of being private and away from other people
Syno: Solitude (अकेलापन) {Solitariness (एकांतता)}

1096 Secrecy (N.) - (गोपनीयता)

The action of keeping something secret or the state of being kept secret

Syno: Mystery (रहस्य)

1097 **Sedulous** (Adj.) - (परिश्रमी)~
Showing dedication and diligence

Syno: Diligent (मेहनती)

1098 **Seek** (V.) - (खोजना)
To attempt to find something

Syno: Pursue (पीछा करना)

1099 **Seizure** (N.) - (जब्ती)
The action of capturing someone or something using force

Syno: Capture (कब्जा)

1100 **Selection** (N.) - (चयन)
The act of carefully choosing the most suitable

Syno: Preference (पसंद)

1101 **Self-Esteem** (N.) - (आत्म-सम्मान)
Confidence in one's own worth or abilities

Syno: Pride (गर्व)

1102 **Self-Possessed** (Adj.) - (आत्मसंयमी)
Calm and in control of one's feelings

Syno: Composed (संयमित)

1103 **Sentient** (Adj.) - (संवेदनशील)
Able to feel or perceive

Syno: Conscious (चेतन)

1104 **Sentiment** (N.) - (भावना)
A view of or attitude toward a situation or event; an opinion

Syno: Feeling (अनुभूति)

1105 **Sentimental** (Adj.) - (भावुक)
Excessively emotional

Syno: Mawkish (भावुकतापूर्ण)

1106 **Sentry** (N.) - (पहरेदार)
A soldier stationed to keep guard or control access to a place

Syno: Guard (रक्षक)

1107 **Sequestered** (Adj.) - (एकांत)
Isolated and hidden away

Syno: Secluded (एकांतप्रिय)

1108 **Serpentine** (Adj.) - (टेढ़ा, घुमावदार)
Curving and twisting like a snake

Syno: Zigzag (टेढ़ा-मेढ़ा)

1109 **Serve** (V.) - (सेवा करना)
To perform duties or services for another person or organization

Syno: Attend (सेवा में उपस्थित होना)

1110 **Severity** (N.) - (गंभीरता)
Seriousness or harshness of something

Syno: Seriousness (गंभीरता)

1111 **Sham** (N.) - (ढोंग)
A false or fake thing

Syno: Fake (नकली)

1112 **Shamefacedly** (Adv.) - (लज्जित होकर)
In an ashamed manner

Syno: Embarrassedly (शर्मिंदा होकर)

1113 **Shapeless** (Adj.) - (अनाकार)
Lacking a clear or definite form or structure

Syno: Amorphous (आकारहीन)

1114 **Sheath** (N.) - (म्यान)~
A close-fitting cover for a sword, knife, or blade

Syno: Coat (आवरण)

1115 **Shimmer** (V.) - (चमकना) *[#R-2]*
To shine with a soft tremulous light

Syno: Shine (चमकना)

1116 **Shine** (V.) - (चमकना) *[#R-2]*
To produce or reflect light

Syno: Glitter (चमकना)

1117 **Shudder** (V.) - (कांपना) *[#R-2]*
To tremble violently from fear or disgust

Syno: Shiver (कंपन, कांपना)

1118 **Shuffle** (V.) - (पैर घसीटकर चलना)
To walk dragging the feet

Syno: Stagger (डगमगाना)

1119 **Signify** (V.) - (संकेत करना)
To be an indication of

Syno: Denote (सूचित करना)

1120 **Silt** (N.) - (कीचड़)
Fine sand, clay, or other material carried by running water and deposited as sediment

Syno: Residue (अवशेष)

1121 **Sinuous** (Adj.) - (टेढ़ा-मेढ़ा)
Having many curves and turns

Syno: Serpentine (टेढ़ा)

1122 **Site** (N.) - (स्थल)
An area of ground on which a town, building, or monument is constructed

Syno: Location (स्थान)

1123 **Slick** (Adj.) - (चिकना)

Impressively smooth and efficient

Syno: Slippery (फिसलन भरा)

1124 Slim (Adj.) - (पतला)
Gracefully thin

Syno: Skinny (दुबला)

1125 **Slither** (V.) - (रेंगना) *[#R-1 (1)]*
To move smoothly over a surface with twisting motion

Syno: Slide (फिसलना) {Crawl (रेंगना)}

1126 **Small** (Adj.) - (छोटा) *[#R-1 (1)]*
Less than normal or usual in size

Syno: Slight (हल्का) {Mini (छोटा)}

1127 **Smear** (V.) - (दाग लगाना) *[#R-1 (1)]*
To mark messily with sticky substance

Syno: Discolour (रंग बिगाड़ना)

1128 **Smudge** (N.) - (धब्बा) *[#R-2]*
A dirty mark

Syno: Stain (दाग)

1129 **Snaky** (Adj.) - (साँप जैसा टेढ़ा-मेढ़ा)
Resembling or suggestive of a snake

Syno: Sinuous (पेचीदा)

1130 **Snooze** (V.) - (झपकी लेना) *[#R-2]*
To take a short, light sleep

Syno: Sleep (नींद, सोना)

1131 **Soar** (V.) - (उड़ना) *[#R-1 (1)]*
To fly or rise high in the air

Syno: Fly (उड़ना)

1132 **Sole** (Adj.) - (एकमात्र)~ *[#R-1 (1)]*
One and only

Syno: Only (केवल) {Solitary (एकांत)}

1133 **Solid** (Adj.) - (ठोस)
Firm and stable in shape

Syno: Firm (मजबूत)

1134 Sparkling (Adj.) - (चमकीला)
Shining brightly with flashes of light

Syno: Gleaming (चमकदार)

1135 Special (Adj.) - (विशेष)
Better or different from the ordinary

Syno: Unique (अद्वितीय)

1136 Species (N.) - (प्रजाति)
A group of similar organisms

Syno: Type (प्रकार)

1137 **Specify** (V.) - (तय करना)
To identify clearly and definitely

Syno: Define (परिभाषित करना)

1138 **Spectrum** (N.) - (वर्णक्रम)
A band of colours; a range of related qualities or ideas

Syno: Range (श्रेणी)

1139 **Spell** (N.) - (अल्प अवधि)
A short period of time

Syno: Moment (क्षण)

1140 **Spike** (N.) - (वृद्धि)
A very high amount, price, or level, usually before a fall

Syno: Increase (बढ़ोतरी)

1141 **Spill** (V.) - (गिराना)
An act of flowing out

Syno: Drop (गिराना)

1142 **Spine** (N.) - (रीढ़) *[#R-2]*
The series of vertebrae extending from the skull to the pelvis; a backbone

Syno: Backbone (रीढ़ की हड्डी), Vertebrae (कशेरुका)

1143 **Spirited** (Adj.) - (उत्साही) *[#R-2]*
Full of energy, enthusiasm, and determination

Syno: Ardent (उत्सुक), Enthusiastic (उत्साही)

1144 Splendid (Adj.) - (शानदार) *[#R-1 (1)]*
Very impressive

Syno: Spectacular (भव्य) {Magnificent (शानदार)}

1145 **Sprightly** (Adj.) - (चंचल) *[#R-1 (2)]*
Lively and full of energy

Syno: Blithe (प्रसन्न)

1146 **Spume** (N.) - (झाग)
Foam or froth on the sea

Syno: Foam (फेन)

1147 **Spunky** (Adj.) - (उत्साही)
Courageous and determined

Syno: Plucky (साहसी)

1148 **Spurn** (V.) - (तिरस्कार करना) *[#R-2]*
To reject with disdain or contempt

Syno: Rebuff (दुत्कारना), Despise (घृणा करना)

1149 **Squalor** (N.) - (गंदगी)
A state of being extremely dirty and unpleasant, especially as a result of poverty or neglect

Syno: Filthiness (मैलापन)

1150 **Squawk** (V.) - (चिल्लाना)~

To make a loud, harsh noise

Syno: Scream (चीखना)

1151 Stamp (V.) - (मुहर लगाना)
To mark with a postage stamp

Syno: Imprint (छापना)

1152 **Stentorian** (Adj.) - (बहुत जोर से)
(Of a person's voice) loud and powerful

Syno: Booming (गरजती हुई)

1153 **Stratified** (Adj.) - (परतदार)
Arranged in layers

Syno: Laminated (परत चढ़ा हुआ)

1154 **Stray** (Adj.) - (आवारा, भटका हुआ) *[#R-2 (1)]*
Having wandered from home or path

Syno: Wandering (भटकता हुआ), Homeless (बेघर) {Aimless (लक्ष्यहीन)}

1155 **Streamline** (V.) - (सुव्यवस्थित करना)
To make more efficient

Syno: Simplify (सरल बनाना)

1156 **Stroll** (V.) - (टहलना)~ *[#R-2 (3)]*
To walk in a leisurely way

Syno: Walk (चलना), Saunter (आराम से चलना) {Roam (घूमना)}

1157 **Stun** (V.) - (स्तब्ध करना)
To knock unconscious or leave dazed

Syno: Shock (झटका देना)

1158 Stupid (Adj.) - (मूर्ख)
Lacking intelligence or common sense

Syno: Dull (मंदबुद्धि)

1159 **Stymie** (V.) - (बाधा डालना) *[#R-2]*
To prevent or hinder the progress of

Syno: Impede (बाधा डालना), Hinder (बाधित करना)

1160 **Submerge** (V.) - (डुबोना)
To place under or cover with water

Syno: Drown (डुबोना)

1161 Submission (N.) - (समर्पण)
The act of yielding to authority or control

Syno: Compliance (अनुपालन)

1162 **Substitute** (N.) - (विकल्प) *[#R-2]*
A person or thing that replaces another

Syno: Replacement (विकल्प)

1163 Substitution (N.) - (अदला-बदली, प्रतिस्थापन)
The action of replacing someone or something with another person or thing

Syno: Exchange (अदला बदली)

1164 **Subsume** (V.) - (सम्मिलित करना)
To include or absorb into a larger whole

Syno: Include (शामिल करना)

1165 Subterranean (Adj.) - (भूमिगत)~ *[#R-1 (1)]*
Existing, occurring, or done under the earth's surface

Syno: Underground (भूमिगत)

1166 Successive (Adj.) - (क्रमानुगत)
Following one another or following others

Syno: Consecutive (लगातार)

1167 **Suffix** (N.) - (प्रत्यय)
A morpheme added at the end of a word to form a derivative

Syno: Ending (अंत)

1168 **Summarise** (V.) - (संक्षेप में कहना)
To give a brief account of something

Syno: Recapitulate (सार दोहराना)

1169 **Superannuated** (Adj.) - (सेवानिवृत्त)
Old, and almost no longer suitable for work or use

Syno: Retired (सेवानिवृत्त)

1170 Supersede (V.) - (प्रतिस्थापित करना, जगह लेना) *[#R-3]*
To take the place of something older or in use

Syno: Supplant (हटाकर जगह लेना), Replace (बदलना)

1171 Superstitious (Adj.) - (अंधविश्वासी)
Having or showing a belief in superstitions

Syno: Irrational (तर्कहीन)

1172 **Surly** (Adj.) - (असभ्य)
Bad-tempered and unfriendly

Syno: Unfriendly (असहयोगी)

1173 **Surmount** (V.) - (पार करना) *[#R-2]*
To overcome a difficulty or obstacle

Syno: Overcome (जीतना)

1174 Surprise (N.) - (आश्चर्य) *[#R-1 (2)]*
A sudden feeling caused by something unexpected

Syno: Shock (चौंकना) {Amazement (आश्चर्य)}

1175 Survey (V.) - (सर्वेक्षण करना) *[#R-2 (1)]*
To examine carefully and record

Syno: Examine (जांचना), Scrutinise (बारीकी से जांचना) {Audit (जाँच करना)}

1176 **Swap** (V.) - (अदला-बदली करना) *[#R-2]*
To exchange one thing for another

Syno: Exchange (लेन-देन करना)

1177 **Sybarite** (N.) - (विलासी)~
A person who loves luxury and pleasure
Syno: Debauchee (ऐयाश)

1178 Sycophant (N.) - (चापलूस)~ *[#R-3 (4)]*
A person who flatters someone powerful for gain
Syno: Fawner (खुशामदी), Flatterer (चापलूस) {Adulator (चाटुकार)}

1179 **Symptomatic** (Adj.) - (लक्षणात्मक)
Serving as a symptom or sign of something undesirable
Syno: Characteristic (खास)

1180 **Taciturnity** (N.) - (कम बोलने की प्रवृत्ति) *[#R-1 (2)]*
The state or quality of being reserved or reticent in conversation
Syno: Silence (मौन) {Reservedness (संकोच)}

1181 Tackle (V.) - (निपटना)
To confront or deal with a problem
Syno: Deal (सामना करना)

1182 **Tag** (N.) - (पहचान-चिह्न, उपनाम)
An identifying label
Syno: Label (पहचान चिह्न)

1183 **Taintless** (Adj.) - (निर्दोष)
Free from fault or impurity
Syno: Faultless (दोषरहित)

1184 **Tale** (N.) - (कहानी) *[#R-1 (1)]*
A story, often imaginary or hard to believe
Syno: Story (कथा)

1185 Tantalise (V.) - (तरसाना)
To tease or torment by showing something desirable but unreachable
Syno: Provoke (उकसाना)

1186 **Teleological** (Adj.) - (लक्ष्यवादी)
Based on explaining things by their purpose or end goal
Syno: Purpose-driven (लक्ष्य-आधारित)

1187 **Temper** (V.) - (नियंत्रित करना) *[#R-2 (1)]*
To make something less strong or severe
Syno: Moderate (संयमित करना), Reduce (कम करना)

1188 **Tenacity** (N.) - (दृढ़ता)~ *[#R-1 (1)]*
The quality of being persistent and firm
Syno: Firmness (मजबूती) {Determination (दृढ़ निश्चय)}

1189 **Tend** (V.) - (देखभाल करना)
To care for; to be likely to behave in a certain way
Syno: Care For (ख्याल रखना)

1190 Tendency (N.) - (प्रवृत्ति) *[#R-2 (2)]*
An inclination towards a particular behaviour or characteristic
Syno: Propensity (प्रवृत्ति), Proneness (झुकाव) {Predisposition (पूर्व-प्रवृत्ति)}

1191 **Tenderness** (N.) - (दयालुता)
The quality of being gentle, loving, or kind
Syno: Kindness (दयालुता)

1192 **Tenet** (N.) - (सिद्धांत)
A fundamental principle or belief
Syno: Belief (विश्वास)

1193 **Tensile** (Adj.) - (लचीला)
Relating to tension; able to be stretched
Syno: Stretchable (लचीला)

1194 Tension (N.) - (तनाव)
The state of being stretched tight; mental or emotional strain
Syno: Strain (जोर)

1195 **Tepid** (Adj.) - (गुनगुना) *[#R-1 (4)]*
Slightly warm; not hot or cold
Syno: Warm (हल्का गर्म) {Dull (नीरस), Lukewarm (गुनगुना), Moderate (मध्यम)}

1196 **Termination** (N.) - (समापन)
The action of bringing something or coming to an end
Syno: Conclusion (समाप्ति)

1197 **Testify** (V.) - (गवाही देना) *[#R-2]*
To give evidence or state something formally
Syno: Affirm (पुष्टि करना), Announce (घोषणा करना)

1198 Thankful (Adj.) - (आभारी)
Feeling grateful
Syno: Obliged (कृतज्ञ)

1199 **Threat** (N.) - (खतरा)
A declaration of harm or a possibility of danger
Syno: Risk (जोखिम)

1200 Threshold (N.) - (दहलीज़) *[#R-2]*
The level or point at which something begins or is entered
Syno: Dawn (भोर), Doorway (द्वार)

1201 **Tidy** (Adj.) - (स्वच्छ)
Neat and orderly

Syno: Orderly (व्यवस्थित)

1202 **Tilt** (N.) - (झुकाव)
A sloping position or movement
Syno: Slant (तिरछा)

1203 **Timetable** (N.) - (समयसारिणी)
A schedule listing events and their times
Syno: Schedule (कार्यक्रम)

1204 **Tinsel** (N.) - (सजावट) *[#R-2]*
Thin shiny strips used as decoration
Syno: Garnish (सजावट), Decoration (सजावट)

1205 **Tirade** (N.) - (तीखी आलोचना)~
A long, angry speech of criticism or accusation
Syno: Rant (गुस्से भरा भाषण)

1206 **Titan** (N.) - (दिग्गज)
A person or thing of very great strength, intellect, or importance
Syno: Giant (विशाल)

1207 **Titanic** (Adj.) - (विशाल)
Extremely large
Syno: Huge (बहुत बड़ा)

1208 **Toddler** (N.) - (शिशु)~
A young child beginning to walk
Syno: Infant (शिशु)

1209 **Toilsome** (Adj.) - (मेहनती कार्य)
Involving hard or tedious work
Syno: Tiresome (थकाऊ)

1210 **Tolerance** (N.) - (सहनशीलता) *[#R-2]*
The willingness to accept differences or ability to endure
Syno: Endurance (धैर्य)

1211 **Tomb** (N.) - (कब्र)
A large structure for burying the dead
Syno: Grave (कब्र)

1212 **Top** (N.) - (शीर्ष)
The highest point or part
Syno: Zenith (चरम)

1213 **Tousled** (Adj.) - (बिखरे हुए)
Untidy or disordered, especially hair
Syno: Disarranged (अव्यवस्थित)

1214 **Toy** (V.) - (खेलना)
To move or handle an object absent-mindedly or nervously
Syno: Play (खेलना)

1215 **Trail** (N.) - (रास्ता, निशानी)
A path or marks left behind
Syno: Path (रास्ता)

1216 **Tranquilizing** (Adj.) - (शांत करने वाला)
Causing calmness or relaxation
Syno: Soothing (शांतिदायक)

1217 **Transcend** (V.) - (पार करना) *[#R-1 (3)]*
To go beyond or rise above a limit or level
Syno: Eclipse (पीछे छोड़ देना) {Surpass (पीछे छोड़ना), Cross (पार करना)}

1218 **Transgression** (N.) - (उल्लंघन)
An act that goes against a law, rule, or code of conduct
Syno: Violation (उल्लंघन)

1219 **Transhistorical** (Adj.) - (इतिहास से परे)
Extending beyond specific historical periods
Syno: Timeless (समय से परे)

1220 **Transition** (N.) - (परिवर्तन)
The process or a period of changing from one state or condition to another
Syno: Change (बदलाव)

1221 **Transmission** (N.) - (प्रसारण) *[#R-2]*
The act or process of sending or broadcasting something
Syno: Conveyance (परिवहन, हस्तांतरण)

1222 **Transmit** (V.) - (प्रसारित करना)
To send or pass something from one place or person to another
Syno: Convey (पहुँचाना)

1223 **Trap** (N.) - (जाल)
A device or situation used to catch
Syno: Ambush (घात)

1224 **Trauma** (N.) - (मानसिक सदमा)
A deeply distressing or disturbing experience
Syno: Emotional Shock (भावनात्मक आघात)

1225 **Travail** (N.) - (कष्ट)
Painful or laborious effort
Syno: Agony (तीव्र पीड़ा)

1226 **Travesty** (N.) - (भद्दा मज़ाक)~
A false or absurd representation
Syno: Mockery (उपहास)

1227 **Tread** (V.) - (चलना)
To walk or step in a particular way
Syno: Walk (चलना)

1228 **Tremble** (V.) - (काँपना)
To shake or quiver slightly, often from fear

or weakness

Syno: Quiver (थरथराना)

1229 **Trembling** (V.) - (कांपना)
To shake due to fear, cold, or weakness

Syno: Shivering (थरथराना)

1230 Trendy (Adj.) - (चलन में)
Very fashionable or up to date

Syno: Popular (लोकप्रिय)

1231 **Tribulation** (N.) - (कष्ट)
A cause of great trouble or suffering

Syno: Suffering (पीड़ा)

1232 **Trimming** (N.) - (छंटाई)
Cutting off excess parts

Syno: Cutting (कटाई)

1233 Trouble (N.) - (परेशानी) *[#R-1 (2)]*
A difficulty or problem

Syno: Complication (जटिलता)

1234 **Truncated** (Adj.) - (छोटा किया हुआ)
Cut short; made shorter than original

Syno: Shortened (संक्षिप्त)

1235 Trust (N./V.) - (भरोसा; विश्वास करना) *[#R-2]*
The belief in reliability or honesty (N.); To rely on or believe in (V.)

Syno: Belief (विश्वास); Believe (विश्वास करना)

1236 **Umpteen** (Adj.) - (अनेक)
Indefinitely many; a large number of

Syno: Countless (अनगिनत)

1237 **Unacknowledged** (Adj.) - (अस्वीकृत)
Not recognized, admitted, or accepted

Syno: Unidentified (अनुस्वीकृत)

1238 Unanimous (Adj.) - (सर्वसम्मत)~ *[#R-1 (1)]*
(Of two or more people) fully in agreement

Syno: Unified (एकमत) {United (एकजुट)}

1239 **Uncharted** (Adj.) - (अज्ञात)
Not mapped, explored, or known

Syno: Undiscovered (अभी तक खोजा न गया)

1240 **Underneath** (Adv.) - (नीचे)
In or to a lower position; below something

Syno: Beneath (नीचे)

1241 **Unfamiliar** (Adj.) - (अपरिचित)
Not known or recognized

Syno: Strange (अनजाना)

1242 **Unhappiness** (N.) - (दुख)
The state of sadness or lack of happiness

Syno: Woe (शोक)

1243 Upbraid (V.) - (फटकारना) *[#R-1 (1)]*
To scold or criticize severely

Syno: Reprimand (डांटना)

1244 **Updated** (Adj.) - (नवीनतम)
To make something more current by adding new information

Syno: Latest (नवीनतम)

1245 **Uplift** (V.) - (उन्नत करना)
To improve something or raise it to a better level

Syno: Improve (सुधारना)

1246 **Upsetting** (Adj.) - (परेशान करने वाला)
Causing distress, worry, or anxiety

Syno: Perturbing (बेचैन करने वाला)

1247 **Useless** (Adj.) - (बेकार)
Not able to achieve the intended purpose

Syno: Worthless (निरर्थक)

1248 **Utmost** (Adj.) - (चरम)
Most extreme or greatest

Syno: Greatest (महानतम)

1249 Vagabond (N.) - (आवारा)~
A person who wanders without home or job

Syno: Tramp (घुमक्कड़)

1250 **Vagrancy** (N.) - (आवारागर्दी) *[#R-2]*
The state of living as a vagrant; homelessness

Syno: Homelessness (बेघरपन), Vagabond (आवारा)

1251 **Valedictory** (Adj.) - (विदाई संबंधी)
Serving as a farewell

Syno: Terminal (अंतिम)

1252 **Valet** (N.) - (निजी सेवक)
A man's personal attendant who looks after clothes and appearance

Syno: Butler (मुख्य पुरुष सेवक)

1253 **Valiance** (N.) - (वीरता)
The quality of being brave or courageous

Syno: Gallantry (शौर्य)

1254 **Vault** (N.) - (तहखाना)
An arched roof or secure storage room

Syno: Crypt (भूमिगत कक्ष)

1255 Velocity (N.) - (वेग)~
The speed of something in a given direction

Syno: Speed (गति)

1256 **Venal** (Adj.) - (भ्रष्ट)

Willing to accept bribes; morally corrupt
Syno: Corrupt (भ्रष्ट)

1257 Venture (N.) - (साहसिक कार्य)~ *[#R-2]*
A risky or uncertain undertaking
Syno: Attempt (प्रयास), Undertaking (कार्य)

1258 **Veracious** (Adj.) - (सत्यवादी)
Speaking or representing the truth
Syno: Accurate (सटीक)

1259 **Verbatim** (Adv.) - (शाब्दिक; हूबहू)~
In exactly the same words as originally used
Syno: Exactly (सटीक रूप से)

1260 Verisimilitude (N.) - (प्रामाणिकता)
The appearance of being true or real
Syno: Authenticity (विश्वसनीयता)

1261 Version (N.) - (संस्करण)
A different form or account of the same thing
Syno: Variation (भिन्नता)

1262 **Vertical** (Adj.) - (लंबवत)
At right angles to the horizontal
Syno: Upright (सीधा)

1263 Vicissitudes (N.) - (उतार-चढ़ाव)
Changes in fortune or circumstances
Syno: Fluctuations (उतार-चढ़ाव)

1264 **Vie** (V.) - (प्रतिस्पर्धा करना)
To compete eagerly to achieve something
Syno: Compete (मुकाबला करना)

1265 Villain (N.) - (खलनायक)~
A character with evil actions or motives in a story
Syno: Antagonist (विरोधी)

1266 **Villainous** (Adj.) - (दुर्जन)
Guilty of wicked or criminal behaviour
Syno: Nefarious (अत्यंत दुष्ट)

1267 Violation (N.) - (उल्लंघन)
An act of breaking a rule, law, or agreement
Syno: Breach (भंग)

1268 Virtuoso (N.) - (कुशल कलाकार)~ *[#R-2]*
A person highly skilled in an art, especially music
Syno: Ace (एक माहिर खिलाड़ी), Maestro (विशेषज्ञ)

1269 **Visceral** (Adj.) - (आंतरिक)
Relating to deep inner feelings, not intellect
Syno: Bodily (शारीरिक)

1270 Visible (Adj.) - (दिखाई देने वाला)
Able to be seen
Syno: Apparent (स्पष्ट)

1271 Visit (V.) - (मिलने जाना)
To go to see someone or a place
Syno: See (मिलने जाना)

1272 Visitor (N.) - (मेहमान)
A person who goes to see a place or person
Syno: Tourist (पर्यटक)

1273 **Vista** (N.) - (दृश्य) *[#R-1 (1)]*
A pleasing view, especially seen through a narrow opening
Syno: Scenery (प्राकृतिक दृश्य) {Landscape (परिदृश्य)}

1274 **Vocation** (N.) - (पेशा) *[#R-2]*
A career or occupation one feels suited for
Syno: Occupation (व्यवसाय)

1275 Vogue (N.) - (प्रचलन, लोकप्रियता) *[#R-3]*
The popular or accepted style at a particular time
Syno: Fashion (प्रचलित शैली)

1276 **Void** (N.) - (रिक्तता)
An empty space
Syno: Gap (रिक्त स्थान)

1277 Voluminous (Adj.) - (विस्तृत)
Occupying much space; large in volume
Syno: Commodious (विशाल)

1278 Wage (N.) - (मजदूरी)
A fixed regular payment for work
Syno: Emolument (वेतन)

1279 **Wager** (N.) - (शर्त)
A bet
Syno: Gamble (जुआ)

1280 **Wake up** (V.) - (जागना)
To awaken from sleep
Syno: Awaken (जागना)

1281 **Wallow** (V.) - (लोटना, गिरते-पड़ते चलना) *[#R-2]*
To roll or lie about in mud, water, or something similar
Syno: Flounder (लड़खड़ाना)

1282 **Wander** (V.) - (भटकना)~ *[#R-5 (1)]*
To move about aimlessly or casually
Syno: Roam (घूमना), Deviate (विचलित होना)

1283 **Waning** (Adj.) - (घटता हुआ) *[#R-1 (2)]*
Becoming less in strength or amount
Syno: Fading (मुरझाता हुआ)

1284 **Wastrel** (N.) - (अपव्ययी) *[#R-1 (1)]*

A person who wastes money or resources
Syno: Spendthrift (फिजूलखर्ची)

1285 Wealth (N.) - (संपत्ति)
An abundance of valuable possessions or money
Syno: Riches (धन)

1286 **Wealthy** (Adj.) - (धनी)
Having a great deal of money or assets
Syno: Affluent (समृद्ध)

1287 **Welter** (N.) - (उथल-पुथल) *[#R-2]*
A confused mass or jumble
Syno: Turmoil (अशांति)

1288 **Whim** (N.) - (सनक) *[#R-1 (2)]*
A sudden and unusual desire
Syno: Fancy (आकस्मिक इच्छा)

1289 Whine (V.) - (शिकायत करना) *[#R-2]*
To complain in an annoying way
Syno: Gripe (शिकायत करना)

1290 **Whinny** (N.) - (हिनहिनाहट)
A gentle high-pitched sound made by a horse
Syno: Neigh (हिनहिनाहट)

1291 **Whirl** (V.) - (तेजी से घूमना)
To move or cause to move rapidly around
Syno: Spin (घूमना)

1292 Whisper (N.) - (फुसफुसाहट)~ *[#R-2 (1)]*
A very soft sound or speech
Syno: Murmur (गुनगुनाहट)

1293 Wholly (Adv.) - (पूर्णतः)
Completely; to the full extent
Syno: Entirely (संपूर्ण रूप से)

1294 **Wistful** (Adj.) - (उदास) *[#R-2]*
Showing a gentle, sad feeling of longing or regret
Syno: Nostalgic (पुरानी यादों से जुड़ा), Sorrowful (दुखी)

1295 **Wobble** (V.) - (डगमगाना)
To move unsteadily from side to side
Syno: Vibrate (काँपना)

1296 **Wonderful** (Adj.) - (अद्भुत)
Extremely good
Syno: Amazing (शानदार)

1297 **Worn** (Adj.) - (घिसा-पिटा)
Damaged or shabby because of much use
Syno: Dilapidated (टूटा फूटा)

1298 **Worse** (Adj.) - (बदतर) *[#R-2]*
More bad than before or another
Syno: Inferior (घटिया), Bad (बुरा)

1299 **Worth** (N.) - (कीमत, उपयोगिता)
The value, importance, or merit of something
Syno: Value (महत्व)

1300 **Wraith** (N.) - (आत्मा)
A ghost or ghostlike image of a person
Syno: Spirit (भूत)

1301 Wreak (V.) - (क्षति पहुंचाना)
To cause something harmful in a violent way
Syno: Cause (कारण बनना)

1302 **Wrench** (V.) - (मोड़ना)
To twist or pull forcefully
Syno: Wrest (छीनना)

1303 **Wry** (Adj.) - (व्यंग्यपूर्ण, विकृत)
Twisted or distorted face or expression
Syno: Crooked (टेढ़ा)

1304 **Xenial** (Adj.) - (मेहमाननवाज़)
Hospitable to strangers
Syno: Friendly (मित्रवत)

1305 Yardstick (N.) - (मापदंड)
A standard or basis used for comparison
Syno: Standard (मानदंड)

1306 Yearn (V.) - (तीव्र इच्छा करना) *[#R-2 (3)]*
To feel a deep longing for something
Syno: Desire (इच्छा करना), Crave (लालसा करना)

*Total **1306** Synonyms asked **2098** times*

C5 Synonyms Practice Sets (Based on Recent SSC Papers)

Practice Set - 1

Direction (Q. 1-10): Select the most appropriate synonym of the given word:

1 Tranquilizing
1) Soothing
2) Irritating
3) Provocative
4) Harsh

2 Extraordinarily
1) Ordinary 2) Incredibly
3) Negligible 4) Enchanting

3 Complaisant
1) Insecure 2) Anxious
3) Alert 4) Submissive

4 Deleterious
1) Harmful
2) Useful
3) Comforting
4) Helpful

5 Disparaging
1) Complimentary
2) Belittling
3) Flattering
4) Kind

6 Circumspect
1) Reckless 2) Brash
3) Carefree 4) Cautious

7 Intransigence
1) Obedience
2) Stubbornness
3) Submission
4) Compliance

8 Carnal
1) Demand 2) Greed
3) Jealousy 4) Earthly

9 Deft
1) Skillful 2) Inept
3) Awkward 4) Clumsy

10 Disconsolate
1) Unhappy 2) Cheerful
3) Content 4) Elated

Practice Set - 2

Direction (Q. 1-10): Select the most appropriate synonym of the given word:

1 Defer
1) Decline 2) Delay
3) Reject 4) Proceed

2 Perspicuous
1) Confused 2) Clear
3) Precarious 4) Muddle

3 Felicitous
1) Odd
2) Irrelevant
3) Unsuitable
4) Appropriate

4 Implacable
1) Soft 2) Unyielding
3) Flexible 4) Gentle

5 Effrontery
1) Audacity 2) Politeness
3) Shyness 4) Courtesy

6 Cadaverous
1) Vibrant 2) Pale
3) Lively 4) Healthy

7 Obfuscation
1) Explanation
2) Clarity
3) Transparency
4) Confusion

8 Capitulate
1) Defend 2) Attack
3) Surrender 4) Resist

9 Malediction
1) Blessing 2) Prophecy
3) plea 4) Curse

10 Gregarious
1) Quiet 2) Sociable
3) Shy 4) Reserved

Practice Set - 3

Direction (Q. 1-10): Select the most appropriate synonym of the given word:

1 Taciturnity
1) Eloquence 2) Talkative
3) Silence 4) Tactic

2 Exiguous
1) Scanty 2) Huge
3) Excessive 4) Abundant

3 Magnanimous
1) Lofty 2) Utter
3) Expressive 4) Brave

4 Dilatory
1) Quick 2) Efficient
3) Prompt 4) Tardy

5 Abnegate
1) Demand 2) Accept
3) Renounce 4) Support

6 Asperity
1) Kindness 2) Harshness
3) Softness 4) Delight

7 Prerogative
1) Bias 2) Satisfaction
3) Privilege 4) Predisposition

8 Munificence
1) Shrewdness
2) Generousness
3) Quietness
4) Liveliness

9 Ignominy
1) Disgrace 2) Respect
3) Fame 4) Honor

10 Apposite
1) Irrelevant 2) Vague
3) Relevant 4) Random

Practice Set - 4

1 Nebulous
1) Vague 2) Precise
3) Obvious 4) Clear

2 Confiscate
1) Titivate 2) Restock
3) Destroy 4) Seize

3 Impartial
1) Nocturnal 2) Neutral
3) Tactile 4) Impressionable

4 Luminous
1) Dull 2) Dim
3) Opaque 4) Radiant

5 Illuminate
1) Explain 2) Darken
3) Destroy 4) Hide

6 Courageous
1) Timid 2) Fearful
3) Gutsy 4) Cowardly

7 Abandon
1) Forsake 2) Cherish
3) Support 4) Accede to

8 Abolish
1) Assist 2) Cancel

3) Subside 4) Worship

9 Exuberance
1) Lethargy
2) Excitement
3) Depression
4) Indifference

10 Neophyte
1) Beginner 2) Veteran
3) Master 4) Expert

Practice Set - 5

Direction (Q. 1-10): Select the most appropriate synonym of the given word:

1 Frugal
1) Lavish
2) Thrifty
3) Extravagant
4) wasteful

2 Apogee
1) Start 2) Peak
3) Nadir 4) Base

3 Grumpy
1) Irritable 2) Friendly
3) Polite 4) Calm

4 Cogent
1) Weak
2) Dubious
3) Convincing
4) Unclear

5 Callow
1) Inexperienced
2) Experienced
3) Wise
4) Mature

6 Abundant
1) Ample 2) Difficult
3) Scarce 4) Barren

7 Abrogate
1) Ratify 2) Repeal
3) Reject 4) Withdraw

8 Eulogy
1) Tribute 2) Criticism
3) Insult 4) Condemnation

9 Infamous
1) Tenable
2) Incomprehensible
3) Notorious
4) Notable

10 Incessant
1) Frequent
2) Recurring
3) Continuous
4) Repetitive

Practice Set - 6

Direction (Q. 1-10): Select the most appropriate synonym of the given word:

1 Blunt
1) Rowdy 2) Adventurous
3) tactful 4) Insensitive

2 Hinder
1) Hide 2) Assist
3) Obstruct 4) Encourage

3 Fasten
1) Undo 2) Loosen
3) Detach 4) Bolt

4 Stunning
1) Plain 2) Gorgeous
3) Hideous 4) Ugly

5 Fondness
1) Brilliance 2) Dislike
3) Liking 4) Mistake

6 Caustic
1) Kind 2) Mild
3) Gentle 4) Sarcastic

7 Edible
1) noisome 2) nutritive
3) noxious 4) mortal

8 Devour
1) Receive 2) Preserve
3) Consume 4) Abstain

9 Gloomy
1) Dismal 2) Buoyant
3) Sticky 4) Vain

10 Frigid
1) Futile 2) Facile
3) Flexible 4) Freezing

Practice Set - 7

Direction (Q. 1-10): Select the most appropriate synonym of the given word:

1 Pernicious
1) Harmless 2) Benevolent
3) Malicious 4) Helpful

2 Dilemma
1) Plight 2) Worn
3) Portion 4) Situation

3 Dodge
1) Trick 2) Opine
3) Display 4) Panic

4 Mythopoeic
1) Destructive
2) Scientific
3) Myth-making
4) Realistic

5 Apportion
1) To allocate 2) To request
3) To confess 4) To complicate

6 Broad
1) Exact 2) Wide
3) Small 4) Particular

7 Jargon
1) Terminology
2) Essay
3) Automobile
4) Music

8 Mask
1) Expose 2) Conceal
3) Enhance 4) Amplify

9 Wanton
1) Habit
2) Obscene
3) Abrogation
4) Prevent

10 Petite
1) Flexible 2) Fit
3) Best 4) Small

Practice Set - 8

Direction (Q. 1-10): Select the most appropriate synonym of the given word:

1 Envy
1) Benign 2) Benevolence
3) Jealousy 4) Abjure

2 Mourn
1) Dread 2) Amuse
3) Approve 4) Grieve

3 Immune
1) Asleep 2) Variable
3) Resistant 4) Safe

4 Warm
1) Unkind 2) Hostile
3) Mean 4) Amicable

5 Eternal
1) Temporary 2) Fleeting
3) Infinite 4) Brief

6 Renounce
1) Adopt 2) Accept
3) Reject 4) Welcome

7 Resign
1) Achieve 2) Insist
3) Stay 4) Surrender

8 Insidious
1) Sudden 2) Deceptive
3) Violent 4) Predictable

9 Envoy
1) Carrier
2) Chief
3) Ambassador
4) Receiver

10 Toxic
1) Lethal 2) Licit
3) Laudatory 4) Lanky

Practice Set - 9

Direction (Q. 1-10): Identify the synonym of the given word:

1 Recalcitrant
1) Compliant
2) Rebellious
3) Submissive
4) Docile

2 Immutable
1) Transient
2) Unchanging
3) Diminishing
4) Fragile

3 Eschew
1) Accept 2) Embrace
3) Avoid 4) Pursue

4 Banish
1) To determine
2) To evaluate
3) To harm
4) To relegate

5 Rancor
1) Amity 2) Goodwill
3) Animosity 4) Harmony

6 Dread
1) Relief 2) Excitement
3) Fear 4) Triumph

7 Ephemeral
1) Everlasting
2) Transient
3) Powerful
4) Fragile

8 Magnificence
1) Grandeur 2) Destroy
3) Dismiss 4) Enormous

9 Wisdom
1) ignorance 2) Cunning
3) Knowledge 4) Foolishness

10 Dingy
1) Pure 2) Dreary
3) Sterile 4) Bright

Practice Set - 10

Direction (Q. 1-10): Identify the synonym of the given word:

1 Innocuous
1) Harmful 2) Harmless
3) Dangerous 4) Toxic

2 Imminent
1) Distant 2) Approaching
3) Delayed 4) Postponed

3 Notorious
1) Famous 2) Unknown
3) Renowned 4) Infamous

4 Ossified
1) Flexible 2) Rigid
3) Synthetic 4) Tangential

5 Mendacious
1) Truthful 2) Dishonest
3) Sincere 4) Honest

6 Plausible
1) Unlikely 2) Unbelievable
3) Believable 4) Incredible

7 Banality
1) Vitality 2) Triviality
3) Versatility 4) Brutality

8 Berserk
1) Stubborn 2) Absurd
3) Demented 4) Lazy

9 Lackluster
1) Brilliant 2) Humdrum
3) Vivid 4) Bright

10 Jeopardy
1) Risk 2) Safety
3) Certainty 4) Security

Practice Set - 11

Direction (Q. 1-10): Identify the synonym of the given word:

1 Quixotic
1) Practical 2) idealistic
3) Realistic 4) Logical

2 Tranquil
1) Restless 2) Peaceful
3) Turbulent 4) Chaotic

3 Flattery
1) Adulation 2) Delegate
3) Friendly 4) Cruelty

4 Juvenile
1) Childish 2) Ancient
3) Grown-up 4) Elder

5 Blatant
1) Subtle 2) Obvious
3) Discreet 4) Hidden

6 Knavery
1) Honesty 2) Integrity
3) Truth 4) Deceit

7 Regret
1) Excitement 2) Sadness
3) Anger 4) Confusion

8 Pristine
1) Polluted 2) Immaculate
3) Dirty 4) Untouched

9 Exculpate
1) Condemn 2) Blame
3) Exonerate 4) Punish

10 Clarity
1) Confusion 2) Lucidity
3) Obscurity 4) Vagueness

Practice Set - 12

Direction (Q. 1-10): Identify the synonym of the given word:

1 Condemn
1) Elevate 2) Tolerate
3) Uphold 4) Denounce

2 Wistful
1) Content 2) Nostalgic
3) Joyful 4) Happy

3 Brisk
1) Lazy 2) Dull
3) Energetic 4) Slow

4 Fickle
1) Constant 2) Unpredictable
3) Reliable 4) Stable

5 Docile
1) Reveal 2) Pliable
3) Exhibit 4) Clarify

6 Absolve
1) Ablute 2) Abate
3) Pardon 4) Give away

7 Endorse
1) Approve 2) Reject
3) Criticize 4) Delay

8 Garrulous
1) Talkative 2) Reserved
3) Silent 4) Listen

9 Assimilation
1) Preservation
2) Segregation
3) Absorption
4) Rejection

10 Xenial
1) Friendly 2) Hostile
3) Warm 4) Cold

Practice Set - 13

Direction (Q. 1-10): Choose the synonym of the given word:

1 Abate
1) Moderate 2) Increase
3) Evil 4) Honest

2 Deteriorate
1) Grow 2) Worsen
3) Revive 4) Improve

3 Fortify
1) Weaken 2) Broke
3) Strengthen 4) Remove

4 Enervate

1) Strengthen 2) Revive
3) Motivate 4) Exhaust

5 Barbarous
1) Dull 2) Calm
3) Matured 4) Brutal

6 Haphazard
1) Organized 2) Intentional
3) Random 4) Planned

7 Bawdy
1) Coarse 2) Support
3) Delay 4) Establish

8 Labyrinth
1) Palace
2) A structure made of pedestals
3) Maze
4) Dungeon

9 Exasperate
1) Distract 2) Inspire
3) Calm 4) Annoy

10 Invective
1) Eulogy 2) Compliment
3) Praise 4) Tirade

Practice Set - 14

Direction (Q. 1-10): Choose the synonym of the given word:

1 Exquisite
1) Crude 2) Harsh
3) Delicate 4) Ordinary

2 Encumbrance
1) Offend 2) Obstacle
3) Ignore 4) Disinterest

3 Abstruse
1) Difficult 2) Obvious
3) Simple 4) Clear

4 Exaggerate
1) Amplify 2) Minimize
3) Suppress 4) Understate

5 Obsequious
1) Defiant 2) Aggressive
3) Proud 4) Submissive

6 Alleviate
1) Worsen 2) Relieve
3) Increase 4) Prolong

7 Alacrity
1) Sluggishness
2) Hesitation
3) Eagerness
4) Delay

8 Relinquish
1) Abandon 2) Maintain
3) Continue 4) Retain

9 Cacophony
1) Harmony 2) Discord
3) Order 4) Silence

10 Diligent
1) Idle 2) Careless
3) Indolent 4) Hardworking

Practice Set - 15

Direction (Q. 1-10): Choose the synonym of the given word:

1 Vicinity
1) Absence 2) Proximity
3) Distance 4) Departure

2 Insolent
1) Disrespectful
2) Gentle
3) Polite
4) Courteous

3 Respect
1) Disrespect 2) Invalidate
3) Attend 4) Honour

4 Reticent
1) Arrogant 2) Reserved
3) Talkative 4) Outspoken

5 Reckless
1) Prudent 2) Cautious
3) Careful 4) Rash

6 Erroneous
1) Accurate 2) Right
3) Fallacious 4) Vital

7 Pinnacle
1) Base 2) Decline
3) Bottom 4) Peak

8 Calumny
1) Truth 2) Slander
3) Praise 4) Compliment

9 Trenchant
1) Blurry 2) Weak
3) Incisive 4) Vague

10 Taciturn
1) Bold 2) Reserved
3) Talkative 4) Noisy

Practice Set - 16

Direction (Q. 1-10): Choose the synonym of the given word:

1 Propitious
1) Doubtful
2) Harmful
3) Favourable
4) Unlucky

2 Perfidious
1) Honest
2) Faithful
3) Treacherous
4) Loyal

3 Feasible
1) Practical 2) Worthless
3) Energetic 4) Tentative

4 Melancholy
1) Excitement
2) Joy
3) Aloof
4) Sadness

5 Palpable
1) Invisible
2) Tangible
3) Theoretical
4) Diminishing

6 Vigilant
1) Inattentive
2) Sleepy
3) Alert
4) Careless

7 Charisma
1) Reputation
2) Charm
3) Atmosphere
4) Influence

8 Nonchalant
1) Anxious 2) Tense
3) Worried 4) Carefree

9 Propitiate
1) Agitate 2) Provoke
3) Appease 4) Enrage

10 Proclivity
1) Impulse 2) Tendency
3) Instinct 4) Habit

Practice Set - 17

Direction (Q. 1-10): Which word is closest in meaning the given word:

1 Frivolous
1) Powerful
2) Essential
3) Significant
4) Trivial

2 Hamstrung
1) Cripple 2) Talkative
3) Jolly 4) Restless

3 Recumbent
1) Upstanding
2) Prostrate
3) Upright
4) Review

4 Conundrum
1) Triumph 2) Celebration
3) Harmony 4) Problem

5 Engendered
1) Eradicated 2) Concealed
3) Generated 4) Challenged

6 Coruscate

1) Blur 2) Dim
3) Sparkle 4) Fade

7 Resignation
1) Protest 2) Acceptance
3) Resistance 4) Denial

8 Gratify
1) Satisfy 2) Insult
3) Displease 4) Annoy

9 Chicanery
1) Truth 2) Deception
3) Honesty 4) Loyalty

10 Eloquent
1) Silent 2) shy
3) Fluent 4) Scattered

Practice Set - 18

Direction (Q. 1-10): Which word is closest in meaning the given word:

1 Egregious
1) Minor 2) Trivial
3) Unnoticed 4) Shocking

2 Dubiously
1) Confidently
2) Definitely
3) sceptically
4) Gladly

3 Impediment
1) Barrier 2) Opportunity
3) Pathway 4) solution

4 Existential
1) Decorative 2) Psychological
3) Cosmic 4) Philosophical

5 Ebullient
1) Depressed
2) Dull
3) Enthusiastic
4) Calm

6 Loathe
1) Hate 2) Like
3) Accept 4) Love

7 Detrimental
1) Unimportant
2) Beneficial
3) Harmful
4) Unpredictable

8 Neglect
1) Support 2) Attention
3) Care 4) Disregard

9 Foster
1) Neglect 2) Reject
3) Promote 4) Oppose

10 Elucidate
1) Confuse
2) Darken
3) Complicate
4) Clarify

Practice Set - 19

Direction (Q. 1-10): Select the most appropriate synonym of the underlined word in the given sentence.

1 The vintage bag was made of <u>coarse</u> black leather.
1) Brief 2) Rough
3) Secure 4) Honest

2 Huxley was an <u>exponent</u> of Darwin's theory of evolution.
1) Cease 2) Terminate
3) Proponent 4) Conclude

3 Farmers wash trees infested with insects with any one of the many insecticides not easily <u>obtainable</u>.
1) Acceptable 2) Accessible
3) Probable 4) Interminable

4 Morality is contextual; therefore, it is foolish to believe that one's moral judgement would be perfect and <u>immaculate</u>.
1) grubby 2) indelicate
3) tarnished 4) impeccable

5 Mr. Satterthwaite was <u>shrewd</u> enough to penetrate her meaning.
1) Innocent 2) Funny
3) Smart 4) Aged

6 The skunk had a <u>conspicuous</u> spinal stripe.
1) faint 2) charming
3) obscure 4) noticeable

7 The disposal of <u>hazardous</u> waste in hospitals and factories is a serious problem and needs to be taken care of urgently.
1) hazy 2) benign
3) belligerent 4) dangerous

8 What makes their jobs even more challenging is the emotional <u>burden</u>.
1) A legal responsibility
2) A financial cost
3) A heavy emotional load
4) A physical task

9 She accused her sister of being <u>vindictive</u> when she was trying to defame her.
1) revengeful 2) venerable
3) vigilant 4) righteous

10 The lockdown during Covid-19 in certain places has imposed threatening <u>constraints</u> on market economy and it will take time to recover from this.
1) Problems 2) Beliefs
3) Faiths 4) Restrictions

Practice Set - 20

Direction (Q. 1-7): Select the most closest in meaning of the word from the sentence.

1 Columbus was <u>convinced</u> that the earth was round.
1) Assured 2) Cynical
3) Sceptical 4) Doubtful

2 The sergeant-major's voice dropped to a whisper, laden with <u>ominous</u> meaning.
1) Cheerful 2) Threatening
3) Uplifting 4) Harmless

3 It's <u>incredible</u> to see him in such good health after the accident.
1) Unimaginable
2) Unremarkable
3) Apparent
4) Unacceptable

4 He made a desperate but only partially successful effort to turn the talk onto a less <u>ghastly</u> topic.
1) Simple 2) Light
3) Gruesome 4) Boring

5 Her voice rose in a crescendo of desperation.
1) Climax 2) Decline
3) Whisper 4) Pause

6 Ramya is an <u>ardent</u> follower of secularism.
1) forced 2) temporary
3) unhappy 4) committed

7 The notion of 'the Author' is a construct of cultural expectation rather than an inherent necessity of literature.
1) Acquired 2) Optional
3) Natural 4) Imaginary

Direction (Q. 8-10): Select the most appropriate synonym of the bracketed word in the following sentence to fill in the blank.

8 The documentary explored the historical and cultural significance of the ______(antique) ruins in the region.
1) obsolete 2) contemporary

3) modern 4) ancient

9 Queen Gulnaar of Arabia mourned her _____ beauty. (waning)
1) frightening 2) futile
3) false 4) fading

10 The elaborate syllabi had to be _____(summarised) to make a presentation in the UGC assessment meeting.
1) prolonged
2) lengthened
3) recapitulated
4) expanded

Answer Key Practice Set - 1:

1 - 1	2 - 2	3 - 4	4 - 1	5 - 2
6 - 4	7 - 2	8 - 4	9 - 1	10 - 1

Answer Key Practice Set - 2:

1 - 2	2 - 2	3 - 4	4 - 2	5 - 1
6 - 2	7 - 4	8 - 3	9 - 4	10 - 2

Answer Key Practice Set - 3:

1 - 3	2 - 1	3 - 1	4 - 4	5 - 3
6 - 2	7 - 3	8 - 2	9 - 1	10 - 3

Answer Key Practice Set - 4:

1 - 1	2 - 4	3 - 2	4 - 4	5 - 1
6 - 3	7 - 1	8 - 2	9 - 2	10 - 1

Answer Key Practice Set - 5:

1 - 2	2 - 2	3 - 1	4 - 3	5 - 1
6 - 1	7 - 2	8 - 1	9 - 3	10 - 3

Answer Key Practice Set - 6:

1 - 4	2 - 3	3 - 4	4 - 2	5 - 3
6 - 4	7 - 2	8 - 3	9 - 1	10 - 4

Answer Key Practice Set - 7:

1 - 3	2 - 1	3 - 1	4 - 3	5 - 1
6 - 2	7 - 1	8 - 2	9 - 2	10 - 4

Answer Key Practice Set - 8:

1 - 3	2 - 4	3 - 3	4 - 4	5 - 3
6 - 3	7 - 4	8 - 2	9 - 3	10 - 1

Answer Key Practice Set - 9:

1 - 2	2 - 2	3 - 3	4 - 4	5 - 3
6 - 3	7 - 2	8 - 1	9 - 3	10 - 2

Answer Key Practice Set - 10:

1 - 2	2 - 2	3 - 4	4 - 2	5 - 2
6 - 3	7 - 2	8 - 3	9 - 2	10 - 1

Answer Key Practice Set - 11:

1 - 2	2 - 2	3 - 1	4 - 1	5 - 2
6 - 4	7 - 2	8 - 2	9 - 3	10 - 2

Answer Key Practice Set - 12:

1 - 4	2 - 2	3 - 3	4 - 2	5 - 2
6 - 3	7 - 1	8 - 1	9 - 3	10 - 1

Answer Key Practice Set - 13:

1 - 1	2 - 2	3 - 3	4 - 4	5 - 4
6 - 3	7 - 1	8 - 3	9 - 4	10 - 4

Answer Key Practice Set - 14:

1 - 3	2 - 2	3 - 1	4 - 1	5 - 4
6 - 2	7 - 3	8 - 1	9 - 2	10 - 4

Answer Key Practice Set - 15:

1 - 2	2 - 1	3 - 4	4 - 2	5 - 4
6 - 3	7 - 4	8 - 2	9 - 3	10 - 2

Answer Key Practice Set - 16:

1 - 3	2 - 3	3 - 1	4 - 4	5 - 2
6 - 3	7 - 2	8 - 4	9 - 3	10 - 2

Answer Key Practice Set - 17:

1 - 4	2 - 1	3 - 2	4 - 4	5 - 3
6 - 3	7 - 2	8 - 1	9 - 2	10 - 3

Answer Key Practice Set - 18:

1 - 4	2 - 3	3 - 1	4 - 4	5 - 3
6 - 1	7 - 3	8 - 4	9 - 3	10 - 4

Answer Key Practice Set - 19:

1 - 2	2 - 3	3 - 2	4 - 4	5 - 3
6 - 4	7 - 4	8 - 3	9 - 1	10 - 4

Answer Key Practice Set - 20:

1 - 1	2 - 2	3 - 1	4 - 3	5 - 1
6 - 4	7 - 3	8 - 4	9 - 4	10 - 3

C6 Top 100 Antonyms (asked in SSC Exams)

1 **Flexible** (Adj.) - (लचीला)~ *[#R-10 (1)]*
Capable of bending easily without breaking
Anto: Rigid (कठोर), Stiff (सख्त)

2 **Bold** (Adj.) - (साहसी, निडर) *[#R-9]*
Showing courage, confidence, or willingness to take risks
Anto: Timid (डरपोक)

3 **Frugality** (N.) - (मितव्ययिता) *[#R-5 (4)]*
The quality of being frugal
Anto: Prodigality (फिजूलखर्ची), Wastefulness (अपव्यय)

4 **Shallow** (Adj.) - (उथला) *[#R-9]*
Having little depth
Anto: Deep (गहरा)

5 **Wicked** (Adj.) - (दुष्ट) *[#R-6 (3)]*
Evil or morally wrong
Anto: Good (अच्छा), Righteous (न्यायसंगत), Moral (नैतिक) {Virtuous (सद्‌गुणी)}

6 **Compulsory** (Adj.) - (अनिवार्य) *[#R-6 (2)]*
Required by law or rule; obligatory
Anto: Optional (ऐच्छिक), Voluntary (स्वैच्छिक)

7 **Denounce** (V.) - (निंदा करना)~ *[#R-6 (2)]*
To publicly declare to be wrong or evil
Anto: Praise (प्रशंसा करना), Compliment (तारीफ करना), Defend (रक्षा करना) {Appreciate (सराहना करना)}

8 **Exonerate** (V.) - (दोषमुक्त करना)~ *[#R-5 (3)]*
To free from blame or declare innocent
Anto: Convict (दोषी सिद्ध करना), Sentence (सजा देना) {Accuse (आरोप लगाना), Incriminate (दोषी ठहराना)}

9 **Captivity** (N.) - (क़ैद) *[#R-6 (1)]*
The condition of being imprisoned or confined
Anto: Liberty (स्वतंत्रता), Freedom (आज़ादी)

10 **Coherent** (Adj.) - (सुसंगत) *[#R-3 (4)]*
Logical and consistent
Anto: Illogical (तर्कहीन), Incomprehensible (समझ से बाहर), Disorganized (अव्यवस्थित) {Inconsistent (असंगत), Disconnected (असंबद्ध), Confused (भ्रमित)}

11 **Refreshing** (Adj.) - (ताज़ा करने वाला) *[#R-3 (4)]*
Pleasantly new or restoring energy
Anto: Stale (बासी) {Wearying (थकाने वाला)}

12 **Accelerate** (V.) - (गति बढ़ाना)~ *[#R-3 (3)]*
To move faster or increase speed
Anto: Delay (विलंब करना) {Slacken (धीमा करना), Impede (बाधा डालना)}

13 **Accessible** (Adj.) - (पहुँचने योग्य) *[#R-5 (1)]*
Easy to reach, approach, or use
Anto: Restricted (प्रतिबंधित) {Inaccessible (पहुँच से बाहर)}

14 **Appoint** (V.) - (नियुक्त करना) *[#R-6]*
To assign a job or role to someone
Anto: Dismiss (बर्खास्त करना)

15 **Clear** (Adj.) - (स्पष्ट) *[#R-5 (1)]*
Easy to perceive, understand, or interpret
Anto: Nebulous (अस्पष्ट), Opaque (अपारदर्शी), Murky (धुंधला), Dim (मंद), Obscure (अबोधगम्य)

16 **Expand** (V.) - (विस्तार करना) *[#R-5 (1)]*
To become or make larger or more extensive
Anto: Contract (संकुचित होना), Shrink (सिकुड़ना), Restrict (सीमित करना)

17 **Florid** (Adj.) - (अत्यधिक सजावटी) *[#R-3 (3)]*
Having a red or flushed complexion; excessively ornate or elaborate
Anto: Plain (सादा), Pale (फीका)

18 **Guilty** (Adj.) - (दोषी) *[#R-6]*
Culpable or responsible for a wrongdoing
Anto: Innocent (निर्दोष)

19 **Material** (Adj.) - (भौतिक) *[#R-1 (5)]*
Relating to physical substance
Anto: Abstract (अमूर्त) {Spiritual (आध्यात्मिक)}

20 **Obfuscate** (V.) - (उलझाना) *[#R-2 (4)]*
To make something unclear or hard to understand
Anto: Clarify (स्पष्ट करना) {Streamline (सरल बनाना), Illuminate (स्पष्ट करना)}

21 **Spiritual** (Adj.) - (आध्यात्मिक) *[#R-4 (2)]*
Relating to or affecting the human spirit or soul as opposed to material or physical

[**#R** denotes repetition of word]

[E.g. in SN 21, #R- **4 (2)** denotes this word has been asked 4 times in SSC and 2 times in other exams]

things

Anto: Physical (भौतिक), Material (भौतिक) {Bodily (शारीरिक)}

22 **Animosity** (N.) - (शत्रुता)~ *[#R-4 (1)]*
A strong feeling of dislike or hostility

Anto: Benevolence (दयालुता), Love (प्रेम), Affection (लगाव) {Comity (सौहार्द)}

23 **Approach** (V.) - (समीप आना) *[#R-5]*
To come near or nearer to someone or something in distance

Anto: Withdraw (वापस लेना), Retreat (पीछे हटना), Recede (दूर हटना), Avoid (बचना)

24 **Concur** (V.) - (सहमत होना) *[#R-5]*
To be of the same opinion; agree

Anto: Disagree (असहमत होना), Differ (भिन्न होना), Resist (विरोध करना)

25 **Critical** (Adj.) - (गंभीर, संकटपूर्ण, आलोचनात्मक) *[#R-1 (4)]*
Very important in a crucial situation; dangerous or serious; expressing severe criticism

Anto: Complimentary (प्रशंसात्मक) {Unimportant (महत्वहीन), Safe (सुरक्षित)}

26 **Curt** (Adj.) - (संक्षिप्त, रूखा) *[#R-1 (4)]*
Rudely brief

Anto: Polite (शिष्ट) {Tactful (व्यवहारकुशल), Courteous (विनीत), Expansive (विस्तृत)}

27 **Dull** (Adj.) - (सुस्त; फीका; कुंद) *[#R-4 (1)]*
Lacking interest or excitement; not bright or shining; not sharp

Anto: Keen (उत्सुक), Exciting (रोमांचक), Bright (उज्ज्वल), Riveting (आकर्षक) {Interesting (दिलचस्प)}

28 **Extensive** (Adj.) - (व्यापक) *[#R-2 (3)]*
Covering a large area or scope

Anto: Limited (सीमित), Intensive (गहन) {Negligible (नगण्य)}

29 **Friendly** (Adj./N.) - (मित्रतापूर्ण; मैत्री मैच) *[#R-3 (2)]*
Kind and pleasant (Adj.); A non-competitive match (N.)

Anto: Hostile (शत्रुतापूर्ण), Unfriendly (अमित्रवत)

30 **Ignorance** (N.) - (अज्ञान) *[#R-5]*
Lack of knowledge or information

Anto: Knowledge (ज्ञान), Acumen (कुशाग्र बुद्धि)

31 **Insatiable** (Adj.) - (अतृप्त)~ *[#R-4 (1)]*
Impossible to satisfy or fully meet desire

Anto: Satiable (संतुष्ट होने योग्य), Satisfiable (संतुष्ट होने योग्य), Content (संतुष्ट), Fulfilled (पूर्ण)

32 **Intentional** (Adj.) - (जानबूझकर) *[#R-5]*
Done on purpose; deliberate

Anto: Accidental (आकस्मिक), Unplanned (अनियोजित)

33 **Liberal** (Adj.) - (उदार) *[#R-4 (1)]*
Open to new ideas and willing to discard traditional values

Anto: Intolerant (असहिष्णु), Stingy (कंजूस), Conservative (रूढ़िवादी) {Bigoted (कट्टर)}

34 **Overt** (Adj.) - (प्रत्यक्ष) *[#R-4 (1)]*
Done or shown openly; clearly visible

Anto: Hidden (छिपा हुआ), Concealed (गुप्त)

35 **Prominent** (Adj.) - (प्रमुख) *[#R-4 (1)]*
Important or easily noticed, well-known

Anto: Obscure (अज्ञात), Unknown (अज्ञात), Inconspicuous (अस्पष्ट)

36 **Scrupulous** (Adj.) - (ईमानदार) *[#R-2 (3)]*
Very careful about what is morally right

Anto: Dishonest (बेईमान), Immoral (अनैतिक)

37 **Success** (N.) - (सफलता) *[#R-1 (4)]*
The achievement of a goal

Anto: Failure (असफलता)

38 **Suppress** (V.) - (दबाना) *[#R-4 (1)]*
To stop or prevent forcefully

Anto: Incite (उकसाना), Reveal (उजागर करना), Release (मुक्त करना) {Stimulate (उत्तेजित करना)}

39 **Suspicious** (Adj.) - (संदिग्ध) *[#R-3 (2)]*
Showing doubt or cautious distrust

Anto: Definitive (निश्चित), Certain (सुनिश्चित), Trustworthy (विश्वसनीय) {Credible (भरोसेमंद)}

40 **Tardy** (Adj.) - (विलंबित) *[#R-4 (1)]*
Arriving or happening later than expected; late

Anto: Prompt (तत्पर), Quick (शीघ्र), Early (जल्दी)

41 **Terminate** (V.) - (समाप्त करना) *[#R-3 (2)]*
To bring to an end

Anto: Begin (शुरू करना), Commence (आरंभ करना) {Introduce (परिचय कराना)}

42 **Vilify** (V.) - (बदनाम करना) *[#R-1 (4)]*
To speak badly about someone to damage reputation

Anto: Commend (प्रशंसा करना)

43 **Virtuous** (Adj.) - (नैतिक) *[#R-4 (1)]*

Having or showing high moral standards

Anto: Vicious (कुटिल), Sinful (पापी), Unethical (अनैतिक), Wicked (दुष्ट)

44 **Vouch** (V.) - (गारंटी देना) *[#R-1 (4)]*
To confirm or guarantee something

Anto: Invalidate (अमान्य करना) {Abjure (त्यागना), Disclaim (अस्वीकार करना)}

45 **Wrath** (N.) - (क्रोध) *[#R-2 (3)]*
Extreme anger

Anto: Glee (आनंद), Composure (संयम) {Happiness (खुशी)}

46 **Abhor** (V.) - (घृणा करना) *[#R-1 (3)]*
To regard with disgust and hatred

Anto: Love (प्रेम करना) {Admire (प्रशंसा करना)}

47 **Alive** (Adj.) - (जीवित) *[#R-3 (1)]*
Living, not dead

Anto: Dead (मृत)

48 **Altercation** (N.) - (झगड़ा) *[#R-2 (2)]*
A noisy argument or disagreement, especially in public

Anto: Compromise (समझौता), Agreement (सहमति) {Concord (सौहार्द)}

49 **Appreciate** (V.) - (मूल्य बढ़ाना; प्रशंसा करना)~ *[#R-3 (1)]*
To recognize the full worth of something; to increase in value

Anto: Disvalue (कम आँकना), Depreciate (मूल्य घटाना) {Decrease (कम होना)}

50 **Artificial** (Adj.) - (कृत्रिम) *[#R-1 (3)]*
Made by humans, not natural or genuine

Anto: Natural (प्राकृतिक) {Genuine (असली)}

51 **Controversial** (Adj.) - (विवादास्पद) *[#R-3 (1)]*
Giving rise to disagreement

Anto: Indisputable (निर्विवाद), Undisputed (अविवादित)

52 **Courtesy** (N.) - (शिष्टाचार) *[#R-2 (2)]*
The showing of politeness toward others

Anto: Rudeness (अशिष्टता), Crudeness (असभ्यता)

53 **Delay** (N./V.) - (देरी; देर करना) *[#R-4]*
A period of waiting (N.); To make something happen later (V.)

Anto: Advance (पहले करना), Haste (जल्दबाजी); Hasten (जल्दी करना)

54 **Dominate** (V.) - (हावी होना) *[#R-4]*
To control or strongly influence

Anto: Liberate (मुक्त करना), Surrender (आत्मसमर्पण करना), Submit (समर्पण करना)

55 **Elegance** (N.) - (भव्यता) *[#R-4]*
The quality of being graceful and stylish

Anto: Vulgarity (अभद्रता), Gracelessness (अशालीनता), Coarseness (रूखापन)

56 **Elevation** (N.) - (ऊंचाई; पदोन्नति) *[#R-2 (2)]*
The act of being raised; A higher level or position

Anto: Depression (गिरावट), Demotion (पदावनति)

57 **Expostulate** (V.) - (विरोध करना) *[#R-2 (2)]*
To argue or protest against something to persuade someone

Anto: Agree (सहमत होना), Laud (प्रशंसा करना)

58 **Expunge** (V.) - (मिटाना)~ *[#R-3 (1)]*
To erase or remove completely

Anto: Insert (डालना), Add (जोड़ना) {Restore (पुनर्स्थापित करना)}

59 **Hollow** (Adj./N.) - (खोखला; गड्ढा) *[#R-3 (1)]*
Having an empty space inside (Adj.); A hole or depression (N.)

Anto: Solid (ठोस), Worthwhile (उपयोगी)

60 **Improve** (V.) - (सुधारना) *[#R-2 (2)]*
To make better

Anto: Spoil (बिगाड़ना), Deteriorate (बिगड़ना) {Diminish (कम करना)}

61 **Incompetent** (Adj.) - (अयोग्य) *[#R-4]*
Lacking ability to do something successfully

Anto: Adept (निपुण)

62 **Infallible** (Adj.) - (अचूक)~ *[#R-2 (2)]*
Incapable of making mistakes or being wrong

Anto: Imperfect (अपूर्ण), Faulty (त्रुटिपूर्ण) {Unreliable (अविश्वसनीय), Erring (त्रुटिशील)}

63 **Inferior** (Adj.) - (घटिया) *[#R-4]*
Lower in rank, status, or quality

Anto: Superior (श्रेष्ठ), Senior (वरिष्ठ)

64 **Linger** (V.) - (देर तक ठहरना)~ *[#R-3 (1)]*
To stay in a place longer than necessary

Anto: Quicken (तेज करना), Hasten (जल्दी करना), Leave (छोड़ देना) {Forge (तेजी से आगे बढ़ना)}

65 **Lively** (Adj.) - (जीवंत) *[#R-3 (1)]*
Full of life, energy, and outgoing spirit

Anto: Sluggish (सुस्त), Gloomy (निस्तेज), Sombre (गंभीर) {Dull (नीरस)}

66 **Myth** (N.) - (मिथक) *[#R-1 (3)]*
A traditional story; a commonly believed but

false idea

Anto: Fact (तथ्य) {Reality (वास्तविकता)}

67 **Often** (Adv.) - (अक्सर) *[#R-2 (2)]*
Frequently; many times

Anto: Seldom (शायद ही कभी), Rarely (कभी कभार)

68 **Opprobrium** (N.) - (अपमान)~ *[#R-2 (2)]*
Harsh public criticism or disgrace

Anto: Honor (सम्मान), Adulation (प्रशंसा) {Praise (प्रशंसा), Encomium (औपचारिक प्रशंसा)}

69 **Originate** (V.) - (उत्पन्न होना) *[#R-2 (2)]*
To have a specified beginning

Anto: Terminate (समाप्त होना) {End (ख़त्म होना)}

70 **Relentless** (Adj.) - (लगातार; निर्दयी) *[#R-3 (1)]*
Continuing without stopping; harsh and unmerciful

Anto: Yielding (लचीला), Intermittent (रुक-रुक कर होने वाला) {Merciful (दयालु)}

71 **Sober** (Adj.) - (संयमित) *[#R-2 (2)]*
Not drunk; calm and serious

Anto: Drunk (नशे में), Agitated (उत्तेजित) {Unreserved (बेझिझक), Excited (उत्साहित)}

72 **Suspend** (V.) - (निलंबित करना) *[#R-3 (1)]*
To temporarily stop or delay something

Anto: Continue (जारी रखना), Resume (फिर से शुरू करना), Persist (बने रहना)

73 **Usurp** (V.) - (हड़पना) *[#R-3 (1)]*
To take power or position illegally or by force

Anto: Surrender (समर्पण करना), Restore (पुनः स्थापित करना), Release (मुक्त करना)

74 **Vehement** (Adj.) - (प्रचंड)~ *[#R-1 (3)]*
Showing strong feeling; intense or passionate

Anto: Mild (हल्का) {Subdued (संयमित), Apathetic (उदासीन)}

75 **Verdant** (Adj.) - (हरा-भरा) *[#R-1 (3)]*
Green with fresh grass or rich vegetation; Flourishing

Anto: Dying (मुरझाया हुआ) {Dry (शुष्क)}

76 **Veteran** (N.) - (अनुभवी)~ *[#R-2 (2)]*
A person who has had long experience in a particular field

Anto: Novice (नौसिखिया)

77 **Widespread** (Adj.) - (व्यापक) *[#R-2 (2)]*
Found or distributed over a large area or number of people

Anto: Limited (सीमित) {Localized (स्थानीय)}

78 **Witty** (Adj.) - (हाजिरजवाबी) *[#R-4]*
Showing quick and clever verbal humour

Anto: Stupid (मूर्ख), Serious (गंभीर), Lame (असंतोषजनक), Unamusing (नीरस)

79 **Abstract** (Adj.) - (अमूर्त, भाववाचक) *[#R-3]*
Existing as an idea, not physical

Anto: Concrete (ठोस)

80 **Acerbic** (Adj.) - (तीखा)~ *[#R-1 (2)]*
Sharp and forthright in speech or comment

Anto: Bland (सौम्य) {Polite (विनम्र), Sweet (मधुर)}

81 **Algid** (Adj.) - (ठंडा) *[#R-3]*
Extremely cold in temperature

Anto: Scorching (झुलसाने वाला), Igneous (आग्नेय, अत्यधिक गर्म)

82 **Amalgamate** (V.) - (एकीकृत करना) *[#R-1 (2)]*
To combine or unite to form one organization or structure

Anto: Dismantle (विघटित करना) {Separate (अलग करना), Disperse (बिखेरना)}

83 **Antecedent** (N.) - (पूर्ववर्ती)~ *[#R-1 (2)]*
A thing or event that existed before or logically precedes another

Anto: Consequence (परिणाम) {Result (नतीजा)}

84 **Antiquated** (Adj.) - (पुराना) *[#R-2 (1)]*
Old-fashioned or outdated

Anto: Contemporary (समकालीन) {Modern (आधुनिक)}

85 **Appearance** (N.) - (उपस्थिति) *[#R-1 (2)]*
An occasion when someone appears in public

Anto: Exit (निकास) {Disappearance (गायब होना)}

86 **Ascent** (N.) - (चढ़ाव) *[#R-3]*
A climb or walk to the summit of a mountain or hill

Anto: Descent (उतराव)

87 **Authorize** (V.) - (अधिकृत करना) *[#R-1 (2)]*
To give official permission or power

Anto: Forbid (मना करना)

88 **Baroque** (Adj.) - (बहुत सजावटी) *[#R-3]*
Very decorative, fancy, and full of elaborate details

Anto: Plain (सादा)

89 **Belittle** (V.) - (छोटा महसूस कराना) *[#R-1 (2)]*
To dismiss or diminish the importance of something

Anto: Extol (प्रशंसा करना) {Praise (तारीफ करना)}

90 **Bestow** (V.) - (प्रदान करना) *[#R-3]*
To give or confer as an honor or gift

Anto: Deny (मना करना)

91 **Better** (Adj.) - (बेहतर) *[#R-3]*
Higher in quality

Anto: Inferior (निम्न), Worse (बदतर)

92 **Betterment** (N.) - (सुधार) *[#R-3]*
The improvement or progress in something

Anto: Deterioration (ह्रास), Worsening (गिरावट)

93 **Bless** (V.) - (आशीर्वाद देना) *[#R-3]*
To give divine favor or express good wishes

Anto: Curse (शाप देना)

94 **Capacious** (Adj.) - (विशाल) *[#R-1 (2)]*
Having a lot of space inside; roomy

Anto: Cramped (तंग) {Limited (सीमित), Confined (परिसीमित)}

95 **Cheap** (Adj.) - (सस्ता) *[#R-3]*
Low in price, especially in relation to similar items

Anto: Expensive (महंगा), Costly (महँगा)

96 **Cheerful** (Adj.) - (प्रसन्न) *[#R-2 (1)]*
Noticeably happy and optimistic

Anto: Gloomy (उदास) {Sad (दुखी)}

97 **Combative** (Adj.) - (लड़ाकू) *[#R-3]*
Ready or eager to fight or argue

Anto: Peaceful (शांतिपूर्ण), Agreeable (सहमत)

98 **Complete** (Adj.) - (पूर्ण) *[#R-2 (1)]*
Having all necessary or appropriate parts

Anto: Partial (आंशिक), Incomplete (अधूरा)

99 **Conform** (V.) - (अनुरूप होना) *[#R-2 (1)]*
To comply with rules, standards, or laws

Anto: Differ (भिन्न होना), Deviate (विचलित होना) {Disobey (अवज्ञा करना)}

100 **Contentment** (N.) - (संतोष) *[#R-2 (1)]*
A state of happiness and satisfaction

Anto: Sadness (दुख), Discomfort (असुविधा) {Agitation (व्याकुलता)}

*Total **100** Antonyms asked **470** times*

C7 Antonyms (asked in SSC Exams)

1 Abase (V.) - (अपमानित करना) *[#R-2]*
To reduce or lower in rank or reputation
Anto: Exalt (ऊँचा उठाना, सम्मान देना)

2 **Abhor** (V.) - (घृणा करना) *[#R-1 (3)]*
To regard with disgust and hatred
Anto: Love (प्रेम करना) {Admire (प्रशंसा करना)}

3 **Above** (Prep.) - (ऊपर) *[#R-2]*
At a higher level or layer than
Anto: Below (नीचे)

4 **Abrasive** (Adj.) - (रूखा)
Showing little concern for others' feelings; harsh
Anto: Delightful (आनंदप्रद)

5 Absence (N.) - (अनुपस्थिति)
The state of being away from a place
Anto: Presence (उपस्थिति)

6 Abstinence (N.) - (परहेज)
The practice of restraining oneself from indulging
Anto: Gluttony (पेटूपन)

7 Abstract (Adj.) - (अमूर्त, भाववाचक) *[#R-3]*
Existing as an idea, not physical
Anto: Concrete (ठोस)

8 **Abutting** (Adj.) - (सटा हुआ)
Being next to or sharing a boundary
Anto: Far (दूर)

9 Accelerate (V.) - (गति बढ़ाना)~ *[#R-3 (3)]*
To move faster or increase speed
Anto: Delay (विलंब करना) {Slacken (धीमा करना), Impede (बाधा डालना)}

10 Accessible (Adj.) - (पहुँचने योग्य) *[#R-5 (1)]*
Easy to reach, approach, or use
Anto: Restricted (प्रतिबंधित) {Inaccessible (पहुँच से बाहर)}

11 **Accommodating** (Adj.) - (सहायक)
Willing to help or please others
Anto: Disobliging (असहायक)

12 Accompany (V.) - (साथ देना)
To go along with someone
Anto: Abandon (छोड़ देना)

13 Acerbic (Adj.) - (तीखा)~ *[#R-1 (2)]*
Sharp and forthright in speech or comment
Anto: Bland (सौम्य) {Polite (विनम्र), Sweet (मधुर)}

14 **Ache** (N.) - (दर्द)
A continuous or prolonged dull pain in the body
Anto: Ease (आराम)

15 **Add** (V.) - (जोड़ना)
To join something to increase size, number, or amount
Anto: Remove (हटाना)

16 **Adipose** (Adj.) - (वसायुक्त)
Relating to or containing fat; fatty
Anto: Lean (दुबला)

17 Adjacent (Adj.) - (सटा हुआ) *[#R-1 (1)]*
Next to or adjoining something else
Anto: Distant (दूर) {Remote (बहुत दूर)}

18 Administer (V.) - (प्रशासन करना)
To manage or run an organization or system
Anto: Neglect (उपेक्षा करना)

19 Admirable (Adj.) - (प्रशंसनीय) *[#R-2]*
Deserving respect or approval
Anto: Unworthy (अयोग्य), Blameworthy (निंदनीय)

20 Admiration (N.) - (प्रशंसा) *[#R-1 (1)]*
A feeling of respect and approval
Anto: Contempt (तिरस्कार) {Disgust (घृणा)}

21 Adopt (V.) - (गोद लेना, अपनाना)
To choose to take up or follow; or to legally take another's child as one's own
Anto: Reject (अस्वीकार करना)

22 **Adultery** (N.) - (व्यभिचार)
Sexual intercourse between a married person and someone other than their spouse
Anto: Purity (पवित्रता)

23 Adventurous (Adj.) - (रोमांचप्रिय)~ *[#R-1 (1)]*
Willing to take risks or try new experiences
Anto: Cautious (सतर्क) {Timid (डरपोक)}

24 Affiliation (N.) - (जुड़ाव)

[**#R** denotes repetition of word]

[E.g. in SN 10, #R- **5 (1)** denotes this word has been asked 5 times in SSC and 1 time in other exams]

The state of being affiliated

Anto: Detachment (अलगाव)

25 **Affordable** (Adj.) - (किफ़ायती)
Cheap enough to buy easily

Anto: Overpriced (अत्यधिक महँगा)

26 **After** (Prep.) - (बाद में)
In the time following an event

Anto: Before (पहले)

27 **Aggressive** (Adj.) - (आक्रामक)~ *[#R-2]*
Ready to attack or confront others

Anto: Peaceful (शांतिपूर्ण), Calm (शांत)

28 **Agility** (N.) - (फुर्ती)
The ability to move quickly and easily

Anto: Stiffness (कठोरता)

29 **Agitated** (Adj.) - (व्याकुल)
Upset or disturbed

Anto: Serene (शांत)

30 **Agree** (V.) - (सहमत होना) *[#R-2]*
To have the same opinion about something

Anto: Oppose (विरोध करना), Refuse (इनकार करना)

31 **Airy** (Adj.) - (हवादार) *[#R-2]*
Open to air and breezes; light and breezy

Anto: Stuffy (घुटन भरा)

32 **Algid** (Adj.) - (ठंडा) *[#R-3]*
Extremely cold in temperature

Anto: Scorching (झुलसाने वाला), Igneous (आग्नेय, अत्यधिक गर्म)

33 **Align** (V.) - (पंक्ति में करना)
To place or arrange things in a straight line

Anto: Disrupt (तितर-बितर करना)

34 **Alike** (Adj.) - (एक समान) *[#R-1 (1)]*
Similar to each other

Anto: Different (अलग)

35 **Alive** (Adj.) - (जीवित) *[#R-3 (1)]*
Living, not dead

Anto: Dead (मृत)

36 **Allegation** (N.) - (आरोप) *[#R-2]*
A claim that someone has done something illegal or wrong, typically without proof

Anto: Exoneration (दोषमुक्ति), Testimony (गवाही)

37 **Allergic** (Adj.) - (एलर्जी संबंधी)
Having an allergy or displaying hypersensitivity to a substance

Anto: Immune (प्रतिरक्षित)

38 **Alliance** (N.) - (संधि)
A union or association formed for mutual benefit, especially between countries or organizations

Anto: Separation (विभाजन)

39 **Alluring** (Adj.) - (आकर्षक)
Very attractive or tempting

Anto: Repulsive (घृणित)

40 **Altercation** (N.) - (झगड़ा) *[#R-2 (2)]*
A noisy argument or disagreement, especially in public

Anto: Compromise (समझौता), Agreement (सहमति) {Concord (सौहार्द)}

41 **Always** (Adv.) - (हमेशा)
At all times; on all occasions

Anto: Never (कभी नहीं)

42 **Amalgamate** (V.) - (एकीकृत करना) *[#R-1 (2)]*
To combine or unite to form one organization or structure

Anto: Dismantle (विघटित करना) {Separate (अलग करना), Disperse (बिखेरना)}

43 **Amazed** (Adj.) - (हैरान) *[#R-1 (1)]*
Feeling great surprise or wonder

Anto: Unimpressed (अप्रभावित) {Unruffled (स्थिर)}

44 **Ambivalent** (Adj.) - (मिले जुले भाव वाला)~ *[#R-1 (1)]*
Having mixed feelings or contradictory ideas about something or someone

Anto: Unequivocal (स्पष्ट) {Resolute (दृढ़ संकल्प)}

45 **Ambrosial** (Adj.) - (सुगंधित)
Extremely pleasing in smell or taste

Anto: Malodorous (बदबूदार)

46 **Amiss** (Adv.) - (गलत)
In a wrong or inappropriate way

Anto: Impeccably (बिना गलती के)

47 **Amuse** (V.) - (मनोरंजन करना)
To make someone laugh or feel entertained

Anto: Bore (ऊबाना)

48 **Anarchic** (Adj.) - (अराजक)
With no controlling rules or principles to give order

Anto: Normal (सामान्य)

49 **Angst** (N.) - (चिंता)
A feeling of deep anxiety or dread; emotional turmoil

Anto: Serenity (शांति)

50 **Anile** (Adj.) - (कमजोर वृद्ध महिला के समान)~
Relating to or resembling an old woman; senile
Anto: Young (युवा)

51 **Animosity** (N.) - (शत्रुता)~ *[#R-4 (1)]*
A strong feeling of dislike or hostility
Anto: Benevolence (दयालुता), Love (प्रेम), Affection (लगाव) {Comity (सौहार्द)}

52 Annex (V.) - (कब्जा करना) *[#R-1 (1)]*
To add or take possession of
Anto: Subtract (घटाना) {Detach (अलग करना)}

53 Annoyance (N.) - (परेशानी)
A feeling of irritation
Anto: Serenity (शांति)

54 Anonymous (Adj.) - (गुमनाम)~
Not identified by name; unknown
Anto: Famous (प्रसिद्ध)

55 Antecedent (N.) - (पूर्ववर्ती)~ *[#R-1 (2)]*
A thing or event that existed before or logically precedes another
Anto: Consequence (परिणाम) {Result (नतीजा)}

56 **Antiquated** (Adj.) - (पुराना) *[#R-2 (1)]*
Old-fashioned or outdated
Anto: Contemporary (समकालीन) {Modern (आधुनिक)}

57 **Antithesis** (N.) - (विपरीत, उलटा)~ *[#R-1 (1)]*
A person or thing that is the direct opposite of someone or something else
Anto: Harmony (सामंजस्य) {Similarity (समानता)}

58 Antonym (N.) - (विलोम)~
A word opposite in meaning to another
Anto: Synonym (पर्यायवाची)

59 **Antsy** (Adj.) - (बेचैन)
Agitated, impatient, or restless
Anto: Collected (संयमित)

60 **Apart** (Adv.) - (अलग)
Separated by a distance in time or space
Anto: Nearby (निकट)

61 Apocryphal (Adj.) - (संदिग्ध) *[#R-1 (1)]*
Of doubtful authenticity, widely circulated as true
Anto: Authentic (प्रामाणिक) {True (सच)}

62 Appearance (N.) - (उपस्थिति) *[#R-1 (2)]*
An occasion when someone appears in public
Anto: Exit (निकास) {Disappearance (गायब होना)}

63 **Appoint** (V.) - (नियुक्त करना) *[#R-6]*
To assign a job or role to someone
Anto: Dismiss (बर्खास्त करना)

64 Appreciate (V.) - (मूल्य बढ़ाना; प्रशंसा करना)~ *[#R-3 (1)]*
To recognize the full worth of something; to increase in value
Anto: Disvalue (कम आँकना), Depreciate (मूल्य घटाना) {Decrease (कम होना)}

65 Apprehensive (Adj.) - (चिंतित)
Anxious or fearful that something bad or unpleasant will happen
Anto: Confident (आत्मविश्वासी)

66 Apprentice (N.) - (प्रशिक्षु)~
A person learning a trade under a skilled worker
Anto: Veteran (अनुभवी)

67 Approach (V.) - (समीप आना) *[#R-5]*
To come near or nearer to someone or something in distance
Anto: Withdraw (वापस लेना), Retreat (पीछे हटना), Recede (दूर हटना), Avoid (बचना)

68 **Approbate** (V.) - (स्वीकार करना)
To approve formally
Anto: Reject (अस्वीकार करना)

69 Approve (V.) - (मंजूरी देना) *[#R-2]*
To officially agree to or accept as satisfactory
Anto: Reject (अस्वीकार करना)

70 **Approximately** (Adv.) - (लगभग)
Close to the actual, but not completely accurate or exact
Anto: Exactly (बिलकुल सही रूप से)

71 Aqueous (Adj.) - (जलीय)
Made from, with, or by water
Anto: Arid (शुष्क)

72 **Arbitrarily** (Adv.) - (मनमाने ढंग से)
Based on random choice rather than reason
Anto: Meticulously (सावधानीपूर्वक)

73 **Arouse** (V.) - (उत्तेजित करना)
To evoke or awaken a feeling, emotion, or response
Anto: Suppress (दबाना)

74 Arrest (V.) - (गिरफ्तार करना) *[#R-2]*
To seize someone by legal authority and take into custody
Anto: Release (रिहा करना), Unbind (मुक्त करना)

75 Arrival (N.) - (आगमन) *[#R-2]*

The action or process of arriving

Anto: Departure (प्रस्थान)

76 **Artifice** (N.) - (चालाकी)
Clever devices used to trick or deceive others

Anto: Truthfulness (सत्यता)

77 Artificial (Adj.) - (कृत्रिम) *[#R-1 (3)]*
Made by humans, not natural or genuine

Anto: Natural (प्राकृतिक) {Genuine (असली)}

78 Ascent (N.) - (चढ़ाव) *[#R-3]*
A climb or walk to the summit of a mountain or hill

Anto: Descent (उतराव)

79 Asset (N.) - (संपत्ति)
A useful or valuable thing, person, or quality

Anto: Liability (देनदारी)

80 Atheist (N.) - (नास्तिक)~
A person who does not believe in God

Anto: Believer (आस्तिक)

81 **Attachment** (N.) - (लगाव)
An added part or emotional bond

Anto: Detachment (विरक्ति)

82 Attend (V.) - (उपस्थित रहना)
To be present at an event or meeting

Anto: Miss (चूकना)

83 Attention (N.) - (ध्यान)
Focusing the mind on something

Anto: Disregard (अनदेखा करना)

84 **Authenticate** (V.) - (सत्यापित करना)
To prove something is real

Anto: Discredit (गलत ठहराना)

85 **Authorize** (V.) - (अधिकृत करना) *[#R-1 (2)]*
To give official permission or power

Anto: Forbid (मना करना)

86 **Avariciousness** (N.) - (लालच)
Extreme greed for wealth

Anto: Generosity (उदारता)

87 **Average** (Adj.) - (औसत)
Neither too high nor too low

Anto: Exceptional (असाधारण)

88 **Avow** (V.) - (स्वीकार करना) *[#R-2]*
To openly admit or declare something

Anto: Deny (इनकार करना), Renounce (त्यागना)

89 **Awake** (Adj.) - (जागा हुआ) *[#R-2]*
Not asleep

Anto: Asleep (सोया हुआ)

90 **Aware** (Adj.) - (जागरूक) *[#R-1 (1)]*
Having knowledge or perception of a situation or fact

Anto: Ignorant (अज्ञानी)

91 Axiom (N.) - (सार्वभौमिक सत्य)~
A statement accepted as true without proof

Anto: Absurdity (बेतुकापन)

92 **Babel** (N.) - (कोलाहल)
A confused noise made by a number of voices

Anto: Quietness (शांति)

93 **Backward** (Adj.) - (अविकसित)
Not developed or advanced

Anto: Forward (विकसित)

94 **Balmy** (Adj.) - (सुखद) *[#R-2]*
Pleasantly warm, mild, and soothing

Anto: Harsh (कठोर), Hard (कठोर)

95 **Baneful** (Adj.) - (हानिकारक)
Causing severe harm, damage, or destruction

Anto: Beneficial (लाभकारी)

96 **Barbarity** (N.) - (अत्यधिक क्रूरता)
Extreme cruelty or brutal behavior

Anto: Compassion (दया)

97 **Baroque** (Adj.) - (बहुत सजावटी) *[#R-3]*
Very decorative, fancy, and full of elaborate details

Anto: Plain (सादा)

98 **Befuddle** (V.) - (भ्रमित करना)
To confuse or make someone unable to think clearly

Anto: Explicate (स्पष्ट करना)

99 **Behemoth** (N.) - (विशालकाय प्राणी)~ *[#R-1 (1)]*
Something enormous

Anto: Midget (बौना)

100 Belittle (V.) - (छोटा महसूस कराना) *[#R-1 (2)]*
To dismiss or diminish the importance of something

Anto: Extol (प्रशंसा करना) {Praise (तारीफ करना)}

101 Beneath (Prep.) - (नीचे) *[#R-2]*
At a lower level or layer than

Anto: Above (ऊपर)

102 **Beneficent** (Adj.) - (परोपकारी)
Generous or doing good

Anto: Cruel (क्रूर)

103 **Benison** (N.) - (आशीर्वाद)
A blessing or good wish
Anto: Execration (अभिशाप)

104 **Bequest** (N.) - (वसीयतनामा)
Property or money left to someone in a will
Anto: Withdrawal (वापसी)

105 **Bestow** (V.) - (प्रदान करना) *[#R-3]*
To give or confer as an honor or gift
Anto: Deny (मना करना)

106 Better (Adj.) - (बेहतर) *[#R-3]*
Higher in quality
Anto: Inferior (निम्न), Worse (बदतर)

107 **Betterment** (N.) - (सुधार) *[#R-3]*
The improvement or progress in something
Anto: Deterioration (ह्रास), Worsening (गिरावट)

108 Bias (N.) - (पक्षपात)
An unfair preference
Anto: Fairness (निष्पक्षता)

109 **Bigot** (N.) - (कट्टरपंथी)~
A person who is intolerant towards those holding different opinions
Anto: Liberal (उदारवादी)

110 **Bland** (Adj.) - (फीका)
Lacking strong features or characteristics and therefore uninteresting
Anto: Exciting (रोमांचक)

111 **Blank** (Adj.) - (खाली)
Empty or clear, or containing no information or mark
Anto: Filled (भरा हुआ)

112 **Blazing** (Adj.) - (जलता हुआ, अत्यधिक गर्म)
Extremely hot or burning brightly
Anto: Frigid (अत्यधिक ठंडा)

113 Blemish (N.) - (दाग)
A mark that spoils appearance
Anto: Perfection (पूर्णता)

114 **Bless** (V.) - (आशीर्वाद देना) *[#R-3]*
To give divine favor or express good wishes
Anto: Curse (शाप देना)

115 **Bloated** (Adj.) - (सूजा हुआ)
Swollen with fluid or gas
Anto: Deflated (पिचका हुआ)

116 **Blooming** (Adj.) - (खिलता हुआ)
In full bloom or flowering
Anto: Fading (मुरझाता हुआ)

117 **Bold** (Adj.) - (साहसी, निडर) *[#R-9]*
Showing courage, confidence, or willingness to take risks
Anto: Timid (डरपोक)

118 **Bondage** (N.) - (दासता)
The state of being a slave
Anto: Liberty (स्वतंत्रता)

119 **Boor** (N.) - (गंवार)
An unrefined, ill-mannered person
Anto: Gentleman (सज्जन)

120 **Border** (N.) - (सीमा)
A line dividing two areas or forming an edge
Anto: Centre (केंद्र)

121 Boring (Adj.) - (उबाऊ)
Not interesting; causing tiredness
Anto: Exciting (रोमांचक)

122 Borrow (V.) - (उधार लेना) *[#R-2]*
To take something with the intention of returning it
Anto: Lend (उधार देना)

123 **Borrowed** (Adj.) - (उधार लिया हुआ)
Taken on loan from someone else
Anto: Lent (उधार दिया हुआ)

124 Boundary (N.) - (सीमा)
The limits of an area or territory
Anto: Core (मुख्य भाग)

125 **Boycott** (V.) - (बहिष्कार करना)
To refuse to buy, use, or participate as a form of protest
Anto: Welcome (स्वागत करना)

126 **Brashness** (N.) - (बेशर्मी, ढिठाई)
Rude or aggressive boldness without respect
Anto: Timidity (कायरता)

127 **Brawny** (Adj.) - (बलिष्ठ)
Physically strong and muscular
Anto: Weak (कमज़ोर)

128 **Breadth** (N.) - (चौड़ाई)
The distance from side to side; width
Anto: Narrowness (संकरापन)

129 **Break** (V.) - (तोड़ना)
To separate into pieces or stop working
Anto: Mend (मरम्मत करना)

130 Bridle (V.) - (नियन्त्रण करना)~

To restrain or control

Anto: Release (मुक्त करना)

131 **Brilliantly** (Adv.) - (चमकदार रूप से)
In a bright or clever way

Anto: Dimly (धुंधले रूप से)

132 **Brindled** (Adj.) - (धब्बेदार)
Having streaks or patches of color

Anto: Unflecked (बिना धब्बों का)

133 Brutality (N.) - (क्रूरता) *[#R-2]*
Savage physical violence; great cruelty

Anto: Humanity (मानवता), Gentleness (सौम्यता)

134 **Budding** (Adj.) - (कलियाँ निकलती हुई; विकसित होता हुआ)
Beginning to develop or show signs of future potential

Anto: Withering (मुरझाता हुआ)

135 **Bulging** (Adj.) - (उभरा हुआ)
Swelling outward

Anto: Contracting (सिकुड़ता हुआ)

136 **Bulk** (N.) - (विशाल मात्रा)
The mass or magnitude of something large

Anto: Handful (मुट्ठी भर)

137 **Bulwark** (N./V.) - (सुरक्षा-दीवार; रक्षा करना) *[#R-1 (1)]*
A defensive wall or protection (N.); To protect or defend (V.)

Anto: Assault (हमला) {Assail (आक्रमण करना)}

138 **Bumpy** (Adj.) - (उबड़-खाबड़)
Uneven, with many patches raised above the rest

Anto: Steady (स्थिर)

139 **Burgeon** (V.) - (फलना-फूलना)
To begin to grow or increase rapidly; flourish

Anto: Shrivel (सिकुड़ना)

140 Burning (Adj.) - (जलता हुआ)
Extremely hot; on fire

Anto: Freezing (अत्यंत ठंडा)

141 Busy (Adj.) - (व्यस्त) *[#R-1 (1)]*
Having a great deal to do

Anto: Idle (निष्क्रिय) {Relaxed (निश्चिंत)}

142 **Calculative** (Adj.) - (चालाक)
Inclined to plan carefully with shrewd intent

Anto: Naive (भोला)

143 **Calm Down** (Ph.) - (शांत करना)
To become quiet or calm after agitation

Anto: Agitate (उत्तेजित करना)

144 **Calmness** (N.) - (शांति)
The state of being free from agitation

Anto: Rage (क्रोध)

145 Camaraderie (N.) - (साथीपन, आपसी मित्रता)
Mutual trust and friendship among people together

Anto: Dislike (नापसंद)

146 **Canonical** (Adj.) - (पारंपरिक) *[#R-1 (1)]*
Conforming to traditional or religious principles

Anto: Unorthodox (अपारंपरिक) {Temporal (सांसारिक)}

147 Capacious (Adj.) - (विशाल) *[#R-1 (2)]*
Having a lot of space inside; roomy

Anto: Cramped (तंग) {Limited (सीमित), Confined (परिसीमित)}

148 **Capital** (Adj.) - (अत्यंत महत्वपूर्ण)
Most important or chief

Anto: Minor (गौण)

149 **Capitalise** (V.) - (लाभ उठाना)
To take the chance to gain advantage from

Anto: Forfeit (गंवाना)

150 **Captivity** (N.) - (क़ैद) *[#R-6 (1)]*
The condition of being imprisoned or confined

Anto: Liberty (स्वतंत्रता), Freedom (आज़ादी)

151 Care (V.) - (ध्यान रखना)
To look after or feel concern

Anto: Disregard (ध्यान न देना)

152 **Careless** (Adj.) - (लापरवाह)
Not giving sufficient attention to avoid harm or errors

Anto: Vigilant (सतर्क)

153 Carry (V.) - (ढोना)
To support and move something from one place to another

Anto: Leave (छोड़ना)

154 **Casuistry** (N.) - (कुतर्क)
The use of clever arguments to trick people

Anto: Honesty (ईमानदारी)

155 **Catastrophic** (Adj.) - (भयानक)~ *[#R-1 (1)]*
Causing sudden great damage or suffering

Anto: Beneficial (लाभकारी)

156 **Cause** (N.) - (कारण) *[#R-1 (1)]*
A reason for an action or condition

Anto: Consequence (परिणाम)

157 **Celebrated** (Adj.) - (प्रसिद्ध) *[#R-2]*
Famous and admired
Anto: Inglorious (अप्रसिद्ध)

158 **Centre** (N.) - (केंद्र) *[#R-2]*
The middle point of something
Anto: Periphery (परिधि), Outskirts (बाहरी इलाका)

159 **Certify** (V.) - (प्रमाणित करना)
To attest or confirm officially
Anto: Disapprove (अस्वीकार करना)

160 **Cessation** (N.) - (समाप्ति) *[#R-1 (1)]*
The process of ending
Anto: Commencement (आरंभ)

161 Characteristic (Adj.) - (विशिष्ट)
Distinctive of a particular person, place, or thing
Anto: Atypical (अविशिष्ट)

162 Charity (N.) - (दान)
The act of giving help, money, or kindness to those in need
Anto: Selfishness (स्वार्थ)

163 **Cheap** (Adj.) - (सस्ता) *[#R-3]*
Low in price, especially in relation to similar items
Anto: Expensive (महंगा), Costly (महँगा)

164 Cheerful (Adj.) - (प्रसन्न) *[#R-2 (1)]*
Noticeably happy and optimistic
Anto: Gloomy (उदास) {Sad (दुखी)}

165 **Chicken Hearted** (Adj.) - (डरपोक)
Lacking courage; cowardly
Anto: Courageous (साहसी)

166 **Chill** (N.) - (ठंड)
A coldness
Anto: Warmth (गर्मी)

167 **Cite** (V.) - (उल्लेख करना)
To refer to or quote
Anto: Forget (भूल जाना)

168 **Civility** (N.) - (शिष्टता)
Polite and respectful behavior
Anto: Insolence (अशिष्टता)

169 **Clammy** (Adj.) - (चिपचिपा)
Unpleasantly damp and sticky to touch
Anto: Dry (सूखा)

170 Classic (Adj.) - (आदर्श)
Of highest quality over time
Anto: Atypical (असामान्य)

171 Clear (Adj.) - (स्पष्ट) *[#R-5 (1)]*
Easy to perceive, understand, or interpret
Anto: Nebulous (अस्पष्ट), Opaque (अपारदर्शी), Murky (धुंधला), Dim (मंद), Obscure (अबोधगम्य)

172 **Clench** (V.) - (मुट्ठी बंद करना)
To close into a tight ball, especially when feeling extreme anger
Anto: Relax (ढीला छोड़ना)

173 **Cloudy** (Adj.) - (बादल छाया हुआ; धुंधला)
Full of or covered with clouds; Not clear or transparent
Anto: Transparent (पारदर्शी)

174 Clutch (V.) - (कसकर पकड़ना)
To hold tightly
Anto: Abandon (त्याग देना)

175 Coax (V.) - (फुसलाना)
To persuade gradually or gently to do something
Anto: Dissuade (हतोत्साहित करना)

176 Coherent (Adj.) - (सुसंगत) *[#R-3 (4)]*
Logical and consistent
Anto: Illogical (तर्कहीन), Incomprehensible (समझ से बाहर), Disorganized (अव्यवस्थित) {Inconsistent (असंगत), Disconnected (असंबद्ध), Confused (भ्रमित)}

177 **Coincide** (V.) - (मेल खाना)
To occur at or during the same time
Anto: Differ (भिन्न होना)

178 Collaboration (N.) - (सहभागिता)
The action of working with someone to produce something
Anto: Division (विभाजन)

179 **Collect** (V.) - (इकट्ठा करना)
To bring or gather together things
Anto: Disperse (बिखेरना)

180 **Colorful** (Adj.) - (रंगीन)
Having bright or varied colors
Anto: Monochrome (एकरंगा)

181 **Combative** (Adj.) - (लड़ाकू) *[#R-3]*
Ready or eager to fight or argue
Anto: Peaceful (शांतिपूर्ण), Agreeable (सहमत)

182 **Comedy** (N.) - (हास्य)
Humorous entertainment or dramatic work with a happy ending

Anto: Tragedy (त्रासदी)

183 **Comfort** (N.) - (आराम)
A physical ease or relief
Anto: Discontentment (असंतोष)

184 **Comical** (Adj.) - (हास्यास्पद) *[#R-2]*
Amusing, especially in a ludicrous or absurd way
Anto: Serious (गंभीर), Tragic (शोकपूर्ण)

185 **Commend** (V.) - (प्रशंसा करना)
To express approval or praise
Anto: Criticise (आलोचना करना)

186 **Commiseration** (N.) - (सहानुभूति) *[#R-1 (1)]*
An expression or feeling of sympathy
Anto: Indifference (उदासीनता)

187 Compatible (Adj.) - (अनुकूल) *[#R-2]*
Able to exist or occur together without conflict
Anto: Incompatible (असंगत), Inconsistent (असंगत)

188 **Compatriot** (N.) - (देशवासी)~
A fellow citizen or national of a country
Anto: Outsider (परदेशी)

189 **Compendium** (N.) - (सारांश)
A collection of concise but detailed information
Anto: Expansion (विस्तार)

190 **Compete** (V.) - (प्रतिस्पर्धा करना)
To try to win against others
Anto: Support (समर्थन करना)

191 Complaint (N.) - (शिकायत)
A statement that something is unsatisfactory
Anto: Praise (प्रशंसा)

192 Complete (Adj.) - (पूर्ण) *[#R-2 (1)]*
Having all necessary or appropriate parts
Anto: Partial (आंशिक), Incomplete (अधूरा)

193 **Compress** (V.) - (दबाना, संकुचित करना)
To flatten by pressure; squeeze; press
Anto: Enlarge (बड़ा करना)

194 Compromise (N.) - (समझौता)
An agreement by mutual concessions
Anto: Dissent (असहमति)

195 Compulsory (Adj.) - (अनिवार्य) *[#R-6 (2)]*
Required by law or rule; obligatory
Anto: Optional (ऐच्छिक), Voluntary (स्वैच्छिक)

196 **Comrade** (N.) - (साथी)
A companion who shares one's activities
Anto: Enemy (शत्रु)

197 Conceive (V.) - (कल्पना करना)
To form a plan or idea in the mind
Anto: Misunderstand (गलत समझना)

198 **Concentrated** (Adj.) - (केंद्रित, गाढ़ा) *[#R-2]*
Wholly directed to one thing; intense
Anto: Diluted (पतला), Dispersed (बिखरा हुआ)

199 Conciliation (N.) - (मेल-मिलाप)
The action of stopping someone from being angry
Anto: Confrontation (टकराव)

200 **Conclusive** (Adj.) - (निर्णायक) *[#R-1 (1)]*
Serving to prove a case; decisive
Anto: Ambiguous (अस्पष्ट) {Indecisive (अनिर्णायक)}

201 Concomitant (Adj.) - (साथ-साथ होने वाला)
Occurring together
Anto: Separate (अलग)

202 **Concur** (V.) - (सहमत होना) *[#R-5]*
To be of the same opinion; agree
Anto: Disagree (असहमत होना), Differ (भिन्न होना), Resist (विरोध करना)

203 **Condense** (V.) - (संक्षेप करना) *[#R-1 (1)]*
To make something denser or more concentrated
Anto: Expand (विस्तार करना)

204 Conform (V.) - (अनुरूप होना) *[#R-2 (1)]*
To comply with rules, standards, or laws
Anto: Differ (भिन्न होना), Deviate (विचलित होना) {Disobey (अवज्ञा करना)}

205 **Conformity** (N.) - (अनुरूपता)
The state of following rules or standards
Anto: Nonconformity (अनुरूपता का अभाव)

206 **Confound** (V.) - (भ्रमित करना)
To confuse or puzzle someone
Anto: Clarify (स्पष्ट करना)

207 **Congested** (Adj.) - (भीड़भाड़ वाला) *[#R-1 (1)]*
So crowded with traffic or people as to hinder freedom of movement
Anto: Cleared (साफ) {Open (खुला)}

208 Connect (V.) - (जोड़ना)
To bring together or into contact so that a link is established
Anto: Detach (अलग करना)

209 **Connive** (V.) - (मिलीभगत करना)
To secretly cooperate in or allow wrongdoing

Anto: Oppose (विरोध करना)

210 **Conquer** (V.) - (जीतना) *[#R-2]*
To defeat and take control by force
Anto: Surrender (आत्मसमर्पण करना)

211 **Consanguinity** (N.) - (एक ही पूर्वज के वंशज, खून का रिश्ता) *[#R-1 (1)]*
The fact of being descended from the same ancestor
Anto: Disunion (फूट) {Estrangement (मनमुटाव)}

212 **Conservative** (Adj.) - (रूढ़िवादी)~
Traditional, resistant to change
Anto: Liberal (उदारवादी)

213 **Consolidated** (Adj.) - (संयुक्त; सुदृढ़) *[#R-1 (1)]*
Combined into a unified whole; made stronger or more solid
Anto: Weakened (कमजोर) {Disjointed (असंगत)}

214 **Constrict** (V.) - (जकड़ना) *[#R-1 (1)]*
To make narrower by encircling pressure
Anto: Stretch (खींचना) {Dilate (फैलाना)}

215 **Consume** (V.) - (उपभोग करना) *[#R-1 (1)]*
To eat, drink, or use up
Anto: Save (बचाना)

216 **Consummate** (Adj.) - (उत्कृष्ट)~
Extremely skilled and accomplished
Anto: Inept (अयोग्य)

217 **Consumption** (N.) - (खपत)
The using up of a resource
Anto: Creation (निर्माण)

218 **Contemplative** (Adj.) - (चिंतनशील) *[#R-1 (1)]*
Expressing prolonged thought
Anto: Unreflective (अचिंतनशील) {Active (सक्रिय)}

219 **Contented** (Adj.) - (संतुष्ट)~ *[#R-2]*
Happy and satisfied
Anto: Dissatisfied (असंतुष्ट)

220 **Contentment** (N.) - (संतोष) *[#R-2 (1)]*
A state of happiness and satisfaction
Anto: Sadness (दुख), Discomfort (असुविधा) {Agitation (व्याकुलता)}

221 **Contest** (V.) - (विरोध करना) *[#R-1 (1)]*
To oppose or challenge
Anto: Concession (स्वीकृति) {Accept (स्वीकार करना)}

222 **Contextual** (Adj.) - (प्रासंगिक)
Relating to or determined by context
Anto: Unrelated (असंबंधित)

223 **Contiguous** (Adj.) - (सटा हुआ)~ *[#R-2]*
Sharing a common border; touching
Anto: Separated (अलग)

224 **Contract** (V.) - (सिकुड़ना)~ *[#R-1 (1)]*
To reduce in size
Anto: Expand (विस्तार करना)

225 **Contribute** (V.) - (योगदान करना)
To give something to help achieve or provide something
Anto: Take (लेना)

226 **Controversial** (Adj.) - (विवादास्पद) *[#R-3 (1)]*
Giving rise to disagreement
Anto: Indisputable (निर्विवाद), Undisputed (अविवादित)

227 **Controversy** (N.) - (विवाद)
A prolonged public disagreement
Anto: Agreement (सहमति)

228 **Contumacious** (Adj.) - (कहना न मानने वाला)
Refusing to obey authority or law
Anto: Obedient (आज्ञाकारी)

229 **Convene** (V.) - (आयोजित करना)
To come or bring together for a meeting; assemble
Anto: Disperse (बिखेरना)

230 **Convenience** (N.) - (सुविधा) *[#R-2]*
The state of proceeding with little effort or difficulty
Anto: Hindrance (बाधा)

231 **Convex** (Adj.) - (उत्तल)
Curved like the exterior of a circle or sphere
Anto: Concave (अवतल)

232 **Convivial** (Adj.) - (खुशनुमा)
Friendly, lively, and enjoyable
Anto: Antisocial (असामाजिक)

233 **Convulsion** (N.) - (ऐंठन)
A violent and involuntary contraction of muscle
Anto: Rest (आराम)

234 **Cosy** (Adj.) - (आरामदायक)
Warm, comfortable and relaxing
Anto: Uncomfortable (असहज)

235 **Countless** (Adj.) - (अनगिनत)
Too many to be counted
Anto: Limited (सीमित)

236 **Courtesy** (N.) - (शिष्टाचार) *[#R-2 (2)]*

The showing of politeness toward others

Anto: Rudeness (अशिष्टता), Crudeness (असभ्यता)

237 **Courtly** (Adj.) - (शिष्ट)
Polite, refined, or elegant

Anto: Rough (अशिष्ट)

238 **Cover** (V.) - (ढकना)
To place something over to hide or protect

Anto: Expose (उजागर करना)

239 **Covert** (Adj.) - (गुप्त) *[#R-2 (1)]*
Not openly acknowledged or displayed

Anto: Public (सार्वजनिक), Overt (खुला)

240 **Covetous** (Adj.) - (लालची)~ *[#R-2]*
Having a great desire to possess something

Anto: Content (संतुष्ट), Benevolent (परोपकारी)

241 Cowardice (N.) - (कायरता) *[#R-2]*
A lack of courage

Anto: Courage (हिम्मत), Boldness (साहस)

242 **Cowardly** (Adj.) - (कायर) *[#R-2 (1)]*
Lacking courage

Anto: Valiant (वीर), Brave (बहादुर) {Courageous (साहसी)}

243 **Coy** (Adj.) - (शर्मीला)
Shy and modest

Anto: Extroverted (मिलनसार)

244 Cozen (V.) - (धोखा देना) *[#R-1 (1)]*
To trick or deceive someone

Anto: Be honest (ईमानदार होना)

245 **Cramped** (Adj.) - (तंग) *[#R-2]*
Confined or restricted in space

Anto: Spacious (विशाल), Extensive (विस्तृत)

246 **Cranky** (Adj.) - (चिड़चिड़ा)
Easily irritated or annoyed

Anto: Cheerful (प्रसन्न)

247 **Craving** (N.) - (लालसा) *[#R-1 (2)]*
A powerful desire for something

Anto: Satisfaction (संतोष) {Dislike (नापसंद)}

248 Create (V.) - (सृजन करना) *[#R-1 (2)]*
To bring something into existence

Anto: Destroy (नष्ट करना)

249 **Credit** (N.) - (जमा धन) *[#R-2]*
Money added or trust given

Anto: Debit (निकाला गया धन)

250 **Crestfallen** (Adj.) - (उदास)
Sad and disappointed

Anto: Triumphant (विजयी)

251 **Crisp** (Adj.) - (कुरकुरा)
Fresh and firm; clear and concise

Anto: Tender (कोमल)

252 Critical (Adj.) - (गंभीर, संकटपूर्ण, आलोचनात्मक) *[#R-1 (4)]*
Very important in a crucial situation; dangerous or serious; expressing severe criticism

Anto: Complimentary (प्रशंसात्मक) {Unimportant (महत्वहीन), Safe (सुरक्षित)}

253 Curiosity (N.) - (जिज्ञासा)~
A desire to know or learn

Anto: Indifference (उदासीनता)

254 Curse (N.) - (अभिशाप)~ *[#R-2]*
An evil spell or cause of suffering

Anto: Boon (वरदान), Praise (प्रशंसा)

255 **Curt** (Adj.) - (संक्षिप्त, रूखा) *[#R-1 (4)]*
Rudely brief

Anto: Polite (शिष्ट) {Tactful (व्यवहारकुशल), Courteous (विनीत), Expansive (विस्तृत)}

256 Customary (Adj.) - (परंपरागत) *[#R-1 (1)]*
According to custom or tradition

Anto: Unusual (असामान्य) {Innovative (नवप्रवर्तक)}

257 **Cynicism** (N.) - (संदेहवाद) *[#R-1 (1)]*
A belief that people are motivated by self-interest

Anto: Hopefulness (उम्मीद) {Optimism (आशावाद)}

258 **Dark** (Adj.) - (अंधेरा)
Having little or no light

Anto: Bright (उज्ज्वल)

259 **Darken** (V.) - (अंधेरा करना) *[#R-1 (1)]*
To make or become dark or darker

Anto: Illuminate (प्रकाशित करना) {Brighten (उज्ज्वल करना)}

260 **Dashed** (Adj.) - (निराश)
Disappointed or let down

Anto: Encouraged (प्रोत्साहित)

261 **Deathly** (Adj.) - (मृत्युपूर्ण)
Resembling or suggestive of death

Anto: Blooming (खिलता हुआ)

262 **Debauched** (Adj.) - (भ्रष्ट)
Morally corrupt; given to excessive sensual pleasure

Anto: Honourable (सम्माननीय)

263 **Decent** (Adj.) - (सभ्य)
Conforming to basic moral standards
Anto: Dishonest (बेईमान)

264 **Deep** (Adj.) - (गहरा) *[#R-1 (2)]*
Extending far down or in
Anto: Shallow (उथला)

265 **Defamatory** (Adj.) - (मानहानिकारक)
Damaging the good reputation of someone
Anto: Complimentary (प्रशंसात्मक)

266 Defence (N.) - (बचाव) *[#R-1 (1)]*
The action of protecting or resisting an attack
Anto: Offence (आक्रमण) {Attack (हमला)}

267 **Deferential** (Adj.) - (आदरपूर्ण) *[#R-1 (1)]*
Polite and showing respect
Anto: Arrogant (घमंडी) {Disrespectful (असम्मानजनक)}

268 Deflate (V.) - (हवा निकालना)
To release air or reduce in size
Anto: Inflate (फुलाना)

269 **Defuse** (V.) - (निष्क्रिय करना) *[#R-1 (2)]*
To make a tense situation safer or calmer
Anto: Agitate (उत्तेजित करना) {Aggravate (बिगाड़ना)}

270 **Degenerate** (V.) - (पतन होना) *[#R-1 (2)]*
To decline or worsen
Anto: Flourish (फलना-फूलना)

271 **Dejection** (N.) - (निराशा)
A state of sadness or low spirits
Anto: Cheer (खुशी)

272 **Delay** (N./V.) - (देरी; देर करना) *[#R-4]*
A period of waiting (N.); To make something happen later (V.)
Anto: Advance (पहले करना), Haste (जल्दबाजी); Hasten (जल्दी करना)

273 **Delectation** (N.) - (आनंद) *[#R-1 (1)]*
Pleasure and delight
Anto: Sorrow (दुःख)

274 **Delinquency** (N.) - (कर्तव्यहीनता)~
Failure to carry out a duty
Anto: Fulfilment (पूर्ति)

275 **Demand** (N.) - (मांग)
An insistent request
Anto: Supply (आपूर्ति)

276 **Demean** (V.) - (नीचा दिखाना)
To lower someone's dignity
Anto: Admire (प्रशंसा करना)

277 **Demote** (V.) - (पद घटाना)
To lower someone's rank or position
Anto: Elevate (पदोन्नत करना)

278 **Demur** (V.) - (असहमति जताना)
To raise objections or hesitate to agree
Anto: Agree (सहमत होना)

279 **Denote** (V.) - (संकेत देना)
To be a sign of; to indicate
Anto: Conceal (छिपाना)

280 Denounce (V.) - (निंदा करना)~ *[#R-6 (2)]*
To publicly declare to be wrong or evil
Anto: Praise (प्रशंसा करना), Compliment (तारीफ करना), Defend (रक्षा करना) {Appreciate (सराहना करना)}

281 Dependence (N.) - (निर्भरता)
The state of relying on someone or something
Anto: Autonomy (स्वायत्तता)

282 **Deport** (V.) - (देश से निकाल देना) *[#R-2]*
To expel from a country
Anto: Permit (अनुमति देना)

283 **Depose** (V.) - (पद से हटाना)
To remove from office
Anto: Promote (पदोन्नत करना)

284 Deposit (V.) - (जमा करना)
To place money in an account or to store something
Anto: Withdraw (निकालना)

285 **Depredation** (N.) - (लूटपाट) *[#R-1 (1)]*
An act of attacking or plundering
Anto: Construction (निर्माण)

286 **Depth** (N.) - (गहराई) *[#R-2]*
The distance from the top or surface to the bottom of something
Anto: Shallowness (उथलापन)

287 **Derelict** (Adj.) - (लापरवाह)~
Neglecting duty or left uncared for
Anto: Attentive (सतर्क)

288 Descent (N.) - (उतार) *[#R-2]*
An action of moving downward, dropping, or falling
Anto: Ascent (चढ़ाव)

289 Desecration (N.) - (अपवित्रीकरण)~ *[#R-2]*
The act of disrespecting something sacred
Anto: Consecration (पवित्रीकरण), Veneration

(आदर)

290 **Deserter** (N.) - (भगोड़ा)
A member of the armed forces who deserts
Anto: Loyalist (वफादार)

291 Desiccate (V.) - (सुखाना)
To remove moisture completely
Anto: Hydrate (पानी देना)

292 **Desiderate** (V.) - (चाहना)
To feel a strong desire for something lacking
Anto: Disregard (अनदेखी करना)

293 **Desist** (V.) - (रोकना)
To stop doing something; to cease or abstain
Anto: Continue (जारी रखना)

294 Desperate (Adj.) - (हताश) *[#R-2 (1)]*
Feeling a hopeless sense that a situation is impossible to deal with
Anto: Hopeful (आशावादी), Content (संतुष्ट)

295 **Despondency** (N.) - (निराशा) *[#R-1 (1)]*
A state of deep discouragement or loss of hope
Anto: Cheerfulness (प्रसन्नता) {Elation (अत्यधिक खुशी)}

296 **Destination** (N.) - (गंतव्य)
The place where a journey ends
Anto: Origin (प्रारंभ)

297 Destruction (N.) - (विनाश) *[#R-2 (1)]*
The process or act of destroying something
Anto: Creation (निर्माण), Preservation (सुरक्षित रखना) {Protection (संरक्षण)}

298 **Destructive** (Adj.) - (विनाशकारी)
Causing great and irreparable harm or damage
Anto: Constructive (रचनात्मक)

299 **Detachment** (N.) - (अलगाव)
The quality of being objective or not emotionally involved
Anto: Subjectivity (पक्षपात)

300 **Developed** (Adj.) - (विकसित)
Advanced or elaborated to a specified degree
Anto: Backward (पिछड़ा)

301 **Dictatorship** (N.) - (तानाशाही)
The government by a dictator
Anto: Democracy (लोकतंत्र)

302 **Differ** (V.) - (भिन्न होना) *[#R-2]*
To be unlike or dissimilar
Anto: Concur (सहमत होना), Conform (अनुरूप होना)

303 Difference (N.) - (अंतर) *[#R-1 (1)]*
A point or way in which people or things are not the same
Anto: Similarity (समानता)

304 Different (Adj.) - (अलग) *[#R-1 (1)]*
Not the same as another; unlike in nature, form, or quality
Anto: Similar (समान)

305 Difficult (Adj.) - (कठिन)
Hard to do or accomplish
Anto: Easy (आसान)

306 **Dig** (V.) - (खोदना)
To break and move earth or ground
Anto: Fill (भर देना)

307 Dignify (V.) - (महत्व देना) *[#R-2]*
To make something seem worthy and impressive
Anto: Degrade (अपमानित करना), Condemn (निंदा करना)

308 Disadvantage (N.) - (हानि, असुविधा) *[#R-2]*
An unfavourable condition reducing success
Anto: Advantage (लाभ), Privilege (विशेष सुविधा)

309 **Disagree** (V.) - (असहमत होना)
To have a different opinion
Anto: Concur (सहमत होना)

310 **Disappointed** (Adj.) - (निराश) *[#R-3]*
Feeling sad because expectations were not met
Anto: Satisfied (संतुष्ट), Encouraged (प्रोत्साहित)

311 Disapprove (V.) - (नापसंद करना, नामंज़ूर करना) *[#R-1 (1)]*
To have or express an unfavourable opinion; To officially refuse or reject
Anto: Commend (प्रशंसा करना) {Accede (सहमत होना)}

312 **Disarming** (Adj.) - (मोहक)
Making someone like you when they had not expected to
Anto: Detestable (घृणित)

313 **Disavowal** (N.) - (अस्वीकार)
The denial of any responsibility or support for something
Anto: Approval (स्वीकृति)

314 Discipline (N.) - (अनुशासन) *[#R-2]*

The training or control of behavior

Anto: Indiscipline (अनुशासनहीनता), Carelessness (लापरवाही)

315 **Discordant** (Adj.) - (असहमत, बेसुरा) *[#R-2 (1)]*
Not in agreement; harsh or unpleasant in sound

Anto: Agreeable (सहमत), Melodious (मधुर) {Harmonious (सामंजस्यपूर्ण)}

316 **Discouraged** (Adj.) - (निराश; हतोत्साहित)
Having lost confidence or enthusiasm; Not given motivation or support

Anto: Inspired (प्रेरित)

317 **Disenfranchise** (V.) - (अधिकार छीनना)
To deprive someone of a legal or civil right

Anto: Authorise (अधिकृत करना)

318 **Disjointed** (Adj.) - (असंगत)
Lacking a coherent sequence or connection

Anto: Connected (संबंधित)

319 **Dismay** (V.) - (निराश करना)~
To fill with fear or disappointment

Anto: Gladden (खुश करना)

320 **Disorder** (V.) - (अव्यवस्थित करना) *[#R-2]*
To disturb the order of

Anto: Regulate (नियंत्रित करना), Arrange (व्यवस्थित करना)

321 **Dispensable** (Adj.) - (अनावश्यक) *[#R-1 (1)]*
Not necessary; can be done without

Anto: Essential (आवश्यक)

322 **Dispose** (V.) - (निपटाना)
To get rid of or deal with something

Anto: Retain (सुरक्षित रखना)

323 **Disputable** (Adj.) - (विवादास्पद)
Open to dispute; contestable

Anto: Indisputable (निर्विवाद)

324 **Disregard** (N.) - (अनदेखी, उपेक्षा) *[#R-2]*
A lack of attention or respect

Anto: Regard (ध्यान, सम्मान)

325 **Dissension** (N.) - (मतभेद)
A disagreement that leads to discord

Anto: Harmony (सामंजस्य)

326 **Dissent** (N./V.) - (असहमति; विरोध करना) *[#R-1 (1)]*
A difference of opinion (N.); To disagree, especially with the majority (V.)

Anto: Agreement (सहमति) {Accede (सहमत होना)}

327 **Dissonance** (N.) - (बेसुरापन) *[#R-1 (2)]*
A lack of harmony among musical notes

Anto: Agreement (सामंजस्य)

328 **Distinctive** (Adj.) - (विशिष्ट) *[#R-1 (1)]*
Having qualities that distinguish from others

Anto: Ordinary (साधारण) {Common (सामान्य)}

329 **Distract** (V.) - (ध्यान हटाना)
To draw attention away from something

Anto: Focus (ध्यान केंद्रित करना)

330 **Distraught** (Adj.) - (व्याकुल) *[#R-2]*
Deeply upset and agitated

Anto: Serene (शांत), Happy (खुश)

331 **Distress** (N.) - (परेशानी)
Extreme anxiety, sorrow, or pain

Anto: Pleasure (आनंद)

332 **Distrustful** (Adj.) - (संदेही)
Not willing to trust others easily

Anto: Ingenuous (भोला)

333 **Diurnal** (Adj.) - (दिवाचर)
Relating to daytime

Anto: Nocturnal (निशाचर)

334 **Diverge** (V.) - (अलग अलग दिशाओं में जाना) *[#R-2]*
To separate and move apart

Anto: Converge (मिलना), Collect (इकट्ठा करना)

335 **Divergence** (N.) - (विचलन) *[#R-2]*
The process or state of diverging

Anto: Convergence (संमिलन), Confluence (संगम)

336 **Divergent** (Adj.) - (विभिन्न) *[#R-1 (1)]*
Tending to be different or develop in different directions

Anto: Similar (समान) {Corresponding (अनुरूप)}

337 **Diversity** (N.) - (विविधता)~ *[#R-2 (1)]*
The state of being diverse; variety

Anto: Uniformity (एकरूपता)

338 **Divest** (V.) - (वंचित करना)
To deprive of power, rights, or possessions

Anto: Vest (अधिकार देना)

339 **Divide** (V.) - (विभाजित करना) *[#R-2]*
To separate into parts

Anto: Unite (जोड़ना), Connect (जोड़ना)

340 **Dominant** (Adj.) - (प्रभावशाली)
Most important, powerful, or influential

Anto: Submissive (अधीन)

341 **Dominate** (V.) - (हावी होना) *[#R-4]*

To control or strongly influence

Anto: Liberate (मुक्त करना), Surrender (आत्मसमर्पण करना), Submit (समर्पण करना)

342 **Douse** (V.) - (भिगोना)
To pour a liquid over; drench

Anto: Dry (सुखाना)

343 **Downcast** (Adj.) - (उदास)
Disheartened; dejected; sad

Anto: Cheerful (प्रसन्न)

344 **Downturn** (N.) - (गिरावट) *[#R-1 (2)]*
A decline in condition, activity, or performance

Anto: Surge (उछाल) {Development (विकास)}

345 **Doze** (V.) - (झपकी लेना)
To sleep lightly for a short time

Anto: Wake (जागना)

346 **Drab** (Adj.) - (फीका)
Lacking brightness or interest; drearily dull

Anto: Bright (उज्ज्वल)

347 **Draining** (Adj.) - (थकाने वाला)
Very tiring or exhausting

Anto: Energizing (ऊर्जादायक)

348 **Drawn** (Adj.) - (थका हुआ)
Looking very tired and worn

Anto: Relaxed (तनावमुक्त)

349 **Dream** (N.) - (सपना)
Images or thoughts during sleep

Anto: Reality (वास्तविकता)

350 **Drenched** (Adj.) - (भीगा हुआ)
Completely wet; soaked through

Anto: Dry (सूखा)

351 **Dull** (Adj.) - (सुस्त; फीका; कुंद) *[#R-4 (1)]*
Lacking interest or excitement; not bright or shining; not sharp

Anto: Keen (उत्सुक), Exciting (रोमांचक), Bright (उज्ज्वल), Riveting (आकर्षक) {Interesting (दिलचस्प)}

352 **Dumb** (Adj.) - (गूंगा)~
Unable to speak; lacking the power of speech

Anto: Vocal (बोलने वाला)

353 **Dummy** (N.) - (नकली)
An imitation or a substitute

Anto: Original (असली)

354 **Duplicate** (N.) - (नक़ल)
An exact copy

Anto: Original (असली)

355 Durable (Adj.) - (टिकाऊ)~ *[#R-1 (1)]*
Able to last a long time without damage

Anto: Fragile (नाजुक) {Perishable (नाशवान)}

356 Duty (N.) - (कर्तव्य)
A moral or legal responsibility

Anto: Exemption (छूट)

357 Dwarf (N.) - (छोटा व्यक्ति)~ *[#R-1 (1)]*
A person of unusually small stature

Anto: Giant (विशालकाय)

358 **Dwell** (V.) - (निवास करना) *[#R-1 (1)]*
To live in or at a specified place

Anto: Leave (छोड़ना)

359 **Dye** (N.) - (रंजक)
A substance used to colour materials

Anto: Bleach (रंग उड़ाना)

360 **Earthly** (Adj.) - (पृथ्वी संबंधी, सांसारिक) *[#R-1 (1)]*
Relating to the earth or human life on the earth

Anto: Celestial (आकाशीय) {Heavenly (स्वर्गीय)}

361 Effective (Adj.) - (प्रभावी) *[#R-1 (1)]*
Successful in producing a desired or intended result

Anto: Fruitless (निष्फल) {Unproductive (अनुत्पादक)}

362 **Effeminacy** (N.) - (नारीत्व) *[#R-1 (1)]*
The quality of having feminine traits or softness

Anto: Manliness (पुरुषत्व)

363 Effeminate (Adj.) - (नारी जैसा)~
(Of a man) showing qualities considered feminine

Anto: Manly (मर्दाना)

364 Effervescent (Adj.) - (जोशीला)~ *[#R-2]*
Giving off bubbles; lively and enthusiastic

Anto: Subdued (दबा हुआ), Stale (बासी)

365 **Egalitarian** (Adj.) - (समानतावादी)~
Supporting equality for all people

Anto: Elitist (अभिजात्यवादी)

366 **Egoist** (N.) - (अहंवादी)~
A person who is excessively self-centered

Anto: Altruist (परोपकारी)

367 **Elasticity** (N.) - (लचीलापन)
The ability to stretch and return to original shape

Anto: Rigidity (कठोरता)

368 Elegance (N.) - (भव्यता) *[#R-4]*
The quality of being graceful and stylish

Anto: Vulgarity (अभद्रता), Gracelessness (अशालीनता), Coarseness (रूखापन)

369 Elementary (Adj.) - (प्राथमिक) *[#R-2]*
Basic or relating to simplest principles of a subject

Anto: Complex (जटिल)

370 **Elevation** (N.) - (ऊंचाई; पदोन्नति) *[#R-2 (2)]*
The act of being raised; A higher level or position

Anto: Depression (गिरावट), Demotion (पदावनति)

371 **Embark** (V.) - (प्रारंभ करना) *[#R-1 (2)]*
To begin an important or difficult course of action

Anto: Finish (समाप्त करना) {Adjourn (स्थगित करना)}

372 **Emigration** (N.) - (उत्प्रवासन)
The act of leaving one's country to live in another

Anto: Immigration (आप्रवासन)

373 **Empowered** (Adj.) - (सशक्त)
Given authority or power to act

Anto: Enslaved (ग़ुलाम बनाया हुआ)

374 **Encircle** (V.) - (घेरना)
To form a circle around; surround

Anto: Exclude (बाहर करना)

375 **End** (N.) - (अंत)
The final or last part of something

Anto: Start (शुरुआत)

376 Endangered (Adj.) - (संकटग्रस्त) *[#R-1 (1)]*
Seriously at risk of extinction

Anto: Protected (संरक्षित) {Preserved (सुरक्षित)}

377 **Endless** (Adj.) - (अनंत)
Having no end

Anto: Limited (सीमित)

378 **Endow** (V.) - (प्रदान करना)
To provide with a quality, ability, or asset

Anto: Deprive (वंचित करना)

379 **Endure** (V.) - (सहना, झेलते रहना) *[#R-1 (1)]*
To suffer something painful or difficult patiently

Anto: Resist (प्रतिरोध करना) {Yield (समर्पण करना)}

380 Enduring (Adj.) - (स्थायी) *[#R-1 (1)]*
Continuing or long-lasting

Anto: Transient (क्षणिक) {Short-Lived (अल्पकालिक)}

381 **Enemy** (N.) - (शत्रु)
A person who opposes or is hostile

Anto: Friend (मित्र)

382 Enlighten (V.) - (ज्ञान देना)
To give someone greater knowledge or understanding

Anto: Befog (भ्रमित करना)

383 **Enlightened** (Adj.) - (ज्ञानवान)
Having or showing a rational, modern, and well-informed outlook

Anto: Confounded (भ्रमित)

384 **Enquire** (V.) - (पूछताछ करना)
To ask for information about something

Anto: Answer (उत्तर देना)

385 Ensue (V.) - (परिणामस्वरूप होना)~ *[#R-1 (1)]*
To happen or occur afterward or as a result

Anto: Precede (पूर्ववर्ती होना)

386 Entrance (N.) - (प्रवेश)
A way in or the act of entering

Anto: Exit (निकास)

387 **Entrap** (V.) - (फंसाना)
To trick or deceive someone into a harmful situation

Anto: Free (मुक्त करना)

388 Equilibrium (N.) - (संतुलन)~ *[#R-3]*
A state where opposing forces are balanced

Anto: Imbalance (असंतुलन)

389 Equivalent (Adj.) - (बराबर)
Equal in value, amount, or meaning

Anto: Dissimilar (भिन्न)

390 Erase (V.) - (मिटाना)~ *[#R-2]*
To remove completely so nothing remains

Anto: Create (सृजन करना)

391 **Eulogistic** (Adj.) - (प्रशंसात्मक)
Highly praising

Anto: Critical (आलोचनात्मक)

392 Euphemism (N.) - (सौम्य अभिव्यक्ति)~ *[#R-2]*
A mild or indirect word used instead of a harsh one.

Anto: Directness (स्पष्टता)

393 **Everlasting** (Adj.) - (शाश्वत)
Lasting forever

Anto: Momentary (क्षणिक)

394 **Everywhere** (Adv.) - (हर जगह)
In all places
Anto: Nowhere (कहीं नहीं)

395 Excel (V.) - (निपुण होना)
To be exceptionally good at something
Anto: Fail (असफल होना)

396 **Excitable** (Adj.) - (उत्तेजनशील)
Easily excited or stimulated
Anto: Placid (शांत)

397 **Exemptions** (N.) - (छूट)
Freedom from a duty, rule, or requirement
Anto: Inclusions (समावेश)

398 **Exert** (V.) - (प्रयास करना)
To apply effort or force
Anto: Relax (आराम करना)

399 Exhaust (V.) - (थकाना) *[#R-2]*
To drain physical or mental energy
Anto: Restore (पुनर्स्थापित करना), Invigorate (स्फूर्ति से भर देना)

400 **Exhaustible** (Adj.) - (समाप्त होने योग्य)
Capable of being used up or exhausted
Anto: Inexhaustible (अक्षय)

401 **Exhume** (V.) - (खोदकर निकालना)
To dig out something buried, especially a corpse
Anto: Bury (दफनाना)

402 **Exist** (V.) - (अस्तित्व में होना)
To be present or real
Anto: Cease (समाप्त होना)

403 **Exit** (N.) - (निकास)
The act of leaving a place
Anto: Entry (प्रवेश)

404 Exonerate (V.) - (दोषमुक्त करना)~ *[#R-5 (3)]*
To free from blame or declare innocent
Anto: Convict (दोषी सिद्ध करना), Sentence (सजा देना) {Accuse (आरोप लगाना), Incriminate (दोषी ठहराना)}

405 **Expand** (V.) - (विस्तार करना) *[#R-5 (1)]*
To become or make larger or more extensive
Anto: Contract (संकुचित होना), Shrink (सिकुड़ना), Restrict (सीमित करना)

406 Expansion (N.) - (विस्तार) *[#R-2]*
The action of becoming larger or more extensive
Anto: Contraction (संकुचन), Compression (संपीड़न)

407 Expel (V.) - (निष्कासित करना)~ *[#R-2]*
To force someone to leave an organization
Anto: Absorb (अवशोषित करना), Accept (स्वीकार करना)

408 **Expostulate** (V.) - (विरोध करना) *[#R-2 (2)]*
To argue or protest against something to persuade someone
Anto: Agree (सहमत होना), Laud (प्रशंसा करना)

409 Expunge (V.) - (मिटाना)~ *[#R-3 (1)]*
To erase or remove completely
Anto: Insert (डालना), Add (जोड़ना) {Restore (पुनर्स्थापित करना)}

410 **Expurgate** (V.) - (अनुचित अंश हटाना)~
To remove objectionable or unsuitable material
Anto: Include (शामिल करना)

411 **Extant** (Adj.) - (मौजूदा, प्रचलित) *[#R-3]*
Still in existence; surviving
Anto: Extinct (विलुप्त), Destroyed (नष्ट)

412 **Extend** (V.) - (बढ़ाना) *[#R-1 (1)]*
To make something longer or larger
Anto: Curtail (कम करना) {Limit (सीमित करना)}

413 Extensive (Adj.) - (व्यापक) *[#R-2 (3)]*
Covering a large area or scope
Anto: Limited (सीमित), Intensive (गहन) {Negligible (नगण्य)}

414 **Extinguished** (Adj.) - (बुझा)
No longer burning or active
Anto: Ignited (प्रज्वलित)

415 Extraneous (Adj.) - (असंगत)~ *[#R-2]*
Irrelevant or unrelated to the subject
Anto: Relevant (संगत), Essential (महत्वपूर्ण)

416 Extreme (Adj.) - (चरम)
Reaching a very high degree
Anto: Mild (हल्का)

417 Extrusion (N.) - (निष्कासन)
The act of forcing out
Anto: Insertion (डालने की क्रिया)

418 **Exultant** (Adj.) - (प्रफुल्लित) *[#R-2 (1)]*
Extremely happy because of success
Anto: Depressed (उदास), Disconsolate (निराश)

419 **Fact** (N.) - (तथ्य)
Something known to be true
Anto: Fiction (कल्पना)

420 **Fade** (V.) - (धुंधला होना)
To gradually disappear
Anto: Appear (प्रकट होना)

421 **Failed** (Adj.) - (असफल) *[#R-3]*
Not successful
Anto: Successful (सफल), Succeeded (सफल हुआ), Passed (उत्तीर्ण)

422 **Faint** (Adj.) - (धुंधला)
Weak or hardly noticeable
Anto: Firm (मजबूत)

423 Fallible (Adj.) - (दोषपूर्ण)~ *[#R-1 (2)]*
Capable of making mistakes or being wrong
Anto: Unerring (अचूक) {Impeccable (निर्दोष), Perfect (दोषरहित)}

424 **Falter** (V.) - (लड़खड़ाना) *[#R-2]*
To start to lose strength or momentum
Anto: Persist (डटे रहना), Stabilise (स्थिर करना)

425 **Fame** (N.) - (प्रसिद्धि) *[#R-3]*
The state of being widely known or recognized
Anto: Obscurity (अज्ञातता), Anonymity (गुमनामी)

426 Familiar (Adj.) - (परिचित)
Well known from long or close association
Anto: Strange (अपरिचित)

427 **Famish** (V.) - (भूखा रहना) *[#R-2 (1)]*
To suffer from extreme hunger
Anto: Satiate (तृप्त करना), Eat (खाना)

428 **Fancy** (Adj.) - (मनोहर)
Decorative, elaborate, or attractive; not plane or simple
Anto: Simple (सरल)

429 **Farce** (N.) - (हास्यप्रद नाटक)
A ridiculous situation
Anto: Tragedy (त्रासदी)

430 **Far-Fetched** (Adj.) - (अविश्वसनीय)
Unlikely and unconvincing; implausible
Anto: Realistic (यथार्थवादी)

431 **Farsighted** (Adj.) - (दूरदर्शी)
Able to see far; having foresight
Anto: Unwise (अविवेकी)

432 **Fat** (Adj.) - (मोटा)
Having a large amount of excess flesh
Anto: Lean (दुबला)

433 **Fatuity** (N.) - (मूर्खता)
Something foolish or stupid
Anto: Sapience (बुद्धिमत्ता)

434 **Fertility** (N.) - (उर्वरता) *[#R-2]*
The ability to produce offspring/crops
Anto: Barrenness (बंजरपन), Infertility (बांझपन)

435 **Fervent** (Adj.) - (उत्साही)
Having or displaying a passionate intensity
Anto: Dispassionate (उदासीन)

436 **Festal** (Adj.) - (उत्सव-संबंधी)~
Relating to a feast or festival
Anto: Solemn (गंभीर)

437 **Fetid** (Adj.) - (दुर्गंधित)
Having a bad smell
Anto: Fragrant (सुगंधित)

438 **Fetter** (V.) - (बेड़ी डालना, रोकना) *[#R-2]*
To restrain or hamper
Anto: Liberate (मुक्त करना)

439 Fiend (N.) - (दुष्ट आत्मा) *[#R-2]*
An evil spirit or demon
Anto: Saint (संत)

440 **Filch** (V.) - (चोरी करना)
To steal small items
Anto: Return (लौटाना)

441 **Finite** (Adj.) - (सीमित) *[#R-2]*
Having limits or bounds
Anto: Infinite (अनंत), Endless (अनंत)

442 Fixation (N.) - (जुनून)~
An obsessive interest in someone or something
Anto: Indifference (उदासीनता)

443 **Flabby** (Adj.) - (पिलपिला)
Soft, loose, and fleshy
Anto: Firm (मजबूत)

444 Flamboyant (Adj.) - (आकर्षक)~ *[#R-2 (1)]*
Attracting attention through exuberance and stylishness
Anto: Understated (सादा), Modest (विनम्र)

445 Flammable (Adj.) - (ज्वलनशील)
Easily set on fire
Anto: Non-Combustible (अज्वलनशील)

446 **Flared** (Adj.) - (तेज़ चमकता हुआ)
Shining brightly
Anto: Darkened (अंधेरा)

447 **Flatter** (V.) - (चापलूसी करना)
To praise somewhat dishonestly

Anto: Insult (अपमान करना)

448 Flee (V.) - (भाग जाना) *[#R-2]*
To run away from a place or situation of danger

Anto: Submit (आत्मसमर्पण करना), Stay (ठहरना)

449 Flexible (Adj.) - (लचीला)~ *[#R-10 (1)]*
Capable of bending easily without breaking

Anto: Rigid (कठोर), Stiff (सख्त)

450 **Flicker** (V.) - (टिमटिमाना)~
To shine or move unsteadily

Anto: Glow (स्थिर चमकना)

451 Flood (N.) - (बाढ़) *[#R-2]*
An overflow of water

Anto: Drought (सूखा)

452 **Florid** (Adj.) - (अत्यधिक सजावटी) *[#R-3 (3)]*
Having a red or flushed complexion; excessively ornate or elaborate

Anto: Plain (सादा), Pale (फीका)

453 **Fluctuate** (V.) - (उतार-चढ़ाव होना) *[#R-3]*
To rise and fall irregularly in number or amount

Anto: Stabilise (स्थिर करना), Steady (स्थिर रखना)

454 **Fluent** (Adj.) - (धाराप्रवाह)
Able to express oneself easily and articulately

Anto: Halting (रुक-रुक कर बोलने वाला)

455 **Focus** (V.) - (केंद्रित करना)
To give attention to one thing

Anto: Disperse (फैलाना)

456 **Fond** (Adj.) - (स्नेही)
Having affection or liking for

Anto: Cold (भावना रहित)

457 **For** (Prep.) - (के लिए)
In support of or in favour of

Anto: Against (के विरुद्ध)

458 **Forbidden** (Adj.) - (वर्जित) *[#R-2]*
Not allowed

Anto: Allowed (अनुमत)

459 Foreign (Adj.) - (विदेशी) *[#R-3]*
Of or from a country other than one's own

Anto: Native (स्थानीय), Domestic (घरेलू)

460 Foreigner (N.) - (विदेशी)
A person from another country

Anto: Native (मूल निवासी)

461 **Foremost** (Adj.) - (सबसे महत्वपूर्ण) *[#R-2]*
Most prominent in rank, importance, or position

Anto: Unimportant (महत्वहीन)

462 **Foresight** (N.) - (दूरदर्शिता)~
The ability to predict future needs

Anto: Shortsightedness (अदूरदर्शिता)

463 **Forever** (Adv.) - (सदा के लिए)
For all time; without end

Anto: Temporarily (अस्थायी रूप से)

464 Forgo (V.) - (त्यागना) *[#R-1 (2)]*
To decline or go without something

Anto: Indulge (भोग करना) {Accept (स्वीकार करना)}

465 Forlorn (Adj.) - (उदास) *[#R-2]*
Pitifully sad and lonely

Anto: Joyful (खुश), Elated (प्रफुल्लित)

466 **Formal** (Adj.) - (औपचारिक) *[#R-2]*
Done according to convention or officially recognized

Anto: Informal (अनौपचारिक)

467 **Formative** (Adj.) - (विकासकारी)
Having a profound influence on development

Anto: Non-influential (प्रभावहीन)

468 **Formerly** (Adv.) - (पहले)
In the past; previously

Anto: Subsequently (बाद में)

469 **Forthcoming** (Adj.) - (आगामी)
About to happen or appear

Anto: Past (बीता हुआ)

470 Forward (Adj.) - (आगे की ओर)
Moving ahead

Anto: Backward (पीछे)

471 **Foul** (Adj./N.) - (गंदा; बेईमानी) *[#R-1 (1)]*
Offensive or unpleasant (Adj.); An unfair act or rule violation (N.)

Anto: Fair (न्यायपूर्ण) {Pleasant (सुखद)}

472 Frailty (N.) - (दुर्बलता)~
The condition of being weak and delicate

Anto: Strength (शक्ति)

473 Frame (V.) - (योजना बनाना)
To construct, plan, or shape

Anto: Disorganise (अव्यवस्थित करना)

474 **Frank** (Adj.) - (स्पष्टवादी) *[#R-1 (1)]*
Open, honest, and direct in speech or manner

Anto: Evasive (टालमटोल करने वाला) {Shy (शर्मीला)}

475 **Frankness** (N.) - (स्पष्टवादिता)
The quality of being open, honest, and direct
Anto: Deception (धोखा)

476 **Fraught** (Adj.) - (भरा हुआ)~
Filled with something undesirable
Anto: Devoid (रिक्त)

477 **Free** (V.) - (मुक्त करना) *[#R-2]*
To release or liberate
Anto: Restrain (रोकना), Imprison (कैद करना)

478 **Freezing** (Adj.) - (अत्यंत ठंडा)
Relating to extremely cold conditions
Anto: Tropical (उष्णकटिबंधीय)

479 **Fret** (V.) - (चिंतित होना) *[#R-2]*
To be constantly or visibly worried
Anto: Delight (प्रसन्न होना), Please (खुश होना)

480 Friend (N.) - (मित्र)
A person with whom one has mutual affection
Anto: Foe (दुश्मन)

481 **Friendly** (Adj./N.) - (मित्रतापूर्ण; मैत्री मैच) *[#R-3 (2)]*
Kind and pleasant (Adj.); A non-competitive match (N.)
Anto: Hostile (शत्रुतापूर्ण), Unfriendly (अमित्रवत)

482 **Frighten** (V.) - (डराना)
To make someone feel afraid
Anto: Comfort (दिलासा देना)

483 **Fritter** (V.) - (व्यर्थ नष्ट करना) *[#R-2]*
To waste time, money, or energy on trifles
Anto: Save (बचाना), Hoard (जमा करना)

484 **Frugality** (N.) - (मितव्ययिता) *[#R-5 (4)]*
The quality of being frugal
Anto: Prodigality (फिजूलखर्ची), Wastefulness (अपव्यय)

485 **Fruitless** (Adj.) - (निष्फल) *[#R-1 (1)]*
Failing to achieve desired results; unproductive
Anto: Successful (सफल) {Effective (प्रभावी)}

486 Fugitive (N.) - (भगोड़ा)~
A person who has escaped from captivity or jail
Anto: Captive (बंदी)

487 Fulfil (V.) - (पूरा करना)
To achieve or realize something desired or promised
Anto: Abandon (त्यागना)

488 **Fulsome** (Adj.) - (चापलूसी भरा)
Excessive or insincere in praise
Anto: Sincere (ईमानदार)

489 **Functional** (Adj.) - (कार्यात्मक) *[#R-1 (1)]*
Practical and working or operating
Anto: Broken (टूटा हुआ) {Useless (अनुपयोगी)}

490 **Gain** (V.) - (प्राप्त करना)
To obtain or acquire something
Anto: Lose (खोना)

491 **Garner** (V.) - (एकत्र करना) *[#R-1 (2)]*
To gather or collect
Anto: Disperse (बिखेरना)

492 **Gaunt** (Adj.) - (दुबला)
Lean and haggard, especially from suffering or hunger
Anto: Plump (मोटा)

493 **Gaze** (V.) - (टकटकी लगाना)
To look steadily
Anto: Glance (सरसरी नज़र डालना)

494 General (Adj.) - (सामान्य)~ *[#R-2]*
Affecting all, not specific
Anto: Particular (विशेष), Specific (विशिष्ट)

495 Generosity (N.) - (उदारता) *[#R-2 (1)]*
The quality of being kind and giving
Anto: Selfishness (स्वार्थ)

496 **Genteel** (Adj.) - (सभ्य)
Polite and refined, often in an affected way
Anto: Uncivilized (असभ्य)

497 **Gentleman** (N.) - (सज्जन)
A chivalrous, courteous, or honourable man
Anto: Boor (गंवार)

498 **Get Back** (Phr.V.) - (वापस पाना)
To recover something lost
Anto: Lose (खोना)

499 **Get On** (Phr.V.) - (आगे बढ़ना)
To make progress or move forward
Anto: Remain (बने रहना)

500 Giant (Adj.) - (विशाल)
Extremely large in size
Anto: Tiny (बहुत छोटा)

501 **Give Away** (Phr.V.) - (दे देना)
To give something for free
Anto: Keep (रखना)

502 **Give Back** (Phr.V.) - (वापस देना)

To return something to its owner

Anto: Keep (रखना)

503 **Glad** (Adj.) - (प्रसन्न) *[#R-3]*
Pleased; delighted

Anto: Gloomy (उदास), Sad (दुखी)

504 Glamour (N.) - (आकर्षण) *[#R-2]*
The attractive charm or appeal

Anto: Repulsiveness (घृणास्पदता), Dullness (नीरसता)

505 Gleaming (Adj.) - (चमकता हुआ) *[#R-1 (2)]*
Shining brightly with reflected light

Anto: Dull (मंद) {Gloomy (अंधकारमय)}

506 Glittering (Adj.) - (चमकदार)
Sparkling or shining brightly

Anto: Dull (फीका)

507 Glory (N.) - (गौरव)
Great honor or praise

Anto: Shame (शर्म)

508 **Glossy** (Adj.) - (चमकीला)
Shiny and smooth

Anto: Dull (मंद)

509 **Go On** (Phr.V.) - (जारी रखना)
To continue doing something

Anto: Stop (रोकना)

510 Gobble (V.) - (भकोसना, जल्दी खाना)
To eat hastily or greedily

Anto: Nibble (कुतरना)

511 **Goodwill** (N.) - (सद्भाव)
Friendly or helpful feelings; benevolence

Anto: Hostility (शत्रुता)

512 **Gradually** (Adv.) - (धीरे-धीरे) *[#R-1 (1)]*
In a gradual way; slowly

Anto: Abruptly (अचानक) {Suddenly (तुरंत)}

513 Grandiose (Adj.) - (आडंबरपूर्ण)
Impressive in appearance, especially pretentiously so

Anto: Moderate (संतुलित)

514 **Grating** (Adj.) - (कर्कश)
Harsh and unpleasant in sound

Anto: Musical (संगीतमय)

515 Group (N.) - (समूह)
A collection of people or things

Anto: Individual (एक व्यक्ति)

516 **Grow** (V.) - (बढ़ना) *[#R-1 (1)]*
To increase in size or cultivate plants

Anto: Shrink (सिकुड़ना) {Shrivel (मुरझाना)}

517 Guilty (Adj.) - (दोषी) *[#R-6]*
Culpable or responsible for a wrongdoing

Anto: Innocent (निर्दोष)

518 **Halcyon** (Adj.) - (शांतिपूर्ण)~ *[#R-1 (2)]*
Very calm and peaceful

Anto: Agitated (उत्तेजित) {Tumultuous (अशांत)}

519 **Hallucinatory** (Adj.) - (भ्रामक)
Resembling or involving hallucinations; seeming unreal or imaginary

Anto: Real (वास्तविक)

520 **Halt** (V.) - (रुकना, रोकना) *[#R-1 (1)]*
To stop or pause; To prevent from continuing

Anto: Trigger (सक्रिय करना)

521 **Harbinger** (N.) - (पूर्वसूचक)~ *[#R-2 (1)]*
A person or thing that signals the coming of something

Anto: Follower (अनुयायी) {Concealer (छिपाने वाला)}

522 **Hardly Ever** (Adv.) - (शायद ही कभी)
Almost never; very rarely

Anto: Frequently (अक्सर)

523 Harness (V.) - (नियंत्रित करना) *[#R-1 (1)]*
To control and use effectively

Anto: Misapply (गलत उपयोग करना)

524 **Hassled** (Adj.) - (परेशान)
Harassed or bothered

Anto: Relaxed (निश्चिंत)

525 Hasten (V.) - (जल्दी करना) *[#R-2 (1)]*
To be quick to do something

Anto: Dawdle (समय बर्बाद करना), Hold (रोकना)

526 Hazy (Adj.) - (धुंधला) *[#R-1 (1)]*
Covered by a haze; not clear or sharply defined

Anto: Clear (स्पष्ट) {Lucid (सुस्पष्ट)}

527 **Hearty** (Adj.) - (उत्साहपूर्ण)
Enthusiastic, energetic, and often loudly expressed

Anto: Aloof (उदासीन)

528 **Heavy** (Adj.) - (भारी) *[#R-2]*
Of great weight; difficult to lift or move

Anto: Light (हल्का)

529 Heed (N.) - (सावधानी)~
Careful attention

Anto: Neglect (अनदेखी)

530 **Heedless** (Adj.) - (लापरवाह) *[#R-1 (1)]*
Showing reckless lack of care or attention
Anto: Observant (सतर्क) {Prudent (समझदार)}

531 Heighten (V.) - (बढ़ाना)
To make or become more intense
Anto: Decrease (घटाना)

532 Heinous (Adj.) - (जघन्य, घृणित) *[#R-2]*
Extremely wicked or morally disgusting
Anto: Virtuous (सदाचारी), Righteous (धर्मात्मा)

533 Hereditary (Adj.) - (आनुवंशिक)
Received or passed on through inheritance
Anto: Acquired (अर्जित)

534 Heresy (N.) - (विधर्म)~
A belief or opinion strongly opposed to accepted doctrine
Anto: Orthodoxy (रूढ़िवाद)

535 **Hidden** (Adj.) - (छिपा हुआ)
Concealed from sight; not visible
Anto: Apparent (स्पष्ट)

536 **High** (Adj.) - (ऊँचा)
At great height
Anto: Low (नीचा)

537 Highlight (V.) - (प्रकाश डालना)
To emphasize or make prominent
Anto: Downplay (कम महत्व देना)

538 Hindrance (N.) - (बाधा) *[#R-2 (1)]*
A thing that causes delay or obstruction
Anto: Advantage (लाभ), Relief (राहत) {Support (सहारा)}

539 **Hit** (V.) - (मारना)
To strike or come into contact forcefully
Anto: Miss (चूकना)

540 Hoarse (Adj.) - (कर्कश)
Sounding rough and harsh in voice
Anto: Smooth (साफ़)

541 **Hollow** (Adj./N.) - (खोखला; गड्ढा) *[#R-3 (1)]*
Having an empty space inside (Adj.); A hole or depression (N.)
Anto: Solid (ठोस), Worthwhile (उपयोगी)

542 **Hopeful** (Adj.) - (आशावादी)
Feeling or inspiring optimism about a future event
Anto: Pessimistic (निराशावादी)

543 Horizontal (Adj.) - (क्षैतिज)
Parallel to the horizon; not vertical
Anto: Vertical (लंबवत)

544 Horrible (Adj.) - (डरावना) *[#R-2]*
Very unpleasant or shocking
Anto: Pleasant (सुखद)

545 Hospitality (N.) - (अतिथि सत्कार)~
The friendly and generous treatment of guests
Anto: Coldness (रूखापन)

546 **Hot** (Adj.) - (गर्म)
Having high temperature
Anto: Frigid (बहुत ठंडा)

547 **How Much** (Det.) - (कितना)
Asking about quantity or degree
Anto: How Little (कितना कम)

548 **Humidity** (N.) - (नमी)
Amount of moisture in the air
Anto: Dryness (सूखापन)

549 **Hype** (V.) - (बढ़ा-चढ़ाकर प्रचार करना) *[#R-2]*
To promote something excessively
Anto: Reduce (कम करना), Understate (कम बताना)

550 **Hysterics** (N.) - (तीव्र उत्तेजना)
A state of uncontrolled emotional excitement
Anto: Calm (शांति)

551 Iconoclast (N.) - (परंपराविरोधी)~
A person who challenges established beliefs
Anto: Conformist (रूढ़िवादी)

552 **Identify** (V.) - (पहचानना)
To establish who or what someone or something is
Anto: Overlook (अनदेखी करना)

553 **Ignite** (V.) - (आग लगाना)~ *[#R-2]*
To catch fire or cause to catch fire
Anto: Extinguish (बुझाना)

554 Ignorance (N.) - (अज्ञान) *[#R-5]*
Lack of knowledge or information
Anto: Knowledge (ज्ञान), Acumen (कुशाग्र बुद्धि)

555 Ignorant (Adj.) - (अज्ञानी)
Lacking knowledge or awareness
Anto: Learned (विद्वान)

556 **Ignore** (V.) - (अनदेखा करना) *[#R-1 (2)]*
To refuse to take notice of
Anto: Recognize (पहचानना) {Consider (विचार करना)}

557 **Illusive** (Adj.) - (मायावी) *[#R-2]*

Deceptive or based on illusion; not real

Anto: Factual (तथ्यात्मक), Real (वास्तविक)

558 Illustrious (Adj.) - (प्रसिद्ध)
Well known and admired for achievements

Anto: Obscure (अज्ञात)

559 Imbroglio (N.) - (उलझन)~ *[#R-2 (1)]*
A very confusing or complicated situation

Anto: Agreement (समझौता), Resolution (समाधान)

560 Immigration (N.) - (आप्रवासन)~
Coming into a foreign country to live

Anto: Emigration (प्रवासन)

561 **Immoral** (Adj.) - (अनैतिक)~
Not conforming to accepted moral standards

Anto: Decent (शालीन)

562 Impatient (Adj.) - (बेचैन)
Having or showing a tendency to be quickly irritated or provoked

Anto: Tolerant (सहनशील)

563 **Impel** (V.) - (प्रेरित करना) *[#R-2 (1)]*
To drive, force, or urge someone to do something

Anto: Repress (दबाना)

564 Impenetrable (Adj.) - (अभेद्य)
Impossible to pass through or enter

Anto: Passable (गुज़रने योग्य)

565 Imperturbable (Adj.) - (शांत)
Unable to be upset or excited; calm

Anto: Excitable (उत्तेजनीय)

566 **Impose** (V.) - (थोपना) *[#R-1 (1)]*
To force something to be accepted or put in place

Anto: Release (छोड़ना)

567 **Impossible** (Adj.) - (असंभव)
Not able to be done or achieved

Anto: Possible (संभव)

568 Impressive (Adj.) - (प्रभावशाली)
Causing admiration because of quality or skill

Anto: Ordinary (सामान्य)

569 **Improve** (V.) - (सुधारना) *[#R-2 (2)]*
To make better

Anto: Spoil (बिगाड़ना), Deteriorate (बिगड़ना) {Diminish (कम करना)}

570 **Impugnable** (Adj.) - (विवादास्पद)
Able to be doubted, challenged, or refuted

Anto: Indubious (निस्संदेह)

571 **Impulsively** (Adv.) - (बिना सोचे-समझे)
In a sudden way, without forethought

Anto: Carefully (सावधानी से)

572 **In Toto** (Adv.) - (संपूर्ण रूप से)
Completely and without exception

Anto: Partially (आंशिक रूप से)

573 Incandescent (Adj.) - (चमकदार)
Emitting light or glowing with heat

Anto: Dusky (धुंधला)

574 **Incarcerate** (V.) - (कैद करना) *[#R-2]*
To imprison or confine someone

Anto: Release (मुक्त करना), Liberate (स्वतंत्र करना)

575 **Inchoate** (Adj.) - (अविकसित) *[#R-2]*
Just begun and not fully formed or developed

Anto: Refined (परिष्कृत, निखरा हुआ)

576 **Incinerate** (V.) - (जलाकर राख करना)
To burn completely

Anto: Extinguish (बुझाना)

577 **Incipient** (Adj.) - (आरंभिक)
Just beginning; in an early stage

Anto: Advanced (विकसित)

578 **Include** (V.) - (शामिल करना) *[#R-2]*
To comprise or contain as part of a whole

Anto: Eliminate (निकालना), Reject (अस्वीकार करना)

579 Inclusion (N.) - (सम्मिलन)
The act of including

Anto: Omission (चूक)

580 Incoherent (Adj.) - (असंगत)~ *[#R-3]*
Not clear or logically connected

Anto: Intelligible (समझने योग्य), Rational (तार्किक), Lucid (स्पष्ट)

581 Incompetent (Adj.) - (अयोग्य) *[#R-4]*
Lacking ability to do something successfully

Anto: Adept (निपुण)

582 Incongruous (Adj.) - (असंगत) *[#R-2]*
Not in harmony with the surroundings

Anto: Harmonious (सामंजस्यपूर्ण), Appropriate (उपयुक्त)

583 **Increase** (V.) - (बढ़ाना) *[#R-1 (2)]*
To become or make greater

Anto: Diminish (कम करना) {Reduce (घटाना)}

584 Indefatigable (Adj.) - (अथक)~

Showing continuous energy and effort without tiring

Anto: Exhausted (थका हुआ)

585 Indefinite (Adj.) - (अनिश्चित)
Lasting for an unknown or unstated length of time

Anto: Bounded (सीमित)

586 **Induce** (V.) - (प्रेरित करना) *[#R-1 (1)]*
To succeed in persuading or leading someone to do something

Anto: Prevent (रोकना)

587 **Inert** (Adj.) - (निष्क्रिय)~ *[#R-1 (2)]*
Lacking the ability or strength to move

Anto: Active (सक्रिय) {Lively (जीवंत)}

588 Infallible (Adj.) - (अचूक)~ *[#R-2 (2)]*
Incapable of making mistakes or being wrong

Anto: Imperfect (अपूर्ण), Faulty (त्रुटिपूर्ण) {Unreliable (अविश्वसनीय), Erring (त्रुटिशील)}

589 Inferior (Adj.) - (घटिया) *[#R-4]*
Lower in rank, status, or quality

Anto: Superior (श्रेष्ठ), Senior (वरिष्ठ)

590 Infertile (Adj.) - (बांझ, उपजहीन)
Unable to conceive children or produce crops

Anto: Fecund (उपजाऊ)

591 Infinite (Adj.) - (अनंत)~ *[#R-2]*
Limitless or endless in space, extent, or size

Anto: Limited (सीमित), Finite (सीमित)

592 **Inflate** (V.) - (फुलाना)
To fill with air or increase in size

Anto: Reduce (घटाना)

593 Influence (V.) - (प्रभावित करना) *[#R-2]*
To affect or change actions or thoughts

Anto: Deter (हतोत्साहित करना)

594 Ingenious (Adj.) - (प्रतिभाशाली)~ *[#R-1 (1)]*
Showing cleverness and originality

Anto: Pedestrian (साधारण) {Uninventive (अविष्कारहीन)}

595 **Ingratiating** (Adj.) - (चापलूसी भरा)
Trying to please others to gain favour

Anto: Proud (घमंडी)

596 **Inhale** (V.) - (साँस लेना)
To breathe in air, gas, or smoke

Anto: Exhale (साँस छोड़ना)

597 **Inhibit** (V.) - (रोकना)~ *[#R-2 (1)]*
To hinder, restrain, or prevent an action

Anto: Allow (अनुमति देना), Encourage (प्रोत्साहित करना) {Promote (बढ़ावा देना)}

598 **Iniquity** (N.) - (अनैतिकता)
Immoral or grossly unfair behaviour

Anto: Good (अच्छाई)

599 **Initial** (Adj.) - (प्रारंभिक) *[#R-2]*
Occurring at the beginning

Anto: Terminal (अंतिम)

600 Innocent (Adj.) - (निर्दोष)~ *[#R-2]*
Not guilty of a crime or offense

Anto: Cunning (चालाक), Guilty (दोषी)

601 Innovate (V.) - (नवाचार करना) *[#R-1 (1)]*
To create something new

Anto: Copy (नकल करना)

602 Inoffensive (Adj.) - (अहानिकर)
Not objectionable or harmful

Anto: Rude (बदतमीज़)

603 Insatiable (Adj.) - (अतृप्त)~ *[#R-4 (1)]*
Impossible to satisfy or fully meet desire

Anto: Satiable (संतुष्ट होने योग्य), Satisfiable (संतुष्ट होने योग्य), Content (संतुष्ट), Fulfilled (पूर्ण)

604 **Insecure** (Adj.) - (असुरक्षित) *[#R-3]*
Not confident or assured; uncertain and anxious

Anto: Confident (आत्मविश्वासी), Firm (दृढ़)

605 Insightful (Adj.) - (सूक्ष्मदर्शी)
Showing deep understanding

Anto: Unperceptive (असंवेदनशील)

606 Install (V.) - (स्थापित करना)
To set up a system or equipment

Anto: Remove (हटाना)

607 **Instinctive** (Adj.) - (स्वाभाविक) *[#R-1 (1)]*
Relating to or prompted by instinct; apparently unconscious or automatic

Anto: Rational (तार्किक) {Acquired (अर्जित)}

608 **Intangible** (Adj.) - (अमूर्त)~
Unable to be touched or grasped; not having physical presence

Anto: Concrete (ठोस)

609 **Intensive** (Adj.) - (गहन)
Concentrated on a single area or subject or into a short time; very thorough or vigorous

Anto: Superficial (ऊपरी)

610 **Intent** (Adj.) - (दृढ़निश्चयी)
Determined and focused

Anto: Uncertain (अनिश्चित)

611 Intentional (Adj.) - (जानबूझकर) *[#R-5]*
Done on purpose; deliberate
Anto: Accidental (आकस्मिक), Unplanned (अनियोजित)

612 **Interact** (V.) - (बातचीत करना)
To communicate or act with others
Anto: Disconnect (संपर्क तोड़ना)

613 Interesting (Adj.) - (दिलचस्प)
Arousing curiosity or attention
Anto: Monotonous (नीरस)

614 **Interim** (Adj.) - (अल्पकालीन) *[#R-2]*
Temporary or provisional
Anto: Permanent (स्थायी)

615 Intermediate (Adj.) - (मध्य)
Coming between two things in time, place, order, character, etc
Anto: Extreme (चरम)

616 Interminable (Adj.) - (अनंत)~
Endless or apparently endless (often used hyperbolically)
Anto: Finite (सीमित)

617 Interpretation (N.) - (व्याख्या)
The action of explaining the meaning of something
Anto: Misinterpretation (गलत व्याख्या)

618 Interruption (N.) - (बाधा)
A break in the flow of something
Anto: Continuation (जारी रखना)

619 **Intimate** (Adj.) - (निकट)
Very close or familiar
Anto: Distant (दूर)

620 **Invaluable** (Adj.) - (अमूल्य)
Extremely useful; indispensable
Anto: Worthless (मूल्यहीन)

621 **Invert** (V.) - (उलटना)
To put upside down or in the opposite position, order, or arrangement
Anto: Straighten (सीधा करना)

622 **Investment** (N.) - (निवेश) *[#R-2]*
The act of investing money to gain profit or benefit
Anto: Divestment (विनिवेश , पूँजी निकालना)

623 **Irk** (V.) - (परेशान करना)
To make someone feel annoyed or irritated
Anto: Please (प्रसन्न करना)

624 Irrational (Adj.) - (तर्कहीन)
Not logical or reasonable
Anto: Reasonable (तार्किक)

625 Irrelevant (Adj.) - (गैरज़रूरी) *[#R-2]*
Not connected with or relevant to something
Anto: Meaningful (अर्थपूर्ण), Consequential (महत्वपूर्ण)

626 Irreverent (Adj.) - (अनादरपूर्ण)~ *[#R-1 (1)]*
Showing lack of respect
Anto: Respectful (सम्मानजनक)

627 Irreversible (Adj.) - (अपरिवर्तनीय)
Not able to be undone or altered
Anto: Repairable (सुधरने योग्य)

628 Jeopardise (V.) - (खतरे में डालना)
To put at risk
Anto: Safeguard (सुरक्षित करना)

629 **Jest** (N.) - (मजाक)
A joke or playful act
Anto: Gravity (गंभीरता)

630 **Jibe** (N.) - (ताना)
A mocking remark
Anto: Consolation (सांत्वना)

631 **Joyless** (Adj.) - (आनंदरहित)
Without happiness
Anto: Blissful (आनंदमय)

632 Joyous (Adj.) - (आनंदित)
Full of happiness and joy
Anto: Melancholic (उदास)

633 **Juicy** (Adj.) - (रसीला)
Full of juice; succulent; (of information) very interesting or exciting
Anto: Dry (सूखा)

634 **Kind** (Adj./N.) - (दयालु; प्रकार) *[#R-2]*
Generous, helpful, and thinking about other people's feelings (Adj.); A category or type (N.)
Anto: Cruel (क्रूर), Mean (कमीना)

635 **Kindness** (N.) - (दयालुता)
The quality of being friendly, generous, and considerate
Anto: Animosity (दुश्मनी)

636 Lachrymose (Adj.) - (रोने वाला) *[#R-1 (2)]*
Tearful or given to weeping
Anto: Jovial (हँसमुख) {Blithe (प्रसन्न)}

637 **Lambency** (N.) - (उज्ज्वलता)
The quality of being softly bright or radiant
Anto: Dullness (मंदता)

638 **Languishing** (Adj.) - (दुर्बल)
Becoming weak; losing strength or vitality
Anto: Flourishing (फलता-फूलता)

639 **Lanky** (Adj.) - (दुबला-पतला)
Tall and thin
Anto: Plump (मोटा)

640 **Large** (Adj.) - (बड़ा)
Big in size
Anto: Tiny (छोटा)

641 **Late** (Adj.) - (देर से आया हुआ)
After the expected or usual time
Anto: Early (जल्दी)

642 **Lawful** (Adj.) - (वैध)
According to law
Anto: Illicit (अवैध)

643 **Lazy** (Adj.) - (आलसी) *[#R-3]*
Unwilling to work or make effort
Anto: Industrious (परिश्रमी), Diligent (लगनशील), Hardworking (मेहनती)

644 **Lead** (V.) - (नेतृत्व करना) *[#R-1 (1)]*
To guide, direct, or be in charge
Anto: Follow (पालन करना)

645 **Learned** (Adj.) - (सीखकर प्राप्त किया हुआ; विद्वान) *[#R-2]*
Gained through learning, training, or experience; A person of great knowledge and learning
Anto: Instinctive (स्वाभाविक), Ignorant (अज्ञानी)

646 **Lechery** (N.) - (व्यभिचार)
Excessive or offensive sexual desire
Anto: Chastity (पवित्रता)

647 **Left** (Adj.) - (बचा हुआ)
Remaining after others are taken or used
Anto: Finished (समाप्त)

648 **Legit** (Adj.) - (वैध)
Allowed by law; legal
Anto: Illegal (अवैध)

649 **Lengthy** (Adj.) - (लंबा)
Very long in time or detail
Anto: Concise (संक्षिप्त)

650 **Leniency** (N.) - (नरमी)
The quality of being merciful or tolerant
Anto: Sternness (कठोरता)

651 **Less** (Adj.) - (कम)
A smaller amount
Anto: More (अधिक)

652 **Lessen** (V.) - (कम करना)
To make or become less; diminish
Anto: Increase (बढ़ाना)

653 **Liable** (Adj.) - (उत्तरदायी)~ *[#R-2]*
Legally responsible or answerable
Anto: Invulnerable (अप्रभावित, सुरक्षित)

654 **Liberal** (Adj.) - (उदार) *[#R-4 (1)]*
Open to new ideas and willing to discard traditional values
Anto: Intolerant (असहिष्णु), Stingy (कंजूस), Conservative (रूढ़िवादी) {Bigoted (कट्टर)}

655 **Liberation** (N.) - (मुक्ति) *[#R-2]*
The act of setting someone free from oppression or slavery
Anto: Bondage (बंधन), Captivity (कैद)

656 **Lifeless** (Adj.) - (निर्जीव) *[#R-2]*
Devoid of life or animation
Anto: Vibrant (जीवंत)

657 **Light** (Adj.) - (हल्का)
Not heavy in weight
Anto: Heavy (भारी)

658 **Linger** (V.) - (देर तक ठहरना)~ *[#R-3 (1)]*
To stay in a place longer than necessary
Anto: Quicken (तेज करना), Hasten (जल्दी करना), Leave (छोड़ देना) {Forge (तेजी से आगे बढ़ना)}

659 **Lively** (Adj.) - (जीवंत) *[#R-3 (1)]*
Full of life, energy, and outgoing spirit
Anto: Sluggish (सुस्त), Gloomy (निस्तेज), Sombre (गंभीर) {Dull (नीरस)}

660 **Local** (Adj.) - (स्थानीय)
Relating to a particular area
Anto: Foreign (विदेशी)

661 **Loitering** (N.) - (बेवजह रुकना) *[#R-2 (1)]*
The act of standing or waiting idly
Anto: Haste (जल्दी), Punctuality (समयनिष्ठता) {Hurry (जल्दबाजी)}

662 **Loosen** (V.) - (ढीला करना)
To make less tight or firm
Anto: Fasten (कसना)

663 **Lordly** (Adj.) - (शानदार)
Grand or proud in manner

Anto: Ignoble (नीच)

664 **Lost** (Adj.) - (खोया हुआ)
Unable to find one's way

Anto: Found (मिला हुआ)

665 **Lovely** (Adj.) - (सुंदर)
Exquisitely beautiful or attractive

Anto: Lousy (बहुत खराब)

666 Luxury (N.) - (विलासिता)
The state of great comfort and extravagant living

Anto: Poverty (गरीबी)

667 **Mad** (Adj.) - (पागल)
Mentally ill; insane. Also, very angry

Anto: Sound (समझदार)

668 **Madden** (V.) - (पागल बनाना)
To make someone very angry; to drive someone to madness

Anto: Calm (शांत करना)

669 Majority (N.) - (बहुमत)
The greater number; more than half of a total

Anto: Minority (अल्पसंख्यक)

670 **Make** (V.) - (बनाना)
To create, produce, or cause something to happen

Anto: Break (तोड़ना)

671 **Maladroit** (Adj.) - (अकुशल) *[#R-2]*
Clumsy or lacking skill in action or behavior

Anto: Skilful (कुशल)

672 **Malaise** (N.) - (अस्वस्थता) *[#R-2]*
A general feeling of discomfort or illness whose cause is hard to identify

Anto: Health (स्वास्थ्य), Wellness (स्वास्थ्य)

673 **Marginal** (Adj.) - (सीमांत, महत्वहीन)
Relating to the edge or margin; minor and not important

Anto: Core (मुख्य)

674 Material (Adj.) - (भौतिक) *[#R-1 (5)]*
Relating to physical substance

Anto: Abstract (अमूर्त) {Spiritual (आध्यात्मिक)}

675 Mature (Adj.) - (समझदार) *[#R-1 (2)]*
Fully developed or sensible

Anto: Immature (अपरिपक्व)

676 Mechanical (Adj.) - (यांत्रिक)
Done by machine

Anto: Manual (हस्तचालित)

677 **Melodramatic** (Adj.) - (अतिनाटकीय)
Exaggerated, sensationalized, or overemotional

Anto: Normal (सामान्य)

678 Melody (N.) - (धुन) *[#R-2]*
A sequence of single notes that is musically satisfying; a tune

Anto: Cacophony (कोलाहल), Disharmony (असंगति)

679 **Memory** (N.) - (स्मृति)
The mental ability to store and remember information

Anto: Oblivion (विस्मृति)

680 **Mental** (Adj.) - (मानसिक) *[#R-1 (1)]*
Relating to the mind

Anto: Physical (शारीरिक) {Balanced (संतुलित)}

681 Merciful (Adj.) - (दयालु)
Showing mercy or compassion

Anto: Cruel (निर्दयी)

682 **Meretricious** (Adj.) - (दिखावटी)
Attractive in appearance but lacking real value

Anto: Natural (प्राकृतिक)

683 **Mesmerised** (Adj.) - (मंत्रमुग्ध)
Completely fascinated

Anto: Abstracted (विचलित)

684 Messy (Adj.) - (गन्दा)
Untidy or dirty; lacking order

Anto: Organised (व्यवस्थित)

685 **Metropolitan** (Adj.) - (महानगरीय)
Relating to a metropolis

Anto: Provincial (प्रांतीय)

686 Mighty (Adj.) - (शक्तिशाली)
Very powerful or strong

Anto: Weak (कमजोर)

687 **Migrate** (V.) - (प्रवास करना) *[#R-2]*
To move from one region or habitat to another according to the seasons

Anto: Stay (ठहरना), Return (वापस आना)

688 Minuscule (Adj.) - (अत्यंत छोटा) *[#R-2 (1)]*
Extremely small; tiny

Anto: Massive (विशाल), Gigantic (विशालकाय)

689 **Misanthropist** (N.) - (मानव विरोधी)
A person who dislikes humankind and avoids human society

Anto: Philanthropist (परोपकारी व्यक्ति)

690 **Misconception** (N.) - (गलतफहमी) *[#R-2]*
A view or opinion that is incorrect
Anto: Understanding (सही समझ)

691 Misdemeanour (N.) - (लघु अपराध)
A minor wrongdoing or offence
Anto: Obedience (आज्ञापालन)

692 **Mislead** (V.) - (भटकाना)
To guide wrongly
Anto: Guide (मार्गदर्शन करना)

693 **Misunderstand** (V.) - (गलत समझना)
To fail to interpret or understand correctly
Anto: Comprehend (समझना)

694 **Mobile** (Adj.) - (गतिशील) *[#R-2]*
Able to move freely
Anto: Stationary (स्थिर), Standing (खड़ा)

695 Moderate (Adj.) - (संयमित) *[#R-2 (1)]*
Average or not excessive
Anto: Extreme (चरम) {Intemperate (असंयमित)}

696 **Moil** (V.) - (परिश्रम करना)
To work hard with continuous effort
Anto: Rest (आराम करना)

697 **Moist** (Adj.) - (नम)
Slightly wet or damp
Anto: Dry (सूखा)

698 **Monstrous** (Adj.) - (विकराल. भयानक) *[#R-1 (2)]*
Extremely cruel, ugly, frightening, or unusually large
Anto: Beautiful (सुंदर) {Tiny (छोटा)}

699 Monumental (Adj.) - (विशाल, अति महत्वपूर्ण) *[#R-1 (1)]*
Great in importance, extent, or size
Anto: Insignificant (महत्वहीन) {Unimpressive (प्रभावहीन)}

700 **Moot** (Adj.) - (विवादास्पद) *[#R-1 (1)]*
Open to debate or uncertainty
Anto: Definite (निश्चित) {Incontestable (अविवादित)}

701 Mortality (N.) - (मरणशीलता, मृत्यु-दर)~
The state of being subject to death; Death rate
Anto: Immortality (अमरता)

702 **Mound** (N.) - (टीला)
A heaped pile or mass of something
Anto: Valley (घाटी)

703 **Mournful** (Adj.) - (शोकपूर्ण) *[#R-2 (1)]*
Feeling, expressing, or inducing sadness, regret, or grief
Anto: Joyous (आनंदित)

704 Movement (N.) - (गतिविधि)
The act of moving or change of position
Anto: Stillness (स्थिरता)

705 **Moving** (Adj.) - (गतिशील)
In motion, not stationary
Anto: Steady (स्थिर)

706 Multifaceted (Adj.) - (बहुमुखी)
Having many facets or aspects
Anto: Simple (सरल)

707 Multiple (Adj.) - (बहुल, एकाधिक)
Having many parts or elements
Anto: Single (एकल)

708 **Mutely** (Adv.) - (चुपचाप)
Without speaking
Anto: Loudly (जोर से)

709 **Mutilate** (V.) - (विकृत करना)
To cause severe damage or disfigurement
Anto: Mend (मरम्मत करना)

710 **Myopic** (Adj.) - (निकटदृष्टि)~ *[#R-2]*
Unable to see far ahead; lacking foresight
Anto: Farsighted (दूरदर्शी)

711 Mysterious (Adj.) - (रहस्यमय) *[#R-1 (1)]*
Difficult or impossible to understand, explain, or identify
Anto: Evident (स्पष्ट) {Straightforward (खुल्लमखुल्ला)}

712 **Myth** (N.) - (मिथक) *[#R-1 (3)]*
A traditional story; a commonly believed but false idea
Anto: Fact (तथ्य) {Reality (वास्तविकता)}

713 Mythical (Adj.) - (पौराणिक, काल्पनिक)
Based on myths; imaginary and not real
Anto: Verifiable (सत्यापित करने योग्य)

714 **Nab** (V.) - (पकड़ना)
To catch someone in the act of doing something wrong
Anto: Free (मुक्त करना)

715 **Nearest** (Adj.) - (सबसे निकट)
At the shortest distance; closest
Anto: Remote (दूरस्थ)

716 **Neat** (Adj.) - (स्वच्छ) *[#R-3]*

Arranged in an orderly, tidy way

Anto: Sloppy (मैला-कुचैला), Messy (अस्त-व्यस्त), Soiled (मैला)

717 Negotiate (V.) - (बातचीत करना) *[#R-2]*
To try to reach an agreement through discussion

Anto: Disagree (असहमत होना)

718 Nervous (Adj.) - (घबराया हुआ) *[#R-2]*
Easily anxious or alarmed

Anto: Courageous (साहसी), Composed (शांत)

719 Never (Adv.) - (कभी नहीं)
At no time; not ever

Anto: Always (हमेशा)

720 Niggardly (Adj.) - (कंजूस) *[#R-2 (1)]*
Not generous; stingy

Anto: Lavish (खर्चीला), Generous (उदार)

721 **Noisily** (Adv.) - (शोर गुल के साथ)
With a lot of noise

Anto: Quietly (चुपचाप)

722 **Noisome** (Adj.) - (बदबूदार; हानिकारक) *[#R-1 (2)]*
Having an extremely offensive smell; also harmful or noxious

Anto: Fragrant (सुगंधित) {Innocuous (हानिरहित)}

723 **Nominate** (V.) - (नामांकित करना)
To propose someone formally for a position or award

Anto: Reject (अस्वीकार करना)

724 **Nonconformist** (Adj.) - (परंपराओं का पालन न करने वाला)~
Not following traditions

Anto: Conventional (परंपरागत)

725 **Nondescript** (Adj.) - (अवर्णनीय, अविशिष्ट) *[#R-1 (1)]*
Lacking clear or distinctive features

Anto: Distinguished (प्रतिष्ठित) {Discernible (पहचानने योग्य)}

726 **Non-Intimidating** (Adj.) - (भयरहित)
Not causing fear or anxiety

Anto: Formidable (डरावना)

727 **Normal** (Adj.) - (सामान्य) *[#R-2]*
Usual or typical in nature

Anto: Strange (विचित्र), Eccentric (अजीब)

728 Noticeable (Adj.) - (ध्यान देने योग्य)
Easy to see or observe

Anto: Hidden (छिपा हुआ)

729 **Novelty** (N.) - (नवीनता)~ *[#R-1 (1)]*
A new or original thing

Anto: Staleness (बासीपन)

730 **Nuanced** (Adj.) - (सूक्ष्म; नाजुक) *[#R-2]*
Having subtle differences; Delicate or refined

Anto: Obvious (स्पष्ट), Sturdy (मजबूत)

731 **Oaf** (N.) - (मूर्ख)~ *[#R-2]*
A stupid or clumsy person

Anto: Genius (प्रतिभाशाली), Intellectual (बुद्धिजीवी)

732 **Obese** (Adj.) - (मोटा) *[#R-3]*
Extremely overweight

Anto: Thin (पतला), Slim (दुबला-पतला), Skinny (दुबला)

733 Obfuscate (V.) - (उलझाना) *[#R-2 (4)]*
To make something unclear or hard to understand

Anto: Clarify (स्पष्ट करना) {Streamline (सरल बनाना), Illuminate (स्पष्ट करना)}

734 **Objurgation** (N.) - (तिरस्कार)
A harsh rebuke or a strong scolding

Anto: Endorsement (समर्थन)

735 **Obligate** (V.) - (बाध्य करना)
To bind or compel someone, legally or morally

Anto: Let Off (छोड़ देना)

736 **Obliging** (Adj.) - (सहायक) *[#R-1 (1)]*
Willing to help or do a kindness

Anto: Unfriendly (अमित्रतापूर्ण)

737 Obsolescence (N.) - (अप्रचलन)~
The process of becoming obsolete or outdated and no longer used

Anto: Modernity (आधुनिकता)

738 Occupied (Adj.) - (व्यस्त)
Busy or being used

Anto: Vacant (खाली)

739 **Offbeat** (Adj.) - (असामान्य)
Different from what is usual or expected

Anto: Conventional (पारंपरिक)

740 Offer (V.) - (प्रस्ताव देना)
To present something for acceptance

Anto: Withhold (रोकना)

741 Officious (Adj.) - (हुकुम चलाने वाला, अफ़सराना) *[#R-2 (1)]*
Domineering or bossy about small matters

Anto: Timid (डरपोक) {Indifferent (उदासीन)}

742 **Offset** (N.) - (संतुलन)

A balancing effect

Anto: Disproportion (असंतुलन)

743 Often (Adv.) - (अक्सर) *[#R-2 (2)]*
Frequently; many times

Anto: Seldom (शायद ही कभी), Rarely (कभी कभार)

744 **Omit** (V.) - (छोड़ देना)
To leave out or exclude something

Anto: Include (शामिल करना)

745 **Opacity** (N.) - (अपारदर्शिता)
The quality of not being clear or transparent

Anto: Visibility (दृश्यता)

746 Opponent (N.) - (प्रतिद्वंद्वी) *[#R-1 (1)]*
A person who competes against or opposes another

Anto: Supporter (समर्थक) {Ally (सहयोगी)}

747 **Opprobrium** (N.) - (अपमान)~ *[#R-2 (2)]*
Harsh public criticism or disgrace

Anto: Honor (सम्मान), Adulation (प्रशंसा) {Praise (प्रशंसा), Encomium (औपचारिक प्रशंसा)}

748 **Oppugn** (V.) - (विरोध करना)
To attack or argue strongly against

Anto: Defend (रक्षा करना)

749 **Optional** (Adj.) - (वैकल्पिक) *[#R-2]*
Available to choose or not required

Anto: Compulsory (अनिवार्य)

750 **Oral** (Adj.) - (मौखिक) *[#R-2]*
Spoken rather than written

Anto: Written (लिखित), Inscribed (अंकित)

751 **Orderly** (Adj.) - (सुव्यवस्थित)
Neat and well arranged

Anto: Chaotic (अव्यवस्थित)

752 **Originate** (V.) - (उत्पन्न होना) *[#R-2 (2)]*
To have a specified beginning

Anto: Terminate (समाप्त होना) {End (ख़त्म होना)}

753 **Outflow** (N.) - (बाहर की ओर प्रवाह)
The movement of something outward from a place

Anto: Influx (अंतर्वाह)

754 **Outgoing** (Adj.) - (मिलनसार, बाहर जाने वाला) *[#R-1 (2)]*
Friendly and socially confident; going away

Anto: Introverted (अंतर्मुखी) {Incoming (आने वाला), Withdrawn (अलग-थलग)}

755 **Outspoken** (Adj.) - (मुँहफट)
Frank in expressing opinions

Anto: Secretive (गुप्त)

756 Outstanding (Adj.) - (शानदार; बकाया) *[#R-2]*
Exceptionally good; something pending

Anto: Ordinary (साधारण)

757 **Overrun** (V.) - (अतिक्रमण करना)
To spread over or occupy a place in large numbers

Anto: Surrender (समर्पण करना)

758 **Overt** (Adj.) - (प्रत्यक्ष) *[#R-4 (1)]*
Done or shown openly; clearly visible

Anto: Hidden (छिपा हुआ), Concealed (गुप्त)

759 **Overweening** (Adj.) - (अत्यधिक आत्मविश्वासी)
Showing excessive confidence or pride

Anto: Modest (विनम्र)

760 **Pacifist** (N.) - (शांतिवादी)~
A person opposed to war or violence

Anto: Warmonger (युद्ध भड़काने वाला)

761 Paltry (Adj.) - (तुच्छ) *[#R-1 (1)]*
Very small or of little value

Anto: Substantial (पर्याप्त)

762 **Panicky** (Adj.) - (घबराया हुआ) *[#R-1 (1)]*
Showing fear or anxiety due to panic

Anto: Calm (शांत)

763 **Paralysed** (Adj.) - (लकवाग्रस्त)
Unable to move or act

Anto: Healthy (स्वस्थ)

764 **Part** (N.) - (भाग)
A piece, portion, or role of something

Anto: Whole (संपूर्ण)

765 Partial (Adj.) - (पक्षपातपूर्ण, अधूरा) *[#R-2 (1)]*
Incomplete or biased toward one side

Anto: Unbiased (निष्पक्ष), Whole (संपूर्ण) {Objective (निष्पक्ष)}

766 Partner (N.) - (साझेदार)
A person sharing work or interest

Anto: Opponent (विरोधी)

767 **Passable** (Adj.) - (स्वीकार्य)
Good enough to be accepted as satisfactory

Anto: Inadequate (अपर्याप्त)

768 Passive (Adj.) - (निष्क्रिय) *[#R-1 (1)]*
Accepting without active response

Anto: Resistant (प्रतिरोधी) {Active (सक्रिय)}

769 **Passivity** (N.) - (निष्क्रियता)
The acceptance without active response or

resistance

Anto: Activity (सक्रियता)

770 **Patchily** (Adv.) - (असमान रूप से)
In an uneven or inconsistent manner

Anto: Consistently (लगातार)

771 **Patriot** (N.) - (देशभक्त)~
A person who strongly supports and defends their country

Anto: Traitor (गद्दार)

772 Peace (N.) - (शांति) *[#R-1 (2)]*
Freedom from disturbance; tranquillity

Anto: Turmoil (उथल-पुथल) {War (युद्ध)}

773 Peer (N.) - (समकक्ष) *[#R-1 (1)]*
A person of equal age or status

Anto: Inferior (हीन)

774 **Penurious** (Adj.) - (कंजूस) *[#R-2 (1)]*
Extremely poor or unwilling to spend money

Anto: Opulent (धनी), Munificent (उदार)

775 Perfect (Adj.) - (उत्तम)
As good as it is possible to be

Anto: Unsatisfactory (असंतोषजनक)

776 **Perfume** (N.) - (इत्र)
A pleasant fragrance

Anto: Stench (दुर्गंध)

777 Periphery (N.) - (घेरा, परिधि)
The outer edge or boundary of something

Anto: Centre (केंद्र)

778 Permanent (Adj.) - (स्थायी)
Lasting forever or for a long time

Anto: Temporary (अस्थायी)

779 **Perpetrate** (V.) - (अपराध करना)~ *[#R-2 (1)]*
To commit a harmful or illegal act

Anto: Prevent (रोकना)

780 Pessimist (N.) - (निराशावादी)~ *[#R-1 (1)]*
A person who expects the worst

Anto: Optimist (आशावादी)

781 **Pestering** (Adj.) - (परेशान करने वाला)
Annoyingly persistent in demands

Anto: Pacifying (शांत करने वाला)

782 Petulant (Adj.) - (चिड़चिड़ा) *[#R-1 (2)]*
Showing sudden irritation or childish anger

Anto: Pleasant (मिलनसार)

783 **Pitiable** (Adj.) - (दयनीय)
Deserving pity or sympathy

Anto: Pleasant (सुखद)

784 **Placatory** (Adj.) - (शांत करने वाला)
Intended to calm anger or hostility

Anto: Aggravating (उत्तेजक)

785 Poor (Adj.) - (गरीब, घटिया)
Lacking enough money, resources or of low quality

Anto: Opulent (धनी)

786 Possess (V.) - (रखना)
To have or own something

Anto: Release (छोड़ना)

787 Powerful (Adj.) - (शक्तिशाली)
Having great strength

Anto: Impotent (शक्तिहीन)

788 **Predecessor** (N.) (पूर्वाधिकारी)~ *[#R-2]*
A person who held a job or office before the current holder

Anto: Successor (उत्तराधिकारी)

789 Predictable (Adj.) - (अनुमान योग्य)
Easy to foresee or expect

Anto: Unexpected (अप्रत्याशित)

790 Premium (Adj.) - (बेहतरीन)
Of superior quality or value

Anto: Inferior (हीन)

791 Prestige (N.) - (प्रतिष्ठा)
Widespread respect and admiration felt for someone based on their achievements

Anto: Disregard (अनादर)

792 **Presumable** (Adj.) - (अनुमानित)
Able to be assumed or taken for granted; likely

Anto: Unlikely (असंभावित)

793 **Presumably** (Adv.) - (संभवतः)~
Probably; based on what is likely or assumed

Anto: Improbably (असंभाव्य रूप से)

794 Pretence (N.) - (दिखावा)
The act of making something false appear true

Anto: Reality (वास्तविकता)

795 **Prevail** (V.) - (जीतना)
To prove more powerful than opposing forces; be victorious

Anto: Surrender (हार मानना)

796 Previous (Adj.) - (पिछला)
Existing or happening before in time or order

Anto: Current (वर्तमान)

797 Prey (N.) - (शिकार) *[#R-1 (1)]*
An animal hunted and killed for food

Anto: Predator (शिकारी)

798 **Pride** (N.) - (गर्व)~
A feeling of self-respect

Anto: Modesty (विनम्रता)

799 **Prim** (Adj.) - (औपचारिक) *[#R-2]*
Stiffly formal and respectable; showing disapproval of impropriety

Anto: Informal (अनौपचारिक), Dishevelled (बिखरा हुआ)

800 **Primed** (Adj.) - (तैयार)
Prepared for action or use; made ready

Anto: Unready (कच्चा)

801 **Primeval** (Adj.) - (अतिप्राचीन)
Of the earliest age; very ancient

Anto: Recent (हाल का)

802 Prior (Adj.) - (पूर्व)
Coming before in time, order, or importance; previous

Anto: Subsequent (आगामी)

803 **Probationer** (N.) - (परखाधीन व्यक्ति)~
A person who is serving a probation period in a job or training

Anto: Master (निपुण)

804 Proceed (V.) - (आगे बढ़ना) *[#R-3]*
To begin or continue an action; move forward

Anto: Recede (पीछे हटना), Withdraw (वापस लेना)

805 **Produce** (V.) - (उत्पादन करना)
To make or manufacture; create or bring about

Anto: Destroy (नष्ट करना)

806 Professional (Adj.) - (पेशेवर) *[#R-2]*
Relating to one's occupation or high standard

Anto: Amateur (शौकिया, गैर-पेशेवर)

807 Prolong (V.) - (अवधि बढ़ाना) *[#R-1 (1)]*
To extend the duration of something

Anto: Shorten (कम करना)

808 Prominent (Adj.) - (प्रमुख) *[#R-4 (1)]*
Important or easily noticed, well-known

Anto: Obscure (अज्ञात), Unknown (अज्ञात), Inconspicuous (अस्पष्ट)

809 Proper (Adj.) - (उचित)
Right or appropriate in a situation

Anto: Unsuitable (अनुपयुक्त)

810 Prosaic (Adj.) - (साधारण, नीरस)~
Ordinary and lacking imagination

Anto: Imaginative (रचनात्मक)

811 Prospect (N.) - (संभावना) *[#R-1 (1)]*
The likelihood of something happening

Anto: Impossibility (असंभवता)

812 Prosper (V.) - (उन्नति करना)
To be successful or flourish

Anto: Decline (गिरना)

813 **Prostration** (N.) - (थकावट)
Complete exhaustion

Anto: Refreshment (ताजगी)

814 **Protean** (Adj.) - (परिवर्तनशील)
Able to change easily; versatile

Anto: Unchanging (अपरिवर्तनीय)

815 Provide (V.) - (प्रदान करना)
To supply or make something available

Anto: Deny (इनकार करना)

816 **Provident** (Adj.) - (किफ़ायती)
Careful in planning and managing resources

Anto: Wasteful (फिजूलखर्च)

817 Provincial (Adj.) - (प्रांतीय)
Relating to a province rather than a major city

Anto: Metropolitan (शहरी)

818 **Provisional** (Adj.) - (अस्थायी) *[#R-2]*
Arranged or existing for the present, possibly to be changed later

Anto: Permanent (स्थायी), Definite (निश्चित)

819 **Public** (Adj.) - (सार्वजनिक)
Relating to everyone

Anto: Private (निजी)

820 **Publicise** (V.) - (प्रचार करना)
To make something widely known

Anto: Withhold (रोकना)

821 **Puissant** (Adj.) - (शक्तिशाली) *[#R-2]*
Having great power; vigorous

Anto: Feeble (कमजोर)

822 Pulchritude (N.) - (सुंदरता)~
The quality of being beautiful

Anto: Ugliness (बदसूरती)

823 **Pulverize** (V.) - (चूर्ण करना)
To crush or grind something into fine particles

Anto: Restore (ठीक करना)

824 Punctual (Adj.) - (समयनिष्ठ)
Doing things at the correct or agreed time
Anto: Late (देरी)

825 Pungent (Adj.) - (तीखा)~
Having a sharply strong taste or smell
Anto: Mild (हल्का)

826 **Pure** (Adj.) - (शुद्ध, पवित्र) *[#R-2 (1)]*
Clean, uncontaminated, and not mixed with anything else
Anto: Indecent (अश्लील), Tainted (दूषित)

827 Purify (V.) - (शुद्ध करना) *[#R-1 (2)]*
To make clean
Anto: Pollute (प्रदूषित करना) {Contaminate (दूषित करना)}

828 Puritanical (Adj.) - (कठोर नैतिक) *[#R-1 (1)]*
Having very strict moral or religious views
Anto: Permissive (उदार) {Liberated (मुक्त)}

829 **Purloin** (V.) - (चुराना)
To steal (something)
Anto: Return (लौटाना)

830 **Purportedly** (Adv.) - (कथित रूप से)
As claimed or said to be true, though not proven
Anto: Certainly (निश्चित रूप से)

831 **Put Forth** (V.) - (प्रस्तुत करना)
To propose for consideration; to publish or produce
Anto: Conceal (छिपाना)

832 **Putrefy** (V.) - (सड़ना)~
To decay or break down, especially due to bacterial action
Anto: Preserve (सुरक्षित रखना)

833 **Quick-Witted** (Adj.) - (तीव्र बुद्धि वाला)
Able to think and respond quickly
Anto: Foolish (मूर्ख)

834 Quiet (Adj./N.) - (शांत; शांति) *[#R-2]*
Making little or no noise; calm; A state of silence or calm
Anto: Noisy (शोरगुल वाला); Commotion (हंगामा)

835 **Quietness** (N.) - (शांति)
The state of being quiet or calm
Anto: Agitation (अशांति)

836 **Quotidian** (Adj.) - (दैनिक) *[#R-1 (2)]*
Occurring every day; ordinary
Anto: Sporadic (कभी-कभार) {Exciting (रोमांचक)}

837 **Raciness** (N.) - (अशोभनीयता)
The quality of being slightly indecent
Anto: Decency (शिष्टता)

838 **Ramify** (V.) - (शाखाओं में बांटना)
To spread out into branches or parts
Anto: Unite (एकजुट करना)

839 **Rampage** (N.) - (हिंसक व्यवहार)~
A period of violent and uncontrollable behaviour
Anto: Harmony (शांति)

840 **Rancid** (Adj.) - (बासी)~ *[#R-3]*
Spoiled with an unpleasant smell or taste
Anto: Fresh (ताज़ा)

841 **Ransack** (V.) - (लूटना)
To violently search and steal, causing damage
Anto: Protect (रक्षा करना)

842 **Rash** (Adj.) - (उतावला) *[#R-2]*
Acting without thinking about consequences
Anto: Careful (सावधान), Considerate (विचारशील)

843 **Ratification** (N.) - (आधिकारिक स्वीकृति)
The formal approval that makes something official
Anto: Disapproval (अस्वीकृति)

844 **Raze** (V.) - (नष्ट करना) *[#R-1 (1)]*
To completely destroy or level
Anto: Build (निर्माण करना)

845 **Realize** (V.) - (समझना)
To understand clearly
Anto: Misunderstand (गलत समझना)

846 **Rear** (N.) - (पीछे का हिस्सा)
The back part
Anto: Front (सामने का हिस्सा)

847 Reasonable (Adj.) - (उचित, तार्किक) *[#R-1 (1)]*
Fair and sensible, based on good judgment
Anto: Outrageous (बेतुका) {Irrational (अतार्किक)}

848 **Reassure** (V.) - (भरोसा दिलाना)
To remove doubts or fears by giving confidence
Anto: Discourage (हतोत्साहित करना)

849 **Rebarbative** (Adj.) - (अप्रिय)
Causing dislike or irritation
Anto: Attractive (आकर्षक)

850 **Rebate** (N.) - (छूट)~
A partial refund or reduction in price

Anto: Increase (वृद्धि)

851 **Rebellion** (N.) - (विद्रोह) *[#R-2 (1)]*
An act of violent or open resistance to an established government or ruler

Anto: Submission (समर्पण), Loyalty (वफादारी)

852 **Rebuff** (V.) - (ठुकराना) *[#R-1 (2)]*
To reject rudely or bluntly

Anto: Praise (प्रशंसा) {Approve (स्वीकृति देना)}

853 **Recalcitrance** (N.) - (जिद)
Stubborn resistance to authority or control

Anto: Compliance (सहमति)

854 **Recall** (V.) - (याद करना)
To remember or bring back to mind

Anto: Forget (भूलना)

855 **Recount** (V.) - (वर्णन करना)
To tell or narrate again in detail

Anto: Suppress (छिपाना)

856 **Recoup** (V.) - (पुनः प्राप्त करना)
To regain something lost or spent

Anto: Lose (खोना)

857 **Rectitude** (N.) - (नैतिकता)
Morally correct behaviour or thinking; righteousness

Anto: Infamy (बदनामी)

858 **Refreshing** (Adj.) - (ताज़ा करने वाला) *[#R-3 (4)]*
Pleasantly new or restoring energy

Anto: Stale (बासी) {Wearying (थकाने वाला)}

859 **Refulgent** (Adj.) - (चमकीला) *[#R-2]*
Shining very brightly

Anto: Dark (अंधेरा), Dull (चमकहीन)

860 **Refuse** (V.) - (मना करना) *[#R-2]*
To decline or reject

Anto: Allow (अनुमति देना), Permit (अनुमति देना)

861 Refute (V.) - (गलत सिद्ध करना) *[#R-1 (1)]*
To prove something wrong or false

Anto: Endorse (समर्थन करना)

862 Reign (V.) - (शासन करना)
To rule

Anto: Yield (समर्पण करना)

863 **Reinforce** (V.) - (मजबूत करना)
To make stronger or support with extra help

Anto: Weaken (कमजोर करना)

864 **Relapse** (V.) - (पुनः पतन होना)~
To fall back into worse condition

Anto: Improve (सुधारना)

865 Relationship (N.) - (संबंध)
The state or manner of being connected

Anto: Opposition (विरोध)

866 **Relaxed** (Adj.) - (तनावमुक्त)
Free from tension and anxiety

Anto: Tense (तनावपूर्ण)

867 Relentless (Adj.) - (लगातार; निर्दयी) *[#R-3 (1)]*
Continuing without stopping; harsh and unmerciful

Anto: Yielding (लचीला), Intermittent (रुक-रुक कर होने वाला) {Merciful (दयालु)}

868 Reminiscent (Adj.) - (याद दिलाने वाला)
Suggesting or reminding one of the past

Anto: Oblivious (बेख़बर)

869 Remnant (N.) - (अवशेष) *[#R-1 (1)]*
A small remaining quantity of something

Anto: Whole (संपूर्ण)

870 **Renew** (V.) - (नवीनीकृत करना)
To resume after an interruption

Anto: Exhaust (समाप्त कर देना)

871 **Repress** (V.) - (दबा देना)
To subdue or restrain by force or authority

Anto: Encourage (बढ़ावा देना)

872 **Reprieve** (N.) - (दण्ड-स्थगन)~ *[#R-2]*
Temporary cancellation or delay of punishment

Anto: Continuation (जारी रहना)

873 **Repulsion** (N.) - (घृणा)
A feeling of intense distaste or disgust

Anto: Attraction (आकर्षण)

874 Reputable (Adj.) - (सम्मानित)
Having a good reputation

Anto: Notorious (बदनाम)

875 Reservation (N.) - (संकोच)
A feeling of doubt or hesitation about something

Anto: Openness (खुलापन)

876 **Reserved** (Adj.) - (अमिलनसार)~ *[#R-2]*
Slow to reveal emotion or opinions

Anto: Communicative (मिलनसार), Friendly (मित्रवत)

877 Resist (V.) - (विरोध करना) *[#R-2 (1)]*
To oppose or refuse to give in to something

Anto: Yield (झुकना), Allow (अनुमति देना) {Submit

(समर्पण करना)}

878 **Resource** (N.) - (संसाधन)
A supply or source that can be used for help or support
Anto: Lack (अभाव)

879 Resourceful (Adj.) - (चतुर)~
Able to find solutions
Anto: Incompetent (अयोग्य)

880 Responsible (Adj.) - (जिम्मेदार)
Having duty, accountability, or being answerable for something
Anto: Irresponsible (गैर जिम्मेदार)

881 Restore (V.) - (सुधारना) *[#R-2 (1)]*
To bring something back to its original or previous state
Anto: Destroy (नष्ट करना), Damage (क्षति पहुंचाना)

882 **Restrictive** (Adj.) - (प्रतिबंधात्मक) *[#R-2 (1)]*
Imposing restrictions or limitations on someone's activities or freedom
Anto: Liberal (उदार), Unbounded (असीमित) {Lenient (नरम)}

883 **Resume** (V.) - (फिर से शुरू करना) *[#R-2 (1)]*
To start again after a pause
Anto: Finish (समाप्त करना), Cease (बंद करना) {Discontinue (बंद करना)}

884 **Retaliation** (N.) - (प्रतिशोध) *[#R-1 (1)]*
The act of attacking back; counterattack
Anto: Reconciliation (सुलह)

885 **Retard** (V.) - (धीमा करना)
To delay or hold back in terms of progress or development
Anto: Hurry (जल्दी करना)

886 **Retention** (N.) - (धारण)
The continued possession, use, or control of something
Anto: Relinquishment (त्याग)

887 **Retrench** (V.) - (कटौती करना)~
To reduce costs or spending in response to economic difficulty
Anto: Recruit (भर्ती करना)

888 **Reward** (V.) - (पुरस्कृत करना)
To give a reward to
Anto: Punish (सजा देना)

889 **Rewarding** (Adj.) - (फलदायी)
Giving satisfaction
Anto: Discouraging (निराशाजनक)

890 **Ribald** (Adj.) - (अश्लील)
Referring to sexual matters in an amusingly rude way
Anto: Clean (शालीन)

891 **Rigidity** (N.) - (कठोरता)
The quality of being stiff or strict
Anto: Flexibility (लचीलापन)

892 **Rise** (V.) - (उठना)
To go up
Anto: Set (अस्त होना)

893 **Risible** (Adj.) - (हास्यास्पद)
Laughable
Anto: Serious (गंभीर)

894 Routine (Adj.) - (नियमित)
Regular and usual; done as part of a normal procedure
Anto: Different (भिन्न)

895 **Rue** (V.) - (पछताना) *[#R-1 (2)]*
To bitterly regret something one has done
Anto: Relish (आनंद लेना) {Delight (आनंद लेना)}

896 **Ruefully** (Adv.) - (उदासी से) *[#R-3]*
In a way that shows sorrow or regret, often slightly humorous
Anto: Cheerfully (प्रसन्नता से), Joyfully (खुशी से)

897 **Rugged** (Adj.) - (खुरदरा)
Having a broken, rocky, and uneven surface
Anto: Smooth (चिकना)

898 Sabotage (V.) - (तोड़-फोड़ करना)~
To deliberately damage or obstruct
Anto: Create (सृजन करना)

899 Sacrifice (V.) - (बलिदान करना)
To give up or surrender something for a cause
Anto: Acquire (अधिग्रहण करना)

900 **Safe** (Adj.) - (सुरक्षित)
Protected from danger
Anto: Insecure (असुरक्षित)

901 **Sage** (Adj.) - (ज्ञानी)
Having or showing profound wisdom
Anto: Foolish (मूर्ख)

902 **Sallow** (Adj.) - (पीला)
Having an unhealthy yellow color
Anto: Flushed (लाल)

903 **Salve** (N.) - (मरहम)

An ointment used to promote healing of the skin

Anto: Irritant (उत्तेजक)

904 **Sanitise** (V.) - (स्वच्छ करना)
To make clean and hygienic; disinfect

Anto: Pollute (प्रदूषित करना)

905 Sarcasm (N.) - (व्यंग्य)~
The use of irony to mock or convey contempt

Anto: Flattery (चापलूसी)

906 **Savant** (N.) - (विद्वान)~ *[#R-2 (1)]*
A person of extensive learning; an eminent scholar

Anto: Dunce (मूर्ख), Amateur (शौकिया) {Ignoramus (अज्ञानी)}

907 Scary (Adj.) - (डरावना)
Causing fear; frightening

Anto: Comforting (आरामदायक)

908 **Scholarly** (Adj.) - (विद्वान)
Involving or relating to serious academic study

Anto: Ignorant (अज्ञानी)

909 **Scoff** (V.) - (उपहास करना)
To mock or treat with contempt

Anto: Praise (प्रशंसा करना)

910 **Scrimp** (V.) - (बचत करना)
To be thrifty or parsimonious; to economize

Anto: Squander (व्यर्थ गवांना)

911 Scrupulous (Adj.) - (ईमानदार) *[#R-2 (3)]*
Very careful about what is morally right

Anto: Dishonest (बेईमान), Immoral (अनैतिक)

912 **Scrutable** (Adj.) - (जांचने योग्य)
Capable of being understood through careful study

Anto: Occult (गुप्त)

913 **Scurrilous** (Adj.) - (अश्लील)~ *[#R-1 (1)]*
Using vulgar or scandalous language to damage reputation

Anto: Complimentary (प्रशंसात्मक) {Admirable (प्रशंसनीय)}

914 **Seamy** (Adj.) - (अनैतिक)
Sordid, disreputable, or unpleasant in nature

Anto: Pure (शुद्ध)

915 **Searing** (Adj.) - (तीव्र गर्म)
Extremely hot

Anto: Freezing (अत्यंत ठंडा)

916 **Seasonable** (Adj.) - (समयानुकूल)
Suitable to or characteristic of the season

Anto: Inappropriate (अनुचित)

917 Secede (V.) - (किसी मंडली से हटना)
To formally withdraw from an organization or union

Anto: Unite (एकजुट होना)

918 **Seclude** (V.) - (एकांत में रहना)
To keep someone away from other people

Anto: Socialize (मेलजोल करना)

919 **Sedate** (Adj.) - (शांत)
Calm, dignified, and unhurried

Anto: Exciting (रोमांचक)

920 Seldom (Adv.) - (शायद ही)
Not often; rarely

Anto: Frequently (अक्सर)

921 **Selective** (Adj.) - (चयनात्मक)
Involving careful choice of the most suitable

Anto: Careless (लापरवाह)

922 **Sell** (V.) - (बेचना)
To exchange for money

Anto: Buy (खरीदना)

923 Semblance (N.) - (समानता)~
An outward appearance, often misleading

Anto: Difference (अंतर)

924 **Sentience** (N.) - (संवेदनशीलता)
The capacity to feel, perceive, or be aware of one's surroundings

Anto: Insensibility (संवेदनहीनता)

925 Servant (N.) - (नौकर)
A person who performs duties for others

Anto: Master (स्वामी)

926 **Servile** (Adj.) - (चापलूस , दास जैसा) *[#R-3]*
Having or showing excessive willingness to serve or please others

Anto: Defiant (अवज्ञाकारी), Arrogant (अहंकारी), Dominant (दबदबे वाला)

927 **Shabby** (Adj.) - (जर्जर) *[#R-2 (1)]*
In poor condition through long use or lack of care

Anto: Nice (अच्छा), Respectable (सम्माननीय) {Smart (सजीला)}

928 **Shallow** (Adj.) - (उथला) *[#R-9]*
Having little depth

Anto: Deep (गहरा)

929 **Shame** (N.) - (शर्म)
A feeling of disgrace
Anto: Pride (गर्व)

930 **Sharp** (Adj.) - (तेज) *[#R-1 (1)]*
Having an edge or point able to cut or pierce
Anto: Blunt (भोथरा)

931 **Shimmering** (Adj.) - (झिलमिलाता हुआ)
Reflecting light to seem sparkly; glimmering
Anto: Gloomy (अंधकारमय)

932 **Short** (Adj.) - (छोटा)
Of small length or duration
Anto: Longest (सबसे लंबा)

933 **Show** (V.) - (दिखाना) *[#R-1 (2)]*
To display or present
Anto: Cover (ढकना)

934 **Shrill** (Adj.) - (तीखा)
Having a high-pitched sound
Anto: Mellow (मधुर)

935 **Shrug** (V.) - (कंधे उचकाना)
To show indifference or lack of concern
Anto: Embrace (स्वीकार करना)

936 **Shun** (V.) - (दूर रहना, बचना)~
To persistently avoid or reject through antipathy
Anto: Cherish (संजोना)

937 **Sickening** (Adj.) - (घृणास्पद)
Causing disgust
Anto: Enticing (आकर्षक)

938 **Simplified** (Adj.) - (सरलीकृत) *[#R-2]*
Made simpler or easier to understand
Anto: Convoluted (पेचीदा), Complex (जटिल)

939 **Sink** (V.) - (डूबना)~
To go down below the surface; to become submerged
Anto: Float (तैरना)

940 **Skeptic** (N.) - (संशयवादी) *[#R-2]*
A person who doubts accepted ideas
Anto: Believer (विश्वासी)

941 **Slave** (N.) - (गुलाम)
A person who is legally owned by someone else and has to work for that person
Anto: Master (मालिक)

942 **Slavish** (Adj.) - (दास जैसा)
Lacking originality or independence
Anto: Assertive (आत्मविश्वासी)

943 **Sleek** (Adj.) - (चिकना)
Smooth and glossy
Anto: Dull (रूखा)

944 **Sloppy** (Adj.) - (लापरवाह, बेढंगा) *[#R-2]*
Careless and untidy; Poorly dressed
Anto: Meticulous (सावधान), Dashing (आकर्षक)

945 **Slur** (N.) - (अपमान)
An insulting remark harming reputation
Anto: Compliment (प्रशंसा)

946 **Sly** (Adj.) - (चालाक)
Cunning and deceitful
Anto: Honest (ईमानदार)

947 **Smart** (Adj.) - (बना-ठना)
Neat and stylish in appearance
Anto: Shabby (फटेहाल)

948 **Smoulder** (V.) - (सुलगना)
To burn slowly with smoke but without flames
Anto: Freeze (जमना)

949 **Smug** (Adj.) - (आत्मसंतुष्ट)~
Excessively proud of oneself or achievements
Anto: Modest (विनम्र)

950 **Snug** (Adj.) - (आरामदायक)~
Warm and cozy
Anto: Uncomfortable (असुविधाजनक)

951 **Sober** (Adj.) - (संयमित) *[#R-2 (2)]*
Not drunk; calm and serious
Anto: Drunk (नशे में), Agitated (उत्तेजित) {Unreserved (बेझिझक), Excited (उत्साहित)}

952 **Sobriety** (N.) - (संयम)~
The state of being sober
Anto: Drunkenness (मदहोशी)

953 **Soft** (Adj.) - (मुलायम)
Not hard
Anto: Hard (कठोर)

954 **Soggy** (Adj.) - (गीला) *[#R-2]*
Very wet and soft
Anto: Dry (सूखा)

955 **Sorcery** (N.) - (जादूगरी)~ *[#R-1 (1)]*
The use of magic, especially black magic
Anto: Reality (वास्तविकता)

956 **Span** (V.) - (फैलाना)
To extend from one side to another

Anto: Concentrate (केंद्रित करना)

957 **Spare** (Adj.) - (अतिरिक्त)
Held in reserve
Anto: Necessary (आवश्यक)

958 **Spat** (N.) - (झगड़ा)
A small argument or dispute
Anto: Agreement (समझौता)

959 Spectacular (Adj.) - (भव्य) *[#R-1 (1)]*
Beautiful in a dramatic and eye-catching way
Anto: Ordinary (साधारण) {Dull (नीरस)}

960 **Spicy** (Adj.) - (मसालेदार)
Having strong flavor
Anto: Mild (हल्का)

961 **Spiritual** (Adj.) - (आध्यात्मिक) *[#R-4 (2)]*
Relating to or affecting the human spirit or soul as opposed to material or physical things
Anto: Physical (भौतिक), Material (भौतिक) {Bodily (शारीरिक)}

962 **Spry** (Adj.) - (चुस्त)~
Especially of an older person, active and lively
Anto: Lethargic (सुस्त)

963 **Squall** (N.) - (आंधी)
A sudden violent gust of wind or a localized storm, especially one bringing rain, snow, or sleet
Anto: Peace (शांति)

964 **Squirm** (V.) - (छटपटाना)
To twist uncomfortably
Anto: Relax (आराम करना)

965 **Stale** (Adj.) - (बासी)~ *[#R-3]*
No longer fresh and pleasant to eat; hard, musty, or dry
Anto: Fresh (ताज़ा)

966 **Stalwart** (Adj.) - (बहादुर)
Loyal, reliable, and hardworking
Anto: Cowardly (कायर)

967 **Stare** (V.) - (घूरना) *[#R-2]*
To look fixedly with eyes wide open
Anto: Glimpse (सरसरी नज़र डालना), Peek (झाँकना)

968 **Starve** (V.) - (भूखा रहना)
To suffer severely or die from hunger
Anto: Stuff (भरना)

969 **Steep** (Adj.) - (खड़ी ढाल)
Rising or falling sharply
Anto: Flat (सपाट)

970 **Stiff** (Adj.) - (कठोर)
Not easily bent or changed in shape; rigid
Anto: Tender (नरम)

971 **Stigmatize** (V.) - (कलंकित करना)
To describe or regard as worthy of disgrace
Anto: Praise (प्रशंसा करना)

972 **Still** (Adj.) - (स्थिर, शांत)
Not moving or quiet
Anto: Active (सक्रिय)

973 Stoic (Adj.) - (भावनाहीन)~
Showing little or no emotion
Anto: Fervent (उत्साही)

974 **Stout** (Adj.) - (मजबूत)
Strongly built; fat; brave
Anto: Thin (पतला)

975 **Straighten** (V.) - (सीधा करना या होना) *[#R-2]*
To make or become straight
Anto: Bend (मोड़ना), Crouch (झुकना)

976 Stratagem (N.) - (चाल)
A plan or scheme used to outwit an opponent or achieve an end
Anto: Frankness (स्पष्टता)

977 Strategic (Adj.) - (रणनीतिक)
Carefully planned to achieve a goal
Anto: Unplanned (अनियोजित)

978 **Strident** (Adj.) - (कर्कश)
Loud and harsh; grating
Anto: Noiseless (शांत)

979 **Strife** (N.) - (संघर्ष)~
Angry or bitter disagreement over fundamental issues; conflict
Anto: Peace (शांति)

980 **Stuck** (Adj.) - (फंसा हुआ)
Unable to move or set in a particular position
Anto: Freed (मुक्त)

981 **Suavity** (N.) - (मधुरता)
The quality of being suave in manner
Anto: Misbehaviour (दुर्व्यवहार)

982 Subjective (Adj.) - (निजी विचारों पर आधारित)
Based on personal feelings or opinions
Anto: Objective (तटस्थ)

983 **Submissively** (Adv.) - (आज्ञाकारी रूप से)
In an obedient manner

Anto: Proudly (गर्व से)

984 **Subordinate** (Adj.) - (अधीनस्थ)
Lower in rank or importance
Anto: Superior (उच्च)

985 Succeed (V.) - (सफल होना) *[#R-1 (1)]*
To achieve the desired aim or result
Anto: Lose (हारना) {Fail (असफल होना)}

986 Success (N.) - (सफलता) *[#R-1 (4)]*
The achievement of a goal
Anto: Failure (असफलता)

987 Successful (Adj.) - (सफल) *[#R-1 (1)]*
Accomplishing an aim or purpose
Anto: Hopeless (निराश) {Vain (व्यर्थ)}

988 **Successor** (N.) - (उत्तराधिकारी)
A person or thing that succeeds another
Anto: Predecessor (पूर्वाधिकारी)

989 **Succinctly** (Adv.) - (संक्षेप में)
In a brief and clear manner
Anto: Elaborately (विस्तार से)

990 Succumb (V.) - (हार मान लेना)
To fail to resist pressure, temptation, or some other negative force
Anto: Overcome (काबू पाना)

991 **Suffice** (V.) - (पर्याप्त होना) *[#R-1 (2)]*
To be enough or adequate
Anto: Lack (कमी होना) {Fall Short (कम पड़ना)}

992 **Sufficiency** (N.) - (पर्याप्तता)
The state of having enough
Anto: Dearth (कमी)

993 Sultry (Adj.) - (उमस भरा)
Hot and humid (of weather or air)
Anto: Frigid (ठंडा)

994 Summary (Adj.) - (संक्षिप्त)~
Brief and concise
Anto: Lengthy (लंबा)

995 **Summit** (N.) - (शिखर)~
The highest point of a mountain
Anto: Bottom (तल)

996 **Sunder** (V.) - (अलग करना)
To split or break apart
Anto: Combine (जोड़ना)

997 Sundry (Adj.) - (विविध)
Of various kinds; several
Anto: Uniform (एकसमान)

998 **Sunny** (Adj.) - (धूप वाला)
Full of sunshine
Anto: Cloudy (बादल वाला)

999 **Superb** (Adj.) - (शानदार)
Extremely good; very impressive
Anto: Inferior (घटिया)

1000 Superior (Adj.) - (श्रेष्ठ) *[#R-2]*
Higher in quality or rank
Anto: Inferior (घटिया)

1001 **Supplant** (V.) - (स्थान लेना)
To take the place of by replacing
Anto: Retain (बनाए रखना)

1002 **Supple** (Adj.) - (लचीला) *[#R-1 (1)]*
Bending and moving easily; flexible
Anto: Brittle (नाज़ुक) {Stiff (अकड़ा हुआ)}

1003 Suppress (V.) - (दबाना) *[#R-4 (1)]*
To stop or prevent forcefully
Anto: Incite (उकसाना), Reveal (उजागर करना), Release (मुक्त करना) {Stimulate (उत्तेजित करना)}

1004 Sure (Adj.) - (निश्चित)
Certain; free from doubt
Anto: Doubtful (संदेहपूर्ण)

1005 **Surplus** (N.) - (अतिरिक्त मात्रा)~
An extra amount more than what is needed
Anto: Dearth (कमी)

1006 Surround (V.) - (घेरना)
To enclose or encircle on all sides
Anto: Free (मुक्त करना)

1007 Survival (N.) - (जीवित रहना)
The state of continuing to live or exist
Anto: Extinction (विलुप्ति)

1008 **Suspend** (V.) - (निलंबित करना) *[#R-3 (1)]*
To temporarily stop or delay something
Anto: Continue (जारी रखना), Resume (फिर से शुरू करना), Persist (बने रहना)

1009 Suspicion (N.) - (संदेह) *[#R-2]*
A feeling that something may be true or wrong
Anto: Trust (विश्वास), Conviction (दृढ़ विश्वास)

1010 Suspicious (Adj.) - (संदिग्ध) *[#R-3 (2)]*
Showing doubt or cautious distrust
Anto: Definitive (निश्चित), Certain (सुनिश्चित), Trustworthy (विश्वसनीय) {Credible (भरोसेमंद)}

1011 Sustainability (N.) - (टिकाऊपन)
The ability to maintain or continue over time

Anto: Instability (अस्थिरता)

1012 **Sweet** (Adj.) - (मीठा) *[#R-2]*
Having a sugary taste; not sour, salty, or bitter

Anto: Sour (खट्टा), Bitter (कड़वा)

1013 **Sweltering** (Adj.) - (भीषण गर्मी वाला)
Extremely and uncomfortably hot

Anto: Freezing (बहुत ठंडा)

1014 **Swerve** (V.) - (मुड़ना)
To change direction suddenly

Anto: Straighten (सीधा करना)

1015 Symbolise (V.) - (प्रतीक बनाना)
To be a symbol of; to represent

Anto: Hide (छुपाना)

1016 Synopsis (N.) - (सारांश)~
A brief summary or general survey of something

Anto: Amplification (विस्तार)

1017 **Taint** (V.) - (दूषित करना)
To contaminate or pollute

Anto: Purify (शुद्ध करना)

1018 Talkative (Adj.) - (बातूनी) *[#R-2]*
Fond of talking a lot

Anto: Withdrawn (कम बोलने वाला), Reticent (संकोची)

1019 Tangible (Adj.) - (वास्तविक; ठोस)~ *[#R-2]*
Perceptible by touch; real and clearly defined

Anto: Abstract (कल्पनात्मक), Intangible (अस्पृश्य)

1020 **Tardy** (Adj.) - (विलंबित) *[#R-4 (1)]*
Arriving or happening later than expected; late

Anto: Prompt (तत्पर), Quick (शीघ्र), Early (जल्दी)

1021 **Tasty** (Adj.) - (स्वादिष्ट) *[#R-3]*
Having a pleasant, distinct flavour

Anto: Insipid (फीका), Bland (बेस्वाद)

1022 **Tawdry** (Adj.) - (भड़कीला)
Cheap and showy in appearance

Anto: Elegant (सलीकेदार)

1023 **Teensy** (Adj.) - (बहुत छोटा)
Extremely small; tiny

Anto: Giant (विशाल)

1024 **Tempestuous** (Adj.) - (उग्र) *[#R-1 (2)]*
Marked by violent emotion or stormy conditions

Anto: Calm (शांत) {Relaxed (आरामदायक), Apathetic (उदासीन)}

1025 Temporary (Adj.) - (अस्थायी)~ *[#R-1 (1)]*
Lasting for only a limited period of time; not permanent

Anto: Lasting (स्थायी) {Permanent (स्थायी)}

1026 **Tempting** (Adj.) - (लुभावना)
Appealing to or attracting someone, even if wrong or unwise

Anto: Repelling (घिनौना)

1027 **Tenebrous** (Adj.) - (अंधकारमय)
Dark or shadowy; lacking light or clarity

Anto: Bright (उज्ज्वल)

1028 **Tensely** (Adv.) - (तनाव से)
In a nervous manner

Anto: Calmly (शांति से)

1029 **Terminate** (V.) - (समाप्त करना) *[#R-3 (2)]*
To bring to an end

Anto: Begin (शुरू करना), Commence (आरंभ करना) {Introduce (परिचय कराना)}

1030 Terrible (Adj.) - (भयानक)
Extremely bad, shocking, or distressing

Anto: Nice (अच्छा)

1031 Testimony (N.) - (गवाही) *[#R-2]*
A formal statement given as evidence, especially in court

Anto: Denial (इनकार), Disproof (खंडन)

1032 Theoretical (Adj.) - (सैद्धांतिक)
Based on theory rather than practical use

Anto: Practical (व्यावहारिक)

1033 Thorough (Adj.) - (संपूर्ण)~ *[#R-2]*
Complete in every detail; not superficial

Anto: Cursory (सतही)

1034 Thoroughly (Adv.) - (पूरी तरह से)
In a thorough or complete manner

Anto: Superficially (सतही रूप से)

1035 Tight (Adj.) - (कसा हुआ)
Firmly fixed or held closely

Anto: Slack (ढीला)

1036 **Tiresome** (Adj.) - (थकानेवाला)
Causing boredom, annoyance, or fatigue

Anto: Energising (ऊर्जावान)

1037 Together (Adv.) - (साथ में)
In the company or proximity of others

Anto: Apart (अलग)

1038 Tolerate (V.) - (सहन करना)
To allow or endure without interference
Anto: Disapprove (अस्वीकार करना)

1039 **Topple** (V.) - (गिराना)
To cause to overbalance and fall
Anto: Stabilize (स्थिर करना)

1040 Torpor (N.) - (सुस्ती)
A state of physical or mental inactivity
Anto: Liveliness (स्फूर्ति)

1041 **Tough** (Adj.) - (कठिन)
Difficult or hard to deal with
Anto: Resolvable (सुलझाने योग्य)

1042 **Tragedy** (N.) - (त्रासदी)
A disastrous event causing great suffering or a sad ending
Anto: Fortune (सौभाग्य)

1043 **Traitorous** (Adj.) - (विश्वासघाती)
Showing disloyalty or betrayal
Anto: Faithful (वफादार)

1044 **Tranquility** (N.) - (शांति) *[#R-1 (1)]*
The quality or state of being calm and peaceful
Anto: Disturbance (अशांति) {Chaos (अराजकता)}

1045 **Transformed** (Adj.) - (परिवर्तित) *[#R-1 (1)]*
Dramatically changed in form or character
Anto: Stagnant (ठहरा हुआ) {Unaltered (अपरिवर्तित)}

1046 **Transience** (N.) - (क्षणभंगुरता)
The state of lasting for a short time
Anto: Eternity (अनन्तता)

1047 **Transitory** (Adj.) - (अस्थायी)~
Lasting for a short time; not permanent
Anto: Eternal (अनन्त)

1048 **Transparency** (N.) - (पारदर्शिता)
The quality of being clear
Anto: Opacity (अपारदर्शिता)

1049 Treachery (N.) - (धोखा)
Betrayal of trust; deceptive action or nature
Anto: Loyalty (वफ़ादारी)

1050 **Tremulous** (Adj.) - (काँपता हुआ)~ *[#R-2]*
Shaking or quivering slightly
Anto: Steady (स्थिर), Stable (स्थायी)

1051 Tropical (Adj.) - (उष्णकटिबंधीय) *[#R-2]*
Relating to or typical of the tropics
Anto: Polar (ध्रुवीय), Cold (ठंडा)

1052 Troublesome (Adj.) - (परेशान करने वाला)
Causing difficulty or annoyance
Anto: Obedient (आज्ञाकारी)

1053 **Truth** (N.) - (सत्य)
The quality or state of being true
Anto: Falsity (मिथ्या)

1054 Truthful (Adj.) - (सत्यवादी)
Telling or expressing the truth; honest
Anto: Deceitful (छली)

1055 Turmoil (N.) - (उथल-पुथल) *[#R-1 (2)]*
A state of great disturbance, confusion, or uncertainty
Anto: Peace (शांति) {Quiet (शांति), Tranquillity (शांति)}

1056 Tyrant (N.) - (अत्याचारी)~
A cruel and oppressive ruler
Anto: Benefactor (हितैषी)

1057 **Tyro** (N.) - (नौसिखिया)~ *[#R-1 (1)]*
A beginner or someone new to an activity
Anto: Professional (पेशेवर) {Expert (विशेषज्ञ)}

1058 **Unanimity** (N.) - (एकमत)
Complete agreement by all involved
Anto: Disagreement (असहमति)

1059 **Unapproachable** (Adj.) - (पहुंच से बाहर का)
Not friendly, easy to talk to, or accessible
Anto: Accessible (सुलभ)

1060 Uncomfortable (Adj.) - (असहज)
Causing or feeling physical or mental discomfort
Anto: Easeful (सुखद)

1061 **Undaunted** (Adj.) - (निडर)
Not intimidated or discouraged by difficulty or danger
Anto: Cowardly (कायर)

1062 **Under** (Prep.) - (के नीचे)
Beneath or at a lower level than
Anto: Over (ऊपर)

1063 **Underestimate** (V.) - (कम आंकना)
To judge something to be less important, smaller, or weaker than it really is
Anto: Exaggerate (बढ़ा-चढ़ाकर कहना)

1064 **Undesirable** (Adj.) - (अनचाहा)
Not wanted or desirable because harmful, objectionable, or unpleasant

Anto: Desirable (वांछनीय)

1065 **Unfair** (Adj.) - (अनुचित)
Not just or not treating people equally
Anto: Just (उचित)

1066 Unfathomable (Adj.) - (अथाह)
Incapable of being fully explored or understood
Anto: Comprehensible (समझने के योग्य)

1067 **Unfavourable** (Adj.) - (प्रतिकूल)
Expressing or showing a negative or disapproving attitude
Anto: Advantageous (लाभकारी)

1068 **Unfeeling** (Adj.) - (भावहीन)
Lacking compassion or sympathy; insensitive
Anto: Affectionate (स्नेही)

1069 **Unfeigned** (Adj.) - (सच्चा)
Genuine and not false or pretended
Anto: Pretended (दिखावटी)

1070 Unforeseen (Adj.) - (आकस्मिक)
Not anticipated or predicted
Anto: Expected (अपेक्षित)

1071 **Unfortunate** (Adj.) - (दुर्भाग्यशाली)
Having bad fortune; unlucky
Anto: Lucky (भाग्यशाली)

1072 **Unholy** (Adj.) - (अपवित्र)
Wicked, immoral, or not sacred
Anto: Sacred (पवित्र)

1073 **Uniform** (Adj.) - (एकरूप) *[#R-2 (1)]*
Consistent or unchanging
Anto: Variable (परिवर्तनशील), Variegated (बहुरंगी)

1074 **Uniformity** (N.) - (एकरूपता)
The state of being the same or consistent
Anto: Variety (विविधता)

1075 **United** (Adj.) - (एकजुट)
Joined together for a common purpose or feeling
Anto: Separated (अलग)

1076 **Unity** (N.) - (एकता)
The state of being united or joined as a whole
Anto: Discord (मतभेद)

1077 **Unleash** (V.) - (मुक्त करना)
To release from restraint or control
Anto: Confine (सीमित करना)

1078 **Unobtrusive** (Adj.) - (नज़र में न आने वाला)
Not attracting attention
Anto: Conspicuous (स्पष्ट)

1079 Unparalleled (Adj.) - (बेजोड़) *[#R-2]*
Having no parallel or equal; exceptional
Anto: Ordinary (सामान्य), Frequent (नियमित)

1080 **Unpredictable** (Adj.) - (अनिश्चित) *[#R-2 (1)]*
Not able to be predicted; likely to change suddenly
Anto: Dependable (विश्वसनीय), Reliable (भरोसेमंद) {Certain (निश्चित)}

1081 **Unsettled** (Adj.) - (अस्थिर; बेचैन) *[#R-1 (2)]*
Not stable or fixed; Anxious or disturbed
Anto: Confident (आत्मविश्वासी) {Composed (शांत)}

1082 **Unsure** (Adj.) - (अनिश्चित) *[#R-2]*
Not confident or certain
Anto: Certain (निश्चित)

1083 **Unsusceptible** (Adj.) - (अप्रभावित)
Not likely to be influenced or harmed
Anto: Vulnerable (संवेदनशील)

1084 **Unsuspecting** (Adj.) - (बेखबर)
Not aware of danger or what is going to happen
Anto: Wary (सतर्क)

1085 **Unusual** (Adj.) - (असामान्य)
Not commonly occurring or done
Anto: Commonplace (साधारण)

1086 **Unworthy** (Adj.) - (अयोग्य) *[#R-2]*
Not deserving effort, attention, or respect
Anto: Noble (महान), Deserving (योग्य)

1087 **Upbraiding** (N.) - (फटकार)
The act of scolding or severe criticism
Anto: Extolling (प्रशंसा)

1088 **Upgrade** (V.) - (उन्नति करना)
To raise or improve to a better standard
Anto: Demote (अवनति करना)

1089 **Uphold** (V.) - (कायम रखना)
To support or maintain despite opposition
Anto: Oppose (विरोध करना)

1090 **Upright** (Adj.) - (ईमानदार) *[#R-2]*
Honest and morally correct
Anto: Immoral (अनैतिक), Corrupt (बेईमान)

1091 **Upshot** (N.) - (परिणाम)
The final result or outcome

Anto: Cause (कारण)

1092 **Urban** (Adj.) - (शहरी) *[#R-2 (1)]*
Relating to or characteristic of a city or town
Anto: Rural (ग्रामीण)

1093 Usurp (V.) - (हड़पना) *[#R-3 (1)]*
To take power or position illegally or by force
Anto: Surrender (समर्पण करना), Restore (पुनः स्थापित करना), Release (मुक्त करना)

1094 **Utterly** (Adv.) - (पूर्णतः)
Completely or to the fullest degree
Anto: Minimally (न्यूनतम रूप से)

1095 **Vaguely** (Adv.) - (अस्पष्ट रूप से)
In an unclear or not exact way
Anto: Distinctly (स्पष्ट रूप से)

1096 **Valor** (N.) - (वीरता) *[#R-1 (2)]*
Great courage in the face of danger
Anto: Cowardice (कायरता)

1097 Valour (N.) - (वीरता)~ *[#R-1 (2)]*
Great courage in the face of danger, especially in battle
Anto: Cowardice (कायरता)

1098 **Vanguard** (N.) - (अग्रगामी)
The forefront group leading new ideas or actions
Anto: Follower (अनुयायी)

1099 **Variance** (N.) - (असहमति)
The state of being different, divergent, or inconsistent
Anto: Harmony (सामंजस्य)

1100 Vehement (Adj.) - (प्रचंड)~ *[#R-1 (3)]*
Showing strong feeling; intense or passionate
Anto: Mild (हल्का) {Subdued (संयमित), Apathetic (उदासीन)}

1101 Veneration (N.) - (आदर) *[#R-2 (1)]*
Great respect or reverence
Anto: Contempt (तिरस्कार), Disrespect (असम्मान)

1102 Vengeance (N.) - (प्रतिशोध)
Punishment or revenge for a wrong or injury
Anto: Forgiveness (क्षमा)

1103 **Verbosity** (N.) - (शब्दाडंबर; अधिक शब्द प्रयोग)~
The quality of using more words than needed
Anto: Succinctness (संक्षिप्तता)

1104 **Verdant** (Adj.) - (हरा-भरा) *[#R-1 (3)]*
Green with fresh grass or rich vegetation; Flourishing
Anto: Dying (मुरझाया हुआ) {Dry (शुष्क)}

1105 **Veteran** (N.) - (अनुभवी)~ *[#R-2 (2)]*
A person who has had long experience in a particular field
Anto: Novice (नौसिखिया)

1106 **Vexatious** (Adj.) - (कष्टप्रद) *[#R-2]*
Causing annoyance, frustration, or worry
Anto: Soothing (सुखद), Pleasant (आनंददायक)

1107 **Viability** (N.) - (व्यवहार्यता, उपयोगिता)
The ability to work successfully or be effective
Anto: Infeasibility (अव्यवहार्यता)

1108 Vibrant (Adj.) - (जीवंत, ऊर्जावान)
Full of energy and enthusiasm
Anto: Listless (उदासीन)

1109 **Victor** (N.) - (विजेता) *[#R-1 (1)]*
A person who defeats an enemy or opponent
Anto: Loser (हारने वाला) {Vanquished (पराजित)}

1110 **Vile** (Adj.) - (नीच)
Extremely unpleasant or morally bad
Anto: Decent (शालीन)

1111 **Vilify** (V.) - (बदनाम करना) *[#R-1 (4)]*
To speak badly about someone to damage reputation
Anto: Commend (प्रशंसा करना)

1112 Virtuous (Adj.) - (नैतिक) *[#R-4 (1)]*
Having or showing high moral standards
Anto: Vicious (कुटिल), Sinful (पापी), Unethical (अनैतिक), Wicked (दुष्ट)

1113 Viscous (Adj.) - (चिपचिपा)
Thick and sticky; having high resistance to flow
Anto: Watery (पानी जैसा)

1114 Visionary (N.) - (दूरदर्शी व्यक्ति)~ *[#R-3]*
A person with imaginative foresight
Anto: Pragmatist (व्यावहारिक व्यक्ति), Realist (यथार्थवादी)

1115 **Vivacity** (N.) - (जीवंतता)
The quality of being lively, animated, and full of energy
Anto: Apathy (उदासीनता)

1116 Vocal (Adj.) - (स्वर-संबंधी; खुलकर बोलने वाला)
Relating to the human voice; expressing opinions freely or loudly
Anto: Silent (चुप)

1117 Voluntary (Adj.) - (स्वैच्छिक)~ *[#R-1 (1)]*
Done by one's own free will
Anto: Mandatory (अनिवार्य) {Necessary (आवश्यक)}

1118 **Vouch** (V.) - (गारंटी देना) *[#R-1 (4)]*
To confirm or guarantee something
Anto: Invalidate (अमान्य करना) {Abjure (त्यागना), Disclaim (अस्वीकार करना)}

1119 **Waggish** (Adj.) - (मजाकिया)
Playfully humorous or joking
Anto: Solemn (गंभीर)

1120 **Waver** (V.) - (डगमगाना) *[#R-1 (1)]*
To hesitate or be indecisive
Anto: Steady (स्थिर रहना) {Resolute (दृढ़ रहना)}

1121 **Wax** (V.) - (बढ़ना) *[#R-2 (1)]*
To grow or increase gradually
Anto: Wane (घटना)

1122 **Weakness** (N.) - (कमजोरी)
The lack of strength
Anto: Strength (शक्ति)

1123 **Wicked** (Adj.) - (दुष्ट) *[#R-6 (3)]*
Evil or morally wrong
Anto: Good (अच्छा), Righteous (न्यायसंगत), Moral (नैतिक) {Virtuous (सद्गुणी)}

1124 **Widespread** (Adj.) - (व्यापक) *[#R-2 (2)]*
Found or distributed over a large area or number of people
Anto: Limited (सीमित) {Localized (स्थानीय)}

1125 **Wilt** (V.) - (मुरझाना)~
To lose freshness, strength, or vitality
Anto: Revive (पुनर्जीवित होना)

1126 **Wisp** (N.) - (छोटा टुकड़ा) *[#R-2]*
A small thin piece or amount
Anto: Lot (बहुत सारा)

1127 Wither (V.) - (मुरझाना) *[#R-2]*
To become dry, weak, or shrivelled
Anto: Bloom (खिलना), Grow (बढ़ना)

1128 Withhold (V.) - (रोकना)
To refuse to give something
Anto: Grant (देना)

1129 **Witty** (Adj.) - (हाजिरजवाबी) *[#R-4]*
Showing quick and clever verbal humour
Anto: Stupid (मूर्ख), Serious (गंभीर), Lame (असंतोषजनक), Unamusing (नीरस)

1130 **Woeful-Eyes** (Adj.) - (दुःखी आंखें)
Having a sad or mournful appearance, often poetic
Anto: Cheerful (प्रसन्न)

1131 Worried (Adj.) - (चिंतित)
Anxious or troubled about actual or potential problems
Anto: Unconcerned (बेफिक्र)

1132 **Worsen** (V.) - (बिगड़ना) *[#R-2]*
To become worse
Anto: Improve (सुधार होना)

1133 **Worthless** (Adj.) - (बेकार; अनुत्पादक)
Having no real value or use; Not producing results
Anto: Productive (उत्पादक)

1134 **Wrath** (N.) - (क्रोध) *[#R-2 (3)]*
Extreme anger
Anto: Glee (आनंद), Composure (संयम) {Happiness (खुशी)}

1135 **Wreck** (V.) - (ध्वस्त करना)
To destroy or severely damage
Anto: Build (बनाना)

1136 **Young** (Adj.) - (युवा) *[#R-2]*
Having lived for only a short time
Anto: Mature (परिपक्व), Ripened (पक्का)

1137 **Zany** (Adj.) - (सनकी) *[#R-3]*
Amusingly unconventional
Anto: Sober (संयमी), Serious (गंभीर), Sensible (समझदार)

*Total **1137** Antonyms asked **1941** times*

C8 Antonyms Practice Sets (Based on Recent SSC Papers)

Practice Set - 1

Direction (Q. 1-10): Select the most appropriate antonym of the given word:

1 Imitate
1) Replicate 2) Copy
3) Innovate 4) Echo

2 Bold
1) Adventurous
2) Brave
3) Timid
4) Fearless

3 Demur
1) Agree 2) Oppose
3) Object 4) Resist

4 Furtive
1) Covert 2) Sneaky
3) Open 4) Stealthy

5 Inflate
1) Increase 2) Reduce
3) Expand 4) Swell

6 Abate
1) Reduce 2) Supply
3) Consume 4) Intensify

7 Fallacy
1) Delusion 2) Mistake
3) Truth 4) Fiction

8 Glut
1) Overload 2) Satiate
3) Stuff 4) Starve

9 Hostile
1) Friendly 2) Aggressive
3) Rude 4) Bitter

10 Fulsome
1) Overdone 2) Sincere
3) Excessive 4) Lavish

Practice Set - 2

Direction (Q. 1-10): Select the most appropriate antonym of the given word:

1 Aloof
1) Detached 2) Reserved
3) Friendly 4) Distant

2 Lucid
1) Transparent
2) Vague
3) Clear
4) Coherent

3 Scary
1) awful 2) bright
3) comforting 4) Pristine

4 Eager
1) Indifferent 2) Keen
3) Interested 4) Enthusiastic

5 Wilt
1) cruel 2) Merciless
3) Revive 4) Strict

6 Axiom
1) Truism 2) Adage
3) Absurdity 4) Principle

7 Fetid
1) Fragrant 2) Fatal
3) False 4) Fatigued

8 Derelict
1) Dilapidated
2) Attentive
3) Deserted
4) Ruined

9 Glory
1) Delight 2) Honour
3) Gluttony 4) Shame

10 Dogmatic
1) Stubborn 2) Flexible
3) Rigid 4) Arrogant

Practice Set - 3

Direction (Q. 1-10): Select the most appropriate antonym of the given word:

1 Differ
1) Conform 2) Question
3) Reject 4) Ignore

2 Barren
1) Sterile 2) Fertile
3) Dry 4) Deserted

3 Assert
1) Deny 2) Maintain
3) Proclaim 4) Declare

4 Quell
1) Suppress 2) Calm
3) Silence 4) Agitate

5 Dainty
1) Demanding
2) Critical
3) Timid
4) Inelegant

6 Dearth
1) Scarcity 2) Abundance
3) Lack 4) Shortage

7 Apathy
1) Indifference
2) Enthusiasm
3) Laziness
4) Carelessness

8 Denial
1) Affirmation
2) Opposition
3) Refusal
4) Liberal

9 Candid
1) Frank 2) Guarded
3) Honest 4) Open

10 Affirm
1) Refuse
2) Accept
3) Acknowledge
4) Support

Practice Set - 4

Direction (Q. 1-10): Select the most appropriate antonym of the given word:

1 Falter
1) Waver 2) Stumble
3) Persist 4) Demur

2 Noxious
1) Beneficial 2) Toxic
3) Poisonous 4) Unhealthy

3 Docile
1) soft 2) Headstrong
3) Gentle 4) Compliant

4 Laconic
1) Elliptical
2) Wordy
3) Compendious
4) Clipped

5 Foment
1) Incite 2) Stir
3) Quash 4) Instigate

6 Insipid
1) Tasteless 2) Dull
3) Vapid 4) Appetizing

7 Flaunt
1) Hide 2) Wide
3) Parade 4) Open

8 Grisly
1) Horrid
2) Disgusting
3) Frightening
4) Attractive

9 Erudite
1) Ignorant 2) Intellectual
3) Wise 4) Scholarly

10 Enmity
1) Friendship 2) Hostility
3) Malignity 4) Antipathy

Practice Set - 5

Direction (Q. 1-10): Select the most appropriate antonym of the given word:

1 Peevish
1) Flat 2) Suave
3) Tedious 4) Dull

2 Obloquy
1) Praise 2) Condemnation
3) Abuse 4) Discredit

3 Heresy
1) Unorthodoxy
2) Dogma
3) Orthodoxy
4) Dissent

4 Obscure
1) Prominent 2) Vague
3) Faint 4) Hidden

5 Prudent
1) Judicious 2) Thoughtless
3) cautious 4) Sensible

6 Jovial
1) Morose 2) Cheerful
3) Happy 4) Joyful

7 Piquant
1) Bland 2) Spicy
3) Zesty 4) Tart

8 Harass
1) Annoy 2) Comfort
3) Disturb 4) Irritate

9 Dominate
1) Rule 2) Submit
3) Govern 4) Control

10 Recount
1) Narrate 2) Retell
3) Suppress 4) Detail

Practice Set - 6

Direction (Q. 1-10): Select the most appropriate antonym of the given word:

1 Slander
1) Mock 2) Praise
3) Blame 4) Abuse

2 Esoteric
1) Abstruse 2) Cryptic
3) Arcane 4) Common

3 Risible
1) Curious 2) Giddy
3) Serious 4) Droll

4 Trivial
1) Lavish 2) Vain
3) Liable 4) Essential

5 Encomium
1) Panegyric
2) Praise
3) Castigation
4) Tribute

6 Abstruse
1) Cryptic
2) Obscure
3) Clear
4) Incomprehensible

7 Denounce
1) Defend 2) Accuse
3) Condemn 4) Blame

8 Malice
1) Cruelty 2) Hatred
3) Kindness 4) Spite

9 Thrifty
1) Extravagant
2) Thankful
3) Intolerant
4) Indifferent

10 Exiguous
1) Meagre 2) Plentiful
3) Sparse 4) Skimpy

Practice Set - 7

Direction (Q. 1-10): Select the most appropriate antonym of the given word:

1 Quixotic
1) Romantic 2) Visionary
3) Pragmatic 4) Idealistic

2 Mythical
1) Imaginary
2) Verifiable
3) Supernatural
4) Symbolic

3 Infernal
1) Wicked 2) Damned
3) Heavenly 4) Accursed

4 Puissant
1) Feeble 2) Robust
3) Powerful 4) Strong

5 Mitigate
1) Diminish 2) Alleviate
3) Intensify 4) Weaken

6 Nugatory
1) Worthless 2) Futile
3) Trivial 4) Significant

7 Penchant
1) Liking 2) Dishonour
3) Dislike 4) Dismissal

8 Oracular
1) Lucid 2) Impress
3) Anxious 4) Idealistic

9 Morbid
1) Cheerful 2) Grim
3) Gloomy 4) Sickly

10 Felicity
1) Anger 2) Despair
3) sorrow 4) Misery

Practice Set - 8

Direction (Q. 1-10): Select the most appropriate antonym of the given word:

1 Barbarous
1) Civilized 2) Cruel
3) Savage 4) Brutal

2 Taciturn
1) Talkative 2) Silent
3) Reserved 4) Quiet

3 Mature
1) Developed 2) Immature
3) Experience 4) Grown

4 Vigilant
1) Attentive 2) Ignore
3) Negligent 4) Alert

5 Redolent
1) Fragrant 2) Evocative
3) Odorous 4) Unscented

6 Proactive
1) Reactive 2) Positive
3) Aggressive 4) Responsible

7 Veracity
1) Falsehood
2) Accuracy
3) Truthfulness
4) Honesty

8 Credulous
1) Trusting 2) Skeptical
3) Gullible 4) Naive

9 Tangible

1) Invisible 2) Real
3) Intangible 4) Definite

10 Sanguine
1) Cheerful 2) Melancholic
3) Confident 4) Buoyant

Practice Set - 9

Direction (Q. 1-10): Identify the antonym of the given word:

1 Exonerate
1) Convict 2) Free
3) Excuse 4) Liberate

2 Disparate
1) Distinct 2) Separate
3) Similar 4) Contrasting

3 Dissemble
1) Disguise 2) Reveal
3) Obscure 4) Pretend

4 Desultory
1) Unmethodical
2) Erratic
3) Methodical
4) Haphazard

5 Opaque
1) Dull 2) Transparent
3) Cloudy 4) Dark

6 Gullibility
1) Trust 2) Skepticism
3) Naivety 4) Innocence

7 Euphemism
1) Directness 2) Ambiguity
3) Politeness 4) Formality

8 Ephemeral
1) Temporary 2) Momentary
3) Eternal 4) Fleeting

9 Elucidate
1) Clarify 2) Explain
3) Obscure 4) Illuminate

10 Extirpate
1) Exterminate
2) Establish
3) Uproot
4) Eradicate

Practice Set - 10

Direction (Q. 1-10): Identify the antonym of the given word:

1 Lassitude
1) Exhaustion
2) Apathy
3) Vigor
4) Lethargy

2 Oppugn
1) Question 2) Defend
3) Dispute 4) Challenge

3 Ineffable
1) Expressible
2) Inarticulate
3) Unfathomable
4) Indescribable

4 Incipient
1) Nascent 2) Developing
3) Advanced 4) Budding

5 Miserable
1) Depressing
2) Cheerful
3) Decorated
4) Wealthy

6 Maladroit
1) Clumsy 2) Awkward
3) skilful 4) Inept

7 Inclusion
1) Omission 2) Boost
3) Accrual 4) Gain

8 Monstrous
1) Beautiful 2) odd
3) Abnormal 4) Strange

9 Imbroglio
1) Entanglement
2) Complication
3) Agreement
4) Dispute

10 Incessant
1) Constant 2) Ceaseless
3) Perpetual 4) Intermittent

Practice Set - 11

Direction (Q. 1-10): Identify the antonym of the given word:

1 Resilient
1) Tough 2) Buoyant
3) Fragile 4) Flexible

2 Refulgent
1) Dull 2) Radiant
3) Gleaming 4) Luminous

3 Reverence
1) Respect 2) Devotion
3) Contempt 4) Worship

4 Placatory
1) Pacifying
2) Soothing
3) Aggravating
4) Conciliatory

5 Perturbed
1) Unsettled 2) Worried
3) Anxious 4) Calm

6 Repudiate
1) Reject 2) Disown
3) Deny 4) Accept

7 Authorize
1) Forbid 2) Allow
3) Empower 4) Permit

8 Reprobate
1) Rogue
2) Virtuous
3) Unprincipled
4) Rakish

9 Obstinate
1) Adamant 2) Stubborn
3) Pliable 4) Headstrong

10 Quaint
1) Humble 2) Ordinary
3) Tolerant 4) Gale

Practice Set - 12

Direction (Q. 1-10): Identify the antonym of the given word:

1 Sagacious
1) Insightful 2) Wise
3) Foolish 4) Prudent

2 Vilify
1) Commend 2) Malign
3) Slur 4) Defame

3 Soporific
1) Stimulating
2) Drowsy
3) Sleep-inducing
4) Sedative

4 Tenacious
1) Persistent 2) Fragile
3) Yielding 4) Firm

5 Venerable
1) Respected 2) Honored
3) Elderly 4) Immature

6 Turbulent
1) Deceptive 2) Humble
3) Calm 4) Satisfied

7 Somnolent
1) Awake 2) Dull
3) Lethargic 4) Sluggish

8 Tenebrous
1) Bright 2) Shadowy
3) Murky 4) Obscure

9 Turpitude
1) Depravity 2) Vice
3) Morality 4) Sin

10 Vexatious
1) Pleasant
2) Annoying
3) Troublesome
4) Irritating

Practice Set - 13

Direction (Q. 1-10): Choose the antonym of the given word:

1 Accentuate
1) Emphasize 2) Highlight
3) Obscure 4) Promote

2 Discipline
1) Commitment
2) Carelessness
3) Determination
4) Focus

3 Vivacious
1) Cheerful 2) Lively
3) Bubbly 4) Unattractive

4 Vindicate
1) Exonerate 2) Accuse
3) Defend 4) Justify

5 Dependence
1) Autonomy
2) Slavery
3) Subordinate
4) Submissiveness

6 Blistering
1) Scorching 2) Chilly
3) Burning 4) Incendiary

7 Degenerate
1) Flourish 2) Perish
3) Dismiss 4) Decay

8 Amiable
1) Friendly 2) Pleasant
3) Hostile 4) Warm

9 Benevolent
1) Humane 2) Generous
3) Kind 4) Malevolent

10 Ameliorate
1) Recondite 2) Motto
3) Exacerbate 4) Succour

Practice Set - 14

Direction (Q. 1-10): Choose the antonym of the given word

1 Fathomable
1) Inauspicious
2) Incoherent
3) Incite
4) Inartistic

2 Zany
1) Sensible
2) Bizarre
3) Clownish
4) Eccentric

3 Lachrymose
1) Tearful 2) Mournful
3) Weepy 4) Jovial

4 Mendacious
1) Dishonest 2) Fraudulent
3) Truthful 4) Deceitful

5 Exaggerate
1) Understate 2) Emphasise
3) Embellish 4) Neglect

6 Impervious
1) Impregnable
2) Permeable
3) Durable
4) Impassive

7 Exacerbate
1) Alleviate 2) Intensify
3) Improve 4) Aggravate

8 Melancholy
1) Miserable 2) Pleasant
3) Profitable 4) Mechanical

9 Evanescent
1) Fleeting 2) Transient
3) Enduring 4) Ephemeral

10 Exhaustion
1) Discouragement
2) Replenishment
3) Establishment
4) Acknowledgement

Practice Set - 15

Direction (Q. 1-10): Choose the antonym of the given word

1 Commend
1) Praise 2) Approve
3) Criticize 4) Applaud

2 Opprobrium
1) Disgrace 2) Contempt
3) Honor 4) Censure

3 Clear
1) Obscure 2) Open
3) Bright 4) Frank

4 Obsequious
1) Assertive 2) Submissive
3) Flattering 4) Servile

5 Meticulous
1) Negligent 2) Thorough
3) Precise 4) Careful

6 Propitiate
1) Appease 2) Mollify
3) Placate 4) Enrage

7 Perfidious
1) Betraying 2) Faithless
3) Loyal 4) Treacherous

8 Pernicious
1) Harmful 2) Detrimental
3) Injurious 4) Beneficial

9 Resistance
1) Tenderness
2) Reliance
3) Awareness
4) Tolerance

10 Prodigious
1) Meagre 2) Phenomenal
3) Enormous 4) Monumental

Practice Set - 16

Direction (Q. 1-10): Choose the antonym of the given word

1 Accumulated
1) Spared 2) Scattered
3) Bunched 4) Garnered

2 Cursory
1) Thorough 2) Brief
3) Hasty 4) Superficial

3 Commendable
1) Notable 2) Blameworthy
3) Laudable 4) Admirable

4 Vociferous
1) Noisy 2) Loud
3) Silent 4) Boisterous

5 Clandestine
1) Open 2) Long
3) secret 4) Boring

6 Egalitarian
1) Fair
2) Biased
3) Democratic
4) Equitable

7 Concomitant
1) Separate
2) Related
3) Independent
4) Detached

8 Transitory
1) Fleeting
2) Eternal
3) Momentary
4) Temporary

9 Deleterious
1) Harmless 2) Dangerous
3) Toxic 4) Poisonous

10 Subterfuge
1) Chicanery 2) Candor
3) Trickery 4) Deception

Practice Set - 17

Direction (Q. 1-10): Which word is opposite in meaning the given word:

1 Impecunious
1) Insolvent 2) Wealthy
3) Indigent 4) Penniless

2 Superficial
1) Shallow 2) Surface
3) External 4) Deep

3 Extravagant
1) Restrained 2) Enrich
3) Lavish 4) Righteous

4 Munificence
1) Stinginess 2) Lavishness
3) Generosity 4) Chanty

5 Eminent
1) Prominent
2) Celebrated
3) Distinguished
4) Obscure

6 Interesting
1) Monotonous
2) Terrible
3) Terrifying
4) Disastrous

7 Ineluctable
1) Unavoidable
2) Preventable
3) Inevitable
4) Inescapable

8 Rebarbative
1) Attractive 2) Repulsive
3) Off-putting 4) Irritating

9 Pulchritude
1) Grace 2) Ugliness
3) Charm 4) Beauty

10 Magnanimous
1) Altruistic 2) Self-absorbed
3) Noble 4) Gracious

Practice Set - 18

Direction (Q. 1-10): Which word is opposite in meaning the given word:

1 Incorrigible
1) Chronic 2) Deep-rooted
3) Habitual 4) Reclaimable

2 Misanthropic
1) Sociable 2) Reclusive
3) Cynical 4) Pessimistic

3 Parsimonious
1) Stingy 2) Frugal
3) Generous 4) Economical

4 Ostentatious
1) Modest 2) Showy
3) Flashy 4) Pretentious

5 Surreptitious
1) Covert 2) Furtive
3) Overt 4) Stealthy

6 Superfluous
1) Redundant 2) Unnecessary
3) Essential 4) Extra

7 Pusillanimous
1) Timid 2) Brave
3) Cowardly 4) Faint-hearted

8 Indefatigable
1) Tenacious 2) Exhausted
3) Dogged 4) Relentless

9 Contumacious
1) Rebellious 2) Unruly
3) Obedient 4) Stubborn

10 Intransigence
1) Obstinacy 2) Compromise
3) Defiance 4) Rigidity

Practice Set - 19

Direction (Q. 1-10): Select the most appropriate antonym of the underlined word in the given sentence.

1 A person with civility impresses the surroundings.
1) Beauty 2) Splendour
3) Comfort 4) Insolence

2 The boss persists with his loyalists even now.
1) retinues 2) discontinues
3) formulates 4) continues

3 His liberal policies were responsible for progress in the community.
1) central 2) ineffectual
3) hysterical 4) conservative

4 Don't meddle with things you don't understand.
1) Dodge 2) Hinder
3) Dabble 4) Disgrace

5 How can you be so joyless on hearing the news?
1) Rapt 2) Dubious
3) Beaming 4) Blissful

6 Two original manuscripts of this text are still extant.
1) extinct 2) drool
3) persist 4) negotiate

7 It was certainly a cowardly act.
1) Believable 2) Brave
3) Fearful 4) Comfortable

8 If you want to be a good detective, it helps to have an inquisitive nature.
1) Comprehensive
2) Itemised
3) Intrusive
4) Disinterested

9 They bestow upon him whatever he wishes.
1) gift 2) intensify
3) deny 4) classify

10 The committee deposed him from his office.
1) Demolished
2) Segregated
3) Interacted
4) Promoted

Practice Set - 20

Direction (Q. 1-7): Select the most opposite meaning of the highlighted word in the sentence.

1 The late secretary of our society was known for his ruthless treatment of all the security personnel of the society.
1) Fragile 2) Compassionate
3) Brutal 4) Startled

2 The athlete demonstrated remarkable agility during the gymnastics routine.
1) Nimbleness
2) Flexibility
3) Stiffness
4) Prowess

3 Maria thinks the animals that live in freedom have a sad look in their eyes.
1) Carefree
2) Liberty
3) Surrendered
4) Captivity

4 The arrival of spring brings an ebullient feeling as flowers bloom and the weather warms.
1) Deciduous 2) Clamant
3) Rude 4) Weary

5 Elisabeth stood at the piano, which did nothing to allay his anxiety.
1) aggravate 2) mitigate
3) simplify 4) mollify

6 The government is proposing to incinerate cattle carcasses at many sites, some of which are in populated areas.
1) Oxidise 2) Blaze
3) Combust 4) Extinguish

7 The explosive used is of my own formulation, and I can vouch for its efficiency.
1) Invalidate 2) Maintain
3) Witness 4) Certify

Direction (Q. 8-10): Select the most appropriate antonym of the bracketed word in the following sentence to fill in the blank.

8 The police thought that the theft was (deliberate), but it was ______.
1) planned 2) expected
3) prepared 4) unintentional

9 (Allies) have always come to his rescue in spite of his ______ attempts to defame him.
1) fellows 2) scholars
3) buddies 4) enemies

10 The patient consumed mushrooms for hallucinatory experiences, but the doctor advised to consume only ______ (hallucinogenic) drugs.
1) regular
2) freaky
3) psychedelic
4) abnormal

Answer Key Practice Set - 1:

1 - 3	2 - 3	3 - 1	4 - 3	5 - 2
6 - 4	7 - 3	8 - 4	9 - 1	10 - 2

Answer Key Practice Set - 2:

1 - 3	2 - 2	3 - 3	4 - 1	5 - 3
6 - 3	7 - 1	8 - 2	9 - 4	10 - 2

Answer Key Practice Set - 3:

1 - 1	2 - 2	3 - 1	4 - 4	5 - 4
6 - 2	7 - 2	8 - 1	9 - 2	10 - 1

Answer Key Practice Set - 4:

1 - 3	2 - 1	3 - 2	4 - 2	5 - 3
6 - 4	7 - 1	8 - 4	9 - 1	10 - 1

Answer Key Practice Set - 5:

1 - 2	2 - 1	3 - 3	4 - 1	5 - 2
6 - 1	7 - 1	8 - 2	9 - 2	10 - 3

Answer Key Practice Set - 6:

1 - 2	2 - 4	3 - 3	4 - 4	5 - 3
6 - 3	7 - 1	8 - 3	9 - 1	10 - 2

Answer Key Practice Set - 7:

1 - 3	2 - 2	3 - 3	4 - 1	5 - 3
6 - 4	7 - 3	8 - 1	9 - 1	10 - 4

Answer Key Practice Set - 8:

1 - 1	2 - 1	3 - 2	4 - 3	5 - 4
6 - 1	7 - 1	8 - 2	9 - 3	10 - 2

Answer Key Practice Set - 9:

1 - 1	2 - 3	3 - 2	4 - 3	5 - 2
6 - 2	7 - 1	8 - 3	9 - 3	10 - 2

Answer Key Practice Set - 10:

1 - 3	2 - 2	3 - 1	4 - 3	5 - 2
6 - 3	7 - 1	8 - 1	9 - 3	10 - 4

Answer Key Practice Set - 11:

1 - 3	2 - 1	3 - 3	4 - 3	5 - 4
6 - 4	7 - 1	8 - 2	9 - 3	10 - 2

Answer Key Practice Set - 12:

1 - 3	2 - 1	3 - 1	4 - 3	5 - 4
6 - 3	7 - 1	8 - 1	9 - 3	10 - 1

Answer Key Practice Set - 13:

1 - 3	2 - 2	3 - 4	4 - 2	5 - 1
6 - 2	7 - 1	8 - 3	9 - 4	10 - 3

Answer Key Practice Set - 14:

1 - 2	2 - 1	3 - 4	4 - 3	5 - 1
6 - 2	7 - 1	8 - 2	9 - 3	10 - 2

Answer Key Practice Set - 15:

1 - 3	2 - 3	3 - 1	4 - 1	5 - 1
6 - 4	7 - 3	8 - 4	9 - 4	10 - 1

Answer Key Practice Set - 16:

1 - 2	2 - 1	3 - 2	4 - 3	5 - 1
6 - 2	7 - 1	8 - 2	9 - 1	10 - 2

Answer Key Practice Set - 17:

1 - 2	2 - 4	3 - 1	4 - 1	5 - 4
6 - 1	7 - 2	8 - 1	9 - 2	10 - 2

Answer Key Practice Set - 18:

1 - 4	2 - 1	3 - 3	4 - 1	5 - 3
6 - 3	7 - 2	8 - 2	9 - 3	10 - 2

Answer Key Practice Set - 19:

1 - 4	2 - 2	3 - 4	4 - 1	5 - 4
6 - 1	7 - 2	8 - 4	9 - 3	10 - 4

Answer Key Practice Set - 20:

1 - 2	2 - 3	3 - 4	4 - 4	5 - 1
6 - 4	7 - 1	8 - 4	9 - 4	10 - 1

C9 Synonyms + Antonyms (Common) List (asked in Other Exams)

1 **Abhorrent** (Adj.) - (घिनौना) *[#R-4]*
Extremely hateful or disgusting
Syno: Offensive (आपत्तिजनक), Hateful (घृणास्पद)
Anto: Attractive (आकर्षक), Adorable (मन मोह लेने वाला)

2 **Abomination** (N.) - (घिनौनी चीज) *[#R-2]*
A thing that causes hatred or disgust
Syno: Detestation (घृणा)
Anto: Adoration (आराधना)

3 **Abstemious** (Adj.) - (संयमी) *[#R-2]*
Eating and drinking in moderation; self-restrained
Syno: Temperate (संयमी)
Anto: Indulgent (विलासी)

4 **Acrimony** (N.) - (कटुता) *[#R-5]*
A feeling of bitterness in speech or manner
Syno: Spleen (गुस्सा), Bitterness (कड़वाहट)
Anto: Courtesy (शिष्टता)

5 **Adherent** (N.) - (समर्थक) *[#R-2]*
A person who supports a particular idea or group
Syno: Follower (अनुयायी)
Anto: Renegade (विद्रोही)

6 **Adjunct** (Adj.) - (सहायक) *[#R-3]*
Added or connected in a secondary way
Syno: Additional (अतिरिक्त)
Anto: Essential (आवश्यक)

7 **Appetizing** (Adj.) - (लुभावना) *[#R-2]*
Appealing to the taste and stimulating the appetite
Syno: Pleasing (मनभावन)
Anto: Distasteful (अरुचिकर)

8 **Aspire** (V.) - (आकांक्षा करना) *[#R-3]*
To have a strong desire to achieve something
Syno: Hope (आशा करना), Endeavour (प्रयास करना)
Anto: Despair (निराश होना)

9 **Astronomical** (Adj.) - (अत्यधिक; खगोलीय) *[#R-2]*
Extremely large; relating to astronomy
Syno: Exorbitant (अत्यधिक)
Anto: Minuscule (सूक्ष्म)

10 **Boost** (V.) - (बढ़ावा देना; प्रोत्साहित करना) *[#R-2]*
To increase, raise, or improve something
Syno: Bolster (सहारा देना)
Anto: Decline (गिरावट आना)

11 **Caution** (N.) - (सावधानी) *[#R-3]*
Care taken to avoid danger or mistakes
Syno: Warn (चेतावनी)
Anto: Rashness (जल्दबाज़ी), Neglect (उपेक्षा)

12 **Ceremonious** (Adj.) - (औपचारिक) *[#R-2]*
Relating to formal ceremonies; very polite
Syno: Formal (औपचारिक)
Anto: Informal (अनौपचारिक)

13 **Coalesce** (V.) - (एक साथ आना)~ *[#R-2]*
To come together and form one whole
Syno: Merge (विलय होना)
Anto: Separate (अलग होना)

14 **Commensurate** (Adj.) - (अनुरूप; समानुपातिक) *[#R-6]*
Corresponding in size or degree; proportional
Syno: Proportionate (आनुपातिक), Equivalent (समकक्ष)
Anto: Disproportionate (असमानुपातिक)

15 **Concerned** (Adj.) - (चिंतित) *[#R-4]*
Feeling worry or anxiety about something
Syno: Apprehensive (चिंतित)
Anto: Indifferent (उदासीन), Uninvolved (असंलग्न)

16 **Consolidate** (V.) - (मजबूत करना) *[#R-5]*
To combine into a single stronger unit
Syno: Integrate (एकीकृत करना), Strengthen (मजबूत करना)
Anto: Weaken (कमजोर करना), Separate (अलग करना), Scatter (बिखेरना)

17 **Contemporary** (Adj.) - (समकालीन, आधुनिक)~ *[#R-5]*
Belonging to the same time period; modern
Syno: Fashionable (प्रचलित), Coincident (एकसाथ घटित), Modern (आधुनिक)
Anto: Outdated (पुराना)

18 **Credence** (N.) - (विश्वास) *[#R-2]*
Belief in something as true

[**#R** denotes repetition of word]

[E.g. in SN 17, #R- **5** denotes this word has been asked 5 times in other exams]

Syno: Belief (विश्वास)
Anto: Disbelief (अविश्वास)

19 Culminate (V.) - (चरम पर पहुंचना) *[#R-3]*
To reach the highest or final point
Syno: Conclude (समाप्त होना)
Anto: Originate (उत्पन्न होना)

20 **Daunting** (Adj.) - (कठिन लगने वाला) *[#R-2]*
Seeming difficult to deal with; intimidating
Syno: Troublesome (परेशान करने वाला)
Anto: Encouraging (हौसला बढ़ाने वाला)

21 Debate (N.) - (वाद-विवाद) *[#R-2]*
A formal discussion
Syno: Discussion (चर्चा)
Anto: Agreement (समझौता)

22 Deceased (Adj.) - (मृत) *[#R-2]*
No longer alive
Syno: Dead (मृत)
Anto: Living (जीवित)

23 **Decelerate** (V.) - (धीमा करना) *[#R-2]*
To reduce speed; to slow down
Syno: Retard (धीमा करना)
Anto: Accelerate (गति बढ़ाना)

24 Decide (V.) - (निर्णय लेना) *[#R-2]*
To make a choice or reach a conclusion
Syno: Choose (चुनना)
Anto: Waver (हिचकिचाना)

25 Deprecate (V.) - (विरोध करना)~ *[#R-2]*
To express disapproval of something
Syno: Disparage (निंदा करना)
Anto: Approve (अनुमोदन करना)

26 **Dilapidate** (V.) - (तबाह करना) *[#R-2]*
To cause a building to fall into disrepair
Syno: Deteriorate (बिगड़ना)
Anto: Renovate (मरम्मत करना)

27 **Dire** (Adj.) - (भयानक) *[#R-3]*
Extremely serious or urgent
Syno: Alarming (चिंताजनक), Urgent (तत्काल)
Anto: Favourable (अनुकूल)

28 **Disdainful** (Adj.) - (तिरस्कारपूर्ण) *[#R-4]*
Showing contempt or lack of respect
Syno: Dismissive (अनदेखा करने वाला)
Anto: Respectful (सम्मानपूर्ण), Reverential (श्रद्धापूर्ण)

29 **Distort** (V.) - (विकृत करना)~ *[#R-2]*
To twist out of the true shape or meaning
Syno: Misrepresent (गलत तरीके से प्रस्तुत करना)
Anto: Correct (सही करना)

30 **Elicit** (V.) - (निकलवाना) *[#R-2]*
To draw out a response or information
Syno: Obtain (प्राप्त करना)
Anto: Suppress (दबाना)

31 **Emerging** (V./Adj.) - (प्रकट होना; उभरता हुआ) *[#R-5]*
To come into view (V.); Newly developed (Adj.)
Syno: Developing (विकसित होना), Growing (बढ़ना)
Anto: Fading (फीका पड़ना), Submerging (डूबना)

32 **Encompass** (V.) - (शामिल करना) *[#R-2]*
To surround or include entirely
Syno: Encircle (घेरना)
Anto: Exclude (बाहर रखना)

33 **Enforce** (V.) - (लागू करना) *[#R-2]*
To compel obedience to a law or rule
Syno: Implement (लागू करना)
Anto: Abandon (त्याग देना)

34 **Engrossed** (Adj.) - (मग्न; ध्यान लगाए हुए) *[#R-2]*
Having all attention fully occupied
Syno: Absorbed (ध्यानमग्न)
Anto: Inattentive (असावधान)

35 **Enhanced** (V.) - (बढ़ाना) *[#R-4]*
To improve or increase
Syno: Improved (सुधारना)
Anto: Decreased (घटाना)

36 **Enthral** (V.) - (मोहित करना) *[#R-2]*
To captivate and hold the attention of
Syno: Mesmerize (मंत्रमुग्ध करना)
Anto: Bore (ऊबाना)

37 **Evaporate** (V.) - (वाष्पित होना) *[#R-2]*
To turn from liquid into vapor
Syno: Vanish (गायब होना)
Anto: Condense (संघनित होना)

38 **Exhausted** (Adj.) - (थका हुआ) *[#R-2]*
Drained of one's physical or mental resources
Syno: Tired (थका हुआ)
Anto: Refreshed (तरोताज़ा)

39 **Expeditious** (Adj.) - (शीघ्र) *[#R-3]*
Done quickly and efficiently
Syno: Prompt (शीघ्र)
Anto: Delayed (विलंबित)

40 Explosion (N.) - (विस्फोट) *[#R-2]*
A violent burst or blowing apart

[Bold SN, indicates that it has been asked in Spelling]

[In Word, ~ indicates that it has been asked in OWS]

Syno: Outburst (विस्फोट)
Anto: Implosion (अंतर्विस्फोट)

41 **Frequently** (Adv.) - (अक्सर) *[#R-2]*
On many occasions; often
Syno: Often (अक्सर)
Anto: Rarely (कभी-कभार)

42 **Galvanise** (V.) - (उत्तेजित करना) *[#R-2]*
To shock or excite someone into action
Syno: Stimulate (उत्तेजित करना)
Anto: Dishearten (निराश करना)

43 **Gusto** (N.) - (उत्साह) *[#R-2]*
Enthusiasm and energy in doing something
Syno: Enthusiasm (उत्साह)
Anto: Apathy (उदासीनता)

44 **Hoist** (V.) - (ऊपर उठाना) *[#R-2]*
To raise or lift something up
Syno: Uplift (ऊपर उठाना)
Anto: Lower (नीचे उतारना)

45 **Imperil** (V.) - (खतरे में डालना) *[#R-2]*
To put in danger or at risk
Syno: Endanger (खतरे में डालना)
Anto: Safeguard (सुरक्षित करना)

46 **Implication** (N.) - (निहितार्थ, आरोप) *[#R-3]*
A possible consequence; something suggested
Syno: Incrimination (आरोप), Consequence (परिणाम)
Anto: Exoneration (दोषमुक्ति)

47 **Inane** (Adj.) - (मूर्खतापूर्ण) *[#R-2]*
Lacking sense or meaning; silly
Syno: Absurd (बेतुका)
Anto: Smart (समझदार)

48 **Indulge** (V.) - (लिप्त होना) *[#R-2]*
To allow oneself to enjoy a pleasure
Syno: Satisfy (संतुष्ट करना)
Anto: Deny (इंकार करना)

49 **Intermittent** (Adj.) - (रुक-रुक कर होने वाला) *[#R-2]*
Occurring at irregular intervals; not constant
Syno: Recurring (आवर्ती)
Anto: Unceasing (लगातार)

50 **Intrinsically** (Adv.) - (अंतर्निहित रूप से) *[#R-2]*
In an essential or fundamental manner
Syno: Fundamentally (मौलिक रूप से)
Anto: Superficially (ऊपर-ऊपर से)

51 **Irksome** (Adj.) - (कष्टप्रद) *[#R-3]*
Annoying or irritating
Syno: Vexing (खीझ उत्पन्न करने वाला)
Anto: Pleasant (सुखद)

52 **Kidnap** (V.) - (अपहरण करना) *[#R-2]*
To take someone away illegally by force
Syno: Abduct (अपहरण करना)
Anto: Liberate (मुक्त करना)

53 **Kindle** (V.) - (प्रज्वलित करना) *[#R-5]*
To light a fire; to arouse emotions
Syno: Incite (उकसाना), Excite (उत्तेजित करना), Ignite (जलाना)
Anto: Extinguish (बुझाना)

54 **Lamentable** (Adj.) - (निराशाजनक) *[#R-2]*
Deserving of grief; very bad
Syno: Deplorable (खेदजनक)
Anto: Desirable (इच्छा योग्य)

55 **Lengthen** (V.) - (बढ़ाना) *[#R-3]*
To make or become longer
Syno: Expand (फैलाना)
Anto: Shorten (घटाना)

56 **Macabre** (Adj.) - (भयंकर) *[#R-2]*
Disturbing and horrifying; gruesome
Syno: Ghastly (भयानक)
Anto: Cheerful (प्रसन्न)

57 **Miserly** (Adj.) - (कंजूस) *[#R-2]*
Unwilling to spend money
Syno: Greedy (लालची)
Anto: Lavish (खर्चीला)

58 **Mutual** (Adj.) - (आपसी; परस्पर)~ *[#R-3]*
Shared by two or more parties
Syno: Reciprocal (पारस्परिक), Joint (संयुक्त)
Anto: Exclusive (विशेष)

59 **Myriad** (Adj.) - (असंख्य) *[#R-2]*
Countless or extremely great in number
Syno: Countless (असंख्य)
Anto: Sole (एकमात्र)

60 **Oblivion** (N.) - (विस्मृति) *[#R-2]*
The state of being forgotten or unaware
Syno: Forgetfulness (भूलने की प्रवृत्ति)
Anto: Consciousness (चेतना)

61 **Oscillate** (V.) - (आगे-पीछे हिलना) *[#R-2]*
To move back and forth regularly
Syno: Swing (हिलना)
Anto: Stabilize (स्थिर करना)

62 **Ostensible** (Adj.) - (दिखावटी) *[#R-4]*

Appearing to be true but possibly not

Syno: Plausible (संभाव्य), Apparent (आभासी)

Anto: Genuine (वास्तविक)

63 **Passe** (Adj.) - (पुराना) *[#R-2]*
Outdated; no longer fashionable

Syno: Obsolete (अप्रचलित)

Anto: Modern (आधुनिक)

64 **Persistent** (Adj.) - (लगातार)~ *[#R-4]*
Continuing firmly despite difficulty

Syno: Tenacious (दृढ़), Continual (निरंतर)

Anto: Irresolute (अस्थिर), Inconsistent (अस्थिर)

65 **Pique** (V.) - (चिढ़ाना, जिज्ञासा जगाना) *[#R-2]*
To irritate; to stimulate curiosity

Syno: Provoke (उकसाना)

Anto: Dampen (शांत करना)

66 **Plenty** (N.) - (बहुतायत) *[#R-4]*
A large amount

Syno: Abundance (प्रचुरता)

Anto: Scarcity (कमी), Paucity (अभाव)

67 **Precaution** (N.) - (सावधानी) *[#R-2]*
A measure taken to prevent harm

Syno: Prevention (रोकथाम)

Anto: Negligence (लापरवाही)

68 **Preceding** (Adj.) - (पूर्ववर्ती) *[#R-3]*
Coming before in order, position, or time

Syno: Previous (पूर्व), Antecedent (पहले का)

Anto: Following (बाद का)

69 **Precipitate** (V.) - (शीघ्र कर देना) *[#R-2]*
To cause to happen suddenly

Syno: Hasten (जल्दी करना)

Anto: Hinder (बाधा डालना)

70 **Propriety** (N.) - (शिष्टता, मर्यादा) *[#R-2]*
The conformity to accepted standards of behaviour

Syno: Rightness (उचितता)

Anto: Indecorum (अशिष्टता)

71 **Prudence** (N.) - (विवेक) *[#R-4]*
The quality of being careful and wise

Syno: Caution (सावधानी), Discretion (विवेकशीलता)

Anto: Recklessness (लापरवाही), Stupidity (मूर्खता)

72 **Qualm** (N.) - (आशंका) *[#R-2]*
A feeling of doubt or uneasiness

Syno: Doubt (संदेह)

Anto: Certitude (निश्चितता)

73 **Reciprocal** (Adj.) - (पारस्परिक) *[#R-3]*
Given or felt by each toward the other

Syno: Mutual (आपसी), Interactive (सहभागितापूर्ण)

Anto: One-Sided (एकतरफा)

74 **Redoubtable** (Adj.) - (प्रभावशाली) *[#R-3]*
Formidable and commanding respect

Syno: Formidable (प्रभावशाली)

Anto: Unimpressive (अप्रभावशाली), Ordinary (साधारण)

75 **Rejuvenation** (N.) - (पुनर्जीवन) *[#R-3]*
The act of making someone feel young again

Syno: Renewal (नवीकरण), Revival (पुनरुत्थान)

Anto: Exhaustion (शक्तिहीनता)

76 **Relegate** (V.) - (पद घटाना) *[#R-4]*
To assign to a lower rank or position

Syno: Demote (पद घटाना)

Anto: Promote (पदोन्नत करना)

77 **Rural** (Adj.) - (ग्रामीण) *[#R-2]*
Relating to the countryside

Syno: Rustic (ग्रामीण)

Anto: Metropolitan (शहरी)

78 **Sagacity** (N.) - (बुद्धिमत्ता) *[#R-2]*
The quality of having good judgment; wisdom

Syno: Insight (सूझ-बूझ)

Anto: Ignorance (अज्ञान)

79 **Salutary** (Adj.) - (लाभकारी) *[#R-3]*
Producing good effects; beneficial

Syno: Beneficial (लाभकारी)

Anto: Unhealthy (हानिकारक)

80 **Schism** (N.) - (मतभेद)~ *[#R-2]*
A division or split within a group

Syno: Split (विभाजन)

Anto: Harmony (सामंजस्य)

81 **Shortcoming** (N.) - (कमी) *[#R-2]*
A fault or failure to meet a standard

Syno: Weakness (कमजोरी)

Anto: Strength (गुण)

82 **Singular** (Adj.) - (अनोखा) *[#R-2]*
Exceptionally good; unusual; being only one

Syno: Peculiar (विचित्र)

Anto: Ordinary (साधारण)

83 **Slapdash** (Adj.) - (लापरवाही से किया गया) *[#R-2]*
Done too quickly and carelessly

Syno: Haphazard (लापरवाह)

Anto: Careful (सावधान)

84 **Solemnity** (N.) - (गंभीरता) *[#R-2]*

The state of being serious and dignified
Syno: Dignity (गरिमा)
Anto: Levity (हल्कापन)

85 Solicitous (Adj.) - (चिंतित) *[#R-3]*
Showing care and concern for someone
Syno: Attentive (ध्यानपूर्वक)
Anto: Indifferent (उदासीन)

86 **Sparsely** (Adv.) - (कम मात्रा में) *[#R-2]*
In a thinly scattered or scarce manner
Syno: Thinly (कम घनत्व में)
Anto: Abundantly (प्रचुर मात्रा में)

87 **Spleen** (N.) - (गुस्सा) *[#R-2]*
A feeling of bad temper or spite
Syno: Temper (खराब मिजाज)
Anto: Cheer (खुशी)

88 **Spur** (V.) - (प्रेरित करना) *[#R-3]*
To encourage
Syno: Stimulate (उत्तेजित करना), Promote (प्रोत्साहित करना)
Anto: Dissuade (हतोत्साहित करना)

89 **Sterling** (Adj.) - (उत्कृष्ट) *[#R-3]*
Excellent in quality
Syno: Genuine (वास्तविक), Outstanding (उत्कृष्ट)
Anto: Atrocious (घटिया)

90 Suppression (N.) - (दमन) *[#R-2]*
The act of putting an end to something by force
Syno: Repression (दमन)
Anto: Encouragement (प्रोत्साहन)

91 **Swathe** (V.) - (लपेटना) *[#R-2]*
To wrap in layers
Syno: Wrap (लपेटना)
Anto: Unwrap (खोलना)

92 Tactical (Adj.) - (योजनाबद्ध) *[#R-2]*
Relating to planned actions for a specific end
Syno: Strategic (रणनीतिक)
Anto: Unplanned (अनियोजित)

93 **Tragic** (Adj.) - (दुखद) *[#R-2]*
Causing great sadness; relating to tragedy
Syno: Appalling (भयावह)
Anto: Comic (हास्य)

94 Tranquillity (N.) - (शांति) *[#R-4]*
The state of being calm and peaceful
Syno: Quietness (शांति), Calm (शांत)
Anto: Uproar (हंगामा), Tumult (कोलाहल)

95 Unruffled (Adj.) - (शांत) *[#R-2]*
Calm and not upset or disturbed
Syno: Calm (शांत)
Anto: Nervous (चिंतित)

96 **Untenable** (Adj.) - (असमर्थनीय) *[#R-3]*
Not able to be defended or maintained
Syno: Illogical (तर्कहीन)
Anto: Logical (तार्किक)

97 Various (Adj.) - (विभिन्न) *[#R-2]*
Of different kinds; several
Syno: Several (कई)
Anto: Similar (समान)

98 Vituperative (Adj.) - (निंदात्मक) *[#R-2]*
Bitter and abusive in language
Syno: Abusive (अपशब्दात्मक)
Anto: Laudatory (प्रशंसात्मक)

99 Worry (N.) - (चिंता) *[#R-3]*
A state of anxiety about problems
Syno: Anxiety (बेचैनी)
Anto: Reassurance (आश्वासन)

*Total **99** Syno+Anto asked **257** times*

C10 Synonyms (asked in Other Exams)

1 **Abash** (V.) - (लज्जित करना)
To make someone feel embarrassed or ashamed
Syno: Shame (शर्मिंदा करना)

2 **Abet** (V.) - (उकसाना)
To help or encourage someone to do something wrong
Syno: Incite (भड़काना)

3 **Abject** (Adj.) - (दयनीय, अत्यंत खराब) *[#R-3]*
Extremely bad; hopeless or without pride
Syno: Miserable (दुखी), Pitiful (दयनीय)

4 **Abyss** (N.) - (गहरी खाई)~ *[#R-2]*
A very deep hole or chasm; a vast emptiness
Syno: Chasm (गहरी खाई), Gorge (घाटी)

5 **Accommodate** (V.) - (ठहराना)
To provide space or lodging; to adjust to meet needs
Syno: Lodge (आवास देना)

6 **Accumulation** (N.) - (संचय)
The gathering or collecting of things over time
Syno: Pile (ढेर)

7 **Achievement** (N.) - (उपलब्धि)
A thing accomplished through effort or skill
Syno: Fulfilment (लक्ष्य-प्राप्ति)

8 **Ad hoc** (Adj.) - (अस्थायी)
Created for a specific purpose; improvised
Syno: Impromptu (तत्काल किया गया)

9 **Adherence** (N.) - (अनुपालन, निष्ठा)
The act of following or supporting rules or beliefs
Syno: Attachment (निष्ठा, लगाव)

10 **Adhesive** (Adj.) - (चिपकने वाला)
Sticky; able to stick to surfaces
Syno: Sticky (चिपचिपा)

11 **Adieu** (N.) - (विदा)
A farewell or goodbye
Syno: Farewell (विदाई)

12 **Admonition** (N.) - (नसीहत)
A warning or piece of advice about behaviour
Syno: Warning (चेतावनी)

13 **Adoration** (N.) - (भक्ति)
A feeling of deep love and respect
Syno: Worship (पूजा)

14 **Aesthetic** (Adj.) - (सौंदर्यपूर्ण)~
Concerned with beauty or artistic taste
Syno: Attractive (आकर्षक)

15 **Affectation** (N.) - (दिखावा)
A pretense or artificial behaviour to impress others
Syno: Artificiality (कृत्रिमता)

16 **Aftermath** (N.) - (परिणाम)
The consequences or results following an event
Syno: Repercussions (परिणाम)

17 **Age** (N.) - (आयु)
The length of time someone has lived; a period in history
Syno: Era (समयावधि)

18 **Aggression** (N.) - (आक्रामकता)
The act of behaving in a hostile or violent manner towards others
Syno: Violence (हिंसा)

19 **Aggrieved** (Adj.) - (पीड़ित)
Feeling resentment at having been unfairly treated
Syno: Wronged (अन्याय पीड़ित)

20 **Agitation** (N.) - (बेचैनी, आंदोलन) *[#R-2]*
A state of anxiety or nervous excitement
Syno: Anxiety (चिंता), Unrest (अशांति)

21 **Allegiance** (N.) - (निष्ठा) *[#R-2]*
A loyalty or commitment to a person or group
Syno: Loyalty (वफादारी)

22 **Alleviation** (N.) - (राहत) *[#R-2]*
The act of making pain or suffering less severe
Syno: Mitigation (कमी)

23 **Allusion** (N.) - (संकेत)
An indirect reference to something
Syno: Intimation (सूचना, संकेत)

24 **Alms** (N.) - (दान) *[#R-3]*
The money or food given to poor people

[**#R** denotes repetition of word]

[E.g. in SN 24, #R- **3** denotes this word has been asked 3 times in other exams]

Syno: Charity (दान), Donation (दान)

25 **Alone** (Adj.) - (अकेला)
Without anyone else
Syno: Solitary (अकेला)

26 **Ambivalence** (N.) - (दुविधा)
The state of having mixed feelings about something
Syno: Uncertainty (अनिश्चितता)

27 **Anathema** (N.) - (अभिशाप / घृणित वस्तु) *[#R-2]*
A thing or person that is intensely disliked or loathed
Syno: Curse (अभिशाप)

28 **Annexure** (N.) - (परिशिष्ट)
An addition or appendix to a document
Syno: Attachment (संलग्नक)

29 **Anonymously** (Adv.) - (गुमनामी में)
In a way that hides one's identity
Syno: Incognito (गुमनाम रूप से)

30 **Antagonistic** (Adj.) - (प्रतिकूल)
Showing opposition or hostility
Syno: Adverse (विरुद्ध)

31 **Apocalyptic** (Adj.) - (प्रलयकारी)~
Relating to catastrophic destruction or the end of the world
Syno: Disastrous (विनाशकारी)

32 **Apology** (N.) - (क्षमायाचना)
An expression of regret for a mistake or offense
Syno: Regret (खेद)

33 **Appendix** (N.) - (अतिरिक्त भाग)
A section of extra information at the end of a book
Syno: Supplement (पूरक)

34 **Appetite** (N.) - (भूख)
A natural desire or craving for food
Syno: Hunger (भूख)

35 **Archaic** (Adj.) - (प्राचीन)~
Very old-fashioned and no longer in common use
Syno: Old-Fashioned (अप्रचलित)

36 **Archetypal** (Adj.) - (आदर्श)
Representing a typical or perfect example
Syno: Prototypical (प्रारूपात्मक)

37 **Armistice** (N.) - (युद्धविराम)
An agreement to stop fighting temporarily
Syno: Ceasefire (युद्धविराम)

38 **Asinine** (Adj.) - (मूर्खतापूर्ण) *[#R-2]*
Extremely stupid or foolish
Syno: Ridiculous (बेवकूफ़ी भरा), Preposterous (बेतुका)

39 **Assistance** (N.) - (सहायता)
The act of helping or support given
Syno: Support (समर्थन)

40 **Assortment** (N.) - (मिश्रित संग्रह)
A collection of different types of things
Syno: Variety (विविधता)

41 **Assured** (Adj.) - (आश्वस्त) *[#R-2]*
Confident, self-possessed, and certain of something
Syno: Confident (विश्वासपूर्ण), Guaranteed (सुनिश्चित)

42 **Astounding** (Adj.) - (आश्चर्यजनक)
Extremely surprising or impressive
Syno: Amazing (अद्भुत)

43 **Attempt** (V.) - (प्रयास करना)
To make an effort to do something
Syno: Try (कोशिश करना)

44 **Attrition** (N.) - (क्रमिक क्षरण)
The gradual reduction in strength or numbers
Syno: Erosion (कटाव)

45 **Augury** (N.) - (भविष्यसूचक चिन्ह)
A sign or omen of what will happen
Syno: Omen (पूर्वसंकेत)

46 **Aureate** (Adj.) - (सुनहरा)
Golden in colour; highly ornamented in style
Syno: Gilded (सोने का पानी चढ़ा हुआ)

47 **Averse** (Adj.) - (अनिच्छुक)
Having a strong dislike or opposition to something
Syno: Unwilling (अनिच्छुक)

48 **Awareness** (N.) - (जागरूकता)
The state of knowing or being conscious of something
Syno: Alertness (सतर्कता)

49 **Backlog** (N.) - (लंबित काम)
An accumulation of unfinished tasks or work
Syno: Accumulation (संचय)

50 **Bamboozle** (V.) - (धोखा देना)
To deceive or trick someone
Syno: Mystify (उलझाना)

51 **Barge** (V.) - (जबरदस्ती घुसना)
To move forcefully or rudely into a place

[Bold SN, indicates that it has been asked in Spelling]

[In Word, ~ indicates that it has been asked in OWS]

Syno: Shove (घुसेड़ना)

52 **Bedevil** (V.) - (परेशान करना)
To cause continuous trouble or distress
Syno: Afflict (कष्ट देना)

53 **Befogged** (Adj.) - (भ्रमित)
Mentally confused or unable to think clearly
Syno: Puzzled (उलझा हुआ)

54 **Beget** (V.) - (उत्पन्न करना)
To cause or produce something
Syno: Create (बनाना)

55 **Behest** (N.) - (आज्ञा)
A command or urgent request
Syno: Command (आदेश)

56 **Bewildered** (Adj.) - (हैरान)
Perplexed and confused; very puzzled
Syno: Stunned (स्तब्ध)

57 **Bewitching** (Adj.) - (मोहक)
Very charming or delightful
Syno: Enchanting (मोहक)

58 **Bibulous** (Adj.) - (शराबी)
Fond of drinking alcohol
Syno: Alcoholic (शराबी)

59 **Bleakness** (N.) - (सूनापन)
The quality of being cold; cheerless and empty
Syno: Desolation (वीरानी)

60 **Blight** (V.) - (नष्ट कर देना)
To spoil or damage something severely
Syno: Blot (बदनाम करना)

61 **Blurred** (Adj.) - (धुंधला)
Not clear or sharp
Syno: Fuzzy (अस्पष्ट)

62 **Bona Fide** (Adj.) - (वास्तविक)
Genuine, sincere, and authentic
Syno: Legitimate (वैध)

63 **Bounce** (V.) - (उछलना)
To spring back after hitting a surface
Syno: Rebound (पलटकर आना)

64 **Bounty** (N.) - (उदारता)
A reward or generous gift
Syno: Largess (उदारता)

65 **Bowdlerize** (V.) - (आपत्तिजनक अंश हटाना)
To remove offensive content from a text
Syno: Censor (जांचकर हटाना)

66 **Breathtaking** (Adj.) - (मनमोहक)
Extremely impressive or beautiful
Syno: Spectacular (भव्य)

67 **Bridge** (V.) - (संबंध स्थापित करना)
To connect two things
Syno: Connect (जोड़ना)

68 **Brigand** (N.) - (डाकू)~
A member of a gang of robbers
Syno: Marauder (लुटेरा)

69 **Briskly** (Adv.) - (फुर्ती से)
In a quick and energetic manner
Syno: Rapidly (तेजी से)

70 **Broach** (V.) - (बात छेड़ना)
To bring up a topic for discussion
Syno: Discuss (चर्चा करना)

71 **Broke** (Adj.) - (कंगाल)
Without money; having no funds
Syno: Bankrupt (दिवालिया)

72 **Browbeat** (V.) - (धमकाना)~
To intimidate someone with stern words
Syno: Bully (धमकाना)

73 **Buffer** (N.) - (मध्यवर्ती)
Something that reduces impact
Syno: Shield (ढाल)

74 **Bunco** (N.) - (धोखाधड़ी)
A swindle or fraud
Syno: Swindle (ठगी)

75 **Bursar** (N.) - (कोषाध्यक्ष)
A person in charge of finances at a school
Syno: Treasurer (कोषाध्यक्ष)

76 **Burst** (V.) - (फटना)
To break open suddenly
Syno: Pop (जोर से फटना)

77 **Caisson** (N.) - (जलरोधी कक्ष)
A watertight chamber used in construction
Syno: Chamber (कक्ष)

78 **Calamitous** (Adj.) - (विपत्तिजनक)
Causing great damage or disaster
Syno: Catastrophic (विनाशकारी)

79 **Caliginous** (Adj.) - (धुंधला) *[#R-4]*
Dark and misty; gloomy
Syno: Dark (अंधकारमय), Misty (धुंधला), Obscure (अस्पष्ट)

80 **Canard** (N.) - (अफवाह)
A false or unfounded story or rumour
Syno: Rumour (अफवाह)

81 **Canonization** (N.) - (आधिकारिक स्वीकृति)

The act of declaring someone a saint
Syno: Recognition (स्वीकृति)

82 Capacity (N.) - (क्षमता)
The maximum amount that can be contained; ability
Syno: Capability (योग्यता)

83 **Captious** (Adj.) - (अवगुण ढूंढ़नेवाला) *[#R-2]*
Tending to find fault; overly critical
Syno: Fault-finding (दोष खोजने वाला)

84 Captivated (Adj.) - (मोहित, आकर्षित)
Strongly attracted or interested
Syno: Fascinated (आकर्षित)

85 **Captive** (N.) - (बंदी) *[#R-3]*
A person held in confinement
Syno: Prisoner (कैदी)

86 **Carte Blanche** (N.) - (पूर्ण स्वतंत्रता) *[#R-2]*
A complete freedom to act as one wishes
Syno: Freedom (स्वतंत्रता), Discretion (विवेकाधिकार)

87 **Catering** (N.) - (खानपान की व्यवस्था)
The business of providing food services
Syno: Supplying (आपूर्ति करना)

88 **Chance** (N.) - (मौका)
An opportunity
Syno: Opportunity (अवसर)

89 **Charm** (N.) - (आकर्षण)
An attractive quality
Syno: Attractiveness (आकर्षण)

90 **Cherished** (Adj.) - (प्रिय)
Beloved or dearly loved
Syno: Valued (मूल्यवान)

91 **Cherubic** (Adj.) - (मासूम)
Having a sweet and innocent appearance like a cherub
Syno: Adorable (प्यारा)

92 **Choleric** (Adj.) - (क्रोधी)
Easily angered; bad-tempered
Syno: Irritable (चिड़चिड़ा)

93 **Circumscribed** (Adj.) - (सीमित)
Restricted within limits
Syno: Constrained (विवश)

94 **Clanking** (Adj.) - (धातु जैसी आवाज़ करने वाला)
Making a loud metallic sound
Syno: Rattling (खनखनाने वाला)

95 **Cleave** (V.) - (चीरना; अलग करना)
To split or divide; or to cling to
Syno: Sever (अलग करना)

96 **Cliched** (Adj.) - (घिसा-पिटा)
Overused and lacking originality
Syno: Hackneyed (घिसा-पिटा)

97 **Cling** (V.) - (चिपकना, कसकर पकड़े रहना)
To hold on tightly to something
Syno: Attach (चिपकना)

98 **Cloak** (N.) - (लबादा, ओढ़नी)
A loose outer garment
Syno: Disguise (भेष)

99 Clock (N.) - (घड़ी)
A device that shows the time
Syno: Watch (कलाई घड़ी)

100 **Cloister** (N.) - (मठ)
A covered walkway in a monastery
Syno: Convent (मठ)

101 **Clutching** (Adj.) - (कसकर पकड़े हुए)
Holding something tightly
Syno: Gripping (मजबूती से पकड़ने वाला)

102 **Cohesive** (Adj.) - (संगठित)
Forming a united whole; sticking together
Syno: Close-Knit (घनिष्ठ)

103 **Colloquy** (N.) - (बातचीत)~
A formal conversation or dialogue
Syno: Conversation (बातचीत)

104 Column (N.) - (स्तंभ)
A vertical pillar; a section in a newspaper
Syno: Pillar (खंभा)

105 Combat (N.) - (युद्ध) *[#R-2]*
A fight or battle
Syno: Fight (लड़ाई)

106 Commencement (N.) - (आरंभ)
The beginning or start of something
Syno: Beginning (शुरुआत)

107 **Commissary** (N.) - (सैनिक भंडार)
A store selling food and supplies
Syno: Canteen (खाद्य भंडार)

108 Communication (N.) - (संचार; संवाद)~
The exchange of information or ideas
Syno: Correspondence (पत्राचार)

109 Competency (N.) - (योग्यता)
The ability to do something successfully
Syno: Capability (क्षमता)

110 Complement (N.) - (पूरक)~
Something that completes or enhances

Syno: Accompaniment (संगत)

111 **Complexity** (N.) - (जटिलता)
The state of being complicated or intricate
Syno: Intricacy (जटिलता)

112 **Comprise** (V.) - (शामिल होना)
To consist of or include
Syno: Contain (समाहित करना)

113 **Conception** (N.) - (धारणा)
The forming of an idea or plan
Syno: Notion (धारणा)

114 **Concourse** (N.) - (लोगों के इकट्ठा होने का स्थान)
A large open area in a public building; a crowd
Syno: Hall (सभा-कक्ष)

115 **Confer** (V.) - (प्रदान करना, विचार-विमर्श करना) *[#R-2]*
To grant or bestow; to consult or exchange views
Syno: Consult (परामर्श करना), Grant (प्रदान करना)

116 **Congruence** (N.) - (सामंजस्य)
The state of being in agreement or harmony
Syno: Agreement (सहमति)

117 **Conquest** (N.) - (विजय)
The act of defeating and taking control
Syno: Victory (विजय)

118 **Containment** (N.) - (नियंत्रण)
The act of keeping something under control
Syno: Confinement (कैद)

119 **Contend** (V.) - (संघर्ष करना; तर्क देना)
To struggle or compete; to assert something
Syno: Compete (प्रतिस्पर्धा करना)

120 **Content** (Adj.) - (संतुष्ट) *[#R-2]*
Satisfied and happy with what one has
Syno: Satisfied (संतुष्ट)

121 **Contention** (N.) - (विवाद)
A heated disagreement; a point argued for
Syno: Dispute (विवाद)

122 **Contrast** (V.) - (अंतर, भेद दिखाना)
To compare differences between things
Syno: Differentiate (अंतर करना)

123 **Contrived** (Adj.) - (कृत्रिम)
Deliberately created rather than arising naturally
Syno: Devised (बनाया हुआ)

124 **Controlling** (Adj.) - (नियंत्रण करने वाला)
Having power to influence or direct behaviour
Syno: Dominating (प्रभुत्व रखने वाला)

125 **Conversational** (Adj.) - (वार्तालाप संबंधी)
Relating to informal spoken communication
Syno: Informal (अनौपचारिक)

126 **Convincing** (Adj.) - (प्रभावशाली)
Able to make someone believe or accept something
Syno: Persuasive (प्रभावशाली)

127 **Convulse** (V.) - (ऐंठन होना)
To shake violently and uncontrollably
Syno: Shiver (काँपना)

128 **Coordinated** (Adj.) - (समन्वित)
Working together smoothly and effectively
Syno: Synchronized (तालमेल में)

129 **Coordination** (N.) - (तालमेल)~
The organization of elements to work together
Syno: Collaboration (सहयोग)

130 **Corporal** (Adj.) - (शारीरिक)
Relating to the human body
Syno: Physical (शारीरिक)

131 **Corral** (V.) - (एक जगह बंद करना)
To gather or confine in an enclosure
Syno: Coop up (कैद करना)

132 **Correspondence** (N.) - (पत्राचार; समानता)
Communication by letters; similarity between things
Syno: Letters (पत्र)

133 **Corrosion** (N.) - (संक्षारण, जंग)
The gradual destruction by chemical reaction
Syno: Decomposition (अपघटन)

134 **Cosmetic** (Adj.) - (सौंदर्य संबंधी) *[#R-2]*
Relating to beauty; superficial in effect
Syno: Superficial (दिखावटी)

135 **Counter** (V.) - (विरोध करना)
To oppose or respond to something
Syno: Oppose (विरोध करना)

136 **Counterpart** (N.) - (समकक्ष)
A person or thing corresponding to another
Syno: Duplicate (प्रतिरूप)

137 **Countervailing** (Adj.) - (जवाबी)
Acting against something to cancel its effect
Syno: Compensating (भरपाई करने वाला)

138 **Covertly** (Adv.) - (गुप्त रूप से)
In a secret or hidden manner

Syno: Surreptitiously (गुप्त रूप से)

139 **Crass** (Adj.) - (असभ्य)
Showing no sensitivity; crude and vulgar
Syno: Coarse (अशिष्ट)

140 **Crave** (V.) - (लालसा करना)~
To feel a strong desire for something
Syno: Yearn (तड़पना)

141 Creditable (Adj.) - (प्रशंसनीय)
Deserving praise or recognition
Syno: Praiseworthy (प्रशंसनीय)

142 **Credulity** (N.) - (भोलापन)
A tendency to believe things too easily
Syno: Naivety (भोलापन)

143 Crevice (N.) - (दरार)
A narrow crack or opening
Syno: Crack (दरार)

144 **Culprit** (N.) - (अपराधी)
A person responsible for a crime or offense
Syno: Criminal (अपराधी)

145 **Curate** (V.) - (संग्रहित करना)
To select and organize content for display
Syno: Compile (संकलित करना)

146 Custody (N.) - (हिरासत)
The legal detention of a person
Syno: Confinement (कैद)

147 **Dampen** (V.) - (गीला करना)
To make slightly wet; to reduce enthusiasm
Syno: Bedew (ओस से भिगोना)

148 **Dazed** (Adj.) - (स्तब्ध)
Unable to think or react properly; confused
Syno: Shocked (चकित)

149 **Deafening** (Adj.) - (कान फाड़ देने वाला)
So loud as to make it impossible to hear anything else
Syno: Thunderous (गरजता हुआ)

150 **Debase** (V.) - (घटाना, ख़राब करना)
To reduce the quality or value of something
Syno: Degrade (नीचा करना)

151 **Debunk** (V.) - (खंडन करना)
To expose the falseness of a claim or belief
Syno: Disprove (खंडन करना)

152 **Decapitated** (V.) - (सिर काटना)
To cut off the head
Syno: Beheaded (सिर काटना)

153 **Decode** (V.) - (अर्थ निकालना)~
To convert a coded message into understandable form
Syno: Decipher (अर्थ समझना)

154 Decorous (Adj.) - (शिष्ट)
Polite and showing good taste
Syno: Seemly (उचित)

155 **De-Facto** (Adj.) - (वास्तविक)
Existing in fact though not officially recognized
Syno: Actual (वास्तविक)

156 Defamation (N.) - (मानहानि)~
The act of damaging someone's reputation
Syno: Calumny (बदनामी)

157 **Deflect** (V.) - (मोड़ना, दिशा बदलना)
To turn aside from a straight course
Syno: Divert (मोड़ना)

158 **Degeneration** (N.) - (पतन)
The process of declining or deteriorating
Syno: Decay (क्षय)

159 **Demagoguery** (N.) - (भड़काऊ राजनीति)
The use of emotional appeals to gain power
Syno: Rabble-rousing (भड़काऊ राजनीति)

160 Demeanour (N.) - (आचरण, व्यवहार)
The outward behaviour or manner of a person
Syno: Attitude (रवैया)

161 **Dent** (N.) - (धँसाव, गड्ढा)
The amount by which something is lessened
Syno: Reduction (कमी)

162 Depression (N.) - (अवसाद)
A mental state of extreme sadness and hopelessness
Syno: Melancholy (उदासी)

163 Derisory (Adj.) - (उपहासजनक)
Ridiculously small or inadequate
Syno: Inadequate (अपर्याप्त)

164 Deserted (Adj.) - (सुनसान)
Abandoned; empty of people
Syno: Uninhabited (निर्जन)

165 Designation (N.) - (पद का नाम)
An official title or name given to someone
Syno: Position (पद)

166 **Desolated** (Adj.) - (उजाड़)
Made bleakly and depressingly empty or bare
Syno: Deserted (वीरान)

167 **Despot** (N.) - (तानाशाह)~ *[#R-2]*
A ruler with absolute power; a tyrant

Syno: Dictator (तानाशाह), Tyrant (अत्याचारी)

168 Devastating (Adj.) - (विनाशकारी)
Causing severe damage, destruction, or shock
Syno: Terrible (भयानक)

169 Deviation (N.) - (विचलन)
The act of departing from an established course
Syno: Aberration (असामान्यता)

170 **Devise** (V.) - (योजना बनाना, ईजाद करना)
To plan or invent something through careful thought
Syno: Contrive (उपाय निकालना)

171 Devoted (Adj.) - (समर्पित)
Very loving or loyal
Syno: Dedicated (निष्ठावान)

172 **Devotee** (N.) - (भक्त)
A person enthusiastically devoted to something
Syno: Worshipper (उपासक)

173 **Digression** (N.) - (भटकाव)
The act of departing from the main subject
Syno: Deviation (विचलन)

174 **Dillydally** (V.) - (टालमटोल करना)
To waste time through indecision
Syno: Dawdle (समय गँवाना)

175 **Diplomat** (N.) - (राजनयिक)
A person who represents their country abroad
Syno: Ambassador (राजदूत)

176 **Disavow** (V.) - (इनकार करना)
To deny any responsibility or connection with
Syno: Repudiate (अस्वीकार करना)

177 **Discernible** (Adj.) - (प्रत्यक्ष)
Able to be seen or recognized
Syno: Perceptible (पहचानने योग्य)

178 Disciple (N.) - (शिष्य)
A follower of a teacher or leader
Syno: Student (विद्यार्थी)

179 **Disclaim** (V.) - (अस्वीकार करना)
To deny responsibility or connection with
Syno: Repudiate (अस्वीकार करना)

180 **Discourteous** (Adj.) - (अशिष्ट)
Rude and lacking good manners
Syno: Brusque (असभ्य)

181 **Dismember** (V.) - (टुकड़ों में काटना)
To cut off the limbs of a person or animal
Syno: Dissect (विच्छेदन करना)

182 **Disorient** (V.) - (उलझन में डालना)
To cause someone to lose sense of direction
Syno: Confuse (उलझाना)

183 **Disowned** (V.) - (त्याग देना)
To reject as one's own
Syno: Abandoned (त्यागना)

184 **Dissect** (V.) - (चीर-फाड़ करना, बारीकी से विश्लेषण करना)
To cut apart for examination; to analyse in detail
Syno: Analyse (विश्लेषण करना)

185 **Divorce** (N.) - (तलाक)
The legal end of a marriage
Syno: Annulment (विवाह रद्द)

186 **Doltish** (Adj.) - (मूर्खतापूर्ण)
Stupid and slow to understand
Syno: Imbecilic (बुद्धिहीन)

187 **Dominance** (N.) - (प्रभुत्व)
The state of having power or control over others
Syno: Influence (प्रभाव)

188 **Dossier** (N.) - (दस्तावेज़ संग्रह)~
A collection of documents about a person or subject
Syno: File (फ़ाइल)

189 **Doughty** (Adj.) - (निर्भीक)
Brave and persistent in effort
Syno: Valiant (वीर)

190 Draconian (Adj.) - (अत्यंत कठोर)~
Extremely harsh and severe
Syno: Vicious (क्रूर)

191 **Dramatic** (Adj.) - (चौंकाने वाला, नाटकीय)
Sudden and striking; relating to drama
Syno: Spectacular (भव्य)

192 Drastic (Adj.) - (कठोर)
Extreme and having a strong effect
Syno: Severe (गंभीर)

193 **Draught** (N.) - (वायु का झोंका)
A current of cool air
Syno: Breeze (हवा का झोंका)

194 **Draw** (V.) - (आकर्षित करना)~
To pull or attract
Syno: Entice (लुभाना)

195 **Drive** (N.) - (प्रेरणा)

A motivation or journey
Syno: Force (बल)

196 **Drown** (V.) - (डूब मरना)
To die by being under water and unable to breathe
Syno: Submerge (डुबोना)

197 **Dry** (Adj.) - (सूखा)
Free from moisture or liquid
Syno: Arid (शुष्क)

198 **Dun** (Adj.) - (मटमैला)
A dull grayish-brown colour
Syno: Drab (फीका)

199 **Duplicity** (N.) - (दोगलापन) *[#R-2]*
Deceitfulness or double-dealing
Syno: Hypocrisy (पाखंड), Deception (धोखा)

200 Earnest (Adj.) - (गंभीर, सच्चा)
Serious and sincere in intention
Syno: Serious (गंभीर)

201 **Ease** (V.) - (हल्का करना)
To make less difficult
Syno: Soften (नरम करना)

202 **Eavesdrop** (V.) - (छिपकर सुनना)
To listen secretly to a private conversation
Syno: Snoop (ताक-झांक करना)

203 Ecological (Adj.) - (पारिस्थितिकीय)
Relating to the environment and living things
Syno: Environmental (पर्यावरणीय)

204 **Educe** (V.) - (प्रकट करना)
To bring out or develop something latent
Syno: Elicit (प्राप्त करना)

205 Effulgent (Adj.) - (चमकदार)
Shining brightly; radiant
Syno: Radiant (चमकीला)

206 **Eject** (V.) - (बाहर निकालना)
To force out or expel suddenly
Syno: Expel (निकाल देना)

207 **Elation** (N.) - (उल्लास)
A feeling of great happiness and excitement
Syno: Ecstasy (परमानंद)

208 **Elderly** (Adj.) - (वृद्ध)
Old or aging; past middle age
Syno: Aged (वृद्ध)

209 **Elevated** (V.) - (ऊपर उठाना)
To raise to a higher position
Syno: Promoted (पदोन्नत करना)

210 Eloquence (N.) - (भाषण-कौशल)~ *[#R-2]*
The art of speaking fluently and persuasively
Syno: Expression (अभिव्यक्ति)

211 Embarrassment (N.) - (शर्मिंदगी)
A feeling of self-consciousness or shame
Syno: Shame (शर्म)

212 **Embolden** (V.) - (हिम्मत देना)
To give someone the courage or confidence to do something
Syno: Encourage (प्रोत्साहित करना)

213 **Enamoured** (Adj.) - (मोहित)
Filled with love or admiration
Syno: Obsessed (जुनूनी)

214 **Endearment** (N.) - (मोह, लाड प्यार) *[#R-2]*
A word or action expressing love or affection
Syno: Affection (स्नेह), Tenderness (कोमलता)

215 **Endowment** (N.) - (अनुदान) *[#R-3]*
A gift of money or property
Syno: Gift (उपहार), Grant (अनुदान)

216 **Enfranchise** (V.) - (मताधिकार देना)
To give the right to vote
Syno: Emancipate (मुक्त करना)

217 Enjoin (V.) - (आदेश देना)
To instruct or urge someone to do something
Syno: Command (आदेश देना)

218 **Enormity** (N.) - (जघन्यता) *[#R-2]*
The extreme seriousness of something bad; great size
Syno: Heinousness (जघन्यता)

219 **Enormously** (Adv.) - (अत्यधिक)
To a very great degree or extent
Syno: Extremely (अत्यंत)

220 **Entitled** (Adj.) - (हकदार)
Having a right or claim
Syno: Privileged (विशेषाधिकार प्राप्त)

221 Entrust (V.) - (सौंपना)
To give responsibility or care to someone
Syno: Assign (सौंपना)

222 **Enuresis** (N.) - (अनैच्छिक मूत्रत्याग) *[#R-2]*
The involuntary passing of urine; bedwetting
Syno: Bed-Wetting (नींद में पेशाब करना)

223 **Epicure** (N.) - (भोजनप्रिय)~
A person who enjoys fine food and drink
Syno: Gourmand (भोजन प्रेमी)

224 Epithet (N.) - (उपाधि)~

A descriptive word or phrase for a person or thing

Syno: Nickname (उपनाम)

225 **Equestrian** (N.) - (अश्वारोही)~
A person who rides horses

Syno: Horseman (घुड़सवार)

226 **Equip** (V.) - (सुसज्जित करना)
To provide with necessary tools or resources

Syno: Furnish (प्रदान करना)

227 Equivocate (V.) - (गोलमोल जवाब देना) *[#R-3]*
To use unclear language to mislead

Syno: Evade (बचना), Prevaricate (टालना)

228 **Ere** (Prep.) - (से पहले; पहले ही)
Before a specified time

Syno: Before (पहले)

229 **Eroded** (V.) - (घिसा हुआ)
To gradually wear away

Syno: Corroded (जंग लगा हुआ)

230 Ethereal (Adj.) - (अलौकिक) *[#R-3]*
Extremely light and delicate; heavenly

Syno: Airy (हल्का), Heavenly (स्वर्गीय), Exquisite (उत्कृष्ट)

231 **Evocative** (Adj.) - (भावोत्तेजक)
Bringing strong images or feelings to mind

Syno: Enchanting (मोहक)

232 Exact (V.) - (वसूल करना)
To demand or obtain forcefully

Syno: Demand (माँगना)

233 **Exaction** (N.) - (वसूली)
The act of demanding payment or obedience

Syno: Extortion (जबरन वसूली)

234 Example (N.) - (उदाहरण)
A thing that illustrates a general rule

Syno: Illustration (उदाहरण)

235 **Excavate** (V.) - (खोदना)
To dig out and remove earth or soil

Syno: Uncover (उजागर करना)

236 Excess (N.) - (अधिकता)
An amount more than necessary

Syno: Profusion (प्रचुरता)

237 **Excommunicate** (V.) - (बहिष्कृत करना)
To officially exclude from membership in a church

Syno: Expel (निकाल देना)

238 Exemplify (V.) - (उदाहरण प्रस्तुत करना)
To serve as a typical example of something

Syno: Demonstrate (प्रदर्शित करना)

239 **Exertion** (N.) - (परिश्रम)
The use of physical or mental effort

Syno: Effort (प्रयास)

240 Exhilarated (Adj.) - (प्रफुल्लित)
Made to feel very happy and excited

Syno: Overjoyed (अति प्रसन्न)

241 **Exhilarating** (Adj.) - (रोमांचकारी) *[#R-2]*
Making one feel very happy and excited

Syno: Exciting (रोमांचक), Thrilling (रोमांचक)

242 Exploratory (Adj.) - (खोज से जुड़ा)
Relating to exploration or investigation

Syno: Investigative (जांचात्मक)

243 Explosive (Adj.) - (विस्फोटक)
Capable of exploding; likely to cause anger

Syno: Eruptive (विस्फोटक)

244 **Extinction** (N.) - (विलुप्ति) *[#R-2]*
The state of no longer existing

Syno: Disappearance (गायब होना)

245 Facade (N.) - (अग्रभाग)
The front of a building

Syno: Front (अग्रभाग)

246 Facet (N.) - (पहलू)
A single side or aspect of something

Syno: Aspect (पहलू)

247 Facetious (Adj.) - (मजाकिया) *[#R-3]*
Treating serious issues with inappropriate humor

Syno: Flippant (लापरवाह), Amusing (मनोरंजक), Jocular (परिहासपूर्ण)

248 **Factitious** (Adj.) - (कृत्रिम) *[#R-2]*
Artificially created rather than natural

Syno: Artificial (कृत्रिम)

249 **Fall** (V.) - (गिरना)
To drop down

Syno: Descend (उतरना)

250 Fallacious (Adj.) - (भ्रामक)
Based on a false or mistaken idea

Syno: Erroneous (गलत)

251 Fashion (V.) - (बनाना)
To give a particular shape or form to

Syno: Make (बनाना)

252 **Faulty** (Adj.) - (त्रुटिपूर्ण)
Having defects or imperfections

Syno: Defective (दोषपूर्ण)

253 **Faux** (Adj.) - (नकली)
Artificial or fake; not genuine
Syno: Simulated (नकली)

254 **Feigned** (V.) - (दिखावा करना)
To pretend
Syno: Pretended (नाटक करना)

255 **Feline** (Adj.) - (बिल्ली जैसा)~
Relating to cats; cat-like
Syno: Catlike (बिल्ली जैसा)

256 **Ferret** (V.) - (खोजना)
To search for something
Syno: Search (खोजना)

257 **Fervid** (Adj.) - (प्रचंड) *[#R-3]*
Intensely enthusiastic or passionate
Syno: Passionate (उत्साही), Ardent (उत्कट)

258 **Fiercely** (Adv.) - (भीषण रूप से)
In a violent or aggressive manner
Syno: Aggressively (आक्रामक रूप से)

259 **Finally** (Adv.) - (अंत में)
At last or after a long time
Syno: Eventually (अंततः)

260 **Fiscal** (Adj.) - (वित्तीय)
Relating to government finances and taxation
Syno: Financial (वित्तीय)

261 **Flag** (V.) - (चिन्हित करना)
To mark an item for attention or treatment
Syno: Highlight (चिन्हित करना)

262 **Flatterer** (N.) - (चापलूस)
A person who gives excessive praise insincerely
Syno: Sycophants (चापलूस)

263 **Flip** (N.) - (पलट)
A quick movement
Syno: Reverse (उलट)

264 **Flurry** (N.) - (हलचल, घबराहट) *[#R-3]*
A brief spell of activity or commotion
Syno: Fluster (घबराहट), Surge (तेज़ बढ़ोतरी), Swirl (भंवर)

265 **Forbearance** (N.) - (सहनशीलता) *[#R-2]*
Patient self-control and tolerance
Syno: Patience (धैर्य), Restraint (संयम)

266 **Force** (V.) - (जबरदस्ती करना)
To compel someone
Syno: Compel (मजबूर करना)

267 **Foreshortened** (V.) - (छोटा करना)
To make appear shorter
Syno: Contracted (संकुचित करना)

268 **Forte** (N.) - (विशेष क्षमता)~
A thing at which someone excels
Syno: Strength (ताकत)

269 **Fragment** (N.) - (टुकड़ा)
A small broken piece of something
Syno: Portion (हिस्सा)

270 **Frazzled** (Adj.) - (थका हुआ)
Completely exhausted and overwhelmed by stress
Syno: Exhausted (थका हुआ)

271 **Frenetic** (Adj.) - (अत्यधिक उत्तेजित)
Fast and energetic in a wild way
Syno: Hectic (व्यस्त)

272 **Furtively** (Adv.) - (गुप्त रूप से)
In a secret or stealthy manner
Syno: Stealthily (चुपके से)

273 **Gaiety** (N.) - (उल्लास)
The state of being cheerful and light-hearted
Syno: Jollity (आनंद)

274 **Garish** (Adj.) - (भड़कीला)
Excessively bright, showy, and tasteless
Syno: Gaudy (भड़कीला)

275 **Ghoulish** (Adj.) - (भयानक)
Morbidly interested in death; gruesome
Syno: Devilish (भयावह)

276 **Gibbous** (Adj.) - (उभरा हुआ)
Having a convex shape; more than half illuminated
Syno: Bulging (उभरा हुआ)

277 **Glean** (V.) - (बटोरना)
To gather information bit by bit
Syno: Gather (एकत्र करना)

278 **Gluttonous** (Adj.) - (पेटू)
Excessively greedy for food
Syno: Greedy (लालची)

279 **Gnarled** (Adj.) - (गाँठदार)
Knobbly, rough, and twisted, especially with age
Syno: Twisted (मुड़ा हुआ)

280 **Goad** (V.) - (उकसाना)
To urge or force someone to act
Syno: Provoke (भड़काना)

281 **God** (N.) - (देवता)
A supreme being worshipped in various

religions
Syno: Deity (देवता)

282 **Gradient** (N.) - (ढाल) *[#R-2]*
The degree of slope
Syno: Slope (ढलान), Incline (झुकाव)

283 **Green** (Adj.) - (अनुभवहीन)
Lacking experience or knowledge
Syno: Naive (भोला)

284 Grievance (N.) - (शिकायत) *[#R-2]*
A complaint about unfair treatment
Syno: Complaint (शिकायत)

285 **Gripe** (V.) - (शिकायत करना)
To complain persistently about something
Syno: Complain (शिकायत करना)

286 Gritty (Adj.) - (साहसी) *[#R-2]*
Showing courage; containing small rough particles
Syno: Courageous (बहादुर), Resolute (दृढ़)

287 **Guest** (N.) - (मेहमान)
A person invited to visit or stay
Syno: Visitor (आगंतुक)

288 **Haggle** (V.) - (मोलभाव करना)
To bargain persistently over a price
Syno: Bargain (सौदा करना)

289 **Hankering** (N.) - (तीव्र इच्छा)
A strong desire or longing for something
Syno: Craving (तीव्र इच्छा)

290 **Hastily** (Adv.) - (जल्दी में)
In a hurried or rushed manner
Syno: Hurriedly (जल्दबाज़ी से)

291 Havoc (N.) - (तबाही)
Widespread destruction or chaos
Syno: Devastation (विनाश)

292 **Haze** (N.) - (धुंध)
A slight obscuring of vision
Syno: Mist (हल्का कोहरा)

293 **Heathen** (N.) - (असभ्य व्यक्ति)
A person who does not belong to a major religion
Syno: Barbarian (जंगली/बर्बर)

294 Heritage (N.) - (विरासत)~
Valued traditions passed down through generations
Syno: Legacy (विरासत)

295 Hiatus (N.) - (अन्तराल)
A pause or gap in a sequence
Syno: Gap (अंतर)

296 **Hobnob** (V.) - (घुलना-मिलना)
To mix socially with people of higher status
Syno: Socialize (मेलजोल करना)

297 **Hone** (V.) - (पैना करना)
To sharpen or improve a skill
Syno: Sharpen (तेज़ करना)

298 **Hopeless** (Adj.) - (निराशाजनक)
Without hope; impossible to achieve
Syno: Despairing (निराश)

299 Hover (V.) - (मंडराना)
To remain in one place in the air; to linger
Syno: Float (तैरना)

300 **Hovering** (Adj.) - (मंडराता हुआ)
Remaining in one place in the air
Syno: Floating (तैरता हुआ)

301 **However** (Adv.) - (फिर भी)
In whatever way
Syno: But (लेकिन)

302 **Howling** (Adj.) - (चीखता हुआ)
Making a loud wailing sound; tremendous
Syno: Wailing (विलाप करता हुआ)

303 **Hubris** (N.) - (अहंकार)
An excessive sense of pride or self-confidence
Syno: Arrogance (अहंकार)

304 **Humanity** (N.) - (मानवता)
All human beings collectively; kindness
Syno: Mankind (मानव जाति)

305 **Hunk** (N.) - (टुकड़ा)
A large piece of something
Syno: Slab (मोटा टुकड़ा)

306 **Hunt** (V.) - (शिकार करना)
To chase and kill animals
Syno: Search (खोजना)

307 **Hurry** (V.) - (जल्दी करना)
To move or act with great speed
Syno: Hasten (जल्दी करना)

308 **Hustle** (V.) - (धक्का-मुक्की करना) *[#R-2]*
To push roughly; to work energetically
Syno: Hurry (जल्दी करना)

309 **Idiocy** (N.) - (मूर्खता)
Extremely stupid behaviour or thinking
Syno: Stupidity (मूर्खता)

310 Idyllic (Adj.) - (मनोहर)~
Extremely peaceful and pleasant

Syno: Blissful (आनंदमय)

311 **Ill-Favoured** (Adj.) - (कुरूप)
Unattractive in appearance
Syno: Ugly (बदसूरत)

312 **Imbecility** (N.) - (मूर्खता)
The state of being very stupid
Syno: Stupidity (मूर्खता)

313 Impact (N.) - (प्रभाव)
A strong effect
Syno: Influence (असर)

314 Impending (Adj.) - (आसन्न)
About to happen very soon
Syno: Imminent (निकट)

315 Imperative (Adj.) - (अनिवार्य) *[#R-3]*
Extremely important and requiring immediate action
Syno: Urgent (तात्कालिक), Essential (जरूरी), Mandatory (अनिवार्य)

316 **Imperceptibly** (Adv.) - (अतिसूक्ष्म रूप से)
In a way that cannot be noticed
Syno: Invisibly (अदृश्य रूप से)

317 **Impish** (Adj.) - (नटखट) *[#R-4]*
Playfully mischievous
Syno: Mischievous (शरारती)

318 **Impound** (V.) - (जब्त करना)
To seize and take legal custody of
Syno: Confiscate (जब्त करना)

319 **Impugn** (V.) - (चुनौती देना)~
To dispute the truth or honesty of
Syno: Challenge (चुनौती देना)

320 **Inaugurate** (V.) - (उद्घाटन करना)
To begin or introduce officially
Syno: Launch (शुरू करना)

321 **Incompatible** (Adj.) - (असंगत) *[#R-4]*
Unable to exist together harmoniously
Syno: Discrepant (विसंगत), Conflicting (विरोधाभासी)

322 Inconceivable (Adj.) - (अकल्पनीय)
Impossible to imagine or believe
Syno: Incredible (अविश्वसनीय)

323 **Incorporated** (V.) - (सम्मिलित करना)
To include as part
Syno: Integrated (एकीकृत करना)

324 **Incorporeal** (Adj.) - (शरीर के बिना, अमूर्त)
Lacking physical form; disembodied
Syno: Bodiless (शरीर रहित)

325 **Incriminate** (V.) - (अपराधी ठहराना)
To make someone appear guilty of a crime
Syno: Prosecute (मुकदमा करना)

326 **Inculcate** (V.) - (दृढ़ता से सिखाना) *[#R-2]*
To instill ideas through persistent instruction
Syno: Infuse (मन में भरना), Instil (अंतर्निहित करना)

327 **Incursion** (N.) - (आक्रमण)
A sudden invasion or attack
Syno: Invasion (आक्रमण)

328 **Indentured** (Adj.) - (बंधुआ)
Bound by a formal legal agreement
Syno: Bonded (बंधुआ)

329 **Indicative** (Adj.) - (सूचक)
Serving as a sign or indication
Syno: Suggestive (संकेतात्मक)

330 **Indiscriminately** (Adv.) - (बिना भेद किए)
In a random manner without distinction
Syno: Randomly (बेतरतीब ढंग से)

331 **Indissolubly** (Adv.) - (अटूट रूप से)
In a way that cannot be separated or dissolved
Syno: Firmly (मजबूती से)

332 Indolence (N.) - (आलस्य) *[#R-2]*
The quality of being lazy; avoiding activity
Syno: Laziness (आलस्य)

333 **Inebriated** (Adj.) - (नशे में) *[#R-2]*
Intoxicated; drunk
Syno: Drunken (नशे में)

334 **Ineptitude** (N.) - (अयोग्यता)~
The lack of skill or ability
Syno: Incompetence (अक्षमता)

335 Inexorable (Adj.) - (अटल)~
Impossible to persuade by request or entreaty
Syno: Merciless (निर्दयी)

336 Infer (V.) - (अनुमान लगाना)
To conclude from evidence or reasoning
Syno: Conclude (निष्कर्ष निकालना)

337 Infinitesimal (Adj.) - (अति सूक्ष्म)
Extremely small or insignificant in size or amount
Syno: Negligible (नगण्य)

338 Infringe (V.) - (उल्लंघन करना)
To actively break the terms of a law or agreement
Syno: Violate (उल्लंघन करना)

339 Innumerable (Adj.) - (असंख्य)
Too many to be counted
Syno: Countless (असंख्य)

340 **Insanity** (N.) - (पागलपन)
The state of being seriously mentally ill
Syno: Madness (पागलपन)

341 Insignificant (Adj.) - (महत्वहीन)
Too small or unimportant to be worth consideration
Syno: Trivial (मामूली)

342 Insolence (N.) - (असभ्यता)
Rude and disrespectful behaviour
Syno: Audacity (दुस्साहस)

343 **Interlocutor** (N.) - (वार्ताकार)
A person who takes part in a conversation
Syno: Dialogist (संवादकर्ता)

344 Intervention (N.) - (हस्तक्षेप) *[#R-2]*
The act of becoming involved to change an outcome
Syno: Intrusion (अतिक्रमण), Interference (हस्तक्षेप)

345 Intrigue (V.) - (दिलचस्पी जगाना)
To arouse curiosity
Syno: Attract (आकर्षित करना)

346 **Introduce** (V.) - (परिचय कराना)
To bring something into use; to present someone
Syno: Initiate (आरंभ करना)

347 **Intrude** (V.) - (घुसपैठ करना)
To enter without permission or welcome
Syno: Interrupt (बाधित करना)

348 **Intrusion** (N.) - (घुसपैठ)
The act of entering without permission
Syno: Trespass (अवैध प्रवेश)

349 **Inured** (V.) - (अभ्यस्त करना)
To accustom
Syno: Accustomed (अभ्यस्त करना)

350 **Inveigh** (V.) - (निन्दा करना)
To speak or write with great hostility
Syno: Criticize (आलोचना करना)

351 Invent (V.) - (आविष्कार करना)
To create something new for the first time
Syno: Devise (ईजाद करना)

352 Invoke (V.) - (आह्वान करना)
To call upon for help or as authority
Syno: Summon (बुलाना)

353 Iridescent (Adj.) - (रंगबिरंगा)
Showing rainbow-like colours that change with angle
Syno: Opalescent (इंद्रधनुषी)

354 **Iterate** (V.) - (दोहराना)
To repeat or state again
Syno: Repeat (दोहराना)

355 **Knock-Down** (V.) - (गिराना)
To strike to the ground; to reduce price
Syno: Demolish (नष्ट करना)

356 **Lambaste** (V.) - (कड़ी आलोचना करना)
To criticize severely
Syno: Criticize (आलोचना करना)

357 **Languor** (N.) - (सुस्ती; थकान)
The state of pleasant tiredness or inactivity
Syno: Lethargy (सुस्ती)

358 Lascivious (Adj.) - (वासना से भरा)
Showing excessive sexual desire
Syno: Lecherous (कामुक)

359 **Lavishly** (Adv.) - (उदारतापूर्वक)
In a generous and extravagant manner
Syno: Generously (उदारतापूर्वक)

360 **Lawsuit** (N.) - (मुकदमा)
A claim brought to a court of law
Syno: Litigation (मुकदमेबाज़ी)

361 **Layoff** (N.) - (छँटनी)~
The dismissal of employees from a job
Syno: Dismissal (छँटनी)

362 Legendary (Adj.) - (पौराणिक)
Described in legends; very famous
Syno: Fabled (काल्पनिक)

363 Legible (Adj.) - (पढ़ने योग्य)
Clear enough to be read
Syno: Readable (पठनीय)

364 **Libelous** (Adj.) - (मानहानिकारक)
Containing a false damaging statement
Syno: Slanderous (बदनामीपूर्ण)

365 **Liberalise** (V.) - (उदार करना)
To remove restrictions on something
Syno: Deregulate (नियंत्रणमुक्त करना)

366 **Limelight** (N.) - (सुर्खियों में)~
The center of public attention
Syno: Prominence (प्रमुखता)

367 **Limited** (Adj.) - (सीमित)
Restricted in size, amount, or extent

Syno: Finite (सीमित)

368 **Literacy** (N.) - (साक्षरता)
The ability to read and write
Syno: Education (शिक्षा)

369 **Literati** (N.) - (विद्वान)
Well-educated people interested in literature
Syno: Intelligentsia (बुद्धिजीवी वर्ग)

370 **Lobby** (V.) - (पैरवी करना)
To try to influence politicians or officials
Syno: Advocate (समर्थन करना)

371 Loose (Adj.) - (ढीला)
Not firmly fixed; not tight
Syno: Slack (ढीला)

372 Lose (V.) - (हारना)
To be deprived of something; to fail to win
Syno: Misplace (खो देना, गलत जगह रख देना)

373 **Lowbrow** (Adj.) - (गैर-बौद्धिक)
Not intellectual or cultured
Syno: Coarse (असभ्य)

374 **Lynch** (V.) - (भीड़ द्वारा हत्या करना) *[#R-2]*
To kill someone illegally by mob action
Syno: Kill (मारना)

375 Magnetic (Adj.) - (चुंबकीय)
Having the power to attract; very attractive
Syno: Captivating (मोहक)

376 **Maiden Speech** (N.) - (पहला भाषण)~
The first speech made by someone in a position
Syno: Inaugural Speech (उद्घाटन भाषण)

377 **Mannerism** (N.) - (हाव-भाव)
A distinctive gesture or way of speaking
Syno: Trait (लक्षण)

378 **Marker** (N.) - (चिन्ह)
An object used to indicate a position
Syno: Indicator (संकेतक)

379 **Marring** (V.) - (खराब करना)
Spoiling or damaging something
Syno: Damaging (नुकसान पहुँचाना)

380 **Mass Murder** (N.) - (सामूहिक हत्या)
The killing of multiple people at once
Syno: Massacre (कत्लेआम)

381 Massacre (N.) - (नरसंहार)
The killing of many people
Syno: Slaughter (वध)

382 **Memorandum** (N.) - (ज्ञापन)
A written message in business or diplomacy
Syno: Missive (पत्र)

383 Memorise (V.) - (याद करना)
To commit something to memory
Syno: Retain (याद रखना)

384 **Mendacity** (N.) - (असत्यता)
The tendency to be untruthful
Syno: Prevarication (टालमटोल)

385 **Mendicant** (N.) - (भिखारी)~
A person who begs for money or food
Syno: Beggar (मांगने वाला)

386 **Mensuration** (N.) - (क्षेत्रमिति)
The measuring of geometric quantities
Syno: Measurement (माप)

387 Meritorious (Adj.) - (प्रशंसनीय)
Deserving reward or praise
Syno: Praiseworthy (प्रशंसनीय)

388 **Mesh** (N.) - (जाल) *[#R-2]*
A material made of interlaced threads
Syno: Netting (जाली)

389 Metaphysics (N.) - (अस्तित्व का अध्ययन)
The branch of philosophy dealing with existence
Syno: Ontology (अस्तित्व शास्त्र)

390 Might (N.) - (ताकत)
Great power or strength
Syno: Strength (शक्ति)

391 **Mitigating** (Adj.) - (कम करने वाला)
Making something less severe or serious
Syno: Extenuating (प्रभाव घटाने वाला)

392 **Modicum** (N.) - (थोड़ा)~
A small quantity of something
Syno: Iota (अल्पांश)

393 **Modulate** (V.) - (नियंत्रित करना)
To adjust or regulate something
Syno: Adjust (समायोजित करना)

394 Monster (N.) - (राक्षस)
A large frightening creature; a cruel person
Syno: Giant (विशालकाय)

395 **Moralisation** (N.) - (नैतिक उपदेश)
Comments about right and wrong behaviour
Syno: Sermonizing (उपदेश)

396 Morning (N.) - (सुबह)
The early part of the day
Syno: Dawn (भोर)

397 **Motivation** (N.) - (प्रेरणा) *[#R-2]*
The reason for acting in a particular way
Syno: Ambition (महत्वाकांक्षा), Inspiration (प्रेरणा)

398 **Motley** (Adj.) - (विविध)
Made up of very different elements; varied
Syno: Diverse (विविध)

399 **Mulish** (Adj.) - (ज़िद्दी)
Stubbornly refusing to change one's mind
Syno: Pigheaded (अड़ियल)

400 **Musty** (Adj.) - (सीलन भरा)
Having a stale or moldy smell
Syno: Stale (बासी)

401 **Narrate** (V.) - (वर्णन करना)
To tell a story or give an account
Syno: Describe (विवरण देना)

402 **Nature** (N.) - (प्रकृति)
The essential character of something
Syno: Character (स्वभाव)

403 **Navigable** (Adj.) - (नौगम्य)
Able to be sailed on by ships
Syno: Passable (गुज़रने योग्य)

404 **Needless** (Adj.) - (अनावश्यक)
Unnecessary; not needed
Syno: Unnecessary (अनावश्यक)

405 **Negate** (V.) - (नकारना)
To make ineffective; to deny
Syno: Cancel Out (रद्द करना)

406 **Nuance** (N.) - (सूक्ष्म अंतर) *[#R-3]*
A subtle difference in meaning or expression
Syno: Distinction (अंतर), Overtone (छुपा हुआ अर्थ)

407 **Nullify** (V.) - (रद्द करना) *[#R-2]*
To make legally void or invalid
Syno: Negate (नकारना), Repeal (रद्द करना)

408 **Obviate** (V.) - (दूर करना)
To remove a difficulty or need
Syno: Preclude (रोकना)

409 **Offence** (N.) - (अपराध)
An illegal act
Syno: Crime (अपराध)

410 **Ooze** (V.) - (रिसना)
To flow slowly out of something
Syno: Exude (रिसना)

411 **Opposition** (N.) - (विरोध)
Resistance or disagreement; a competing group
Syno: Resistance (प्रतिरोध)

412 **Oppress** (V.) - (अत्याचार करना)
To treat people cruelly or unfairly
Syno: Maltreat (दुर्व्यवहार करना)

413 **Oracle** (N.) - (देववाणी)
Divine advice or prophecy
Syno: Prophecy (भविष्यवाणी)

414 **Oratory** (N.) - (भाषणकला)~
The art of public speaking
Syno: Eloquence (वाकपटुता)

415 **Organic** (Adj.) - (जैविक)
Relating to living matter; produced naturally
Syno: Natural (प्राकृतिक)

416 **Organize** (V.) - (आयोजित करना)
To arrange systematically; to plan
Syno: Arrange (व्यवस्थित करना)

417 **Oriented** (Adj.) - (केंद्रित)
Adjusted or tailored to specified circumstances
Syno: Directed (निर्देशित)

418 **Outlast** (V.) - (अधिक समय तक चलना)
To live or last longer than something
Syno: Survive (जीवित रहना)

419 **Outlook** (N.) - (दृष्टिकोण)
A person's attitude or point of view
Syno: Prospect (संभावना)

420 **Outrage** (N.) - (आक्रोश)
An extremely strong reaction of anger
Syno: Anger (क्रोध)

421 **Overcome** (V.) - (जीत हासिल करना)
To succeed in dealing with a problem
Syno: Surmount (जीतना)

422 **Overrule** (V.) - (खारिज करना)
To reject a decision by authority
Syno: Veto (निषेध करना)

423 **Overwrought** (Adj.) - (बहुत बेचैन)
In a state of excessive nervousness
Syno: Agitated (उत्तेजित)

424 **Painful** (Adj.) - (पीड़ादायक)
Causing physical or emotional pain
Syno: Excruciating (तीव्र पीड़ादायक)

425 **Pall** (V.) - (फीका पड़ना, ऊबाऊ होना)
To become less interesting over time
Syno: Bore (ऊबाना)

426 **Palpitate** (V.) - (धड़कना)
To beat rapidly or tremble

Syno: Tremble (कांपना)

427 **Panoramic** (Adj.) - (विस्तृत दृश्य)
Showing a wide view of an area
Syno: Extensive (विस्तृत)

428 Paradigm (N.) - (प्रतिमान)~ *[#R-2]*
A typical example or model of something
Syno: Model (नमूना), Exemplar (उदाहरण)

429 Parapet (N.) - (सुरक्षा दीवार)
A low wall along the edge of a roof or bridge
Syno: Fortification (किलेबंदी)

430 Paraphernalia (N.) - (सहायक वस्तुएँ)
The miscellaneous equipment or items needed for an activity
Syno: Accessories (सहायक उपकरण)

431 **Parson** (N.) - (पादरी)
A member of the clergy; a minister
Syno: Priest (पादरी)

432 **Patriarchal** (Adj.) - (पुरुष-प्रधान)
Relating to a male-dominated society
Syno: Male-Dominated (पुरुष प्रधान)

433 Patronage (N.) - (संरक्षण) *[#R-3]*
The support or sponsorship given by a patron
Syno: Support (समर्थन)

434 **Peerless** (Adj.) - (अतुलनीय)
Having no equal; unmatched
Syno: Unequalled (अतुलनीय)

435 **Penalize** (V.) - (दंडित करना)
To punish for breaking a rule
Syno: Punish (सज़ा देना)

436 Penetrate (V.) - (घुसना)~
To go through or into something
Syno: Permeate (भीतर तक समा जाना)

437 **Peripatetic** (Adj.) - (घुमक्कड़)
Traveling from place to place
Syno: Itinerant (घूमते रहने वाला)

438 Persuasive (Adj.) - (प्रेरक)
Good at convincing others
Syno: Influential (प्रभावशाली)

439 **Phenomenal** (Adj.) - (असाधारण)
Remarkable or exceptional
Syno: Remarkable (उल्लेखनीय)

440 Philistine (Adj.) - (संस्कृतिहीन)~
Hostile or indifferent to culture and the arts
Syno: Uncultivated (असभ्य)

441 **Phony** (Adj.) - (नकली)
Not genuine; fake
Syno: Fake (नकली)

442 Picturesque (Adj.) - (मनोरम)
Visually attractive; quaint
Syno: Scenic (सुंदर दृश्य वाला)

443 **Pine** (V.) - (तरसना)
To yearn deeply
Syno: Crave (तरसना)

444 **Pirate** (V.) - (लूटपाट करना)~
To plunder or attack; to copy illegally
Syno: Raid (छापा मारना)

445 Plagiarize (V.) - (साहित्यिक चोरी करना) *[#R-2]*
To copy another's work and claim it as one's own
Syno: Copy (नकल करना)

446 Plebeian (Adj.) - (सामान्य जन का)
Relating to ordinary people; not refined
Syno: Common (सामान्य)

447 **Pleonexia** (N.) - (लोभ)
An excessive desire for wealth or possessions
Syno: Greed (लालच)

448 **Plow** (V.) - (खेत जोतना)
To turn over soil; to move forward steadily
Syno: Cultivate (खेती करना)

449 **Ploy** (N.) - (चाल)
A cunning plan to achieve something
Syno: Ruse (चाल)

450 **Plucky** (Adj.) - (साहसी)
Having courage and determination
Syno: Gutsy (निडर)

451 **Plummet** (V.) - (तेज़ी से गिरना) *[#R-2]*
To fall rapidly straight down
Syno: Decline (गिरना), Nosedive (तेज़ी से गिरना)

452 **Poise** (N.) - (आत्मसंयम)~
A graceful composure and self-assurance
Syno: Equanimity (समभाव)

453 **Poltroon** (N.) - (कायर)
A coward; a person without courage
Syno: Pusillanimous (कायर)

454 **Potentate** (N.) - (शासक)
A ruler with great power
Syno: Monarch (सम्राट)

455 Potentially (Adv.) - (संभाव्यतः)
With the capacity to develop or happen
Syno: Possibly (संभवतः)

456 **Prankish** (Adj.) - (शरारती)
Inclined to play tricks or pranks
Syno: Mischievous (शरारती)

457 **Prattle** (V.) - (बकबक करना)
To talk at length about trivial matters
Syno: Chatter (बकबक करना)

458 Precede (V.) - (पहले होना)
To come before in time or order
Syno: Antecede (पूर्व में होना)

459 Precipitation (N.) - (वर्षा)
The falling of rain or snow
Syno: Rainfall (वर्षा)

460 Preconception (N.) - (पूर्वधारणा)
An idea formed before having evidence
Syno: Notion (धारणा)

461 **Predisposition** (N.) - (प्रवृत्ति)
A tendency to behave in a certain way
Syno: Inclination (झुकाव)

462 **Predominantly** (Adv.) - (मुख्य रूप से)
Mainly or for the most part
Syno: Mainly (मुख्य रूप से)

463 **Preemptive** (Adj.) - (पूर्व-निवारक)
Done to prevent an expected action
Syno: Preventive (निवारक)

464 Prerequisite (N.) - (अनिवार्य शर्त)
Something required beforehand
Syno: Necessity (आवश्यकता)

465 Preservation (N.) - (संरक्षण)
The act of keeping something safe from harm
Syno: Conservancy (संरक्षण)

466 Presume (V.) - (मान लेना)
To suppose something is true without proof
Syno: Suppose (मान लेना)

467 Prevaricate (V.) - (टालमटोल करना)~
To avoid telling the truth directly
Syno: Deceive (धोखा देना)

468 **Prioritize** (V.) - (प्राथमिकता देना)
To arrange in order of importance
Syno: Organize (क्रमबद्ध करना)

469 **Prison** (N.) - (जेल)
A building where criminals are confined
Syno: Confinement (कैद)

470 **Privation** (N.) - (अभाव)
The lack of basic necessities of life
Syno: Deprivation (कमी)

471 Probable (Adj.) - (संभावित)
Likely to happen or be true
Syno: Likely (संभावित)

472 Procurement (N.) - (खरीद)
The act of obtaining goods or services
Syno: Acquisition (अधिग्रहण)

473 **Profusely** (Adv.) - (प्रचुर मात्रा में)
In large amounts; abundantly
Syno: Amply (भरपूर)

474 Propensity (N.) - (झुकाव)
A natural tendency to behave in a certain way
Syno: Bias (पक्षपात)

475 **Prorogue** (V.) - (स्थगित करना)
To discontinue a session of parliament
Syno: Adjourn (स्थगित करना)

476 **Proselytise** (V.) - (मत परिवर्तन कराना, धर्म बदलना)
To convert someone to a religion or belief
Syno: Convert (परिवर्तित करना)

477 **Protected** (Adj.) - (संरक्षित)
Kept safe or shielded from harm or injury
Syno: Secured (सुरक्षित)

478 **Protracted** (Adj.) - (दीर्घकालीन; अपेक्षा से अधिक लंबा)
Lasting longer than expected or usual
Syno: Extensive (लंबा फैला हुआ)

479 **Provocative** (Adj.) - (उत्तेजक)
Causing anger or strong reaction; arousing
Syno: Exciting (रोमांचक)

480 **Quibble** (V.) - (छोटी बातों पर बहस करना)
To argue about minor details
Syno: Argue (बहस करना)

481 Quick (Adj.) - (तेज)
Moving fast; happening in a short time
Syno: Expeditious (शीघ्र)

482 **Radiate** (V.) - (उत्सर्जित करना)
To emit energy; to spread out from a center
Syno: Emanate (निकलना)

483 **Ramp** (N.) - (ढलान)
A sloping surface
Syno: Incline (ढलान)

484 **Rancour** (N.) - (द्वेष) *[#R-3]*
A feeling of bitterness or resentment lasting a long time
Syno: Spite (द्वेष), Hatred (घृणा), Animosity (शत्रुता)

485 **Rapacity** (N.) - (लालच)
An aggressive greed
Syno: Greed (लोभ)

486 Rapport (N.) - (तालमेल) *[#R-2]*
A close and harmonious relationship
Syno: Harmony (सामंजस्य), Affinity (लगाव)

487 **Rashness** (N.) - (उतावलापन)
The quality of acting without careful thought
Syno: Hastiness (जल्दबाजी)

488 **Raspy** (Adj.) - (कर्कश)
Having a rough or harsh sound
Syno: Gravelly (कर्कश)

489 **Rebound** (V.) - (वापस उछलना)
To bounce back after hitting a surface
Syno: Recover (उबरना)

490 Reciprocate (V.) - (समान प्रतिक्रिया देना)~
To respond to an action with a similar one
Syno: Respond (जवाब देना)

491 Reconnaissance (N.) - (टोह, सैन्य सर्वेक्षण) *[#R-2]*
A military observation to gather information
Syno: Investigation (जांच), Survey (सर्वेक्षण)

492 **Recreancy** (N.) - (कायरता)
The quality of being cowardly or disloyal
Syno: Cowardice (कायरता)

493 Recuperate (V.) - (स्वस्थ होना)
To recover from illness or exhaustion
Syno: Recover (ठीक होना)

494 **Redress** (V.) - (सुधार करना)
To remedy or set right a wrong
Syno: Restore (पुनः स्थापित करना)

495 Refurbish (V.) - (नवीनीकृत करना)
To renovate and redecorate something
Syno: Renovate (नवीनीकरण करना)

496 Regulate (V.) - (नियंत्रित करना)
To control or maintain by rules
Syno: Control (नियंत्रण करना)

497 **Reiteration** (N.) - (पुनरावृत्ति, दोहराव)
The act of saying or doing something again
Syno: Repetition (दोहराव)

498 **Reject** (V.) - (अस्वीकार करना)
To refuse to accept or consider
Syno: Refuse (इनकार करना)

499 **Rekindle** (V.) - (पुनर्जीवित करना)
To revive or renew something
Syno: Reawaken (पुनः जागृत करना)

500 **Relieved** (Adj.) - (निश्चिंत, राहत पाया हुआ)
No longer feeling distressed or anxious
Syno: Reassured (आश्वस्त)

501 Remittance (N.) - (भेजी गई राशि)
A sum of money sent as payment
Syno: Payment (भुगतान)

502 **Repast** (N.) - (भोजन)
A meal
Syno: Meal (भोजन)

503 **Represent** (V.) - (प्रस्तुत करना)
To act for someone officially or show something in a particular way
Syno: Portray (चित्रित करना)

504 **Repressive** (Adj.) - (दमनकारी)
Preventing freedom of expression; oppressive
Syno: Oppressive (दमनकारी)

505 **Reprisal** (N.) - (प्रतिशोध) *[#R-2]*
An act of retaliation for injury
Syno: Retaliation (जवाबी हमला)

506 Rescue (V.) - (बचाना) *[#R-2]*
To save from danger or harm
Syno: Help (मदद करना)

507 Residue (N.) - (अवशेष)
A small amount remaining after the main part
Syno: Remainder (शेष)

508 **Resonant** (Adj.) - (प्रभावशाली, गुंजायमान)
Deep and continuing to sound; evocative
Syno: Deep (गंभीर)

509 Resonate (V.) - (गूँजना)
To produce a deep continuing sound; to evoke
Syno: Echo (गूँजना)

510 **Respond** (V.) - (जवाब देना)
To react or reply to something
Syno: Answer (उत्तर देना)

511 **Rigour** (N.) - (कड़ाई, सख्ती) *[#R-2]*
The quality of being thorough and strict
Syno: Strictness (कड़ाई)

512 **Ripe** (Adj.) - (पका हुआ)
Fully developed and ready to eat; mature
Syno: Mature (परिपक्व)

513 **Risky** (Adj.) - (जोखिम भरा)
Involving the possibility of danger
Syno: Dangerous (खतरनाक)

514 Rivalry (N.) - (प्रतिस्पर्धा)
A competition for the same goal
Syno: Competition (प्रतियोगिता)

515 **Roam** (V.) - (घूमना)
To move about without a fixed destination
Syno: Wander (भटकना)

516 **Root** (N.) - (जड़, मूल)
The basic cause or origin
Syno: Base (नींव)

517 **Rostrum** (N.) - (मंच)~
A platform for public speaking
Syno: Podium (मंच)

518 Ruminate (V.) - (मनन करना)
To think deeply about something
Syno: Think (सोचना)

519 **Saturnine** (Adj.) - (उदास)
Slow and gloomy in temperament
Syno: Glum (उदास)

520 **Saunter** (V.) - (टहलना)~ *[#R-2]*
To walk in a slow relaxed manner
Syno: Stroll (टहलना)

521 **Scamper** (V.) - (तेजी से भागना)
To run with quick light steps
Syno: Scurry (जल्दी में चलना)

522 **Scarcely** (Adv.) - (मुश्किल से)
Barely or almost not at all
Syno: Hardly (मुश्किल से)

523 **Schlep** (V.) - (मेहनत से ढोना)
To carry or drag with difficulty
Syno: Trek (कठिन रास्ते से जाना)

524 Scholar (N.) - (विद्वान)
A person devoted to academic study
Syno: Expert (विशेषज्ञ)

525 Scintillate (V.) - (चमकना)
To sparkle or shine brightly
Syno: Gleam (चमकना)

526 **Scorching** (Adj.) - (अत्यधिक गर्म) *[#R-2]*
Very hot
Syno: Searing (झुलसाने वाला), Torrid (अत्यधिक गर्म)

527 **Scribble** (V.) - (जल्दी-जल्दी लिखना)
To write or draw carelessly
Syno: Doodle (बिना सोचे-समझे बनाना)

528 **Secretive** (Adj.) - (छिपाने वाला)
Inclined to conceal feelings or information
Syno: Reticent (अल्पभाषी)

529 **Seething** (Adj.) - (क्रोध से भरा)
Filled with intense but unexpressed anger
Syno: Agitated (उत्तेजित)

530 **Semantic** (Adj.) - (अर्थ संबंधी)
Relating to meaning in language
Syno: Meaningful (अर्थपूर्ण)

531 **Sequel** (N.) - (अगली कड़ी)
A continuation of an earlier work
Syno: Continuation (निरंतरता)

532 Serendipitous (Adj.) - (आकस्मिक लाभ)
Occurring by happy chance
Syno: Accidental (आकस्मिक)

533 Shield (N.) - (ढाल)~
A protective barrier
Syno: Screen (आड़)

534 **Shocked** (Adj.) - (स्तब्ध) *[#R-2]*
Caused to feel surprised and upset
Syno: Appalled (स्तब्ध)

535 **Shrewdly** (Adv.) - (चालाकी से)
In a clever and perceptive manner
Syno: Astutely (चतुराई से)

536 Sieve (N.) - (छलनी) *[#R-2]*
A utensil with holes for straining
Syno: Filter (छलनी)

537 Silhouette (N.) - (छाया आकृति)~
A dark outline seen against a lighter background
Syno: Profile (रूपरेखा)

538 **Skimpy** (Adj.) - (बहुत थोड़ा)
Providing less than needed; scanty
Syno: Modest (थोड़ा)

539 **Slanderous** (Adj.) - (बदनामी वाला)~
Containing false statements damaging reputation
Syno: Abusive (अपमानजनक)

540 **Slap** (V.) - (थप्पड़ मारना)
To hit with the flat of the hand
Syno: Beat (मारना)

541 **Slavery** (N.) - (गुलामी)
The state of being owned by another person
Syno: Bondage (बंधन)

542 **Sleuth** (N.) - (जासूस)
A detective who investigates crimes
Syno: Detective (जासूस)

543 **Slumberous** (Adj.) - (निद्रालु)

Sleepy or inducing sleep
Syno: Lethargic (सुस्त)

544 **Smash** (V.) - (तोड़ना)
To break violently into pieces
Syno: Crush (कुचलना)

545 **Smother** (V.) - (ढककर बुझाना)~
To suffocate or extinguish by covering
Syno: Douse (पानी डालकर बुझाना)

546 **Smouldering** (Adj.) - (सुलगता हुआ)
Showing barely suppressed anger or desire
Syno: Simmering (सुलगता हुआ)

547 **Snag** (N.) - (अड़चन)
An unexpected difficulty
Syno: Hitch (रुकावट)

548 Sovereignty (N.) - (संप्रभुता)
The supreme power or authority
Syno: Administration (प्रशासन)

549 **Sparkle** (N.) - (उल्लास, चमक)
A flash of light; liveliness or vivacity
Syno: Cheerfulness (प्रसन्नता)

550 **Specious** (Adj.) - (भ्रामक)~ *[#R-3]*
Superficially plausible but actually wrong
Syno: Deceptive (धोखेबाज़)

551 **Spray** (N.) - (छिड़काव)
A liquid flying in small drops
Syno: Mist (धुंध)

552 **Spread** (V.) - (फैलाना)
To extend over an area; to distribute
Syno: Expand (विस्तार करना)

553 **Staggering** (Adj.) - (चौंकाने वाला)
Extremely surprising or hard to believe
Syno: Astounding (चकित करने वाला)

554 **Stalemate** (N.) - (गतिरोध)
A situation where no progress can be made
Syno: Deadlock (गतिरोध)

555 **Stamina** (N.) - (सहनशक्ति) *[#R-2]*
The ability to sustain prolonged effort
Syno: Endurance (सहनशक्ति), Power (शक्ति)

556 **Startled** (Adj.) - (चौंका हुआ)
Feeling or showing sudden shock or alarm
Syno: Surprised (आश्चर्यचकित)

557 Starvation (N.) - (भूखमरी)
The suffering or death caused by lack of food
Syno: Hunger (भूख)

558 **Starved** (V.) - (भूखा रहना)
To suffer from hunger
Syno: Deprived (वंचित करना)

559 **Stately** (Adj.) - (राजसी)
Dignified and impressive in manner
Syno: Distinguished (प्रतिष्ठित)

560 Statutory (Adj.) - (वैधानिक)
Required or permitted by law
Syno: Legal (कानूनी)

561 **Steal** (V.) - (चुराना)
To take without permission
Syno: Embezzle (गबन करना)

562 **Stellar** (Adj.) - (तारकीय, शानदार) *[#R-2]*
Relating to stars; exceptionally good
Syno: Starry (तारों भरा), Extraordinary (असाधारण)

563 **Stifle** (V.) - (दम घोंटना)
To suppress or hold back; to suffocate
Syno: Smother (दम घोंटना)

564 **Strafe** (V.) - (विमान से हमला करना)
To attack with gunfire from aircraft
Syno: Attack (हमला करना)

565 **Stylish** (Adj.) - (आकर्षक)
Fashionable and elegant
Syno: Fashionable (प्रचलित)

566 **Subliminal** (Adj.) - (चेतना की सीमा से नीचे)
Below the level of conscious awareness
Syno: Subconscious (अवचेतन)

567 Submit (V.) - (समर्पण करना)
To accept authority
Syno: Concede (हार मानना)

568 **Subversive** (Adj.) - (विध्वंसकारी)
Seeking to undermine authority
Syno: Insurgent (विद्रोही)

569 Subvert (V.) - (तख्ता पलट देना)
To undermine the power of an institution
Syno: Overturn (पलटना)

570 Supplement (N.) - (पूरक)
Something added to complete or enhance
Syno: Addition (जोड़)

571 **Suppliant** (N.) - (विनती करने वाला) *[#R-2]*
A person who asks humbly
Syno: Petitioner (याचक)

572 **Surrogate** (N.) - (प्रतिस्थापक)
A substitute
Syno: Substitute (विकल्प)

573 **Swell** (V.) - (सूजना)

To become larger or rounder; to increase
Syno: Enlarge (बढ़ाना)

574 **Sycophancy** (N.) - (चापलूसी)
The excessive flattery to gain advantage
Syno: Flattery (चापलूसी)

575 Sycophantic (Adj.) - (चापलूस)
Seeking favor through excessive flattery
Syno: Flattering (चापलूसी भरा)

576 **Tarnished** (Adj.) - (कलंकित)
Damaged in purity, reputation, or appearance
Syno: Tainted (दूषित)

577 **Taskmaster** (N.) - (कठोर प्रबंधक)
A person who assigns hard work to others
Syno: Chief (मुख्य)

578 **Tattered** (Adj.) - (फटा-पुराना)
Torn and in poor condition
Syno: Dilapidated (जर्जर)

579 **Teeming** (Adj.) - (भरा हुआ)
Full of or swarming with people or things
Syno: Busy (भीड़-भाड़ वाला)

580 **Temperance** (N.) - (संयम)
The moderation or self-restraint
Syno: Abnegation (त्याग, परहेज)

581 Tenor (N.) - (मूल भाव)
The general meaning or character of something
Syno: Purport (अभिप्राय)

582 Tenure (N.) - (कार्यकाल)~
The holding of an office; guaranteed employment
Syno: Incumbency (पदभार)

583 Terminal (Adj.) - (लाइलाज)
Relating to the end; causing death eventually
Syno: Incurable (न ठीक होने वाला)

584 **Testament** (N.) - (वसीयत)~
A will; evidence or proof of something
Syno: Will (वसीयत)

585 Think (V.) - (सोचना)
To use one's mind to form ideas
Syno: Contemplate (विचार करना)

586 **Thrift** (N.) - (किफ़ायत)
The careful use of money; economical management
Syno: Frugality (कमखर्ची)

587 **Throng** (N.) - (भीड़)
A large crowd
Syno: Crowd (भीड़)

588 **Tie** (V.) - (बाँधना)
To fasten with string or rope; to connect
Syno: Tether (बाँधना)

589 **Timbre** (N.) - (स्वर-गुण)
The quality of sound that distinguishes voices
Syno: Resonance (गूँज)

590 **Top-Notch** (Adj.) - (उत्कृष्ट)
Of the highest quality; excellent
Syno: Excellent (उत्कृष्ट)

591 **Tormented** (Adj.) - (उत्पीड़ित) *[#R-2]*
Experiencing severe physical or mental suffering
Syno: Distressed (परेशान), Agonised (पीड़ित)

592 **Torture** (V.) - (यातना देना)
To inflict severe pain
Syno: Excruciate (यातना देना)

593 **Totter** (V.) - (लड़खड़ाना)
To move unsteadily; to be about to collapse
Syno: Wobble (डगमगाना)

594 **Traduce** (V.) - (बदनाम करना)
To speak badly of someone falsely
Syno: Defame (बदनाम करना)

595 **Trailblazing** (Adj.) - (नया रास्ता बनाने वाला)
Introducing new ideas or methods
Syno: Pioneering (मार्गदर्शक)

596 **Trait** (N.) - (लक्षण) *[#R-2]*
A distinguishing quality or characteristic
Syno: Characteristic (विशेषता)

597 **Trajectory** (N.) - (मार्ग)
The path followed by a moving object
Syno: Path (रास्ता)

598 **Transgress** (V.) - (उल्लंघन करना) *[#R-3]*
To violate a law or moral standard
Syno: Trespass (सीमा लाँघना), Violate (उल्लंघन करना)

599 Transpire (V.) - (घटित होना; सामने आना)
To become known; to happen
Syno: Emerge (प्रकट होना)

600 **Truancy** (N.) - (अनुपस्थिति)
The act of staying away from school without permission
Syno: Absenteeism (अनुपस्थिति)

601 Tumultuous (Adj.) - (अशांत) *[#R-2]*
Loud and confused; turbulent

Syno: Violent (प्रचंड), Disorderly (अव्यवस्थित)

602 **Turbidity** (N.) - (धुंधलापन)
The state of being cloudy or murky
Syno: Murkiness (गंदलापन)

603 Turbulence (N.) - (अशांति)~ *[#R-2]*
A state of violent or unsteady movement; instability
Syno: Commotion (हंगामा), Disturbance (अशांति)

604 **Unabated** (Adj.) - (निरंतर)
Without any reduction in intensity
Syno: Incessant (निरंतर)

605 **Unadorned** (Adj.) - (सादा)
Not decorated; plain and simple
Syno: Austere (सादा)

606 Unassuming (Adj.) - (विनम्र) *[#R-2]*
Modest and not drawing attention
Syno: Modest (विनम्र)

607 **Unaware** (Adj.) - (बेख़बर)
Not conscious of something; ignorant
Syno: Oblivious (ध्यान न देने वाला)

608 Unceremonious (Adj.) - (अशिष्ट)
Rude or abrupt in manner without proper respect
Syno: Impolite (अशिष्ट)

609 **Uncompromising** (Adj.) - (अटल)
Unwilling to change one's position
Syno: Inflexible (अडिग)

610 **Underwrite** (V.) - (आर्थिक गारंटी देना)
To support financially; to accept insurance risk
Syno: Sponsor (आर्थिक सहायता देना)

611 **Universal** (Adj.) - (सार्वभौमिक)~
Relating to all people or things
Syno: Global (वैश्विक)

612 **Unorthodox** (Adj.) - (अपरंपरागत, असामान्य)
Not following traditional methods
Syno: Innovative (नवीन)

613 **Unprocessed** (Adj.) - (कच्चा)
Not treated or prepared; raw
Syno: Crude (कच्चा)

614 **Unscrupulousness** (N.) - (बेईमानी)
The quality of having no moral principles
Syno: Corruption (भ्रष्टाचार)

615 Unsuitable (Adj.) - (अनुपयुक्त)
Not right or appropriate for a purpose
Syno: Improper (अनुचित)

616 Untamed (Adj.) - (अनियंत्रित)
Not domesticated or controlled; wild
Syno: Wild (अनियंत्रित)

617 **Unyielding** (Adj.) - (अडिग)
Not giving way to pressure; firm
Syno: Firm (मजबूत)

618 **Utilize** (V.) - (उपयोग करना)
To make practical use of something
Syno: Harness (काम में लाना)

619 **Vagary** (N.) - (अनियमित परिवर्तन)
An unpredictable change or action
Syno: Whims (सनक)

620 Validation (N.) - (पुष्टि)
The act of confirming something as valid
Syno: Attestation (प्रमाणन)

621 **Vantage** (N.) - (लाभप्रद स्थिति, व्यापक दृष्टिकोण की स्थिति) *[#R-2]*
A position giving a good view; an advantage
Syno: Outlook (दृष्टिकोण), Perspective (दृष्टिकोण)

622 **Vapid** (Adj.) - (नीरस)
Lacking liveliness or interest; dull
Syno: Dull (नीरस)

623 **Vaulted** (Adj.) - (गुंबददार)
Having an arched roof or ceiling
Syno: Arched (धनुषाकार)

624 Vaunt (V.) - (डींग मारना)
To boast about something proudly
Syno: Boast (डींग हांकना)

625 **Vehemently** (Adv.) - (जोश के साथ)
In a forceful and passionate manner
Syno: Forcefully (बलपूर्वक)

626 **Vendor** (N.) - (विक्रेता)
A person or company selling goods
Syno: Seller (बेचने वाला)

627 **Verge** (N.) - (किनारा)
The edge or border of something
Syno: Threshold (दहलीज)

628 **Verify** (V.) - (सत्यापित करना)
To make sure something is true or accurate
Syno: Confirm (पुष्टि करना)

629 Veritable (Adj.) - (वास्तविक)
Used for emphasis; genuine
Syno: Genuine (वास्तविक)

630 **Versatility** (N.) - (बहुमुखी प्रतिभा)

The ability to adapt to many different functions

Syno: Creativity (रचनात्मकता)

631 **Verve** (N.) - (जोश) *[#R-3]*
A great energy, enthusiasm, and spirit

Syno: Buoyancy (उत्साह), Enthusiasm (उत्साह)

632 **Vilification** (N.) - (निंदा)
The act of speaking evil of someone

Syno: Denigration (निंदा)

633 **Vitriolic** (Adj.) - (कटु)
Filled with bitter criticism or hatred

Syno: Abusive (गाली गलौज)

634 **Vividness** (N.) - (स्पष्टता)
The quality of being bright or clear

Syno: Clarity (स्पष्टता)

635 **Waft** (V.) - (हवा में उड़ना)
To pass gently through the air

Syno: Drift (बहना)

636 **Wandering** (V.) - (भटकना)
To move without direction

Syno: Roving (घूमना)

637 **Warning** (N.) - (चेतावनी) *[#R-3]*
A statement that something bad may happen

Syno: Caution (चेतावनी), Presage (पूर्वसूचना), Caveat (चेतावनी)

638 **Warrior** (N.) - (योद्धा) *[#R-2]*
A brave or experienced fighter

Syno: Soldier (सैनिक)

639 **Whole** (Adj.) - (पूरा)
Entire or complete without any part removed

Syno: Complete (पूरा)

640 **Woe** (N.) - (दुःख)~
A state of great sorrow or distress

Syno: Misery (दुख)

641 **Worship** (V.) - (पूजा करना)
To show religious devotion; to admire greatly

Syno: Adore (आराधना करना)

642 **Wrest** (V.) - (जबरन ले लेना) *[#R-2]*
To forcibly take something from someone

Syno: Seize (जब्त करना)

643 **Wrestle** (V.) - (संघर्ष करना)
To struggle with someone

Syno: Battle (युद्ध करना)

644 **Yearly** (Adj.) - (वार्षिक)
Happening once a year; annual

Syno: Annual (वार्षिक)

*Total **644** Synonyms asked **745** times*

C11 Synonyms Practice Sets
(Based on Recent Other Exam Papers)

Practice Set - 1

Direction (Q. 1-10): Select the most appropriate synonym of the given word.

1 Ethereal
1) Mundane 2) Heavenly
3) Earthly 4) Fruitful

2 Languor
1) Ambition 2) Vim
3) Boredom 4) Bear

3 Rejuvenation
1) Regret 2) Revival
3) Death 4) Treat

4 Unaware
1) Conscious 2) Taught
3) Oblivious 4) Unwanted

5 Achievement
1) Fulfilment 2) Disaster
3) Failure 4) Loss

6 Preservation
1) Conservancy
2) Neglect
3) Destruction
4) Endangerment

7 Scorching
1) Snappy 2) Rigid
3) Torrid 4) Glacial

8 Emerging
1) Growing
2) Following
3) Sequencing
4) Ending

9 Hustle
1) Whistle 2) Humble
3) Hurry 4) Inertia

10 Pirating
1) Raiding 2) Sneezing
3) Seizing 4) Rehearsing

Practice Set - 2

Direction (Q. 1-10): Select the most appropriate synonym of the given word

1 Fortunate
1) Angry 2) Lucky
3) Careless 4) Sad

2 Deceased
1) Dead 2) Misplace
3) Unwell 4) Extended

3 Accommodate
1) Proof 2) Lodge
3) Inform 4) Feature

4 Turbulence
1) Easy Ease
2) Peace
3) Disturbance
4) Quietness

5 Vividness
1) Clarity 2) Mildness
3) Weakness 4) Ambiguity

6 Covertly
1) Affluence
2) Gulf
3) Surreptitiously
4) Amalgam

7 Defamation
1) Approval
2) Praise
3) Compliment
4) Calumny

8 Degeneration
1) Decay 2) Unattainable
3) Recreate 4) Delve

9 Aesthetic
1) Attractive 2) Plain
3) Hideous 4) Ugly

10 Worry
1) Promotion 2) Addiction
3) Anxiety 4) Loneliness

Practice Set - 3

Direction (Q. 1-10): Select the most appropriate synonym of the given word

1 Flurry
1) Fast 2) Soothe
3) Surge 4) Quick

2 Equip
1) Practice 2) Furnish
3) Affect 4) Influence

3 Devotee
1) Sentry 2) Delicate
3) Atheist 4) Worshipper

4 Trajectory
1) Path 2) Function
3) Force 4) Angle

5 Explosive
1) Innocent 2) Injurious
3) Eruptive 4) Delicious

6 Dossier
1) Folder 2) Rim
3) Drawer 4) File

7 Embarrassment
1) Dilemma 2) Neglect
3) Fault 4) Hardship

8 Enjoined
1) Debarred 2) Advised
3) Observed 4) Let

9 Demeanour
1) Attitude 2) Probable
3) Stable 4) Grave

10 Extinction
1) Disappearance
2) Spread
3) Expertise
4) Excellence

Practice Set - 4

Direction (Q. 1-10): Select the most appropriate synonym of the given word

1 Salutary
1) Adversarial
2) Lively
3) Beneficial
4) Solely

2 Lacunae
1) Characteristic
2) Cavity
3) Prominent Portion
4) Speciality

3 Garner
1) Collect 2) Distribute
3) Send 4) Co-Exist

4 Nuance
1) Nuisance 2) Distinction
3) Brightness 4) Information

5 Plagiarize
1) Create 2) Copy
3) Originate 4) Invent

6 Heathen
1) Natural 2) Old
3) Primitive 4) Barbarian

7 Redoubtable
1) Flimsy 2) Perplexing
3) Formidable 4) Voluble

8 Imperil
1) Destroy 2) Elaborate
3) Endanger 4) Influence

9 Relegate
1) Demote 2) Keep
3) Deny 4) Disapprove

10 Haze
1) Rain 2) Cold
3) Mist 4) Summer

Practice Set - 5

Direction (Q. 1-10): Select the most appropriate synonym of the given word

1 Disorient
1) Distract 2) Disburse
3) Dissolve 4) Distort

2 Bedevil
1) Deliver 2) Assist
3) Afflict 4) Relieve

3 Buffer
1) Limited 2) Intense
3) Sufficient 4) Intermediate

4 Contemporary
1) Kaput 2) Remote
3) Coincident 4) Disused

5 Vagaries
1) Calculations
2) Encounters
3) Whims
4) Chances

6 Brigand
1) Tactician 2) Marauder
3) Peasant 4) Diplomat

7 Devoted
1) Extended 2) Dedicated
3) Devastated 4) Gratified

8 Subliminal
1) Divine
2) Clear
3) Subconscious
4) Subjective

9 Snag
1) Hazard 2) Hitch
3) Surprise 4) Decoy

10 Draconian
1) Lenient 2) Clement
3) Benignant 4) Vicious

Practice Set - 6

Direction (Q. 1-10): Select the most appropriate synonym of the given word

1 Cautioned
1) Reasoned 2) Admitted
3) Warned 4) Refused

2 Resonant
1) Soft 2) Harsh
3) Deep 4) Quivering

3 Rebuffed
1) Took 2) Rejected
3) Criticized 4) Granted

4 Disowned
1) Accepted 2) Abandoned
3) Allowed 4) Questioned

5 Exhilarating
1) Peaceful 2) Prominent
3) Thrilling 4) Eager

6 Banished
1) Deported 2) Called Back
3) Accepted 4) Notified

7 Tarnished
1) Enhanced 2) Tainted
3) Restored 4) Assigned

8 Schlep
1) Trek 2) Beach
3) Rock 4) A Mineral

9 Doltish
1) Wise 2) Imbecilic
3) Clever 4) Precocious

10 sparkle
1) Lethargy 2) Cheerfulness
3) Blandness 4) Lifelessness

Practice Set - 7

Direction (Q. 1-10): Choose the word nearest in meaning to the given word.

1 Glance
1) Stare 2) Gaze
3) Glimpse 4) Flash

2 Abhorrent
1) Stinking 2) Violent
3) Jealous 4) Hateful

3 Universal
1) Admirable 2) Particular
3) Global 4) Versatile

4 Averse
1) Indifferent 2) Unwilling
3) Angry 4) Jealous

5 Literacy
1) Education 2) Respect
3) Industry 4) Mercy

6 Sleuth
1) Convict 2) Enemy
3) Detective 4) Policeman

7 Irreverent
1) Unnecessary
2) Disdainful
3) Erroneous
4) Irrelevant

8 Lobbying
1) Pressurising
2) Advertising
3) Advocating
4) Restricting

9 Earnest
1) Serious 2) Lonely
3) Odd 4) Grateful

10 Adoration
1) Liking
2) Worship
3) Admiration
4) Respect

Practice Set - 8

Direction (Q. 1-5): Select the option that is the nearest meaning of the given word.

1 Expeditious
1) Fast 2) Slow
3) Happy 4) Sad

2 Backlog
1) Surpass
2) Surmise
3) Innate
4) Inventory

3 Hastily
1) Hurriedly 2) Abruptly
3) Patiently 4) Carefully

4 Ostensible
1) Strong 2) Desirable
3) Apparent 4) Fateful

5 Fallacious
1) Erroneous 2) Logical
3) Sensible 4) Rational

Direction (Q. 6-10): Select the most appropriate synonym of the highlighted word in the given sentence.

6 Today, distance has become <u>insignificant</u> in terms of time, and travel for business, military or diplomatic reasons has become virtually immediate.
1) Consequential
2) Trivial
3) Substantial
4) Meaningful

7 After the scandal broke, the company's stock prices began to <u>plummet</u> overnight.
1) Rebound 2) Nose-Dive
3) Spearhead 4) Fluctuate

8 To prevent Tutu from <u>wandering</u> about on the train.
1) Carrying 2) Concerning
3) Flipping 4) Roving

9 No person is allowed to <u>transgress</u> beyond the line of control.
1) Offend 2) Seize
3) Trespass 4) Exempt

10 The annual inflation rate, coupled with the <u>unscrupulousness</u> of some employers, has led to a situation where many people are not able to earn enough to cover their.
1) Corruption 2) Hardwork
3) Faith 4) Honesty

Practice Set - 9

Direction (Q. 1-10): Select the most appropriate synonym for the underlined word in the given sentence.

1 The government's policies have <u>alienated</u> a large section of the

society.
1) Separated 2) Deactivated
3) Validated 4) Divorce

2 The Korean War lasted from 1950 to 1953, ending in armistice.
1) Dispute 2) Bloodshed
3) Hostility 4) Ceasefire

3 The movie star's biography is a glossy, sycophantic portrayal.
1) Cowardly
2) Domineering
3) Insolent
4) Flattering

4 That irksome window you can't open because it has a ripped screen.
1) Valuable 2) Instrumental
3) Tedious 4) Swinging

5 The politician was well-known for his ability to make a convincing public speech.
1) Implausible
2) Outrageous
3) Hushed
4) Persuasive

6 The mystery of India's ancient port of Muziris has captivated archaeologists for decades.
1) Fascinated
2) Distracted
3) Preoccupied
4) Consumed

7 Mr. Dattani had a trailblazing role in the world of Indian drama.
1) Living 2) Pioneering
3) Small 4) Big

8 She was goaded into starting the fight with the manager.
1) Provoked 2) Hated
3) Aided 4) Lied

9 The agenda of the meeting was to nullify the Reform Act of 1833.
1) Rectify 2) Ratify
3) Repeal 4) Amend

10 The new cameras provide a panoramic view, capturing number plates and tracking traffic movement.
1) Patchy
2) Precise
3) Circumscribed
4) Extensive

Practice Set - 10

Direction (Q. 1-10): Select the most appropriate synonym of the underlined word in the given sentence

1 Despite his accomplishments, he maintained an unassuming demeanour at the event.
1) Confident 2) Modest
3) Boastful 4) Pretentious

2 The government wants to spread the importance of education in rural areas.
1) Remote 2) Rustic
3) Cultured 4) Urban

3 It was certain that riots will precede civil war.
1) Intensify 2) Prolong
3) Cease 4) Antecede

4 Rana lay on the ground, clutching his chest, sure his heart was going to jump right out of it.
1) Bandaging 2) Gripping
3) Dropping 4) Wetting

5 Nina could hear the pots and pans clanking in the kitchen.
1) Rattling 2) Poking
3) Lingering 4) Dragging

6 Young people tend to be so mulish that elders find it difficult to strike a conversation with them.
1) Indiscipline
2) Pig Headed
3) Lazy
4) Animalistic

7 The sudden announcement of the company's bankruptcy had a profound (impact) on the stock market.
1) Influence 2) Gain
3) Detriment 4) Advantage

8 The army retreated after facing heavy resistance.
1) Fathom 2) Withdrew
3) Excuse 4) Flourish

9 The harsh and untamed horse galloped away, and the startled and confused rider fell off.
1) Nervous 2) Delicious
3) Obedient 4) Wild

10 The best that the paparazzi had managed to get was a smudgy silhouette about to board a jet.
1) Selfie 2) Profile
3) Autograph 4) Mugshot

Answer Key Practice Set - 1:

1 - 2	2 - 3	3 - 2	4 - 3	5 - 1
6 - 1	7 - 3	8 - 1	9 - 3	10 - 1

Answer Key Practice Set - 2:

1 - 2	2 - 1	3 - 2	4 - 3	5 - 1
6 - 3	7 - 4	8 - 1	9 - 1	10 - 3

Answer Key Practice Set - 3:

1 - 3	2 - 2	3 - 4	4 - 1	5 - 3
6 - 4	7 - 1	8 - 2	9 - 1	10 - 1

Answer Key Practice Set - 4:

1 - 3	2 - 2	3 - 1	4 - 2	5 - 2
6 - 4	7 - 3	8 - 3	9 - 1	10 - 3

Answer Key Practice Set - 5:

1 - 1	2 - 3	3 - 4	4 - 3	5 - 3
6 - 2	7 - 2	8 - 3	9 - 2	10 - 4

Answer Key Practice Set - 6:

1 - 3	2 - 3	3 - 2	4 - 2	5 - 3
6 - 1	7 - 2	8 - 1	9 - 2	10 - 2

Answer Key Practice Set - 7:

1 - 3	2 - 4	3 - 3	4 - 2	5 - 1
6 - 3	7 - 2	8 - 3	9 - 1	10 - 2

Answer Key Practice Set - 8:

1 - 1	2 - 4	3 - 1	4 - 3	5 - 1
6 - 2	7 - 2	8 - 4	9 - 3	10 - 1

Answer Key Practice Set - 9:

1 - 1	2 - 4	3 - 4	4 - 3	5 - 4
6 - 1	7 - 2	8 - 1	9 - 3	10 - 4

Answer Key Practice Set - 10:

1 - 2	2 - 2	3 - 4	4 - 2	5 - 1
6 - 2	7 - 1	8 - 2	9 - 4	10 - 2

C12 Antonyms (asked in Other Exams)

1 **Abatement** (N.) - (कमी)
The act of reducing or lessening something
Anto: Accumulation (संचयन)

2 **Abhorrence** (N.) - (घृणा) *[#R-2]*
A feeling of strong hatred or disgust
Anto: Admiration (प्रशंसा)

3 **About** (Adv.) - (लगभग; इधर-उधर)
In a general or approximate manner; in every direction
Anto: Exactly (सटीक रूप से)

4 **Absently** (Adv.) - (अनमने ढंग से)
In a distracted or inattentive manner
Anto: Alertly (सतर्कता से)

5 **Accelerated** (Adj.) - (त्वरित)
Increased in speed, amount, or extent
Anto: Retarded (मंद)

6 **Acceptance** (N.) - (स्वीकृति) *[#R-2]*
The act of receiving or agreeing to something
Anto: Denial (इनकार), Rejection (अस्वीकृति)

7 **Accidental** (Adj.) - (आकस्मिक)
Happening by chance; not planned
Anto: Intentional (जानबूझकर किया गया)

8 **Acme** (N.) - (शिखर, चरमोत्कर्ष)
The highest point or peak of something
Anto: Base (आधार)

9 **Activity** (N.) - (गतिविधि)
The state of being active or doing things
Anto: Dormancy (निष्क्रियता)

10 **Actual** (Adj.) - (वास्तविक)
Existing in fact; real
Anto: Hypothetical (काल्पनिक)

11 **Addition** (N.) - (जोड़)
The act of adding something; an extra part
Anto: Subtraction (घटाव)

12 **Adjudicate** (V.) - (निर्णय करना)
To make a formal judgment or decision
Anto: Equivocate (टालना)

13 **Adulteration** (N.) - (मिलावट)
The act of making something impure by adding inferior substances
Anto: Purification (शुद्धिकरण)

14 **Affection** (N.) - (स्नेह) *[#R-2]*
A feeling of fondness or liking for someone
Anto: Aversion (घृणा)

15 **Aggrandisement** (N.) - (आत्म-उत्कर्ष)
The act of promoting one's own importance
Anto: Humility (विनम्रता)

16 **Alarming** (Adj.) - (चिंताजनक)
Causing worry or fear due to potential danger
Anto: Reassuring (आश्वस्त करने वाला)

17 **Allurement** (N.) - (आकर्षण)
The quality of being attractive or tempting
Anto: Repulsion (विकर्षण)

18 **Altercate** (V.) - (झगड़ना)
To argue or dispute angrily
Anto: Coexist (मिलजुलकर रहना)

19 **Amateurish** (Adj.) - (अनाड़ी)
Done without skill or expertise
Anto: Competent (सक्षम)

20 **Ambiguity** (N.) - (अस्पष्टता) *[#R-2]*
The state of having more than one possible meaning
Anto: Certainty (निश्चितता)

21 **Ancillary** (Adj.) - (सहायक)
Providing support to the main activities
Anto: Primary (प्रमुख)

22 **Angelical** (Adj.) - (दिव्य)
Resembling an angel in beauty or purity
Anto: Diabolical (शैतानी)

23 **Animated** (Adj.) - (ऊर्जावान)
Full of energy or enthusiasm
Anto: Lifeless (निर्जीव)

24 **Appeasable** (Adj.) - (संतुष्ट होने योग्य)
Capable of being calmed or satisfied
Anto: Implacable (जो शांत न हो सके)

25 **Appellant** (N.) - (अपीलकर्ता)
A person who appeals a court decision
Anto: Respondent (प्रत्यर्थी)

26 **Append** (V.) - (जोड़ना)
To add something to the end of a document

[**#R** denotes repetition of word]

[E.g. in SN 20, #R- **2** denotes this word has been asked 2 times in other exams]

Anto: Remove (हटाना)

27 **Apprehensible** (Adj.) - (समझ में आने योग्य)
Capable of being understood or grasped
Anto: Incomprehensible (समझ से परे)

28 **Approbation** (N.) - (अनुमोदन, मंजूरी)
An approval or praise for something
Anto: Disapproval (अस्वीकृति)

29 **Arbitration** (N.) - (मध्यस्थता)~
The process of settling a dispute by a neutral party
Anto: Litigation (कानूनी मुकदमा)

30 **Aromatic** (Adj.) - (सुगंधित)
Having a pleasant and distinctive smell
Anto: Putrid (बदबूदार)

31 **Arrant** (Adj.) - (पूर्ण, बिल्कुल)
Complete and utter, typically in a negative sense
Anto: Partial (आंशिक)

32 **Artless** (Adj.) - (सरल)
Natural and simple, without any deception or guile
Anto: Crafty (चालाक)

33 **Ascetic** (Adj.) - (तपस्वी, संयमी)~
Practicing strict self-denial
Anto: Hedonistic (भोगवादी)

34 **Asceticism** (N.) - (तपस्या)
The practice of severe self-discipline and avoidance of pleasure
Anto: Excess (अधिकता)

35 **Askew** (Adv.) - (टेढ़ा; तिरछा)
In a crooked or tilted manner
Anto: Straight (सीधे)

36 **Aspiring** (Adj.) - (महत्वाकांक्षी)
Having ambitions to achieve something
Anto: Uninterested (उदासीन)

37 **Assumption** (N.) - (धारणा)
A thing accepted as true without proof
Anto: Proof (प्रमाण)

38 **Atrocious** (Adj.) - (भयानक)
Extremely bad or cruel
Anto: Admirable (प्रशंसनीय)

39 **Attach** (V.) - (संलग्न करना) *[#R-2]*
To fasten or join one thing to another
Anto: Detach (अलग करना)

40 **Attractive** (Adj.) - (आकर्षक) *[#R-2]*
Pleasing to look at; appealing
Anto: Repulsive (घृणित)

41 **Authority** (N.) - (अधिकार)
The power to give orders or make decisions
Anto: Weakness (कमजोरी)

42 **Baffling** (Adj.) - (हैरान करने वाला)
Impossible to understand; perplexing
Anto: Simple (सरल)

43 **Balk** (V.) - (हिचकिचाना)
To hesitate or refuse to proceed
Anto: Accept (स्वीकार करना)

44 **Barring** (Prep.) - (को छोड़कर)
Except for; unless there is
Anto: Including (समेत)

45 **Basic** (Adj.) - (बुनियादी)
Fundamental or essential
Anto: Complex (जटिल)

46 **Beacon** (N.) - (प्रकाशस्तंभ)
A light or signal used for guidance or warning
Anto: Obscurity (अस्पष्टता)

47 **Beatific** (Adj.) - (आनंदित)
Showing great happiness or blessedness
Anto: Sorrowful (दुखी)

48 **Beauty** (N.) - (सुंदरता)
A quality that gives pleasure to the senses
Anto: Ugliness (कुरूपता)

49 **Bedlam** (N.) - (कोलाहल)
A scene of chaos and confusion
Anto: Tranquility (शांति)

50 **Beguiling** (Adj.) - (आकर्षक)
Pleasantly attractive, often misleading
Anto: Repelling (प्रतिकर्षी)

51 **Beleaguered** (Adj.) - (दबाव में)
Surrounded or under constant pressure
Anto: Carefree (निश्चिंत)

52 **Besiege** (V.) - (घेराबंदी करना)~
To surround with armed forces; to overwhelm
Anto: Defend (बचाव करना)

53 **Bestiality** (N.) - (क्रूरता)
A savage or cruel behaviour like an animal
Anto: Gentleness (नम्रता)

54 **Biased** (Adj.) - (पक्षपातपूर्ण)
Unfairly prejudiced for or against someone
Anto: Impartial (निष्पक्ष)

55 **Blandishment** (N.) - (चापलूसी)
The use of flattering words to persuade

someone
Anto: Admonishment (फटकार)

56 Blithesome (Adj.) - (प्रसन्न)
Cheerful and light-hearted
Anto: Sullen (उदास)

57 **Blocked** (Adj.) - (अवरुद्ध)
Completely obstructed or closed off
Anto: Clear (साफ)

58 **Boggle** (V.) - (घबरा जाना)
To be startled or overwhelmed with amazement
Anto: Comprehend (समझना)

59 **Booming** (Adj.) - (तेज़ी से बढ़ता हुआ)
Growing rapidly and successfully
Anto: Declining (गिरता हुआ)

60 **Boon** (N.) - (वरदान)~ *[#R-2]*
A thing that is helpful or beneficial
Anto: Bane (अभिशाप), Curse (श्राप)

61 **Bore** (V.) - (ऊबाना)
To make someone feel weary
Anto: Charm (मोहित करना)

62 **Boundless** (Adj.) - (असीमित)
Unlimited or without limits
Anto: Finite (सीमित)

63 **Brainy** (Adj.) - (बुद्धिमान)
Very intelligent or clever
Anto: Stupid (मूर्ख)

64 Build (V.) - (निर्माण करना)
To construct or create something
Anto: Demolish (ढहा देना)

65 **Bulldoze** (V.) - (बलपूर्वक गिरा देना)
To clear land with force; to push through aggressively
Anto: Construct (निर्माण करना)

66 **Buoy** (V.) - (उत्साहित करना)~
To keep afloat; to encourage or uplift
Anto: Depress (निराश करना)

67 **Burgeoning** (Adj.) - (उभरता हुआ)
Beginning to grow or increase rapidly; flourishing
Anto: Dwindling (घटता हुआ)

68 Burlesque (N.) - (व्यंग्यात्मक नकल)
A comic or exaggerated imitation
Anto: Tribute (सम्मान)

69 **Burly** (Adj.) - (हट्टा-कट्टा)
Large and strong in build
Anto: Skinny (दुबला)

70 **Bustling** (Adj.) - (चहल-पहल भरा)
Full of busy activity
Anto: Quiet (शांत)

71 Cacophonous (Adj.) - (शोरगुल, शोरयुक्त) *[#R-2]*
Having harsh and unpleasant sounds
Anto: Melodious (मधुर)

72 **Canonise** (V.) - (संत घोषित करना)
To declare someone a saint officially
Anto: Abominate (घृणा करना)

73 Celebrity (N.) - (प्रसिद्ध व्यक्ति)
A famous person
Anto: Mediocrity (साधारण व्यक्ति)

74 **Childish** (Adj.) - (बचकाना)
Silly and immature like a child
Anto: Mature (परिपक्व)

75 **Chimerical** (Adj.) - (काल्पनिक)
Imaginary or fanciful; unrealistic
Anto: Feasible (संभव)

76 **Chivalry** (N.) - (वीरता और शिष्टाचार)
A quality of courtesy, honor, and gallantry
Anto: Discourtesy (असभ्यता)

77 Circumlocution (N.) - (घुमावदार भाषा)~
The use of many words when fewer would do
Anto: Conciseness (संक्षिप्तता)

78 Clemency (N.) - (दया)~
A merciful or lenient treatment of an offender
Anto: Severity (कठोरता)

79 **Clique** (N.) - (गुट)~
A small exclusive group of people
Anto: Outsiders (बाहरी लोग)

80 Coercive (Adj.) - (जबरन) *[#R-2]*
Using force or threats to make someone act
Anto: Gentle (नम्र)

81 Cognate (Adj.) - (समान उत्पत्ति वाला; समान मूल का शब्द)
Related by origin; a word related to another
Anto: Unrelated (असंबंधित)

82 **Cohesion** (N.) - (एकता, जुड़ाव)
The act of sticking together as a united whole
Anto: Disintegration (विखंडन)

83 **Collective** (Adj.) - (सामूहिक)
Done by a group
Anto: Individual (व्यक्तिगत)

84 **Commissioned** (Adj.) - (नियुक्त)
Authorized or assigned to perform duties

Anto: Unauthorized (अनधिकृत)

85 Compelling (Adj.) - (प्रभावशाली, प्रेरक)
Very strong and persuasive
Anto: Unconvincing (अप्रभावी)

86 **Compendious** (Adj.) - (संक्षिप्त)
Containing the essential facts in a brief form
Anto: Verbose (शब्दाडंबरपूर्ण)

87 **Complainant** (N.) - (शिकायतकर्ता)
A person who makes a formal complaint
Anto: Defendant (प्रतिवादी)

88 Compliment (N.) - (प्रशंसा)~ *[#R-4]*
An expression of praise
Anto: Insult (अपमान), Denunciation (निंदा)

89 Complimentary (Adj.) - (प्रशंसात्मक)
Expressing praise; given free of charge
Anto: Disparaging (निंदात्मक)

90 Component (N.) - (घटक)
A part or element of a larger whole
Anto: Whole (सम्पूर्ण)

91 Composure (N.) - (संयम) *[#R-2]*
The state of being calm and in control
Anto: Agitation (उत्तेजना), Turbulence (अशांति)

92 **Comprehensible** (Adj.) - (समझने के योग्य)
Able to be understood; clear
Anto: Unclear (अस्पष्ट)

93 **Concealed** (Adj.) - (छिपा हुआ)
Kept secret; hidden
Anto: Revealed (प्रकट किया)

94 **Conciliate** (V.) - (शांत करना)
To make peace or reconcile differences
Anto: Provoke (भड़काना)

95 **Condensation** (N.) - (संघनन)
The process of vapor turning into liquid
Anto: Evaporation (वाष्पीकरण)

96 Confession (N.) - (अपराध-स्वीकार)
The act of admitting a fault or crime
Anto: Denial (इनकार)

97 **Confidant** (N.) - (विश्वसनीय मित्र)
A person trusted with private matters
Anto: Opponent (प्रतिद्वंद्वी)

98 Confidence (N.) - (आत्मविश्वास)
A feeling of self-assurance; trust in someone
Anto: Diffidence (हिचकिचाहट)

99 **Conflation** (N.) - (एकीकरण)
The merging of two or more things into one
Anto: Split (विभाजन)

100 **Confute** (V.) - (खंडन करना, गलत सिद्ध करना)
To prove a statement or person to be wrong
Anto: Confirm (पुष्टि करना)

101 **Consanguine** (Adj.) - (रक्त-संबंधी)
Related by blood; having a common ancestor
Anto: Unrelated (असंबंधित)

102 Conscientiously (Adv.) - (ईमानदारी से)
In a careful and thorough manner
Anto: Carelessly (लापरवाही से)

103 **Consecrate** (V.) - (पवित्र करना)
To declare something sacred or dedicate to a purpose
Anto: Desecrate (अपवित्र करना)

104 Consistency (N.) - (स्थिरता)
The quality of being uniform or constant
Anto: Variation (परिवर्तन)

105 **Conspire** (V.) - (षड्यंत्र करना)
To plan secretly with others to do something wrong
Anto: Disassociate (संबंध तोड़ना)

106 Continual (Adj.) - (लगातार)
Happening repeatedly over time
Anto: Occasional (कभी-कभी)

107 **Conversant** (Adj.) - (परिचित)
Familiar with or knowledgeable about
Anto: Ignorant (अज्ञानी)

108 **Conversely** (Adv.) - (विपरीत रूप से)
In an opposite way or manner
Anto: Similarly (समान रूप से)

109 Cooperation (N.) - (सहयोग) *[#R-2]*
The act of working together for a common purpose
Anto: Division (विभाजन), Hostility (शत्रुता)

110 **Copy** (N.) - (नकल)
A thing made to be similar to another; a duplicate
Anto: Original (मूल)

111 Corporeal (Adj.) - (शारीरिक) *[#R-2]*
Having a physical body; material
Anto: Spiritual (आध्यात्मिक), Mental (मानसिक)

112 **Costly** (Adj.) - (महंगा)
Expensive; causing great loss or suffering
Anto: Economical (किफ़ायती)

113 **Coterie** (N.) - (मंडली)
A small exclusive group with shared interests

Anto: Loner (एकांतप्रिय)

114 **Counteract** (V.) - (प्रतिकार करना)
To act against and reduce the effect of
Anto: Exacerbate (और खराब करना)

115 **Coward** (N.) - (कायर)
A person who lacks courage
Anto: Hero (वीर)

116 **Criminate** (V.) - (आरोप लगाना)
To accuse someone of a crime
Anto: Vindicate (निर्दोष साबित करना)

117 Criticism (N.) - (आलोचना)
Expression of disapproval based on faults
Anto: Appreciation (प्रशंसा)

118 **Cruelty** (N.) - (क्रूरता)
The quality of causing pain or suffering
Anto: Kindness (दयालुता)

119 **Crumble** (V.) - (बिखरना, टूटना)~
To break into small pieces
Anto: Build (बनाना)

120 **Cumulatively** (Adv.) - (संचयी रूप से)
In a way that increases by successive additions
Anto: Individually (व्यक्तिगत रूप से)

121 Curable (Adj.) - (इलाज के योग्य)
Able to be healed or remedied
Anto: Terminal (प्राणघातक)

122 Decisive (Adj.) - (निर्णायक)
Settling an issue; showing determination
Anto: Doubtful (संदिग्ध)

123 Decorum (N.) - (शिष्टाचार) *[#R-2]*
Proper behaviour and good manners in society
Anto: Impropriety (अनुचितता)

124 **Defendant** (N.) - (प्रतिवादी, आरोपी)
A person accused of a crime in court
Anto: Plaintiff (वादी, मुकदमा दायर करने वाला)

125 **Deflated** (Adj.) - (पिचका हुआ, हतोत्साहित)
Having lost air or confidence
Anto: Inflated (फूला हुआ)

126 **Defray** (V.) - (खर्च उठाना)
To provide money to pay costs or expenses
Anto: Charge (वसूल करना)

127 **Degrade** (V.) - (अपमानित करना) *[#R-2]*
To lower in dignity or quality
Anto: Dignify (सम्मान देना), Promote (पदोन्नति देना)

128 Delete (V.) - (मिटाना)
To remove or erase something
Anto: Insert (सम्मिलित करना)

129 Deprived (Adj.) - (वंचित)
Lacking basic needs, rights, or opportunities
Anto: Privileged (विशेषाधिकार प्राप्त)

130 Despised (V.) - (तिरस्कार करना)
To feel contempt for
Anto: Loved (प्रेम करना)

131 **Destitution** (N.) - (दरिद्रता)
The state of extreme poverty
Anto: Affluence (समृद्धि)

132 **Determine** (V.) - (निर्धारित करना)
To establish or decide something firmly
Anto: Hesitate (हिचकिचाना)

133 Develop (V.) - (विकसित करना)
To grow or improve
Anto: Wane (घटना)

134 **Deviant** (Adj.) - (असामान्य)
Departing from normal or accepted standards
Anto: Typical (सामान्य)

135 Devilish (Adj.) - (शैतानी)
Resembling a devil; wicked or mischievous
Anto: Angelic (दैवीय)

136 **Dextrous** (Adj.) - (निपुण) *[#R-3]*
Showing skill and ease in physical movement
Anto: Inept (अयोग्य), Clumsy (अनाड़ी)

137 Diaphanous (Adj.) - (पारदर्शी)
Light and almost transparent; delicate
Anto: Opaque (अपारदर्शी)

138 **Differential** (Adj.) - (विभेदक)
Relating to a difference or distinction
Anto: Homogeneous (एकरूप)

139 **Digital** (Adj.) - (डिजिटल)
Relating to electronic technology using binary code
Anto: Analog (एनालॉग)

140 Dilapidated (Adj.) - (जर्जर)
Badly damaged or fallen into ruin
Anto: Renovated (नवीनीकृत)

141 **Disability** (N.) - (विकलांगता)
A physical or mental condition that limits activity
Anto: Capability (योग्यता)

142 **Disband** (V.) - (तितर-बितर करना)
To break up a group or organization

Anto: Assemble (इकट्ठा करना)

143 **Disconcerting** (Adj.) - (परेशान करने वाला)
Causing confusion, unease, or embarrassment
Anto: Soothing (शांत करने वाला)

144 **Discontinue** (V.) - (बंद करना)
To stop permanently
Anto: Resume (फिर से शुरू करना)

145 **Discount** (N.) - (छूट)
A reduction in price
Anto: Premium (अधिमूल्य)

146 Discrepancy (N.) - (भिन्नता)
A difference between things that should be the same
Anto: Consistency (संगति)

147 Discriminatory (Adj.) - (भेदभावपूर्ण)
Showing unfair treatment based on prejudicc
Anto: Equitable (निष्पक्ष)

148 Dishevelled (Adj.) - (अव्यवस्थित) *[#R-2]*
Having an untidy or messy appearance
Anto: Tidy (साफ-सुथरा)

149 **Disinclination** (N.) - (अनिच्छा)
A reluctance or lack of enthusiasm
Anto: Propensity (झुकाव, रुझान)

150 Disinterested (Adj.) - (निष्पक्ष)
Impartial and free from bias
Anto: Partisan (पक्षपाती)

151 **Dismantle** (V.) - (अलग-अलग करना)~ *[#R-2]*
To take apart piece by piece
Anto: Assemble (जोड़ना)

152 Disparage (V.) - (नीचा दिखाना)
To speak of as unimportant; to belittle
Anto: Applaud (प्रशंसा करना)

153 **Disparagement** (N.) - (निंदा)
The act of criticizing unfairly
Anto: Admiration (प्रशंसा)

154 **Disproof** (N.) - (खंडन) *[#R-2]*
A piece of evidence that shows something is not true
Anto: Proof (प्रमाण), Evidence (सबूत)

155 **Disreputable** (Adj.) - (बदनाम)
Having a bad reputation; not respectable
Anto: Prestigious (प्रतिष्ठित)

156 **Distinction** (N.) - (विशिष्टता) *[#R-2]*
A mark of excellence or honor; a difference
Anto: Insignificance (महत्वहीनता)

157 **Distinctly** (Adv.) - (स्पष्ट रूप से)
In a clear or unmistakable manner
Anto: Vaguely (अस्पष्ट रूप से)

158 Disturbance (N.) - (अशांति)
An interruption of peace or normal condition
Anto: Calm (शांति)

159 **Disturbed** (Adj.) - (विचलित)
Showing signs of mental illness or emotional distress
Anto: Peaceful (शांतिपूर्ण)

160 Divert (V.) - (मोड़ना)
To turn from one course to another; to amuse
Anto: Concentrate (केंद्रित करना)

161 **Dogma** (N.) - (मतवाद)
A set of beliefs held as unquestionable truth
Anto: Skcpticism (संशयवाद)

162 **Downsize** (V.) - (कम करना)
To reduce the number of employees or size
Anto: Expand (विस्तार करना)

163 Downtrodden (Adj.) - (शोषित)
Oppressed and treated badly by those in power
Anto: Respected (सम्मानित)

164 Duress (N) - (दबाव)
A threat, pressure, or coercion used to force someone
Anto: Volition (इच्छा)

165 **Dusk** (N.) - (संध्या, सांझ)~
The time of day just before night
Anto: Dawn (भोर)

166 **Dusky** (Adj.) - (सांवला)
Somewhat dark in colour; shadowy
Anto: Pale (गोरा)

167 **Educated** (Adj.) - (शिक्षित)
Having knowledge acquired through learning
Anto: Ignorant (अज्ञानी)

168 **Effusive** (Adj.) - (अत्यधिक भावुक) *[#R-3]*
Expressing feelings freely and openly
Anto: Reticent (संकोची), Reserved (संयमी)

169 **Egress** (N.) - (निकास)
The act of going out; an exit
Anto: Entrance (प्रवेश)

170 **Eloquently** (Adv.) - (वाक्पटुता से)
In a fluent and persuasive manner
Anto: Inarticulately (अस्पष्ट रूप से)

171 **Emancipated** (Adj.) - (मुक्त)

Freed from control or restriction
Anto: Restrained (नियंत्रित)

172 **Endanger** (V.) - (खतरे में डालना)
To put at risk or in danger
Anto: Protect (सुरक्षित करना)

173 **Endeared** (V.) - (प्रिय बनाना)
To make beloved
Anto: Alienated (अलग करना)

174 **Enervated** (V.) - (कमजोर करना) *[#R-2]*
To drain of energy
Anto: Energized (ऊर्जित करना), Pumped (उत्साहित करना)

175 **Enrich** (V.) - (समृद्ध करना) *[#R-3]*
To make richer
Anto: Impair(क्षतिग्रस्त करना)

176 **Ensuing** (Adj.) - (आगामी)
Happening or occurring afterward or as a result
Anto: Preceding (पूर्ववर्ती)

177 **Equanimous** (Adj.) - (स्थिर-चित्त)
Calm and composed in temperament
Anto: Anxious (चिंतित)

178 **Equipoise** (N.) - (संतुलन)
A state of balance between opposing forces
Anto: Imbalance (असंतुलन)

179 **Erratic** (Adj.) - (अनियमित) *[#R-5]*
Unpredictable and inconsistent in behaviour
Anto: Normal (सामान्य), Regular (नियमित), Consistent (सुसंगत)

180 **Escape** (N.) - (पलायन) *[#R-2]*
The act of fleeing
Anto: Encounter (मुठभेड़), Arrest (गिरफ्तारी)

181 **Established** (V.) - (स्थापित करना)
To set up
Anto: Demolished (ध्वस्त करना)

182 **Eulogise** (V.) - (प्रशंसा करना)~
To praise highly in speech or writing
Anto: Criticize (आलोचना करना)

183 **Evacuate** (V.) - (खाली करना)~
To remove people from a dangerous place
Anto: Fill (भरना)

184 **Excoriate** (V.) - (कड़ी निंदा करना)
To criticize someone severely
Anto: Commend (प्रशंसा करना)

185 **Execrable** (Adj.) - (घृणित)
Extremely bad or unpleasant
Anto: Excellent (उत्कृष्ट)

186 **Expatiate** (V.) - (विस्तार से चर्चा करना)
To speak or write at length about something
Anto: Summarise (सारांशित करना)

187 **Expert** (N.) - (विशेषज्ञ)~
A person with great knowledge
Anto: Amateur (नौसिखिया)

188 **Explicitly** (Adv.) - (स्पष्ट रूप से)
In a clear and direct manner
Anto: Equivocally (अस्पष्ट रूप से)

189 **Exploit** (V.) - (शोषण करना)
To use selfishly for profit
Anto: Protect (रक्षा करना)

190 **Exponential** (Adj.) - (घातांकीय)
Increasing rapidly at a growing rate
Anto: Gradual (क्रमिक)

191 **Exposed** (Adj.) - (उजागर) *[#R-2]*
Not covered or hidden from view
Anto: Protected (संरक्षित)

192 **Express** (V.) - (व्यक्त करना)
To convey a thought or feeling in words
Anto: Conceal (छिपाना)

193 **Extended** (Adj.) - (विस्तारित)
Made larger; enlarged in area, volume, or scope
Anto: Curtailed (सीमित)

194 **External** (Adj.) - (बाहरी)
Relating to the outside; coming from outside
Anto: Internal (आंतरिक)

195 **Extinguish** (V.) - (बुझाना)~
To put out a fire; to end something
Anto: Inflame (भड़काना)

196 **Fabrication** (N.) - (मनगढ़ंत)~
The act of inventing false information
Anto: Truth (सत्य)

197 **Failure** (N.) - (विफलता)
The lack of success; a person who fails
Anto: Success (सफलता)

198 **Faint-hearted** (Adj.) - (कायर)
Lacking courage or determination
Anto: Gallant (वीर)

199 **Falling off** (N.) - (कमी, गिरावट)
A decline or decrease in something
Anto: Improvement (सुधार)

200 **Favourable** (Adj.) - (अनुकूल)

Expressing approval; giving an advantage
Anto: Inauspicious (अशुभ)

201 **Fawning** (Adj.) - (खुशामदी)
Displaying exaggerated flattery or affection
Anto: Aloof (उदासीन)

202 **Feckless** (Adj.) - (निकम्मा)
Lacking purpose or determination; irresponsible
Anto: Responsible (जिम्मेदार)

203 **Fiasco** (N.) - (पूर्ण विफलता) *[#R-2]*
A complete and embarrassing failure
Anto: Success (सफलता)

204 **Fine** (Adj.) - (उत्तम)
Of high quality; thin or delicate
Anto: Coarse (खुरदुरा)

205 **Foolhardy** (Adj.) - (दुस्साहसी)
Recklessly bold or rash
Anto: Cautious (सतर्क)

206 Forbidding (Adj.) - (डरावना)
Unfriendly or threatening in appearance
Anto: Mild (कोमल)

207 **Fraternity** (N.) - (भाईचारा) *[#R-3]*
A brotherhood; a group with shared interests
Anto: Strife (संघर्ष), Quarrel (झगड़ा), Feud (पुरानी दुश्मनी)

208 **Fretting** (Adj.) - (चिंतित)
Constantly worried or anxious about something
Anto: Calm (शांत)

209 **Fulmination** (N.) - (कड़ी निंदा)
An expression of strong protest
Anto: Compliment (प्रशंसा)

210 **Furthest** (Adj.) - (सबसे दूर)
At the greatest distance
Anto: Nearest (सबसे निकट)

211 **Fussy** (Adj.) - (बहुत नखरे वाला)
Excessively particular or difficult to please
Anto: Careless (लापरवाह)

212 **Fuzzy** (Adj.) - (धुंधला) *[#R-2]*
Unclear or indistinct; covered with fuzz
Anto: Clear (स्पष्ट)

213 **Gainsay** (V.) - (इनकार करना) *[#R-2]*
To deny or contradict something
Anto: Accept (स्वीकार करना)

214 **Gentleness** (N.) - (कोमलता)
The quality of being kind and mild
Anto: Sternness (कठोरता)

215 Germane (Adj.) - (प्रासंगिक) *[#R-3]*
Relevant and appropriate to the subject
Anto: Irrelevant (अप्रासंगिक)

216 **Gimcrack** (Adj.) - (भड़कीला लेकिन घटिया)
Showy but cheap and poorly made
Anto: Outstanding (बहुत बढ़िया)

217 **Gingerly** (Adv.) - (सावधानी से)
In a careful or cautious manner
Anto: Heedlessly (लापरवाही से)

218 Gratifying (Adj.) - (संतोषजनक)
Giving satisfaction or pleasure
Anto: Dreary (नीरस)

219 **Guileless** (Adj.) - (निष्कपट)
Without deceit; honest and innocent
Anto: Wily (चालाक)

220 **Hale** (Adj.) - (तंदुरुस्त)
Strong and healthy
Anto: Debilitated (कमजोर)

221 Handsome (Adj.) - (सुंदर; आकर्षक)
Attractive in appearance; generous
Anto: Ugly (बदसूरत)

222 **Hardy** (Adj.) - (मजबूत)
Capable of enduring difficult or harsh conditions
Anto: Delicate (नाजुक)

223 **Hatred** (N.) - (घृणा)~
An intense feeling of dislike
Anto: Liking (पसंद)

224 Haughtiness (N.) - (घमंड)
The quality of being arrogantly proud
Anto: Humility (विनम्रता)

225 **Hearten** (V.) - (हौसला देना)
To make someone feel more cheerful
Anto: Depress (उदास करना)

226 Hectic (Adj.) - (व्यस्त)
Full of busy activity
Anto: Relaxing (आरामदायक)

227 Heretical (Adj.) - (विधर्मी)
Opposing accepted religious beliefs
Anto: Orthodox (रूढ़िवादी)

228 **Heroism** (N.) - (वीरता)
Great bravery or courage
Anto: Timidity (कायरता)

229 **Hirsute** (Adj.) - (रोयेंदार, बालदार)

Having much hair; hairy
Anto: Bald (गंजा)

230 Homogeneous (Adj.) - (समान प्रकृति का)~
Consisting of parts or elements that are all the same kind
Anto: Heterogeneous (मिश्रित, अलग-अलग प्रकार का)

231 Honesty (N.) - (ईमानदारी) *[#R-2]*
The quality of being truthful and sincere
Anto: Deceit (छल)

232 Humongous (Adj.) - (विशाल)
Extremely large in size or amount
Anto: Tiny (छोटा)

233 **Hurried** (Adj.) - (जल्दबाजी में)
Done more quickly than usual
Anto: Measured (सोचा-समझा)

234 **Hypocritical** (Adj.) - (पाखंडी)
Pretending to have virtues one does not possess
Anto: Sincere (ईमानदार)

235 **Hypothetical** (Adj.) - (काल्पनिक)
Based on a possible situation; imagined
Anto: Factual (वास्तविक)

236 **Icy** (Adj.) - (बर्फीला)
Extremely cold or covered with ice
Anto: Warm (गर्म)

237 Idol (N.) - (आदर्श व्यक्ति)~
A greatly admired person
Anto: Nobody (तुच्छ व्यक्ति)

238 Illusion (N.) - (भ्रम) *[#R-2]*
A false impression of reality
Anto: Reality (वास्तविकता)

239 Immature (Adj.) - (अपरिपक्व) *[#R-2]*
Not fully developed; childish in behaviour
Anto: Seasoned (अनुभवी), Mellowed (परिपक्व)

240 **Immersion** (N.) - (निमज्जन; पूर्ण संलग्नता)
The act of being deeply involved or submerged
Anto: Detachment (अलगाव)

241 **Impecuniousness** (N.) - (निर्धनता)
The state of having little money; poverty
Anto: Affluence (समृद्धि)

242 **Impenitent** (Adj.) - (अपश्चातापी)
Not feeling shame or regret for wrongdoing
Anto: Repentant (पश्चातापी)

243 **Imprison** (V.) - (कैद करना)
To put someone in prison
Anto: Release (रिहा करना)

244 **Improbable** (Adj.) - (असंभाव्य)
Not likely to happen or be true
Anto: Likely (संभावित)

245 **Inaccessible** (Adj.) - (अप्राप्य)~
Impossible to reach or enter
Anto: Accessible (सुलभ)

246 **Inauspicious** (Adj.) - (अमंगल)
Not promising success; unlucky
Anto: Propitious (शुभ)

247 **Incidental** (Adj.) - (गौण)
Happening as a minor part of something
Anto: Essential (आवश्यक)

248 **Incisive** (Adj.) - (पैना, स्पष्ट)
Impressively sharp, clear, and direct in thought or expression
Anto: Vague (अस्पष्ट)

249 Inclusive (Adj.) - (समावेशी) *[#R-3]*
Including all groups or elements
Anto: Exclusive (अनन्य)

250 Inconvenience (N.) - (असुविधा)
Trouble or difficulty
Anto: Comfort (आराम)

251 **Indeterminate** (Adj.) - (अनिश्चित)
Not exactly known or defined; vague
Anto: Definite (निश्चित)

252 **Indifference** (N.) - (उदासीनता) *[#R-2]*
Lack of interest or concern
Anto: Inclination (झुकाव), Affection (स्नेह)

253 Indulgent (Adj.) - (उदार)
Allowing excessive freedom; lenient
Anto: Strict (सख्त)

254 **Inequitable** (Adj.) - (अन्यायपूर्ण) *[#R-2]*
Unfair and not treating people equally
Anto: Fair (निष्पक्ष)

255 **Inequity** (N.) - (अन्याय) *[#R-2]*
Lack of fairness or justice
Anto: Fairness (निष्पक्षता)

256 **Infantile** (Adj.) - (बचकाना)
Relating to infants; childish
Anto: Mature (परिपक्व)

257 **Infatuated** (Adj.) - (मोहित)
Possessed with an intense but short-lived passion
Anto: Detached (अलग थलग)

258 Infectious (Adj.) - (संक्रामक)
Capable of spreading disease; spreading easily
Anto: Noncontagious (असंक्रामक)

259 Inflammatory (Adj.) - (भड़काऊ)
Arousing strong feelings of anger
Anto: Calming (शांत करने वाला)

260 Influential (Adj.) - (प्रभावशाली)
Having great influence on others
Anto: Insignificant (महत्वहीन)

261 **Infraction** (N.) - (उल्लंघन)
A violation of a law or rule
Anto: Compliance (पालन)

262 **Inhuman** (Adj.) - (अमानवीय)
Lacking human qualities; cruel
Anto: Compassionate (दयालु)

263 **Iniquitous** (Adj.) - (अन्यायपूर्ण) *[#R-2]*
Grossly unfair and immoral
Anto: Just (न्यायपूर्ण), Virtuous (चरित्रवान)

264 **Inserted** (V.) - (सम्मिलित करना)
To place inside
Anto: Removed (हटाना)

265 Insinuate (V.) - (इशारा करना)~
To suggest something unpleasant indirectly
Anto: Declare (घोषित करना)

266 **Instigator** (N.) - (उकसाने वाला)
A person who causes something to happen
Anto: Peacemaker (शांतिदूत)

267 **Insubstantial** (Adj.) - (तुच्छ)
Lacking strength or reality; flimsy
Anto: Appreciable (ध्यान देने योग्य)

268 **Insurgent** (Adj.) - (विद्रोही)~
Rising in active revolt against authority
Anto: Compliant (आज्ञाकारी)

269 Intellectual (Adj.) - (बौद्धिक)~ *[#R-2]*
Relating to the mind and understanding
Anto: Ignorant (अज्ञानी)

270 Intelligent (Adj.) - (बुद्धिमान)
Having good mental ability; smart
Anto: Dull (मंदबुद्धि)

271 **Intimidating** (Adj.) - (भयभीत करने वाला) *[#R-2]*
Frightening or threatening
Anto: Friendly (मित्रतापूर्ण)

272 **Intricacy** (N.) - (जटिलता) *[#R-2]*
The quality of being complex with many details
Anto: Simplicity (सादगी)

273 Irresistible (Adj.) - (अत्यंत सम्मोहक)
Too attractive or powerful to be resisted
Anto: Repulsive (घृणित)

274 **Jaundiced** (Adj.) - (पक्षपातपूर्ण)
Having a distorted or prejudiced view of things
Anto: Unbiased (निष्पक्ष)

275 **Jeer** (V.) - (मज़ाक उड़ाना) *[#R-2]*
To mock or ridicule loudly
Anto: Praise (प्रशंसा करना), Acclaim (प्रशंसा करना)

276 Joyful (Adj.) - (आनंदित)
Feeling or expressing great happiness
Anto: Sad (दुखी)

277 **Jubilate** (V.) - (जश्न मनाना)
To show great joy and triumph
Anto: Mourn (शोक मनाना)

278 **Jumbo** (Adj.) - (विशाल)
Very large
Anto: Miniature (लघु)

279 **Kindred** (Adj.) - (समान स्वभाव का, सजातीय)
Similar in kind
Anto: Unrelated (असंबंधित)

280 **Lack** (N.) - (कमी)
The state of being without something needed
Anto: Adequacy (पर्याप्तता)

281 Languish (V.) - (दुर्बल होना)
To become weak; to suffer neglect
Anto: Flourish (प्रगति करना)

282 **Laudatory** (Adj.) - (प्रशंसात्मक)
Expressing praise and approval
Anto: Derogatory (अपमानजनक)

283 **Lend** (V.) - (उधार देना)
To give something temporarily to another
Anto: Borrow (उधार लेना)

284 **Level up** (V.) - (स्तर बढ़ाना)
To increase to the higher standard or level
Anto: Regress (पीछे हटना)

285 **Libel** (N.) - (मानहानि)
A published false statement damaging reputation
Anto: Flattery (चापलूसी)

286 **Likeness** (N.) - (समानता) *[#R-2]*
The quality of being alike; a portrait
Anto: Difference (अंतर), Dissimilarity (भिन्नता)

287 **Liquidated** (Adj.) - (समाप्त)
Wound up; converted to cash
Anto: Flourishing (समृद्ध)

288 Loathsome (Adj.) - (घृणास्पद)
Causing hatred or disgust
Anto: Delightful (आनंददायक)

289 **Logically** (Adv.) - (तार्किक रूप से)
In a way that follows reason
Anto: Irrationally (तर्कहीन रूप से)

290 Lopsided (Adj.) - (एकतरफ़ा, असंतुलित)
Unequal on different sides; not balanced
Anto: Balanced (संतुलित)

291 **Lucre** (N.) - (अनुचित धन)
Money gained in a dishonourable way
Anto: Poverty (गरीबी)

292 **Magniloquent** (Adj.) - (शब्दाडंबरपूर्ण)
Using grand or pompous language
Anto: Terse (संक्षिप्त)

293 Malodorous (Adj.) - (बदबूदार)
Having an unpleasant smell
Anto: Fragrant (सुगंधित)

294 **Mar** (V.) - (खराब करना)
To spoil or damage something
Anto: Enhance (बढ़ाना)

295 **Maraud** (V.) - (लूटपाट करना)
To attack and loot violently
Anto: Defend (रक्षा करना)

296 **Marginalise** (V.) - (महत्वहीन बनाना)
To treat as insignificant or push to the edge
Anto: Integrate (एकीकृत करना)

297 **Marked** (Adj.) - (स्पष्ट, उल्लेखनीय)
Clearly noticeable; evident
Anto: Imperceptible (न मालूम पड़ने वाला)

298 Master (N.) - (मालिक)
A person with authority or skill
Anto: Slave (दास)

299 **Metaphorical** (Adj.) - (रूपकीय)
Using language in a non-literal way
Anto: Literal (शाब्दिक)

300 Microscopic (Adj.) - (सूक्ष्म)
So small as to be visible only with a microscope
Anto: Enormous (विशाल)

301 Middle (Adj.) - (मध्य; बीच में)
At an equal distance from extremes
Anto: Extreme (चरम)

302 **Minimise** (V.) - (न्यूनतम करना) *[#R-2]*
To reduce to the smallest amount
Anto: Enlarge (बढ़ाना), Increase (वृद्धि करना)

303 **Miracle** (N.) - (चमत्कार)
An extraordinary event attributed to divine power
Anto: Normality (सामान्यता)

304 Mischievous (Adj.) - (शरारती) *[#R-2]*
Playfully causing trouble
Anto: Obedient (आज्ञाकारी), Behaved (शिष्ट)

305 **Modesty** (N.) - (विनम्रता)
The quality of being humble; moderation
Anto: Ostentation (दिखावा)

306 Momentary (Adj.) - (अल्पकालिक)~
Lasting for a very short time
Anto: Lasting (टिकाऊ)

307 Momentum (N.) - (गति)
The force gained by movement; driving force
Anto: Stagnation (ठहराव)

308 Monologue (N.) - (एकालाप)~
A long speech by one person
Anto: Dialogue (संवाद)

309 **Mortify** (V.) - (लज्जित करना)
To cause great embarrassment or shame
Anto: Console (सांत्वना देना)

310 **Mount** (V.) - (चढ़ना)
To climb up
Anto: Descend (उतरना)

311 **Move** (V.) - (चलना)
To change position
Anto: Stay (रुकना)

312 **Muted** (V.) - (कम करना)
To make less intense
Anto: Amplified (प्रवर्धित करना)

313 **Mutinous** (Adj.) - (विद्रोही) *[#R-2]*
Refusing to obey authority; rebellious
Anto: Obedient (आज्ञाकारी)

314 **Noisy** (Adj.) - (शोरगुल भरा)
Making a lot of noise; loud
Anto: Quiet (शांत)

315 **Noteworthy** (Adj.) - (ध्यान देने योग्य)
Deserving attention; remarkable
Anto: Insignificant (महत्वहीन)

316 Obscurity (N.) - (अस्पष्टता)
The state of being unknown or unclear

Anto: Definiteness (स्पष्टता)

317 **Obverse** (N.) - (सामने का भाग)
The front side of a coin
Anto: Reverse (पीछे का भाग)

318 **Omnipotent** (Adj.) - (सर्वशक्तिमान)~
Having unlimited power; all-powerful
Anto: Impotent (शक्तिहीन)

319 Order (N.) - (व्यवस्था)
An arrangement; a command or instruction
Anto: Confusion (अव्यवस्था)

320 **Overdue** (Adj.) - (विलंबित)
Not having arrived or happened on time
Anto: Punctual (समयनिष्ठ)

321 **Pagan** (N.) - (पारंपरिक धर्म से अलग आस्था रखने वाला व्यक्ति) *[#R-2]*
A person holding religious beliefs other than major religions
Anto: Believer (आस्तिक)

322 **Pang** (N.) - (टीस)
A sudden sharp feeling of pain or emotion
Anto: Solace (सांत्वना)

323 **Parable** (N.) - (शिक्षाप्रद कथा)~
A simple story teaching a moral lesson
Anto: Fact (तथ्य)

324 Parallel (Adj.) - (समांतर)
Side by side and having the same distance apart
Anto: Divergent (अपसारी)

325 **Parch** (V.) - (सुखा देना)
To make extremely dry from heat
Anto: Wet (गीला करना)

326 Particular (Adj.) - (विशेष)
Specific rather than general; very exact
Anto: Vague (अस्पष्ट)

327 Passionate (Adj.) - (उत्साही)
Showing strong feelings or beliefs
Anto: Apathetic (उदासीन)

328 **Paunchy** (Adj.) - (मोटे पेट वाला)
Having a large belly
Anto: Slim (पतला)

329 **Pauperise** (V.) - (गरीब कर देना)
To make someone very poor
Anto: Enrich (समृद्ध बनाना)

330 Perfection (N.) - (पूर्णता)
The state of being without flaw
Anto: Deficiency (कमी)

331 **Perigee** (N.) - (उपग्रह की कक्षा का पृथ्वी से निकटतम बिंदु)
The point in orbit closest to Earth
Anto: Apogee (पृथ्वी से सबसे दूर का बिंदु)

332 Perspicacity (N.) - (समझदारी) *[#R-2]*
The quality of having keen mental perception
Anto: Dullness (मंदबुद्धि), Obtuseness (समझ की कमी)

333 Pertinacious (Adj.) - (हठी)~
Holding firmly to an opinion; stubborn
Anto: Yielding (झुकने वाला)

334 **Picayune** (Adj.) - (तुच्छ)
Of little value or importance; petty
Anto: Consequential (महत्वपूर्ण)

335 **Pioneering** (Adj.) - (अग्रणी)
Introducing or using new ideas, methods, or approaches
Anto: Traditional (परंपरागत)

336 **Pivotal** (Adj.) - (अत्यंत महत्वपूर्ण)~
Of crucial importance; central
Anto: Irrelevant (असंबंधित)

337 **Plague** (N.) - (महामारी)
A deadly disease
Anto: Reprieve (राहत)

338 **Plaintive** (Adj.) - (दुःखभरा) *[#R-2]*
Sounding sad and mournful
Anto: Gleeful (प्रसन्न), Cheerful (हंसमुख)

339 **Platonic** (Adj.) - (अशारीरिक)
Intimate but not sexual
Anto: Physical (शारीरिक)

340 Poverty (N.) - (गरीबी)
The state of being extremely poor
Anto: Prosperity (समृद्धि)

341 **Praiseworthy** (Adj.) - (प्रशंसनीय)
Deserving approval and admiration
Anto: Blameworthy (निंदनीय)

342 **Predator** (N.) - (शिकारी)~
An animal that hunts others; an exploiter
Anto: Prey (शिकार)

343 Preliminary (Adj.) - (प्रारंभिक) *[#R-2]*
Done in preparation for something main
Anto: Final (अंतिम)

344 **Prepossessing** (Adj.) - (आकर्षक)
Attractive in appearance
Anto: Unattractive (अनाकर्षक)

345 Pressing (Adj.) - (अत्यावश्यक)

Requiring immediate attention or action
Anto: Undemanding (कम माँग वाला)

346 **Pretense** (N.) - (दिखावा)
An attempt to make something appear true when it is not
Anto: Reality (सच्चाई)

347 Pretension (N.) - (दिखावटी दावा)
A claim to have a skill or quality
Anto: Humility (विनम्रता)

348 Pretentious (Adj.) - (बनावटी)~
Attempting to impress by affecting importance
Anto: Modest (विनम्र)

349 **Probate** (N.) - (वसीयत की पुष्टि)
The official process of proving a will valid
Anto: Intestacy (वसीयत के बिना मृत्यु)

350 **Proffer** (V.) - (पेश करना)
To offer something for acceptance
Anto: Withhold (रोकना)

351 Progression (N.) - (प्रगति)
The process of moving forward gradually
Anto: Relapse (गिरावट)

352 **Promptly** (Adv.) - (शीघ्रता से)
Without delay; immediately
Anto: Tardily (देरी से)

353 Provision (N.) - (आपूर्ति, प्रावधान)
The act of supplying something; a condition in an agreement
Anto: Removal (कटौती)

354 **Puerile** (Adj.) - (बचकाना)
Childishly silly and immature
Anto: Mature (परिपक्व)

355 Punishment (N.) - (दंड)
A penalty for wrongdoing
Anto: Reward (पुरस्कार)

356 **Purgatorial** (Adj.) - (कष्टकारी)
Relating to suffering or purification
Anto: Blissful (आनंदमय)

357 Purposefully (Adv.) - (उद्देश्यपूर्वक)
In a determined and intentional manner
Anto: Inadvertently (अनजाने में)

358 Pursuit (N.) - (पीछा)
The act of chasing; an activity one engages in
Anto: Avoidance (परहेज़)

359 **Query** (N.) - (प्रश्न)
A question
Anto: Answer (उत्तर)

360 **Quisling** (N.) - (गद्दार)
A traitor who collaborates with an enemy
Anto: Patriot (देशभक्त)

361 **Raid** (N.) - (छापा)
A sudden attack or search
Anto: Retreat (पीछे हटना)

362 Rancorous (Adj.) - (द्वेषपूर्ण)~
Characterized by bitterness and resentment
Anto: Forgiving (क्षमाशील)

363 Rapidly (Adv.) - (जल्दी)
Very quickly; at a fast rate
Anto: Slowly (धीरे-धीरे)

364 Readable (Adj.) - (पठनीय)
Easy or enjoyable to read
Anto: Illegible (अपठनीय)

365 Recession (N.) - (मंदी)
A period of economic decline
Anto: Boom (तेजी)

366 **Reclaim** (V.) - (पुनः प्राप्त करना)
To retrieve or recover something; to convert land
Anto: Desert (छोड़ देना)

367 Recognisable (Adj.) - (पहचानने योग्य)
Able to be identified or known
Anto: Imperceptible (न मालूम पड़ने वाला)

368 **Recollection** (N.) - (स्मरण)
The action of remembering something
Anto: Forgetfulness (भूलने की आदत)

369 **Reduce** (V.) - (कम करना)
To make smaller in size or amount
Anto: Amplify (बढ़ाना)

370 Refusal (N.) - (इनकार) *[#R-2]*
The act of declining to accept or do something
Anto: Consent (सहमति)

371 **Related** (Adj.) - (संबंधित)
Connected by relationship, similarity, or association
Anto: Unlike (अलग)

372 **Reluctance** (N.) - (अनिच्छा) *[#R-3]*
An unwillingness or hesitation to do something
Anto: Eagerness (उत्सुकता), Enthusiasm (उत्साह)

373 Reluctantly (Adv.) - (अनिच्छा से)
In an unwilling or hesitant manner
Anto: Willingly (खुशी से)

374 Remonstrate (V.) - (विरोध करना) *[#R-2]*

To make a forceful protest
Anto: Agree (स्वीकार करना), Laud (प्रशंसा)

375 Remuneration (N.) - (पारिश्रमिक)~
The payment for work or services
Anto: Nonpayment (भुगतान न होना)

376 **Repellent** (Adj.) - (अरुचिकर)
Causing strong disgust or aversion
Anto: Attractive (आकर्षक)

377 **Reprehensible** (Adj.) - (निंदनीय)
Deserving condemnation; very bad
Anto: Commendable (प्रशंसनीय)

378 **Restiveness** (N.) - (बेचैनी)
The quality of being restless or uneasy
Anto: Docility (आज्ञाकारिता)

379 Resuscitate (V.) - (पुनर्जीवित करना)
To revive from unconsciousness
Anto: Extinguish (बुझाना)

380 **Retrograde** (Adj.) - (पीछे जाने वाला (अवनतिशील))
Moving backward; becoming worse
Anto: Progressive (प्रगतिशील)

381 Reverberate (V.) - (गूंजना) *[#R-2]*
To be repeated as an echo; to have lasting effect
Anto: Quieten (शांत करना)

382 Reverse (V.) - (उलटना)
To move backward; to change to the opposite
Anto: Advance (आगे बढ़ना)

383 **Revival** (N.) - (पुनर्जीवन)
The act of bringing back to life or use
Anto: Extinction (विलुप्ति)

384 **Revolting** (Adj.) - (घिनौना)
Causing intense disgust
Anto: Delightful (मनोहर)

385 **Rickety** (Adj.) - (अस्थिर)
Poorly made and likely to collapse
Anto: Stable (स्थिर)

386 **Rimy** (Adj.) - (बर्फ से ढका हुआ)
Covered with frost
Anto: Thawed (पिघला हुआ)

387 **Romantic** (Adj.) - (प्रेमपूर्ण, कल्पनाशील)
Relating to love; idealistic
Anto: Realistic (यथार्थवादी)

388 **Rudely** (Adv.) - (अशिष्टता से)
In an impolite or offensive manner
Anto: Politely (विनम्रतापूर्वक)

389 **Run-down** (Adj.) - (थका हुआ, जर्जर) *[#R-2]*
Exhausted or in poor condition
Anto: Energetic (ऊर्जावान)

390 **Salvation** (N.) - (मोक्ष)
The act of being saved from harm or sin
Anto: Damnation (नरकवास)

391 Sartorial (Adj.) - (पोशाक सौंदर्य संबंधी)
Relating to clothing or tailoring
Anto: Slovenly (मैला-कुचैला)

392 **Scathing** (Adj.) - (तीखा, कटु)
Expressing very strong criticism or scorn
Anto: Gentle (नरम)

393 **Scintilla** (N.) - (नाममात्र)
A tiny trace or amount of something
Anto: Abundance (प्रचुरता)

394 **Scornful** (Adj.) - (तिरस्कारपूर्ण) *[#R-2]*
Feeling or expressing contempt
Anto: Courteous (विनम्र)

395 **Seamlessly** (Adv.) - (बिना रुकावट)
In a smooth and continuous manner
Anto: Intermittently (रुक-रुक कर)

396 **Secret** (Adj.) - (गुप्त)
Kept hidden from others; confidential
Anto: Open (खुला)

397 **Sedentary** (Adj.) - (बैठा रहने वाला) *[#R-2]*
Involving much sitting and little physical activity
Anto: Active (सक्रिय)

398 **Senility** (N.) - (बुढ़ापा (मानसिक क्षीणता))
The condition of mental decline in old age
Anto: Youthfulness (युवापन)

399 **Sensitivity** (N.) - (संवेदनशीलता)
The quality of being easily affected or hurt
Anto: Imperviousness (कठोरता)

400 Sentence (V.) - (सज़ा देना)
To officially state the punishment decided by a court
Anto: Acquit (बरी करना)

401 **Sentinel** (N.) - (पहरेदार)
A guard or watchman
Anto: Intruder (घुसपैठिया)

402 Separate (V.) - (विभाजित करना)
To divide
Anto: Conjoin (जोड़ना)

403 **Servitude** (N.) - (गुलामी)
The state of being a slave or servant

Anto: Freedom (स्वतंत्रता)

404 **Set Free** (V.) - (मुक्त करना)
To release from captivity or restraint
Anto: Confine (बंद करना)

405 **Shattered** (V.) - (तोड़ देना)
To break into pieces
Anto: Patched (जोड़ना)

406 Shortage (N.) - (कमी)
A lack or scarcity of something needed
Anto: Abundance (प्रचुरता)

407 Significantly (Adv.) - (महत्वपूर्ण रूप से)
In a way that is important or meaningful
Anto: Minimally (नाममात्र)

408 **Sketchy** (Adj.) - (अपूर्ण)
Not thorough or detailed; questionable
Anto: Complete (पूर्ण)

409 **Slimy** (Adj.) - (चिपचिपा, घिनौना)
Covered with slime; disgustingly dishonest
Anto: Clean (साफ)

410 **Slump** (V.) - (गिर पड़ना)
To fall or sink down heavily
Anto: Rise (उठना)

411 **Smitten** (Adj.) - (मोहित)
Strongly attracted to someone or something
Anto: Unaffected (अप्रभावित)

412 **Sobering** (Adj.) - (गंभीर)
Making a person serious and aware
Anto: Trivial (मामूली)

413 **Sojourner** (N.) - (अस्थायी यात्री)
A person who stays temporarily in a place
Anto: Resident (स्थायी निवासी)

414 Spoil (V.) - (खराब करना) *[#R-2]*
To damage or ruin something
Anto: Embellish (सजाना)

415 Spoilage (N.) - (खराबी)
The decay or rotting of food
Anto: Conservation (संरक्षण)

416 **Squeamish** (Adj.) - (जल्दी घिन करने वाला)
Easily disgusted or made uncomfortable
Anto: Unflinching (अविचलित)

417 **Stained** (Adj.) - (दागदार)
Marked with spots or discoloration
Anto: Spotless (बेदाग)

418 Start (V.) - (शुरू करना)
To begin
Anto: Halt (रोकना)

419 **Stereotypical** (Adj.) - (रूढ़िबद्ध)
Following a typical or fixed pattern
Anto: Unconventional (अपरंपरागत)

420 **Stimulant** (N.) - (उत्तेजक)
A substance that increases activity or energy
Anto: Tranquilizer (प्रशांतक)

421 **Stimulating** (Adj.) - (उत्तेजक)
Encouraging or arousing interest or enthusiasm
Anto: Boring (उबाऊ)

422 **Strait** (Adj.) - (संकीर्ण)
Narrow or restricted; tight
Anto: Wide (चौड़ा)

423 **Striking** (Adj.) - (आकर्षक)
Attracting attention by being unusual or prominent
Anto: Unimpressive (प्रभावहीन)

424 **Stumble** (V.) - (ठोकर खाना)
To trip while walking
Anto: Stride (लंबे कदमों से चलना)

425 Stupefy (V.) - (चकित कर देना)
To make someone unable to think clearly
Anto: Enliven (जीवंत करना)

426 **Stupidity** (N.) - (मूर्खता)
The quality of lacking intelligence
Anto: Acumen (सूझबूझ)

427 **Subjugation** (N.) - (अधीनता)
The act of bringing under control or domination
Anto: Independence (स्वतंत्रता)

428 Subsequently (Adv.) - (बाद में)
After a particular time
Anto: Formerly (पहले)

429 Subservient (Adj.) - (आज्ञाकारी)~
Prepared to obey others without question
Anto: Aggressive (आक्रामक)

430 Supporter (N.) - (समर्थक)
A person who approves of and encourages
Anto: Critic (आलोचक)

431 **Swiftly** (Adv.) - (तेजी से)
In a fast and sudden manner
Anto: Leisurely (आराम से)

432 **Swingeing** (Adj.) - (कठोर)
Severe or extreme in effect
Anto: Mild (हल्का)

433 Sympathetic (Adj.) - (दयालु)
Feeling or showing concern for others
Anto: Antagonistic (शत्रुतापूर्ण)

434 **Synthesize** (V.) - (संयोजित करना)
To combine elements into a coherent whole
Anto: Separate (अलग करना)

435 **Tangentially** (Adv.) - (ऊपरी तौर से)
In a way that only slightly relates to something
Anto: Directly (सीधे तौर पर)

436 **Thick Skinned** (Adj.) - (गैर-संवेदनशील)
Not easily hurt by criticism
Anto: Sensitive (संवेदनशील)

437 **Timidity** (N.) - (डरपोकपन)
The quality of being easily frightened; shyness
Anto: Boldness (साहस)

438 **Torment** (N.) - (पीड़ा)
Severe suffering
Anto: Comfort (आराम)

439 **Tout** (V.) - (प्रचार करना)
To promote or praise enthusiastically
Anto: Criticise (आलोचना करना)

440 **Tractable** (Adj.) - (आज्ञाकारी)
Easy to control or influence
Anto: Stubborn (जिद्दी)

441 **Transfer** (V.) - (स्थानांतरित करना)
To move from one place to another
Anto: Retain (बनाए रखना)

442 **Treat** (V.) - (व्यवहार करना)
To behave towards someone in a certain way; to give medical care
Anto: Afflict (पीड़ित करना)

443 **Tricky** (Adj.) - (कठिन, पेचीदा)
Difficult to deal with; requiring skill
Anto: Effortless (सहज)

444 Ultimate (Adj.) - (अंतिम)
Being the final or most extreme point of something
Anto: Initial (प्रारंभिक)

445 **Unbigoted** (Adj.) - (उदार)
Free from prejudice; tolerant
Anto: Intolerant (कट्टर)

446 **Unbridled** (Adj.) - (अनियंत्रित)
Uncontrolled or unrestricted
Anto: Controlled (नियंत्रित)

447 **Undeterred** (Adj.) - (अटल)
Not discouraged by difficulties
Anto: Discouraged (हतोत्साहित)

448 **Undulating** (Adj.) - (लहरदार)
Moving with a smooth wavelike motion
Anto: Flat (सपाट)

449 **Uneasy** (Adj.) - (बेचैन)
Feeling anxious or uncomfortable
Anto: Comfortable (आरामदायक)

450 **Unequal** (Adj.) - (असमान)
Not the same in size or value; unfair
Anto: Commensurate (अनुरूप)

451 **Unfold** (V.) - (खोलना)
To open or spread out; to reveal
Anto: Conceal (छिपाना)

452 **Unfriendly** (Adj.) - (अमित्रतापूर्ण)
Not pleasant or kind
Anto: Warm (स्नेही)

453 **Ungainly** (Adj.) - (भद्दा) *[#R-2]*
Clumsy and awkward in movement
Anto: Graceful (सुंदर), Attractive (आकर्षक)

454 **Unhinged** (Adj.) - (असंतुलित)
Mentally unstable or irrational
Anto: Rational (तर्कसंगत)

455 **Unite** (V.) - (एकजुट होना)
To come together for a common purpose
Anto: Separate (अलग होना)

456 **Unjust** (Adj.) - (अन्यायी) *[#R-2]*
Not fair or right
Anto: Fair-Minded (न्यायप्रिय), Just (न्यायसंगत)

457 **Unknown** (Adj.) - (अपरिचित)
Not known or familiar
Anto: Renowned (प्रसिद्ध)

458 **Unlikely** (Adj.) - (असंभावित)
Not likely to happen or be true
Anto: Probable (संभावित)

459 Unmindful (Adj.) - (बेखबर)
Not conscious or aware of
Anto: Vigilant (सतर्क)

460 Unnecessary (Adj.) - (अनावश्यक)
Not needed; more than required
Anto: Vital (आवश्यक)

461 **Unrest** (N.) - (अशांति)
A state of dissatisfaction and disturbance
Anto: Calm (शांति)

462 **Untrammelled** (Adj.) - (स्वतंत्र)
Not restricted or hampered

Anto: Restricted (प्रतिबंधित)

463 Unveil (V.) - (प्रकट करना)
To remove a covering; to reveal
Anto: Conceal (छिपाना)

464 **Unviable** (Adj.) - (असंभव)
Not capable of working successfully
Anto: Feasible (संभव)

465 **Unwind** (V.) - (आराम करना, लपेट खोलना)
To relax after tension; to undo something twisted
Anto: Strain (तनाव देना)

466 **Urgent** (Adj.) - (अत्यावश्यक)
Requiring immediate attention
Anto: Trivial (मामूली)

467 **Variation** (N.) - (विविधता)
A change or difference in condition
Anto: Uniformity (समानता)

468 **Varied** (Adj.) - (विविध)
Having many different types or elements
Anto: Monotonous (एकरस/नीरस)

469 **Veil** (V.) - (छुपाना, ढकना)
To cover or conceal
Anto: Show (दिखाना)

470 **Vestibule** (N.) - (प्रवेशद्वार)
An entrance hall or passage
Anto: Exit (निकास)

471 **Vexation** (N.) - (परेशानी)
The state of being annoyed or worried
Anto: Comfort (आराम)

472 **Vexing** (V.) - (परेशान करना)
To cause annoyance
Anto: Placating (शांत करना)

473 Vicissitude (N.) - (उतार चढ़ाव)
A change in circumstances or fortune
Anto: Stability (स्थिरता)

474 Victory (N.) - (विजय) *[#R-3]*
Success in a battle or competition
Anto: Defeat (हार)

475 Vigorously (Adv.) - (जोरदार ढंग से)
In a strong and active manner
Anto: Softly (धीरे से)

476 **Vigour** (N.) - (जोश)~
Physical strength and good health; energy
Anto: Lethargy (सुस्ती)

477 Violence (N.) - (हिंसा)
Behaviour involving physical force to hurt
Anto: Restraint (संयम)

478 Volatility (N.) - (अस्थिरता)
The quality of changing rapidly and unpredictably
Anto: Stability (स्थिरता)

479 **Waive** (V.) - (त्यागना)
To refrain from insisting on a right
Anto: Claim (दावा करना)

480 **Warily** (Adv.) - (सावधानी से)
In a cautious and watchful manner
Anto: Carelessly (लापरवाही से)

481 **Warmer** (Adj.) - (ज़्यादा गर्म)
Comparative for warm; slightly hot
Anto: Colder (ज़्यादा ठंडा)

482 **Waylay** (V.) - (घात लगाकर रोकना)
To stop and attack someone; to intercept
Anto: Permit (अनुमति देना)

483 Welfare (N.) - (कल्याण, सुख)
The health and happiness of a person or group
Anto: Misery (दुख)

484 **Wield** (V.) - (धारण करना, प्रयोग करना)
To hold and use a weapon or tool
Anto: Relinquish (त्यागना)

485 **Willing** (Adj.) - (इच्छुक)
Ready and eager to do something
Anto: Reluctant (अनिच्छुक)

486 **Woebegone** (Adj.) - (दुखी)
Looking sad or miserable
Anto: Cheerful (प्रसन्न)

487 **Woeful** (Adj.) - (दुखी)
Characterized by sorrow; very bad
Anto: Cheerful (प्रसन्न)

488 **Yesteryear** (N.) - (बीता हुआ समय)
A period of time in the past
Anto: Future (भविष्य)

*Total **488** Antonyms asked **563** times*

C13 Antonyms Practice Sets (Based on Recent Other Exam Papers)

Practice Set - 1

Direction (Q. 1-10): Identify the most appropriate ANTONYM of the given word.

1 Significantly
1) Deeply
2) Largely
3) Tremendously
4) Minimally

2 Inexorable
1) Relentless 2) Inevitable
3) Relenting 4) Unavoidable

3 Rejuvenation
1) Exhaustion
2) Preservation
3) Stimulation
4) Vitality

4 Prompted
1) Facilitated
2) Accelerated
3) Encouraged
4) Discouraged

5 Inaccessible
1) Obstructed
2) Remote
3) Difficult
4) Convenient

6 Minimise
1) Diminish 2) Equal
3) Increase 4) Lower

7 Tranquillity
1) Chaos 2) Peace
3) Calmness 4) Serenity

8 Explicitly
1) Recklessly
2) Diligently
3) Equivocally
4) Occasionally

9 Tricky
1) Subtle 2) Intricate
3) Sublime 4) Effortless

10 Elevated
1) High 2) Raised
3) Lowered 4) Increased

Practice Set - 2

Direction (Q. 1-10): Identify the most appropriate ANTONYM of the given word.

1 Reclaimed
1) Deserted 2) Noble
3) Intrigue 4) Survived

2 Rapidly
1) Softly 2) Quickly
3) Fast 4) Slowly

3 Recognisable
1) Imperceptible
2) Noticeable
3) Distinguishable
4) Identifiable

4 Inclusive
1) Diverse 2) Collaborative
3) Accessible 4) Exclusive

5 Cooperation
1) Hostility
2) Dialogue
3) Collaboration
4) Interaction

6 Conciliate
1) Assimilate 2) Appease
3) Provoke 4) Coordinate

7 Adventurous
1) Daring
2) Bold
3) Courageous
4) Timid

8 Idol
1) Hero
2) Role Model
3) Insignificant
4) Icon

9 Beacon
1) Illuminate 2) Radiate
3) Emblaze 4) Obscure

10 Bustling
1) Lively 2) Crowded
3) Vibrant 4) Quiet

Practice Set - 3

Direction (Q. 1-10): Select the most appropriate Antonym of the given word.

1 Plague
1) Smite 2) Reprieve
3) Burgeon 4) Excruciate

2 Caution
1) Watchfulness
2) Rashness
3) Restraint
4) Attention

3 Intrinsically
1) Ultimately
2) Fundamentally
3) Superficially
4) Eventually

4 Sympathetic
1) Oppressive 2) Antagonistic
3) God-Like 4) Feministic

5 Pretense
1) Intensity
2) Reality
3) Exasperation
4) Impatience

6 Amazed
1) Surprised 2) Astonished
3) Arcane 4) Unruffled

7 Insurgent
1) Revolting 2) Rcbcllious
3) Dissident 4) Compliant

8 Revival
1) Ease 2) Eliminate
3) Recover 4) Build

9 Deflated
1) Increased 2) Impressed
3) Appraised 4) Perused

10 Remonstrated
1) Protested 2) Agreed
3) Completed 4) Argued

Practice Set - 4

Direction (Q. 1-10): Select the most appropriate Antonym of the given word.

1 Diaphanous
1) Frail 2) Sheer
3) Opaque 4) Contaminated

2 Attach
1) Detach 2) Connect
3) Affix 4) Adhere

3 Immersion
1) Attraction 2) Engagement
3) Expansion 4) Detachment

4 Expert
1) Master 2) Amateur
3) Reverent 4) Professional

5 Consolidate
1) Scatter
2) Solidify
3) Incorporate
4) Amalgamate

6 Touting
1) Criticising 2) Endorsing
3) Advertising 4) Praising

7 Distinctly
1) Explicitly 2) Differently
3) Variedly 4) Implicitly

8 Transfer
1) Retainment

2) Launch
3) Entrust
4) Bequeath

9 Beguiling
1) Wizening 2) Smoothening
3) Tempting 4) Repelling

10 Escape
1) Encounter 2) Refrain
3) Confuse 4) Borrow

Practice Set - 5

Direction (Q. 1-10): Select the most appropriate Antonym of the given word.

1 Instigator
1) Innovator 2) Rebel
3) Pacifier 4) Activist

2 Mutual
1) Exclusive 2) Generic
3) Modified 4) Bilateral

3 Plaintive
1) Cheerful
2) Sorrowful
3) Melancholy
4) Mournful

4 Query
1) Doubt 2) Question
3) Answer 4) Objection

5 Intellectual
1) Rational 2) Highbrow
3) Ignorant 4) Scholarly

6 Parch
1) Scorch 2) Wet
3) Desiccate 4) Dry

7 Victory
1) War 2) Peace
3) Defeat 4) Failure

8 Reverberate
1) Repeat 2) Loud
3) Quieten 4) Resound

9 Mitigating
1) Worsening 2) Softening
3) Reducing 4) Easing

10 Infectious
1) Dangerous 2) Problematic
3) Gloomy 4) Harmless

Practice Set - 6

Direction (Q. 1-10): What is the most appropriate ANTONYM of the word.

1 Variation
1) Uniformity 2) Deviation
3) Mutation 4) Novel

2 Summoned
1) Subpoena 2) Convene
3) Dismiss 4) Sanction

3 Unhinged
1) Strange 2) Rational
3) Supported 4) Classified

4 Sketchy
1) Unreliable 2) Illustrative
3) Complete 4) Uncreative

5 Sojourner
1) Visitor 2) Customer
3) Patron 4) Owner

6 Treat
1) Employ 2) Address
3) Afflict 4) Travel

7 Rural
1) Natural
2) Suburban
3) Metropolitan
4) Agricultural

8 Torment
1) Comfort 2) Ascertain
3) Torture 4) Mistreat

9 Shortcoming
1) Advantage 2) Drawback
3) Temporary 4) Apology

10 Squeamish
1) Critical 2) Delicate
3) Prudish 4) Uncritical

Practice Set - 7

Direction (Q. 1-10): Select the most appropriate ANTONYM of the underlined word in the given sentence.

1 In the age of AI, human souls too have become <u>enervated</u>.
1) Petrified 2) Fatigued
3) Pumped 4) Devitalized

2 Despite his initial <u>reluctance</u> , he eventually nailed the task.
1) Doubt
2) Hesitation
3) Enthusiasm
4) Caution

3 After years of <u>obscurity</u> , the artist catapulted into the spotlight.
1) Darkness 2) Uncertainty
3) Dimness 4) Definiteness

4 Indian fans of K-pop <u>canonise</u> their ideals to their core.
1) Deify 2) Adulate
3) Abominate 4) Revere

5 Both the parties agreed to go for an <u>arbitration</u>.
1) Mediation
2) Adjustment
3) Adjudication
4) Disagreement

6 He had no <u>qualms</u> about speaking his mind with confidence and honesty.
1) Shame 2) Inhibition
3) Censor 4) Certitude

7 Mili's <u>execrable</u> performance on stage made her rethink her passion.
1) Stupendous
2) Terrible
3) Lacklustre
4) Formidable

8 Even though they had a deep bond, their relationship was strictly <u>platonic</u>.
1) Celibate 2) Chaste
3) Asexual 4) Physical

9 The lawyer Suresh was able to <u>confute</u> the witness's testimony with irrefutable evidence.
1) Controvert 2) Contradict
3) Confound 4) Concede

10 He accepted the invitation <u>reluctantly</u>.
1) Willingly 2) Sadly
3) Doubtfully 4) Cautiously

Practice Set - 8

Direction (Q. 1-10): Select the most appropriate ANTONYM of the underlined word in the given sentence.

1 The crowd <u>jeered</u> at the person's inability to speak clearly.
1) Scouted 2) Jibed
3) Acclaimed 4) Derided

2 The defendant's behaviour was quite <u>erratic</u>.
1) Irregular 2) Unstable
3) Capricious 4) Consistent

3 The forecast was that we would experience <u>intermittent</u> rain.
1) Sporadic 2) Refined
3) Enlivening 4) Unceasing

4 The new version includes many <u>enhanced</u> features.
1) Aggravated 2) Decreased
3) Improved 4) Augmented

5 The <u>burlesque</u> version of Bieber's hit song Baby also trended on the internet.
1) Acoustic 2) Parody
3) Tribute 4) Emulate

6 One minute traffic control rule has only <u>exacerbated</u> the city's traffic issue.
1) Mitigated 2) Aggravated
3) Deepened 4) Complicated

7 The artist's work was characterised by its <u>subtlety</u> and nuance, requiring careful observation to appreciate its full meaning.
1) Modernity 2) Understated
3) Overt 4) Complexity

8 Smoking is considered as a <u>loathsome</u> habit.

1) Hoarse 2) Delightful
3) Noxious 4) Nasty

9 The ground needed to be cleared of malodorous heap of garbage.
1) Rotting 2) Frowsy
3) Noisome 4) Savoury

10 The rancorous debate between the two politicians was filled with bitter accusations and personal attacks, leaving the audience feeling unsettled.
1) Altruistic 2) Cantankerous
3) Malevolent 4) Acrimonious

Practice Set - 9

Direction (Q. 1-10): Select the most appropriate ANTONYM of the underlined word in the given sentence.

1 The popular fiction of young writer has enriched our literature in many ways.
1) Improvised
2) Impaired
3) Undervalued
4) Overvalued

2 We need a disinterested mediator to assist us with this thorny issue.
1) Partisan
2) Disinclined
3) Distinguished
4) Bored

3 Without my glasses everything looks fuzzy.
1) Useful 2) Vague
3) Clear 4) Misty

4 The client's demands were somewhat vexing , but the interiors were adjusted accordingly.
1) Irksome 2) Persecuting
3) Placating 4) Nettlesome

5 The teacher assigned the group activity to pique the students' interest in the lesson.
1) Dampen 2) Invigorate
3) Vivify 4) Enkindle

6 The village was marauded during the invasion.
1) Looted 2) Pitied
3) Guarded 4) Inhabited

7 This atmosphere of solemnity dissolved into songs and laughter.
1) Ceremony 2) Humility
3) Levity 4) Sobriety

8 Sharnali's lifestyle has always been ascetic.
1) Pragmatic 2) Hedonist
3) Pietist 4) Dynamic

9 The team members approach to problem-solving was highly homogeneous .
1) Divergent 2) Convergent
3) Insurgent 4) Indulgent

10 I was scrupulous in reviewing my actions, for I believed that true integrity required relentless honesty.
1) Circumspect
2) Impetuous
3) Emphatic
4) Conscientious

Practice Set - 10

Direction (Q. 1-10): In the given sentence, identify the antonym for the bracketed word.

1 It was a hypothetical condition which he had never even considered.
1) Suspect 2) Casual
3) Vague 4) Factual

2 My husband and I previously agreed that we didn't want children, but we were young and immature.
1) Unfledged 2) Idiosyncratic
3) Mellowed 4) Callow

3 Despite facing setbacks, the team remained persistent in their pursuit of the project goals.
1) Stubborn 2) Tenacious
3) Relentless 4) Inconsistent

4 Doctors say the patient's condition has ameliorated.
1) Expanded 2) Deteriorated
3) Moderated 4) Faltered

5 The employees deserve to have their representation adjudicated within the time frame.
1) Discussed 2) Equivocated
3) Forwarded 4) Gauged

6 The dish garnished with fried parsley looks delicious.
1) Brandish 2) Luscious
3) Marred 4) Decorated

7 Despite his reputation for being tight-fisted, he surprised everyone with a miserly donation to the charity.
1) Avaricious 2) Lavish
3) Churlish 4) Paltry

8 The committee members approached the stranger warily.
1) Suspiciously
2) Cautiously
3) Carefully
4) Carelessly

9 His constant disparagement of his colleagues affected team morale.
1) Distraction
2) Temptation
3) Apprehension
4) Admiration

10 Her circumlocution made it difficult to understand the main point of her argument.
1) Euphemism
2) Conciseness
3) Periphrasis
4) Tautology

Answer Key Practice Set - 1:

1 - 4	2 - 3	3 - 1	4 - 4	5 - 4
6 - 3	7 - 1	8 - 3	9 - 4	10 - 3

Answer Key Practice Set - 2:

1 - 1	2 - 4	3 - 1	4 - 4	5 - 1
6 - 3	7 - 4	8 - 3	9 - 4	10 - 4

Answer Key Practice Set - 3:

1 - 2	2 - 2	3 - 3	4 - 2	5 - 2
6 - 4	7 - 4	8 - 2	9 - 1	10 - 2

Answer Key Practice Set - 4:

1 - 3	2 - 1	3 - 4	4 - 2	5 - 1
6 - 1	7 - 4	8 - 1	9 - 4	10 - 1

Answer Key Practice Set - 5:

1 - 3	2 - 1	3 - 1	4 - 3	5 - 3
6 - 2	7 - 3	8 - 3	9 - 1	10 - 4

Answer Key Practice Set - 6:

1 - 1	2 - 3	3 - 2	4 - 3	5 - 4
6 - 3	7 - 3	8 - 1	9 - 1	10 - 4

Answer Key Practice Set - 7:

1 - 3	2 - 3	3 - 4	4 - 3	5 - 4
6 - 4	7 - 1	8 - 4	9 - 4	10 - 1

Answer Key Practice Set - 8:

1 - 3	2 - 4	3 - 4	4 - 2	5 - 3
6 - 1	7 - 3	8 - 2	9 - 4	10 - 1

Answer Key Practice Set - 9:

1 - 2	2 - 1	3 - 3	4 - 3	5 - 1
6 - 3	7 - 3	8 - 2	9 - 1	10 - 2

Answer Key Practice Set - 10:

1 - 4	2 - 3	3 - 4	4 - 2	5 - 2
6 - 3	7 - 2	8 - 4	9 - 4	10 - 2

PART - D

(HOMONYMS & HOMOPHONES)

Contents:-

* *Additional non-PYQ Homonyms are included in Chapter F2.*

Updated and Additional Content: -

1. Combined vocabulary for Homonyms, Homophones and confusing words provided in a single chapter.
2. Though a relatively new exam topic, the chapter offers comprehensive coverage of all important Homonyms, Homophones, and Confusing Words from PYQs.

Additional Symbols for smarter and efficient preparation: -

1. **#R (Repetition Count)**: The #R tag, used to show how many times an Idiom has been asked in competitive exams.

HOMONYMS, HOMOPHONES & CONFUSING WORDS

Introduction

Homonyms are words that look or sound the same but carry different meanings. For instance, **Well** can mean "in good health" or "a source of water." In Delhi Police 2022: *"She is not keeping ______ these days"*, here Well means healthy, not a water well.

Homophones are words that sound alike but are spelled differently and mean different things. Like **Bare** (uncovered) and **Bear** (to carry/tolerate). SSC CHSL 2023 asked: *"Even animals find it difficult to ______ the loss of their loved ones"* with options bare, where, bear, wear.

Confusing Words are pairs that students often mix up even though they are neither homonyms nor homophones. Words like **Accept/Except**, **Ceased/Seized**, **Scent/Sense/Cents/Cense** fall in this category.

How Exams Test Homonyms, Homophones & Confusing Words

In real competitive exams, there is no strict line between homonyms and homophones. Exams use these terms loosely and often interchangeably. For example, in SSC CGL Tier 2 (2024), the question says "Select the most appropriate homophone" but the words being tested are actually homonyms. Similarly, in CHSL Tier 1 (2024), the question asks for a "homonym" but the options include homophones like Career and Carrier.

On top of that, exams sometimes throw in garbage or non-existing words as options to confuse you. In CGL Tier 2 (2024), one question had "sause" as an option (not a real word). CHSL 2024 had "carreer" (a misspelling) sitting right next to the correct answer. So do not panic if you see an unfamiliar option, it might just be a made-up distractor.

Questions mostly come in two formats:

1. Fill in the blank: This is the more common type. SSC CGL Tier 2 (2022) asked, *"The wind ______ so powerfully that the door closed."* Options: blow, blues, blue, blew. Or from Delhi Police 2022, *"In case of a snake ______, villagers do not go to the hospital."* Options: byte, bite, bight, bait.

2. Pick the nearest homonym/homophone: SSC CGL 2023 asked, "Select the nearest homonym of: Accept" with options Accent, Expert, Expect, Except. Here you just need to identify which word sounds closest or is most commonly confused.

How to Study This Chapter

Part 1 - PYQ Based (646 words, 242 groups): Words picked directly from previous year's questions of SSC, DSSSB, CDS, Delhi Police and other exams. These are your top priorities.

Part 2 - Non PYQ (720 words, 309 groups): Important words that have not appeared yet but match the pattern and difficulty level of recent papers. Your safety net for new questions.

- **Read in groups.** Words are arranged in confusing pairs/sets. Always study them together, not one by one.
- **Meaning + Hindi meaning.** Read both. For Hindi Medium students the Hindi meaning often makes the difference click faster than the English one.
- **Revise regularly.** Do not try to finish everything in one sitting. Cover a few groups daily and keep revisiting the tough ones.

D1 HOMONYMS + HOMOPHONES
(Asked in SSC & Other Exams)

1 **Accept** (V.) - To receive (स्वीकार करना)
Aspect (N.) - The way something appears or is viewed (दृष्टिकोण)
Except (Prep.) - Not including (सिवाय)
Expect (V.) - To anticipate or look forward to (अपेक्षा करना) *[#R-11]*

2 **Access** (N.) - The opportunity or right to use something (पहुँच)
Excess (N.) - An amount more than necessary (अतिरिक्त) *[#R-1]*

3 **Ad** (N.) - A short form of advertisement (विज्ञापन)
Add (V.) - To put something extra into something (जोड़ना) *[#R-2]*

4 **Address** (N.) - The number of a building, name of the street, and place where somebody lives or works (पता)
Address (V.) - To speak to (a person or an assembly) (संबोधित करना) *[#R-2]*

5 **Advance** (N.) - Development or improvement (प्रगति)
Advance (Adj.) - Done or provided beforehand; prior (अग्रिम)
Advance (V.) - To move forward (आगे बढ़ना) *[#R-3]*

6 **Affect** (V.) - To influence (प्रभावित करना)
Effect (N.) - A result (परिणाम) *[#R-2]*

7 **Air** (N.) - The invisible gas (हवा)
Ere (Conj.) - Before (पहले) *[#R-3]*

8 **Alleviate** (V.) - To make pain, suffering, or a problem less severe (कम करना)
Elevate (V.) - To lift up (उठाना, ऊंचा करना) *[#R-2]*

9 **Allowed** (V.) - Gave permission (अनुमति देना)
Aloud (Adv.) - Spoken out loud (ऊँची आवाज़ में)
Loud (Adj.) - Producing powerful sound (ऊँचा स्वर)
Loudly (Adv.) - In a loud manner (जोर से) *[#R-2]*

10 **Allusion** (N.) - An indirect reference (परोक्ष संदर्भ; इशारा)
Elusion (N.) - The act of escaping or avoiding cleverly (चतुराई से बच निकलना)
Illusion (N.) - A false idea or misleading appearance (भ्रम; झूठा आभास) *[#R-7]*

11 **Altar** (N.) - A sacred platform or place (पूजा या बलि का स्थान)
Alter (V.) - To change (बदलना) *[#R-2]*

12 **Ambulatory** (N.) - A covered walkway in a monastery or cathedral (गलियारा, परिक्रमा-पथ)
Ambulatory (Adj.) - Able to walk; relating to walking (चलने-फिरने योग्य) *[#R-2]*

13 **Amice** (N.) - A general scarf or neck covering (गमछा)
Amice (N.) - A white linen vestment worn by priests during worship (धार्मिक वस्त्र) *[#R-2]*

14 **Antiphonary** (N.) - A liturgical book that contains chants (भजन-संग्रह)
Antiphony (N.) - Alternate singing (प्रत्युत्तर गायन) *[#R-2]*

15 **Any Way** (N.) - Any manner or method (किसी भी तरीके से)
Anyway (Adv.) - Regardless; in spite of everything (फिर भी) *[#R-2]*

16 **Appraise** (V.) - To estimate the value or quality of something (आंकना)
Apprise (V.) - To inform or tell (सूचना देना) *[#R-2]*

17 **Arms** (N.) - The two upper limbs of the human body (भुजा)
Arms (N.) - Weapons (हथियार) *[#R-2]*

18 **Assure** (V.) - To guarantee (आश्वासन देना)
Ensure (V.) - To make certain that something will happen (सुनिश्चित करना)
Insure (V.) - To provide insurance (बीमा करना) *[#R-2]*

19 **Ate** (V.) - Past tense of eat; consumed food (खाना)
Eight (N.) - The numeral representing 8 (आठ) *[#R-2]*

20 **Back** (N.) - The rear part of the body or of something (पीठ / पिछला हिस्सा)
Back (V.) - To support, help, or give approval to something (समर्थन करना) *[#R-2]*

21 **Bailey** (N.) - A farmyard or enclosed yard for animals (बाड़ा)
Bailey (N.) - The enclosed courtyard of a

[**#R** denotes repetition of word]

[E.g. in SN 7, #R- **3** denotes this word has been asked 3 times in SSC and other exams]

castle (किला-आंगन) *[#R-2]*

22 **Bait** (N.) - Something used to lure or entice (प्रलोभन)
Bight (N.) - A curve or recess in a coastline (खाड़ी)
Bite (V.) - To cut or tear with teeth (काटना)
Byte (N.) - A unit of digital information (बाइट (कंप्यूटर मेमोरी की एक इकाई)) *[#R-3]*

23 **Bald** (Adj.) - Having little or no hair on the head (गंजा)
Baled (V.) - Packed goods tightly into bundles (लपेटना)
Balled (V.) - Formed into a ball (गोल किया)
Bawled (V.) - Cried or shouted loudly (चिल्लाया) *[#R-4]*

24 **Band** (N.) - A group of musicians (संगीतकारों का समूह)
Band (N.) - A range of frequencies (आवृत्ति सीमा)
Band (N.) - A thin strip of material used for binding (पट्टी) *[#R-3]*

25 **Bank** (N.) - A store of things, which you keep to use later (कोष)
Bank (N.) - A financial institution for saving money (बैंक (वित्तीय संस्था))
Bank (N.) - The edge/side of a river or lake (नदी का किनारा, तट) *[#R-3]*

26 **Bare** (Adj.) - Without covering or clothing; naked or nude (नंगा; बिना ढका)
Bear (V.) - To tolerate something (सहना)
Bear (N.) - A large heavy mammal with thick fur (भालू) *[#R-10]*

27 **Bark** (N./V.) - A loud sound made by a dog (भौंकना)
Bark (N.) - The outer covering of a tree (छाल) *[#R-3]*

28 **Bases** (N.) - Base layers applied before makeup (आधार परत)
Bases (N.) - Military places where armed forces are stationed (सैन्य ठिकाने) *[#R-2]*

29 **Basil** (N.) - A type of plant (तुलसी)
Basilica (N.) - A large public or religious building (विशाल गिरजाघर) *[#R-2]*

30 **Bass** (N.) - A type of fish (बास मछली)
Bass (N.) - Low-pitched sound or voice (नीचा सुर) *[#R-2]*

31 **Bat** (N.) - A cricket or baseball implement (बल्ला)
Bat (N.) - A flying mammal (चमगादड़)
Bat (V.) - To support or defend someone (Idiomatic) (पक्ष लेना) *[#R-3]*

32 **Beat** (N.) - A rhythmic pattern in music (ताल, संगीत की लय)
Beat (V.) - To defeat someone in a contest (पराजित करना)
Beet (N.) - A red-coloured root vegetable (चुकंदर)
Bit (N.) - A small piece (थोड़ा-सा) *[#R-3]*

33 **Beer** (N.) - A carbonated, fermented alcoholic beverage (एक प्रकार की मदिरा)
Bier (N.) - A stand or platform used to carry a coffin (अर्थी) *[#R-7]*

34 **Bellow** (V.) - To shout in a loud voice (गरजना)
Below (Prep.) - Lower in place, rank, or value (नीचे)
Blow (V.) - To be moving or to cause something to move (फूँकना) *[#R-3]*

35 **Berth** (N.) - A fixed bed/bunk on a ship or train (शयनस्थान, बर्थ)
Birth (N.) - The process of being born (जन्म) *[#R-4]*

36 **Bi** (Adj.) - Occurring every two; twice (द्वि)
Buy (V.) - To purchase (खरीदना)
By (Prep.) - Near; through the agency of (समीप)
Bye (N.) - A farewell greeting; short form of goodbye (अलविदा) *[#R-16]*

37 **Blew** (V.) - Past tense of blow; moved as an air current (बहना)
Blue (Adj.) - Having the color of a clear sky (नीला) *[#R-2]*

38 **Boar** (N.) - A wild male pig (सूअर)
Bore (V.) - To drill a hole through (छेदना)
Bore (V.) - To make someone feel weary/ uninterested (ऊबाना) *[#R-2]*

39 **Board** (N.) - A long, thin, flat piece of wood (तख़्ता)
Board (V.) - To get on a ship, aircraft, or vehicle (सवार होना, चढ़ना) *[#R-1]*
Bored (Adj.) - Feeling uninterested (ऊबा हुआ)

40 **Boarder** (N.) - A person who lives in a boarding house or hostel (छात्रावासी)
Border (N.) - The dividing line between two countries or regions (सीमा) *[#R-2]*

41 **Born** (V.) - Brought into life (जन्म लेना)
Borne (V.) - To have endured; Past participle of bear (सहा हुआ) *[#R-4]*

42 **Boat** (N.) - A small vessel for travelling on water (नाव; नौका)
Bote (N.) - Compensation paid for injury (क्षतिपूर्ति; हर्जाना) *[#R-2]*

43 **Brake** (N.) - A device for slowing or stopping

motion (गतिरोधक)
Break (V.) - To separate into pieces (तोड़ना)
Break (N.) - A pause, rest, or interval (विराम, अवकाश) [#R-8]

44 **Can** (V.) - To be able to (कर सकना)
Can (N.) - A sealed metal container for food/ drink (धातु का डिब्बा) [#R-2]

45 **Capital** (N.) - The primary city of a country or region (राजधानी)
Capital (N.) - Money or assets invested or available for investment (पूँजी)
Capitol (N.) - The building where a legislative assembly meets (संसद भवन) [#R-2]

46 **Carat** (N.) - A unit of weight used for gemstones (कैरेट (रत्नों के वजन की इकाई))
Caret (N.) - A proofreading or writing symbol (^) indicating insertion (सुधार-चिह्न)
Carrot (N.) - An orange root vegetable (गाजर)
Karat (N.) - A measure of gold purity (शुद्धता) [#R-7]

47 **Career** (N.) - A profession or long-term work path in life (पेशा)
Carrier (N.) - A person or thing that carries goods, people (वाहक) [#R-2]

48 **Carry** (V.) - To hold, move, or transport something (उठाना)
Curry (N.) - A dish with spices (करी) [#R-2]

49 **Case** (N.) - A box or holder (डिब्बा)
Case (N.) - A lawsuit or court proceeding (मुकदमा)
Case (N.) - A set of circumstances requiring action or decision (मामला) [#R-3]

50 **Cast** (N.) - Actors in a play/film (कलाकार)
Cast (V.) - To throw something forcefully (फेंकना)
Cast (V.) - To form something by pouring liquid into a mold (सांचे में ढालना)
Caste (N.) - A hereditary social class (जाति) [#R-3]

51 **Cease** (V.) - To stop or discontinue (रोकना, समाप्त करना)
Seas (N.) - Large bodies of salt water (समुद्र)
Sees (V.) - To perceive with the eyes (देखना)
Seize (V.) - To take hold of suddenly or forcibly (कब्जा करना) [#R-7]

52 **Ceiling** (N.) - The upper interior surface of a room (भीतरी छत)
Sealing (N.) - The process of making inaccessible or secret (सीलबंदी) [#R-4]

53 **Cense** (V.) - To perfume with incense (सुगंधित करना)
Sense (N.) - A faculty by which the body perceives stimuli (समझ) [#R-4]

54 **Cent** (N.) - A monetary unit equal to one-hundredth of a dollar (मुद्रा की छोटी इकाई)
Saint (N.) - A holy person recognized for great virtue (संत)
Scent (N.) - A distinctive smell (खुशबू)
Sent (V.) - Dispatched; caused to go or be delivered (भेजा) [#R-9]

55 **Cere** (N.) - The wax-like covering at the base of a bird's beak (चोंच का मोमी आवरण)
Sear (V.) - To burn or scorch a surface with intense heat (जलाना)
Seer (N.) - A person who can supposedly see into the future (भविष्यद्रष्टा)
Sere (Adj.) - Dried up or withered (मुरझाया हुआ) [#R-4]

56 **Cereal** (N.) - A grain used for food (अनाज)
Serial (Adj.) - Occurring in a series (क्रमिक)
Serial (N.) - A program made up of multiple episodes (धारावाहिक) [#R-3]

57 **Chair** (N.) - A seat with a back (कुर्सी)
Chair (V.) - To preside over or conduct a meeting (अध्यक्षता करना) [#R-2]

58 **Change** (N.) - Coins returned after payment (छुट्टे)
Change (V.) - To make something different (परिवर्तन करना)
Change (V.) - To move from one place, vehicle, or system to another (स्थानांतरित होना)
Change (V.) - To replace or exchange one thing for another (बदलना) [#R-4]

59 **Charge** (N.) - A price asked for goods or services; a fee (शुल्क, कीमत)
Charged (V.) - Filled with power or electricity (ऊर्जित)
Charged (V.) - Formally accused of a crime (आरोप लगाना) [#R-2]

60 **Cheat** (V.) - To deceive or trick (धोखा देना)
Chit (N.) - A signed note, voucher, or receipt (परची) [#R-2]

61 **Cite** (V.) - To quote or mention as evidence or support (समर्थन, प्रमाण या पुष्टि के लिए प्रस्तुत करना)
Cyte (suffix) - A suffix meaning - cell (used in biology e.g. Leukocyte, Erythrocyte) (कोशिका)
Sight (N.) - The ability to see; something worth seeing (दृष्टि; देखने योग्य स्थान)
Site (N.) - A location or place (physical or online) (स्थान; जगह (भौतिक या वेबसाइट)) [#R-19]

62 **Cleared** (Adj.) - Free from blame or accusation (निर्दोष)
Cleared (V.) - Made free of dirt or obstruction (साफ़ किया)
Cleared (V.) - Taken away or emptied (हटाया) *[#R-3]*

63 **Climactic** (Adj.) - Relating to a moment of heightened excitement or climax (चरम)
Climatic (Adj.) - Relating to the climate of a particular area (जलवायु संबंधी) *[#R-2]*

64 **Clipped** (V.) - Cut something short or trim (काटा)
Clipped (Adj.) - Shortened or spoken in a brief, abrupt manner (संक्षिप्त) *[#R-2]*

65 **Close** (Adj.) - Emotionally near; intimate (घनिष्ठ)
Close (V.) - To shut (बंद करना)
Close (Adj.) - Near in distance or time (निकट, पास) *[#R-2]*

66 **Coaled** (V.) - Provided with a supply of coal (कोयला भरना)
Cold (Adj.) - Having a low temperature (ठंडा)
Cowled (Adj.) - (Of a piece of clothing) with a hood (हुड वाला, टोपीदार) *[#R-3]*

67 **Coarse** (Adj.) - Rough and not smooth (खुरदुरा)
Course (N.) - A path or series of lessons (पाठ्यक्रम, मार्ग) *[#R-4]*

68 **Coast** (N.) - The edge of land near the sea (तट)
Cost (N.) - The price paid for something (कीमत) *[#R-2]*

69 **Codex** (N.) - A system, code, or structured data set (संहिता)
Codex (N.) - An ancient handwritten book or manuscript (पांडुलिपि) *[#R-2]*

70 **Compact** (N.) - A formal agreement or treaty (संधि)
Compact (Adj.) - Having a small and dense structure (छोटा लेकिन घना)
Compact (N.) - A small cosmetic case (मेकअप-डिब्बा) *[#R-2]*

71 **Compare** (V.) - To estimate or measure by examining similarities or differences (तुलना करना)
Compere (N.) - A person who introduces performers; an emcee/host (संचालक) *[#R-2]*

72 **Complacent** (Adj.) - Too satisfied with oneself or a situation, showing lack of concern or effort (आत्मसंतुष्ट, लापरवाह)
Complaisant (Adj.) - Willing to please others; overly polite or obliging (मिलनसार, विनम्र,) *[#R-2]*

73 **Complement** (N.) - Something that completes or makes perfect (पूरक)
Compliment (N.) - An expression of praise, commendation, or admiration (प्रशंसा) *[#R-10]*

74 **Condition** (N.) - A rule or requirement (शर्त)
Condition (N.) - The physical or mental state (स्थिति)
Condition (V.) - To train or accustom someone (अभ्यस्त करना) *[#R-3]*

75 **Content** (Adj.) - Satisfied and at peace (संतुष्ट)
Content (N.) - Amount of a substance present (मात्रा)
Content (N.) - Topics or information included in a book, broadcast, or media (विषय) *[#R-3]*

76 **Council** (N.) - An elected/appointed governing body (परिषद्; समिति)
Counsel (N.) - Advice; a lawyer in court (सलाह; वकील)
Consul (N.) - An official representing a country abroad (विदेश में देश का प्रतिनिधि) *[#R-5]*

77 **Court** (N.) - A place where legal cases are heard (न्यायालय)
Court (N.) - A playing area (मैदान)
Court (N.) - The household or circle of a ruler (दरबार) *[#R-3]*

78 **Creak** (V.) - To make a sharp, harsh, or squeaking sound (चरमराना)
Creek (N.) - A small narrow stream or river (नाला, छोटी नदी)
Crick (N.) - A painful stiffness in the neck or back (अकड़न) *[#R-3]*

79 **Crews** (N.) - Groups of people who work on a ship, aircraft, etc. (जहाज़, विमान आदि के सभी कर्मचारी)
Cruise (V.) - To travel by boat as a holiday (समुद्र-पर्यटन करना)
Crus (N.) - The shin bone (tibia) between the knee and ankle (पिंडली)
Cruse (N.) - A small vessel (such as a jar or pot) for holding a liquid (प्याली) *[#R-7]*

80 **Crosier** (N.) - A bishop's ceremonial staff (धर्मदंड)
Crosier (N.) - The coiled young shoot of a fern (कुंडली) *[#R-2]*

81 **Currant** (N.) - A small dried or fresh fruit (किशमिश)
Current (N.) - A movement or stream, especially of water or air (धारा)
Current (Adj.) - Existing or happening now (वर्तमान) *[#R-6]*

82 **Cygnet** (N.) - A young swan (हंस का बच्चा)

Signet (N.) - A ring bearing a seal or monogram (मुहरदार अंगूठी) *[#R-2]*

83 **Cymbal** (N.) - A concave brass percussion plate that clashes loudly (झांझर)
Symbol (N.) - A thing that represents or stands for something else (प्रतीक) *[#R-2]*

84 **Dare** (V.) - To have the courage to do something (साहस करना)
Their (Pron.) - Belonging to or associated with the people or things previously mentioned or easily identified (उनका)
There (Adv.) - In, at, or to that place or position (वहाँ)
They're (Cont.) - Contraction of "they are" (वे हैं) *[#R-6]*

85 **Dash** (N.) - A short, fast run or sprint (दौड़)
Dash (N.) - A small quantity (थोड़ी-सी मात्रा) *[#R-2]*

86 **Date** (N.) - A romantic meeting between two people (प्रेमी-प्रेमिका की मुलाकात)
Date (N.) - The fruit of the date palm tree (खजूर)
Date (N.) - A specific day of the month or year (तारीख, दिनांक) *[#R-3]*

87 **Deal** (N.) - An advantageous offer or a large amount (सौदा)
Deal (V.) - To give out, especially cards (बाँटना)
Deal (V.) - To handle, manage, or cope with (निपटना, संभालना) *[#R-2]*

88 **Dear** (Adj.) - Beloved or cherished (प्रिय, प्यारा)
Deer (N.) - A hoofed grazing animal (हिरण)
Dear (Adj.) - Expensive; costly (महंगा) *[#R-3]*

89 **Deem** (V.) - To think or judge something in a particular way (समझना)
Dim (Adj.) - Not bright; unclear (धुंधला) *[#R-2]*

90 **Defuse** (V.) - To reduce danger, tension, anger, or conflict (शांत करना)
Diffuse (V.) - To spread out gradually in all directions (फैलाना) *[#R-2]*

91 **Defy** (V.) - To disobey (अवहेलना)
Deify (V.) - To worship or regard as a god (पूजा करना) *[#R-2]*

92 **Desert** (V.) - To leave someone who needs protection (साथ छोड़ देना)
Desert (N.) - A dry, hot, sandy region with little rain (रेगिस्तान)
Dessert (N.) - A sweet course served at the end of a meal (मिठाई) *[#R-4]*

93 **Dew** (N.) - Water droplets condensed from air (ओस)
Do (V.) - To perform an action (करना)
Due (Adj.) - Having to be paid (बक़ाया) *[#R-4]*

94 **Digest** (N.) - A condensed collection or summary of information or laws (संक्षेप)
Digest (V.) - To break down food in the body (पचाना) *[#R-2]*

95 **Discreet** (Adj.) - Careful not to attract attention (विवेकपूर्ण)
Discrete (Adj.) - Separate and distinct (अलग-अलग) *[#R-2]*

96 **Dispatch** (N.) - An official message or news report sent from a place (आधिकारिक संदेश)
Dispatch (N.) - Speed and efficiency in doing something (फुर्ती, तत्परता)
Dispatch (V.) - To send goods, messages, or someone to a destination (भेजना, रवाना करना) *[#R-3]*

97 **Does** (N.) - Plural of doe (female deer) (हिरणियाँ)
Does (V.) - Third-person singular form of do (करता है)
Dose (N.) - A measured amount of medicine or drug (खुराक, मात्रा)
Doze (V.) - To sleep lightly (झपकी लेना) *[#R-3]*

98 **Dove** (N.) - A type of bird (कबूतर)
Dove (V.) - To plunge or rush into something (कूद पड़ना, गोता लगाना) *[#R-2]*

99 **Draft** (N.) - A preliminary written version of a document (प्रारूप)
Draught (N.) - A cold current of air (हवा का झोंका)
Drought (N.) - A period of dry weather (सूखा) *[#R-2]*

100 **Dual** (Adj.) - Having two parts or aspects (दोहरी)
Duel (N.) - A formal fight between two people (द्वंद्वयुद्ध) *[#R-2]*

101 **Duck** (N.) - A water bird (बतख)
Duck (V.) - To lower the head or body quickly to avoid something (झुकना) *[#R-2]*

102 **Dung** (N.) - Animal waste used as manure (गोबर)
Dunk (V.) - To dip or plunge something quickly into liquid (डुबोना, भिगोना) *[#R-2]*

103 **Elicit** (V.) - To draw out (प्रकाश में लाना)
Illicit (Adj.) - Illegal, forbidden (अवैध) *[#R-4]*

104 **Elude** (V.) - To escape or avoid cleverly (चालाकी से बच निकलना)
Allude (V.) - To refer to something indirectly (इशारा करना) *[#R-2]*

105 **Eminent** (Adj.) - Prominent (प्रख्यात)
Immanent (Adj.) - Inherent (अन्तर्निहित)
Imminent (Adj.) - About to happen (आसन्न) *[#R-2]*

106 **Enquiry** (N.) - The act of asking for information (पूछताछ)
Inquiry (N.) - A formal investigation or systematic search for facts (जाँच) *[#R-2]*

107 **Fair** (Adj.) - Light-skinned (गोरा)
Fair (N.) - An exhibition, carnival, or market (मेला)
Fair (Adj.) - Just, equitable, impartial (न्यायसंगत, उचित)
Fare (N.) - The money paid for transportation (किराया)
Fear (N.) - The feeling when scared or in danger (भय)
Fere (N.) - A companion (साथी) *[#R-6]*

108 **Fait** (N.) - Something already done or completed (हो चुका काम)
Fate (N.) - Destiny; the predetermined course of events (भाग्य) *[#R-2]*

109 **Fall** (V.) - To be beaten or defeated (हारना)
Fall (V.) - To come at a particular time or happen in a particular place (घटित होना)
Fall (V.) - To go down onto the ground suddenly (गिरना) *[#R-3]*

110 **Fanon** (N.) - A ceremonial cloth worn by the Pope during Mass (पोप का अनुष्ठानिक वस्त्र)
Fanon (N.) - Fan-created stories or details outside the official canon (प्रशंसकों द्वारा बनाई गई कल्पनाएँ) *[#R-2]*

111 **Farther** (Adj.) - More distant (दूर)
Further (Adv.) - In addition; to a greater degree (आगे) *[#R-2]*

112 **Faze** (V.) - To disturb or bother (चिंतित या परेशान कर देना)
Phase (N.) - A stage in the development of something (अवस्था) *[#R-4]*

113 **Feat** (N.) - An achievement showing great skill or strength (करतब)
Feet (N.) - The plural of 'foot' (पैर)
Fit (Adj.) - Being in good health or physical condition (स्वस्थ)
Fit (V.) - To be the right size and shape for someone or something (उपयुक्त) *[#R-2]*

114 **Fief** (N.) - Land granted by a lord to a vassal in feudal times (सामंती भूमि)
Fief (N.) - A personal domain of power or control (figurative) (अधिकार-क्षेत्र) *[#R-2]*

115 **File** (N.) - A folder or collection of documents (काग़ज़ात)
File (V.) - To arrange or place in order (क्रमबद्ध करना)
File (V.) - To smooth or shape something (घिसना) *[#R-3]*

116 **Fillet** (N.) - A boneless cut of fish or meat (मांस का टुकड़ा)
Fillet (N.) - A narrow band or line used in manuscript or book decoration (पतली पट्टी) *[#R-2]*

117 **Fine** (N.) - A sum of money paid as penalty (जुर्माना)
Fine (Adj.) - Of good quality; satisfactory (अच्छा, बढ़िया)
Fine (Adj.) - Very thin or delicate (बारीक, महीन)
Find (V.) - To discover or locate something (ढूंढना; खोजना) *[#R-4]*

118 **Flair** (N.) - A natural talent (विशेष योग्यता)
Flare (N.) - A fire or blaze of light (चमक) *[#R-2]*

119 **Flea** (N.) - A very small jumping insect that lives on animals (पिस्सू)
Flee (V.) - To run away or escape from danger (भाग जाना)
Fly (V.) - To move through the air (उड़ना)
Fly (N.) - A small flying insect (मक्खी) *[#R-2]*

120 **Flour** (N.) - Ground grain used in baking (आटा, मैदा)
Flower (N.) - The reproductive structure of some plants (फूल, पुष्प) *[#R-4]*

121 **Found** (V.) - To come across or obtain by searching (पाया)
Found (V.) - To set up or start something (स्थापित करना) *[#R-2]*

122 **Gait** (N.) - A manner of walking (चाल)
Gate (N.) - A barrier that can be swung or drawn aside (दरवाज़ा/फाटक) *[#R-2]*

123 **Gallon** (N.) - A unit of liquid measurement (गैलन)
Galloon (N.) - A narrow ornamental braid or metallic lace for garments (सजावटी फीता) *[#R-1]*

124 **Gild** (V.) - To cover with a thin layer of gold; to make attractive (सोने का पानी चढ़ाना)
Gilled (Adj.) - Having gills (गलफड़ों वाला)
Guild (N.) - An association of persons with similar interests or pursuits (श्रेणी)
Guilt (N.) - A feeling of responsibility for wrongdoing (अपराध-बोध) *[#R-3]*

125 **Gradual** (N.) - A church book containing

chants for the Mass (भजन-पुस्तक)
Gradual (Adj.) - Happening slowly; step by step (क्रमिक) *[#R-2]*

126 **Groan** (V.) - To make a deep sound of pain, sorrow, or displeasure (कराहना)
Grown (Adj.) - Having reached full development (विकसित) *[#R-3]*

127 **Hair** (N.) - Fine, threadlike strands growing from the skin (बाल)
Hare (N.) - A fast-running long-eared mammal (खरहा)
Heir (N.) - A person inheriting property or a title (वारिस) *[#R-4]*

128 **Hall** (N.) - A large room or passage (सभागार)
Haul (V.) - To pull or drag with effort (घसीटना)
Hole (N.) - An opening or hollow space (छेद)
Whole (Adj.) - Entire; complete (पूरा) *[#R-4]*

129 **Hatch** (N.) - A movable cover or access door (ढक्कन)
Hatch (V.) - To emerge from an egg after development (निकलना) *[#R-2]*

130 **Heal** (V.) - To become healthy again (ठीक करना)
Heel (N.) - The back part of the foot (एड़ी)
He'll (Cont.) - Contraction of 'he will' (वह करेगा) *[#R-2]*

131 **Hear** (V.) - To perceive with the ear (सुनना)
Here (Adv.) - In, at, or to this place (यहाँ) *[#R-1]*

132 **Heard** (V.) - Perceived sound; past tense of hear (सुना)
Herd (N.) - A group of animals (झुंड) *[#R-4]*

133 **Hoard** (N.) - A hidden fund or supply (संग्रह)
Horde (N.) - A large group or crowd (भीड़) *[#R-2]*

134 **Hook** (N.) - A curved metal object used to catch, hang or attach things (कुंडा)
Hook (N.) - A curved punching blow in boxing (घुमावदार घूंसा) *[#R-2]*

135 **Idle** (Adj.) - Not active or in use (निष्क्रिय, निठल्ला)
Idol (N.) - An image or statue worshipped as a god (मूर्ति)
Idol (N.) - A person or thing greatly admired (आदर्श)
Idyll (N.) - A short poem or scene describing a simple, peaceful, rural life (ग्रामीण जीवन का शांत, सुखद चित्रण) *[#R-6]*

136 **Inapt** (Adj.) - Not suitable or appropriate (अनुचित)
Inept (Adj.) - Lacking skill or ability (अकुशल) *[#R-2]*

137 **Keen** (Adj.) - Having or showing eagerness or enthusiasm (इच्छुक)
Kin (N.) - Relatives (रिश्तेदार) *[#R-1]*

138 **Kenosis** (N.) - Emptying or draining out of contents (रिक्तीकरण)
Kenosis (N.) - Self-emptying; especially Christ's renunciation (आत्मत्याग) *[#R-2]*

139 **Kind** (N.) - A sort or class of something (प्रकार)
Kind (Adj.) - Friendly; caring; or considerate toward others (दयालु) *[#R-2]*

140 **Knight** (N.) - An armored warrior in medieval times (मध्यकालीन कवचधारी योद्धा)
Knight (N.) - A chess piece shaped like a horse (शतरंज में घोड़ा)
Night (N.) - The dark period after sunset (रात) *[#R-3]*

141 **Knot** (N.) - A fastening made by tying a piece of string or rope (गाँठ, फंदा)
Knot (N.) - A unit of speed for ships (nautical mile/hr) (नॉट (गति की इकाई))
Naught (N.) - Nothing; zero (शून्य)
Not (Adv.) - Negation (नहीं)
Nought (N.) - Zero or nothing (शून्य) *[#R-4]*

142 **Last** (Adj.) - Coming after all others; final (अंतिम)
Last (V.) - To continue or remain for a period of time (टिके रहना)
Least (Adj.) - Smallest in amount or degree (न्यूनतम)
Lost (Adj.) - Unable to be found (खोया हुआ)
Lust (N.) - Strong sexual desire (वासना) *[#R-3]*

143 **Lay** (V.) - To put or set down (रखना)
Lei (N.) - A Hawaiian garland of flowers worn around the neck (फूलों की माला)
Lie (V.) - To be in a horizontal or resting position (लेटना)
Lye (N.) - A strong alkaline solution used in soap making (क्षार घोल) *[#R-4]*

144 **Lead** (N.) - A heavy, soft metal (सीसा)
Lead (V.) - To guide, direct, or be in charge (नेतृत्व करना) *[#R-1]*

145 **Letter** (N.) - A written message sent to someone (पत्र)
Letter (N.) - A symbol of the alphabet (अक्षर; वर्ण)
Later (Adv.) - After the expected or usual time (बाद में)
Latter (Adj.) - The second of two things mentioned (बाद वाला, दूसरा) *[#R-3]*

146 **Levered** (Adj.) - Using borrowed money to increase potential return (ऋण-समर्थित)

Levered (V.) - To lift, move, or open something using a lever (टेक लगाकर खोला) *[#R-2]*

147 **Light** (N.) - Natural or artificial radiance; illumination (रोशनी)
Light (Adj.) - Not serious or profound (सतही)
Light (Adj.) - Not severe; gentle or mild (हल्का)
Light (V.) - To ignite or set on fire (जलाना) *[#R-3]*

148 **Loan** (N.) - Money or something given to be returned later (उधार)
Lone (Adj.) - Alone; without companions (अकेला) *[#R-2]*

149 **Loon** (N.) - A large water bird (जल पक्षी)
Lune (N.) - A crescent-shaped figure; the shape of a new moon (चंद्र-कोर) *[#R-2]*

150 **Loose** (Adj.) - Not firmly fixed (ढीला)
Lose (V.) - To be deprived of or cease to have (खोना) *[#R-6]*

151 **Main** (Adj.) - Chief, most important (मुख्य)
Mane (N.) - Long hair on the neck of a lion or horse (शेर या घोड़े की गर्दन के लंबे बाल) *[#R-2]*

152 **Maize** (N.) - Corn (मक्का)
Maze (N.) - A complicated network of paths (भूल-भुलैया) *[#R-4]*

153 **Marshal** (N.) - A high-ranking military officer (उच्च सैन्य अधिकारी)
Martial (Adj.) - Related to war, soldiers, fighting, or the military (सैन्य)
Martial (Adj.) - Showing aggression or readiness to fight (लड़ाकू) *[#R-3]*

154 **Match** (N.) - A competition between opponents (मुक़ाबला)
Match (N.) - A small stick used to light fire (माचिस की तीली)
Match (V.) - A person or thing equal to another (बराबरी, समान) *[#R-1]*

155 **Medium** (N.) - A means or system for conveying information (माध्यम)
Medium (N.) - A substance or material through which something passes (द्रव्य, बीच का पदार्थ) *[#R-2]*

156 **Mensa** (N.) - An international society for people with high IQs (बुद्धिजीवी-संघ)
Mensa (N.) - The flat top of a church altar (वेदी का ऊपरी भाग) *[#R-2]*

157 **Mitre** (N.) - A bishop's ceremonial headgear (बिशप की धार्मिक टोपी)
Mitre (N.) - A joint or angled cut; especially at 45° (कोना) *[#R-2]*

158 **Modal** (Adj.) - Related to mode or manner (प्रकारगत)
Model (N.) - A representation of shape or design (नमूना)
Model (V.) - To shape or design something (ढालना) *[#R-3]*

159 **Motion** (N.) - (Parliamentary) a proposal put forward for discussion or decision (प्रस्ताव)
Motion (N.) - The act of moving (गति) *[#R-2]*

160 **Nail** (N.) - A small metal spike used to join or hang things (कील)
Nail (N.) - The thin, hard area covering the end of each finger and toe (नाखून)
Nail (V.) - To catch or apprehend a wrongdoer (पकड़ना)
Nail (V.) - To do something successfully or perfectly (सफल करना) *[#R-7]*

161 **Notes** (N.) - Musical sounds (स्वर)
Notes (N.) - Paper money or banknotes (मुद्रा)
Notes (N.) - Written information or messages (लिखित जानकारी) *[#R-3]*

162 **Oar** (N.) - A long pole with a flat blade used for rowing a boat (चप्पू)
O'Er (Prep.) - Over (archaic or poetic) (ऊपर)
Or (Conj.) - Used to link alternatives (अथवा)
Ore (N.) - A naturally occurring solid material from which metal can be extracted (अयस्क) *[#R-3]*

163 **Oriel** (N.) - A projecting window built out from a wall (बाहर निकली खिड़की)
Oriel (N.) - A small chapel, gallery, or prayer space (rare/old usage) (प्रार्थना-कक्ष) *[#R-2]*

164 **Pair** (N.) - A set of two matching things (जोड़ा (दो समान चीज़ें))
Pare (V.) - To trim or cut away the outer edges (छीलना; छिलका उतारना)
Pear (N.) - A sweet fruit, wider at base (नाशपाती (फल))
Peer (N.) - A person of equal rank or status (समकक्ष व्यक्ति; बराबरी का व्यक्ति)
Peer (V.) - To look closely or with difficulty (ध्यान से देखना; झांककर देखना)
Pier (N.) - A platform extending into water for boats (जेटी; जहाज बाँधने का घाट) *[#R-8]*

165 **Pallium** (N.) - A ceremonial woolen band worn by certain bishops (ऊनी धार्मिक पट्टा)
Pallium (N.) - The outer layer of the cerebrum (मस्तिष्क की बाहरी परत) *[#R-2]*

166 **Park** (N.) - A public area with grass, trees, and open space for recreation (उद्यान)
Park (V.) - To station a vehicle in a designated

spot (वाहन खड़ा करना) *[#R-2]*

167 **Pars** (N.) - A standard score or unit, mainly used in golf (मानक-स्कोर)
Parse (V.) - To analyze a sentence grammatically (व्याकरणिक विश्लेषण करना) *[#R-2]*

168 **Pass** (V.) - To formally announce a decision or judgment (पारित करना)
Pass (V.) - To go across or hand over something (सौंपना)
Pass (V.) - To succeed in an exam (उत्तीर्ण होना)
Pass (N.) - A narrow route through mountains (दर्रा) *[#R-3]*

169 **Patina** (N.) - A superficial appearance suggesting age, elegance, or respectability (बनावटी छवि)
Patina (N.) - A thin layer that forms on metal or stone over time (परत) *[#R-2]*

170 **Pause** (V.) - To stop temporarily (विराम लेना)
Paws (N.) - The feet of an animal having claws (पंजे) *[#R-4]*

171 **Peace** (N.) - A state of tranquillity or quiet (शांति)
Piece (N.) - A portion or part of a whole (टुकड़ा) *[#R-2]*

172 **Peak** (N.) - The highest or most important point or level (चोटी, शिखर)
Peek (V.) - To look quickly or furtively (झांकना)
Pique (N./V.) - A feeling of annoyance; to stimulate interest (चिढ़ाना) *[#R-2]*

173 **Pick** (V.) - To choose or select (चुनना)
Pike (N.) - A large freshwater fish (पाइक मछली)
Pike (N.) - A long spear used by soldiers also a military formation (भाला) *[#R-3]*

174 **Plain** (Adj.) - Simple; Clear; easy to understand (सादा, सहज, स्पष्ट)
Plain (N.) - A large flat area of land (मैदान; समतल भूमि)
Plane (N.) - An aircraft that flies in the sky (हवाई जहाज़)
Plane (V.) - To make a surface flat or smooth using a tool (समतल बनाना) *[#R-4]*

175 **Pore** (V.) - To study or look at something very carefully (गहराई से पढ़ना)
Pore (N.) - A tiny opening in skin or a surface (रोमछिद्र)
Pour (V.) - To cause liquid to flow from a container (उड़ेलना; डालना (तरल पदार्थ))
Pour (V.) - To rain heavily (मूसलाधार बारिश होना)
Poor (Adj.) - Lacking money; in poverty (गरीब)
Poor (Adj.) - Of low quality; below standard (घटिया; निम्न स्तर का) *[#R-6]*

176 **Precede** (V.) - To come before in time or order (पहले होना)
Proceed (V.) - To continue or go forward (आगे बढ़ना) *[#R-2]*

177 **Precipitate** (V.) - To cause something to happen suddenly or too quickly (शीघ्रता से घटित करना)
Precipitate (V.) - To make a solid form and separate from a liquid (अवक्षेपित करना) *[#R-2]*

178 **Principal** (Adj.) - First in order of importance (मुख्य)
Principle (N.) - A fundamental truth or proposition (सिद्धांत) *[#R-4]*

179 **Quiet** (Adj.) - Making little or no noise (शांत)
Quite (Adv.) - To the greatest extent; completely (बिल्कुल) *[#R-2]*

180 **Rack** (V.) - To strain, torture, or exert intensely (used in idioms) (पीड़ित करना)
Wrack (N.) - Debris, or wreckage washed ashore by the sea (मलबा) *[#R-2]*

181 **Racket** (N.) - A fraudulent or extortion-based scheme (धोखाधड़ी)
Racket (N.) - A light frame with net used to hit a ball (रैकेट)
Racket (N.) - A loud, unpleasant sound (शोर) *[#R-3]*

182 **Rain** (N.) - Water falling from clouds in drops (बारिश, वर्षा)
Reign (N.) - The period during which a sovereign occupies the throne (शासन)
Rein (N.) - A long, narrow strap attached at one end to a horse's bit (लगाम) *[#R-6]*

183 **Raise** (V.) - To lift or move to a higher position or level (उठाना)
Rase (V.) - To erase, scrape, or level something (मिटाना)
Rays (N.) - Narrow beams of light or other radiant energy (किरणें)
Raze (V.) - To completely destroy or demolish something (पूरी तरह नष्ट करना) *[#R-4]*

184 **Real** (Adj.) - Genuine or true (असली)
Reel (N.) - Cylinder for winding thread or film (रील, धागा या फिल्म लपेटने की नली) *[#R-2]*

185 **Record** (N.) - A written account of facts or events (अभिलेख)
Record (N.) - The best or highest result in a field (कीर्तिमान)
Record (V.) - To capture audio or video (रिकॉर्ड करना) *[#R-3]*

186 **Register** (N.) - A book or list used to record information (रजिस्टर)
Register (V.) - To sign up or enroll (पंजीकरण करना). *[#R-2]*

187 **Resolution** (N.) - A firm decision to do or not do something (संकल्प)
Resolution (N.) - The act of solving a dispute or issue (समाधान)
Resolution (N.) - The degree of detail or sharpness of an image (स्पष्टता) *[#R-3]*

188 **Rest** (V.) - To relax or cease activity (आराम करना)
Wrest (V.) - To take something by force or effort (छीनना) *[#R-2]*

189 **Right** (Adj.) - Correct / just / proper (सही / उचित)
Right (N.) - A moral or legal entitlement to have or do somcthing (अधिकार)
Rite (N.) - A religious or other solemn ceremony or act (अनुष्ठान/रिवाज)
Wright (N.) - A maker or builder (कारीगर)
Write (V.) - To compose letters or symbols on a surface (लिखना) *[#R-23]*

190 **Righting** (V.) - Correcting something; restoring to a proper position (सुधारना)
Rioting (V.) - Taking part in violent public disorder (दंगा करना)
Writing (N.) - The act of forming letters by hand or composing text (लेखन) *[#R-3]*

191 **Ring** (V.) - To make a clear resonant or vibrating sound (घंटी बजाना)
Ring (N.) - A circular band worn on the finger (अंगूठी)
Wring (V.) - To twist and compress (मरोड़ना) *[#R-2]*

192 **Road** (N.) - A path or street for travel (सड़क)
Rode (V.) - Sat on and controlled a vehicle or animal (सवारी की)
Rowed (V.) - Moved a boat using oars (चप्पू चलाया) *[#R-3]*

193 **Roast** (V.) - To cook by exposing to dry heat (भुनना)
Roost (N.) - A place where birds rest or sleep (बसेरा) *[#R-2]*

194 **Rock** (V.) - To move or sway back and forth or side to side (झकझोर देना)
Rock (N.) - A large piece of stone; a boulder (चट्टान, पत्थर) *[#R-1]*

195 **Roe** (N.) - A small Eurasian deer (एक प्रकार का छोटा हिरण)
Roe (N.) - The mass of eggs found in a female fish (मछली के अंडे)
Row (N.) - A number of people or things in a line (पंक्ति)
Row (N.) - A noisy argument or quarrel (झगड़ा)
Row (V.) - To propel a boat using oars (नाव खेना) *[#R-5]*

196 **Role** (N.) - A function played by a person in a situation (भूमिका)
Roll (V.) - To move by turning over (लुढ़कना) *[#R-2]*

197 **Root** (N.) - The underground part of a plant that absorbs water (मूल/जड़)
Root (V.) - To cheer or support enthusiastically (उत्साहित करना, समर्थन करना)
Rot (V.) - To undergo decomposition; decay (सड़ना)
Rout (V.) - To defeat decisively (हराना)
Route (N.) - A way or course taken to reach a destination (मार्ग) *[#R-2]*

198 **Rose** (N.) - A thorny shrub bearing fragrant flowers (गुलाब)
Rose (V.) - Got up; increased; moved upward (उठा, बढ़ा) *[#R-2]*

199 **Rubric** (N.) - A set of criteria or instructions for assessing work (मूल्यांकन-मानदंड)
Rubric (N.) - Directions or rules governing religious rituals (अनुष्ठान-नियम) *[#R-2]*

200 **Sauce** (N.) - A liquid or semi-liquid food used to add flavor (चटनी)
Saws (N.) - Cutting tools with a toothed blade (आरी) *[#R-2]*

201 **Scale** (N.) - A device used for measuring weight (मापने का यंत्र)
Scale (N.) - A series of musical notes in order (सुरों का पैमाना)
Scale (N.) - The size, extent, or level of something (स्तर, परिमाण)
Scale (V.) - To climb or ascend (चढ़ना) *[#R-4]*

202 **Scales** (N.) - A device used to measure weight (तराजू)
Scales (N.) - A series of musical notes in ascending or descending order (स्वरक्रम)
Scales (N.) - Levels or ranges used for measurement or comparison (मापक्रम) *[#R-3]*

203 **Sconce** (N.) - A wall-mounted holder, especially for a candle or light (दीवारदीप)
Sconce (V.) - To punish, eject, or settle someone forcibly (दंडित करना) *[#R-2]*

204 **Sea** (N.) - The expanse of salt water that covers most of the earth's surface (समुद्र)

See (V.) - To perceive with the eyes (देखना) *[#R-2]*

205 **Seal** (N.) - An official stamp or emblem (मुहर, सरकारी सील)
Seal (N.) - A marine animal that lives in cold water (सील (समुद्री जीव))
Seal (V.) - To close or fasten something tightly (कसकर बंद करना) *[#R-1]*

206 **Seam** (N.) - A line where two pieces of fabric are sewn together (सिलाई)
Seem (V.) - To give the impression of being something (प्रतीत होना) *[#R-2]*

207 **Sentence** (N.) - A group of words expressing a complete idea (वाक्य)
Sentence (N.) - A punishment declared by a judge (दंड) *[#R-2]*

208 **Show** (N.) - A public entertainment or event (प्रदर्शन)
Show (V.) - To present, exhibit, or make visible (दिखाना) *[#R-2]*

209 **Sided** (V.) - Aligned with a position (पक्ष लिया)
Sighed (V.) - Exhaled audibly, expressing sadness or relief (गहरी साँस छोड़ी) *[#R-1]*

210 **Sol** (N.) - The Sun (Latin) (सूर्य)
Sole (Adj.) - Being the only one (एकमात्र, केवल)
Sole (N.) - The underside of a foot or shoe (तलवा)
Soul (N.) - The spiritual part of a person (आत्मा) *[#R-4]*

211 **Stage** (N.) - A distinct period or phase in a process (अवस्था)
Stage (N.) - A raised platform used for performances or public events (मंच)
Stage (V.) - To organize or present something publicly (आयोजित करना) *[#R-3]*

212 **Stalk** (N.) - The main stem of a plant (डंठल)
Stalk (V.) - To follow or watch someone secretly or persistently (पीछा करना)
Stock (N.) - A supply of something accumulated for future use (भंडार) *[#R-4]*

213 **Stationary** (Adj.) - Not moving or not intended to be moved (स्थिर)
Stationery (N.) - Writing materials, such as paper, envelopes, and pens (लेखन सामग्री)*[#R-4]*

214 **Steep** (Adj.) - Having a sharp incline or very high degree (खड़ा)
Steep (V.) - To leave something in liquid to extract flavour (भिगोना) *[#R-2]*

215 **Stern** (Adj.) - Strict; serious in manner (कठोर)
Stern (N.) - The rear (back) part of a ship (जहाज़ का पिछला भाग) *[#R-2]*

216 **Still** (Adv.) - Even now; up to this time (अभी भी)
Still (Adj.) - Not moving; quiet (स्थिर) *[#R-2]*

217 **Storm** (N.) - A sudden forceful assault (धावा)
Storm (N.) - Violent weather with wind; rain (तूफ़ान) *[#R-2]*

218 **Swell** (Adj.) - Excellent; very good (बढ़िया)
Swell (V.) - To grow larger or fuller (फूलना) *[#R-2]*

219 **Tableau** (N.) - A scene or dramatic representation (often a still visual scene) (दृश्य)
Tableau (N.) - A structured arrangement or lineup, especially of positions or members (व्यवस्था) *[#R-2]*

220 **Tail** (N.) - The rear part of an animal (पूँछ)
Tale (N.) - A story or narrative (कहानी)
Tell (V.) - To inform or narrate (बताना)
Toil (N.) - Hard work; to work hard (कठिन परिश्रम) *[#R-4]*

221 **Tau** (N.) - (Religious) The Tau Cross; a T-shaped Christian symbol (ताऊ-क्रॉस)
Tau (N.) - A numerical indicator or coefficient used in analysis or markets (गुणांक) *[#R-2]*

222 **Tear** (V.) - To pull apart or in pieces by force (फाड़ना)
Tear (N.) - A drop of liquid from the eye (आँसू) *[#R-1]*

223 **Tend** (V.) - To regularly or frequently behave in a particular way or have a certain characteristic (प्रवृत्ति या झुकाव होना)
Tent (N.) - A portable shelter made of cloth, supported by poles and ropes (तम्बू)
Tenth (Adj.) - Constituting number ten in a sequence (दसवां) *[#R-3]*

224 **Tenor** (N.) - A singing voice or the meaning of something (गायक, स्वर, भाव)
Tenure (N.) - The period of holding a job or office (कार्यकाल) *[#R-1]*

225 **Throne** (N.) - (Power) Royal rule or sovereignty (राजसत्ता)
Throne (N.) - (Seat) A ceremonial chair used by a monarch (सिंहासन) *[#R-2]*

226 **Tier** (N.) - A row or level of a structure (स्तर)
Tire (V.) - To become weary or bored (थकना)
Tyre (N.) - A rubber covering, typically inflated, placed around the rim of a wheel to form a soft contact with the road (पहिया (टायर)) *[#R-2]*

227 **To** (Prep.) - Indicating the place, person,

or thing that someone or something moves toward (को)
Too (Adv.) - More than what is needed or wanted (बहुत ज़्यादा, अत्यधिक)
Too (Adv.) - Also; in addition (भी)
Two (Num.) - Equivalent to the sum of one and one (दो) *[#R-3]*

228 **Toe** (N.) - Any of the five digits on the front of the foot (पैर की अंगुली (अँगूठा))
Tow (V.) - To pull a car or boat behind another vehicle (खींचकर ले जाना) *[#R-2]*

229 **Track** (N.) - A course or route along which something moves (पटरी)
Tract (N.) - An expanse of land or water (क्षेत्र)
Tract (N.) - A short pamphlet on a topic (पुस्तिका) *[#R-1]*

230 **Trip** (N.) - A journey or excursion (यात्रा)
Trip (V.) - To stumble or catch one's foot (ठोकर खाना) *[#R-1]*

231 **Tripos** (N.) - A three-legged stool or table (तीन पाये की कुर्सी)
Tripos (N.) - An academic examination system (परीक्षा प्रणाली) *[#R-2]*

232 **Vain** (Adj.) - Having excessive pride in appearance; or futile (घमंडी)
Vane (N.) - A device used to find which way the wind is blowing (पवन दिशा सूचक)
Vein (N.) - A blood vessel; or a streak/line in material (नस)
Wane (V.) - To decrease gradually; become weaker (घटते जाना)
When (Adv./Conj.) - At what time; the time at which (कब / जब) *[#R-4]*

233 **Vault** (N.) - A curved roof, chamber, or underground room (तहखाना)
Vault (V.) - To leap or jump, especially using hands or equipment (छलांग लगाना) *[#R-2]*

234 **Wait** (V.) - To stay in one place until something happens (प्रतीक्षा करना, इंतज़ार करना)
Weight (N.) - A body's relative mass (वजन, भार) *[#R-2]*

235 **Waiter** (N.) - A person who serves food and drinks in a restaurant (परोसने वाला)
Whither (Adv.) - To what place or state (कहाँ पर)
Wither (V.) - To lose freshness or vitality (मुरझाना) *[#R-2]*

236 **Waive** (V.) - To refrain from claiming or insisting on; give up (छोड़ देना)
Wave (V.) - To move the hand in greeting or farewell (हाथ हिलाना)
Wave (N.) - A moving swell of water in the sea or ocean (लहर) *[#R-2]*

237 **Watch** (N.) - A time-keeping device worn on the wrist (घड़ी)
Watch (V.) - To observe or look at carefully (देखना) *[#R-2]*

238 **Wear** (N.) - Damage or change caused by use over time (घिसावट)
Wear (V.) - To have clothes or accessories on the body (पहनना)
Were (V.) - Past tense of "are" (थे)
Where (Adv./Conj.) - At or in what place (कहाँ) *[#R-3]*

239 **Weather** (N.) - The state of the atmosphere at a particular place and time (मौसम)
Wether (N.) - A castrated male sheep (बधिया नर भेड़)
Whether (Conj.) - Expressing a doubt or choice between alternatives (चाहे) *[#R-2]*

240 **Well** (N.) - A deep hole from which water is drawn (कुआँ)
Well (Adv.) - In a good or satisfactory way (अच्छी तरह से)
Well (Adj.) - In good health; not ill (स्वस्थ) *[#R-4]*

241 **Will** (N.) - A written document stating how property is distributed after death (वसीयत)
Will (N.) - Strong intention or mental resolve (इच्छा) *[#R-2]*

242 **Wind** (N.) - Moving air; a natural force (हवा)
Wind (V.) - To twist or rotate something by hand or a tool (लपेटना) *[#R-2]*

*Total **242** Homonym Sets asked **738** times*

D2 Homonyms Practice Sets
(Based on Recent SSC & Other Exam Papers)

Practice Set - 1

Direction (Q. 1-10): Select the most appropriate option to fill in the blank.

1 The mother couldn't ______ such an insult from her son in front of the others.
1) bier 2) bear
3) beer 4) bare

2 Many new ideas are ______ when challenges are bravely ______by those who dare to think differently.
1) born, borne
2) born, bourn
3) borne, born
4) bourn, bourne

3 After realizing their leader had planned to ______ them in the middle of the vast ______ , the people refused to follow him any further.
1) dessert, desert
2) dessert, dessert
3) desert, dessert
4) desert, desert

4 He had to ______ his brains trying to remember how he came to be on the shore strewn with ______ and driftwood.
1) wrack, rack
2) rack, rack
3) rack, wrack
4) wrack, wrack

5 As the lonely ______ wailed over the lake, the pale ______ rose slowly, casting silver ripples on the water.
1) lune, loon
2) loon, loon
3) lune, lune
4) loon, lune

6 The ______ in my shoelace created a lot of trouble.
1) not 2) naught
3) knot 4) nought

7 She ______ the obligation of attending the kitty party with patience, but soon the mindless chatter began to ______ her.
1) bore, boar
2) boar, boar
3) boar, bore
4) bore, bore

8 She is going through a challenging ______, but these problems cannot ______ her.
1) model; modal
2) modal; model
3) phase; faze
4) faze; phase

9 The group of travellers were wonderstruck by the ______ of the coin.
1) white 2) wide
3) weight 4) wait

10 As his ______ ring slipped from his finger and sank into the pond, a curious ______ paddled over and, mistaking it for food, swallowed it whole.
1) symbol, cymbal
2) signet, cygnet
3) cygnet, signet
4) cymbal, symbol

Practice Set - 2

Direction (Q. 1-10): Choose the correct option that correctly explains the meanings of the given words:

1 Stationery and Stationary
1) Stationery means standing still and stationery means immobile
2) Stationery means writing and office material and stationary means in station
3) Stationery means writing and office material and stationary means immobile
4) Stationery means standing still and stationery means writing and office material

2 Complaisant and Complacent
1) Complaisant means overconfident and complacent means eager to please
2) Complaisant means confident and complacent means overconfident
3) Complaisant means eager to please and complacent means to manifest universally
4) Complaisant means eager to please and complacent means over-confident

3 Boarder and Border
1) Boarder means a food-and-lodge resident and border means boundary
2) Boarder means boundary and border means a food-and-lodge resident
3) Boarder means one who fits planks on the surfaces and border means boundary
4) Boarder means wider and border means one who fits planks on the surfaces

4 Enquiry and Inquiry
1) Enquiry means to seek information and inquiry means to investigate
2) Enquiry means to investigate and inquiry means to seek information
3) Enquiry means to seek information and inquiry means act of investiture
4) Enquiry means act of investiture and inquiry means to investigate

5 Masterful and Masterly
1) Masterful means imperious and masterly means autocratic
2) Masterful means skilful and masterly means imperious
3) Masterful means leader-like and masterly means skilful
4) Masterful means imperious and masterly means highly skilful

6 Compliment and Complement
1) Compliment means to synthesise and complement means to praise
2) Compliment means to go well with and complement means to praise
3) Compliment means to praise and complement means to blend well with
4) Compliment means to blend well with and complement means to praise

7 Deify and Defy
1) Deify means to confer upon one the status of god and defy means to oppose
2) Deify means to oppose and defy means to confer upon one the status of god
3) Deify means to define and defy means to oppose
4) Deify means to deny and defy means to oppose

8 Concurrent and Consecutive
1) Concurrent means occurring at the same time and consecutive means occurring one after the other
2) Concurrent means occurring non-simultaneously and consecutive means occurring one after the other
3) Concurrent means occurring at the same time and consecutive means occurring thereafter
4) Concurrent means occurring thereafter and consecutive means occurring at the same time

9 Epitaph and Epithet
1) Epitaph means a tombstone and epithet means a phrase expressing an attribute
2) Epitaph means words written on a tombstone and epithet means a phrase expressing an attribute
3) Epitaph means unspoken words and epithet means a phrase expressing an attribute
4) Epitaph means words written on a tombstone and epithet means an epigram

10 Discomfort and Discomfit
1) Discomfort means disturb and discomfit means unfit
2) Discomfort means unease and discomfit means to embarrass
3) Discomfort means to embarrass and discomfit means unfit
4) Discomfort means unfit and discomfit means to make comfortable

Practice Set - 3

Direction (Q. 1-10): Select the sentence containing the homonym of the highlighted word.

1 The bishop condemned the act as simony, citing canonical law.
1) The preacher was accused of simony for charging for blessings.
2) The court equated indulgence-selling with simony.
3) The alchemist failed to explain the simony in his formulas.
4) Simony was rampant in medieval ecclesiastical courts.

2 She refused to bark at strangers.
1) The bark echoed through the forest.
2) Dogs usually bark at night.
3) His bark was worse than his bite.
4) The rough bark of the tree peeled off easily.

3 He ran a 100-meter dash to the finish line.
1) The recipe calls for a dash of salt and pepper.
2) The dog made a sudden dash for the ball.
3) He made a quick dash to the store for some milk.
4) The marathon runner put on a final dash of speed.

4 The ancient sconce held a flickering torch along the corridor.
1) The thief smashed the wall sconce and fled.
2) The student was sconced for violating tradition.
3) The bronze sconce was engraved with floral motifs.
4) The hallway featured a new LED sconce.

5 He could not lead the team under pressure.
1) They used lead pipes in old construction.
2) He tried to lead the meeting professionally.
3) She leads the choir every Sunday.
4) He wrote a report on leadership styles.

6 He put the fish on the hook and threw it into the water.
1) He used a small hook to hang the picture.
2) He needed a small hook to attach the keychain.
3) The boxer threw a right hook.
4) The latch on the gate was a simple hook.

7 Please make sure to write your full home address...
1) The celebrity requested that her residential address be kept private and removed

from all public search directories for security reasons.
2) After living in the city for ten years, Sarah had to notify the post office that her permanent address was changing to a rural farmhouse.
3) The delivery driver called me because he was having trouble finding my address on the GPS due to the new construction in the neighborhood.
4) Millions of people tuned in to watch the president's televised address regarding the new economic policies.

8 The ancient patera was discovered near the temple ruins.
1) The curator displayed a silver patera from Hellenistic Syria.
2) The historian cited a patera in a Latin votive inscription.
3) The botanist studied the shape of the leaf's patera.
4) The archaeologist cataloged a bronze patera for libation.

9 He offered a great deal on the used car.
1) The two countries signed a new trade deal.
2) The magician will deal out the cards for the trick.
3) I found a great deal on airline tickets.
4) The business deal was finalized this morning.

10 The architect discussed the vault beneath the cathedral.
1) The gymnast performed a perfect vault over the horse.
2) The treasury vault was secured with biometric locks.
3) The earthquake cracked the stone vault supporting the nave.
4) The nobles were interred in the family vault.

Practice Set - 4

Direction (Q. 1-10): Select the sentence containing the homonym of the highlighted word.

1 The knight raised his pauldron before mounting.
1) The blacksmith polished the steel pauldron until it gleamed.
2) The art historian admired the engraved pauldron of the effigy.
3) The biology student dissected the pauldron Of the sea slug.
4) The museum displayed a 15th-century Italian pauldron.

2 The historian referenced a bailey in Norman military architecture.
1) The shepherd gathered his sheep in the bailey.
2) The bailey was reinforced with wooden palisades.
3) The outer bailey surrounded the motte.
4) The king's guard patrolled the lower bailey.

3 The legal scholar revised the digest of civil statutes.
1) The magazine's monthly digest reached a million readers.
2) He took a tablet to aid his digest after the meal.
3) The editor proofread the tax digest overnight.
4) The court referenced an old digest of maritime law.

4 The Latin rubric directed the priest to genuflect.
1) The rubric specified the font and spacing for the essay.
2) The rubric on the scroll was highlighted in red ink.
3) The rubric guided the monk through the psalmody.
4) The rubric dictated the feast-day procedures.

5 The manuscript bore a colophon detailing the scribe's name.
1) The typesetter inserted a printer's colophon on the final page.
2) The insect's antenna ended in a segmented colophon.
3) The medieval colophon praised the patron.
4) The librarian studied the Syriac colophon.

6 The scholar examined the chancel at the east end of the church.
1) The chancel was elevated above the nave by a few steps.
2) The concert began in the chancel with chamber musicians.
3) The builder reinforced the chancel arch using steel ties.
4) The chemist analyzed the properties of a synthetic chancel.

7 The conservator repaired the fillet on the old manuscript binding.
1) The chef pan-seared a salmon fillet with herbs.
2) The bookbinder stitched the leather fillet tightly.
3) The fillet was traced in gold on the spine.
4) The medieval fillet indicated title divisions.

8 The guards stood in pike formation along the causeway.
1) The angler pulled a large pike from the icy lake.
2) The rebel was punished by being placed on the pike.
3) The infantry pike split the enemy's front line.
4) The pike gleamed beside the veteran's armor.

9 The illuminated antiphonary contained Advent chants.
1) The singer read directly from the antiphonary.

2) The musicologist translated a medieval antiphonary.
3) The engineer downloaded an antiphonary for circuit patterns.
4) The archivist restored the parchment antiphonary.

10 The manuscript contained a siglum to denote a textual variant.
1) The editor inserted the siglum before the footnote.
2) The lab technician cleaned the siglum from the sample slide.
3) The scholar decoded each siglum used in the Vulgate.
4) The margin displayed an unknown siglum.

Practice Set - 5

Direction (Q. 1-5): Select the most appropriate option to fill in the blank.

1 A sailor was ______through the high tides.
1) selling 2) ceiling
3) swelling 4) sailing

2 The ______ was decorated with candles and chocolates everywhere.
1) flower 2) flour
3) floor 4) flor

3 The ointment will help to ______ the wound.
1) heal 2) heel
3) he'll 4) kneel

4 The mechanics tried a lot to get that car ______ from the accident spot.
1) toad 2) told
3) toed 4) towed

5 I ______ that he has been promoted to the post of ______ officer.
1) heard; ceiling
2) herd; ceiling
3) herd; sealing
4) heard; sealing

Direction (Q. 6-10): Which of the following options is NOT one of the meanings of the homonym.

6 Condition
1) To improve the hardness and elasticity of things
2) The physical state of something or someone
3) to train someone to behave in a certain way
4) A requirement that must be met for something to happen

7 Advance
1) Move forward
2) Progress
3) Special benefits
4) Ahead of time

8 Medium
1) A channel or system of communication or information
2) The lowest scale in an evaluation
3) A substance through which something is transmitted
4) A person who claims to communicate with spirits

9 Precipitate
1) To cause something to happen suddenly or unexpectedly
2) A solid substance that forms and settles out of a liquid solution
3) A steep or abrupt slope or cliff
4) To fall or drop suddenly, especially from a height

10 Content
1) The topics or material included within a book or broadcast
2) A state of satisfaction or peaceful happiness
3) The amount of a particular substance in something
4) A container used for storing liquids

Answer Key Practice Set - 1:

1 - 2	2 - 1	3 - 4	4 - 3	5 - 4
6 - 3	7 - 4	8 - 3	9 - 3	10 - 2

Answer Key Practice Set - 2:

1 - 3	2 - 4	3 - 1	4 - 1	5 - 4
6 - 3	7 - 1	8 - 1	9 - 2	10 - 2

Answer Key Practice Set - 3:

1 - 3	2 - 4	3 - 1	4 - 2	5 - 1
6 - 3	7 - 4	8 - 3	9 - 2	10 - 1

Answer Key Practice Set - 4:

1 - 3	2 - 1	3 - 2	4 - 1	5 - 2
6 - 4	7 - 1	8 - 1	9 - 3	10 - 2

Answer Key Practice Set - 5:

1 - 4	2 - 3	3 - 1	4 - 4	5 - 4
6 - 1	7 - 3	8 - 2	9 - 3	10 - 4

PART - E
(SPELLING)

Contents:-

Updated and Additional Content: -

1. **New SSC Spellings:** Added new words from **417 sets** asked by SSC after the publication of the last edition (May 2024).

2. **Expanded Spelling Coverage:** Added new words from 470 sets of other competitive exams. The 2026 edition now covers a total of 1,277 additional sets (470 + 807) from other exams since the 2023 edition.

Additional Symbols for smarter and efficient preparation: -

1. **#R (Repetition Count):** The #R tag, used to show how many times an Idiom has been asked in competitive exams.

SPELLING

Introduction

Correct spelling is an essential scoring area in competitive examinations such as **SSC, DSSSB, Banking, Defence**, and other government recruitment exams. Every year, candidates lose easy marks not because of lack of knowledge but due to minor spelling errors. Since competitive exams demand both **accuracy and speed**, strong familiarity with frequently asked spellings becomes a decisive advantage.

In examinations, candidates are tested not only on knowledge of words but also on their ability to recognise incorrect forms, distinguish between similar-looking options, and avoid pronunciation-based mistakes. They take seconds to answer if you have revised, and seconds to lose marks if you have not. No reasoning, no calculation, no elimination. Pure recall

How Exams Test SPELLING

You are given four similar-looking words and asked to pick the correctly spelled one (or the incorrectly spelled one). The trap is simple: all four options look almost right. One letter is swapped, doubled, or dropped. Here are real patterns from SSC papers:

- "Identify the correctly spelled word." Options: Vaccum, Vacume, Vacuum, Vacuom. Answer: Vacuum (double u, not double c)
- "Identify the incorrectly spelled word." Options: Accommodation, Environment, Occassion, Government. Answer: Occassion (correct: Occasion — one s, not two)
- "Identify the correctly spelled word." Options: Maintainance, Maintenance, Maintenence, Maintainence. Answer: Maintenance (not maintain + ance)
- "Identify the correctly spelled word." Options: Pronounciation, Pronunciation, Pronunsiation, Pronuncation. Answer: Pronunciation (no "o" after "n")

Notice the pattern: examiners target the exact letter where students hesitate. If you have seen the word enough times, you spot the correct one instantly. That is what this chapter trains you to do.

How to Use This Chapter

Every word in this chapter has been included because it was asked in a real examination. Nothing here is filler. The words are marked by #R how frequently they have been tested. Start from the top and work your way down.

#R (Repetition Count): Each spelling is accompanied by **#R**, indicating how many times that word has appeared in competitive examinations, especially SSC. For example, **Committee (35)** means ths word *Committee* has been asked **35 times** in various SSC and other examinations. In **"200 Most Repeated Spellings in SSC Exams,"** words are arranged according to repetition frequency, the higher the repetition, the higher the position. This allows students to focus first on **exam-proven words** instead of random vocabulary lists.

High #R spellings must be your top priority since they repeatedly appear across shifts, exam cycles, and various competitive exams.

Key Spelling Rules

Most misspellings are not random. They follow patterns. These ten rules cover the majority of spelling errors tested in competitive exams:

SN	Rule	Pattern	Examples
1	**ie or ei**	i before e, except after c	believe, achieve / receive, perceive Exceptions: weird, seize, foreign
2	**s or es**	Add -es after ch, sh, ss, x, z endings	arches, classes, boxes, quizzes hero > heroes; but piano > pianos
3	**y to i**	Consonant + y: change y to i before suffix Keep y before -ing	try > tried, tried; study > studies try > trying, study > studying
4	**Drop final e**	Drop e before vowel suffix Keep e after ce / ge	save > saving, use > usable traceable, manageable, noticeable
5	**Double t**	Short vowel + t, stress on last syllable: double t	commit > committed, forget > forgetting but treat > treating (long vowel)
6	**Double r**	Single vowel + r, stress on last syllable: double r	occur > occurred, prefer > preferred but preference (stress shifts)
7	**Double l**	Single vowel before l: double l	cancel > cancelled, travel > travelling but conceal > concealing (double vowel)
8	**Dropped letters**	Some words lose letters when suffix is added	argue > argument, humour > humorous proceed > procedure
9	**-able / -ible** **-ant / -ent**	No reliable rule — memorise these	negligible, sensible, admirable, suitable attendance, independence, intelligence
10	**Silent letters**	Letters written but not pronounced	debt, knife, column, rhythm, subtle mortgage, pneumonia, island

E1 Spelling Word List (asked in SSC Exams)

SN Correct Spelling (#R)

1 Abacus
2 **Abandoned (2)**
3 Abbreviated
4 Abdomen
5 Abductor
6 Aberrance
7 **Aberrant (2)**
8 Abnormality
9 Abolished
10 Abroad
11 Abruptly
12 **Abscess (2)**
13 Abscission
14 Absent
15 **Abstinent (2)**
16 Abyssal
17 Academician
18 Academy
19 Acceleration
20 Accent
21 Accentuation
22 **Acceptable (4)**
23 **Accessibility (2)**
24 Accessories
25 **Accidentally (4)**
26 **Accommodation (12)**
27 **Accommodative (2)**
28 **Accompanied (2)**
29 **Accompaniment (2)**
30 **Accompany (4)**
31 **According (2)**
32 Accost
33 Accountability
34 **Accountancy (2)**
35 Accreditation
36 **Accredited (3)**
37 Accretion
38 Accuracy
39 Accurately
40 Aced
41 **Achieved (2)**
42 Achieving
43 **Acknowledgment (5)**
44 **Acquaintance (6)**
45 **Acquainting (2)**
46 **Acquiescence (2)**
47 Acreage
48 **Across (3)**
49 **Activities (3)**
50 **Actually (4)**
51 Actuation
52 Adaptability
53 Added
54 Addiction
55 **Additional (2)**
56 Addressed
57 Addressee
58 Adequacy
59 Adjournment
60 **Administration (4)**
61 **Administrator (2)**
62 **Admired (2)**
63 Admirer
64 **Admissible (2)**
65 **Admission (5)**
66 **Admittance (2)**
67 **Adolescent (3)**
68 Adorned
69 **Adrenaline (2)**
70 Adroitness
71 Adulterant
72 Adulterous
73 **Advancement (2)**
74 **Adventure (6)**
75 Adventurer
76 **Advertise (5)**
77 **Advertisement (7)**
78 Advertising
79 **Advice (2)**
80 **Advisable (4)**
81 **Advisory (3)**
82 Aerodynamic
83 Aeronautical
84 Aeroplane
85 Aerosol
86 Aerospace
87 Aestivation
88 Affected
89 **Affiliate (6)**
90 Affirmation
91 **Affordable (2)**
92 **Afforestation (2)**
93 Agent
94 Ago
95 Agrarian
96 Agreeable
97 Agriculture
98 Ahead
99 Aircraft
100 Airdrome
101 Airliner
102 Airplane
103 Alacritous
104 **Alarmed (2)**
105 Alcoholism
106 Alerted
107 **Algebra (2)**
108 Algorithm
109 Alibi
110 Alighted
111 **Alignment (2)**
112 Alimentary
113 Alkali
114 **Allegorical (2)**
115 **Allergy (3)**
116 **Alligator (2)**
117 Alliterate
118 Allocation
119 Allopathy
120 Allotment
121 **Allotted (2)**
122 Allotting
123 **Allowance (3)**
124 Allowed
125 **Almighty (6)**
126 **Almost (2)**
127 Alphabet
128 Alpine
129 **Already (4)**
130 Altering
131 **Alternate (2)**
132 Alternative
133 **Although (2)**
134 Altogether
135 Aluminium
136 Amalgamation
137 **Ambience (2)**
138 Ambient
139 Ambiguities
140 Ambulance
141 Ambush
142 **Amendment (4)**
143 **Ammunition (2)**
144 Amount
145 **Amplification (2)**
146 Amplified
147 Anaesthesia
148 Analogue
149 Analysable
150 Analysed
151 Analytically
152 Ancestral
153 Anchoring
154 Aneurysm
155 **Angel (3)**
156 Angiography
157 Angriest
158 Annexation
159 **Annotate (2)**
160 **Announcement (7)**
161 Annoyed
162 Annual
163 Annunciation
164 Anomalies
165 Answered
166 Antarctic
167 Anthropomorphous
168 Antibodies

[**#R** denotes repetition of word]

[E.g. in SN 160, **(7)** denotes this word has been asked 7 times in SSC exams]

169 Antic
170 Antioxidant
171 **Antiseptic (2)**
172 Aphrodisiac
173 Apothegm
174 **Apparatus (2)**
175 **Apparel (3)**
176 **Apparently (9)**
177 Appealing
178 Appeared
179 Appeasement
180 Appended
181 Appliance
182 Applicable
183 Applying
184 Appointment
185 **Appreciating (2)**
186 Approachable
187 Appropriately
188 Appropriation
189 **Approval (2)**
190 Approximate
191 Arachis
192 Arbitrate
193 Archery
194 Archetype
195 Architect
196 Argumentation
197 Arie
198 **Aristocrat (2)**
199 Armature
200 **Arrangement (6)**
201 Arrhythmia
202 Arrived
203 Arrogate
204 **Artefact (3)**
205 Artery
206 **Article (4)**
207 Artiest
208 Artillery
209 Artistic
210 Ascendance
211 Ascendant
212 Ascended
213 Ascension
214 Ashes
215 Aspect
216 Asphyxiate
217 Aspirant
218 Aspirate
219 **Assassinate (6)**
220 **Assassination (9)**
221 **Assembly (4)**
222 Asserted
223 **Assessment (6)**
224 **Assigned (2)**
225 **Assignment (6)**
226 **Assimilate (2)**
227 Assimilated
228 Assisting
229 **Associate (4)**
230 **Association (4)**
231 Assorted
232 Assurable
233 **Assurance (3)**
234 Assure
235 **Assuredly (3)**
236 Asthma
237 Astonishingly
238 **Athlete (7)**
239 **Atmosphere (4)**
240 Attacked
241 **Attendance (5)**
242 Attendant
243 **Attention (8)**
244 **Attitude (6)**
245 **Attorney (2)**
246 Attribution
247 Auction
248 Audition
249 Augustan
250 Aureus
251 **Austerity (2)**
252 Autarky
253 Authenticity
254 **Authorities (2)**
255 Automated
256 **Automatic (3)**
257 **Autonomous (2)**
258 **Autumn (3)**
259 **Auxiliary (4)**
260 Avail
261 Available
262 Avenue
263 Avid
264 Avigation
265 Avoidance
266 Awakening
267 Award
268 **Awesome (2)**
269 Awfully
270 Awkwardly
271 Baffled
272 Bagel
273 **Baggage (2)**
274 Bail
275 Bailout
276 **Balloon (3)**
277 Bamboo
278 Bandicoot
279 Bangle
280 Banker
281 Bankruptcies
282 Banquet
283 Barbarian
284 Barbecue
285 **Barely (2)**
286 Barrage
287 **Barricade (3)**
288 Barrister
289 Bas
290 Based
291 Bastion
292 Batch
293 **Battalion (3)**
294 Beach
295 Bead
296 Beaker
297 Beam
298 Bear
299 Beast
300 Beaten
301 Beautician
302 Beautifully
303 Because
304 Becoming
305 Bedridden
306 Beer
307 **Beggar (8)**
308 Beggarly
309 Begged
310 Begger
311 Begin
312 **Beginner (2)**
313 **Beginning (18)**
314 **Behave (3)**
315 **Beige (3)**
316 Belated
317 **Believe (18)**
318 **Believed (3)**
319 Believing
320 Bellowing
321 Bellwether
322 Belly
323 Bemoan
324 Bemoaning
325 Bench
326 Benchmark
327 Benefited
328 Bequeath
329 Berate
330 Bereave
331 Bereaving
332 Berry
333 **Betray (2)**
334 Bewitched
335 Biannual
336 **Biases (2)**
337 Bicycle
338 Bier
339 **Billion (2)**
340 Binocular
341 Biodiversity
342 Biologist
343 Biopic
344 Biosphere
345 **Biscuit (3)**
346 **Bitter (2)**
347 Black
348 Blackboard
349 **Blade (2)**
350 Blandness
351 Blare
352 Blessing
353 Blockage
354 Blonde
355 Bloomed
356 Blossom
357 Boasting
358 Boldly
359 Bombshell
360 **Bonafide (2)**
361 Booking
362 **Booty (2)**
363 Boredom
364 Borrowing
365 **Bothering (2)**
366 Bough
367 Bouncing
368 Bound

369 **Bourgeoisie (2)**
370 **Bowlegged (2)**
371 Boxing
372 Bracelet
373 Brag
374 Braggart
375 Brainstorm
376 **Brake (2)**
377 Braking
378 Branches
379 **Brand (2)**
380 Branding
381 Brandish
382 Bravado
383 Bravely
384 Brawling
385 Breaching
386 **Bread (2)**
387 Breakage
388 Breath
389 Breathe
390 **Briefcase (2)**
391 Briefing
392 Brighten
393 Brilliance
394 **Brilliant (4)**
395 **Brinjal (2)**
396 **Bristle (3)**
397 Britain
398 Broadcaster
399 Broadcasts
400 Broccoli
401 Brochure
402 Bronze
403 Broom
404 Brought
405 Brush
406 Bubble
407 **Budgetary (2)**
408 Buffett
409 Bugle
410 **Building (3)**
411 Bulb
412 **Bulletin (3)**
413 Bullying
414 Bureau
415 **Bureaucrat (8)**
416 **Bureaucratic (4)**
417 **Burning (2)**
418 Busiest
419 **Business (21)**
420 **Businessman (3)**
421 Butterflies
422 **Buying (2)**
423 Bypass
424 **Cabbage (2)**
425 **Cactus (4)**
426 Cadre
427 Cafe
428 Calamities
429 **Calculate (4)**
430 **Calendar (19)**
431 Calligraphic
432 Calling
433 Camera
434 Camphor
435 **Cancellation (4)**
436 Cancelled
437 Candescent
438 Candidate
439 Cannot
440 Canteen
441 Canvas
442 Capabilities
443 Capillary
444 **Capitulation (2)**
445 Carbonated
446 Carcinogen
447 **Career (5)**
448 Carefully
449 Caribbean
450 **Carousel (2)**
451 **Carriage (3)**
452 **Carrier (5)**
453 **Carrying (2)**
454 Cashier
455 Cassel
456 **Cassette (2)**
457 Caste
458 Castigated
459 Castle
460 Casualty
461 Categorical
462 Categorically
463 Categories
464 **Category (5)**
465 **Caterpillar (2)**
466 Cathedral
467 Cattle
468 Cauliflower
469 Causeway
470 Causing
471 Causticity
472 Cautiously
473 Ceasing
474 **Ceiling (3)**
475 Celebrant
476 Celebrating
477 **Celebration (4)**
478 Censorship
479 Centenary
480 Central
481 **Century (3)**
482 Cereal
483 Cereals
484 Ceremonies
485 **Ceremony (6)**
486 Certainly
487 Certainty
488 **Certificate (3)**
489 Chain
490 **Challenging (3)**
491 **Chameleon (2)**
492 **Champagne (2)**
493 **Champion (2)**
494 Championship
495 Chancellery
496 **Chancellor (2)**
497 Chandelier
498 **Changeable (6)**
499 Changed
500 Channel
501 Chapter
502 Characteristics
503 Chargeable
504 Chariot
505 Charitable
506 Charmingly
507 Chastisement
508 Chauffer
509 **Chef (3)**
510 Chemical
511 Chemist
512 **Chemistry (3)**
513 Chew
514 Chief
515 Childhood
516 **Children (2)**
517 Chinese
518 **Chirpy (2)**
519 Chlorophyll
520 **Chocolate (4)**
521 Choice
522 **Cholera (2)**
523 **Choose (2)**
524 Chorography
525 Christmas
526 **Cigarette (2)**
527 Circadian
528 Circle
529 **Circuit (3)**
530 Circular
531 **Circulation (2)**
532 **Circumference (2)**
533 Circumventing
534 **Circus (2)**
535 **Citation (2)**
536 Citizen
537 Citizenry
538 Civics
539 **Civilisation (5)**
540 Claim
541 Classical
542 Classicist
543 **Classification (3)**
544 Clattering
545 Click
546 Climate
547 Climbed
548 Climber
549 Clinical
550 Closure
551 Cloth
552 Clothed
553 Clothes
554 Clover
555 Clown
556 Cloying
557 Club
558 Coadunation
559 **Coalescence (3)**
560 **Coalition (3)**
561 Cobblestone
562 Cognizant
563 Coherence
564 Collaboratively
565 Collage
566 **Collectable (2)**
567 Collection
568 Collector

569 College
570 **Collide (4)**
571 Colloquium
572 **Colonel (3)**
573 Colonial
574 Colonize
575 **Combination (9)**
576 **Combustion (2)**
577 **Comedian (3)**
578 **Comfortable (3)**
579 **Commendation (4)**
580 Commended
581 Comment
582 **Commentary (4)**
583 Commercial
584 Commercially
585 Commissariat
586 Commissioner
587 **Commit (9)**
588 **Committee (35)**
589 Commodious
590 Commodities
591 Commodity
592 Communicate
593 Communique
594 Communities
595 **Community (6)**
596 Commuter
597 **Company (3)**
598 Comparable
599 **Comparative (2)**
600 **Comparison (7)**
601 **Competition (5)**
602 **Competitive (2)**
603 **Competitor (5)**
604 Complacency
605 Complaisance
606 Complemented
607 **Completely (3)**
608 Completion
609 **Composition (3)**
610 Comprehension
611 Comprehensive-ness
612 Compression
613 Computation
614 **Concentrate (4)**
615 **Concentration (3)**
616 Concert
617 Conciliatory
618 Concisely
619 Conclusion
620 **Concrete (2)**
621 **Concurrently (3)**
622 Concussion
623 **Condemnation (2)**
624 Condensing
625 Condescend
626 **Condition (4)**
627 Condom
628 Conduct
629 **Conductor (2)**
630 Confectionery
631 **Conference (6)**
632 Confide
633 **Confirmed (2)**
634 Confrontation
635 Congratulate
636 Congratulation
637 Congregate
638 Coniferous
639 Conjectural
640 **Conjoined (2)**
641 Conjugate
642 **Conjuror (2)**
643 Connected
644 **Connivance (4)**
645 **Connotation (3)**
646 **Conscientious-ness (3)**
647 Consequently
648 Consider
649 **Consideration (2)**
650 Considered
651 **Consignment (2)**
652 Consistently
653 **Consolation (2)**
654 Consolidation
655 Consonant
656 Conspicuously
657 **Constipation (2)**
658 Constituency
659 **Constitute (2)**
660 **Constitution (3)**
661 **Constitutional (2)**
662 **Construction (2)**
663 Constructive
664 Consultancy
665 **Consumerism (2)**
666 Consumerist
667 Consummation
668 Contain
669 **Contained (3)**
670 **Container (2)**
671 Contestant
672 Context
673 **Continent (2)**
674 **Continuance (3)**
675 **Continuation (3)**
676 Continuity
677 **Continuous (3)**
678 **Continuously (2)**
679 Continuum
680 Contortion
681 Contour
682 Contraction
683 **Contractor (2)**
684 Contradictory
685 Contraption
686 Contributed
687 **Contribution (2)**
688 Contusion
689 Convener
690 **Convenient (3)**
691 **Convergence (3)**
692 **Conversation (2)**
693 Conversion
694 Convertible
695 Convey
696 **Conveyance (2)**
697 Convincible
698 **Cooking (2)**
699 **Cooperate (4)**
700 Coordinate
701 **Copulate (2)**
702 Copyright
703 Cordially
704 Corporate
705 **Corporation (2)**
706 Correction
707 Correlate
708 Correlative
709 **Correspond (2)**
710 **Correspondent (2)**
711 Corresponding
712 Corrigible
713 Corrupted
714 **Corruption (4)**
715 Corvette
716 Coterminous
717 Could
718 Council
719 **Councillor (3)**
720 Count
721 **Countenance (8)**
722 Counter march
723 Countermove
724 Counteroffensive
725 Counterpane
726 **Countries (2)**
727 Country
728 Couple
729 Courageously
730 **Courier (2)**
731 **Course (3)**
732 Cousin
733 Cracker
734 Cradle
735 Cramp
736 Crater
737 Crayon
738 Crazy
739 Cream
740 **Creativity (3)**
741 **Creator (3)**
742 Creature
743 Credential
744 Credo
745 Cremation
746 Cremator
747 Crescent
748 **Cricketer (2)**
749 Crime
750 Criminal
751 Cringe
752 **Criteria (2)**
753 **Critique (2)**
754 **Critiqued (2)**
755 Crockery
756 Crop
757 Cropping
758 Croton
759 Crouching
760 **Crowded (2)**
761 **Cruelly (3)**
762 Crunch
763 Crunchy
764 Crushing
765 Crystal

766 Crystallisation
767 Cube
768 Cubicle
769 Cuddle
770 **Culinary (3)**
771 **Cultural (2)**
772 **Cumulative (2)**
773 **Currently (2)**
774 Curricular
775 **Curriculum (5)**
776 Curry
777 **Cursor (2)**
778 Curtsy
779 Curvaceous
780 **Cushion (3)**
781 **Custard (2)**
782 **Customer (2)**
783 Cyclist
784 Cylinder
785 Cytochrome
786 Cytokinesis
787 Cytotoxicity
788 Dabbled
789 Daily
790 Dalmatian
791 Damaged
792 Dampness
793 Dare
794 Data
795 Dataset
796 Daughter
797 Daylight
798 Deadliest
799 **Deadline (2)**
800 Dealer
801 Dearest
802 **Debatable (2)**
803 Debauchery
804 Debris
805 Debt
806 Debtor
807 Decaffeinated
808 **Decease (2)**
809 Deceitful
810 Deceived
811 Decibel
812 Decided
813 Decimal
814 **Decision (8)**
815 Declared
816 Declination
817 Declivity
818 Decorated
819 Decorative
820 Dedicating
821 Deduction
822 Defective
823 Defenestrate
824 **Definitely (23)**
825 **Definition (11)**
826 **Deforestation (2)**
827 Deform
828 Defrauded
829 Degree
830 Deities
831 Deleted
832 Delible
833 **Delicacy (2)**
834 Deliciously
835 Delighted
836 **Delightful (2)**
837 Delightfully
838 **Deliquescence (2)**
839 Delirious
840 Deliverance
841 Delivery
842 Delusional
843 Demanded
844 Demarcation
845 Demolished
846 Demonian
847 **Demonstrated (3)**
848 Demonstrating
849 Demonstration
850 Demoralize
851 Dental
852 Deodorize
853 Deontological
854 Department
855 **Dependent (3)**
856 Deployments
857 Depravity
858 Derived
859 **Descendant (5)**
860 **Describe (4)**
861 Descriptive
862 Desensitising
863 Deserve
864 Designated
865 Desired
866 Despatch
867 **Despite (5)**
868 **Despotic (3)**
869 **Dessert (2)**
870 Destabilised
871 **Destiny (2)**
872 Destress
873 Destructively
874 **Detach (3)**
875 **Detail (2)**
876 Detailed
877 Detainee
878 **Detergent (2)**
879 Deteriorating
880 Determining
881 **Determinism (2)**
882 **Deterred (2)**
883 Deterrent
884 Devastated
885 **Device (2)**
886 Devotion
887 Diabetes
888 Diagonal
889 Diagram
890 **Dialogue (3)**
891 **Diamond (2)**
892 **Diaphragm (3)**
893 **Diarrhoea (3)**
894 Diary
895 Dictate
896 **Diesel (2)**
897 **Dietician (2)**
898 Differentiate
899 Differently
900 Diffraction
901 **Diffusion (2)**
902 Dignitaries
903 Dignitary
904 Dilution
905 **Dimension (3)**
906 Diminution
907 Dimple
908 Dining
909 Dinner
910 **Dinosaur (2)**
911 Dip
912 Diphtheria
913 Diploma
914 Directed
915 Director
916 Disabilities
917 Disabled
918 Disallow
919 Disambiguate
920 **Disappear (7)**
921 **Disappointment (4)**
922 **Disapproval (2)**
923 Discerning
924 **Disciplinarian (2)**
925 **Disciplinary (2)**
926 Discomfiture
927 **Discomfort (3)**
928 Disconcerted
929 Discourse
930 Discovered
931 **Discovery (3)**
932 **Discrepancies (3)**
933 Discrete
934 **Discrimination (6)**
935 Discursive
936 Discussed
937 **Discussion (6)**
938 Disenchantment
939 Disenfranchised
940 Disguising
941 **Disgusting (2)**
942 Disharmony
943 Disillusionment
944 Disintegrated
945 Disinterest
946 Dislodge
947 Disobedient
948 Disobey
949 Disorientation
950 Dispensary
951 Disposable
952 Disposal
953 Dissatisfaction
954 **Dissatisfied (3)**
955 Disseminating
956 Dissentient
957 Dissertation
958 Dissidence
959 Dissimulation
960 Dissociation
961 Dissonant
962 **Distance (2)**
963 Distillation

964 Distinguishes
965 Dithering
966 **Dive (2)**
967 Diversification
968 **Diversified (2)**
969 Diversifying
970 Dividend
971 Divinity
972 **Doctor (6)**
973 Doctrine
974 Documentation
975 Doldrums
976 Domineering
977 Donation
978 Doppelganger
979 Dosage
980 **Doubt (2)**
981 Doubtfully
982 Downfall
983 **Drainage (3)**
984 Drape
985 Drawing
986 Dreamy
987 Dredge
988 Dress
989 Dressed
990 **Dribble (2)**
991 Dribbling
992 Drifter
993 **Drunkenness (2)**
994 Dry-clean
995 Duality
996 Duly
997 **Dumbbell (3)**
998 Dumping
999 Dungeon
1000 **Duration (2)**
1001 Duties
1002 Dutiful
1003 **Dwelling (4)**
1004 Dyeing
1005 Dying
1006 Dynamics
1007 Dysentery
1008 Dysfunction
1009 Eagle
1010 Earlier
1011 Earnestness
1012 Earning
1013 Earring
1014 Earthiness
1015 **Earthquake (2)**
1016 Easier
1017 **Ecclesiastical (2)**
1018 Echolalia
1019 **Eclipse (2)**
1020 **Economic (4)**
1021 **Economy (4)**
1022 Ecumenical
1023 Eczema
1024 Edge
1025 Edition
1026 Educational
1027 **Effectively (2)**
1028 Effervescence
1029 Efflorescence
1030 Effluent
1031 Effluvium
1032 Effort
1033 Effusively
1034 Egalitarianism
1035 Egotism
1036 Egyptian
1037 **Eighth (4)**
1038 **Eighty (2)**
1039 Elaborately
1040 **Election (5)**
1041 **Electric (3)**
1042 **Electrician (2)**
1043 **Electricity (2)**
1044 Electrolyte
1045 Electron
1046 Electron-beam
1047 **Electronic (2)**
1048 Eleemosynary
1049 Element
1050 Elephant
1051 Elephantine
1052 Elevate
1053 Elevating
1054 Eleven
1055 **Eligibility (2)**
1056 Elite
1057 Elliptical
1058 Elopement
1059 **Embankment (3)**
1060 **Embarrass (21)**
1061 **Embarrassing (5)**
1062 Embassy
1063 Embattle
1064 Embedded
1065 **Embodiment (4)**
1066 Embroidered
1067 Embroidery
1068 Emerald
1069 Emerged
1070 **Emergency (4)**
1071 **Emigrate (3)**
1072 Eminently
1073 **Emission (3)**
1074 **Emitted (2)**
1075 Emolument
1076 Emphasised
1077 Empiricism
1078 **Employed (3)**
1079 **Employee (2)**
1080 Emporium
1081 En masse
1082 Enable
1083 Enchantment
1084 Enclosed
1085 **Encyclopaedia (4)**
1086 Enervating
1087 Enfeebled
1088 Enfranchisement
1089 **Engineer (4)**
1090 Engineering
1091 Engraving
1092 Enhancement
1093 Enjambement
1094 Enjoying
1095 Enlightenment
1096 Enlist
1097 Enmeshment
1098 **Ensure (7)**
1099 **Enterprise (3)**
1100 Enterprising
1101 **Entertainment (3)**
1102 Entirely
1103 Entity
1104 Entrant
1105 Entreat
1106 **Entrepreneur (22)**
1107 **Entrepreneurial (3)**
1108 **Entrepreneur-ship (2)**
1109 Entwine
1110 **Envelope (2)**
1111 **Environment (11)**
1112 **Environmental (3)**
1113 Ephemera
1114 Epigram
1115 **Epiphany (2)**
1116 Episcopal
1117 Epistemological
1118 **Equality (2)**
1119 Equally
1120 Equation
1121 Equilateral
1122 Equine
1123 **Equipment (9)**
1124 **Equipped (2)**
1125 **Equitable (2)**
1126 Equitably
1127 **Equivocation (2)**
1128 Eradicated
1129 **Eradication (6)**
1130 Eraser
1131 Erected
1132 Erosion
1133 Erupt
1134 Escalade
1135 Escalator
1136 **Esoterica (2)**
1137 Especially
1138 Essay
1139 **Essence (4)**
1140 **Essentially (2)**
1141 Establishment
1142 Estimation
1143 Eternally
1144 Ethereality
1145 Eudaimonia
1146 European
1147 Evacuation
1148 **Evaluation (2)**
1149 Evanescence
1150 Evaporation
1151 Evasion
1152 Everyone
1153 Everything
1154 Evidently
1155 **Evocation (3)**
1156 **Evolutionary (2)**

1157 Exacerbating
1158 Exaggerated
1159 Examination
1160 Exasperated
1161 Excavation
1162 **Excellence (6)**
1163 **Excellent (9)**
1164 **Except (2)**
1165 **Exception (2)**
1166 Exceptionable
1167 **Exchange (2)**
1168 **Excite (3)**
1169 **Exclaim (2)**
1170 **Exclamation (4)**
1171 Exclamatory
1172 Exclusionary
1173 Excretory
1174 Excruciate
1175 Excuse
1176 Execution
1177 **Executive (5)**
1178 **Exercise (2)**
1179 Exercising
1180 **Exhibition (2)**
1181 Exhibitionist
1182 **Exhilarate (11)**
1183 **Existence (11)**
1184 **Existentialism (3)**
1185 Expansive
1186 **Expect (3)**
1187 Expectation
1188 Expected
1189 Expediency
1190 **Expedient (2)**
1191 Expenditure
1192 Expense
1193 **Experience (7)**
1194 **Experiment (8)**
1195 Experimental
1196 Expertly
1197 Experts
1198 Expiry
1199 Explained
1200 **Explanation (10)**
1201 **Expletive (2)**
1202 Explode
1203 **Exploitation (2)**
1204 Exploitative
1205 Exploration
1206 Explored
1207 Exploring
1208 Exposition
1209 Expostulation
1210 **Exposure (2)**
1211 **Expression (3)**
1212 Extemporaneous
1213 Extemporise
1214 **Extension (3)**
1215 **Exterminated (2)**
1216 Externalism
1217 Extragalactic
1218 **Extraordinary (2)**
1219 Extravert
1220 **Extremely (3)**
1221 Extroversion
1222 Exuberantly
1223 Facilitation
1224 Factories
1225 Fahrenheit
1226 **Faithfully (2)**
1227 Falcon
1228 Falsification
1229 Falsified
1230 Faltering
1231 Family
1232 Farther
1233 Fascinated
1234 Fascism
1235 Fascist
1236 Fasting
1237 Fatality
1238 **Fatally (2)**
1239 Fattening
1240 Fault
1241 Favour
1242 **Favourite (4)**
1243 **Feather (2)**
1244 **Feature (3)**
1245 Featured
1246 **February (2)**
1247 Feedable
1248 Feedback
1249 Feeling
1250 Feisty
1251 **Femininity (2)**
1252 Fencing
1253 **Fermentation (2)**
1254 Festival
1255 Feudal
1256 **Field (5)**
1257 **Fiery (4)**
1258 Fifteenth
1259 **Fifty (2)**
1260 Fighting
1261 Figure
1262 Filial
1263 Filled
1264 Filling
1265 Finance
1266 **Financial (2)**
1267 Financially
1268 Finery
1269 Fiona
1270 Fished
1271 Fishing
1272 Fission
1273 **Fitter (3)**
1274 Flame
1275 Flapped
1276 Flare
1277 **Flashy (2)**
1278 **Flavour (2)**
1279 Flexibility
1280 Flickered
1281 Floccinaucinihili-pilification
1282 Floor
1283 Floppiest
1284 Floral
1285 **Flour (2)**
1286 **Flower (4)**
1287 Floweriest
1288 Flowing
1289 Flown
1290 Fluffy
1291 **Fluorescence (2)**
1292 Fluttering
1293 Focal
1294 Focused
1295 Fodder
1296 Fold
1297 Followed
1298 Follower
1299 Fomentation
1300 Foolproof
1301 Foot
1302 **Forcibly (3)**
1303 Forcing
1304 Forebear
1305 **Forecast (3)**
1306 Forecasted
1307 Foresee
1308 **Foreseeable (5)**
1309 Foretell
1310 Forewarned
1311 **Forfeit (4)**
1312 Forgetful
1313 Forgotten
1314 Form
1315 Formed
1316 Formulae
1317 Fortieth
1318 Fortified
1319 **Forty (3)**
1320 Found
1321 Fourteenth
1322 Fourth
1323 Fracking
1324 **Fraction (3)**
1325 Fractional
1326 Fractious
1327 Fractural
1328 Fragmentation
1329 Frankly
1330 Fraudster
1331 **Freeze (2)**
1332 Freighter
1333 Frenetically
1334 Frenzied
1335 Frequency
1336 Freshen
1337 Fridge
1338 Frieze
1339 Frigidity
1340 Frisk
1341 Frolicked
1342 Front
1343 Frost
1344 **Frosty (2)**
1345 Frothiest
1346 **Frown (3)**
1347 Frowned
1348 Frustrated
1349 Frying
1350 Fuchsia
1351 Fugacious
1352 Fulcrum

1353 **Fulfilment (2)**
1354 **Function (4)**
1355 Fundamentally
1356 Funereal
1357 Fungal
1358 Furl
1359 Furnace
1360 Furnish
1361 Further
1362 Fusible
1363 **Future (2)**
1364 **Futuristic (2)**
1365 Gadget
1366 Gained
1367 Gait
1368 Galaxies
1369 Galaxy
1370 Gallantry
1371 **Gallery (4)**
1372 Galley
1373 Gallop
1374 Gang
1375 **Gangster (2)**
1376 **Garbage (2)**
1377 Gardener
1378 Gargantuan
1379 Garment
1380 **Garrison (2)**
1381 Gathered
1382 **Gathering (2)**
1383 **Gauche (3)**
1384 Gauze
1385 Gazelle
1386 **Gazette (2)**
1387 Genealogical
1388 Generated
1389 **Generation (2)**
1390 Generously
1391 Gentile
1392 Gentry
1393 Genuinely
1394 **Geography (3)**
1395 Geospatial
1396 Geostationary
1397 Gesticulate
1398 Ghost
1399 **Giant (2)**
1400 Giddyap
1401 Gifted
1402 Giggle
1403 **Gimmick (2)**
1404 **Ginger (2)**
1405 **Girdle (2)**
1406 Glade
1407 Glider
1408 Glitch
1409 Glitter
1410 **Global (2)**
1411 **Gloss (2)**
1412 **Glove (2)**
1413 Gnawing
1414 Goal
1415 Goddess
1416 Godly
1417 Goggle
1418 **Gorilla (2)**
1419 Gothic
1420 Gourd
1421 Gourmandize
1422 **Governance (2)**
1423 **Government (11)**
1424 **Governor (3)**
1425 Grabbed
1426 Gradation
1427 Graduate
1428 **Grammar (15)**
1429 Grammatic
1430 **Grammatical (2)**
1431 Grandiloquent
1432 Grandiosity
1433 Grandly
1434 Granting
1435 Gravely
1436 Grease
1437 Greater
1438 Greatness
1439 Greave
1440 Greenery
1441 Greengrocer
1442 Gridlock
1443 Grip
1444 Groggy
1445 **Groom (2)**
1446 Groove
1447 **Groovy (3)**
1448 Gross
1449 **Ground (2)**
1450 Grower
1451 Grown
1452 **Guarantee (13)**
1453 Guaranteed
1454 Guaranty
1455 **Guard (4)**
1456 **Guardian (4)**
1457 Gud
1458 Guerrilla
1459 **Guidance (6)**
1460 Guide
1461 Guidelines
1462 Guiled
1463 Guillotine
1464 Gunner
1465 Gutter
1466 Gymnastic
1467 **Gynaecology (2)**
1468 Gypsy
1469 Habitation
1470 Habitude
1471 Haematite
1472 Haemoglobin
1473 **Haemorrhage (2)**
1474 Hagiography
1475 Hallowed
1476 **Halloween (2)**
1477 Hallucinating
1478 Handful
1479 Handicapped
1480 **Handkerchief (7)**
1481 Handled
1482 **Handling (2)**
1483 Happen
1484 **Happened (2)**
1485 Happening
1486 **Happily (2)**
1487 Harassed
1488 **Harassment (8)**
1489 Haughtily
1490 Haunted
1491 Haunting
1492 **Headache (2)**
1493 Headmaster
1494 **Headmistress (2)**
1495 Headquartered
1496 Healing
1497 Health
1498 Healthiest
1499 **Healthy (2)**
1500 **Heard (2)**
1501 Heartbeat
1502 Hearted
1503 Heave
1504 Heaven
1505 Heavenly
1506 Heavily
1507 Heering
1508 **Height (4)**
1509 **Heiress (2)**
1510 Heist
1511 **Helicopter (3)**
1512 **Helpful (2)**
1513 Hemoglobinopathy
1514 **Hermeneutics (2)**
1515 **Hesitancy (2)**
1516 **Hierarchical (2)**
1517 **Hierarchy (14)**
1518 Hiked
1519 Hilarity
1520 Hippocampus
1521 **Hippopotamus (2)**
1522 Histories
1523 Hitch
1524 Hoisting
1525 Hold
1526 Holiday
1527 Holistically
1528 Hollered
1529 Homage
1530 Homely
1531 Homeopathy
1532 **Homoeopath (2)**
1533 Honestly
1534 Hopelessness
1535 Horoscope
1536 Horrific
1537 **Horror (4)**
1538 **Hospital (2)**
1539 **Hostel (2)**
1540 Hotel
1541 **Household (2)**
1542 **Humanitarian (3)**
1543 Humanitarianism
1544 Humbly
1545 **Humiliate (2)**
1546 Humiliating
1547 **Humour (2)**
1548 Hundred

1549 Hungary
1550 Hungry
1551 Hunting
1552 **Hygiene (9)**
1553 **Hygienic (3)**
1554 **Hypnotic (2)**
1555 **Hypnotist (2)**
1556 Hypnotized
1557 Hysterically
1558 Icicle
1559 Idealize
1560 Ideate
1561 **Identically (2)**
1562 Identifiable
1563 **Identification (2)**
1564 **Idiotic (3)**
1565 Igneous
1566 **Ignition (2)**
1567 **Illegal (3)**
1568 Illegally
1569 **Illegitimate (8)**
1570 **Illicitly (2)**
1571 Illnesses
1572 Illuminating
1573 **Illumination (3)**
1574 **Illustrate (2)**
1575 Ill-will
1576 Imagery
1577 Imagination
1578 Imitated
1579 **Immediacy (2)**
1580 **Immediate (9)**
1581 **Immediately (10)**
1582 Immersive
1583 **Immigrate (2)**
1584 Immorality
1585 Immovable
1586 Immunize
1587 Impacted
1588 Impassionate
1589 Impassive
1590 **Impeach (2)**
1591 Impersonate
1592 Impersonator
1593 Implant
1594 **Implement (3)**
1595 **Implementation (2)**
1596 Implementing
1597 Importance
1598 **Impoverish (2)**
1599 **Impractical (2)**
1600 Impressed
1601 Impressing
1602 **Impression (4)**
1603 Impressionable
1604 Imprint
1605 Impropriety
1606 **Improvement (2)**
1607 **Imprudence (2)**
1608 Impudence
1609 Inability
1610 **Inaccuracies (3)**
1611 Inaccurate
1612 Inactivity
1613 Inadequate
1614 Inadvertently
1615 Inapplicable
1616 **Inappropriate (3)**
1617 Inattentive
1618 **Inaugural (2)**
1619 Incautious
1620 Incendiary
1621 **Incidentally (4)**
1622 Incision
1623 Incoherence
1624 Incommunicable
1625 Inconclusive
1626 Incongruent
1627 Inconsequential
1628 **Inconsistent (2)**
1629 **Inconspicuous (2)**
1630 Inconvenient
1631 Incorrect
1632 Increased
1633 Increasingly
1634 **Incredibly (2)**
1635 **Incredulous (3)**
1636 **Increment (2)**
1637 Incremental
1638 **Incriminating (2)**
1639 Incubate
1640 Indecisiveness
1641 **Independence (5)**
1642 **Independent (9)**
1643 Independently
1644 Indicate
1645 Indication
1646 Indicator
1647 **Indigestion (2)**
1648 **Indisposition (2)**
1649 Indisputably
1650 **Individual (8)**
1651 Individualise
1652 Individuality
1653 Industrial
1654 **Industries (2)**
1655 **Ineffectual (2)**
1656 Inefficacious
1657 Inefficiency
1658 Inefficient
1659 Inequality
1660 Inexpressible
1661 **Infection (2)**
1662 Infest
1663 Infidel
1664 Infiltrate
1665 Infinitely
1666 Infinitive
1667 **Inflation (2)**
1668 Inflection
1669 Influenced
1670 Informal
1671 **Information (3)**
1672 Informational
1673 **Informative (2)**
1674 **Infrastructure (3)**
1675 **Ingenuity (2)**
1676 Ingratitude
1677 Inhabitant
1678 Inherit
1679 Inheriting
1680 Initially
1681 **Initiative (4)**
1682 Injection
1683 Injury
1684 Inkling
1685 Inky
1686 **Innocence (3)**
1687 **Innovation (2)**
1688 **Innovative (2)**
1689 Innovatively
1690 Inoculated
1691 Inoculation
1692 Inquieted
1693 Inquietude
1694 Inquire
1695 Inquiry
1696 **Insect (2)**
1697 Insecurities
1698 Insertion
1699 **Insight (5)**
1700 **Insistence (2)**
1701 **Insoluble (2)**
1702 Insolvency
1703 **Insouciant (3)**
1704 Inspector
1705 Inspirative
1706 Inspiring
1707 **Install (2)**
1708 Installation
1709 **Instalment (3)**
1710 Instance
1711 **Instantaneous (4)**
1712 Instantaneously
1713 Instantly
1714 Instead
1715 Instil
1716 Instinctual
1717 **Institute (2)**
1718 **Institution (2)**
1719 **Institutional (3)**
1720 Institutionalized
1721 Instruct
1722 Instructive
1723 Instructor
1724 Instrument
1725 Instrumental
1726 Insurance
1727 Insure
1728 **Insurmountable (2)**
1729 **Intelligence (6)**
1730 Intelligibility
1731 Intend
1732 Intensity
1733 Intention
1734 Intentionally
1735 Interactive
1736 Intercede
1737 Interdicted
1738 **Interdisciplinary (2)**

1739 **Interest (2)**
1740 **Intermingled (2)**
1741 Intermittence
1742 Intermittently
1743 International
1744 Internet
1745 Interrelated
1746 **Interrogation (2)**
1747 Interrogative
1748 **Interrupt (8)**
1749 **Interrupted (2)**
1750 **Interruption (2)**
1751 **Intertextuality (2)**
1752 Intertwine
1753 **Intertwined (2)**
1754 **Interview (4)**
1755 **Interwoven (2)**
1756 Intimation
1757 **Intoxication (2)**
1758 Intricately
1759 Intrigued
1760 Introduction
1761 Introductory
1762 Intubate
1763 Intuition
1764 Invader
1765 Inveigle
1766 Invention
1767 Inventor
1768 Investigating
1769 Investments
1770 **Invitation (2)**
1771 **Invite (3)**
1772 **Inviting (4)**
1773 Involve
1774 Inward
1775 Iodine
1776 Ironically
1777 Ironing
1778 Irradiate
1779 **Irreconcilable (2)**
1780 Irregularity
1781 Irreligious
1782 Irreplaceable
1783 **Irrespective (3)**
1784 **Irresponsible (5)**
1785 Irretrievable
1786 **Irrigation (2)**
1787 **Irritable (4)**
1788 Irritably
1789 Irritant
1790 **Irritating (3)**
1791 Irritation
1792 Isle
1793 **Issue (2)**
1794 Issued
1795 Itch
1796 Jailor
1797 **January (2)**
1798 Jarring
1799 Jasmine
1800 Jaundice
1801 Javelin
1802 **Jealousy (3)**
1803 Jeweller
1804 **Jewellery (5)**
1805 Jigsaw
1806 Jingoistic
1807 **Jocular (2)**
1808 Jocularly
1809 Journal
1810 **Judgement (2)**
1811 Judicial
1812 Juggle
1813 Jugglery
1814 **Juncture (2)**
1815 **Junior (2)**
1816 Jurist
1817 **Justice (3)**
1818 Juxtaposed
1819 **Juxtaposition (3)**
1820 **Kaleidoscope (5)**
1821 Kangaroo
1822 Kelp
1823 Kerbstone
1824 Ketchup
1825 **Kettle (2)**
1826 **Kicked (2)**
1827 Kilometre
1828 **Kindergarten (3)**
1829 **Kinetic (2)**
1830 **Kingdom (2)**
1831 **Kitchen (2)**
1832 Kitten
1833 Knead
1834 Kneel
1835 **Knight (5)**
1836 Knives
1837 Knock
1838 Knowing
1839 **Knowledgeable (4)**
1840 Known
1841 **Label (2)**
1842 Labelled
1843 Labelling
1844 **Laboratory (5)**
1845 Labourer
1846 Labrador
1847 Lackadaisically
1848 Lacquer
1849 Ladybug
1850 Laid Off
1851 Lamppost
1852 Landmass
1853 Landscape
1854 **Language (4)**
1855 **Lantern (2)**
1856 Laparoscopy
1857 **Lapped (2)**
1858 **Lapse (3)**
1859 **Largesse (3)**
1860 Laser
1861 Lastly
1862 Lateral
1863 **Latitude (2)**
1864 Lauded
1865 **Laughable (2)**
1866 **Laughed (2)**
1867 Laughing
1868 **Laughter (2)**
1869 Launderette
1870 Lay
1871 **Layer (2)**
1872 **Leader (3)**
1873 Leading
1874 Leaf
1875 Leaning
1876 Leather
1877 Lecherousness
1878 **Lecture (5)**
1879 Legendry
1880 Legerdemain
1881 **Legionnaire (6)**
1882 Legislation
1883 Legislator
1884 Legislature
1885 **Legitimacy (3)**
1886 Lemonade
1887 Leopard
1888 Lepidopterology
1889 **Lesson (2)**
1890 **Letter (2)**
1891 **Liaison (15)**
1892 Liberian
1893 **License (10)**
1894 Licentious
1895 Liege
1896 **Lieutenant (9)**
1897 Lifelessness
1898 **Lightning (2)**
1899 Limber
1900 Limitedness
1901 Lingered
1902 **Liquefier (2)**
1903 Liquidity
1904 List
1905 Listen
1906 Listener
1907 Listening
1908 **Literal (2)**
1909 Literally
1910 **Literary (3)**
1911 **Literature (5)**
1912 Litigant
1913 Litigation
1914 Littered
1915 Liturgy
1916 Liveable
1917 **Livelihood (3)**
1918 Livelike
1919 Living
1920 Lizard
1921 Loafer
1922 **Location (4)**
1923 Locker
1924 Logarithm
1925 Logic
1926 **Loneliness (2)**
1927 **Longitude (2)**
1928 Longitudinal
1929 **Loophole (2)**
1930 Loot
1931 Loquacity
1932 Loser
1933 Losing
1934 Loss

1935 Loud
1936 **Loudly (2)**
1937 **Lovable (2)**
1938 Lubricant
1939 **Luggage (4)**
1940 **Luminescent (2)**
1941 **Lustrous (2)**
1942 Luxuries
1943 **Luxurious (5)**
1944 Lyre
1945 Lyricist
1946 **Machiavellian (5)**
1947 **Machinery (4)**
1948 **Macroeconomic (2)**
1949 Made
1950 **Maelstrom (2)**
1951 Magazine
1952 Magic
1953 Magisterial
1954 **Magistrate (2)**
1955 **Maintained (2)**
1956 **Maintenance (31)**
1957 **Majestic (2)**
1958 Majestical
1959 Maladjusted
1960 Malfunctioned
1961 Maligned
1962 Malnourished
1963 Malt
1964 Mammography
1965 **Manageable (3)**
1966 **Management (3)**
1967 Manager
1968 Manger
1969 Mangled
1970 Manhandle
1971 **Manifestation (2)**
1972 Manifesting
1973 **Manipulate (8)**
1974 **Manipulation (3)**
1975 **Manner (3)**
1976 Mannered
1977 Mantel
1978 Mantelpiece
1979 Mantle
1980 **Manufacturer (2)**
1981 **Manufacturing (2)**
1982 **Marathon (2)**
1983 Marginalised
1984 Marigold
1985 Marijuana
1986 **Marriage (7)**
1987 Marriageable
1988 Married
1989 Marshal
1990 Marshmallow
1991 Marvelous
1992 **Marzipan (2)**
1993 Mascot
1994 Masculine
1995 Massage
1996 Match
1997 Matchless
1998 Maternal
1999 Maternity
2000 Mathematical
2001 **Mathematician (3)**
2002 **Mathematics (7)**
2003 Mathematise
2004 Matriculation
2005 Matrix
2006 **Matter (5)**
2007 Mattress
2008 Maturity
2009 Maudlin
2010 **Maximum (2)**
2011 Meaningful
2012 **Measurement (2)**
2013 **Mechanism (2)**
2014 Medal
2015 **Medallion (2)**
2016 Media
2017 **Medicine (3)**
2018 Meditation
2019 Meditative
2020 Mediterranean
2021 **Mellifluence (2)**
2022 Melodies
2023 Melting
2024 **Member (2)**
2025 Membrane
2026 **Memorable (2)**
2027 Memorial
2028 Memories
2029 Menorah
2030 Mention
2031 Mentioned
2032 Meritocratic
2033 Merriment
2034 Mesing
2035 **Messenger (2)**
2036 Metabolic
2037 Metabolism
2038 Metal
2039 Metallic
2040 **Metamorphic (2)**
2041 Metaphor
2042 Meteorological
2043 Meteorology
2044 Methodology
2045 Metropolises
2046 Mice
2047 Microscopical
2048 Midday
2049 Midget
2050 Midst
2051 Migraine
2052 **Mileage (2)**
2053 **Milieu (4)**
2054 Militant
2055 Military
2056 **Millennia (4)**
2057 **Million (2)**
2058 **Millionaire (7)**
2059 Millipede
2060 Minaret
2061 Mined
2062 Minimal
2063 Minimum
2064 **Mining (7)**
2065 **Minister (3)**
2066 Ministry
2067 Minus
2068 Mirror
2069 Misaligned
2070 Misalliance
2071 Miscalculation
2072 **Mischief (4)**
2073 Miscreant
2074 Miserably
2075 Misinterpret
2076 Misinterpretation
2077 Misinterpreting
2078 Misled
2079 Mismatch
2080 Misogynous
2081 Misrepresent
2082 **Missing (2)**
2083 **Mission (2)**
2084 **Missionary (3)**
2085 Mississippi
2086 **Misspell (5)**
2087 Misspelling
2088 Misspelt
2089 Mistaken
2090 Mitochondria
2091 Moan
2092 Mockery
2093 Mocking
2094 Model
2095 Modification
2096 Modified
2097 **Moisture (3)**
2098 Molest
2099 Molestation
2100 **Moment (3)**
2101 Momentarily
2102 Money
2103 Monitor
2104 Monitoring
2105 Monkey
2106 Monolith
2107 Monologued
2108 Monotheistic
2109 Montage
2110 **Morality (2)**
2111 Mortally
2112 Mortified
2113 Mosquito
2114 Mosquitoes
2115 **Motivate (2)**
2116 Motivated
2117 **Motivational (2)**
2118 Motto
2119 **Mountain (2)**
2120 Mountaineer
2121 Mountaineering
2122 **Mourning (2)**
2123 Mouse
2124 **Moustache (4)**
2125 Mousy
2126 Muesli
2127 Multifarious
2128 Multilateral

2129 Multinational
2130 Multiprocessor
2131 Mumble
2132 Municipal
2133 Municipality
2134 Mural
2135 Murderous
2136 Murmur
2137 **Murmuring (2)**
2138 Muscle
2139 Mushy
2140 **Musician (4)**
2141 Musk
2142 **Mutineer (2)**
2143 Mutter
2144 Myocardial
2145 Mysteries
2146 Mythography
2147 Narratological
2148 Narrator
2149 Narrowest
2150 Nasal
2151 **Nation (2)**
2152 National
2153 Nationalise
2154 **Nationalist (2)**
2155 Natural
2156 Naturalism
2157 Naturalistic
2158 Naturally
2159 Naturopathy
2160 **Nausea (2)**
2161 Nautical
2162 **Necessitate (2)**
2163 **Necessity (8)**
2164 Need
2165 Negation
2166 Negative
2167 **Negativity (2)**
2168 **Negligence (3)**
2169 **Neighbour (2)**
2170 Neighbourhood
2171 Neighbouring
2172 **Neither (4)**
2173 Neoliberalism
2174 Neolithic
2175 Neoplasm
2176 **Nephew (2)**
2177 Nerve
2178 Netiquette
2179 **Neurological (2)**
2180 Neuron
2181 Neuroplasticity
2182 Neuropsychology
2183 Neurosurgeon
2184 **Neutral (5)**
2185 Neutralise
2186 Neutrality
2187 Neutron
2188 Newest
2189 Nibble
2190 **Niece (7)**
2191 Nightingale
2192 **Nineteen (2)**
2193 **Nineteenth (3)**
2194 **Ninety (2)**
2195 Ninth
2196 Nipped
2197 Nitrocellulose
2198 **Nobility (2)**
2199 Noctambulism
2200 Nonchalantly
2201 **Non-commis-sioned (3)**
2202 Noncommittal
2203 Noodle
2204 **Normally (2)**
2205 North
2206 Nosy
2207 Notably
2208 Notation
2209 Noticing
2210 Notification
2211 Notional
2212 **Notoriety (2)**
2213 Noun
2214 **Nourishment (3)**
2215 Novelist
2216 **November (2)**
2217 Nozzle
2218 Nuclear
2219 Number
2220 Numinous
2221 Nuptial
2222 Nutrition
2223 **Obeisance (2)**
2224 Obesity
2225 Objectionable
2226 **Oblique (2)**
2227 Obliquely
2228 Obscurantist
2229 Observance
2230 Observer
2231 Obsess
2232 **Obsessive (2)**
2233 Obsolescing
2234 Obstipation
2235 Obviously
2236 **Occasion (32)**
2237 **Occasional (5)**
2238 **Occasionally (9)**
2239 Occupancy
2240 Occupant
2241 **Occurred (5)**
2242 **Occurrence (29)**
2243 Occurring
2244 October
2245 Ocular
2246 Odorous
2247 Odour
2248 Oeuvre
2249 **Offered (2)**
2250 Offering
2251 **Official (2)**
2252 Officiate
2253 Offshoot
2254 Offspring
2255 Ointment
2256 Older
2257 **Olfactory (5)**
2258 **Oligopoly (2)**
2259 **Omelette (2)**
2260 **Omitted (3)**
2261 Once*
2262 **Onomatopoeia (6)**
2263 Opened
2264 Opening
2265 Operator
2266 Opine
2267 Opportunities
2268 **Opportunity (12)**
2269 **Oppression (3)**
2270 Optical
2271 Optimism
2272 **Option (2)**
2273 Orange
2274 **Ordinance (4)**
2275 Ordinarily
2276 Ordination
2277 Organisation
2278 Organometallic
2279 **Orientation (3)**
2280 **Original (3)**
2281 **Ornamental (3)**
2282 Ornate
2283 **Orthopaedic (2)**
2284 Otorhinolaryngol-ogy
2285 Ought
2286 Outage
2287 Outburst
2288 **Outcome (2)**
2289 Outsource
2290 Overall
2291 Overflow
2292 **Overreact (4)**
2293 **Override (2)**
2294 Overruns
2295 Overthrow
2296 Overview
2297 **Overwhelming (2)**
2298 Packet
2299 Pageantry
2300 Paint
2301 Paired
2302 Palace
2303 Palaeolithic
2304 Palanquin
2305 Palate
2306 Palimpsest
2307 Palladium
2308 Palliative
2309 Palmistry
2310 **Pamphlet (3)**
2311 Pancake
2312 Pancreas
2313 Panellist
2314 Panicked
2315 Panther
2316 Paper
2317 **Parachute (4)**
2318 Paraconsistent
2319 Parakeet
2320 Parallelism
2321 Parallelogram
2322 Paralysis
2323 Parameter
2324 Paramilitary

2325 Parapodia
2326 Parcel
2327 Pare
2328 Parent
2329 Parentage
2330 Parlay
2331 **Parliament (5)**
2332 Parody
2333 Participant
2334 Participate
2335 **Participation (2)**
2336 Particle
2337 **Particulate (2)**
2338 Partisanship
2339 Partly
2340 Party
2341 Pasion
2342 **Passage (3)**
2343 **Passenger (6)**
2344 Password
2345 Pasta
2346 Paste
2347 **Pastime (2)**
2348 **Pastor (2)**
2349 Pasture
2350 **Patient (3)**
2351 Patriotic
2352 **Patriotism (2)**
2353 Patronise
2354 Pattern
2355 **Peaceful (6)**
2356 Pearl
2357 Peasant
2358 Peccadillo
2359 Peddle
2360 Pedestal
2361 Peekaboo
2362 Peel
2363 Penetrating
2364 **People (2)**
2365 Perceivable
2366 perceived
2367 Percentage
2368 Percolation
2369 Percussion
2370 **Percussive (2)**
2371 Perennially
2372 Perfectionist
2373 Perfectly
2374 **Perform (2)**
2375 **Performance (11)**
2376 Performing
2377 **Peripheral (3)**
2378 Perishable
2379 Permafrost
2380 **Permissible (2)**
2381 Permitting
2382 Perpetrator
2383 **Perpetuity (3)**
2384 Perseverant
2385 Persevered
2386 Persisted
2387 **Persistence (4)**
2388 Persistency
2389 **Personal (5)**
2390 **Personality (5)**
2391 Perspiration
2392 **Persuasion (3)**
2393 Pertaining
2394 Pervade
2395 Perversion
2396 Perverted
2397 **Pessimism (2)**
2398 Pestilence
2399 Pestilential
2400 **Phallocentrism (2)**
2401 **Pharaoh (3)**
2402 **Pharmaceutical (3)**
2403 Phenomena
2404 **Phenomenological (2)**
2405 Phenomenology
2406 Philosophical
2407 **Philosophy (6)**
2408 **Phlegm (2)**
2409 Phonology
2410 Photograph
2411 Photography
2412 Photolithography
2413 **Photosynthesis (3)**
2414 Phylloxera
2415 **Physics (2)**
2416 Physiologist
2417 Physiotherapist
2418 Phytoplankton
2419 Phytoremediation
2420 **Piano (2)**
2421 Picking
2422 Pickle
2423 **Picnic (2)**
2424 Picnicked
2425 Pictography
2426 **Pictorial (2)**
2427 **Picture (5)**
2428 Pie
2429 **Piece (4)**
2430 **Pierce (4)**
2431 Piercing
2432 **Piety (2)**
2433 **Pigeon (2)**
2434 **Pilgrimage (2)**
2435 Pitch
2436 Piteous
2437 Pitiful
2438 Pizza
2439 Placard
2440 Plagued
2441 Plane
2442 **Planning (3)**
2443 Plantain
2444 Plasmodia
2445 Plastic
2446 **Plateau (3)**
2447 Platform
2448 Platinum
2449 Platter
2450 Player
2451 **Playful (3)**
2452 **Playwright (4)**
2453 **Please (2)**
2454 Plenary
2455 Plenipotentiary
2456 Pluckiness
2457 Plural
2458 Plus
2459 Pneumatic
2460 **Pneumonia (4)**
2461 Poem
2462 **Poetry (2)**
2463 Poison
2464 Polarization
2465 Policeman
2466 **Policies (2)**
2467 **Politician (4)**
2468 Pollen
2469 Pollination
2470 Pollutant
2471 Polysemy
2472 **Pomegranate (3)**
2473 Pondering
2474 Pontifical
2475 Popularly
2476 Porcelain
2477 Porphyroblastic
2478 Portative
2479 **Portion (3)**
2480 **Portuguese (2)**
2481 Position
2482 Possessed
2483 **Possesses (2)**
2484 **Possession (13)**
2485 **Possibility (3)**
2486 **Possible (5)**
2487 Posthumously
2488 Postmodernism
2489 Postponed
2490 Postulate
2491 **Posture (3)**
2492 **Potassium (2)**
2493 **Potatoes (2)**
2494 Potentiality
2495 Power
2496 Practically
2497 Practitioner
2498 Praised
2499 Prankster
2500 Precariously
2501 Precipitously
2502 Precursor
2503 Predicated
2504 Predicator
2505 **Predominant (2)**
2506 **Preferable (4)**
2507 Preferential
2508 Prehistoric
2509 Premature
2510 **Premier (5)**
2511 **Preparation (2)**
2512 **Prepared (2)**
2513 **Preparing (2)**
2514 Prescience
2515 Prescribed
2516 **Prescription (2)**
2517 **Presence (4)**
2518 **Present (2)**
2519 Presentable

2520 Presentation
2521 Presented
2522 Presenter
2523 Presentiment
2524 Presidential
2525 **Pressure (4)**
2526 Pressurised
2527 **Prestigious (2)**
2528 Prettier
2529 Prevailed
2530 Preventable
2531 Prevented
2532 Preventing
2533 **Prevention (4)**
2534 **Preview (2)**
2535 Previously
2536 Pried
2537 Priest
2538 Priestly
2539 Primarily
2540 Primate
2541 Prime
2542 Primitivism
2543 **Primordial (2)**
2544 Prince
2545 Princely
2546 Princess
2547 Principality
2548 Principally
2549 Printed
2550 Priorities
2551 Prisoner
2552 Private
2553 **Privileged (2)**
2554 Proactivity
2555 **Problem (3)**
2556 Problematic
2557 **Procedure (7)**
2558 Proceeding
2559 **Process (3)**
2560 Processes
2561 Processing
2562 **Procession (5)**
2563 **Processor (2)**
2564 Proclaiming
2565 Producing
2566 Production
2567 **Productivity (2)**
2568 **Profession (5)**
2569 **Professor (13)**
2570 Profitable
2571 Profoundly
2572 **Programme (2)**
2573 **Project (3)**
2574 Projection
2575 Promise
2576 **Promotional (2)**
2577 **Promulgate (2)**
2578 Pronounce
2579 **Pronunciation (14)**
2580 Propagation
2581 **Propeller (2)**
2582 **Properly (3)**
2583 Property
2584 Prophesy
2585 Prophylaxis
2586 **Proportion (2)**
2587 Proportionate
2588 **Propose (2)**
2589 Proprioception
2590 **Prosecutor (2)**
2591 **Prosperous (2)**
2592 Protag
2593 **Protection (2)**
2594 **Protein (10)**
2595 Protestor
2596 Protuberance
2597 Proved
2598 Proverbial
2599 **Providence (3)**
2600 Provoking
2601 Proximate
2602 Prudently
2603 Psalm
2604 Pseudonymous
2605 Pseudopodia
2606 Psychiatrist
2607 **Psychiatry (3)**
2608 Psychic
2609 Psychological
2610 **Psychometric (3)**
2611 Psychopharma-cology
2612 Psychotherapist
2613 **Publication (2)**
2614 **Publicly (3)**
2615 Published
2616 **Puddle (2)**
2617 Punch
2618 Punctilio
2619 Punctuate
2620 **Punctuation (2)**
2621 Puppeteer
2622 Puppies
2623 **Purchase (3)**
2624 Purchasing
2625 Purity
2626 Purport
2627 **Purpose (2)**
2628 Purvey
2629 Puzzling
2630 Pyramid
2631 Pyrrhonism
2632 **Quadrant (2)**
2633 Quadruple
2634 Quagmire
2635 Qualification
2636 **Qualities (2)**
2637 **Quality (2)**
2638 Quantify
2639 **Quantitative (2)**
2640 Quantity
2641 Quantum
2642 **Quarrelled (3)**
2643 Quasi
2644 Quench
2645 Querulousness
2646 **Question (3)**
2647 Questionable
2648 Questioned
2649 **Questionnaire (15)**
2650 **Queue (4)**
2651 **Quickly (2)**
2652 **Quiescence (2)**
2653 **Quieten (3)**
2654 **Quietly (3)**
2655 Quinine
2656 Quinoa
2657 **Quintessence (2)**
2658 Quizzes
2659 Quizzical
2660 Quotable
2661 **Quotation (2)**
2662 **Quote (2)**
2663 Quotient
2664 Radar
2665 Radiator
2666 Radicalism
2667 Radius
2668 Raged
2669 Rainbow
2670 Raisin
2671 Rambunctious
2672 Range
2673 Rankle
2674 Rascal
2675 Rated
2676 Rather
2677 Rationalisation
2678 Rationing
2679 Reachable
2680 Reached
2681 Reactive
2682 Reading
2683 Realised
2684 **Reality (3)**
2685 Rebuttal
2686 Recapture
2687 **Receipt (16)**
2688 **Received (10)**
2689 Receiving
2690 **Recent (2)**
2691 Reception
2692 Receptionist
2693 Receptive
2694 Recipe
2695 Reciprocating
2696 Reckoned
2697 Recognise
2698 **Recognition (3)**
2699 **Recommenda-tion (4)**
2700 **Reconciliation (2)**
2701 Reconsider
2702 Reconsidered
2703 Reconstructive
2704 Recopies
2705 Record
2706 Recourse
2707 **Recruit (4)**
2708 Recruiting
2709 **Recruitment (2)**
2710 Recuperation
2711 Recurrence
2712 Reduced
2713 Reduction
2714 Reef

2715 **Refer (5)**
2716 **Referee (4)**
2717 **Reference (11)**
2718 **Referred (7)**
2719 **Reflect (2)**
2720 Reflected
2721 **Reflection (3)**
2722 Reformation
2723 Reformed
2724 Refrain
2725 Refrigeration
2726 **Refrigerator (6)**
2727 Refused
2728 Refutation
2729 Regardless
2730 Regimental
2731 Regina
2732 **Region (2)**
2733 Regional
2734 Register
2735 Registration
2736 Regrettable
2737 **Regularization (2)**
2738 **Regulation (2)**
2739 Regulator
2740 **Rehabilitation (4)**
2741 **Rehearsal (5)**
2742 **Reimbursement (4)**
2743 **Reinforcement (2)**
2744 Reinstate
2745 Rejection
2746 Released
2747 Relevance
2748 **Reliance (4)**
2749 **Reliant (2)**
2750 **Relieve (4)**
2751 **Religiosity (2)**
2752 **Religious (5)**
2753 Remained
2754 Remark
2755 **Remembrance (4)**
2756 Reminder
2757 Remitted
2758 Remoteness
2759 Removal
2760 **Remunerative (2)**
2761 Render
2762 Rendered
2763 **Renewable (2)**
2764 Renewal
2765 Repair
2766 Repent
2767 Repentant
2768 **Repertoire (2)**
2769 **Repetition (4)**
2770 Repetitive
2771 Replaceable
2772 Replacement
2773 Reply
2774 Repositories
2775 Repository
2776 **Representation (2)**
2777 Reprography
2778 Repurposed
2779 Reputed
2780 **Require (4)**
2781 **Required (2)**
2782 Requite
2783 **Research (5)**
2784 **Researcher (2)**
2785 **Resemblance (3)**
2786 **Resemble (4)**
2787 Resettlement
2788 **Reside (2)**
2789 Residence
2790 Residual
2791 Resistivity
2792 Resonance
2793 Resort
2794 Resources
2795 Respectable
2796 Respectively
2797 Respiratory
2798 Resplendence
2799 Responded
2800 Response
2801 **Responsibilities (2)**
2802 **Responsibility (2)**
2803 **Restaurant (19)**
2804 Restrained
2805 Restriction
2806 Resultant
2807 **Resurrect (2)**
2808 **Resurrection (3)**
2809 Retail
2810 Retinal
2811 **Retrospect (3)**
2812 **Revealed (2)**
2813 Reveller
2814 **Reverberation (2)**
2815 Reversal
2816 **Review (3)**
2817 **Revise (2)**
2818 Revision
2819 **Revolutionise (2)**
2820 Revolutionize
2821 Revolve
2822 Rewind
2823 Rhapsodic
2824 **Rhetorical (2)**
2825 **Rhinoceros (2)**
2826 **Rhyme (4)**
2827 Rhythmic
2828 Rialising
2829 Ride
2830 Ridge
2831 Ridiculously
2832 Rifle
2833 **Righteous (4)**
2834 Riot
2835 Rising
2836 Road
2837 **Roast (3)**
2838 Roaster
2839 **Robber (2)**
2840 **Robbery (2)**
2841 Rockery
2842 Rocket
2843 Rocking
2844 Rodent
2845 Rolling
2846 Romanticism
2847 Roofline
2848 Rope
2849 Rotation
2850 Rotational
2851 Rotten
2852 Round
2853 **Rubber (2)**
2854 Rubbing
2855 Rubbish
2856 Rule
2857 **Rumble (2)**
2858 Running
2859 Rupee
2860 Rusk
2861 Rustle
2862 Ruthlessness
2863 Sabbatical
2864 Saccharine
2865 Sacrament
2866 **Sacrilegious (3)**
2867 Sacrosanct
2868 Sadly
2869 Safety
2870 Salary
2871 Saleable
2872 Salt
2873 Salute
2874 Sanctimonious
2875 **Sanctuaries (7)**
2876 **Sandwich (2)**
2877 Satirical
2878 Saucer
2879 Saviour
2880 Savoured
2881 Scandalous
2882 Scarf
2883 **Scattered (2)**
2884 Scavenger
2885 Scenario
2886 Scene
2887 **Scenery (6)**
2888 **Scenic (3)**
2889 **Scheduled (2)**
2890 **Scheme (3)**
2891 Schist
2892 **Schizophrenia (2)**
2893 Schizotypal
2894 **Science (3)**
2895 **Scientific (2)**
2896 **Scientist (10)**
2897 Scimitar
2898 **Scintillator (2)**
2899 **Scissors (2)**
2900 **Scoreboard (2)**
2901 Scorpion
2902 Scratched

2903 **Scripture (4)**
2904 **Scrutinize (2)**
2905 **Sculpture (2)**
2906 Scurvy
2907 Seafood
2908 **Search (2)**
2909 **Season (2)**
2910 Seasonal
2911 Secluded
2912 **Secondary (3)**
2913 **Secretariat (2)**
2914 **Secretary (7)**
2915 Secrete
2916 Secretion
2917 Secretly
2918 Securities
2919 Security
2920 **Sediment (2)**
2921 Sedimentary
2922 Sedition
2923 Seditious
2924 Seduction
2925 Seed
2926 Seeing
2927 Seemed
2928 Segment
2929 Segregation
2930 Segued
2931 Seismic
2932 Seizing
2933 Semester
2934 **Sensation (3)**
2935 **Sensational (2)**
2936 **Sense (2)**
2937 Senseless
2938 Sensible
2939 Sentimentalist
2940 Sentimentally
2941 **Separable (2)**
2942 **Separately (2)**
2943 **Separation (3)**
2944 **Sequence (2)**
2945 **Serenity (3)**
2946 **Sergeant (12)**
2947 Seriously
2948 Sermonise
2949 **Serpent (2)**
2950 **Serrated (2)**
2951 Serum
2952 **Service (4)**
2953 **Session (2)**
2954 **Setback (3)**
2955 Settle
2956 Settler
2957 Seventeenth
2958 Seventy-Two
2959 Several
2960 Shade
2961 **Shadow (2)**
2962 Shameful
2963 Shareholders
2964 Sharpen
2965 Sheet
2966 Shelf
2967 Shepherd
2968 **Shining (2)**
2969 Shocker
2970 Shoddy
2971 Shook
2972 Shopaholic
2973 Shopping
2974 Shortfall
2975 Shoulder
2976 **Shout (2)**
2977 Shouted
2978 Showpiece
2979 Shrine
2980 Shrinkage
2981 **Shrubbery (2)**
2982 Shuddering
2983 Siege
2984 Signage
2985 **Signature (2)**
2986 **Significance (2)**
2987 Similitude
2988 Simplify
2989 Simulation
2990 Simultaneously
2991 Sincerely
2992 Sincerity
2993 **Single (2)**
2994 Sinhalese
2995 Situation
2996 Sizable
2997 **Size (2)**
2998 Sizeable
2999 Sketches
3000 Skewed
3001 Skidded
3002 Skilful
3003 Skilled
3004 Skyscraper
3005 **Slaughter (3)**
3006 Slaughtered
3007 Sledge
3008 **Slice (2)**
3009 Slide
3010 Sliding
3011 Slip
3012 Slipper
3013 Slippery
3014 Slogan
3015 Slope
3016 Sloth
3017 Slough
3018 Slowly
3019 Slurry
3020 Smallish
3021 Smelled
3022 Smelly
3023 Smoothy
3024 Snatch
3025 Snatching
3026 Sneak
3027 Sobriquet
3028 Sociable
3029 Social
3030 Socialite
3031 Sock
3032 Software
3033 **Solicitation (2)**
3034 Solipsism
3035 **Soluble (2)**
3036 **Solution (5)**
3037 Solve
3038 Some
3039 Something
3040 Son
3041 Soothing
3042 Sorry
3043 Source
3044 Spanning
3045 Sparrow
3046 **Special (3)**
3047 **Specialist (2)**
3048 **Speciality (2)**
3049 Specified
3050 Specifying
3051 Specs
3052 Spectacle
3053 Spectator
3054 Spectroscopy
3055 Speculative
3056 **Speech (2)**
3057 Speed
3058 Spelling
3059 Spiteful
3060 Splatter
3061 Splendour
3062 Spoken
3063 Sponge
3064 Sponsor
3065 **Spontaneity (2)**
3066 Spoonful
3067 Spouse
3068 Sprang
3069 Sprawled
3070 Sprinkler
3071 Sprout
3072 Squadron
3073 Square
3074 Squawked
3075 Squirrel
3076 Staggered
3077 **Stagnation (2)**
3078 Stake
3079 Stakeholder
3080 Staple
3081 Staring
3082 Starting
3083 Statesmen
3084 Station
3085 **Stationery (3)**
3086 **Statistical (2)**
3087 Statistician
3088 Statistics
3089 Statue
3090 Steam
3091 Stepping
3092 Stere
3093 Stereo
3094 Sternly
3095 Stigmatic
3096 Stigmatisation
3097 **Stiletto (2)**
3098 Stipulate
3099 Stipulated
3100 **Stock (2)**
3101 Stocked
3102 Stoically

3103 Stoichiometric
3104 Stomach
3105 Stomata
3106 **Stone (2)**
3107 Stooped
3108 Stopped
3109 Storage
3110 Straight
3111 Straightest
3112 Straightway
3113 Strain
3114 **Strangely (3)**
3115 Strangled
3116 Strangulate
3117 Strategies
3118 **Stratification (3)**
3119 Stratigraphic
3120 Streaming
3121 Street
3122 **Strengthen (2)**
3123 Strepitous
3124 **Stressed (2)**
3125 Stretching
3126 Stridency
3127 **Strike (2)**
3128 Striker
3129 **String (2)**
3130 Stripe
3131 Strived
3132 Stroke
3133 Struck
3134 **Structural (3)**
3135 **Structuralism (2)**
3136 **Structure (3)**
3137 **Struggle (3)**
3138 Struggler
3139 **Stubble (2)**
3140 Student
3141 Studied
3142 **Studious (2)**
3143 Study
3144 Studying
3145 Stupefaction
3146 Stylistics
3147 Subjected
3148 Subjugator
3149 **Submitted (3)**
3150 Subsequence
3151 **Subservience (2)**
3152 Substance
3153 Substantially
3154 **Substantive (5)**
3155 Subtleties
3156 Subtropical
3157 **Subway (2)**
3158 Succeeded
3159 **Successfully (3)**
3160 **Succession (2)**
3161 **Sudden (2)**
3162 Suddenly
3163 Suddenness
3164 Suffered
3165 **Suffering (2)**
3166 Suggest
3167 **Suggested (2)**
3168 **Suggestion (2)**
3169 Sully
3170 Summer
3171 Summery
3172 Sunrise
3173 Superintend
3174 **Superintendent (3)**
3175 **Superiority (3)**
3176 Supernumerary
3177 Supervision
3178 **Supplementary (3)**
3179 Supplication
3180 Supply
3181 Supporting
3182 Suppose
3183 Supposed
3184 Supposition
3185 Suppressant
3186 Suppressing
3187 Suppressor
3188 **Surely (2)**
3189 Surgeon
3190 Surgeries
3191 **Surgery (2)**
3192 Surpassing
3193 Surrealism
3194 Surrogacy
3195 **Surrounding (5)**
3196 Survived
3197 Susceptibility
3198 Suspense
3199 **Suspension (2)**
3200 Swallow
3201 Swear
3202 **Sweater (2)**
3203 Swim
3204 Swimmer
3205 **Swimming (2)**
3206 **Swivelling (2)**
3207 Sword
3208 Swum
3209 Sycophants
3210 Syllabi
3211 Symbiotic
3212 Symbolical
3213 Symbolism
3214 **Symmetry (3)**
3215 Sympathize
3216 Symptom
3217 Symptomatically
3218 Synchronize
3219 Synchronous
3220 Syncopation
3221 Syndrome
3222 Synergism
3223 Syringe
3224 Syrup
3225 System
3226 **Systematic (2)**
3227 Syzygy
3228 Tabular
3229 Tactfully
3230 Tactic
3231 **Tailor (2)**
3232 Talent
3233 Talon
3234 Tamarind
3235 Tamper
3236 **Tapestry (2)**
3237 Targeted
3238 Tariff
3239 Task
3240 Tattle
3241 Taught
3242 **Teacher (6)**
3243 **Technical (2)**
3244 Technically
3245 **Technician (2)**
3246 **Technique (3)**
3247 Technological
3248 **Technology (5)**
3249 Tech-Savvy
3250 **Television (2)**
3251 Temerarious
3252 **Temperament (6)**
3253 **Temperature (7)**
3254 **Temple (2)**
3255 **Temptation (2)**
3256 Tennessee
3257 Tenth
3258 Terabyte
3259 Terminator
3260 **Terminology (2)**
3261 Termite
3262 Terracide
3263 Terracotta
3264 Terrestrial
3265 Terrifying
3266 Territorial
3267 **Territory (5)**
3268 **Terrorism (4)**
3269 Terrorist
3270 Tertial
3271 Tertiary
3272 Texture
3273 Thanksgiving
3274 Their
3275 Thenceforth
3276 Theorise
3277 Theorised
3278 Therapist
3279 Thermodynamic
3280 Thermodynamics
3281 **Thesaurus (2)**
3282 Thespian
3283 **Thief (2)**
3284 Thing
3285 **Though (3)**
3286 **Thought (2)**
3287 Thoughtful
3288 Thought-Provoking
3289 **Thousand (2)**
3290 Thrashed
3291 Thrashing
3292 **Threatened (3)**
3293 Threatening
3294 Thrilled
3295 Thriller
3296 Thrilling
3297 Throat

3298 Throttle
3299 Throttled
3300 Through
3301 **Throughout (2)**
3302 Throw
3303 Thrust
3304 **Thunder (3)**
3305 Thunderous
3306 Thyroid
3307 Tightened
3308 Tightrope
3309 Timely
3310 Tinderbox
3311 **Tinker (2)**
3312 Tissue
3313 **Titillate (2)**
3314 Toast
3315 **Tobacco (2)**
3316 Today
3317 Toffee
3318 Token
3319 **Tolerant (3)**
3320 Tomato's
3321 Tomatoes
3322 **Tomorrow (7)**
3323 Tonality
3324 **Tongue (4)**
3325 Tonsure
3326 Torches
3327 Tornado
3328 Totalitarian
3329 Toughness
3330 Tour
3331 Tourism
3332 Tournament
3333 Traceable
3334 Tractor
3335 **Tradition (2)**
3336 Traditionally
3337 **Traffic (3)**
3338 Trafficking
3339 Trailer
3340 Traipse
3341 Tram
3342 Tranchant
3343 Tranquillize
3344 **Transcendental (2)**
3345 Transferred
3346 **Transformative (2)**
3347 Translate
3348 Translucent
3349 Transmissible
3350 Transmitted
3351 Transportation
3352 **Traumatic (3)**
3353 **Traveller (3)**
3354 Travelling
3355 **Treasure (5)**
3356 Treatment
3357 Treaty
3358 **Treble (2)**
3359 Trial
3360 **Triangular (2)**
3361 Triangulation
3362 Tribe
3363 Tribunal
3364 Tribute
3365 Trickery
3366 Trickster
3367 Trifle
3368 Triple
3369 Trisomy
3370 Trousers
3371 **Truly (6)**
3372 Trunk
3373 Trusted
3374 **Trustworthy (2)**
3375 Truthfully
3376 **Tuition (6)**
3377 Tumble
3378 Tumbler
3379 **Tunnel (2)**
3380 Turmeric
3381 Turtle
3382 Tweak
3383 **Twelfth (6)**
3384 Twinkle
3385 Twisted
3386 Typical
3387 Tyrannical
3388 Ubiquity
3389 **Ultimately (2)**
3390 Umbilical
3391 Umbrella
3392 Unacceptable
3393 Unaffected
3394 Unambiguous
3395 **Unassailable (2)**
3396 Unattractiveness
3397 Unbreakable
3398 Uncertain
3399 Unchallenged
3400 Unchecked
3401 **Uncle (2)**
3402 Unclean
3403 **Unconscious (2)**
3404 Unconsciously
3405 Uncontroversial
3406 Unconventional
3407 Uncovered
3408 Unction
3409 Unctuous
3410 Undergarment
3411 Underprivileged
3412 **Underrated (3)**
3413 **Understanding (2)**
3414 Understood
3415 Undertow
3416 **Undoubtedly (2)**
3417 Undulate
3418 Unduly
3419 Unexpected
3420 Unflappable
3421 Unforgettable
3422 **Unfortunately (2)**
3423 Unhappy
3424 Unintended
3425 Unintentionally
3426 Uninterruptedly
3427 Unison
3428 Universalities
3429 Universe
3430 **University (3)**
3431 Unkempt
3432 Unlawful
3433 Unmanageable
3434 Unmistakable
3435 Unnatural
3436 Unnerve
3437 Unnerving
3438 Unorganised
3439 **Unpretentious (4)**
3440 Unquestionable
3441 **Unravel (3)**
3442 Unreasonable
3443 Unsavoury
3444 Unscientific
3445 Unshielded
3446 Unsuited
3447 Unsurpassable
3448 Unsustainable
3449 Untie
3450 **Until (3)**
3451 Untouchability
3452 **Unwavering (4)**
3453 Unwearied
3454 Unwilling
3455 Upcoming
3456 Update
3457 **Uproar (2)**
3458 Uprooted
3459 Upstairs
3460 Urbanisation
3461 Urchin
3462 Usable
3463 Usual
3464 **Usually (3)**
3465 **Utilitarianism (3)**
3466 **Utterance (2)**
3467 Vacancies
3468 Vacation
3469 Vaccinate
3470 **Vaccination (5)**
3471 **Vaccine (2)**
3472 Vacuous
3473 **Vacuum (14)**
3474 Vacuum-Cleaner
3475 **Valediction (4)**
3476 Validity
3477 Valorous
3478 Value
3479 Valuing
3480 Variability
3481 Vassal
3482 Vastness
3483 Veer
3484 Vegetable
3485 **Vegetation (2)**
3486 **Vehemence (2)**
3487 **Vehicle (5)**
3488 Vein
3489 Venison
3490 Venomous
3491 Ventilation

3492 Ventilator
3493 Ventriculoperito-neal
3494 Veranda
3495 Verbal
3496 Verifiability
3497 Verification
3498 Vermilion
3499 Verminous
3500 Versus
3501 Very
3502 Vessel
3503 Vestibular
3504 **Veterinary (4)**
3505 Vial
3506 Vibe
3507 Vicariousness
3508 Viceregal
3509 Vicereine
3510 Victim
3511 Victories
3512 **Video (2)**
3513 Vigilante
3514 Vilifying
3515 **Village (5)**
3516 Vindication
3517 Violating
3518 **Violin (5)**
3519 Virtually
3520 Vise
3521 **Visibility (3)**
3522 Vision
3523 **Visualise (2)**
3524 Vitality
3525 Vituperation
3526 Vividly
3527 **Vocabulary (3)**
3528 **Volcano (2)**
3529 Volume
3530 Volunteered
3531 Volunteering
3532 **Voluptuous (2)**
3533 Vomitus
3534 Voracity
3535 Vulnerabilities
3536 Vulnerability
3537 Wafted
3538 Waiter
3539 Waiting
3540 Waitress
3541 Wakeful
3542 Wantonly
3543 Wariness
3544 Warranty
3545 **Washing (2)**
3546 Wass
3547 Wasted
3548 Watercourse
3549 Wave
3550 Wealthiest
3551 Wearily
3552 Wearing
3553 **Weather (10)**
3554 Weave
3555 **Website (2)**
3556 Wedding
3557 **Wednesday (3)**
3558 Week
3559 Weekend
3560 Welcoming
3561 Welded
3562 Well-Deserved
3563 Wellhead
3564 Wench
3565 Wherefore
3566 **Whether (3)**
3567 **While (2)**
3568 Whimper
3569 Whip
3570 Whisked
3571 Whistle
3572 Whiten
3573 Whither
3574 Wholeness
3575 Whorl
3576 Wider
3577 Wiggle
3578 Wildernesses
3579 **Wilful (4)**
3580 Willingness
3581 Winch
3582 Winning
3583 Winter
3584 Wired
3585 Wish
3586 **Wit (2)**
3587 Witch
3588 Withdrawal
3589 Withering
3590 **Witness (3)**
3591 Witnesses
3592 Wondered
3593 Woollen
3594 Working
3595 Worsened
3596 **Worshipped (2)**
3597 Worthwhile
3598 Wrap Up
3599 Wrapped
3600 Wreathe
3601 Wrecked
3602 Wrestler
3603 **Wrinkle (2)**
3604 **Write (2)**
3605 **Writing (3)**
3606 **Written (2)**
3607 Wrongdoing
3608 Xenotransplanta-tion
3609 **Xylophone (2)**
3610 **Yacht (2)**
3611 **Yesterday (2)**
3612 Yeti
3613 Yoghurt
3614 Younger
3615 Youthful
3616 Zealously
3617 Zestful
3618 **Zoologist (2)**
3619 Zucchini

*Total **3619** Spellings asked **6235** times*

SN	Correct Spelling (#R)
1	Accommodate (38)
2	Committee (35)
3	Separate (35)
4	Occasion (32)
5	Maintenance (31)
6	Privilege (31)
7	Occurrence (29)
8	Bureaucracy (29)
9	Necessary (27)
10	Conscientious (27)
11	Millennium (26)
12	Definitely (23)
13	Mischievous (23)
14	Perseverance (23)
15	Entrepreneur (22)
16	Connoisseur (22)
17	Business (21)
18	Embarrass (21)
19	Conscious (21)
20	Embarrassment (20)
21	Calendar (19)
22	Restaurant (19)
23	Beginning (18)
24	Believe (18)
25	Argument (18)
26	Knowledge (18)
27	Receive (18)
28	Leisure (18)
29	Recommend (17)
30	Receipt (16)
31	Address (16)
32	Aesthetic (16)
33	Exaggerate (16)
34	Grammar (15)
35	Liaison (15)
36	Questionnaire (15)
37	Manoeuvre (15)
38	Consensus (15)
39	Deceive (15)
40	Parallel (15)
41	Supersede (15)
42	Colleague (15)
43	Dilemma (15)
44	Efficient (15)
45	Magnanimous (15)
46	Hierarchy (14)
47	Pronunciation (14)
48	Vacuum (14)
49	Conscience (14)
50	Acquire (14)
51	Discipline (14)
52	Miscellaneous (14)
53	Camouflage (14)
54	Indispensable (14)
55	Magnificent (14)
56	Guarantee (13)
57	Possession (13)
58	Professor (13)
59	Achieve (13)
60	Perceive (13)
61	Relevant (13)
62	Meticulous (13)
63	Accommodation (12)
64	Opportunity (12)
65	Sergeant (12)
66	Cemetery (12)
67	Schedule (12)
68	Conceive (12)
69	Foreign (12)
70	Grateful (12)
71	Humorous (12)
72	Resplendent (12)
73	Amateur (12)
74	Definition (11)
75	Environment (11)
76	Exhilarate (11)
77	Existence (11)
78	Government (11)
79	Performance (11)
80	Reference (11)
81	Audience (11)
82	Dictionary (11)
83	Acquiesce (11)
84	Delicious (11)
85	Fabulous (11)
86	Irrelevant (11)
87	Noticeable (11)
88	Omission (11)
89	Vicious (11)
90	Gregarious (11)
91	Surveillance (11)
92	Ubiquitous (11)
93	Explanation (10)
94	Immediately (10)
95	License (10)
96	Protein (10)
97	Received (10)
98	Scientist (10)
99	Weather (10)
100	Acoustic (10)
101	Bouquet (10)
102	Etiquette (10)
103	Inoculate (10)
104	Pseudonym (10)
105	Psychology (10)
106	Absence (10)
107	Acclaim (10)
108	Achievement (10)
109	Acknowledge (10)
110	Aggravate (10)
111	Apparent (10)
112	Appearance (10)
113	Benevolent (10)
114	Precious (10)
115	Tyranny (10)
116	Weird (10)
117	Appreciate (10)
118	Apparently (9)
119	Assassination (9)
120	Combination (9)
121	Commit (9)
122	Equipment (9)
123	Excellent (9)
124	Hygiene (9)
125	Immediate (9)
126	Independent (9)
127	Lieutenant (9)
128	Occasionally (9)
129	Personnel (9)
130	Architecture (9)
131	Cautious (9)
132	Commitment (9)
133	Definite (9)
134	Desperate (9)
135	Eminent (9)
136	Essential (9)
137	Grandeur (9)
138	Irresistible (9)
139	Jealous (9)
140	Permanent (9)
141	Rhythm (9)
142	Belligerent (9)
143	Endeavour (9)
144	Ephemeral (9)
145	Harass (9)
146	Attention (8)
147	Beggar (8)
148	Bureaucrat (8)
149	Countenance (8)
150	Decision (8)
151	Experiment (8)
152	Harassment (8)
153	Illegitimate (8)
154	Individual (8)
155	Interrupt (8)
156	Manipulate (8)
157	Necessity (8)
158	Abundance (8)
159	Approach (8)
160	Appropriate (8)
161	Benign (8)
162	Challenge (8)
163	Colloquial (8)
164	Consequence (8)
165	Courteous (8)
166	Evidence (8)
167	Exuberant (8)
168	Inadvertent (8)
169	Minuscule (8)
170	Mysterious (8)
171	Pernicious (8)
172	Precision (8)
173	Professional (8)
174	Pursuit (8)
175	Quarantine (8)
176	Recalcitrant (8)
177	Successful (8)
178	Journey (8)
179	Ambiguous (8)
180	Contemporary (8)
181	Idiosyncrasy (8)
182	Inevitable (8)
183	Innocuous (8)
184	Voluntary (8)
185	Advertisement (7)
186	Announcement (7)
187	Athlete (7)
188	Comparison (7)
189	Disappear (7)
190	Ensure (7)
191	Experience (7)
192	Handkerchief (7)
193	Marriage (7)
194	Mathematics (7)
195	Millionaire (7)
196	Mining (7)
197	Niece (7)
198	Procedure (7)
199	Referred (7)
200	Sanctuaries (7)

*Total **200** Spellings asked **2441** times*

E3 Spellings Practice Sets

(Based on Recent SSC Papers)

Practice Set - 1

Direction (Q. 1-10): Choose the correctly spelt word:

1 1) Grotesque
2) Grosteasque
3) Grostasque
4) Growtesque

2 1) Parliment 2) Pailament
3) Parliament 4) Parlaiment

3 1) Aggregate 2) Aggergate
3) Agregate 4) Aggegrate

4 1) Accomadate
2) Accomodate
3) Accommodate
4) Accomodet

5 1) Cholera 2) Choleraa
3) Chorlla 4) Cyholera

6 1) Thermodinamick
2) Thermadynamic
3) Thermodynnamic
4) Thermodynamic

7 1) Forcast 2) Forecase
3) Forcaust 4) Forecast

8 1) Cigarette 2) Cigerette
3) Cigartte 4) Cigarate

9 1) Enviorment
2) Envirmnet
3) Environment
4) Envirrent

10 1) Guarantee 2) Guarantiy
3) Guarentee 4) Guarantie

Practice Set - 2

Direction (Q. 1-10): Choose the correctly spelt word:

1 1) Accelerate 2) Accellerate
3) Accelarate 4) Accellrate

2 1) Gragarous 2) Gragerious
3) Gregarious 4) Gregareous

3 1) Aberrant 2) Abberant
3) Abberrent 4) Abberrant

4 1) Business 2) Buisness
3) Bussiness 4) Buseness

5 1) Beaurocrat 2) Burocrat
3) Bureaucrat 4) Buroucrat

6 1) Iresistible 2) Irresistable
3) Irresistible 4) Irresistble

7 1) Accessories
2) Accesories
3) Acceories
4) Acceseries

8 1) Extroversion
2) Extroversoin
3) Extroverssion
4) Extroversin

9 1) Facsimily 2) Facsmile
3) Facsimile 4) Facsimele

10 1) Lieutenant 2) Lieutennant
3) Lutennant 4) Ltuenant

Practice Set - 3

Direction (Q. 1-10): Choose the correctly spelt word:

1 1) Neccessary 2) Necessary
3) Nessessary 4) Neccesary

2 1) Government
2) Goverment
3) Govarnment
4) Goverenment

3 1) Conspicous
2) Conspequos
3) Conspqcuous
4) Conspicuous

4 1) Personnel 2) Personel
3) Personeel 4) Persnell

5 1) Milenium 2) Millennium
3) Millenniam 4) Milennium

6 1) Assets 2) Assests
3) Assetts 4) Asests

7 1) Acknowledgement
2) Acknoledgement
3) Acknowlegdment
4) Acknowlegement

8 1) Commite 2) Commtee
3) Committee 4) Committe

9 1) Effervescence
2) Effervescense
3) Efferescence
4) Effervesance

10 1) Delussion 2) Dilusion
3) Delusion 4) Delusian

Practice Set - 4

Direction (Q. 1-10): Choose the correctly spelt word:

1 1) Embillish 2) Imbellish
3) Embelish 4) Embellish

2 1) Questionnair
2) Questionnare
3) Questionnaire
4) Questronnaire

3 1) Exhilarate 2) Exilerate
3) Exhilerate 4) Exhillarate

4 1) Occasional
2) Occational
3) Occassiona
4) Occasionale

5 1) Humorus 2) Humourous
3) Humorous 4) Humurous

6 1) Grateful
2) Greatful
3) Gratefull
4) Greitful

7 1) Mishevious
2) Mischievious
3) Mischeivous
4) Mischievous

8 1) Magnanemous
2) Magnanimus
3) Magnanamous
4) Magnanimous

9 1) Discipline 2) Discpline
3) Disipline 4) Discepline

10 1) Entreprenure
2) Entroprenure
3) Entrepreneur
4) Enterprenuer

Practice Set - 5

Direction (Q. 1-10): Choose the correctly spelt word:

1 1) Easthetic 2) Aesthetic 3) Aesthatic 4) Aesthettic
2 1) Xenotransplantion 2) Xenotransplantation 3) Zenotransplantation 4) Xenotransplantasion
3 1) Collectible 2) Collecteble 3) Colletible 4) Collectibel
4 1) Warent 2) Varrant 3) Warant 4) Warrant
5 1) Sphygmomannometer 2) Sphygmomanometer 3) Sphygmamanometre 4) Sphygmomamometer
6 1) Palete 2) Palet 3) Palate 4) Pelate
7 1) Consensus 2) Concensus 3) Consencus 4) Consenus
8 1) Forein 2) Foriegn 3) Foreign 4) Forign
9 1) Cemetery 2) Cemetary 3) Cemetry 4) Semetary
10 1) Phonology 2) Phonnology 3) Phonollogy 4) Phonelogy

Practice Set - 6

Direction (Q. 1-10): Select the INCORRECTLY spelt word.

1 1) Garrulous 2) Grateful 3) Guarantee 4) Garulous
2 1) Malfeasance 2) Magnanimous 3) Perserverance 4) Insatiable
3 1) Vicereine 2) Floccinaucinihilipilification 3) Defenestrate 4) Quintessance
4 1) Exagerate 2) Leisure 3) Colleague 4) Maintenance
5 1) Ephemera 2) Preposterous 3) Alterior 4) Paraphernalia
6 1) Supersede 2) Perseverance 3) Priviledge 4) Assassinate
7 1) Preposterous 2) Prepostrous 3) Legitimate 4) Kneel
8 1) Perspicacious 2) Perspicasious 3) Loneliness 4) Lightning
9 1) Acquiescence 2) Bourgeoisie 3) Consciencious 4) Epitome
10 1) Beligerant 2) Excellent 3) Existence 4) Belligerent

Practice Set - 7

Direction (Q. 1-10): Select the INCORRECTLY spelt word.

1 1) Hermeneutics 2) Phallocentrisim 3) Structuralism 4) Metafiction
2 1) Acheived 2) Accessible 3) Committee 4) Accommodate
3 1) Impetuous 2) Imperial 3) Impetunent 4) Implication
4 1) Pedagogy 2) Psephology 3) Hagiography 4) Psephallogy
5 1) Apparent 2) Practitionaire 3) Recommend 4) Memento
6 1) Acknowledge 2) Connoissuer 3) Acquire 4) Absence
7 1) Asceticism 2) Iconoclast 3) Antideluvian 4) Neoliberalism
8 1) Administration 2) Genaelogical 3) Investigations 4) Pertaining
9 1) Obsolesence 2) Scrumptious 3) Vanquish 4) Capitulation
10 1) Prophecy 2) Tobacco 3) Questionaire 4) Procession

Practice Set - 8

Direction (Q. 1-10): Find the word with a spelling mistake.

1 1) Pseudonym 2) Epitaph 3) Circumlocution 4) Inoccuous
2 1) Irregular 2) Irresponsible 3) Irrelevent 4) Irritable
3 1) Intuition 2) Instinctual 3) Implusive 4) Initiative
4 1) Liason 2) Manoeuvre 3) Reservoir 4) Camouflage
5 1) Idiosyncracy 2) Incredible 3) Idiosyncrasy 4) Guidance
6 1) Influential 2) Magnanimous 3) Magnanimos 4) Intelligent
7 1) Embarrassment 2) Lndispensible 3) Camouflage 4) Rendezvous
8 1) Obstinate 2) Odorous 3) Occasional 4) Observence
9 1) Avaricious 2) Temerarious 3) Inadvertant 4) Penitent
10 1) Hurdle 2) Humour 3) Hundred 4) Hungery

Practice Set - 9

Direction (Q. 1-10): Which of the following is the correct spelling of the word?

1 1) Twelfth 2) Twelth
3) Twelvth 4) Twelft

2 1) Sacrilegious
2) Sacriligeous
3) Sacreligious
4) Secreligeous

3 1) Voug 2) Vogue
3) Vougue 4) Vog

4 1) Reconcile 2) Reconsile
3) Reconeile 4) Reconcil

5 1) Unforesen
2) Unforeseen
3) Unphorseen
4) Unforsean

6 1) Servillance 2) Survailance
3) Survilance 4) Surveillance

7 1) Supresede 2) Superceed
3) Supersede 4) Supercede

8 1) Unianimous
2) Unanimous
3) Uninamous
4) Unanimus

9 1) Voluntary 2) Voluntry
3) Volontary 4) Vouluntary

10 1) Vacum 2) Vacuum
3) Vaccum 4) Vaccuum

Practice Set - 10

Direction (Q. 1-10): Fill in the blank with the correctly spelt word.

1 The scientist was awarded for her work in _____ chemistry.
1) organometallic
2) organomettalic
3) organomettallik
4) organometalic

2 The study examined the _____ bias in eyewitness testimony.
1) reconstrutive
2) recontructive
3) reconstructive
4) reconsturctive

3 The _____ theory revolutionized the field of anthropology.
1) evoluttionary
2) evolutionary
3) evolusionary
4) evvolutionary

4 The patient's _____ behavior indicated a severe disorder of thought processes.
1) ideosyncratic
2) idiosyncrasic
3) idiosyncratic
4) idiosyncrotic

5 Their explanation was filled with _____ making it hard to discern the truth.
1) obfuscation
2) obfusscation
3) obfascation
4) obfescation

6 His _____ remarks showed a blatant disrcgard for professional courtesy.
1) causstic 2) caustic
3) caustick 4) causticc

7 His _____ disregard for protocol annoyed his superiors.
1) blatant 2) blaetant
3) blatennt 4) blattant

8 The leader's _____ behavior eventually alienated even his staunchest supporters.
1) imperrious 2) imparious
3) imperious 4) impirious

9 Despite overwhelming evidence, he remained _____ in his beliefs.
1) obstinatte 2) obstinate
3) obsteinate 4) obbstinate

10 The species showed remarkable _____ to extreme conditions.
1) adaptibility
2) adaptability
3) adaptibilitye
4) adaptabilitty

Practice Set - 11

Direction (Q. 1-10): Choose the INCORRECTLY spelt word in the given sentence.

1 The shedule followed by my sister ultimately leads to stress and other adverse effects.
1) Adverse 2) Followed
3) Ultimately 4) Shedule

2 It may seem pretintious to say so but I cannot live without my essential articles.
1) Articles 2) Essential
3) Cannot 4) Pretintious

3 Mesing up your laundry or being late for work is not very important when you consider your entire life.
1) Entire 2) Important
3) Mesing 4) Laundry

4 Fungal diseases in the lungs are often similar to other illnesses such as bacterial or viral pneumoniia.
1) Fungal 2) Pneumoniia
3) Illnesses 4) Often

5 This catagory may include information to support secondary statements, anecdotes, and wordiness, as shown below.
1) Anecdotes 2) Secondary
3) Catagory 4) Information

6 I took out a water tumbler for a drink, but found the water in the metal container had frozen so I couldn't quanch my thirst. I ate some biscuits and offered some to Hillary.
1) Offered 2) Tumbler
3) Quanch 4) Container

7 The project aims to coordinate the efforts of millions of people who are aprehensive about the impact of micro plastics on the oceans.
1) Coordinate 2) Aprehensive
3) Millions 4) Impact

8 Everyone admired her because of her charesma, but she was a narcissist full of self-admiration and treachery.
1) Treachery
2) Narcissist
3) Self-Admiration
4) Charesma

9 It's better to think about what you are doing right now—without worying about the unknown.
1) Without 2) Worying
3) Better 4) About

10 Life requires great sacrifices and an understanding of the duoality of the universe; this makes us happier.
1) Understanding
2) Duoality
3) Universe
4) Sacrifices

Practice Set - 12

Direction (Q. 1-10): Choose the INCORRECTLY spelt word in the given sentence.

1 Her aesthetic sense and meticulos attention to detail conferred an unparalleled distinction to her work.
1) Meticulos
2) Aesthetic
3) Unparalleled
4) Conferred

2 Comprehensiveness constitues wisdom and many examples from history illustrate this fact.
1) Comprehensiveness
2) Illustrate
3) Wisdom
4) Constitues

3 Enthusiasm is one of those vital elements that transforms an indivdual and his failures into victories and success.
1) Success 2) Victories
3) Indivdual 4) Failures

4 The chef used a special recepie for the gourmet dish.
1) Special 2) Gourmet
3) Chef 4) Recepie

5 After receiving the parcel, she immedietely opened it.
1) Receiving 2) Opened
3) Parcel 4) Immedietely

6 You need to be concious enough to listen to the question.
1) Listen 2) Concious
3) Enough 4) Question

7 Clear communicetion is essential for effective collaboration and successful completion of complex projects at work.
1) Communicetion
2) Collaboration
3) Completion
4) Effective

8 Generousity is a godly feature among many individuals on the earth.
1) Feature 2) Godly
3) Individuals 4) Generousity

9 The company's policy on employee benefits is quite comprehensve.
1) Company's
2) Benefits
3) Comprehensve
4) Policy

10 The diplomat's erudition was matched only by his arrogance and recalcitrent attitude towards compromise.
1) Erudition
2) Recalcitrent
3) Compromise
4) Arrogance

Practice Set - 13

Direction (Q. 1-10): Identify the INCORRECTLY spelt word in the following sentence and select its correct spelling from the given options.

1 You shall recieve proper pay for your work.
1) Propeer 2) Resieve
3) Propper 4) Receive

2 It is his previlage to present all the candidates for ordination to the bishop of the diocese.
1) Odination 2) Deocease
3) Prevalage 4) Privilege

3 This will sound weired, but bear with me.
1) Wired 2) Bier
3) Weird 4) Beer

4 The calandar was reformed during the time of Julius Caesar.
1) Calendar 2) Celender
3) Riformed 4) Reeformed

5 Wether we want to admit it or not, we all wish everyone would like us.
1) Addmit 2) Whither
3) Admitt 4) Whether

6 There are a number of artists currently creating unique, collectble teapots.
1) Currintly 2) Collectibile
3) Currantly 4) Collectable

7 Every year, students plagerize without realising it because they just don't understand the research process and proper methods of citation.
1) Rializing 2) Plagiarise
3) Citetion 4) Propper

8 His acquiantance with the author led to many fruitful collaborations.
1) Aquaintance
2) Acquaintance
3) Acquaintence
4) Acuiantance

9 The teacher assessed the student's flyer for writing.
1) Fire 2) Flare
3) Flair 4) Friar

10 The occurence of this phenomenon is quite rare.
1) Occurrence
2) Occurance
3) Occerence
4) Occurrance

Practice Set - 14

Direction (Q. 1-10): Choose the sentence that contains correct spellings.

1 1) The audiance applauded the musicans performance.
2) The audiance applauded the musician's perfomance.
3) The audience applauded the muzicians performance.
4) The audience applauded the musician's performance.

2 1) The athlete's acheivements are impressive.
2) The athlete's achievements are impressive.
3) The athletees achievements are impressive.
4) The athlete's achievements are imprressive.

3 1) The resteraunt serves delicious meals.
2) The resturant serves deliscious meals.
3) The restaurant serves delicious meals.
4) The resturaunt serves delisious meals.

4 1) He is wimsical by nature. No one can seek an explanation from him for his absurd attitude towards others.
2) He is whimsical by natur. No one can seek an explanation from him for his absurd attitude towards others.
3) He is whimsical by nature. No one can seek an explanation from him for his absurd atitude towards others.
4) He is whimsical by nature.

No one can seek an explanation from him for his absurd attitude towards others.

5 1) The liberian told the childrean to return their boooks by Friday.
2) The librarian told the children to return their books by Friday.
3) The libraian told the childrean to return their books by Friday.
4) The librarian told the childern to return their books by Fryday.

6 1) I will definitely attend the conference.
2) I will definetely attend the conference.
3) I will definately attend the conference.
4) I will definitly attend the conference.

7 1) The athlete ran quickley across the finish line.
2) The athlete ran quickly across the finish line.
3) The athlet ran quicly across the finnish line.
4) The athelete ran quicly across the finish line.

8 1) Harshita's expectations aleinated her in her office.
2) The children's behaviour alienated their mother.
3) Teachers alnieate talkative students in the class.
4) Poor children sometimes feel alianeted in society.

9 1) Esha risembles her mother very much.
2) Esha resimbles her mother very much.
3) Esha resembles her mother very much.
4) Esha risimbles her mother very much.

10 1) The gardner planted colorfull flowers in the garden.
2) The gardner planted colorful flowers in the gardin.
3) The gardener planted colourfull flowers in the gardin.
4) The gardener planted colourful flowers in the garden.

Practice Set - 15

Direction (Q. 1-10): Select the correct spelling of the word to fill in the blank in the given sentence.

1 The speaker was lauded for her ______ delivery, responding without notes.
1) extemporanious
2) exemporaneous
3) extemporaneous
4) extemporeaneous

2 His ______ is a brilliant student.
1) sun 2) sone
3) sune 4) son

3 The king's ______ reign led to widespread unrest among the people.
1) despotick 2) despppotic
3) despotic 4) disspotic

4 The essay was ______ with references to obscure literary movements.
1) repllete 2) replete
3) repleat 4) rpelite

5 Uttarakhand has faced many natural ______ in recent years.
1) calamities 2) kalaimites
3) qalimities 4) clamities

6 The citizens of Iraq wanted ______ after years of war.
1) pease 2) piece
3) peace 4) peice

7 The ______ of the ancient manuscript was a painstaking process.
1) resurection
2) ressurection
3) resurrection
4) resurraction

8 The new theory was dismissed as ______ by the mainstream scientific community.
1) prepostrous
2) preposterous
3) preposturous
4) preposteruos

9 Fill in the blank with the correctly spelt word. We should schedule an appointment with our ______ to get a checkup for our baby.
1) paediatrician
2) pediatricean
3) pidiatrician
4) pediotrician

10 He lost his most valuable ______ during the move.
1) posession 2) possesion
3) possession 4) posesssion

Practice Set - 16

Direction (Q. 1-5): Choose the correct spelling to complete the sentence.

1 The scholar's interpretation was based on a ______ understanding of the philosophy.
1) superficial 2) supperficial
3) supurficial 4) supperficiall

2 After 35 years of service, Mr. Das finally retired and began receiving his ______ benefits every month.
1) supcranution
2) superanuation
3) superannuation
4) superanualtion

3 It is my ______ that municipal employees handle their jobs with great professionalism.
1) bilief 2) belief
3) beleif 4) beleaf

4 The professor emphasized the ______ nature of literary interpretation.
1) subjectif 2) subgective
3) subjective 4) subjuctive

5 She roasted a ______ over the campfire.
1) marshmellow
2) marshmallo
3) marshmallow
4) marshmelloe

Direction (Q. 6-10): Choose the option that completes the sentence using the correct spelling.

6 The lights of the Aurora Borealis are a natural ______.
1) phenomenon
2) phenominnon
3) phenominon
4) phinominon

7 all of a sudden, they found themselves in a terrible ______.
1) dilemna 2) dilemma
3) dilema 4) dilemmae

8 The scientists had to do an ______ amount of research on the project.
1) extraordinary
2) extraordinery

3) extrordinary
4) ecstraordinary

9 The newly fallen snow transformed the landscape ______ .
1) magicaly 2) magically
3) magickelly 4) majicelly

10 I ______ some great change in her attitude.
1) perceived 2) received
3) percieived 4) precieved

Practice Set - 17

Direction (Q. 1-10): Choose the correctly spelt word that means.

1 Abundant in growth, especially vegetation
1) Luxurient 2) Luxuirant
3) Luxuriant 4) Luxureant

2 Opposite in nature
1) Contrary 2) Countary
3) Contrery 4) Contreryy

3 Formal disapproval
1) Censure 2) Censhur
3) Senssure 4) Senshure

4 Basic or fundamental
1) Rudimentry
2) Rudimentary
3) Rudementary
4) Rudamentary

5 Easily broken
1) Brittel 2) Brittle
3) Brittle 4) Brittle

6 Concise and forcefully expressive
1) Pithy 2) Pithey
3) Pithhy 4) Pithi

7 Witty, clever, and verbally skillful
1) Persiphledge
2) Persiflage
3) Pursiflage
4) Persiflagee

8 Harmless
1) Innocuous 2) Inoccuous
3) Innocous 4) Innocuouss

9 To express disapproval or disappointment
1) Reproove 2) Reprove
3) Reprovve 4) Repruve

10 A person of high rank or title
1) Nobble 2) Noblie
3) Noble 4) Nobel

Practice Set - 18

Direction (Q. 1-10): Choose the correct spelling of the word meaning.

1 A long adventurous journey
1) Odessay 2) Odyssey
3) Odessy 4) Oddysey

2 Inappropriate or unsuitable
1) Incongruous
2) Incongreous
3) Incongrus
4) Inkongruous

3 Extremely poor or impoverished
1) Impecuneous
2) Imppecunious
3) Impecunius
4) Impecunious

4 Study of the mind
1) Sychology
2) Psychology
3) Psychollogy
4) Psycology

5 The theory that all knowledge comes from sensory experience
1) Empiricisim
2) Empiricalism
3) Empiricism
4) Empiricicm

6 Excessively talkative, especially on trivial matters
1) Garrulous 2) Garullous
3) Garulous 4) Garrullus

7 Clumsy or awkward in movement or manner
1) Gauche 2) Gosh
3) Goush 4) Gauch

8 Mild disapproval
1) Expossulation
2) Expostulation
3) Expostelation
4) Expostullation

9 Temporary stay or visit
1) Soejourn 2) Sojourn
3) Sajourn 4) Sojurn

10 Based on reason
1) Rational 2) Rashonal
3) Rationel 4) Rashanal

Practice Set - 19

Direction (Q. 1-10): Find the correct spelling of a word describing.

1 Disloyal betrayal
1) Perphidy 2) Perfidy
3) Perfedee 4) Perfody

2 Complex and obscure knowledge
1) Esoterica 2) Esoterrica
3) Esottirica 4) Esotorica

3 Moral philosophy
1) Ethicks 2) Ethiques
3) Ethics 4) Ethikz

4 A leadership role
1) Lieutenant 2) Lieutanant
3) Leuitenant 4) Luitenant

5 Reasoning method
1) Logic 2) Logik
3) Logick 4) Logiq

6 Theory of knowledge
1) Epistemology
2) Epistomology
3) Eppistemology
4) Epistemollogy

7 An official who supervises an exam
1) Envigilator 2) Invigilator
3) Invegilator 4) Invagelator

8 Extreme frugality
1) Parsimonious
2) Parsimmonious
3) Parsimonius
4) Parcimonious

9 An educational qualification
1) Diplumma 2) Diploma
3) Dipluma 4) Dipploma

10 Having a harmful effect
1) Deleterious
2) Deliterious
3) Deleterous
4) Deletrious

Practice Set - 20

Direction (Q. 1-5): Find the word that is spelled correctly and means.

1 A rule or principle
1) Axiom 2) Axion
3) Axom 4) Axiome

2 A skilled craftsman or builder
1) Artizan 2) Artisan
3) Artesan 4) Artisen

3 Not important
1) Triveal 2) Trivial
3) Triveel 4) Triviel

4 Questioning everything
1) Pyrrhonism
2) Pyrhonism
3) Pyrhhonism
4) Pirronism

5 The quality of being sarcastic in

a bitter way
1) Causticity 2) Costicity
3) Cawstic 4) Caustisity

Direction (Q. 6-10): In the following, there are four different words, out of which only one word is correctly spelt.

6 1) Magnitic 2) Enigmatic
3) Autometic 4) Puzling

7 1) Fabulous 2) Beautifal
3) Marvelus 4) Charmeng

8 1) Downfal 2) Decilne
3) Debacle 4) Discomfeture

9 1) Flimsy 2) Funy
3) Irational 4) Partisen

10 1) Jubletion
2) Depresion
3) Desperation
4) Fascinetion

Answer Key Practice Set - 1:

1 - 1	2 - 3	3 - 1	4 - 3	5 - 1
6 - 4	7 - 4	8 - 1	9 - 3	10 - 1

Answer Key Practice Set - 2:

1 - 1	2 - 3	3 - 1	4 - 1	5 - 3
6 - 3	7 - 1	8 - 1	9 - 3	10 - 1

Answer Key Practice Set - 3:

1 - 2	2 - 1	3 - 4	4 - 1	5 - 2
6 - 1	7 - 1	8 - 3	9 - 1	10 - 3

Answer Key Practice Set - 4:

1 - 4	2 - 3	3 - 1	4 - 1	5 - 3
6 - 1	7 - 4	8 - 4	9 - 1	10 - 3

Answer Key Practice Set - 5:

1 - 2	2 - 2	3 - 1	4 - 4	5 - 2
6 - 3	7 - 1	8 - 3	9 - 1	10 - 1

Answer Key Practice Set - 6:

1 - 4	2 - 3	3 - 4	4 - 1	5 - 3
6 - 3	7 - 2	8 - 2	9 - 3	10 - 1

Answer Key Practice Set - 7:

1 - 2	2 - 1	3 - 3	4 - 4	5 - 2
6 - 2	7 - 3	8 - 2	9 - 1	10 - 3

Answer Key Practice Set - 8:

1 - 4	2 - 3	3 - 3	4 - 1	5 - 1
6 - 3	7 - 2	8 - 4	9 - 3	10 - 4

Answer Key Practice Set - 9:

1 - 1	2 - 1	3 - 2	4 - 1	5 - 2
6 - 4	7 - 3	8 - 2	9 - 1	10 - 2

Answer Key Practice Set - 10:

1 - 1	2 - 3	3 - 2	4 - 3	5 - 1
6 - 2	7 - 1	8 - 3	9 - 2	10 - 2

Answer Key Practice Set - 11:

1 - 4	2 - 4	3 - 3	4 - 2	5 - 3
6 - 3	7 - 2	8 - 4	9 - 2	10 - 2

Answer Key Practice Set - 12:

1 - 1	2 - 4	3 - 3	4 - 4	5 - 4
6 - 2	7 - 1	8 - 4	9 - 3	10 - 2

Answer Key Practice Set - 13:

1 - 4	2 - 4	3 - 3	4 - 1	5 - 4
6 - 4	7 - 2	8 - 2	9 - 3	10 - 1

Answer Key Practice Set - 14:

1 - 4	2 - 2	3 - 3	4 - 4	5 - 2
6 - 1	7 - 2	8 - 2	9 - 3	10 - 4

Answer Key Practice Set - 15:

1 - 3	2 - 4	3 - 3	4 - 2	5 - 1
6 - 3	7 - 3	8 - 2	9 - 1	10 - 3

Answer Key Practice Set - 16:

1 - 1	2 - 3	3 - 2	4 - 3	5 - 3
6 - 1	7 - 2	8 - 1	9 - 2	10 - 1

Answer Key Practice Set - 17:

1 - 3	2 - 1	3 - 1	4 - 2	5 - 2
6 - 1	7 - 2	8 - 1	9 - 2	10 - 3

Answer Key Practice Set - 18:

1 - 2	2 - 1	3 - 4	4 - 2	5 - 3
6 - 1	7 - 1	8 - 2	9 - 2	10 - 1

Answer Key Practice Set - 19:

1 - 2	2 - 1	3 - 3	4 - 1	5 - 1
6 - 1	7 - 2	8 - 1	9 - 2	10 - 1

Answer Key Practice Set - 20:

1 - 1	2 - 2	3 - 2	4 - 1	5 - 1
6 - 2	7 - 1	8 - 3	9 - 1	10 - 3

SECTION -II
(VOCAB BOOSTER)

Contents:-

Updated and Additional Content: -

1. **Phrasal Verbs**: The phrasal verb list has been split into two categories, PYQ-based (covered in Chapter **B8**) and Non-PYQ-based. This section covers the Non-PYQ-based phrasal verbs as vocabulary boosters.
2. **Homonyms**: The homonym list has also been split into two categories, PYQ-based (covered in Chapter **D1**) and Non-PYQ-based. This section covers the Non-PYQ-based collection.
3. **Fixed Prepositions**: Important usage rules have been added along with a handpicked selection of fixed prepositions to strengthen your preparation.
4. **The Hindu Vocabulary**: Words already covered in the OWS or Synonyms-Antonyms chapters have been removed to avoid repetition and replaced with a fresh set of The Hindu vocabulary, complete with definitions, Hindi meanings, and synonyms.
5. **Foreign Words**: This chapter has been revised and enhanced with **197** important foreign words.
6. **Root Words**: The chapter has been revised and expanded to cover Root Words, Prefixes, and Suffixes, enabling you to understand and derive thousands of words with ease.

F1 Phrasal Verbs (Additional List)

1 **Abide by** - To follow a rule, law, or decision (नियम का पालन करना)

2 **Account for** - i) To explain the reason for something (कारण बताना)
ii) To form a particular proportion (हिस्सा बनाना)

3 **Act as** - To perform the role of something (की भूमिका निभाना)

4 **Act for** - To represent someone on their behalf (किसी की ओर से काम करना)

5 **Act on (or upon)** - To take action based on advice/information (सलाह पर अमल करना)

6 **Act out** - i) To perform a story with actions (अभिनय करना)
ii) To express emotions through bad behaviour (उग्र व्यवहार करना)

7 **Act up** - i) To behave badly (person) (बदतमीज़ी करना)
ii) To malfunction (machine/body part) (ठीक से काम न करना)

8 **Add in** - To include something as part of a total (शामिल करना)

9 **Add on** - To include something extra (अतिरिक्त जोड़ना)

10 **Add to** - To increase something (बढ़ाना)

11 **Add up** - i) To calculate the total (जोड़ना / कुल निकालना)
ii) To seem logical or reasonable (तर्कसंगत होना)
iii) To amount to a total or result (कुल मिलाकर होना)

12 **Advise against** - To recommend not doing something (कुछ न करने की सलाह देना)

13 **Agree with** - i) To have the same opinion (सहमत होना)
ii) To suit (food/climate) (रास आना)

14 **Aim at** - i) To point towards a target (निशाना लगाना)
ii) To intend to achieve (लक्ष्य रखना)

15 **Allow for** - To consider something when planning (ध्यान में रखना)

16 **Answer back** - To reply rudely to someone in authority (बदतमीज़ी से जवाब देना)

17 **Answer for** - To be responsible/accountable for something (ज़िम्मेदार होना)

18 **Appeal to** - i) To make a formal request (अपील करना)
ii) To attract or interest someone (आकर्षित करना)

19 **Apply for** - To make a formal request for something (आवेदन करना)

20 **Attend on (or upon)** - To serve or wait upon someone (सेवा करना)

21 **Attend to** - i) To deal with something (निपटाना)
ii) To pay attention to (ध्यान देना)

22 **Back away** - To move backwards from someone/something (पीछे हटना)

23 **Back down** - To withdraw from a position or argument (अपनी बात से पीछे हटना)

24 **Back off** - i) To retreat (पीछे हटना)
ii) To stop interfering or pressuring (दखल देना बंद करना)

25 **Bail on** - To abandon someone or break a commitment (बीच में छोड़ देना)

26 **Bail out** - i) To rescue from difficulty (esp. financial) (मुश्किल से बचाना)
ii) To pay bail for someone (ज़मानत देना)
iii) To jump from an aircraft using a parachute (विमान से पैराशूट के जरिए कूदना)

27 **Bank on** - To rely or depend on something (भरोसा करना)

28 **Bank up** - To pile up or accumulate (ढेर लगाना)

29 **Be in for** - To be about to experience something (किसी चीज़ का सामना होने वाला होना)

30 **Bear away** - To carry something away (साथ ले जाना)

31 **Bear on (or upon)** - To be relevant to or affect something (संबंधित होना)

32 **Beat up** - To attack and injure by hitting repeatedly (बुरी तरह पीटना)

33 **Become of** - To happen to someone/something (used in questions) (का क्या हुआ)

34 **Beef up** - To strengthen or increase something (मज़बूत करना / बढ़ाना)

35 **Begin with** - To start with something (से शुरू करना)

36 **Believe in** - i) To have faith in the existence

of (अस्तित्व में विश्वास करना)
ii) To trust in the value of something (भरोसा रखना)

37 **Bet on** - To gamble on or rely on something happening (दाँव लगाना / भरोसा करना)

38 **Bite off** - To remove something by biting (दाँत से काट कर अलग करना)

39 **Block off** - To close or obstruct an area (रास्ता बंद करना)

40 **Blow away** - i) To be carried away by wind (हवा से उड़ जाना)
ii) To greatly impress someone (बहुत प्रभावित करना)

41 **Blow off** - i) To ignore or skip something (नज़रअंदाज़ करना / टालना)
ii) To release steam/pressure (भाप छोड़ना)
iii) To release anger or energy (गुस्सा निकालना)

42 **Boil over** - i) To overflow while boiling (उबल कर बाहर आना)
ii) To erupt in anger (गुस्से में फूटना)

43 **Boot up** - To start a computer (कंप्यूटर चालू करना)

44 **Bottle up** - To suppress emotions (भावनाओं को दबाना)

45 **Bounce back** - To recover quickly from a setback (जल्दी उबरना)

46 **Bow out** - To withdraw gracefully (शालीनता से अलग होना)

47 **Brace for** - To prepare for something difficult (कठिनाई के लिए तैयार होना)

48 **Branch out** - To expand into new areas or activities (नए क्षेत्र में विस्तार करना)

49 **Break even** - To have no profit or loss (न लाभ न हानि की स्थिति)

50 **Break forth** - To suddenly emerge or burst out (अचानक प्रकट होना)

51 **Break open** - To open by force (ज़बरदस्ती खोलना)

52 **Break through** - To overcome an obstacle or barrier (बाधा पार करना)

53 **Breeze through** - To accomplish something easily (आसानी से पूरा करना)

54 **Bring along** - To bring someone/something with you (साथ लाना)

55 **Bring back** - i) To return something (वापस लाना)
ii) To revive memories (यादें ताज़ा करना)

56 **Bring down** - i) To cause to fall (गिराना)
ii) To reduce (कम करना)
iii) To overthrow (सत्ता से हटाना)

57 **Bring forth** - To produce or give rise to (उत्पन्न करना)

58 **Bring in** - i) To introduce (law, system) (लागू करना)
ii) To earn money (कमाना)

59 **Bring off** - To succeed in doing something difficult (मुश्किल काम पूरा करना)

60 **Bring on** - i) To cause or trigger something (उत्पन्न करना)
ii) To introduce someone into action (किसी को मैदान में उतारना)

61 **Bring over** - To bring someone to one's home (घर लाना)

62 **Bring round (or around)** - i) To persuade someone (राज़ी करना)
ii) To revive someone who fainted (होश में लाना)

63 **Bring under** - To bring under control (नियंत्रण में लाना)

64 **Brush aside** - To dismiss or ignore something (नज़रअंदाज़ करना)

65 **Brush up** - i) To improve or refresh one's knowledge or skill (सुधारना / दोहराना)
ii) To tidy or smarten up one's appearance (साफ-सुथरा करना)
iii) To clean by brushing (ब्रश से साफ करना)

66 **Build in** - To include as an integral part (अंतर्निहित करना)

67 **Build on** - To use as a foundation for further progress (आधार बनाकर आगे बढ़ना)

68 **Build up** - i) To increase gradually (धीरे-धीरे बढ़ना)
ii) To develop (विकसित करना)

69 **Bulk up** - To gain muscle mass (मांसपेशियाँ बढ़ाना)

70 **Bump into** - To meet someone by chance (अचानक मिलना, टकरा जाना)

71 **Burn down** - To destroy completely by fire (जलकर राख होना)

72 **Burn out** - i) To become exhausted from overwork (थककर चूर होना)
ii) To stop working due to overheating or damage (अत्यधिक गर्मी या क्षति से काम बंद कर देना)

73 **Burn through** - To use up something quickly (जल्दी खर्च करना)

74 **Burn up** - i) To destroy by fire (जला देना)
ii) To make very angry (गुस्सा दिलाना)

75 **Burst out** - i) To suddenly start (laughing,

crying) (अचानक शुरू होना)
ii) To exclaim (चिल्ला उठना)

76 **Butt out** - To stop interfering (दखल देना बंद करना)

77 **Buy into** - i) To believe in an idea (विश्वास करना)
ii) To buy shares in a company (हिस्सेदारी खरीदना)

78 **Buy off** - To bribe someone to stop opposition or trouble (रिश्वत देकर चुप कराना)

79 **Buy out** - To purchase someone's share in a business (हिस्सा खरीद लेना)

80 **Buy up** - To buy all available stock of something (सारा माल खरीद लेना)

81 **Buzz off** - To go away (rude) (भाग जाओ)

82 **Call after** - i) To name someone after another person (किसी के नाम पर नाम रखना)
ii) To shout to someone who is leaving (पीछे से पुकारना)

83 **Call back** - i) To return a phone call (वापस फ़ोन करना)
ii) To ask someone to return (वापस बुलाना)

84 **Call by** - To visit briefly (थोड़ी देर के लिए मिलना)

85 **Call forth** - To evoke or summon something into action (किसी भावना या शक्ति को उत्पन्न करना, आह्वान करना)

86 **Call in** - i) To telephone (workplace) (फ़ोन करना)
ii) To summon an expert (विशेषज्ञ बुलाना)

87 **Call round (or around)** - i) To telephone several people (कई लोगों को फ़ोन करना)
ii) To visit briefly (थोड़ी देर के लिए मिलना)

88 **Call up** - i) To telephone (फ़ोन करना)
ii) To summon for military service (सेना में बुलाना)
iii) To bring to mind (याद दिलाना)

89 **Calm down** - To become or make someone less agitated (शांत होना)

90 **Camp out** - To sleep outdoors in a tent (तंबू में रहना)

91 **Care for** - i) To look after someone (देखभाल करना)
ii) To like something (पसंद करना)

92 **Carry away** - To get overly excited or emotional (भावनाओं में बह जाना)

93 **Carry forward** - To transfer to the next period (accounting) (आगे ले जाना)

94 **Carry off** - i) To win a prize (जीतना)
ii) To succeed despite difficulty (सफलतापूर्वक करना)

95 **Carry over** - To transfer to next period (आगे ले जाना)

96 **Carry through** - To complete something despite difficulties (अंत तक पूरा करना)

97 **Carve out** - To create through effort (मेहनत से बनाना)

98 **Cash in** - i) To exchange something for money, esp. chips or bonds (भुनाना)
ii) To profit or take advantage of a situation (फायदा उठाना)

99 **Cast away** - i) To throw away (फेंक देना)
ii) To be stranded after a shipwreck (जहाज़ डूबने के बाद तट पर फँस जाना)

100 **Cast down** - To make someone feel sad or discouraged (निराश करना)

101 **Cast off** - i) To untie a boat (नाव खोलना)
ii) To discard (त्यागना)

102 **Cast out** - To expel or drive out (निकाल देना)

103 **Catch on** - i) To become popular (लोकप्रिय होना)
ii) To understand (समझ आना)

104 **Catch out** - To discover someone's mistake/deception (गलती पकड़ना)

105 **Cater to** - To provide what someone wants (ज़रूरतें पूरी करना)

106 **Change into** - i) To transform (बदलना)
ii) To put on different clothes (कपड़े बदलना)

107 **Change over** - To switch from one system to another (एक प्रणाली से दूसरी पर जाना)

108 **Charge with** - To formally accuse of a crime (आरोप लगाना)

109 **Cheat on** - i) To be unfaithful in a relationship (बेवफ़ाई करना)
ii) To act dishonestly in exam (नकल करना)

110 **Cheat out of** - To deprive someone through deception (धोखे से वंचित करना)

111 **Check in** - To register at a hotel or airport (चेक-इन करना)

112 **Check on** - To verify someone's condition or progress (हाल-चाल देखना)

113 **Check out** - i) To leave a hotel (होटल छोड़ना)
ii) To examine (जाँचना)
iii) To borrow from library (किताब लेना)

114 **Check through** - To examine thoroughly (अच्छी तरह जाँचना)

115 **Check up** - i) To examine or verify (जाँच करना)
ii) To have a medical examination (चिकित्सा जाँच करवाना)

116 **Cheer on** - To encourage with shouts (उत्साहवर्धन करना)

117 **Cheer up** - To become or make happier (खुश

होना / खुश करना)

118 **Chicken out** - To withdraw due to fear (डर से पीछे हटना)

119 **Chip away** - i) To break small pieces off something (टुकड़े-टुकड़े तोड़ना)
ii) To gradually reduce or erode (धीरे-धीरे कम करना)

120 **Chip in** - To contribute money or help (योगदान देना)

121 **Chop up** - To cut into small pieces (टुकड़े-टुकड़े करना)

122 **Chuck out** - i) To throw away (फेंकना)
ii) To force someone to leave (निकालना)

123 **Clamp down** - i) To take strict action to suppress something (सख्ती करना)
ii) To become stricter about enforcement (कड़ाई से लागू करना)

124 **Clap back** - To respond sharply or wittily to criticism (तीखा जवाब देना)

125 **Clean out** - i) To empty completely (पूरा खाली करना)
ii) To take all someone's money (पैसे लूट लेना)

126 **Clean up** - i) To make clean (साफ करना)
ii) To make large profits (खूब कमाना)
iii) To remove corruption or improve a system (भ्रष्टाचार हटाना / सुधार करना)

127 **Clear out** - i) To empty a place (खाली करना)
ii) To leave quickly (निकल जाना)

128 **Clear up** - i) To tidy (साफ करना)
ii) To resolve (सुलझाना)
iii) To become bright or sunny (weather) (मौसम साफ होना)

129 **Clock in (or on)** - To record arrival time at work (आने का समय दर्ज करना)

130 **Clock out (or off)** - To record departure time from work (जाने का समय दर्ज करना)

131 **Clog up** - To block or become blocked (अवरुद्ध करना / जाम होना)

132 **Close down** - To stop operating permanently (स्थायी रूप से बंद करना)

133 **Close in** - i) To approach threateningly (घेरना)
ii) (Of days) To become shorter (दिन छोटे होना)
iii) (Of time/event) To draw nearer (समय या घटना का करीब आना)

134 **Close off** - To block access to an area (प्रवेश बंद करना)

135 **Close out** - To sell remaining stock at reduced prices (बाकी माल सस्ते में बेचना)

136 **Close up** - i) To shut completely (पूरी तरह बंद करना)
ii) To move closer together (पास-पास आना)
iii) A photograph taken from a short distance (नज़दीकी दृश्य (फ़ोटो / फ़िल्म में))

137 **Come along** - i) To make progress (तरक्की करना)
ii) To accompany someone (साथ आना)
iii) To arrive or appear (आना)

138 **Come apart** - To break into pieces (टूट जाना)

139 **Come back** - To return (वापस आना)

140 **Come clean** - To confess the truth (सच उगल देना)

141 **Come down** - i) To decrease in price or level (कम होना / गिरना)
ii) To descend (उतरना)
iii) To be passed down (tradition) (विरासत में आना)

142 **Come forward** - To offer help, information, or support voluntarily (मदद या जानकारी के लिए सामने आना)

143 **Come from** - To originate (से आना / से होना)

144 **Come in** - i) To enter (अंदर आना)
ii) To become fashionable (फैशन में आना)
iii) To finish a race in a position (स्थान पाना)

145 **Come of** - To result from (परिणाम होना)

146 **Come off it** - Stop pretending or lying (exclamation) (बकवास बंद करो)

147 **Come on** - i) Hurry up (Exclamation) / encouragement (चलो / जल्दी करो)
ii) To start (illness, show, rain) (शुरू होना)
iii) To make progress (प्रगति करना)

148 **Come to** - i) To regain consciousness (होश आना)
ii) To amount to (total) (कुल होना)
iii) To realize or understand something (किसी बात का एहसास होना)

149 **Come upon** - To find or meet unexpectedly (अचानक पाना / मिलना)

150 **Con out of** - To obtain through deception (धोखे से हासिल करना)

151 **Cool down** - i) To become less hot (ठंडा होना)
ii) To become calmer (शांत होना)

152 **Cool off** - i) To become less hot (ठंडा होना)
ii) To calm down after anger (गुस्सा शांत होना)
iii) To lose interest or excitement (उत्साह या रुचि कम हो जाना)

153 **Cope with** - To deal with something challenging successfully (किसी कठिन स्थिति का

सामना करना)

154 **Count down** - To count backwards to zero (उलटी गिनती करना)

155 **Count in** - To include someone (शामिल करना)

156 **Count on** - To rely on someone/something (भरोसा करना)

157 **Count out** - i) To exclude someone (बाहर रखना)
ii) To count one by one (गिनकर निकालना)

158 **Count up** - To calculate the total (कुल गिनना)

159 **Cover for** - To do someone's work in their absence (किसी की जगह काम करना)

160 **Cozy up** - i) To make oneself comfortable (आराम से बैठना)
ii) To snuggle (सिमटकर बैठना)

161 **Crack on** - To continue quickly with a task (जल्दी-जल्दी काम करना)

162 **Crack open** - To open (bottle) for celebration (खोलना)

163 **Crash out** - To fall asleep quickly from exhaustion (थककर सो जाना)

164 **Creep out** - To make someone feel uncomfortable or scared (डरावना लगना)

165 **Creep up** - i) To increase gradually (धीरे-धीरे बढ़ना)
ii) To move slowly upward (धीरे-धीरे ऊपर जाना)

166 **Crop up** - To appear unexpectedly (अचानक आ जाना)

167 **Cross off** - To remove from a list (सूची से काटना)

168 **Cross over** - To change sides or genres (पक्ष बदलना)

169 **Cry out** - To shout or scream loudly (ज़ोर से चिल्लाना, पुकारना)

170 **Curl up** - To sit or lie in a curled position (सिमटकर बैठना)

171 **Cut across** - i) To take a shorter route (छोटा रास्ता लेना)
ii) To affect different groups equally (सबको प्रभावित करना)

172 **Cut back** - i) To reduce in amount, size, or expenditure (कटौती करना / कम करना)
ii) To prune plants or bushes (छंटाई करना)
iii) To reverse direction suddenly while running (अचानक दिशा बदलना)

173 **Cut off** - i) To disconnect (काट देना)
ii) To isolate (अलग कर देना)
iii) To interrupt someone speaking (बीच में टोकना)

174 **Cut out** - i) To stop doing something (बंद करना)
ii) To remove by cutting (काटकर निकालना)
iii) (Engine) to suddenly stop working (बंद हो जाना)

175 **Cut up** - i) To cut into pieces (टुकड़े करना)
ii) To be very upset (बहुत दुखी होना)

176 **Date back** - To have existed since a particular time in the past (पुराना होना / किसी समय से होना)

177 **Deal in** - To buy and sell a particular product (व्यापार करना)

178 **Deal with** - i) To handle a problem or situation (निपटना)
ii) To be about (topic) (संबंधित होना)

179 **Decide on** - To choose after consideration (चुनना / तय करना)

180 **Delight in** - To take great pleasure in (आनंद लेना)

181 **Depend on (or upon)** - i) To rely on (निर्भर होना)
ii) To be determined by (भरोसा करना)

182 **Deter from** - To discourage from doing something (रोकना)

183 **Devote to** - To dedicate time or effort to (समर्पित करना)

184 **Die away** - To gradually become weaker and disappear (धीरे-धीरे कम होना)

185 **Die down** - To become less intense (शांत होना)

186 **Die for** - To want something very much (बहुत चाहना)

187 **Die off** - To die one by one until none remain (एक-एक करके मरना)

188 **Die out** - To become extinct (विलुप्त होना)

189 **Dig in** - i) To start eating enthusiastically (खाने पर टूट पड़ना)
ii) To entrench oneself / refuse to change position (अड़ जाना)
iii) To reach into a bag or pocket (हाथ डालना)

190 **Dig up** - To discover information (खोज निकालना)

191 **Dish out** - i) To serve food (परोसना)
ii) To give criticism freely (आलोचना करना)

192 **Dispose of** - To get rid of (निपटाना)

193 **Dive in** - i) To start doing something with enthusiasm (जोश से शुरू करना)
ii) To jump into water (पानी में कूदना)
iii) To start eating eagerly (खाने पर टूट पड़ना)

194 **Do for** - i) To ruin or kill (बरबाद करना)

ii) To be enough or sufficient (पर्याप्त होना)

195 **Do over** - i) To do again (दोबारा करना)
ii) To redecorate (सजाना)

196 **Do up** - i) To fasten (buttons, zip) (बंद करना)
ii) To renovate (मरम्मत करना)

197 **Do with** - To need or want (ज़रूरत होना)

198 **Do without** - To manage without something (बिना काम चलाना)

199 **Double up** - To share a room or space (साथ रहना / बाँटना)

200 **Drag on** - To continue for too long (लंबा खिंचना)

201 **Drag out** - To make something last longer than necessary (बेवजह लंबा करना)

202 **Draw back** - To move away from something (पीछे हटना)

203 **Draw in** - i) (Days) To become shorter (दिन छोटे होना)
ii) To attract (आकर्षित करना)

204 **Draw on** - i) To use a resource (उपयोग करना)
ii) To approach (time) (नज़दीक आना)
iii) To put on or put on clothes (कपडे पहनना)

205 **Draw out** - i) To prolong (लंबा करना)
ii) To encourage someone to talk (बुलवाना)

206 **Dream of** - To imagine or hope for (सपना देखना)

207 **Dream up** - To invent or imagine something (सोच निकालना)

208 **Dress up** - i) To wear formal clothes (अच्छे कपड़े पहनना)
ii) To wear a costume (भेष बदलना)

209 **Drift apart** - To gradually become less close (दूर हो जाना)

210 **Drift off** - To gradually fall asleep (धीरे-धीरे सो जाना)

211 **Drive at** - To suggest or imply (इशारा करना)

212 **Drive away** - To force to leave (भगा देना)

213 **Drive out** - To force to leave a place (निकाल देना)

214 **Drive through** - To pass through without stopping (बिना रुके गुज़रना)

215 **Drive up** - To increase (prices) (बढ़ाना)

216 **Drop by** - To visit informally (अचानक मिलने आना)

217 **Drop off** - i) To leave someone somewhere (छोड़ना)
ii) To fall asleep (सो जाना)
iii) To decrease (कम होना)

218 **Drop out** - i) To withdraw or quit from a course, competition, or activity (बीच में छोड़ देना)
ii) To reject conventional society and live alternatively (समाज से कटना)
iii) To fall out or become dislodged (गिर जाना)

219 **Drum in** - i) To teach something by constant repetition (बार-बार दोहराकर सिखाना)
ii) To instill an idea firmly (मन में बैठाना)

220 **Drum up** - To generate or encourage interest, support, or business (रूचि, समर्थन या व्यवसाय जुटाना)

221 **Dry off** - To become dry or make something dry (सुखाना)

222 **Dry out** - i) To become completely dry (पूरा सूखना)
ii) To recover from alcoholism (शराब छुड़ाना)

223 **Dry up** - i) To become completely dry (सूख जाना)
ii) To stop talking (forget lines) (चुप हो जाना)

224 **Duck out** - i) To leave quickly or quietly (चुपके से निकल जाना)
ii) To avoid a duty or responsibility (जिम्मेदारी से बचना)

225 **Dwell on** - To think or talk about something for too long (सोचते रहना)

226 **Ease in** - i) To gradually introduce or settle into something (धीरे-धीरे शुरू करना)
ii) To gently insert or fit something (आराम से डालना / बैठाना)

227 **Ease off** - To reduce in intensity or pressure (कम होना)

228 **Ease up** - i) To become less intense or reduce in pressure (नरम पड़ना, कम होना)
ii) To slow down or relax effort (धीमा पड़ना, आराम करना)

229 **Eat away** - i) To erode or gradually destroy by chemical or physical action (क्षरण करना / घुलाना)
ii) To consume or diminish gradually (धीरे-धीरे खत्म करना)
iii) To gnaw or worry persistently at some-one's mind (मन को कचोटना)

230 **Eat into** - To gradually reduce or use up (धीरे-धीरे खत्म करना)

231 **Eat out** - To have a meal at a restaurant (बाहर खाना)

232 **Eat up** - i) To eat completely (खा जाना)
ii) To consume resources (खर्च कर देना)

233 **Edge out** - i) To gradually defeat or replace (धीरे-धीरे हराना)

ii) To narrowly defeat or surpass (मामूली अंतर से हराना)

234 **Embark on (or upon)** - To start a new project or journey (शुरू करना)

235 **Empty out** - To remove everything from inside (पूरा खाली करना)

236 **End in** - To have as a result (परिणाम होना)

237 **End up** - To finally be in a situation (अंत में होना)

238 **End with** - To have something at the end (से खत्म होना)

239 **Engage in** - To participate in an activity (में शामिल होना)

240 **Enter into** - To begin (agreement, discussion) (में प्रवेश करना)

241 **Entrust to** - To give responsibility to someone (सौंपना)

242 **Entrust with** - To give someone a responsibility (ज़िम्मेदारी देना)

243 **Even out** - To become equal or level gradually (धीरे-धीरे बराबर होना)

244 **Even up** - To make something equal or balanced (बराबर करना)

245 **Expose to** - i) To make someone experience something (किसी को कुछ अनुभव कराना)

246 **Face down** - To confront and defeat through intimidation (डराकर हराना)

247 **Face off** - To confront in competition (आमने-सामने होना)

248 **Fade away** - To gradually disappear (धीरे-धीरे गायब होना)

249 **Fall apart** - i) To break into pieces (टूट जाना)
ii) To fail completely (plan, relationship) (बिखर जाना)

250 **Fall behind** - To fail to keep up (पिछड़ जाना)

251 **Fall flat** - i) To fail completely (पूरी तरह असफल होना)
ii) To have no effect (बेअसर होना)

252 **Fall in** - i) To collapse inward (अंदर धंसना, गिरना)
ii) To form a military line (कतार में लगना)

253 **Fall over** - To trip and fall (गिर पड़ना)

254 **Fall to** - i) To begin doing something eagerly (करने लगना)
ii) To be assigned or come as a responsibility (ज़िम्मेदारी आना)

255 **Fan out** - To spread out in different directions (फैल जाना)

256 **Farm out** - To send work to be done by others (काम बाहर भेजना)

257 **Feel for** - i) To have sympathy for (सहानुभूति रखना)
ii) To try to find something by touching (टटोलना / हाथ से ढूँढना)

258 **Feel like** - To want to do something (मन करना)

259 **Feel up** - To touch someone inappropriately (अनुचित तरीके से छूना)

260 **Ferret out** - To discover through searching (खोज निकालना)

261 **Fight back** - i) To resist (प्रतिरोध करना)
ii) To suppress (tears, emotions) (रोकना)

262 **Fight off** - To resist and defeat (लड़कर भगाना)

263 **Fight out** - To settle by fighting or arguing (लड़कर निपटाना)

264 **Figure on** - To expect or plan for (उम्मीद करना)

265 **Fill in** - i) To complete a form (भरना)
ii) To inform someone (बताना)
iii) To substitute for someone (किसी की जगह लेना)

266 **Fill out** - i) To complete a form (भरना)
ii) To become fuller (body) (भरा होना)

267 **Fill up** - To make completely full (पूरा भरना)

268 **Find out** - To discover information (पता लगाना)

269 **Finish off** - i) To complete (पूरा करना)
ii) To kill (मार डालना)

270 **Finish up** - i) To complete (पूरा करना)
ii) To end up (अंत में होना)

271 **Fire away** - i) To begin speaking or asking questions freely (बोलना या सवाल पूछना शुरू करना)
ii) To shoot repeatedly (गोली चलाना)

272 **Fire up** - i) To start an engine (चालू करना)
ii) To excite or motivate (उत्साहित करना)

273 **Firm up** - To make more definite or stronger (पक्का करना)

274 **Fish for** - To try to obtain indirectly (घुमाकर पूछना)

275 **Fish out** - To pull out from a container (निकालना)

276 **Fit in** - i) To belong socially (घुलना-मिलना)
ii) To find time for (समय निकालना)
iii) To be suitable as part of something (में फिट होना)

277 **Fix up** - i) To arrange (व्यवस्था करना)
ii) To repair (ठीक करना)

278 **Fizzle out** - To gradually fail or end weakly (धीरे-धीरे खत्म होना)

279 **Flake out** - To fall asleep from exhaustion (थककर सो जाना)

280 **Flare up** - i) To suddenly become worse (भड़कना)
ii) To become angry suddenly (गुस्सा होना)

281 **Flick through** - To look quickly through pages (सरसरी नज़र डालना)

282 **Flip out** - To suddenly become very angry, excited, or emotionally upset (अचानक बहुत गुस्सा या भावुक हो जाना)

283 **Flirt with** - i) To behave romantically with (इश्कबाज़ी करना)
ii) To consider casually (idea, danger) (विचार करना)

284 **Float around** - To circulate (idea, rumor) (फैलना)

285 **Flood in** - To arrive in large numbers (उमड़ पड़ना)

286 **Focus on** - To concentrate attention on (ध्यान केंद्रित करना)

287 **Follow through** - To complete an action (पूरा करना)

288 **Fool around** - i) To behave playfully (मज़ाक करना)
ii) To have casual affairs (छेड़छाड़ करना)

289 **Force into** - To compel someone to do something (मजबूर करना)

290 **Fork out** - To pay reluctantly (मजबूरन देना)

291 **Freak out** - To become very upset or excited (घबरा जाना)

292 **Free up** - To make available (उपलब्ध कराना)

293 **Freeze over** - To become completely covered with ice (जम जाना)

294 **Freshen up** - To wash and make oneself look fresh (ताज़ा होना)

295 **Gain ground** - i) To make progress (प्रगति करना)
ii) To become more popular (लोकप्रिय होना)

296 **Gain on** - To get closer to someone you are chasing (दूरी कम करना)

297 **Gang up** - i) To form a group to intimidate or oppose someone (गिरोह बनाना / एकजुट होना)
ii) To join together against a common target (मिलकर विरोध करना)

298 **Gather around** - To come together in a group around something (इकट्ठा होना)

299 **Get about (or around)** - i) To move from place to place (इधर-उधर घूमना)
ii) (Of news) To spread (खबर फैलना)

300 **Get across** - To communicate an idea successfully (बात समझाना, विचार पहुँचाना)

301 **Get ahead** - i) To make progress, especially in career (तरक्की करना, आगे बढ़ना)
ii) To surpass or move in front of others (आगे निकलना)

302 **Get around to** - To finally do something after delay (समय निकालना)

303 **Get at** - i) To reach or access something (पहुँचना, हासिल करना)
ii) To imply or suggest indirectly (इशारा करना, संकेत करना)
iii) To criticize repeatedly (बार-बार आलोचना करना)

304 **Get behind** - To support someone or something (समर्थन करना)

305 **Get by** - To manage with limited resources (गुज़ारा करना, काम चलाना)

306 **Get down** - i) To descend or dismount (उतरना, नीचे आना)
ii) To depress or discourage someone (उदास करना, हतोत्साहित करना)
iii) Write something down (लिखना शुरू करना)

307 **Get down to** - To begin doing something seriously (गंभीरता से शुरू करना)

308 **Get hold of** - i) To obtain something (प्राप्त करना)
ii) To contact someone; (संपर्क करना)

309 **Get in** - i) To enter a vehicle or place (अंदर आना, घुसना)
ii) To arrive at a destination (पहुँचना)
iii) To be admitted or elected (दाखिला मिलना, चुना जाना)

310 **Get into** - i) To be admitted to an institution (में दाखिला पाना)
ii) To enter a vehicle, building or situation (में घुसना)
iii) To become involved in an activity (में लगना, शामिल होना)

311 **Get out** - i) To leave a place or vehicle (बाहर निकलना)
ii) (Of news or secret) To become known (राज़ खुलना)
iii) To avoid doing something (बचना, टालना)

312 **Get round (or around)** - i) To find a way to avoid a problem (रास्ता निकालना)
ii) To persuade someone by being nice (फुसलाना, मना लेना)

313 **Get to** - i) To arrive at a place (पहुँचना)
ii) To annoy or affect emotionally (परेशान करना)

314 **Get together** - i) To meet socially (मिलना-जुलना)
ii) To collect or gather things (इकट्ठा करना)

315 **Get up** - i) To rise from bed (बिस्तर से उठना)
ii) To stand up (खड़ा होना)

316 **Get up to** - To be involved in something, usually bad (में लगा होना)

317 **Give back** - To return something to its owner (वापस करना)

318 **Gloss over** - To treat a problem as less serious than it is (नज़रअंदाज़ करना, छुपाना)

319 **Go after** - To chase or pursue (पीछा करना, हासिल करने की कोशिश)

320 **Go against** - i) To oppose or act contrary to (के खिलाफ जाना)
ii) (Of decision) To be unfavorable (विरुद्ध होना)

321 **Go ahead** - i) To proceed with something (आगे बढ़ना)
ii) (Expression) Permission to proceed (कीजिए, आगे बढ़िए)

322 **Go at** - i) To attack energetically (जोश से हमला करना)
ii) To start doing something energetically (जोश से लग जाना)
iii) To try to deal with a problem forcefully (डटकर सामना करना)

323 **Go away** - i) To leave a place (चले जाना)
ii) To disappear (खत्म हो जाना)

324 **Go back** - To return to a place or state (वापस जाना)

325 **Go back on** - To break a promise or agreement (वादे से मुकरना)

326 **Go beyond** - To exceed a limit or expectation (से आगे जाना)

327 **Go by** - i) To pass (time) (बीतना, गुज़रना)
ii) To follow or be guided by (के अनुसार चलना)
iii) To be known as (name or nickname) (किसी नाम से जाना जाना)

328 **Go for** - i) To choose or prefer (चुनना, पसंद करना)
ii) To attack physically (पर हमला करना)
iii) To try to achieve (हासिल करने की कोशिश)

329 **Go into** - i) To enter a profession or business (में जाना, में आना)
ii) To examine or investigate in detail (जाँच करना, विस्तार से देखना)

330 **Go on** - i) To continue (जारी रखना)
ii) To happen (होना)
iii) To proceed to the next thing (आगे बढ़ना)
iv) To continue talking, often for a long time (लगातार बोलते रहना)

331 **Go out** - i) To leave home for entertainment (बाहर जाना, घूमने जाना)
ii) (Of fire/light) To stop burning (बुझ जाना)
iii) To date someone romantically (डेट करना)

332 **Go overboard** - To do something excessive or extreme (हद से ज़्यादा कर देना)

333 **Go round (or around)** - i) To be enough for everyone (सबके लिए पर्याप्त होना)
ii) To visit someone casually (किसी के घर जाना)

334 **Go together** - To be suitable or look good as a combination (साथ जाना)

335 **Go under** - (Of business) To fail (डूबना, बंद होना)

336 **Go up** - i) To increase in price or level (बढ़ना)
ii) To be built or constructed (बनना)

337 **Go with** - i) To match or suit (से मेल खाना)
ii) To choose or accept an option (चुनना)
iii) To agree with or support (सहमत होना / समर्थन करना)

338 **Go without** - To manage without having something (के बिना गुज़ारा करना)

339 **Goof around** - To behave in a silly way, waste time (मज़ाक करना, समय बर्बाद करना)

340 **Goof up** - To make a mistake (गलती करना, गड़बड़ करना)

341 **Grapple with** - i) To struggle to deal with a difficult problem (किसी कठिन समस्या से जूझना)
ii) To hold onto someone and fight physically (किसी से जकड़ कर लड़ना)

342 **Gross out** - To disgust or make someone feel sick or very uncomfortable (घिन दिलाना, बेहद असहज करना)

343 **Grow apart** - To become less close over time (दूर होना, अलग होना)

344 **Grow back** - To regrow after being removed (फिर से उगना)

345 **Grow into** - i) To become big enough to fit (बड़े होकर फिट होना)
ii) To develop into (में विकसित होना)

346 **Grow on** - To gradually become liked (धीरे-धीरे पसंद आना)

347 **Grow out** - i) To grow outward or become too long (बाहर की ओर बढ़ना)
ii) To let a hairstyle grow to its natural state (बालों को बढ़ने देना)

348 **Grow up** - i) To become an adult (बड़ा होना)
ii) To behave maturely (imperative) (बड़े बनो, समझदार बनो)

349 **Hack into** - To gain unauthorized access to a computer system (कंप्यूटर में सेंध लगाना)

350 **Hand back** - To return something to its owner (वापस करना)

351 **Hand on** - To pass something to the next person (आगे देना)

352 **Hand round** - To distribute something to a group (बांटना)

353 **Hang back** - To hesitate or be reluctant to act (पीछे रहना, हिचकिचाना)

354 **Hang on** - i) To wait for a short time (थोड़ा रुकिए)
ii) To hold tightly (कसकर पकड़ना)
iii) To persist despite difficulties (टिके रहना)

355 **Hang onto** - i) To keep something (संभालकर रखना)
ii) To hold tightly (पकड़े रहना)

356 **Hang out** - To spend time relaxing with friends (दोस्तों के साथ समय बिताना)

357 **Hang over** - (Of threat/problem) To remain unresolved (लटका रहना, मंडराना)

358 **Hang up** - i) To end a phone call (फोन रखना, कॉल काटना)
ii) To put on a hook or hanger (टांगना)

359 **Harp on (about)** - To talk repeatedly and annoyingly about something (एक ही बात बार-बार कहना)

360 **Hash out** - To discuss thoroughly until resolved (विस्तार से चर्चा करना)

361 **Have against** - To have a reason to dislike someone (के खिलाफ होना)

362 **Have on** - i) To be wearing something (पहना होना)
ii) To trick or tease someone (मज़ाक करना, उल्लू बनाना)
iii) To have something arranged or planned (कुछ तय या आयोजित होना)

363 **Head back** - To return to a place (वापस जाना)

364 **Head for** - i) To move towards a destination (की ओर जाना)
ii) To be likely to experience (की ओर बढ़ना)

365 **Head off** - i) To prevent something from happening (रोकना, टालना)
ii) To start a journey (रवाना होना)

366 **Head out** - To leave for a destination (निकलना)

367 **Head toward** - To move in the direction of (की ओर जाना)

368 **Head up** - To lead or be in charge of (नेतृत्व करना)

369 **Hear about** - To receive information about something (के बारे में सुनना)

370 **Hear from** - To receive news or communication from (से खबर मिलना)

371 **Hear of** - To know about the existence of (के बारे में सुनना)

372 **Heat up** - i) To become warmer or more intense (गरम होना, तीव्र होना)
ii) To warm food (गरम करना)

373 **Help out** - To assist someone with work or problems (मदद करना)

374 **Hide away** - i) To put something in a secret place (छुपाना)
ii) To isolate oneself (एकांत में रहना)

375 **Hit back** - To respond to criticism or attack (जवाबी हमला करना)

376 **Hit on (or upon)** - i) To discover by chance (अचानक पता लगाना)
ii) To talk to someone with romantic or sexual interest (लाइन मारना)

377 **Hit out** - i) To strike out wildly or aggressively (जोर से वार करना)
ii) To criticize or attack verbally (कड़ी आलोचना करना)
iii) To bat powerfully in cricket/baseball (जोरदार शॉट खेलना)

378 **Hold against** - To blame someone for something (दोष देना)

379 **Hold back** - i) To restrain, control, or prevent progress (आगे बढ़ने से रोकना)
ii) To withhold information (जानकारी छुपाना)

380 **Hold down** - i) To keep a job for a long time (नौकरी बनाए रखना)
ii) To keep at a low level (नीचे रखना)

381 **Hold forth** - To speak at length about something (लंबा भाषण देना)

382 **Hold off** - i) To delay or postpone (टालना, रोकना)
ii) To resist an attack (हमला रोकना)
iii) (Of bad weather) to fail to occur (न आना, टला रहना)

383 **Hold onto** - To keep possession of something (अपने पास रखना)

384 **Hold over** - To postpone to a later date (आगे के लिए टालना)

385 **Hold with** - To agree with or approve of (से सहमत होना)

386 **Home in** - i) To move toward a target or destination (लक्ष्य की ओर बढ़ना)

ii) To focus attention on something (ध्यान केंद्रित करना)

387 **Hook up** - To connect to a system or equipment (जोड़ना)

388 **Hunt down** - To search for and find after much effort (खोजकर पकड़ना)

389 **Hurry up** - To do something more quickly (जल्दी करना)

390 **Identify with** - To feel connection or sympathy with (से जुड़ाव महसूस करना)

391 **Impact on** - To have an effect on (पर प्रभाव डालना)

392 **Impose on (or upon)** - To take unfair advantage of kindness (का फायदा उठाना)

393 **Impress on** - To emphasize something to someone (पर जोर देना)

394 **Improve on (or upon)** - To achieve better than previous result (से बेहतर करना)

395 **Indulge in** - To allow oneself to enjoy something, often excessively (किसी चीज़ में ज़रूरत से ज़्यादा लिप्त होना)

396 **Infer from** - To conclude from evidence (से अनुमान लगाना)

397 **Insist on** - To demand firmly (पर ज़ोर देना)

398 **Interfere with** - i) To prevent from working properly (में दखल देना)
ii) To cause problems or disrupt (बाधा डालना)

399 **Invest in** - To put money or effort into something (में निवेश करना)

400 **Iron out** - To resolve problems or difficulties (समस्याएँ सुलझाना)

401 **Jack up** - i) To raise with a jack (जैक से उठाना)
ii) To increase prices sharply (अचानक बढ़ाना)

402 **Jam into** - To force into a small space (ठूंसना)

403 **Jam up** - To become blocked or stuck (जाम होना)

404 **Join in** - To participate in an activity (में शामिल होना)

405 **Join up** - i) To enlist in the military (सेना में भर्ती होना)
ii) To connect (मिलाना)

406 **Jot down** - To write quickly (जल्दी से नोट करना)

407 **Jump at** - To accept eagerly (तुरंत स्वीकार करना)

408 **Jump in** - i) To enter quickly (जल्दी से घुसना)
ii) To interrupt a conversation (बीच में बोलना)

409 **Jump on** - i) To criticize harshly (कड़ी आलोचना करना)
ii) To take advantage of an opportunity eagerly (मौका लपक लेना)

410 **Jump out** - i) To leap out suddenly (अचानक बाहर कूदना)
ii) To be immediately noticeable (तुरंत नज़र आना)

411 **Jump to** - To reach hastily without proper thought (जल्दबाज़ी में पहुंचना)

412 **Keel over** - To fall down suddenly (अचानक गिर पड़ना)

413 **Keep at** - To continue doing despite difficulty (लगे रहना)

414 **Keep away** - i) To stay at a distance or prevent someone from coming near (दूर रहना, दूर रखना)
ii) To avoid contact with something (किसी चीज़ से बचना)

415 **Keep back** - i) To withhold information (छुपाना)
ii) To stay at a distance (पीछे रहना)

416 **Keep down** - i) To prevent from increasing (बढ़ने से रोकना)
ii) To manage to eat and not vomit (उल्टी रोकना)

417 **Keep from** - i) To prevent or refrain from (रोकना, बचना)
ii) To withhold information from someone (कोई बात छुपाना / न बताना)

418 **Keep off** - i) To stay away from (से दूर रहना)
ii) To avoid a topic (विषय से बचना)

419 **Keep on** - i) To continue doing something (जारी रखना)
ii) To persist (लगे रहना)

420 **Keep out** - i) To prevent from entering (बाहर रखना)
ii) To stay outside (बाहर रहना)

421 **Keep to** - i) To adhere to or follow (का पालन करना)
ii) To limit oneself (तक सीमित रहना)

422 **Key in** - To enter data using keyboard (टाइप करना)

423 **Kick against** - To resist or oppose strongly (विरोध करना)

424 **Kick around** - To discuss informally (अनौपचारिक चर्चा करना)

425 **Kick back** - To relax and take it easy (आराम करना)

426 **Kick in** - i) To start to have effect (असर होना)
ii) To contribute money (पैसे देना)

427 **Kick off** - To begin (especially sports or events) (शुरू होना)

428 **Kick out** - To force someone to leave (निकाल देना)

429 **Kill off** - To destroy completely (पूरी तरह खत्म करना)

430 **Kneel down** - To go down on knees (घुटने टेकना)

431 **Knock about (or around)** - To spend time aimlessly (इधर-उधर घूमना)

432 **Knock back** - i) To drink quickly (जल्दी से पीना)
ii) To cost a lot (महँगा पड़ना)

433 **Knock off** - i) To stop working (काम बंद करना)
ii) To reduce a price or amount (मूल्य कम करना)

434 **Knock out** - i) To make unconscious (बेहोश करना)
ii) To eliminate from competition (प्रतियोगिता से बाहर करना)

435 **Knock over** - i) To cause to fall by hitting (टक्कर से गिराना)
ii) To rob a place (किसी जगह को लूटना)

436 **Knock up** - i) To wake someone by knocking (जगाना)
ii) To make quickly (जल्दी बनाना)

437 **Know about** - To have information regarding (के बारे में जानना)

438 **Know of** - To be aware of the existence of (के बारे में पता होना)

439 **Land in** - i) To arrive at a place (में पहुंचना)
ii) To get into a difficult situation (मुसीबत में पड़ जाना)

440 **Land on** - To discover or choose something (पर उतरना)

441 **Land up** - To end up in a place or situation (में पहुंच जाना)

442 **Lash out** - i) To attack suddenly and violently, physically or verbally (अचानक हमला करना / भड़कना)
ii) To spend money extravagantly (खुलकर खर्च करना) {British informal}
iii) To kick or strike out wildly (बेतहाशा मारना)

443 **Laugh at** - To mock or ridicule someone (पर हंसना)

444 **Laugh off** - To dismiss something by laughing (हँसकर टाल देना)

445 **Launch into** - To begin enthusiastically (जोश से शुरू करना)

446 **Lay aside** - To save for future use (बचाकर रखना)

447 **Lay down** - i) To establish rules or principles (नियम बनाना)
ii) To put down or stop carrying (नीचे रखना)
iii) To surrender or give up (आत्मसमर्पण करना)

448 **Lay in** - To stock up supplies (भंडार करना)

449 **Lay into** - To attack or criticize severely (कड़ी आलोचना करना)

450 **Lay on** - To provide or supply (प्रबंध करना)

451 **Laze about (around)** - To spend time relaxing and doing nothing (आराम से बैठे समय बिताना, कुछ न करना)

452 **Laze around** - To spend time idly (आराम से समय बिताना)

453 **Lead on** - To deceive by false hopes (झूठी उम्मीद दिलाना)

454 **Lead to** - To result in or cause (का कारण बनना)

455 **Lead up** - i) To gradually approach or introduce (धीरे-धीरे आगे बढ़ना)
ii) To precede (पहले आना)

456 **Leaf through** - To turn pages quickly (जल्दी-जल्दी पन्ने पलटना)

457 **Leak out** - To become known despite secrecy (बाहर आ जाना)

458 **Lean on** - i) To depend on for support (का सहारा लेना)
ii) To pressure someone (दबाव डालना)

459 **Leap at** - To accept eagerly (तुरंत स्वीकार करना)

460 **Learn about** - To acquire knowledge of something (के बारे में सीखना)

461 **Learn of** - To become aware of (के बारे में पता चलना)

462 **Leave behind** - i) To forget to bring (भूल जाना)
ii) To depart from permanently (पीछे छोड़ना)

463 **Leave off** - To stop doing something (बंद करना)

464 **Leave out** - To omit or exclude (छोड़ना, शामिल न करना)

465 **Leave to** - To let someone handle something (पर छोड़ देना)

466 **Let alone** - i) Much less (तो दूर की बात)
ii) Not to mention (छोड़ो भी / कहना ही क्या)

467 **Let go** - i) To release (छोड़ देना)
ii) To dismiss from employment (नौकरी से निकाल देना)

468 **Let in** - i) To allow to enter (अंदर आने देना)
ii) To admit (प्रवेश देना)

469 **Let into** - i) To allow entry (अंदर आने देना)
ii) To share a secret (राज़ बताना)

470 **Let on** - To reveal a secret (राज़ खोलना)

471 **Let out** - i) To release (बाहर निकलने देना)
ii) To make clothing bigger (ढीला करना)
iii) To make a sound (आवाज़ निकालना)
iv) To reveal a secret (राज़ खोलना)

472 **Let up** - To become less intense (कम होना)

473 **Lie ahead** - To be in the future (आगे होना)

474 **Lie around** - To be scattered untidily; to relax lazily (इधर-उधर पड़ा रहना)

475 **Lie behind** - i) To be the reason for (के पीछे का कारण)
ii) To remain in a place after someone has left (पीछे रह जाना)

476 **Lie down** - To recline (लेटना)

477 **Lie in** - To stay in bed longer than usual (देर तक सोना)

478 **Lie low** - i) To avoid attention (नज़र में न आना)
ii) To stay hidden (छिपकर रहना)

479 **Lift up** - i) To raise something or someone (ऊपर उठाना)
ii) To encourage or make someone feel better (उत्साहित करना)

480 **Light up** - i) To illuminate (रोशन करना)
ii) To start smoking (सिगरेट जलाना)
iii) (Of face) To show happiness (खुशी से चमकना)

481 **Lighten up** - i) To become less serious (गंभीर न होना)
ii) To make something less heavy (तनाव कम करना)

482 **Line up** - i) To arrange in a row (कतार में लगाना)
ii) To organize or arrange (व्यवस्था करना)

483 **Link up** - To connect or join (जोड़ना)

484 **Listen in** - i) To listen secretly to a conversation (चोरी-छुपे सुनना)
ii) To tune in to a broadcast or listen as a passive participant (रेडियो सुनना, श्रोता बनकर सुनना)

485 **Listen out** - To listen attentively and be alert for a particular sound or signal (ध्यान से सुनना, किसी आवाज़ के लिए सतर्क रहना)

486 **Live by** - i) To follow principles strictly (के अनुसार जीना)
ii) To survive by (doing something) (जीविका चलाना)

487 **Live for** - To regard as main purpose in life (के लिए जीना)

488 **Live off** - To depend on for money or food (पर निर्भर रहना)

489 **Live on** - i) To survive on (पर गुज़ारा करना)
ii) To continue to exist (जीवित रहना)

490 **Live with** - i) To accept an unpleasant situation (स्वीकार करके जीना)
ii) Stay or reside with someone (किसी के साथ रहना)

491 **Load up** - i) To fill or pack with a large quantity of goods (लादना / भरना)
ii) To acquire or consume large amounts of something (बहुत सारा लेना / भर लेना)
iii) To load a vehicle, weapon, or software (लोड करना)

492 **Lock away** - To put in a secure place (सुरक्षित जगह रखना)

493 **Lock down** - To confine; to secure completely (बंद करना)

494 **Lock in** - To secure a rate or price (पक्का करना)

495 **Lock out** - To prevent entry by locking (बाहर बंद कर देना)

496 **Lock up** - i) To secure by locking (ताला लगाना)
ii) To imprison (जेल में बंद करना)

497 **Log in (or on)** - To start a computer session (लॉग इन करना)

498 **Log off (or out)** - To end a computer session (लॉग आउट करना)

499 **Long for** - To want very much (की बहुत इच्छा होना)

500 **Look ahead** - To think about the future (भविष्य के बारे में सोचना)

501 **Look around (or round)** - To explore a place; to search (चारों ओर देखना)

502 **Look at** - i) To direct eyes toward (देखना)
ii) To examine (जांचना)

503 **Look back** - i) To think about or reflect on the past (अतीत को याद करना / पीछे मुड़कर देखना)
ii) To turn and look behind oneself (पीछे देखना)
iii) To suffer a setback after progress (used in negative: 'never looked back') (पीछे मुड़कर न देखना)

504 **Look for** - To search for (खोजना)

505 **Look forward to** - To await with pleasure (किसी चीज़ की उत्सुकता से प्रतीक्षा करना)

506 **Look in** - i) To make a brief visit (थोड़ी देर के लिए मिलने जाना)
ii) To watch a TV programme briefly (झलक देखना)

507 **Look on** - i) To watch without participating (देखते रहना)
ii) To regard or consider (मानना, समझना)

508 **Loom over** - To dominate threateningly

(मंडराना)

509 **Loosen up** - To relax and become less tense (ढीला पड़ना, आराम करना)

510 **Lose out** - To fail to benefit (नुकसान में रहना)

511 **Luck into** - To obtain something by good fortune (भाग्य से मिलना)

512 **Luck out** - To be very fortunate (बहुत भाग्यशाली होना)

513 **Make for** - i) To move towards a place (की ओर जाना)
ii) To contribute to or result in (में योगदान देना)

514 **Make into** - To transform into something different (में बदलना)

515 **Make of** - To understand or have opinion about (के बारे में सोचना)

516 **Map out** - To plan in detail (विस्तार से योजना बनाना)

517 **Mark down** - i) To reduce the price (दाम कम करना)
ii) To record in writing (लिख लेना)

518 **Mark off** - To separate by drawing a line; to tick off (निशान लगाना)

519 **Mark out** - i) To indicate boundaries (सीमाएँ चिह्नित करना)
ii) To distinguish someone as special (अलग पहचान देना)

520 **Match up** - To be equal or compatible (मेल खाना)

521 **Max out** - To reach the maximum limit (अधिकतम सीमा तक पहुंचना)

522 **Meet up** - i) To meet socially by arrangement (मिलना / भेंट करना)
ii) To come together at an agreed place (इकट्ठा होना)
iii) To encounter or converge (मिल जाना)

523 **Meet with** - To experience or receive (सामना होना)

524 **Melt away** - To disappear gradually (धीरे-धीरे गायब होना)

525 **Melt down** - i) To melt something for recycling (गलाना, पिघलाना)
ii) To lose emotional control (भावनात्मक रूप से टूट जाना)

526 **Mess about (or around)** - i) To behave in silly or time-wasting way (मज़ाक करना, समय बर्बाद करना)
ii) Handle something carelessly or incorrectly (गलत तरीके से छेड़छाड़ करना)

527 **Mess up** - To spoil or do badly (खराब करना, गड़बड़ करना)

528 **Mess with** - To interfere with; to provoke (से छेड़छाड़ करना)

529 **Miss out** - i) To fail to experience or take advantage of something (किसी चीज़ से वंचित रहना)
ii) To omit or skip something (छोड़ देना)
iii) To lose an opportunity (मौका गँवाना)

530 **Mistake for** - To wrongly identify as someone else (समझ लेना)

531 **Mix in** - i) To combine (मिलाना)
ii) To socialize (घुलना-मिलना)

532 **Mix up** - To confuse one thing with another (गड़बड़ करना)

533 **Mock up** - To make a model for testing (नमूना बनाना)

534 **Mop up** - i) To clean liquid with mop or cloth (पोंछना)
ii) To complete remaining tasks (बचा-खुचा काम निपटाना)

535 **Mount up** - To increase gradually to large amount (बढ़ते जाना)

536 **Mouth off** - To speak rudely or complain loudly (बकवास करना)

537 **Move along** - i) To keep moving (आगे बढ़ना)
ii) To progress (प्रगति करना)

538 **Move away** - To go to live in a different place (कहीं और जाना)

539 **Move in** - i) To start living in a new home (नए घर में जाना)
ii) To approach a place or person, often quickly or aggressively (तेज़ी से नज़दीक आना, घुस आना)

540 **Move on** - To stop doing something and start new (आगे बढ़ना)

541 **Move out** - To leave a home permanently (घर खाली करना)

542 **Move over** - To change position to make room (हटना)

543 **Move up** - To advance to a higher position (तरक्की करना)

544 **Mow down** - i) To kill many people (सभी को मार देना)
ii) To cut grass (काट डालना)

545 **Muddle through** - To manage despite confusion (किसी तरह निकालना)

546 **Muddle up** - To confuse or mix wrongly (गड़बड़ करना)

547 **Nag at** - To criticize or complain persistently (खीजना)

548 **Nail down** - i) To finalize or settle definitely (पक्का करना)
ii) To define precisely (स्पष्ट करना)

549 **Name after** - To give the same name as someone else (के नाम पर रखना)

550 **Narrow down** - To reduce number of options (विकल्प कम करना)

551 **Nod off** - To fall asleep briefly (झपकी लेना, ऊँघना)

552 **Note down** - To write something for future reference (नोट करना)

553 **Object to** - To express disapproval of (पर आपत्ति करना)

554 **Occur to** - To come into someone's mind suddenly (अचानक दिमाग़ में आना)

555 **Open out** - To spread or unfold; to become more communicative (खुलना)

556 **Open up** - To start talking freely; to become available (खुलकर बात करना)

557 **Opt for** - To choose or select (चुनना)

558 **Opt in** - To choose to participate (शामिल होने का विकल्प चुनना)

559 **Opt out** - i) To choose not to participate or be involved (भाग न लेना)
ii) To withdraw from something (हटना / पीछे हटना)
iii) To decline or refuse involvement (इनकार करना)

560 **Order about (or around)** - To keep giving orders in bossy way (हुक्म चलाना)

561 **Order off** - To tell someone to leave a playing field (मैदान से बाहर भेजना)

562 **Owe to** - To be indebted for (का आभारी होना)

563 **Own up** - i) To confess or admit responsibility (स्वीकार करना)
ii) To acknowledge wrongdoing (गलती मानना)
iii) To come clean about something (सच बोलना)

564 **Pack away** - To put items into storage (संभालकर रखना)

565 **Pack in** - i) To stop doing something (बंद करना)
ii) To attract large audiences (भीड़ खींचना)
iii) To fit many things in a limited space (ठूंसना)

566 **Pack off** - To send someone away hastily (जल्दी से भेजना)

567 **Pack up** - i) To put things in containers for moving (सामान बाँधना)
ii) To stop working (machine) (काम करना बंद करना)

568 **Pan out** - To develop or turn out (होना, निकलना)

569 **Paper over** - To hide problems superficially (समस्याएँ छुपाना)

570 **Part from** - To leave or separate from someone (से अलग होना)

571 **Part with** - To give up or hand over reluctantly (मन मारकर देना)

572 **Pass around** - To distribute to a group (बांटना)

573 **Pass by** - To go past (गुज़रना)

574 **Pass down** - To transfer from generation to generation (पीढ़ी-दर-पीढ़ी देना)

575 **Pass for** - To be accepted as (के रूप में स्वीकार होना)

576 **Pass into** - To become part of (में शामिल होना)

577 **Pass on** - i) To give to next person (आगे देना)
ii) To die (euphemism) (गुज़र जाना)

578 **Pass over** - To ignore or overlook for promotion (नज़रअंदाज़ करना)

579 **Pass through** - To travel through a place (से गुज़रना)

580 **Pass up** - To decline an opportunity (अच्छा मौका छोड़ देना, मौका गँवाना)

581 **Patch together** - To assemble hastily from various parts (जोड़-तोड़ कर बनाना)

582 **Patch up** - i) To repair temporarily (जुगाड़ से ठीक करना)
ii) To settle a quarrel (सुलह करना)

583 **Pay back** - i) To return borrowed money (वापस करना)
ii) To take revenge on (बदला लेना)

584 **Pay for** - i) To give money in exchange (के लिए पैसे देना)
ii) To suffer consequences (भुगतना)

585 **Pay off** - i) To clear a debt completely (पूरा कर्ज़ चुकाना)
ii) To be successful or worthwhile (सफल होना)
iii) To bribe someone (घूस देना)

586 **Pay out** - To pay money from a fund (भुगतान करना)

587 **Pay up** - To pay what is owed (बकाया चुकाना)

588 **Peel off** - To remove by peeling (छीलकर उतारना)

589 **Perk up** - To become more cheerful or lively (खुश होना, चुस्त होना)

590 **Peter out** - To gradually diminish and stop (धीरे-धीरे खत्म होना)

591 **Phase in** - To introduce gradually (धीरे-धीरे लागू करना)

592 **Pick at** - i) To eat in small amounts without appetite (थोड़ा-थोड़ा खाना, बिना भूख खाना)
ii) To keep criticizing or annoying someone repeatedly (लगातार ताने देना)

593 **Pick out** - i) To choose from a group (चुनना)
ii) To recognize or identify (पहचानना)

594 **Pick over** - To examine carefully to select the best (छांटना)

595 **Pick up** - i) To lift from a surface (उठाना)
ii) To collect someone or something (लेने जाना)
iii) To learn informally (सीखना)
iv) To improve or increase (सुधरना, बढ़ना)

596 **Pig out** - To eat a lot greedily (खूब खाना)

597 **Pile up** - To accumulate in large quantities (ढेर लगना)

598 **Pin down** - i) To identify precisely (पक्का करना)
ii) To force to make decision (निर्णय लेने पर मजबूर करना)

599 **Pipe down** - To be quiet (शांत होना)

600 **Piss off** - i) To annoy greatly (परेशान करना)
ii) To leave or go away (हट जाओ!)

601 **Pitch in** - To contribute effort or money (मदद करना)

602 **Plan for** - To prepare for something expected (की योजना बनाना)

603 **Plan on** - To intend to do something (का इरादा रखना)

604 **Play along** - i) To cooperate or pretend to agree (साथ देना / सहमति जताना)
ii) To go along with a plan or pretence (नाटक में साथ देना)
iii) To humor someone (किसी की हाँ में हाँ मिलाना)

605 **Play around** - i) To do in a careless, experimental, or casual way (खेल-खेल में करना)
ii) To spend time idly (फालतू समय बिताना)

606 **Play at** - To pretend to do something casually without seriousness (शौक या मज़े के लिए करना)

607 **Play back** - To replay recorded sound or video (रिकॉर्ड की गई आवाज़ या वीडियो फिर से चलाना)

608 **Play off** - i) To set one person or group against another for advantage (एक-दूसरे के खिलाफ खड़ा करना)
ii) To compete in a tiebreaker or playoff (निर्णायक मुकाबला खेलना)
iii) To exploit rivalry between parties (प्रतिद्वंद्विता का फायदा उठाना)

609 **Play out** - To happen in a particular way (घटित होना)

610 **Play up** - i) To exaggerate (बढ़ा-चढ़ाकर बताना)
ii) To cause problems (machine/child) (परेशान करना)
iii) To emphasize (ज़ोर देना)

611 **Plod along** - To make slow, steady progress (धीरे-धीरे चलना)

612 **Plod on** - To continue slowly despite difficulty (धीरे-धीरे जारी रखना)

613 **Plough through (or plow)** - To proceed with difficulty (मुश्किल से निकलना)

614 **Plug away** - To work hard and steadily (लगे रहना)

615 **Plug in** - To connect to electrical supply (प्लग लगाना)

616 **Plug up** - To block something completely (बंद करना)

617 **Point to** - To suggest, indicate, or provide evidence for something (की ओर इशारा करना)

618 **Polish off** - To finish quickly (जल्दी खत्म करना)

619 **Polish up** - To improve or refine (सुधारना, चमकाना)

620 **Pony up** - To pay money that is owed (पैसे देना)

621 **Pop in** - To visit briefly (थोड़ी देर के लिए आना)

622 **Pop out** - i) To leave briefly (थोड़ी देर के लिए बाहर जाना)
ii) To appear suddenly (अचानक दिखाई देना)

623 **Pop up** - To appear suddenly and unexpectedly (अचानक प्रकट होना)

624 **Pour in** - i) To arrive in large numbers (बड़ी संख्या में आना)
ii) To flow continuously and heavily (तेज़ी से लगातार बहना)

625 **Pour out** - To express emotions freely (मन की बात कहना)

626 **Power through** - To complete something with determination (पूरे जोश से करना)

627 **Press ahead (or on)** - To continue determinedly (दृढ़ता से जारी रखना)

628 **Press for** - To demand firmly (माँग करना)

629 **Press on** - To continue despite difficulties (आगे बढ़ते रहना)

630 **Prey on** - To exploit or victimize someone (किसी का शिकार करना, शोषण करना)

631 **Print out** - To produce printed copy from computer (प्रिंट निकालना)

632 **Prop up** - To support or keep from falling

(सहारा देना)

633 **Provide for** - i) To supply needs of (भरण-पोषण करना)
ii) To make arrangements for (प्रावधान करना)

634 **Pry into** - To try to find out about private matters (में ताक-झांक करना)

635 **Pry out** - To obtain information with difficulty (जानकारी निकालना)

636 **Psych out** - To intimidate someone mentally (मानसिक रूप से डराना)

637 **Pull apart** - i) To separate forcefully (अलग करना)
ii) To criticize harshly (कड़ी आलोचना करना)

638 **Pull away** - To start moving (vehicle) (चलना शुरू करना)

639 **Pull back** - To withdraw or retreat (पीछे हटना)

640 **Pull down** - To demolish a building (गिराना, तोड़ना)

641 **Pull in** - i) (Of vehicle) To stop at roadside (किनारे रुकना)
ii) To attract audience (दर्शक खींचना)

642 **Pull out** - i) To withdraw from participation (हटना, निकलना)
ii) (Of vehicle) To move out (बाहर निकलना)

643 **Pull over** - To stop vehicle at roadside (गाड़ी रोकना)

644 **Pull round (around)** - To recover from illness (बीमारी से स्वस्थ होना)

645 **Pull through** - To survive a serious illness (बीमारी से उबरना)

646 **Punch in** - To record arrival time at work (काम पर आने की हाज़िरी लगाना)

647 **Punch out** - To record departure time from work (काम से जाने की हाज़िरी लगाना)

648 **Punch up** - To make more interesting or lively (रोचक बनाना)

649 **Push ahead** - i) To proceed determinedly despite obstacles (दृढ़ता से आगे बढ़ना)
ii) To continue making progress (प्रगति जारी रखना)
iii) To move forward forcefully (ज़ोर से आगे बढ़ना)

650 **Push around** - To bully or treat roughly (धौंस जमाना)

651 **Push for** - To demand or advocate strongly (ज़ोर देना)

652 **Push off** - To leave (चले जाना)

653 **Push on** - To continue despite difficulty (जारी रखना)

654 **Push through** - To force acceptance of (मंज़ूर करवाना)

655 **Put about** - To spread rumours or information (फैलाना)

656 **Put aside** - i) To save for later use (बचाकर रखना)
ii) To ignore temporarily (अलग रखना)

657 **Put away** - i) To store in proper place (रखना, जमाना)
ii) To eat large amounts (खूब खाना)
iii) To save money to spend later (भविष्य के लिए पैसे बचाना)

658 **Put back** - i) To return to original place (वापस रखना)
ii) To postpone (टालना)

659 **Put forward** - To propose or suggest (प्रस्ताव रखना)

660 **Put past** - To consider someone capable of (usually negative) (से ऐसी उम्मीद रखना)

661 **Put through** - i) To connect by telephone (फोन लगाना)
ii) To cause to experience (से गुज़ारना)

662 **Put together** - To assemble, build, or prepare something (जोड़ना, बनाना, व्यवस्थित करना)

663 **Quarrel with** - To disagree with (से असहमत होना)

664 **Queue up** - To wait in a line (कतार में लगना)

665 **Quiet down** - To become calmer or less noisy (शांत होना)

666 **Quieten down** - To become or make quiet (शांत होना)

667 **Quit on** - To stop supporting or helping someone (साथ छोड़ देना)

668 **Race through** - To do something very quickly (जल्दी-जल्दी करना)

669 **Rack up** - To accumulate or score a large amount of something (बड़ी मात्रा में इकट्ठा करना, अंक या जीत हासिल करना)

670 **Rain down** - i) To fall in large quantities from above (बड़ी मात्रा में गिरना)
ii) To pour or shower heavily (बरसना)
iii) To descend abundantly, often of blows or criticism (वार बरसाना)

671 **Rake in** - To earn money in large amounts (खूब कमाना)

672 **Rake over** - To examine past events in detail (पुरानी अप्रिय बातों को फिर से उठाना)

673 **Rake up** - To bring up unpleasant past

matters (पुरानी बात उखाड़ना)

674 **Rally around (or round)** - To come together for support (समर्थन में आना)

675 **Ramble on** - To talk at length aimlessly (बेमतलब बोलते रहना)

676 **Ramp up** - To increase significantly (तेज़ी से बढ़ाना)

677 **Rattle off** - To say quickly from memory (झटपट बोलना)

678 **Rattle on** - To talk quickly and at length (बकबक करना)

679 **Rattle through** - To do something very quickly (जल्दी-जल्दी निपटाना)

680 **Reach out** - i) To make contact or communicate (संपर्क करना)
ii) To extend a hand or offer help (मदद का हाथ बढ़ाना)
iii) To stretch or extend physically (हाथ फैलाना)

681 **Read into** - To find more meaning than intended (ज़्यादा मतलब निकालना)

682 **Read out** - To read aloud (ज़ोर से पढ़ना)

683 **Read through** - To read completely and carefully (पूरा पढ़ना)

684 **Read up** - i) To study a subject by reading extensively (पढ़कर जानकारी लेना)
ii) To research or learn about something (किसी विषय पर पढ़ाई करना)

685 **Reason with** - To persuade by logical argument (समझाना)

686 **Reckon on** - To expect or count on (उम्मीद करना)

687 **Reckon with** - To take into account (ध्यान में रखना)

688 **Refer to** - i) To mention or speak about (का उल्लेख करना)
ii) To consult for information (देखना, संदर्भ लेना)

689 **Reflect on** - To think carefully about (पर विचार करना)

690 **Rein in** - To control or restrain (नियंत्रित करना)

691 **Remind of** - To cause to remember (याद दिलाना)

692 **Report to** - To be responsible or answerable to someone (किसी के प्रति जवाबदेह होना)

693 **Resign oneself to** - To accept something unpleasant that cannot be changed (किसी अप्रिय बात को मजबूरी में स्वीकार कर लेना)

694 **Resort to** - To use when other options fail (का सहारा लेना)

695 **Rest on** - To depend on (पर निर्भर होना)

696 **Rest with** - To be the responsibility of (की जिम्मेदारी होना)

697 **Result in** - To cause as outcome (का परिणाम होना)

698 **Return to** - To go back to a place or activity (वापस लौटना)

699 **Rev up** - To increase speed or activity (तेज़ करना)

700 **Revert to** - To go back to a former state (पर वापस आना)

701 **Rig up** - To make or set up quickly (जुगाड़ करना)

702 **Ring back** - To return a phone call (वापस फोन करना)

703 **Ring off** - To end a phone call (फोन रखना)

704 **Ring out** - To sound loudly and clearly (गूंजना)

705 **Ring up** - i) To telephone someone (फोन करना)
ii) To record sale on cash register (कैश रजिस्टर पर दर्ज करना)

706 **Rip apart** - i) To tear into pieces (चीर देना)
ii) To criticize severely (तीव्र आलोचना करना)

707 **Rip into** - To attack or criticize fiercely (जमकर आलोचना करना)

708 **Rip off** - i) To cheat or overcharge (ठगना)
ii) To tear away (फाड़ना)
iii) To copy or imitate dishonestly (नकल करना)

709 **Rip up** - To tear into pieces (फाड़कर टुकड़े करना)

710 **Rise above** - To overcome or not be affected by (से ऊपर उठना)

711 **Rise up** - To revolt or rebel (विद्रोह करना)

712 **Roll in** - To arrive in large numbers (बड़ी संख्या में आना)

713 **Roll out** - i) To launch or introduce officially (लॉन्च करना)
ii) To spread something out by rolling (बेलना/फैलाना)

714 **Roll over** - i) To turn over onto the other side (पलटना)
ii) To renew or transfer a financial investment (वित्तीय निवेश को आगे बढ़ाना)
iii) To submit without resistance (बिना विरोध के झुक जाना)

715 **Roll up** - To arrive casually (आ पहुँचना)

716 **Root for** - To support enthusiastically (का समर्थन करना)

717 **Root out** - To find and remove completely (जड़ से खत्म करना)

718 **Rope in** - To persuade to participate (शामिल करना)

719 **Round off** - i) To complete satisfactorily (अच्छी तरह समाप्त करना)
ii) To approximate a number (राउंड ऑफ करना)

720 **Round up** - i) To gather together (इकट्ठा करना)
ii) To raise to higher number (ऊपर की तरफ पूर्णांक करना)

721 **Rub in** - To emphasize something hurtful (चोट पर नमक छिड़कना)

722 **Rub off** - i) To be transferred through contact or influence (प्रभाव पड़ना / असर होना)
ii) To erase or remove by rubbing (रगड़कर मिटाना)
iii) To wear away by friction (घिसकर हटना)

723 **Rub out** - To erase (मिटाना)

724 **Rule out** - To exclude as possibility (बाहर करना)

725 **Run after** - To chase (पीछे भागना)

726 **Run against** - i) To compete against (प्रतिस्पर्धा करना)
ii) To encounter (टकराना)

727 **Run around** - To be very busy (दौड़-भाग करना)

728 **Run by** - To tell someone about something for approval (से पूछना)

729 **Run in** - To use gently at first (new vehicle) (नई गाड़ी को धीरे-धीरे चलाना)

730 **Run off** - i) To flee or escape (भाग जाना)
ii) To print copies (प्रतियाँ छापना)

731 **Run on** - i) To continue longer than expected (ज़्यादा देर चलना)
ii) To work using a particular fuel or power (पर निर्भर होना)

732 **Run through** - i) To rehearse or review (अभ्यास करना)
ii) To use up wastefully (उड़ा देना)

733 **Run to** - To amount to (तक पहुँचना)

734 **Run up** - i) To accumulate a bill or debt (कर्ज़ या बिल जमा करना)
ii) To make something quickly (जल्दी से बनाना)
iii) To raise a flag (झंडा फहराना)
iv) To approach someone by running (दौड़कर किसी के पास जाना)

735 **Rush into** - To do hastily without thinking (जल्दबाज़ी में करना)

736 **Sail through** - To succeed easily (आसानी से पास करना)

737 **Save up** - To accumulate money by saving (बचत करना)

738 **Scale back** - To reduce in size or extent (कम करना)

739 **Scale down** - To make smaller (छोटा करना)

740 **Scare away (or off)** - To frighten away (डराकर भगाना)

741 **Scrape by** - To manage with very little money (मुश्किल से गुज़ारा करना)

742 **Scrape through** - To barely succeed (बमुश्किल पास होना)

743 **Scrape together** - To collect with difficulty (बड़ी मुश्किल से जमा करना)

744 **Screen off** - To separate by screen (परदे से अलग करना)

745 **Screen out** - To filter or eliminate (छांटना)

746 **Screw up** - To make a serious mistake (गड़बड़ करना)

747 **Seal off** - To close an area to prevent access (बंद कर देना)

748 **See about** - To deal with or arrange (का प्रबंध करना)

749 **See off** - i) To go to airport/station to say goodbye (विदाई देना)
ii) To deal with successfully (निपटना)

750 **See to** - To attend to or deal with something (किसी काम का ध्यान रखना, संभालना)

751 **Seek out** - To search for and find (खोजना)

752 **Sell off** - To sell remaining stock cheaply (सस्ते में बेचना)

753 **Sell out** - i) To sell all tickets or stock (सब बिक जाना)
ii) To betray principles for money (सिद्धांत बेचना)

754 **Send back** - To return something (वापस भेजना)

755 **Send for** - To summon or request to come (बुलवाना)

756 **Send in** - To submit by post or email (भेजना)

757 **Send out** - To distribute widely (वितरित करना)

758 **Set apart** - To distinguish from others (अलग करना)

759 **Set back** - i) To delay progress (प्रगति में रुकावट डालना)
ii) To cost a certain amount of money (खर्च होना)

760 **Set to** - To begin doing something with energy (जोश से शुरू करना)

761 **Settle down** - i) To start living stable life (बस जाना)

ii) To become calm (शांत होना)

762 **Settle for** - To accept less than desired (से संतोष करना)

763 **Settle in** - To become comfortable in new place (जमना)

764 **Settle on** - To decide or choose (तय करना)

765 **Settle up** - To pay what is owed (हिसाब करना)

766 **Shake up** - i) To upset or shock (हिला देना)
ii) To reorganize drastically (पुनर्गठन करना)

767 **Shape up** - i) To develop or progress (आकार लेना)
ii) To improve behaviour (सुधरना)

768 **Shell out** - To pay reluctantly (खर्च करना)

769 **Ship off** - To send away (भेज देना)

770 **Ship out** - i) To send goods (भेजना)
ii) To leave a place (किसी जगह को छोड़ कर चले जाना)

771 **Shoot down** - i) To destroy aircraft in flight (गिराना)
ii) To reject an idea (खारिज करना)

772 **Shoot up** - To increase rapidly (तेज़ी से बढ़ना)

773 **Shop round (or around)** - To compare prices before buying (तुलना करके खरीदना)

774 **Shore up** - To support or strengthen (सहारा देना)

775 **Shout down** - To silence by shouting louder (चिल्लाकर चुप कराना)

776 **Show around** - To take someone on tour of place (घुमाना)

777 **Show off** - To display proudly (दिखावा करना)

778 **Show up** - i) To arrive or appear (आना)
ii) To be clearly visible (नज़र आना)
iii) To embarrass by outperforming (शर्मिंदा करना)

779 **Shrink from** - To be reluctant to do (से कतराना)

780 **Shrug off** - To dismiss as unimportant (नज़रअंदाज़ करना)

781 **Shut down** - To stop operating permanently (बंद करना)

782 **Shut in** - To confine indoors (अंदर बंद करना)

783 **Shut off** - To stop the flow or supply (बंद करना)

784 **Shut out** - To exclude or keep out (बाहर रखना)

785 **Shut up** - i) To stop talking (चुप होना)
ii) To close securely (अच्छी तरह बंद करना)

786 **Side with** - To support in a dispute (का पक्ष लेना)

787 **Sign in** - To register arrival (रजिस्टर करना)

788 **Sign off** - i) To conclude a broadcast (कार्यक्रम समाप्त करना)
ii) To approve officially (मंज़ूरी देना)

789 **Sign on** - i) To register as unemployed (बेरोज़गारी भत्ता के लिए पंजीकरण)
ii) To hire or enlist (भर्ती करना)

790 **Sign out** - To register departure (जाते समय रजिस्टर करना)

791 **Sign up** - To enrol or register (पंजीकरण करना)

792 **Simmer down** - To become less angry (शांत होना)

793 **Single out** - To select for special attention (चुनना)

794 **Sink in** - To be fully understood (समझ में आना)

795 **Sit around** - To sit idly without doing anything (बैठे रहना)

796 **Sit back** - To relax and do nothing (आराम से बैठना)

797 **Sit down** - To take a seat (बैठना)

798 **Sit in** - i) To attend as an observer without active participation (दर्शक के रूप में बैठना)
ii) To occupy a place as a form of protest (धरना देना)
iii) To substitute temporarily for someone (अस्थायी रूप से जगह लेना)

799 **Sit on** - i) To delay dealing with something (टालना)
ii) To be a member of a committee or group (समूह का सदस्य होना)

800 **Sit out** - To not participate (हिस्सा न लेना)

801 **Sit through** - To stay until the end of something boring (झेलना)

802 **Sit up** - i) To move to upright position (सीधे बैठना)
ii) To pay attention (ध्यान देना)

803 **Size up** - To assess or evaluate (आकलन करना)

804 **Skim through** - To read quickly (सरसरी नज़र डालना)

805 **Skip over** - To omit or pass by (छोड़ना)

806 **Slap on** - To add hastily or carelessly (जल्दी से लगाना)

807 **Sleep in** - To sleep longer than usual (देर तक सोना)

808 **Sleep on** - To postpone decision until next day (सोचने के लिए रात गुज़ारना)

809 **Sleep over** - To spend night at someone's

house (रात रुकना)

810 **Slip away** - To leave quietly (चुपके से जाना)

811 **Slip by** - To pass quietly or without being noticed (चुपचाप या बिना ध्यान दिए निकल जाना)

812 **Slip in** - i) To enter quietly or unobtrusively (चुपके से अंदर आना)
ii) To insert casually into conversation (बात में डालना)

813 **Slip up** - To make a careless mistake (गलती करना)

814 **Slow down** - To reduce speed or pace (धीमा करना)

815 **Smooth over** - To make problem seem less serious (सुलझाना)

816 **Snap out** - i) To say something sharply or abruptly (तेज़ी से बोलना)
ii) To break free from a state (किसी स्थिति से बाहर आना)

817 **Snap up** - To buy or take quickly (झट से खरीदना)

818 **Sneak in** - To enter secretly (चोरी-छिपे घुसना)

819 **Sneak out** - To leave quietly and secretly (चुपके से निकलना)

820 **Soak up** - i) To absorb (सोखना)
ii) To enjoy atmosphere (माहौल का आनंद लेना)

821 **Sort out** - To organize or resolve (सुलझाना)

822 **Sound out** - To try to discover opinions (राय जानना)

823 **Space out** - To become dreamy and lose focus (बेध्यान होना)

824 **Spark off** - To trigger or cause to start (भड़काना)

825 **Speak out** - To express opinion openly (खुलकर बोलना)

826 **Speak up** - i) To speak louder (ज़ोर से बोलना)
ii) To express opinion (बोलना)

827 **Speed up** - To increase speed (तेज़ करना)

828 **Spell out** - i) To explain something in detail (विस्तार से समझाना)
ii) To say or write each letter of a word (अक्षर-अक्षर बोलना या लिखना)

829 **Spill over** - To spread beyond boundaries (फैलना)

830 **Spin off** - To create as separate entity (अलग करना)

831 **Spin out** - To prolong unnecessarily (लंबा खींचना)

832 **Spit out** - i) To say something quickly (जल्दी बोल देना)
ii) To eject from mouth (थूकना)

833 **Splash out** - To spend money extravagantly (खूब खर्च करना)

834 **Split up** - To separate or end relationship (अलग होना)

835 **Spread out** - To extend over a large area (फैलना)

836 **Spring up** - To appear suddenly (अचानक उभरना)

837 **Spy on** - To watch secretly (जासूसी करना)

838 **Square up** - i) To prepare to fight (भिड़ने को तैयार होना)
ii) To settle a debt (हिसाब चुकाना)

839 **Squeeze in** - To fit in despite lack of space/ time (समय निकालना)

840 **Stack up** - i) To accumulate (जमा होना)
ii) To compare (तुलना में होना)

841 **Stamp out** - To eliminate completely (जड़ से मिटाना)

842 **Stand around** - To stand without doing anything (खड़े रहना)

843 **Stand back** - To move away from something (पीछे हटना)

844 **Stand down** - To resign from position (पद छोड़ना)

845 **Stand in** - To substitute or deputize for someone temporarily (किसी की अनुपस्थिति में उसकी जगह लेना)

846 **Start off** - To begin (शुरू करना)

847 **Start out** - To begin a journey or career (शुरू करना)

848 **Start over** - To begin again from scratch (नए सिरे से शुरू करना)

849 **Start up** - To begin operating (शुरू होना)

850 **Stay away** - i) To keep one's distance or avoid (दूर रहना)
ii) To not attend or not come (न आना)
iii) To remain absent (अनुपस्थित रहना)

851 **Stay behind** - To remain after others leave (पीछे रुकना)

852 **Stay in** - To remain at home (घर पर रहना)

853 **Stay off** - To not go on; to avoid (से दूर रहना)

854 **Stay on** - To remain in position (बने रहना)

855 **Stay out** - To remain outside or away from home (बाहर रहना)

856 **Stay up** - To remain awake (जागते रहना)

857 **Stem from** - To originate from (से उत्पन्न होना)

858 **Step aside** - To move out of the way (एक तरफ होना)

859 **Step back** - To move backwards (पीछे हटना)

860 **Step down** - To resign from position (पद छोड़ना)

861 **Step in** - To intervene (बीच में आना)

862 **Step on** - i) To place foot on (पैर रख देना)
ii) To offend someone (ठेस पहुँचाना)

863 **Step out** - To leave briefly (थोड़ी देर के लिए बाहर जाना)

864 **Step up** - i) To increase (बढ़ाना)
ii) To take responsibility (ज़िम्मेदारी लेना)

865 **Stick around** - To stay in place (रुके रहना)

866 **Stick by** - To remain loyal to (के साथ रहना)

867 **Stick out** - i) To protrude (बाहर निकलना)
ii) To be very noticeable (अलग दिखना)

868 **Stick to** - To continue with; not change (पर अडिग रहना)

869 **Stick together** - To remain united (एकजुट रहना)

870 **Stick up** - i) To rob at gunpoint (बंदूक की नोक पर लूटना)
ii) To protrude upward (ऊपर खड़ा होना)

871 **Stick with** - To continue with (के साथ रहना)

872 **Stock up** - To accumulate or buy large quantities of supplies (बड़ी मात्रा में सामान इकट्ठा करना, भंडार करना)

873 **Stop by** - To visit briefly (थोड़ी देर के लिए आना)

874 **Stop over** - To stay briefly during journey (रास्ते में ठहरना)

875 **Storm out** - To leave angrily (गुस्से में बाहर जाना)

876 **Straighten out** - To resolve or clarify (सुलझाना)

877 **Stress out** - To make extremely worried or anxious (तनाव में डालना)

878 **Strike back** - To retaliate (जवाबी हमला करना)

879 **Strike down** - To declare invalid (law) (खारिज करना)

880 **Strike off** - To remove from a list or register (नाम काटना)

881 **Strike out** - To start independently (अपना रास्ता बनाना)

882 **Strike up** - To begin (conversation/ friendship) (शुरू करना)

883 **Strip down** - To remove all covering (सब उतारना)

884 **Stumble across (or upon)** - To find by chance (संयोग से मिलना)

885 **Stumble on** - To discover accidentally (गलती से पता चलना)

886 **Suck up to** - To flatter to gain advantage (चापलूसी करना)

887 **Sum up** - To summarize (सारांश देना)

888 **Swear by** - To have complete confidence in (पर पूरा भरोसा होना)

889 **Sweep up** - To clean by sweeping (झाड़ू लगाना)

890 **Switch off** - To turn off (बंद करना)

891 **Switch on** - i) To turn on a device (किसी उपकरण को चालू करना)
ii) To suddenly display a particular quality or behaviour at will (अचानक किसी गुण या व्यवहार को प्रदर्शित करना)

892 **Switch over** - To change to different system (बदलना)

893 **Take away** - i) To remove (हटाना)
ii) To subtract (घटाना)

894 **Take down** - i) To write down (लिखना)
ii) To remove from position (उतारना)

895 **Take for** - To mistake for (समझना)

896 **Take on** - i) To undertake responsibility (ज़िम्मेदारी लेना)
ii) To employ (नौकरी पर रखना)
iii) To compete against (का मुकाबला करना)

897 **Take to** - i) To develop liking for (पसंद करना)
ii) To begin as habit (आदत डालना)

898 **Talk back** - To reply rudely (उल्टा जवाब देना; बदतमीज़ी से जवाब देना)

899 **Talk down** - i) To persuade someone not to do something dangerous (समझा-बुझाकर रोकना)
ii) To belittle or minimize (कम करके बताना)

900 **Talk into** - To persuade (मनाना)

901 **Talk out** - i) To discuss thoroughly to resolve (बातचीत से सुलझाना)
ii) To talk until time runs out (बोलते रहना)

902 **Talk through** - To explain step by step (समझाना)

903 **Tamper with** - To interfere with or alter (छेड़छाड़ करना)

904 **Tap into** - To use or access a resource (का उपयोग करना)

905 **Taper off** - To decrease gradually in activity or intensity (गतिविधि/तीव्रता का धीरे-धीरे कम होना)

906 **Team up** - To join forces with others (मिलकर काम करना)

907 **Tear apart** - To destroy violently (तबाह करना)

908 **Tear down** - To demolish (गिराना)

909 **Tear into** - To attack or criticize fiercely (कड़ी आलोचना करना)

910 **Tear off** - To remove by pulling roughly (नोचकर निकालना)

911 **Tear up** - To rip into pieces (फाड़ना)

912 **Tell apart** - To distinguish between (अंतर करना)

913 **Tell off** - To scold or reprimand (डाँटना)

914 **Tell on** - To inform against (की शिकायत करना)

915 **Thaw out** - To warm and become unfrozen (पिघलना)

916 **Thin out** - To become less dense or crowded (कम होना)

917 **Think about** - To consider carefully (के बारे में सोचना)

918 **Think ahead** - To plan for the future (आगे की सोचना)

919 **Think back** - To recall or reflect on past events or times (पुरानी बातें याद करना, अतीत पर विचार करना)

920 **Think of** - To consider or have opinion about (के बारे में सोचना)

921 **Think over** - To consider carefully (सोच-विचार करना)

922 **Think through** - To consider thoroughly (पूरी तरह सोचना)

923 **Think up** - To invent or devise (सोचकर निकालना)

924 **Throw away** - i) To discard (फेंक देना)
ii) To waste an opportunity (गँवाना)

925 **Throw in** - i) To include something as extra (मुफ्त में देना, अतिरिक्त जोड़ना)
ii) To give up and stop trying (हार मान लेना)

926 **Throw off** - To get rid of (छुटकारा पाना)

927 **Throw out** - i) To discard or expel (बाहर निकालना)
ii) To reject a proposal (खारिज करना)

928 **Throw up** - To vomit (उल्टी करना)

929 **Tick off** - i) To mark as checked (टिक करना)
ii) To annoy (चिढ़ाना)

930 **Tidy up** - To make a place neat (साफ-सुथरा करना)

931 **Tie down** - To restrict freedom (बाँधकर रखना)

932 **Tie in** - i) To be connected or consistent with something (मेल खाना / जुड़ा होना)
ii) To coordinate or link together (तालमेल बिठाना)
iii) To relate or correspond (संबंधित होना)

933 **Tie up** - i) To fasten securely (बाँधना)
ii) To keep busy (व्यस्त रखना)

934 **Tip off** - To give secret information (सूचना देना)

935 **Tire out** - To exhaust completely (थका देना)

936 **Top off** - To complete or finish something in a final and satisfying way (किसी काम को अंतिम रूप देना)

937 **Top up** - To fill to maximum (भरना)

938 **Touch down** - (Of aircraft) To land (उतरना)

939 **Touch off** - To trigger (भड़काना)

940 **Touch up** - To make small improvements (सुधार करना)

941 **Toy with** - i) To consider casually (किसी विचार को हल्के में लेना)
ii) To play with someone's feelings (किसी की भावनाओं से खेलना)

942 **Track down** - To find after searching (खोज निकालना)

943 **Trade in** - To exchange old item for new (एक्सचेंज करना)

944 **Trade off** - To accept something by giving up another (किसी लाभ के बदले कुछ छोड़ना)

945 **Trail off** - To become quieter and quieter until stopping completely (voice/speech) (आवाज़/बात का धीरे-धीरे धीमा होकर बंद हो जाना)

946 **Trick into** - To deceive someone into doing something (धोखे से करवाना)

947 **Trigger off** - To cause something to start (भड़काना; शुरू कर देना)

948 **Trip up** - i) To make a mistake (गलती करना)
ii) To stumble (ठोकर खाना)

949 **Try on** - To put on clothing to check fit (पहनकर देखना)

950 **Try out** - To test or experiment with (आज़माना)

951 **Tuck in** - To push edges neatly under something (किनारों को अंदर दबाना)

952 **Turn around (or round)** - i) To reverse direction (पलटना)
ii) To improve a situation (स्थिति सुधारना)

953 **Turn away** - To refuse entry or service (वापस भेजना)

954 **Turn back** - To return the way you came (वापस जाना)

955 **Turn into** - To transform into (में बदलना)

956 **Turn off** - i) To switch off (बंद करना)
ii) To disgust or repel (नापसंद)

957 **Turn on** - i) To switch on (चालू करना)
ii) To attack suddenly (पर हमला करना)

958 **Turn to** - To seek help from (की ओर मुड़ना)

959 **Type up** - To type a document (टाइप करना)

960 **Urge on** - To encourage strongly (उकसाना, प्रोत्साहित करना)

961 **Use up** - To exhaust supply of (खत्म करना)

962 **Usher in** - To mark the beginning of (की शुरुआत करना)

963 **Veg out** - To relax and do nothing (पूरी तरह आराम करना; कुछ न करना)

964 **Venture out** - To go somewhere despite risk (बाहर निकलना)

965 **Verge on** - To be close to a particular state (के करीब होना)

966 **Vote in** - To elect (चुनना)

967 **Vote out** - To remove by voting (मतदान से हटाना)

968 **Vouch for** - To guarantee or confirm (की गारंटी देना)

969 **Wade through** - To deal with with difficulty (मुश्किल से निपटना)

970 **Wait around** - To wait doing nothing (इंतज़ार करते रहना)

971 **Wait on** - To serve (सेवा करना)

972 **Wait up** - To stay awake waiting (जागकर इंतज़ार करना)

973 **Wake up** - i) To stop sleeping (जागना)
ii) To become aware (जागरूक होना)

974 **Walk away** - i) To leave or depart on foot (चलकर जाना / छोड़कर जाना)
ii) To abandon or quit a situation (किसी स्थिति को छोड़ देना)
iii) To escape unharmed (बच निकलना)

975 **Walk in** - i) To enter a place (अंदर आना)
ii) To arrive unexpectedly (बिना पूर्व सूचना आना)

976 **Walk into** - i) To collide with (टकराना)
ii) To get (job) easily (आसानी से पाना)

977 **Walk off** - i) To leave suddenly in anger (नाराज़ होकर जाना)
ii) To get rid of by walking (चलकर उतारना)

978 **Walk out** - i) To leave in protest (विरोध में बाहर जाना)
ii) To go on strike (हड़ताल पर जाना)

979 **Walk through** - To explain step by step (समझाना)

980 **Ward off** - To prevent or repel (रोकना, दूर रखना)

981 **Warm to** - To begin to like (पसंद करने लगना)

982 **Warm up** - i) To exercise lightly before activity (शरीर गरम करना)
ii) To become warmer (गर्म होना)
iii) To become friendlier (घुलना-मिलना)

983 **Warn off** - To advise to stay away (दूर रहने की चेतावनी देना)

984 **Wash away** - To remove or carry away with water (पानी से बहा ले जाना)

985 **Wash off** - To remove by washing (धोकर निकालना)

986 **Wash out** - To be cancelled due to rain (बारिश से रद्द होना)

987 **Wash up** - To clean dishes (बर्तन धोना)

988 **Watch out** - i) To be alert for danger (सावधान रहना)
ii) To keep an eye open for something (नज़र रखना)

989 **Watch over** - To guard or protect (निगरानी करना)

990 **Water down** - To dilute by adding water (पानी मिलाकर पतला करना)

991 **Wave off** - i) To dismiss casually (टाल देना)
ii) To say goodbye by waving (हाथ हिलाकर विदा करना)

992 **Wear away** - To erode gradually (घिसना)

993 **Wear down** - To gradually exhaust (थका देना)

994 **Wear off** - To gradually disappear (असर कम होना)

995 **Weed out** - To remove unwanted elements (छाँटना)

996 **Weigh down** - To burden or depress (बोझ डालना)

997 **Weigh in** - To add one's opinion (राय देना)

998 **Weigh up** - To assess carefully (आकलन करना)

999 **While away** - To pass time idly (समय बिताना)

1000 **Whip up** - i) To prepare quickly (जल्दी से बनाना)
ii) To stir up emotions (भड़काना)

1001 **Whittle down** - To reduce gradually (धीरे-धीरे कम करना)

1002 **Win back** - To regain (वापस पाना)

1003 **Win out** - To succeed eventually (अंत में जीतना)

1004 **Win over** - To gain support of (राज़ी करना)

1005 **Wind up** - i) To end up in a situation (किसी स्थिति में पहुँचना)

ii) To conclude (समाप्त करना)
iii) To tease or irritate (चिढ़ाना)
iv) To wind a toy or watch (चाबी देना)

1006 **Wipe away** - To remove by wiping (पोंछकर साफ करना)

1007 **Wipe off** - i) To clean by wiping (पोंछकर साफ करना)
ii) Eliminate completely (समाप्त करना)

1008 **Wipe out** - i) To destroy completely (पूरी तरह खत्म करना)
ii) To exhaust (थका देना)

1009 **Wipe up** - To clean a spilled liquid (पोंछकर सुखाना)

1010 **Wise up** - To become aware (समझदार बनना)

1011 **Work in** - To include something (शामिल करना)

1012 **Work off** - To get rid of something (fat, energy, anger) through physical activity (कसरत/मेहनत करके (चर्बी, गुस्सा आदि) निकाल देना)

1013 **Work on** - To try to improve (पर काम करना)

1014 **Work round** - To find a way to avoid a problem (समस्या से बचते हुए हल निकालना)

1015 **Work through** - To deal with problems methodically (सुलझाना)

1016 **Work up** - i) To develop gradually (विकसित करना)
ii) To make excited or upset (उत्तेजित करना)

1017 **Wrap up** - i) To complete or finish (समाप्त करना)
ii) To cover with wrapping (लपेटना)
iii) To dress warmly (गर्म कपड़े पहनना)

1018 **Write back** - To reply by letter/email (जवाब लिखना)

1019 **Write down** - To record in writing (लिखना)

1020 **Write out** - To write something in full or complete form (पूरा लिखना)

1021 **Write up** - To write full version of notes (विस्तार से लिखना)

1022 **Yearn for** - To long for (की तड़प होना)

1023 **Yell out** - To shout loudly (ज़ोर से चिल्लाना)

1024 **Yield to** - To give way to (के आगे झुकना)

1025 **Zip up** - To close with zipper (ज़िप बंद करना)

1026 **Zone out** - To lose concentration (ध्यान पूरी तरह भटक जाना)

1027 **Zoom in** - To magnify image (ज़ूम करना)

1028 **Zoom out** - To show wider view (ज़ूम आउट करना)

F2 HOMONYMS + HOMOPHONES (Additional List)

1 **Abate** (V.) - To become less strong, diminish (कम होना, घटना)
Abet (V.) - To encourage or support someone in a criminal act (उकसाना, अपराध आदि में सहायक होना)
Abut (V.) - To be next to or share a boundary with something (सटा हुआ होना)

2 **Abjure** (V.) - To formally reject or not accept a belief (त्यागना)
Adjure (V.) - To solemnly command or advise someone to do something (अनुरोध करना)

3 **Accede** (V.) - To agree or consent (सहमत होना)
Exceed (V.) - To be greater in number or size than something (अधिक होना)

4 **Accessary** (N.) - A person who helps in a crime (अपराध में सहायक व्यक्ति)
Accessory (N.) - Something extra that is not necessary but is attractive or useful (सहायक उपकरण)

5 **Accident** (N.) - An unfortunate happening that occurs unintentionally (दुर्घटना)
Incident (N.) - An individual occurrence or event (घटना)

6 **Adversary** (N.) - An enemy or opposing force (प्रतिद्वंद्वी, विरोधी)
Adversity (N.) - An unfavorable situation (विपत्ति)

7 **Advice** (N.) - An opinion offered as a guide (सलाह)
Advise (V.) - To give advice (सलाह देना)

8 **Adapt** (V.) - To adjust to new conditions (अनुकूल होना)
Adept (Adj.) - Skilled, proficient (निपुण)
Adopt (V.) - To choose or take as one's own (गोद लेना)

9 **Addition** (N.) - The act of adding something (जोड़, वृद्धि)
Edition (N.) - A particular form or version of a published text (संस्करण)

10 **Adore** (V.) - To regard with the utmost esteem, love, and respect (बहुत चाहना)
Adorn (V.) - To decorate or add beauty (सजाना)

11 **Adverse** (Adj.) - Unfavorable (प्रतिकूल)
Averse (Adj.) - Having a strong dislike or disinclination (विरुद्ध, अनिच्छुक)

12 **Afflict** (V.) - To cause pain or suffering (कष्ट देना)
Inflict (V.) - To impose (something unpleasant or harmful) (थोपना)

13 **Ail** (V.) - To be sick or unwell (बीमार होना)
Ale (N.) - A type of beer (शराब)

14 **Aid** (V.) - To help or assist (मदद करना)
Aide (N.) - An assistant (सहयोगी)

15 **Aisle** (N.) - A space between rows (गलियारा)
I'll (Cont.) - Contraction of 'I will' (मैं करूँगा/करूँगी)
Isle (N.) - An island (द्वीप)

16 **Amiable** (Adj.) - Pleasant and friendly (सुशील)
Amicable (Adj.) - Friendly (मैत्रीपूर्ण)

17 **All ways** (Adv.) - In every manner possible (सभी तरह से)
Always (Adv.) - At all times; every time (हमेशा)

18 **Alteration** (N.) - A change (परिवर्तन)
Altercation (N.) - A dispute or quarrel (तकरार)
Alternation (N.) - The act of switching back and forth (अदल-बदल)

19 **Apposite** (Adj.) - Suitable, well adapted (उचित)
Opposite (Adj.) - Completely different (विपरीत)

20 **Apprehend** (V.) - To catch somebody (पकड़ना)
Comprehend (V.) - To understand (समझना)

21 **Admission** (N.) - An act of admitting or being accepted (दाखिला)
Admittance (N.) - Permission to enter a place (प्रवेश की अनुमति)

22 **Allay** (V.) - To reduce or calm (fear, worry) (शांत करना, कम करना)
Alley (N.) - A narrow passage between buildings (गली)
Ally (N.) - A friend or supporter (मित्र, सहयोगी)

23 **Allude** (V.) - To make an indirect reference to (संकेत करना)
Elude (V.) - To avoid (टालना)

24 **All ready** (Ph.) - Everyone or everything is ready (सब तैयार)
Already (Adv.) - By this time (पहले से ही)

25 **All right** (Ph.) - Completely right or okay (बिल्कुल ठीक)
Alright (Adv.) - Informal variant of "all right" often used to denote that something is satisfactory but not necessarily perfect (ठीक है)

26 **Alternate** (Adj.) - Every other; happening by turns (एकांतर, बारी-बारी का)
Alternate (V.) - To switch between two things in turn (बारी-बारी करना)
Alternative (N.) - A possibility of choice (विकल्प)

27 **All together** (Ph.) - Everyone/everything in one place (सब मिलकर)
Altogether (Adv.) - Thoroughly (पूरी तरह से)

28 **A lot** (Ph.) - A large quantity; many of something (बहुत ज्यादा)
Allot (V.) - To divide or portion out (आवंटित करना)

29 **Angel** (N.) - A supernatural being; a good person (फरिश्ता)
Angle (N.) - A shape made by joining 2 straight lines (कोण)

30 **Antic** (N.) - Funny or silly behaviour (मसखरापन, अजीब हरकत)
Antique (Adj.) - Very old and therefore unusual and valuable (प्राचीन)

31 **Annual** (Adj.) - Occurring or happening every year (वार्षिक)
Annul (V.) - To make void or null (निरस्त करना)

32 **Any one** (P.) - Refers to a single person or thing in a group (कोई एक)
Anyone (P.) - Refers to any person or any member of a group (कोई भी)

33 **A part** (N.) - One of the pieces into which something can be divided (हिस्सा)
Apart (Adv.) - Separated (टुकड़ों में)

34 **Artful** (Adj.) - Crafty or cunning (चालाक, धूर्त)
Artistic (Adj.) - Characteristic of art or artists (कलात्मक)

35 **Artisan** (N.) - A worker who practices a trade or handicraft (शिल्पकार)
Artist (N.) - Someone who creates things with great skill and imagination (कलाकार)
Artiste (N.) - A professional performer (singer, dancer, etc.) (कलाकार (गायक, नर्तक आदि))

36 **Aesthetic** (Adj.) - Related to beauty or art (सौंदर्य संबंधी)
Ascetic (Adj.) - Practicing strict self-denial (तपस्वी)

37 **Accent** (N.) - A way of saying words that shows where a person is from (लहजा)
Ascent (N.) - The act of rising or climbing (चढ़ाई)
Assent (N.) - Consent, agreement (सहमति)

38 **Assistance** (N.) - Help (सहायता)
Assistants (N.) - Helpers (सहायक)

39 **Auger** (N.) - A sharp tool that is used for making holes (बरमा)
Augur (V.) - To make a prediction about (भविष्यवाणी करना)

40 **Affectation** (N.) - Speech or conduct not natural to oneself (बनावटी व्यवहार, दिखावा)
Affection (N.) - A feeling of liking and caring (प्यार)

41 **Adulteration** (N.) - The act of making something impure by mixing (मिलावट)
Adultery (N.) - Being unfaithful to one's spouse (व्यभिचार)

42 **Aspersion** (N.) - A false charge meant to harm someone's reputation (कलंक, निंदा)
Aspiration (N.) - A strong desire or ambition (अभिलाषा)

43 **Aspire** (V.) - To want something very much (महत्वाकांक्षा रखना)
Expire (V.) - To end or terminate (समाप्त होना)

44 **Advert** (N.) - An advertisement (विज्ञापन)
Advert (V.) - To refer to or draw attention to (उल्लेख करना, संदर्भ देना)
Avert (V.) - To turn away or to prevent (टालना)

45 **Are** (V.) - Plural form of "to be" (हैं)
Hour (N.) - A period of 60 minutes (एक घंटा)
Our (Det.) - Belonging to us (हमारा)

46 **A while** (N.) - A period of time (थोड़ी देर)
Awhile (Adv.) - For a short time (कुछ समय के लिए)

47 **Ball** (N.) - A spherical object (गेंद, बॉल)
Bawl (V.) - To cry loudly (चिल्लाना, रोना)
Bowl (N.) - A deep round container with a wide open top (कटोरा)

48 **Billed** (V.) - Charged or invoiced (बिल किया गया)
Build (V.) - To construct (निर्माण करना, बनाना)

49 **Bath** (N.) - A tub for washing; the act of bathing (स्नान; नहाने का टब)
Bathe (V.) - To wash someone (especially a child) (नहलाना)

50 **Baleful** (Adj.) - Expressing harmful intentions (हानिकारक)

Baneful (Adj.) - Poisonous or fatal (घातक)

51 **Baited** (V.) - Deliberately annoy or taunt someone (ताना देना)
Bated (Adj.) - Very anxious or excited (बहुत चिंतित या उत्साहित)

52 **Bridal** (Adj.) - Related to a bride or a wedding (शादी/वधू का)
Bridle (N.) - Headgear used to control a horse (लगाम)
Bridle (V.) - To restrain or control (नियंत्रित करना)

53 **Beneficent** (Adj.) - Helping people and doing good acts (परोपकारी)
Beneficial (Adj.) - Helpful, useful (फायदेमंद)

54 **Bail** (N.) - The temporary release of a prisoner in exchange for security (जमानत)
Bale (N.) - A bound-up bundle (गांठ)

55 **Balmy** (Adj.) - Mild and refreshing (सुहावना)
Barmy (Adj.) - Very foolish (पागल)

56 **Beside** (Prep.) - Close to; next to (के बग़ल में)
Besides (Prep.) - Except for; in addition to (अलावा)

57 **Biannual** (Adj.) - Happening twice a year (अर्धवार्षिक)
Biennial (Adj.) - Happening once every two years (द्विवार्षिक)

58 **Breath** (N.) - Air inhaled and exhaled (noun) (सांस)
Breathe (V.) - To inhale and exhale air (verb) (सांस लेना)

59 **Chord** (N.) - A group of notes sounded together (तार, स्वर समूह)
Cord (N.) - A thin, flexible string or rope (रस्सी, डोरी)

60 **Chute** (N.) - A sloping channel or slide (नाली, धारा)
Shoot (V.) - To fire a gun (निशाना लगाना, गोली चलाना)

61 **Canvas** (N.) - A heavy, coarse cloth (चित्रफलक (कैनवास))
Canvass (V.) - To survey; to examine (परखना, जांचना)

62 **Childish** (Adj.) - Immature; not behaving like an adult (बचकाना)
Childlike (Adj.) - Innocent and trusting like a child (बच्चों के जैसा)

63 **Choose** (V.) - To pick or select (चुनना)
Chose (V.) - To select freely, Past tense of "choose" (चुना)

64 **Clothes** (N.) - Garments worn to cover the body (कपड़े)
Cloths (N.) - Pieces of fabric (कपड़े के टुकड़े)

65 **Cemetery** (N.) - A burial ground (कब्रिस्तान)
Symmetry (N.) - Balanced proportions (समरूपता)

66 **Cannon** (N.) - A large gun that fires heavy projectiles (तोप)
Canon (N.) - A rule or law, typically religious (धार्मिक नियम, सिद्धांत)

67 **Cession** (N.) - The formal giving up of rights, property, or territory (हक छोड़ना)
Session (N.) - A meeting or series of meetings (सत्र)

68 **Check** (V.) - To verify or examine (जाँच करना)
Cheque (N.) - A written order directing a bank to pay money (चेक)

69 **Clip** (N.) - A small object, usually made of metal or plastic, used for holding things together (चिमटी)
Clip (V.) - The act of cutting something to make it shorter (छोटा करना)

70 **Credible** (Adj.) - That you can believe (विश्वसनीय)
Creditable (Adj.) - Praiseworthy (प्रशंसनीय)
Credulous (Adj.) - Easily fooled; too ready to believe (भोला, आसानी से विश्वास करने वाला)

71 **Coma** (N.) - A state of unconsciousness (अचेत दशा)
Comma (N.) - A punctuation mark used to separate words or phrases (अल्पविराम)

72 **Cooperation** (N.) - Working together (सहयोग)
Corporation (N.) - A large company or group of companies (निगम)

73 **Corporal** (Adj.) - Relating to the body (दैहिक)
Corporeal (Adj.) - Having a physical body (शारीरिक)

74 **Comprehensible** (Adj.) - Able to be understood (समझने के योग्य)
Comprehensive (Adj.) - Covering completely or broadly (विस्तृत)

75 **Contagious** (Adj.) - Capable of being transmitted by contact (संक्रामक)
Contiguous (Adj.) - Next to or touching another (मिला/सटा हुआ)

76 **Confidant** (N.) - A person with whom you share secrets (विश्वासपात्र)
Confident (Adj.) - Full of conviction; certain

(आत्मविश्वासी)

77 **Continual** (Adj.) - Repeated with breaks in between (नियमित)
Continuance (N.) - The state of continuing to exist or function (नित्यता)
Continuation (N.) - An act or the state of continuing (विस्तार)
Continuous (Adj.) - Without stopping (निरंतर)

78 **Censor** (V.) - To remove inappropriate parts from media (काट-छांट करना)
Censure (N.) - Strong criticism or disapproval (निंदा)
Sensor (N.) - A device that responds to a physical stimulus (ज्ञानेंद्री)

79 **Collision** (N.) - An instance of two or more things striking violently against each other (टक्कर)
Collusion (N.) - Secret illegal cooperation (मिलीभगत)

80 **Contemptible** (Adj.) - Not worthy of respect or approval (घिनौना)
Contemptuous (Adj.) - Showing deep hatred or disapproval (तिरस्कारपूर्ण)

81 **Considerable** (Adj.) - Large or of noticeable importance (विचारणीय)
Considerate (Adj.) - Thoughtful of the needs of others (विचारशील)

82 **Ceremonial** (Adj.) - Relating to or used in a ceremony (अनुष्ठानिक)
Ceremonious (Adj.) - Very formal or polite (औपचारिक)

83 **Confirm** (V.) - To establish the truth or accuracy of something (पुष्टि करना)
Conform (V.) - To follow rules or standards (अनुरूप होना, पालन करना)

84 **Conscientious** (Adj.) - Very careful and thorough in one's work (ईमानदार)
Consensus (N.) - General agreement (सर्वसम्मति)

85 **Coherent** (Adj.) - Logical and consistent; easy to understand (स्पष्ट)
Inherent (Adj.) - Existing as a natural or permanent part (जन्मजात)

86 **Collaborate** (V.) - To work together (सहयोग करना)
Corroborate (V.) - To support a statement with evidence (समर्थन करना)

87 **Casual** (Adj.) - Not formal (अनौपचारिक)
Causal (Adj.) - Relating to or acting as a cause (करणीय)

88 **Councillor** (N.) - An elected member of a council (सभा का सदस्य)
Counsellor (N.) - An adviser (सलाहकार)

89 **Centenary** (N.) - The 100th anniversary of an event (शताब्दी)
Century (N.) - A period of 100 years (शतक)

90 **Conservation** (N.) - Protection of natural resources or the environment (संरक्षण)
Conservatism (N.) - Preference for traditional values; resistance to change (रूढ़िवाद)

91 **Conscience** (N.) - Moral sense of right and wrong (अंतरात्मा, विवेक)
Conscious (Adj.) - Awake and aware (सचेत)

92 **Capability** (N.) - The ability to do something (योग्यता)
Capacity (N.) - The ability to understand or do something (क्षमता)

93 **Commandeer** (V.) - To take property for official or military use (अधिग्रहण करना)
Commander (N.) - A person who commands (सेनाध्यक्ष)

94 **Corps** (N.) - A body of troops (दल)
Corpse (N.) - A dead body (लाश)

95 **Days** (N.) - Periods of 24 hours (दिनों)
Daze (V.) - To stun or bewilder (चकराना, घबराना)

96 **Dairy** (N.) - A place where milk products are processed (डेयरी)
Diary (N.) - A personal journal (डायरी)

97 **Dependant** (N.) - A person who relies on another for support (आश्रित)
Dependent (Adj.) - Relying on someone else for support (निर्भर)

98 **Deprecate** (V.) - To express disapproval of (विरोध/निंदा करना)
Depreciate (V.) - To decrease in value over time (मूल्य कम करना)

99 **Descent** (N.) - Downward movement (अवरोहण, उतराई)
Dissent (N.) - Disagreement (असहमति)

100 **Device** (N.) - An object or machine designed for a specific purpose (उपकरण)
Devise (V.) - To plan or invent (योजना बनाना)

101 **Disinterested** (Adj.) - Unbiased; not taking sides (निष्पक्ष)
Uninterested (Adj.) - Lacking interest (रुचिहीन)

102 **Dominant** (Adj.) - Commanding, controlling over all others; very powerful (प्रभावी)

Dominate (V.) - To control or have power over (हावी होना)

103 **Die** (V.) - To stop living (मरना)
Die (N.) - One of a pair of dice (पासा)
Dye (V.) - To change or add colour (रंगना)

104 **Drop** (V.) - To fall or allow to fall (गिराना)
Drop (V.) - To become lower or less (गिरावट)
Drop (N.) - A small round mass of liquid (बूंद)

105 **Deferment** (N.) - A temporary postponement (मोहलत)
Deference (N.) - Respect or courtesy (सम्मान)
Difference (N.) - The state of being dissimilar (अंतर)

106 **Defective** (Adj.) - Faulty, having a flaw (दोषपूर्ण)
Deficient (Adj.) - Not having enough of something (अपर्याप्त, कम)

107 **Decease** (V.) - To die (मृत्यु)
Disease (N.) - Illness (बीमारी)

108 **Divers** (N.) - People who dive underwater (गोताखोर)
Diverse (Adj.) - Differing from one another (विविध)

109 **Deduce** (V.) - To derive as a conclusion (परिणाम निकालना)
Deduct (V.) - To subtract (काटना)

110 **Deliverance** (N.) - Setting free; rescue or release (मुक्ति)
Delivery (N.) - Act or manner of delivering something (वितरण)

111 **Decry** (V.) - To publicly criticize (दोष देना)
Descry (V.) - To see or notice something or someone (पता लगा लेना)

112 **Done** (V.) - To communicate that something has ended (समाप्त)
Dun (Adj.) - Of a dull greyish-brown colour (भूरा-धूसर रंग)

113 **Dam** (N.) - A barrier to obstruct the flow of water (बांध)
Damn (V.) - To condemn (निंदा करना, धिक्कारना)

114 **Doll** (N.) - A child's toy that looks like a small person or a baby (गुड़िया)
Dull (Adj.) - Not interesting or exciting; boring (सुस्त)

115 **Effective** (Adj.) - Producing the desired result (असरदार)
Efficient (Adj.) - Working in a way that does not waste a resource (कुशल)

116 **Emigrant** (N.) - A person who leaves one place or country (अपने देश को छोड़ने वाला)
Immigrant (N.) - A person who comes to live in a new country (प्रवासी, आप्रवासी)

117 **Emigrate** (V.) - To leave one country or region to settle in another (अपने देश को छोड़ना)
Immigrate (V.) - To enter another country and reside there (विदेश में आकर बसना)

118 **Every day** (Ph.) - Each day, succession (adj. + noun) (हर दिन)
Everyday (Adj.) - Routine, commonplace, ordinary (adj.) (रोज़ का)

119 **Enviable** (Adj.) - Very desirable (लोभ्य)
Envious (Adj.) - Jealous (ईर्ष्या)

120 **Envelop** (V.) - To surround (ढंक लेना)
Envelope (N.) - A container for a letter (पत्र का लिफ़ाफ़ा)

121 **Exception** (N.) - Exclusion (अपवाद)
Exceptionable (Adj.) - Liable to objection or debate (आपत्तिजनक)
Exceptional (Adj.) - Standing out from the others in a positive way (असाधारण)

122 **Eligible** (Adj.) - Qualified (योग्य)
Illegible (Adj.) - Difficult or impossible to read (अस्पष्ट)

123 **Exceedingly** (Adv.) - Extremely (अत्यधिक)
Excessively (Adv.) - Exceeding normal or proper limits (अधिकता से)

124 **Exhausted** (Adj.) - Very tired (थका हुआ)
Exhausting (Adj.) - Causing fatigue or weariness (थकाने वाला)
Exhaustive (Adj.) - Very thorough and complete (संपूर्ण)

125 **Economic** (Adj.) - Relating to trade, industry, or money (आर्थिक)
Economical (Adj.) - Avoiding waste or extravagance (किफ़ायती)
Economics (N.) - The study of money, trade, and industry (अर्थशास्त्र)

126 **Final** (Adj.) - Not to be changed (अंतिम)
Finale (N.) - The end or closing part (समापन)

127 **Forbear** (V.) - To refrain or abstain from (रोकना)
Forebear (N.) - An ancestor (पूर्वज)

128 **Formally** (Adv.) - In a conventional or ceremonial manner (औपचारिक रूप से)
Formerly (Adv.) - Previously (पहले)

129 **Forth** (Adv.) - Forward (आगे)

Fourth (Adj.) - Number four in a series (चौथा)

130 **Incite** (V.) - To encourage or stir up (उकसाना, भड़काना)
Insight (N.) - The ability to understand inner qualities or relationships (अन्तर्दृष्टि)

131 **Expedient** (Adj.) - Convenient, Suitable for achieving (उचित साधन, सुविधाजनक)
Expedition (N.) - A journey undertaken for a specific purpose (अभियान)

132 **Esteem** (N.) - Great respect (सम्मान)
Estimate (N.) - An approximate calculation (अनुमान)
Estimation (N.) - Opinion or judgement (विचार या परख)

133 **Exposition** (N.) - A comprehensive description or explanation (विस्तृत व्याख्या)
Exposure (N.) - The state of being vulnerable or at risk (खुलासा)

134 **Egoist** (N.) - An egoist, on the other hand, acts primarily out of self-interest, prioritizing their own well-being (स्वार्थी)
Egotist (N.) - A person who talks too much about themselves (अहंवादी)

135 **Emerge** (V.) - To come into view (उभरना)
Immerse (V.) - To become deeply involved (डुबो देना)

136 **Eruption** (N.) - A sudden and violent release (विस्फोट)
Irruption (N.) - A sudden, often violent, entry (आक्रमण)

137 **Elemental** (Adj.) - Basic or essential (मौलिक)
Elementary (Adj.) - Introductory or basic (प्राथमिक)

138 **Excursion** (N.) - A short trip or outing (सैर)
Incursion (N.) - A hostile entrance into a territory (धावा)

139 **Entrance** (N.) - An opening, such as a door (प्रवेश द्वार)
Entry (N.) - The act of entering (प्रवेश)

140 **Fatal** (Adj.) - Causing death (घातक)
Fatalist (N.) - A person who believes in fate (भाग्यवादी)
Fateful (Adj.) - Having far-reaching consequences (विनाशक)

141 **Effeminate** (Adj.) - (of a man) having traits traditionally associated with women (नारी जैसा)
Feminine (Adj.) - Associated with women or girls (स्त्री)
Feminist (N.) - A person who supports equal rights for women (नारीवादी)

142 **Forceful** (Adj.) - Powerful and assertive (शक्तिशाली, प्रभावशाली)
Forcible (Adj.) - Achieved by force (प्रबल)

143 **Fain** (Adv.) - Gladly or willingly (इच्छुक, प्रसन्नता से)
Feign (V.) - To pretend (ढोंग करना)

144 **Forego** (V.) - To precede or go before (पहले होना)
Forgo (V.) - To abstain or refrain from (त्यागना)

145 **Facilitate** (V.) - To make easier (आसान करना)
Facility (N.) - A building, service, or equipment provided for a specific purpose (सुविधा)
Felicitate (V.) - To congratulate (बधाई देना)
Felicity (N.) - Happiness (परम सुख)

146 **Formalism** (N.) - Strict adherence to prescribed forms (नियम-निष्ठता)
Formality (N.) - The quality of being formal (औपचारिकता)

147 **Forthright** (Adj.) - Direct and honest (स्पष्टवादी)
Forthwith (Adv.) - Immediately (तत्काल)

148 **Financial** (Adj.) - Pertaining to money (वित्तीय)
Fiscal (Adj.) - Related to financial matters (राजकोषीय)

149 **Foreword** (N.) - An introduction to a book (प्रस्तावना)
Forward (Adj.) - Directed toward the front (आगे)

150 **Foul** (Adj.) - Very dirty, smelly, or unpleasant; unfair (गंदा, अनुचित)
Fowl (N.) - A bird, especially one used as food (पक्षी)

151 **Great** (Adj.) - very good or excellent (महान, शानदार)
Grate (V.) - To shred food using a rough surface (कद्दूकस करना, घिसना)
Grate (N.) - A metal framework in a fireplace (अँगीठी की जाली)

152 **Genteel** (Adj.) - Polite, refined, or respectable (सज्जन)
Gentle (Adj.) - Kind and mild (कोमल)

153 **Gamble** (V.) - Play games of chance for money; bet. (जुआ)
Gambol (V.) - To skip about playfully (हँसते खेलते दौड़ना)

154 **Gaol** (N.) - Prison (British spelling) (कारागार)
Goal (N.) - An aim or desired result (लक्ष्य)

155 **Ghastly** (Adj.) - Frightful or horrible (अत्यंत

अप्रिय या हानिकर)
Ghostly (Adj.) - Eerie or mysterious (प्रेतात्मा जैसा)

156 **God-like** (Adj.) - Resembling a deity (भगवान जैसा)
Godly (Adj.) - Devoutly religious (ईश्वरीय जीवन)

157 **Gorilla** (N.) - A large ape (गोरिल्ला (बड़े बन्दर की एक प्रजाति))
Guerrilla (N.) - A member of a small, independent combat unit (छापामार सैनिक)

158 **Graceful** (Adj.) - Elegantly beautiful in form or manner (सुंदर)
Gracious (Adj.) - Kind and courteous (दयालु)

159 **Gravitation** (N.) - Movement toward a center of attraction, especially the earth (आकर्षण-शक्ति)
Gravity (N.) - The force that attracts objects with mass toward each other (गुरुत्वाकर्षण बल)

160 **Hangar** (N.) - A large building for housing aircraft (विमान शाला)
Hanger (N.) - A shoulder-shaped frame for hanging clothes (कपड़े टाँगने की फ्रेम)

161 **Higher** (Adj.) - Greater in height or elevation (उच्चतर, ऊँचा)
Hire (V.) - To employ for payment (किराये पर लेना, नौकरी देना)

162 **Historic** (Adj.) - Famous or important in history (ऐतिहासिक)
Histrionic (Adj.) - Overly dramatic or emotional (अभिनय-संबंधी)

163 **Humiliation** (N.) - The state of being humiliated or disgraced (निरादर)
Humility (N.) - The quality of being humble (विनम्रता)

164 **Homely** (Adj.) - Simple in appearance. (घरेलू/साधारण)
Homily (N.) - A moral discourse, usually delivered during a church service (धर्मोपदेश)

165 **Honorable** (Adj.) - Deserving of respect (माननीय)
Honorary (Adj.) - Holding a title or position without the associated duties (अवैतनिक)

166 **Hail** (N.) - Pellets of frozen rain (ओला)
Hail (V.) - To greet or acclaim (जयजयकार करना)
Hale (Adj.) - Free from disease or infirmity (हट्टा कट्टा)
Hell (N.) - A place of suffering or torment (नरक)

167 **Hero** (N.) - A person admired for brave deeds (नायक, हीरो)
Heroin (N.) - A powerful illegal drug (हेरोइन (नशे का पदार्थ))
Heroine (N.) - A female character in a book or film (नायिका)

168 **Horn** (N.) - A hard, pointed growth on an animal's head (सींग)
Horn (N.) - A wind instrument or warning device (भोंपू (हार्न))

169 **Hypercritical** (Adj.) - Excessively critical (अतिआलोचनात्मक)
Hypocritical (Adj.) - Characterized by hypocrisy (पाखंडी)

170 **Humanism** (N.) - A philosophical stance emphasizing human values and concerns (मानवतावाद)
Humanities (N.) - Academic disciplines studying human culture (मानविकी)
Humanity (N.) - The quality of being humane (इंसानियत)

171 **Hallow** (V.) - To make holy (पवित्र)
Halo (N.) - A ring of light around a person's head (प्रभामंडल)
Hollow (Adj.) - Having an empty space inside (खोखला)

172 **Human** (Adj.) - Relating to or characteristic of people (इंसान)
Humane (Adj.) - Kind, compassionate (दयालु)

173 **Industrial** (Adj.) - Related to industry (औद्योगिक)
Industrious (Adj.) - Diligent, hard-working (मेहनती)

174 **Impassable** (Adj.) - Not able to be passed or crossed (अगम्य)
Impossible (Adj.) - Not able to occur or be done (असंभव)

175 **Indigenous** (Adj.) - Native to a particular region (स्वदेशी)
Indigent (Adj.) - Poor, needy (दरिद्र)

176 **Ingenious** (Adj.) - Clever, original, inventive (प्रतिभा-सम्पन्न)
Ingenuous (Adj.) - Showing innocent or childlike simplicity (सरल)

177 **Imaginary** (Adj.) - Existing only in the imagination (काल्पनिक)
Imaginative (Adj.) - Having or showing creativity (कल्पनाशील)

178 **Intelligent** (Adj.) - Having or showing intelligence (बुद्धिमान)

Intelligible (Adj.) - Able to be understood (समझ में आने योग्य)

179 **Immoral** (Adj.) - Not conforming to accepted standards of morality (भ्रष्ट)

Amoral (Adj.) - Lacking a moral sense (नीतिहीन)
Unmoral (Adj.) - Not concerned with moral standards (अनैतिक)

180 **Incomparable** (Adj.) - Without an equal in quality or extent; matchless; beyond comparison (बेमिसाल)
Uncomparable (Adj.) - Not able to be compared (तुलना न हो सकने वाला)

181 **Interminable** (Adj.) - Endless or apparently endless (अनंत)
Intermittent (Adj.) - Occurring at irregular intervals (रुक-रुक कर)

182 **Inert** (Adj.) - Lacking the ability to move (निष्क्रिय)
Invert (V.) - To turn upside down (पलटना)

183 **Accidental** (Adj.) - Occurring unexpectedly or by chance (दुर्घटनावश, अनजाने में)
Incidental (Adj.) - Occurring as a minor or secondary consequence of something else (आकस्मिक)

184 **Its** (P.) - Possessive form of 'it' (इसका)
It's (Cont.) - Contraction of 'it is' (यह है)

185 **I** (P.) - A subject pronoun (मैं)
Me (P.) - An object pronoun (मुझे)

186 **Jealous** (Adj.) - Feeling envy or resentment toward someone (ईर्ष्या)
Zealous (Adj.) - Filled with enthusiasm (उत्साही)

187 **Knead** (V.) - To massage or squeeze dough (गूँथना, मसलना)
Need (N.) - A requirement or necessity (आवश्यकता, ज़रूरत)

188 **Knave** (N.) - A dishonest or unscrupulous man (धूर्त)
Naïve (Adj.) - Showing a lack of experience or wisdom (अनुभवहीन)

189 **Judicial** (Adj.) - Of or relating to the administration of justice (अदालती)
Judiciary (N.) - The branch of government that interprets and applies the law (न्यायतंत्र)
Judicious (Adj.) - Having or showing good judgement (न्यायसंगत)

190 **Gnu** (N.) - A large African antelope; wildebeest (नू (एक अफ्रीकी हिरन))
Knew (V.) - To have information in your mind (जानता था)
New (Adj.) - Recently made, invented, or discovered (नया)

191 **Know** (V.) - To be aware of through observation or information (जानना)
No (Adv.) - A negative response or vote (नहीं)

192 **Leak** (N.) - An accidental hole that allows something to escape (रिसाव, लीक)
Leek (N.) - A vegetable related to onions (हरा प्याज़)

193 **Later** (Adv.) - After the expected or usual time (बाद में)
Latter (Adj.) - The second of two things mentioned (बाद वाला, दूसरा)

194 **Lessen** (V.) - To reduce or diminish (कम करना)
Lesson (N.) - Something learned through experience (सबक)

195 **Lightening** (V.) - Becoming lighter in color or mood (हल्का करना)
Lightning (N.) - A flash of light in the sky caused by electricity (बिजली, तड़ित)

196 **Luxuriant** (Adj.) - Abundant, lush (प्रचुर)
Luxurious (Adj.) - Providing great comfort and pleasure (विलासितापूर्ण)

197 **Limit** (N.) - A point beyond which something cannot go (सीमा)
Limitation (N.) - A limiting condition or measure (बाधा)

198 **Loathe** (V.) - To feel intense dislike or disgust for (नापसंद करना)
Loth (Adj.) - Unwilling; reluctant (also spelled "loath") (अनिच्छुक)

199 **Learned** (Adj.) - Possessing or displaying knowledge (विद्वान)
Learnt (V.) - Gain knowledge or skills, Past tense of 'learn' (सीखा)

200 **Literal** (Adj.) - Taking words in their most basic sense (यथाशब्द, शब्दशः)
Literary (Adj.) - Concerning the writing or study of literature (साहित्यिक)

201 **Liable** (Adj.) - Legally responsible (उत्तरदायी)
Libel (N.) - A published false statement damaging to a person's reputation (निंदलेख)

202 **Lovable** (Adj.) - Inspiring or deserving love (प्यारा)
Lovely (Adj.) - Beautiful or attractive (प्रिय)

203 **Might** (N.) - Strength or power (शक्ति, बल)
Mite (N.) - A small amount or a tiny insect

(दीमक, कीड़ा)

204 **Moose** (N.) - A large deer with palmate antlers (बारहसिंगा (विशेष प्रकार का बड़ा हिरण))

Mousse (N.) - A light, fluffy dessert or hair styling foam (फेंटा हुआ पदार्थ, जमाई हुई क्रीम)

205 **Mail** (N.) - Letters and parcels sent by post (डाक, मेल)

Male (N.) - Of or denoting the sex that produces sperm (पुरुष, नर)

206 **Missed** (V.) - Failed to hit, reach, or catch (खो दिया, चूक गया)

Mist (N.) - A cloud of tiny water droplets (कुहासा, धुंध)

207 **Manner** (N.) - A way of doing or being (शैली)

Manor (N.) - A landed estate (जागीर)

208 **Mantel** (N.) - A shelf above a fireplace (अँगीठी के ऊपर का शेल्फ)

Mantle (N.) - A cloak or covering (आवरण)

209 **Match** (N.) - A person or thing equal to another (बराबरी, समान)

Match (N.) - A competition between opponents (मुक़ाबला)

210 **May be** (Ph.) - To express that something is possible (हो सकता है)

Maybe (Adv.) - Used to indicate uncertainty or possibility (शायद)

211 **Mean** (V.) - To intend to convey (इरादा करना)

Mean (Adj.) - Not generous or kind (निर्दय, नीच)

Mean (N.) - The average of a set of numbers (औसत)

212 **Meat** (N.) - The flesh of an animal used as food (मांस)

Meet (V.) - To come together at a particular time or place (मिलना)

Mete (V.) - To give out or distribute (especially punishment) (सजा या पुरस्कार बाँटना)

213 **Immemorial** (Adj.) - Originating in the distant past; very old (पुरातन)

Memorable (Adj.) - Worth remembering or easy to remember (यादगार)

Memorial (Adj.) - Serving to preserve remembrance (स्मारक)

214 **Momentary** (Adj.) - Lasting only for a short time (क्षणिक)

Momentous (Adj.) - Having great significance (अत्यंत महत्वपूर्ण)

Momentum (N.) - The impetus gained by a moving object (संवेग)

215 **Marine** (Adj.) - Related to the sea or sea transport (समुद्र से संबंधित)

Maritime (Adj.) - Connected with human activity at sea (समुद्री)

216 **Manifest** (Adj.) - Clearly apparent or obvious (स्पष्ट)

Manifestation (N.) - The action or fact of showing something (अभिव्यक्ति, प्रकटीकरण)

217 **Medal** (N.) - A metal disk with a design awarded as a honor (पदक)

Metal (N.) - A solid material that is typically shiny and conducts electricity and heat (धातु)

Mettle (N.) - A person's ability to cope well with difficulties (साहस)

218 **Miner** (N.) - A person who works in a mine (खदान में काम करने वाला व्यक्ति)

Minor (N.) - A person under the legal age of full responsibility (नाबालिग)

Minor (Adj.) - Lesser in importance, size, or degree (मामूली)

219 **Miser** (N.) - A person who hoards money and spends as little as possible (कंजूस)

Misery (N.) - A state of great unhappiness and emotional distress (कष्ट)

220 **Morale** (N.) - The confidence and enthusiasm of a person or group (आत्मविश्वास, मनोबल)

Moral (Adj.) - Concerned with principles of right and wrong behaviour (नैतिक)

Moral (N.) - The lesson or principle taught by a story or event (नैतिकता)

221 **Knows** (V.) - Has knowledge or information (जानता/जानती है)

Noes (N.) - Plural of 'no'; negative votes (नहीं के उत्तर)

Nose (N.) - The part of the face used for smelling (नाक)

222 **None** (P.) - Not any (कोई नहीं, एक भी नहीं)

Nun (N.) - A member of a religious community of women (साध्वी, भिक्षुणी)

223 **Neglectful** (Adj.) - Characterized by neglect (बेपरवाह)

Negligent (Adj.) - Failing to take proper care (असावधान)

Negligible (Adj.) - So small as to be meaningless (बहुत कम)

224 **Overdo** (V.) - To exaggerate or be excessive (अतिशयोक्ति करना, हद से ज़्यादा करना)

Overdue (Adj.) - Late or past an appointed time (समय पर न हुआ, विलंबित)

225 **Observance** (N.) - The practice of observing a

law, custom, or religious ritual (अनुपालन)
Observation (N.) - The action or process of observing something (निगरानी)

226 **Ordinance** (N.) - A law or regulation made by a local authority (अध्यादेश)
Ordnance (N.) - Mounted guns; artillery (युद्ध-सामग्री)

227 **Official** (N.) - A person holding a position of authority (अधिकारी)
Official (Adj.) - Of or relating to an authority (आधिकारिक)
Officious (Adj.) - Assertive of authority in an annoyingly domineering way (परेशान करने वाला)

228 **Organic** (Adj.) - Relating to or derived from living matter (जैविक)
Organisation (N.) - A group of people with a particular purpose (संगठन)
Organism (N.) - An individual living thing (जीव)

229 **Pole** (N.) - A long, slender piece of wood or metal (खंभा, ध्रुव)
Poll (N.) - To cast a vote or take a survey (मतदान, सर्वेक्षण)

230 **Praise** (V.) - To express approval or admiration (प्रशंसा करना)
Prays (V.) - To offer prayers or make earnest requests to God (प्रार्थना करना)

231 **Passed** (V.) - Having received a passing grade on an examination (उत्तीर्ण)
Past (N.) - Having happened or existed before now (अतीत)

232 **Pastor** (N.) - A Christian minister in charge of a church (पादरी)
Pasture (N.) - Land covered with grass for grazing animals (चरागाह)

233 **Patience** (N.) - The capacity to tolerate delay or problems without becoming annoyed (धैर्य)
Patients (N.) - People receiving medical treatment (रोगी)

234 **Pedal** (N.) - A lever operated by the foot (पैडल)
Peddle (V.) - To sell goods, typically by going from place to place (फेरी लगा कर बेचना)
Petal (N.) - A segment of the corolla of a flower (पंखुड़ी)

235 **Patrol** (N.) - The action of moving around an area to keep watch (पहरा)
Petrol (N.) - Gasoline (पेट्रोल)

236 **Personal** (Adj.) - Relating or belonging to a particular person (व्यक्तिगत)
Personnel (N.) - A body of persons usually employed (कर्मचारी)

237 **Practice** (N.) - The actual application of an idea or method (अभ्यास)
Practise (V.) - To perform an activity repeatedly to improve skill (अभ्यास करना)

238 **Presence** (N.) - The state of being present (उपस्थिति)
Presents (N.) - Gifts (उपहार)

239 **Providence** (N.) - Divine guidance or care (परमात्मा)
Provident (Adj.) - Making provision for the future; frugal (किफ़ायती)
Providential (Adj.) - Occurring or taking place by divine foresight or intervention (भाग्यशाली)

240 **Practicable** (Adj.) - Able to be done or put into practice (संभव)
Practical (Adj.) - Concerned with actual use or practice (व्यावहारिक)

241 **Prescribe** (V.) - To lay down as a rule or guide (निर्धारित करना)
Proscribe (V.) - To forbid or prohibit (मना करना)

242 **Popular** (Adj.) - Liked or admired by many people (लोकप्रिय)
Populous (Adj.) - Having many inhabitants (घनी आबादी वाला)

243 **Pale** (Adj.) - Light in color (फीका)
Pale (N.) - A wooden stake or fence (घेरा)
Pail (N.) - A bucket (बाल्टी)

244 **Pain** (N.) - Physical or emotional suffering (पीड़ा)
Pane (N.) - A single sheet of glass in a window or door (खिड़की आदि में जड़ा शीशा)

245 **Peel** (V.) - To remove the outer covering or skin (छीलना)
Peel (N.) - The outer skin or rind (छिलका)
Peal (N.) - A loud ringing of a bells (घंटियों की गूँज)
Pill (N.) - A small, round or oval medicine (गोली, टैबलेट)

246 **Punctilious** (Adj.) - Showing great attention to detail or correct behaviour (अति शिष्टाचारी)
Punctual (Adj.) - Happening or doing something at the agreed or proper time (समयपालक)

247 **Prudent** (Adj.) - Acting with or showing care and thought for the future (विवेकी)
Prudential (Adj.) - Involving or showing careful thought about the future (दूरदर्शितापूर्ण)

248 **Precedent** (N.) - An earlier event or action that is regarded as an example or guide to be considered in subsequent similar circumstances (पूर्ववर्ती)
President (N.) - The elected head of a republican state (राष्ट्रपति/अध्यक्ष)

249 **Physic** (N.) - A medicine that purges; especially a cathartic (औषधि)
Physics (N.) - The science of matter and energy and their interactions (भौतिक विज्ञान)
Physique (N.) - The form, size, and development of a person's body (कद-काठी)

250 **Pray** (V.) - To address a solemn request or expression of thanks to a deity or other object of worship (प्रार्थना करना)
Prey (N.) - An animal taken by a predator as food (शिकार)

251 **Politic** (Adj.) - Shrewd or prudent in practical matters; tactful (नीति-चतुर)
Political (Adj.) - Of or relating to government, a government, or the conduct of government (राजनीतिक)

252 **Point** (N.) - A particular spot, place, or position in an area or on a map, object, or surface (बिन्दु)
Point (V.) - To indicate the position or direction of something (संकेत करना)

253 **Persecute** (V.) - To harass or punish in a manner designed to injure, grieve, or afflict (सताना)
Prosecute (V.) - To institute legal proceedings against someone (अभियोग लगाना)

254 **Pitiable** (Adj.) - Deserving or arousing pity (दयनीय)
Pitiful (Adj.) - Evoking or deserving pity (करुणामय)

255 **Policy** (N.) - A course or principle of action adopted or proposed by a government, party, business, or individual (नीति)
Polity (N.) - A form of government of a nation, state, church, or organization (राज्यतन्त्र)

256 **Prescription** (N.) - A doctor's written order for medicine (नुस्खा, दवा का पर्चा)
Proscription (N.) - The action of forbidding something (प्रतिबंध)

257 **Petrify** (V.) - To change into stone or a stony substance (पत्थर बनाना)
Putrefy (V.) - To rot or decay with an offensive smell (सड़ना)

258 **Prodigal** (Adj.) - Spending money or resources freely and recklessly; wastefully extravagant (फिजूल खर्च)
Prodigious (Adj.) - Remarkably or impressively great in extent, size, or degree (असाधारण)
Prodigy (N.) - A person, especially a young one, endowed with exceptional qualities or abilities (विलक्षणता)

259 **People** (N.) - Human beings in general; a group of humans (लोग)
Pupil (N.) - The apparently black circular opening in the center of the iris of the eye (आँखों की पुतली)
Pupil (N.) - A student under the direct supervision of a teacher or professor (विद्यार्थी)

260 **Quail** (N.) - A small, short-tailed Old World game bird (बटेर)
Quail (V.) - To draw back in fear; cower (भयभीत होना)

261 **Rap** (V./N.) - To strike or hit sharply (थपथपाना, दस्तक)
Wrap (V.) - To cover or enclose (लपेटना, समेटना)

262 **Rational** (Adj.) - Based on or in accordance with reason or logic (तर्कसंगत)
Rationale (N.) - A set of reasons or a logical basis for a course of action or belief (तर्काधार)

263 **Respectfully** (Adv.) - In a way that shows politeness and deference (विनम्रता पूर्वक)
Respectively (Adv.) - In the order given (क्रमशः)

264 **Respectable** (Adj.) - Having a good reputation; decent (सम्मानित)
Respectful (Adj.) - Showing deference and respect (आदरपूर्ण)
Respective (Adj.) - Relating or belonging to each separately (संबंधित)

265 **Reverend** (N.) - A member of the clergy (पादरी)
Reverend (Adj.) - Worthy of reverence; deserving respect (पूज्य, आदरणीय)
Reverent (Adj.) - Feeling or showing deep and solemn respect (श्रद्धालु)

266 **Rapt** (Adj.) - Completely fascinated or absorbed by what one is seeing or hearing (मोहित)
Wrapt (Adj.) - Fully absorbed or deeply interested in something (मग्न, पूरी तरह ध्यान में डूबा हुआ)

267 **Recourse** (N.) - A source of help in a difficult situation (सहारा)
Resource (N.) - A source of supply or support for particular work (संसाधन)

268 **Ruler** (N.) - A person exercising government or dominion (शासक)
Ruler (N.) - A strip or cylinder of wood, metal, or plastic used for measuring length or drawing straight lines (मापक)

269 **Steal** (V.) - To take without permission (चोरी करना)
Steel (N.) - A strong, hard metal alloy (इस्पात)

270 **Sell** (V.) - To give something in exchange for money (बेचना)
Cell (N.) - A small room (कोठरी)
Cell (N.) - A biological unit (कोशिका)
Sail (V.) - To travel on water in a ship or boat (नौकायन करना, जहाज़ चलाना)
Sail (N.) - A piece of fabric on a ship that catches wind (पाल)

271 **Stair** (N.) - A step in a flight of stairs (सीढ़ी, पायदान)
Stare (V.) - To look fixedly at something (घूरना, टकटकी लगाना)

272 **Scene** (N.) - The place where an incident in real life or fiction occurs (दृश्य)
Seen (V.) - Perceive with the eyes (देखा)

273 **Serf** (N.) - A member of the lowest feudal class (कृषि-मज़दूर)
Surf (N.) - The swell of the sea that breaks upon a shore or reef (लहर)

274 **Sensible** (Adj.) - Acting with or showing good sense (समझदार)
Sensitive (Adj.) - Quick to detect or respond to slight changes or influences (संवेदनशील)

275 **Shear** (V.) - To cut or clip hair or wool (बाल या ऊन काटना)
Sheer (Adj.) - Very thin or transparent (शुद्ध)

276 **Ship** (N.) - A vessel larger than a boat for transporting people or goods by sea (जहाज़)
Ship (V.) - To transport by ship (ढोना)

277 **Sink** (V.) - To go downward in quality, state, or condition (घटना/डूबना)
Sink (N.) - A fixed basin with a water supply and a drain (हौज/नाली)

278 **Soar** (V.) - To fly or rise high into the air (बहुत वृद्धि होना)
Sore (Adj.) - Feeling or affected by pain or discomfort (पीड़ादायक)
Sour (Adj.) - Having an acid taste, like lemon or vinegar (खट्टा)

279 **Sociable** (Adj.) - Enjoying the company of others; friendly (मिलनसार)
Social (Adj.) - Relating to society or its organization (सामाजिक)

280 **Sensual** (Adj.) - Relating to or consisting in the gratification of the senses or the indulgence of appetite (कामुक)
Sensuous (Adj.) - Of or relating to the senses or sensible objects (इंद्रियगत)

281 **Spacious** (Adj.) - Having a lot of space (विशाल)
Specious (Adj.) - Seeming to be right or true, but really wrong or false (दिखावटी)

282 **Spiritual** (Adj.) - Relating to or affecting the human spirit or soul as opposed to material or physical things (आध्यात्मिक)
Spirituous (Adj.) - Containing or impregnated with alcohol obtained by distillation (शराब सम्बन्धी)

283 **Stimulant** (N.) - Something that causes increased activity or efficiency, especially of the body or mind (उत्तेजक)
Stimulus (N.) - Something that causes a response or reaction (प्रोत्साहन)

284 **Storey** (N.) - A level or floor of a building (मंज़िल)
Story (N.) - An account of imaginary or real people and events told for entertainment (कहानी)

285 **Special** (Adj.) - Distinguished by some unusual quality (विशेष)
Especial (Adj.) - Particularly great or notable (विशेष रूप से, खास)

286 **Spring** (V.) - To move or jump suddenly or rapidly upward or forward (छलाँग मारना)
Spring (N.) - The season between winter and summer (बसंत ऋतु)

287 **Son** (N.) - A male child or person in relation to either or both of his parents (पुत्र)
Sun (N.) - The star round which the earth orbits (सूर्य)

288 **Suit** (N.) - A set of clothes to be worn together (कपड़ों का एक सेट)
Suite (N.) - A set of connected rooms, typically in a hotel (कमरों का सेट)

289 **Sham** (N.) - Something that is not what it purports to be (ढोंगी)
Shame (N.) - A painful feeling of humiliation or distress caused by consciousness of wrong or foolish behaviour (लज्जा/शर्म)

290 **Sever** (V.) - To divide or separate (अलग करना)
Severe (Adj.) - Very great; intense (गंभीर)

291 **Statue** (N.) - A carved or cast figure of a person or animal (प्रतिमा)
Statute (N.) - A written law passed by a legislative body (नियम या क़ानून)

292 **Straight** (Adj.) - Without a bend, angle, or curve (सीधा)
Strait (N.) - A narrow passage of water connecting two seas or two other large areas of water (जलडमरूमध्य)

293 **Counterfeit** (Adj.) - Made in exact imitation of something valuable with the intention to deceive or defraud (नक़ली)
Forfeit (N.) - Something that is lost or given up as punishment or because of a rule or agreement (जुरमाना, हारना)
Surfeit (N.) - An excessive amount of something (आधिक्य (अधिक होना))

294 **Taught** (V.) - Past tense of teach (पढ़ाया)
Taut (Adj.) - Stretched or pulled tight; not slack (तना हुआ)

295 **Temperament** (N.) - A person's nature, especially as it permanently affects their behaviour (व्यक्ति का स्वभाव)
Temperance (N.) - Moderation or self-restraint, especially in eating and drinking (संयम)

296 **Tolerable** (Adj.) - Able to be endured or tolerated (संतोषजनक)
Tolerant (Adj.) - To allow or accept something that you do not like or agree with (सहनशील)

297 **Temporal** (Adj.) - Relating to worldly as opposed to spiritual affairs (सांसारिक)
Temporary (Adj.) - Lasting for only a limited period of time; not permanent (अल्पकालिक)

298 **Tamper** (V.) - To interfere with something in order to cause damage or make unauthorized alterations (हस्तक्षेप करना)
Temper (N.) - The state of the mind with regard to being annoyed or calm (स्वभाव)

299 **Team** (N.) - A group of players forming one side in a competitive game or sport (दल)
Teem (V.) - To be full of or swarming with (बड़ी संख्या में व्यक्तियों या वस्तुओं का चलना-फिरना)

300 **Than** (Conj.) - Used in expressions introducing an exception or contrast (की अपेक्षा)
Then (Adv.) - At that time (उस वक़्त)

301 **Thorough** (Adj.) - Complete with regard to every detail (पूरी तरह, गहराई से)
Threw (V.) - Past tense of 'throw' (फेंका)
Through (Prep.) - Moving in one side and out of the other side of an opening or hole (के माध्यम से)

302 **Tortuous** (Adj.) - Full of twists and turns (जटिल)
Torturous (Adj.) - Involving or causing torture (यातनापूर्ण)

303 **Throes** (N.) - Intense or violent pain and struggle (तीव्र पीड़ा)
Throws (V.) - Propel through the air (फेंकना)

304 **Tie** (N.) - A necktie (टाई)
Tie (V.) - To bind or fasten (बाँधना)
Tie (N.) - An equality of score in a game or contest (बराबर अंको पर समाप्त करना)

305 **Union** (N.) - The act or fact of joining together, especially in a political or organizational context (संयोजन, मेल-जोल)
Unity (N.) - The state of being united or joined as a whole (एकता)

306 **Upright** (Adj.) - Sitting or standing with the back straight (सीधा)
Uptight (Adj.) - Anxious or angry in a tense way (तनावग्रस्त, चिड़चिड़ा)

307 **Urban** (Adj.) - In, relating to, or characteristic of a city or town (शहरी)
Urbane (Adj.) - Courteous and refined in manner (शिष्ट)

308 **Vale** (N.) - A valley (घाटी)
Veil (N.) - A piece of cloth worn to cover the face (पर्दा, आवरण)

309 **Variance** (N.) - The state or fact of disagreeing or being different (असहमति, विसंगति)
Variation (N.) - A change or slight difference in condition, amount, or level, typically within certain limits (भिन्नता)

310 **Verses** (N.) - Writing that is arranged in short lines with a regular rhythm (छंद)
Versus (Prep.) - As opposed to; in contrast to (बनाम)

311 **Vacation** (N.) - An extended period of recreation, especially one spent away from home or traveling (छुट्टी)
Avocation (N.) - A hobby or minor occupation (शौक, उप-व्यवसाय)
Vocation (N.) - A strong feeling of suitability for a particular occupation (व्यवसाय)

312 **Virtual** (Adj.) - Being on or simulated on a computer (अप्रत्यक्ष)
Virtuous (Adj.) - Having or showing high

moral standards (धार्मिक)

313 **Veracity** (N.) - Conformity to facts; accuracy (सच्चाई)

Voracity (N.) - The quality of being ravenously hungry or insatiable (पेटूपन, अत्यधिक लालच)

314 **Vassal** (N.) - Someone who is subordinate or dependent on another (अधीनस्थ, निर्भर व्यक्ति)

Vessel (N.) - A ship or large boat (पानी का जहाज)

Vessel (N.) - A hollow container, especially one used to hold liquid (पात्र)

315 **Venal** (Adj.) - Showing or motivated by susceptibility to bribery (घूसख़ोर)

Venial (Adj.) - Not very serious and able to be forgiven (मामूली)

316 **Venerable** (Adj.) - Respected because of age, wisdom, or character (आदरणीय)

Vulnerable (Adj.) - Able to be easily physically or mentally hurt (असुरक्षित, कमजोर)

317 **Veracious** (Adj.) - Speaking or representing the truth (ईमानदार)

Voracious (Adj.) - Having a great appetite for something (पेटू)

318 **Verbal** (Adj.) - Expressed in spoken words (मौखिक)

Verbose (Adj.) - Using or containing more words than necessary (शब्दबहुल)

319 **Way** (N.) - A method, direction, or path (रास्ता, तरीका)

Weigh (V.) - To determine the weight of something (तौलना, विचार करना)

Whey (N.) - The watery part of milk left after making cheese (मट्ठा, छाछ)

320 **Wilful** (Adj.) - Intentional; done on purpose (स्वेच्छाचारी)

Willing (Adj.) - Ready, eager, or prepared to do something (इच्छुक)

321 **Vet** (N.) - A veterinarian; an animal doctor (पशु चिकित्सक)

Vet (V.) - To check or evaluate for accuracy or authenticity (जाँचना)

Wet (Adj.) - Covered or saturated with water or another liquid (गीला)

Whet (V.) - To excite or stimulate (उत्तेजित करना)

322 **Waist** (N.) - The part of the human body between the ribs and the hips (कमर)

Waste (V.) - To use or expend carelessly (बर्बाद करना)

323 **Wary** (Adj.) - Cautious; watchful (सावधान)

Weary (Adj.) - Exhausted; tired (थका हुआ)

324 **Weak** (Adj.) - Lacking physical strength or energy (कमजोर)

Week (N.) - A period of seven days (सप्ताह)

325 **Which** (P.) - Asking for or specifying one of a group (जो)

Witch (N.) - A woman thought to have magic powers (डायन)

326 **Who's** (Cont.) - Contraction of 'who is' or 'who has' (कौन है)

Whose (P.) - Belonging to or associated with which person (किसका)

327 **Womanish** (Adj.) - Characteristic of a woman, often used disparagingly to imply weakness (जनाना)

Womanly (Adj.) - Having qualities traditionally associated with women, in an admiring sense (नारीसुलभ, महिला जैसा)

328 **Wraith** (N.) - A ghost or ghost-like image of someone (भूत-प्रेत, साया)

Wrath (N.) - Extreme anger (क्रोध)

329 **Wreak** (V.) - To cause a large amount of damage or harm (बदला लेना)

Wreck (V.) - To severely damage or destroy (नष्ट करना, तबाह करना)

330 **Yore** (N.) - Time long past (पुराने समय, प्राचीन काल)

Your (P.) - Belonging to or associated with you (आपका)

You're (Cont.) - Contraction of 'you are' (आप हैं)

FIXED PREPOSITIONS

Definition:
Fixed Prepositions are specific prepositions that are conventionally used with verbs, adjectives, or nouns. These combinations are fixed by convention, and **no logical grammar rule is followed**. They cannot be changed or substituted with other prepositions. Examples: Afraid of; Interested in; Married to; Different from; Depend on; Similar to

Types: Fixed prepositions may be classified as Adjective (Afraid of), Verb (Listen to) and Noun (Effect on) prepositions.

Fixed Prepositions vs Other Concepts

Aspect	Fixed Prepositions	Phrasal Verbs	Idioms
Structure	Word + fixed preposition	Verb + particle	Group of words with figurative meaning
Meaning	Predictable from components	Changes completely	Cannot be understood literally
Example	Afraid of; Depend on	Give up; Break down	Kick the bucket; Bite the bullet
Flexibility	Cannot change preposition	Separable/Inseparable	Entire phrase is fixed
Exam focus	Grammar error spotting	Vocabulary-based	Vocabulary-based

Same Word + Different Prepositions = Different Meanings

Usage 1		Usage 2	
Agree with	Agree with a person or opinion	**Agree to**	Accept a proposal or plan
Angry with	Angry at a person	**Angry at/about**	Angry at a thing or situation
Think of	Idea comes to mind	**Think about**	Consider something deeply
Good at	Skilled in something	**Good for**	Beneficial for something
Die of	Disease (internal cause)	**Die from**	Injury (external cause)

Why Fixed Prepositions Are Important for Competitive Exams

Fixed Prepositions are among the most frequently tested grammar topics in competitive exams. Questions rarely ask for definitions; instead, candidates are tested on identifying incorrect prepositions in sentences. Error Spotting, Sentence Correction, Fill in the Blanks, Sentence Improvement, and Cloze Tests regularly include fixed preposition errors. This makes the topic a high-scoring area with relatively low preparation effort.

Example: Married to (correct) vs ~~Married with~~ (incorrect)

COMMONLY CONFUSED FIXED PREPOSITIONS

SN	Correct ✓	Incorrect X	Explanation & Similar Examples
1	**Afraid OF**	Afraid from	OF is used with fear-related adjectives, not FROM. Similar: Scared of, Frightened of, Terrified of, Fearful of, Petrified of, Nervous of, Wary of, Apprehensive of
2	**Different FROM**	Different than/to	FROM shows contrast or distinction. Similar: Distinct from, Separate from, Apart from, Dissimilar from, Divergent from, Detached from
3	**Married TO**	Married with	TO shows relationship bond. Similar: Engaged to, Related to, Attached to, Connected to, Allied to, Bound to, Linked to
4	**Superior TO**	Superior than	Latin-origin comparatives always take TO, never THAN. Similar: Inferior to, Senior to, Junior to, Prior to, Posterior to, Preferable to, Anterior to
5	**Depend ON**	Depend upon/from	ON shows reliance or support. Similar: Rely on, Count on, Based on, Hinge on, Rest on, Bank on, Lean on, Build on
6	**Consist OF**	Consist from	OF shows composition or parts. Similar: Composed of, Made up of, Comprised of (informal), Full of, Devoid of, Bereft of
7	**Interested IN**	Interested for	IN shows involvement or engagement in a topic. Similar: Absorbed in, Engaged in, Involved in, Immersed in, Engrossed in, Wrapped up in, Caught up in
8	**Good AT**	Good in	AT is used for skills and abilities. Similar: Bad at, Clever at, Brilliant at, Excellent at, Skilled at, Expert at, Adept at, Proficient at, Quick at
9	**Listen TO**	Listen at	TO shows direction of attention. Similar: Attend to, Pay attention to, Respond to, React to, Object to, Refer to, Appeal to
10	**Wait FOR**	Wait to	FOR shows expectation of something/someone. Similar: Hope for, Long for, Wish for, Ask for, Search for, Look for, Apply for, Care for
11	**Angry WITH person**	Angry on person	WITH is used for emotions directed at people. Similar: Annoyed with, Furious with, Upset with, Displeased with, Irritated with, Fed up with, Cross with, Disgusted with
12	**Pleased WITH**	Pleased from	WITH shows satisfaction towards something/someone. Similar: Satisfied with, Delighted with, Content with, Happy with, Thrilled with, Impressed with, Comfortable with
13	**Congratulate ON**	Congratulate for	ON is used for achievements and occasions. Similar: Compliment on, Comment on, Insist on, Focus on, Concentrate on, Reflect on, Decide on, Rely on
14	**Accuse OF**	Accuse for	OF is used for allegations and charges. Similar: Suspect of, Convict of, Acquit of, Guilty of, Innocent of, Capable of, Aware of, Conscious of
15	**Blame FOR**	Blame of	FOR shows reason or cause of fault. Similar: Punish for, Criticize for, Scold for, Praise for, Thank for, Forgive for, Apologize for, Responsible for

SN	Correct ✓	Incorrect X	Explanation & Similar Examples
16	**Prevent FROM**	Prevent to	FROM + gerund shows stopping an action. Similar: Prohibit from, Stop from, Restrain from, Discourage from, Deter from, Refrain from, Abstain from, Desist from
17	**Agree WITH (Someone)**	Agree to person	WITH is used when sharing same opinion as a person. Similar: Disagree with, Concur with, Side with, Sympathize with, Comply with, Coincide with, Associate with
18	**Agree TO (Proposal)**	Agree with proposal	TO is used for accepting proposals, terms, or conditions. Similar: Consent to, Accede to, Submit to, Yield to, Succumb to, Resort to, Adhere to
19	**Capable OF**	Capable to	OF + gerund shows ability. Similar: Incapable of, Fond of, Tired of, Sick of, Proud of, Ashamed of, Aware of, Jealous of, Suspicious of
20	**Able TO**	Able of	TO + infinitive shows ability. Similar: Unable to, Willing to, Ready to, Eager to, Reluctant to, Liable to, Prone to, Subject to, Due to
21	**Prefer X TO Y**	Prefer X than Y	TO is used in preference comparisons, not THAN. Similar: Preferable to, Superior to, Inferior to, Senior to, Junior to, Prior to
22	**Proud OF**	Proud on	OF is used for feelings of pride. Similar: Ashamed of, Jealous of, Envious of, Fond of, Tired of, Sick of, Weary of, Scared of, Aware of
23	**Fond OF**	Fond with	OF shows liking or affection. Similar: Tired of, Sick of, Weary of, Proud of, Ashamed of, Jealous of, Envious of, Suspicious of, Aware of
24	**Aware OF**	Aware about	OF shows knowledge or consciousness. Similar: Conscious of, Mindful of, Ignorant of, Regardless of, Irrespective of, Devoid of, Bereft of, Short of
25	**Solution TO**	Solution of/for	TO shows answer or remedy to a problem. Similar: Answer to, Key to, Clue to, Secret to, Threat to, Damage to, Objection to, Exception to, Reaction to
26	**Effect ON**	Effect to	ON shows impact or influence. Similar: Impact on, Influence on, Impression on, Attack on, Ban on, Restriction on, Hold on, Grip on
27	**Addicted TO**	Addicted of/with	TO shows dependency or attachment. Similar: Accustomed to, Habituated to, Used to, Devoted to, Dedicated to, Committed to, Opposed to, Exposed to
28	**Based ON**	Based upon/in	ON shows foundation or basis. Similar: Depend on, Rely on, Count on, Insist on, Focus on, Concentrate on, Comment on, Reflect on, Decide on
29	**Discuss (no prep)**	Discuss about	Transitive verb - takes direct object without preposition. Similar: Describe, Mention, Enter (physical), Await, Comprise, Attack, Reach, Resemble, Marry
30	**Enter (no prep)**	Enter into room	Physical entry needs no preposition; Enter into = agreements. Similar: Discuss, Describe, Mention, Await, Comprise, Reach, Approach, Contact, Address

SN	Correct ✓	Incorrect X	Explanation & Similar Examples
31	**Die OF (Disease)**	Die from disease	OF is used for illness or internal causes. Similar: Die of cancer, fever, hunger, thirst, old age, heart attack, natural causes, starvation
32	**Die FROM (Injury)**	Die of injury	FROM is used for external causes or wounds. Similar: Die from wounds, injuries, accident, bleeding, trauma, gunshot, poisoning, drowning
33	**Arrive AT (Small place)**	Arrive to station	AT is used for specific points or small places. Similar: Arrive at airport, hotel, office, school, hospital, station, bus stop, destination
34	**Arrive IN (Large place)**	Arrive at city	IN is used for large areas like cities and countries. Similar: Arrive in Delhi, London, India, France, Europe, Asia, the country, town
35	**Jealous OF**	Jealous from	OF is used for envy. Similar: Envious of, Suspicious of, Proud of, Ashamed of, Fond of, Tired of, Aware of, Conscious of, Scared of
36	**Tired OF**	Tired from	OF shows boredom or being fed up. Similar: Sick of, Weary of, Bored with, Fed up with, Fond of, Proud of, Ashamed of, Aware of
37	**Search FOR**	Search of	FOR shows seeking something. Similar: Look for, Hunt for, Ask for, Apply for, Wait for, Hope for, Long for, Care for, Wish for
38	**Angry AT (Thing)**	Angry on thing	AT/ABOUT is used for situations or things. Similar: Annoyed at, Surprised at, Shocked at, Amazed at, Alarmed at, Astonished at, Delighted at
39	**Focus ON**	Focus at/in	ON shows concentration. Similar: Concentrate on, Insist on, Depend on, Rely on, Comment on, Reflect on, Decide on, Dwell on, Elaborate on
40	**Insist ON**	Insist for	ON shows firm demand. Similar: Persist in, Depend on, Rely on, Focus on, Concentrate on, Comment on, Reflect on, Decide on, Dwell on
41	**Inferior TO**	Inferior than	Latin-origin comparative - always TO. Similar: Superior to, Senior to, Junior to, Prior to, Posterior to, Preferable to, Anterior to
42	**Senior TO**	Senior than	Latin-origin comparative - always TO. Similar: Junior to, Superior to, Inferior to, Prior to, Posterior to, Elder to, Preferable to
43	**Junior TO**	Junior than	Latin-origin comparative - always TO. Similar: Senior to, Superior to, Inferior to, Prior to, Posterior to, Preferable to
44	**Scared OF**	Scared from	OF is used with all fear-related adjectives. Similar: Afraid of, Frightened of, Terrified of, Fearful of, Petrified of, Horrified at, Alarmed at
45	**Frightened OF**	Frightened from	OF is used for fear. Similar: Afraid of, Scared of, Terrified of, Fearful of, Petrified of, Apprehensive of, Nervous of
46	**Key TO**	Key of/for	TO shows means or solution. Similar: Solution to, Answer to, Clue to, Secret to, Threat to, Damage to, Objection to, Reaction to

SN	Correct ✓	Incorrect X	Explanation & Similar Examples
47	**Access TO**	Access of	TO shows entry or availability. Similar: Admission to, Approach to, Entrance to, Solution to, Key to, Answer to, Objection to, Reaction to
48	**Impact ON**	Impact to	ON shows effect or influence. Similar: Effect on, Influence on, Impression on, Attack on, Ban on, Hold on, Grip on, Emphasis on
49	**Damage TO**	Damage of	TO shows harm caused. Similar: Injury to, Threat to, Danger to, Harm to, Solution to, Key to, Answer to, Objection to, Reaction to
50	**Devoted TO**	Devoted for	TO shows dedication. Similar: Dedicated to, Committed to, Attached to, Addicted to, Accustomed to, Opposed to, Exposed to, Subjected to

KEY MEMORY RULES

Rule	Always Use	Never Use	Examples
Latin comparatives	TO	THAN	Superior to, Inferior to, Senior to, Junior to, Prior to, Preferable to
Fear adjectives	OF	FROM	Afraid of, Scared of, Frightened of, Terrified of, Fearful of
Emotions towards person	WITH	ON	Angry with, Annoyed with, Pleased with, Satisfied with, Furious with
Emotions towards thing	AT / ABOUT	ON	Angry at, Surprised at, Shocked at, Annoyed about
No-preposition verbs	(no prep)	about/to/for	Discuss, Describe, Enter, Await, Comprise, Mention, Reach, Resemble
Composition	OF	FROM	Consist of, Composed of, Made up of, Full of
Skills & abilities	AT	IN	Good at, Bad at, Clever at, Expert at, Skilled at
Dependency	ON	UPON/FROM	Depend on, Rely on, Count on, Based on, Focus on

F3 Fixed Prepositions
(Important for SSC and Other Exams)

1 **Ability to** (की क्षमता) - The capacity or skill to do something
2 **Abound in** (से भरपूर होना) - To exist in large quantities or numbers
3 **Abound with** (से भरपूर होना) - Plentiful or full of something
4 **Absolve from** (से मुक्त करना) - To free from guilt, blame, or responsibility
5 **Abstain from** (से परहेज करना) - To refrain from doing something
6 **Abstinence from** (से परहेज) - The practice of restraining oneself from indulging in something
7 **Accede to** (को स्वीकार करना) - To agree to a demand, request, or treaty
8 **Acceptable to** (को स्वीकार्य) - Satisfactory or allowed; Suitable
9 **Access to** (तक पहुँच) - The means or opportunity to approach or enter a place
10 **Accessible to** (के लिए उपलब्ध; सुलभ) - Able to be reached or entered
11 **Accompanied by** (के साथ) - Occurring or going together with something or someone
12 **Accomplice to** (का सहभागी; अपराध में सहयोगी) - A person who helps another commit a crime
13 **According to** (के अनुसार) - As stated or reported by
14 **Accountable to** (के प्रति जवाबदेह) - Responsible to someone for one's actions
15 **Accuse of** (पर आरोप लगाना) - To charge someone with wrongdoing
16 **Accused of** (का आरोपित) - Charged with a wrongdoing or crime
17 **Accustomed to** (के आदी) - Familiar with something due to prolonged experience
18 **Acquaintance with** (से परिचय) - Knowledge or familiarity with something
19 **Acquainted with** (से परिचित होना) - To be familiar with or aware of something
20 **Acquit of** (से बरी करना) - To free someone from a criminal charge
21 **Adapt to** (के अनुसार ढलना) - To adjust to new conditions
22 **Addicted to** (का आदी) - Physically or mentally dependent on something
23 **Addiction to** (की लत) - A state of physical or psychological dependence on something
24 **Adept at** (में निपुण) - Very skilled or proficient at something
25 **Adept in** (में निपुण) - Very skilled or proficient at something
26 **Adequate for** (के लिए पर्याप्त) - Sufficient for a particular purpose
27 **Adhere to** (का पालन करना (नियम)) - To follow or stick to rules
28 **Adjacent to** (से सटा हुआ) - Next to or adjoining something
29 **Admiration for** (के लिए प्रशंसा) - Respect and approval for someone or something
30 **Admit into** (में प्रवेश देना) - To allow someone to enter a place or institution
31 **Admit of** (की अनुमति देना) - To allow something or make it possible
32 **Admit to** (को स्वीकार करना) - To confess or acknowledge something
33 **Advantage of** (का फायदा) - A favourable position or benefit from something
34 **Advantage over** (पर बढ़त) - A superior position compared to others
35 **Advice on** (पर सलाह) - Guidance or recommendation about something
36 **Advise on** (पर सलाह देना) - To give guidance or recommendations about something
37 **Affable to** (के प्रति मिलनसार) - Friendly and easy to talk to
38 **Affection for** (के प्रति लगाव) - Fondness or liking for someone or something
39 **Affectionate towards** (के प्रति स्नेहपूर्ण) - Showing love and fondness towards someone
40 **Affiliated to** (से संबद्ध) - Officially attached or connected to an organization
41 **Affiliated with** (से संबद्ध) - Closely associated with a particular group or organization
42 **Afflicted with** (से पीड़ित) - Suffering from something unpleasant, like a disease
43 **Afraid of** (से डरना) - Feeling fear or anxiety about something
44 **Agree on** (पर सहमत होना) - To have the same opinion about
45 **Agreeable to** (के लिए सहमत) - Willing to do

something

46 **Agreement on** (पर सहमति) - A consensus about

47 **Agreement with** (के साथ सहमति; मतैक्य) - An accordance with

48 **Aim at** (पर निशाना लगाना) - To point or direct towards a target

49 **Aim for** (का लक्ष्य रखना) - To try to achieve

50 **Akin to** (के समान) - Similar to something

51 **Alarmed at** (चौंक जाना; चिंतित या भयभीत हो जाना) - Frightened or disturbed by something

52 **Alien to** (के लिए अजनबी) - Unfamiliar, strange, or unrelated to something

53 **Alight at** (पर उतरना) - To step down onto something

54 **Alight from** (से उतरना) - To step down from a vehicle

55 **Alive to** (के प्रति जागरूक) - Aware of or responsive to something

56 **Allegiance to** (के प्रति निष्ठा; वफादारी) - A loyalty or commitment to a person or cause

57 **Allergic to** (से एलर्जी) - Having an allergy to

58 **Alliance with** (के साथ गठबंधन) - A partnership or association with someone or something

59 **Allowance for** (के लिए प्रावधान) - A provision or consideration for something

60 **Aloof from** (से अलग) - Distant or detached from a situation

61 **Alternative to** (का विकल्प) - Another option or possibility instead of something

62 **Amazed at** (पर चकित) - Greatly surprised by

63 **Amazed by** (से चकित) - Greatly surprised by

64 **Ambition for** (के लिए महत्वाकांक्षा) - A strong desire to achieve something

65 **Amuse with** (से मनोरंजन करना) - To entertain or occupy pleasantly

66 **Amused by** (से आनंदित; पर हँसना) - Finding something funny or entertaining

67 **Analogous to** (के समान) - Similar or comparable to something

68 **Anger at** (पर क्रोध) - Anger towards

69 **Angry about** (के बारे में नाराज़) - Feeling anger regarding

70 **Angry at** (पर नाराज़) - Feeling anger towards

71 **Angry with** (से नाराज़) - Feeling anger towards

72 **Annoyed about** (के बारे में नाराज़) - Slightly angry about

73 **Annoyed at** (पर नाराज़) - Slightly angry at

74 **Annoyed with** (से नाराज़) - Slightly angry with someone

75 **Answer by** (के माध्यम से जवाब देना) - To respond to something through a particular means

76 **Answer to** (को जवाब देना) - Accountable to someone

77 **Answerable to** (के प्रति जवाबदेह) - Responsible to someone or required to explain actions

78 **Antidote to** (के विरुद्ध औषधि; का इलाज) - A remedy that counteracts poison or something harmful

79 **Anxiety about** (के बारे में चिंता) - A worry about

80 **Anxiety for** (के लिए चिंता) - Worry or unease about something

81 **Anxious about** (के बारे में चिंतित) - Worried about

82 **Apologise to a person** (किसी व्यक्ति से माफी मांगना) - To express regret to someone for an action

83 **Apology for** (के लिए माफी) - An expression of regret for

84 **Appeal for** (के लिए अपील करना) - To make a serious or urgent request for something

85 **Appeal to** (से अपील करना) - To make a serious request; to attract

86 **Appetite for** (की भूख) - A strong desire or liking for something

87 **Applicable to** (पर लागू होना) - Relevant or appropriate to something

88 **Application for** (के लिए आवेदन) - A formal request for

89 **Apply to** (पर लागू होना) - Relevant to; to make a request to

90 **Appoint to a post** (किसी पद पर नियुक्त करना) - To assign someone to a particular job or position

91 **Apprentice to** (का प्रशिक्षु; के लिए शिष्य) - Someone who works for another to learn a trade

92 **Apprise of** (से अवगत कराना) - To inform someone of something

93 **Approach to** (किसी चीज़ से निपटने का तरीका) - A way of dealing with something

94 **Appropriate to** (के लिए उपयुक्त) - Suitable or proper for something

95 **Approval of** (की स्वीकृति) - Formal permission or official acceptance of something

96 **Approve of** (को स्वीकृति देना) - To agree to or accept officially

97 **Aptitude for** (के लिए योग्यता) - A natural ability or skill at doing something

98 **Argue about** (के बारे में बहस करना) - To have a disagreement about

99 **Argument about** (के बारे में बहस) - A disagreement or discussion about something

100 **Argument with** (से बहस) - A dispute with someone

101 **Arrival at** (पर पहुँचना) - Reaching a destination or place

102 **Arrival in** (में आगमन) - Reaching a city or country
103 **Arrive at** (पर पहुँचना) - To reach a place or conclusion
104 **Ashamed of** (से शर्मिंदा) - Embarrassed or guilty about something
105 **Ask for** (माँगना) - To request something
106 **Aspirant to** (का आकांक्षी) - A person who aspires to a particular position or status
107 **Aspire to** (की आकांक्षा रखना) - To have a strong ambition to achieve something
108 **Assent to** (को सहमति देना) - To agree to or approve of something
109 **Assiduous in** (में मेहनती) - Showing great care and perseverance in something
110 **Associated with** (से जुड़ा हुआ) - Connected with something or someone else
111 **Assurance of** (का आश्वासन) - A promise or guarantee of something
112 **Assure of** (का आश्वासन देना; किसी को निश्चिंत करना) - To confidently tell someone something
113 **Assured by** (के द्वारा विश्वास दिया गया) - Given confidence by someone
114 **Astonished at** (से आश्चर्यचकित) - Greatly surprised by something
115 **Astonished by** (से आश्चर्यचकित) - Very surprised by
116 **Attach to** (से जोड़ना) - To fasten or connect to
117 **Attachment to** (के प्रति लगाव) - A strong affection or connection to something
118 **Attack on** (पर हमला) - An assault on
119 **Attempt at** (का प्रयास) - An effort to do
120 **Attend upon** (की सेवा करना) - To accompany or serve someone
121 **Attending on** (की देखभाल करना) - Accompanying or serving someone
122 **Attention to** (पर ध्यान देना; की ओर ध्यान केंद्रित करना) - Focusing on or considering something carefully
123 **Attitude to (towards)** (के प्रति रवैया, दृष्टिकोण) - A way of thinking or feeling about something
124 **Attraction for** (के प्रति आकर्षण) - A liking or interest in something
125 **Avail of** (का लाभ उठाना) - To make use of an opportunity or offer
126 **Available for** (के लिए उपलब्ध) - Free or obtainable for
127 **Award for** (के लिए पुरस्कार) - A prize given in recognition of achievement
128 **Aware of** (से अवगत) - Having knowledge or realization of something
129 **Awareness of** (की जागरूकता) - A knowledge of
130 **Bad for** (के लिए बुरा) - Harmful to
131 **Bargain for** (की उम्मीद करना) - To expect or anticipate
132 **Bargain with** (से सौदा करना) - To negotiate with someone
133 **Base on** (पर आधारित होना) - To use as a foundation
134 **Based on** (पर आधारित) - Founded on
135 **Basis for** (का आधार) - A foundation for
136 **Bathe in** (में नहाना) - To immerse oneself in a liquid
137 **Bearing on** (पर प्रभाव) - Relevance or influence on something
138 **Beg of** ((किसी से) विनम्रतापूर्वक मांगना) - To ask someone for something humbly
139 **Beg pardon of** (से क्षमा मांगना) - To apologize to someone
140 **Belief in** (में विश्वास) - A faith in
141 **Believe in** (में विश्वास करना) - To have faith in
142 **Beneficial to** (के लिए लाभदायक) - Helpful or advantageous for something
143 **Benefit by** (से लाभ उठाना) - To gain an advantage from something
144 **Benefit from** (से लाभ प्राप्त करना) - To gain an advantage from something
145 **Benefit of** (का लाभ) - An advantage of
146 **Bent on** (पर अड़ा हुआ) - Determined to do something
147 **Beset with** (कठिनाइयों से घिरा हुआ) - Continuously troubled by something
148 **Bestow upon** (सम्मान या उपहार के रूप में कुछ देना) - To give something as an honour or gift
149 **Beware of** (से सावधान रहना) - Cautious or wary of something
150 **Bigoted against** (के प्रति कट्टर; के खिलाफ पूर्वाग्रही) - Showing intolerance or prejudice against a group
151 **Blame for** (के लिए दोष) - A responsibility for something bad
152 **Blessed with** (से धन्य) - Endowed with something desirable
153 **Blind to** (के प्रति अनजान) - Unable or unwilling to notice something
154 **Blush at** (में शर्मिंदा महसूस करना) - To feel embarrassed or ashamed about something
155 **Blush for** (के लिए शर्माना) - To feel embarrassed or ashamed on behalf of someone
156 **Boast of** (पर घमंड करना) - To speak with excessive pride about something
157 **Border on** (से सटा होना) - Close to an

undesirable condition or quality

158 **Bored with** (से ऊबा हुआ) - Feeling uninterested in

159 **Borrow from** (किसी व्यक्ति से उधार लेना) - To take or receive something from someone with the intention of returning it

160 **Bother about** (की चिंता करना) - To worry about

161 **Bound for** (की ओर जा रहा; गंतव्य की ओर) - Traveling or heading towards a destination

162 **Brilliant at** (में प्रतिभाशाली) - Very skilled at

163 **Burdened with** (से लदा हुआ) - Weighed down by something oppressive

164 **Busy with** (में व्यस्त) - Actively engaged in doing something

165 **But for** (अगर न होता; के बिना) - If it were not for; except for

166 **Candidate for** (के लिए उम्मीदवार) - A person being considered for a position or role

167 **Capable of** (के लिए सक्षम) - Having the ability or qualities necessary to do something

168 **Capacity for** (की क्षमता) - The maximum amount that something can contain or produce

169 **Care about** (की परवाह करना) - To feel concern for

170 **Careful about** (के बारे में सावधान) - Cautious or particular about something

171 **Careful of** (से सावधान) - Cautious about

172 **Careful with** (के साथ सावधान) - Cautious when handling

173 **Careless about** (के बारे में लापरवाह) - Not giving sufficient attention to something

174 **Cater for** (के लिए व्यवस्था करना) - To provide what is needed or required

175 **Cause of** (का कारण) - A reason for

176 **Cautious about** (के बारे में सावधान) - Careful and avoiding potential problems

177 **Certain about** (के बारे में निश्चित) - Sure about

178 **Certain of** (के बारे में निश्चित) - Completely sure about something

179 **Change in** (में बदलाव) - An alteration in

180 **Characteristic of** (की विशेषता) - A feature or quality belonging typically to a person, place, or thing

181 **Charge against** (के खिलाफ आरोप) - A formal accusation of wrongdoing

182 **Charge of** (का आरोप) - An accusation of a crime

183 **Choice between** (के बीच चुनाव) - Selecting between two or more alternatives

184 **Claim on** (पर दावा) - A right to something

185 **Claim to** (पर दावा) - A right to

186 **Clamour against** (के खिलाफ शोर मचाना) - A loud and persistent demand, often in opposition to something

187 **Clamour for** (के लिए शोर मचाना) - A loud and persistent demand for something, usually an action

188 **Clear about** (के बारे में स्पष्ट) - Having no doubt about

189 **Clever at** (में चतुर) - Skilled at doing

190 **Cling to** (से चिपके रहना) - To hold onto something tightly

191 **Close to** (के नजदीक) - Near to something in distance or time

192 **Comment on** (पर टिप्पणी) - To remark about

193 **Commit to** (के प्रति प्रतिबद्ध होना) - To pledge or bind to a certain course of action

194 **Committed to** (के प्रति प्रतिबद्ध) - Dedicated to

195 **Common to** (के लिए सामान्य) - Shared by two or more people or things

196 **Comparable to** (से तुलनीय) - Similar or equivalent to something else

197 **Compare to** (से तुलना करना (असमान चीज़ों में समानता दिखाना)) - To point out similarities between two unlike things

198 **Compare with** (से तुलना करना (समान चीज़ों की तुलना करना)) - To examine differences between two similar things

199 **Comparison between** (के बीच तुलना) - An evaluation of similarities

200 **Comparison with** (से तुलना) - An examination of two or more items to establish similarities and dissimilarities

201 **Compassion for** (के लिए करुणा) - A concern for the sufferings or misfortunes of others

202 **Compatible with** (के साथ संगत) - Able to exist or perform in harmonious or agreeable combination

203 **Compensate for** (की भरपाई करना) - To make up for something

204 **Compete with** (से प्रतिस्पर्धा करना) - To try to be better than

205 **Complain about** (के बारे में शिकायत करना) - To express dissatisfaction

206 **Complaint about** (के बारे में शिकायत) - An expression of dissatisfaction

207 **Compliment on** (पर बधाई देना; प्रशंसा व्यक्त करना) - To express praise, commendation, or admiration to someone about something

208 **Comply with** (का पालन करना) - To act in accordance with a request, command, or instruction

209 **Composed of** (से बना हुआ) - Made up of specified elements or parts
210 **Compromise with** (से समझौता करना) - To arrive at an agreement by making concessions
211 **Concede to** (को मानना) - To yield or admit to something
212 **Concentrate on** (पर ध्यान केंद्रित करना) - To focus attention on
213 **Concentration on** (पर एकाग्रता) - A focus on
214 **Concern about** (के बारे में चिंता) - A worry about
215 **Concern for** (के लिए चिंता) - Worry or anxiety about something
216 **Concerned about** (के बारे में चिंतित) - Worried about
217 **Concerned with** (से संबंधित) - Involved with or affected by something
218 **Concession to** (को रियायत) - Allowing or yielding to something
219 **Condemn to** (को दंडित करना) - Sentence someone to a particular punishment
220 **Condole with** (के साथ संवेदना व्यक्त करना) - To express sympathy for someone in grief
221 **Confer honour on** (पर सम्मान प्रदान करना) - To bestow an honour on someone
222 **Confide in** (पर भरोसा करना; को बताना) - To tell something to someone in confidence
223 **Confidence in** (में विश्वास) - Trust or belief in someone or something
224 **Confident about** (के बारे में आश्वस्त) - Sure about
225 **Confident of** (के बारे में आश्वस्त) - Having strong belief or full assurance about something
226 **Confine to** (तक सीमित रखना) - To restrict to a particular area
227 **Conform to** (के अनुरूप होना) - To comply with rules, standards, or laws
228 **Conformity with** (के अनुरूप) - Correspondence in form, manner, or character
229 **Confused about** (के बारे में भ्रमित) - Uncertain about
230 **Confused by** (से भ्रमित) - Made uncertain by
231 **Connect to** (से जोड़ना) - To link or join together
232 **Connected to** (से जुड़ा) - Linked to
233 **Connected with** (से संबंधित) - Associated with
234 **Connection between** (के बीच संबंध) - A link among
235 **Connection with** (से संबंध) - An association with
236 **Conscious of** (के प्रति सचेत) - Aware of something
237 **Consent to** (को सहमति देना) - To give permission for or approval of something
238 **Consist of** (से मिलकर बना होना) - Made up of
239 **Consistent with** (के अनुरूप) - In agreement or harmony with something
240 **Contact with** (से संपर्क) - A communication with
241 **Contempt for** (के प्रति अवमानना) - A strong feeling of lack of respect for someone or something
242 **Content with** (से संतुष्ट) - In a state of peaceful happiness with something
243 **Contented with** (से संतुष्ट) - Satisfied with
244 **Contrary to** (के विपरीत) - Opposite in nature or character to something
245 **Contrast with** (से अंतर करना) - To differ strikingly from something else
246 **Contribute to** (में योगदान देना) - To give towards a common purpose
247 **Contribution to** (में योगदान) - Giving or adding to something
248 **Control of** (का नियंत्रण) - A power over
249 **Control over** (पर नियंत्रण) - The power or authority to direct something
250 **Convert to** (में परिवर्तित करना) - To change from one form to another
251 **Convicted of** (का दोषी ठहराना) - Having been found guilty of a criminal offense
252 **Convinced of** (के बारे में आश्वस्त) - Completely certain about something
253 **Convulsed with** (अनियंत्रित हँसी या मनोभाव से प्रभावित) - Affected by uncontrollable laughter or emotion
254 **Cope with** (से निपटना) - To deal with difficulties
255 **Copy of** (किसी चीज़ की प्रतिलिपि) - A reproduction or imitation of something
256 **Correspond to** (के अनुरूप होना) - Equivalent to
257 **Count on** (पर भरोसा करना) - To rely on someone
258 **Courteous to** (के प्रति विनम्र) - Polite and respectful to someone
259 **Cover with** (से ढकना) - To place something over or on top of something else
260 **Covered with** (से ढका हुआ) - Having a layer of something on top
261 **Crave for** (की तीव्र इच्छा रखना) - To have an intense desire for something
262 **Crazy about** (का दीवाना) - Very enthusiastic about
263 **Criticism of** (आलोचना) - A negative assessment or remark about something
264 **Crowded with** (से भरा हुआ) - Full of people
265 **Cruel to** (के प्रति क्रूर) - Causing pain to
266 **Cruelty to** (के प्रति क्रूरता) - Deliberately cruel or

harsh treatment of a person or animal

267 **Cure for** (उपचार या इलाज) - Something that removes a disease or solves a problem

268 **Curious about** (के बारे में उत्सुक) - Eager to know about

269 **Dabble in** ((शौक के तौर पर) में हाथ आजमाना) - To take part in an activity in a casual or superficial way

270 **Damage to** (को नुकसान) - A harm to

271 **Danger of** (का खतरा) - A risk of

272 **Deaf to** (के प्रति बहरा) - Unwilling or unable to listen or respond to something

273 **Deal with** (से निपटना) - To handle or manage

274 **Dear to** (किसी के लिए प्रिय) - Regarded with deep affection by someone

275 **Decamp with** (के साथ भाग जाना) - To leave suddenly, taking something with you

276 **Decide on** (का निर्णय करना) - To make a choice about

277 **Decline in** (में गिरावट होना) - To become smaller, fewer, or less

278 **Decrease in** (में कमी) - A reduction in

279 **Dedicate to** (को समर्पित करना) - To devote to a purpose

280 **Dedicated to** (को समर्पित) - Devoted to

281 **Dedication to** (के प्रति समर्पण) - A commitment to

282 **Defective in** (में दोषपूर्ण) - Having a fault or flaw

283 **Deficient in** (में कमी) - Lacking in

284 **Delay in** (में देरी) - A postponement in

285 **Delight at** (पर प्रसन्न होना) - To feel or express great pleasure in something

286 **Delighted at** (पर प्रसन्न) - Very pleased at

287 **Delighted by** (से प्रसन्न) - Very pleased by

288 **Delighted with** (से प्रसन्न) - Feeling or expressing great pleasure about something

289 **Deliverance from** (से मुक्ति) - Being freed or saved from something unpleasant

290 **Deluged with** (बड़ी संख्या में चीजों से अभिभूत होना) - Overwhelmed by a large number of things

291 **Demand for** (की मांग) - A need for

292 **Departure from** (से प्रस्थान) - A leaving from

293 **Depend upon** (पर निर्भर होना) - To rely on

294 **Dependent on** (पर निर्भर) - Relying on or influenced by something

295 **Deprive of** (से वंचित करना) - To prevent someone from having or doing something

296 **Deprived of** (से वंचित) - Lacking or deprived of something

297 **Derive from** (से प्राप्त करना) - To obtain from a source

298 **Derived from** (से व्युत्पन्न) - Obtained from

299 **Descent from** (वंशानुगत) - The origin or background of someone in terms of family or nationality

300 **Description of** (का वर्णन) - An account of

301 **Desire for** (की इच्छा) - A strong wish to have or do something

302 **Desist from** (से परहेज करना) - To stop doing something

303 **Despair of** (से निराश होना) - To lose or give up hope

304 **Destined for** (के लिए नियत) - Intended for or certain to have a particular fate

305 **Destined to** (के लिए निश्चित) - Certain to do or have something

306 **Detach from** (से अलग करना) - To separate or disconnect from something

307 **Determined to** (के लिए दृढ़ संकल्प) - Firmly resolved to

308 **Devote to** (को समर्पित करना) - To give time or attention to

309 **Devoted to** (के प्रति समर्पित) - Feeling or displaying strong affection or dedication towards something

310 **Differ from** (से भिन्न होना) - Unlike or dissimilar to something

311 **Differ with** (से असहमत होना) - To disagree with someone

312 **Difference between** (के बीच अंतर) - A point or way in which people or things are not the same

313 **Difference in** (में अंतर) - A variation in

314 **Different from** (से भिन्न) - Not the same as something else

315 **Difficult for** (के लिए कठिन) - Hard for someone

316 **Difficulty in** (में कठिनाई) - A problem or trouble in doing something

317 **Difficulty with** (के साथ कठिनाई) - A trouble with

318 **Diligent in** (में मेहनती) - Showing persistent effort in doing something

319 **Disadvantage to** (के लिए नुकसानदायक) - Something that puts someone in an unfavourable position

320 **Disagree with** (से असहमत होना) - To have a different opinion

321 **Disappointed at** (पर निराश) - Sad because of unmet expectations

322 **Disappointed by** (से निराश) - Let down by

323 **Disappointed in** (में निराश) - Let down by someone

324 **Disappointed with** (से निराश) - Unhappy because someone or something was not as good as expected
325 **Disapprove of** (को अस्वीकार करना) - To have an unfavourable opinion
326 **Disastrous to** (के लिए विनाशकारी) - Extremely harmful or damaging
327 **Discriminate against** (के खिलाफ भेदभाव करना) - To treat a person or group worse than others
328 **Discriminate between** (के बीच भेदभाव करना) - To recognize or perceive the difference between things
329 **Discrimination in** (में भेदभाव) - The practice of treating one person or group differently from another in an unfair way
330 **Discussion about** (के बारे में चर्चा) - A conversation about
331 **Disgrace to** (के लिए कलंक) - A person or thing that brings shame or discredit
332 **Disgust at** (से घृणा; के लिए घृणा) - A strong feeling of dislike or disapproval caused by something unpleasant
333 **Disgust with** (से घृणा; के लिए घृणा) - A strong feeling of dislike or disapproval caused by something unpleasant
334 **Disgusted at** (पर घृणा महसूस करना; से बेहद घिन आना) - Feeling revulsion at
335 **Disgusted by** (से घृणा महसूस करना; से बेहद घिन आना) - Feeling strong disapproval or revulsion caused by something
336 **Disgusted with** (से घृणा महसूस करना; से तीव्र अरुचि होना) - Feeling revulsion towards
337 **Dislike of** (से नापसंदगी) - An aversion to
338 **Dispense with** (के बिना काम चलाना) - To forgo or do without something
339 **Displeased with** (से नाराज़) - Feeling or showing irritation or dissatisfaction towards something
340 **Dispose of** (का निपटारा करना) - To get rid of
341 **Disposed to** (के लिए तैयार) - Inclined or willing to do something
342 **Dissolve in** (में घुलना) - To become absorbed in a liquid and form a solution
343 **Distance from** (से दूरी) - The amount of space between two points or places
344 **Distinguish between** (के बीच अंतर करना) - To recognize or identify the difference between two things
345 **Distinguish one thing from another** (एक चीज़ को दूसरे से अलग करना) - To recognize or identify the difference between two specific things
346 **Distinguished from** (से अलग) - Different from others
347 **Divide into** (में बाँटना) - To separate into parts
348 **Divorce from** (से तलाक लेना) - To legally end a marriage with someone
349 **Doubt about** (के बारे में संदेह) - Uncertainty about something
350 **Doubtful about** (के बारे में संदिग्ध) - Uncertain about
351 **Drag into** (में घसीटना) - To involve someone in an unpleasant situation
352 **Dream of** (का सपना देखना) - To imagine or hope for
353 **Drenched with** (से भीगा हुआ) - Completely soaked or saturated with a liquid
354 **Dressed in** (में सजा हुआ) - Wearing
355 **Due to** (के कारण) - Caused by or ascribable to something
356 **Duty to** (के प्रति कर्तव्य) - A moral or legal obligation towards someone
357 **Dwell in** (में रहना) - To live or reside in a place
358 **Eager for** (के लिए उत्सुक) - Very keen to have
359 **Easy for** (के लिए आसान) - Not difficult for
360 **Effect on** (पर प्रभाव) - An impact on
361 **Eligible for** (के लिए योग्य) - Qualified to participate in or receive something
362 **Embarrassed about** (के बारे में शर्मिंदा) - Feeling shame about
363 **Embarrassed by** (से शर्मिंदा) - Made to feel shame by
364 **Emphasis on** (पर जोर) - A stress on
365 **Enamoured with** ((किसी व्यक्ति) से मोहित) - Filled with love for or fascinated by a person
366 **Enchant with** (से मंत्रमुग्ध) - To fill with delight or charm
367 **Endowed with** (से संपन्न) - Provided with a quality, ability, or asset
368 **Engaged in** (में व्यस्त) - Busy or occupied with an activity
369 **Engaged to** (सगाई करना) - Committed to marry someone
370 **Enlarge on** (पर विस्तार से बताना) - To speak or write about something in more detail
371 **Enmity against** (के खिलाफ शत्रुता) - A state of active hostility against someone
372 **Enmity towards** (के प्रति शत्रुता) - A state of deep hostility towards someone
373 **Enquire of** ((किसी व्यक्ति) से पूछताछ करना) - To ask someone for information
374 **Enraged at** (पर क्रोधित होना) - Extremely angry

about something

375 **Enraged with** (से क्रोधित होना) - Extremely angry with someone

376 **Enter upon** (आरंभ करना; शुरू करना) - To begin or undertake a task or duty

377 **Enthusiasm for** (के लिए उत्साह) - An eagerness for

378 **Enthusiastic about** (के बारे में उत्साहित) - Very interested in

379 **Entitled to** (का हकदार) - Having the right to do or have something

380 **Enveloped in** (में लिपटा हुआ) - Completely surrounded or covered by something

381 **Envious of** (से ईर्ष्या करना) - Feeling or showing envy towards someone

382 **Equal to** (के बराबर) - Having the same value, measure, or importance as something

383 **Equipped with** (से सुसज्जित) - Provided with

384 **Equivalent to** (के समतुल्य) - Equal in value, amount, meaning, or importance

385 **Eradicate from** (को पूरी तरह से हटाना) - To completely remove or destroy something from a place

386 **Essential for** (के लिए आवश्यक) - Absolutely necessary for something

387 **Essential to** (के लिए अनिवार्य) - Necessary to

388 **Example of** (का उदाहरण) - An instance of

389 **Excellent at** (में उत्कृष्ट) - Very good at

390 **Exception to** (अपवाद) - A person or thing excluded from a general rule

391 **Exchange for** (के बदले में) - To give or receive something in return for another thing

392 **Excited about** (के बारे में उत्साहित) - Feeling enthusiasm about

393 **Excited by** (से उत्साहित) - Made enthusiastic by

394 **Excuse for** (का बहाना) - A reason given for

395 **Exempt from** (से मुक्त) - Free from an obligation

396 **Exemption from** (से मुक्त होना) - The state of being released from an obligation or liability

397 **Expect from** (से अपेक्षा करना) - To anticipate from someone

398 **Experience in** (में अनुभव) - Knowledge or skill gained through involvement in something

399 **Experience of** (का अनुभव) - Practical contact with or observation of facts or events

400 **Experienced in** (में अनुभवी) - Having experience in

401 **Expert at** (में विशेषज्ञ) - Very skilled at something

402 **Expert in** (में निपुण) - A person having special knowledge or skill in a field

403 **Explanation for** (का स्पष्टीकरण) - A reason for

404 **Explanation of** (की व्याख्या) - A description of

405 **Expose to** (के संपर्क में लाना) - To make vulnerable to

406 **Exposed to** (के संपर्क में) - Made vulnerable to

407 **Exposure to** (के संपर्क में आना) - The state of being in contact with something

408 **Exult at** (पर बहुत खुश होना) - To feel or show triumphant elation about something

409 **Exult over** (पर जश्न मनाना) - To rejoice or celebrate something

410 **Faced with** (का सामना करना) - To confront a situation

411 **Fail in** (में असफल होना) - Unsuccessful in

412 **Failed in** (में असफल होना) - Having been unsuccessful in achieving something

413 **Failure in** (में असफलता) - A lack of success in

414 **Failure of** (की विफलता) - The lack of success in doing or achieving something

415 **Faith in** (में आस्था) - A trust in

416 **Faithful to** (के प्रति वफादार) - Remaining loyal and steadfast to someone or something

417 **Fall in** (में गिरावट) - A decrease in number, amount, or level

418 **Fall into** (में गिर जाना; में पड़ जाना) - To drop into; to enter a particular state

419 **False to** (के प्रति बेवफा; अविश्वसनीय) - Not faithful or loyal to someone or something

420 **Familiar to** (के लिए परिचित) - Well known or easily recognized by someone

421 **Familiar with** (से परिचित) - Having good knowledge of or being well acquainted with something

422 **Famous for** (के लिए प्रसिद्ध) - Known or recognized by many people for something

423 **Far from** (से दूर) - At a great distance in space or time from something

424 **Fascinated by** (से मंत्रमुग्ध) - Strongly attracted or interested in something

425 **Fascinated with** (से आकर्षित) - Strongly attracted or interested in something

426 **Fatal to** (के लिए घातक) - Causing death or disaster to someone or something

427 **Fatigued by** (से थका हुआ) - Made tired or exhausted by something

428 **Fault with** (में दोष ढूंढना) - A weakness or imperfection in someone or something

429 **Favourable to** (के अनुकूल) - Expressing approval or support for someone or something

430 **Fear of** (का डर) - The feeling of being scared

or afraid of something

431 **Fearful of** (से डरा हुआ) - Feeling afraid or anxious about the possibility of something

432 **Fed up with** (से परेशान) - Annoyed or unhappy because you have had too much of something

433 **Feed on** (पर जीना, का भोजन करना) - To eat or survive on something as a regular source of food

434 **Felicitated on** (पर बधाई पाना) - To express or offer congratulations for something

435 **Fight for** (के लिए लड़ना) - To struggle to achieve

436 **Fill with** (से भरना) - To put a large amount of something into a space

437 **Filled with** (से भरा हुआ) - Full of

438 **Fined for** (के लिए जुर्माना भरना) - Required to pay an amount of money as a penalty

439 **Fit for** (के योग्य) - Suitable for

440 **Fit to** (के योग्य) - Suitable to do something

441 **Focus on** (पर ध्यान देना) - To concentrate attention on

442 **Fond of** (का शौक़ीन) - Having an affection or liking for someone or something

443 **Fondness for** (के लिए प्रेम) - An affection or liking for someone or something

444 **Forgive for** (के लिए क्षमा करना) - To pardon someone for

445 **Fortunate in** (में भाग्यशाली होना) - Having good luck or success in something

446 **Free from** (से मुक्त) - Released or exempt from something unpleasant or restrictive

447 **Free of** (से रहित, से खाली) - Not containing something harmful or unwanted

448 **Friendly to** (के प्रति मित्रवत) - Kind towards

449 **Friendly with** (के साथ मित्रवत) - Behaving in a pleasant, kind way towards someone

450 **Frightened of** (से डरा हुआ) - Scared of

451 **Full of** (से भरा हुआ) - Containing a lot of

452 **Generous to** (के प्रति उदार) - Giving freely to

453 **Generous with** (के साथ उदार) - Willing to give

454 **Gentle with** (के साथ कोमल) - Careful and kind with

455 **Gifted with** (से प्रतिभाशाली, से संपन्न) - Naturally having a special talent or quality

456 **Glad about** (के बारे में खुश) - Pleased about something

457 **Glad of** (के लिए खुश) - Pleased about

458 **Glance at** (पर नज़र डालना) - To look briefly at

459 **Good at** (में निपुण, में कुशल) - Having ability or skill in something

460 **Good for** (के लिए अच्छा, के लिए उपयुक्त) - Beneficial or suitable for someone or something

461 **Grateful for** (के लिए आभारी) - Thankful for

462 **Grateful to** (के प्रति आभारी) - Thankful to

463 **Greedy for** (के लिए लालची) - Having a strong desire for

464 **Guard against** (से बचाव करना) - To take precautions against

465 **Guilty of** (का दोषी) - Responsible for wrongdoing

466 **Habituated to** (का आदी) - Accustomed to

467 **Hanker after** (की लालसा रखना) - To have a strong desire for

468 **Happy about** (के बारे में खुश) - Pleased about

469 **Happy with** (से खुश) - Satisfied with

470 **Harmful to** (के लिए हानिकारक) - Damaging to

471 **Hatred for** (किसी चीज़ के प्रति नफ़रत) - An intense dislike for something

472 **Heartbroken over** (पर दिल टूटा हुआ; से अत्यंत दुखी) - Extremely sad and upset about something

473 **Heir to** (का उत्तराधिकारी) - An inheritor of

474 **Hinge on** (पर निर्भर होना) - To depend entirely on

475 **Honest with** (के साथ ईमानदार) - Truthful with

476 **Hope for** (की आशा करना) - To expect and desire something to happen

477 **Hopeful of** (के लिए आशावान) - Optimistic about

478 **Hostile to** (के प्रति शत्रुतापूर्ण) - Antagonistic toward

479 **Identical to** (के समान) - Exactly the same as

480 **Ignorant of (about)** (से अनजान, से अपरिचित) - Lacking knowledge about something

481 **Ill with** (से बीमार) - Sick with

482 **Impatient with** (से अधीर) - Lacking patience with

483 **Important for** (के लिए महत्वपूर्ण) - Significant for

484 **Impossible for** (के लिए असंभव) - Not possible for

485 **Impressed by** (से प्रभावित) - Favorably affected by

486 **Improvement in** (में सुधार) - A change that makes something better

487 **In contrast to** (से विपरीत) - Strikingly different from something

488 **Incapable of** (में असमर्थ) - Unable to do

489 **Inclined to** (के प्रति झुका हुआ) - Tending toward

490 **Independent of** (से स्वतंत्र) - Not relying on

491 **Indifferent to** (के प्रति उदासीन) - Lack of interest in

492 **Inferior to** (की तुलना में हीन) - Lower in quality or rank

493 **Influence on** (पर प्रभाव) - An effect on

494 **Inquire into** (की जाँच करना) - To investigate something

495 **Insist on** (पर जोर देना) - To demand firmly

496 **Inspired by** (से प्रेरित) - Motivated by something

497 **Intent on** (पर तुला हुआ) - Determined to do something

498 **Interest in** (में रुचि) - A curiosity about

499 **Interested in** (में रुचि रखना) - Wanting to know or learn about

500 **Interfere with** (में हस्तक्षेप करना) - To get involved in others' matters

501 **Introduce to** (से परिचित कराना) - Present (someone) to another person

502 **Invest in** (में निवेश करना) - To put money into

503 **Involved in** (में शामिल) - Taking part in

504 **Jealous of** (से ईर्ष्यालु) - Envious of

505 **Junior to** (उम्र में छोटा) - Lower in rank or status

506 **Keen on** (का शौक़ीन) - Eager or excited about

507 **Kind to** (के प्रति दयालु) - Behaving in a caring way towards

508 **Knock at** (पर खटखटाना) - To strike (a door) to attract attention

509 **Known for** (के लिए जाना जाता है) - Famous for

510 **Lack of** (की कमी) - The state of being without or not having enough of something

511 **Liable for** (के लिए उत्तरदायी) - Legally responsible for

512 **Limit to** (तक सीमित) - To restrict something to a particular amount or scope

513 **Listen to** (को सुनना) - To pay attention to sounds

514 **Look after** (की देखभाल करना) - To take care of

515 **Look at** (को देखना) - To direct eyes towards

516 **Look for** (को ढूंढना) - To search for

517 **Loyal to** (के प्रति वफादार) - Faithful to

518 **Married to** (से विवाहित) - Wedded to

519 **Opposite to** (के विपरीत) - Contrary to

520 **Proud of** (पर गर्व करना) - Pleased with

521 **Qualified for** (के लिए योग्य) - Having qualifications for

522 **Responsible for** (के लिए जिम्मेदार) - Having duty for

523 **Satisfied with** (से संतुष्ट) - Content with

524 **Similar to** (के समान) - Resembling

525 **Sorry for** (के लिए क्षमा चाहना) - Feeling regret for

526 **Superior to** (से बेहतर) - Better than

527 **Sure of** (के बारे में निश्चित) - Certain of

528 **Surprised at** (पर आश्चर्यचकित) - Amazed at

529 **Suspicious of** (पर संदेह करना) - Distrustful of

530 **Tired of** (से थका हुआ) - Weary of

531 **Wait for** (का इंतज़ार करना) - To stay expecting someone

532 **Worried about** (के बारे में चिंतित) - Anxious about

The Hindu Editorial Vocabulary

If you have ever prepared for any competitive exam in India, you have heard this advice at least once: ***"Read The Hindu daily."*** Every topper says it. Every coaching institute recommends it. But have you ever wondered why *this* newspaper specifically?

The answer is simple. The Hindu uses a level of English that is a step above everyday language. Its editorials are written with precision, and the vocabulary is rich but not unnecessarily complex. These are exactly the kind of words that appear in SSC, Banking, Defense, DSSSB, and other competitive examinations. Whether the question is a Cloze Test, Reading Comprehension, Synonyms-Antonyms, One Word Substitutions or Fill in the Blanks, the words are often picked from the same pool that newspapers like The Hindu use regularly.

Here is a real example. Suppose you read a headline: **"The government faced criticism for the abrogation of the agreement."** If you know that **Abrogation** means the formal cancellation of a law or agreement (निराकरण), you understood the headline. Now the same word shows up in your exam as an OWS or Synonym-Antonym question. You already know it. Not because you crammed it the night before, but because you had seen it, understood it, and remembered it naturally.

And the benefit does not stop at exams. These words will help you write better essays, speak more confidently in interviews, and understand news, articles, and reports without reaching for a dictionary every few minutes. When you use words like **Acquiescence**, **Pragmatic**, or **Unprecedented** in the right context, it reflects a level of command over the language that sets you apart.

But let us face it. Not everyone has the time or habit to read The Hindu every single day. And even those who do, often skip the difficult words or forget them within a week. That is exactly why this chapter exists.

This chapter is a ready-made collection of **over 1000 words** picked from The Hindu editorials. Each word comes with:

- Hindi meaning for quick understanding
- Clear English definition
- Synonyms and Antonyms for exam-style questions

It is worth noting that **many frequently used editorial words have already been covered in the OWS and Synonyms-Antonyms chapters of this book**. Words that have appeared directly in previous exam papers are likely to be found there. The words in this chapter are the remaining ones, equally important but not yet covered elsewhere. Together, these chapters give you a complete editorial vocabulary bank.

Study 15 to 20 words a day. Read the meaning, go through the synonyms and antonyms, and try to use at least a few in your own sentences. If you combine this with the Root Words chapter, you will not just memorise these words but actually understand why they mean what they mean. That is when vocabulary truly becomes yours.

F4 The Hindu Vocabulary
(Important for SSC & Other Exams)

1 **Abetment** (N.) - उकसावा, बहकावा
Encouraging or helping someone commit a wrongful act
Syno: Assistance, Aid, Support

2 **Ablation** (N.) - शरीर के हिस्से को काटकर निकालना
Surgical removal of tissue or melting away of a surface by heat
Syno: Removal, Excision, Resection

3 **Abolition** (N.) - उन्मूलन
Formal ending of a system, practice, or institution
Syno: Repeal, Dissolution, Abolishment

4 **Abrogation** (N.) - रद्दीकरण
Formal repeal or cancellation of a law or agreement
Syno: Abolition, Repeal, Abolishment

5 **Absenteeism** (N.) - अनुपस्थिति
Habitual absence from work or duty
Syno: Truancy, Nonattendance, Absence

6 **Abstention** (N.) - परहेज
Deliberately refraining from doing something
Syno: Abnegation, Avoidance, Eschewal

7 **Accrete** (V.) - साथ-साथ बढ़ना
Grow by gradual accumulation or coalescence
Syno: Accumulate, Gather, Collect

8 **Acquaintance** (N.) - परिचित
A person one knows slightly; familiarity with something
Syno: Familiarity, Experience, Involvement

9 **Acquiescence** (N.) - मौन सहमति
Reluctant acceptance of something without protest
Syno: Obedience, Assent, Compliance

10 **Activism** (N.) - सक्रियतावाद
Vigorous campaigning for political or social change
Syno: Advocacy, Campaigning, Militancy

11 **Actuarial** (Adj.) - बीमा गणित संबंधी
Relating to insurance risk and premium calculation
Syno: Statistical, Probabilistic, Insurance-related

12 **Adaptability** (N.) - ढलने की क्षमता, अनुकूल होने की योग्यता
Ability to adjust to new conditions
Syno: Elasticity, Flexibility, Workability

13 **Addictive** (Adj.) - व्यसनकारी, लत लगाने वाला
Causing a strong, hard-to-break habit or dependency
Syno: Addicting, Habit-forming, Narcotic

14 **Adjournment** (N.) - स्थगन
Suspension of a meeting or session to a later time
Syno: Discontinuance, Suspension, Lapse

15 **Adjudication** (N.) - न्यायनिर्णय
Formal judgment or decision on a disputed matter
Syno: Sentence, Ruling, Disposition

16 **Advisability** (N.) - उचितता
Quality of being sensible and worth recommending
Syno: Desirability, Feasibility, Expediency

17 **Affirmative** (Adj.) - सकारात्मक, स्वीकारात्मक
Agreeing with or consenting to a statement or request
Syno: Positive, Approving, Confirmatory

18 **Agglomeration** (N.) - ढेर
A collected mass or jumbled assemblage of things
Syno: Assortment, Variety, Jumble

19 **Agrarian** (Adj.) - कृषि संबंधी
Relating to farming or cultivation of land
Syno: Agricultural, Farming, Rural

20 **Alarmist** (Adj.) - भय फैलाने वाला, डर दिखाने वाला
Exaggerating dangers to cause needless worry or panic
Syno: Sensationalist, Scaremongering

21 **Albeit** (Conj.) - हालांकि
Even though
Syno: Although, Though, But

22 **Alcoholism** (N.) - शराब की लत
Addiction to alcohol consumption
Syno: Drunkenness, Intemperance, Insobriety

23 **Alibi** (N.) - कहीं और होने का सबूत
Proof of being elsewhere when a crime occurred
Syno: Excuse, Justification, Reason

24 **Alienation** (N.) - अलगाव

Feeling of isolation or estrangement from a group
Syno: Estrangement, Disaffection, Divorce

25 **Allegations** (N.) - आरोप
Claims or assertions made without proof
Syno: Accusations, Indictments, Charges

26 **Amalgamation** (N.) - विलय
Combining or merging multiple entities into one
Syno: Amalgam, Mixture, Mix

27 **Ambit** (N.) - सीमा
The scope, extent, or bounds of something
Syno: Scope, Realm, Confines

28 **Ambush** (N./V.) - घात; घात लगाना
A hidden sudden attack (N.); To attack from hiding (V.)
Syno: Attack, Ambushment, Trap

29 **Amicus Curiae** (N.) - न्यायमित्र
An adviser to a court on a case they are not party to
Syno: Friend of the court

30 **Ammunition** (N.) - गोला-बारूद
A supply of bullets, shells, and other projectiles
Syno: Munitions, Ordnance, Shells

31 **Analysed** (V.) - विश्लेषण किया
Examined in detail
Syno: Dissect, Examine, Assess

32 **Animus** (N.) - दुश्मनी
Strong dislike or hostile attitude
Syno: Hostility, Grudge, Hatred

33 **Annexation** (N.) - अधिग्रहण
Forcible takeover and incorporation of territory
Syno: Confiscation, Expropriation, Takeover

34 **Anoint** (V.) - तेल लगाकर पवित्र करना; चुनना/नियुक्त करना
Apply oil ceremonially; formally choose or appoint
Syno: Smear, Paint, Coat

35 **Anonymity** (N.) - गुमनामी
State of being unknown or unidentifiable
Syno: Obscurity, Silence, Oblivion

36 **Anticipation** (N.) - पूर्वानुमान
Expectation or prediction of something future
Syno: Expectation, Expectancy, Expectance

37 **Antifederalist** (Adj.) - संघवाद-विरोधी
Opposing a strong centralized federal government
Syno: Decentralist

38 **Antiquity** (N.) - प्राचीनता, बहुत पुराना समय
The ancient past, especially before the Middle Ages
Syno: Ancientness, Antiquation, Age

39 **Apologist** (N.) - पक्ष समर्थक
One who defends or argues in favour of something controversial
Syno: Defender, Supporter, Advocate

40 **Appeasement** (N.) - तुष्टीकरण
Making concessions to avoid conflict
Syno: Pacification, Conciliation, Placation

41 **Appellate** (Adj.) - अपीलीय
Relating to legal appeals, especially in court
Syno: Revisory, Reviewing

42 **Apportion** (V.) - बाँटना
Divide and distribute among several parties
Syno: Allot, Assign, Allocate

43 **Appreciable** (Adj.) - उल्लेखनीय
Large enough to be noticed or measured
Syno: Distinguishable, Noticeable, Audible

44 **Aquifer** (N.) - जलाधार
Underground rock layer that holds or transmits groundwater
Syno: Water table, Underground reservoir

45 **Arbitrage** (N.) - अंतर बाज़ार सौदा
Profiting by buying and selling the same asset in different markets
Syno: Speculation, Trading, Exploitation

46 **Arbitrate** (V.) - मध्यस्थता करना
Settle a dispute as a neutral third party
Syno: Decide, Settle, Determine

47 **Archetype** (N.) - मूल प्रतिरूप
An original model or most typical example of something
Syno: Original, Prototype, Source

48 **Arguable** (Adj.) - विवादास्पद
Open to disagreement; debatable
Syno: Questionable, Debatable, Disputable

49 **Artillery** (N.) - तोपखाना
Large-calibre guns used in warfare on land
Syno: Guns, Weapons, Ordnance

50 **Ascension** (N.) - ऊपर चढ़ना, उच्च पद पर पहुँचना
Rising to an important position or higher level
Syno: Ascent, Climb, Rising

51 **Aspersion** (N.) - कलंक, बदनामी
A damaging remark attacking someone's reputation
Syno: Criticism, Dart, Attack

52 **Assassinate** (V.) - हत्या करना
To murder an important person, often for

political reasons
Syno: Murder, Slay, Execute

53 **Assessment** (N.) - मूल्यांकन
Evaluation of the nature, quality, or ability of something
Syno: Evaluation, Appraisal, Estimation

54 **Assimilate** (V.) - अपने में मिला लेना, घुल-मिल जाना
To absorb and integrate into a wider group or culture
Syno: Absorb, Integrate, Incorporate

55 **Asymmetric** (Adj.) - असमान, विषम
Not equal or balanced in shape, size, or arrangement
Syno: Oblique, Uneven, Unsymmetrical

56 **Asymmetry** (N.) - असमानता, असंतुलन
Lack of symmetry or balance between parts
Syno: Imbalance, Disproportion, Tension

57 **Atmosphere** (N.) - वायुमंडल, माहौल
The layer of gases surrounding a planet; overall mood of a place
Syno: Ambience, Mood, Environment

58 **Attendant** (Adj.) - साथ आने वाला, संबंधित
Occurring together with or as a result of something
Syno: Resultant, Consequent, Due (to)

59 **Auspices** (N.) - संरक्षण, देखरेख
Guidance, support, or patronage of a person or organization
Syno: Sponsorship, Patronage, Aegis

60 **Authenticity** (N.) - प्रामाणिकता
The quality of being genuine or real
Syno: Truth, Genuineness, Verity

61 **Authoritarian** (Adj./N.) - सत्तावादी; निरंकुश शासक
Demanding strict obedience (Adj.); A person who demands obedience (N.)
Syno: Dictatorial, Totalitarian, Autocratic

62 **Backslide** (V.) - पतन होना
To revert to a worse condition; relapse
Syno: Relapse, Regress, Lapse

63 **Bald claim** (N.) - निराधार दावा
An assertion made without any supporting evidence
Syno: Bare assertion, Unsubstantiated claim, Unsupported allegation

64 **Bankruptcy** (N.) - दिवालियापन
State of being unable to repay one's debts
Syno: Ruin, Failure, Insolvency

65 **Bar** (V.) - रोकना
To prevent, prohibit, or block entry or action
Syno: Prevent, Prohibit, Exclude

66 **Barbarism** (N.) - बर्बरता
Extreme cruelty or brutality
Syno: Savagery, Brutality, Cruelty

67 **Barrage** (N.) - बौछार, गोलाबारी
An overwhelming quantity of something; concentrated bombardment
Syno: Flurry, Bombardment, Volley

68 **Barricade** (N./V.) - अवरोध, बैरिकेड लगाना
A barrier erected to block passage; to block with a barrier
Syno: Fence, Barrier, Wall

69 **Baseless** (Adj.) - निराधार
Without any factual foundation; groundless
Syno: Unreasonable, Unfounded, Groundless

70 **Bastion** (N.) - गढ़
A stronghold or fortified place; a defender of something
Syno: Stronghold, Fortress, Citadel

71 **Battalion** (N.) - बटालियन, सैन्य टुकड़ी
A large organized body of troops
Syno: Army, Troops, Soldiers

72 **Bedrock** (N.) - आधारशिला, नींव
The fundamental basis or foundation of something
Syno: Foundation, Basis, Cornerstone

73 **Beeline** (N.) - सीधा रास्ता
A straight, direct route between two places
Syno: Shortcut

74 **Befall** (V.) - घटित होना
(Of something bad) to happen to someone
Syno: Happen, Occur, Be

75 **Befit** (V.) - उपयुक्त होना
To be appropriate for; to suit
Syno: Suffice, Fit, Serve

76 **Beleaguer** (V.) - घेराबंदी करना, तंग करना
To surround with forces; to harass or trouble greatly
Syno: Besiege, Attack, Encircle

77 **Belied** (V.) - झुठलाया
Gave a false impression of; disguised or contradicted
Syno: Misrepresented, Obscured, Concealed

78 **Belittling** (V.) - तुच्छ समझना, छोटा दिखाना
Making someone or something seem unimportant
Syno: Slighting, Insulting, Demeaning

79 **Belligerence** (N.) - उग्रता, युद्धप्रियता
Aggressive or hostile behaviour; readiness to fight

Syno: Aggression, Aggressiveness, Hostility

80 **Benchmark** (N.) - मानक
A standard or reference point for comparison
Syno: Standard, Criterion, Measure

81 **Bereaved** (Adj.) - शोक में डूबा हुआ, किसी अपने को खोने का दुख झेलने वाला
Grieving the death of a close person
Syno: Grieving, Bereft, Widowed

82 **Bicker** (V.) - तकरार करना
To argue over petty, trivial matters
Syno: Squabble, Quarrel, Argue

83 **Bilateral** (Adj.) - द्विपक्षीय
Involving or affecting two sides or parties
Syno: Two-sided, Mutual, Reciprocal

84 **Billow** (N./V.) - लहर; उमड़ना, फूलना
A large swelling wave or rolling mass (N.); To swell outward or surge like a wave (V.)
Syno: Wave, Swell, Surge

85 **Blaze** (N./V.) - ज्वाला, भड़कना
A large fiercely burning fire (N.); To burn intensely (V.)
Syno: Flame, Inferno, Conflagration

86 **Blithely** (Adv.) - बेफिक्री से, लापरवाही से
In a casually cheerful and carefree manner
Syno: Breezily, Laughingly, Joyfully

87 **Bloat** (V.) - फूलना
To swell or puff up
Syno: Inflate, Distend, Swell

88 **Bloodbath** (N.) - नरसंहार, हत्याकांड
An event involving widespread killing or slaughter
Syno: Massacre, Slaughter, Carnage

89 **Blueprint** (N.) - खाका, योजना
A detailed plan or design for something
Syno: Plan, Strategy, Program

90 **Bluff** (N./V.) - धोखा, झांसा देना
An attempt to deceive someone about one's intentions or abilities (N.); To deceive or mislead by pretending confidence (V.)
Syno: Deception, Pretense, Fraud

91 **Blurb** (N.) - संक्षिप्त प्रचार-विवरण
A short promotional description of a book, film, etc.
Syno: Synopsis, Summary, Write-up

92 **Bluster** (N./V.) - शेखी, डींग मारना
Loud aggressive talk with little effect (N.); To talk loudly and aggressively with little effect (V.)
Syno: Rhetoric, Bombast, Braggadocio

93 **Bollard** (N.) - सड़क या बंदरगाह पर लगा मोटा खंभा
A short thick post used to secure ropes or block traffic
Syno: Post, Pillar, Stanchion

94 **Bombardment** (N.) - बमबारी, गोलाबारी
A continuous attack with bombs, shells, or missiles
Syno: Barrage, Flurry, Volley

95 **Botch** (V.) - बिगाड़ना
To carry out a task badly or carelessly
Syno: Fumble, Blow, Bungle

96 **Botched up** (Adj.) - गड़बड़ किया हुआ
Spoiled by poor or careless work; messed up
Syno: Mishandled, Bungled, Messed up

97 **Bravura** (N.) - कुशलता, बेहतरीन कला-प्रदर्शन
Great technical skill and brilliance in a performance
Syno: Virtuosity, Brilliance, Mastery

98 **Brazenness** (N.) - निर्लज्जता, ढिठाई
Shameless and impudent boldness
Syno: Gall, Nerve, Arrogance

99 **Breathless** (Adj.) - हाँफता हुआ, साँस फूलना
Gasping for breath; feeling suffocated or airless
Syno: Close, Suffocating, Stifling

100 **Breed** (V.) - उत्पन्न करना, पैदा करना
To produce offspring; to give rise to something
Syno: Generate, Produce, Engender

101 **Brink** (N.) - कगार
The very edge of a steep place or boundary
Syno: Verge, Cusp, Edge

102 **Briquettes** (N.) - ईंधन की ईंटें
Small compressed blocks of coal dust or charcoal used as fuel
Syno: Blocks

103 **Buff** (N.) - शौकीन
A person very enthusiastic and knowledgeable about a subject
Syno: Lover, Sucker, Fan

104 **Bumbling** (Adj.) - अनाड़ी
Clumsy and ineffectual; incompetent
Syno: Clumsy, Inept, Incompetent

105 **Bureaucrat** (N.) - नौकरशाह
A government official, especially one rigidly following procedures
Syno: Clerk, Official, Functionary

106 **Burgeoned** (V.) - तेज़ी से बढ़ा
Grew or increased rapidly
Syno: Increased, Rose, Swelled

107 **Buttress** (N./V.) - सहारा / मज़बूत करना
A support structure for a wall; to strengthen or reinforce
Syno: Anchor, Pillar, Backbone

108 **By-election** (N.) - उपचुनाव
An election held to fill a vacancy during a term
Syno: By-poll, Special election

109 **Byproduct** (N.) - उपउत्पाद
A secondary product resulting from a manufacturing process
Syno: Derivation, Derivative, Derivate

110 **Cadaver** (N.) - शव
A dead body, especially one used for dissection
Syno: Corpse, Remains, Carcass

111 **Calibrated** (Adj.) - सही तरीके से मापा हुआ, जाँचा-परखा
Carefully measured or adjusted to a standard
Syno: Measured, Computed, Calculated

112 **Caliphate** (N.) - ख़िलाफ़त (ख़लीफ़ा का शासन)
An Islamic state ruled by a caliph
Syno: Islamic state

113 **Callousness** (N.) - संवेदनहीनता; निर्दयता
Cruel insensitivity and disregard for others
Syno: Heartlessness, Coldness, Insensitivity

114 **Campaigner** (N.) - अभियानकर्ता
A person who actively works for a cause or goal
Syno: Activist, Advocate, Crusader

115 **Canister** (N.) - डिब्बा
A cylindrical container, usually metal, for storing things
Syno: Barrel, Tin, Drum

116 **Capitalism** (N.) - पूँजीवाद
Economic system where trade and industry are privately owned for profit
Syno: Free market, Private enterprise, Laissez-faire

117 **Capsized** (V.) - पलट गया
Overturned in water (of a boat)
Syno: Overturned, Collapsed, Keeled

118 **Carcasses** (N.) - शव (जानवरों के)
Dead bodies of animals
Syno: Corpses, Stiffs, Relics

119 **Carnivore** (N.) - मांसाहारी
An animal that feeds on flesh
Syno: Predator, Meat-eater

120 **Case scenario** (N.) - संभावित स्थिति
A hypothetical situation or possible outcome
Syno: Hypothetical situation, Possible outcome, Eventuality

121 **Casteless** (Adj.) - जातिविहीन
Not belonging to or recognizing any caste
Syno: Classless, Egalitarian, Unclassified

122 **Cataclysmic** (Adj.) - प्रलयंकारी
Causing sudden, violent destruction; disastrous
Syno: Disastrous, Fatal, Unfortunate

123 **Catchment** (N.) - जलग्रहण
An area from which rainfall drains into a river or reservoir
Syno: Drainage basin, Watershed, Collection area

124 **Causality** (N.) - कार्य-कारण संबंध
The relationship between cause and effect
Syno: Cause, Causation, Determinant

125 **Cavalcade** (N.) - जुलूस
A formal procession of vehicles or people on horseback
Syno: Fleet, Convoy, Parade

126 **Caveat** (N.) - चेतावनी
A warning or condition attached to something
Syno: Warning, Caution, Admonition

127 **Censorship** (N.) - अभिव्यक्ति पर नियंत्रण
Suppression of speech or information deemed objectionable
Syno: Suppression

128 **Centrist** (Adj.) - मध्यमार्गी
Having moderate political views; neither left nor right
Syno: Moderate, Central, Middle-of-the-road

129 **Cereals** (N.) - अनाज
Grains used for food, such as wheat, rice, or corn
Syno: Grains, Crops, Food staples

130 **Certitude** (N.) - निश्चितता
Complete certainty or firm conviction
Syno: Certainty, Assurance, Confidence

131 **Charade** (N.) - दिखावा; नाटक
An absurd pretense or hollow act presented as genuine
Syno: Pretense, Facade, Farce

132 **Chariness** (N.) - सावधानी
Caution or wariness
Syno: Care, Carefulness, Caution

133 **Checkpoint** (N.) - चौकी, नाका
A manned barrier where travellers undergo security checks
Syno: Inspection point, Control point,

Roadblock

134 **Chequered** (Adj.) - उतार-चढ़ाव भरा
Marked by varied fortunes; having both good and bad periods
Syno: Varied, Diverse, Uneven

135 **Chink** (N.) - दरार
A narrow opening or crack, especially one admitting light
Syno: Crack, Gap, Fissure

136 **Chip away** (V.) - धीरे-धीरे कम करना
To gradually reduce or weaken something
Syno: Erode, Wear down, Diminish

137 **Chirpy** (Adj.) - खुशमिज़ाज
Cheerful and lively
Syno: Perky, Vivacious, Sprightly

138 **Choreograph** (V.) - नृत्य निर्देशन करना
Plan the steps for a dance; coordinate an event in detail
Syno: Plan, Prepare, Organize

139 **Chunk** (N.) - टुकड़ा
A thick, solid piece of something
Syno: Piece, Lump, Hunk

140 **Churn** (V.) - मथना
To agitate vigorously; to swirl or stir forcefully
Syno: Swirl, Stir, Agitate

141 **Citation** (N.) - संदर्भ
A reference or quotation from a source
Syno: Reference, Quotation, Mention

142 **Civilisation** (N.) - सभ्यता
An advanced stage of human society with developed culture
Syno: Lifestyle, Culture, Society

143 **Civilization** (N.) - सभ्यता
An advanced stage of human social and cultural development
Syno: Lifestyle, Culture, Society

144 **Claims** (V.) - दावा करना
To state or assert something as true
Syno: Alleges, Insists, Asserts

145 **Clairvoyance** (N.) - भविष्य देखने की शक्ति, पारलौकिक दृष्टि
The supposed ability to perceive things beyond normal senses
Syno: Sixth sense, Telepathy, Second sight

146 **Clamour for** (V.) - ज़ोरदार माँग करना
To demand something loudly or urgently
Syno: Demand, Call (for), Press (for)

147 **Clampdown** (N.) - कड़ी कार्रवाई
A strict action to suppress or restrict something
Syno: Crackdown, Suppression, Repression

148 **Clause** (N.) - खंड, धारा
A specific provision or condition in a document or law
Syno: Provision, Stipulation, Term

149 **Clutter** (N.) - अव्यवस्था
A messy, untidy collection of things
Syno: Disorder, Mess, Jumble

150 **Coalescence** (N.) - आपस में मिलकर एक होना
The merging of separate elements into one whole
Syno: Fusion, Synthesis, Mixture

151 **Coalition** (N.) - गठबंधन
A temporary alliance, especially of political parties or states
Syno: Alliance, Union, Partnership

152 **Coarser** (Adj.) - अधिक मोटा, अधिक खुरदरा
Rougher in texture; consisting of large particles
Syno: Grained, Sandy, Granular

153 **Codify** (V.) - नियमों को व्यवस्थित रूप से लिखना
Arrange laws or rules into a systematic code
Syno: Classify, Rank, Distinguish

154 **Coexistence** (N.) - साथ-साथ रहना, एक साथ मौजूद होना
The state of existing together at the same time or place
Syno: Occurrence, Coincidence, Concurrence

155 **Cognisant** (Adj.) - अवगत, जानकार
Aware or having knowledge of something
Syno: Aware, Conscious, Mindful

156 **Cognition** (N.) - समझने-जानने की प्रक्रिया
The mental process of gaining knowledge and understanding
Syno: Perception, Observation, Intellection

157 **Cognitive** (Adj.) - सोचने-समझने से जुड़ा
Relating to mental processes like perception, memory, and reasoning
Syno: Reasonable, Empirical, Analytic

158 **Coherence** (N.) - तालमेल, तर्कसंगत जुड़ाव
The quality of being logical and consistent
Syno: Consistency, Logic, Unity

159 **Collaborating** (V.) - सहयोग करना
Working jointly on an activity or project
Syno: Cooperating, Partnering

160 **Collegium** (N.) - कॉलेजियम
A body of people with a shared professional or academic purpose
Syno: Association, Society, Academy

161 **Collision** (N.) - टक्कर
A violent impact between two moving objects
Syno: Crash, Shock, Impact

162 **Colourless** (Adj.) - रंगहीन, नीरस
Lacking colour; dull and uninteresting
Syno: Dull, Drab, Bland

163 **Commensurable** (Adj.) - तुलनीय
Measurable by a common standard; proportionate
Syno: Proportional, Commensurate, Comparable

164 **Commissioning** (V.) - चालू करना, नियुक्त करना
Ordering or authorizing the production of something
Syno: Authorizing, Appointing, Inaugurating

165 **Communalise** (V.) - सांप्रदायिक बनाना
To give a communal character; create communal divisions
Syno: Polarize, Sectarianize

166 **Communally** (Adv.) - सामूहिक रूप से
In a shared or collective manner
Syno: Collectively, Jointly, Cooperatively

167 **Communiqué** (N.) - सरकारी बयान / आधिकारिक घोषणा
An official announcement or statement, especially to the media
Syno: Posting, Release, Advertisement

168 **Comorbidity** (N.) - एक साथ कई बीमारियाँ होना
The presence of additional diseases alongside a primary one
Syno: Coexisting condition, Concurrent disorder, Co-occurring illness

169 **Complacence** (N.) - आत्मसंतोष
Smug, uncritical satisfaction with oneself
Syno: Self-satisfaction, Smugness, Contentment

170 **Complication** (N.) - जटिलता
A difficulty that makes something harder
Syno: Difficulty, Problem, Obstacle

171 **Complicit** (Adj.) - मिलीभगत में शामिल
Involved with others in wrongdoing or illegal activity
Syno: Involved, Implicated, Culpable

172 **Complicity** (N.) - मिलीभगत
Involvement as an accomplice in wrongdoing
Syno: Conspiracy, Collusion, Connivance

173 **Comprising** (V.) - से मिलकर बना होना
Consisting of; being made up of
Syno: Containing, Including, Consisting (of)

174 **Concordance** (N.) - सामंजस्य
Agreement or harmony between people or things
Syno: Understanding, Concord, Compliance

175 **Concurrent** (Adj.) - समकालिक, एक साथ होने वाला
Happening or existing at the same time
Syno: Synchronous, Synchronic, Simultaneous

176 **Condemnable** (Adj.) - निंदनीय
Deserving strong disapproval or censure
Syno: Abhorrent, Abominable, Detestable

177 **Condemnation** (N.) - कड़ी निंदा
Expression of very strong disapproval
Syno: Reprimand, Censure, Punishment

178 **Conditioned** (Adj.) - अभ्यस्त, प्रशिक्षित
Trained or accustomed to behave in a certain way
Syno: Prepared, Primed, Ripe

179 **Conduit** (N.) - नाली, माध्यम
A channel or pipe for conveying fluids or as a passage
Syno: Pipe, Tube, Channel

180 **Confrontational** (Adj.) - टकरावपूर्ण
Tending to deal with situations aggressively; hostile
Syno: Aggressive, Militant, Hostile

181 **Connived** (V.) - मिलीभगत की
Secretly allowed something wrong to happen
Syno: Winked, Ignored, Tolerated

182 **Connotation** (N.) - छिपा हुआ अर्थ, अप्रत्यक्ष मतलब
An implied or associated meaning beyond the literal sense
Syno: Implication, Sense, Meaning

183 **Conservatism** (N.) - रूढ़िवाद
Preference for traditional values and resistance to change
Syno: Conservativeness, Traditionalism, Ultraconservatism

184 **Consigned** (V.) - सौंपा, हवाले किया
Delivered or handed over to someone's custody
Syno: Sent, Transported, Shipped

185 **Consolation** (N.) - सांत्वना
Comfort received after a loss or disappointment
Syno: Comforting, Reassurance, Consoling

186 **Consonance** (N.) - सामंजस्य
Agreement or harmony between opinions or actions
Syno: Harmony, Agreement, Accord

187 **Consortium** (N.) - संघ
An association of several companies or organizations
Syno: Organization, Institute, Association

188 **Constituent** (Adj./N.) - घटक
A component or integral part of a whole
Syno: Member, Component, Ingredient

189 **Constructive** (Adj.) - सृजनात्मक, सुधारात्मक
Serving a useful purpose; helpful and productive
Syno: Creative, Productive, Causal

190 **Construed** (V.) - व्याख्या की
Interpreted a word or action in a particular way
Syno: Interpreted, Understood, Perceived

191 **Consulate** (N.) - वाणिज्य दूतावास
The office or building of a consul in a foreign city
Syno: Legation, Diplomatic mission

192 **Consultation** (N.) - परामर्श
A meeting to seek advice or discuss something
Syno: Discussion, Consult, Debate

193 **Containing** (V.) - नियंत्रित या शामिल करना
Holding back or restraining something
Syno: Restraining, Curbing, Controlling

194 **Contends** (V.) - तर्क करना
Argues or asserts firmly
Syno: Argues, Asserts, Maintains

195 **Contestation** (N.) - विवाद
The act of disputing or challenging something
Syno: Dispute, Controversy, Disputation

196 **Context** (N.) - संदर्भ
The circumstances surrounding an event or statement
Syno: Environment, Surroundings, Atmosphere

197 **Continuance** (N.) - निरंतरता
The state of continuing to exist or operate
Syno: Duration, Lifespan, Life

198 **Continuum** (N.) - लगातार चलने वाली श्रृंखला, निरंतर क्रम
A continuous sequence where extremes differ but adjacent parts blend
Syno: Spectrum, Scale, Sequence

199 **Contracted** (V.) - सिकुड़ा, छोटा हुआ
Became smaller, shorter, or decreased in size
Syno: Shrunk, Diminished, Reduced

200 **Contraction** (N.) - सिकुड़ना, सिकुड़ाव
The process of becoming smaller or shorter
Syno: Compression, Squeezing, Contracting

201 **Convened** (V.) - एकत्रित किया
Called together for a meeting or assembly
Syno: Summoned, Mustered, Called

202 **Convergence** (N.) - एक बिंदु पर आना, एक साथ मिलना
The act of coming together from different directions
Syno: Confluence, Convergency, Merging

203 **Conversion** (N.) - परिवर्तन
The act of changing from one form or state to another
Syno: Transformation, Transition, Shift

204 **Convocation** (N.) - दीक्षांत समारोह
A formal assembly, especially a university graduation ceremony
Syno: Assembly, Conference, Meeting

205 **Coquettishly** (Adv.) - नखरे से
In a playfully flirtatious manner
Syno: Flirtatiously, Teasingly, Playfully

206 **Cordon** (N.) - घेराबंदी, सुरक्षा घेरा
A line of guards or barriers blocking access to an area
Syno: Barricade, Bumper, Buffer

207 **Coronal** (Adj.) - मुकुटाकार
Relating to a crown or crown-like structure
Syno: Crown-like

208 **Cosponsor** (V.) - सह-प्रायोजन करना
Jointly sponsor a project or proposal
Syno: Co-fund

209 **Coterminous** (Adj.) - एक ही सीमा वाला
Sharing the same boundaries, extent, or duration
Syno: Coinciding, Congruent, Contiguous

210 **Counterproductive** (Adj.) - उलटा असर करने वाला
Having the opposite of the desired effect
Syno: Unsuccessful, Inefficient, Ineffective

211 **Covet** (V.) - लालच करना
Eagerly desire something, especially belonging to another
Syno: Crave, Want, Desire

212 **Coyness** (N.) - लज्जा
Shyness or reluctance to reveal details or commit
Syno: Shyness, Modesty, Demureness

213 **Crackdown** (N.) - कड़ी कार्रवाई
Strict action to suppress undesirable or illegal activity
Syno: Clampdown, Repression, Suppression

214 **Crematoria** (N.) - श्मशान घाट

Places where dead bodies are cremated
Syno: Crematoriums, Cremation facilities

215 **Crippling** (Adj.) - अपंग करने वाला
Causing severe damage or disability; debilitating
Syno: Debilitating, Incapacitating, Paralyzing

216 **Crosshairs** (N.) - निशाना
Intersecting lines in an optical sight used for aiming
Syno: Sight

217 **Crunch** (N.) - संकट
A critical period of shortage or severe difficulty
Syno: Shortage, Lack, Deficiency

218 **Cryosphere** (N.) - हिममंडल
The frozen water regions of Earth's surface
Syno: Ice cap, Frozen zone

219 **Cull** (V.) - छाँटना
Select and remove from a larger group
Syno: Select, Choose, Pick

220 **Culpability** (N.) - दोष का दायित्व
Responsibility for a fault or wrongdoing; blame
Syno: Blame, Guilt, Onus

221 **Cumulative** (Adj.) - बढ़ता हुआ (जमा होने वाला)
Increasing gradually by successive additions
Syno: Accumulative, Additive, Incremental

222 **Cyclical** (Adj.) - चक्रीय
Occurring in regular, repeated cycles
Syno: Recurring, Periodic, Repetitive

223 **Dabble** (V.) - किसी काम को सरसरी तौर पर करना
Take part in an activity casually or superficially
Syno: Toy with, Tinker with

224 **Damn** (V.) - धिक्कारना
Condemn or express strong disapproval of
Syno: Condemn, Denounce, Curse

225 **Dastard** (N.) - कायर
A mean and contemptible coward
Syno: Coward, Craven, Chicken

226 **Deaddiction** (N.) - नशामुक्ति
The process of curing someone of an addiction
Syno: Rehabilitation, Detoxification, Recovery

227 **Debatable** (Adj.) - विवादास्पद
Open to argument or dispute; questionable
Syno: Questionable, Disputable, Arguable

228 **Debutant** (N.) - नवागंतुक
A person making their first public appearance
Syno: Novice, Newcomer, Beginner

229 **Deceitful** (Adj.) - धोखेबाज़
Deliberately misleading or dishonest
Syno: Fraudulent, Dishonest, Deceptive

230 **Deceleration** (N.) - गति में कमी
A reduction in speed or rate
Syno: Decline, Braking, Slowdown

231 **Decennially** (Adv.) - दस साल में एक बार
Once every ten years
Syno: Every decade, Once per decade

232 **Decipherable** (Adj.) - समझने योग्य
Able to be read, understood, or decoded
Syno: Analyzable, Soluble, Explainable

233 **Deescalate** (V.) - तनाव कम करना
Reduce the intensity or severity of a conflict
Syno: Reduce, Decrease, Minimize

234 **Deescalation** (N.) - तनाव में कमी
Reduction in the intensity of a conflict or tension
Syno: Reduction, Decrease, Deflation

235 **Defection** (N.) - दलबदल
Abandoning one's country, party, or cause for another
Syno: Apostasy, Schism, Scission

236 **Defenceless** (Adj.) - रक्षाहीन
Without any defence; unable to protect oneself
Syno: Vulnerable, Helpless, Susceptible

237 **Defensive** (Adj.) - रक्षात्मक
Used or intended for defence or protection
Syno: Protective, Self-protective, Preventive

238 **Deferment** (N.) - टालना, देरी
The act of postponing something to a later time
Syno: Deferral, Postponement, Delay

239 **Deficient** (Adj.) - अपर्याप्त
Lacking in a required quality or amount
Syno: Incomplete, Partial, Flawed

240 **Definitive** (Adj.) - निर्णायक
Done with authority; final and conclusive
Syno: Authoritative, Classical, Comprehensive

241 **Deflation** (N.) - मुद्रा-संकुचन (कीमतों में गिरावट)
A general decline in prices due to reduced money supply
Syno: Downturn, Shrinkage, Slump

242 **Deflationary** (Adj.) - कीमतें गिराने वाला
Causing or relating to a decline in general prices
Syno: Contractionary, Recessionary

243 **Dehydration** (N.) - निर्जलीकरण
The loss or removal of water from something

Syno: Dryness, Aridity, Dehumidification

244 **Deinduction** (N.) - पद से हटाना
Removal from a position or reversal of induction
Syno: Removal, Reversal, Withdrawal

245 **Deislamise** (V.) - इस्लामीकरण समाप्त करना
Remove or reduce Islamic influence from a society
Syno: Secularise

246 **Deity** (N.) - देवता
A god or goddess
Syno: God, Divinity, Angel

247 **Delegitimise** (V.) - अवैध ठहराना
Destroy or undermine the legitimacy of something
Syno: Invalidate, Nullify, Disenfranchise

248 **Deletion** (N.) - हटाना, मिटाना
The act of removing or erasing something
Syno: Omission, Elimination, Elision

249 **Deliberative** (Adj.) - विचार-विमर्श वाला
Involving careful thought or formal discussion
Syno: Thoughtful, Reflective, Contemplative

250 **Delimitation** (N.) - सीमा तय करना
The act of fixing boundaries or limits
Syno: Demarcation, Delineation, Boundary-setting

251 **Delineation** (N.) - चित्रण, रेखांकन
Precise description or portrayal of something
Syno: Sketch, Drawing, Depiction

252 **Demand-driven** (Adj.) - माँग-आधारित
Driven primarily by consumer or market demand
Syno: Market-driven, Consumer-led

253 **Demarcation** (N.) - सीमा निर्धारण
Fixing of a boundary or limit between things
Syno: Distinction, Separation, Discrimination

254 **Demilitarisation** (N.) - सेना हटाना
Removal of military forces and weapons from an area
Syno: Disarmament, Demobilization, Denuclearization

255 **Democratise** (V.) - लोकतांत्रिक बनाना
Make something accessible to everyone
Syno: Standardize, Normalize, Equalize

256 **Demolishment** (N.) - ध्वंस, विध्वंस
The act of pulling down or destroying a structure
Syno: Destruction, Demolition, Devastation

257 **Demolition** (N.) - विध्वंस
The act of destroying or tearing down a structure
Syno: Destruction, Devastation, Havoc

258 **Demonetise** (V.) - नोटबंदी करना
Withdraw currency from use as legal tender
Syno: Invalidate, Withdraw

259 **Demonic** (Adj.) - राक्षसी, आसुरी
Resembling or characteristic of a demon; fiendishly evil
Syno: Sinister, Satanic, Malicious

260 **Demonise** (V.) - बदनाम करना
Portray someone as wicked or threatening
Syno: Vilify, Malign, Denigrate

261 **Demonstrable** (Adj.) - साबित किया जा सकने वाला
Able to be clearly proved or shown
Syno: Verifiable, Confirmable, Empirical

262 **Demoralise** (V.) - हतोत्साहित करना
Cause someone to lose confidence or hope
Syno: Paralyze, Intimidate, Frighten

263 **Demotion** (N.) - पद में गिरावट
Reduction in rank or status
Syno: Firing, Dismissal, Reduction

264 **Depletion** (N.) - कमी, घटाव
Reduction or exhaustion of a resource
Syno: Decrease, Reduction, Decline

265 **Deploy** (V.) - तैनात करना
Position troops, equipment, or resources for action
Syno: Station, Position, Locate

266 **Depreciation** (N.) - मूल्यह्रास
Decrease in the value of an asset over time
Syno: Devaluation, Reduction, Decline

267 **Deprivation** (N.) - वंचना, अभाव
Lack of basic material necessities or comforts
Syno: Lack, Loss, Privation

268 **Derail** (V.) - पटरी से उतारना; बाधित करना
Cause to leave tracks; obstruct or disrupt a process
Syno: Distract, Disturb, Bother

269 **Desirability** (N.) - चाहत, ज़रूरत की अहमियत
Quality of being worth having or wanting
Syno: Feasibility, Advisability, Desirableness

270 **Destabilise** (V.) - अस्थिर करना
Upset the stability of a region or system
Syno: Unsettle, Disturb, Undermine

271 **Destabilise** (V.) - अस्थिर करना
Upset the stability of a region or system
Syno: Undermine, Disrupt, Unsettle

272 **Deterrent** (N.) - निवारक

Something that discourages or prevents an action
Syno: Obstacle, Hurdle, Barrier

273 **Detriment** (N.) - हानि, नुकसान
A cause of harm or damage
Syno: Harm, Damage, Injury

274 **Dexterously** (Adv.) - कुशलतापूर्वक
With skill and cleverness
Syno: Skillfully, Deftly, Adroitly

275 **Diabolism** (N.) - शैतानियत
Devil worship; sorcery or extreme wickedness
Syno: Satanism, Vileness, Wickedness

276 **Diaspora** (N.) - प्रवासी समुदाय
People scattered from their original homeland
Syno: Dispersion, Scattering

277 **Dictate** (N./V.) - आदेश / हुक्म चलाना
An authoritative order; to command or lay down rules
Syno: Order, Command, Decree

278 **Dictum** (N.) - कथन, उक्ति
A formal authoritative pronouncement or statement
Syno: Principle, Rule, Doctrine

279 **Diffusion** (N.) - प्रसार
The spreading of something more widely
Syno: Spreading, Dissemination, Dispersion

280 **Dignitary** (N.) - गणमान्य व्यक्ति
A person of high rank or official importance
Syno: Pillar, Celebrity, Monument

281 **Diktat** (N.) - फरमान
A harsh order imposed by someone in power
Syno: Decree, Edict, Ruling

282 **Dilation** (N.) - फैलाव
The process of becoming wider or more open
Syno: Expansion, Widening, Enlargement

283 **Diligence** (N.) - परिश्रम
Careful and persistent effort in work
Syno: Effort, Assiduity, Persistence

284 **Dilution** (N.) - कमज़ोर करना, पतला करना
Making something weaker or less effective
Syno: Weakening, Thinning, Attenuation

285 **Diorama** (N.) - छोटा 3D मॉडल (दृश्य)
A three-dimensional miniature model of a scene
Syno: Model, Tableau, Display

286 **Diplomacy** (N.) - कूटनीति
Skill in dealing with people tactfully; the management of international relations
Syno: Manners, Tact, Statesmanship

287 **Directive** (N.) - निर्देश
An official or authoritative instruction
Syno: Instruction, Edict, Order

288 **Directives** (N.) - निर्देश
Official or authoritative instructions
Syno: Instructions, Edicts, Orders

289 **Disadvantageous** (Adj.) - प्रतिकूल
Creating unfavourable or harmful conditions
Syno: Unfavorable, Adverse, Negative

290 **Disaffection** (N.) - असंतोष, नाराज़गी
Dissatisfaction or disloyalty, especially towards authority
Syno: Estrangement, Alienation, Schism

291 **Disagreement** (N.) - असहमति
Difference of opinion; lack of consensus
Syno: Dispute, Controversy, Debate

292 **Disarmament** (N.) - हथियार कम करना / निशस्त्रीकरण
Reduction or withdrawal of military forces and weapons
Syno: Demilitarization, Demobilization, Denuclearization

293 **Disassociate** (V.) - संबंध तोड़ना
Disconnect or separate oneself from something
Syno: Separate, Divide, Disconnect

294 **Disbursal** (N.) - वितरण, भुगतान
Payment or distribution of money from a fund
Syno: Distribution, Allocation, Apportionment

295 **Discomfit** (V.) - असहज करना
Make someone feel uneasy, embarrassed, or frustrated
Syno: Frustrate, Baffle, Thwart

296 **Disconcertingly** (Adv.) - विचलित करने वाले ढंग से
In a disturbing or unsettling manner
Syno: Disturbingly, Alarmingly, Unsettlingly

297 **Discrepancies** (N.) - गड़बड़ियाँ, फ़र्क
Inconsistencies or unexpected differences
Syno: Difference, Distinctness, Distinctiveness

298 **Discrete** (Adj.) - अलग, पृथक
Individually separate and distinct
Syno: Single, Separate, Detached

299 **Discretionary** (Adj.) - अपनी मर्ज़ी पर आधारित
Left to individual choice or judgment
Syno: Optional, Voluntary, Elective

300 **Disgruntle** (V.) - असंतुष्ट करना
Make someone angry or dissatisfied
Syno: Anger, Infuriate, Outrage

301 **Disincentive** (N.) - हिम्मत तोड़ने वाली बात
A factor that discourages a particular action
Syno: Counterincentive

302 **Disinflation** (N.) - महँगाई की दर में कमी
A reduction in the rate of inflation
Syno: Deceleration, Moderation

303 **Disingenuous** (Adj.) - कपटी, छलपूर्ण
Insincere; pretending ignorance or naivety
Syno: Dishonest, Deceitful, Untruthful

304 **Disjoint** (V.) - अलग करना, तोड़ना
To disconnect or separate into parts
Syno: Separate, Divide, Split

305 **Dismaying** (Adj.) - निराशाजनक
Causing concern and distress
Syno: Disconcerting, Disheartening, Discouraging

306 **Dismissive** (Adj.) - तिरस्कारपूर्ण, उपेक्षापूर्ण
Treating something as unworthy of consideration
Syno: Contemptuous, Disdainful, Scornful

307 **Dispassion** (N.) - भावशून्यता, तटस्थता
Calm detachment; absence of strong emotion
Syno: Detachment, Objectivity, Coldness

308 **Dispensation** (N.) - छूट, विशेष अनुमति
Exemption from a rule or special permission
Syno: Exemption, Permission, Authorization

309 **Dispersal** (N.) - बिखराव
The act of scattering over a wide area
Syno: Dispersion, Scattering, Dissipation

310 **Dispossess** (V.) - बेदखल करना
To deprive someone of land or property
Syno: Evict, Deprive, Expropriate

311 **Disruption** (N.) - रुकावट, बाधा
A disturbance or interruption to a process
Syno: Disturbance, Dislocation, Upheaval

312 **Disruptive** (Adj.) - विघ्नकारी
Causing disturbance or interruption
Syno: Disturbing, Unsettling, Troublesome

313 **Dissection** (N.) - चीर-फाड़, विश्लेषण
Detailed analysis or cutting apart to examine
Syno: Analysis, Examination, Investigation

314 **Dissenter** (N.) - असहमतिकर्ता, मतभेदी
A person who opposes or disagrees with the majority
Syno: Dissident, Renegade, Dissentient

315 **Dissidence** (N.) - मतभेद
Opposition to official policy or authority
Syno: Discord, Strife, Friction

316 **Dissipate** (V.) - तितर-बितर करना
To scatter, disperse, or squander
Syno: Disperse, Dispel, Scatter

317 **Dissolution** (N.) - विघटन
Formal ending or breaking up of an institution
Syno: Breakup, Split, Partition

318 **Distinguish** (V.) - अंतर करना
To recognize or perceive as different
Syno: Differentiate, Discern, Discriminate

319 **Dither** (V.) - दुविधा में होना
To be indecisive; to hesitate
Syno: Hesitate, Vacillate, Waver

320 **Diversion** (N.) - मोड़
Turning something aside from its course; a detour
Syno: Detour, Deflection, Deviation

321 **Diverted** (V.) - मोड़ दिया गया
Redirected or turned aside from a course
Syno: Redirected, Rerouted, Deflected

322 **Dizzying** (Adj.) - चक्कर देने वाला, भ्रमित करने वाला
Causing dizziness or bewilderment
Syno: Giddy, Whirling, Woozy

323 **Doldrums** (N.) - मंदी
A state of stagnation or depression
Syno: Stagnation, Slump, Lull

324 **Dole** (N.) - भत्ता
Government benefit paid to the unemployed
Syno: Philanthropy, Charity, Welfare

325 **Drudgery** (N.) - कठिन और नीरस काम
Hard, menial, or dull work
Syno: Labor, Effort, Toil

326 **Drumbeat** (N.) - नगाड़े की थाप
A persistent, rhythmic pounding or pressure
Syno: Barrage, Flurry, Bombardment

327 **Durability** (N.) - टिकाऊपन
Ability to withstand wear, pressure, or damage
Syno: Longevity, Resilience, Toughness

328 **Dynamism** (N.) - गतिशीलता
Vigorous energy and forcefulness
Syno: Vigor, Energy, Life

329 **Easterly** (Adj.) - पूर्वी
Facing, moving toward, or coming from the east
Syno: Eastern, Eastbound, Eastward

330 **Echelon** (N.) - स्तर
A level or rank in an organization or society
Syno: Level, Ranking, Rank

331 **Ectomorphic** (Adj.) - दुबले-पतले शरीर वाला
Having a lean, slender body type

Syno: Willowy, Lanky, Spindly

332 **Edifice** (N.) - भव्य इमारत
A large, imposing building
Syno: Tower, Cathedral, Structure

333 **Eerily** (Adv.) - भयानक ढंग से
In a strange and frightening manner
Syno: Uncannily, Weirdly, Spookily

334 **Egregiously** (Adv.) - अत्यंत निंदनीय रूप से
In a shockingly bad or flagrant manner
Syno: Grossly, Flagrantly, Unspeakably

335 **Elimination** (N.) - उन्मूलन
Complete removal or getting rid of something
Syno: Removal, Withdrawal, Suspension

336 **Elongated** (Adj.) - लम्बोतरा, खिंचा हुआ
Unusually long or stretched in shape
Syno: Lengthened, Extended, Stretched

337 **Emanate** (V.) - निकलना
To issue or spread out from a source
Syno: Radiate, Emit, Cast

338 **Emblematic** (Adj.) - प्रतीकात्मक
Serving as a symbol of something
Syno: Symbolic, Representative, Representational

339 **Emotive** (Adj.) - भावोत्तेजक
Arousing intense feeling or emotion
Syno: Emotional, Provocative, Stirring

340 **Emphasised** (V.) - ज़ोर दिया, बल दिया
Gave special importance or stress to something
Syno: Stressed, Highlighted, Underscored

341 **Empowerment** (N.) - सशक्तिकरण
Granting authority or power to someone
Syno: Mandate, Accreditation, Authorization

342 **Enactment** (N.) - कानून बनाना, कानून लागू करना
The process of passing a law into effect
Syno: Act, Law, Bill

343 **Enamour** (V.) - मोहित करना
To charm or fill with love and admiration
Syno: Captivate, Enchant, Charm

344 **Enclave** (N.) - घिरा हुआ क्षेत्र
A distinct area enclosed within a larger territory
Syno: District, Neighborhood, Ghetto

345 **Enclosure** (N.) - घेरा, बाड़ा
An area sealed off by a barrier or fence
Syno: Courtyard, Patio, Yard

346 **Encroachment** (N.) - अतिक्रमण
Intrusion on someone's territory or rights
Syno: Intrusion, Invasion, Infringement

347 **Enfeeble** (V.) - दुर्बल बनाना
To make weak or feeble
Syno: Weaken, Soften, Waste

348 **Enforceable** (Adj.) - लागू करने योग्य
Capable of being enforced by law
Syno: Binding, Applicable, Executable

349 **Enmeshed** (Adj.) - उलझा हुआ
Entangled in a difficult situation; trapped
Syno: Trapped, Tangled, Ensnared

350 **Ensconced** (Adj.) - आराम से जमा हुआ
Comfortably and securely settled in a place
Syno: Nestled, Lodged, Perched

351 **Enshroud** (V.) - ढकना
To cover completely; to hide from view
Syno: Conceal, Hide, Obscure

352 **Entourage** (N.) - सेवकों/साथियों का दल
A group of attendants surrounding an important person
Syno: Crew, Suite, Staff

353 **Entrapped** (V.) - फंसाया गया
Caught in a trap; ensnared
Syno: Trapped, Tangled, Ensnared

354 **Entreaties** (N.) - विनती
Earnest requests or appeals
Syno: Pleas, Appeals, Prayers

355 **Entrench** (V.) - मजबूती से स्थापित करना
To establish so firmly that change becomes very difficult
Syno: Root, Embed, Lodge

356 **Enumeration** (N.) - गणना
The act of counting or listing items one by one
Syno: List, Listing, Inventory

357 **Enumerator** (N.) - गणनाकार
A person who counts or lists things, especially officially
Syno: Counter, Tallier, Census-taker

358 **Epicentre** (N.) - भूकंप का केंद्र, मुख्य केंद्र
The central point of something, especially an earthquake
Syno: Focus, Centre, Heart

359 **Equitable** (Adj.) - न्यायसंगत
Fair and impartial
Syno: Impartial, Equal, Objective

360 **Equivocation** (N.) - गोल-मोल बात
Use of ambiguous language to avoid the truth
Syno: Ambiguity, Shuffle, Circumlocution

361 **Errant** (Adj.) - भटकता हुआ
Straying from the accepted course or

standards
Syno: Wayward, Deviant, Straying

362 **Erred** (V.) - गलती की
Made a mistake; was incorrect
Syno: Blundered, Misjudged, Slipped

363 **Erroneously** (Adv.) - गलत तरीके से
In a wrong or incorrect manner
Syno: Mistakenly, Incorrectly, Inaccurately

364 **Euthanise** (V.) - इच्छा मृत्यु देना
Put to death humanely to end suffering
Syno: Mercy kill

365 **Evacuation** (N.) - निकासी
Removal of people from a dangerous place
Syno: Exodus, Emigration, Withdrawal

366 **Eventful** (Adj.) - घटनापूर्ण
Full of notable events or incidents
Syno: Momentous, Significant, Memorable

367 **Eventuality** (N.) - संभावना
A possible event or outcome, especially an unpleasant one
Syno: Possibility, Potential, Prospect

368 **Eviction** (N.) - बेदखली
Legal expulsion of someone from a property
Syno: Removal, Deposition, Ouster

369 **Evocation** (N.) - स्मरण
The act of bringing a feeling, memory, or image to mind
Syno: Recall, Summoning, Conjuring

370 **Evocatively** (Adv.) - भावोत्तेजक ढंग से
In a way that strongly evokes images, memories, or feelings
Syno: Suggestively, Reminiscently, Hauntingly

371 **Evolution** (N.) - विकास, धीरे-धीरे बदलाव
Gradual development or change over time
Syno: Progress, Development, Progression

372 **Exalted** (Adj.) - उच्च
Held in high regard; elevated in rank or status
Syno: Glorious, Famous, Celebrated

373 **Excavator** (N.) - खुदाई मशीन
A large machine for digging and moving earth
Syno: Digger, Backhoe, Earthmover

374 **Exchequer** (N.) - राजकोष
The treasury or funds of a government or institution
Syno: Pocket, Finances, Resources

375 **Excluded** (V.) - बाहर रखा गया
Denied access to; barred from
Syno: Barred, Prohibited, Banned

376 **Exclusivist** (Adj.) - बहिष्कारवादी, दूसरों को बाहर रखने वाला
Favouring exclusion of others from rights or privileges
Syno: Sectarian, Separatist, Elitist

377 **Executive** (Adj.) - कार्यकारी
Having the power to put plans or actions into effect
Syno: Administrative, Managerial, Directorial

378 **Exemplified** (V.) - उदाहरण प्रस्तुत किया
Served as a typical example of
Syno: Illustrated, Demonstrated, Explained

379 **Exhaustively** (Adv.) - संपूर्ण रूप से
In a thorough and comprehensive manner
Syno: Systematically, Thoroughly, Extensively

380 **Exhortation** (N.) - जोशीला आह्वान, प्रेरणा
An earnest urging or strong encouragement to do something
Syno: Recommendation, Suggestion, Warning

381 **Exoneration** (N.) - दोषमुक्ति
Official clearing of someone from blame or guilt
Syno: Pardon, Forgiveness, Clearing

382 **Expansive** (Adj.) - विस्तृत
Covering a wide area; extensive
Syno: Extensive, Broad, Wide

383 **Expediency** (N.) - सुविधावाद
Prioritizing convenience or practicality over principles
Syno: Expedience, Desirability, Feasibility

384 **Expedient** (Adj.) - सुविधाजनक, उचित (भले ही नैतिक न हो)
Convenient and practical, though possibly improper
Syno: Prudent, Desirable, Wise

385 **Expeditiously** (Adv.) - शीघ्रता से
Quickly and efficiently
Syno: Quickly, Swiftly, Rapidly

386 **Exploitative** (Adj.) - शोषणकारी
Unfairly using others for one's own advantage
Syno: Abusive, Manipulative, Predatory

387 **Exposition** (N.) - विवरण
A detailed explanation of an idea or theory
Syno: Explanation, Elucidation, Clarification

388 **Expulsion** (N.) - निष्कासन
The act of forcing someone out of an organization or place
Syno: Deportation, Displacement, Migration

389 **Extrapolate** (V.) - अनुमान लगाना

Estimate or conclude from known facts or trends
Syno: Derive, Understand, Decide

390 **Extremism** (N.) - अतिवाद
Holding extreme political or religious views
Syno: Excessiveness, Excess, Radicalism

391 **Extremist** (N.) - उग्रवादी
A person holding extreme or fanatical political or religious views
Syno: Radical, Extreme, Rabid

392 **Fag** (N.) - कठिन काम
A tedious or exhausting task
Syno: Struggle, Labor, Work

393 **Fait accompli** (N.) - हो चुकी घटना
Something already done that cannot be changed
Syno: Done deal, Foregone conclusion

394 **Falsified** (V.) - झूठा साबित किया, जाली बनाया
Altered information or evidence to mislead
Syno: Distorted, Misrepresented, Misinterpreted

395 **Fanaticism** (N.) - कट्टरता
Excessive and obsessive zeal or enthusiasm
Syno: Zeal, Obsession, Infatuation

396 **Fanciful** (Adj.) - काल्पनिक
Overimaginative and unrealistic
Syno: Bizarre, Absurd, Foolish

397 **Farcical** (Adj.) - हास्यास्पद
Absurdly laughable or ridiculous
Syno: Humorous, Comedic, Funny

398 **Fatalities** (N.) - मौतें
Deaths, especially from accidents or disasters
Syno: Casualties, Victims, Losses

399 **Fearmongering** (N.) - भय फैलाना
Deliberately arousing public fear about an issue
Syno: Scaremongering, Alarmism

400 **Federalism** (N.) - संघवाद
A system of government with power shared between central and regional authorities
Syno: Decentralization, Devolution, Regionalism

401 **Federalist** (Adj.) - संघवादी
Supporting or relating to a federal system of government
Syno: Federal, Unionist

402 **Federation** (N.) - संघ
A union of states with a central government but internal autonomy
Syno: Union, Confederacy, Coalition

403 **Festering** (Adj.) - सड़ता हुआ
Becoming infected and producing pus; worsening over time
Syno: Putrefying, Suppurating, Oozing

404 **Festoons** (N.) - माला
Decorative garlands of flowers, leaves, or ribbons hung in curves
Syno: Garlands, Wreaths, Streamers

405 **Fiddle** (V.) - छेड़छाड़ करना
Fidget or tinker with something restlessly or nervously
Syno: Fidget, Toss, Twitch

406 **Fiefdom** (N.) - जागीर
A domain or area under someone's personal control
Syno: Area, Realm, Domain

407 **Filibuster** (N.) - अवरोधी भाषण
A prolonged speech to obstruct legislative proceedings
Syno: Temporize, Obstruct , Stall

408 **Fiscal deficit** (N.) - राजकोषीय घाटा
Gap between a government's spending and its revenue
Syno: Budget deficit, Budgetary shortfall

409 **Flak** (N.) - आलोचना
Strong criticism
Syno: Criticism, Opposition, Hostility

410 **Flank** (V.) - बगल में होना
Be positioned on the side of something or someone
Syno: Border, Adjoin, Skirt

411 **Flashpoint** (N.) - संकट का बिंदु
A place or moment where violence or conflict erupts
Syno: Volcano, Time bomb, Powder keg

412 **Foibles** (N.) - कमज़ोरियाँ
Minor weaknesses or quirks in someone's character
Syno: Weaknesses, Faults, Shortcomings

413 **Foil** (V.) - नाकाम करना
Prevent someone or something from succeeding
Syno: Frustrate, Thwart, Baffle

414 **Foist** (V.) - थोपना
Impose something unwanted on someone
Syno: Impose, Inflict, Wish

415 **Foray** (N.) - छापा
A sudden raid or first attempt into a new area
Syno: Raid, Incursion, Sortie

416 **Forcible** (Adj.) - बलपूर्वक
Done by or involving physical force
Syno: Forceful, Powerful, Potent

417 **Forecaster** (N.) - पूर्वानुमानकर्ता
A person who predicts future events or trends
Syno: Diviner, Prophet, Prognosticator

418 **Foregone** (Adj.) - पूर्व निर्धारित
Predictable; inevitable
Syno: Predetermined, Inevitable, Predictable

419 **Foresee** (V.) - पूर्वाभास करना
Predict or know something before it happens
Syno: Anticipate, Predict, Divine

420 **Foreseeable** (Adj.) - अनुमान लगाने योग्य
Able to be predicted or expected
Syno: Inevitable, Foreseen, Predictable

421 **Forgettable** (Adj.) - भूलने लायक
Easily forgotten; not memorable
Syno: Unremarkable, Unmemorable, Unexceptional

422 **Formative** (Adj.) - निर्माणकारी
Having a strong influence on character or development
Syno: Creative, Productive, Constructive

423 **Fortress** (N.) - किला
A large, strongly built military stronghold
Syno: Stronghold, Citadel, Fortification

424 **Fracas** (N.) - हंगामा
A noisy disturbance or quarrel
Syno: Skirmish, Clash, Battle

425 **Fractious** (Adj.) - चिड़चिड़ा
Irritable, quarrelsome, and hard to control
Syno: Contentious, Controversial, Feisty

426 **Fractured** (Adj.) - टूटा हुआ
Broken, cracked, or disrupted
Syno: Broken, Shattered, Smashed

427 **Fraternal** (Adj.) - भाईचारे का
Brotherly; of or like a brother
Syno: Familial, Brotherly, Friendly

428 **Fray** (N.) - झगड़ा
A competitive struggle, fight, or conflict
Syno: Battle, Struggle, Fight

429 **Fretful** (Adj.) - चिड़चिड़ा
Anxious, worried, and easily irritated
Syno: Irritable, Anxious, Troubled

430 **Frisk** (V.) - तलाशी लेना
Search someone by patting over their clothing
Syno: Search, Pat down, Examine

431 **Frivolously** (Adv.) - बिना गंभीरता के
In a silly, unserious, or irresponsible manner
Syno: Foolishly, Trivially, Irresponsibly

432 **Frontload** (V.) - शुरुआत में अधिक भार डालना
Allocate most effort or cost to the beginning of a process
Syno: Prioritize, Concentrate

433 **Frontrunner** (N.) - अग्रणी
The leading candidate or competitor in a contest
Syno: Leader, Favourite, Top contender

434 **Fudge** (V.) - टाल-मटोल करना
Avoid making a clear decision; evade the issue
Syno: Evade, Hedge, Dodge

435 **Full-blown** (Adj.) - पूर्ण विकसित
Fully developed; complete in all aspects
Syno: Ripe, Complete, Mature

436 **Furlough** (N.) - छुट्टी
A temporary leave of absence, especially from military duty
Syno: Leave, Vacation, Sabbatical

437 **Furore** (N.) - तहलका
An outbreak of public anger or excitement
Syno: Commotion, Stir, Disturbance

438 **Gaffe** (N.) - चूक
An embarrassing blunder or social mistake
Syno: Blunder, Mistake, Error

439 **Gallows** (N.) - फाँसी का तख़्ता
A wooden frame used for hanging criminals
Syno: Scaffold, Gibbet

440 **Gamut** (N.) - पूरी श्रृंखला
The complete range or scope of something
Syno: Spectrum, Range, Scale

441 **Gargantuan** (Adj.) - विशाल
Enormous; extremely large
Syno: Gigantic, Huge, Enormous

442 **Gauntlet** (N.) - दस्ताना; कठिन परीक्षा
A severe ordeal or challenge; also a heavy glove
Syno: Ordeal, Fire, Trial

443 **Genocidal** (Adj.) - नरसंहारात्मक
Relating to the deliberate mass killing of an ethnic or national group
Syno: Murderous, Homicidal, Exterminatory

444 **Geopolitical** (Adj.) - भू-राजनीतिक
Relating to politics influenced by geographical factors
Syno: Geostrategic, Politico-geographic

445 **Geopolitics** (N.) - भू-राजनीति
International politics shaped by geographical

factors
Syno: International relations, Political geography

446 **Gestation** (N.) - गर्भावस्था
The period of development in the womb; also gradual development of a plan or idea
Syno: Pregnancy, Breeding, Spawning

447 **Ghettos** (N.) - बस्ती
Poor, segregated city areas inhabited by minority groups
Syno: Enclaves, Districts, Barrios

448 **Giggle** (V.) - खिलखिलाना
Laugh lightly and repeatedly in a silly way
Syno: Titter, Snicker, Chuckle

449 **Gimmick** (N.) - तरकीब
A clever trick or device to attract attention or business
Syno: Ruse, Scheme, Trick

450 **Gleefully** (Adv.) - खुशी-खुशी
With great joy or delight
Syno: Cheerfully, Delightedly, Merrily

451 **Glimmer** (N.) - झिलमिलाहट
A faint or wavering light
Syno: Glint, Flicker, Sparkle

452 **Granular** (Adj.) - दानेदार
Resembling small grains; highly detailed
Syno: Coarse, Grained, Granulated

453 **Graveness** (N.) - गंभीरता
Seriousness or solemnity
Syno: Intentness, Gravity, Seriousness

454 **Gravitate** (V.) - आकर्षित होना
Be naturally drawn or attracted toward something
Syno: Prefer, Choose, Tend

455 **Grievous** (Adj.) - गंभीर
Very severe or serious
Syno: Harsh, Searing, Severe

456 **Grub** (N.) - खाना
Food
Syno: Food, Provisions, Eats

457 **Gusty** (Adj.) - झोंकेदार
Blowing in strong, sudden bursts of wind
Syno: Windy, Blustery, Breezy

458 **Gutted** (Adj.) - अत्यंत निराश
Extremely disappointed and upset
Syno: Devastated, Destroyed

459 **Hailed** (V.) - प्रशंसा की गई
Praised or acclaimed enthusiastically
Syno: Praised, Applauded, Saluted

460 **Hallmarks** (N.) - विशेषताएँ
Distinctive features, especially of excellence
Syno: Characteristics, Traits, Features

461 **Halving** (V.) - आधा करना
Reducing to half
Syno: Bisecting, Dividing, Splitting

462 **Ham-handed** (Adj.) - अनाड़ी
Clumsy and lacking skill
Syno: Clumsy, Awkward, Heavy-handed

463 **Harangues** (N.) - लंबे-चौड़े भाषण
Lengthy, aggressive speeches
Syno: Tirades, Diatribes, Attacks

464 **Hardliner** (N.) - कट्टरपंथी
A person with firm, uncompromising views
Syno: Hawk, Zealot, Diehard

465 **Haulage** (N.) - ढुलाई, माल परिवहन
Commercial transport of goods
Syno: Transport, Carriage, Conveyance

466 **Haunting** (Adj.) - भुतहा; मन से न जाने वाला
Evocative and hard to forget; eerie
Syno: Eerie, Creepy, Weird

467 **Haywire** (Adj.) - गड़बड़
Out of control; malfunctioning
Syno: Down, Malfunctioning, Broken

468 **Headscarf** (N.) - सिर का दुपट्टा
A cloth covering worn over the head
Syno: Hijab, Veil, Kerchief

469 **Hearken** (V.) - ध्यान से सुनना
To listen attentively
Syno: Listen, Hear, Heed

470 **Heartening** (Adj.) - उत्साहवर्धक
Encouraging; giving hope or optimism
Syno: Promising, Bright, Optimistic

471 **Heist** (N.) - डकैती
A robbery, especially of a bank or institution
Syno: Theft, Grab, Burglary

472 **Heliborne** (Adj.) - हेलिकॉप्टर द्वारा ले जाया गया
Transported by helicopter
Syno: Airlifted, Helicopter-transported

473 **Hijacking** (N.) - अपहरण
Illegally seizing a vehicle, aircraft, or ship in transit
Syno: Commandeering, Seizing, Skyjacking

474 **Hillock** (N.) - टीला
A small hill or mound
Syno: Knoll, Hummock, Foothill

475 **Hindsight** (N.) - बाद की समझ
Understanding of an event only after it has occurred

Syno: Retrospect, Retrospection, Afterthought

476 **Hinterlands** (N.) - भीतरी इलाके
Remote, less developed areas away from cities
Syno: Countryside, Bush, Country

477 **Homage** (N.) - श्रद्धांजलि
Public honour or respect; a tribute
Syno: Tribute, Commendation, Citation

478 **Hooch** (N.) - अवैध शराब
Cheap or illegally made liquor
Syno: Liquor, Booze, Alcohol

479 **Hosting** (V.) - मेज़बानी करना
Organizing and providing a venue for an event
Syno: Accommodating, Housing, Entertaining

480 **Humanitarian** (Adj.) - मानवतावादी
Concerned with promoting human welfare
Syno: Philanthropic, Charitable, Benevolent

481 **Hurl** (V.) - जोर से फेंकना
Throw with great force
Syno: Throw, Fling, Toss

482 **Hypertensive** (Adj.) - उच्च रक्तचाप से संबंधित
Having or relating to abnormally high blood pressure
Syno: High-pressured

483 **Ideological** (Adj.) - वैचारिक
Based on or relating to a set of ideas or beliefs
Syno: Philosophical, Theoretical, Opinionative

484 **Illegality** (N.) - अवैधता
The state of being against the law
Syno: Criminality, Unlawfulness, Abuse

485 **Ill-gotten** (Adj.) - बेईमानी से प्राप्त
Acquired illegally or dishonestly
Syno: Illicit, Stolen, Fraudulent

486 **Imagers** (N.) - तस्वीर लेने वाले उपकरण
Devices used to capture images
Syno: Sensors, Scanners, Cameras

487 **Imaginative** (Adj.) - कल्पनाशील
Creative and full of new ideas
Syno: Inventive, Creative, Innovative

488 **Imbalance** (N.) - असंतुलन
Lack of balance or proportion
Syno: Inequality, Difference, Contrast

489 **Immortality** (N.) - अमरत्व
The state of living forever or lasting fame
Syno: Eternity, Afterlife, Hereafter

490 **Immunise** (V.) - टीका लगाना
Make immune, especially by vaccination
Syno: Vaccinate, Inoculate, Protect

491 **Immunologist** (N.) - प्रतिरक्षा विज्ञानी
A scientist who studies the immune system
Syno: Immunobiologist

492 **Impartiality** (N.) - निष्पक्षता
Fairness without bias or favouritism
Syno: Objectivity, Neutrality, Neutralism

493 **Impend** (V.) - नज़दीक होना / होने वाला होना
Be about to happen
Syno: Loom, Brew, Approach

494 **Impertinence** (N.) - गुस्ताख़ी / बदतमीज़ी
Rudeness or lack of respect
Syno: Disrespect, Insolence, Impudence

495 **Impinge** (V.) - दख़ल देना / असर डालना
Encroach on or negatively affect something
Syno: Encroach, Infringe, Trespass

496 **Implacably** (Adv.) - अटल रूप से
In an unrelenting, uncompromising manner
Syno: Unrelentingly, Inexorably, Uncompromisingly

497 **Implead** (V.) - मुकदमे में पक्ष बनाना
Make someone a party to a lawsuit
Syno: Sue

498 **Implosion** (N.) - भीतरी धमाका / अंदर की ओर धँसना
A violent inward collapse
Syno: Collapse, Contraction

499 **Imposition** (N.) - थोपना; ज़बरदस्ती लागू करना
The act of forcing something unwelcome on someone
Syno: Enforcement, Infliction, Burden

500 **Impractical** (Adj.) - अव्यावहारिक
Not sensible or realistic for actual use
Syno: Useless, Unsuitable, Unusable

501 **Imprimatur** (N.) - अनुमोदन
Official approval or authorization
Syno: Approval, Blessing, Favor

502 **Impropriety** (N.) - अनुचित आचरण / गलत व्यवहार
Behaviour that is improper or socially unacceptable
Syno: Unfitness, Inappropriateness, Disrespect

503 **In question** (Adj. phrase) - विचाराधीन, जिसकी बात हो रही है
Being discussed or under dispute
Syno: Disputed, Debated, Contested

504 **Inaction** (N.) - निष्क्रियता
Lack of action where some is expected
Syno: Inertia, Inactivity, Nonaction

505 **Inactiveness** (N.) - निष्क्रियता
State of not being active or engaged

Syno: Passivity, Dormancy, Inactivity

506 **Inadequacy** (N.) - अपर्याप्तता
Insufficiency or lack of what is needed
Syno: Shortage, Lack, Deficiency

507 **Inaugural** (Adj.) - उद्घाटन संबंधी
Marking the beginning of something
Syno: First, Initial, Original

508 **Incapacitation** (N.) - अक्षम बनाना / असमर्थ होना
State of being made unable to function normally
Syno: Incapacity, Debilitation, Injury

509 **Incarceration** (N.) - कारावास
Imprisonment; confinement in prison
Syno: Captivity, Internment, Imprisonment

510 **Incitement** (N.) - उकसावा
Act of provoking or urging someone to act
Syno: Excitement, Encouragement, Stimulus

511 **Inclusivity** (N.) - समावेशिता
Practice of including all types of people
Syno: Inclusion, Openness, Accessibility

512 **Incoherence** (N.) - असंगति
Lack of logical connection or clarity
Syno: Illogic, Irrationality, Absurdity

513 **Incompetence** (N.) - अयोग्यता
Inability to do something successfully
Syno: Inability, Incompetency, Ineptitude

514 **Inconclusive** (Adj.) - अनिर्णायक
Not leading to a definite result or conclusion
Syno: Indecisive, Uncertain, Open-ended

515 **Inconsistent** (Adj.) - असंगत, अनियमित
Not staying the same; contradictory
Syno: Conflicting, Incompatible, Contradictory

516 **Inconsolable** (Adj.) - जिसे दिलासा न दिया जा सके
So distressed that no comfort is possible
Syno: Heartbroken, Sad, Unhappy

517 **Incredulity** (N.) - अविश्वास
Unwillingness or inability to believe something
Syno: Disbelief, Skepticism, Doubt

518 **Incur** (V.) - झेलना
To bring something unpleasant upon oneself
Syno: Seek, Contract, Pursue

519 **Incursion** (N.) - आक्रमण
A sudden attack or raid into enemy territory
Syno: Invasion, Raid, Foray

520 **Indignity** (N.) - अपमान
Treatment that causes shame or loss of dignity
Syno: Insult, Sarcasm, Outrage

521 **Indiscriminate** (Adj.) - अंधाधुंध
Done randomly without careful judgment
Syno: Random, Haphazard, Arbitrary

522 **Indisputable** (Adj.) - निर्विवाद
Impossible to challenge or deny
Syno: Unquestionable, Undeniable, Irrefutable

523 **Induction** (N.) - प्रवेश, दीक्षा
Formal introduction or admission into a role or position
Syno: Inauguration, Inaugural, Initiation

524 **Inebriate** (V.) - नशे में धुत करना
To make someone drunk; intoxicate
Syno: Intoxicate, Befuddle, Stupefy

525 **Inefficient** (Adj.) - अकुशल
Not achieving maximum productivity; wasteful
Syno: Unsuccessful, Ineffective, Counterproductive

526 **Inequality** (N.) - असमानता
Lack of equality in status, rights, or opportunities
Syno: Difference, Diversity, Distance

527 **Inescapable** (Adj.) - अनिवार्य, जिससे बचा न जा सके
Impossible to avoid or deny
Syno: Inevitable, Necessary, Unavoidable

528 **Inexorably** (Adv.) - अटलता से
In an unstoppable, relentless manner
Syno: Relentlessly, Uncompromisingly, Unalterably

529 **Infamous** (Adj.) - कुख्यात, बदनाम
Well known for something bad; notorious
Syno: Notorious, Shady, Criminal

530 **Infidelity** (N.) - विश्वासघात
Unfaithfulness to a partner or commitment
Syno: Adultery, Betrayal, Disloyalty

531 **Infiltrating** (V.) - घुसपैठ करना
Secretly entering or gaining access to a group or place
Syno: Sneaking, Inserting, Slipping

532 **Infiltration** (N.) - घुसपैठ
Secret entry into a group or place to gain information
Syno: Penetration, Intrusion, Permeation

533 **Inflation** (N.) - महंगाई, मुद्रास्फीति
General rise in prices reducing purchasing power
Syno: Escalation

534 **Infliction** (N.) - प्रहार, थोपना

Act of imposing something unpleasant on someone
Syno: Imposition, Administration, Delivery

535 **Influx** (N.) - प्रवाह
Arrival of large numbers of people or things
Syno: Flow, Flood, Inflow

536 **Informal** (Adj.) - अनौपचारिक
Relaxed, casual, or unofficial
Syno: Unconventional, Unofficial, Unorthodox

537 **Infrequent** (Adj.) - कभी-कभार, विरल
Not occurring often; rare
Syno: Occasional, Sporadic, Odd

538 **Infringement** (N.) - उल्लंघन
Violation of a law, agreement, or right
Syno: Violation, Breach, Trespass

539 **Infusing** (V.) - भरना, समाहित करना
Filling with a particular quality or feeling
Syno: Suffusing, Imbuing, Investing

540 **Infusion** (N.) - समावेश, मिलावट
Introduction of a new element into something
Syno: Introduction, Injection, Instillation

541 **Ingenuity** (N.) - सूझबूझ, चतुराई
Cleverness and originality in solving problems
Syno: Creativity, Creativeness, Imagination

542 **Ingratitude** (N.) - एहसान-फ़रामोशी, कृतघ्नता
Lack of gratitude; unthankfulness
Syno: Ungratefulness, Thanklessness, Unappreciation

543 **Inhabitant** (N.) - निवासी
A person or animal that lives in a particular place
Syno: Resident, Occupant, Resider

544 **Innovative** (Adj.) - नवीन
Introducing new ideas, methods, or products
Syno: Inventive, Creative, Innovational

545 **Inoperative** (Adj.) - निष्क्रिय, अचल
Not working or taking effect
Syno: Dormant, Off, Vacant

546 **Inpatient** (N.) - भर्ती मरीज़
A patient who stays in hospital during treatment
Syno: Resident, Admitted patient

547 **Inquire** (V.) - पूछताछ करना
To ask for information or investigate
Syno: Ask, Examine, Question

548 **Inseparable** (Adj.) - अविभाज्य, अभिन्न
Unable to be separated; always together
Syno: Familiar, Close, Intimate

549 **Insinuation** (N.) - घुमा-फिराकर आरोप, इशारों में लांछन
An indirect hint suggesting something bad
Syno: Innuendo, Imputation, Suggestion

550 **Instability** (N.) - अस्थिरता
State of being unstable and prone to change
Syno: Unsteadiness, Precariousness, Unstableness

551 **Insularity** (N.) - संकीर्णता
Narrow-mindedness; state of being isolated or detached
Syno: Parochialism, Provincialism, Intolerance

552 **Insulate** (V.) - बचाव करना, सुरक्षित रखना
To protect from heat, cold, noise, or external influence
Syno: Isolate, Separate, Segregate

553 **Insulation** (N.) - रोधन; ताप/ध्वनि/विद्युत-रोधन
Material or process preventing loss of heat, sound, or electricity
Syno: Protection, Shielding, Isolation

554 **Insurgency** (N.) - विद्रोह
A rebellion or uprising against authority
Syno: Insurrection, Revolt, Uprising

555 **Insurrection** (N.) - विद्रोह
A violent uprising against a government or authority
Syno: Revolt, Uprising, Mutiny

556 **Intensity** (N.) - तीव्रता
The quality of being extremely strong or forceful
Syno: Enthusiasm, Emotion, Intenseness

557 **Intercept** (V.) - अवरोध करना
To stop or catch something before it reaches its destination
Syno: Grab, Capture, Block

558 **Internalise** (V.) - आत्मसात करना
To absorb attitudes or behaviour into one's nature
Syno: Absorb, Assimilate, Incorporate

559 **Internalize** (V.) - आत्मसात करना
To absorb attitudes or behaviour into one's nature
Syno: Absorb, Assimilate, Incorporate

560 **Interplanetary** (Adj.) - अंतरग्रहीय
Existing or travelling between planets
Syno: Celestial, Cosmic, Extraterrestrial

561 **Interstate** (Adj.) - अंतरराज्यीय
Existing or carried on between states
Syno: Cross-state, Interregional

562 **Intolerant** (Adj.) - असहनशील
Unwilling to accept differing views, beliefs, or behaviour
Syno: Impatient, Complaining, Uncompromising

563 **Intractable** (Adj.) - ज़िद्दी, हठी, काबू में न आने वाला
Hard to control, manage, or resolve
Syno: Rebellious, Rebel, Stubborn

564 **Intrusion** (N.) - अतिक्रमण
The act of entering without permission or welcome
Syno: Encroachment, Incursion, Invasion

565 **Intrusive** (Adj.) - दखलंदाज़
Unwelcomely interfering or disturbing
Syno: Busy, Intruding, Obtrusive

566 **Invalidate** (V.) - अमान्य करना
To make something legally or officially void
Syno: Abolish, Repeal, Cancel

567 **Invalidation** (N.) - अमान्यकरण
The act of making something null or void
Syno: Abolition, Repeal, Nullification

568 **Invasion** (N.) - आक्रमण
Entry into a country or region with armed force
Syno: Incursion, Raid, Foray

569 **Invasive** (Adj.) - आक्रामक
Tending to spread harmfully; intruding on privacy or space
Syno: Intrusive, Encroaching, Aggressive

570 **Inversion** (N.) - उलटाव
The act of reversing the position or order of something
Syno: Reversal, Transposition, Interchange

571 **Ironical** (Adj.) - व्यंग्यात्मक
Happening contrary to what is expected; using irony
Syno: Wry, Sardonic, Paradoxical

572 **Irreparable** (Adj.) - जिसकी भरपाई न हो सके
Impossible to repair or fix
Syno: Irreversible, Irremediable, Irretrievable

573 **Irrevocably** (Adv.) - अपरिवर्तनीय रूप से
In a way that cannot be changed or reversed
Syno: Permanently, Irreversibly, Unalterably

574 **Irrigation** (N.) - सिंचाई
The artificial supply of water to land or crops
Syno: Watering, Sprinkling, Hydration

575 **Iteration** (N.) - पुनरावृत्ति
The repetition of a process; a repeated version
Syno: Repetition, Repeat, Replay

576 **Jester** (N.) - मसखरा, भांड
A professional clown or fool, especially at a medieval court
Syno: Comedian, Jokester, Humorist

577 **Jugglery** (N.) - छल-कपट
Trickery or deception; the art of juggling
Syno: Deception, Trickery, Treachery

578 **Juncture** (N.) - मोड़
A critical point in time or events
Syno: Point, Moment, Minute

579 **Juxtaposition** (N.) - आमने-सामने रखना, तुलनात्मक स्थिति
Placing two things close together for contrasting effect
Syno: Proximity, Abutment, Immediacy

580 **Kerfuffle** (N.) - हंगामा
A commotion or fuss, especially over conflicting views
Syno: Commotion, Stir, Disturbance

581 **Lag** (V./N.) - पिछड़ना, पिछड़न
To fall behind in movement or progress (V.); a delay or interval between events (N.)
Syno: Trail, Straggle, Dawdle

582 **Laggards** (N.) - पिछड़ने वाले
Those who fall behind or are slow to progress
Syno: Snails, Stragglers, Laggers

583 **Lambast** (V.) - कड़ी आलोचना करना
To criticize someone or something harshly
Syno: Scold, Criticize, Lecture

584 **Landmark** (N.) - महत्वपूर्ण स्थान
A significant or historically notable feature or event
Syno: Milestone, Climax, Watershed

585 **Launder** (V.) - कपड़े धोना; धन शोधन करना
To wash clothes; to make illegal money appear legitimate
Syno: Cleanse, Wash, Purify

586 **Laxity** (N.) - ढिलाई, लापरवाही
Lack of strictness or care
Syno: Slackness, Looseness, Negligence

587 **Leeway** (N.) - गुंजाइश
Freedom or flexibility to act within limits
Syno: Slack, Latitude, Space

588 **Legislative** (Adj.) - विधायी
Relating to the making of laws
Syno: Lawmaking, Statutory, Parliamentary

589 **Legislator** (N.) - विधायक
A person who makes laws; a member of a legislature

Syno: Senator, Lawmaker, Lawgiver

590 **Legitimise** (V.) - वैध बनाना
To make something lawful or acceptable
Syno: Enable, Authorize, Validate

591 **Levelling** (V./N.) - समतल बनाना
Making or becoming flat, even, or equal
Syno: Balancing, Equating, Adjusting

592 **Levy** (V.) - वसूल करना
To impose or collect a tax or fee
Syno: Impose, Exact, Collect

593 **Liaise** (V.) - समन्वय करना
To cooperate and communicate with others on a matter
Syno: Communicate, Coordinate, Cooperate

594 **Limbo** (N.) - अनिश्चित स्थिति
A state of uncertainty while awaiting a decision
Syno: Purgatory, Inferno, Underworld

595 **Liquidity** (N.) - तरलता (नकदी उपलब्धता)
Availability of cash or easily convertible assets
Syno: Solvency, Convertibility

596 **Litigate** (V.) - मुकदमा करना
To take a legal dispute to court
Syno: Sue, Prosecute, Contest

597 **Liturgy** (N.) - पूजा विधि
A fixed form of public religious worship or ceremony
Syno: Ritual, Rite, Ceremony

598 **Lofting** (V.) - ऊपर उछालना / फेंकना
Launching or throwing something high into the air
Syno: Throwing, Tossing, Hurling

599 **Loggerhead** (N.) - मतभेद की स्थिति
A state of disagreement or dispute (at loggerheads)
Syno: Impasse, Stalemate, Deadlock

600 **Lumpen** (Adj.) - वंचित और असामाजिक
Dispossessed, degraded, and cut off from society
Syno: Low, Proletarian, Unwashed

601 **Lynching** (N.) - भीड़ द्वारा हत्या
Killing someone by a mob without legal trial
Syno: Execution, Hanging, Killing

602 **Mace** (N.) - गदा
A heavy spiked club used as a weapon
Syno: Cane, Nightstick, Baton

603 **Machination** (N.) - षड्यंत्र
A crafty scheme or plot with sinister intent
Syno: Conspiracy, Scheme, Plot

604 **Maelstrom** (N.) - भंवर
A powerful whirlpool; a turbulent situation
Syno: Vortex, Gulf, Whirlpool

605 **Maintainable** (Adj.) - रखरखाव योग्य
Capable of being maintained or kept in good condition
Syno: Serviceable, Manageable

606 **Mala fide** (Adj./Adv.) - बदनीयत; बदनीयती से
In bad faith; with intent to deceive
Syno: Dishonest, Fraudulent, Deceitful

607 **Mantle** (V.) - ढकना
To cover or envelop
Syno: Cloak, Cover, Shroud

608 **Mapping** (N./V.) - मानचित्रण
Charting, surveying, or establishing correspondences
Syno: Planning, Designing, Shaping

609 **Marginally** (Adv.) - थोड़ा सा
Slightly; to a small extent
Syno: Slightly, Barely, Narrowly

610 **Marshal** (N./V.) - सेना नायक; व्यवस्थित करना
A high-ranking officer; to organize or arrange systematically
Syno: Organize, Mobilize, Summon

611 **Martyrs** (N.) - शहीद
People who suffer or die for a cause
Syno: Victims, Sufferers

612 **Marxist** (Adj./N.) - मार्क्सवादी
Relating to Karl Marx's political and economic theories
Syno: Bolshevik, Leninist, Trotskyite

613 **Materialise** (V.) - साकार होना
To become real or actually happen
Syno: Begin, Originate, Arise

614 **Maul** (V.) - बुरी तरह नोचकर घायल करना
To attack and injure by scratching and tearing
Syno: Abuse, Attack, Manhandle

615 **Maven** (N.) - विशेषज्ञ
An expert or connoisseur
Syno: Expert, Master, Scholar

616 **Maximalist** (Adj./N.) - अधिकतमवादी
One who holds extreme views and refuses to compromise
Syno: Extremist, Radical, Fundamentalist

617 **Meaningless** (Adj.) - अर्थहीन
Having no meaning, purpose, or significance
Syno: Pointless, Absurd, Stupid

618 **Meddled** (V.) - हस्तक्षेप किया
Interfered in others' affairs without invitation
Syno: Interfered, Messed, Snooped

619 **Merchandise** (N.) - व्यापारिक माल
Goods bought and sold in business
Syno: Goods, Commodities, Stock

620 **Messianic** (Adj.) - मसीहाई
Fervent and idealistic, as if driven by a divine mission
Syno: Zealous, Impractical, Unrealistic

621 **Mete** (V.) - (दंड या न्याय) देना; बाँटना
To distribute or dispense (punishment or justice)
Syno: Distribute, Dispense, Administer

622 **Meteorology** (N.) - मौसम विज्ञान
The scientific study of weather and atmosphere
Syno: Climatology, Aerology

623 **Microcosm** (N.) - लघु रूप
A miniature representation of something larger
Syno: Representative, Sample, Example

624 **Milestone** (N.) - मील का पत्थर (महत्वपूर्ण उपलब्धि)
A significant stage or event in development
Syno: Climax, Landmark, Watershed

625 **Milieu** (N.) - परिवेश
A person's social environment or surroundings
Syno: Environment, Surroundings, Environs

626 **Militancy** (N.) - उग्रवाद
Aggressive behaviour in support of a cause
Syno: Aggression, Aggressiveness, Hostility

627 **Militant** (Adj.) - उग्रवादी
Aggressively active in pursuing a political or social cause
Syno: Aggressive, Hostile, Belligerent

628 **Millennial** (Adj./N.) - सहस्राब्दी संबंधी; युवा पीढ़ी का
Relating to a millennium or the generation born around 1981-1996
Syno: Thousand-year, Generational

629 **Mindless** (Adj.) - विचारहीन
Done without thought or concern
Syno: Dumb, Stupid, Slow

630 **Mire** (N.) - कीचड़; दलदल
Swampy ground; a difficult situation hard to escape
Syno: Bog, Quagmire, Swamp

631 **Miscreant** (N.) - दुराचारी
A person who behaves badly or breaks the law
Syno: Villain, Brute, Offender

632 **Misinterpret** (V.) - गलत समझना
To understand or explain something wrongly
Syno: Misrepresent, Distort, Misstate

633 **Moiety** (N.) - आधा भाग
One of two equal halves of something
Syno: Half, Part, Section

634 **Mongers** (N.) - विक्रेता; फैलाने वाला
Dealers or promoters, often of something undesirable
Syno: Dealers, Traders, Peddlers

635 **Mongrelised** (V./Adj.) - मिश्रित
Made mixed or hybrid in character
Syno: Hybrid, Mixed, Cross

636 **Monitored** (V.) - निगरानी की
Observed or checked over a period of time
Syno: Watched, Covered, Observed

637 **Monomaniacal** (Adj.) - जुनूनी
Obsessively fixated on a single subject or idea
Syno: Obsessed, Fixated, Monomaniac

638 **Moratorium** (N.) - रोक
A temporary ban or suspension of an activity
Syno: Suspension, Suspense, Abeyance

639 **Morbidity** (N.) - बीमारी की दर
The state or incidence of disease in a population
Syno: Unhealthiness, Sickness, Illness

640 **Morphed** (V.) - रूपांतरित हुआ
Changed or transformed into something different
Syno: Transformed, Mutated, Metamorphosed

641 **Muckraking** (N.) - घोटाले उजागर करना
Exposing misconduct or scandals, especially of public figures
Syno: Mudslinging, Scandal-mongering, Exposure

642 **Mucky** (Adj.) - गंदा
Dirty or messy
Syno: Muddy, Slimy, Filthy

643 **Mulling** (V.) - विचार करना
Thinking deeply and at length about something
Syno: Pondering, Contemplating, Reflecting

644 **Multipolar** (Adj.) - बहुध्रुवीय
Having power distributed among multiple centres
Syno: Polycentric, Pluralistic, Distributed

645 **Multitiered** (Adj.) - बहुस्तरीय

Having several tiers or levels
Syno: Multilevel, Hierarchical, Stratified

646 **Mummified** (Adj.) - ममीकृत (संरक्षित शव)
Preserved by drying or embalming, especially a dead body
Syno: Shriveled, Dried, Wizened

647 **Muzzle** (N.) - मुँह पर लगाया जाने वाला बंधन
A strap fitted over an animal's mouth to prevent biting
Syno: Gag, Restraint, Bridle

648 **Mystic** (N.) - रहस्यवादी
A person who seeks spiritual union with the divine
Syno: Contemplative, Spiritualist, Seer

649 **Nausea** (N.) - मतली, जी मिचलाना
A feeling of sickness with an urge to vomit
Syno: Sickness, Queasiness, Nauseousness

650 **Negligence** (N.) - लापरवाही
Failure to take proper care
Syno: Neglectfulness, Carelessness, Neglect

651 **Neofascist** (Adj.) - नव फ़ासीवादी
Relating to a modern movement resembling fascism
Syno: Ultranationalist, Authoritarian, Fascistic

652 **Neutrality** (N.) - तटस्थता
State of not supporting either side in a conflict
Syno: Objectivity, Neutralism, Objectiveness

653 **Nip** (V.) - चुटकी काटना
To pinch sharply; to stop something early
Syno: Snip, Clip, Pinch

654 **Nomination** (N.) - नामांकन
The act of formally proposing someone for a position
Syno: Election, Selection, Destination

655 **Nonchalance** (N.) - बेपरवाही
Calm indifference or lack of concern
Syno: Disregard, Indifference, Casualness

656 **Noninclusive** (Adj.) - सबको शामिल न करने वाला
Not including all types of people or things
Syno: Exclusive, Restrictive, Discriminatory

657 **Nonstate** (Adj.) - गैर-राजकीय
Not affiliated with or belonging to a government
Syno: Non-governmental, Private, Unofficial

658 **Notoriety** (N.) - कुख्याति
Fame for something bad or negative
Syno: Infamy, Disrepute, Ill repute

659 **Nutshell** (N.) - संक्षेप, सार
A very brief summary; the fewest possible words
Syno: Summary, Synopsis

660 **Obeisance** (N.) - प्रणाम, नमन
A gesture or act of respectful reverence
Syno: Homage, Respect, Salute

661 **Objectivity** (N.) - निष्पक्षता
Freedom from bias or personal prejudice
Syno: Neutrality, Objectiveness, Neutralism

662 **Obscurantism** (N.) - अज्ञानवाद
Deliberate prevention of facts from becoming known
Syno: Mystification

663 **Obsessive** (Adj.) - जुनूनी
Excessively preoccupied with a thought or activity
Syno: Impulsive, Compulsive, Obsessional

664 **Offending** (Adj.) - आपत्तिजनक
Causing displeasure, insult, or offence
Syno: Insulting, Offensive, Abusive

665 **Oligopoly** (N.) - कुछ कंपनियों का बाज़ार पर कब्जा
A market dominated by a small number of firms
Syno: Cartel, Syndicate

666 **Ominously** (Adv.) - अशुभ रूप से
In a way suggesting something bad will happen
Syno: Threateningly, Menacingly, Forebodingly

667 **Onslaught** (N.) - हमला
A fierce or destructive attack
Syno: Attack, Assault, Offensive

668 **Opaqueness** (N.) - अपारदर्शिता (पारदर्शिता की कमी)
Lack of transparency or clarity
Syno: Ambiguity, Ambiguousness, Mysteriousness

669 **Opportunist** (N./Adj.) - अवसरवादी
One who exploits circumstances for selfish gain
Syno: Chameleon, Chancer, Weathercock

670 **Oppressive** (Adj.) - दमनकारी
Unjustly harsh and burdensome
Syno: Harsh, Brutal, Tough

671 **Oratorial** (Adj.) - भाषण कला संबंधी
Relating to the art of public speaking
Syno: Rhetorical, Declamatory

672 **Ousted** (V.) - बेदखल किया गया
Expelled or removed from a position or place

Syno: Dismissed, Ejected, Outed

673 **Outcry** (N.) - चीख-पुकार
A strong public expression of anger or disapproval
Syno: Roar, Noise, Howl

674 **Outmanoeuvre** (V.) - चतुराई से हराना
Defeat an opponent by being cleverer or more skilful
Syno: Outflank, Outfox, Outsmart

675 **Outpost** (N.) - चौकी
A remote military camp or distant settlement
Syno: Village, Settlement, Hamlet

676 **Overhaul** (V.) - पूरी मरम्मत करना
Thoroughly examine and repair or renovate
Syno: Renovate, Revamp, Refurbish

677 **Over-reliance** (N.) - अत्यधिक निर्भरता
Excessive dependence on something
Syno: Overdependence

678 **Overtures** (N.) - प्रस्ताव
Initial approaches or proposals to open negotiations
Syno: Preludes, Preliminaries, Curtain-raisers

679 **Paddy** (N.) - धान
Unhusked rice or a field where rice is grown
Syno: Unhusked rice, Rice paddy

680 **Paeans** (N.) - स्तुति गीत
Songs of praise or triumph
Syno: Tributes, Commendations, Citations

681 **Palanquin** (N.) - पालकी
A covered seat carried on poles by bearers
Syno: Litter, Sedan chair, Doolie

682 **Partisanship** (N.) - पक्षपात
Strong biased support for a particular cause or side
Syno: Bias, Prejudice, Tendentiousness

683 **Passthrough** (N./Adj.) - हस्तांतरण (आगे भेजना)
Transfer of funds or costs from one party to another
Syno: Transfer, Conveyance, Transmission

684 **Patronise** (V.) - कृपा दिखाना
Treat someone with condescending kindness
Syno: Condescend, Lord (it over), Cut

685 **Pauperize** (V.) - निर्धन बनाना
Make someone extremely poor; impoverish
Syno: Impoverish, Bankrupt, Ruin

686 **Payload** (N.) - पेलोड (ले जाया जाने वाला माल)
The cargo carried by a vehicle, aircraft, or spacecraft
Syno: Cargo, Load, Loading

687 **Peg** (N./V.) - खूंटी, निश्चित करना
A pin or bolt used to fasten or hang things (N.); to fix a price, rate, or amount at a set level (V.)
Syno: Pin, Hook , Fix, Set

688 **Perceptible** (Adj.) - प्रत्यक्ष
Able to be seen, heard, or noticed
Syno: Distinguishable, Audible, Noticeable

689 **Percolate** (V.) - रिसना
Filter gradually through a porous surface
Syno: Drip, Seep, Flow

690 **Percolation** (N.) - छनन, रिसाव
The process of liquid slowly filtering through
Syno: Drip, Seep, Flow

691 **Peremptory** (Adj.) - हुक्म चलाने वाला, सख्त
Insisting on immediate obedience; bossy and imperious
Syno: Authoritarian, Domineering, Arrogant

692 **Perishable** (Adj.) - नाशवान
Liable to decay or spoil quickly
Syno: Fragile, Sensitive, Delicate

693 **Permissible** (Adj.) - अनुमति योग्य, जायज़
Allowed or permitted by rules or law
Syno: Allowable, Acceptable, Permitted

694 **Perpetrator** (N.) - अपराधी
A person who commits a harmful or illegal act
Syno: Offender, Perp, Criminal

695 **Perpetuity** (N.) - अनंत काल
The state of lasting forever; eternity
Syno: Eternity, Infinity, Foreverness

696 **Pertinently** (Adv.) - प्रासंगिक रूप से
In a directly relevant manner
Syno: Sensibly, Relevantly, Meaningfully

697 **Pessimism** (N.) - निराशावाद
Tendency to expect the worst outcome
Syno: Negativity, Defeatism, Cynicism

698 **Phalanx** (N.) - व्यूह, दल
A tightly packed group of people or things
Syno: Group, Brigade, Platoon

699 **Piecemeal** (Adj./Adv.) - टुकड़ों में
Done in stages; not as a whole
Syno: Gradual, Phased, Incremental

700 **Pilgrimage** (N.) - तीर्थयात्रा
A journey to a sacred or revered place
Syno: Travel, Trek, Journey

701 **Placard** (N.) - तख्ती, पोस्टर
A poster or sign for public display

Syno: Poster, Billboard, Sign

702 **Plantain** (N.) - पकाने वाला केला; कच्चा केला
A starchy banana-like fruit, typically cooked before eating
Syno: Cooking banana

703 **Plenum** (N.) - पूर्ण सत्र
A meeting attended by all members
Syno: Assembly, Gathering, Congregation

704 **Plexus** (N.) - नसों/नाड़ियों का जाल
A network of nerves or vessels in the body
Syno: Meshwork, Web, Mesh

705 **Plunder** (V.) - लूटना
To steal or rob using force, especially during conflict
Syno: Loot, Pillage, Sack

706 **Pneumonia** (N.) - निमोनिया
Lung infection causing inflammation and fluid buildup
Syno: Bronchopneumonia, Pulmonitis

707 **Pogrom** (N.) - नरसंहार
An organized massacre of a particular ethnic group
Syno: Genocide, Massacre, Slaughter

708 **Polarised** (Adj.) - ध्रुवीकृत
Sharply divided into two opposing groups or views
Syno: Divided, Split, Splintered

709 **Pomp** (N.) - भव्यता, ठाट-बाट
Ceremony and splendid display
Syno: Spectacle, Fanfare, Parade

710 **Populist** (Adj.) - लोकलुभावन
Appealing to the interests of ordinary people
Syno: Demagogic, Rabble-rousing

711 **Portentous** (Adj.) - अशुभसूचक
Ominous; warning of something momentous or calamitous
Syno: Ominous, Sinister, Menacing

712 **Posit** (V.) - मान लेना
To assume or put forward as a basis of argument
Syno: Assert, Postulate, Hypothesize

713 **Post-arrival** (Adj.) - आगमन के बाद
Occurring after arrival
Syno: Post-landing

714 **Posterity** (N.) - भावी पीढ़ियाँ
All future generations of people
Syno: Offspring, Progeny, Fruit

715 **Post-facto** (Adj.) - घटना के बाद का, बाद में किया गया
Done or made after the fact; retrospective
Syno: Retrospective, Retroactive, Ex post facto

716 **Postulate** (V.) - मान लेना
To assume or suggest something as true without proof
Syno: Assume, Hypothesize, Presuppose

717 **Powerhouse** (N.) - शक्ति केंद्र
A person or thing of great energy or strength
Syno: Achiever, Hustler, Highflier

718 **Precarity** (N.) - अनिश्चितता
The state of being insecure or unstable
Syno: Insecurity, Instability, Uncertainty

719 **Precinct** (N.) - क्षेत्र, इलाक़ा
A defined administrative or police district; an area
Syno: Area, Department, Element

720 **Precipitous** (Adj.) - अत्यंत खड़ा, तीव्र
Extremely steep; or sudden and dramatic
Syno: Steep, Abrupt, Sudden

721 **Precondition** (N.) - पूर्वशर्त
A condition that must be met before something can happen
Syno: Requirement, Necessity, Condition

722 **Precursor** (N.) - अग्रदूत
A forerunner; something that comes before another
Syno: Forerunner, Harbinger, Symptom

723 **Prediction** (N.) - भविष्यवाणी
A forecast about what will happen in the future
Syno: Predicting, Forecast, Forecasting

724 **Predominant** (Adj.) - प्रमुख
Most influential, powerful, or important
Syno: Main, Dominant, Greatest

725 **Preelection** (Adj.) - चुनाव-पूर्व
Occurring before an election
Syno: Pre-poll, Pre-vote

726 **Preeminence** (N.) - सर्वश्रेष्ठता
The state of surpassing all others; supreme excellence
Syno: Excellence, Excellency, Superiority

727 **Preeminent** (Adj.) - सर्वश्रेष्ठ
Surpassing all others; outstanding
Syno: Greatest, Main, Highest

728 **Preemptive** (Adj.) - पहले से किया गया (रोकने के लिए), अग्रिम
Taken in advance to prevent an anticipated event
Syno: Preventive, Precautionary, Anticipatory

729 **Premature** (Adj.) - समय से पूर्व
Happening before the proper or expected time; too early
Syno: Early, Untimely, Unexpected

730 **Preparedness** (N.) - तत्परता
The state of being ready for something
Syno: Readiness, Preparation, Carefulness

731 **Prescribes** (V.) - निर्धारित करना
Lays down rules; advises or authorizes officially
Syno: Specifies, Defines, Directs

732 **Prestigious** (Adj.) - प्रतिष्ठित
Having high status; inspiring respect and admiration
Syno: Respected, Respectable, Reputable

733 **Preventable** (Adj.) - रोकथाम योग्य
Able to be stopped or avoided
Syno: Avoidable, Avertible, Stoppable

734 **Prima facie** (Adj./Adv.) - प्रथम दृष्टया
At first sight; accepted as correct until proved otherwise
Syno: Presumed, Apparent, Possible

735 **Princely** (Adj.) - राजसी, शाही
Resembling a prince; magnificent or lavishly generous
Syno: Regal, Royal, Aristocratic

736 **Probabilistic** (Adj.) - संभावना पर आधारित
Based on or involving probability
Syno: Stochastic, Random, Chance

737 **Proceedings** (N.) - कार्यवाही
Legal actions or a series of steps in a formal process
Syno: Lawsuits, Actions, Suits

738 **Profligacy** (N.) - फ़िज़ूलख़र्ची
Reckless extravagance or wastefulness
Syno: Extravagance, Wastefulness, Prodigality

739 **Prohibitive** (Adj.) - निषेधात्मक
So high or restrictive as to discourage or forbid
Syno: Forbidding, Restrictive

740 **Prominently** (Adv.) - प्रमुख रूप से
In a noticeable or conspicuous way
Syno: Conspicuously, Noticeably, Strikingly

741 **Promulgate** (V.) - घोषित करना
To officially announce or make widely known
Syno: Publish, Announce, Proclaim

742 **Propagandist** (N.) - प्रचारक
A person who spreads biased information to promote a cause
Syno: Promoter, Campaigner, Advocate

743 **Propagation** (N.) - प्रसार
The act of spreading or transmitting something widely
Syno: Transmission, Distribution, Dissemination

744 **Proponent** (N.) - समर्थक
A person who advocates or supports a theory or proposal
Syno: Advocate, Supporter, Advocator

745 **Proportion** (N.) - अनुपात
A part or share relative to the whole; a ratio
Syno: Ratio, Fraction, Percentage

746 **Prospective** (Adj.) - संभावित, भावी
Expected or likely to happen or become in the future
Syno: Potential, Future, Possible

747 **Prosperous** (Adj.) - समृद्ध, संपन्न
Wealthy and successful; flourishing
Syno: Thriving, Prospering, Successful

748 **Prostrate** (V./Adj.) - दंडवत लेटना; अत्यंत कमज़ोर
Lying face down in submission or reverence; utterly exhausted
Syno: Flatten, Submit, Bow down

749 **Proto state** (N.) - अधूरा राज्य, आरंभिक राज्य
An entity with some but not all features of a sovereign state
Syno: Quasi-state, Pre-state

750 **Provenance** (N.) - उत्पत्ति
The origin or source of something
Syno: Origin, Source, Derivation

751 **Proviso** (N.) - शर्त
A condition or stipulation in a document
Syno: Provision, Requirement, Stipulation

752 **Provocation** (N.) - उकसावा
An action or speech meant to arouse anger
Syno: Incitement, Instigation, Goading

753 **Proximate** (Adj.) - निकटतम
Closest in space, time, or relationship
Syno: Nearest, Adjacent, Immediate

754 **Psephological** (Adj.) - चुनाव-विश्लेषण संबंधी
Relating to the statistical study of elections and voting
Syno: Electoral

755 **Pulverise** (V.) - चूर-चूर करना
Crush or destroy completely
Syno: Destroy, Demolish, Shatter

756 **Punitive** (Adj.) - दंडात्मक
Inflicting or intended as punishment

Syno: Correctional, Penal, Corrective

757 **Purport** (V.) - दावा करना (प्रायः झूठा)
Claim or appear to be something, often falsely
Syno: Claim, Profess, Allege

758 **Purported** (Adj.) - कथित
Alleged but not proven to be true
Syno: Hypothetical, Supposed, Conjectural

759 **Putative** (Adj.) - कथित, माना हुआ
Generally assumed or believed to be
Syno: Apparent, Presumed, Probable

760 **Quantifiable** (Adj.) - मापने योग्य
Able to be measured or counted
Syno: Measurable, Calculable, Computable

761 **Quashed** (V.) - निरस्त किया, रद्द किया
Rejected or declared void, especially legally
Syno: Quelled, Suppressed, Subdued

762 **Questionable** (Adj.) - संदिग्ध
Doubtful in honesty, truth, or quality
Syno: Dubious, Disputable, Problematic

763 **Quibbling** (V.) - छोटी बातों पर बहस करना
Arguing over trivial matters
Syno: Cavilling

764 **Quickening** (N.) - तेज़ होना; गर्भ में पहली हलचल
Acceleration; first fetal movement felt in pregnancy
Syno: Stirring, Acceleration, Hastening

765 **Quirky** (Adj.) - विचित्र
Unusual or peculiar in an interesting way
Syno: Bizarre, Funny, Strange

766 **Radioactive** (Adj.) - रेडियोधर्मी
Emitting harmful radiation from atomic decay
Syno: Irradiated, Nuclear, Contaminated

767 **Ratcheted** (V.) - धीरे-धीरे बढ़ाया
Increased or intensified steadily and progressively
Syno: Increased, Intensified, Escalated

768 **Rationalise** (V.) - तर्कसंगत बनाना
Justify with logical-sounding but questionable reasons
Syno: Explain, Justify, Account (for)

769 **Reallocate** (V.) - पुनः आवंटित करना
Distribute or assign resources differently
Syno: Allocate, Provide, Distribute

770 **Realpolitik** (N.) - व्यावहारिक राजनीति
Politics based on practical rather than moral considerations
Syno: Pragmatism, Practicality, Expediency

771 **Reassess** (V.) - पुनर्मूल्यांकन करना
Evaluate or reconsider something again
Syno: Assess, Evaluate, Reevaluate

772 **Reassurance** (N.) - आश्वासन
Words or actions that remove doubt or fear
Syno: Comforting, Consolation, Consoling

773 **Rebuttal** (N.) - खंडन
A counterargument that challenges a claim
Syno: Refutation, Disproof, Confutation

774 **Recapture** (V.) - पुनः प्राप्त करना
Regain possession of something lost
Syno: Regain, Retrieve, Recover

775 **Reciprocity** (N.) - आपसी लेन-देन, परस्पर सहयोग
Mutual exchange of things for shared benefit
Syno: Mutuality, Exchange, Give-and-take

776 **Reckoning** (N.) - हिसाब
The act of calculating or estimating
Syno: Calculation, Estimation, Appraisal

777 **Recombinant** (Adj.) - पुनः संयोजित, नये संयोजन वाला
Formed by genetic recombination
Syno: Hybrid, Chimeric

778 **Reconciliation** (N.) - सुलह
Restoration of friendly relations
Syno: Acceptance, Reconcilement, Conciliation

779 **Reconvert** (V.) - पुनः परिवर्तित करना
Convert back to a previous state
Syno: Revert, Retransform

780 **Recourse** (N.) - सहारा
A source of help in a difficult situation
Syno: Opportunity, Resource, Resort

781 **Recurrence** (N.) - पुनरावृत्ति
The act of happening again
Syno: Outbreak, Renewal, Burst

782 **Recuse** (V.) - (न्यायिक कार्यवाही से) स्वयं को अलग करना
Withdraw oneself from judging due to conflict of interest
Syno: Disqualify, Withdraw, Abstain

783 **Reestablish** (V.) - पुनः स्थापित करना
Establish or restore something again
Syno: Restore, Reinstate, Revive

784 **Refashion** (V.) - नये सिरे से बनाना
Remake or reshape something differently
Syno: Remodel, Modify, Alter

785 **Reflective** (Adj.) - चिंतनशील
Given to deep or careful thought
Syno: Thoughtful, Melancholy, Contemplative

786 **Reformist** (N.) - सुधारवादी
One who advocates gradual reform
Syno: Progressivist, Modernizer, Ameliorator

787 **Regressive** (Adj.) - पिछड़ेपन की ओर ले जाने वाला
Moving backward to a less developed state
Syno: Decremental, Degressive, Decrescent

788 **Regularise** (V.) - नियमित करना
Make something regular, lawful, or standard
Syno: Standardize, Normalize, Organize

789 **Regulator** (N.) - नियामक
A body or device that controls or supervises a process
Syno: Controller, Control, Selector

790 **Regurgitate** (V.) - बिना समझे दोहराना
Repeat information without understanding it
Syno: Repeat, Reiterate, Recycle

791 **Reification** (N.) - किसी विचार को ठोस चीज़ मानना
Treating an abstract idea as a concrete thing
Syno: Objectification, Materialization, Concretization

792 **Reimburse** (V.) - प्रतिपूर्ति करना (भुगतान लौटाना)
Repay money that someone has spent or lost
Syno: Repay, Compensate, Refund

793 **Reimpose** (V.) - पुनः लागू करना
Impose something again
Syno: Reapply, Relay, Inflict

794 **Reinstate** (V.) - बहाल करना
Restore someone or something to a former position
Syno: Restore, Reestablish, Rehabilitate

795 **Reintroduce** (V.) - पुनः प्रस्तुत करना
Bring something back into use or existence
Syno: Restore, Reinstate, Revive

796 **Reinvigorate** (V.) - पुनर्जीवित करना
Give new energy or strength to
Syno: Revitalize, Revive, Rejuvenate

797 **Reiterated** (V.) - दोहराया, बार-बार कहा
Said again for emphasis or clarity
Syno: Repeated, Replicated, Renewed

798 **Rejig** (V.) - पुनर्व्यवस्थित करना
Rearrange or reorganize something
Syno: Rearrange, Reorganize, Reshuffle

799 **Relent** (V.) - नरम पड़ना
Become less severe; yield or give in
Syno: Succumb, Concede, Submit

800 **Relocate** (V.) - स्थानांतरित करना
Move to a new place or position
Syno: Move, Remove, Transfer

801 **Reminiscent** (Adj.) - याद दिलाने वाला
Suggestive of or reminding one of something past
Syno: Suggestive, Revealing, Evocative

802 **Remunerative** (Adj.) - लाभप्रद
Financially rewarding; lucrative
Syno: Lucrative, Profitable, Economic

803 **Render** (V.) - प्रस्तुत करना
To provide, give, or deliver something
Syno: Relinquish, Deliver, Surrender

804 **Renege** (V.) - मुकर जाना
Go back on a promise or commitment
Syno: Withdraw, Recall, Back out

805 **Renunciatory** (Adj.) - त्यागपूर्ण
Relating to or involving giving up something
Syno: Ascetic, Abnegatory, Renouncing

806 **Reorganise** (V.) - पुनर्गठित करना
To organise again or differently; restructure
Syno: Restructure, Rearrange, Overhaul

807 **Reorient** (V.) - नई दिशा देना
To change the focus or direction of something
Syno: Redirect, Refocus, Realign

808 **Reparation** (N.) - क्षतिपूर्ति
Compensation for a wrong or damage done
Syno: Damages, Compensation, Restitution

809 **Repatriate** (V.) - स्वदेश वापस भेजना
Send someone back to their own country
Syno: Return, Restore

810 **Replicate** (V.) - प्रतिलिपि बनाना
Make an exact copy of something; reproduce
Syno: Reproduce, Copy, Render

811 **Repo rate** (N.) - रेपो दर
Rate at which a central bank lends to commercial banks
Syno: Repurchase rate, Policy rate

812 **Repossession** (N.) - पुनः अधिग्रहण
Retaking possession of property, especially for non-payment
Syno: Reclamation, Recovery, Retrieval

813 **Repression** (N.) - दमन
Subduing or suppressing someone or something by force
Syno: Restraint, Discipline, Suppression

814 **Resonance** (N.) - गूँज, गहरा प्रभाव
A quality that evokes deep emotional response
Syno: Echo, Reverberation

815 **Respective** (Adj.) - क्रमशः संबंधित
Belonging separately to each one mentioned
Syno: Different, Separate, Individual

816 **Respondent** (N.) - जवाब देने वाला (कानूनी: प्रत्यर्थी)
A person who replies, especially in a survey or legal case
Syno: Interviewee, Responder, Answerer

817 **Resultant** (Adj.) - परिणामस्वरूप
Occurring as a result or consequence
Syno: Consequent, Accompanying, Attendant

818 **Resumption** (N.) - पुनः आरंभ
The act of beginning something again after a pause
Syno: Recommencement, Renewal, Resuscitation

819 **Resurgent** (Adj.) - फिर से उभरता हुआ
Rising or becoming active again after decline
Syno: Reviving, Renascent, Reawakening

820 **Resurrect** (V.) - पुनर्जीवित करना
Revive something inactive, forgotten, or disused
Syno: Revive, Renew, Reanimate

821 **Retraumatise** (V.) - फिर से सदमा पहुँचाना
Cause someone to experience trauma again
Syno: Reinjure, Revictimize

822 **Returnable** (Adj.) - वापसी योग्य
Able to be returned or given back
Syno: Refundable, Redeemable, Exchangeable

823 **Revanchism** (N.) - प्रतिशोधवाद
Policy of seeking to recover lost territory or status
Syno: Irredentism

824 **Revanchist** (Adj./N.) - प्रतिशोधवादी
Seeking retaliation, especially to recover lost territory
Syno: Vengeful, Retaliatory, Vindictive

825 **Reversion** (N.) - पुरानी स्थिति में लौटना
A return to a previous state or condition
Syno: Regression, Retrogression, Decline

826 **Revictimise** (V.) - पुनः पीड़ित करना
Subject someone to victimisation again
Syno: Retraumatise

827 **Revictimize** (V.) - दोबारा पीड़ित करना
Make someone a victim again
Syno: Retraumatize

828 **Review Petition** (N.) - पुनर्विचार याचिका
A legal plea asking a court to review its own decision
Syno: Reconsideration plea, Rehearing application

829 **Revisionary** (Adj.) - संशोधनात्मक
Relating to or involving revision or correction
Syno: Amendatory, Corrective, Modifying

830 **Revisit** (V.) - पुनर्विचार करना
To consider or examine something again
Syno: Reconsider, Review, Reexamine

831 **Rig** (V.) - हेराफेरी करना
Manipulate or control fraudulently
Syno: Manipulate, Fix, Tamper with

832 **Riposte** (N.) - जवाबी प्रहार
A quick, sharp reply to an insult or criticism
Syno: Retort, Insult, Repartee

833 **Ripple** (V.) - लहराना
Form or flow with small waves on the surface
Syno: Splash, Wash, Bubble

834 **Riven** (Adj.) - विभाजित
Split or torn apart violently
Syno: Disrupted, Broken, Fractured

835 **Rivulet** (N.) - छोटी नदी
A very small stream
Syno: Brook, Creek, Stream

836 **Rubble** (N.) - मलबा
Broken fragments of stone, brick, or concrete; debris
Syno: Debris, Wreckage, Ruins

837 **Ruckus** (N.) - हंगामा
A noisy disturbance or commotion
Syno: Brawl, Altercation, Clash

838 **Ruinous** (Adj.) - विनाशकारी
Causing or likely to cause destruction or disaster
Syno: Disastrous, Fatal, Unfortunate

839 **Rumbling** (N.) - गड़गड़ाहट
A continuous deep sound like distant thunder
Syno: Thundering, Roaring, Booming

840 **Sacrosanct** (Adj.) - अतिपवित्र
Too important or sacred to be changed or interfered with
Syno: Sacred, Holy, Inviolable

841 **Sanctioning** (V.) - अनुमोदन करना
Giving official permission or approval
Syno: Approving, Authorizing, Endorsing

842 **Sanitation** (N.) - स्वच्छता
Public health practices, especially clean water and sewage disposal
Syno: Hygiene, Cleanliness, Disinfection

843 **Sarcophagus** (N.) - पत्थर का ताबूत, शवपेटिका
A decorated stone coffin from ancient times
Syno: Casket, Coffin, Tomb

844 **Scandal** (N.) - घोटाला
An action or event causing public outrage or disgrace
Syno: Disgrace, Reflection, Stain

845 **Scaremonger** (N.) - भय फैलाने वाला
A person who spreads fear or alarming

rumours
Syno: Alarmist, Fearmonger, Doomsayer

846 **Scholastic** (Adj.) - शैक्षिक
Relating to schools and education
Syno: Educational, Academic, Scholarly

847 **Screen** (V.) - जाँच करना
To examine or test for suitability
Syno: Examine, Vet, Check

848 **Scruples** (N.) - नैतिक संकोच
Moral doubts or hesitation about doing something
Syno: Qualms, Misgivings, Compunctions

849 **Scrutinise** (V.) - जाँचना
Examine or inspect closely and thoroughly
Syno: Examine, Review, Scan

850 **Scuffle** (N.) - हाथापाई
A short, confused fight at close quarters
Syno: Skirmish, Clash, Fight

851 **Secession** (N.) - अलगाव, विलगाव
Formal withdrawal from a federation or political body
Syno: Withdrawal, Separation, Disaffiliation

852 **Sectarian** (Adj.) - सांप्रदायिक
Relating to a sect; narrow-minded or partisan
Syno: Parochial, Petty, Small

853 **Secularism** (N.) - धर्मनिरपेक्षता
Principle of separating religion from government or public affairs
Syno: Laicism

854 **Seditious** (Adj.) - राजद्रोही
Inciting rebellion against the authority of a state
Syno: Inflammatory, Provocative, Incendiary

855 **Seeded** (Adj.) - बोया गया; वरीयता प्राप्त
Having seeds planted; ranked or placed in a tournament draw
Syno: Planted, Ranked, Embedded, Positioned

856 **Sensitively** (Adv.) - संवेदनशीलता से
With awareness and consideration for others' feelings
Syno: Thoughtfully, Lovingly, Considerately

857 **Separatist** (N.) - अलगाववादी
One who advocates separation of a group from a larger body
Syno: Sectarian, Schismatic, Apostate

858 **Sequential** (Adj.) - क्रमबद्ध
Following in a logical order or sequence
Syno: Consecutive, Successive, Straight

859 **Sequester** (V.) - अलग करना
Isolate or hide away
Syno: Isolate, Separate, Remove

860 **Setback** (N.) - बाधा, धक्का, विफलता
A reversal or check in progress
Syno: Reversal, Reverse, Lapse

861 **Shambles** (N.) - अव्यवस्था, गड़बड़ी
A state of total disorder or chaos
Syno: Dump, Mess, Hole

862 **Shambolic** (Adj.) - अव्यवस्थित
Chaotic, disorganized, or mismanaged
Syno: Chaotic, Disorderly, Disordered

863 **Shanty** (N.) - झोपड़ी
A small, crudely built shack
Syno: Hut, Camp, Shack

864 **Shoddy** (Adj.) - घटिया
Badly made or done
Syno: Poor, Terrible, Cheap

865 **Shortchange** (V.) - ठगना
Cheat someone by giving less than what is due
Syno: Cheat, Squeeze, Pluck

866 **Showcase** (V.) - प्रदर्शन करना
Display or exhibit
Syno: Show, Display, Exhibit

867 **Simulacrum** (N.) - नकल, प्रतिरूप
An image or imitation of someone or something
Syno: Imitation, Likeness, Semblance

868 **Skew** (V.) - तिरछा करना, विकृत करना
Distort or bias in a particular direction
Syno: Tilt, Veer, Slope

869 **Skilling** (V./N.) - कौशल विकास
The process of learning or teaching practical skills
Syno: Training, Educating, Instructing

870 **Skip** (V.) - छोड़ना
Pass over or omit
Syno: Omit, Bypass, Overlook

871 **Skirmish** (N.) - झड़प
A brief fight or minor conflict
Syno: Encounter, Brush, Fight

872 **Skirted** (V.) - बचना
Avoided or evaded
Syno: Bypassed, Circumvented, Avoided

873 **Skullduggery** (N.) - कपट, छल
Underhanded trickery or dishonest behaviour
Syno: Deception, Treachery, Chicanery

874 **Skyrocket** (V.) - आसमान छूना
Increase very steeply or rapidly

Syno: Soar, Increase, Rocket

875 **Slackness** (N.) - ढिलाई, लापरवाही
Lack of care, discipline, or tightness; negligence
Syno: Negligence, Neglectfulness, Neglect

876 **Slain** (V.) - मारा गया
Killed violently
Syno: Killed, Destroyed, Murdered

877 **Sleuths** (N.) - जासूस
Detectives or investigators
Syno: Detectives, Investigators, Operatives

878 **Slew** (N.) - बहुत सारे
A large number or quantity of something
Syno: Loads, Ton, Multitude

879 **Slippage** (N.) - गिरावट, चूक
A gradual decline or failure to meet a standard or deadline
Syno: Decline, Deterioration, Regression

880 **Slush** (N.) - पिघली हुई बर्फ़, कीचड़
Partially melted snow or ice
Syno: Slurry, Mush, Sludge

881 **Smacked** (V.) - थप्पड़ मारा
Hit sharply or forcefully
Syno: Slapped, Knocked, Hit

882 **Smorgasbord** (N.) - विविध संग्रह
A wide variety or assortment
Syno: Variety, Assortment, Medley

883 **Snowballed** (V.) - तेज़ी से बढ़ गया
Increased rapidly in size, intensity, or importance
Syno: Increased, Swelled, Rose

884 **Snub** (V.) - तिरस्कार करना, उपेक्षा करना
Reject or ignore someone disdainfully
Syno: Ignore, Slight, Rebuff

885 **Socialist** (Adj./N.) - समाजवादी
Relating to or advocating collective ownership and social equality
Syno: Communist, Commie, Red

886 **Solemnise** (V.) - विधिवत संपन्न करना
Perform a ceremony officially, especially a marriage
Syno: Consecrate, Honor, Celebrate

887 **Solidarity** (N.) - एकजुटता
Unity and mutual support within a group
Syno: Sympathy, Empathy, Kinship

888 **Sowing** (V.) - बुआई करना
Planting seeds in the ground for growing
Syno: Planting, Seeding, Scattering

889 **Spacefaring** (Adj.) - अंतरिक्ष यात्रा करने वाला
Capable of or engaged in space travel
Syno: Astronautical, Cosmonautical, Interplanetary

890 **Spate** (N.) - बाढ़, भरमार
A sudden large number of things occurring at once
Syno: Flood, Torrent, Influx

891 **Speculative** (Adj.) - अनुमानित, सट्टेबाज़ी संबंधी
Based on conjecture rather than knowledge; involving risk
Syno: Hypothetical, Theoretical, Conjectural

892 **Spigot** (N.) - टोंटी (पानी का नल)
A faucet or tap
Syno: Valve, Tap, Faucet

893 **Spiralling** (Adj.) - तेज़ी से बढ़ता हुआ
Rapidly and continuously increasing or decreasing
Syno: Escalating, Mounting, Soaring

894 **Splurge** (V.) - फ़िज़ूलख़र्ची करना
Spend money freely or extravagantly
Syno: Consume, Lose, Spend

895 **Spotlight** (N.) - सुर्खियाँ, सार्वजनिक ध्यान
Intense public attention or scrutiny
Syno: Limelight, Attention, Center stage

896 **Spree** (N.) - होड़, उन्माद
A bout of unrestrained activity or indulgence
Syno: Fling, Lark, Binge

897 **Spurt** (V.) - फूट निकलना
Gush out in a sudden, forceful stream
Syno: Burst, Gush, Surge

898 **Squandered** (V.) - बर्बाद किया
Wasted recklessly, especially money or time
Syno: Spent, Lost, Wasted

899 **Staffer** (N.) - कर्मचारी
A member of staff; an employee
Syno: Employee, Worker, Personnel

900 **Stagflation** (N.) - महँगाई के साथ मंदी
Economic condition of high inflation, slow growth, and high unemployment
Syno: Recession, Stagnation, Economic decline

901 **Stance** (N.) - दृष्टिकोण
An attitude or position on an issue
Syno: Posture, Attitude, Carriage

902 **Stand** (N.) - रुख
Opinion or attitude towards something
Syno: Position, Viewpoint, Opinion

903 **Standalone** (Adj.) - स्वतंत्र
Operating independently without needing

other systems
Syno: Independent, Self-contained, Freestanding

904 **Standardize** (V.) - मानकीकरण करना
Make something conform to a standard
Syno: Organize, Normalize, Formalize

905 **Staples** (N.) - मुख्य खाद्य पदार्थ
Basic or essential items, especially food
Syno: Essentials, Basics, Necessities

906 **Stark** (Adj.) - कठोर, बिलकुल स्पष्ट
Severe in appearance; sharply evident
Syno: Grim, Gruff, Fierce

907 **Stationed** (V.) - तैनात किया गया
Assigned or posted at a particular place
Syno: Appointed, Placed, Posted

908 **Status** (N.) - स्थिति
The position or standing of someone or something
Syno: Situation, Deal, Story

909 **Stealth** (N.) - गोपनीयता, चोरी-छिपे कार्य
Cautious, secretive action or movement
Syno: Secrecy, Slyness, Furtiveness

910 **Sterilise** (V.) - जीवाणुरहित बनाना
Make free from bacteria or microorganisms
Syno: Disinfect, Sanitize, Purify

911 **Stewardship** (N.) - प्रबंधन
Responsible supervision and care of something
Syno: Management, Supervision, Handling

912 **Straddle** (V.) - दोनों ओर पैर रखना
Sit or stand with one leg on either side of
Syno: Perch, Sit, Bestride

913 **Strain** (N.) - तनाव
Pressure or tension causing stress
Syno: Stress, Tension, Pressure

914 **Streamlined** (Adj.) - सुव्यवस्थित
Made efficient and easy to use
Syno: Efficient, Simplified, Optimized

915 **Strewn** (V.) - बिखरा हुआ
Scattered untidily over a surface
Syno: Spray, Sprinkle, Dot

916 **Strides** (N.) - लंबे निर्णायक कदम
Long, decisive steps; significant progress
Syno: Marches, Steps, Paces

917 **Strings** (N.) - शर्तें
Conditions or restrictions attached to something
Syno: Conditions, Stipulations, Provisos

918 **Structuralist** (Adj.) - संरचनावादी
Relating to structuralism as an analytical approach
Syno: Formalist

919 **Stubble** (N.) - ठूँठ, छोटी दाढ़ी
Short stalks left after harvest; short regrown hair after shaving
Syno: Bristle

920 **Stultify** (V.) - हतोत्साहित करना, निरर्थक बनाना
Cause to lose enthusiasm or become ineffective
Syno: Inhibit, Restrain, Impede

921 **Stutterer** (N.) - हकलाने वाला
A person who stammers while speaking
Syno: Stammerer

922 **Subservience** (N.) - अधीनता
Willingness to obey others unquestioningly
Syno: Servility, Subserviency, Obsequiousness

923 **Subsidence** (N.) - धंसाव
Gradual sinking or settling of ground
Syno: Sinking, Settling, Descent

924 **Substantiate** (V.) - प्रमाणित करना, पुष्टि करना
Provide evidence to prove the truth of something
Syno: Prove, Establish, Demonstrate

925 **Substantive** (Adj.) - ठोस, महत्वपूर्ण
Meaningful, important, and having real substance
Syno: Substantial, Significant, Considerable

926 **Succour** (N.) - सहारा
Help and support in times of distress
Syno: Assistance, Support, Encouragement

927 **Suitability** (N.) - उपयुक्तता
The quality of being right or appropriate for a purpose
Syno: Appropriateness, Applicability, Relevance

928 **Summative** (Adj.) - अंतिम मूल्यांकन संबंधी
Assessing overall learning at the end of a period
Syno: Cumulative, Aggregate

929 **Supplements** (N.) - पूरक
Additions that improve or complete something
Syno: Increases, Additions, Boosts

930 **Surfeit** (N.) - अति, अतिरेक
An excessive amount of something
Syno: Surplus, Excess, Abundance

931 **Symbolism** (N.) - प्रतीकवाद
Use of symbols to represent ideas or qualities
Syno: Allegory, Imagery, Representation

932 **Tableau** (N.) - झाँकी
A scene or group arranged for artistic effect
Syno: Mise-en-scène, Backdrop, Scenery

933 **Tantamount** (Adj.) - बराबर, के समान
Equivalent to; virtually the same as
Syno: Analogous, Comparable, Similar

934 **Tantrum** (N.) - नखरा, गुस्से का आवेश
An uncontrolled outburst of anger or frustration
Syno: Huff, Outburst, Scene

935 **Tardiness** (N.) - देरी
Delay or lateness
Syno: Lateness, Delinquency, Belatedness

936 **Tatters** (N.) - फटे कपड़े
Torn and ragged pieces of cloth or material
Syno: Tears, Rips, Shreds

937 **Teem** (V.) - भरा हुआ
Be full of or swarming with
Syno: Burst, Buzz, Abound

938 **Temptation** (N.) - प्रलोभन
A desire to do something, especially something unwise
Syno: Seduction, Lure, Appeal

939 **Terminology** (N.) - शब्दावली
Specialized terms used in a particular field or subject
Syno: Vocabulary, Dialect, Language

940 **Terrestrial** (Adj.) - पृथ्वी संबंधी
Relating to the earth or land; worldly
Syno: Temporal, Mundane, Physical

941 **Testbed** (N.) - परीक्षण स्थल
A platform or environment for experimental testing
Syno: Proving ground, Testing ground, Laboratory

942 **Testy** (Adj.) - चिड़चिड़ा
Easily irritated or annoyed
Syno: Irritable, Fiery, Peevish

943 **Theatrical** (Adj.) - नाटकीय, दिखावटी
Exaggerated and overly dramatic in manner
Syno: Dramatic, Staged, Melodramatic

944 **Thrash** (V.) - पीटना
Beat someone or something repeatedly and violently
Syno: Flog, Whip, Beat

945 **Threadbare** (Adj.) - घिसा-पिटा
Worn out and shabby from overuse
Syno: Dilapidated, Neglected, Tattered

946 **Tinker** (V.) - छोटी मोटी मरम्मत करना
Casually attempt to repair or adjust something
Syno: Horse around, Diddle (with), Clown (around)

947 **Tizzy** (N.) - घबराहट
A state of nervous excitement or agitation
Syno: Panic, Huff, Fuss

948 **Topography** (N.) - भू-आकृति विज्ञान
The physical features and layout of an area
Syno: Geography, Landscape, Terrain

949 **Torpedo** (V.) - नष्ट करना, बर्बाद करना
Destroy or sabotage something deliberately
Syno: Destroy, Wreck, Sabotage

950 **Totalitarian** (Adj.) - निरंकुश
Of a dictatorial government demanding complete obedience
Syno: Oppressive, Authoritarian, Domineering

951 **Traction** (N.) - पकड़; रफ़्तार पकड़ना
Grip or hold on a surface; gaining momentum
Syno: Grip, Purchase, Footing

952 **Trample** (V.) - रौंदना
Tread on and crush
Syno: Stomp, Stamp, Kick

953 **Tranche** (N.) - हिस्सा, किश्त
A portion of something, especially money
Syno: Portion, Segment, Instalment

954 **Transmissive** (Adj.) - संचारी; आर-पार जाने देने वाला
Allowing passage or transmission of something
Syno: Transparent, Permeable

955 **Transnational** (Adj.) - देशों की सीमाओं से परे; बहुराष्ट्रीय
Extending across national boundaries
Syno: International, Multinational, Foreign

956 **Traumatic** (Adj.) - आघातपूर्ण
Emotionally disturbing or distressing
Syno: Horrible, Painful, Terrible

957 **Travails** (N.) - कठिनाइयाँ; कष्ट
Painful struggles or hardships
Syno: Pains, Distresses, Agonies

958 **Trawler** (N.) - ट्रॉलर; जाल से मछली पकड़ने वाली नाव
A fishing boat that drags a large net
Syno: Angler, Troller, Fly fisherman

959 **Tremors** (N.) - कंपन; झटके
Involuntary shaking or quivering movements
Syno: Quakes, Earthquakes, Shakes

960 **Trial** (N.) - मुकदमा
Formal examination of evidence in a court
Syno: Hearing, Proceeding, Litigation

961 **Trifle** (N.) - मामूली बात; तुच्छ वस्तु
A thing of little value or importance
Syno: Bagatelle, Triviality, Trinket

962 **Trimester** (N.) - तिमाही
A period of three months
Syno: Quarter, Term

963 **Trough** (N.) - गड्ढा; नीचा स्तर; नाँद
A low point in a cycle; a long open container
Syno: Dip, Slump, Nadir

964 **Trounced** (V.) - बुरी तरह हराया
Defeated heavily in a contest
Syno: Bombed, Whipped, Overcame

965 **Trudge** (V.) - भारी कदमों से चलना
Walk slowly with heavy, weary steps
Syno: Shuffle, Stumble, Stomp

966 **Tug** (V.) - खींचना
Pull something hard or suddenly
Syno: Pull, Yank, Jerk

967 **Tussle** (N.) - हाथापाई; संघर्ष
A vigorous struggle or scuffle
Syno: Clash, Skirmish, Battle

968 **Tweak** (V.) - सुधारना; बेहतर बनाना
Make small adjustments to improve something
Syno: Adjust, Modify, Fine-tune

969 **Uber-liberal** (Adj.) - अति उदारवादी
Extremely liberal in politics or philosophy
Syno: Ultraliberal, Radical

970 **Unabashed** (Adj.) - निःसंकोच; बेशर्म
Not embarrassed or ashamed
Syno: Unashamed, Proud, Unembarrassed

971 **Uncritical** (Adj.) - अविवेकी
Lacking critical judgment or analysis
Syno: Naive, Innocent, Simple

972 **Unctuosity** (N.) - चिकनाई; चापलूसी
Oiliness or greasy quality; smarmy insincerity
Syno: Oiliness, Greasiness, Sycophancy

973 **Undeniable** (Adj.) - अकाट्य; निर्विवाद
Impossible to deny; unquestionably true
Syno: Unquestionable, Indisputable, Irrefutable

974 **Undergird** (V.) - सहारा देना
Provide support or a firm basis for
Syno: Sustain, Support, Carry

975 **Underscore** (V.) - बल देना; रेखांकित करना
Emphasize or highlight something
Syno: Emphasize, Reinforce, Underline

976 **Uneasiness** (N.) - बेचैनी
A feeling of anxiety or discomfort
Syno: Turmoil, Unrest, Unease

977 **Unencumbered** (Adj.) - भारमुक्त; निर्बाध
Free from burden or impediment
Syno: Unhindered, Unimpeded, Unburdened

978 **Unenviable** (Adj.) - जिससे ईर्ष्या न हो; कठिन
Difficult, undesirable, or unpleasant
Syno: Undesirable, Abominable, Horrid

979 **Unfazed** (Adj.) - बेपरवाह; जो घबराए नहीं
Not disturbed or troubled; calm
Syno: Undaunted, Composed, Untroubled

980 **Unfettered** (Adj.) - बंधनमुक्त; पूरी तरह आज़ाद
Free and unrestrained
Syno: Unleashed, Escaped, Unchained

981 **Unflappable** (Adj.) - जो विचलित न हो; शांतचित्त
Remaining calm and composed in a crisis
Syno: Nonchalant, Calm, Imperturbable

982 **Unforgivable** (Adj.) - जिसे माफ़ न किया जा सके
Too bad to be forgiven or excused
Syno: Unacceptable, Inexcusable, Unpardonable

983 **Unfurl** (V.) - खोलना; फैलाना
Spread out from a rolled or folded state
Syno: Expand, Extend, Unfold

984 **Unification** (N.) - एकीकरण
The process of uniting into a whole
Syno: Merger, Merging, Consolidation

985 **Unlaundered** (Adj.) - बिना धुला हुआ
Not washed or cleaned
Syno: Dirty, Soiled, Unwashed

986 **Unnerving** (Adj.) - घबराहट में डालने वाला
Causing anxiety or unease; unsettling
Syno: Disturbing, Uneasy, Unsettling

987 **Unravel** (V.) - सुलझाना
Undo or solve something complicated
Syno: Fray, Untangle, Disentangle

988 **Unreasonable** (Adj.) - अनुचित; अतर्कसंगत
Beyond what is fair or sensible
Syno: Irrational, Unwarranted, Unfounded

989 **Unrepentant** (Adj.) - बेपछतावा; बिना पछतावे का
Showing no regret for wrongdoings
Syno: Ruthless, Impenitent, Cruel

990 **Unsavoury** (Adj.) - अप्रिय; भद्दा
Disagreeable or distasteful
Syno: Distasteful, Unappetizing, Unpalatable

991 **Unseemly** (Adj.) - अशिष्ट; बेढंगा; अनुचित
Not proper or appropriate; indecent
Syno: Inappropriate, Unsuitable, Improper

992 **Untruthful** (Adj.) - असत्यवादी; झूठा
Not telling the truth; dishonest

Syno: Dishonest, Deceitful, Mendacious

993 **Unveiled** (V.) - पर्दा उठाया; सामने लाया
Revealed or made public for the first time
Syno: Revealed, Disclosed, Exposed

994 **Upbringing** (N.) - परवरिश; पालन-पोषण
The way a child is raised and educated
Syno: Rearing, Parenting, Parenthood

995 **Usurious** (Adj.) - सूदखोरी वाला
Charging excessively high interest rates
Syno: Exorbitant, Extortionate, Excessive

996 **Usurpation** (N.) - हड़प; ज़बरदस्ती कब्जा
Seizing power or property by force
Syno: Takeover, Appropriation, Seizure

997 **Utterance** (N.) - कथन; बात; कही गई बात
A spoken word, statement, or remark
Syno: Voice, Expression, Formulation

998 **Vacillating** (Adj.) - डाँवाडोल; अस्थिर
Wavering between opinions; indecisive
Syno: Irresolute, Uncertain, Unsure

999 **Vainglorious** (Adj.) - घमंडी; दंभी
Excessively proud or boastful
Syno: Smug, Arrogant, Proud

1000 **Valorise** (V.) - महत्त्व देना; मान बढ़ाना
Give value to; enhance the status of
Syno: Value, Esteem, Appreciate

1001 **Veneer** (N.) - दिखावटी आवरण
A superficial or deceptive outward appearance
Syno: Facade, Gloss, Window dressing

1002 **Vetted** (V.) - जाँचा-परखा गया
Carefully examined or investigated
Syno: Screened, Investigated, Verified

1003 **Violative** (Adj.) - उल्लंघनकारी
In violation of a law, rule, or principle
Syno: Infringing, Transgressive, Breaching

1004 **Votary** (N.) - भक्त; समर्थक
A devoted follower or advocate
Syno: Adherent, Follower, Disciple

1005 **Wafer-thin** (Adj.) - अत्यंत पतला
Extremely thin
Syno: Paper-thin, Flimsy, Insubstantial

1006 **Wake-up call** (N.) - चेतावनी
An event that alerts to danger or a problem
Syno: Warning, Red flag, Red light

1007 **War-battered** (Adj.) - युद्ध से तबाह
Damaged or devastated by war
Syno: War-torn, Devastated, Battle-scarred

1008 **Warmth** (N.) - गरमाहट; अपनापन
Heat or friendly affection
Syno: Warmness, Glow, Lukewarmness

1009 **Wean** (V.) - दूध छुड़ाना; आदत छुड़ाना
Gradually withdraw someone from a dependency
Syno: Detach, Disengage, Separate

1010 **Whiff** (N.) - हलकी गंध; झलक
A brief, faint smell; a slight trace
Syno: Hint, Glimmer, Flicker

1011 **Whip** (V.) - कोड़े से मारना
Beat with a whip or similar instrument
Syno: Lash, Flog, Scourge

1012 **Whistleblower** (N.) - मुखबिर; भंडाफोड़ करने वाला
A person who exposes wrongdoing in an organization
Syno: Reporter, Spy, Informant

1013 **Winnowed** (V.) - छाँटा गया
Sifted to separate the good from the bad
Syno: Sifted, Filtered, Screened

1014 **Withdrawal** (N.) - वापसी; निकासी
The act of pulling back or retreating
Syno: Retreat, Retirement, Pullout

1015 **Year-on-year** (Adv.) - साल-दर-साल
Compared with the same period last year
Syno: Annually, Year over year

Foreign Words & Phrases

Introduction

Foreign words and phrases are borrowed expressions from languages like Latin, French, German and Italian that are commonly used in English. Words like Ad hoc (for a specific purpose, or temporary), Faux pas (a social blunder), Status quo (the current situation), Carpe diem (seize the day) are all foreign in origin but used widely in everyday English, Government offices, legal language, journalism and of course, competitive exams.

These words are tested regularly in SSC, DSSSB, Defense and other competitive exams. They may look intimidating because of their unusual spellings, but once you learn the meaning, they become some of the easiest marks in the vocabulary section.

How Exams Test These

Questions on foreign words usually come in these formats:

1. Direct meaning: SSC CPO asked, *"Carpe diem means"* with options: Ignore the sadness, Currently using, Converse directly, Seize the moment. You simply need to know that Carpe diem means "seize the day."

2. Sentence substitution: SSC GD Constable 2022 asked, *"The treaty was signed by both the parties to retain the status-quo."* Options: previous condition, unnatural behaviour, current situation, class of societies. Here you need to understand how the foreign word fits in context.

3. Idiom/Phrase meaning: SSC CGL asked, *"Choose the meaning of: Fait accompli"* with options: one who complains a lot, an irreversible change, a reversible change, to struggle. The answer is "an irreversible change" since fait accompli means something already done that cannot be undone.

4. Synonym matching: SSC CGL tested **Persona non grata** (an unwelcome person) as a synonym option for "Pariah." So sometimes you will not even see the question framed as a foreign word question, it just appears as a vocabulary option.

Reality

The biggest trap with foreign words is that they often look like they mean something they do not. "In camera" has nothing to do with a camera, it means "in private." "De facto" does not mean "based on facts," it means "in reality." In an exam, when asked the meaning of "Ex gratia," one option was "A government by ex officials," which sounds logical but is completely wrong. It actually means "without legal obligation." If you go by the look or feel of the word instead of the actual meaning, you will lose easy marks.

How to Study This Chapter

- **Learn the origin.** Knowing whether a word is Latin or French helps you remember it. Latin words are more common in legal and formal contexts (prima facie, suo motu), while French words appear more in everyday usage (debut, elite, detour).
- **Meaning + Hindi meaning.** Read both. For Hindi medium students the Hindi meaning often makes it click faster.
- **Revise regularly.** Do not try to memorise all 197 words in one go. Cover a few daily and keep revisiting.

Chapter Structure

Part 1: PYQ Based (81 words): Words picked directly from previous year questions of SSC, CDS, and other competitive exams. These are your top priority.

Part 2: Non PYQ (116 words): Important words that have not appeared yet but match the pattern and difficulty of recent papers. Your safety net for new questions.

F5 Foreign Words & Phrases (Italian, French, Latin, & German)

Foreign Words Asked in Competitive Exams

1 **À la carte** *{French}* - On the menu; according to the menu card (मेनू से अलग-अलग व्यंजन चुनकर मंगाना)
2 **À la mode** *{French}* - In fashion (प्रचलन में)
3 **Ab initio** *{Latin}* - From the beginning (प्रारंभ से)
4 **Ad hoc** *{Latin}* - Arranged or improvised for a specific purpose as needed, without prior planning (अस्थायी, विशेष उद्देश्य के लिए)
5 **Ad interim** *{Latin}* - In the meantime (इस बीच)
6 **Alibi** *{Latin}* - A plea or proof that a person charged with a crime was elsewhere when it was committed (इस बात का सबूत कि अपराध के समय व्यक्ति कहीं और था)
7 **Alumni** *{Latin}* - Graduates or former students (पूर्व छात्र)
8 **Anno Domini (AD)** *{Latin}* - Years counted after Christ's birth; In the year of the Lord (ईसा मसीह के जन्म के बाद का वर्ष; ईस्वी सन्)
9 **Apéritif** *{French}* - Alcoholic drink taken before meals to stimulate appetite (भूख जगाने वाली मदिरा जो भोजन से पहले पी जाती है)
10 **Arbiter/Arbitrium** *{Latin}* - A judge/ judgment (मध्यस्थ/निर्णय)
11 **Attaché** *{French}* - Diplomatic support staff (दूतावास का सहायक अधिकारी)
12 **Avant-garde** *{French}* - New, experimental and innovative ideas, especially in art or fashion (बहुत नए और अलग प्रयोग करने वाला (विशेषकर कला/विचारों में))
13 **Beret** *{French}* - A round, flat cap (गोल, चपटी टोपी)
14 **Biennium** *{Latin}* - A period of two years (दो वर्षों की अवधि)
15 **Bon voyage** *{French}* - Have a good journey (शुभ यात्रा)
16 **Bourgeoisie** *{French}* - The capitalist or property-owning middle class (संपन्न मध्यम वर्ग)
17 **Carpe diem** *{Latin}* - Seize the day; Enjoy the present moment (वर्तमान का लाभ उठाओ)
18 **Connoisseur** *{French}* - An expert in matters of taste and art (कला, स्वाद या गुणवत्ता का जानकार विशेषज्ञ)
19 **Cul-de-sac** *{French}* - A dead-end street; a street closed at one end (बंद गली)
20 **De facto** *{Latin}* - In fact; in practice (वस्तुतः; व्यवहार में)
21 **Débris** *{French}* - Scattered remains; scattered pieces of broken materials (टूटे-फूटे अवशेष)
22 **Début** *{French}* - A first public appearance or performance (पहला सार्वजनिक प्रदर्शन)
23 **Déjà vu** *{French}* - The feeling of having experienced the present situation before (पहले देखा या अनुभव किया हुआ लगना)
24 **Détente** *{French}* - Easing of strained relations (तनाव में कमी; संबंधों में सुधार)
25 **Détour** *{French}* - A longer alternative route to avoid an obstacle (सीधे रास्ते के बजाय लिया गया लंबा रास्ता)
26 **Dossier** *{French}* - A collection of documents on someone or something (किसी व्यक्ति या विषय से संबंधित दस्तावेज़ों का संकलन)
27 **Double entendre** *{French}* - A phrase with a double meaning, especially one that is suggestive (दोहरा अर्थ वाला वाक्यांश)
28 **Élan** *{French}* - Enthusiastic vigour and flair (उत्साह या जीवंतता)
29 **Élite** *{French}* - A select group (चुनिंदा समूह)
30 **En bloc** *{French}* - All together as a group (सब एक साथ)
31 **En masse** *{French}* - All together; in a large group (बड़ी संख्या में एक साथ)
32 **Entourage** *{French}* - A group of attendants or associates (सहायकों का समूह)
33 **Et al. / Et alia** *{Latin}* - And others (एवं अन्य)
34 **Ex gratia** *{Latin}* - Given voluntarily, not legally required; as a matter of grace (बिना कानूनी बाध्यता के (विशेषतः भुगतान))
35 **Façade** *{French}* - The principal front of a building; a deceptive outward appearance (इमारत का सामने वाला हिस्सा; बाहरी दिखावा)
36 **Facta non verba** *{Latin}* - Deeds, not words; actions matter more than words (बोलो नहीं, करके दिखाओ)
37 **Fait accompli** *{French}* - Something already

done and beyond alteration (जो हो चुका हो और बदला न जा सके)

38 **Faux pas** *{French}* - A social blunder or breach of etiquette (सामाजिक भूल)

39 **Fiancé** *{French}* - Engaged man (मंगेतर (पुरुष))

40 **Fiancée** *{French}* - Engaged woman (मंगेतर (महिला))

41 **Forte** *{French}* - Strong point (ख़ूबी; मज़बूत पक्ष)

42 **Homo sapiens** *{Latin}* - The species of human beings (मानव प्रजाति)

43 **Ibid.** *{Latin}* - In the same place (used in references) (उसी स्थान पर)

44 **In camera** *{Latin}* - In private; in a judge's chambers (एकांत में, न्यायाधीश के कक्ष में)

45 **In situ** *{Latin}* - In the original place (मूल स्थान पर)

46 **Inter alia** *{Latin}* - Among other things; to indicate that something is only one part of a larger group (अन्य बातों के साथ-साथ)

47 **Je ne sais quoi** *{French}* - An indefinable quality (अवर्णनीय आकर्षण)

48 **Laissez-faire** *{French}* - A policy of non-interference, especially in economic matters (अहस्तक्षेप की नीति (विशेषकर आर्थिक मामलों में))

49 **Liaison** *{French}* - A communication link between groups; a person who serves as such a link (दो पक्षों के बीच संपर्क; संपर्क सूत्र)

50 **Locus standi** *{Latin}* - The right to bring an action or be heard in court (दिए गए मामले में मुकदमा करने या सुनवाई का अधिकार)

51 **Maisonette** *{French}* - A set of rooms with a separate entrance in a building (अलग प्रवेश द्वार वाला छोटा मकान)

52 **Matinée** *{French}* - An afternoon performance of a play, film, or concert (दोपहर का प्रदर्शन या शो (विशेषकर नाटक, फ़िल्म या संगीत कार्यक्रम का))

53 **Mêlée** *{French}* - A confused fight or scuffle (लड़ाई या धक्का-मुक्की)

54 **Mutatis mutandis** *{Latin}* - With the necessary changes having been made (आवश्यक बदलाव करने के बाद)

55 **Persona non grata** *{Latin}* - An unacceptable person (अस्वीकार्य व्यक्ति)

56 **Pococurante** *{Italian}* - Caring little about anything; indifferent and nonchalant (उदासीन; बेपरवाह)

57 **Post meridiem (PM)** *{Latin}* - After midday; Time after noon (दोपहर बाद)

58 **Pot-pourri** *{French}* - A mixture of dried petals and spices; a miscellaneous collection (सुगंधित फूलों की पंखुड़ियों और मसालों का मिश्रण; विविध मिश्रण)

59 **Prima facie** *{Latin}* - At first sight; on the face of it (प्रथम दृष्टया)

60 **Pro forma** *{Latin}* - For the sake of form (औपचारिकता के लिए)

61 **Pro rata** *{Latin}* - In proportion (अनुपात में)

62 **Proletarian** *{Latin}* - A member of the working class (श्रमिक वर्ग का सदस्य)

63 **Quid pro quo** *{Latin}* - Something given in return for something (कुछ के बदले कुछ)

64 **R.S.V.P. (Répondez s'il vous plaît)** *{French}* - Please respond; request for confirmation of attendance (कृपया उत्तर दें (आमंत्रण का))

65 **Rendezvous** *{French}* - Meeting at a prearranged time and place (पूर्व-निर्धारित समय और स्थान पर मिलना)

66 **Riposte** *{French}* - A quick return thrust in fencing; a retort (जवाबी प्रहार)

67 **Sang-froid** *{French}* - The ability to stay calm in a difficult or dangerous situation (खतरे या कठिन परिस्थितियों में शांत रहने की क्षमता)

68 **Sobriquet** *{French}* - A person's nickname (किसी व्यक्ति का उपनाम)

69 **Status quo** *{Latin}* - The existing state of affairs (यथास्थिति; मौजूदा स्थिति)

70 **Sui generis** *{Latin}* - Unique, of its own kind (अपनी तरह का; अद्वितीय)

71 **Suo motu** *{Latin}* - On one's own initiative (especially in legal contexts) (स्वतः संज्ञान (विशेषकर कानूनी संदर्भ में))

72 **Tête-à-tête** *{French}* - A private conversation between two people (दो लोगों के बीच निजी बातचीत)

73 **Ultra vires** *{Latin}* - Beyond the powers (शक्तियों से परे)

74 **Versus (vs./v.)** *{Latin}* - Against (के विरुद्ध)

75 **Via** *{Latin}* - By way of (के माध्यम से)

76 **Vice versa** *{Latin}* - The other way round (और इसका उलटा भी)

77 **Vide** *{Latin}* - See; Refer to (देखें, संदर्भ लें)

78 **Viva voce** *{Latin}* - By word of mouth; orally (मौखिक रूप से)

79 **Viz.** *{Latin}* - Namely; that is to say (used to introduce a specific list) (अर्थात्, यानी)

80 **Volte-face** *{French (from Italian)}* - A complete reversal of opinion or position (रुख बदलना)

81 **Zeitgeist** *{German}* - Spirit of the age; Intellectual or cultural climate of a period (युग की भावना; किसी समय विशेष की मानसिकता या सोच)

Other Important Foreign Words

1 **A cappella** *{Italian}* - Without instrumental accompaniment (बिना किसी वाद्य-यन्त्र के (केवल स्वर में))
2 **À deux** *{French}* - Of or for two; performed or done by two people (especially in dance) (दो व्यक्तियों के लिए / द्वारा)
3 **A fortiori** *{Latin}* - With even stronger reason (मजबूत तर्क से)
4 **A posteriori** *{Latin}* - Based on experience or observation (अनुभव के आधार पर)
5 **A priori** *{Latin}* - Based on theoretical reasoning rather than experience (तर्क के आधार पर (अनुभव के बिना))
6 **Ab antiquo** *{Latin}* - From ancient times (प्राचीन काल से)
7 **Ab origine** *{Latin}* - From the origin (उत्पत्ति से)
8 **Ad infinitum** *{Latin}* - Endlessly; without limit (अंतहीन; बिना अंत के)
9 **Ad libitum (ad lib)** *{Latin}* - At one's pleasure; done freely without preparation, especially as improvisation in music (इच्छानुसार, मनमाने ढंग से)
10 **Ad nauseam** *{Latin}* - To a sickening or excessive degree (उबकाई आने तक; बहुत ज़्यादा)
11 **Ad referendum** *{Latin}* - To be referred; for further consideration (आगे विचार के लिए)
12 **Ad valorem** *{Latin}* - According to value; referring to a tax or duty based on the value of goods (मूल्यानुसार (कर))
13 **Addendum** *{Latin}* - An addition or supplement to a book or document (जोड़ा जाने वाला)
14 **Al dente** *{Italian}* - Cooked just enough to retain a firm texture when bitten (हल्का कड़ा रहने तक पकाया हुआ (दाँत से काटने पर))
15 **Alfresco** *{Italian}* - In the open air (खुली हवा में)
16 **Ante meridiem (A.M.)** *{Latin}* - Before noon (पूर्वाह्न (दोपहर से पहले))
17 **Au naturel** *{French}* - In the natural state (प्राकृतिक अवस्था में)
18 **Beau idéal** *{French}* - Perfect type or model (सर्वोत्तम उदाहरण)
19 **Beau monde** *{French}* - Fashionable society (उच्च समाज)
20 **Beaux arts** *{French}* - Fine arts (ललित कलाएँ)
21 **Belles-lettres** *{French}* - Literary works valued for their aesthetic qualities (ललित साहित्य; सौंदर्यपरक साहित्यिक रचनाएँ)
22 **Billet-doux** *{French}* - A love letter (प्रेम पत्र)
23 **Blitzkrieg** *{German}* - Sudden, swift military attack (आकस्मिक, तीव्र सैन्य आक्रमण)
24 **Bon mot** *{French}* - A witty remark (हाज़िरजवाब टिप्पणी)
25 **Bon vivant** *{French}* - One who enjoys the good life (ऐशो-आराम का शौकीन)
26 **Brasserie** *{French}* - An informal restaurant serving beer and food (अनौपचारिक भोजनालय)
27 **Chic** *{French}* - Stylish and fashionable (सुरुचिपूर्ण; शैलीदार)
28 **Circa** *{Latin}* - Around; Approximately (used in dates) (लगभग (समय या तिथि के संदर्भ में))
29 **Coiffeur** *{French}* - A hairdresser (male) (नाई (पुरुष))
30 **Coiffure** *{French}* - A hairstyle (बालों का सँवारा हुआ रूप)
31 **Cosa nostra** *{Italian}* - The Sicilian Mafia; organized crime syndicate (संगठित अपराध गिरोह (इतालवी माफ़िया))
32 **Coup de grâce** *{French}* - A final blow that brings death or ends something (अंतिम प्रहार)
33 **Coup de main** *{French}* - A surprise attack (आकस्मिक आक्रमण)
34 **Couturier** *{French}* - A fashion designer (male) (वस्त्र-डिज़ाइनर (पुरुष))
35 **Couturière** *{French}* - A fashion designer (female) (वस्त्र-डिज़ाइनर (महिला))
36 **Cui bono?** *{Latin}* - For whose benefit? (किसके लाभ के लिए?)
37 **De jure** *{Latin}* - By law; according to law (क़ानूनन)
38 **De trop** *{French}* - Unwelcome; superfluous; not wanted (अनावश्यक; अवांछित)
39 **Débutant** *{French}* - A male beginner (पदार्पण करने वाला (पुरुष))
40 **Débutante** *{French}* - A female beginner (पदार्पण करने वाली (महिला))
41 **Dei gratia** *{Latin}* - By the grace of God (ईश्वर की कृपा से)
42 **Démarche** *{French}* - A political move or diplomatic action (राजनीतिक या कूटनीतिक कदम)
43 **Deo gratias** *{Latin}* - Thanks be to God (ईश्वर को धन्यवाद)
44 **Deo volente** *{Latin}* - God willing (यदि ईश्वर ने चाहा तो)
45 **Deus ex machina** *{Latin}* - An unexpected saviour or solution, especially in a story or drama (अचानक प्रकट होने वाला अप्रत्याशित समाधान (विशेषकर साहित्य/नाटक में))
46 **Dolce vita** *{Italian}* - A life of pleasure and luxury (ऐशो-आराम का जीवन)

47 **Doppelgänger** *{German}* - A ghostly double or exact look-alike of a living person (हमशक्ल; किसी जीवित व्यक्ति का प्रतिरूप)
48 **En banc** *{French}* - By the full court (पूर्ण न्यायालय द्वारा)
49 **En famille** *{French}* - With one's family (अपने परिवार के साथ)
50 **En passant** *{French}* - In passing; incidentally (चलते-चलते; संयोगवश)
51 **En route** *{French}* - On the way (रास्ते में)
52 **Entente** *{French}* - An understanding or alliance (समझौता या गठबंधन)
53 **Entre nous** *{French}* - Between ourselves; confidentially (हमारे बीच; गोपनीय रूप से)
54 **Ex parte** *{Latin}* - On behalf of only one party (केवल एक पक्ष की ओर से)
55 **Ex post facto** *{Latin}* - After the fact; retroactively (घटना के बाद लागू)
56 **Exempli gratia (e.g.)** *{Latin}* - For example (उदाहरण के लिए)
57 **Femme fatale** *{French}* - Dangerously attractive woman (घातक सुंदरी)
58 **Folie des grandeurs** *{French}* - Delusions of greatness (स्वयं को बहुत महान समझने का भ्रम)
59 **Force majeure** *{French}* - Superior force, unforeseeable event (अप्रत्याशित घटना, अपरिहार्य बल)
60 **Gîte** *{French}* - A holiday home or lodge (अवकाश गृह)
61 **Grande dame** *{French}* - A woman of high respect or prestigious position (प्रतिष्ठित महिला)
62 **Haut monde** *{French}* - High society (उच्च समाज)
63 **Haute couture** *{French}* - High-end fashion; exclusive custom-fitted clothing (उच्च श्रेणी की वस्त्र-सज्जा)
64 **Haute cuisine** *{French}* - Sophisticated or high-quality cooking (उच्च स्तरीय पाक-कला)
65 **Hauteur** *{French}* - An arrogant manner; a superior attitude toward others (घमंडी रवैया, अहंकारी व्यवहार)
66 **Id est (i.e.)** *{Latin}* - That is (used to clarify) (अर्थात)
67 **In absentia** *{Latin}* - In the absence of the person concerned (संबंधित व्यक्ति की अनुपस्थिति में)
68 **In extremis** *{Latin}* - At the point of death; in an extreme situation (मृत्यु की कगार पर; अत्यंत कठिन स्थिति में)
69 **In propria persona** *{Latin}* - In one's own person (स्वयं)
70 **Infra dig (infra dignitatem)** *{Latin}* - Beneath one's dignity (शान के खिलाफ़, प्रतिष्ठा से नीचे)
71 **Ipso facto** *{Latin}* - By the fact itself (उसी कारण से; स्वतः)
72 **Leitmotif** *{German}* - A recurring theme (बार-बार आने वाला विषय)
73 **Manqué** *{French}* - Having failed to become what one could have been (जो बन सकता था पर नहीं बना)
74 **Mea culpa** *{Latin}* - My fault (मेरी गलती)
75 **Mélange** *{French}* - A mixture or assortment (मिश्रण; विविधता)
76 **Memento mori** *{Latin}* - A reminder of the inevitability of death (मृत्यु का स्मरण; मौत को याद रखो)
77 **Ménage** *{French}* - Household (घर-परिवार)
78 **Modus vivendi** *{Latin}* - A practical arrangement for coexistence (साथ रहने की व्यावहारिक व्यवस्था)
79 **Mot juste** *{French}* - The exact right word (एकदम सही शब्द)
80 **Ne plus ultra** *{Latin}* - Nothing further beyond; the ultimate point of perfection (परम उत्कृष्टता, चरम सीमा)
81 **Née** *{French}* - Born as (used to indicate a married woman's maiden name) (जन्म नाम (महिला का विवाह से पहले का नाम))
82 **Noblesse oblige** *{French}* - Privilege entails responsibility (विशेषाधिकार के साथ ज़िम्मेदारी आती है)
83 **Nom de plume** *{French}* - Pen name, pseudonym (लेखक का काल्पनिक नाम)
84 **Non sequitur** *{Latin}* - A conclusion that does not logically follow from what preceded it (तर्कहीन बात)
85 **Nonpareil** *{French}* - Having no equal; unparalleled (अद्वितीय)
86 **Nota bene** *{Latin}* - Note well (ध्यान दें)
87 **Objet d'art** *{French}* - Work of art (कला कृति)
88 **On dit** *{French}* - A piece of gossip; a rumour (अफ़वाह; सुनी-सुनाई बात)
89 **Outré** *{French}* - Bizarre; beyond what is proper or conventional (सामान्य मर्यादा से परे; विचित्र; असामान्य)
90 **Papabile** *{Italian}* - Likely or possible candidate for the Pope (पोप पद के लिए संभावित या संभव उम्मीदवार)
91 **Par excellence** *{French}* - Outstandingly good of its kind; the best (सर्वश्रेष्ठ; बेजोड़)
92 **Per annum** *{Latin}* - Per year; annually (प्रति वर्ष)

93 **Per capita** *{Latin}* - Per head; for each person (प्रति व्यक्ति)

94 **Per centum** *{Latin}* - By the hundred; percent (प्रतिशत)

95 **Per se** *{Latin}* - By itself; intrinsically (अपने आप में)

96 **Persona grata** *{Latin}* - An acceptable person (स्वीकृत व्यक्ति)

97 **Protégé** *{French}* - One who is protected or trained by another (किसी के द्वारा संरक्षित या प्रशिक्षित व्यक्ति)

98 **Religio loci** *{Latin}* - The religious awe or sanctity of a place (किसी स्थान की धार्मिक पवित्रता)

99 **Renvoi** *{French}* - Referral of a legal matter to another jurisdiction (किसी विधिक विवाद को दूसरे क्षेत्राधिकार में भेजना)

100 **Résumé** *{French}* - A summary or brief account; a CV (संक्षिप्त विवरण; जीवन-वृत्त)

101 **Sanctum sanctorum** *{Latin}* - The holiest of places; a very private or secret place (पवित्रतम स्थान, गोपनीय कक्ष)

102 **Sans** *{French}* - Without (के बिना)

103 **Savoir-faire** *{French}* - The ability to act or speak appropriately in social situations (सामाजिक परिस्थितियों में उचित व्यवहार या बात करने का कौशल)

104 **Sine qua non** *{Latin}* - An essential condition; indispensable requirement (अनिवार्य शर्त)

105 **Sotto voce** *{Italian}* - In a low voice (धीमी आवाज़ में)

106 **Sua sponte** *{Latin}* - Of one's own accord (अपनी इच्छा से)

107 **Sub rosa** *{Latin}* - Secretly; confidentially (गुप्त रूप से)

108 **Summum bonum** *{Latin}* - The highest good (परम कल्याण)

109 **Terra firma** *{Latin}* - Solid ground (ठोस जमीन)

110 **Terra incognita** *{Latin}* - Unknown land (अज्ञात भूमि)

111 **Tour de force** *{French}* - An outstanding achievement or performance (ताकत, कौशल या सूझ-बूझ का कारनामा)

112 **Tout de suite** *{French}* - Immediately, at once (तुरंत, फ़ौरन)

113 **Ubique** *{Latin}* - Everywhere (हर जगह)

114 **Verboten** *{German}* - Forbidden; prohibited by rule or law (निषिद्ध, प्रतिबंधित)

115 **Vers libre** *{French}* - Free verse; poetry without regular metre or rhyme (छंदमुक्त कविता; बिना छंद या तुक की कविता)

116 **Via media** *{Latin}* - A middle way (बीच का रास्ता)

Root Words, Prefixes & Suffixes

You already know the word **Incredible** (अविश्वसनीय). But what about **Credence**? Looks unfamiliar? Both these words come from the same root: **"Cred"**, which means **to believe**. Once you know this one root, both words become simple.

Let us break **Incredible** apart. It has three parts:

In (Prefix: not) + **Cred** (Root: believe) + **ible** (Suffix: able to)
= not able to believe = unbelievable (अविश्वसनीय)

That is it. A **prefix** is added before the root. A **suffix** is added after it. And the **root** in the middle carries the core meaning. Together, they build the word. Most of these roots come from Latin and Greek, which form over 60% of English vocabulary.

Now here is where it gets powerful. From this single root **"Cred" (believe)**, look how many words open up:

- **Credible** – able to believe; believable (विश्वसनीय)
- **Incredible** – not + able to believe; unbelievable (अविश्वसनीय)
- **Credulous** – someone who believes too easily (विश्वासी, अंधविश्वासी)
- **Incredulous** – not willing to believe; doubtful (अविश्वासी, संदेहशील)
- **Credence** – belief that something is true (प्रत्यय, विश्वास)
- **Credential** – proof of one's qualification or trustworthiness (प्रमाण पत्र)
- **Discredit** – to take away belief; to damage reputation (बदनाम करना)
- **Creed** – a set of beliefs or principles (मत, आस्था)
- **Credo** – a statement of personal beliefs (व्यक्तिगत विश्वास का विवरण)
- **Accredit** – to officially recognize or authorize (मान्यता प्रदान करना)

One root. Ten words. You did not memorise any of them. You *understood* them. That is the difference between cramming a word list and actually building vocabulary. When you learn roots, the words stay with you because they make sense.

Competitive exams, whether SSC, Banking, Defense, DSSSB, or other exams, will always throw words you have never seen before. You cannot memorise the entire dictionary. But you *can* learn the building blocks that make up those words. That is exactly what this chapter gives you.

This chapter contains **over 400 root words, prefixes, and suffixes**, each with its meaning in English and Hindi, along with exam-relevant examples. Study 5 to 10 roots a day. Look at the examples. Try thinking of more words from the same root, prefix or suffix from OWS or Syno-Anto chapters of Blackbook. Within a few weeks, unfamiliar words will start making sense on their own.

F6 Root words, Prefixes and Suffixes (Important for SSC & Other Exams)

SN	Root Word	Meaning	Examples
1	**ac, acr**	sharp (तीखा), bitter (कड़वा)	1. Acerbic - expressing harsh or sharp criticism in a clever way; tasting sour or bitter (कठोर, तीखा; कड़वा) 2. Acrid - smell or taste is strong and sharp, and usually unpleasant (तीखा)
2	**acer, acri**	bitter (कड़वा), unpleasant (अप्रिय)	1. Acerophobia - fear of sour tastes (खटाई से डर) 2. Acrimonious - full of anger and strong bitter feelings (उग्र, कटृता)
3	**aer, aero**	air (वायु)	1. Aerate - to let air reach something (वायु-प्रसार करना, हवा भरना) 2. Aerodynamics - the branch of mechanics that deals with the motion of gases (especially air) and their effects on bodies in the flow (वायुगति विज्ञान)
4	**agog**	leading (नेतृत्व करना), curiosity (जिज्ञासा)	1. Demagogue - an orator who appeals to the passions and prejudices of his audience (जनोत्तेजक नेता) 2. Haemagogue - promoting the flow of blood (रक्त के प्रवाह को बढ़ावा देना)
5	**agr, agri, agro**	farming (कृषि)	1. Agrarian - relating to the management of land (कृषि-संबंधी) 2. Agriculture - practice of growing crops or raising animals (कृषि) 3. Agroforestry - agriculture incorporating the cultivation and conservation of trees (कृषि वानिकी)
6	**alg, algo**	pain (दर्द)	1. Analgesic - a drug that makes one pain free (दर्दनाशक) 2. Nostalgia - a wistful desire to return in thought (बीते वक्त की याद, उदासी) 3. Algophobia - fear of pain (दर्द का भय)
7	**ali, alter**	other (अन्य), another (एक और, किसी दूसरे)	1. Alien - foreigner; strange and not familiar; relating to creatures from another planet (विदेशी) 2. Alternative - A thing that you can choose to do from any other (विकल्प)
8	**ambul, amble**	walk (टहलना), move (कदम)	1. Amble - to walk in a slow relaxed manner (टहलना) 2. Ambulance - a vehicle that moves a patient (रोगी वाहन)
9	**ami**	love (प्यार), friendly (दोस्ताना)	1. Amiable - friendly and lovable (मिलनसार) 2. Amity - friendly and peaceful relations (मेल-जोल)
10	**andr, andro**	man (आदमी), male (पुरुष)	1. Androgynous - being both male and female (उभयलिंगी) 2. Android - a type of machine that looks like a real person (मानव जैसी मशीन) 3. Misandry - hatred towards men (आदमी के प्रति घृणा)

SN	Root Word	Meaning	Examples
11	**anim**	life (ज़िंदगी), spirit (आत्मा)	1. Animal - a living organism (जानवर) 2. Animate - to make alive (चेतन, सजीव)
12	**ann, enn**	year (वर्ष)	1. Anniversary - a date observed once a year (सालगिरह) 2. Annual - happening once a year (वार्षिक) 3. Millennium - 1,000 years (हज़ार वर्ष)
13	**anthrop, anthropo**	human (इंसान)	1. Anthropology - the study of mankind (मनुष्य जाति का विज्ञान) 2. Philanthropy - love for mankind (लोकोपकार, मानव-प्रेम)
14	**api**	bees (मधुमक्खी)	1. Apiary - where bees are reared (मधुमक्खियों के पालने का स्थान) 2. Apiculture - rearing of bees (मधुमक्खी पालन)
15	**apt, ept**	skill (कौशल), ability (क्षमता)	1. Aptitude - Natural ability or skill at doing something (कौशल) 2. Inept - Having no skill; not good at doing something (अयोग्य)
16	**aqu, aqua, aqui**	water (पानी)	1. Aquarium - a water container for fish (मछलीघर) 2. Aquatic - relating to water (जलीय) 3. Aquifer - an underground layer of water-bearing rock (भूमिगत जलस्रोत)
17	**arbor**	tree (पेड़)	1. Arbor - a shady area formed by trees (वृक्षों द्वारा निर्मित छायादार क्षेत्र) 2. Arborist - someone working with trees (पेड़ों की देखभाल और रख-रखाव में विशेषज्ञ)
18	**art**	skill (कौशल)	1. Artifact - object made by a person's skill (विरूपण साक्ष्य, शिल्पकृति) 2. Artist - a person who creates skillfully (कलाकार)
19	**arthr, arthro**	joint (जोड़)	1. Arthritis - inflammation of a joint (वात रोग, गठिया) 2. Arthroscope - a tool to see inside a joint (जोड़ों के अंदर देखने का एक उपकरण)
20	**astro, aster**	star (तारा), outer space (बाहरी अंतरिक्ष)	1. Astronaut - a person traveling to the stars (अंतरिक्षयात्री) 2. Astronomer - someone who studies the stars (खगोलविद) 3. Asterisk - a star-shaped symbol (तारांकन चिहन)
21	**aud, audi, audio**	hear (सुनना)	1. Audible - loud enough to be heard (सुनाई देने योग्य) 2. Audience - people who listen to a program (श्रोता) 3. Audiovisual - relating to sound and vision (दृश्य-श्रव्य)
22	**aug, aux, auc**	increase (बढ़ोतरी), growth (विकास), assist (सहायता देना)	1. Augment - to increase the amount, value, size, etc (बढ़ाना) 2. Auxiliary - a person who is employed to assist other people in their work (सहायक) 3. Auction - a public sale in which goods or property are sold to the highest bidder (नीलामी)
23	**avi, avia**	bird (चिड़िया), flight (उड़ान)	1. Aviary - A place for keeping birds (पक्षीशाला) 2. Aviation - the art of designing or operating aircraft (विमानन)

SN	Root Word	Meaning	Examples
24	**bar, baro**	pressure (दबाव), weight (वज़न)	1. Barometer - an instrument that measures air pressure (वायुमान यंत्र) 2. Isobaric - by constant or equal pressure (समदाब रेखीय)
25	**bell, belli**	war (युद्ध), fight (लड़ाई)	1. Bellicose - warlike (लड़ाकू) 2. Belligerent - hostile, ready to fight (युद्धरत)
26	**bibli, biblio**	book (किताब)	1. Bibliography - a list of books used as sources (ग्रन्थसूची) 2. Bibliophile - a person who loves books (पुस्तकों को प्यार करनेवाला)
27	**bri, brev**	brief (संक्षिप्त), short (छोटा)	1. Abridge - piece of writing shorter by removing details and information that is not important (संक्षेप करना) 2. Brevity - the state of being short or quick (संक्षिप्तता)
28	**cand**	glowing (प्रकाश से युक्त), shine (चमक), white (सफ़ेद)	1. Candid- free from bias, prejudice, or malice (स्पष्टवादी) 2. Incandescent- white, glowing, or luminous with intense heat (सफ़ेद, चमकीला, या तेज़ गर्मी से चमकने वाला)
29	**cant, cent, chant**	to sing (गाने के लिए), charm (आकर्षण)	1. Accent - a distinctive way of pronouncing language (लहज़ा) 2. Enchant - to attract somebody strongly or please someone very much (मंत्रमुग्ध करना, प्रसन्न करना) 3. Cantata - a musical composition for voices and instruments (कण्ठ-संगीत, गायन-रचना)
30	**cap, cip, cept**	to take (लेने के), receive (प्राप्त करना), get (पाना)	1. Captivating - exciting and pleasant (मनोरम) 2. Accept - to take willingly something that is offered (स्वीकार करना) 3. Percipient - good at noticing and understanding things (समझने वाला)
31	**cardi, cardio**	heart (दिल)	1. Cardiac - relating to the heart (हृदय सम्बन्धी) 2. Cardiologist - a heart doctor (हृदय रोग विशेषज्ञ)
32	**carn, carni**	flesh (मांस), meat (मांस)	1. Carnal - pertaining to the body or flesh (कामुक) 2. Carnivorous - flesh-eating (मांसभक्षी)
33	**caust, caut**	to burn (जलाना)	1. Caustic - capable of burning or eating away (दाहक) 2. Cauterize - to burn with a hot instrument (दाग़ना)
34	**centr, centro, centri**	center (केंद्र)	1. Centrifugal - moving outward from a center (अपकेंद्री :- केंद्र से बाहर की ओर) 2. Egocentric - self-centered (अहंकारपूर्ण) 3. Centroid - the center point of a geometric figure (किसी ज्यामितीय आकृति का केंद्र बिंदु)
35	**cerebr, cerebro**	brain (दिमाग)	1. Cerebral - pertaining to the brain (सेरिब्रल, दिमाग़ी) 2. Cerebrospinal - pertaining to the brain and the spinal cord (मस्तिष्कमेरु)
36	**chrom, chromo, chromat, chromato**	color (रंग), pigment (रंग)	1. Achromatic - without color (बिना रंग का) 2. Chromatics - the study of color (रंग-विज्ञान) 3. Chromatophores - cells that produce color (वर्णक कोशिकाएँ) 4. Chromoplast - a type of plastid in plant cells containing color pigments (रंग वर्णक युक्त प्लास्टिड)

SN	Root Word	Meaning	Examples
37	**chron, chrono**	time (समय)	1. Chronic - lasting for a long time (दीर्घकालिक) 2. Chronological - arranging events in time order (कालक्रमबद्ध, समय के अनुसार)
38	**clam, claim**	to shout (चिल्लाना), to cry for something (किसी चीज़ के लिए रोना)	1. Acclaim - to praise or welcome somebody, something publicly (प्रशंसा करना) 2. Clamour - A loud cry (कोलाहल)
39	**cli**	to lean toward (की ओर झुकना)	1. Climax - the most exciting or important event or point in time (चरम बिन्दु) 2. Inclination - a feeling that makes somebody want to behave in a particular way (झुकाव)
40	**cogn**	know (जानना)	1. Cognition - process of acquiring knowledge (ज्ञान प्राप्त करने की प्रक्रिया) 2. Recognize - to discover that one knows (पहचानना)
41	**corp**	body (शरीर)	1. Corporal - pertaining to the body (शारीरिक) 2. Corpse - a dead body (लाश)
42	**cosm**	universe (ब्रह्मांड)	1. Cosmonaut - a Russian astronaut (अंतरिक्ष यात्री) 2. Cosmos - the universe (ब्रह्मांड)
43	**cranio**	skull (खोपड़ी)	1. Cranial - pertaining to the skull (कपाल) 2. Cranium - skull of vertebrates (कशेरुकियों की खोपड़ी)
44	**cred**	belief (आस्था), believe (विश्वास)	1. Credence - belief that something is true or valid (प्रत्यय, विश्वास) 2. Incredible - unbelievable (अविश्वसनीय)
45	**culp**	blame (दोष), fault (गलती)	1. Culpable - deserving to be blamed or considered responsible for something wrong (दोषी, आपराधिक) 2. Culprit - A person who has been blamed for something wrong or against the law (अपराधी)
46	**cycl**	circle (घेरा)	1. Cycle - repeated sequence of events (चक्र) 2. Cyclone -a violent tropical storm (चक्रवात)
47	**dem, demo**	people (लोग)	1. Democracy - government of the people (प्रजातंत्र) 2. Demography - the study of populations (जनसांख्यिकीय)
48	**dendr, dendro, dendri**	tree (पेड़)	1. Dendriform - in the shape of a tree (वृक्ष के समान आकार का) 2. Dendrochronology - dating events by studying growth rings in trees (वृक्षवलय कालक्रम) 3. Philodendron - a climbing plant that grows on trees (ऊपर की तरफ बढ़ने वाला पौधा जो पेड़ों पर उगता है)
49	**dent, dont**	tooth (दाँत)	1. Dental - relating to teeth (दंत-संबंधी) 2. Dentist - a doctor for the teeth (दाँतों का डॉक्टर) 3. Orthodontist - a specialist dentist who straightens teeth (दंत-संशोधन विशेषज्ञ)
50	**derm, derma**	skin (त्वचा)	1. Dermatitis - inflammation of the skin (त्वचा पर लालिमा के साथ सूजन) 2. Dermatologist - a doctor for the skin (त्वचा विशेषज्ञ)

SN	Root Word	Meaning	Examples
51	**dexter**	right hand (दायाँ हाथ)	1. Ambidextrous - one who uses both hands equally well (दोनों हाथों का समान सहजता या निपुणता से उपयोग करना) 2. Dexterity - ability to use hands skillfully (निपुणता)
52	**dict**	to speak (बात करने के लिए), say (कहना)	1. Abdicate - to formally declare to relinquish or renounce the power or position. (त्यागना) 2. Predict - to say something in advance that will happen in the future (भविष्यवाणी करना)
53	**diction**	say (कहना), speak (बोलना)	1. Contradiction - a lack of agreement between facts (विरोधाभास) 2. Dictionary - a book of collection of words and their definitions (शब्दकोष)
54	**dign**	worth (लायक)	1. Dignified - controlled, graceful and deserving respect (गरिमापूर्ण, प्रतिष्ठित) 2. Dignity - calm, serious and controlled behaviour that makes people respect you (गरिमा)
55	**dol**	suffer (पीड़ित), pain (दर्द)	1. Condolence - sympathy or sadness that you feel for somebody (शोक) 2. Doleful - very sad (मातमी, उदास)
56	**domin**	master (मालिक), control (नियंत्रण)	1. Dominate - to be the master of; domineering (हावी होना) 2. Predominate - to have more power than others (प्रबल होना)
57	**dorm**	to sleep (सोने के लिए), motionless (स्तब्ध)	1. Dormancy - state of being static or dormant; motionless (निद्रा) 2. Dormitory - a building of sleeping rooms (छात्रावास)
58	**dox**	belief (आस्था), praise (प्रशंसा), opinions (राय)	1. Orthodox - When someone has the same opinions and beliefs acceptable by most people (रूढ़िवादी) 2. Paradox - self contradictory statement (विरोधाभास)
59	**duc, duct**	to lead (नेतृत्व करना)	1. Conduct - to organize particular activity (संचालन करना) 2. Educate - to develop, teach, lead out from ignorance (शिक्षित)
60	**dura**	long lasting (दीर्घकाल तक चलने वाला)	1. Durability - the ability to last over time (सहनशीलता) 2. Endure - to continue to exist in the same state or condition (सहन करना)
61	**ego**	self (खुद)	1. Alter ego - a person's secondary or alternative personality (दूसरा व्यक्तित्व) 2. Egoistic - self-centered (आत्म केन्द्रित)
62	**enn, enni, anni**	years (साल)	1. Bicentennial - a 200th anniversary (दो सौ साल का) 2. Anniversary -returning or recurring each year (सालगिरह, वर्षगाँठ)
63	**equ, equi, equus**	horse (घोड़ा)	1. Equestrian - related with the riding of horses (घुड़सवार) 2. Equerry - an officer who takes care of horses for royalty (शाही अश्वपाल)

SN	Root Word	Meaning	Examples
64	**erg, ergo**	work (काम)	1. Energy - the power to accomplish work (ऊर्जा) 2. Ergonomics - study of the working environment (कर्मचारी परिस्थिति विज्ञान)
65	**err**	wander (घूमना), transgress (उल्लंघन करना), make a mistake (भूल करना)	1. Aberrant - not usual or not socially acceptable (धर्मपथ से हटनेवाला) 2. Erratic - not happening at regular times (अनियमित)
66	**esth, aesth**	feeling (अनुभूति), sensation (सनसनी), beauty (सुंदरता)	1. Aesthetic - pertaining to a sense of beauty (सौंदर्य संबंधी) 2. Kinesthesia - the sensation of bodily movement. (गतिबोध, शारीरिक गति संवेदना)
67	**fab, fam**	speak (बोलना)	1. Affable - pleasant, kind, friendly and easy to talk to (मिलनसार) 2. Fabulous - Excellent, wonderful (आश्चर्यजनक) 3. Defame - to damage the reputation of a person by saying bad things (बदनाम करना)
68	**fac, fic, fig**	to do (करने के लिए), to make (बनाने के लिए)	1. Artifice - a clever trick intended to deceive someone (चाल, चालाकी) 2. Facile - produced without effort or careful thought (सुगम) 3. Configuration - the way in which parts of something are arranged (संरचना, विन्यास)
69	**fact, fac, fic**	made (बनाया), produce (उत्पादन करना)	1. Benefaction - the act of giving something, such as money (दान) 2. Manufacture - to produce (उत्पादन) 3. Factory - a place where things are made (कारखाना)
70	**fer**	to carry (ले जाना), to bear (सहना), to bring (लाना)	1. Aquifer - an underground layer of water-bearing permeable rock (जलवाही स्तर) 2. Transfer - moved from one place to another (स्थानांतरण)
71	**ferv**	boil (उबलना), glow (चमकना), to burn (जलाना)	1. Fervent - having or showing great warmth or feeling (जोशीला, उत्साही) 2. Fervor - very strong feeling about something (जोश)
72	**fid**	faith (आस्था), trust (विश्वास)	1. Confide - place trust in someone (विश्वास करना) 2. Fidelity - faithfulness (सत्य के प्रति निष्ठा)
73	**fin**	end (अंत), finish (खत्म करना)	1. Finale - the last part of a show or a piece of music (समापन) 2. Finish - to complete something (खत्म करना)
74	**flam, flagr**	to burn (जलाना)	1. Aflame - burning on fire (जलता हुआ) 2. Flammable - capable of being easily set on fire (ज्वलनशील) 3. Conflagration - an extensive and destructive fire (भीषण आग)
75	**flect, flex**	to bend (मोड़ने के लिए), curve (वक्र)	1. Flexible - able to bend easily (लचीला) 2. Retroflex - bent or curved backward (टेढ़ा, पीछे की ओर

SN	Root Word	Meaning	Examples
			झुका या मुड़ा हुआ) 3. Reflect - to bend back light or thought (परावर्तित करना)
76	**flict**	to strike (चोट मारना)	1. Afflict - to make someone or something suffer physically or mentally (पीड़ा देना) 2. Inflict - To cause something injurious or harmful (पीड़ा पहुंचाना)
77	**flu, flux**	to flow (प्रवाह)	1. Confluence - the place where two rivers flow together and gathering at one point (संगम, मेल) 2. Flux - a continuous movement (प्रवाह)
78	**fort**	strength (ताकत), strong (मज़बूत)	1. Fortify - to make defensible (मजबूत) 2. Forte - something that a person excels (प्रधान गुण)
79	**fra, frac, frag**	to break (तोड़ने के लिए)	1. Fracture - a crack or break in a bone (भंग) 2. Fragment - pieces of something (टुकड़ा) 3. Fragile - easily broken or damaged (कमज़ोर)
80	**fund, found**	bottom (तल), basis (आधार)	1. Founder - Someone who establishes an organization (संस्थापक) 2. Fundamental - basic and important (मौलिक, बुनियादी)
81	**fur, fury**	anger (गुस्सा), rage (क्रोध)	1. Furore - angry reaction to something by a lot of people; a public outburst (हंगामा) 2. Infuriate - to make extremely angry (क्रोधित करना)
82	**fus**	to pour (उँडेलना)	1. Circumfuse - To pour or spread (उँडेलना) 2. Infuse — to pour in (डालना, भरना)
83	**gam, gamy**	marriage (शादी), union (मिलन)	1. Monogamy - the practice of marrying one person at a time (एकविवाह-प्रथा) 2. Polygamy - the practice or custom of having more than one wife or husband at the same time (बहुविवाह)
84	**gastr, gastro**	stomach (पेट)	1. Gastric - pertaining to the stomach (पेट सम्बन्धी) 2. Gastronomy - serving the stomach by providing good food (पौष्टिक भोजन बनाने की कला या विज्ञान)
85	**gen, geno, gene**	birth (जन्म), production (उत्पादन), origin (मूल)	1. Generation - all the people born at approximately the same time (पीढ़ी) 2. Genealogy - the study of the history of a family (वंशावली अध्ययन)
86	**ger**	old age (बुढ़ापा, वृद्ध अवस्था)	1. Gerontocracy - the rule of the elders (वृद्ध-शासन) 2. Gerontology - the science of aging (वृद्धावस्था)
87	**gnos, gnom, cogn**	knowledge (ज्ञान)	1. Agnostic - one who believes that the existence of God is unknown (अज्ञेयवाद; अनीश्वरवादी) 2. Cognitive - relating to or involving the processes of thinking and reasoning (संज्ञानात्मक) 3. Gnomology - a collection of wise sayings (सूक्तिसंग्रह)
88	**gon**	angle (कोण)	1. Decagon - a plane polygon of 10 angles and 10 sides (दसभुज) 2. Pentagon - a polygon of five angles and five sides (पंचकोण)

SN	Root Word	Meaning	Examples
89	**gram**	letter (पत्र), written (लिखा हुआ)	1. Diagram - a simple drawing (आरेख) 2. Grammar - rules of how to write words in sentences (व्याकरण)
90	**grand**	big (बड़ा), great (महान), large (बड़ा)	1. Grandeur - the quality or state of being grand (शान) 2. Grandiose - larger and containing more detail than necessary (दिखावटी)
91	**graph, graphy, graphein**	to write (लिखना, लेखन)	1. Cacography - Bad handwriting or spelling (बूरी लिखावट) 2. Epigraphy - the study of written materials recorded on inscriptions (प्रालेख-विद्या)
92	**grat**	pleasing (मनभावन), joy (आनंद)	1. Gratitude - the feeling of being grateful and wanting to express your thanks (कृतज्ञता) 2. Gratify - to please or satisfy somebody (संतुष्ट करना, प्रसन्न करना)
93	**greg**	group (समूह)	1. Congregate - to gather into a crowd, group, or assembly (एकत्रित होना) 2. Gregarious - living in group; sociable (झुण्ड में रहनेवाला)
94	**gress, grad, grade, gradi**	to step (कदम बढ़ाने के लिए), to go (चल देना)	1. Gradient - inclination, slope (ढलान) 2. Gradual - step by step (क्रमिक) 3. Progress - movement forward or onward (प्रगति)
95	**gyn, gyno, gyne**	woman (महिला), female (महिला)	1. Gynecology - the science of female reproductive health (स्त्रीरोग विज्ञान) 2. Gynephobia - fear of women (महिलाओं का डर)
96	**heli, helio**	sun (सूरज)	1. Heliograph - apparatus used to send message with the help of sunlight (सूर्य के प्रकाश की सहायता से संदेश भेजने के लिए प्रयुक्त उपकरण) 2. Heliotropism - movement or growth in relating to the sun (सूर्य की ओर मुड़ना)
97	**helic, helico**	spiral (कुंडली), circular (गोलाकार)	1. Helicopter - an aircraft with horizontal rotating wing (हेलीकॉप्टर) 2. Helix - a spiral form (कुंडलित वक्रता)
98	**hem, hemo, haema, hemato**	blood (रक्त, खून)	1. Hemoglobin - red blood particle (हीमोग्लोबिन) 2. Hemorrhage - excessive bleeding or loss of blood from a damaged blood vessel (रक्तस्राव) 3. Hematology - the branch of medicine focused on the study of blood (रक्त विज्ञान)
99	**hydr, hydro**	liquid (तरल), water (पानी)	1. Hydrate - to add water to (जलयोजित करना) 2. Hydrophobia - intense fear of water (जल का डर)
100	**iatr, iatro**	medicine (दवा), healer (आरोग्य करनेवाला)	1. Podiatry - medical care for feet. (पदचिकित्सा) 2. Psychiatric - the branch of medicine that focuses on mental, emotional, and behavioral disorders (मानसिक रोग सम्बन्धी)
101	**icon, icono**	image (छवि, प्रतिमा)	1. Icon - an (often religious) image, in modern usage a simplified graphic of high symbolic content (मूर्ति, प्रतिमा) 2. Iconology - science of symbols and icons (प्रतिमा विज्ञान)

SN	Root Word	Meaning	Examples
102	**imag**	likeness (समानता), idea (कल्पना)	1. Imaginative - able to think up new ideas or images (कल्पनाशील) 2. Imagine - to form a picture or likeness in the mind. (कल्पना करना)
103	**ject**	throw (फेंक)	1. Eject - to throw someone, something out (निकालना) 2. Project - to cast or throw something (कुछ डालना या फेंकना)
104	**jud**	law (कानून)	1. Judgement - a decision of a court of law (निर्णय) 2. Judiciary - a system of courts of law. (न्यायतंत्र)
105	**junct**	join (जोड़ना)	1. Adjunct - something joined to another thing but not necessarily a part of it (सहायक) 2. Junction - a place where things, especially roads or railways, come together (संगम)
106	**juven**	young (युवा)	1. Juvenile - a person who is not old enough to be considered an adult (किशोर) 2. Rejuvenate - to bring back to youthful strength or appearance. (फिर से युवा करना)
107	**kine, kinemat**	motion (गति)	1. Kinematics - the study of objects without considering the cause of motion (गतिकी, गति विज्ञान) 2. Kinetics - study of the force of motion (गति के बल का अध्ययन)
108	**lab**	work (काम)	1. Collaborate - to work with a person (सहयोग) 2. Laborious - requiring a lot of hard work (श्रमसाध्य, कठिन)
109	**lact, lacto**	milk (दूध)	1. Lactometer - device used to measure the cleanliness or quality of milk (दूध की शुद्धता नापने का यंत्र) 2. Lactose - the sugar contained in milk (दूध में मौजूद चीनी)
110	**latry**	worship (पूजा)	1. Anthropolatry - worship of human beings (मनुष्य की पूजा) 2. Iconolatry - worship of icons or images (प्रतिमा-पूजा)
111	**lev, levi**	light in weight (वजन में हल्के), to raise (बढ़ाना), to rise (ऊपर उठना)	1. Elevate - to lift (something) up (उठाना, ऊपर करना) 2. Levity - humour or lack of seriousness (छिछोरापन, गंभीरता की कमी)
112	**lex**	word (शब्द), law (कानून), reading (पढ़ना)	1. Lexicographer - a person who writes or compiles a dictionary (शब्दकोषकार) 2. Alexia - partial or complete inability to read (पठन अक्षमता)
113	**lib, liber**	to free (आज़ाद, मुक्त करना)	1. Liberate - to set free (मुक्त करना) 2. Liberty - freedom (स्वतंत्रता)
114	**lingu**	language (भाषा), tongue (जीभ)	1. Bilingual - a person who speaks two languages equally well (द्विभाषी) 2. Multilingual - able to communicate in multiple languages (बहुभाषी)

SN	Root Word	Meaning	Examples
115	**lip, lipo**	fat (वसा)	1. Lipase - enzyme that breaks down fat (एंजाइम जो वसा को तोड़ता है) 2. Liposuction - the mechanical removal of fat reserves in the tissue (वसा हटाने की प्रक्रिया)
116	**litho**	stone (पत्थर)	1. Lithology - the study of rocks (चट्टानों का अध्ययन) 2. Monolith - a very large, upright piece of stone (एकाश्म)
117	**loc**	place (जगह)	1. Location - a place (जगह) 2. Relocate - to move to a new place (स्थानांतरित होना)
118	**log, logy**	word (शब्द), doctrine (सिद्धांत), study (अध्ययन)	1. Analogy - similarity, especially between things otherwise dissimilar. (समानता, समरूपता) 2. Logic - correct reasoning (तर्क)
119	**loqu, loqua, locu**	speak (बोलना)	1. Elocution - art of public speaking (सार्वजनिक स्थान पर बोलने की कला) 2. Eloquent - speaking beautifully and forcefully (सुवक्ता) 3. Loquacious - very talkative (बातूनी)
120	**lu, luc**	light (रोशनी), clarity (स्पष्टता)	1. Illuminate - To shine light on something (प्रकाश डालना) 2. Lucid - Clearly expressed; easy to understand (स्पष्ट अर्थ का)
121	**lud**	game or play (खेल या क्रीड़ा)	1. Ludic - playful (शोख़ी) 2. Ludicrous - foolish, ridiculous, idiotic (ऊटपटांग)
122	**lud, lus**	to play (क्रीड़ा करना), trick (चाल)	1. Allude - to refer to something indirectly (संकेत करना) 2. Illusion - something that tricks the mind or perception (भ्रम, छल)
123	**lumin**	light (रोशनी)	1. Lumen - unit measuring light (प्रकाश मापने वाली इकाई) 2. Luminescent - producing light without being heated (संदीप्तिशील; कम तापमान पर उत्सर्जित होने वाले प्रकाश)
124	**lun, luna, luni**	moon (चंद्रमा)	1. Lunar - relating to the moon (चाँद सम्बन्धी) 2. Lunitidal - relating to tidal phenomena caused by the moon (चंद्रमा के कारण होने वाली ज्वारीय घटनाएं) 3. Lunarscape - the surface of the moon (चाँद की सतह)
125	**lustre**	shine (चमक), bright (चमकदार)	1. Lacklustre - lacking brilliance or radiance (मंद) 2. Lustrous - shining (चमकदार)
126	**lut, lug, luv**	to wash (धोना)	1. Ablution - The act of washing yourself (स्नान) 2. Deluge - A sudden very heavy fall of rain (बाढ़) 3. Alluvium - A deposit of sand, mud etc. formed by flowing water (जलोढ़क, मिट्टी इत्यादि)
127	**magn, magna, magni**	great (महान), large (बड़ा)	1. Magnificent - grand (शानदार) 2. Magnify - make larger (बड़ा करना, आवर्धित करना) 3. Magnate - a powerful person, especially in business or industry (रईस, पूंजीपति)
128	**man, mani, manu**	hand (हाथ)	1. Manual - done with the hands (हस्तचालित, हाथ से किया गया) 2. Manuscript - a book written by hand (हस्तलिपि) 3. Maneuver - to move by hand (पैंतरेबाज़ी)
129	**mar, mari**	sea (समुद्र)	1. Aquamarine - color of sea water (समुद्र के पानी का रंग) 2. Submarine - an undersea boat (पनड़ब्बी)

SN	Root Word	Meaning	Examples
130	**max**	greatest (महानतम)	1. Maximal - the best or greatest possible (अधिक से अधिक) 2. Maximum - the greatest amount. (अधिकतम)
131	**medi**	middle (मध्य)	1. Medieval - pertaining to the middle ages (मध्यकालीन) 2. Medium - in the middle (मध्यम)
132	**melan, melano**	black (काला), dark (गहरा, अंधेरा)	1. Melancholy - a state of dark emotions (उदासी) 2. Melanoma - malignant dark tumor of the skin (सबसे ख़तरनाक स्किन कैंसर का प्रकार)
133	**memor, memori**	remember (याद करना)	1. Memorial - related to remembering a person or event (घटना को याद करने से संबंधित) 2. Memory - an ability to retain knowledge or an individual's stock of retained knowledge (याद)
134	**meter, metr, metry**	measure (माप)	1. Audiometer- an instrument that measures hearing acuteness (श्रवण शक्ति मापने का यंत्र) 2. Metric - measured (मापा) 3. Chronometry- the science of accurate time measurement (काल-मापन)
135	**migr**	wander (भटकना), move (स्थानांतरित करना)	1. Immigrant - a person who moves to a new country to settle (आप्रवासी) 2. Migration - the process of moving. (प्रवास)
136	**misein**	hate (नफरत करना)	1. Misogynist - a person who hates women (महिलाओं से घृणा करने वाला) 2. Misanthropy - a dislike of humankind (मानव जाति से अरुचि)
137	**miss, mit**	send (भेजना), let go (जाने देना)	1. Dismiss - to send someone away (नकार देना) 2. Admittance - entry (प्रवेश) 3. Emit - to send something out (उत्सर्जित करना)
138	**mob**	move (हिलना)	1. Mobile - able to move freely (गतिमान) 2. Immobilize - to stop from moving (स्थिर)
139	**morph, morpho**	shape (आकार), form (रूप)	1. Amorphous - without distinct shape or form (आकारहीन) 2. Morphology - scientific study of the structure and form of animals and plants (आकृति विज्ञान)
140	**mort**	death (मृत्यु)	1. Mortal - certain to die (मरणशील) 2. Mortician - an undertaker (अंत्येष्टि कर्मचारी, शव-सज्जाकार) 3. Immortal - living forever, unable to die (अमर)
141	**mot, mov**	move (हिलना)	1. Motivate - to move someone to action (उत्साहित करना, प्रेरित करना) 2. Removable - able to be taken or carried away. (हटाने योग्य)
142	**mut**	change (बदलना)	1. Immutable - not changing (अपरिवर्तनीय) 2. Mutate - to undergo a change (रूप बदलना)
143	**my, myo**	muscle (मांसपेशी)	1. Myasthenia - muscle fatigue or weakness (मांसपेशियों की कमजोरी)

SN	Root Word	Meaning	Examples
			2. Myosin - common protein in muscle tissue (मांसपेशियों के ऊतकों में सामान्य प्रोटीन)
144	**narr**	tell (बताना), relate (संबंधित करना)	1. Narrate - to tell a story (बयान करना) 2. Narrator - a person who tells a story (कथावाचक)
145	**nat**	born (जन्म)	1. Innate - included since birth (जन्मजात) 2. Natural - gotten at birth, not afterward (प्राकृतिक)
146	**nav**	ship (जहाज)	1. Naval - relating to a navy or warships (नौसेना या युद्धपोतों से संबंधित) 2. Navigate - to sail a ship through a place (नौचालन करना)
147	**necr, necro**	corpse (शव), dead (मृत)	1. Necrology - a list of persons who have recently died. (मृतों की सूची) 2. Necrophilia - an irresistible sexual attraction to dead body (शवकाम्कता)
148	**neg**	no (नहीं), not (नहीं), deny (इनकार करना)	1. Negate - to say it didn't happen (इंकार कर देना) 2. Renege - to go back on a promise (इनकार)
149	**nephr, nephro**	kidney (गुर्दा)	1. Nephritis - inflammation of the kidneys (गुर्दे में सूजन हो जाना) 2. Nephrotomy - surgical incision of a kidney (किडनी का सर्जिकल चीरा)
150	**neur, neuro**	nerve (तंत्रिका), nervous system (तंत्रिका तंत्र)	1. Neuralgia - pain along a nerve (नसों का दर्द) 2. Neurotic - mental disorder that usually does not include an impaired perception of reality. (अति चिंतित)
151	**noc, nox, nec**	harm (हानि), kill (मारना), poison (ज़हर)	1. Necropsy - The examination of dead body (शव-परीक्षा) 2. Noxious - Deadly injurious; Harmful (हानिकारक)
152	**nom, nomin**	name (नाम), appoint (नियुक्त करना)	1. Misnomer - an error in naming a person or thing (मिथ्यानाम) 2. Nominate - to name for election or appointment, to designate. (नियुक्त करना)
153	**nom, nomo**	law (कानून), custom (रिवाज)	1. Agronomics - The science of soil management and crop production (कृषि विज्ञान) 2. Nomology - The science of law and lawmaking (कानूनों का विज्ञान)
154	**noun, nunc**	declare (घोषित करना), announce (घोषणा करना)	1. Announce - to declare in public (सार्वजनिक घोषणा) 2. Enunciate - to speak or declare something clearly. (उच्चारित करना)
155	**nov**	new (नया)	1. Novelty - something new (नवीनता) 2. Renovate - to make something like new again (अच्छी अवस्था में लाना)
156	**nox, noct**	night (रात)	1. Nocturnal - active at night (रात में सक्रिय) 2. Equinox - the time when day and night are of equal length (दिन-रात बराबर होने का समय)
157	**numer**	number (संख्या)	1. Enumerate - to name a number of items on a list (गिनना, गणना) 2. Numerous - a large number (बहुत ज्यादा)

SN	Root Word	Meaning	Examples
158	**nuptial**	wedding (विवाह), marriage (शादी)	1. Antenuptial - a contract made between two people before they marry agreeing on the distribution of their assets (विवाह से पूर्व होनेवाला) 2. Prenuptial - made or occurring before marriage (विवाह पूर्व)
159	**obstetric**	midwifery (दाई का काम)	1. Obstetrician - a doctor who is specially trained to deal with pregnant women (प्रसूति विशेषज्ञ) 2. Obstetrics - the branch of medicine dealing with childbirth (प्रसूति विज्ञान)
160	**ocu**	eye (आंख)	1. Ocular - related to the eyes or sight (आंख सम्बन्धी) 2. Oculist - an eye doctor (नेत्र-विशेषज्ञ)
161	**odonto**	tooth (दांत)	1. Orthodontics - the treatment of irregularities in the teeth (दंत संशोधन) 2. Periodontal - pertaining to bone and tissue around a tooth (दांत के आसपास के ऊतकों से संबंधित)
162	**odor**	smell (गंध), scent (महक)	1. Deodorant - a substance that helps prevent body odor (दुर्गन्ध दूर करनेवाला) 2. Odoriferous- something that bears or diffuses a scent (सुगंधित)
163	**onym**	name (नाम), word (शब्द)	1. Anonymous - Without a known or acknowledged name (गुमनाम) 2. Synonym - A word with a similar meaning (समानार्थी शब्द)
164	**opt**	wish (इच्छा), best (श्रेष्ठ)	1. Optimal - most favourable condition for growth (इष्टतम) 2. Optimum - most favourable point, amount or degree etc. (अनुकूलतम)
165	**osteo**	bone (हड्डी)	1. Osteoporosis - a medical condition in which the bones become brittle and fragile (एक चिकित्सा स्थिति जिसमें हड्डियां भंगुर और नाज़ुक हो जाती हैं) 2. Osteology - the study of bones (अस्थिविज्ञान)
166	**ovi**	egg (अंडा)	1. Oviform - having the shape of an egg (अंडे के आकार का) 2. Oviparous - species that lay eggs (वे प्रजातियाँ जो अंडे देती हैं)
167	**pac, peac**	peace (शांति), agree (सहमत होना)	1. Pacify - To make calm and quiet somebody who is angry or upset (शांत करना) 2. Pacific - peaceful in character or intent (चरित्र या इरादे में शांतिपूर्ण) 3. Peaceable - inclined toward peace; friendly and non-aggressive (शांतिप्रिय, मिलनसार)
168	**pater, patr, patri**	father (पिता), chief (मुखिया), ancestor (पूर्वज)	1. Paternal - relating to fathers (पैतृक) 2. Patricide - the act of killing one's father (पिता का वध) 3. Patriarch - the male head of a family (कुलपति, कुल प्रमुख)
169	**path**	feeling (अनुभूति), emotion (भावना)	1. Antipathy - a feeling of strong dislike, opposition, or anger (घृणा) 2. Psychopath - a mentally unstable person (मनोरोगी)

SN	Root Word	Meaning	Examples
170	**ped, padi, pade**	foot (पैर), feet (पैर)	1. Pedal - a lever pushed by the foot (पैडल) 2. Pedicure - cosmetic treatment of feet and toes. (पादचिकित्सक, पैरों की सफ़ाई करना)
171	**pel**	to force, push (जबरदस्ती करना)	1. Expel - to officially force someone to leave (निष्कासित) 2. Impel - to force to move forward (प्रेरित करना)
172	**pept, peps**	digestion (पाचन)	1. Pepsin - a digestive enzyme (पित्त का एक प्रधान अंश) 2. Dyspepsia - indigestion or an upset stomach (अपच या पेट खराब होना)
173	**pet, pit**	seek (तलाश), attack (आक्रमण करना), to go (चल देना)	1. Compete - to try to be more successful than someone or something else (प्रतिस्पर्धा करना) 2. Perpetual - Continuing for a long period of time without interruption (लगातार)
174	**phag, phage**	to eat (खाने के लिए)	1. Anthropophagy or sarcophagy - cannibalism (नरमांस-भक्षण) 2. Oesophagus - the passage leading from the throat to the stomach (गले से पेट तक जाने वाला मार्ग) 3. Bacteriophage - a virus that destroys bacteria (जीवाणुभोजी)
175	**phem**	saying, speech (कहावत, भाषण)	1. Blasphemy - the act of insulting or showing contempt for God (ईश्वर-निंदा) 2. Dysphemism - an offensive or disparaging expression that is substituted for an inoffensive one (निन्दा)
176	**phil, philo**	love (प्यार), friend (दोस्त)	1. Bibliophile - loving books (किताबों से प्यार) 2. Philology - the love of words (भाषाशास्त्र)
177	**phon, phono, phone, phony**	sound (ध्वनि), voice (आवाज़), speech (भाषण)	1. Homophone - a word that sounds the same as another word but has a different meaning (समध्वनीय भिन्नार्थक शब्द) 2. Cacophony - a harsh, unpleasant 'sound' (अप्रिय 'ध्वनि') 3. Phonetic - relating to human speech sounds (ध्वनि-विज्ञान) 4. Phonograph - a device for recording and playing sound (ध्वनि-लेखक, ग्रामोफोन)
178	**phot, photo**	light (रोशनी)	1. Photogenic - caused by light (प्रकाश उत्पन्न करने वाला) 2. Photosynthesis - the process by which green plants use sunlight to synthesize nutrients (प्रकाश संश्लेषण)
179	**phyll, phyllo**	leaf (पत्ता)	1. Chlorophyll - the green pigment in plants that absorbs light energy for photosynthesis (पौधों में हरा वर्णक जो प्रकाश संश्लेषण के लिए प्रकाश ऊर्जा को अवशोषित करता है) 2. Phyllotaxis - the arrangement of leaves on a plant stem (किसी पौधे के तने या शाखा पर पत्तियों के पैटर्न या व्यवस्था)
180	**phys**	nature (प्रकृति), medicine (दवा), the body (शरीर)	1. Physical - relating to the body (भौतिक) 2. Physique - nature and shape of one's body (किसी के शरीर की प्रकृति और आकार)

SN	Root Word	Meaning	Examples
181	**phyt, phyto, phyte**	plant (पौधा), to grow (विकसित करने के लिए)	1. Chrysophyte - a group of algae commonly found in lakes (शैवालों का एक समूह जो आमतौर पर झीलों में पाया जाता है) 2. Epiphyte - a plant that grows on another plant but is not parasitic (एक पौधा जो किसी अन्य पौधे पर बढ़ता है लेकिन परजीवी नहीं होता) 3. Phytology - the study of plants (वनस्पति विज्ञान)
182	**plac**	peace or please (शांति या कृपया)	1. Placate - To make somebody feel less angry about something (शांत करना) 2. Placid - having a calm appearance; free from disturbance (सौम्य)
183	**pliant**	flexible (लचीला)	1. Pliancy - the quality of being willing to accept change (लचीलापन) 2. Compliant - ready to conform to rules or orders (नियमों या आदेशों का पालन करने के लिए तैयार)
184	**pneum, pneumo**	breathing (साँस लेने), lung (फेफड़ा), air (वायु)	1. Pneumatic - using the force of air (वायवीय) 2. Pneumonia - inflammation of the lungs (निमोनिया)
185	**pod, pode**	foot (पैर)	1. Podiatrist - a doctor for the feet (पैरो और टखनों के विकारों के विशेषज्ञ) 2. Tripod - a stand or frame with 3 legs. (तिपाई)
186	**polis**	city (शहर)	1. Cosmopolis - A large city inhabited by people from many different countries (सार्वभौम नगर) 2. Metropolis - a very large or busy city (प्रधान नगर, प्रमुख नगर)
187	**pon, pos**	put (रखना), place (स्थान)	1. Apposite - Very appropriate and suitable for a particular situation (उचित) 2. Postpone - to defer or delay something to a later time (स्थगित करना)
188	**pop**	people (लोग)	1. Popular - appealing to a lot of people (लोकप्रिय) 2. Populist - a supporter of the rights of people (लोकवादी)
189	**port**	carry (ढोना)	1. Export - to carry goods out of a place to another (निर्यात) 2. Porter - a person who carries luggage (बोझ ढोनेवाला)
190	**psych, psycho**	mind (मन), soul (आत्मा)	1. Psychology - the study of the mind (मनोविज्ञान) 2. Psyche - the human spirit or soul (मानस)
191	**pugn, pugna, pung**	fight (लड़ाई)	1. Pugnacious - eager or quick to argue, quarrel, or fight (झगड़ालू) 2. Repugnant - extremely distasteful or unpleasant (अत्यंत अरुचिकर या अप्रिय)
192	**pul**	urge (प्रेरित करना), drive (चालित करना)	1. Impulsive - having a spontaneous urge to do something (आवेगशील) 2. Compulsive - resulting from or relating to an irresistible urge (एक अप्रतिरोध्य प्रेरणा के कारण या उससे संबंधित)

SN	Root Word	Meaning	Examples
193	**purg**	clean (साफ करना)	1. Purge - remove anything undesirable (साफ करना) 2. Expurgate - remove objectionable passages from a publication (छाँटना, परिशोधन करना)
194	**pyr, pyro**	heat (गर्मी), fire (आग), light (प्रकाश)	1. Pyrometer - a thermometer for measuring high temperature (उष्णता के कारण वस्तुओं का प्रसार नापने का यंत्र) 2. Pyrotechnics - a firework display (एक आतिशबाजी प्रदर्शन) 3. Pyromania - an obsessive desire to set things on fire (आगज़नी का जूनून)
195	**radic, radix**	root (जड़), origin (मूल)	1. Eradicate - pull out at the roots (उन्मूलन करना, जड़ से उखाड़ना) 2. Radical - relating to or affecting the fundamental nature of something (किसी चीज के मौलिक स्वरूप से संबंधित या प्रभावित करने वाला)
196	**rage**	anger (क्रोध)	1. Outrage - an extremely strong reaction of anger, shock, or indignation (क्रोध, सदमे या रोष की एक अत्यंत मजबूत प्रतिक्रिया) 2. Enrage - to make very angry (बहुत गुस्सा करना)
197	**ram, rami**	branch (शाखा)	1. Ramification - a complex or unwelcome consequence of an action or event (जटिलता) 2. Ramify - to form branches or offshoots; split into two or more parts (शाखाएँ या उपशाखाएँ बनाना; दो या अधिक भागों में विभाजित होना)
198	**rect**	straight (सीधा), right (सही)	1. Rectification - the act of correcting something or making something right (संशोधन) 2. Correct - free from error; in accordance with fact or truth (गलती से मुक्त; तथ्य या सत्य के अनुसार)
199	**rhin, rhino**	nose (नाक)	1. Rhinoceros - a species of animals with a big horn on the snout (गैंडा) 2. Rhinoplasty - plastic surgery performed on the nose (नाक पर की जाने वाली प्लास्टिक सर्जरी)
200	**rhod, rhodo**	red (लाल)	1. Rhododendron - a flower with red, pink flowers (बुरूंश का फूल, एक प्रकार की सदाबहार झाड़ी) 2. Rhodophytes - red-colored algae (लाल शैवाल)
201	**rid, ris**	to laugh (हँसना), to mock (उपहास करना)	1. Derision - cruel mockery or scornful ridicule (उपहास, तिरस्कार) 2. Risible - provoking laughter; laughable or ridiculous (हास्यास्पद)
202	**rog**	to ask (पूछना), to claim (दावा करना)	1. Arrogant - having an exaggerated sense of self-importance (अभिमानी) 2. Derogatory - showing disrespect or criticism; belittling (अपमानजनक, निंदनीय)
203	**rupt**	break (तोड़ना), burst (फोड़ना)	1. Bankrupt - not having enough money to pay your debts (दिवालिया) 2. Rupture - a break in something. (टूटना)
204	**san**	health (स्वास्थ्य)	1. Sanitary - relating to cleanliness and health (स्वास्थ्य-संबंधी)

SN	Root Word	Meaning	Examples
			2. Sanitation - maintenance of public health and cleanliness (स्वच्छता)
205	**sanct, sacr, secr**	sacred (पवित्र), holy (पवित्र)	1. Desecrate - To violate the sacredness (अपवित्रता) 2. Sacrifice - The act of offering something to a god (त्याग करना)
206	**scend**	climb (चढ़ना), go (जाना)	1. Ascend - to climb upward (चढ़ना) 2. Descend - to go or climb down (उतरना)
207	**sci**	know (जानना)	1. Conscience - sense of knowing right from wrong (अंतरात्मा की आवाज) 2. Omniscient - knowing everything. (सर्वज्ञ)
208	**scop, scope, scopy**	see (देखना), examine (परीक्षण करना), observe (निरीक्षण)	1. Periscope - a seeing instrument on a submarine (पनडुब्बी पर देखने वाला एक यंत्र) 2. Telescope - a device used to see over a distance. (दूरबीन) 3. Endoscopy - a medical procedure to look inside the body (दूरबीन दवारा शरीर के अंदर देखने की चिकित्सा प्रक्रिया)
209	**scrib, script**	to write (लिखना), written (लिखा हुआ)	1. Inscribe - to write or engrave letters on a surface (अंकित करना) 2. Scribe - a person who copies out documents (लिपिक) 3. Manuscript - a handwritten text or document (पांडुलिपि) 4. Inscription - writing engraved or carved on a surface (अभिलेख)
210	**sec, sequ**	to follow (अनुकरण करना)	1. Consequence - a result of a particular action or situation (परिणाम) 2. Sequel - A book, movie, play, etc. that follows the story of a previous one (अगली कड़ी; परिणाम)
211	**sect**	cut (काटना)	1. Bisect - to cut into two equal parts. (द्विभाजित करना) 2. Dissect - to cut apart piece by piece (काटना)
212	**sen**	old (वृद्ध), old age (बुढ़ापा)	1. Senex - an old man (वृद्ध पुरुष) 2. Senile - having poor mental ability due to old age (जराजन्य मानसिक दुर्बलता) 3. Senescence - the process of growing old (बूढ़े होने की प्रक्रिया)
213	**sens, sent**	to feel (महसूस करने के लिए)	1. Sensory - relating to sensation or the physical senses (संवेदना या शारीरिक इंद्रियों से संबंधित) 2. Sentimental - having an excessive gentle emotions (भावुक)
214	**soci**	companion (साथी), group (समूह), society (समाज)	1. Social - relating to society or interaction among people (सामाजिक) 2. Sociology - the study of human social relationships and institutions (समाज शास्त्र)
215	**sol**	alone (अकेला)	1. Solitary - done alone, by yourself (अकेला) 2. Desolate - lonely, dismal, gloomy (सुनसान)
216	**somn, somni, somna**	sleep (नींद)	1. Insomnia - habitual sleeplessness or inability to sleep (नींद न आने का रोग) 2. Somnolent - feeling drowsy or sleepy (नींद से भरा हुआ,

SN	Root Word	Meaning	Examples
			ऊँघता हुआ) 3. Somniloquy - the act of talking in one's sleep (नींद में बात करना) 4. Somnambulist - a person who walks in their sleep (नींद में चलने वाला व्यक्ति)
217	**son**	sound (आवाज़)	1. Consonant - a speech sound (व्यंजन) 2. Supersonic - faster than sound (पराध्वनिक)
218	**soph**	wise (बुद्धिमान, ज्ञानी)	1. Philosopher - a wise person (दार्शनिक) 2. Sophisticated - having a refined knowledge of the ways of the world (दुनिया के तरीकों का परिष्कृत ज्ञान रखने वाला)
219	**spec, spect, spic**	see (देखना), look (देखना)	1. Spectator - a person who sees an event. (दर्शक) 2. Conspicuous - clearly visible (स्पष्ट रूप से दिखाई देने वाला)
220	**spir**	breathe (साँस लेना)	1. Aspire - to "breathe" towards a set goal (महत्वाकांक्षा करना) 2. Respiration - "breathing" in and out, again and again (श्वसन)
221	**sta**	stand (खड़ा होना)	1. Stable - firmly fixed or not likely to move or change (स्थिर) 2. Stationary - at a standstill, fixed. (अचल)
222	**stell**	star (तारा)	1. Constellation - a group of stars that forms a pattern (तारामंडल) 2. Interstellar - between the stars (तारे के बीच का)
223	**struct**	build (निर्माण)	1. Construct - to build or make (something) by putting parts together (निर्माण) 2. Structure - something built (संरचना)
224	**sua**	smooth (चिकना), advice (सलाह), sweet (मीठा)	1. Dissuade - To advise somebody not to do something (न करने के लिए समझाना) 2. Persuasive - Able to persuade somebody through advice (प्रेरक)
225	**sum**	highest (उच्चतम)	1. Summation - the total, highest amount (योग) 2. Summit - the highest point or top (उच्चतम बिंदु)
226	**taci**	silent (मौन), to be silent (चुप रहना)	1. Taciturn - not to speak much, reserved (अल्पभाषी) 2. Reticent - not revealing one's thoughts or feelings readily (मौन रहने वाला)
227	**temp, tempor**	time (समय)	1. Temporal - relating to time (लौकिक) 2. Temporary - lasting for only a limited period of time; not permanent (अस्थायी)
228	**ten, tens, tent, tenu**	thin (पतला), slender (पतला-दुबला), stretched tight (कसकर खिंचा हुआ)	1. Tenuous - very slender or fine; insubstantial (बहुत पतला या महीन; अवास्तविक) 2. Extend - to stretch something (बढ़ाना) 3. Attenuate - to make something less or weaker (दुर्बल होना) 4. Attention - focusing the mind on something (ध्यान)

SN	Root Word	Meaning	Examples
229	**terr, terra, terri**	land (भूमि), earth (धरती)	1. Terrain - ground or land (भूभाग) 2. Territory - an area of land (इलाका) 3. Extraterrestrial - existing outside the earth (पृथ्वी के बाहर विद्यमान)
230	**the, theo**	god (ईश्वर)	1. Atheist - a person who disbelieves or lacks belief in the existence of God or gods (नास्तिक) 2. Theology - the study of religion, god, etc. (धर्मशास्त्र)
231	**therm, thermo**	heat (गर्मी)	1. Thermal - relating to heat (ऊष्मा-संबंधी) 2. Thermostat - a device that controls heat. (तापस्थापी)
232	**tort**	twist (मोड़)	1. Contort - to twist or bend out of the normal shape (सामान्य आकार से मोड़ना या झुकाना) 2. Distort - to give a misleading or false account or impression of (बिगाड़ना)
233	**tox**	poison (ज़हर)	1. Toxic - containing or being poisonous material (विषाक्त) 2. Toxicology - the study of poisons (ज़हर का ज्ञान)
234	**tract**	pull (खींचना), drag (खींचना)	1. Attract - to pull objects nearer (आकर्षित करना) 2. Distract - to drag attention away from something (विचलित) 3. Tractor - a powerful vehicle used for pulling (ट्रैक्टर)
235	**trepido**	fearful (भयभीत), alarmed (चिंतित)	1. Intrepid - fearless (निडर) 2. Trepidation - a feeling of fear or anxiety about something that may happen (घबराहट)
236	**turb, turba**	disorder (विकार), confusion (भ्रम), turmoil (उथल-पुथल)	1. Disturb - To cause someone to be anxious or upset (परेशान करना) 2. Turbulent - characterized by conflict, disorder, or confusion (उपद्रवी)
237	**urb**	city (शहर)	1. Urban - relating to a city (शहरी) 2. Urbanology - the study of city life. (शहरी विज्ञान)
238	**uxor**	wife (पत्नी)	1. Uxoricide - killing of one's wife (पत्नी की हत्या) 2. Uxorious - having or showing an excessive or submissive fondness for one's wife (पत्नी-परस्त, जोरू का ग़ुलाम)
239	**vac**	empty (खाली)	1. Vacate - to leave (a place that one previously occupied) (खाली करना) 2. Vacation - a time without work (छुट्टी)
240	**vacill**	to waver (लड़खड़ाना), to hesitate (संकोच करना)	1. Vacillate - to waver indecisively between choices (दुविधा में रहना) 2. Vacillation - the state of being indecisive (अनिर्णय की स्थिति, दुविधा)
241	**ven, vent**	come (आना)	1. Convene - to come or bring together for a meeting or activity (बुलाना) 2. Intervene - to come between (हस्तक्षेप करना) 3. Advent - the arrival of something important or notable (आगमन)

SN	Root Word	Meaning	Examples
242	**ventr**	belly (पेट), hollow cavity (खोखली गुहा)	1. Ventriloquism - the art of projecting one's voice so it appears to come from another source (पेट बोली) 2. Ventricle - a small hollow cavity in an organ (किसी अंग की खोखली गुहा)
243	**ver, veri**	truth (सच)	1. Veracity - the truth (सच्चाई) 2. Verify - to make sure that something is true. (सत्यापित करना)
244	**verb**	word (शब्द)	1. Proverb - a short saying that expresses a well-known truth (कहावत) 2. Verbalize - to put into words (क्रिया बनाना)
245	**vers, vert**	turn (मोड़)	1. Reverse - to turn something to the opposite side or direction (पलटना / विपरीत करना) 2. Controversy - a prolonged public disagreement or heated debate (विवाद) 3. Revert - to return to a previous state or condition (वापस लौटना)
246	**vid, vis**	to see (देखना)	1. Vista - a scene, view, or panorama (परिदृश्य) 2. Invisible - unable to be seen (अदृश्य) 3. Provident - making careful provision for the future; showing foresight (दूरदर्शी)
247	**vince, vic**	conquer (जीतना)	1. Convince - to win someone over (राजी करना) 2. Victory - a success or triumph over an enemy in battle or war (विजय)
248	**vir**	male (पुरुष)	1. Virile - having strength, energy, and a strong sex drive (पौरुषयुक्त) 2. Virtuoso - a person who is extremely skilled at something (कला प्रवीण व्यक्ति) 3. Triumvirate - a group of three powerful men (तीन शक्तिशाली पुरुषों का समूह)
249	**viv, vit**	live (रहना), life (ज़िंदगी)	1. Revival - the act of bringing back to life (पुनः प्रवर्तन) 2. Vital - absolutely necessary or important (अत्यावश्यक)
250	**vivi**	alive (जीवित)	1. Revivification - renewal or restoration of life (पुनरुत्थान) 2. Viviparous - species that give birth to their young ones (जो प्रजाति शिशु को जन्म देती है)
251	**voc, voci**	voice (आवाज़), call (पुकारना)	1. Advocate - to speak in favor of (समर्थन करना, पक्ष लेना) 2. Vociferous - vehement or clamorous (कोलाहलपूर्ण)
252	**vol**	wish (इच्छा), will (इच्छा शक्ति)	1. Volunteer - a person who voluntarily undertakes or expresses a willingness to undertake a service (स्वयं सेवक) 2. Volition - the faculty or power of using one's will (इच्छाशक्ति)
253	**volv, volu**	roll (लुढ़कना), turn (घूमना)	1. Revolve - to move in a circular orbit around (घूमना) 2. Convoluted - (of an argument, story, sentence, etc.) extremely complex and difficult to follow (पेचीदा)
254	**vor, vour, vore**	eat (भोजन करना)	1. Voracious - wanting or devouring great quantities of food (पेटू) 2. Carnivore - an animal that feeds on other animals

SN	Root Word	Meaning	Examples
			(मांसाहारी) 3. Devour - to eat up greedily or hungrily (भूख या लालच से खाना)
255	**xer, xero, xeri**	dry (सूखा)	1. Xerophyte - a plant that needs very little water (एक पौधा जो शुष्क जलवायु में उगता है) 2. Xerography - a dry photocopying process (एक सूखी फोटोकॉपी प्रक्रिया) 3. Xeric - requiring small amounts of moisture (सूखा)

SN	Prefix	Meaning	Examples
256	**a**	without (बिना)	1. Abyss - without bottom (अतल क्षेत्र, गहरी खाई) 2. Amoral - without moral sense (नीतिहीन, अनैतिक)
257	**a**	on (पर)	1. Afire - on fire (जलता हुआ) 2. Ashore - on the shore (किनारे पर, तट पर)
258	**ab**	away from (दूर, अलग)	1. Abduct - to take someone away illegally (अवैध रूप से ले जाना) 2. Abnormal - departing from what is normal or usual (असामान्य) 3. Aberration - a departure from what is normal or expected (सामान्य से भटकाव / पथभ्रष्टता) 4. Absent - away from a place; not present (अनुपस्थित)
259	**acro**	height (ऊंचाई), beginning (शुरुआत)	1. Acrobat - a high walker (कलाबाज) 2. Acrophobia - fear of height (ऊँचाई का डर)
260	**ad**	to (को), toward (की ओर)	1. Adapt - to change or adjust to different conditions (अनुकूल बनाना) 2. Adhere - follow a rule, comply with (मानना, पालन करना)
261	**ambi, amphi**	both (दोनों), on both sides (दोनों तरफ)	1. Amphibians - any animal that can live both on land and in water (उभयचर) 2. Ambiguous - more than one possible meaning (अस्पष्ट)
262	**ante**	before (पहले), in front (सामने)	1. Antecede - to come before something in time (पूर्ववर्ती) 2. Anteroom- a small room before the main room (उपकक्ष, प्रतीक्षा-कक्ष)
263	**anti**	against (ख़िलाफ़), opposite of (से उल्टा)	1. Antibody - a substance that destroys micro-organisms (रोग-प्रतिकारक) 2. Antiseptic - preventing infection (सड़न रोकने वाली दवा)
264	**apo**	away from (से दूर), separate (अलग)	1. Apology - to express regret for something done or said (क्षमायाचना) 2. Apostate - One who abandons his faith (स्वधर्मत्यागी)
265	**arch, archi**	rule (शासन), chief (प्रमुख), beginning (आरंभ)	1. Monarch - a sovereign ruler such as a king or queen (सम्राट) 2. Archbishop - the chief bishop of a region (प्रधान पादरी) 3. Oligarchy - a system of government ruled by a small powerful group (अल्पतंत्र)

SN	Prefix	Meaning	Examples
			4. Archive - a collection of historical records or documents (प्रालेख)
266	**archa, archaio**	ancient (प्राचीन), primitive (पुरातन)	1. Archaeology - the study of ancient cultures (पुरातत्त्व) 2. Archaic - belonging to an earlier period; outdated and no longer in use (पुराना और अप्रचलित)
267	**auto**	self (खुद)	1. Autocrat - a person who governs with absolute power (तानाशाह) 2. Automatic - moving by itself (स्वचालित)
268	**bene**	good (अच्छा), well (अच्छी तरह से)	1. Beneficial - producing a good effect (फायदेमंद) 2. Benevolent - showing kindness or goodwill (परोपकारी)
269	**bi, bin**	two (दो), twice (दो बार)	1. Biannual - happening twice a year (साल में दो बार) 2. Binoculars - optical device with two lenses (दूरबीन)
270	**bio**	life (ज़िंदगी), living thing (जीवित वस्तु)	1. Biography- a life story written by another person (जीवनी) 2. Biology - the science of life (जीवविज्ञान)
271	**caco**	bad (खराब), ill (बीमार), unpleasant (अप्रिय)	1. Cacoethes - an uncontrollable urge or desire (बुरी आदत, लत) 2. Cacophony - unpleasant, harsh sound (कोलाहल)
272	**calli**	beautiful (सुंदर)	1. Calligraphy - the art of beautiful hand writing (सुलेख) 2. Calliphony - beautiful or elegant sound, euphony (श्रुतिमधुरता, मधुर ध्वनि)
273	**cata**	intensive (गहन), completely (पूरी तरह से)	1. Cataclysm - a flood or other disaster, deluge (प्रलय) 2. Catastrophe - turning for the worst, a substantial disaster (तबाही)
274	**cent, centi**	hundred (सौ), hundredth (सौवां)	1. Centenarian- a person between 100 and 109 years old (सौ वर्ष का) 2. Century - 100 years (शतक) 3. Centimeter - a unit of length equal to one hundredth of a meter (मीटर का सौवाँ भाग)
275	**chiro**	hand (हाथ)	1. Chiromancy - the art of reading palms to tell someone's future (हस्तरेखा विद्या) 2. Chiropractor - a medical person trained to treat pain and injury by spinal manipulation (दर्द और चोट का इलाज करने के लिए प्रशिक्षित एक चिकित्सा व्यक्ति)
276	**circum, circle**	around (आस-पास), about (के बारे में)	1. Circumnavigate - to sail around (परिभ्रमण करना, पूरा चक्कर लगाना) 2. Circumscribe - to draw around (रेखा से घेरना)
277	**co**	with (साथ), together (एक साथ)	1. Coauthor - writer who collaborates with another author (सह-लेखक) 2. Cooperate - to act or work with another or others (सहयोग)
278	**col**	together (एक साथ), jointly (संयुक्त रूप से)	1. Collision - smashing together (टक्कर) 2. Collusion - secret agreement or cooperation especially for an illegal or deceitful purpose (आपसी साँठ - गाँठ)

SN	Prefix	Meaning	Examples
279	**com**	together (एक साथ), common (सामान्य)	1. Commission - a group of persons directed to perform some duty (आयोग) 2. Composition - an arrangement or putting together of parts (संघटन)
280	**con**	with (साथ), jointly (संयुक्त रूप से)	1. Concur - to agree with someone (सहमत होना) 2. Convoy - a group of vehicles or ships travelling together (काफिले)
281	**contra, contro**	against (ख़िलाफ़), opposite (विलोम)	1. Contradict - to argue against (खंडन) 2. Contrast - an obvious difference between two or more things (अंतर) 3. Controversy - a prolonged public disagreement (विवाद)
282	**counter**	oppose (का विरोध), contrary (इसके विपरीत), against (ख़िलाफ़)	1. Counteract - to oppose the effects of an action (प्रतिकार करना) 2. Counteroffensive - attack against an attack (जवाबी हमले)
283	**crypt, crypto**	hidden (छिपा हुआ), secret (गुप्त)	1. Cryptic - having a mysterious or obscure meaning (रहस्यमय, गूढ़) 2. Cryptography - the science of writing and deciphering secret codes (कूटलिपि विद्या)
284	**de**	reduce (कम करना), remove (निकालना)	1. Debug - to remove bugs (दोष मुक्त करना) 2. Dethrone - to remove from power (राज-गद्दी से उतारना)
285	**dec, deca, deka**	ten (दस)	1. Decade - a period of ten years (दशक) 2. Decahedron - a three-dimensional solid having ten faces (दशफलक) 3. Dekagram - a unit of mass equal to ten grams (दस ग्राम)
286	**deci**	one tenth (दसवें भाग)	1. Decimal - numbered or proceeding by tens (दशमलव) 2. Decibel - one tenth of the sound volume unit bel (ध्वनि आयतन इकाई बेल का दसवां हिस्सा)
287	**demi**	half (आधा), less than (से कम)	1. Demi god - half god (अर्ध-देव) 2. Demitasse - a small cup of coffee (एक छोटा कप कॉफी)
288	**di, diplo**	two (दो), twice (दो बार)	1. Dichromatic - displaying two colors (दो रंग वाला) 2. Diplococcus - bacteria that usually occur in pairs (बैक्टीरिया जो आमतौर पर जोड़े में होते हैं)
289	**dia**	across (आर-पार), through (के माध्यम से)	1. Dialogue - communicative process between two or more people (वार्ता) 2. Diameter - line segment that passes through the centre of the circle (व्यास)
290	**dipso**	thirsty (प्यासा), alcoholic thirst (शराबी प्यास; लत)	1. Dipsomania - an uncontrollable craving for alcoholic drinks (शराब की लत) 2. Dipsophobia - fear of alcoholic drinks (शराब पीने का एक असामान्य और लगातार डर)
291	**dis**	not (नहीं)	1. Disagree - different opinion; dispute (असहमत) 2. Disobey - not comply or refuse to follow (अवज्ञा; आज्ञा का उल्लंघन करना)

SN	Prefix	Meaning	Examples
292	**du, duo**	two (दो), twice (दो बार)	1. Duet - a musical composition for two voices or instruments (युगल, जुगलबंदी) 2. Duplicate - make an identical copy (नक़ल) 3. Duo - a pair normally thought of as being together (जोड़ी)
293	**dys**	abnormal (असामान्य), bad (खराब), difficult (कठिन)	1. Dyslexia - a learning disability that makes reading and language-related tasks harder (अपपठन, पढ़ने में सीखने की अक्षमता) 2. Dystopia - an imaginary place of total misery (तबाह देश)
294	**em, en**	in (में), within (अंदर)	1. Empathy - ability to share someone else's feelings (समानुभूति) 2. Empower - to give power or authority (सशक्तिकरण) 3. Encircle - to form a circle around; surround (घेर लेना)
295	**endo**	within (अंदर), inside (अंदर)	1. Endocrine - relating to glands that secrete directly into the blood or lymph (अंत: स्रावी) 2. Endotherm - a creature that can keep its inside temperature fairly constant (एक प्राणी जो अपने अंदर का तापमान काफी स्थिर रख सकता है)
296	**ep, epi**	on (पर), over (ऊपर), after (बाद)	1. Epitome - a standard or typical example of something (प्रतीक) 2. Epilogue - a short speech delivered after a play (उपसंहार)
297	**equ, equi**	equal (बराबर), equally (समान रूप से)	1. Equation - a statement of equality (समीकरण) 2. Equilibrium - a state of balance between opposing forces or actions (संतुलन)
298	**ethno**	race (जाति; वर्ग), people (लोग)	1. Ethnic - pertaining to a defined group of people (जातीय) 2. Ethnology - the science of people and races (मानव जाति विज्ञान)
299	**eu**	good (अच्छा), well (अच्छी तरह से)	1. Euphemism - replacing an offensive word with an inoffensive one (शिष्टोक्ति, कठोर बात को कोमल रीति से कहना) 2. Euphoria - feeling of well-being (उत्साह)
300	**ex**	from (से), out (बाहर)	1. Excavate - to dig out (खोदना) 2. Extract - to pull out (निकालना)
301	**extra, extro**	outside (बाहर), beyond (आगे)	1. Extraordinary - beyond ordinary (असाधारण) 2. Extrovert - an outgoing person (बहिर्मुखी व्यक्ति, मिलनसार और अनारक्षित व्यक्ति)
302	**flor, flora, fleur**	flower (फूल)	1. Flora - the plant life of a particular time or area (वनस्पति) 2. Florist - someone working with flowers (फूल वाला)
303	**fore**	in front of (के सामने), previous (पहले का), earlier (पहले)	1. Forefather - ancestor, forbear (पूर्वज) 2. Forecast - a prediction of future events (पूर्वानुमान)

SN	Prefix	Meaning	Examples
304	**geo**	earth (धरती), soil (मिट्टी)	1. Geography - study of the earth's surface (भूगोल) 2. Geology - study of the structure of the earth (भूगर्भ शास्त्र)
305	**giga**	a billion (एक अरब)	1. Gigabyte - unit of computer storage space (डेटा भंडारण क्षमता की एक इकाई) 2. Gigawatt - unit of electric power (one billion watts) (बिजली की एक इकाई)
306	**hect, hecto, hecat**	hundred (सौ)	1. Hectare - metric unit equaling 100 ares or 10,000 square meters (हैक्टर) 2. Hectometer - 100 meters (हेक्टोमीटर)
307	**hemi**	half (आधा), partial (आंशिक)	1. Hemisphere - one half of the earth (गोलार्द्ध) 2. Hemistich - half a line of poetry (कविता की आधी पंक्ति)
308	**hepa**	liver (यकृत)	1. Hepatitis - inflammation of the liver (हेपेटाइटिस) 2. Hepatotoxic - toxic and damaging to the liver (यकृतविषकारी)
309	**hept, hepta**	seven (सात)	1. Heptagon - a shape with seven angles and seven sides (सातकोणक) 2. Heptateuch - the first seven books of the old testament (प्रानी धर्म-प्स्तक की प्रथम सप्त प्स्तकें)
310	**herbi**	grass (घास), plant (पौधा)	1. Herbicide - any chemical used to kill unwanted plants, etc. (खरपतवारनाशक) 2. Herbivory - the state or condition of feeding on plants (शाकाहारी)
311	**hetero**	different (अलग), other (अन्य)	1. Heterodox - not conforming to traditional beliefs (पाखंडपूर्ण, धर्म-विरूद्ध) 2. Heteronyms - words with same spelling but different meanings (विषमार्थी शब्द) 3. Heterogeneous - consisting of different types (विजातीय, विषमांगी)
312	**hex, hexa**	six (छह)	1. Hexagon - a shape with six angles, sides (षट्भ्ज) 2. Hexapod - having six legs (षट्पद)
313	**homo, homeo**	like (समान), alike (एक जैसे), same (वही)	1. Homogeneous - of the same nature or kind (सजातीय) 2. Homonym - sounding alike (समनाम, एक जैसे लगने वाले)
314	**hyp, hypo**	under (अंतर्गत), low (कम)	1. Hypoglycemia - an abnormally low level of sugar in the blood (रक्त में शर्करा का असामान्य रूप से कम स्तर) 2. Hypothesis - a theory that is unproven but used under the assumption that it is true. (परिकल्पना)
315	**hyper**	too much (बहृत अधिक), over (ऊपर), beyond (आगे)	1. Hyperactive - very restless (अति सक्रिय) 2. Hypertension - above normal pressure. (उच्च रक्तचाप)
316	**idio**	peculiar (विचित्र), personal (निजी), distinct (विशिष्ट)	1. Idiomatic - peculiar to a particular language (मुहावरेदार) 2. Idiot - someone who is distinctly foolish or stupid (बेवकूफ़)

SN	Prefix	Meaning	Examples
317	**il, im, in, ig, ir**	not (नहीं), without (बिना)	1. Illegal - not legal (गैरकानूनी) 2. Inappropriate - not appropriate (अनुचित) 3. Impossible - not possible (असंभव) 4. Ignore - to refuse to take notice (अनदेखा करना) 5. Irregular - not regular, even, or consistent (अनियमित)
318	**incend**	to set fire (आग लगाना), to inflame (भड़काना)	1. Incendiary - designed to cause fire; or tending to inflame strong feelings (आग लगाने वाला / भड़काऊ) 2. Incense - to make someone extremely angry (क्रोधित करना / भड़काना)
319	**infra**	beneath (नीचे), below (नीचे)	1. Infrared - below the regular light spectrum (अवरक्त) 2. Infrastructure - underlying framework of a system (आधारभूत संरचना)
320	**inter**	between (बीच में), among (के बीच)	1. Interval - a pause or break in activity (मध्यान्तर, अंतराल) 2. Intersection - place where roads come together (चौराहा)
321	**intra, intro**	within (अंदर), inside (अंदर)	1. Intranet - a local or restricted communications network (आंतरिक नेटवर्क) 2. Intravenous - inside or into a vein (नसों में) 3. Introspection - a reflective looking inward (आत्ममंथन)
322	**iso**	equal (बराबर)	1. Isobar - a line on a map connecting points of equal barometric pressure (समदाब-रेखा) 2. Isothermal - having equal or constant temperature. (समतापीय)
323	**kilo**	thousand (हज़ार)	1. Kilograms - 1,000 grams (किलोग्राम) 2. Kilometer - 1,000 meters (किलोमीटर)
324	**klepto**	theft (चोरी)	1. Kleptomaniac - who cannot control their desire to steal things (चोरी करने की बीमारी से पीड़ित) 2. Kleptophobia - the fear of stealing (चोरी का डर)
325	**macro**	big (बड़ा), large (बड़ा)	1. Macroeconomics - study of the overall forces of economy. (समष्टि अर्थशास्त्र) 2. Macromolecule - a large molecule (एक बड़ा अणु)
326	**mal**	bad (खराब), ill (बीमार), wrong (गलत)	1. Malicious - showing a desire to cause harm to someone (दुर्भावनापूर्ण) 2. Malware - Malicious software (मैलवेयर)
327	**mater, matr, matri**	mother (माँ)	1. Maternal - relating to motherhood (मातृ) 2. Matriarch - a woman head of a household. (कुलमाता)
328	**mega**	great (महान), huge (विशाल)	1. Megalopolis - an area with many nearby cities (महानगर) 2. Megastructure - huge building or other structure. (एक बहुत बड़ी बहुमंजिला इमारत)
329	**meta**	change (परिवर्तन), after (बाद), beyond (आगे)	1. Metamorphosis - a complete change of form (कायापलट) 2. Metaphysics - study of nature and reality (प्रकृति और वास्तविकता का अध्ययन)
330	**micro**	small (छोटा)	1. Microbe - a very small living thing (सूक्ष्म जीव) 2. Microscope - a device to see very small things. (सूक्ष्मदर्शी)

SN	Prefix	Meaning	Examples
331	**mid**	middle (मध्य)	1. Midriff - the area between the chest and the waist (मध्य झिल्ली, पट) 2. Midway - halfway between. (बीच का रास्ता)
332	**milli**	one-thousandth (एक हज़ारवाँ)	1. Milliliter - one thousandth of a liter (मिलीलीटर) 2. Millimeter - one thousandth of a meter (मिलीमीटर)
333	**min, mini**	small, less (छोटा, कम)	1. Mini - something that is very small (छोटा) 2. Minutiae - very small or trivial details. (ज़रा सी बात)
334	**mis, miso**	hatred, wrong (घृणा, गलत)	1. Misappropriate - dishonest or inappropriate use of others' money, data (दुरुपयोग करना) 2. Misprint - an error in printing (छापे की गलती)
335	**mon, mono**	one, single (एक, एकल)	1. Monochromat - having one color (एक ही रंग का होना) 2. Monotheism - belief in one god (एकेश्वरवाद)
336	**multi**	many, multiple (कई, अनेक)	1. Multicolored - having many colors (सारंग) 2. Multitasking - doing many things at once (बहुकार्यन)
337	**neo**	new (नया), recent (हाल ही का)	1. Neocolonialism - the control of less-developed countries by the developed countries (नव-उपनिवेशवाद) 2. Neophyte - someone who is new to a particular activity (नौसिखिया)
338	**non**	not (नहीं)	1. Nondescript - with no special characteristics (गुमनाम, अवर्णित) 2. Nonsense - without sense (बकवास)
339	**ob, op**	against (विपरीत), in front of (के सामने)	1. Object - to be against something (आपत्ति व्यक्त करना) 2. Opposition - the act of resistance or action against. (विरोध)
340	**oct, octa, octo**	eight (आठ)	1. Octave - a series of eight notes in a musical scale (आठ सुरों की एक श्रृंखला) 2. Octopus - sea animal with 8 arms (ऑक्टोपस)
341	**omni**	all (सभी)	1. Omnipotent - with all the power (सर्वशक्तिमान) 2. Omnivorous - eating all foods (सर्व-भक्षक, सर्वाहारी)
342	**ortho**	straight (सीधा), correct (सही), right (ठीक)	1. Orthodontist - a dentist that straightens teeth (दंत संशोधक) 2. Orthography - the correct way of writing. (लिखने का सही तरीका)
343	**over**	excessive (अत्यधिक)	1. Overconfident - more confident than is appropriate (अति आत्मविश्वास का जोखिम) 2. Overestimate - estimate something to be better or larger (अधिक मूल्य लगाना)
344	**pale, paleo**	ancient (प्राचीन)	1. Paleography - the study of ancient forms of writing (प्राचीन शिलालेखों का अध्ययन) 2. Paleontology - study of ancient fossils (जीवाश्म विज्ञान)
345	**pan**	all (सभी), any (कोई), everyone (सब लोग)	1. Pandemic - affecting all (महामारी) 2. Panacea - a cure for all diseases or problems (रामबाण, सर्वरोगहारी)
346	**para**	beside (के बगल में), beyond (आगे), assistant (सहायक)	1. Parallel - alongside and always an equal distance apart (समानांतर)

SN	Prefix	Meaning	Examples
			2. Parasite - an organism that lives on and off another living being (परजीवी)
347	**ped, pedo**	child (बच्चा)	1. Pedagogue - a teacher, usually a very strict one (अध्यापक) 2. Pediatrician - a doctor who treats the diseases of children (बच्चों का चिकित्सक)
348	**pent, penta**	five (पाँच)	1. Pentagon - shape having 5 angles and 5 sides (पंचभूज) 2. Pentavalent - having a valency of five (पाँच की संयोजकता वाला)
349	**per**	through (के माध्यम से), throughout (लगातार)	1. Permeable - allowing liquids or gases to pass through (द्रव या गैसों को पास करने की अनुमति देना) 2. Persist - to continue for a long time (दृढ़ रहना)
350	**peri**	around (आस-पास), enclosing (संलग्न)	1. Perimeter - the outer boundary of an area. (परिमाप) 2. Perihelion - the point in the orbit of a planet, asteroid, or comet at which it is closest to the sun (उपसौर)
351	**poly**	many (अनेक), more than one (एक से अधिक)	1. Polychrome - with many colors (कई रंगों के साथ) 2. Polygon - shape with 3 or more straight sides. (बहुभुज)
352	**post**	after (बाद में), behind (पीछे)	1. Posthumous - after someone's death (मरणोपरांत) 2. Postscript - an additional remark at the end of a letter, after the signature (हस्ताक्षर के बाद, पत्र के अंत में एक अतिरिक्त टिप्पणी)
353	**pre**	before (पहले)	1. Preamble - a part in front of a formal document (प्रस्तावना) 2. Prepare - to get ready in advance (पहले से तैयार होना)
354	**pro**	forward (आगे), in favor of (के पक्ष में)	1. Prognosis - a prediction of what will happen (पूर्वानुमान) 2. Proponent - a person who advocates a theory, proposal, or course of action (एक व्यक्ति जो सिद्धांत, प्रस्ताव, या कार्रवाई के क्रम का समर्थन करता है)
355	**prot, proto**	first (पहला), original (मूल)	1. Prototype - the first of a kind (मूलरूप) 2. Protocol - a first draft from which a document is prepared (मूल लिपि)
356	**pseud, pseudo**	false (झूठा)	1. Pseudonym - a fictitious name (काल्पनिक नाम) 2. Pseudopodia - false feet (पादाभ)
357	**quad, quadr, quadri**	four (चार)	1. Quadrant - each of four quarters of a circle (वृत्त का चतुर्थ भाग) 2. Quadruple - increased fourfold (चौगुना) 3. Quadrilateral - a closed two-dimensional figure that has 4 sides, 4 angles, and 4 vertices (चतुर्भुज)
358	**quart**	one-fourth (एक-चौथाई)	1. Quart - a fourth of a gallon (चौथाई गेलन) 2. Quarter - one fourth (एक चौथाई)
359	**quin, quint**	five (पाँच)	1. Quintet - a composition for 5 voices or instruments (पंचवादक संगीत; पाँच वस्तुओं का समूह) 2. Quintuple - multiplied by five (पांच से गुणा)

SN	Prefix	Meaning	Examples
360	**radio**	radiation (विकिरण), ray (किरण)	1. Radioactive - emitting radiation (रेडियोधर्मी) 2. Radiologist - someone diagnosing or treating via radiation (विकिरण चिकित्सक)
361	**re**	again (फिर), back (वापस)	1. Reaction - a response (प्रतिक्रिया) 2. Revert - return to (a previous state, practice, topic, etc.) (एक पिछली स्थिति, अभ्यास, विषय आदि में लौटना)
362	**retro**	backward (पीछे), behind (पीछे की ओर)	1. Retroactive - relating to something in the past (पूर्वव्यापी) 2. Retrograde - directed or moving backward (पीछे की ओर निर्देशित या गतिमान)
363	**se**	apart (अलग)	1. Secede - to formally break away from (किसी मंडली से हटना) 2. Serum - a liquid isolated out of another (वह स्पष्ट तरल जिसे रक्त से अलग किया जाता है)
364	**semi**	half (आधा), partial (आंशिक)	1. Semicircle - half of a circle (एक वृत्त का आधा) 2. Semiconscious - only partially conscious (केवल आंशिक रूप से सचेत)
365	**sept, septi**	seven (सात)	1. September - this used to be the seventh month in the roman calendar (रोमन कैलेंडर में सातवाँ महीना) 2. Septuagenarian - a person who is from 70 to 79 years old (एक व्यक्ति जो 70 से 79 वर्ष का है)
366	**sub**	under (अंतर्गत), lower than (से कम), inferior to (अधीनस्थ)	1. Submerge - to put underwater (डूबना) 2. Substandard - inferior to accepted standards (स्वीकृत मानकों से कमतर)
367	**super**	higher in quality or quantity (गुणवत्ता या मात्रा में उच्चतर)	1. Supervise - observe and direct the execution of (a task or activity) (निरीक्षण और निर्देशन करना) 2. Superior - above average, better in quality (बेहतर)
368	**sur**	over (ऊपर), above (से अधिक)	1. Surpass - to exceed or go beyond someone in achievement or quality (बढ़कर होना / पीछे छोड़ देना) 2. Surplus - an amount that is more than what is needed (आधिक्य)
369	**syn, sym, syl, sys**	together (एक साथ), same (वही)	1. Sympathy - feelings of support or agreement (सहानुभूति) 2. Systole - The rhythmical contraction of the heart (हृदय का संकुचन) 3. Asynchronous - Not occurring or happening at the same time (अतुल्यकालिक, एक ही समय में घटित न होना)
370	**tact, tang**	touch (छूना)	1. Tangible - able to be touched (छूने योग्य) 2. Tactile - relating to the sense of touch (स्पर्शनीय)
371	**tel, tele, telo**	far (दूर), distant (दूरस्थ), complete (पूरा)	1. Telecommuting - working remotely, bridging the distance via virtual devices. (संचारण) 2. Television - a device to receive pictures from afar (टेलीविजन) 3. Telephone - a device to talk to a distant person (टेलीफ़ोन)

SN	Prefix	Meaning	Examples
372	**ter, trit**	rub (रगड़ना)	1. Attrition- the act of rubbing together or wearing down (संघर्षण) 2. Trite- used or occurring so often as to have lost interest, freshness, or force (घिसे-पिटे)
373	**tetra**	four (चार)	1. Tetrapod - having 4 legs (चौपाया) 2. Tetrarchy - government by 4 rulers (चतुर्थ खण्ड के राज्यपाल का क्षेत्र)
374	**trans**	across (आर-पार), beyond (आगे), through (के माध्यम से)	1. Transcontinental - across the continent (किसी महाद्वीप का विस्तार करना या उसके आर-पार जाना) 2. Transport - to carry something across a space. (परिवहन)
375	**tri**	three (तीन)	1. Trilogy - a group of three related novels, plays, films, operas, or albums (तीन संबंधित उपन्यासों, नाटकों, फिल्मों, ओपेरा, या एल्बमों का एक समूह) 2. Triangle - a figure with 3 sides and 3 angles (त्रिभुज)
376	**ultra**	beyond (आगे), extreme (चरम), more than (इससे अधिक)	1. Ultraviolet - light waves that are beyond the visible light spectrum at its violet end (पराबैंगनी) 2. Ultrasonic - sound waves beyond human hearing. (पराश्रव्य, पराध्वनिक)
377	**un**	not (नहीं), opposite of (से उल्टा), lacking (अभाव)	1. Unbelievable - difficult to believe; extraordinary (अविश्वसनीय) 2. Unfriendly - lacking friendliness. (अमित्र)
378	**uni**	one (एक), single (अकेला)	1. Unilateral - decided by only one person or nation (एक तरफा) 2. Unique - the only one of its kind (अद्वितीय)
379	**xen, xeno**	foreign (विदेशी)	1. Xenophile - attracted to foreigners (विदेशी चीज़ों (जैसे शैलियों या लोगों) के प्रति आकर्षित होना) 2. Xenophobic - afraid of foreigners (विदेशी चीज़ (लोगों) से डर और घृणा)
380	**zo, zoo**	animal (जानवर)	1. Saprozoic - Animals or plants that feed on dead and decaying organic matter (मृतजीवी) 2. Zootomy - the branch of zoology concerned with the dissection and anatomy of animals (पशुओं के शरीर की चीर-फाड़)

SN	Suffix	Meaning	Examples
381	**able, ible**	capable of (सक्षम, करने योग्य)	1. Breakable - broken easily (भंगुर, नाज़ुक) 2. Visible - able to be seen (दृश्यमान)
382	**aholic, oholic**	obsession for something (किसी चीज़ के प्रति जुनून)	1. Alcoholic - obsession for alcohol (शराबी, पियक्कड़) 2. Workaholic - obsession for work (काम में डूबे रहना)
383	**al**	relating to (से संबंधित)	1. Factual - contain facts (वास्तविक) 2. Herbal - made from herbs (जड़ी बूटी संबन्धी)

SN	Suffix	Meaning	Examples
384	**arium, orium, ary**	a place for (के लिए एक जगह)	1. Auditorium - A place for the gathering of an audience (सभागार, सभाभवन) 2. Planetarium - a building in which moving images of the sky at night are shown using a special machine (नक्षत्र-भवन) 3. Library - a building or organization that has a collection of books, documents, music, etc. for people to borrow (पुस्तकालय)
385	**cede, ceed, cess**	to go (चल देना), yield (उपज)	1. Accessible - easily entered, approached, or obtained (पहुंच योग्य, सुगम) 2. Recede - to go back (दूर जाना) 3. Exceed - to go beyond the limits (अधिक होना)
386	**cide, cise**	cut (काटना), kill (मारना)	1. Homicide - murder (मानव हत्या) 2. Insecticide - a chemical used to kill insects (कीटनाशक) 3. Incisor - a sharp tooth for cutting food (कृन्तक दाँत, काटने वाले दाँत)
387	**cracy**	rule (नियम), government (सरकार), power (शक्ति)	1. Aristocracy - government by nobility (श्रेष्ठ जनों के द्वारा राज्य शासन; अभिजात वर्ग) 2. Bureaucracy - government by state officials (नौकरशाही)
388	**ectomy**	surgical removal of (का शल्य चिकित्सा द्वारा निष्कासन)	1. Appendectomy - a surgical operation to remove the appendix (अपेंडिक्स को हटाने के लिए किया जाने वाला ऑपरेशन) 2. Hysterectomy - a surgical operation to remove all or part of the uterus (गर्भाशय को हटाने के लिए सर्जिकल ऑपरेशन)
389	**ence, ance**	state (अवस्था), condition (स्थिति)	1. Conference - a large formal meeting (सम्मेलन) 2. Performance - act of performing (प्रदर्शन)
390	**ful**	full of (पूर्ण)	1. Helpful - willing to assist others (मददगार) 2. Thoughtful - thinking deeply about something (विचारमग्न)
391	**graph, graphy**	writing (लिखना), recording (रिकॉर्डिंग), written (लिखित)	1. Graphology - the study of handwritings (हस्तलेख का विज्ञान) 2. Seismograph - a machine noting strength and duration of earthquakes (भूकंप-सूचक यंत्र)
392	**ian**	related to (से संबंधित)	1. Historian - a person who specializes in the study of history (इतिहासकार) 2. Pedestrian - a person who is walking (पैदल यात्री)
393	**ic, tic**	relating to a process or state (किसी प्रक्रिया या स्थिति से संबंधित)	1. Metallic - metal nature (धातुमय, धात्विक) 2. Realistic - able to see things as they really are (वास्तविक)
394	**ile**	related to (से संबंधित)	1. Domicile - housing that someone is living in (आवास) 2. Sterile - incapable of producing fruit or young ones; barren; infertile (बाँझ)
395	**ism**	belief or doctrine (विश्वास, विचारधारा), practice or	1. Racism - discriminating against people based on their race or background (नस्लवाद / जातिवाद)

SN	Suffix	Meaning	Examples
		system (अभ्यास, प्रणाली)	2. Tourism - the practice of travelling to places for pleasure or recreation (पर्यटन)
396	**ist**	a specialist or professional in a field (किसी क्षेत्र का विशेषज्ञ, जानकार)	1. Cyclist - a person who rides a bicycle (साइकिल-सवार) 2. Soloist - a musician who performs a solo (एकल कलाकार)
397	**ity**	state of being (होने की स्थिति)	1. Creativity - the ability to produce new things using imagination (रचनात्मकता) 2. Equality - The state of being equal (समानता)
398	**less**	without (बिना)	1. Homeless - people who do not have a home (बेघर) 2. Wireless - without wire (तार रहित)
399	**ly**	in a particular way (किसी विशेष तरीके से)	1. Carefully - With great attention (सावधानी से) 2. Quickly - fast; rapidly (जल्दी से)
400	**mancy**	divination (भविष्यवाणी, अटकल)	1. Geomancy - divination by interpreting patterns in earth or soil (भू-आकृति द्वारा भविष्यकथन) 2. Pyromancy - divination by interpreting fire or flames (अग्नि ज्योतिष)
401	**mania**	madness (पागलपन), insanity (पागलपन), excessive desire (अत्यधिक इच्छा)	1. Maniac - an insane person (पागल) 2. Melomania - craze for music (संगीत के प्रति दीवानगी) 3. Megalomania - obsession with power or greatness (सत्ता या महानता का जुनून)
402	**ology**	study of (का अध्ययन)	1. Entomology - the study of insects (कीटविज्ञान) 2. Pedology - the study of the formation, characteristics, and distribution of soils (मिट्टी-संबंधी विद्या)
403	**pathy**	feelings (भावना)	1. Anthropopathy - ascription of human passions or feelings to a being or beings not human (मानवीय भावनाओं को जिम्मेदार ठहराना) 2. Pathetic - causing feelings of sadness (दयनीय)
404	**phobia**	fear (डर)	1. Claustrophobia - extreme or irrational fear of confined places (बंद स्थानों का अत्यधिक या अतार्किक भय) 2. Logophobia - fear of words (शब्दों से डर)
405	**simulo, similis**	like (समान), resembling (मिलते-जुलते), of the same kind (एक ही तरह के)	1. Assimilate - to learn and understand something (अपनाना) 2. Verisimilar - having the appearance of truth (मुमकिन, संभावित)
406	**term**	end (अंत), limit (सीमा, हद)	1. Determine - to establish or decide something conclusively (निर्धारित करना) 2. Terminate - to bring something to an end (समाप्त करना)

APPENDIX*

G1. Special Word Lists (2300+ words)

i. Words list with root Phobia
ii. Words list with root Mania
iii. Words list with root Phile
iv. Words list with root Ism
v. Words list with root Logy
vi. Words list with root Graphy
vii. Words list with root Mancy
viii. Words list with root Loquy
ix. Words list with root Phagy
x. Words list with root Culture
xi. Words list with root Somnia
xii. Words list with root Sophy
xiii. Words list with root Theo
xiv. Words related to Government
xv. Words related to Killing/Killer
xvi. Words related to Places
xvii. Words related to Home
xviii. Words related to Marriage/Children
xix. Words related to Group
xx. Words related to Age
xxi. Words related to Worship
xxii. Words related to Professions
xxiii. Words related to Literature
xxiv. Words related to Scientific Instruments

https://bit.ly/BBEV4_G